Routledge International Handbook of Sex Industry Research

The *Routledge International Handbook of Sex Industry Research* unites 57 contributions from researchers, sex workers, activists, and practitioners who live and work in 28 countries throughout the world.

Focusing tightly on the contemporary state of sex industry research through eight carefully selected themes, this volume sets a clear agenda for future research, activism, and policymaking. Approaching the topic from a multidisciplinary perspective on an expanding field frequently divided by political and ideological conflicts, the handbook clearly establishes the parameters of the field while also showcasing the most vibrant contemporary empirical and theoretical work.

Unprecedented in its global scope, the *Routledge International Handbook of Sex Industry Research* will appeal to students, researchers, and policymakers interested in fields such as sociology of gender and sexuality; crime, justice, and the sex industry; sociology of work and professions; and sexual politics.

Susan Dewey is Associate Professor of Gender and Women's Studies at the University of Wyoming, USA.

Isabel Crowhurst is Senior Lecturer in Sociology and Criminology at the University of Essex, UK.

Chimaraoke Izugbara is Director of Global Health, Youth and Development research at the International Center for Research on Women, USA.

Routledge International Handbooks

Routledge Handbook of the History of Women's Economic Thought *ed. Kirsten Madden*

The Routledge Handbook of Contemporary Feminism *ed. Tasha Oren, Andrea Press*

Routledge Handbook of Global Populism *ed. Carlos de la Torre*

Handbook of Indigenous Environmental Knowledge *ed. Thomas Thornton, Shonil Bhagwat*

The Routledge Handbook to Museums, Media and Communication *ed. Kirsten Drotner, Vincent Dziekan, Ross Parry, Kim Christian Schrøder*

Routledge International Handbook of Sex Industry Research *ed. Susan Dewey, Isabel Crowhurst, and Chimaraoke Izugbara*

Routledge Handbook of Cultural Sociology 2nd Edition *ed. Laura Grindstaff, Ming-Cheng Lo, John R. Hall*

The Routledge Handbook of Latin American Development *ed. Julie Cupples, Marcela Palomina-Schalscha and Manuel Prieto*

The Routledge International Handbook of Embodied Perspectives in Psychotherapy: Approaches from Dance Movement and Body Psychotherapies *ed. Helen Payne, Sabine Koch, Jennifer Tantia and Thomas Fuchs*

The Routledge Handbook of Teaching Landscape *ed. Elke Mertens, Nilgül Karadeniz, Karsten Jørgensen, Richard Stiles*

For more information about this series, please visit: www.routledge.com/Routledge-International-Handbooks/book-series/RIHAND

Routledge International Handbook of Sex Industry Research

Edited by Susan Dewey, Isabel Crowhurst, and Chimaraoke Izugbara

cost
EUROPEAN COOPERATION
IN SCIENCE AND TECHNOLOGY

Routledge
Taylor & Francis Group

LONDON AND NEW YORK

First published 2019
by Routledge
2 Park Square, Milton Park, Abingdon, Oxon OX14 4RN

and by Routledge
711 Third Avenue, New York, NY 10017

Routledge is an imprint of the Taylor & Francis Group, an informa business

British Library Cataloguing-in-Publication Data
A catalogue record for this book is available from the British Library

Library of Congress Cataloging-in-Publication Data
A catalog record has been requested for this book

ISBN: 978-0-815-35412-3 (hbk)
ISBN: 978-1-351-13391-3 (ebk)

Typeset in Bembo
by Swales & Willis Ltd, Exeter, Devon, UK

Contents

Contents

Contents

Contents

Contributors

Oluwakemi Abiodun Adesina was educated at the University of Ibadan (Nigeria), where she obtained her BA (Hons.), MA, and PhD degrees in History. She is a 2013 Fellow of the American Council of Learned Society's (ACLS), African Humanities Program. Her research interests include: girls', gender, and women's history, youth cultures, migrations, commercial sex trade, and social and economic history. She is a member of the International Federation for Research in Women's History (United Kingdom) and the Women's Research and Documentation Centre.

Shovita Dhakal Adhikari is a PhD candidate at the Department of Sociology, University of Essex. Her research explores the application of global anti-trafficking framework in the national context. Prior to pursuing her PhD she worked for five years as a development practitioner in Nepal.

Kaoru Aoyama is a sociologist who has been conducting participatory action research in Japan with a sex worker-led advocacy group engaged in outreach with migrant sex workers and surveys with Japanese sex workers.

Lynzi Armstrong is Lecturer in Criminology at Victoria University of Wellington in New Zealand. Lynzi completed her PhD on decriminalization and the management of risks of violence among street-based sex workers in New Zealand in 2012. Her ongoing research focuses on sex worker rights, stigma, anti-trafficking policy, and sex work law reform.

David S. Bimbi is a social psychologist who began his career as a HIV peer educator as an undergraduate college student. During graduate school, he served in leadership roles in local LGBT and HIV/AIDS organizations and helped develop programming and organize community events. Dr. Bimbi's research and publications have mostly focused on behavioral health and wellness among stigmatized populations specifically persons living with HIV/AIDS, LGB individuals, persons of transgender experience, and male sex workers.

Thaddeus Gregory Blanchette is an anthropologist at the Federal University of Rio de Janeiro, Macaé. He has been studying sex work, trafficking, and sex tourism in Brazil for over 13 years. He is a founding member of Prostitution Policy Watch and a representative for the Davida sex workers' rights association on the Rio de Janeiro state and Brazilian federal anti-trafficking councils.

Hilary Caldwell is a PhD candidate at UNSW Sydney, Australia, sex therapist in private practice and, a feminist and sex worker ally. Her master's degree via research project examined men who buy sex and she has an additional master's degree in Health Science (Sexual Health).

Rosie Campbell, Jane Scoular, Teela Sanders, Jane Pitcher, and Stewart Cunningham are all members of the Beyond the Gaze research team, which examines online commercial sex markets in the UK.

Moshoula Capous-Desyllas is Associate Professor of Sociology at California State University. She engages in qualitative and arts-based research and has published her research in the area of sex work in the journals *Sexualities, Qualitative Social Work, Journal of Community Practice*, as well as book chapters in *Queer Sex Work* (Routledge, 2015), *Feminisms in Social Work Research* (Routledge, 2014), and *Creative Arts in Research for Community and Cultural Change* (Detselig Enterprises, 2011). She was also an activist and member of SWOC (Sex Worker Outreach Coalition) in Portland, Oregon.

Irina Churakova is a PhD student at the National Research University Higher School of Economics in Moscow and holds a Master of Arts in Counseling from the University of Manchester. Her dissertation focuses on predictors of mental health and psychosocial conditions of victimization of sex trafficking survivors, and is based a study conducted at the International Organization for Migration (IOM) diplomatic mission in Moscow, where she has worked as a counseling psychologist.

Rob Comber is Lecturer in Computer Mediated Communications and researcher in human–computer interaction at Open Lab, Newcastle University. He specializes in design for Collective Action, including co-design of services with and for communities and citizens.

Isabel Crowhurst is Senior Lecturer in Sociology and Criminology at the University of Essex, UK. Her research is concerned with the intersection of sexual practices, intimate lives, and socio-legal structures. Recent publications include *Reproducing Citizens: Family, State and Civil Society* (Routledge, 2015, with Sasha Roseneil, Ana Cristina Santos, and Mariya Stoilova) and *Sexualities Research: Critical Interjections, Diverse Methodologies and Practical Applications* (Routledge, 2017, with Andrew King and Ana Cristina Santos). Isabel was Chair of COST Action Prospol "Comparing European Prostitution Policies" from 2013 to 2017.

Ana Paula da Silva is an anthropologist at the Federal Fluminense University, coordinated the ethnographic component of the Prostitution Policy Watch's Olympics and World Cup research project in the Vila Mimosa, and participated in the WhatsApp group and photography component of the project. Ana Paula has conducted ethnographic research on the Rio de Janeiro sex markets since 2005 with a focus on sex tourism, race, gender, sexuality, and trafficking, and is also a member of the Davida collective.

Susan Dewey's research focuses on the intersections between violence, sexuality, and the feminization of poverty in women's criminal justice system involvement. She is the author or lead editor of nine books and is currently co-authoring her tenth, *Outlaw Women: Prison, Rural Violence, and Poverty on the New American Frontier* (under contract, New York University Press), with a team of community-based researchers. She is Associate Professor of Gender and Women's Studies at the University of Wyoming, where she leads the Wyoming Pathways from Prison project.

John de Wit is Professor of Interdisciplinary Social Science at Utrecht University, the Netherlands, and Professor of Social Research in Health at UNSW Sydney, Australia. Trained in social psychology, he is a leading international expert in theory-based research and intervention development in social and behavior aspects of health. John is particularly passionate about HIV prevention, sexual health promotion, and well-being in marginalized communities.

Angela Donini is Professor in the Philosophy Department at the Federal University of the State of Rio de Janeiro. She is a visual artist and filmmaker, with work that addresses questions about art, politics, the body, subjectivity, resistance, and creation. She is a member of the sex worker rights' collective Davida and directed the award-winning documentary *Corpos que Escapam* (*Bodies that Escape*) (2015), which features prostitute rights activist Gabriela Leite and trans activist João Nery.

Agata Dziuban is Assistant Professor at the Institute of Sociology at the Jagiellonian University, Poland, and has been working as a policy officer at the International Committee on the Rights of Sex Workers in Europe (ICRSE) since 2014. She has conducted numerous consultations with sex worker communities in Europe, is the co-founder of Sex Work Polska, Coalition for the Rights of Sex Workers in Poland, and has been engaged in the design and implementation of peer-education programmes for sex workers in Poland.

Mfon Umoren Ekpootu is Professor of History at the University of Port Harcourt, Nigeria with research interests in gender and sexuality. She has published articles on human trafficking and the colonial policing of sexuality in southern Nigeria's Cross River region.

Valentine C. Ezeh is an experimental psychologist in the Department of Psychology, University of Nigeria, Nsukka and currently working on the psychology of adolescent sexuality in Nsukka Zone, South Eastern Nigeria.

Mira Fey is a PhD candidate in Geneva where her doctoral field research focuses on the translation of the Geneva Prostitution Law into everyday police action and the effects of this translation on the sex workers' labor conditions.

Jessica Hernandez is a graduate of the Sociology Department at California State University Northridge, where she earned her bachelor's degree with an emphasis on social welfare and social justice. Influenced by anti-oppressive social work, she has worked with hundreds of sex workers as a case manager and facilitator of an art therapy class at a non-profit organization.

Chimaraoke Izugbara directs the Global Health, Youth and Development Program at the International Center for Research on Women (ICRW). He holds PhDs in Health Anthropology and in Social Work, Gender, and Health from the University of Gothenburg, Sweden, and has taught in universities in Africa, Europe, and the United States. With research interests spanning sexuality, gender, development, and reproductive health, Dr. Izugbara has authored over a hundred peer-reviewed papers in leading social science and public health journals. His most recent book is *Women's Health in Africa: Issues, Challenges, and Opportunities* (Routledge, 2015).

Elena Jeffreys is a PhD student currently pursuing a project entitled "Sex Worker Organizations and Funding." She works closely with sex worker organizations in her feminist research.

Juline A. Koken is a social psychologist specializing in the health of LGBT individuals and sex workers of all genders; her research focuses on HIV prevention, substance use (treatment and harm reduction approaches), and sexual health. Dr. Koken is also an expert in motivational interviewing and does training and treatment fidelity monitoring with research and service programs implementing MI. Dr. Koken is an Assistant Professor of Health Sciences at LaGuardia Community College, CUNY.

Alexander Kondakov is Assistant Professor in the Department of Political Science and Sociology at the European University at St. Petersburg and researcher at the Centre for Independent Social Research in St. Petersburg, Russia. He is also the deputy editor-in-chief for the *Journal of Social Policy Studies*. Currently, he is a Wisconsin Russia Project Research Associate at the University of Wisconsin–Madison. For a decade, Kondakov's work has been primarily focused on law and sexuality studies, more specifically on queer sexualities in Russia. He has also published articles in *Sexualities*, *Social and Legal Studies*, and *Feminist Legal Studies*, among others.

Mary Laing is Senior Lecturer in Criminology at Northumbria University and is interested in the regulation and criminalization of sex work. She is on the board of National Ugly Mugs and is currently undertaking research utilizing digital technologies with Open Lab at Newcastle University on trans sex work.

Rachel Lennon has a master's degree in Public Health with Melbourne University and is currently completing her PhD at Western Sydney University. Rachel's thesis explores the impacts of stigma and discrimination on female street-based sex workers. Rachel has worked in the not-for-profit sector for over a decade and her expertise lies in public health, health promotion, and working with vulnerable communities such as Aboriginal communities, women living with HIV/AIDS, and women experiencing family violence.

Pranee Liamputtong is Professor of Public Health at the School of Science and Health, Western Sydney University, Australia. Pranee has a particular interest in issues related to cultural and social influences on women's reproductive and sexual health. She works mainly with refugee and migrant women in Melbourne and with women in Asia. Pranee has also worked with, and written about, marginalized/vulnerable individuals in her research. Pranee is a qualitative researcher and has also published several method books including *Qualitative Research Methods* (4th ed., Oxford University Press, 2012); *Research Methods in Health* (3rd ed., Oxford University Press, 2017), and *Handbook of Research Methods in Health Social Sciences* (Springer, 2018).

Samantha Majic is Associate Professor of Political Science at John Jay College, City University of New York. Their most recent publication together is *Negotiating Sex Work: The Unintended Consequences of Policy & Activism* (University of Minnesota, 2014).

Lawrence Lekau Mamabolo is passionate about issues related to marginalized groups, resilience, key populations, and presently works as a mentor by training clinical and non-clinical staff on health issues in South Africa.

Lauren Martin is Director of Research at the University of Minnesota's Urban Research Outreach-Engagement Center and a lecturer at the Humphrey School of Public Affairs. She has been conducting community-based action research on sex trading and sex trafficking that she started in 2006.

Gregory Mitchell is Associate Professor of Women's, Gender, and Sexuality Studies at Williams College. His book *Tourist Attractions: Performing Race and Masculinity in Brazil's Sexual Economy* (University of Chicago Press, 2016) is an ethnography of male sex workers and their clients. His current research is about sex work, police violence, moral panics, and global sporting events such the Olympics and World Cup. His work has appeared in *American Ethnologist, Wagadu, Brasiliana, Plural, Journal of Popular Music Studies*, and several edited volumes in the United States and Brazil.

Santiago Morcillo is a sociologist who conducts research on issues related to sexuality, the sex industry, gender, health, and subjectivity. He has also been collaborating with local sex workers' organizations in Buenos Aires and in San Juan.

Jerald L. Mosley is a retired Supervising Deputy Attorney General with the Office of the California Attorney General, where he worked for over 17 years from 1996 to 2014 managing trials and appeals in state and federal courts. Prior to attending law school at UCLA, he graduated with a PhD in Philosophy from the University of California Davis.

Laura Murray coordinated the photography project as an executive researcher with Prostitution Policy Watch, a research and activist collaborative based at the Institute of Research on Urban and Regional Planning at the Federal University of Rio de Janeiro, Brazil. Laura is also a postdoctoral researcher at the Institute of Social Medicine at the State University of Rio de Janeiro, member of the sex worker rights collective Davida, and directed the documentary *A Kiss for Gabriela* (2013) about the late and legendary sex worker activist Gabriela Leite.

Georgina Yaa Oduro is Senior Lecturer at the Department of Sociology and Anthropology at the University of Cape Coast, Ghana. She holds a PhD in Sociology of Education from the University of Cambridge and is a Takemi fellow in International Health at the Harvard School of Public Health.

José Miguel Nieto Olivar has been a researcher at the Center for Gender Studies at the State University of Campinas in Brazil since 2010. Working on social programs and in anthropological projects in Colombia and Brazil on issues of gender, sexuality, human rights, sex work/sexual markets, sexual and reproductive health, young people's sexuality, human trafficking, and sexual exploitation in the borderlands and the Amazon region, he also collaborates with the Centro de Investigaciones en Sociedad, Salud y Cultura (Colombia), the Brazilian Network of Sex Workers, and the Gender-Based Violence Watch on Amazon.

Alexandra Oliveira is Professor at the University of Porto, where she has been researching the subject of commercial sex for more than 20 years. She is the author of two books in addition to being a health educator with sex workers in the area of HIV/AIDS/STDs prevention.

Cristiane Oliveira coordinated the Vila Mimosa photography project. Cristiane has worked as a sex worker in the Vila for over a decade, and during that time, collaborated on a variety of research and health-related projects. During the 2014 World Cup, she documented her daily experiences using an audio and video recorder, an inspiration for the project realized during the Olympic Games.

Elsa Oliveira is the co-coordinator of the MoVE method:visual:explore project and a researcher at the African Centre for Migration and Society at the University of the Witwatersrand.

Treena Orchard is Associate Professor in the School of Health Studies and an Affiliate in Women's Studies and Feminist Research at Western University. An anthropologist with cultural and medical expertise, she has conducted ethnographic research with women in sex work, people with HIV/AIDS, indigenous populations, and those of sexual minority status across Canada and in India. She lives in London, Ontario with her two cats, Mr. Marbles and Shiva, and visits her family in Saskatoon, Saskatchewan as often as possible.

Denice Palacios has a master's degree in Social Work from California State University, Fullerton. She engages in qualitative research that explores the lives of women, men, and trans folks working in the sex industry. As a former sex worker and activist, she uses her life experiences and education to empower others to share their stories.

Subadra Panchanadeswaran is Associate Professor and Director of the PhD program at Adelphi University School of Social Work. Her area of practice and research is primarily in gender-based violence and her work examines the intersections of violence, HIV/AIDS, and substance use disorders both in the United States and internationally. She studies female sex workers and sexual minorities, substance-using populations, and immigrant women in the United States especially South Asian women. Her most recent research project examined the impact of mobile phone technology on female sex workers' lives in India.

Jo Phoenix is Professor of Criminology at the Open University. She has numerous publications on subjects ranging from prostitution policy reform, child sexual exploitation, women's involvement in sex work, youth justice, and youth justice practice. Her research interests also include gender, crime, justice, professional ethics and knowledge, and criminological and sociological theory. Her most recent publications include: "The Politics of Sexuality: Alternative Vision of Sex and Social Change" in P. Carlen and L. Ayres (Eds.) *Alternative Criminologies* (Routledge, 2018), and "Child-Friendly Youth Justice?" in R. Little and T. Bateman (Eds.) *Youth Justice Compendium* (Sage, 2018).

Adriana Piscitelli is a feminist anthropologist, professor, and senior researcher at the State University of Campinas (Unicamp) in Brazil. During the past 17 years she has carried out studies about the transnationalization of sex and marriage markets and about human trafficking.

Patrick Preston is a sex worker and a PhD candidate in English Literature at the University of East Anglia whose research explores twentieth-century queer writing, in particular how contemporary literature stages the contingencies of queer sex work.

Helen Rand is currently in the third year of her PhD with the Department of Sociology at the University of Essex. She is supervised by Dr. Isabel Crowhurst and Professor Joan Busfield. The working title for her thesis is "Providers and 'Punters' of Technology Mediated Sexual Services in Britain: A Sociological Study of Sex Work in the Digital Age." Helen has combined work with academic study throughout her adult life, graduating from the School of Oriental and African Studies in 2002 with a BA in Religions and Politics, and later completing a master's degree in International Development at the University of Manchester in 2010.

Patricia Rivas is a graduate of California State University, Northridge, where she received her bachelor's degree in Sociology with an emphasis on social justice. Her interests are primarily centered upon the importance of strengthening the foundation of mental health in the human psychological developmental process.

Caroline Sambai researches in the areas of health communication and popular culture. Her PhD thesis was on depictions of HIV/AIDS and sexuality in Kenyan television dramas. She lectures full time in the Department of Literature, Theatre, and Film studies at Moi University, Kenya.

Greta Schuler is the researcher and facilitator of the *Izwi Lethu: Our Voice* newsletter project, a collaboration between the African Centre for Migration and Society and the Sisonke National Sex Worker Movement in South Africa. Greta is working toward her PhD in Creative Writing at the University of the Witwatersrand.

Giulia Selmi holds a PhD in Sociology and Social Research at the University of Trento (Italy) and she's currently post-doc research fellow at the Department of Human Sciences of the University of Verona (Italy) where she's member of the Politesse Research Center on Politics and Theories of Sexuality. Her research is concerned with the social studies of sexualities and with the new form of intimacy.

Carisa R. Showden is Senior Lecturer in Sociology and Director of the Board of Gender Studies at the University of Auckland.

Peter Simatei is Professor of Comparative Literature and Culture, an area in which he has published widely. He is currently working on a project titled "Sexual Metaphor and Innuendo in Kalenjin Popular Music."

May-Len Skilbrei is Professor of Criminology at the Department of Criminology and Sociology of Law at the University of Oslo, Norway. Skilbrei has researched prostitution and prostitution policies since the mid-1990s. In 2013 she published a book with Ashgate on Nordic prostitution policy together with Charlotta Holmström. In the last ten years she has been involved in research on human trafficking, migration, and gender, and has published articles in *Crime & Justice, Women & Criminal Justice, Sexuality Research & Social Policy, Ethnos*, and *British Journal of Criminology*. She also co-edited the book *Prostitution Research in Context: Methodology, Representation and Power* with Marlene Spanger (Routledge, 2017).

Marlene Spanger is Associate Professor in the Department of Culture and Global Studies at Aalborg University in Denmark. Her research fields include the policy fields of prostitution and human trafficking, transnational intimacies, and migration, with special attention to gender, sexuality, racialization, and affective practices.

P.J. Starr is a filmmaker, photographer, and researcher. She has directed numerous short films about the experience of sex workers and allied communities, and most recently released the feature documentary *No Human Involved*. P.J. has been involved in curating film selections for the last decade and has also reviewed films for several festivals. She holds a doctorate in Anthropology and has contributed to several community research projects globally in Australia, Latin America, and the United States.

Elfriede Steffan, Barbara Kavemann, and Tzvetina Arsova Netzelmann are social scientists who draw on long-term experience in research on sex work, violence, social inclusion, and access to support services.

Luca Stevenson is a male sex worker and coordinator of the International Committee on the Rights of Sex Workers in Europe (ICRSE), a network of 90 organizations in 33 countries in Europe and Central Asia. As a member of several sex worker-led organizations in the UK and France—including Sex Worker Open University, SCOT-PEP and the French Union of Sex Workers (STRASS)—Luca has a vast knowledge of sex workers' self-organization and has been coordinating large-scale advocacy campaigns focusing on sex workers' access to human, labor, and civil rights.

Angelika Strohmayer is an interdisciplinary researcher exploring the ways in which digital technologies are utilized by and designed with sex work support services to facilitate support in fragmented and centralized contexts. Currently she is based at Open Lab, Newcastle University.

Cecilia Varela is a researcher from the National Counsel of Scientific and Technical Researches from Argentina (CONICET) and Professor at the University of Buenos Aires, where she received her PhD.

Hendrik Wagenaar is Professor at the Department of Urban Studies and Planning at the University of Sheffield. He publishes in the areas of participatory democracy, prostitution policy, interpretive policy analysis, and practice theory. He is author of *Meaning in Action: Interpretation and Dialogue in Policy Analysis* (M.E. Sharpe, 2011), and editor of the seminal *Deliberative Policy Analysis* (Cambridge University Press, 2003). In the area of prostitution research he published *Designing Prostitution Policy: Intention and Reality in Regulating the Sex Trade* (with Helga Amesberger and Sietske Altink, Policy Press, 2017) and *Assessing Prostitution Policies in Europe* (with S. Jahnsen, Routledge, 2017).

Ronald Weitzer is Professor of Sociology at George Washington University. He has published extensively on sex work, including his two books: *Sex for Sale* (2nd ed., Routledge, 2010) and *Legalizing Prostitution* (New York University Press, 2012). An early paper on the sex workers' rights movement was followed by studies of erotic businesses, clients, media representations, regulatory policies, and human trafficking. He was an expert witness in the seminal court case that challenged the constitutionality of Canada's prostitution laws, *Bedford v. Canada*.

Yo-Hsin Yang is a PhD candidate in Human Geography at Durham University. His doctoral thesis explores Asian gay men's multiple sexual practices in different Bangkok gay scenes such as clubs, saunas, and erotic massage, with a focus on the entanglement between body, power, space, and intimacy.

Per Jørgen Ystehede works as research adviser at the Department of Criminology and Sociology of Law, University of Oslo. Ystehede has published in the field of historical criminology, history of science, literature, and law. Together with Paul Knepper, he is the editor of *The Cesare Lombroso Handbook* (Routledge, 2014).

Daniil Zhaivoronok's research is focused on genealogy and politics of feminists' engagements with the complex field of commercial sexuality. In his research, he tries to show how competing feminist discourses about commercial sex are assembled, how they work, and what effects they produce. He has published several articles in Russian peer-reviewed journals and is a junior research assistant in the Gender Studies Program, European University at St. Petersburg (Russia).

Tiantian Zheng is the author and co-author of nine books. *Red Lights* (University of Minnesota Press, 2009) is the Winner of the 2010 Sara A. Whaley Book Prize from the National Women's Studies Association. *Ethnographies of Prostitution in Contemporary China* (Palgrave, 2009) is the Winner of the 2011 Research Publication Book Award from the Association of Chinese Professors of Social Sciences in the United States. *Tongzhi Living* (University of Minnesota Press, 2015) was awarded the Outstanding Academic Title by *Choice* in 2016, selected for its excellence in scholarship and presentation, the significance of its contribution to the field, and value as important treatment of the subject. It was also nominated for three additional awards.

Acknowledgments

This collection was inspired by the pioneering work of COST Action IS1209 ProsPol, an established international network of over 90 members from 25 countries that remains very active through publishing, conference, and other circuits. Funded through COST by the European Commission, ProsPol was the first truly international network to unite researchers and activists with the goal of expanding understandings of the complexities of commercial sex to promote better-informed prostitution law and policy. The Handbook builds upon ProsPol's collective wisdom while also bridging significant cultural, national, and geographic divides through the three editors' breadth of expertise in Africa, Europe, and North America.

◯cost

EUROPEAN COOPERATION
IN SCIENCE AND TECHNOLOGY

1

Introduction

Susan Dewey, Isabel Crowhurst, and
Chimaraoke Izugbara

Introduction

Uniting contributions from researchers, sex workers, activists, and professional practitioners worldwide, *The Routledge International Handbook of Sex Industry Research* represents the coalescence of a vibrant epistemic community. This community has emerged in the past four decades since the sex industry first became the focus of consistent and widespread global critical inquiry among researchers. The Handbook clearly establishes the contemporary state of this multidisciplinary field of study while also including some of the most exciting contemporary empirical and theoretical work with the broader goal of setting a clear agenda for the development of future research, public policy, and activism. Unprecedented in its global scope and tightly presented around eight carefully selected themes that exemplify the current state of sex industry research, this volume explores an expanding field that is all too frequently divided by fraught political and ideological conflicts and cultural sensitivities.

Sex industry research critically engages with the broad spectrum of behaviors, actors, and socio-cultural beliefs that surround the exchange of sex for money and, in so doing, illuminates complex and multi-faceted aspects of the broader socio-cultural contexts within which such exchanges take place. Studying transactional sex offers unique insights into areas of the human experience that otherwise remain obscured by the veil of propriety that, in most societies, protects a status quo that systematically places women and members of other historically oppressed groups at a distinct socio-economic disadvantage. Scholarly and other forms of critical engagement with the sex industry often reveal that even the most seemingly straightforward sex-for-money exchanges take place at the gendered intersections of sexuality, class, migrant, or citizenship status, and ethnic, racial, or cultural identities that suffuse many forms of transactional sexual exchange.

Studies of the sex industry featured in the Handbook, as in the field more generally, analyze the characteristics and consequences of dominant socio-cultural norms that both undergird and stigmatize the industry's existence. Inequalities of gender, race, class, sexual orientation, place of origin, citizenship status, and identity-related factors inform the experiences of sex industry involvement among sex workers, clients, and third parties alike. These inequalities likewise shape the perspectives of services providers, criminal justice professionals, and others tasked with regulatory oversight or other forms of professional engagement with people in the sex industry. Dominant socio-cultural norms regarding intimacy, marriage, and other sexual/affective relationships directly inform the types of activities classified as transactional sex in a given context, as do cultural beliefs about labor and other forms of economic exchange. These dominant norms—as well as their negotiation and contestation—are also evident in the politics and ethics of knowledge production about the sex industry and how such knowledge circulates and is accepted and received globally.

Most sex workers throughout the world face significant marginalization as women and men, and generally as people, whose primary or ancillary income generation strategies involve transactional sex. Their stigmatization is the direct result of culturally conflicted attitudes about sexuality, intimacy, and gender norms in many, if not all, societies. Yet despite the universality of sex workers' marginalization and stigmatization, researchers disagree profoundly about the nature of transactional sex and approaches to its regulation. Parties interested in these issues typically position themselves along a continuum between those who regard sex work as a legitimate labor form and those who regard such exchanges as morally reprehensible. These disagreements, and their global political consequences, are discussed at length in Chapter 2, "Sex industry research: key theories, methods, and challenges."

Despite perspectival differences, almost all researchers, activists, and others concerned with this issue agree that the sex industry is an enduring global reality that encompasses an extraordinarily diverse set of practices, venues, and people subject to equally variant legal and regulatory frameworks. They also agree that sex work continues to evoke major religious, moral, ethical, socio-cultural, and medical concerns and remains highly stigmatized. The sex industry encompasses a broad umbrella of transactional sexual exchanges that vary tremendously in terms of participants' motivations and expectations regarding price, physical contact, emotional labor, level of discretion, self-perception, and likelihood of negative experiences such as arrest or violence. For instance, a university student who provides no-contact sexual services to webcam clients she will most likely never meet in person has a very different set of both life and sex industry experiences from a woman who engages in street prostitution to support her addiction. Likewise, exotic dancers in a legal venue may see themselves as artists and entertainers, whereas teenage runaways who perform survival sex in exchange for shelter may regard these exchanges as akin to the sexual abuse that made them leave home in the first place.

As in so many other industries, the circumstances in which sex workers, their clients, third parties, and those tasked with regulating sexual labor operate depend on the legal status of their income generation strategies, the amount of control they exercise over their working conditions, and their occupational expertise in each niche market. A third party with the citizenship status, capital, and business acumen necessary to obtain licenses and manage a brothel in a context where prostitution is legal has a very different set of concerns than an undocumented woman who shares her apartment with other migrant sex workers while evading police and unscrupulous people who may wish to exploit her vulnerabilities as a person without citizenship rights. An older woman who facilitates younger sex workers' journeys to Western Europe may envision her activities as enabling others to have a better life, whereas as an anti-trafficking or migrant rights activist may decry her profiting from other women's sexual labor as exploitative.

The sex industry is at best a slippery concept, and yet the diversity of the sex industry and its participants is matched in equal measure by the sheer breadth of actors who concern themselves with its existence. Those interested in the sex industry and its participants attribute such interest to a set of motivations, goals, and ideological-political reasons that span a continuum from supporters of sex worker rights to neo-abolitionism. Such sharp perspectival distinctions are well known in the field, to the extent that peer-reviewed articles, monographs, and the introductions of edited collections on this subject nearly always include a requisite section delineating the major "camps" or ideological stances on the sex industry. Each stance uses its own distinctive language to describe who and what the sex industry entails and also to advocate for specific legal and policy approaches to the regulation of transactional sex.

Supporters of sex worker rights generally regard transactional sex as a legitimate form of work worthy of respect and labor protections like any other job, although they often acknowledge that significant stigma accrues to transactional sex in almost all its forms. Sex worker rights advocates often frame their arguments within a discourse of international human rights by emphasizing the socio-economic constraints and other inequalities that contribute to many people's involvement in the sex industry. In this way of thinking, sex workers and their clients are entitled to equal protections under the law and should not be arrested or otherwise stigmatized for their activities. On the other side of the continuum, neo-abolitionists regard the sex industry as morally reprehensible and/or abusive, and generally do not distinguish between voluntary participation in prostitution or other forms of transactional sex and sex trafficking. Adherents to this approach accordingly use terms such as "prostituted" or "trafficked" to indicate the lack of agency experienced by individuals, who trade sex for money and who are almost always assumed to be women. Within this school of thought prostitution is viewed as violence against all women.

Such wide-ranging interests across a continuum of perspectives on the sex industry have given rise to associated activist and professional practices that likewise span an ideological gamut well documented throughout the Handbook. In many ways, the research enterprise itself is no different. The sheer magnitude of both the sex industry and those interested in it for various reasons is in itself reason enough to study this phenomenon empirically. Yet an even more significant contribution that the multidisciplinary field of sex industry research offers to the world lies in its great potential to offer meaningful suggestions for law and policy. Suggestions derived from such research and that engage with the concerns of those with sex industry experiences tend to be the exception rather than the rule throughout the world. All too often, regulatory measures governing the sex industry derive from dominant cultural values and associated assumptions regarding the dangers to public health and morality that sex workers (and, albeit far less frequently, their clients) are thought to pose to society.

Attempts to translate sex work research into policy in a meaningful and systematic fashion accordingly present significant challenges. Yet this Handbook is itself indicative of the persistent determination of researchers and activists in this field to build bridges between communities that otherwise often remain locked in ideological and professional silos. This collection was inspired by a pioneering example of such work: COST Action ProsPol, an established international network of over 90 members from 25 countries and chaired by Handbook co-editor Isabel Crowhurst. Funded by the European Union programme COST, ProsPol was the first truly international network to unite researchers and activists with the goal of expanding understandings of the complexities of commercial sex to promote better-informed prostitution law and policy. The Handbook builds upon ProsPol's collective wisdom while also bridging significant cultural, national, and geographic divides through the three co-editors' breadth of expertise and experience in Africa, Europe, and the Americas. Above all, however, this volume acknowledges the epistemic community of sex work researchers, activists, and others who, with their long history of intellectual and activist engagement, have endeavored to advance knowledge about the much-misunderstood cultural practices that constitute the sex industry.

Knowledge production at the interstices of research and advocacy

Sex industry research has its roots in the rights-based activist movements for equal socio-sexual rights that first emerged in North America and Western Europe during the 1970s. Research presented throughout the Handbook has its inception in the feminist and queer activism that gradually became integrated into both mainstream academia as well as public policy in many countries throughout the world. It is no coincidence that the first systematic studies of the sex industry began to occur in large numbers in the 1980s, when researchers inspired by or involved in these activist movements came into professional maturity as tenured professors, leaders of third-sector organizations tasked with sex workers' rights, or activists who regarded transactional sex, especially prostitution, as the most fundamental manifestation of male domination over women.

Sex industry research is in many ways unique because of its location at the interstices of research and advocacy. Yet it also occupies a unique place among the various forms of knowledge production that usually emerge from universities. Sex industry research remains stigmatized as an intellectual pursuit because its results often directly call into question many of the embedded moral, legal, and economic principles that form the basis of social inequalities such as sexism, racism, classism, and xenophobia. Universities exist, in part, to critically examine these very principles as part of their mission to contribute to the societies of which they are a part, and yet university administrations and departments are often dominated by relatively class-privileged individuals who may be uneasy with research topics that dominant cultural values position as controversial in ways that may reflect poorly on the university's reputation.

Researchers of the many complexities of transactional sex who aspire to make a real and meaningful difference in the lives of those who participate in their academic studies and who generally are relegated to the margins of society, may accordingly find that their efforts are institutionally dismissed, questioned, or criticized as outside the purview of the research enterprise. Researchers may also find that the rewards they and their sex worker or other activist colleagues receive for their efforts far outweigh mainstream academic accolades. Working at the interstices of research and activism, as with any professionally unconventional choice, presents benefits and challenges that can produce potentially dynamic results. In this respect, the multidisciplinary field of sex industry research offers many potential lessons to academics who wish to pursue theoretical and methodological avenues of inquiry designed to bring about meaningful social change.

Envisioning research with people in sex work as inseparable from the possibilities for real-world social change provides numerous benefits, most notably in terms of democratizing the research enterprise as a whole. Drawing on feminist praxis that envisions research as productive of inclusive community-based collaboration, many working in this field acknowledge the inherently flawed positivist notion of neutral, value-free research as the product of a long history of exclusionary practices within the knowledge-production enterprise. Such exclusionary practices stem from the historically disproportionate value assigned to the opinions expressed by those with academic credentials or other socio-institutionally recognized forms of expertise. These practices silence the people variously involved in transactional sex in ways that further reinforce their socio-economic marginalization by denying them the right to produce knowledge about their own lives and experiences.

Many studies in this Handbook emphasize the importance of allowing the community, however defined, to help set the terms of the study in ways designed to foster positive social change rather than placing sole control within the hands of researchers who may or may not have lived experience with the subject under study. Doing so, many of our authors argue, pushes researchers, sex workers, and others involved in this work to actively question the values and assumptions that they bring to collaborative projects, and such questioning can further support community engagement. Recognizing the critical importance of including multiple vantage points, experiences, and ways of knowing—especially because sex workers have expertise that researchers do not always share—helps to move research from a cold, clinical abstraction relegated to academic journals into a meaningful community product designed to benefit all concerned by promoting justice for greater numbers of people on their own terms.

Yet working at the interstices of research and activism presents challenges from critics who dismiss community-based projects as agenda-laden, less rigorous, and less scientific. Such criticisms have direct, and potentially devastating, professional consequences such as tenure denial or exclusion from publication in top peer-reviewed venues. With a few exceptions such as social work and community development, academia tends not to value community-based work or, at best, to regard it as a decorative garnish to the real academic substance of peer-reviewed publications, grant funding, and other institutionally supported markers of academic success. In many academic fields the term "activism" has negative connotations for researchers because it implies the type of bias that scientific research, from the European Enlightenment forward, claims to avoid.

Researchers also face challenges outside the academy because of the compartmentalization of identities and standpoints that often accompanies community-based collaboration by locking individuals into artificially bifurcated categories such as either "sex worker," "researcher," or "activist." Such bifurcations usually fail to acknowledge that a person may publicly or privately self-identify with more than one of these categories. Likewise, such bifurcation belies the complexities of individual lived experiences both past and present in potentially destructive ways. An academic with previous sex industry experience, for instance, may not wish to disclose those experiences because of the real professional consequences, such as stigmatization and not being taken seriously by some academic peers or policymakers, that could accompany such disclosure. Similarly, a person who has worked in one sex industry sector but becomes involved in a research project on another may face accusations from other sex workers of not adequately understanding the issues at stake in their sector.

As is evident in many of the Handbook's chapters, sex industry researchers face challenges from multiple sides, including academia, sex workers, and activists of various political persuasions. Often these challenges center on questions and criticisms related to age-old questions regarding the validity of claims to knowledge, expertise, and authority, such as whether individual lived experiences outweigh empirically derived knowledge. Researchers often face accusations of silencing some perspectives while giving voice to others, and struggle with the best way to give equal weight to different forms of knowledge, all while working within a global research enterprise that skeptically regards research and activism as discrete entities that ought not to merge.

Although the field of sex industry research is multidisciplinary and has origins in activist struggles for justice, published studies tend to be concentrated in academic disciplines that risk further stigmatizing and pathologizing sex workers. Public health, criminology, social work, and criminal justice—the primary fields in which studies of the sex industry often appear—tend to focus the scope of analytical inquiry on aspects of sex workers' lives that may reify dominant cultural stereotypes that position them as vectors of disease, perpetrators and victims of crime, and as suffering from addictions, compromised mental health, and other social problems. Some sex workers certainly do contend with these issues, just like their peers who have no sex industry experience, yet it is problematic to focus on these issues if doing so precludes portraying sex workers in the full and complex contexts of their lives.

Such problems of representation stem in large part from the fact that knowledge production about the sex industry remains largely shaped by academia, which itself is subject to market forces that allocate funding, resources, and jobs according to perceived demands for specific areas of study. One example of how these market forces impact academia is the popularity of criminology and its practitioner-focused subsidiary, criminal justice, as an area of study among university students. The increasing corporatization of higher education along a market model in many parts of the world envisions tuition-paying university students as consumers whose preferences help determine the disciplines targeted for university administrators' investment in academic positions, institutional funding, and other forms of support. Larger numbers of tuition-paying students, in other words, result in more faculty positions in certain fields, larger numbers of graduate students choosing areas of study they hope will guarantee them future tenure-track or otherwise permanent academic work, and resulting research targeted toward "high-growth" disciplines.

Available grant funding also plays a significant role in the politics of knowledge production, with government, foundation, or other institutional priorities shaped in part by popular conceptions of social problems. Chapter 18, "Globally circulating discourses on the sex industry: a focus on three world regions," discusses this issue at length by exploring the complex historical, cultural, and economic forces that inform knowledge production. Many contributors to this Handbook acknowledge the explicitly political nature of the research enterprise, which takes unique national, regional, and global forms. Yet, as many contributions to this volume illustrate, the research enterprise itself is also informed by globally circulating conceptions regarding human rights, best practices, development, and activist concerns that often extend far beyond the scope of the sex industry.

The Handbook reflects the multidisciplinary state of the field by encompassing a wide range of academic fields that, taken together, represent the extraordinary diversity of both the sex industry and research about it. Readers will find representatives from a broad spectrum of social and behavioral sciences, humanities, activism, art, and practitioner-oriented fields, including sociology, anthropology, psychology, human geography, history, sex worker rights organizing, film studies, public health, gender studies, literature, creative writing, criminology, law, urban planning, social work, and sex therapy. The fact that so many academic, creative, and practitioner-oriented fields have an interest in the sex industry underscores both the importance of the research presented here and the significant role played by context in shaping it.

Context matters

As is evident in the depth and breadth of chapters featured here, the field of sex industry research continues to expand in ways that emphasize the complex intricacies of social, economic, and other phenomena at work in the contexts under study. Context indisputably does matter, both in shaping or otherwise regulating the sex industry's everyday operations and in determining the conditions in which individual sex workers earn an income. Much contemporary research in this field accordingly and appropriately emphasizes the importance of carefully examining the specific contextual aspects of different sex industry forms. These generally include analytical attention to the venue type, geographic area, legislative and/or regulatory framework, and cultural norms.

Numerous studies address significant, and important, distinguishing characteristics with respect to where, between whom, and other particularities of how transactional sex occurs. Critical attention to sex industry venues tends to focus on differences between indoor and outdoor settings of varying legal statuses, costs, points of commonality among those who work, patronize, or act as third parties within them, and the role state agents, services providers, and others play in regulating such venues. Research also carefully distinguishes between how these venue-based differences manifest in specific geographic regions, especially with respect to how legal or regulatory frameworks both intersect with and reflect the cultural, political, religious, or other norms that govern everyday life within them.

Devoting analytical attention to these differences is essential to understanding the interplay between various sex industry forms and the cultures in which they operate. Yet such intent focus on these specificities may overemphasize the uniqueness of each research site in ways that isolate and compartmentalize forms of knowledge by preventing meaningful comparisons. Such focused intensity risks falling into the kind of paralytic academic solipsism that prohibits ready translation of empirical research into clear and concise policy recommendations. Context matters a great deal to sex industry researchers, yet the policymakers who are accountable to the public—whoever and wherever they are—tend to want easily implemented solutions to what is often cast as "the problem" of sex industry regulation. Researchers must avoid becoming so mired in context that they are unable to speak clearly and confidently to policymakers about the implications of their findings or lose sight of the larger theoretical implications of their work.

Academia tends to discourage generalizations in favor of focusing on highly specialized findings that distinguish, sometimes in relatively superficial ways, one study from the next. Yet uniting so many different studies from such diverse geographic and cultural areas in the Handbook emphasizes that there are, in fact, many shared circumstances and experiences even within and across the tremendous diversity of the global sex industry. Researchers may disagree, sometimes vehemently, about the particularities of these circumstances and experiences, but most would acknowledge that five important similarities constitute a "red thread" through a vast labyrinth of studies conducted on the global sex industry.

First, research consistently indicates that sex workers across the extremely diverse spectrum of sex industry sectors all face stigmatization and marginalization that often negatively impact their overall well-being. Such negative impacts take social, interpersonal, and legal forms that can include isolation from peers outside the sex industry, the psychological toll of hiding sex work involvement from family members or other loved ones, and, for those who work in criminalized sectors, the ever-present threat of arrest, incarceration, or deportation. Some individuals certainly regard their sex industry involvement as a career choice consciously made over other attractive work opportunities available to them, but economic need generally remains the strongest determinant of sex industry participation. As a result, the lower-autonomy, lower-income sex industry sectors disproportionately involve people who are marginalized because of racism, xenophobia, sexism, transphobia, and other forms of socio-economic exclusion.

Second, regulatory approaches to the sex industry have a direct and far-reaching impact on the labor conditions, practices, and associated risks sex workers face as they go about earning a living. Part of the reason that legal and regulatory approaches to the sex industry are subject to so much debate is because of the immediate consequences they pose to sex workers, especially when such approaches derive from prevailing moral norms or assumptions and are enforced unevenly, with those sex workers who have higher education and class status less likely to work in venues where they face arrest and other negative sanctions. While all legal and regulatory approaches to sex work present potential costs and benefits, research consistently demonstrates that criminalization only further marginalizes sex workers worldwide by relegating their activities to less safe and less well-lit areas where they exercise limited autonomy and fear arrest. Sex workers in legal settings may also struggle with these issues if they lack appropriate documents or health certificates, creating a de facto form of criminalization.

Third, sex worker activists worldwide continue to advocate for human rights approaches that seek to move beyond outdated "risk group" paradigms by shining a bright spotlight on the legal, political, and cultural stances that often pose the greatest risks to sex workers' well-being.

Contemporary sex workers' rights movements emphasize the multiple concerns that sex workers face, including pervasive stigmatization leading to issues with child custody, relationships, difficulties finding other work, and also the myriad dangers to health, safety, and autonomy associated with criminalization. In this view, the real risks come not from sex work itself but from the conditions imposed by stigma, social marginality, and criminalization. These arguments are significant because sex worker rights activism has significantly shaped the field of sex industry research, including by encouraging researchers, and the funders that support their work, to shift the discourse away from health-related vulnerabilities to focus on other relevant issues.

Fourth, concerns about sex trafficking now dominate prevailing global discourse about and approaches to sex industry regulation as part of a criminal justice paradigm that neatly collapses sex industry participants into victims/criminals in ways that do not reflect reality for the majority of sex workers. Law enforcement, social services providers, and many others throughout the world now commonly refer to sex trafficking, with its connotations of coercion and victimization, to describe voluntary sex workers, who are thought to engage in transactional sex because of negative psycho-social experiences. This shift toward viewing sex workers as victims/criminals has taken place in the context of increased global concerns about securitization, which in turn subjects sex workers to increased socio-legal scrutiny and mandatory therapeutic intervention in the name of rescuing them. Such discourse also positions sex workers who are criminalized as "foreign prostitutes," "addicts," "street people," or "unwanted migrants," as especially in need of such therapeutic interventions.

Fifth, calls for evidence-based law and policy, while well intentioned, neglect the reality that those tasked with the sex industry's regulation are almost always able to mobilize evidence that supports their position. Ideology produces its own evidence, especially when government and other major granting agencies support avenues of inquiry in research that are likely to substantiate the status quo. Neo-abolitionists are accordingly able to mobilize ample evidence in support of their claims that the sex industry is morally reprehensible and inherently abusive, just as some sex worker rights activists can present a significant body of research that presents sex work as a space of relative freedom within what, for many sex workers, are a highly constrained set of economic alternatives.

All Handbook contributors, and hopefully all sex industry researchers, support the goal of evidence-based policymaking. However, it is important to acknowledge that "evidence" typically derives from prevailing discourses and their associated performative powers. Such powers may derive from a variety of sources, including highly lauded and often country-specific models for sex industry regulation in Europe or the United Nations Sustainable Development Goals that help to guide policies about sex workers in the developing world. Context does matter, quite profoundly, given the political, legal, and socio-cultural structures that both create and inform the global sex industry. Yet researchers, activists, policymakers, and others concerned for whatever reasons with the sex industry must find ways to unite the wealth of shared knowledge they possess in order to critically examine the lessons offered by their respective municipal, national, or regional experiences with sex industry. Doing so has great potential to assist with the emergence of law, policy, and associated practices in productive ways, meant to benefit all members of society.

Organization and scope of the book

The scope and content of this volume acknowledges the importance of context without losing sight of the pressing need to highlight commonalities of both experience and circumstance among many sex workers throughout the world. The Handbook is accordingly organized around the most pressing questions of interest to sex industry researchers, policymakers, sex workers, and activists today. Carefully selected by the co-editors after our many respective years in the field, the Handbook tackles eight specific areas of inquiry associated with questions that remain relatively unexplored: the research enterprise, socio-legal practices, global knowledge flows, families and intimate relationships, clients, third parties, cultural representations, and technologies. To address these areas, the chapters that follow unite an unprecedentedly expansive international collection of empirical, theoretical, and artistic pieces to actively make a statement about the field of sex industry research and its future.

The eight thematic chapter sections are preceded by concise introductions that contextualize the questions posed in each within the history of global sex industry research past and present while also exploring possibilities for future research. These concise introductions also attend to how the cultural, temporal, and geographic specificities of each chapter's featured case study reflect enduring themes in this field of research while also offering fresh perspectives on them. Perhaps most importantly, these introductions emphasize how, taken together, these case studies contribute to global understandings of the sex industry with a view to making meaningful contributions to this burgeoning field of study.

Part I, "The research enterprise," addresses fundamental questions regarding what aspects of the sex industry are empirically knowable given the myriad contextual and individual elements at work within it, including the institutional and social forces that shape what scholars in this field can accomplish. This section sets the stage for subsequent sections through case studies that critically examine the politics of how researchers obtain research funding, engage with theoretical frames designed to elicit new perspectives, resolve ethical dilemmas, and carry out collaborative or participatory projects with sex workers. This section's case studies include contributions from researchers living and working in Ghana, the United States, Portugal, Japan, Canada, and New Zealand underscoring the universality of the issues addressed.

In Part II, "Socio-legal practices," contributors who have conducted research in Nigeria, the Netherlands, New Zealand, South Africa, Belgium, and Germany, explore the factors that account for significant gaps between empirical evidence and socio-legal practice in some countries, regions, or contexts but not others. This section also questions whether certain socio-legal practices facilitate certain types of living and working conditions for people involved in transactional sex and examines how sex industry participants manage the impacts of such practices on their everyday lives. By critically engaging with these issues, this section provides crucial real-world insights into the complex dynamics involved in translating law and policy into practice.

Part III, "Global knowledge flows," builds directly upon the previous two sections through critical analysis of the intersections between the construction of knowledge and the socio-legal practices that emerge from certain ideologies. As such, this section raises questions regarding what fosters the development and global circulation of "best practices" for sex industry knowledge production and regulatory instruments. Drawing upon case studies of Argentina, Nepal, South Africa, Brazil, Russia, England, and Wales, as well as a regional comparison of how these knowledge flows maneuver through and between Europe, the Americas, and sub-Saharan Africa, this section also examines how various actors respond to practical and ethical questions that arise from these global knowledge circuits.

In Part IV, "Families and intimate relationships," chapters document how people in the sex industry financially and emotionally support their children, family members, and intimate partners. This section also examines how legal, policy, and available support structures inform, constitute, or otherwise shape these relationships as well as the forms of support that sex industry workers receive from family members, intimate partners, and others. Case studies derive from research in Chile, Denmark, Thailand, Brazil, Spain, Denmark, and the United States, with many carefully attuned to the multiple forms of family and intimate relationships in sex workers' lives.

Part V, "Clients," unites research from Brazil, Australia, the United States, Nigeria, and China to examine the cultural, interpersonal, individual, and socio-legal factors that motivate sex industry patronage and govern the interactions that take place between sex workers and their clients. This section also examines how sex workers select and/or cultivate various forms of relationships with their clients with a view to more fully understanding the dynamics of such relationships. Chapters also question some of the assumptions made by researchers, policymakers, and others about the nature of sex worker–client interactions, with a view to understanding how the significant stigmatization of the sex industry impacts those who patronize it.

Part VI, "Third parties," builds upon the preceding two sections' explorations of sex workers' socio-economic and affective ties to analyze the role of third parties in organizing and managing transactional sexual exchanges. It asks whether certain types of third-party relationships and/or the socio-legal contexts in which they operate influence sex industry working conditions in certain ways. Engaging with research findings from the Amazon, Russia, Poland, Switzerland, and the United States, this section sheds light on a misunderstood and maligned sector of the sex industry.

Part VII, "Cultural representations," engages with historical and contemporary research from colonial West Africa, Australia, Thailand, Brazil, the United Kingdom, and Norway. Chapters in this section examine how literary, artistic, cinematic, and other cultural products historically represented sex workers and the industry of which they are a part. In so doing, these analyses remain carefully attuned to what these representations reveal about the cultural and historical contexts that produced them by examining how and in what ways these artistic and other cultural products mobilize transactional sexual exchange for socio-political, rights-based, religious, or other purposes.

Part VIII, "Technologies," unites research from Italy, the United Kingdom, India, and the United States to address one of the more recent developments in sex industry research with many exciting possibilities for future avenues of inquiry. Chapters in this section explore how increasingly pervasive technologies have facilitated new sex industry forms as well as how such technologies shape identities, foster increased visibility, and potentially increased surveillance of sex industry participants. Likewise, these chapters also examine how the sex industry has itself facilitated technological innovation.

Taken together, the Handbook's eight sections present a comprehensive portrait of the state of sex industry research. No other volume to date has explored such diverse issues in a focused manner that sets a clear agenda for the future of the field.

2

Sex industry research

Key theories, methods, and challenges

Susan Dewey, Isabel Crowhurst, and Chimaraoke Izugbara

Introduction

This chapter offers a "state-of-the-field" introduction to sex industry research. It is written to familiarize graduate students, professional practitioners, and others new to the field with key theories and methods in a burgeoning area of academic inquiry. Specialist readers will also find the chapter helpful as it concisely describes the key theories, methods, and challenges that span the vast array of academic disciplines that critically engage with the diverse global practices and actors comprising the sex industry. The first section reviews the various feminist, Marxist, social movement, queer, sociological, social psychological, and public health perspectives that most commonly inform research in this field. Next, this chapter introduces and provides examples of survey, ethnographic, participatory, arts-based, digital, textual, social mapping, archival, and clinical methods that are essential components of research designs in the field. The final section engages with the socio-political and institutional gatekeeping, mutual mistrust generated by enduring ideological silos, and under-acknowledged hierarchies that present challenges for research in the field and discusses how researchers endeavor to overcome them.

Theories

In this chapter we explore seven key theoretical perspectives that we have identified as central in defining and framing inquiries into commercial sex over the past four decades since critical engagement with the sex industry first emerged in a systematic manner. True to its Greek root word—*theoria*, meaning to see and to know—theory provides a set of key perspectives that guide the interpretation and study of data, allowing researchers to unite different theories as a mode of critical inquiry. Theory need not over-determine approaches to research in a dogmatic manner, as all sound theoretical perspectives encompass sufficient analytical space for application to data in unique ways. While sex industry researchers utilize a wide array of theories, a vast majority of studies frame their insights using one or more feminist, Marxist, social movement, queer, sociological, social psychological, or public health theoretical perspectives.

Feminist theorists generally take positions on a continuum between radical and liberal approaches to their studies of the sex industry and the manifestations of the sex-gender system operative within it.

Radical feminist theorists advocate for a fundamental restructuring of society to eliminate patri-archy, generally defined as a political economy of gender-based structural inequalities that create and sustain women's subservient status to men. Some radical feminists regard the sex industry as the ultimate manifestation of women's oppression by men and accordingly advocate for its aboli-tion (MacKinnon, 2011). Other radical feminists, known as sex-radical (or sex-positive) feminists, argue that the kind of "outlaw" sexuality expressed by some sex industry participants constitutes a form of destabilizing resistance to patriarchy and the restrictive heteronormative ethos it supports (Rubin, 2011). Liberal feminists regard sex work as a choice made within broader restrictions on women's socio-economic and sexual agency, a central tenet of the sex worker rights movement (Leigh, 1997). Liberal feminists generally acknowledge commercial sex as a form of labor that represents the marketization of women's sexuality as an aspect of the complex contextual processes that constitute the social reproduction of gender (Wardlow, 2004).

For Marxists, the sex industry is a manifestation of the capitalist oppression that creates and sustains the class inequality that is essential to the operations of the capitalist market economy. Engels used prostitution both as a metaphor for the exploitative nature of capitalist exchange and the bourgeois family that emerged within the Industrial Revolution, both of which sought to control women, the laboring classes, and other oppressed groups, referring to marriage and monogamy as "inseparable opposites, poles of the same social conditions" (Engels, 1884, p. 92). Marxists regard the sex industry as central to the sustenance of the political economy of capi-talism through a specific form of labor exploitation that produces and reproduces women as a subjugated socio-economic group (Beloso, 2012). By envisioning the sex industry as an aspect of capitalist exploitation, Marxists conceptualize it as part of the same illusory framework that characterizes other "free" and "equal" commodity transactions under capitalism (Bhattacharya, 2016). Considering the political economy of sexual labor and desire has proved particularly use-ful for scholars interested in linking global processes to the sex industry's existence, particularly as a response to national economic crises and the reproduction of colonial and postcolonial inequities (Pope, 2005; Allen, 2007).

Social movements theorists tap into more recent Marxist interpretations that build on the clarion call for all oppressed peoples to build a collective movement to end their oppression. While traditional Marxism envisaged that sex work would end with socialism or communism, more recent radical social movements call for new rules of engagement with sex work by drawing on this oppression-based argument. This approach envisions sex workers as political actors who can advance their human rights and overcome stigmatization and marginalization through collective action. Central to this perspective is the notion that sex industry participants are both agentive and authorities on their own experiences—as reflected in "nothing about us without us," the popular sex worker rights maxim regarding research and other forms of representation—and that the development of a collective sex worker identity and networks of peer support are essential components of generating positive social change (Mgbako, 2016). This theoretical perspective actively supports sex workers as producers of knowledge, with the understanding that no group understands the issues facing sex workers better than sex workers themselves (Empower Foundation, 2012). Social movements theorists envision sex workers and researchers as partners in raising awareness about socio-economic injustices and developing strategies to facilitate long-term transformative social and legal change (Graca, Goncalves, & Martin, 2017).

Queer theory envisions sexuality as a social construction and sexual identity as a performance that reflects dominant cultural norms regarding gender and sexuality, with great potential for social and sexual liberation existing in transgression from or rejection of such norms (Sedgwick, 1990; Edelman, 2004). Queer theorists emphasize the importance of considering the various meanings ascribed to sex work, which for some sex workers are a space of validation and personal freedom from constraints experienced in homophobic family, neighborhood, and national contexts (Mai, 2012). Queer theory opens a vista in which "sex worker" is not an affixed identity but a fluid performance in which we are all participants; in so doing, this theoretical approach encourages considerations of the full spectrum of experiences among people in the sex industry. Hence scholars have argued for the importance of considering the experiences of male, transgender, and other queer-identified sex workers—despite their small numbers relative to women in sex work—as a means to shift dominant academic discourse away from the decades-old debates about consent, coercion, abuse, self-esteem, and risk that remain prevalent in discussions of women in sex work (Comte, 2014). Queer theorists likewise note how critical engagement with the cultural forces that sexualize some bodies, and not others, offers great potential to lend theoretical insights into the sex-gender system as a whole and how particular bodies are sites for its contestation (Smith, 2012).

Theories of stigma stem largely from sociologist Erving Goffman's pioneering work on how individuals manage devalued or discredited identities in society (Goffman, 1963), which occurred at a time when many sociologists began a shift toward understanding what, then as now, many sociologists and criminologists referred to as "deviance." Sociological theories of deviance likewise remain important today, with the academic journal *Deviant Behavior* publishing many highly acclaimed studies in this field. Contemporary theories often coalesce around why women enter and/or leave the sex industry, the sources, forms, and dynamics of sex work-related stigma; sex workers' strategies for managing stigma, relationships between sex workers and clients, and the impact of sex work on other aspects of sex workers' lives. This body of knowledge derived from theorizing on stigma emphasizes that individuals negotiate their stigmatized identities in conjunction with dominant cultural constructions of their work as well as cultural ideals regarding gender and sexual norms (Hannem & Bruckert, 2016). Stigma has been theorized as intersectional (Levey & Pinsky, 2014) and as negatively impacting sex workers' labor conditions, health, and safety (Benoit, Jansson, Smith, & Flagg, 2017), and ability to seek out needed services, such as health care (Lazarus et al., 2012).

Social psychological theories of the sex industry focus on how individuals' conceptions of themselves and the world change in response to their treatment by, and social interactions with, other people. Scholars with this theoretical orientation tend to focus on reasons for entering or leaving prostitution and patterns of interpersonal interactions that shape the lives of people in the sex industry. This includes consideration of sex workers' experiences before and after their involvement in the industry, often with the goal of offering models or recommendations for assisting individual sex workers who seek therapeutic treatment or other services. Such theorists acknowledge a "complex structure of causation" (Sinha, 2015) comprising limiting factors such as constrained socio-economic opportunities or supports along with attracting factors such as flexible hours, higher pay, and other benefits impossible to obtain without performing sex work. Hence this theoretical focus frames some of the patterns at work in individual experiences of entering and working in the sex industry as negative or otherwise problematic yet requiring social services or other assistance that is unavailable (Firmin, Lee, Firmin, Deakin, & Holmes, 2013). Individual, relational, structural, and cultural barriers to leaving the sex industry also emerge in many studies using this theoretical perspective, with exit becoming more difficult due to entrenched marginalization and the fact that other jobs do not pay as well, which is often a motivation for sex industry participation in the first place (Baker, Dalla, & Williamson, 2010; Cimino, 2012). These theories engage with social work approaches that focus on how to help sex workers either leave or stay safe in the profession, and offer a non-oppressive focus on how to mobilize sex workers' agency to support sex workers in making decisions for themselves, rather than traditional social work framings of sex work as a social problem resulting from lack of opportunities and individual maladjustment.

Public health theories examine the sex industry through a lens that focuses on protecting and improving the health of communities and understanding the patterns and causes at work in health-related disparities. Understanding how to best prevent disease transmission or worsening health conditions among individuals with particular characteristics—who are generally referred to as "populations" and "risk groups" in public health's prevention theory parlance—is the primary driving force behind such inquiries (Rose, 1985; Doyle, Furey, & Flowers, 2006). Public health theories explore the barriers and supports that facilitate or compromise individual health through work with individuals in contexts that bear a higher disease burden relative to the general population, leading to considerations of the social determinants of health at work in those contexts (Rhodes et al., 2012). Taking health risks and potential interventions to foster the self-efficacy, practical knowledge, and situational changes thought necessary to reduce them as its primary targets, public health theories examine both individual and structural factors in sex workers' health-related decision-making (Safika, Levy, & Johnson, 2013; Vasylyeva, Friedman, Gensburg, & Smyrnov, 2017).

Researchers and activists alike frequently unite these seven major theoretical perspectives in designing research and analyzing data in ways that promote novel interpretations of empirical phenomena related to the sex industry. Marxist feminists, for instance, may locate the feminization of poverty and women's reduced earning power relative to men as the central "problem" in prostitution. A researcher interested in how the development of collective sexual identities exerts a positive impact among members of queer communities may unite social movement theory and queer theory to examine related research questions. Likewise, uniting the lenses of social psychology and public health might prove very effective for a research team concerned with the prevalence of violence in sex workers' lives in order to determine long-term interventions to reduce it. In all instances, theories are perspectives meant to guide, rather than determine, a study's research design and interpretation of results.

Methods

Here we discuss nine primary methods that we identified as structuring the mode of inquiry of sex industry researchers who, across a wide range of academic disciplines, use them to answer research questions. Survey, ethnographic, participatory, arts-based, digital, textual, social mapping, archival, and clinical methods all provide a set of systematic tools to guide researchers throughout data collection, a process that reflects the origin of the word "methods" in the Greek *hodos*, meaning path. Researchers typically select methods that reflect a theoretical or discipline-specific framework, such that those working in public health are much more likely to adopt clinical methods than those in the humanities, which will likely adopt textual or arts-based approaches. Methods can be either qualitative in their focus on a phenomenon's substance or scope or quantitative in their exploration of a phenomenon's frequency or extent, or a mixture of both qualitative and quantitative approaches applied to the issue under study. This section focuses exclusively on prevailing methods for data collection rather than methods that sex industry researchers utilize to access research sites, sample participants, or analyze data, since these topics are discussed at length elsewhere (Dewey & Zheng, 2013).

Survey methods differ with respect to the amount of time involved, flexibility available in terms of subject matter, and amount of direction provided by the participant and the researcher. These methods occupy a spectrum that includes, on one extreme, life histories in which one or a few participants set the tone by choosing how to discursively represent their life trajectories, to another extreme of structured questionnaires that focus on gathering a specific set of researcher-determined variables from a large group. Structured questionnaires may be administered anonymously, whereas semi-structured interviews and other survey methods usually involve a researcher and participants meeting face to face to discuss the subject of research for an extended period of time. Increasingly, however, researchers in this field are using digital-mediated technologies such as texting, Skype, and instant messaging to conduct rich qualitative interviews with their participants involved in the sex industry (see for example Rand, Chapter 54 in this volume). This not only facilitates anonymity, but it also reflects the expanding online commercial sex sector.

Structured surveys can be useful in assessing public opinion about the sex industry, such as prevailing perceptions regarding whether a history of victimization informs general public assessments of sex workers' culpability or blameworthiness for engaging in stigmatized labor (Menaker & Franklin, 2013). These surveys can also collect large amounts of information around a specific topic, such as whether age of entry into prostitution impacts women's sex trade experiences overall relative to other variables, such as race, motherhood, and social class (Martin, Hearst, & Widome, 2010). Semi-structured interviews emphasize individual experiences with a particular issue, whereas focus groups highlight perspectives on the prevalence of shared experiences as peers validate or contradict each other's statements. Both approaches may demonstrate a coalescence of institutional and interpersonal forms of marginalization by using the participants' own words (Scorgie et al., 2013).

Ethnographic methods are long term, often extending into a year or more of immersion in ways that seek to mimic as closely as possible the conditions of everyday life for research participants by habitually visiting, residing, or even working in the sex industry venues they study. Ethnographic research closely mirrors the socialization process that takes place through observation and experience in other arenas of life, thus allowing for validation and corroboration of results by observing individuals in multiple social contexts over a period of time (Zheng, 2009). Ethnography captures the sex industry's nuances with its keen attention to how the shifting social relationships at work within it reveal broader cultural anxieties, for instance about migrant and national identities (Ndjio, 2017). The long-term nature of this method also emphasizes the disconnections between popular perceptions and sex workers' lived experiences, as is the case in a great deal of ethnographic research on migration and sex work (Parreñas, 2011; Plambech, 2017). Yet the meaning of ethnographic participation is also changing in response to the burgeoning online sex industry sector, with more researchers focused on Internet sex markets where they conduct participant observation without any physical presence.

Participatory research methods approach researchers and community members as equal partners in praxis, defined as the process by which theory or ideology becomes realized in the form of concrete action. Sometimes also called community-based participatory action research, action research, mutual inquiry, or feminist participatory research, these methods are very time-consuming because of the consensus-building required to work across what can be very different lived experiences and circumstances, prompting many researchers to wait until after tenure or other stable points in their careers to pursue such work. Participatory methods prioritize work *with*, rather than *on*, sex workers as a means to democratize knowledge production and also as a means to gain deeper knowledge of sex workers' lives and the dynamics of their work (van der Meulen, 2011). Such methods may prove fruitful by actively involving sex workers in guiding, developing, and conducting research on issues that directly impact them and offer potential for interventions, including occupational health and safety concerns, while emphasizing to researchers the numerous privacy and confidentiality concerns that sex workers have about participating in research (Shannon et al., 2007). These methods also prompt researchers to carefully consider the composition and boundaries of the community under study, as significant stigma discourages sex workers from collectively working together, and ideally facilitate a greater sense of cohesive identity once the participatory project is complete (Graca et al., 2017).

Arts-based methods examine and analyze aspects of research participants' experiences through visual, theatrical, written, or performative creative works. Researchers who use arts-based methods often regard them as especially inclusive and accessible because while not everyone can easily read and interpret the results of research presented in a highly specialized field, almost anyone can appreciate visual, textual, and performative representations of a social issue. Arts-based methods also give individuals who are part of stigmatized groups an opportunity to come together and validate their set of shared experiences through creative expression (Clover, 2011). Projects that work with sex workers to use photography, whether exclusively or with other methods, to document the everyday minutiae of sex workers' lives resist dominant cultural constructions that often dehumanize sex workers and deny them the ability to define themselves (Capous Desyllas, 2013; Cheng, 2013). Performance art, whether derived from interviews with sex workers or developed directly with them, can evocatively express safety and other concerns (O'Neill, 2002), while artistic representations of the body's experiences with compromised health through body mapping can be a powerful tool of community mobilization and health advocacy (Orchard, 2017).

Digital methods use technology to study virtual social networks, online media platforms, and other electronic means of transmitting information. Such methods can also include data mining to track the frequency with which individuals in specific cities or regions utilize online sex industry fora (Cunningham & Shah, 2014) and can also comprise more contemporary versions of traditional archival methods that utilized paper copies of police records, court documents, and social work case files that today are digitized in many countries. Researchers use digital methods to examine online fora where sex workers' clients congregate by posting their experiences with providers of sexual services and avoiding arrest or negative police encounters as a means to provide advice to one another (Holt & Blevins, 2006). Online discussions organized by and for sex workers' clients play an important role in socializing new clients as well with respect to norms for conduct that purchasers of sexual services ought to expect or observe (Horswill & Weitzer, 2018). Other digital methods include the observation of online sex industry performers to ascertain how they attract, retain, and interact with their clients (Weiss, 2017).

Textual methods critically examine how language—often referred to as discourse—constructs and/or advances particular perspectives about sex work through examinations of such representations in mass media, interpersonal communication, public policy or law/municipal ordinances, research reports or other documents for public consumption produced by activist groups, governments, or others. Juxtaposing sex workers' descriptions of their own lives with dominant cultural portrayals can identify significant disconnects, such as the differences between constructions of trafficked victims and the actual experiences of undocumented migrants (Jacobsen & Skilbrei, 2010). Content analysis of advertising for sexual services can help to illuminate how language, cultural framings, and visual representations generate or sustain particular inequalities of gender, race, and class, as is evident in analyses of sex tourism marketing materials (Gezinski, Karandikar, Levitt, & Ghaffarian, 2016). Likewise, systematic analyses of how sex workers share accounts of their work experiences with colleagues and others can offer meaningful insights into interventions and outreach measures designed to assist sex workers (Roche, Neaigus, & Miller, 2005).

Social mapping methods explore how physical spaces and the relationships that take place within and across them—including their governance through zoning, licensing, and policing practices—contribute to or influence the subject of study. In the form of social network analysis, this method can also focus on how relationships between people shape patterns with respect to various forms of social relationships, violence, and disease transmission. Working with participants to physically map out the spatial practices that surround the sale and purchase of sex in "red-light" areas provides insight into the conditions surrounding these exchanges and accordingly improve outreach or regulatory efforts (Atkins & Laing, 2012). Identifying "hot spots" for social interactions in which sex workers report client violence or being pressured for sex without a condom can likewise draw attention to policing and zoning practices that increase sex workers' risk of contracting infections (Shannon et al., 2009). Such insights can also be gleaned by examining the configurations and expressions of the various forms of structural, symbolic, and interpersonal violence experienced in indoor and outdoor settings among sex workers during their work and free time (Ribeiro & Sacramento, 2005).

Archival methods examine original records produced by institutions, governments, or other entities during a particular time period of interest to the researcher in order to provide insights on the historical processes that informed particular constructions of, and responses to, the sex industry. These records typically were first generated by state authorities, such as police, health services, or municipalities, or by third-sector organizations led and staffed by private citizens, and accordingly require interpretation within the context that produced them. Researchers using archival methods may examine colonial documents, such as social workers' records, government reports, police files, newspaper articles, and travel accounts, to determine the insights that particular approaches to the sex industry offer into relations between colonizers and colonized (Tambe, 2005). Archival methods also offer insights into how war shifts legal and popular discourse on prostitution, particularly with respect to perceptions about threats posed to local women by enemy forces, soldiers' sexual practices, and state security as a whole (Roger & Debruyne, 2016). Examining municipal government records related to the sex industry's regulation, including practices of taxation and legal measures used to enforce order, can reflect significant regional differences in how state approaches to sex industry regulation reflect the institutionalization of dominant gender norms in ways that transform the state via official endorsement of these norms (Remick, 2014).

Clinical methods assess a variety of issues related to health, including the prevalence of particular health issues, factors, and correlates associated with such prevalence, and test the effectiveness of health-related interventions among a group of people with shared characteristics. Such methods often utilize questionnaires and health screenings with large numbers of participants, necessitating the division of these large groups into smaller ones, as occurs in randomized controlled trials that arbitrarily assign individuals to two or more groups to determine outcomes of interest to the researchers. Researchers using clinical methods may adopt a cohort approach, also referred to as a prospective observational study, in which a study follows a group of sex workers over time to investigate correlations between particular variables, such as migration and health (Goldenberg et al., 2014). Cross-sectional studies utilize observations conducted with a defined population of sex workers over a specific time interval to measure particular health outcomes, such as associations between sex workers' collective agency and utilization of public health services (Parimi, Mishra, Tucker, & Saggurti, 2012). Another common public health method is the case control study, which compares the odds of a health experience among two or more groups using interviews, medical records or both, such as the likelihood that sex workers face a higher risk of a particular health condition than their peers who are not involved in sex work (Alvarado-Esquivel et al., 2017).

All nine of these methods typically employ a case study approach that focuses research attention on a particular sex industry venue type in a specific city or region. Depending on the academic discipline, personal preferences, and other factors, some researchers work in one geographic area and/or with one sex industry type for many years or even throughout their entire career, whereas others explore many different ones within the context of their broader scholarly interests in health, social inequalities, migration, or other issues. Researchers adopt a combination of methods following careful consideration of their research questions, sites, or particular aspects of the phenomena under study. For example, a researcher interested in facilitating sex workers' representations of themselves to counter dominant cultural representations might use a combination of arts-based and textual methods, while a public health study could incorporate clinical and participatory methods to determine the best means to reduce incidence of health problems among sex workers. Yet even the most carefully planned research design will face challenges in the course of its implementation, making it useful to reflect on how sex industry researchers confront and overcome these challenges.

Confronting and overcoming challenges

Even the most carefully selected theories and methods cannot protect sex industry researchers from some of the most common ethical and practical challenges they must confront and overcome in their work. Foremost among these challenges are socio-political and institutional gatekeeping, mutual mistrust generated by enduring ideological silos, and under-acknowledged hierarchies.

Socio-political and institutional gatekeeping

Socio-political and institutional limitations on meaningful, long-term collaboration between sex workers, researchers, and other potential community partners can undermine or even sabotage the potential for empirical inquiry that could inform evidence-based law and policy. These limitations are a form of gatekeeping designed to reproduce the ideological status quo on sex work and take numerous forms, but most profoundly manifest in restrictions imposed by the dynamics of institutional research and the granting of disproportionate financial and professional rewards to researchers who endorse prevailing ideological frameworks. Gatekeeping occurs as part of limitations imposed by the research enterprise itself, which is a hierarchically governed system that prioritizes formal credentials and restricted pathways to tenure, promotion, and publication with particularly prestigious journals or presses. The academic enterprise requires that researchers follow these restricted pathways to survive professionally, and be prepared to face institutional dismissal of their work with sex worker rights or other advocacy groups as little more than "volunteering" at best or, at worst, evidence of bias that impedes empirical inquiry.

Sex work-related stigma adheres to research on the subject, as is evident in the ghettoization of sex work research to academic disciplines that further pathologize, even if unintentionally, sex workers as criminal vectors of disease. Consider, for example, how much of sex work research comes from the fields of public health, criminal justice, and criminology, and derives from state or foundation funders concerned primarily with health or the criminal justice system. The availability of funding for particular types of research directly influences research design, methods, and sharing of findings in ways compounded by the existence of divisive camps that force researchers to politically align themselves with a dominant ideological perspective as they conduct their work and share results. We need only "follow the money" to see the powerful ways in which gatekeeping governs sex work research; consider, for instance, the efflorescence of North American and Western European work in the late 1980s and 1990s on street-involved women struggling with addiction, as a result of increased grant funding available for HIV/AIDS research. In sub-Saharan Africa, sex workers also only became a critical population group for research because of the HIV epidemic. While this research was certainly essential to address a public health crisis among some sex workers, the result was a predominant research focus on sex workers' mental and sexual health (Vanwesenbeeck, 2001), with little known about their children, families, and other parts of their lives that sex workers themselves consider far more important than their struggles with addiction and the prostitution they use to support it. The result is an echo chamber of grant funding or institutional support available and subsequent truths produced about the sex industry, to the degree that many funders regard sex workers as the "hard to reach" category. All too often this phrase is but a polite way of conveying its true meaning of "hard to reach from my desk at the university or research institute, where none of my colleagues or friends turn tricks, are incarcerated, or struggle with debilitating addictions or untreated mental health issues." Activist or religious organizations may also practice gatekeeping by demanding rigid philosophical or political alignment with their goals; in such instances, a researcher's response to the question "what are your politics?" may derail the possibility of working together.

Successfully overcoming gatekeeping often begins with asking some potentially difficult questions to clearly ascertain the actors, conditions, and forces with which researchers and sex workers must contend in their work. What are our goals? Who can we work with, and why? Who can we not work with, and why? What are the political consequences of doing this work, especially in academic contexts where collaborative, community-based work can be subject to condescension? The more honest that researchers and sex workers, both between and among themselves, can be about their answers, the more likely they are to succeed in their endeavors. Researchers do need to be willing to do the educational work required to overcome the preconceived notions about sex work held by ethics board members or other institutional figures by demonstrating the cultural norms at work in particular sex work or services provision settings. Accordingly, researchers may consider joining forces to document global, national, and local-institutional ethics board standards as a means to identify new ways to infuse ethical standards for the use of research in evidence-based law and policy initiatives. This may take the form of recommendations for standard, or good, research practices readily translatable to various contexts (Allman & Ditmore, 2009), yet the need to do so emphasizes the highly contested nature of sex for sale.

Researchers and sex workers know that, in most instances, the resources at our disposal will be limited due to the numerous forms that gatekeeping takes and the many contexts in which it manifests. Hence, they must tread very carefully in thinking about how they wish to engage in collaborative or participatory work, what it might involve, and how they intend to navigate potentially challenging issues that may (or may not) be apparent from the outset (van der Meulen, 2011). It may be a good idea to observe relationships between groups and individuals involved in or connected with issues related to transactional sex in the community of interest. Paying close attention to existing difficulties, fractiousness, or other problems can provide researchers with a sense of what potential for collaboration may exist, and which groups or individuals might be best positioned to fully participate in such work (Crowhurst, 2012).

Mutual mistrust generated by enduring ideological silos

Fraught social, legal, and prevailing moral stances on sex work force researchers and sex workers into ideological silos that complicate or even undermine the establishment of sustainable trust and rapport relationships as well as possibilities for social change-oriented dialogue. The result is a tense, and often unspoken, undercurrent of mutual mistrust both between and among researchers and sex workers that stems directly from their various ideological, moral, and culture-bound perspectives on sex work. Commercial sex, like other ways of making a living in the service industry, is a fundamentally economic issue that reflects various forms of structural violence and social exclusion; the most marginalized sex workers are often poor members of historically oppressed groups. It is difficult for academic researchers to establish trust with individuals who feel (and are) consistently marginalized by authority figures who hold powerful sway in their lives, including police, social workers, and other street-level bureaucrats responsible for the daily reinforcement of socio-legal structures.

Sex workers, irrespective of the legal status of commercial sex, are generally well aware of the potential for research to further stigmatize and sustain social prejudices against historically oppressed groups. Hence sex workers may not trust authority for good reason and accordingly choose not to be completely open and forthcoming with researchers (Agustín, 2004), as the decision to do so might include potential for retribution following involuntary or voluntary disclosure of data and segregation into areas that zoning ordinances, policing practices, and poverty render what sex workers themselves regard as unsafe, dilapidated, or isolated working areas. It is likewise difficult for individuals involved in various forms of transactional sex to trust one another or advocate for their rights as a community when they do not regard themselves as sharing anything in common beyond a means of earning a living that they may regard as unsavory. Sex workers also mistrust each other, with those who are most active in rights-based movements sometimes seeking to dissociate themselves from those whose struggles with addiction, homelessness, and violence reify the worst sex industry stereotypes and potentially undermine their political cause. Grassroots organizations and other activist groups, irrespective of their perspective on the sex industry, make enormous (and often poorly paid or unpaid) demands on their staff, and overburdened individuals, who may dismiss other organizations' or groups' goals and regard academics as privileged parties interested in preserving a status quo that they regard as ethically reprehensible. This is compounded by the reality that some grassroots organizations may reflect deeply embedded street and social hierarchies that regard sex work as a low-status activity, resulting in the sidelining of sex worker rights as peripheral to broader issues considered more relevant to larger numbers of people, such as addictions or incarceration.

Researchers and sex workers alike need to make their agenda and methods transparent from the outset of communications to alleviate mistrust, which unfortunately can sometimes mean being forced to "take sides" before a project even begins. As these relationships deepen over time, researchers need to remain mindful that informed consent to participate in research is an ongoing process, and must remain vigilant to the secretive and sensitive contents that participants reveal to them and seek further consent to include these contents in the research data. Reciprocity plays a critical role both in sustaining long-term collaborative relationships and in alleviating mistrust between and among researchers and sex workers. This includes willingness to engage in the emotional reciprocity of listening and to think creatively about how collaboration can mutually benefit all concerned. Researchers can add legitimacy to sex worker rights groups by providing institutional support and endorsement, just as collaboration with sex workers can add great depth to research and more readily identify practical possibilities for social change.

Researchers and sex workers must be willing to challenge their own assumptions about individual orientations and room to ideologically maneuver within each framework. At a minimum, though, researchers should expect that they will be questioned about their agenda and stance and that sex workers should have input into research in ways that reflect their needs and goals (Stella, 2006; SWOP, n.d.). Sharing previous publications and related materials may help to minimize risks of ideological conflicts later in the research process, but it may also abruptly derail any possibilities for collaborative research. Even before formulating research questions or goals, researchers must be completely honest with themselves about their own ideological stance and prepare for organizations and individuals based on this stance. Recognizing the inevitability of ideological dogmatism among all groups, and being willing to actively listen to all concerned parties before formulating the research, can go a long way to alleviate mistrust. It is essential to avoid idealizing any particular ideological position and be willing to actively listen to what the needs may be in a particular context, from all sides (and determine what sides are available to take), before starting the work.

Under-acknowledged hierarchies

In academic, sex industry, and policy or services provision circles alike, socio-economic hierarchies that regard particular institutions, sex work venues, or approaches as more prestigious or enlightened can replicate and reinforce the very exclusionary forces their members purport to contest. These hierarchies often remain unspoken because it can be uncomfortable to talk about the reasons why particular individuals, and not others, receive invitations to speak or otherwise set the tone of events. Academia, as an intensely hierarchical and sometimes even nepotistic cultural system, rewards association with prestigious universities, publication in particular venues, and grants from specific funders. Work that is "applied," meaning that it is of immediate practical use to people impacted by the issue under study, is generally regarded as the low-status realm of technicians rather than true intellectuals.

These hierarchies are evident among individuals in other professions as well, as are occupational norms that restrict or even outright prohibit dialogue with members of a different group. Such hierarchies also exist among people in sex work due to the fundamental class, citizenship, ethno-racial, and cultural differences that directly inform the experiences of individuals in sex industry venues as well as their abilities to speak openly and affect change. The sex industry, like all occupational sectors, is rife with highly stratified cultural systems comprised of their own norms, procedures, and moral orientations. Sex workers with greater privileges—of citizenship in the country where they reside, of relative choice, and multiple other identity factors—inevitably dominate rights-based movements to the exclusion (however unintentional) of those who lack rights and hence do not feel safe, able, or inclined to engage in activist organizing (Cwikel & Hoban, 2005). Sex worker rights activists, like academics, thus face the very challenging task, and associated accusations, of speaking for less privileged others.

In conjunction with these challenges, hierarchies of expertise inevitably impact the sharing of research results and their interpretation by mass media. Research design demands focus and clear definitions of the social issue or so-called "population" under study yet may also, in subsequent publications or media coverage, generalize the experiences of those featured to all sex workers. Hence, academics who work with street-involved women may be disheartened, but not surprised, to see that journalists may extend their findings from work with this very specific group to all people in the sex industry. The result is that readers in the general audience take away a skewed perception of an inevitably very complex issue; in some instances, these perspectives may derive directly from the dominant ideological framework governing the topic or geographical area of study.

The fact that most researchers have disproportionate access, relative to most sex workers, to wider audiences makes researchers doubly responsible for identifying meaningful categories within sex worker hierarchies as well as ways to convey findings in an indisputably hierarchical academic and other social settings. This raises the question of who gets to define "community," particularly in circumstances where individual sex workers may not identify with each other due to competition and independent work ethos. The environment/venue in which sex work is carried out constitutes a critical element of how women experience it and researchers and participants must respect how individuals self-identify, including when this means that sex workers from different venues do not wish to work together. Occupational segregation occurs along the lines of gender, class, sexual orientation, ethno-racial identity, and socio-economic status, such that sex workers may have little in common with those in other venues and hence not see any kind of collaboration or identification as positive; another way in which the sex industry is indistinct from other capitalist forms.

Hierarchy is almost always inherent to organizations and researchers must remain cognizant of the need to operate within these hierarchies, even while attempting to devise more inclusive visions of the future. Overcoming hierarchies, in some instances, is simply a matter of researchers being willing to also commit themselves to the everyday work of organizing, in ways deemed appropriate by the organization or individuals involved. Collaboration and consultation with sex workers is essential to overcome these hierarchies and ensure full representation of the complexities of their lives, yet practical realities can severely undermine such work because stigmatization and criminalization can threaten to expose and harm sex workers who participate in such research or even make them targets for retribution. Hence no matter how restricted a project might be in terms of funding, team members should be equally rewarded. This can be accomplished through clear discussions about individual goals as a means to identify forms of compensation, which could include: an official title to list on a resume, co-authoring publications or other materials, joint presentations, sharing grant-writing skills, knowledge of where to find low-cost or pro bono legal services, or assistance in navigating social services application processes. Such honesty encourages individuals to draw connections between their own experiences while becoming familiar with the unique skills each member can contribute to the project and encourage working relationships that may help to keep individuals connected to their fellow participants.

Sex workers and researchers can, and regularly do, overcome the significant ethical and practical challenges that the socio-economic and political conditions in which they live and work pose to their collaborative efforts. The work of conveying sex workers' diverse perspectives and experiences on their own terms remains a political act, as research findings do not always correspond with state law or policy and may even indicate the need for significant socio-legal and political change. In this and myriad other ways, engaging or participating in sex work research requires courage, fortitude, and, above all, a willingness to speak the truth to power.

References

Agustín, Laura María. 2004. Alternate Ethics, or: Telling Lies to Researchers. *Research for Sex Work* 7: 6–7.

Allen, Jafari. 2007. Means of Desire's Production: Male Sex Labor in Cuba. *Identities* 14(1/2): 183–202.

Allman, Dan and Melissa Ditmore. 2009. Good Practice for Sex Workers' Participation in Biomedical HIV Prevention Trials. *Research for Sex Work* 7: 3–5.

Alvarado-Esquivel, Cosme, Sanchez-Anguiano, Luis, Hernandez-Tinoco, Jesus, Estrada-Martinez, Sergio, Perez-Alamos, Alma, Ramos-Nevarez, Agar, Cerrillo-Soto, Sandra Margarita, and Guido-Arreola, Carlos Alberto. 2017. *Entamoeba Histolytica* Infection in Female Sex Workers: A Matched Case-Control Study in Durango, Mexico. *Journal of Clinical Medical Research* 9(7): 624–627.

Atkins, Michael and Laing, Mary. 2012. Walking the Beat and Doing Business: Exploring Spaces of Male Sex Work and Public Sex. *Sexualities* 15(5/6): 622–643.

Baker, Lynda, Dalla, Rochelle, and Williamson, Celia. 2010. Exiting Prostitution: An Integrated Model. *Violence Against Women* 16(5): 579–600.

Beloso, Brooke Meredith. 2012. Sex, Work, and the Feminist Erasure of Class. *Signs: Journal of Women in Culture & Society* 38(11): 47–70.

Benoit, Cecilia, Jansson, S. Mikael, Smith, Michaela, and Flagg, Jackson. 2017. Prostitution Stigma and Its Effects on the Working Conditions, Personal Lives, and Health of Sex Workers. *Journal of Sex Research* 55(4/5): 457–471. doi: https://doi-org.libproxy.uwyo.edu/10.1080/00224499.2017.1393652.

Bhattacharya, Malini. 2016. Neither "Free" nor "Equal" Work: A Marxist-Feminist Perspective on Prostitution. *ANTYAJAA: Indian Journal of Women and Social Change* 1(1): 82–92.

Capous Desyllas, Moshoula, 2013. Representations of Sex Workers' Needs and Aspirations: A Case for Arts-Based Research. *Sexualities* 16(7): 772–787.

Cheng, Sealing. 2013. Private Lives of Public Women: Photos of Sex Workers (Minus the Sex) in South Korea. *Sexualities* 16(1/2): 30–42.

Cimino, Andrea. 2012. A Predictive Theory of Intentions to Exit Street-Level Prostitution. *Violence Against Women* 18: 1235–1252.

Clover, Darlene. 2011. Successes and Challenges of Feminist Arts-Based Participatory Methodologies with Homeless/Street-Involved Women in Victoria. *Action Research* 9(1): 12–26.

Comte, Jacqueline. 2014. Decriminalization of Sex Work: Feminist Discourses in Light of Research. *Sexuality & Culture* 18(1): 196–217.

Crowhurst, Isabel. 2012. The Fallacy of the Instrumental Gate? Contextualising the Process of Gaining Access Through Gatekeepers. *International Journal of Social Research Methodology* 16(6): 463–475.

Cunningham, Scott and Manisha Shah. 2014. *Decriminalizing Indoor Prostitution: Implications for Sexual Violence and Public Health.* Washington, DC: National Bureau of Economic Research. http://scunning.com/w20281.pdf.

Cwikel, Julie and Elizabeth Hoban. 2005. Contentious Issues in Research on Trafficked Women Working in the Sex Industry: Study Design, Ethics, and Methodology. *Journal of Sex Research* 42(4): 306–316.

Dewey, Susan and Zheng, Tiantian. 2013. *Ethical Research with Sex Workers: Anthropological Approaches.* New York: Springer.

Doyle, Yvonne, Furey, Ambrose, and J. Flowers. 2006. Sick Individuals and Sick Populations: 20 Years Later. *Journal of Epidemiology & Community Health* 60(5): 396–399.

Edelman, Lee. 2004. *No Future: Queer Theory and the Death Drive.* Durham, NC: Duke University Press.

Empower Foundation. 2012. Hit and Run: Sex Workers' Research on Anti trafficking in Thailand. www.empowerfoundation.org/sexy_file/Hit%20and%20Run%20%20RATSW%20 Eng%20online.pdf.

Engels, Friedrich. 1884. *Origins of the Family, Private Property and the State.* New York: Penguin.

Firmin, Michael, Lee, Alisha, Firmin, Ruth, Deakin, Lauren, and Holmes, Hannah. 2013. Qualitative Perspectives Toward Prostitution's Perceived Lifestyle Addictiveness. *Journal of Behavioral Addictions* 2(4): 231–238.

Gezinski, Lindsay, Karandikar, Sharvari, Levitt, Alexis, and Ghaffarian, Roxane. 2016. "Total Girlfriend Experience": Examining Marketplace Mythologies on Sex Tourism Websites. *Culture, Health & Sexuality* 18(7): 785–798.

Goffman, Erving. 1963. *Stigma: Notes on the Management of Spoiled Identity.* New York: Simon & Schuster.

Goldenberg, Shira, Chettiar, Jill, Nguyen, Paul, Dobrer, Sabina, Montaner, Julio, and Shannon, Kate. 2014. Complexities of Short-Term Mobility for Sex Work and Migration Among Sex Workers: Violence and Sexual Risks, Barriers to Care, and Enhanced Social and Economic Opportunities. *Journal of Urban Health* 91(4): 736–751.

Graca, Marta, Manuela Goncalves, and Antonio Martins. 2017. Action Research with Street-Based Sex Workers and an Outreach Team: A Co-Authored Case Study. *Action Research* 1–29. doi: 10.1177/1476750316685877.

Hannem, Stacey and Bruckert, Chris. 2016. "I'm Not a Pimp but I Play One on TV": The Moral Career and Identity Negotiations of Third Parties in the Sex Industry. *Deviant Behavior* 38(7): 824–836.

Holt, Thomas and Blevins, Kristie. 2006. Examining Sex Work from the Client's Perspective: Assessing Johns Using Online Data. *Deviant Behavior* 28(4): 333–354.

Horswill, Abbe and Weitzer, Ron. 2018. Becoming a Client: The Socialization of Novice Buyers of Sexual Services. *Deviant Behavior* 39(2): 148–158.

Jacobsen, Christine and Skilbrei, May-Len. 2010. "Reproachable Victims?" Representations and Self-Representations of Russian Women Involved in Transnational Prostitution. *Ethnos* 75(2): 190–212.

Lazarus, Lisa, Deering, Kathleen, Nabess, Rose, Gibson, Kate, Tyndall, Mark, and Shannon, Kate. 2012. Occupational Stigma as a Primary Barrier to Health Care for Street-Based Sex Workers in Canada. *Culture, Health, and Sexuality* 14: 139–150.

Leigh, Carol. 1997. Inventing Sex Work. In J. Nagle (Ed.), *Whores and Other Feminists* (pp. 225–231). New York: Routledge.

Levey, Tania and Pinsky, Dina. 2014. A Constellation of Stigmas: Intersectional Stigma Management and the Professional Dominatrix. *Deviant Behavior* 36(5): 347–367.

MacKinnon, Catherine. 2011. Trafficking, Prostitution, and Inequality. *Harvard Civil Rights Civil Liberties Law Review* 46: 271–309.

Mai, Nicola. 2012. The Fractal Queerness of Non-Heteronormative Migrants Working in the UK Sex Industry. *Sexualities* 15(5/6), 570–585.

Martin, Lauren, Hearst, Mary, and Widome, Rachael. 2010. Meaningful Differences: Comparison of Adult Women Who First Traded Sex as a Juvenile Versus as an Adult. *Violence Against Women* 16(11): 1252–1269.

Menaker, Tasha and Franklin, Cortney. 2013. Commercially Sexually Exploited Girls and Participant Perceptions of Blameworthiness: Examining the Effects of Victimization History and Race Disclosure. *Journal of Interpersonal Violence* 28(10): 2024–2051.

Mgbako, Chi. 2016. *To Live Freely in this World: Sex Worker Activism in Africa*. New York: New York University Press.

Ndjio, Basile. 2017. Sex and the Transnational City: Chinese Sex Workers in the West Africa City of Douala. *Urban Studies* 54(4): 999–1015.

O'Neill, Maggie. 2002. Renewed Methodologies for Social Research: Ethno-Mimesis as Performative Praxis. *Sociological Review* 50(1): 75–88.

Orchard, Treena. 2017. *Remembering the Body: Ethical Issues in Body Mapping Research*. New York: Springer.

Parimi, Prabhakar, Mishra, Ram, Tucker, Saroj, and Saggurti, Niranjan. 2012. Mobilizing Community Collectivization Among Female Sex Workers to Promote STI Service Utilization from the Government Healthcare System in Andhra Pradesh, India. *Journal of Epidemiology & Community Health* 66: ii62–ii68.

Parreñas, Rhacel Salazar. 2011. *Illicit Flirtations: Labor, Migration, and Sex Trafficking in Tokyo*. Stanford, CA: Stanford University Press.

Plambech, Sine. 2017. Sex, Deportation, and Rescue: Economies of Migration Among Nigerian Sex Workers. *Feminist Economics* 23(3): 134–159.

Pope, Cynthia. 2005. The Political Economy of Desire: Geographies of Female Sex Work in Havana, Cuba. *Journal of International Women's Studies* 6(2): 99–118.

Remick, Elizabeth. 2014. *Regulating Prostitution in China: Gender and Local Statebuilding 1900–1937*. Stanford, CA: Stanford University Press.

Rhodes, Tim, Wagner, Karla, Strathdee, Steffanee, Shannon, Kate, Davidson, Peter, and Bourgois, Philippe. 2012. Structural Violence and Structural Vulnerability within the Risk Environment: Theoretical and Methodological Perspectives for a Social Epidemiology of HIV Risk Among Injection Drug Users and Sex Workers. In P. O'Campo and J. Dunn (Eds.), *Rethinking Social Epidemiology: Towards a Science of Change* (pp. 205–230). New York: Springer.

Ribeiro, Manuela and Sacramento, Octavio. 2005. Violence Against Prostitutes: Findings of Research in the Spanish-Portuguese Frontier Region. *European Journal of Women's Studies* 12(1): 61–81.

Roche, Brenda, Neaigus, Alan, and Miller, Maureen. 2005. Street Smarts and Urban Myths: Women, Sex Work, and the Role of Storytelling in Risk Reduction and Rationalization. *Medical Anthropology Quarterly* 19(2): 149–170.

Roger, Maren and Emmanuel Debruyne. 2016. From Control to Terror: German Prostitution Policies in Eastern and Western European Territories During Both World Wars. *Gender and History* 28(3): 687–708.

Rose, Geoffrey. 1985. Sick Individuals and Sick Populations: *International Journal of Epidemiology* 14: 32–38.

Rubin, Gayle. 2011. Blood Under the Bridge: Reflections on "Thinking Sex." *GLQ: A Journal of Lesbian and Gay Studies* 17(1): 15–48.

Safika, Iko, Levy, Judith, and Johnson, Timothy. 2013. Sex Work Venue and Condom Use Among Female Sex Workers in Senggigi, Indonesia. *Culture, Health & Sexuality* 15(5): 598–613.

Sedgwick, Eve Kosofsky. 1990. *Epistemology of the Closet*. Berkeley, CA: University of California Press.

Scorgie, Fiona, Vasey, Katie, Harper, Eric, Richter, Marlise, Nare, Prince, Maseko, Sian, and Chersich, Matthew. 2013. Human Rights Abuses and Collective Resilience Among Sex Workers in Four African Countries: A Qualitative Study. *Globalization & Health* 9(33): 1–13.

Shannon, Kate, Bright, Vicki, Allinott, Shari, Alexon, Debbi, Gibson, Kate, Tyndall, Mark, and Maka Project Partnership. 2007. Community-Based HIV Prevention Research Among Substance-Using Women in Survival Sex Work: The Maka Project Partnership. *Harm Reduction Journal* 4: 20–26.

Shannon, Kate, Strathdee, Stefanee, Shoveller, Jean, Rusch, Melanie, Kerr, Thomas, and Tyndall, Mark. 2009. Structural and Environmental Barriers to Condom-Use Negotiation with Clients Among Female Sex Workers: Implications for HIV-prevention Strategies and Policies. *American Journal of Public Health* 99: 659–665.

Sinha, Sunny. 2015. Reasons for Women's Entry into Sex Work: A Case Study of Kolkata, India. *Sexuality & Culture* 19(1): 216–235.

Smith, Nicola. 2012. Body Issues: The Political Economy of Male Sex Work. *Sexualities* 15(5/6): 586–603.

Stella, by and for Sex Workers in Montreal. 2006. *Sex Workers and Research Ethics*. Montreal: Stella. www.chezstella.org/docs/ConsSIDArechEthiA.pdf.

SWOP/Sex Workers Outreach Project. n.d. *How to Be an Ally to Sex Workers*. Chicago: SWOP. http://redlightchicago.wordpress.com/how-to-be-an-ally-to-sex-workers.

Tambe, Ashwini. 2005. The Elusive Ingénue: A Transnational Feminist Analysis of European Prostitution in Colonial Bombay. *Gender and Society* 19(2): 160–179.

Van der Meulen, Emily. 2011. Action Research with Sex Workers: Dismantling Barriers, Building Bridges. *Action Research* 9: 370–384.

Vanwesenbeeck, Ine. 2001. Another Decade of Social Scientific Work on Sex Work: A Review of Research 1990–2000. *Annual Review of Sex Research* 12: 242–287.

Vasylyeva, Tetyana, Friedman Samuel, Gensburg, Lenore, and Smyrnov, Pavlo. 2017. Engagement in Sex Work Does Not Increase HIV Risk for Women Who Inject Drugs in Ukraine. *Journal of Public Health* 39(3): e103–e110.

Wardlow, Holly. 2004. Anger, Economy, and Female Agency: Problematizing "Prostitution" and "Sex Work" Among the Huli of Papua New Guinea. *Signs: Journal of Women in Culture & Society* 29(4): 1017–1040.

Weiss, Benjamin. 2017. Patterns of Interaction in Webcam Sex Work: A Comparative Analysis of Female and Male Broadcasters. *Deviant Behavior*. doi: 10.1080/01639625.2017.1304803.

Zheng, Tiantian. 2009. *Red Lights: The Lives of Sex Workers in Postsocialist China*. Minneapolis, MN: University of Minnesota Press.

Part I
The research enterprise

3

The research enterprise

An introduction

Susan Dewey, Isabel Crowhurst, and Chimaraoke Izugbara

Introduction

The research enterprise is a formidable socio-political force that directly shapes knowledge production and political action across academic disciplines and areas of professional practice that engage with the sex industry. Existing literature extensively documents challenges facing researchers and practitioners, including ideological debates about evidence, democratizing knowledge production, reproducing dominant norms in research, widespread stigma, and the ethics of the knowledge production process. Chapters in this section engage with these ongoing challenges while offering clear directions for future research.

Key themes in existing literature

Ideological debates often center on the concern that researchers may mobilize evidence to substantiate a set of a priori assumptions about the sex industry. Those who regard the sex industry as a morally reprehensible form of violence against women present evidence of widespread and flagrant abuse within it while dismissing supporters of sex worker labour rights as members of a "pro-prostitution lobby" (Farley, 2004). Such approaches have been widely critiqued by researchers concerned with the potential for such work to eschew basic tenets of scientific inquiry in order to further a specific political agenda (Weitzer, 2010; Ellison, 2017). Researchers and practitioners, especially those who are new to the field, accordingly find themselves squarely located in the midst of these debates while attempting to make meaningful contributions that advance evidence-based public policy and associated practices (Fedina, 2014).

Participatory research is widely embraced in this field of study as a means to overcome long-standing traditions of research "on" rather than "with" members of groups that face significant marginalization and stigmatization. Personal experiences with the sex industry provide valuable insights into the knowledge production process and numerous researchers and practitioners accordingly emphasize the potentially transformative power of including current or former sex workers in research (O'Neill, 2010; Kim & Jeffreys, 2013). The potential to democratize the knowledge production process is often touted as an alternative to the public silencing of those who work in the sex industry (Macioti & Geymonat, 2016). Yet tensions can emerge within such areas of research when sex worker participation is confined to a minor role designed to instrumentally demonstrate community involvement or, conversely, when sex workers regard academic partners without sex industry experience as naïve or unable to understand their issues (Nencel, 2017).

Research in this field has historically focused almost exclusively on heterosexual women who sell sexual services to heterosexual men because such individuals constitute the majority of sex industry participants. Work with these populations pioneered theoretical connections between prostitution, gender inequality, and exploitative economic systems (Walkowitz, 2017). Yet focusing exclusively on these heteronormative sexual exchanges risks reification of dominant stereotypes regarding gender and sexuality by excluding the various meanings ascribed to commercial sex in queer communities and the associated insights provided into dominant cultural conceptualizations of, and legal approaches to, the sex industry (Comte, 2014). Researchers have accordingly noted that the relative lack of attention to men as providers of sexual services functions to naturalize dominant cultural conceptions of men's hyper-sexuality in contrast to women's supposed sexual vulnerability (Dennis, 2008), while also neglecting the considerable diversity of men's involvement as providers in the sex industry (Minichiello & Denton, 2013).

Widespread stigmatization of the sex industry also impacts researchers across academic fields of inquiry through "courtesy stigma" (Sanders, 2006) that associates their work with prurient interests that are usually not discussed in professional settings. Such stigmatization can also harm researchers' professional and personal lives through public association with a taboo and politically charged topic that, in some cultural contexts and professional settings, may result in ostracism (Hammond & Kingston, 2014). Such pervasive stigma also directly informs dominant cultural representations of sex workers, social workers, and others who might be considered stakeholders in research or interventions with sex workers (Hannem & Tigchelaar, 2016). Within this fraught ideological and practical terrain, researchers must balance the goal of raising awareness about issues facing those in the sex industry with the reality that speaking for others can further entrench the stigma with which sex workers already struggle (Cunningham, 2015).

In many ways, these challenges coalesce in critical engagement with the ethics and politics of the research and knowledge production process. Researchers must scrutinize their study designs and remain attuned throughout their work to potential ethical issues that may arise throughout the research process, including how to engage in local projects that respect sex workers' rights to privacy while participating in research (Shaver, 2005). It is normal in research of this kind for research participants to disclose information to researchers that is often reserved for extremely close relationships, which requires researchers to constantly reevaluate how to utilize information gained through research, particularly when such information may have been shared by a participant who regards the researcher as a friend or confidante because of their long-term relationship (O'Connell Davidson, 2008; Dewey & Zheng, 2013). The array of criminal justice and social services interventions that target sex workers can prompt researchers to speak out against such initiatives when they violate basic human rights to freedom from coercive interventions (Wahab & Panichelli, 2013), thus placing researchers at the intersections of scholarship and activism.

Chapter overview

Chapters in this section engage with and build upon this work. Bimbi and Koken (Chapter 4) detail how policy and funding streams direct the research enterprise through preferred pedagogical, theoretical, and empirical lenses that limit the scope of critical inquiry. Majic and Showden (Chapter 5) question the value of both criminal justice interventions and prevailing academic approaches in this field and recommend feminist reflexivity to correct the ongoing disconnect between narratives, policies, and outcomes. Orchard (Chapter 6) builds on a rich historical tradition of autobiographical writings by women in the sex industry to explore how street-involved women's writings, while rare, offer great potential for the democratization of, and critical reflection on, the knowledge production process.

Oduro, Otoo, and Asiama (Chapter 7) explore the ethical and pragmatic dimensions of designing and conducting research with minors in the sex industry by discussing the tensions, contradictions, practicalities, and lessons learned in a successfully completed project. Oliveira (Chapter 8) uses a case study approach to analyze the strengths and weaknesses participatory methods offer to this field by linking scientific research and socio-political intervention. Aoyama (Chapter 9) examines the dual marginalization of participatory action and sex industry research within the knowledge production enterprise through a case study illustrating how this marginalization manifests in terms of gatekeeping by sex worker participants and dominant cultural/political resistance to sex work-related policy change.

Future directions

Researchers rarely engage in an explicit manner with the means by which funding, political, and cultural dynamics shape research and knowledge production about the sex industry, which is curious given the tremendous power these forces wield in their professional lives. One potentially productive area for future research might lie in interrogating the frameworks and assumptions that undergird the research enterprise, with the goal of systematically engaging with dominant forms of knowledge production as cultural systems with their own norms and practices. Difficult questions arising within such a project might include the following. Where does research focus its empirical laser beam? How do funders' priorities sharpen this focus? How might new theoretical frameworks, approaches, and multidisciplinary alliances in projects help to overcome challenges researchers face in this field? What is the goal of sex industry research? Is it merely to pay lip service to social transformation—whether in the specific areas of improved health and safety, implementation of particular legal or policy frameworks, or "giving voice" to sex workers—with the instrumental goal of facilitating the knowledge production machine's smooth operations through peer-reviewed publications in particular venues, obtaining research grants from highly regarded funders, and receiving tenure? What have researchers been able to accomplish in terms of meaningful change in sociopolitical climates globally characterized by hostility toward their work?

Researchers may likewise pursue critical inquiry into the democratization of the research process with the goal of developing new methods and frameworks for analysis. Inclusive, participatory methods are commonly used in sex industry research to work against empiricist modes of inquiry. Yet democratization of the research process, like more "mainstream" research forms, makes some assumptions as well, most specifically that research participants will be inherently interested in rights-based inquiry and advocacy based on particular aspects of their identity, such as earning money through trading sex. The "rosy glow" of participatory research does not always sufficiently acknowledge significant differences in orientation, perspectives, and personality among participants, which risks replicating the same kind of Othering/distancing that participatory methods explicitly attempt to combat. Future research in this field will likely question how researchers might move past this dilemma through new methods and approaches that do not simply incorporate the views and energies of a vocal minority of sex workers whose experiences and goals may or may not represent those of their peers. Doing so would occur in dialogue with the reality that a wealth of evidence-based reports and studies have already been produced by scholars, advocacy groups, and others, yet policymakers and academic researchers tend to be rather fixed in where and how they locate sources of evidence, leading them to overlook these rich resources (Jahnsen & Wagenaar, 2017).

References

Comte, Jacqueline. 2014. Decriminalization of Sex Work: Feminist Discourses in Light of Research. *Sexuality & Culture* 18(1): 196–217.

Cunningham, Stewart. 2015. Reinforcing or Challenging Stigma? The Risks and Benefits of "Dignity Talk" in Sex Work Discourse. *International Journal for the Semiotics of Law* 29(1): 1–21.

Dennis, Jeffery. 2008. Women Are Victims, Men Make Choices: The Invisibility of Men and Boys in the Global Sex Trade. *Gender Issues* 25(1): 11–25.

Dewey, Susan and Zheng, Tiantian. 2013. *Ethical Research with Sex Workers: Anthropological Approaches.* New York: Springer.

Ellison, Graham. 2017. Who Needs Evidence? Radical Feminism, the Christian Right and Sex Work Research in Northern Ireland. In Sarah Armstrong, Jarrett Blaustein, and Alistair Henry (Eds.), *Reflexivity and Criminal Justice* (pp. 289–314). London: Palgrave MacMillan.

Farley, Melissa. 2004. Bad for the Body, Bad for the Heart: Prostitution Harms Women Even if Legalized or Decriminalized. *Violence Against Women* 10(10): 1087–1125.

Fedina, Lisa. 2014. Use and Misuse of Research in Books on Sex Trafficking: Implications for Interdisciplinary Researchers, Practitioners, and Advocates. *Trauma, Violence & Abuse* 16(2): 188–198.

Hammond, Natalie and Kingston, Sarah. 2014. Experiencing Stigma as Sex Work Researchers in Professional and Personal Lives. *Sexualities* 17(3): 329–347.

Hannem, Stacey and Tigchelaar, Alex. 2016. Doing It in Public: Dilemmas of Images, Voice, and Constructing Publics in Public Sociology on Sex Work. *Symbolic Interaction* 38: 634–653.

Jahnsen, Synnove and Wagenaar, Hendrik. 2017. *Assessing Prostitution Policy in Europe.* London: Routledge.

Kim, Jules and Jeffreys, Elena. 2013. Migrant Sex Workers and Trafficking: Insider Research For and By Migrant Sex Workers. *ALARj: Action Learning and Action Research Journal* 19(1): 62–96.

Macioti, P.G. and Geymonat, Giulia Garofolo, Eds. 2016. *Sex Workers Speak. Who Listens?* Open Democracy. https://drive.google.com/file/d/0B2lN4rGTopsaSldZNW4tUzVEUFk/edit.

Minichiello, Victor and Denton, John. 2013. New Pleasures and Old Dangers: Reinventing Male Sex Work. *Journal of Sex Research* 50(3/4): 263–275.

Nencel, Lorraine. 2017. Epistemologically Privileging the Sex Worker: Uncovering the Rehearsed and Presumed in Sex Work Studies. In Marlene Spanger and May-Len Skilbrei (Eds.), *Prostitution Research in Context: Methodology, Representation and Power* (pp. 67–84). London: Routledge.

O'Connell Davidson, Julia. 2008. If No Means No, Does Yes Mean Yes? Consenting to Research Intimacies. *History of the Human Sciences* 21(4): 49–67.

O'Neill, Maggie. 2010. Cultural Criminology and Sex Work: Resisting Regulation Through Radical Democracy and Participatory Action Research (PAR). *Journal of Law and Society* 37(1): 210–232.

Sanders, Teela. 2006. Sexing Up the Subject: Methodological Nuances in Researching the Female Sex Industry. *Sexualities* 9(4): 449–468.

Shaver, Frances. 2005. Sex Work Research: Methodological and Ethical Challenges. *Journal of Interpersonal Violence* 20(3): 296–319.

Wahab, Stéphanie and Panichelli, Meg. 2013. Ethical and Human Rights Issues in Coercive Interventions with Sex Workers. *Affilia* 28: 344.

Walkowitz, Judith. 2017. The History and Politics of Prostitution: Prostitution and the Politics of History. In Marlene Spanger and May-Len Skilbrei (Eds.), *Prostitution Research in Context: Methodology, Representation and Power.* London: Routledge.

Weitzer, Ron. 2010. The Mythology of Prostitution: Advocacy Research and Public Policy. *Sexuality Research and Social Policy* 7(1): 15–29.

4

Selective vision

How disciplinary frames, funding streams, and social policy shape research on sex work

David S. Bimbi and Juline A. Koken

Introduction

In 2004, the "Traditional Values Coalition," a group claiming to represent thousands of Christian churches in the United States, compiled a list of over 150 researchers receiving federal funding that the group complained appealed to "prurient" interests (Brower 2004). The researchers listed (the authors' team among them) were primarily investigating topics relating to sexuality. The list was presented to the US Congress with a demand that the funding for these scientists be investigated or halted. The list was compiled using key word searches (i.e. "prostitution," "sex work," "homosexuality," etc.) on publicly available information about federally funded research. Scientists defended the legitimacy of their research, and the group was unsuccessful in their demand that this type of work be halted. Yet many researchers in the field of sexual science described ways in which they altered their approach to research work in the wake of this and many other attacks on sexuality research that effectively "chilled" the research environment. Our own research team changed the language we used in research grant abstracts, removing any mention of sex work, homosexuality, or transgender identity in an effort to avoid future negative attention from conservative groups on our work. This is just one small example of the intersection between research science, culture, and sex work and the ways in which our research—and thus, what is "knowable" or documentable—is constrained within the social context of sex work research.

Such constraints on "knowledge" result in and perpetuate disciplinary blind spots. Research questions that funding agencies will not support, and work that is constrained or rendered impossible within the context of social policy that refuses to acknowledge sex work as a form of labor, are just a few of the ways knowledge on sex work has been limited. Although some might argue that the evolution of sex work research mirrors socio-historical changes in cultural attitudes towards the meaning of sexual behavior (Bimbi 2007), it is questionable how much this research ultimately reflects the experiences of sex workers themselves.

In this chapter we will describe the intersection between sex work research and social policy, funding streams, and academic disciplines while exploring the ways in which what is "knowable" about sex work is constrained by the social, policy, funding, and disciplinary context within which research is conducted. It is not our intent to detail a review of the literature in all of these areas but rather to highlight the ways in which the research enterprise is shaped by and reflects the social, cultural, and economic context within sex work research is conducted. We will conclude with some comments about the ways in which the research enterprise is expanding its scope beyond these limitations and recommend further strategies for promoting research outside of traditional frames.

Alternative facts and social policy

In the United States, morality about sex work leads to a resistance to data-driven policy. *Morality policy* (Weitzer 2010) is not only "resistant to facts" (Wagenaar & Altink 2012) but is resistant to any line of inquiry that would produce evidence to challenge the status quo. Morality policy is framed by anecdotal evidence and distorted interpretation of data (see Lowthers et al. 2017 for a description of how one Brazilian researcher, Adriana Piscitelli, had her data interpreted through conflicting lenses to support diverging views on sex work). This morality frame is then compounded by media reports that do not challenge misreported data. Further, research is frequently only funded or cited by policy advocates or media sources when it confirms the a priori hypothesis of morality policy (e.g., sex work is always bad with negative consequences).

Morality policy has its basis in the "oppression paradigm" (Weitzer 2010), which defines prostitution as inherently exploitative and harmful to workers. The Western abolitionist stance (to outlaw sex work) is inexorably intertwined with patriarchal Christian beliefs and political activism against same-sex marriage, abortions, sex education, and access to birth control (Fitzgerald 2015). The neo-abolitionist view permeates advocacy groups and services providers throughout the world, including Melissa Farley and the Prostitution Research and Education advocacy group, Shared Hope International, and others like it (Fitzgerald 2015; Weitzer 2010).

What is known about sex work is also limited by the refusal of governing bodies to permit questions about sex work to be asked—for example, currently the United States will not permit questions about sex work to be included in national surveys (Forbes 2015). One federal funding branch in the United States required that applications for research funding (whether situated in the United States or abroad) be accompanied by a statement certifying that the applicant did not support prostitution or the legalization of prostitution (Fitzgerald 2015). Morality policy thus has bled into funding streams for sex work research, and publications resulting from studies funded by these streams have tended to conflate sex work with trafficking, limiting what can be known about sex work through biased research frames seeking to confirm grantees' a priori beliefs about the meaning of sex work (Fitzgerald 2015).

Non-governmental institutions may also embrace morality policy intellectually or out of fear of reprisals from donors, alumni, and funders (Weitzer 2010). One recent piece describing the linkages between morality policy and academic approaches to sex work related the experience of one researcher who was unable to meet with local agencies who were afraid to collaborate with her due to her work being viewed as too "pro sex work" and thus potentially endangering their grant funding (Fitzgerald 2015). The same research team (Brents & Hausbeck 2005) described having a publication rejected by a federally funded anti-trafficking program because the results—which described the safety of workers in brothels in the US state of Nevada—were perceived as too close to promoting prostitution (described in Lerum & Brents 2016).

Our own research team has had manuscripts on male sex work that received highly positive reviews rejected by journal editors on more than one occasion for reasons that appear to be driven by cultural bias more than scientific merit. One editor of a journal stated our manuscript portrayed the experiences of some male sex workers in too positive a light. Another editor argued that even if men in the study described positive aspects of their work or currently enjoyed their work that they believed in the future the men would come to regret their participation in sex work, thus calling into question how much the narratives of sex workers can be believed. While these manuscripts were later published, the first in a peer-reviewed journal (Koken et al. 2004) and another as a book chapter (Koken & Bimbi 2014), journal editors act as powerful scientific gatekeepers. If data that is viewed as "too positive" about sex work is not regarded as credible or worthy of publication, it cannot be disseminated in the field or, as in our case, will be slowed or limited in dissemination. In this way certain kinds of knowledge on sex work may be actively kept out of the frame.

Additionally, the act of researching sex work (and sex itself) may be viewed as "morally questionable" and under-valued by the institutions where researchers are based (Irvine 2012), such as colleges, universities, or non-governmental service organizations. In academia, where tenure and promotion decisions often hinge on a faculty's grant and publication activity, sex work scholars may need to diversify or alter their research agenda to include less controversial subjects to protect their careers—limiting the body of knowledge on sex work due to a need to protect researcher's career prospects. Many researchers who also have had experience as sex workers also report keeping their sex work experience secret in order to protect their academic careers (Fitzgerald 2015). Thus, while many academics and advocates (ourselves included) have called for greater inclusion of sex workers in research programs, sex workers (or former sex workers) who work in academia often feel they cannot be open about their sex work experience. In this way the voices of sex workers continue to be elided in many research projects and publications. Thus, the stigma associated with sex work often extends to those who study or provide services to sex workers. Academics may be pressured to cease research on sex work overtly ("do not do this research at this institution") or passively ("no direct support will be provided for this kind of work and you may not include students"). The stigma of sex work may also reach into the personal lives of researchers (and service providers) working with this population (Hammond & Kingston 2014; Weitzer 2017).

For practical and conceptual reasons, precise and reliable numbers on sex work are hard to obtain (Shaver 2005). Practical reasons include high mobility of sex workers and a difficult to access social milieu; conceptual reasons include ill-defined categories such as "forced prostitution" or "trafficking" (Weitzer 2015). This oppression paradigm (Weitzer 2010) and associated limitations in surveys of sex work lead to a persistent lack of reliable data as well as the promulgation of distorted data (Kessler 2015; Wagenaar et al. 2017). By comparison, in nations and states in which sex work is decriminalized or legalized, researchers may be less stigmatized for focusing on sex work and programs and services for sex workers can be promoted without fear of government reprisal. Morality policy may still apply but without the added burden of researching an illegal activity.

New Zealand is often presented as the alternative to morality policy. In 2003, the Prostitution Reform Act (PRA) was finally passed and replaced previous laws criminalizing sex work. Evaluation of the impact of such sweeping changes in the law regarding sex work was mandated as part of the legislation. The Prostitution Law Review Committee (PLRC) was set up to evaluate the PRA. Researchers from the University of Otago partnered with the New Zealand Prostitutes Collective using a community-based participatory approach (Abel et al. 2007). The resulting publication (Abel et al. 2007), highlighted the positive impacts of the legislation for sex workers noting few negative consequences for the health and safety of sex workers after passage of the act. The authors did note that stigmatization and marginalization of sex workers is still widespread. The researchers also reported that there did not seem to be an increase in the number of sex workers as a result of the legislation, which perhaps could be viewed as a positive outcome of those opposed to the PRA (relaxing prostitution policy did not lead to a detected increase in the number of sex workers). Regardless, morality policy is clearly evidenced in this report by the following disclaimer:

> This project was part-funded by the Ministry of Justice. However, the views, opinions, findings and conclusions or recommendations expressed in this publication are strictly those of the author/s. They do not necessarily reflect the views of the Ministry of Justice. The Ministry of Justice takes no responsibility for any errors or omissions in, or for the correctness of, the information contained in this publication.
>
> *(Abel et al. 2007, p. 2)*

This disclaiming statement clearly illustrates some continued discomfort on behalf of the government to be perceived as in any way promoting or condoning prostitution. The disclaimer also attempts to distance the government from public critique of the study and its findings. Aside from examining the impact of policy changes, what is known about sex work is further limited by the policy or researcher focus on an individual's status as a "sex worker" while neglecting the contextual, intersectional, and multiple forces that effect an individual sex worker's decisions, working conditions and well-being (Agustín 2007; Pisani 2008). Gender and sexual identity, race, ethnicity, legal residency status, age, social class, and local culture are not unique considerations but points of intersection that defy broad generalizations about sex work, as well as relationships between workers, clients, and involved third parties (Pisani 2008).

Academic visions and disciplinary frames

Within academic disciplines research on sex work is often situated and examined within contextual silos. Public health focuses mostly on HIV/STD transmission (sex workers as "vectors of disease" hypothesis), with limited concern for the holistic well-being of individual sex workers (Bimbi & Koken 2014). Psychology frequently limits investigations to documentation of traumas or personal characteristics that "predict" entering sex work as well as the traumas that result from performing sex work (Koken & Bimbi 2014). Sociology historically framed sex work as deviant behavior, resulting from problems in home life and as a social process in which individuals are channeled into "deviant occupations" through the social influence of peers or grooming from predatory members of the local community (Bimbi 2007). In criminal justice studies of trafficking, exploitation, and the association of sex work with other "criminal" activities are the prime areas of interest (Fitzgerald 2015). The voices of sex workers themselves as well as clients and other involved parties are largely unheard across disciplines.

Researchers may not only have to assess the climate at their institution to pursue inquiry into sex work but may also have to navigate and negotiate the positionality, politics and moral values of their academic peers. The ability to engage in research relies on acquiring funding that is dependent upon agencies with their own set of beliefs and agendas. For example, the National Institutes of Health and other funding streams release requests for proposals (RFPs) to fund research. These RFPs rarely if ever, focus on sex work outside of coercive sex work (e.g., trafficking), and fail to consider the needs of the sex worker and the client. At other times, researchers may even opt to use alternative phrases in grant applications (e.g., "vulnerable women" "at risk youth") such as our team did to avoid triggering implicit and explicit biases against sex work among grant reviewers and grant funders while avoiding scrutiny from public groups such as the Traditional Values Coalition.

Public health and sex work

Sex work has long been equated with disease in public health from nineteenth-century efforts to curb the spread of "venereal diseases" to late twentieth-century efforts to halt the spread of HIV. The "vectors of disease" transmission hypothesis led to a marked increase of research on sex work since the 1980s (Bimbi 2007) mostly with funds earmarked for HIV or substance abuse research. The focus is less often on the client's role in disease transmission (e.g., demands for sex without a condom) and lays the burden of responsiblity for safer sex on the sex workers. Regardless, much of what is presently known about sex workers was information gathered in the context of HIV or drug research and is therefore not generalizable to many populations and sub-populations of sex workers.

Further, the public health goal of improving the health of individuals and communities has been restricted by US public policy. The United States Leadership against HIV/AIDS, Tuberculosis, and Malaria Act of 2003 established the President's Emergency Plan for AIDS Relief (PEPFAR) that explicitly included the provision that agencies and organizations that promoted or supported sex workers would be ineligible to receive funds. This came to be known as the "anti-prostitution pledge" and has had a marked impact on public health programming globally. Ditmore and Allman (2013) presented the case story of a hypothetical agency impacted by PEPFAR based on reports from 25 projects and organizations in 14 non-Western nations. They offer the example of organizations being directly told by USAID that drop-in centers for sex workers are definitely not permitted under PEPFAR. Another agency allowed sex workers to meet, but clandestinely, with no public promotion allowing the agency to hide the group from USAID.

Morality policies such as PEPFAR and others meant to curb sex work have been demonstrated to be ineffective in reducing demand, while controls and regulations frequently make things worse for the sex worker and are directly at odds with public health and human rights principles. For example, Shannon et al. (2015) reviewed 87 studies on sex workers and HIV risk and argues that decriminalization of sex work would have the greatest effect of all in reducing female sex workers' HIV risk. Shannon suggests that decriminalization could avert 33–46% of HIV infections, if accompanied by sex worker-led interventions and community empowerment.

In nations where policies on sex work are more progressive (i.e. sex work is legalized, decriminalized, or legally tolerated in other ways) more participatory research approaches are possible. For example, the European Network Male Prostitution (ENMP) began in the Netherlands with funding from Dutch HIV/AIDS and health organizations in 1997 (Sanders et al. 2009, 72). In 2000, the ENMP became the first EU-funded program specific to male sex workers and their needs, but with a mandate to focus on HIV and STD prevention and health promotion. The network eventually expanded to include 24 nations. The ENMP published several reports and then merged into the European Network for the Promotion of Rights and Health among Migrant Sex Workers (TAMPEP) when the EU declined to continue funding due to objections from the Swedish government (Mattson 2016, 44). The Swedish government objected to the projects goals, its funding, and the participation of a Swedish NGO in the network because the Swedish approach criminalizes the purchase of sex but not the sale. Unfortunately, morality policy again imposed limitations on the practice of participatory research approaches and partnerships between sex workers and researchers by restricting funding streams.

Sociology, criminology, and sex work

Historically, sociology has approached sex work through a deviance frame (Weitzer 2009), frequently casting sex workers (and sometimes clients as well) as antisocial agents who participate in actions that harm the community. However, in recent decades there has been an explosion of sociological research expanding the lens on sex work to include explorations of sex work as labor, as embedded within larger cultural approaches to gender and sexuality, and as an activity within a larger economic and global context (see Lerum & Brent 2016 for a review). This expansion of sociological research on sex work has increased what is knowable about sex work to include many areas of focus that were previously neglected or seen only through a deviance lens and resisted reductionist theorisation of sex work involved parties.

The field of research on trafficking has been shaped largely by the morality policies and the oppression paradigm that often conflates sex work with trafficking (Weitzer 2015). Within the field of criminology there has been a focus on sex work as crime, victimization, and as an industry depending on the exploitation of minors. US federal government funding streams in this area have been channeled towards uncovering juvenile delinquency and youth exploitation. Even within this relatively traditional frame, however, some studies exploring the involvement of minors in sex work or third parties involved in sex work transactions ("market facilitators") have resisted easy categorization in older deviance paradigms, instead using rigorous sampling methodology to collect data that offered evidence that was counter to previous assumptions about the involvement of minors and "pimps" in sex work (Marcus et al. 2014). This is an example of how asking broader questions and questioning previous theories about sex work may broaden what is knowable about sex work even when funding from traditionally conservative government sources provides the foundation for study.

In the United Kingdom, where selling sex is not criminalized per se, although other aspects of sex work are, a recent study (Sanders et al. 2017) funded by the Economic and Social Research Council demonstrates how a slightly more relaxed policy environment combined with government willingness to fund participatory research on sex work can produce knowledge on sex work that expands the frame beyond the oppression paradigm. For the "Beyond the Gaze" project, a collaborative team of criminology, sociology, legal, and other scholars partnered with sex workers, activists, and local police to produce a multi-method research programme aiming to understand the impact of technology use on sex work, with a focus on the health and safety of sex workers. This program used a participatory approach and has recently begun to release their groundbreaking findings demonstrating the ways in which the Internet is used by sex workers to manage their business and increase their safety on the job (Cunningham et al. 2017).

Psychology and sex work

Unfortunately, the field of psychology has often reinforced and perpetuated stereotypes of sex workers—particularly women sex workers, as men and transgender sex workers are underrepresented in psychological research—with a particular focus on trauma as both a reason for entering sex work (e.g. the theory of repetition compulsion or reenactments; Levy 1998) as well as a result of participation in sex work (e.g. Farley et al. 1998; Farley & Barkan 1998 and many others working from a neo-abolitionist stance). Research in this area often seems to collect only data that will confirm the a priori assumptions of the researchers doing the work, such as by asking questions only about the frequency of assault, history of childhood abuse, and so on, without exploring other reasons for entering sex work or allowing for the possibility of positive experiences within sex work (Koken 2010). The assumption driving these selectively focused surveys seems to be that only individuals who suffered from trauma and neglect would be sex workers, leaving unknowable other reasons for entering sex work or experiences within sex work.

When psychological studies exploring mental health, resiliency, or well-being among sex workers have been published, they are often from researchers and samples within nations where sex work is legal or decriminalized, potentially demonstrating the possibility of expanding "what is knowable" when the cultural and policy context allows for and acknowledges a multiplicity of experiences within sex work. For example, Dutch researcher Ine Vanwesenbeeck has collected and reported data from large, diverse samples of sex workers in the Netherlands, which have allowed for identification of similarities and differences in sex workers' mental health by venue, migration status, income, and other factors (Vanwesenbeeck 1994). Vanwesenbeeck also pioneered a psychological study of sex work burnout (Vanwesenbeeck 2005), which normalized a range of levels of well-being by comparing sex worker burnout to a comparable sample of women professionals performing emotional labor (such as nursing) and a sample of persons with work-related psychological problems. A recent study exploring women sex workers' romantic relationships and coping strategies for working with clients (Bellhouse et al. 2015) drew on an Australian sample where sex work has some legal status depending on the territory. These studies demonstrate the potential for expanding what is knowable about sex work when research is conducted in a social context where sex work is less criminalized (and potentially less stigmatized) and when researchers approach the work as a form of labor comparable to other forms of labor.

Conclusion

The selective visions of social policy, funding streams, and disciplinary frames have created, promulgated, and disseminated a limited constellation of facts about sex workers resulting in stereotypes so pervasive as to be accepted as fact by large proportions of individuals. The diverse experiences and voices of sex workers themselves as well as clients and other involved parties are frequently excluded or ignored. Advocates for sex work, public health, and human rights have repeatedly called for policy based on best practices and prioritizing research on sex work that involves participatory approaches and does not rely solely on HIV or criminal justice funding. Some organizations of sex workers, advocates, and researchers have begun collecting and publishing work that centers the experiences of sex workers as both subject and author (for one example, see the many publications released in editions of Research for Sex Work put out by the Network of Sex Work Projects: www.nswp.org/resources/types/research-sex-work).

In states where sex work policy can be characterized as more relaxed because sex work is decriminalized, legalized, or otherwise tolerated, opportunities for collaborations between sex workers, advocates, government agencies, and researchers have emerged. State-funded research programmes such as the "Beyond the Gaze" project in the UK (Sanders et al. 2017) and others in New Zealand (Abel et al. 2007) illustrate the potential for the expansion of knowledge on sex work through participatory and inclusive approaches. The fruit of such research may support improvement of social policy informed by evidence and the involvement of sex workers themselves.

Regardless, improvement in research-funding streams would be inconsequential without a cultural shift in academic and policymaking institutions. Overcoming the stigma and resistance to conducting sex work research is a critical aspect of reducing the stigma attached to sex work at the societal level (Weitzer 2017). Institutions should concern themselves solely with the protection of human subjects and the scientific merit of the research methodology and permit scholars the academic freedom to choose the topic and population of their study. While funding is important, not all research requires multi-year, multi-million dollar budgets, instead only requiring qualified researchers and community partners with the time and the minimal resources (e.g., computers, software, research assistants) necessary to conduct the study, hopefully without opposition from their home institution. Finally, and most importantly, academic disciplines must examine how morality policy, pedagogical silos, and resistance to the inclusion of non-academic parties (such as sex workers and other community members) have restricted the knowledge produced about sex work. Only when research programmes are informed by multiple perspectives—sex workers and involved parties, community members, academics across disciplines, and policy makers—and are free from institutional, funder, and disciplinary blindness may a more representative picture of sex work begin to emerge.

References

Abel, G., L. Fitzgerald, and C. Brunton. 2007. *The Impact of the Prostitution Reform Act on the Health and Safety Practices of Sex Workers: Report to the Prostitution Law Review Committee.* Christchurch, New Zealand: University of Otago.

Agustín, L. 2007. *Sex at the Margins: Migration, Labour Markets and the Rescue Industry.* London: Zed Books.

Bellhouse, C., S. Crebbin, C. Fairley, and J. Bilardi. 2015. The impact of sex work on women's personal romantic relationships and the mental separation of their work and personal lives: A mixed methods study. *PLoS One,* 10, #10: e0141575. https://doi.org/10.1371/journal.pone.0141575.

Bimbi, D. 2007. Male prostitution: Pathology, paradigms and progress in research. *Journal of Homosexuality,* 53: 7–35.

Bimbi, D. and J. Koken. 2014. Public health and male sex work. In V. Minichiello and J. Scott, eds., *Male Sex Work and Society,* 200–222. New York: Harrington Park Press.

Brents, Barbara, and Kathryn Hausbeck. 2005. Violence and legalized brothel prostitution in Nevada: Examining safety, risk, and prostitution policy. *Journal of Interpersonal Violence,* 20(3): 270–295.

Brower, V. 2004. List of "prurient" research stirs fear, anger among US scientists. *Nature Medicine,* 10: 104–107.

Cunningham, et al. 2017. Behind the screen: Commercial sex, digital spaces and working online. *Technology in Society,* epub ahead of print: 1–8. https://doi.org/10.1016/j.techsoc.2017.11.004.

Ditmore, Melissa Hope, and Dan Allman. 2013. An analysis of the implementation of PEPFAR's anti-prostitution pledge and its implications for successful HIV prevention among organizations working with sex workers. *Journal of the International AIDS Society,* 16(1): 17354.

Farley, M., I. Baral, M. Kiremire, and U. Sezgin. 1998. Prostitution in five countries: Violence and post-traumatic stress disorder. *Feminism and Psychology,* 8: 415–426.

Farley, M., and H. Barkan. 1998. Prostitution, violence, and posttraumatic stress disorder. *Women and Health,* 27: 37–49.

Fitzgerald, J. 2015. How the government and the Christian lobby quash real research on sex workers. *Pacific Standard.* https://psmag.com/news/government-christian-lobby-quashes-real-research-on-sex-workers.

Forbes, A. 2015. Speaking of sex workers: How suppression of research has distorted the United States' Domestic HIV response. *Reproductive Health Matters,* 23(45): 21–29.

Hammond, Natalie, and Sarah Kingston. 2014. Experiencing stigma as sex worker researchers. *Sexualities,* 17(3): 329–347.

Irvine, J. 2012. Can't ask, can't tell: How institutional review boards keep sex in the closet. *Contexts,* 11: 8–33.

Kessler, G. 2015. The bogus claim that 300,000 U.S. children are "at risk" of sexual exploitation. *Washington Post.* www.washingtonpost.com/news/fact-checker/wp/2015/05/28/the-bogus-claim-that-300000-u-s-children-are-at-risk-of-sexual-exploitation/?utm_term=.bd6fc44387fd.

Koken, J. 2010. The meaning of the "whore": How feminist theories on prostitution shape research on female sex workers. In M. Ditmore, A. Levy, and A. Willman, eds., *Sex Work Matters: Power and Intimacy in the Global Sex Industry,* 28–64. London: Zed Books.

Koken, J., and D. Bimbi. 2014. Mental health and male sex work. In V. Minichiello and J. Scott, eds., *Male Sex Work and Society,* 224–239. New York: Harrington Park Press.

Koken, J., D. Bimbi, J. Parsons, and P. Halkitis. 2004. The experience of stigma in the lives of male internet escorts. *Journal of Psychology and Human Sexuality,* 16: 13–32.

Lerum, K., and B.G. Brents. 2016. Sociological perspectives on sex work and human trafficking. *Sociological Perspectives,* 59: 17–26.

Levy, M.S. 1998. A helpful way to conceptualize and understand reenactments. *Journal of Psychotherapy Practice and Research,* 7: 227–235.

Lowthers, M., M. Sabat, E.M. Durisin, and K. Kempadoo. 2017. A sex work research symposium: Examining positionality in documenting sex work and sex workers' rights. *Social Sciences*, 6: 39–45.

Marcus, A. et al. (2014). Conflict and agency among sex workers and pimps: A closer look at domestic minor sex trafficking. *The ANNALS of the American Academy of Political and Social Science*, 653(1): 225–246.

Mattson, G. 2016. *The Cultural Politics of European Prostitution Reform*. New York: Palgrave Macmillan.

Pisani, E. 2008. *The Wisdom of Whores: Bureaucrats, Brothels and the Business of AIDS*. New York: Norton & Company.

Sanders, T., M. O'Neill, and J. Pitcher. 2009. *Prostitution: Sex Work, Policy and Politics*. London: Sage.

Sanders, T., J. Scoular, J. Pitcher, and R. Campbell. 2017. *Beyond the Gaze: Summary Briefing on Internet Sex Work*. Leicester: University of Leicester. www.beyond-the-gaze.com/wp-content/uploads/2018/01/BtGbriefingsummaryoverview.pdf, accessed 7/17/17.

Shannon, K., S. Strathdee, S. Goldenberg, P. Duff, P. Mwangi, M. Rusakova, S. Reza-Paul, J. Lau, K. Deering, M. Pickles, and M. Boily, M. 2015. Global epidemiology of HIV among female sex workers: Influence of structural determinants. *Lancet*, 385(9962): 55–71.

Shaver, F.M. 2005. Sex work research: Methodological and ethical challenges. *Journal of Interpersonal Violence*, 20: 296–319.

United States Leadership against HIV/AIDS, Tuberculosis, and Malaria Act of 2003. 22 U.S.C. 7601. Public Law 108–25, 108th Congress. 117 Stat. 711. 2003. www.gpo.gov/fdsys/pkg/PLAW-108publ25/pdf/PLAW-108publ25.pdf.

Vanwesenbeeck, I. 1994. *Prostitutes' Well Being and Risk*. Amsterdam: University Press.

Vanwesenbeeck, I. 2005. Burnout among indoor female sex workers. *Archives of Sexual Behavior*, 34: 627–639.

Wagenaar, Hendrik, and Sietske Altink. 2012. Prostitution as morality politics or why it is exceedingly difficult to design prostitution policy. *Sexuality Research and Social Policy*, 9(3): 279–292.

Weitzer, Ronald. 2009. Sociology of sex work. *Annual Review of Sociology*, 35: 213–234.

Weitzer, R. 2010. The mythology of prostitution: Advocacy research and public policy. *Sexuality Research and Social Policy*, 7: 15–29.

Weitzer, R. 2015. Human trafficking and contemporary slavery. *Annual Review of Sociology*, 41: 223–242.

Weitzer, R. 2017. Resistance to sex work stigma. *Sexualities*, epub ahead of print: 1–13. doi: 10.1177/1363460716684509.

5

Redesigning the study of sex work

A case for intersectionality and reflexivity

Samantha Majic and Carisa R. Showden

Introduction

Sex work has long sparked debates among feminists, from the sex wars of the 1980s to their reinvigoration in the early 2000s when public and political attention to sex trafficking escalated in the United States and internationally. Currently, in the United States and large parts of Western Europe, the dominant policy narrative about sex work is in fact a story of sex *trafficking* (Johnston et al. 2015; Kempadoo 2005). This story involves a young, innocent (and frequently) white girl who is tricked and trapped by a (predatory, older, often black or brown) man into a life of sexual slavery. In the end, the girl must be rescued and the man must be punished (Bernstein 2012; Chuang 2010; Musto 2016). With its adherence to certain gender tropes (e.g., women are sexually passive and imperilled); its convergence with radical feminist commitments, in particular to ending violence against women; and its individualizing focus, this story has had important effects on public policy, as local, state, and national governments have devoted millions of dollars to fight sex trafficking (Weitzer 2011, 2015; US Department of State 2013). However, the relatively low numbers of victims rescued and traffickers prosecuted raises questions about the accuracy of this narrative, the utility of prevailing US criminal justice interventions, and, more broadly, the methods by which scholars study sex work, particularly among young people (Lutnick 2016).

Our goal in this chapter is to explore how feminist research may both contribute to and potentially correct this ongoing disconnect between narratives, policies, and outcomes. To accomplish this, we reflect on our recent comprehensive narrative analysis of 128 academic studies conducted since 2000 about young people who trade sex in North America (Showden & Majic forthcoming 2018), in which we seek to understand the prominence and validity of the dominant narrative by examining *what* researchers know about young people's experiences of domestic minor sex trafficking and *how* we, as academics, have come to know it. We critically reflect on feminist research on prostitution and sex trafficking to argue for an intersectional approach that maintains fidelity to central feminist concerns about both resisting essentializing narratives and ending sexual and gender-based violence and exploitation. In so doing, we connect current debates in research on sex trafficking with core second-wave radical feminist concerns, specifically feminist theorist and activist Charlotte Bunch's (1979) clarion call to feminist praxis. Bunch argued that such praxis requires feminists to consciously question the root of our fear of making certain arguments, encouraging feminist researchers to rethink our assumptions and how they shape our perspective on politics.[1]

To unpack our argument, we contextualize our study of young people[2] who trade sex within the broader feminist-ideological debates that frame this research and explain how we arrived at our proposed intersectional approach to, and understanding of, research about young people who trade sex. The model we developed encourages reflexivity in the process of research design; consideration of the impact of data collection and analysis on current knowledge and future research; and the use of more robust data to offer policy recommendations that do not generate further harms against sex workers. We advocate for an intersectional approach because it allows us to capture experiences and needs currently missing from much research and policy for youth who trade sex. Over the past 30 years, intersectionality has become a critical tool in generating more inclusive social science research, and it is well suited to policymaking for social justice. This usefulness rests on intersectionality's insistence on foregrounding differences while aiming to circumvent the "oppression Olympics" by maintaining that axes of oppression and identities are interactive rather than additive. Its usefulness also stems from its capaciousness, as it serves as both a method and an interpretative framework while being firmly rooted in feminist praxis fighting domination through counter-hegemonic and transformative knowledge production (Bilge 2013).[3]

Project background

The dominant narrative about young people who trade sex has captured public and political attention through repeated media stories and sparked numerous policy responses in the United States and internationally, such as the federal Trafficking Victims Protection Act (TVPA), which defines any person under the age of 18 who engages in a sex trade as a victim of domestic minor sex trafficking. Yet even with the laws passed and resources expended,[4] there are no reliable estimates of the total numbers of girls (or boys, or transgender youth) who trade sex, consensually or otherwise.[5] Given the influence of the dominant narrative and its questionable effects, we examined whether it is substantiated by peer-reviewed studies that have emerged on the topic since the TVPA's initial passage in 2000. To do so, we undertook a comprehensive narrative analysis (CNA) of 128 peer-reviewed sex trafficking studies in the United States that were conducted by researchers working from neo-abolitionist, sex workers' rights, public health, and other perspectives.[6] Our findings showed that the unitary dominant narrative cited by politicians and police is divorced from a more complex reality. While a small subset of sex trade-involved youth have experiences that fit this narrative, it erases many of the vulnerabilities that often inform the experiences of minors who trade sex.

As we and others (Lutnick 2016; Weitzer 2005; Zhang 2009) have found, one main reason for this erasure is that the narrative's supporting research is often plagued by methodological deficits that arise, in part, from attempts to "prove" pre-determined outcomes through research designs or narrow interpretative frames. In response, to try to improve research and policy design, we developed a four-fold "matrix of agency and vulnerability" to capture the intersecting mix of individual, social, economic, and political structures that variously push youth into the sex trades and shape their experiences therein (Figure 5.1).

This matrix places young people and their needs at the centre of sex trafficking analyses and policies rather than focusing exclusively on dominant cultural beliefs about young people's sexuality and the morality of prostitution. Following from our book's matrix and analysis, in

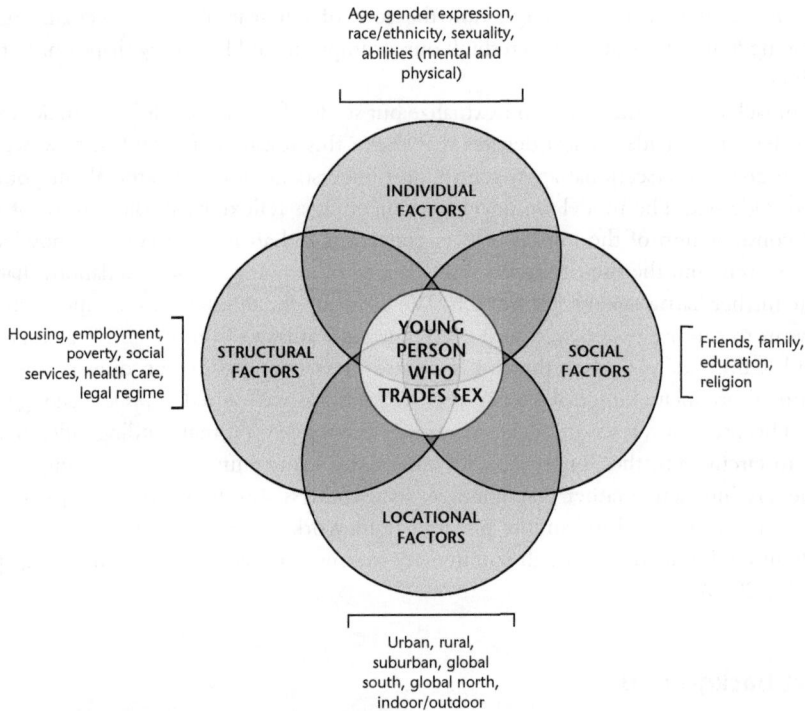

Figure 5.1 Matrix of agency and vulnerability. Created by Elspeth Tory of RedFish Graphics.

Source: Showden and Majic (forthcoming 2018).

this chapter we examine how methodological and ideological orientations can distort research on important and sensitive topics that matter to feminists, and we raise "conscious questions" (Bunch 1979) to again orient feminist sex work research toward collective action, social justice, and privileging the voices of the marginalized.

Dominant trafficking narratives: ideology, research, and policy

Four central claims constitute "conventional wisdom" and justify legislation regarding all forms of human trafficking: (1) the number of trafficking victims both worldwide and domestically is huge; (2) the global magnitude of trafficking is steadily growing; (3) sex trafficking is one of the largest organized criminal enterprises in the world, after illegal drugs and weapons trading; and (4) sex trafficking is more serious and prevalent than labor trafficking (Weitzer 2015). As Laura Agustín (2005) writes, the last of these claims is commonly affirmed by governmental and non-governmental social forums, the communications media, and in scholarly writings, although, as Everett and Charlton (2014) point out, data from the International Labour Organization and the Global Alliance Against Trafficking in Women contradict this claim.

The empirical foundation that supports these four claims remains thin due to the numerous challenges to conducting research about human trafficking. First, the traits identifying someone as a victim or perpetrator of human trafficking are unclear, as not all individuals or experiences fit into the categories and narratives set out in policies and treaties; and not all people who do fit self-identify as trafficking victims (Hua & Nigorizawa 2010). Second, human trafficking and sex trafficking are not always easily distinguishable, as some people knowingly cross borders to engage in domestic or similar work and then voluntarily begin sex work once they are in a new country, while some young people engage in a mix of quasi-legal and illegal activities that don't involve border crossing but may involve some degree of sexual activity (Ditmore et al. 2012; Marcus et al. 2014). Hence, a third and related challenge: victims and perpetrators of trafficking typically constitute a "hidden" population (Lee & Renzetti 1990; Tyldum & Brunovskis 2005) that is difficult to identify and access via traditional social science research methods. And fourth, victims and perpetrators may be unwilling to speak with researchers about their experiences because of trauma, stigma, fear of deportation and/or other retaliation, or a myriad of other concerns. Consequently, the number of human trafficking victims and their "typical" situations are difficult to estimate and describe.

The bulk of published research focuses on sex trafficking, due in part to anti-prostitution advocates' access to policymakers through the late twentieth and early twenty-first centuries. Working in coalition with the religious right and conservative politicians, these advocates convinced the Bush Administration that sex trafficking was the most prevalent and damaging form of trafficking and secured support for research to investigate (and bolster) these claims (Weitzer 2015). While the rhetoric emphasizing sex trafficking at the expense of other forms of trafficking began to shift in the Obama administration, Bush-era anti-trafficking policies largely continued intact. As a result, the majority of research-based journal articles, reports, and books dealing with all forms of human trafficking of both adults and minors since 2000 focused on sex trafficking of women and girls, with little consideration of men and boys and other forms of work (Gozdziak & Bump 2008). Many US government-funded sex work/trafficking studies likewise reflect what Ronald Weitzer terms an "oppression paradigm," whereby domination and subordination are presumed to be core ontological features of sexual commerce (Weitzer 2011). This paradigm is more psychological than structural, and is often unilateral in both diagnosis ("bad men" are the problem) and prescription ("end men's demand for paid sex").

Since much high-profile research falls within the oppression paradigm, a second and related problem is the scarcity and low-visibility of other empirical research. Most writing on sex trafficking is based on "anecdotal evidence, dubious data sources, or unverifiable global generalizations" (Lerum & Brents 2016, 18; see also critiques by Hoang & Parreñas 2014; Zhang 2009). For example, a content analysis of 42 recent books on sex trafficking found that 79% of them approvingly cite and base their own analyses on at least one of the three flawed sources of data about the prevalence of human trafficking, including the US State Department and Kevin Bales (the author, professor, and co-founder of the global anti-trafficking campaign, Free the Slaves), both of which have failed to disclose the methods behind their statistical pronouncements and conclusions, and a 2001 University of Pennsylvania study by Estes and Weiner that misclassified large portions of their sample as involved in commercial sex. Moreover, these books also fail to acknowledge the discrepancies among the statistics in these sources or discuss the lack of data that results from the subversive and hidden nature of human trafficking (Fedina 2015).

In a perfect world, research about sex trafficking generally, and about young people who engage in the sex trades more specifically, would avoid these limitations. Such studies would sample widely and ethically, avoid making unfounded generalizations, and include varied voices from people of all gender identities and sexual orientations in the sex trades so that knowledge *about* them was produced *with* them. And all studies of human trafficking would be more carefully peer reviewed. However, we do not live in a perfect world: there are ongoing debates in the social and physical sciences about the extent to which research is ever truly "objective" or "value free" (Harding 1991, 2015), and peer review processes are not flawless (see e.g., Balietti 2016). That said, there is research available that meets some of these standards. But this research is scattered across academic journals and ignored by most policymakers and the media, both because scholars often do not disseminate their research in ways that are accessible to the general public and because it often fails to confirm preconceived norms about gender, sex, and sex work.

Feminist scholars have been at the forefront of research into prostitution and sex trafficking since the 1970s, but this has not unified understandings of or approaches to studying these issues. Without re-treading the extensive histories of the feminist "sex wars," one outcome was that feminists who view sex work as violence against women prevailed in US policy debates. By aligning with an array of "strange bedfellows" (Bernstein 2007) that have variously included political conservatives, the religious right, law enforcement, and military agencies such as the State Department, they have promoted a "law and order" approach to combating prostitution and sex trafficking rather than the consciousness-raising and community organizing approach that animated radical feminist praxis around domestic violence and health care in the 1970s and 1980s.[7] Termed "carceral feminism" (Bernstein 2010), this approach empowers various state actors with a fraught relationship to communities of color—including police and federal immigration enforcement authorities—to find and prosecute individuals, with less attention to supporting grassroots activism or addressing the neoliberal economic dynamics that lead many people to trade sex or cross borders in the first place (Andrijasevic & Mai 2016; Bumiller 2008).

So how can scholars "do" sex trafficking research in a way that returns feminist praxis to *challenging* gender norms, empowering women and communities, and disengaging from the neoliberal, patriarchal, and militarized state? Building on feminist research methods, we share some lessons learned that we hope can build a more intersectionally feminist approach to sex work and trafficking research.

Reflexivity and intersectionality in research design

An intersectional approach to and understanding of research about young people who trade sex requires reflexivity, defined as the "process of a continual internal dialogue and critical self-evaluation of researcher's positionality as well as active acknowledgment and explicit recognition that this position may affect the research process and outcome" (Berger 2013, 2). We link reflexivity to the standpoint epistemologies first articulated by Black feminist theorists (e.g., Hill Collins 1990; hooks 1990, 1999). These epistemologies de-centered dominant white women's experiences and made diverse women's experiences the focus of any research or political agenda (see also Crenshaw 1995). Reflexivity calls on scholars to acknowledge how their research participants are variously positioned (and possibly marginalized), and to also consider how *their own* race, class, gender, and sexuality, among other factors, intersects and interacts with their research process.

In the context of sex work research, reflexivity may involve considering how, for example, a scholar's own sex work experience (or lack thereof) informs her decisions about sites to study. Or the researcher might ask if her personal opinions about sex workers' capacities for self-advocacy deterred her from including them in the process of research design and implementation. By pushing researchers to continually interrogate the relationship between their own positionality and their research project, this standpoint-informed reflexivity asks scholars to re-evaluate their own biases and challenge the notion that they are objective, disembodied "observers" who "produce" knowledge free from personal or other influences (Kournay 2009; Rouse 2009).

Such reflexivity is not without professional and research-related consequences. Lynzi Armstrong (2012, 7) writes that when she spoke of the sex workers she encountered in the field "in a positive and respectful way," she faced stigma from non-sex workers that was difficult to challenge. Michelle Tracy Berger and Kathleen Guidroz (2014) explain how they faced professional stigma and were explicitly sexualized and propositioned by both professors and peers in the course of conducting sex work research. They note that while their reflexive "politics-of-location" approach helped them cope with this stigma and harassment, it also facilitated harassment by linking them more closely with their research subjects as they gave up the protective veneer of objectivity. But reflexivity was not "optional" for them, because they understood that "researcher and respondent sexualities [are] shifting positions vis-à-vis each other and the knowledge they are (co)producing" (Berger & Guidroz 2014, 5).

These consequences may be even more acute for less privileged scholars, particularly graduate students, untenured professors, those who are "out" about their sex industry involvement, and/or those who are debt-laden from obtaining an education. In short, their positionality will influence their research, as precarity in an increasingly tenuous academic profession can affect how research gets produced. For example, precarity may implicitly shape a felt need to rely on "mainstream," "positivist/objective" and quantitative research methods (as opposed to more qualitative and reflexive methods) in order to prove one's worth in an academic system emphasizing quantity of research outputs and "numbers-driven" research projects.

Still, our own research about young people who trade sex highlights the value of reflexivity. For both of us, our own positions and experiences as white, cisgender, and relatively privileged, feminist-identified women without direct sex work experience would have made it easy to omit and ignore (or prioritize and privilege) certain perspectives. Through our previous research about agency in sex work, domestic violence, and the use of assisted reproduction technology (Showden 2011), and the sex worker rights movement in the United States (e.g., Majic 2014), we came to believe that sex workers are a diverse group whose capacities for agency are shaped by their personal standpoints and the broader political, economic, and social structures of their lives (see the Introduction in Showden & Majic 2014). But as we began to conceptualize our project that considered *young* people who trade sex, we regularly had to be reflexive about our own standpoints and understandings of sex work. Even as our previous research complicated the dominant narrative that all sex work constitutes violence against women, we could not ignore that many sex workers *do* experience violence, and that our previous work only considered adult sex workers.

As we developed and worked on a project that studied *young people* who trade sex, we had to keep certain questions in mind—for example: how might young people's capacity for agency and consent be shaped by different factors than adults? And might youths and adults experience different forms of exploitation? Furthermore, we also had to be reflexive about our ideological orientations. Given our evidence-based support for the decriminalization of consensual commercial sexual activity among adults, a non-reflexive approach risked excluding studies conducted by scholars who do not share this perspective. However, eliminating such studies could be problematic. Studying youths rather than adults changes the legal and social stakes, and researchers who oppose prostitution's decriminalization are not necessarily more biased, or conduct poorly designed studies, than other researchers. Therefore, we regularly queried our own methods and relied on broad inclusion criteria such as peer review. Despite problems with the peer review process (for discussion, see Lee et. al. 2013), it does ensure that some scrutiny is applied to research methods and findings.[8] As a result of this reflexive stance, we ultimately included studies conducted by scholars from a range of disciplines, who hold varied ideological positions. Though our process was not flawless, we believe our reflexivity made us more open to potentially surprising or uncomfortable results.

Reflexivity and intersectionality in data collection and analysis

As standpoint theory indicates, starting research from the lives of marginalized people will generate illuminating insights and questions that are less likely to arise from the lives and experiences of those in dominant positions (Harding 1993). Of course, questions of epistemic privilege are fraught and not all marginalized positions are equally informative in any given situation (Nencel 2017). Intersectionality theory usefully counters the urge to make reductive claims that any one axis of identity determines how a person's or group's experiences are shaped. In short, to generate an intersectional understanding of an issue, multiple standpoints need to be accounted for, and an interpretative frame centering the interactive effects of structural inequalities needs to be in place. Our CNA indicated that viewing youths' experiences in the sex trades through an intersectional lens highlights the crosscutting effects of structural marginalization for young people.

Yet an intersectional picture does not simply "emerge" from the data. One has to *do* intersectionality as a research method to see how crosscutting axes of power shape the experiences of research subjects, research project development, and researchers themselves. In short, it wasn't sufficient for us to acknowledge our own positions as we attempted to collect the "best" data out there on young people who trade sex; we had to dig into the data to understand the details it provided. We systematically analyzed the "meta details" of the studies, for example: who were the researchers (i.e., what were their disciplinary or advocacy areas); how were they funded; what methods did they use; how and where did they sample; what terms did they use to describe both buyers and sellers in commercial sex markets and in sex trafficking chains; did they ask about sexuality; did they sample youth of different racial and ethnic backgrounds; what age range did they include in their definition of "youth"; and so on.

In reviewing the data and metadata from these studies, we found that all of these elements intersect. For example, neo-abolitionist researchers define all sex work and sex trafficking as violence against women and, thus, have a gendered analysis of sex work as male violence against women. These researchers were most likely to purposively sample from carceral and victim services settings (e.g., jails and hospitals), and so they were most likely to identify a third party ("trafficker"), boyfriend, or predatory adult as the most common recruiter of young people into the sex trades and to hear the more negative descriptions of sex industry experiences. Therefore, such studies may over-represent third-party recruitment because police are more likely to ascribe victimhood if they can identify an exploiter. In these studies, researchers also often sample cis-gender girls, who are over-represented and therefore accessible in the carceral and victim services settings from which neo-abolitionist researchers prefer to recruit.[9]

In contrast, critical trafficking scholars (CTS) include researchers who study sex work and sex trafficking through the lens of particular social problems (e.g., homelessness) or through different identity positions (e.g., LGBTQ research). These researchers were more likely to use *in situ* methods, like ethnographic and respondent-driven sampling, where participants are voluntarily recruited from their social networks and locations of daily life. As a result, their studies tended to sample broadly across genders and sexualities, and their findings indicated a that wider range of forces beyond individual men/traffickers motivated young people to trade sex. Yet even with these broader sampling practices and findings, we found important omissions and exclusions. For example, researchers of homelessness examine sexual subjectivity in terms of homophobia and social exclusion from families of origin, while much of the LGBTQ research focuses on gender but downplays sexual subjectivity. This omission may be explained by their emphasis on socio-structural factors as more important than sex or sexuality in trafficking research, but as a consequence, they tend to avoid investigating related issues such as sexual abuse, unlike neo-abolitionist scholars, who pay significant attention to sexual abuse as a causal mechanism in sex trafficking of young people. Additionally, in contrast to neo-abolitionist scholars, critical trafficking scholars who focus on homelessness, for example, are most likely to identify recruitment by peers, while researchers of LGBTQ youth are most likely to identify self-recruitment into the sex trades. In some cases (Maitra 2002; Raible 2011) this emphasis on self-recruitment reflects a romanticizing of queer subcultural milieus in sex trades, but most CTS studies make clear that discrimination in employment or schools, for example, drives participation in sex trades.[10]

These different research focuses result from the intersections of recruitment methods, disciplinary biases, and ideological positions. So, what does all of this mean for the feminist commitment to tackling sexual violence and sex trafficking? First, it is clear that even as sexual violence, sex trafficking, and the sex trades are deeply feminist issues, scholars explicitly aligned with feminist, women's, or gender studies are not the only ones with a prolonged and dedicated interest in studying young people who trade sex. Researchers in fields ranging from public health to anthropology—whether or not they identify as feminist scholars—have helped to bring a complex understanding of gender as intersectional—and essential—to studying and addressing the issues faced by these young people.

Further, the methods scholars employ vary considerably depending upon their ideological and disciplinary positions. We learn a number of inconsistent and often contradictory "truths" about gender and commercial sex through the research, often because neo-abolitionists especially (in our view) have failed to uphold certain feminist methodological commitments as they drifted from standpoint and other feminist methods and praxis in the 1970s and 1980s. The main tension that became clear from our study was between foundational feminist commitments and the challenges of the evidence. On the one hand, the feminist commitment to learn about an issue by listening to the marginalized and to challenge gender-based oppression means that feminists need to *listen to women and others who are in the sex trades*. But some researchers do a better job than others of listening to a range of voices and contextualizing results. For example, Melissa Farley and colleagues (2003, 35) draw from their single-location study with street-based sex workers to state that "violence is *the norm* [emphasis added] for women in prostitution" in the United States. Street-based workers are most likely of all sex workers to experience violence (Weitzer 2005), and it is important to document their experiences. But generalizing this as "the norm" for all forms of sex work is problematic: conclusions need to be calibrated and contextualized so as not to erase other voices and experiences, such as trans youth who experience violence or indoor workers who report far less violence (Weitzer 2005).

Still, the evidence we do have about youth in the sex trades indicates how difficult it is to tackle the complexities of gender oppression in an intersectional way. Shifting methods and embracing reflexivity in future research on this topic would acknowledge multiple biases in current research, and would also enable scholars to address gaps in the research, e.g., the role of mental health and disability in structuring vulnerability to sex trafficking, or the ways that youth sometimes use commercial sex strategically to cope with the homophobia, transphobia, and/or misogyny of current social service providers (see e.g., Corliss et al. 2007; Williamson & Prior 2009).

Policy recommendations

Our discussion here is informed by an understanding of research as transformative, where the goal is to empower and change the lives of the people studied (Chilisa 2012). With this in mind, we urge scholars to view varied (and often contradictory) data on a topic as an opportunity to identify common themes and suggest policies that address them and their intersections in new and productive ways. Data about young people who trade sex varies greatly, particularly when it comes to understanding the category of "young people." This label could mean all persons under 18, persons under 16, individuals aged 16 to 24, and multiple variations on this theme. Given this disparity, how could policy be developed to transform the lives of young people if there is no consensus about what this category includes? After all, a 10-year-old and an 18-year-old, for example, are positioned very differently, both personally and structurally; thus, they have disparate policy needs. Yet these varied needs could still be used to develop helpful policy if one considers the broader common themes that emerge from and across research on youth in the sex trades. For example, even as there was no concrete definition (and, by extension, sampling) of "young people" across studies, we found that youth status—no matter how this was defined—often meant limited education and job and income opportunities, which made it difficult for them to secure housing. These factors make young people vulnerable to engaging in sex trades or being exploited by sex traffickers. From a policy perspective, then, it seems like more accessible housing options for young people who struggle with homelessness, whether due to transphobia, poverty, disability, or any of the other myriad challenges they face, would lessen vulnerabilities to, and empower and transform the lives of, this group of people.

A second example concerns gender. Gender representation is not uniform among young people who trade sex: this population also includes boys, transgender, and gender non-conforming individuals; however, we can learn and develop better policy from this variation. Currently, police often arrest more cis-gender girls than other groups of young people (Lutnick 2016; Peters 2015). Police and abolitionist organizations characterize these as "arrests for the girls' own protection" (Musto 2016, 39)—a response premised upon a paternalism steeped in heteronormative gender ideology. Understanding the gender variation among young people who trade sex may help to reform these practices so that "trafficking victims" are understood inclusively, and the interventions developed to help them are less likely to reinforce a deeply entrenched view of girls as unable to articulate their own needs, or of boys as invulnerable, or of queer youth as sexual experimenters who primarily benefit from trading sex.

In stating this, we are not suggesting that more youth (including boys and trans youth) need to be arrested. Instead, by expanding understandings of this population, we can target policy and service development towards a wider range of young people in need. In short, by adopting a more reflexive and intersectional approach to sex work and sex trafficking research, we can see opportunities for interventions that challenge researchers' own ideological biases and are more wide-ranging in how they define and address the problem of sex trafficking.

Conclusion

Our call for greater reflexivity in sex work and sex trafficking research is aimed at all of us in the field, rather than at any single group of scholars. We see this reflexivity as a contribution to broader feminist discussions of intersectionality as both method and interpretive framework (e.g., Bowleg 2008) and to sex work-specific research. While there are many critiques of inter-sectionality, we find it best suited to the kind of reflexive research we're promoting, in part because of the positive possibilities for both social justice and inclusive research generated in, for example, participant-driven sex work research and the policy and data interpretation suggestions that emerged from our intersectional frame.

Furthermore, intersectionality draws renewed attention to the need for more critical self-awareness about feminist methods and ideological blind spots. Asking conscious questions guides us to seeing where our gender assumptions or investments in patriarchal power structures are impeding our own feminist praxis goals. In this way, we are also suggesting a broader re-thinking of those feminist goals and commitments because the outcomes of feminist research and advocacy have, to date, largely been carceral and, consequently, often harmful to women and girls. Undoubtedly, an important part of sexual and domestic violence activism was getting the criminal justice system to take victims seriously. But if our efforts to combat gender oppression involve continually empowering the very institutions that perpetuate rape culture and gender violence—such as the police, immigration enforcement, the military—then we, as feminists, need to think about how much our solutions to a specific gender problem (a) distort the ways in which the problem is gendered and (b) enhance the militaristic and moralistic arms of the state.

We hope our suggestions encourage reflexivity in future research through, among other things, engaging in better sampling practices, listening to study participants, and forming more multi-disciplinary research partnerships. Better yet—in the spirit of earlier feminist models of politics and praxis that operated through community organizing and (critical) self-help such as early domestic violence shelters and feminist health care groups—these studies should be undertaken with the help of, or in partnership with, former or current sex workers.[11] After all, feminists have long argued that women's voices matter , and the same can be said for sex workers of all genders. In the research process, persons who trade sex can help shape study questions and designs in ways helpful for more people rather than in ways that create other forms of exploitation.

Notes

1 Others have written since about the requirements of feminist praxis. See Naples (2003) for an exemplary recent work in this extensive field.

2 As we discuss below, "young people" is an imprecise concept typically defined by researchers to include those under the age of 16 or 18, but it can include older individuals up to age 29.

3 Despite its usefulness, there have been engaged critiques of intersectionality as both method and interpretative framework: e.g., its expansiveness can be read as incoherence (Davis 2008); its roots in Black feminist politics may seem to prioritize "race" (Lewis 2013) and essentialize Black women (Nash 2008); its (early) focus on identities could over-invest it in stabilizing subject positions and reasserting the centrality of white women's subjectivity (Puar 2012); and the turn to a structural critique from a positive project of reclaiming identities arguably leaves it insistently negative (*anti*-oppression) so that "positive moments of difference" (Singh 2015, 668) and "creative conformity" (663) get lost in a relentless dismantling of and resistance to domination.

4 Between 2001 and 2010 the US government authorized a total of $1.45 billion for domestic and international anti-trafficking programs—allocations that increased dramatically each year during this time period (Siskin & Wyler 2013, pp. 55–60, cited in Weitzer 2015, 224).

5 The oft-repeated claim that 100,000 to 300,00 young people are trafficked annually has been widely debunked. See discussion in Lutnick (2016).

6 A comprehensive narrative analysis combines the tools of methodological, systematic, narrative, and theoretical contribution reviews. For more information about each of these, see Elsevier Guide (2016). For more information about the method and data collection in our CNA, see Showden and Majic (forthcoming 2018).

7 Lorna Bracewell (2016) looks at how the sex radical side of the sex wars also failed to live up to its radical roots as it aligned with liberal anti-censorship activists in the "porn wars" of the 1980s.

8 For more information on the limits of peer review, and the application of reflexive methods to arrive at our final dataset, see Showden and Majic (forthcoming 2018, Ch. 2).

9 For more sources and further discussion, see Showden and Majic (forthcoming 2018). In addition to this implicit gender bias in sampling within carceral settings, a number of neo-abolitionist researchers explicitly excluded cis boys and transgender youth from their analyses, even though they had been recruited in their original samples (Clarke, et. al. 2012; Martin et al. 2010; Williams 2010). Similarly,

some researchers of homelessness also excluded cis boys and transgender youth (e.g., Chen et al. 2004). To our knowledge only one study excluded cis girls from its sample, and this was because most of those who were recruited did not identity as LGBTQ, which was a major focus of the study (Hein 2011). Please note that not all of these studies made it into our final CNA.

10 Note that these two studies were part of our original (n = 497) dataset, but not part of the final CNA.

11 For two examples of such research, see Lutnick (2014) and Bowen and O'Doherty (2014).

References

Agustín, Laura. 2005. Migrants in the Mistress' House: Other Voices in the "Trafficking" Debate. *Social Politics: International Studies in Gender, State & Society*, 12(1), 96–117.

Andrijasevic, Rutvica, & Mai, Nicola. 2016. Editorial: Trafficking (in) Representations: Understanding the Recurring Appeal of Victimhood and Slavery in Neoliberal Times. *Anti-Trafficking Review*, 1–10.

Armstrong, Lynzi. 2012. Reflections on a Research Process: Exploring Violence Against Sex Workers from a Feminist Perspective. *Women's Studies Journal*, 26(1), 2–10.

Balietti, Stefano. 2016. Science Is Suffering Because of Peer Review's Big Problems. *New Republic*, August 9.

Berger, Michele Tracy, & Guidroz, Kathleen. 2014. Researching Sexuality: The Politics-of-Location Approach for Studying Sex Work. In Showden, C.R. & Majic, S. *Negotiating Sex Work: Unintended Consequences of Policy and Activism*. Minneapolis, MN: University of Minnesota Press.

Berger, Roni. 2013. Now I See It, Now I Don't: Researcher's Position and Reflexivity in Qualitative Research. *Qualitative Research*, 15(2), 219–234. doi:10.1177/1468794112468475.

Bernstein, Elizabeth. 2007. *Temporarily Yours: Intimacy, Authenticity, and the Commerce of Sex*. Chicago, IL: University of Chicago Press.

Bernstein, Elizabeth. 2010. Militarized Humanitarianism Meets Carceral Feminism: The Politics of Sex, Rights, and Freedom in Contemporary Anti-trafficking Campaigns. *Signs*, 36, 45–71.

Bernstein, Elizabeth. 2012. Carceral Politics as Gender Justice? The "Traffic in Women" and Neoliberal Circuits of Crime, Sex, and Rights. *Theory and Society*, 41, 233–259.

Bilge, Sirma. 2013. Intersectionality Undone: Saving Intersectionality from Feminist Intersectionality Studies. *DuBois Review*, 10, 405–424.

Bowen, R., & O'Doherty, T. 2014. Participant-Driven Action Research (PDAR) with Sex Workers in Vancouver. In Showden, C.R. & Majic, S. *Negotiating Sex Work: Unintended Consequences of Policy and Activism*. Minneapolis, MN: University of Minnesota Press.

Bowleg, Lisa. 2008. When Black + Lesbian + Woman ≠ Black Lesbian Woman: The Methodological Challenges of Qualitative and Quantitative Intersectionality Research. *Sex Roles*, 59, 312–325.

Bracewell, Lorna N. 2016. Beyond Barnard: Liberalism, Antipornography Feminism, and the Sex Wars. *Signs: Journal of Women in Culture and Society*, 42, 23–48.

Bumiller, Kirsten. 2008. *In an Abusive State: How Neoliberalism Appropriated the Feminist Movement Against Sexual Violence*. Durham, NC: Duke University Press.

Bunch, Charlotte. 1979. Not By Degrees: Feminist Theory and Education. *Quest: A Feminist Quarterly*, 5, 7–18.

Chen, Xiaojin, Tyler, Kimberly A., Whitbeck, Les B., & Hoyt, Dan R. 2004. Early Sexual Abuse, Street Adversity, and Drug Use Among Female Homeless and Runaway Adolescents in the Midwest. *Journal of Drug Issues*, 34, 1–21.

Chilisa, Bagele. 2012. *Indigenous Research Methodologies*. Thousand Oaks, CA: Sage.

Chuang, Janie. 2010. Rescuing Trafficking from Ideological Capture: Prostitution Reform and Anti-Trafficking Law And Policy. *University of Pennsylvania Law Review*, 158, 1656–1725.

Clarke, R.J., Clarke, E., Roe-Sepowitz, D., & Fey, R. 2012. Age at Entry into Prostitution: Relationship to Drug Use, Race, Suicide, Education Level, Childhood Abuse, and Family Experiences. *Journal of Human Behaviour in the Social Environment*, 22, 270–289.

Corliss, H.L., Belzer, M., Forbes, C., & Wilson, E.C. 2007. An Evaluation of Service Utilization Among Male to Female Transgender Youth: Qualitative Study of a Clinic-Based Sample. *Journal of LGBT Heath Research*, 3, 49–61.

Crenshaw, Kimberlé. 1995. *Critical Race Theory: The Key Writings that Formed the Movement*. New York: New Press, distributed by W.W. Norton & Co.

Davis, Kathy. 2008. Intersectionality as Buzzword: A Sociology of Science Perspective on What Makes a Feminist Theory Successful. *Feminist Theory*, 9, 67–85.

Ditmore, M., Maternick, A., & Zapert, K. 2012. *The Road North: the Role of Gender, Poverty, and Violence in Trafficking from Mexico to the US*. New York: Sex Workers Project.

Elsevier Guide. 2016. *Education Research Review: Guide for Authors*. www.elsevier.com/journals/educational-research-review/1747-938x/guide-for- authors.

Estes, Richard, & Weiner, Neil. 2001. *The Commercial Sexual Exploitation of Children in the U.S., Canada, and Mexico: Executive Summary of the U.S. National Study*. Philadelphia, PA: University of Pennsylvania.

Everett, J., & Charlton, S.E. 2014. Debates and Dilemmas: Global Sex Trafficking. In Everett, J. M. & Charlton, S. E. 2014. *Women Navigating Globalization: Feminist Approaches to Development*. Lanham, MD: Rowman & Littlefield.

Farley, M., Cotton, A., Lynne, J., Zumbeck, S., Spiwak, F., Reyes, M., Alvarez, D., & Sezgin, U. 2003. Prostitution and Trafficking in Nine Countries: An Update on Violence and Post-Traumatic Stress Disorder. In Farley, M. (ed.), *Prostitution, Trafficking and Traumatic Stress*. Binghamton, NY: Haworth Press.

Fedina, Lisa. 2015. Use and Misuse of Research in Books on Sex Trafficking. *Trauma, Violence, and Abuse*, 16, 188–198.

Gozdziak, E., & Bump, M. 2008. *Data and Research on Human Trafficking: Bibliography of Research-Based Literature*. Washington, DC: Institute for the Study of International Migration.

Harding, Sandra. 1991. *Whose Science? Whose Knowledge? Thinking from Women's Lives*. Ithaca, NY: Cornell University Press.

Harding, Sandra. 1993. Rethinking Standpoint Epistemology: What Is Strong Objectivity? In Alcoff, Linda (ed.) *Feminist Epistemologies*. London: Routledge.

Harding, Sandra. 2015. *Objectivity and Diversity: Another Logic of Scientific Research*. Chicago, IL: University of Chicago Press.

Hein, Laura C. 2011. Survival Strategies of Male Homeless Adolescents. *Journal of the American Psychiatric Nurses Association*, 17, 274–282.

Hill Collins, Patricia. (1990). *Black Feminist Thought*. New York: Unwin Hyman.

Hoang, K.K., & Parreñas, R.S. 2014. *Human Trafficking Reconsidered: Rethinking the Problem, Envisioning New Solutions*. New York: London, International Debate Education Association.

hooks, bell. 1990. *Yearning: Race, Gender and Cultural Politics*. Toronto, ON: Between the Lines.

hooks, bell. 1999. *Feminist Theory: From Margin to Centre*. Cambridge, MA: South End Press.

Hua, J., & Nigorizawa, H. 2010. US Sex Trafficking, Women's Human Rights and the Politics of Representation. *International Feminist Journal of Politics*, 12, 401–423.

Johnston, A., Friedman, B., & Sobel, M. 2015. Framing an Emerging Issue: How U.S. Print and Broadcast News Media Covered Sex Trafficking, 2008–2012. *Journal of Human Trafficking*, 1, 235–254.

Kempadoo, Kamala. 2005. From Moral Panic to Global Justice: Changing Perspectives on Trafficking. In Kempadoo, K., Sanghera, J., & Pattanaik, B. (eds.) *Trafficking and Prostitution Reconsidered: New Perspectives on Migration, Sex Work and Human Rights*. Boulder, CO: Paradigm Books.

Kournay, Janet A. 2009. The Place of Standpoint Theory in Feminist Science Studies. *Hypatia*, 24, 209–218.

Lee, C., Sugimoto, C., Zhang, G., & Cronin, B. 2013. Bias in Peer Review. *Journal of the American Society for Information Science and Technology*, 64, 2–17.

Lee, R.M., & C. Renzetti. 1990. The Problems of Researching Sensitive Topics. *American Behavioral Scientist*, 33 (5): 510–528.

Lerum, K., & Brents, B. 2016. Sociological Perspectives on Sex Work and Human Trafficking. *Sociological Perspectives*, 59, 17–26.

Lewis, Gail. 2013. Unsafe Travel: Experiencing Intersectionality and Feminist Displacements. *Signs*, 38, 869–892.

Lutnick, Alexandra. 2014. Beyond Prescientific Reasoning: The Sex Worker Environmental Assessment Team Study. In Showden, C.R. and Majic, S. (eds.) *Negotiating Sex Work: Unintended Consequences of Policy and Activism*. Minneapolis, MN: University of Minnesota Press.

Lutnick, Alexandra. 2016. *Domestic Minor Sex Trafficking: Beyond Victims and Villains*. New York: Columbia University Press.

Maitra, Rob. 2002. The Homeless Community of the Piers. *Gay and Lesbian Review Worldwide*, 9 (2): 8–11.

Majic, Samantha. 2014. *Sex Work Politics: From Protest to Service Provision* (1st edition). Philadelphia, PA: University of Pennsylvania Press.

Marcus, A., Horning, A., Curtis, R., Sanson, J., & Thompson, E. 2014. Conflict and Agency Among Sex Workers and Pimps: A Closer Look at Domestic Minor Sex Trafficking. *Annals of the American Academy of Political and Social Science*, 653, 225–246.

Martin, L., Hearst, M., & Widome, R. 2010. Meaningful Differences: Comparison of Adult Women Who First Traded Sex as a Juvenile Versus as an Adult. *Violence Against Women*, 16, 1252–1269.

Musto, Jennifer. 2016. *Control and Protect: Collaboration, Carceral Protection, and Domestic Sex Trafficking in the United States*. Berkeley, CA: University of California Press

Naples, Nancy A. 2003. *Feminism and Method: Ethnography, Discourse Analysis, and Activist Research*. New York: Routledge.

Nash, Jennifer C. 2008. Rethinking Intersectionality. *Feminist Review*, 89, 1–15.

Nencel, Lorraine. 2017. Epistemologically Privileging the Sex Worker: Uncovering the Rehearsed and Presumed in Sex Work Studies. In Spanger, M. & Skilbrei, M. L. (eds.) *Prostitution Research in Context: Methodology, Representation and Power*. London: Routledge.

Peters, Alicia. (2015). *Responding to Human Trafficking: Sex, Gender, and Culture in the Law*. Philadelphia, PA: University of Pennsylvania Press.

Puar, Jasbir K. 2012. "I Would Rather Be a Cyborg Than a Goddess": Becoming-Intersectional in Assemblage Theory. *Philosophia*, 2, 49–66.

Raible, John. 2011. Queering the Adult Gaze: Young Male Hustlers and Their Alliances with Older Gay Men. *Journal of LGBT Youth*, 8, 260–280.

Rouse, Joseph. 2009. Standpoint Theories Reconsidered. *Hypatia*, 24, 200–209.

Showden, C.R. 2011. *Choices Women Make: Agency in Domestic Violence, Assisted Reproduction, and Sex Work*. Minneapolis, MN: University of Minnesota Press.

Showden, C.R., & Majic, S. 2014. *Negotiating Sex Work: Unintended Consequences of Policy and Activism*. Minneapolis, MN: University of Minnesota Press.

Showden, C.R., & Majic, S. Forthcoming 2018. *Youth Who Trade Sex in the U.S.: Intersectionality, Agency, and Vulnerability*. Philadelphia, PA: Temple University Press.

Singh, Jakeet. 2015. Religious Agency and the Limits of Intersectionality. *Hypatia*, 30, 657–674.

Siskin A., & Wyler L.S. 2013. *Trafficking in Persons: U.S. Policy and Issues for Congress*. Washington, DC: Congressional Research Service.

Tyldum, G. & Brunovskis, A. 2005. Describing the Unobserved: Methodological Challenges in Empirical Studies on Human Trafficking. *International Migration*, 43, 17–34.

US Department of State. 2013. USG TIP Projects with Funds Obligated in FY2012. Washington, DC. https://2009-2017.state.gov/documents/organization/229068.pdf.

Weitzer, Ronald. 2005. The Growing Moral Panic over Prostitution and Sex Trafficking. *The Criminologist*, 30, 2–5.

Weitzer, Ronald. 2011. Sex Trafficking and the Sex Industry: The Need for Evidence-Based Theory and Legislation. *Journal of Criminal Law and Criminology*, 101, 1337–1369.

Weitzer, Ronald. 2015. Human Trafficking and Contemporary Slavery. *Annual Review of Sociology*, 41, 223–242.

Williams, Linda M. 2010. Harm and Resilience Among Prostituted Teens: Broadening our Understanding of Victimisation and Survival. *Social Policy and Society*, 9, 243–254.

Williamson, C., & Prior, M. 2009. Domestic Minor Sex Trafficking: A Network of Underground Players in the Midwest. *Journal of Child and Adolescent Trauma*, 2, 46–61.

Zhang, Sheldon. 2009. Beyond the "Natasha" Story: A Review and Critique of Current Research on Sex Trafficking. *Global Crime*, 10, 178–195.

6

First-person singular(s)

Teasing out multiple meanings in sex work autobiographies

Treena Orchard

Introduction

> Why do we write? A chorus erupts. Because we cannot simply live.
>
> *(Patti Smith 2017, 93)*

Women organize different systems of sex work and the material items and relationships that inform these exchanges into their lives in ways that are complex and mutable over time. As an anthropologist I explore these issues through interviews, participant observation, social mapping, arts-based methods, and fieldnotes, all of which are recognized epistemologically as 'data.' However, I am also interested in how women in the sex trade document their own lives in ways that fall off the page and bleed into less explored margins of what is considered 'research.' Over the past two decades, women have marked themselves in my life and offered deeper clues about theirs through photos, a bracelet, notes scrawled on scraps of paper, as Facebook friends, and in endless memories that stack up like sacred texts in my limbic system. After completing my first collaborative project with women in sex work in London, Ontario (Orchard et al. 2012, 2013, 2014) one participant, Sheila (a pseudonym), imparted to me a particularly special gift.

In the summer of 2010, over cups of coffee in her small apartment she handed me two written documents, which she described as her 'life story.' Sheila did not indicate why they were written or what I should do with them, she just pressed the powerful information into my hands. She has since moved away from London and I have felt haunted by her writings, which I have poured over and then returned to the filing cabinet countless times. What do I do with them? Why are there two stories? What do they reveal about how Sheila sees the world and her place in it? Do I analyze them as ethnographic or literary material? Informed by critical ethnographic and feminist theory, along with interpretive approaches from the auto/biography literature, this chapter problematizes these questions. I begin by unpacking the structure and content of each life story, then provide a comparative analysis of the two works, and conclude with a reflection on Sheila's writing as a righteous expression of subjectivity as well as a powerful gift of human solidarity.

The dual biographies at the heart of this discussion are part of a rich history of writing by women in sex work, which began in the 'Western' cultural context during the eighteenth century alongside the rise of the European novel and erotica focusing on prostitutes and courtesans (Booth 2008; Peakman 2006). Referred to as the "whore biography" this diverse genre includes accounts of women who 'fell' into prostitution following rape or seduction and those who rose above their disenfranchised socio-sexual status through strategic alliances with powerful men. Although often penned by scrupulous men who profited considerably, a handful of these narratives were written by the women themselves, which focused less on their moral slide and more on resisting or avenging the sexual and gendered inequities of the time (Peakman 2009).

The 1980s marked the next significant period during which women from different parts of the world and sex work fields were writing about their lives and forging ahead with the global sex workers' rights movements (Bell 1987; Delacoste and Alexander 1987; Pheterson 1989). These writings illuminate women's ideas about sexuality, power, and the importance of pleasure as well as the complicated emotional and physical outcomes of being involved in work that has yet to be fully recognized as valid, legal, and socially important. While similar themes are present in later writings (Bruckert 2002; Frank 2002; Jeffrey and MacDonald 2006; Kempadoo and Doezema 1998; Nagle 1997; Oakley 2007; Sterry 2009; van der Meulen et al. 2013), the more recent works also include discussions of clients (Christina 2004; Sycamore 2000), how to become a successful professional in the trade (Meretrix 2001; Montenegro 2014), and other genres, including poetry and memoir (Febos 2011; Werhurn and Bazuin 2017).

Many types of sex work are documented in this literature but accounts from women in street-based settings are relatively rare, despite the fact they remain the most documented group of sex trade workers (Dewey and St. Germain 2016; Hail-Jares et al. 2017). Of those that do exist, very few shed light or focus on these writings from a literary standpoint (see Dawn 2013 for an exception). Online blogs and other writings by and for women in the trades are more diverse in terms of writing styles and content compared to traditional book formats. Yet, even here entries by those in street-level sex work and whose lives are shaped by poverty, racism, and addictions are significantly less common. Sheila addresses these complex themes head on and in doing so makes a unique contribution to the existing literature, particularly in relation to issues of subjectivity, everyday survival, the politics of health, and the therapeutic power of writing. Her work includes sentences that are incomplete and words that are abbreviated, which are left uncorrected in the interest of preserving the original form and style of her work.

Laying out the bones: structure and technique in the autobiographies

The way that Sheila writes is animated, complicated, and while the conceptual thread is not always clear what is evident is that she structures her writings in a literary way and not 'simply' as a chronological telling of life events. With beautiful lines like: "anger and fear flowed through my veins like something I couldn't explain," "men became muscle to me and a source of money," and evocative often uncomfortable questions like: "why do we, as people who do try, throw our hands up?" she demonstrates her aesthetic skills and desire to (re)create her life through the written word.

Structure

There are two autobiographies, the first is 14 pages and the second is 27 pages. The two writings are recoded on letterhead from Ontario Works, the provincial government agency that provides economic support or 'welfare' (see Figure 6.1). She writes on both sides of each piece of paper, denotes the page numbers with a handwritten encircled number in the top left of each side of paper, and she writes with a heavy pen that impresses each letter into the page. The back pages contain more writing than the front pages because the letterhead text and images are not present. The material featured on the letterhead side is written in the 15 lines allotted to the "Message" to the caseworker. Seeing those words atop each piece of paper produces a powerful feeling and it is one of the ways that her work haunted me. While I am not the caseworker I am the one she has left these pages, these messages to, which amplifies my sense of obligation to put forward her work. Using the letterhead of the government agencies she critiques to lay bare their hypocrisy, as discussed in detail below, is particularly compelling and admirable.

Technique

In autobiographies, the author is the 'narrating I' and the 'narrated I' and often shifts between first- and third-person perspectives to distinguish between describing an experience/exteriority and the subjective account of that experience/interiority (Perselli 2005; Sutin and Robins 2008). Sheila often blurs these narrative boundaries and is both subject and object of her own inquiry. The most compelling example of this is the "alkie-addict" or "the addict," figurative terms that are used interchangeably to reference people with addictions and herself as someone who has fought these demons. They are employed to illuminate the central theme in her work: the detrimental effects of the inequitable distribution of power in society on vulnerable people. The "alkie-addict" anchors her critique of how those running social institutions (i.e., doctors, police, social services) often feed upon the suffering of the poor and keep each other afloat through greed and structural violence: "Now we earn money on the weakness of addicts all across the board." Shifting from third to first person, Sheila reveals the sad fact that she has few options but to enter this hypocritical system: "I know if I want to make a living out there in today's society, the suffering alkie-addict is the way to go." Cognizant of the structural binds

Figure 6.1 Institutional letterhead used in Sheila's writings.

Message to caseworker

Date:	
Caseworker's name:	Caseworker #:
Your name:	Member ID:

Message:

that tether her to a life of dependence and highlighting the fallacy of needing to exploit/use her addictions to access social services, she is both a symbol of injustice and a fleshly survivor of this inhumane system.

Another device that surfaces in Shelia's work is that of "hmmm," which is employed five or six times in the second autobiography to preface certain statements or questions and generate a sense of interaction between the text and the reader. After a scathing commentary on how "the addict" in government-funded methadone programs (where clients are mandated to undergo urine tests to detect banned substances) often circumvent the medical system by using substances like Ritalin that evade detection, Sheila uses "hmmm" in the following way: "Yes, a bunch of Ritalin addicts running around on methadone but [they] got away with fucking the system . . . hmmm, you scared yet?" This question follows information that she provides about the penetrability of the system and the prowess of the "addict," two things many people do not typically think about in a causal way. Does she want to scare me or is her intention to remind me of our shared vulnerability, as members of a society that prides itself on the strength of its 'systems' to keep out the dangerous/undesirable/weakened—the 'alkie-addict'? Using this device reveals her creativity and the "hmmm" forces the reader to pause, thus slowing down the reading of the work and generating a pensive connection between writer and reader and reader and text.

Her use of humour is brilliant and the way she makes certain tragic situations hilarious is not only engaging, it renders them indelible. Take the following critique of the snack bar, an essential part of any harm reduction or outreach worker's tool kit, and the pathetic client on the receiving end of these food items: "And we won't forget about the fucking nutrition bars, hell no. Just a good gesture to keep the sad bastards going." Sheila's blacker comedic insights are revealed when she discusses the dangers of trusting a system (i.e., disability/social services) that does not provide adequate care, in life and/or death: "If I was to trust today's society . . . well all I see is a tombstone. And even then, I'm not sure what disability gives us lifers on disability for a grave site. HA HA." Her use of "lifers," a word associated with prison and living a life shaped by institutional time, connects with the recurring theme of systemic violence against the vulnerable or the 'alkie-addicts,' which she views as a crime.

Adding flesh to the bones: analyzing the autobiographies

I knew a great deal about Sheila's life prior to receiving her writings and analyzing them should have been relatively straightforward, but it was not. It was challenging for two primary reasons, the first of which is the hybrid nature of the work, which intersects ethnographic life history and literary autobiography. Do I conduct thematic/inductive coding often used in ethnographic research (Madden 2010; Naples 2003) or 'surface reading' (Best and Marcus 2009) employed by literary scholars? These approaches are distinct and the former considers overt meanings within a text alongside insights gleaned from in-person observation and accumulated knowledge of an individual/cultural setting over time. Surface reading, on the other hand, foregrounds what is evident and apprehensible in texts to stay as close as possible to the author's original intentions (McNeill and Douglas 2017). I tried to thread both perspectives into the analysis and knowing about her life prior to seeing the writings reduced the likelihood of misinterpretation of her work, which can be quite confusing in places. Doing this also maintains the integrity of the immediately discernable meaning (the surface) and brings a richness to the analysis that would not have been possible without my pre-existing knowledge of her life to (thick description). The analysis involved multiple readings of both autobiographies, line-by-line coding to identify themes/ideas as well as seminal quotations and literary devices and tabulating the key themes according to the frequency with which they appear (see Tables 6.1 and 6.2 below).

The second reason analyzing Sheila's work has been difficult is linked with the profoundly personal form it takes, recorded in her own handwriting with its unique rounded look. I have run my hand over the pages countless times, feeling the way her heavy pressing on the pen made the letters sink into the paper like inverted braille. There is no escaping her authorial presence because she is literally and figuratively *in* these pages, which is comforting and intimidating. Working with this embodied physical record also generates feelings of responsibility regarding how Sheila and her writings are represented, which is important considering how 'over-represented' women in street-based sex work are by others within the realm of research, the media, and society in general (Dewey and St. Germain 2016, 42–43). This sense of obligation is a quintessential feature of what anthropologists call the gift economy, a framework used to understand the exchange of material items and power relations that shape relationships and cultural systems (Mauss 1950). While the term 'gift' sounds patently benevolent, it can also engender or reproduce certain inequities that exist between the parties that gift and those that receive. Relative to Sheila, I have more power to get her work into the wider social universe where it belongs, which I imagine she was cognizant of and perhaps banking on. In some ways, without this sense of discomfort Sheila's writings might cease to be a true gift, which is a useful way of thinking about her writings that continue to have "a soul" long after they have left the hands of their creator (ibid., 66).

Autobiography 1: "chapters, chapters, chapters"

This is the shorter of the two pieces and its content, organization, and length lead me to believe it was written first. It includes additional insights into Sheila's childhood and family life that are not included the second narrative and is structured more succinctly along her life chronology, two structural features that characterize beginnings in auto/biographical writing (Brockmeier, 2001; Fivush 2008) Given its brevity and organizational structure, she likely

Table 6.1 Primary themes in Autobiography 1[1]

5	4	3	2
Life statements	Health (physical, mental)	Government hypocrisy	Feeling depressed, exhausted
Booze/dope	Desire to do something different, to help others	General comments about insufficient social services	Desire for family
Feeling sad/lost	Institutions	Corrupt, stigmatizing Dr. practices	Running away
Critique of harm reduction		The farm	Her kids
		Men	
		Housing	
		Feeling angry	
		Desire for structure	
		Being an addict	
		Sex work	

used it as a jumping-off point versus creating the longer piece first and then writing this one. Spatial limitations do not permit an in-depth analysis of this work and my aim here is to flesh out some of her salient insights regarding the key issues of subjectivity, addictions, institutional forces, and harm reduction.

Sheila opens with her first name, age, status as "clean and off drugs and alcohol," and where she is from. She then describes her 'blended' family (i.e., multiple half and full siblings with different fathers and mothers), sexual abuse by her father and other men, being raised by older siblings, and the lifelong sadness associated with losing her mother when she was 4 years old. Sheila was kidnapped before the age of 10 and provides arresting details of her 12-month captivity as a sex slave, a terrifying experience that reinforced the powerlessness and depleted self-worth she experienced at home. This traumatic event and the drugs that were injected into her, cocaine specifically, also laid the groundwork for her struggle with addictions: "Cocaine became my friend and allowed me to do anything I was told . . . I did a lot needles and drank to escape." In these opening pages, she moves frequently between different time periods and says: "Chapters are my life . . . I will be doing a lot of jumping around as my life, I really do feel, were and are chapters." She repeats the phrase "chapters, chapters, chapters" and uses it later like a dinkus, a row of asterisks used to break up the text in a book or article, to delineate her formative years and her present life.

This narrative focuses primarily on early traumas, institutional responses to addictions and mental health (i.e., medical system, police/criminal justice, and social services), and Sheila's desire for a better life: "From being alone a lot in life without the real sense of family, I guess I want to have structure and growth the last half of life." Her insights into a life "run on institutions," including group homes, a draconian school for "wayward children" in the 1960s (e.g. Bonneville Training School), Child's Aid Society, psychiatric institutions, jail, and various social services, reflect her keen awareness of the unfortunate fact that these systems do not always operate with the best interests of the 'client' at heart. She critiques the harm reduction approach most severely because it seems to perpetuate the hurt that people in pain do to themselves, it lets people off the hook without doing the hard work of healing, and it allows institutional players (i.e., government, pharmaceutical companies, prescribing physicians) to make money from the 'alkie-addict': "Running around in vans and giving out needles, crack pipes is just contributing to helping us die . . . The government's living off addicts in addiction."[2]

This narrative also includes a specific critique of those in the medical system, with whom Sheila has had intimate and exploitative interactions. Given these experiences, it makes sense that she refers to the "Medical system as the pimp . . . 10 years having a Dr. give me my pills while doing the oldest profession known to mankind." However, she does more than rail against harm reduction and the health system, she offers a therapeutic alternative. Shaped by her restorative experiences of living on a commune before coming to London, Sheila advocates for

[a] farm for women who appreciate their recovery and want to live with others who enjoy company and living in a positive structure. Self-care, long-term housing, education living off the land. Projects to make a difference to build a proper inner foundation in life.

Autobiography 2: "life on life's terms"

This writing begins with Sheila stating her first name, age, and where she is from and unlike the other autobiography there is no statement about being clean and sober. She then launches into a tangled discussion of her abusive childhood and early as well as current interactions with socio-medical and criminal justice systems, painful experiences she refers to as "facing life on life's terms." She is cognizant that this account is somewhat jumbled and instead of starting over or shifting to a more organized style of writing, she owns this aspect of her work and where she is at during this recollective process: "Sorry I am jumping around but that's how my thoughts are." Many of the issues explored are also featured in the first narrative (see Table 6.2 below), but they are communicated with greater emotive force and she employs more questions ("why isn't my thinking okay?") and imperative statements ("do the math"), which enrich the sense of immediacy and uncertainty that stream through this autobiography.

Addictions, personal and structural conditions that have shaped her suffering, and Sheila's dismay with harm reduction dominate this discussion. She got sober in the late 1990s and early 2000s through 12-step programs (i.e., Alcoholics Anonymous) and the grit of hard personal work, a tough love, individual-oriented strategy she sums up with the phrase "get busy livin or get busy dyin."[3] She highlights several differences between this approach and harm reduction, including the inequity of service provision for people within the addictions spectrum: "There is more for those active addicts than us clean ones . . . What about the chickadee out here who's already faced the battle and have [sic] put using to a back seat and want [sic] to live a healthy productive life?" Sheila also lays out the labyrinth-like conditions of harm reduction, which promotes dependency (on service systems and substances like methadone) and individual responsibility (to take methadone daily, secure housing, meet appointments). One outcome of this seemingly contradictory strategy is that the 'addict-alkie' is set up to believe that 'meeting them where they are at'—a key tenet of harm reduction—affords them greater power over their lives. She exclaims: "I CAN'T BELIEVE THE ADDICT-ALKIE RUNS THE BEAT" and then unpacks the hollowness of this 'power' by drawing attention to how it exacerbates people's already difficult lives while trapping them in a series of systems designed to offer only band-aid solutions:

> Rehab isn't methadone, dude . . . Empathy for stupidity doesn't fly. Have we all slept and then woke up to this? Addiction has over-populated our society, giving the addict no real freedom even if they want to stop. 21 days here then to leave and become homeless.

At one point, Sheila draws parallels between methadone maintenance therapy and 'The Final Solution': "We all didn't like what Hitler done but we abuse his knowledge and methadone's been the biggest gate to Hell." This is a rather extreme analogy, but it aligns with how she refers to methadone throughout the narrative: "It's the same as junk [heroin] itself" and "it shouldn't be a life sentence." I wonder if she knows that methadone was created in Germany or that it was designed to circumvent morphine addiction. First marketed under the name *Dolphine* in honour of Adolf Hitler (Smith 1982) methadone and other powerful drugs like the stimulant Pervitin, which was consumed by German troops at staggering rates (833,000 per day at one point), were part of the Third Reich's war machine and hastened the country's global pharmaceutical dominance (Ohler 2016).

Along with these sharp critiques, Sheila's writing is also hilarious and penetrating on a more interior, emotional level with respect to how she presents herself. The following description of a former boyfriend reminds us that life has not only been about struggle, she too has had hot love and excitement: "A bad boy who rode a Harley-Davidson and thrilled the shit out of me." Feeling "macaronied out" is another phrase that sticks in my mind because it is such an original and funny way of poking fun at the over-abundance of cheap, starchy foods offered at soup kitchens and church-sponsored lunches for the poor. In this autobiography Sheila also talks about who she is and how she feels about herself, often within the context of her ongoing healing journey, as these powerful passages illuminate:

Table 6.2 Primary themes in Autobiography 2

13	12	10	8	7	6	5	4	3	2
Institutions	Critiques of harm reduction; "alkie-addict"	Physical health	Sex work	Sobriety	Addiction	The work of life	Methadone	Farm	Lost
	Mental health				Don't give up	Trust		Men	Kids
	Social services				Self and life desires	Corrupt doctors		Healing	Roommate
								Angry	OD
								Sexual abuse	
								Hard to get help	
								Death	
								Quest statements	

I tell myself daily that I'm okay. I need help but have flown on some strong virtues that have kept me alive. 48 years of shit off and on and believe me I've run all my life and wonder how I make it. Strong virtues and high standards on myself has been a blessing.

I have a long healing path and do see it as a struggle . . . Strength, honour and truth has become my model. Chapters in recovery are hard and this round I've had no escape except to heal the body. The mind's there but always questioning the real deal. I have not got all the puzzle's pieces together.

Comparative analysis

In both sets of writings, Sheila provides rich descriptions of the diverse emotional landscape she inhabits and has had to walk through over the course of her life. In the first story feelings of being sad/lost dominate, whereas in the second piece she focuses more on betrayal and anger, which she frames as a useful feeling: "At least anger was an emotion that people can feel, hear, and be aware of immediately." She discusses prostitution in both life stories, but the way she discusses this theme differs. In the first autobiography she refers to it several times as "the oldest work in the world" and focuses primarily on her exploitation as a child sex slave. In the second piece Shelia concentrates on the need to legalize prostitution and demonstrates a complex array of feelings about sex work and herself as woman who has done this, namely fear, shame, lack of self-respect, and a resource she can count on to survive. Physical ailments and mental health issues are not really mentioned in the first story, yet they are among the most frequently cited issues in the second narrative. Wanting to help others and desiring a family/familial structure are spoken about many times in the first story, yet they do not surface in the second one.

The most significant difference between the two writings involves the relationship between her life trajectory and her sense of self. The first autobiography is rooted in a detailed chronology of events, people, and institutions that have profoundly shaped her life trajectory. Here, Sheila highlights the devastating impact of these things *on* her and the first person is rarely seen: "life was very sad"; "starting life locked up." The second piece is more introspective and creative in its interpretation of how different individuals and social forces have shaped, but not wholly determined, who she is as a woman. Take this statement: "I see myself as damaged but with skills," which registers her presence and value. This and other instances of Sheila making sense of life as well as herself align with "quest narratives" (Pugh and Tietjen 1997, ix), which are about self-expression, self-knowledge, and a physical and emotional place where the authors belong. The following examples reflect these elements of quest narratives: "All my life I have been fighting with addiction, self-esteem, wondering why I am here and wondering really my purpose"; "We fall, we get back up and move on hoping not to fall again. Daily trying to make sense of where I belong has been trying."

The second story also includes ruminations on what Sheila wants her life to be about or to mean, along with discussions about the literal and figurative work that is required to 'simply' be in the world. Referred to as "life desires" and "the work of life," these emotive reflections evoke qualities associated with the "'hope-to-die-with-my-boots-on righteous dopefiend' who is tough but also vulnerable to the structural violence she seeks to resist and survive in spite of" (Bourgois and Schonberg 2009, 212; Pearson and Bourgois 1995). Take the following 'life desires' examples, both of which are summative and somewhat affirmative: "I hope I die clean and no matter what society does, I keep my chin up"; "I am not perfect nor do I strive for perfection. I do strive to have freedom and peace and positive hand on my journey." The 'work of life' material is rooted more firmly in the concrete-ness of life and includes phrases like "doggy dog world," "putting in time," and "survival armour," which she uses to describe the psycho-emotional preparation she needs to engage in to feel protected from the harms she encounters in daily life.

Sheila's gift: communication, power, and a subjectivity of her own

Women have long written about their lives to assert or insert themselves within larger social narratives about gender, race, sexuality, class, family life, as well as the arts and the politics of being human. This includes a small but robust body of work by women and others in the sex trade that first emerged in the eighteenth century (Breashears 2003; Peakman 2006) and then again with considerable force in the 1980s as part of third-wave/sex-positive feminism (Delacoste and Alexander 1987; Pheterson 1989). The books, online pieces, and other forms of artistic and political expression created by these groups of women explore a multitude of fascinating, important issues that intersect with and inform diverse lived sex work experiences (Nagle 1997; Oakley 2007; Red Umbrella Project 2013, 2014). Sheila's writings align with this literature and are at the same time distinctive from them because she writes from a socio-economic and sexual location that remains under-represented in sex work autobiography—the street level—and unlike many of the works cited above that concentrate on their lives in sex work, for Sheila that is not the definitive subject. Her narratives focus primarily on the people and systems that have conspired to govern her across time and space: the men who kidnapped her, the abusive teachers at the Bonneville Training School, corrupt physicians who pushed pills and their bodies into her, and social service industries that distribute their 'help' in deeply inequitable ways. She also engages in several parallel tasks that are fundamental to autobiography: the translation and creation of the self (Champagne 1999; Smith 1987); the performance of the self (Greenleaf 2004); and the quest for self-expression, self-knowledge, and a place to belong (Pugh and Tietjen 1997; Turner and Ehlers 2003). She writes her self and her life, on her own terms.

Sheila's work is an agential expression of her complex, fluid subjectivity and it functions as potent gift within the moral economy that structures our relationship and gives it meaning. Through the anthropological lens, gifts are often discussed as literal and figurative trade items through which existing power structures and social ideologies are reproduced, often in ways that reify the inequities between giver and receiver. Alongside this traditional interpretation of Mauss' seminal work (1950), it is important to remember the magical spirit and transformative force that gifts can also contain, transmit, and symbolize. By giving her writings to me Sheila is not simply bowing under or reconstituting the power inequities embedded in our respective status as women from different classes or social groups, she is contesting the conditions upon which those differences are constructed. The pages she handed to me are not filled with a victim narrative or a singularly sad story, as one might expect from a 'marginalized' woman, but with smart, hilarious, and deeply moving critiques of power itself and her orbit within life's cosmos. Gifting them to me binds us in solidarity that is dictated, in part, by the inequities of the gift economy but also by the political power of communication and the shared consciousness that is possible through creativity: "Only through communication can human life hold meaning" (Freire 1973/2000, 58).

These writings and the project of diving their substance once haunted me, yet now I do not want to leave them—sweet irony and evidence of the abiding significance of Sheila's gift. Her work matters for many reasons, including what Eakin (1992, 3) calls being "touched by knowledge through the experiences of others to whom we bear some responsibility." We need to care about one another better and encouraging creativity and communication is a powerful, democratic place to start. This work also raises questions about the meaning and value assigned to different subjects and experiences: What does it mean to have a life worth reading and who decides? (McNeill and Douglas 2017, 7). Without asking these questions and devising innovative ways to make sense of formerly 'unseen' narratives or 'data' that defy easy analysis or classification, these autobiographies may have remained asleep in my filing cabinet. Solidarity is stronger than apprehension and this is something I am indebted to Sheila for making me remember.

Notes

1 The numbers in both Tables 6.1 and 6.2 refer to the frequency with which Sheila mentions the theme at hand in her writing.
2 An example she uses often is methadone, which the government promotes to control opiate addiction and profits handsomely from because it is not covered by many provincial health care plans. Her repeated jab at methadone as "just another fucking bandage" (or "the dragon") that often traps people in the cycle of addiction and makes the government money also aligns with what drug policy researchers in Canada have argued for decades (Fischer 2000). The profits to be made from methadone are tremendous and in Ontario alone the government stands to make $10, 950,000 annually from the estimated 50,000 clients, each of whom pay 6.00 per "drink" per day (Blackwell 2016).
3 Which is the title of a 2005 song by Fall Out Boy about hard living and loving on the street, and is a phrase used by several women in my ongoing research in London.

References

Bell, L. 1987. *Good Girls/Bad Girls: Feminists and Sex Trade Workers Face to Face*. Toronto, ON: The Women's Press.

Best, S. and Marcus, S. 2009. Surface Reading: An Introduction. *Representations* 108: 1–21.

Blackwell, T. 2016. Critics Question Methadone Usage as Patient Numbers Soar in Canada. *National Post* [online]. Available at: http://news.nationalpost.com/news/canada/critics-question-methadone-usage-as-patient-numbers-soar-in-canada [Accessed November 13, 2017].

Booth, M. 2008. Whore Biographies 1700–1825. *Biography* 31(3): 466–473.

Bourgois, P. and Schonberg, J. 2009. *Righteous Dopefiend*. Berkeley, CA: University of California Press.

Breashears, C. 2003. Scandalous Categories: Classifying the Memoirs of Unconventional Women. *Psychological Quarterly* 82(2): 187–212.

Brockmeier, J. 2001. From the End to the Beginning Retrospective Teleology in Autobiography. In J. Brockmeier and D. Carbaugh, Eds., *Narrative and Identity* (pp. 247–280). Amsterdam and Philadelphia, PA: John Benjamins.

Bruckert, C. 2002. *Taking It Off, Putting It On: Women in the Strip Trade*. Toronto, ON: Women's Press.

Champagne, L. 1999. Notes on Autobiography and Performance. *Women & Performance: A Journal of Feminist Theory* 19(10): 155–172.

Christina, G. 2004. *Paying for It: A Guide by Sex Workers for Their Clients*. Emeryville, CA: Greenery Press.

Dawn, A. 2013. *How Poetry Saved My Life: A Hustler's Memoir*. Vancouver, BC: Arsenal Press.

Delacoste, F. and Alexander, P., Eds. 1987. *Sex Work: Writings by Women in the Sex Industry*. San Francisco, CA: Cleis Press.

Dewey, S. and St. Germain, T. 2016. *Women of the Street: How the Criminal Justice Social Service Alliance Fails Women in Prostitution*. New York: New York University Press.

Eakin, P. 1992. *Touching the World: Reference in Autobiography*. Princeton, NJ: Princeton University Press.

Febos, M. 2011. *Whip Smart: The True Story of a Secret Life*. New York: St. Martins Griffin.

Fischer, B. 2000. Prescriptions, Power and Politics: The Turbulent History of Methadone Maintenance in Canada. *Journal of Public Health Policy* 21(2): 187–210.

Fivush, R. 2008. Remembering and Reminiscing: How Individual Lives Are Constructed in Family Narratives. *Memory Studies* 1(1): 49–58.

Freire, P. [1973] 2000. *Pedagogy of the Oppressed*. New York: Continuum.

Frank, K. 2002. *G-Strings and Sympathy: Strip Club Regulars and Male Desire*. Durham, NC: Duke University Press.

Greenleaf, M. 2004. Performing Autobiography: The Multiple Memoirs of Catherine the Great (1756–1796). *The Russian Review* 63: 407–426.

Hail-Jares, K., Shdaimah, C., and Leon, C., Eds. 2017. *Challenging Perspectives on Street-Based Sex Work*. Philadelphia, PA: Temple University Press.

Jeffrey, L. and MacDonald, G. 2006. *Sex Workers in the Maritimes Talk Back*. Vancouver, BC: UBC Press.

Kempadoo, K. and Doezema, J., Eds. 1998. *Global Sex Workers: Rights, Resistance, and Redefinition*. New York: Routledge.

McNeill, L. and Douglas, K. 2017. Heavy Lifting: The Pedagogical Work of Life Narratives. *a/b: Auto/Biography Studies* 32(1): 5–14.

Madden, R. 2010. *Being Ethnographic: A Guide to the Theory and Practice of Ethnography*. Los Angeles, CA and London: Sage.

Mauss, M. 1950 (1990 translation by W.D. Halls). *The Gift: The Form and Reason for Exchange in Archaic Societies*. New York: W.W. Norton.

Meretrix. M. 2001. *A Guide to Sex Work for the Ambitious and Intrigued*. Emeryville, CA: Greenery Press.

Montenegro, G. 2014. *10,000 Men and Counting*. Bloomington, IN: Xlibris.

Nagle, J. Ed. 1997. *Whores and Other Feminists*. New York: Routledge.

Naples, N. 2003. *Feminism and Method: Ethnography, Discourse Analysis and Activist Research*. New York and London: Routledge.

Oakley, A., Ed. 2007. *Working Sex: Sex Workers Write About a Changing Industry*. Emeryville, CA: Seal Press.

Ohler, N. 2016. *Blitzed: Drugs in Nazi Germany*. London: Alan Lane.

Orchard, T., Farr, S., Macphail, S., Wender, C., and Wilson, C. 2013. Resistance, Negotiation, and Management of Identity Among Women in the Sex Trade in London, Ontario. *Culture, Health & Sexuality* 15(2): 191–204.

Orchard, T., Farr, S., Macphail, S., Wender, C., and Wilson, C. 2014. Expanding the Scope of Inquiry: Exploring Accounts of Childhood and Family Among Canadian Sex Workers. *Canadian Journal of Human Sexuality* 23(1): 9–18.

Orchard, T., Farr, S., Macphail, S., Wender. C., and Young, D. 2012. Sex Work in the Forest City: Sex Work Beginnings, Types, and Clientele Among Women in London, Ontario. *Sexuality Research and Social Policy* 9(4): 350–362.

Peakman, J., Ed. 2006. *Whore Biographies 1700–1825*. London: Pickering & Chatto.

Peakman, J. 2009. Blaming and Shaming in Whores' Memoirs. *History Today* 59(8): 33–39.

Pearson, C. and Bourgois, P. 1995. Hope to Die a Dope Fiend. *Cultural Anthropology* 10(4): 1–7.

Perselli, V. 2005. Heavy Fuel: Memoire, Autobiography, and Narrative, In C. Mitchell, S. Weber, and K. O'Reilly-Scanlon, Eds., *Just Who Do We Think We Are?* (pp. 22–33). London: Routledge.

Pheterson, G., Ed. 1989. *A Vindication of the Rights of Whores*. Seattle, WA: Seal Press.

Pugh, D. and Tietjen, J. 1997. *I Have Arrived Before My Words: Autobiographical Writings of Homeless Women*. Alexandria, VA: Charles River Press.

Red Umbrella Project. 2013. *Prose & Lore: Memoir Stories About Sex Work. Issue 2*. New York: New York Foundation.

Red Umbrella Project. 2014. *Prose & Lore: Memoir Stories About Sex Work. Issues 3 & 4*. New York: New York Foundation.

Smith, P. 2017. *Devotion*. New Haven, CT: Yale University Press.

Smith, S. 1987. *A Poetics of Women's Autobiography: Marginality and the Fictions of Self-Representation*. Bloomington, IN: Indiana University Press.

Smith, W. 1982. Chemistry and the Holocaust. *Journal of Chemical Education* 59(10): 836–838.

Sterry, D. Ed. 2009. *Hos, Hookers, Call Girls, and Rent Boys: Professionals Writing on Life, Love, Money, and Sex*. Berkeley, CA: Soft Skull Press.

Sutin, A. and Robins, R. 2008. When the "I" Looks at the "Me": Autobiographical Memory, the Visual, and the Self. *Conscious Cognition* 17(4): 1386–1397.

Sycamore, M., Ed. 2000. *Tricks and Treats: Sex Workers Write About Their Clients*. Binghamton, NY: Harrington Park Press.

Turner, S. and Ehlers, T. 2003. *Sugar's Life in the Hood: The Story of a Former Welfare Mother*. Austin, TX: University of Texas Press.

van der Meulen, E., Durisin, E., and Love, V. 2013. *Selling Sex: Experience, Advocacy, and Research on Sex Work in Canada*. Vancouver, BC: UBC Press.

Werhurn, A. and Bazuin, N. 2017. *Modern Whore: A Memoir*. Impulse[b:] Publishing.

7

"Sisters of the night"[1]

Ethical and practical challenges in researching prostitution among minors in Ghana

Georgina Yaa Oduro, Samuel Otoo, and Aikins Amoako Asiama

Introduction

For quite some time now, child prostitution (those below 18 years) has attracted the attention of researchers, activists, service providers, and policymakers. Yet, limited consensus exists on the characteristics, experiences, and needs of minors involved in prostitution.[2] Even less is known about the dynamics of child[3] prostitution in sub-Saharan Africa. The departure point of the current study is the ethical and practical challenges associated with research on prostitution by minors. The study, conducted in Ekutuase,[4] Ghana, involved girls aged between 14 and 17 years. It examined a wide range of issues including the family backgrounds of the girls, factors that influenced their entry into prostitution, and the age at which they did so, their clients, working conditions, and challenges. Our study highlights the considerable ethical and practical challenges that may emerge during research on child prostitution as well as the legal and policy implications of such research.

Research, activism, and socio-legal practice related to the sex industry are fraught with contestations, debates, and polemics resulting in divergent ways of conceptualizing and engaging with prostitution. Existing discourses on transactional sexual exchanges involving minors use different concepts including "prostitution," "sex work," "commercial sexual exploitation," and "prostituted children." Each term reflects deeply rooted views that surround and inform the involvement of minors in prostitution. The term "sex work," for example, is generally perceived as a form of labour, while "prostitution" typically connotes exploitation and victimization. Irrespective of these discursive differences, international law regards prostitution involving minors (persons below the age of 18 years) as an abuse of the right of the child (ECPAT 2014; UNCRC 1989). Following this definition, discussions regarding commercial sex among minors often strive to emphasize it as exploitative, devoid of agency, and coercive (O'Connell Davidson 2005; Willis & Levy 2002).

Globally, laws in many countries reflect provisions in international law that regard prostitution involving minors as a violation of their rights and as a punishable criminal act (Reid & Piquero 2014). Law and policy typically distinguish the involvement of minors in prostitution from sexual abuse because the former involves commercial exploitation on a larger scale of individuals who have not yet reached the age of consent. Such minors are often considered victims but not sex workers or child labourers (Bakirci 2007). These dynamics present an extraordinary set of ethical and practical challenges to researchers. The following analysis highlights some of the complexities inherent in researching prostitution involving minors in an African context. It offers lessons to researchers, activists, and practitioners interested in exploring how to engage with, and overcome challenges associated with minors' involvement in prostitution research in sub-Saharan Africa.

The study context

Ghana, a West African English-speaking country surrounded by Francophone countries is flanked in the east by Togo, west by Cote d'Ivoire, and north by Burkina Faso. On the south of the country lies the Gulf of Guinea and Atlantic Ocean. Half of the country's 28 million residents are young people (aged 15 to 24 years), with 42% of the population under 15 years of age (Ghana Living Standard Survey 2008; Ghana Statistical Service 2010; MOWAC/UNICEF 2009). As is the case in most of sub-Saharan Africa, Ghanaian cultural norms and practices strongly value children, with families frequently compelling their married male relatives to either divorce or marry a second wife if a marriage does not produce children[5] (Nukunya 2003). The cultural imperative for adults to marry and give birth to children has a pragmatic aspect as well, given that the Ghanaian state offers limited welfare benefits to elderly people, who consequently must rely on their children to support them until their death. Children are widely regarded as essential to ensuring the perpetuation of families' lineages, culture, and society more generally (Assimeng 2006; Nukunya 2003; Oduro 2012).

Given the intense cultural value associated with children, it is unsurprising that successive Ghanaian governments have continued to profess a commitment to the promotion and protection of children's welfare (MOWAC/UNICEF 2009). These commitments have found expression in initiatives such as the National Commission of Children, established in 1979 to advance children's interests and rights; extensive Constitutional protections guaranteeing children's rights; the Ministry of Gender, Children and Social Protection; a National Youth Policy and Adolescent Reproductive and Health Policy, and the Children's Act are all in place to ensure minors' well-being (MOWAC/UNICEF 2009). Ghana was also the first African country to sign the United Nations Charter on Children's Rights (UNHCR) in 1990. The government also regularly asserts its commitment to children's rights through the celebration of the International Day of the Family, the World Day against Child Labour, African Union Day of the African Child, the World Day for the Prevention of Child Abuse, and Activism Days against Gender Violence (MOWAC/UNICEF 2009; Oduro 2012), all of which emphasize the protection of children against all forms of abuse. These efforts notwithstanding, some children in Ghana engage in prostitution and experience different forms of abuse.

Interestingly, silence on matters of sexuality is one way that most Ghanaian cultural groups demonstrate their value for, and protection of children (Awusabo-Asare et al. 2017; Bochow 2012; Oduro 2010). Accurate and comprehensive sexuality education is therefore hardly provided at most homes and schools in Ghana leading one researcher to observe that many Ghanaian children learn about sex and sexuality through equally uninformed peers, the Internet, jokes, songs, humour, and euphemisms (Anarfi et al. 2009).

The HIV/AIDS pandemic and widespread social media have increasingly altered the way sexuality-related information is accessed in Ghana. Some form of sex education has been introduced in schools and other informal settings throughout the country (Awusabo-Asare et al. 2017; Miedema & Oduro 2017). Youth in Ghana also use social media to discuss sex, watch pornography, and exchange sexuality-related information. These cultural shifts notwithstanding, most adults in Ghana still regard children as asexual, and express opposition to the public discussion of sexuality (Bochow 2012; Oduro 2010; Oduro & Miedema forthcoming).

It is in this context that we studied the involvement of Ghanaian minors in prostitution. The study took place over a period of three months in 2016 through interviews and informal conversations with 30 participants made up of 15 minors involved in prostitution and third parties who alternately protect the girls and sometimes coerce them and profit from their commercial sexual labor. These third parties comprised of three adult prostitutes who entered the trade as children and two male pimps. We also collected data from ten stakeholders mainly health policy makers, social workers, journalists, law enforcement officers, traditional leaders, staff of youth-focused non-governmental organizations (NGOs), and community leaders.

In what follows, we address the ethical and practical challenges we faced in our work as well as what we learned about the dynamics of this type of research. We also emphasize the lessons offered by our study for future inquiries in the field.

Ethical challenges

The ethical issues and challenges associated with research on sexuality, minors, and prostitution have been discussed extensively in the literature (cf. Izugbara 2012; Kelly & Coy 2016; Melrose 2002; O' Connell Davidson 2005; Oduro 2012; Willis & Levy 2002). However, this ever-growing body of literature is silent on ethical challenges and experiences that specifically emerge in the context of prostitution by minors in Africa and Ghana. This is not surprising since research on minors is a difficult and sensitive endeavor with three major ethical implications. First, minors are perceived to lack the capacity to take informed decisions. Second, minors are expected to be naïve, innocent, and to embody virtue and acceptable behavior. Third, prostitution is a highly stigmatized subject. Additional ethical challenges relate to how to engage with the violence, abuse, and exploitation that minors in prostitution often face (Aldridge 2014; Rittenhouse & Felicini 2015). Our study secured ethical clearance from two institutions. First, from the host university in Ghana and, second from the Harvard School of Public Health (HSPH), Harvard University, US, where the first author undertook a fellowship program to analyze and write up the study.

Ethical considerations on informed consent and voluntary participation require participants to freely consent to participation in a study and in the case of minors, consent of parents, guardians, caregivers, or gatekeepers are needed. Even though most of the minors involved in this research fit the description of emancipated minors (more on this later), consent was still needed from the guardians and parents of the few participants who were in such custody. However, these young people were involved in a stigmatized behavior without their parents' or guardians' knowledge and creating awareness of it through the mandatory consent of their parents or guardians could expose and jeopardize the future and marriage prospects of these girls (Greydamus & Patel 1991; Melrose 2002). The clustered nature of housing in the Ekutuase community, reflected in compound houses with close-knit neighbors and extended family members, highlights the tensions that could emerge in securing consent in communal communities. It therefore raises the subject of consent in collectivist versus individualistic societies. How we addressed the dilemma of securing consent is discussed in detail later.

Socio-demographic characteristics of the prostituted minors

The background of the girls in our study is shown in Table 7.1. Most of them became sex workers at very early ages and had little or no education. While many were from single-parent

Table 7.1 Socio-demographic characteristics of prostituted minors

Pseudonyms	Current age	Age of entry	Living arrangement	Level of education	Introduction to the trade
Ewurama (has a child who was staying with her mum)	16 years	11 years	Lives with mum	Primary	Self-initiated
Aggie	15 years	13 years	Lives alone	Completed JHS[6] but could not continue because of poverty	Introduced by friends
Ashie	14 years	13 years	Lives with mum	JHS level dropout	Introduced by a friend
Vida	17 years	15 years	Lives in another town and moves from place to place for the trade. Stays with friends	No education	Introduced by a senior sister
Selma	16 years	16 years (started 3 months ago)	Lives with an absentee brother so feels like she lives alone	Primary	Self-initiated
Baby	14 years	12 years	Lives with a rich dad	Still in JHS	Introduced by friends
Abi	15 years	15 years (started 5 months ago)	Has rented a place with her friends	High school dropout	Introduced by school mates
Sweetie	14 years	11 years	Lost both parents, was living with an uncle but ran away due to maltreatment. Lives with a boyfriend	Junior high school dropout	Introduced by boyfriend
Lucky	15 years	13 years	Lives with grandma	Primary school dropout	Self-initiated
Naami	17 years	14 years	Lives alone	Completed JHS	Was doing it at a former place and has now relocated to study context. Got the idea from a boyfriend
Anowa	14 years	12 years	Lives with dad	Still in school (JHS 3)	Introduced by schoolmates
Adjeley	16 years	15 years	Lives with a cousin who is also in the business	Learning hairdressing	Introduced by cousin
Elorm	15 years	14 years	Lives with friends	Not working	Introduced by friends. Not permanent at current place
Rabi	16 years	14 years	Orphaned. Has a child and lives with grandma	Not working or schooling but want capital for petty trading	Introduced by a friend
Dela	15 years	15 years (4 months ago)	Lives with both parents	In a vocational school	Lives with both parents. Parents not aware of her involvement in the trade. Introduced by a friend

Source: Fieldwork by authors, Ghana 2016.

homes, others lived on their own, or with friends and/or boyfriends. Lack or weak parental support and presence is a commonly mentioned factor in child sex work in Africa. (Leclerc-Madlala 2003; Mgbako & Smith 2009; Oduro 2012; Oyeoku & Azikewe 2013; Vanwesenbeek 2001). Some of the minors lived with siblings and other relatives. Only one 15-year-old girl, Dela, reported living with both parents. Two of the minors, Rabi and Aggie, were mothers.

Data on the family background of the girls highlight the difficulties associated with reaching their parents or guardians for permission to involve them in the study since most of them easily fit the description of emancipated minors. Hofmann (1980) defines emancipated minors as persons below 18 years who are no longer under parental control either by legitimate emancipation or more ambiguous and self-proclaimed separation from their families based on parental non-availability or neglect.

While most of the girls were emancipated minors, few were still under the partial control of their single mums, single dads, and other relatives. For example, 16-year-old Rabi lived with her grandmother who was unable to keep watch or have full control over her thereby enabling her to slip out at night to work as a prostitute. Moreover, the Ekutuase community where the study took place is highly communal with clustered houses and neighbors and community members who all know each other. Therefore, lack of caution in reaching out to the guardians/parents of the girls for consent or leakage of information about their activities may result in serious repercussions and resultant stigmatization. Buttressing the potential for research to expose the minors to public knowledge, one stakeholder observed, "our society is different from elsewhere since everyone knows the other, people therefore hide and ply their sex trade with associated consequences such as spreading diseases since we don't know who is a prostitute and who is not." Thus, the collective and close-knit nature of the study context meant successes, failures, and shameful behaviors move beyond the individual to the collective level, or what Assimeng (2009) calls "collective consciousness." This notion of collective consciousness and associated repercussions was seriously taken into consideration in our data-gathering process with conscious effort made to prevent any mishaps.

The challenge of safeguarding the anonymity and privacy of our study participants was managed by seeking their own consent rather than their parents/guardians. Also, parents/guardians were not at the hotspots where the minors plied their trade hence securing their consent would have meant following-up with the girls at their home with possible unwelcome consequence. We therefore defied the ethical requirement for parental/guardian consent since seeking parental and guardian consent would have amounted to betrayal. Also, most of the participants were emancipated minors who could grant their own consent (Greydanus & Patel 1991; Hofmann 1980; Knecht 1981; Roemer 1985). Kelly and Coy's (2016) argument that deeper, wider, and critical decisions that aim at prioritizing the safety and well-being of study participants above other factors should be considered in such situations was paramount in our decision to concentrate on the minors instead of their parents though the few accessed through NGOs were granted consent by the NGO workers (see more on access negotiation and gaining access to the girls later).

In our interactions with the girls, we prioritized their safety, well-being, and right to participation without coercion. They had the right to voluntary participation and withdrawal. We respected them and did what we could to protect their identities. We were also alert to the need to use ethical routes to report any risks that the girls might be exposed to. We had a professional counsellor from the host institution on the research team.

Another ethical challenge we experienced relates to power relations and inequalities between participants and the researchers. Such power dimensions centered on the competence of the study participants based on their age, gender, social class, and issues of vulnerability.

However, the power differentials between researchers and study participants in sex research have not received much attention in the literature. We experienced some level of power inequalities in our study with the minors we studied at Ekutuase. They regularly demonstrated their ability to make or mar research projects as demonstrated in the following quote by 14-year-old Sweetie, who entered the sex industry at 11 years old:

> Ahhh, we are fed up with you people, you are always asking questions. What benefit do we get from such questions? I am going to tell the others not to respond to you, "yɛ abrɛ mo" [we are tired of you].

Sweetie's point demonstrated to us the powerful position of participants in the success of research projects. Their willingness or unwillingness to respond to interviews had implications for the success or failure of our study. As a difficult-to-reach population, in a stigmatized and illegal trade, it was initially difficult gaining access to them. It was important therefore to find ways to ensure that the sentiments expressed by Sweetie did not prevent the participation of others in the study. So, our assurances and explanations of the ultimate benefit of such studies to young people's health and well-being helped study participants to be more cooperative. As we later learned, Sweetie's response was critical and pragmatic. Prostitution in Ghana is illegal and minors who engage in the practice risk stigma and social sanctions. They risk losing marriage prospects and face ostracization. Given this understanding, we agreed with the respondents that we would not re-contact them for additional information for the study. One of the girls noted: "Okay, we will talk to you people but don't come back for more information. Also, no one should know that we have talked to you or [been] involved in this business" (Lucky, 15 years). It is therefore worthy to note that though the participants were minors, they wielded much power.

Remuneration or payment for participants' time and involvement in research projects is another thorny ethical issue in the research enterprise, especially in the case of children. Maddy Coy (2006) for example, has raised questions about the parallel transactions between paying women for sex and paying them for participation in research. The ethical dilemmas with payment center on whether payments are tokens of appreciation, compensations, or an incentive for participation. While giving tokens for participants' time in research is not a new thing, the point at which the token is introduced in the research process, the amount of money, size of gifts, and type of tokens given to research participants may make a difference. For example, giving participants drugs, alcohol, and other self-harming tokens, or huge amounts of money is unethical (Alderson & Morrow 2011; Cwikel & Hoban 2005; Kelly & Coy 2016; Melrose 2002; Willis & Levy 2002). In our case, informed by the practice in similar research projects, we gave participants 20 Ghana cedis (GhȻ20.00), which is the equivalent of 5 US dollars ($5.00) for their participation in the study. This amount was enough for a pack of food (either fried rice and chicken or jollof rice and chicken). We also engaged them at times when the market was quiet and they had no client with them to forestall any lost labor time. We agreed from the onset of every interview that they had the right to leave and attend to a customer whenever one came around. There were few interviews that were truncated because customers showed up during the interviews and the girls left to attend to them. Aside the ethical issues, we also grappled with some practical challenges.

Practical challenges

In this section, we discuss practical issues related to research on minors in prostitution such as access negotiation procedures, some risks encountered by the research team, challenge with the venue used for interviews, identity issues, inability to follow up on participants, and lastly belated participation refusals. We make a case for reflexivity in research on sensitivity issues.

As a difficult-to-reach population, minors involved in sex work may not easily be recruited into research projects. Prior to data collection and participant recruitment, we spent two weeks processing the places and hotspots where the girls worked and could be located. Melrose's (2002) access negotiation strategies suggest two key ways of reaching minors in prostitution: networking and outcropping strategies. Networking involves gaining access to the prostitutes through networks and organizations associated with sex workers while "outcropping" refers to going to the operation sites of prostitutes to interview them. These strategies were employed with the assistance of two male graduate students of the host university in Ghana. We gathered data at prostitution sites and from one NGO working with young sex workers. The NGO was identified a bit later in our study and it greatly facilitated our fieldwork activities. Our outcropping strategy led to the collection of data during the night at the operation sites of the girls while free of clients.

The girls were initially skeptical and declined to participate in the study when approached by Georgina Oduro. Oduro was probably perceived by the girls as a mature woman and a mother figure, and therefore an unlikely person to discuss sex work with. Following this experience, we decided that the interviews would be best conducted by the young men. The first author interviewed some of the girls at the NGO site during the day while the second and third authors interviewed them at night at their operation sites. The male students were accepted by the girls who initially thought they were potential clients. When the students explained that they were conducting research, the girls asked to see their identity cards. As one of the girls noted: "*mo ma menhwe hom ID, eto dabia na journalist fo no abe record hen na won akobo wo radio do a hen enyim*" literally translated as, "let me have a look at your ID, sometimes these journalists come and record us and play our voices on radio without our knowledge or consent" (Ashie, 14 years).

Research has documented sex workers as highly at risk for violence (cf. Izugbara 2007, 2012; Mgbako & Smith 2009; Ndijo 2017; Oduro 2012). There is, however, little research on the risk encountered by researchers involved in prostitution studies. All too often, researchers are viewed as privileged and insulated from risks (Edmonds 2003; Shaw et al. 2011; Warr 2004). Maguire (2005), for example, contends that before embarking on interviews or related research activities, the researcher has a responsibility to ensure that no harm befall the children as a result of their participation in the research process. However, the hidden and illegal activities in which children in the worst forms of child labor are involved may sometimes put the researcher at greater risk. For instance, in Nepal, some researchers were threatened by traffickers with knives when investigating the process of trafficking Nepalese girls and boys across the border to India (Kumar et al. 2001). In our study, however, the young men who conducted fieldwork at night encountered serious risks from pimps and clients who intimidated, threatened, and tried to rob them. They also experienced smoke fumes and loud music from the pubs and hotspots where the minors/sisters operated. Further, fieldworkers had to commute at night through lonely and dangerous routes to the hotspots for interviews. In some instances, fieldworkers had difficulty finding taxis to drive them home. We managed this challenge by arranging for daily pick-up services for the two male fieldworkers after data collection.

Venue for interviews conducted at night posed major challenges. Often, the streets, bars, and pubs where the girls worked were noisy, which affected the quality of our recordings. Whereas, the interviews arranged and conducted at the NGO offices elsewhere in the Ekutuase community were better.

Another practical challenge experienced in the study relates to the inability to build enough rapport with participants because of the clandestine nature of their trade, and their fluid and mobile lifestyle from one hotspot to another. Most qualitative studies are undertaken over a longer period to enable the building of rapport and trust with participants for the production of high-quality data. Additionally, sensitive research projects are often undertaken by practitioners such as health personnel or NGO workers who work directly with such clients and have easy access, good rapport, and longer relationships with them, instead of academics who are often perceived as outsiders. As observed by Edmonds (2003), small talk, play, recurrent visits, patience, and time are some of the major ingredients needed when obtaining reliable data from children on delicate or sensitive issues. This was, however, impossible with our study because of the points mentioned earlier.

Implications and conclusion

This chapter examined the challenges of undertaking ethically sensitive studies. Sieber and Stanley (1988) and Lee and Renzetti (1993) in different studies describe sensitive research as studies with potential consequences or implications, either directly for participants or for the class of individuals represented by the research. Sensitive studies may cover taboo and deviant topics, intrude the private sphere, and delve into deeply personal experiences of people and therefore call for extreme tact and sensitivity in the research process. Our study was therefore characterized by many tensions. Specifically, we explored the tensions encountered in researching the experiences of minors involved in sex work in a Ghanaian metropolis. The challenges among other things led to the collection of some data at night, which was a new experience for Oduro in her research career. The experience informed the title of this chapter: "Sisters of the night."

Findings from our study draw attention to the knowledge and practice of securing informed consent in individualistic versus communal societies (Agulanna 2008). Written informed consent is comparatively easier to secure in Western liberalized individualistic societies than their collectivist counterparts. The Ekutuase community where this study took place was more communalistically inclined with an oral culture, people knowing each other, and showing concern or interest in each other's affairs (Gyekye 1996). It is therefore common to enter a house in search of someone but find neighbors responding and showing interest in you in the absence of the person. Some would go to the extent of enquiring about your mission and be ready to take messages on the person's behalf. Securing consent in such a context requires extra caution compared to societies where people are more autonomous and have privacy in their dealings. It was therefore not surprising that the few minors who lived with single parents and relatives cautioned us against following them up, but rather personally consented to their participation in the study. Our study also shows the importance of the concept of emancipated minors in research. Even though Ekutuase was a communal society, it still had minors who were sexually active and involved in sex work. Social change and the complexity of African society is gradually impacting on communal personhood and contributing to minors who are on their own or in charge of their lives and doing work that is often perceived as unsafe for minors (Oduro 2012).

The role of context, location, and specificities of some African realities became extremely critical in our research project. For instance, though sex work is generally stigmatized by many societies, the stigma is a little overwhelming in most African societies because first, prostitution is illegal and criminalized in a number of African countries; second, the communal nature of the society coupled with the concept of collective consciousness (Assimeng 1999) makes perceptions about prostitution shameful as it deviates from social norms and values and negatively affects not only the individual prostitute but her family as well. The involvement of minors is highly unacceptable and/or even forbidden in lieu of the concept of childhood innocence and need for sex to take place only within marriage. The pervasive nature of stigma on sensitive topics in Ghana, for example, led Oduro and Otsin (2014) into recruiting participants for an abortion research study from NGO assisted abortion clinics instead of public health facilities where patients refused to participate by assigning other reasons for their presence at the facility instead of abortion.

Another issue worthy of discussion in such an ethically sensitive project relates to the positionality of the researcher vis-à-vis access to participants and data. Whereas health personnel and some NGO workers can have easy access to sex workers, the same cannot be said of researchers who are often outside such zones. Negotiating research access to such a difficult-to-reach study population can be challenging, though we were successful as discussed earlier. Whereas some participants easily give valid information to the stranger-outsider who knows nothing about them and who they might not encounter again, others prefer insiders who they have grown to know and trust such as health personnel or NGO workers. A researcher's position as an insider or outsider, gender, age, and sometimes ethnicity, all have implications for access to participants and quality of data. For example, as members of the same ethnic group that is governed by norms of decency and good moral conduct (Gyekye 1996), child sex workers viewed a mature female researcher suspiciously with some level of hostility since she could harbor some judgmental attitudes towards them.

The issue of payment for participants' time or tokens for their participation and the comparatively easy access by the male researchers on the streets and hotspots in this study have been highlighted. However, as noted by Kelly and Coy (2016), such issues should be carefully thought through from the inception to the completion of the study with researchers trained on the ethics and expectations of such projects. The two male researchers involved in this study were fully trained in research and ethics as part of their graduate program. They were also trained specifically for this study even though they have much experience from other research projects.

Additionally, the emotional challenges extensively discussed by Melrose (2002) in such sensitive studies experienced not only by the participants or girls but also by researchers because of the difficult, exploitative, abusive, and violent experiences of the child prostitutes or minors thereby depriving them of their chance to live as normal children or adolescents also came up in our research project and this makes the researcher equally vulnerable. As identified by Nilan (2002), research ethics committees are concerned about danger and risk, but with a focus on the participants' well-being, and not that of the researcher. This oversight could be viewed as embodying Lather's (2012) argument about subjectivity and its real value in research acknowledges the human status of the researcher in the same way that participants' humanness is considered, with an implicit assumption that issues surrounding the researcher's experiences do not impact on the research and pose no risk to either the researcher or the outcomes of the research. Yet, the risk involved in undertaking sensitive research with vulnerable communities can be both physical and emotional for the researcher.

Finally, the risks, illegality, spectra of vulnerabilities, and marginalized positions of minors involved in clandestine activities, organized crime, and such "closed and guarded activities and spaces" risk being neglected or overlooked in the research enterprise because of the sensitivities and layers of ethics associated with such endeavours that could deter potential researchers. Yet, the best way to empower such marginalized and vulnerable children and youth is to project their voices through research. However, in so doing, we must respect them, protect their dignity, and prioritize their safety and well-being above the research project. In sum, we should note that realities or practicalities sometimes clash with ethics as laid out by review boards (IRBs) and the like, yet we should observe such ethics with some attention to contextual realities and practicalities. We should also be reflexive throughout the research journey with layers of responsibilities thereby making the research a process instead of a one-off event. As articulated by Kelly and Coy (2016), the complexities of undertaking such sensitive research projects call for high levels of reflexivity, since the demands require the operationalization of ethics both as a process and practice. Such research helps us to understand and appreciate the application of ethics in research projects in its entirety since they call for critical and pragmatic decisions, which may be summed up in what Guillemin and Gillam (2004, cited in Kelly & Coy 2016, 33) describe as "ethically important moments that must be negotiated in real time with real people."

Acknowledgment

We wish to thank all participants for making this study possible by sharing their experiences on a very sensitive issue. We further thank the Ford Foundation for funding the analysis and writing up of this study through a Takemi Fellowship at the Harvard School of Public Health. Dr. Jesse Bump and Dr. Theresa Betancourt of the HSPH deserve our appreciation for their mentorship during the first author's Takemi Fellowship at Harvard and their input in the analysis and writing up of the research. And most importantly, our reviewers for giving us constructive input that has helped to improve the chapter.

Notes

1 The girls and young women who participated in this study did not have an emic term they used to refer to their involvement in prostitution and instead called themselves the "sisters of the night," which we accordingly adopt here.
2 For key voices in these debates, see O' Connell Davidson (2005) and ECPAT (2014).
3 Child prostitution, minors involved in prostitution, child sex workers, and prostituted girls are used interchangeably in the chapter in reference to the involvement, trading, and exchange of sexual services by girls below 18 years old.
4 Ekutuase is a pseudonym for the city in which the study was undertaken.
5 Unfortunately, this cultural practice operates under the assumption that infertility is a woman's fault.
6 JHS and SHS represent junior high school and senior high school respectively.

References

Agulanna, C., 2008. *Informed consent in sub-Saharan African communal culture: The "multi-step" approach.* Masters thesis in Applied Ethics submitted to Linkoping universitet. Accessed on April 15, 2018 from https://pdfs.semanticscholar.org/cb0f/1e2dde77556e0a99c29641c22e9bf44be4ba.pdf.
Alderson, P. and Morrow, V., 2011. *The ethics of research with children and young people: A practical handbook.* London: Sage.
Aldridge, J., 2014. Working with vulnerable groups in social research: Dilemmas by default and design. *Qualitative Research, 14*(1), pp. 112–130.
Anarfi, J., Ahiadeke, C., Ampofo, W., and Addo, K., 2009. *Female sex workers behavioural surveillance survey in Accra and Kumasi, Ghana.* Accra, Ghana: ISSER, NMIMR, Prolink.
Assimeng, J.M., 1999. *Social structure of Ghana: A study in persistence and change.* Accra, Ghana: Ghana Publishing Corporation.
Assimeng, J.M., 2006. *Understanding society: An introduction to sociology for African students* (vol. 87). Ghana: Woeli Publishing Services.
Awusabo-Asare, K., Stillman, M., Keogh, S., Doku, D.T., Kumi-Kyereme, A., Esia-Donkoh, K., Leong, E., Amo-Adjei, J., and Bankole, A., 2017. *From paper to practice: Sexuality education policies and their implementation in Ghana.* New York: Guttmacher Institute.
Bakirci, K., 2007. Child pornography and prostitution: Is this crime or work that should be regulated? *Journal of Financial Crime, 14*(1), pp. 5–11.

Bochow, A., 2012. Let's talk about sex: Reflections on conversations about love and sexuality in Kumasi and Endwa, Ghana. *Culture, Health & Sexuality, 14*(suppl. 1), pp. S15–S26.

Coy, M., 2006. This morning I'm a researcher, this afternoon I'm an outreach worker: Ethical dilemmas in practitioner research. *International Journal of Social Research Methodology, 9*(5), pp. 419–431.

Cwikel, J. and Hoban, E., 2005. Contentious issues in research on trafficked women working in the sex industry: Study design, ethics, and methodology. *Journal of Sex Research, 42*(4), pp. 306–316.

ECPAT International, 2014. The commercial sexual exploitation of children in Latin America. Accessed March 16, 2017, www.ecpat.org/wp-content/uploads/2016/04/Regional%20CSEC%20Overview_Latin%20America%20(English).pdf.

Edmonds, C.N., 2003. *Ethical considerations when conducting research on children in the worst forms of child labour in Nepal.* Geneva: ILO-IPEC.

Ghana Living Standards Survey, 2008. *Ghana Statistical Service: Report of the fifth round* (GLSS 5). Accra, Ghana: Ghana Publishing Corporation.

Ghana Statistical Service, 2010. *2010 Population and housing census.* Ghana, GSS.

Greydanus, D.E. and Patel, D.R., 1991. Consent and confidentiality in adolescent health care. *Pediatric Annals, 20*(2), pp. 80–84.

Gyekye, K., 1996. *African cultural values.* Accra, Ghana: Sankofa.

Hofmann, A.D., 1980. A rational policy toward consent and confidentiality in adolescent health care. *Journal of Adolescent Health Care, 1*(1), pp. 9–17.

Izugbara, C.O., 2007. Constituting the unsafe: Nigerian sex workers' notions of unsafe sexual conduct. *African Studies Review, 50*(3), pp. 29–49.

Izugbara, C.O., 2012. Client retention and health among sex workers in Nairobi, Kenya. *Archives of Sexual Behavior, 41*(6), pp. 1345–1352.

Kelly, L. and Coy, M., 2016. Ethics as process, ethics in practice: Researching the sex industry and trafficking. In Siegel, D. and de Wildt, R. (Eds.), *Ethical concerns in research on human trafficking* (pp. 33–50). New York: Springer.

Knecht, L.D.A., 1981. Consent and confidentiality. *Journal of School Health, 51*(9), pp. 606–609.

Kumar, K.C.B., Adhikari, K.P., Subedi, G., and Gurun, Y.B., 2001. *Situation of child porters: A rapid assessment.* Investigating the worst forms of child labour series, 6. Geneva: International Labor Office.

Lather, P., 2012. The ruins of neo-liberalism and the construction of a new (scientific) subjectivity. *Cultural Studies of Science Education, 7*(4), pp. 1021–1025.

Leclerc-Madlala, S., 2003. Protecting girlhood? Virginity revivals in the era of AIDS. *Agenda, 17*(56), pp. 16–25.

Lee, R.M. and Renzetti, C.M., 1993. The problems of researching sensitive topics. In Renzetti, C.M. and Lee. R.M. (Eds.), *Researching sensitive topics.* Thousand Oaks, CA: Sage.

Maguire, M.H., 2005, January. What if you talked to me? I could be interesting! Ethical research considerations in engaging with bilingual/multilingual child participants in human inquiry. *Forum Qualitative Sozialforschung/Forum: Qualitative Social Research, 6*(1).

Melrose, M., 2002. Labour pains: Some considerations on the difficulties of researching juvenile prostitution. *International Journal of Social Research Methodology, 5*(4), pp. 333–351.

Mgbako, C. and Smith, L.A., 2009. Sex work and human rights in Africa. *Fordham International Law Journal, 33*, p. 1178.

Miedema, E. and Oduro, G.Y., 2017. Sexuality education in Ghana and Mozambique: An examination of colonising assemblages informing school-based sexuality education initiatives. In Allen, L. & Rasmussen, M.L. (Eds.), *The Palgrave Handbook of Sexuality Education* (pp. 69–93). London: Palgrave.

Ministry of Women and Children's Affairs/United Nations Children's Fund (MOWAC/UNICEF), 2009. *Children in Ghana.* Accra, Ghana: UNICEF.

Ndjio, B., 2017. Sex and the transnational city: Chinese sex workers in the West African city of Douala. *Urban Studies, 54*(4), pp. 999–1015.

Nilan, P., 2002. Dangerous fieldwork re-examined: The question of researcher subject position. *Qualitative Research, 2*(3), pp. 363–386.

Nukunya, G.K., 2003. *Tradition and change in Ghana: An introduction to sociology.* Accra, Ghana: Ghana Universities Press.

O'Connell Davidson, J., (2005). *Children in the global sex trade.* Cambridge: Polity.

Oduro, G.Y., 2010. *Gender relations, sexuality and HIV/AIDS education: A study of Ghanaian youth cultures* (Doctoral dissertation, University of Cambridge, UK).

Oduro, G.Y., 2012. "Children of the street": Sexual citizenship and the unprotected lives of Ghanaian street youth. *Comparative Education, 48*(1), pp. 41–56.

Oduro. G.Y. and Miedema, E., forthcoming. "We have sex, but we don't talk about it": Examining silence in teaching and leaning about sex and sexuality in Ghana and Ethiopia. In Nyeck, S.N. (Ed.), *The Routledge handbook of gender and sexualities in Africa*. London: Routledge.

Oduro, G.Y. and Otsin, M.N.A., 2014. "Abortion—it is my own body": Women's narratives about influences on their abortion decisions in Ghana. *Health Care for Women International, 35*(7–9), pp. 918–936.

Oyeoku, E.K. and Azikewe, U., 2013. Peer group influence and family standard of living as correlates of prostitution tendencies among university undergraduates in South East Nigeria. *Research on Humanities and Social Sciences, 3*(11), pp. 2222–2863.

Reid, J.A. and Piquero, A.R., 2014. On the relatoinships between commercial sexual exploitation/prostitution, substance dependency, and delinquency in youthful offenders. *Child Maltreatment, 19*(3–4), pp. 247–260.

Rittenhouse, R.H. and Felicini, E., 2015. *Researching the sexual exploitation of children*. Bangkok: ECPAT International.

Roemer, R., 1985. Legislation on contraception and abortion for adolescents. *Studies in Family Planning, 16*(5), pp. 241–251.

Shaw, C., Brady, L.M., and Davey, C., 2011. *Guidelines for research with children and young people*. London: National Children's Bureau.

Sieber, J.E. and Stanley, B., 1988. Ethical and professional dimensions of socially sensitive research. *American Psychologist, 43*(1), pp. 49–55

UNCRC, 1989. *The Convention on the Rights of the Child*. A/RES/44/25. New York: UNRC.

Vanwesenbeeck, I., 2001. Another decade of social scientific work on sex work: A review of research 1990–2000. *Annual Review of Sex Research, 12*(1), pp. 242–289.

Warr, D.J., 2004. Stories in the flesh and voices in the head: Reflections on the context and impact of research with disadvantaged populations. *Qualitative Health Research, 14*(4), pp. 578–587.

Willis, B.M. and Levy, B.S., 2002. Child prostitution: Global health burden, research needs, and interventions. *Lancet, 359*(9315), pp. 1417–1422.

8

An action research project with sex worker peer educators in Lisbon, Portugal

Collaboration as a key issue for empowerment

Alexandra Oliveira[1]

Introduction

Participatory action research (PAR) has been extensively used by many researchers[2] to ensure that collaborative projects are carried out *with* sex workers rather than *on* them. Through their active participation in the research process, sex workers can help to define and shape the parameters of an investigation to combat the exclusion, stigma, and silencing that sex workers so often experience (Mathieu 2003; van der Meulen 2011). It could be argued, as several contributors to this volume have, that participatory action and other forms of community-based research are now methodological best practices in projects that involve sex workers. This chapter retrospectively analyzes the challenges faced and strengths that the Peer Education Project with Sex Workers (PREVIH) encountered in the design, implementation, and collection of results of a sex worker peer education project.

Peer education is a community-based intervention in which members of the target community are trained in health-related knowledge and communication skills in order to promote healthy behaviors among peers, and is an internationally proven strategy for behavior change among groups that are difficult to reach (Jones et al. 2011). This project had both research and external evaluation components led by the author and was the first time in Portugal that a non-governmental organization (NGO) supported a training course for sex workers that focused on supporting their role as peer educators in harm reduction or health promotion projects. A secondary goal of the project stimulated the development of the first association of sex workers in Portugal, with the broader goal of encouraging the peer educators to become activists for sex worker rights. Reflecting on the challenges faced in this project as well as the attempts to overcome them, this chapter critically reflects on the possible links between scientific research and socio-political intervention.

Action research and participatory methodology in sex work research

From its inception as a methodology, action research has been inherently oriented toward the application of scientific knowledge to social change (Lewin 1946). Action research is a step-by-step process that emerges over time and is open to modifications, adjustments, changes of direction, and redefinitions that meet people's needs. Action research regards the research process as an interactive spiral with a set of phases that develop continuously through constant readjustments. Action research is adaptable, so that researchers can adjust the method to suit the particular context and actors involved in the research.

Practitioners of action research typically involve community members who are most affected by the issues under study from the inception of the project, especially through the definition of objectives. Our project was unsuccessful with this initial phase due to a lack of local precedent for sex worker participation in intervention research[3] and the absence of an organized sex worker rights group. Thus, rather than applying a prescribed model of action research, I and my colleagues at a the health organizations that provide services to sex workers defined the project's objectives a priori, without assessing the sex workers' needs and without their collaboration. This initial setback made our team even more committed to the participatory research principles of community involvement, re-evaluation, and readjustment throughout the development of training for sex worker peer educators, with the goal of helping them to mobilize politically.

PAR can help sex work researchers to overcome many of the ethical concerns identified within this field of academic inquiry. Many researchers have commented that sex work researchers focus on particular venues due to ease of access or dominant concerns about public health, leading to an overrepresentation of research on women in street prostitution (Weitzer 2005) and in the prevalent association between prostitution and misery (Vanwesenbeeck 2001). Concerns regarding confidentiality, stigmatization, and power dynamics between researchers and participants are common in this type of research (Hart 1998; Sanders 2006; Shaver 2005). Participatory methods have been widely adopted by sex work researchers because of their enormous emancipatory potential for democratizing the research process (Boog 2003; Hubbard 1999) through the adoption of participant-centered guidelines that protect sex workers (Shaver 2005), including sex workers as co-researchers (Graça 2015; O' Neill 2010; van der Meulen 2011; Wahab 2003), and addressing what sex workers regard as their real needs while fostering human dignity (Sanders 2006).

The Peer Education Project with Sex Workers (PREVIH)

The Group of Activists for HIV/AIDS (GAT), an organization dedicated to the prevention and treatment of HIV/AIDS, developed PREVIH's central goal of training sex workers to be peer educators and future sex worker activists in response to the absence of an organized sex worker rights movement in Portugal. GAT established a partnership with Piaget's Agency for Development (APDES), a harm reduction organization that works with illicit drug users and sex workers, to model the peer education training course for sex workers on a similar program that APDES led with illicit drug users (APDES 2011; Marques et al. 2012). GAT also established a partnership with the University of Porto, where the author works, to develop a research methodology for adapting APDES' approach to the unique issues facing sex workers. Action research proved best suited to this goal.

PREVIH comprised two phases that involved 15 sex workers with diverse characteristics and sex industry experiences, including 9 cisgender women, 5 cisgender men, and 1 transwoman. Participants included sex workers born in Portugal as well as migrants who made their living in indoor and outdoor contexts in various parts of the country, although mostly based in Lisbon and Porto. The actions took place in these two cities and the project included the payment of travel to all participants. Although some results described here are specific to the first phase and others to the second phase, this chapter presents the two phases together without distinguishing between them.

Training sex workers as peer educators

Training sex workers as peer educators took place in three phases. First, GAT, APDES, and another two NGOs that work with sex workers in outreach projects identified sex workers who showed great potential to work as successful peer educators. Each one of the four partner organizations identified potential peer educators based on their field experience with sex workers. The criteria were free and defined by each of them. However, this selection used the same criteria that are defined in other peer education experiences with sex workers, i.e. a sex worker peer educator must be leader of the group and, therefore, should be seen as a reference model for the peers, having a high level of motivation, namely being motivated to assume their role as sex worker and as peer educator, have pedagogical abilities and excellent communication skills, hold basic knowledge on health issues, and have a didactic role based on their experience, being able to transmit the knowledge acquired (Borlone and Macchieraldo, 2004; Mongard et al. 1997). Next, sex workers participated in a training to develop peer education and harm reduction skills, adapted from the APDES model used with illicit drug users, including communication and conflict management, teamwork and decision-making, and sexual health. Although it was adapted from the APDES model, an initial evaluation survey was conducted with the selected sex workers, which revealed their training needs. From the results of this survey, a greater number of hours was allocated to the modules considered more important by the trainees, namely the module of citizenship, the module of protection and promotion of sex workers' rights, and the module on sexually transmitted infections. The training lasted 40 hours in the first phase and 66 hours in the second phase of the project.[4] The training sessions were evaluated by the trainers, the research team, and sex workers through discussion groups. The evaluation was done through focus groups in which the trainees expressed their opinion about the training. Although the opinion was generally positive, the pairs mentioned the need for improvement in the training, suggesting that it should be more dynamic and use more illustrative techniques that would appeal to visual memory. In this way, the trainees alerted us to the need to use teaching methods that reinforced the probability of transferring the learning to the real contexts, as well as techniques that could help in the memorization of knowledge. Finally, the integration of peer educators in outreach projects, which involved monitoring and evaluating their integration alongside them and their supervisors. The supervisor was a professional from the outreach team in which the peer educator was integrated and was tasked with helping them in their integration, the close monitoring of peer educators, and the mediation between them, other professionals involved, and the network of services (like health or social services). This is one of the most relevant aspects in sex worker peer educators' training and has been recommended by peer educators' manuals (e.g. Mongard et al. 1997). These manuals argue that the supervision encompasses a multitude of advantages, in particular because it helps in the management of the roles between professional and personal life, promotes moments of reflection that increase feelings of self-esteem and confidence, and helps in the construction of solutions to overcome difficulties, among others. It establishes a proximity relationship that facilitates integration, also because the supervisor serves as mediator between the peer educator and the team or institution, and can contribute to the definition of rules and organizational dynamics that are more flexible and adjusted to their characteristics and specificities.

The integration was evaluated in APDES-led discussion groups with sex workers and supervisors. The indicators for assessing their integration, defined by their supervisors in a focus group, were the capacity of knowledge transmission, establishing new contacts and intervening in new territories, and the skills to give complementary responses to questions from the project team. The meetings for evaluation took place on a bimonthly basis and were conducted by two people from APDES, having a member of the university monitoring their progress and recording the audiofiles for subsequent transcription and content analysis. After these analyses, the peers' and the supervisors' contributions produced changes that led to improvements in their integration. For example, in the first discussion group, stress and frustration appeared as negative aspects of the peer educators' work. Stress arose as a result of emotional exhaustion linked with the impossibility of responding to all the requests and to the lack of a more organized schedule. These cases were in part related to the very high expectations that some of them had in relation to their role and functions, resulting in stress, frustration, and demotivation. Thus, the sex worker peer educators suggested that it would be advantageous to carry out a prior negotiation and definition of their tasks. Following this, the APDES gave all supervisors a list of recommendations for the reception of peer educators and stressed the importance of presenting and describing the dynamics and functioning of the institution. It was also suggested to supervisors that they should set a timetable for peer educators, as well as a clear and detailed plan of their tasks, which would be negotiated. The supervisors' effort to prioritize the tasks and contributions of peer educators at the time of their integration contributed to the decrease in stress and frustration associated with their work.

The first general assessment was carried out approximately one month after the integration of peer educators and was very positive. Peer educators were evaluated by their supervisors and self-evaluated as being well-integrated, motivated, and having autonomy to carry out their tasks, as well as to bring new contributions to the outreach project. All of them had distributed condoms and other preventive and informative materials, provided health education, and clarified about lower-risk sexual practices and other information. Furthermore, some of them made referrals and follow-ups to health institutions, participated in team meetings, addressed issues related to citizenship and activism, and surveyed the needs of sex workers. Some even organized sessions for raising awareness of sex workers' rights, gave support in areas such as family planning with adolescents and drug using, and organized a website on the issue of sex work legalization.

Empowerment and political activism of sex workers as peer educators

To achieve the empowerment and political activism of sex workers, we had three objectives. The first was strengthening the sense of belonging and identification with both the group of peer educators and the group of sex workers, raising awareness for the importance of activism as a way of achieving social and political changes, and encouraging militancy for the rights of sex workers. The second was to facilitate the involvement of sex worker peer educators in joint actions and in different activism tasks. Finally, to lay the foundations for setting up an organization—this began in the first phase of the project and continued in the second phase.

This component focused on community empowerment and stimulation of political activism. In the already mentioned initial evaluation, the sex workers pointed to lack of knowledge and willingness to learn about various topics, such as citizenship and activism. To achieve this purpose, alongside the training sessions of the first component, the author included a module on "Citizenship, protection, and promotion of sex workers' rights" that targeted the needs set out by sex workers during the evaluation. This module focused on the advantages and disadvantages of different forms of activism, the knowledge about the international movement of sex workers,[5] and the knowledge and understanding of the lack of a sex workers' movement in Portugal.

Later, the author led several focus groups that aimed to strengthen the sense of belonging and identification with the group of sex workers, the importance of activism, the consolidation of the concept of sex work as work, and the concept of the sex workers themselves as activists.

They discussed their relationship with other sex workers, including the contributions of that relationship to their identity and their sense of belonging to the group. Discussions about the importance of activism as a way of achieving social and political changes and encouraging militancy for sex workers' rights, as well as the possible contribution of each of them in this struggle, led to the idea of carrying out specific actions that will be addressed in the next section. These focus groups contributed both to strengthening the knowledge learned in the training on citizenship and activism and on the struggle for sex workers' rights, and to carry out specific actions. With this, we could raise awareness to fight for their rights, including labour rights, and, eventually, the development of an organization.

Outcomes and discussion

The inclusion of sex workers in outreach projects as peer educators, with different types and degrees of contribution, has been recommended as a good practice (TAMPEP 2009). This process was evaluated by all the participants as effective and peer educators were well integrated and recognized as adding value to the outreach projects. Challenges and difficulties associated with the process, with sex workers' commitment and compliance, and with the tasks resulting from their integration as peer educators were overcome. Some of the difficulties associated with the integration of peer educators were in part related to the very high expectations of their role and functions, resulting in stress, frustration, and demotivation. Once these difficulties were identified, they were solved through group discussions, suggesting that it is advantageous to invest in better prior negotiation and more effective definition of the tasks.

In addition to the integration of sex workers as peer educators in each one of the four partner organizations, the main results seem to be the participation in community activities and activist actions and the foundations of an organization. These result in working together to address obstacles and respond to challenges. Having identified the problems of this group, sex workers and the research team evolved to find solutions and overcome constraints in order to achieve common goals. That is, in fact, a trait of PAR: an orientation to common goals and "ethics," for the emancipation, individual and social empowerment, and participatory democracy (Boog 2003). Consequently, another result was social and personal empowerment.

To achieve the objectives of participation in community activities and activist actions, we organized a set of activities, including the participation in a conference, a demonstration, and a lecture, among others.

Regarding the participation in the conference, we (the research team, the promoter entity, and peer educators) decided to propose the presentation of two communications (one poster and one oral communication) at the second International PREVIH Conference.[6] Considering its feasibility and advantages, the peer educators prepared these communications with enthusiasm.

The poster was titled: "The peers' voice: Reflections of a group of sex worker peer educators about their work" (Ferreira et al. 2013). Its contents comprised of what is peer education, what are the required personal characteristics and the role of peer educators. The oral presentation consisted of the presentation by a cis woman about her experience as a sex worker. The contents of the poster were also presented in a plenary session by the transwoman involved in the project.

As for the evaluation of participating in the conference, all the peer educators considered themselves experienced something they felt was enriching and well appreciated. The aspects they highlighted can be divided into two main ideas: the possibility of meeting persons and institutions involved in sex work, intervenors, researchers, or activists; and the fact that they felt they were at the same level as the other participants and that their contribution was seen in the same way, even if there were people with very different professional and social statuses, most of them having much higher valorization. If the former idea may be linked to the isolation to which the sex workers are often subjected, the latter connects with the stigma. Stigma is an attribute that leads to deep discredit (Goffman 1963). The stigmatization process requires the co-occurrence of labelling, stereotyping, separation, loss of status, and discrimination (Link and Phelan 2001). Even more, stigma's internalization generates feelings of being devalued and negatively marked. This activity therefore projected the opposite effect, having a positive impact on their self-esteem and self-confidence.

The main difficulty of this activity was related to the lack of skills to make the poster, which was considered a complex task. This was overcome through the support at preparatory meetings where the author made her resources available so that the peers could successfully create a poster for the conference.

Another planned and realized activity was the participation in the May Day march, together with a group of precarious workers, both in Lisbon and Porto. All the peer educators welcomed this idea and showed willingness to participate. After the commitment to participate in both the march and its promotion, the peer educators had an enthusisastic set of ideas and they proposed that advertising should be done orally and using leaflets, and suggested the use of red umbrellas[7] during the demonstration and the creation of common slogans, among others. During the demonstrations, they carried banners with slogans, such as "No crime, no disease. Sex work is work," distributed leaflets, and carried red umbrellas. Two of them even wrote a text to be read out before the beginning of the march. When evaluating their participation in the May Day march, they considered it was undoubtedly an important moment.

Although all sex worker peer educators collaborated in the organization of the demonstration, not all of them attended. The fear of publicly assuming her status as a sex worker prevented one woman from participating in the march. This fear, which is common among sex workers, is related to the stigma associated with commercial sex and has been documented in the scientific literature (e.g. Mathieu 2003; Oliveira 2011). People endeavor to cover up their activities because they feel threatened by stigma if their commercial sex practices are discovered by those who are outside their sphere of work (Aggleton and Parker 2015). Invisibility is a stigma management strategy and a way to avoid social rejection. Therefore, having publicly assumed their identity as sex workers was a political and empowered act.

Another activity, which emerged as a suggestion at the end of the first phase, referred to the need to contact other audiences/people outside the sex industry and was achieved through the collaboration of a lecture given to students on the Master's Degree in Psychology course at the University of Porto. Two of the peer educators, a cis woman and a cis man, came to one of the author's courses and presented the Peer Education Project with Sex Workers. Their testimony focused on their experience as trainees, peer educators, and sex workers.

Activism, public assumption as sex workers, becoming visible rather than hiding, having an active voice, being affirmative, and seeing their experiences as valid are clear signs of sex workers' empowerment. When all these aspects go beyond the scope of training and extend to other contexts and activities, such as going to university to speak in a class, we can conclude that this process has expanded and may continue to do so. Taking Zimmerman's (1995) concept of empowerment, we can mention the presence of both community empowerment, as individuals worked together in an organized way to improve the life of the collective; and also psychological empowerment, concerning the individual level.

With regard to the creation of an organization, we were interested in creating the conditions to allow this to emerge from the group, which eventually happened. During one of the focus groups, a trainee suggested the establishment of an organization, which the others endorsed and therefore launched the foundations for that organization.

To this end, the peer educators began by identifying obstacles to the mobilization of sex workers, namely the great number of immigrant sex workers currently in Portugal, the lack of self-motivation for mobilization, and the reluctance to publicly disclose the fact that they are sex workers.

To overcome these constraints, as suggested by one of the peer educators, each of them set out their level of interest in assuming the commitment to continue the group to create an association. In this manifestation of intentions, all agreed on the will to continue this plan, albeit with different degrees of commitment—for example, while some had no trouble in unveiling their identity, others just would do back-office work that would keep their identity hidden. What is noteworthy is that even the most reticent took the common goal of, as one of peers stated, "creating solutions to the needs of sex workers, be it in a direct and immediate way through peer educators' outreach work, whether in the struggle for their rights." Following this commitment, the peer educators put forward some proposals to carry out this project, namely the agreement to hold fortnightly meetings, defining their needs and getting ideas to be discussed in the group.

After this, the group wrote a text outlining some basic aspects of the future organization. To produce the text, they answered three questions: Who are we? What are our problems? What are the solutions we propose?

After replying to the questions, we built a text in which they advocate the following:

> We are a group of sex workers and former sex workers fighting for our rights and aiming to promote equality.
> Our main problem is the lack of recognition of sex work as work.
> Our specific problems are [among others]: (i) prejudice, discrimination, and stigma; (ii) violence against sex workers; (iii) lack of occupational safety and health; (iv) problems with access to health care by migrant sex workers; (v) lack of adequate responses by the police to sex workers' complaints.
> We propose: (i) to raise sex workers' awareness of their rights and their duties and the need to fight for the recognition of their work; (ii) to fight against stigma, prejudice, and discrimination; (iii) to fight for dignity and respect for sex workers; (iv) to contribute to the visibility of sex workers; (v) to value sex work, particularly emphasizing its relevance to society.

This text was a sort of working program to materialize the idea of a future sex workers' organization. The text was produced during the first phase of the project and the peer educators tried to maintain and achieve this objective during the second phase. There were several meetings with this aim and the peer educators still continued and had several meetings after the end of the project with this objective in mind. They almost achieved that ambition, however, a series of events resulted in this idea being aborted. Among them, one of the sex workers returned to their country, two of them withdrew, and, above all else, there were increasing disagreements concerning the group's leadership.

The unfeasibility of creating an association of sex workers in this case can find some justification in difficulties that have already been identified as obstacles to the mobilization of sex workers, such as preferring to remain anonymous, safeguarding privacy, and fear related to legal status as well as identifying themselves as temporary workers in the case of migrants (Lopes 2006). Nevertheless, the lack of formal and sustained sex worker mobilization in Portugal must be understood within the context of a generally weak social movement culture (Lopes and Oliveira 2006). Moreover, this lack of mobilization may also be related to the legal situation of sex work in Portugal. In contrast to other European countries, the act of selling or buying sex in itself is not a crime in Portugal, and sex workers therefore face less immediate persecution by police forces, except if they are immigrants in an irregular situation. Obviously, this does not mean that they do not suffer other kinds of discrimination and harassment but can explain, at least partially, the fact that there is still not a sex workers' association in Portugal.

Concluding thoughts

The sex worker peer educators' involvement in various actions, including their participation in the conference, May Day demonstrations, and lecture made possible and materialized their political and social activism.

The text produced by sex worker peer educators during the project was a big step in, based on the awareness of lack of social and legal recognition of their activity. This is even more important because it emerges as self-mobilization. Our role was simply to provide them with knowledge on activism and to contribute to their political consciousness.

This exercise provided much learning in methodologies to engage, commit, and empower sex workers. This participatory methodology proved to be efficient in overcoming obstacles and finding solutions to problems even if there are some recognized obstacles to the emergence and development of sex worker movements—such as the lack of structure and organization of the world of commercial sex, the low level of pragmatic competencies for collective action, the existing stigma, the low level of political competence, and the commercial logic of the world of sex work that stimulates competition and not solidarity (Mathieu 2003).

All these actions required the group's involvement in specific tasks, which meant the organization of a common project and what that entailed for group cohesion and empowerment. We know that participating in activities and community organizations has been consistently associated with empowerment, specifically psychological empowerment (Zimmerman and Rappaport 1988). This became obvious when the participants publicly declared their status as sex workers, became visible instead of hiding themselves, had a voice, were assertive, and validated their experiences. Also, we must emphasize that all these aspects went beyond the scope of the training and were expanded to other contexts and activities.

The effective sex workers' integration in harm reduction projects, sex workers' activism and political conscience, and planting the seeds for a sex workers' association are the strengths of the project. Some restriction to sex workers' participation can be seen as a limitation.

This process can be seen as a good example of the importance of the participation and continuous involvement of sex workers in particpatory action research studies; it can be viewed as a method of redistributing power to the participants and a tool for empowerment, which can be extended through its replication in other contexts. As O' Neill (2010, 227) argued, "it creates a space for the voices of the marginalized to become involved actively in change or transformation." PAR is a theoretical approach to action that is inherently critical and grounded in an emancipatory worldview (Boog 2003). Participatory methods may be seen as a contribution to social justice.

This methodology implies the importance of listening to sex workers and giving them a leading role, recognizing them as the experts and placing their lived experiences at the center of the investigation (Wahab 2003). It recognizes sex workers as the legitimate producers of knowledge about their own lives, which, for those who are marginalized and are not used to have a voice, is an important step.

Furthermore, action research is associated with the application of scientific knowledge to social change and can potentially establish a link between scientific research and socio-political intervention.

To hear from sex workers and to collaborate with them is to give them back the voice that has been denied, to put them at the center, and to realize the real needs of sex workers. Stimulating participatory practices could contribute to more social equity and justice and to a more democratic society (Graça 2015). Thus we can conclude that this exercise provided insights about methodologies for social change and challenged the way we traditionally conceive research. Above all, the relevance of this project lies in understanding the contributions of the participatory methodological approach to the field of sex work.

Notes

1 The author would like to thank the multiple authors of the collaborative project, namely: A. Timóteo, A. Lourenço, A. Malheiros, C. Silva, C. Bono, C. Oliveira, E. Santos, I. Oliveira, Inês Rego, J. Ferreira, L. Tavares, M. Mota, M. Santos, M. Trindade, and T. Ferreira.
2 For examples of this work, see Cornish (2006), Graça (2015), Lopes (2006), Martin (2013), van der Meulen (2011), O'Neill (2010), and Shagi et al. (2008). For the full results, in Portuguese, of the study presented in this chapter, see Oliveira and Mota (2012, 2013).
3 As far as I know, this was the first experience of PAR with sex workers in Portugal. Subsequently, Graça (2015) developed a PAR case study with street-based female sex workers and an outreach team.
4 The greater number of hours of the second phase resulted from the evaluation of the first phase in which the trainees suggested that a greater number of hours should be assigned to the modules they considered the most important.
5 The module highlighted the history of the modern movement of sex workers, including their emergence almost simultaneously in the 1970s in the United States and Europe; the initial objectives and strategies; its landmarks and remarkable dates; how the movement became global; the diversity of forms it has been assuming (e.g. unions, associations, networks, etc.); and the current struggles (e.g. fight against clients' criminalization).
6 The second International Conference on HIV among hidden groups, namely men that have sex with men and commercial sex workers, organized by GAT in partnership with the Institute of Hygiene and Tropical Medicine of the New University of Lisbon on March 25 and 26, 2013.
7 Red umbrellas have been used since 2001 as a symbol of the struggle of sex workers in various parts of the world. This was one of the subjects addressed in the training session on citizenship, activism, and the struggle for the rights of sex workers, which indicates the importance of political awareness.

References

Aggleton, Peter and Richard Parker. 2015. Male sex work: current characteristics and recent transformations. In Peter Aggleton and Richard Parker, Eds., *Men who sell sex: global perspectives*, 1–14. London: Routledge.

APDES. 2011. *Projecto InPar: Resultados da investigação relativos à integração de utilizadores de drogas enquanto educadores de pares em equipas de redução de riscos*. Porto: APDES.

Boog, Ben. 2003. The emancipatory character of action research, its history and the present state of the art. *Journal of Community & Applied Social Psychology* 13: 426–438.

Borlone, Pierfranca and Grazia Macchieraldo. 2004. *Fenarete project: professional training for peer educators in prostitution field*. Pordenone: Comitato per i Diritti Civili delle Prostitute.

Cornish, Flora. 2006. Empowerment to participate: a case study of participation by Indian sex workers in HIV prevention. *Journal of Community and Applied Social Psychology* 16: 301–315. doi: 10.1002/casp.866.

Ferreira, J., T. Ferreira, A. Lourenço, C. Oliveira, C. Silva, M. Santos, L. Tavares, A. Timóteo, J. Santos, Mafalda Mota, Inês Rego, Alexandra Oliveira, and Cristiana Pires. 2013. A voz dos pares: Reflexões de um grupo de educadores de pares trabalhadores do sexo sobre o seu trabalho. Poster presented at II International Conference on HIV among hidden groups, Lisbon, March 26.

Goffman, Erving. 1963. *Stigmate: Les usages sociaux des handicaps*. Paris: Les Editions de Minuit.

Graça, Marta. 2015. *Intervenção socioeducativa: investigação-ação participativa com trabalhadoras do sexo de rua e uma equipa de outreach*. PhD dissertation, University of Aveiro.

Hart, Angie. 1998. *Buying and selling power: anthropological reflections on prostitution on Spain*. Boulder, CO: Westview Press.

Hubbard, Phil. 1999. Researching female sex work: reflections on geographical exclusion, critical methodologies and "useful" knowledge. *Area* 31: 229–237.

Jones, Amanda, Alan Flisher, and Catherine Mathews. 2011. Who are the peer educators? HIV prevention in South Africa schools. *Health Education Research* 26: 563–571.

Lewin, Kurt. 1946. Action research and minority problems. *Journal of Social Issues* 2: 34–46.

Link, Bruce and Jo Phelan. 2001. Conceptualizing stigma. *Annual Review of Sociology* 27: 363–385.

Lopes, Ana. 2006. *Trabalhadores do sexo uni-vos! Organização laboral na indústria do sexo.* Lisboa: D. Quixote.

Lopes, Ana and Alexandra Oliveira. 2006. Sex worker mobilization in Portugal: slow awakenings. In Colin Barker and Mike Tyldesley, Eds., *Conference papers of the Eleventh International Conference on Alternative Futures and Popular Protest* (Vol. III), Manchester, April 19–21.

Marques, Joana, Ana Sofia Mora, and Alina Santos. 2012. *O trabalho primeiro: manual para a promoção da empregabilidade dos utilizadores de drogas e recomendações para a integração pela educação de pares.* Vila Nova de Gaia: APDES.

Martin, Lauren. 2013. Sampling and sex trading: lessons on research design from the street. *Action Research* 11: 220–235.

Mathieu, Lilian. 2003. The emergence and uncertain outcomes of prostitutes' social movements. *European Journal of Women's Studies* 10: 29–50. doi: 10.1177/1350506803010001788.

Mongard, Hanka, Licia Brussa, and Miek Jong. 1997. *Peer educators' manual.* Amsterdam: TAMPEP.

Oliveira, Alexandra. 2011. *Andar na vida: Prostituição de rua e reacção social.* Coimbra: Almedina.

Oliveira, Alexandra and Ana Mafalda Mota. 2012. *Implementação e avaliação de um modelo de educação de pares para trabalhadores(as) do sexo. Relatório final da supervisão científica.* Porto: FPCEUP.

Oliveira, Alexandra and Ana Mafalda Mota. 2013. *Desenvolvimento e Avaliação de um Modelo de Educação de Pares para Trabalhadores(as) do Sexo. Relatório final da supervisão científica da 2ª fase do projeto.* Porto: FPCEUP.

O'Neill, Maggie. 2010. Cultural criminology and sex work: resisting regulation through radical democracy and participatory action research (PAR). *Journal of Law and Society* 37: 210–232.

Sanders, Teela. 2006. Sexing up the subject: methodological nuances in researching the female sex industry. *Sexualities* 9: 449–468.

Shagi, Charles, A. Vallely, S. Kasindi, C. Betty, S. Soteli, N. Kavit, L. Vallely, S. Lees, R. Hayes, D. Ross, and N. Desmond. 2008. A model for community representation and participation in HIV prevention trials among women who engage in transactional sex in Africa. *AIDS Care* 20: 1039–1049.

Shaver, Frances. 2005. Sex work research: methodological and ethical challenges. *Journal of Interpersonal Violence* 20: 296–319. doi: 10.1177/0886260504274340.

TAMPEP. 2009. *Work safe sex work: a European manual on good practices in work with and for sex workers.* Amsterdam: TAMPEP International Foundation.

van der Meulen, Emily. 2011. Action research with sex workers: dismantling barriers and building bridges. *Action Research* 9: 370–384. doi: 10.1177/1476750311409767.

Vanwesenbeeck, Ine. 2001. Another decade of social scientific work on sex work: a review of research 1990–2000. *Annual Review of Sex Research* 12: 242–289.

Wahab, Stéphanie. 2003. Creating knowledge collaboratively with female sex workers: insights from a qualitative, feminist and participatory study. *Qualitative Inquiry* 9: 625–642.

Weitzer, Ronald. 2005. New directions in research on prostitution. *Crime, Law & Social Change* 43: 211–235. doi: 10.1007/s10611-005-1735-6.

Zimmerman, Marc. 1995. Psychological empowerment: issues and illustrations. *American Journal of Community Psychology* 23: 581–599.

Zimmerman, Marc and Julian Rappaport. 1988. Citizen participation, perceived control, and psychological empowerment. *American Journal of Community Psychology* 16: 725–750.

9

Researchers and gatekeepers in participatory action research in Japan's sex industry

Kaoru Aoyama

Introduction

Participatory action research (PAR) is recognised by sociologists, anthropologists, social workers and others as an innovative and authentic method of research into marginalised sections of society including the sex industry. It needs to be centred on the marginalised community and requires researchers to be aware of their roles as facilitators and supporters towards changing the structure and reality of the particular marginalisation for the better, including scientific research and knowledge production as a whole (Chevalier and Buckles 2013; Dewey and Zheng 2013; Hubbard 1999; O'Neill and Campbell 2006).

However, the ethical, political and personal challenges of PAR in this subject area are as well recognised as its applicability. These challenges are related to the criminalisation and regulation of the industry, ideological divisions among feminists over sex work, the way in which human rights discourse is disseminated (or not) in a particular society and, of course, relationships between the researcher and the researched, to name only a few representative issues. Similar challenges have been recorded in different parts of the world, at least in English writings, and interweave to form a larger picture of stigma attached to sex work (Dewey and Zheng 2013; Pérez-y-Pérez and Stanley 2011; Sanders 2006; Shaver 2005; Sinha 2016). What this suggests is that as a result sex work PAR faces certain universal obstacles to gaining access to mainstream academic and policymaking mechanisms or even to get off the ground at all. We could say that this type of sex work research is as marginalised as its subject. If the research is so marginalised that it does not have influence on mainstream knowledge production and policymaking, the larger problem for the researcher is that s/he cannot fulfil the intended role as a facilitator towards any major shift, or even find ways to circumvent, so to speak, the power at work.

This chapter reconsiders this potentially universal dilemma: PAR is crucial to overcome marginalisation *and* difficult to conduct so as to achieve its goal precisely because of the subject's marginalisation, and stigma attached in the case of sex work. In doing so, I will refer to what I have experienced while conducting such research with a network of (former) sex workers and their supporters in Japan during the past decade. I will focus on the gatekeeper issue, stemming from the complicated relationship between a researcher and a key mediator to gain access to a field and respondents in marginalised communities (Eide and Allen 2005). This focus has two advantages: first, it will clarify how exactly marginalisation and stigma function within the research process; and second, it will serve, although as a postscript, the critical and reflexive ideal of PAR to shift the macro power relationships, through a negative example of not being able to transfer the change in the micro one.

The chapter begins by introducing the legal and the ideological frameworks of sex work in Japan and then introduces SWASH, the sex worker and supporter network, and examines their coping strategy under these circumstances. Using SWASH's involvement in PAR with myself as a researcher as a case study, the chapter then goes into details of the relationship between one member acting as a gatekeeper and the researcher, which led to the 'failure' of the project. There are elements where this is influenced by time- and place-specific politics and economics, such as the nation's HIV prevention policy setting the paradigm and funding of the project. However, this chapter on the whole argues that the 'failure' is not an idiosyncratic happening of this project or this relationship, and in conclusion, explores a way to use the 'failure' to still approach the ultimate purpose of PAR: deriving new knowledge for policy and practice from the whole process to change the current structure.

The law's impact on sex work

Criminalisation and regulation

Japan is one of the many countries that employ both criminalisation and regulation policies on sex work (Overs 2015). The Prostitution Prevention Law and the Entertainment Business Law work together to technically prohibit prostitution (although only directly penalising public solicitation and third-party beneficiaries) while allowing registered entertainment premises to trade various sexual services perfectly legally, as I have explored elsewhere (Aoyama 2015). Thus the two laws serve to set boundaries between what is 'good' and what is 'bad' for 'public order and morals' in Japan and allow a quasi-criminal, quasi-legal grey area between them. The Entertainment Business Law has gone through frequent amendments. Each time a new service comes into fashion the precise contents of the grey area between regulated legal activities and criminal activities also shifts. In other words, the sex industry has been both normalised through legalisation under the Entertainment Business Law and ostracised through criminalisation under the Prostitution Prevention Law. This combination strongly influences sex workers' participation in action research or not by altering their self-definition and their agency.

Regarding criminalisation and sex workers' self-definition, Dewey and Zheng (2013) show that criminalisation further complicates the will to and reality of participating in action research. Unsurprisingly, sex workers who engage in illegal types of work are unwilling to disclose who they are and what they are doing while legal sex workers would avoid being associated with illegal counterparts (Dewey and Zheng 2013: 59–60). All participants have to protect themselves from being stigmatised as sex workers but the legal ones would make extra effort to distance themselves from being criminalised. This is a typical coping strategy of the socially deviant: trying to distance themselves from the label, or observable identity, of stigma as far as possible, sometimes by differentiating themselves from the more stigmatised (here, criminal) in order to relatively assimilate themselves with the 'normal' (c.f. Clifton D. Bryant 1990: 440).

However, if the line between the deviant (illegal sex worker) and the less deviant (legal sex worker) is often redrawn at the hands of the normalising power of jurisdiction, it becomes difficult to differentiate themselves as less (or more) deviant. This is one effect of the grey area between criminalisation and normalisation for Japanese sex workers. They cannot quite use the coping strategy described by Dewey and Zheng's workers, even though the two groups share a similar hierarchy between kinds of work, because it is never clear who are relatively further from stigma. Stigma distance management is not in the hands of sex workers. As a result, the reduced agency in this matter makes Japanese workers even less ready to identify themselves as sex workers, even if they are defined as legal at that particular moment.

SWASH and their coping strategy

When sex workers cannot or do not identify themselves as sex workers, as the subjects of their rights, the road to assert the rights is long and winding. This was the case even in Europe, the United States, Australia and other Asian countries where sex workers' rights movements are currently well established and/or unionised (Dewey and Zheng 2013; Brewis and Linstead 2000: Ch. 8–10; Kempadoo and Doezema 1998; Mitrovic and Muller 2009). In Japan, SWASH is the only sex worker-led and identified network, which has constantly been vocal and publishing for two decades. It started as a *tôjisha* movement in 1999 – *tôjisha* means the person(s) central to the social issue at hand who is actually doing/being it, precisely the agent in the context of PAR[1] – in order to address sex workers' particular and practical needs such as protecting occupational health and safety under stigmatisation (SWASH 2014).

It is noteworthy that they use an opposite, group-based, stigma coping strategy compared with the above, individual-based, distancing strategy (see different coping strategies in different minority situations in Dovidio et al. 2010: 417). They have no written organisational rules but when publicising their activities, for instance, 'non-outing' is a golden rule: anyone involved pays special attention not to disclose who, among the members, have been sex workers in what kinds of work unless a *tôjisha* member discloses this information about and by her/himself. Based strictly on the right to determine oneself, this rule also works to protect those who could be criminalised at the same time as sharing, if only minimally, the burden of stigma by not specifying individual targets and by those who could be defined as less stigmatised intentionally not distancing themselves. The grey area between the laws – blurred boundaries between legal and illegal sex workers and between sex workers and non-sex-workers through simultaneous normalisation and criminalisation – also provides leeway for 'non-outing'. 'Non-outing' can be non-labelling. Although the hurdle might be very high, it is possible in theory to invite non-sex workers and those who are selling sexual services but do not currently identify as sex workers to cooperate with this strategy, i.e. to identify themselves as sex workers and share the burden and solidarity towards improving the *tôjisha*'s situation.

Participatory action research in the sex industry

The researcher and the gatekeeper

SWASH as a *tôjisha* network and I as a researcher had been thinking that advocating for sex workers' rights as workers' rights was necessary to enable stigma management and the agency to normalise themselves as workers to deal with their problems at hand, as well as to further extend the solidarity between the stigmatised and the 'normal'. In order to gain more social recognition that this advocacy was sound, that sex workers would be capable of becoming the subjects of rights, as well as to determine and overcome the problems practically, the need for research participated in by *tôjisha* leading to action became the link between SWASH and myself.

A clear-cut example of trial and error here that I will use as a case study is from a team project to prevent HIV infection among sex workers between 2009 and 2011, which was called for by the Ministry of Health, Labour and Welfare as sex workers had become a national target group for HIV/AIDS prevention following the same global trend (Ministry of Health and Welfare 1999; Scarlet Alliance 2014). My role as a researcher was to find ways to develop and disseminate an intervention programme among migrant sex workers. To start with, we needed to grasp the contemporary conditions of both Japanese and migrant sex workers to compare them. However, access to migrant sex workers was even more limited than their Japanese counterparts, mostly because they were more severely criminalised: working in the sex industry is prohibited, with some exceptions, by immigration control laws and regulations for non-Japanese nationals (Aoyama 2014a).

As Teela Sanders, Tiantian Zheng and myself have argued from our fieldwork experience in different parts of the world (Aoyama 2009; Dewey and Zheng 2013: Ch. 3; Sanders 2006), it is usually necessary for a non-sex worker researcher to first find a third party, such as a sex work activist or an outreach project, who is trustworthy and trusted within the *tôjisha* community, to introduce them to the community. Whether this gatekeeper becomes a propelling collaborator or an extra barrier to the project depends on the quality of rapport the researcher establishes with her/him. Because I had known them for several years by then, attending their meetings and social events and travelling together to attend international sex workers' conferences, and had already experienced an aborted commissioned research together,[2] I thought we had a good rapport already. I invited SWASH members to conduct PAR and consulted them about the best access to migrant workers, and one of them became a crucial gatekeeper.

To jump to the conclusion, the project failed in two ways: it stopped short as PAR; and it did not lead to an intervention programme for HIV prevention among migrant sex workers. The causes can be largely rendered to the gatekeeper issue (NB: not the gatekeeper herself), or the power politics at work in between the researcher and the gatekeeper are perhaps never surmountable even if there is a sense of rapport. A more in-depth exploration of the causes is mapped out below in line with the priorities, necessities and difficulties of PAR practised in predecessors' work not only in the sex industry: defining the participating *tôjisha* community and its boundaries; democratic participation by the researcher and *tôjisha*; breaking down the mainstream academic distinction between the objective 'knowers' and subjective 'not-knowers'; and the more concrete issues of funding and research paradigms being a stumbling block (Boontinand 2005: 182; Dewey and Zheng 2013: Ch. 4; Lawson 2015: ix; Sanders 2006). Following this mapping shows that the Japanese phenomena are not isolated from wider sex work research contexts.

The tôjisha community and its boundaries

For the first step, realistically, our definition of the *tôjisha* community needed to be quite narrow vis-à-vis the fact that the sex industry is diverse in Japan, as in other parts of the world (Dewey and Zheng 2013; Overs 2015; Spanger and Skilbrei 2017). The focus of the HIV prevention project was on those who have strong probability of conducting prostitution, which by the Prostitution Prevention Law and its application in Japan involves penis–vagina intercourse and is illegal. Then, we had to focus on workers in in-house premises as Internet services were too difficult to track down and street workers had become much more on guard and thus invisible since the 2005 'clean-up' activities in red-light districts due to the Anti-Trafficking Action Plan (Aoyama 2014b). In-house premises are represented by 'rejuvenating massage parlours' or 'fashion health' where clients would expect sexual 'massage', and 'soap land', defined by the Entertainment Businesses Law as a 'public bath house with private compartments where services are provided to clients of the opposite gender'. This 'opposite gender' and the 'penis–vagina' application above divide the industry sharply by gender of the workers and clients, and also made us focus on female sex workers as the laws' assumption, which more or less reflects the reality, and excludes men as workers.[3]

Whether migrants were employed or not depended heavily on whether the particular premises were aiming, at least on the surface, to be law abiding or not. Then, migrants' legal disadvantages (see Aoyama 2014a for details) divided the industry roughly by nationalities or ethnicities of workers. As a consequence, we limited our migrant research to Chinese and Korean workers, who had become visible in red-light districts by that time, in the sexual massage parlours by the names of 'Chinese health' and 'Korean health', and our Japanese research to 'soap land' where we expected most workers would be Japanese.

The Japanese part was relatively straightforward as some of the members had direct contacts and knowledge of working conditions and feelings attached to 'soap land' work. To conduct the migrant part, however, we needed to invent another method, as migrant workers had never been a part of the sex worker movement in Japan and this meant that the community that SWASH represented was not the migrants' *tôjisha* community. Someone in SWASH called Oki (pseudonym) got an idea and volunteered to become a semi-*tôjisha* by working as a sex worker in both Chinese and Korean premises to have access to co-workers, insider information and a comparative perspective. She thought this was feasible as she already knew some managers working for Chinese and Korean parlours who would not mind employing a Japanese worker as their non-regular clients would not realise if she pretended to be Chinese or Korean, and she would not have to conduct illegal services. Furthermore, this would be a good action for SWASH's network to bridge between the Japanese and migrant communities.

The issue of the boundary of the *tôjisha* community went beyond the technical boundaries between different target communities at this stage; another aspect of the boundary came forward, between *tôjisha* and the researcher especially around consent (Dewey and Zheng 2013: 98). It could be argued that the researcher and the team accepting Oki's idea at face value was exploitative to Oki: it could never be clear how much pressure Oki felt to make the research succeed; how on the researcher's/my side the same pressure worked to minimise the ethical question and led me to readily accept this idea; and how the pressure we felt from our wish to stand up against the discourse that denies sex workers' agency to volunteer worked on Oki, the team and myself. Moreover, there was an implied consensus between SWASH members and I directly about different positionalities of the researcher and *tôjisha* that I myself was not a sex worker and therefore I was never the one doing sex work for the purpose of research either. This last point brings us to the question of democracy within a team of PAR in a complex way.

Democratic participation by the researcher and tôjisha: power politics upside down

Democratic participation is a hard-to-actualise key concept in PAR. Nominally, it should be inclusive of both *tôjisha* and the researcher, equally participated in by both sides. In real terms, however, the expected equality is the basis of a dilemma, one of the main questions of this chapter; as it is the researcher's side that is required to change, to assimilate itself with the *tôjisha*'s, to challenge mainstream academia to equalise the terms of participation, thus leading to marginalising itself within academia. In other words, the researcher's change in the long run involves the loss of their own prerogatives vis-à-vis the marginalised as they try to change the power structure that gives them the prerogatives, *but* they need to stay inside the prerogatives to activate these changes.

The loss of prerogatives, however, can happen in short-term micro power politics in the very process of PAR. The prerogatives can be challenged by the socially marginalised precisely because of the epistemology of PAR that the power structure of the society that makes the distinction between the centre and the margin needs to be overturned by the marginalised (Boontinand 2005; Sanders et al. 2009: 168–170). Thus, the researcher not being a sex worker (not socially marginalised) in our case worked for the sex worker gatekeeper to demonstrate her power, though micro, to override the power of the researcher. The interaction between the researcher, the team and Oki below explicates this well.

To make our research democratic, the team tried to follow *tôjisha*-centred procedural principles of PAR: data/information collection and dissemination of the results being led and/or at least evaluated by *tôjisha* who are fairly representative of their community (Dewey and Zheng 2013: Ch. 4). Fair representation was the first problem in connection with the strong presence of a gatekeeper, Oki. Oki was employed in Chinese and Korean parlours despite being a Japanese national, while other ways we tried to minimise bias via multiple methods to recruit interviewees such as by outreach or by random flyer all failed. Oki as a semi-*tôjisha* became the almost sole contact within the *tôjisha* community. She did her very best to bridge between the migrants and Japanese sex workers by becoming their colleague, chatting at the parlours whenever possible, going shopping or eating out together with them. She also got acquainted with barkers and drivers. Yet, the limitations are clear. The problem of bias caused by the difficulty of access overlaps with some of the previous research (Sanders et al. 2009: 176–177; Shaver 2005). It should be noted, however, that the problems were caused not so much by her background of being Japanese but by being after all protective about insider information as a semi-*tôjisha* on behalf of *tôjisha*. Oki spoke with only those who spoke Japanese in the community as she thought that there was no way translators could be involved. She could neither record any conversations nor ask for a formal interview with any of the informants, possibly because of the 'non-outing' policy of SWASH so embedded in her thoughts and actions. Oki wrote reports to the team instead but did not include her own work experiences in them either. As the gatekeeper, she had the power to select what she would report, who she would introduce and gently request us not to record.

At the stage of analysing the data and writing up the project report, we had to admit that much of the research aim – to find ways to develop and disseminate an intervention programme to prevent HIV infection among migrant sex workers – was not fulfilled as the first step of fact-finding was not successful enough to provide enough valid data. What we agreed then was to write about the hindrances to PAR in this area as a result of meta-analysis of the research itself, and to do this through me writing and asking other members to check. From this, as a conclusion, we deduced and suggested points to develop and disseminate HIV prevention programmes by working with the sex worker community.

SWASH's critical evaluation of their participation in this project was explicitly included in the final report. They reflected that they actively participated in the research by agreeing with its outline and purposes. In conclusion, however, they felt that it was difficult to incorporate their lived experiences and situated knowledge into academic research because, in short, our PAR was not democratic enough (Aoyama et al. 2011). SWASH did not feel that the research process failed because it lacked democratic representation or that the research team had not gathered varied enough data because the gatekeeper's power overrode the multi-method measures and the researcher's power to direct the research. It was about an ultimate question from *tôjisha* to the current structure of academia and the researcher's power that belongs to that.

Breaking down the mainstream distinction: the dilemma of not losing academic value

One member stated the feeling as: 'I want the partnership between researchers and sex workers to be either "democracy" or "fascism".' If it was a 'democracy', it should have started by discussing with *tôjisha* 'what sort of research, for what purpose, with what method, and how long time will be spent' would be possible or not. Then, we could have drawn up a research plan together. If not, she continued, 'the participation becomes more like a part-time job' and, if so, '"fascism" with everything decided, led, commanded and concluded by the researcher who also bears all the responsibility would be better, less demanding, and with clearer parameters to consent to or not' (Aoyama et al. 2011: 8–9).

As in Dewey and Zheng (2013: Ch. 4), research would not be valued as participatory from the *tôjisha* side if they are not involved from the beginning of the design, defining qualitative and quantitative questions. Our project could not start as such due mainly to its funding condition and fixed research paradigm, which will be discussed later, but still aimed for PAR and got a half-baked cake between 'democracy' and 'fascism' in the end. The *tôjisha* power that criticised and overrode the researcher's in the micro process of the project was actually also challenging the larger-scale academic structure – to break down the mainstream distinction between the assumed 'knowers' and 'not-knowers'. As the researcher, however, I could not transfer this micro power struggle to the macro arena. Instead, I was immobilised in trying to be both democratic, on one hand, in order to overturn the power structure in favour of the marginalised within the research process, and simultaneously to follow rigorous academic and administrative rules and regulations ('fascism') on the other, in order to ultimately gain access to influence on mainstream knowledge to facilitate change.

The complex part is that *tôjisha* could exercise, willingly or not, their power *not* to pursue the struggle to reach the macro power structure. On one hand, if PAR is still considered academic, although academia is a large part of the mainstream knowledge production it challenges, it cannot completely undermine the status of being academic, at least in one go. This was reflected in SWASH's original aim in our project, which was clear in the final report also, that they wanted their own activism to be persuasive and gain social status with research evidence to expand their network. At the same time, and resonating again with Dewey and Zheng's (2013: Ch. 4) summary regarding stigmatisation and criminalisation, SWASH members were at best suspicious about academic research for good reasons. Because they thought research might breach the privacy of the researched, might even lead to persecution especially for migrant workers, might bring nothing good back to sex workers in the end, they might be misinformed about it and consent to something wrong, Oki's gatekeeping power to control access and information was more or less supported by other SWASH members, too. They did not proactively contribute to the 'fact finding' in the form considered as valid evidence from the researcher's viewpoint and challenged the hitherto 'knower' and the way of knowing, but, as a result, hindered, at least at that time, the research process aiming to challenge the larger social structure. They also experienced a dilemma between utilising general academic value possibly leading to social status and undermining a certain part of that value.

Research paradigms and funding: concrete stumbling blocks

The way we aimed to gain social status might be more compliant than fighting against the mainstream. Both SWASH and I acknowledged that sex workers' voices did not have the same social or academic status as professional researchers in Japan. During the project, it was not unusual for us to actually and quite publicly face this. Upon a presentation of qualitative analysis of conversations with sex workers for the interim evaluation of the funding board for HIV prevention, which was also an influential body in policymaking, a board member remarked, 'Well, that was a good story. Where is your data, by the way?' A public servant administrator of this board kindly hinted that we needed immunological statistics input to continue getting funding, etc.

Considering research 'evidence' as important was central to the project gaining social and academic status but it was a hindrance at the same time. Oki argued that her report to the team was 'evidence' to back up the political conviction – 'sex work as work' – which SWASH, and myself, had had before conducting the research, as empowering and necessary for HIV prevention. As an activist, she needed *to deduce* from the conviction as premise and explain what she witnessed and the *tôjisha* community said. As an empirical sociologist, however, I decided that this would not stand the kind of evaluation of the HIV board – 'where is the data?' – and to use Oki's report as hearsay material only as opposed to the primary 'evidence' *to induce* a workable rule to prevent HIV infection. The fundamental issue here is the research paradigm, which is strongly influenced by another big issue of funding research in the real world, especially when its goal is policymaking such as creating HIV prevention measures.

Our research was funded and thus regulated by the Ministry of Health, Labour and Welfare's scheme for HIV prevention, which is a research instrument of its Health Service Bureau. It is medically oriented, positivist and objectivist in terms of its research paradigm, as the aims are advancing basic, clinical, socio-medical, immunological science research and achieving results that can be utilised to implement necessary measures against HIV infection (MHLW 2003). MHLW's medical orientation, however, does not just dismiss a naturalist or subjectivist research paradigm as the 1999 new policy guideline is renowned for stating, 'It is necessary to gain *tôjisha*'s understanding and cooperation to conduct immunological and social-scientific research on [. . .] [their] social background while paying attention to human rights' (Ministry of Health and Welfare 1999). Nevertheless, sociological researchers and *tôjisha* groups involved including myself have always been minorities in medical policymaking especially when we are conducting phenomenological qualitative research. We are burdened with long standing debates regarding positivist versus naturalist paradigms and quantitative versus qualitative methodologies in science (Lincoln and Guba 1985; Zeinaloo 2004). In our project, we could not dialectically challenge the evaluation of medicine – 'where is the data?' None of us had the chance to design the research from the *tôjisha* perspective as SWASH described, or to decide whether this way or this time frame would be feasible at all in the macro power politics of academic and policy paradigms set by the funding body.

Also, some local and general university rules and regulations to implement the macro research paradigms are too bureaucratic to make our research possible. In our case, just to take one basic example, a rule restricting cash transactions in the process of research was a problem. This rule exists for a good reason to prevent fraud. In practice, however, we are required to give the official name, address, e-mail and other contact address, bank details, and recently, the personal number (social security and tax number for the state to identify an individual) of those who we want to pay remuneration, honoraria or per-diem. Not only sex workers but any minority, such as migrants, transgender people or anyone involved with them would instantly realise that this is impossible, if not unethical; this kind of so-called bureaucratic transparency is nothing but a threat to their privacy and right to not disclose personal information that could lead to discrimination, bullying, economic and social loss or interrogation by law enforcement. This was exactly what SWASH was suspicious about. As a result, participants we could recruit were very limited and this reduced the number and variety of views of the team.

These mismatches of paradigms and practices seriously restricted what we could realistically imagine we could do from the start. That also meant that those who were not used to navigating bureaucratic rules and regulations, let alone those who already hated them, felt that they were forced to be under this power even if they did voluntarily participate. If a research plan is to be truly centred on the *tôjisha* standpoint, researchers receiving funding within academic institutions need to constantly negotiate with the administration to make some leeway in the too strict rules. Ironically, however, the negotiation can still only take place *within* the physical and discursive space of the institution, within its vocabulary, etiquette and timing, which prevents non-academic *tôjisha* from participating much.

Conclusion: 'failure' as knowledge towards useful policy and practice

The failure of our project could still be used as knowledge derived from PAR as a new knowledge production process. Quoting Jenny Muir on the bias of PAR, Sanders et al. (2009: 177) state,

> given the diversity within the sex industry, as with other groups, it is unlikely that one research study will represent the population as a whole and thus it is important to be explicit about the limitations of methods used. [. . .] 'the general lessons that can be drawn [. . .] in relation to bias are to assume that it will occur, to be alert for it, and to use it as data (Muir 2008: 126)'.

To approach a general lesson, the specific lessons learnt in our case are as follows.

Regarding specifying or even creating *tôjisha* communities, to make *tôjisha* identification and participation in research more feasible for a variety of people involved in the industry, it would be ideal for sex work research itself to be more widely conducted, and then to combine this variety of outcomes to seek ways to de-stigmatise sex work. This is also a move towards sex workers' identification as the subjects of their rights by expanding the solidarity among them to include legal and illegal, stigmatised and less stigmatised sex workers, to take over the normalising power of jurisdiction. More widely, linking with those who are involved with other minority issues would support those who are concerned with sex work issues. The link could be made through the focus on *tôjisha*, the person(s) central to the social issue at hand who is actually doing/being it, as the term is encompassing beyond sex workers and bridges to all those who are marginalised within the current social structure. The link could also be sustained by feminist standpoint theory in which the marginalised 'can learn to identify their distinctive opportunities to turn an oppressive feature of the group's conditions into a source of critical insight' and thus 'into an epistemological, scientific, and political advantage' (Harding 2004: 7–8).

Regarding democratic participation leading to breaking down the mainstream academic distinction between 'knowers' and 'not-knowers', both *tôjisha* and researchers need first and repeatedly to break down their own perceptions about key ideas. These would include 'research', 'democracy', '*tôjisha*', 'subject', 'evidence' and 'which information should be protected by whom and against whom' that set our sense of ownership of knowledge. The ideas would draw a map of practical conditions of the research, defining, as SWASH critically pointed out in our final report, what, which, who, where, when and how they do the collaboration. Then, even if there was a crucial gatekeeper for a piece of PAR, the necessary knowledge from the *tôjisha* side would be able to be shared with necessary parties, not be kept unknown to make all immobilised.

Continuing to seek multiple methods as a group is another important dimension to strengthen the aim of fairer representation as well as to have more open relationships within the participants and towards relevant supporters outside. Multiple methods are also necessary to ensure a variety of people and perspectives, from *tôjisha*, researchers and the industry, are involved in sex work research.

The research paradigm and funding, a seemingly insurmountable structural condition, might also offer an opening for multiple methods. Researchers aiming to find multiple methods could, for example, cooperate with immunologists willing to try inter-paradigm research between quantitative, qualitative, social, natural and phenomenological sciences. Funding opportunities, although shrinking everywhere in the world in sex work research, could still be sought and gained in the area of sociology and humanities, not only health and medicine.

All in all, in order to make the new knowledge gained from PAR, including its failure like ours, into 'data' to contribute to policy and practice to ease *tôjisha*'s marginalisation and stigmatisation in the long run, the micro power struggle between *tôjisha*, represented by the gatekeeper, and the researcher needs to be transferred to a macro one. There is no one or easy solution, of course, but the researcher first and repeatedly needs to come back to the principle that s/he is a facilitator for the *tôjisha*-centred structural change for de-marginalisation and de-stigmatisation. S/he also needs to let this be known inside and out of the research circle to show that s/he is in compliance with *tôjisha* identification and solidarity beyond the stigmatised and the 'normal'. Then through the researcher's facilitation, the participating *tôjisha* should be clearly and practically notified, in understandable terms, about the project's research conditions including the expected and conflicting paradigms, funding requirements, administrative rules and regulations. This is not just in order to obey or rebel against the rules and regulations but to develop skills to negotiate with or outwit academia and induce changes in it. Whether *tôjisha*'s voices will become 'evidence' or not depends on whether the above kinds of collaboration can be accumulated by a wider variety of sex work research communities. If *tôjisha*'s voices become 'evidence' as a result, it will be a significant paradigm change related to the macro power structure, not least reflecting and also furthering a significant change/overturning of the positionalities and power relationship between *tôjisha* and the researcher.

Notes

1 *Tôjisha* is gradually becoming known as a global term in some areas of research. Its dissemination started from Shinichiro Kumagaya, a leading 'science of self' researcher on autism spectrum disorders (Kumagaya 2016).
2 UNODC commissioned SWASH to empirically research migrant sex workers in Japan for comparative studies between India, Thailand and Japan in 2006. SWASH contacted me and we launched the three-year project. In the second year, however, the Japanese part was abruptly cancelled by the UN. The reason was not disclosed but one of the officers in charge 'privately' phoned me to explain that that was because the then Japanese ambassador to the UN complained about our research saying that there were no foreign 'sex workers' in Japan as they were legally not allowed to exist so there were no grounds to conduct the research. As a UN organisation, the Office could not force a project in a country if the state representative disapproved. Before hanging up, he added, 'This conversation did not happen. Good luck.'
3 Other HIV prevention research programmes funded by the same ministry within this decade have included many MSM participatory action research projects but no team has so far incorporated male sex workers. The invisibility of male sex workers is also a global issue. The Global Network of Sex Work Projects (NSWP) analyses the universal contributing factors, implicated in local discourses and laws, as their percentage is small, male sex workers do not fit the narrative of sex work as a form of violence against women, and double stigma towards homosexuality and sex work (NSWP 2014: 2–3).

References

Aoyama, Kaoru. 2009. *Thai Migrant Sex Workers from Modernisation to Globalisation*. London: Palgrave Macmillan.
Aoyama, Kaoru. 2014a. Moving from Modernisation to Globalisation: Migrant Sex Workers in Japan. In Emiko Ochiai and Kaoru Aoyama, eds. *Asian Women and Intimate Work*, 263–288. Leiden and Boston: Brill.

Aoyama, Kaoru. 2014b. Grôbaru-ka to sekkusu wâku: shinka suru risuku/kakudai suru undô (Globalisation and Sex Work: Deepening Risk/Widening Movement). *Shakai-gaku hyôron* (Japanese Sociological Review), 65(2): 224–238.

Aoyama, Kaoru. 2015. The Sex Industry in Japan: The Danger of Invisibility. In Mark McLelland and Vera Mackie, eds. *The Routledge Handbook of Sexuality Studies in East Asia*, 281–293. London and New York: Routledge.

Aoyama, Kaoru, Yukiko Kaname and Kasumi Yagi. 2011. Sekkusu wâku tono kyôdô ni yoru yobô kainyû puroguramu no kaihatsu to fukyû (Development and Dissemination of Preventative Intervention Programme through Working with Sex Workers). Higashi, Yuko (Principle) *Kobetsu shisaku-sô (tokuni seifûzoku ni kakawaru hitobito/ijû-rôdôsha) no HIV kansen yobô taisaku to sono kainyû kôka ni kansuru kenkyû – heisei 23 nendo sôkatsu/buntan kenkyû hôkokusho* (Research on HIV Prevention Strategy and Effectiveness of Intervention Among the Key Populations, Especially Those Who Are Involved in Sexual Entertainment and Migrants: Summary and Project Reports for FY 2011), 5–12. Kôsê-rôdô kagaku kenkyû hojokin eizu taisaku kenkyû jigyô (Research Project on HIV/AIDS, Health Labour Sciences Research Grant).

Boontinand, Jan. 2005. Feminist Participatory Action Research in the Mekong Region. In Kamala Kempadoo et al., eds. *Trafficking and Prostitution Reconsidered: New Perspectives on Migration, Sex Work, and Human Rights*, 175–197. Boulder, CO and London: Paradigm.

Brewis, Joanna and Stephen Linstead. 2000. *Sex, Work and Sex Work: Eroticizing Organization*. London and New York: Routledge.

Chevalier, Jacques M. and Daniel J. Buckles. 2013. *Participatory Action Research: Theory and Methods for Engaged Inquiry*. London and New York: Routledge.

Clifton, D. Bryant. 1990. *Deviant Behavior: Readings in the Sociology of Norm Violation*. New York, Washington, Philadelphia and London: Hemisphere Publishing.

Dewey, Susan and Tiantian Zheng. 2013. *Ethical Research with Sex Workers: Anthropological Approaches*. New York, Heidelberg, Dordrecht and London: Springer.

Dovidio, John F., Miles Hewstone, Peter Glick and Victoria M. Esses. 2010. *The SAGE Handbook of Prejudice, Stereotyping and Discrimination*. London: Sage.

Eide, Phyllis and Carol B. Allen. 2005. Recruiting Transcultural Qualitative Research Participants: A Conceptual Model. *International Journal of Qualitative Methods*, 4(2): 44–56.

Harding, Sandra, ed. 2004. *The Feminist Standpoint Theory Reader*. London and New York: Routledge.

Hubbard, Phil. 1999. Researching Female Sex Work: Reflections on Geographical Exclusion, Critical Methodologies and 'Useful' Knowledge. *Area*, 31(3): 229–237.

Kempadoo, Kamala and Jo Doezema. 1998. *Global Sex Workers: Rights, Resistance, and Redefinition*. London and New York: Routledge.

Kôsê-rôdô-sho (MHLW). 2003. Kôsê-rôdô kagaku kenkyû hojokin kenkyû jigyô no gaiyô (The Outlook of Research Project by Health Labour Sciences Research Grant). At www.mhlw.go.jp/shingi/2003/05/s0509-6c13.html, accessed on 31/10/2017.

Kôsê-sho (Ministry of Health and Welfare). 1999. Kokuji dai-217-go: kôtensê meneki fuzen shôkôgun ni kansuru tokutei kansen-shô yobô shishin (Public Notice No. 217: the Prevention Policy against Specified Infectious Diseases on AIDS). At www1.mhlw.go.jp/topics/kansensyou/tp1116-1_11.html, accessed on 31/10/2017.

Kumagaya, Shinichiro. 2016. An Invitation to Tojisha-Kenkyu: A New Science Focusing on Oneself. At www.u-tokyo.ac.jp/en/whyutokyo/indpt_tojisha_018.html, accessed on 31/10/2017.

Lawson, Hal, A. 2015. Introduction. In H.A. Lawson et al. *Participatory Action Research*, ix–xxvii. Oxford and New York: Oxford University Press.

Lincoln, Yvonna S. and Egon G. Guba. 1985. *Naturalistic Inquiry*. London and New Delhi: Sage.

Mitrovic, Emilija and Dorothea Muller, eds. 2009. *Working in the Sex Industry: Jobs with Representation of Interest?* Marburg: Forum Wissenschaft Studien 57.

NSWP. 2014. Briefing Paper No. 8: The Needs and Rights of Male Sex Workers. At https://docs.google.com/viewer?url=http%3A%2F%2Fwww.nswp.org%2Fsites%2Fnswp.org%2Ffiles%2FMale%2520SWs.pdf, accessed on 5/4/2018.

O'Neill, Maggie and Rosie Campbell. 2006. Street Sex Work and Local Communities: Creating Discursive Spaces for Genuine Consultation and Inclusion. In Rosie Campbell and Maggie O'Neill, eds. *Sex Work Now*, 33–61. Cullompton, UK: Willan.

Overs, Cheryl. 2015. Map of Sex Work Law by Sexuality, Poverty and Law Programme, Institute of Development Studies. At http://spl.ids.ac.uk/sexworklaw, accessed on 15/3/2018.

Pérez-y-Pérez, Maria and Tony Stanley. 2011. Ethnographic Intimacy: Thinking Through the Ethics of Social Research in Sex Worlds. *Sociological Research Online*, 16(2): 1–10.

Sanders, Teela. 2006. Sexing Up the Subject: Methodological Nuances in Researching the Female Sex Industry. *Sexualities*, 9(4): 449–468.

Sanders, Teela, Maggie O'Neil and Jane Pitcher. 2009. *Prostitution: Sex Work, Policy and Politics*. Los Angeles, London, New Delhi, Singapore and Washington, DC: Sage.

Scarlet Alliance. 2014. *The Principles for Model Sex Work Legislation*. Sydney: Redfern.

Shaver, Frances M. 2005. Sex Work Research: Methodological and Ethical Challenges. *Journal of Interpersonal Violence*, 20(3): 296–319.

Sinha, Sunny. 2016. Ethical and Safety Issues in Doing Sex Work Research: Reflections from a Field-Based Ethnographic Study in Kolkata, India. *Qualitative Health Research*, 27(6): 893–908.

Spanger, Marlene and May-Len Skilbrei. 2017. *Prostitution Research in Context: Methodology, Representation and Power*. Oxon and New York: Routledge.

SWASH. 2014. SWASH no katudô: 1999–2014 (Activities of SWASH: 1999–2014). At https://docs.google.com/viewer?url=http%3A%2F%2Fswashweb.sakura.ne.jp%2Ffile%2FABOUT_SWASH.pdf, accessed on 31/10/2017.

Zeinaloo, Tavakol M. 2004. Medical Research Paradigms: Positivistic Inquiry Paradigm versus Naturalistic Inquiry Paradigm. *Journal of Medical Education*, 5(2): 75–80.

Part II
Socio-legal practices

10

Socio-legal practices

An introduction

Susan Dewey, Isabel Crowhurst, and Chimaraoke Izugbara

Introduction

Legal and regulatory approaches to the sex industry vary dramatically by country, region, context, and venue, and tend to be informed by prevailing public sentiments in ways that directly impact labor practices, safety, and the ability of sex industry participants to drive or respond to the socio-legal conditions in which they earn a living. Key themes in existing literature related to socio-legal practices include disconnects between legislation and practice, labor conditions produced by particular socio-legal approaches, heterogeneity and variance in law enforcement practices, calls for grassroots input into socio-legal practices, and the reflection of prevailing political sentiments in prostitution policy. Chapters in this section engage with these ongoing challenges while offering clear directions for future research.

Key themes in existing literature

Researchers note the prevalence with which significant gaps exist between the clarity of law and policy as written and the quotidian messiness of its implementation. Assessments of prostitution policies emphasize the considerable national and contextual variations that span governance of the sex industry even within in a single region or country (Jahnsen & Wagenaar, 2017). Yet gaps between policy and practice are perhaps most evident with respect to socio-legal constructions of sex trafficking, which increasingly dominates discussions of the sex industry and particularly of prostitution in ways that do not often reflect the experiences and perspectives of those targeted by anti-trafficking efforts (Mai, 2014). Police, social workers, and other practitioners tasked with the enforcement of related law and policy accordingly must utilize their discretion regarding who to arrest, who to identify as a victim of trafficking, and, in the case of undocumented migrant sex workers, who to deport (Ham, Segrave, & Pickering, 2013; Pickering & Ham, 2013).

Prevailing legislation or policy and social norms directly influence sex industry labour practices and conditions to the degree that these codified, normative approaches have implications for sex workers' safety and welfare (Pitcher & Wijers, 2014). Criminalization is widely regarded as being conducive to exploitative working conditions, particularly among undocumented migrant sex workers who face pressure to appease both third parties and police by engaging in commercial sex in ways that diminish their autonomy and control over their earnings and working conditions (Baye & Heumann, 2014). Criminalization and its associated need to evade police detection is a source of significant stress for sex workers, whose associated poor working conditions have consequences for other aspects of their lives (O'Doherty, 2011; Duff et al., 2017). Social stigma significantly impacts sex workers in all legal and regulatory contexts through negative consequences in personal and/or intimate relationships, working conditions, and work–life balance (O'Doherty, 2011; Benoit et al., 2017).

Disconnects between socio-legal policy and practice are particularly evident in the heterogeneity and variance in law enforcement priorities, such that the most socio-economically vulnerable individuals in the sex industry are most likely to face arrest and other negative consequences (Dank, Yahner, & Yu, 2017). Regulation occurs at multiple national, state/provincial, and municipal levels (McCarthy et al., 2012), and is applied to an equally diverse set of actors and communities. The result is, unsurprisingly, considerable variance in enforcement practices so that, for example, arrests are not as common in neighborhood contexts where residents are unconcerned with the presence of those engaged in commercial sex (Cooper, 2016). Likewise, police harassment and abuse of sex workers is relatively common in settings that criminalize prostitution and especially rife when individuals involved in sex trading also struggle with addiction, homelessness, and related issues (Odinokova et al., 2014). Concerns about such practices have prompted sex workers worldwide to advocate for inclusion in legal and policymaking decisions about their lives and working conditions (Fassi, 2015).

Prostitution policy reflects prevailing political sentiments in ways that some scholars regard as constitutive of prostitution itself as an act. From this perspective, the law creates the concept of prostitution even as it actively polices it (Scoular, 2017). Historically as today, prostitution is a political lightning rod that reflects prevailing concerns about public morality, order, and sexuality, such that all too often concerns for sex worker rights fall by the wayside in the name of maintaining a desired social order (Roos, 2002). Hence rigid systems of control may govern the sex industry even when law and policy appear relatively relaxed (Pates, 2012) and sex workers in neighboring countries or regions may experience very different working conditions and forms of governance (Van Meir, 2017).

Chapter overview

Chapters in this section engage with and build upon this work. Wagenaar (Chapter 11) analyzes the key challenges facing policymakers with respect to control and oversight of the sex industry to conclude that collaborative governance with sex worker advocacy groups' full participation in policy design and implementation is a best practice. Weitzer (Chapter 12) identifies best practices for the regulation of indoor prostitution with potential for global implementation in ways that respect significant similarities and differences between and among contexts and venues. Armstrong (Chapter 13) explores how sex worker activism has successfully enabled decriminalization in ways that prioritize occupational health and safety as well as human rights for sex workers.

Ekpootu (Chapter 14) examines the disconnects between the law on paper and its everyday implementation and how sex workers resist and renegotiate their relationships with society and the state to foster particular living and working conditions. Netzelmann, Steffan, and Kavemann (Chapter 15) analyze case files from a support center for women exiting prostitute to identify the obstacles they face, including anticipated stigmatization, access to non-judgmental counseling and other support services, and anxiety surrounding the transition to the 'conventional' world more generally. Mamabolo (Chapter 16) focuses on criminalized sex workers' resiliency to emphasize the psychological strategies they employ as they face pervasive violence, stigmatization, and various forms of marginalization.

Future directions

Most sex work researchers take for granted the assumption that sex workers are authorities of their own experiences and that their voices are crucial to the development of evidence-based socio-legal practices. Yet the same level of respect is often not accorded to police, policymakers, community members, and others who wield significant power and authority relative to sex workers. Including such perspectives—especially the diversity within and among them—is critical to a balanced and holistic approach to this topic. Related future research in this field will likely explore the cultural, economic, and other conditions that have proven conducive to socio-legal practices that respect sex worker human rights while also according the same respect to the significant majority of people who object to the sex industry's physical manifestations in their neighborhoods through advertising, loitering, and other practices that generally reduce a locale's desirability.

Researchers may likewise pursue critical inquiry into systematic ways to draw parallels between what is now well established in existing literature as the highly contextualized nature of both the sex industry and research about it. Considerations of the processes by which the global pervasiveness of criminalization and stigmatization have taken such firm hold cross-culturally will likely offer insights into how alternative socio-legal practices might also establish themselves. Moving beyond context to focus on globally prevalent concerns will help facilitate research-based advocacy for evidence-based socio-legal practices with respect to the sex industry's socio-legal management and oversight.

References

Baye, Eneze Modupe-Oluwa and Heumann, Silke. 2014. Migration, Sex Work and Exploitative Labor Conditions Experiences of Nigerian Women in the Sex Industry in Turin, Italy and Counter-Trafficking Measures. *Gender, Technology and Development* 18(1): 77–105.

Benoit, Cecilia, Jansson, Mikael S., Smith, Michaela, and Flagg, Jackson. 2017. Prostitution Stigma and Its Effect on the Working Conditions, Personal Lives, and Health of Sex Workers. *Journal of Sex Research* 55(4/5): 1–15.

Cooper, Emily. 2016. "It's Better Than Daytime Television": Questioning the Socio-Spatial Impacts of Massage Parlors on Residential Communities. *Sexualities* 19(5/6): 547–566.

Dank, Meredith, Yahner, Jennifer, and Yu, Lilly. 2017. *Consequences of Policing Prostitution: An Analysis of Individuals Arrested and Prosecuted for Commercial Sex in New York City*. New York: Urban Institute.

Duff, S., Sou, J., Chapman, S., Dobrer, M., Braschel, S., Goldenberg, K., and Shannon, Kate. 2017. Poor Working Conditions and Work Stress Among Canadian Sex Workers. *Occupational Medicine* 67(7): 512–521.

Fassi, Marisa. 2015. Sex Work and the Claim for Grassroots Legislation. *Culture, Health & Sexuality* 17(1): 74–84.

Ham, Julie, Segrave, Marie, and Pickering, Sharon. 2013. In the Eyes of the Beholder: Border Enforcement, Suspect Travelers and Trafficking Victims. *Anti-Trafficking Review* 2: 51–66.

Jahnsen, Synnove and Wagenaar, Hendrik. 2017. *Assessing Prostitution Policy in Europe*. London: Routledge.

McCarthy, Bill, Benoit, Cecilia, Jansson, Mikael, and Kolar, Kat. 2012. Regulating Sex Work: Heterogeneity in Legal Strategies. *Annual Review of Law and Social Science* 8: 255–271.

Mai, Nicola. 2014. Too Much Suffering: Understanding the Interplay Between Migration, Bounded Exploitation and Trafficking Through Nigerian Sex Workers' Experiences. *Sociological Research Online Special Section: Exploitation and its Opposite: Researching the Quality of Working Life in the Sex Industries* 21(4): 13.

Odinokova, Veronika, Rusakova, Maia, Urada, Lianne, Silverman, Jay, and Raj, Anita. 2014. Police Sexual Coercion and Its Association with Risky Sex Work and Substance Use Behaviors Among Female Sex Workers in St. Petersburg and Orenburg, Russia. *International Journal on Drug Policy 25*(1): 96–104.

O'Doherty, Tamara. 2011. Criminalization and Off-Street Sex Work in Canada. *Canadian Journal of Criminology and Criminal Justice 53*(2): 217–245.

Pates, Rebecca. 2012. Liberal Laws Juxtaposed with Rigid Control: an Analysis of the Logics of Governing Sex Work in Germany. *Sexuality Research and Social Policy 9*(3): 212–222.

Pickering, Sharon and Ham, Julie. 2013. Hot Pants at the Border: Sorting Sex Work from Trafficking. *British Journal of Criminology 54*(1): 2–19.

Pitcher, Jane and Wijers, Marjan. 2014. The Impact of Different Regulatory Models on the Labor Conditions, Safety, and Welfare of Indoor-Based Sex Workers. *Criminology & Criminal Justice 14*(5): 549–564.

Roos, Julia. 2002. Backlash Against Prostitutes' Rights: Origins and Dynamics of Nazi Prostitution Policies. *Journal of the History of Sexuality 11*(1): 67–94.

Scoular, Jane. 2017. *The Subject of Prostitution: Sex Work, Law and Social Theory*. London: Routledge.

Van Meir, Jessica. 2017. Sex Work and the Politics of Space: Case Studies of Sex Workers in Argentina and Ecuador. *Social Sciences 6*(2): 42–82.

11

Understanding prostitution policy

The challenges to regulating prostitution and how to harness them

Hendrik Wagenaar

Introduction: the enduring entanglement of prostitution and the state

In most European countries since the middle of the nineteenth century, prostitution as a social phenomenon cannot be seen apart from the efforts of authorities to prohibit, contain, or regulate it (Corbin 1990; de Vries 1997; Gibson 1986; Jahnsen and Wagenaar 2017; Walkowitz 1982) The sites and modes of the sex trade within the urban environment, and the place of sex workers in society, are the joint outcome of autonomous socio-economic forces, government intervention and civil society reactions. Prostitution, in all its manifestations, is deeply entangled with the state. While trade liberalization and the ensuing structural adjustments, poverty, migration trends, education and employment possibilities, and global connectedness through the Internet influence the "supply" of sex workers, an array of government interventions shapes the nature, organization, and location of prostitution markets. Zoning laws determine which urban spaces are designated for prostitution purposes, national laws determine the legal position and civil rights of sex workers, the mandate, skills, and expertise of professionals and administrators influence their health and work conditions, police procedure impacts the security situation of sex workers, immigration laws influence their mobility, and labor law influences work conditions and worker rights for sex workers. And, while policymakers do not by themselves determine society's attitude towards prostitution, their rhetoric and pronouncements exert a strong influence on the public's understanding and acceptance of the sex trade.

However, given the entanglement of policy and prostitution, public policy is remarkably underrepresented in the rich and varied literature on prostitution. Much of the prostitution literature prefers to discuss prostitution either in non-policy terms or to reduce public policy towards prostitution to only one element of the policy process. Each academic field develops its own traditions; its own preferred foci of attention, problem definitions, and styles of writing. More specifically, in the academic literature, prostitution is predominantly discussed as shaped by society-wide extraneous influences (Bernstein 2007), as broad (national) policy regimes (Agustín 2008), in terms of feminism governance (Halley et al. 2006), as discourse (Doezema 2010), as a series of rational economic transactions that aggregate into a market for sexual services (Edlund and Korn 2002), and as the outcome of broad shifts in governmentality (Scoular 2010). Scholarly writing on prostitution, even when it purportedly discusses public policy, overwhelmingly moves within a legal framework, supported by a smattering of sociology to explain the need to adapt law to extraneous developments. The foundational assumption of the field is that law is the paramount instrument of change, and hard battles are fought over the proper constitution of the legal regime pertaining to prostitution. A good example is a recent article by Holmström and Skilbrei (2017) in which the authors assess the intended and unintended effects of the Swedish Sex Purchase Act. In their careful weighing of a wide range of evidence that estimates the law's effect on the prevalence of prostitution, attitudes towards prostitution, the extent of trafficking, and social stigma, the authors never stray from a largely legal framework. Even when they conclude that Swedish officials understand the law as working independently of other social processes (Holmström and Skilbrei 2017, 91), or that research is needed to investigate the conceptual and instrumental links between law and outcomes (ibid., 103), they never once refer to policy theory. The effect is that certain phenomena that characterize the contemporary sex trade, are hard to explain or escape the analyst's attention altogether. In contrast to policy domains such as health, education, or climate change, most of the prostitution literature is oblivious to the core texts of policy theory as well as its key concepts such as agenda setting, policy formulation, policy implementation, or policy instruments. Yet, the discipline of policy analysis offers exactly what Holmström and Skilbrei (2017) admonish the field to consider: a coherent body of theory and research that shows how law comes into being and is subsequently transformed into policy practices and societal impact.

The purpose of this chapter therefore is to use concepts and insights from policy theory to elucidate the state's conduct towards prostitution. In addition, the policy literature, as we will see in the conclusion of this chapter, also provides suggestions for solving some of the stubborn problems that flow from the entanglement of prostitution and the state. While this chapter draws predominantly on the European experience with prostitution policy, some of the themes discussed in this chapter, such as the importance of national discourse, and (local) decentered policy implementation for the impact of prostitution, the intrinsic difficulty of collecting reliable statistics on the sex trade, the moral nature of prostitution policy, or the benefits of collaborative policymaking, might well transcend the geographical boundaries of this chapter.

Themes in the analysis of prostitution policy

From the middle of the nineteenth century European states have attempted to control prostitution by restricting the freedom of movement of sex workers and suspending certain basic rights. Prostitutes (I use the terminology of the times) were sequestered in designated districts or houses (*maisons de tolerance*), they had to wear clothing that singled them out as sex workers, they were subjected to frequent mandatory STD testing, and they could be quarantined indefinitely in hospitals without due process (Corbin 1990). Prostitutes were subject to extensive extra-judicial and custodial powers of the police. They could be arrested for minor rule infractions, banned from certain parts of the city, and, upon suspicion of harboring an STD locked up in a hospital for indefinite time. Many European countries had adopted this so-called French system (Jahnsen and Wagenaar 2017). The overt purpose of these measures was to contain the spread of STDs; however, as historians of prostitution observe, the latent aim was to assuage the fears of the upcoming bourgeoisie of the corrupting influence of unrestrained female sexuality on family and society.

Originally, the regulationist project was rooted in a strong stereotype of the prostitute. Prostitutes were considered to be lazy, intemperate, profligate and immature, idle and impulsive (Corbin 1990, 6–7). Her condition was a combination of innate temperament and family heritage. This combination of traits called out for supervision and surveillance. In addition, nineteenth-century middle-class reformers were obsessed with the lifestyle of the poor, in particular their alleged profligate sexual habits (Stedman Jones 2014). This obsession found epistemological expression in bringing the tools of the nascent social sciences in the form of categorization and survey projects to bear on the poor and what were considered the criminal classes (Thompson 2013). It also resulted in ambitious programs of state intervention aimed at "improving" slum housing (mostly by their erasure) and "moralizing" the poor (Stedman Jones 2014). The impetus of this middle-class project was a deep-seated fear of insurrection and disorder, as well as contagion by loose morals. Around the turn of the century these fears would supplant geneticist images of the prostitute with fears of spreading disorder; regulationism was no longer seen as a sufficient remedy for containing prostitution and calls for abolitionism began to be heard (Corbin 1990; Walkowitz 1982).

The upshot of this brief and simplified summary of the history of nineteenth-century regulation is that the state's involvement in the regulation of prostitution represented a complex crosscurrent of larger images, ideas, and sentiments about social class and sexual conduct. As Corbin (1990, 24) summarizes it: "(T)he regulationist discourse had become . . . the reflection and crossroads of all the bourgeois obsessions of the time." These "obsessions" were hidden beneath scientific theories and formal policy schemes whose overt aim was to understand and contain prostitution and improve the situation of the prostitute. Although the language has changed, the essential configuration of prostitution policy—a combination of obsessive attention, out of proportion to the size of the social phenomenon, which is driven by middle-class obsessions with the poor, with migrants, and with heterodox sexual conduct, a feverish desire by state authorities to intervene and regulate, the application of scientific theories and instruments that give a gloss of authority to discursive images, and the ignoring of the rights of sex workers as the acceptable collateral effects of regulation—remains by and large unchanged. Under the veneer of national law, policy instruments, "scientific" research reports commissioned by government agencies, and international agreements, contemporary prostitution policy still reflects the obsessions of the "respectable" middle classes.

This short summary of the state's involvement with prostitution contains a welter of policy themes. First, the example demonstrates an astonishing continuity in the approach to prostitution. Control, sequestration, surveillance, registration, and the restriction of movement and settlement of sex workers have been the policy strategies of choice throughout almost two centuries and across at least 22 European countries (Jahnsen and Wagenaar 2017). Second, this continuity is to a large extent decentered. It is not the result of some large, centrally orchestrated anti-prostitution initiative or the inexorable forces of structural oppression, but instead it occurs through a myriad of low-level, mundane, administrative decisions about policy instruments. Almost by default authorities opt for authoritative instruments (Wagenaar et al. 2017, Ch. 3). *Authoritative instruments* "involve, and rely primarily on, the ability of governments to direct or steer targets in the directions they would prefer them to go through the use of the real or perceived threat of state-enforced sanctions" (Howlett 2011, 83). While nineteenth-century authorities used the (extra-) judicial powers of the police, twenty-first-century administrators employ so called "enforcement schemes" to detect and ensnare traffickers, "administrative measures" to close down brothels suspected of violating regulations, or social work interventions to discipline sex workers (Skilbrei and Holmström 2013). The disciplinarian motive of authoritative policy instruments are complemented by financial, organizational, and information instruments. For example (the threat of) sanctions and fines are commonplace in the regulation of prostitution. Instead of STD hospitals, the officials now impose mandatory STD testing requirements. Instead of surveys of the poor, modern societies institute the office of the "Rapporteur" to collect and report figures on trafficking in prostitution, thereby guaranteeing the continued visibility of the issue (Wagenaar et al. 2017). Then as now, registration of sex workers is still one of the information instruments of choice. In addition, more sophisticated instruments that capitalize on the vast information processing capacities of contemporary IT are mobilized in the control of the sex trade. On the other hand, we must be careful not to overinterpret the similarities between the present and the past. Many European countries nowadays engage in serious scientific evaluations of public policy that inform the (inter-)national debate about the merits of different approaches to prostitution policy (for examples, see Abel et. al 2010; Skilbrei and Holström 2013). Policy instruments such as social work or public health are cornerstones in a harm-reduction approach to sex workers. In New Zealand and Vancouver authorities have engaged in genuine horizontal deliberation with sex workers and their advocates to collaboratively design and implement prostitution policy (Abel et al. 2010; Johnson 2015).

Third, this re-description of prostitution policy in terms of policy instruments demonstrates the importance of policy implementation for understanding prostitution policy. For national laws, no matter how morally ambitious, to have any effect "on the ground," requires careful translation into action. This raises a host of normative, political, administrative, and practical questions. The work of policy translation does not start from scratch. While designing new regulation calls for a lot of creativity, much of the work of implementation is mundane and mechanistic. It is always a fortuitous alliance between the habitual and the imaginative. For example, policy implementation requires that funding must be allocated to specific agencies and programs, that personnel is hired or assigned, and that rules are formulated and procedures developed (Howlett and Ramesh 2003, 185). In most of the countries on which this chapter draws this work has been delegated to a professional administrative bureaucracy. Or rather *bureaucracies*, as agencies at all levels and in different societal sectors have been authorized with designing policy implementation. That extends to NGOs, charities, and businesses (when public service delivery is contracted out). Civil and administrative law regulates the relationship between political decision makers and public administration. A variety of statutes designate which administrative level is assigned with the implementation of a policy, which agency is assigned with what task, what type of regulation needs to be followed, how agencies and administrators deal with social organizations and citizens, and how appeal to administrative decisions is organized. The result is a densely interconnected, complex policy field, where many actors use their practical judgement and administrative discretion to make rules and regulations work (Maynard-Moody and Musheno 2003; Vinzant and Crothers 1998; Wagenaar et al. 2017, Ch. 3).

A focus on policy implementation, with its densely networked character is important for two reasons. First, it explains policy variety and divergence. For example, Skilbrei and Holmström (2013) convincingly demonstrate that the Nordic model of client criminalization shows considerable variation in its realization in different countries. Or, the federal German *Prostitutions Gesetz* of 2001 that decriminalized brothels was never implemented by the "*Länder*" and cities, many of which in effect introduced more repressive schemes (Hünecke 2017). Second, a focus on policy implementation allows for a collective discussion about the success or failure of the law. Implicit in the very idea of policy implementation is a notion of an "end state or policy achievement" and an associated understanding of the moral ambition that is expressed by the law. It is the responsibility of elected officials, administrators, and professionals to realize that end state (Lane 1987, 528). Differently put, the understanding that policy implementation is in reality a complex set of discretionary actions by local actors, does not mean that we should lose sight of the normative "glue" that holds the policy process together and forms its justification. Lane makes a helpful distinction between the responsibility and the trust dimensions of the implementation process. The first refers to an accountability norm that puts certain constraints on the implementation process. Differently put, no matter how interactive, improvisational, and discretionary the implementation process is, we are always justified to inquire to what extent objectives have been accomplished, and what outcomes mean in light of the law's intentions (Lane 1987, 542). The trust aspect of policy implementation refers to the public power entrusted to politicians, administrators, and professionals in a democratic system to realize policies (Lane, 1987, 542). The trust aspect balances autonomy, necessary for making the judgments to design regulation, and accountability, with the constraints that follow from the intent of the law and from an administrative ethos of fairness, justice, and equality. Taken together, the responsibility and trust dimensions of policy implementation uphold the idea that we can assess policies on their achievements. Not in the unrealistic, centralistic sense of deviation from a clear instruction, but in a more subtle sense of comparing the normative intention of a policy with its actual effects on the ground. This does not only imply the assessment of policy outcome relative to the policy's normative intent, but also the rightness or feasibility of moral goals in light of the policy's (unintended) outcomes. Such a fine-grained evaluation counts as an improvement over the ubiquitous but ultimately futile debates about the merits of different aggregate prostitution regimes. We will return to this point at the end of this chapter.

However, a focus on policy implementation and policy instruments does not explain the remarkable continuity in policy approach across history and time. What makes this continuity particularly puzzling is that the contain-and-control approach has largely failed in terms of its self-professed goals. Not a single country in our 22-country study has succeeded in eradicating prostitution (Jahnsen and Wagenaar 2017). For reasons to be explained later in this chapter, we cannot establish on the basis of data the number of sex workers if the authorities have succeeded in containing or diminishing the sex trade in a particular locale. What we do know is that throughout history every major city in the countries under study had considerable prostitution scenes, even under the most repressive political regimes, and that the contain-and-control approach has had considerable negative effects on the human rights of sex workers. What then explains the stubborn persistence of policy strategy in the face of repeated failure? Three important policy concepts, discourse, morality politics, and symbolic policymaking, go a long way to explain this seeming puzzle.

As we have seen, discourse is a trope in the contemporary academic prostitution literature. The central concepts in discourse analysis are myth, meaning, and power. Its purpose is not so much to confront certain myths about prostitution (in particular the myth about trafficking as an epidemic worldwide phenomenon) with the reality of sex workers' lives, but to trace the genealogy of these images, and how they succeed in convincing the larger world of their truth claims (Doezema 2010, 10). By placing the discourse on trafficking in a historical perspective, the analyst discerns larger patterns of meaning-making and the coalitions and mechanisms (such as funding decisions, organizational design, media attention) that fuel those meanings and succeed in imposing them upon the larger public. It explains the naturalization of certain images and understandings through the repeated use of certain narrative tropes that are owned and supported by actors who claim political, academic, and moral authority (Fairclough 2003).

The challenge of discourse analysis is that although it bears an intuitive relationship with policy formulation and implementation, that relationship is far from obvious. From one perspective the laws, bylaws, ordinances, administrative arrangements, and officials that regulate prostitution *are* discourse; that is they are the organizational expression of the power elite's beliefs, images, and sentiments towards prostitution. These arrangements and professional roles form the sedimentation of a society's attitudes towards prostitution, gender relations, and immigration. For example, the Swedish laws that criminalize clients who solicit paid sex are the direct expression of the discourse on gender relationships, sexuality, prostitution, and the Swedish tradition of paternalistic welfare statism that gives the state the right to intervene in personal life-style and individual moral choice (Dodillet and Östergren 2013; Halley et. al 2006). However, the relationship between discourse and policy is neither linear nor unidirectional. Discourse is rarely a monolithic, unassailable, ideological bloc that exhaustively determines political, administrative, and professional arrangements. In fact, regulatory schemes also shape, consolidate, and give legitimacy to different elements of the reigning discourse, while resistance to such schemes shapes the arguments of their supporters. Discourse is itself a "child of social experience" (Walkowitz 1982, 5).

Every policy domain is cognitively and emotionally shaped by discourse, but in some the pushback from experience is weaker than in others. One reason that phantasmatic schemes and ideologies (Glynos and Howarth 2007) have relatively free reign in prostitution policy is the fact that it is a prime example of morality politics. In the policy literature the concept of moral politics refers to policies in which first principles are at stake, over which exists deep conflict among the public, and which do not necessarily coincide with the left–right, liberal–conservative political divide (Engeli et al. 2012; Mooney 1999, 675). This usually results in a denotative definition, the ubiquitous list of life, body, and "sin" issues that are considered to belong to the class of morality politics: abortion, contraception, gambling, same-sex marriage, drugs, pornography, physician-assisted suicide, and prostitution. Wagenaar and Altink (2012) considered this definition too restrictive. They argued that all policies can be construed as struggle over the interpretation and realization of key values (Stone 1997) and that policies may move in and out of moral territory over the course of a policy's life cycle (before the advent of austerity politics macro-economic policy was more technical and less determined by moral arguments). We therefore decided to speak of morality *politics*, instead of policy, to indicate that the issue has moved from the realm of policymaking (which despite unavoidable conflicts over ideas and instruments has the moral and instrumental aim to resolve or ameliorate a collective problem) to that of deep and intractable conflict (in which the struggle over the prevalence of symbolic positions takes precedence over resolving collective problems). Differently put, morality politics indicates a situation where the minimum common ground that is the condition for engaging in effective collective problem solving, has broken down into irreconcilable conflict over moral positions about what is right or virtuous with regard to the issue at hand. In light of this conceptualization we also suggested that it is more fruitful to define morality politics by its effects on policymaking. Using the case of prostitution policy, we distinguished six such effects: morality politics is ruled by ideology (often the issue at hand is a proxy for a larger ideological project); it is lay policy (it is owned by ordinary people and everyone has an opinion about it); it is emotionally charged; it is impervious to evidence; it is impatient with the tedious, hard work of policy implementation; and instead is prone to grand policy gestures and sudden policy reversals (Wagenaar and Altink 2012; Wagenaar et al. 2017, Ch. 2).

The moral nature of prostitution policy goes a long way in explaining some of the characteristics of contemporary prostitution policy. One of its characteristics, for example, is a cavalier attitude towards evidence. Not only is policy driven by inflated data on trafficking (Weitzer 2015) or the size of the sex trade (Wagenaar et al. 2013), policymakers and activists regularly make up evidence through rhetorical devices such as inflated figures or the melodramatic story (Vance 2011; Wagenaar et al. 2017). Prostitution policy is vulnerable to this; because of the extreme mobility of sex workers, precise, reliable data are exceedingly hard to obtain (Wagenaar et al. 2013, 2017). Highly exaggerated claims about the extent of "forced prostitution" or of a trend towards "invisible illegal prostitution" as the alleged result of a relaxing of surveillance or enforcement, go unopposed, and through constant repetition by persons of authority in the media take on the aura of truth claims.[1] This then is followed by calls for even more repression, more extensive surveillance, or stricter enforcement. The fact that these schemes have hardly any effect, except a further erosion of the human rights of sex workers, does not deter their proponents. Within the universe of morality politics their purpose is largely symbolic (Edelman 1985). In a nutshell, symbolic politics is about conveying a particular message or meaning to an audience that is not in a position to assess the validity of truth claims about a policy. Edelman realised that in mass democracies most people's (and many politicians') experience with policy issues is almost exclusively through the mass media (and nowadays through the filter bubbles of social media). Clever politicians use this circumstance to their advantage. They use mass and social media to push a topic up the political agenda by disseminating alarmist stories about the issue at hand (Kingdon 2011). To this purpose they employ narrative tropes such as stories of decline ("the situation rapidly gets worse unless we intervene now," or "the situation is much worse than we always assumed") or helplessness and control ("if we don't act now, the situation will get out of hand") (Stone 1997). For example, opponents of the legalization of brothels in the Netherlands used the helplessness and control trope by claiming that the proposed measure would attract hordes of foreign prostitutes from Eastern Europe (Outshoorn 2004). In a climate of morality politics it does not matter that the predicted surge in immigrant prostitution never materialized. The next step is the proposal and enactment of policies that aim to counter these alarming situations to convey the message to the public that the authorities are in control of a bad situation. For example, when the city of Vienna proposed a 7-step plan to reform prostitution policy, the authorities, led by right-wing political parties, hostile media, and the police, quickly zoomed in on only one of these aims: the reform of street prostitution. Although there were fewer outdoor sex workers in Vienna than there were brothels (which were largely left alone then), elected officials and the media exaggerated the size of the phenomenon, allowing the police to crack down in a highly visible way on outdoor sex workers (by harassing and arresting them and relegating them to the outskirts of the city). The action sent the desired message to the public (Wagenaar et al. 2013, Ch. 3).

Challenges to prostitution policy

In a general sense, public policy is a purposive course of action, authorized, though not necessarily initiated or implemented, by government, to deal with a problem or matter of concern (Anderson 1984, 3; Howlett and Ramesh 2003, 7). Policy domains such as prostitution policy are sometimes characterized as belonging to the class of "wicked problems" (Rittel and Webber 1973). Wicked problems are problems for which there is no immediate solution, where the explanation determines the solution, where every problem is a symptom of another problem, and for which no true or false but only better or worse solutions exist (ibid.) Because of its intuitive appeal, the concept of wicked problem enjoyed considerable popularity among policy analysts. However, as it is so general that it applies to more or less every policy issue, and as it does not suggest strategies to deal with "wickedness" in a constructive manner, the concept has lost some of its lustre. Instead I propose to use the concepts of "challenge" and "complexity." All public policies face certain general challenges, or key tasks that need to be adhered to to realize a policy, any policy. Think of the challenge of setting a policy agenda and creating support for it (Kingdon 2011), addressing the intractable nature of the problem (Rittel and Webber 1973), moving a bill through parliament, translating policy intentions into policy design and implementation (Howlett 2011), and navigating networks of policy actors at different scalar levels (Rhodes 1996). For example, although supported by a powerful network of feminist actors who occupied key institutional positions in the heart of the Dutch government, the 2000 repeal of brothels in the Netherlands, at the time hailed (or condemned) as a remarkable example of progressive policymaking in prostitution, was voted down and re-admitted to parliament several times over a ten-year period, before it managed to overcome some particularly stubborn Christian-Democratic veto points (John 2012; Outshoorn 2004). These general challenges can best be regarded as the generic tasks that policymakers face and the requisite skills that experienced policymakers need to possess to successfully formulate, design, and implement public policy.

In addition to general challenges, every policy presents a number of domain-specific challenges to the policymaker and analyst alike. A domain-specific challenge is a circumstance or characteristic of a specific policy field that heavily influences the nature of, and possibilities for, concerted action in that field. While a general policy challenge represents a necessary and inescapable task, domain-specific challenges act more like constraints in a policy field, setting the limits of what is possible and imaginable. Both are important because they displace the analytic gaze away from grand moral claims towards the everyday political and administrative tasks of designing and implementing effective policies, in this instance in the domain of prostitution.

The domain-specific challenges of prostitution policy are the following. Prostitution is *stigmatized*. Trading sex for money is considered to be demeaning to women and involving an unacceptable commodification of female sexuality (Nussbaum 1998; Radin 1996). The stigma on prostitution results in its public condemnation, or at the very minimum, public distrust, lack of acceptance, and a generalized anxiety about prostitution's effects on marriage and community. It also leads to sex work taking place at the margins of society, usually in designated urban spaces, engaged in by persons, such as low-income immigrants, who are at a far remove from the general public, or by ordinary women working and living among us who conceal their work as a sex worker. Stigmatization transforms female prostitution into an unspecified threat from an unknown Other; a contagious activity that affects the morals of our daughters, sons, and husbands, and threatens public health, morality, and the status of women (Chuang 2010; Corbin 1990; Nussbaum 1998, 709). This combination of fear, approbation, and ignorance leads to an urge among authorities to control prostitution.

In addition to the stigmatized, covert nature of prostitution, and partly as a result of it, *precise and reliable numbers are hard to come by*. Prostitution is an occupation that is characterized by, sometimes extreme, mobility, which makes it almost impossible to collect numbers about basic categories such as the daily number of sex workers in a specific geographically bounded location. Another reason for the lack of reliable statistics is the difficulty of precisely defining core policy categories, in particular nowadays central categories such as "trafficking," or "forced prostitution" (Wagenaar et al. 2017, Ch. 2 note 3 for a concrete example). The combination of the cultural ignorance about prostitution and sex workers, and the lack of numbers, creates a situation in which, even in the best of circumstances, policymakers are "sailing blind," without a solid base of evidence to guide their assessments and decisions.

But these are not the best of circumstances. Prostitution policy is an archetypical case of *morality politics* as we argued above with all its attendant problems for temperate, deliberate policymaking. Finally, *prostitution policy is hard to disentangle from immigration policy*. In this world of large population movements, and with most sex workers being immigrants, there is a close political and legal association of prostitution policy with immigration policy. This association has a predominantly restrictive character. Nations do not like poor immigrants; they certainly do not like poor immigrants who choose to work in prostitution. Despite the right to free movement of labor within the constitutional space of the EU, nation states still try to discourage and unsettle sex worker migrants from EU countries after they have habituated to the destination country. This dynamic is reinforced by the trafficking discourse. Vance (2011) rightly admonishes the observer of contemporary prostitution policy to distinguish between "law in the books" and "law in action." Where the first is clear about human rights, labor rights, and the free movement of labor within the EU, the second focuses on criminal codes to police borders, on the criminalization of prostitution even in the licensed sector, on the fight against "forced prostitution," and on labor laws that disempower immigrants.

Breaking through the contain-and-control cycle: towards collaborative governance in prostitution policy

What does all this add up to? We have observed that prostitution policy is realized at the local level. In the light of the preceding challenges, I would characterize the task that local policy officials dealing with the regulation of prostitution face, as follows: *How can local officials design and implement an effective and humane prostitution policy that is cognizant of the global and moral forces that shape prostitution in contemporary society?* In our 2017 book we argue that policymakers have to navigate what in effect is a complex policy field that defies control and that the most optimal strategy in dealing with the kind of complexity that follows from the domain-specific challenges of policymaking is to harness it. Harnessing complexity boils down to three broad strategies: increase variation, change interaction, and select and nurture solutions that work (Axelrod and Cohen 2000). Concretely I will suggest that policymakers need to organize the policy process in such a way that it provides space for the voice of the sex worker to be heard where it counts (change interactions), and create operating routines to allow sex workers' experience to influence policy design and implementation (increase variation). The technical term for this form of policy design is "collaborative governance."

What is collaborative governance? It is a mode of governance in which public agencies engage with various stakeholders to jointly deliberate about public problems (Ansell 2011, 167). It is intended to overcome the limitations of adversarial and managerialist forms of governance (Ansell and Gash 2008, 547). Collaborative governance differs from the more generic term "governance" in that it requires more stringent, more demanding standards of working together. Or, to put it differently, collaborative governance requires reflection on the *design* of the collaborative relationship. Just inviting people over and sitting around a table in a meeting room will not necessarily result in a productive exchange of ideas. Ansell and Gash (2008, 544) express this in the following, more demanding definition of collaborative governance: "A governing arrangement where one or more public agencies directly engage non-state stakeholders in a collective decision-making process that is formal, consensus-oriented, and deliberative and that aims to make or implement public policy or manage public programs or assets." This definition covers various types of collaborative arrangements, from conflict resolution platforms in which parties who are locked in intransigent conflict try to find mutually acceptable accommodations (Innes and Booher 2010) to the kind of long-standing contractual relationships that the NZPC in New Zealand or the Scarlet Alliance in Australia holds with public health agencies (Abel et al. 2011; Gall 2016). But whatever the nature of the arrangement, to designate it as collaborative, to allow it to build effective governing capacity, it needs to have the following characteristics.

First, it is essential that actors from civil society who are affected by the policy, who are stakeholders in other words, are involved in the governing arrangement. But this in itself is not sufficient. To infuse the collective problem-solving situation with genuinely new insights and knowledge, it is particularly important that peripheral, marginal, or vulnerable groups, such as sex workers, are involved. Inclusiveness is essential to secure legitimacy (this forum represents all stakeholders), diversity (a precondition for dealing with social and technical complexity) (Axelrod & Cohen, 2000 32; Innes and Booher 2010, 36), and mutual recognition as genuine participants in the policy process. Recognition is particularly important for the most peripheral and vulnerable partners, as they have felt isolated in their struggle to get heard.

Second, the collaborative arrangement needs to be *authoritative*. That is, it must be aimed at, and have the mandate for, decision-making. It must be exclusive in the sense that it cannot be a sideshow to the "real" political process of decision-making. The time and energy that participants put into the process must result in genuine influence.

Third, a condition for authority is that the collaborative arrangement has a formal and not a casual character. This implies a minimum of organization and formalization, such as agreeing on rules and procedures for meeting and decision-making, a contractual arrangement with accountability procedures for situations where services are delivered, transparency (meetings are reported), an insistence on exclusivity (no forum hopping), and the sharing of resources.

Fourth, and perhaps most important, the actors need to engage in "authentic dialogue." Authentic dialogue is a technical term that signifies a process of communication that observes the requirements of accuracy, comprehensibility, sincerity, and legitimacy (Innes and Booher 2010, 97–99). Authentic dialogue can only be achieved in situations of face-to-face dialogue. It represents the hard-to-capture communicative process that forms the beating heart of every collaborative dialogue. It is the necessary condition for mutually learning new ways to think and act together and to develop trust (Ansell and Gash 2008, 558). Finally, successful collaborative governance requires leadership. In the literature on collaborative governance, leadership is usually discussed in terms of facilitation. Facilitative leadership helps to navigate conflicting parties through the ups and downs of conflict resolution. Facilitative leaders engage in "assisted negotiation" by mediating, or when the parties are stuck in a conflict and cannot reach a consensus, draft a solution in nonbinding arbitration (ibid., 554). "Leadership is crucial for setting and maintaining clear ground rules, building trust, facilitating dialogue, and exploring mutual gains" (ibid.). In addition, facilitative leadership is essential in empowering the weaker stakeholders in the collaborative platform, both to protect the democratic rights of the weaker parties to influence decisions that affect them, as to guarantee the requisite diversity that is required to "think out of the box" and arrive at genuinely creative solutions.

On first sight, these requirements might be seen as too demanding or not realistic in a highly adversarial policy domain as prostitution policy where trust is exceedingly low. However, we have observed several real-world examples where officials and sex workers were able to work together constructively over longer periods of time and overcome the ineffectiveness and animosity of contain-and-control policies (Johnson 2015; Wagenaar et al. 2017, Ch. 6.5).

In this chapter I have demonstrated the importance of policy theory for understanding and improving prostitution policy. A grasp of policy theory allows the analyst to understand and overcome both the unending and futile ideological debates about the best policy regime to deal with prostitution as the stagnation in actual policymaking. In addition, policy theory can be a progressive force in the state's dealings with sex work. Prostitution policy is a domain in which state institutions do not always operate in a righteous way. Sex workers and third parties are often treated as second-class citizens (Wagenaar 2015). The unstated goal of many policies is to discourage prostitution by making life difficult for sex workers, particularly so for migrant sex workers and the third parties they have enlisted to settle in the country of arrival. The stigma of prostitution (and in the case of migrants the additional stigma of being a migrant) pervades every aspect of public policy, even in countries where prostitution and/or brothels are legalized (Jeffrey 2015). The neo-abolitionist mindset of authorities, pundits, and the media only reinforces this dynamic.

The Israeli philosopher Avishai Margalit makes an important distinction in this respect between a civilized and a decent society. "A civilized society" he says, "is a society whose members do not humiliate one another, while a decent society is one in which the institutions do not humiliate people" (Margalit 1998, 1). In many of the countries under study, state institutions fail this basic standard of decency towards sex workers. The focus in the prostitution literature is mostly on rights, but humiliation is an equally important but overlooked and essential value in the government's interaction with its citizens. "Humiliation is any sort of behavior or condition that constitutes a sound reason for a person to consider his or her self-respect injured" (ibid., 9). The problem with humiliation is that, although it might only pertain to a small and peripheral group, it is corrosive to the social relations and moral dignity of a society. Humiliation is contagious (ibid., 32). We either identify with the humiliated person or we do not and accept it, but in both cases we are negatively implicated. Humiliation has an adverse effect on the moral fabric of society. In many European countries (and in the United States as well) prostitution policy is affected by a corrosive mixture of deceit about statistics and claims about the extent of trafficking and coercion in prostitution on the one hand, and institutional behavior that is humiliating to sex workers on the other (Chuang 2010). This has moral implications that far exceed the relatively constricted realm of the sex trade and discussion about what constitutes better or worse public policy. It implies a statement about the kind of society we aspire to be. A sober and dispassionate analysis of the most effective and humane strategies of policymaking goes a long way in achieving decency in prostitution policy.

Note

1 In a recent blog Felicia Anna, a sex worker in Amsterdam, and her partner demonstrated how the Dutch National Rapporteur seriously inflated numbers of victims of trafficking in prostitution in her official reports. By counting instances of suspected trafficking, often reported anonymously by the public, and not distinguishing between exploitation in prostitution and other industries, the Rapporteur counted 6,250 victims in the Netherlands in 2016. Anna reports that the Dutch criminal justice system handles 250–300 cases that year. The number of 6,250 has been widely and uncritically reported in the Dutch media and cited over and over again by politicians as evidence of a catastrophic prostitution problem in the Netherlands, of the failure of the legalization of brothels and of the need to abolish prostitution from Dutch society. The fact that the source was an official report of the National Rapporteur gave the numbers authority
(http://behindtheredlightdistrict.blogspot.com.au/2017/10/overestimating-trafficking-victims-to.html. Accessed, February 15, 2018).

References

Abel, G., Fitzgerald, L., Healy, C., and Taylor, A. (eds.). 2010. *Taking the Crime Out of Sex Work: New Zealand's Sex Workers' Fight for Decriminalisation*. Bristol: Policy Press.
Agustín, L. 2008. Sex and the Limits of Enlightenment: The Irrationality of Legal Regimes to Control Prostitution. *Sexuality Research and Social Policy*, 5: 73–86.
Anderson, J.E. 1984. *Public Policy-Making: An Introduction*. Boston, MA: Houghton Mifflin.
Ansell, C.K. 2011. *Pragmatist Democracy: Evolutionary Learning as Public Philosophy*. Oxford: Oxford University Press.
Ansell, C.K. and Gash, A. 2008. Collaborative Governance in Theory and Practice. *Journal of Public Administration Theory and Practice*, 18: 543–571.
Axelrod, R. and Cohen, M.D. 2000. *Harnessing Complexity: Organizational Implications of a Scientific Frontier*. New York: Basic Books.
Bernstein, E. 2007. *Temporarily Yours: Intimacy, Authenticity and the Commerce of Sex*. Chicago, IL: University of Chicago Press.
Chuang, J.A. 2010. Rescuing Trafficking from Ideological Capture: Prostitution Reform and Anti-Trafficking Law and Policy. *University of Pennsylvania Law Review*, 158: 1655–1728
Corbin, A. 1990. *Women for Hire: Prostitution and Sexuality in France After 1850*. Cambridge, MA: Harvard University Press.

Dodillet, S. and Östergren P. 2013. The Swedish Sex Purchase Act: Claimed Success and Documented Effects, in H. Wagenaar, S. Altink, and H. Amesberger. *Final Report of the International Comparative Study of Prostitution Policy in the Netherlands, Austria and the Netherlands*, 107–130. The Hague: Platform 31.

Doezema, J. 2010. *Sex Slaves and Discourse Masters: The Construction of Trafficking*. London: Zed Books.

Edelman, M. 1985. *The Symbolic Uses of Politics*. Urbana IL: University of Illinois Press.

Edlund, L. and Korn, E. 2002. A Theory of Prostitution. *Journal of Political Economy*, 110: 181–214.

Engeli, I., Green-Pedersen, C., and Larsen, L.T. (eds.) 2012. *Morality Politics In Western Europe: Parties, Agendas and Policy Choices*. Basingstoke, UK: Palgrave Macmillan.

Fairclough, N. 2003. *Analysing Discourse: Textual Analysis for Social Research*. Abingdon, UK: Routledge.

Gall, Gregor. 2016. *Sex Worker Unionization: Global Developments, Challenges and Possibilities*. Basingstoke, UK: Palgrave Macmillan.

Gibson, M. 1986. *Prostitution and the State in Italy, 1860–1915*. New Brunswick, NJ: Rutgers University Press.

Glynos, J. and Howarth, D. 2007. *Logics of Critical Explanation in Social and Political Theory*. Abingdon, UK: Routledge.

Halley, J., Kotiswaran, P., Shamir, H., and Thoms, C. 2006. From the International to the Local in Feminist Legal Responses to Rape, Prostitution/Sex Work, and Sex Trafficking: Four Studies in Contemporary Governance Feminism. *Harvard Journal of Law and Gender*, 29: 335–429.

Holmström, C. and Skilbrei, M.L. 2017. The Swedish Sex Purchase Act: Where Does it Stand. *Oslo Law Review*, 4(2): 82–104.

Hooghe, L. and Marks, M. 2003. Unraveling the Central State, But How? Types of Multi- Level Governance. *American Political Science Review*, 97: 233–243.

Howlett, M. 2011. *Designing Public Policies: Principles and Instruments*. Abingdon, UK: Routledge.

Howlett, M. and Ramesh, M. 2003. *Studying Public Policy: Policy Cycles and Policy Subsystems* (2nd ed.). Oxford: Oxford University Press.

Innes, J.I. and Booher, D.E. 2010. *Planning with Complexity: An Introduction to Collaborative Rationality for Public Policy*, Abingdon, UK: Routledge.

Jahnsen, S.Ø. and Wagenaar, H. (eds.) 2017. *Assessing Prostitution Policies in Europe*. Abingdon, UK: Routledge.

Jeffrey, L.A. 2015. *Cave! Hic Dragones: Negotiating the Contradictory Pressures of Sex Work Policy Making: Lessons for Canadian Policymakers*. Paper for the Second international Conference on Public Policy. Milan, Italy, July 1–3.

John, P. 2012. *Analyzing Public Policy*. Abingdon, UK: Routledge.

Johnson, G.F. 2015. Governing Sex Work: An Agonistic Policy Community and its Relational Dynamics. *Critical Policy Studies*, 9: 259–277.

Kingdon, J.W. 2011. *Agendas, Alternatives, and Public Policies* (2nd ed.). Boston, MA: Longman.

Lane, J.E. 1987 Implementation, Accountability and Trust. *European Journal of Political Research*, 15: 527–546.

Margalit, Avishai. 1998. *The Decent Society*. Cambridge, MA: Harvard University Press.

Maynard-Moody, M. and Musheno, M. 2003. *Cops, Teachers, Counsellors: Stories from the Front-Line of Public Services*. Ann Arbor, MI: University of Michigan Press.

Mooney, C.S. 1999. The Politics of Morality Policy: Symposium Editor's Introduction. *Policy Studies Journal*, 27: 675–680.

Nussbaum, M.C. 1998. "Whether From Reason or Prejudice": Taking Money For Bodily Services. *Journal of Legal Studies*, 27: 693–724.

Outshoorn, J.V. 2004. Voluntary and Forced Prostitution: The "Realistic Approach" of the Netherlands, in J. Outshoorn (ed.) *The Politics of Prostitution: Women's Movements, Democratic States and the Globalisation of Sex Commerce*, 185–204. Cambridge: Cambridge University Press.

Radin, M.J. 1996. *Contested Commodities: The Trouble with Trade in Sex, Children, Body Parts, and Other Things*. Cambridge, MA: Harvard University Press.

Rittel, H.W. and Webber, M. 1973. Dilemmas in a General Theory of Planning. *Policy Sciences*, 4: 155–169.

Scoular, J. 2010. What's Law Got to Do With It? How and Why Law Matters in the Regulation of Sex Work. *Journal of Law and Society*, 37: 12–39.

Skilbrei, M.L. and Holmström, C. 2013. *Prostitution Policy in the Nordic Region: Ambiguous Sympathies*. Farnham, UK: Ashgate.

Stedman Jones, Gareth. 2014. *Outcast London: A Study in the Relationships Between Classes in Victorian Society*. London: Verso.

Stone, D. 1997. *Policy Paradox: The Art of Political Decision-Making*. New York: W.W. Norton & Company.

Thompson, E.P. 2013. *The Making of the English Working Class*. London: Penguin.

Vance, C.S. 2011. States of Contradiction: Twelve Ways to Do Nothing about Trafficking While Pretending to. *Social Research: An International Quarterly*, 78: 933–948.

Vinzant, J.C. and Crothers, L. 1998. *Street-Level Leadership: Discretion and Legitimacy in Front-Line Public Service*. Washington, DC: Georgetown University Press

Vries, P. de 1997. *Kuisheid voor mannen, vrijheid voor vrouwen: de reglementering en bestrijding van prostitutie in Nederland 1850–1911* (Doctoral thesis). Hilversum, the Netherlands: Uitgeverij Verloren.

Wagenaar, H. 2015. Governance-Driven Conflict: Policy, Reason of State and Authoritarian Governmentality, in E. Gualini, J. Mourato, and M. Allegra (eds.) *Conflict in the City: Contested Urban Spaces and Local Democracy*, 112–132. Berlin: Jovis Verlag.

Wagenaar, H. and Altink, S. 2012. Prostitution as Morality Politics or Why It Is Exceedingly Difficult to Design and Sustain Effective Prostitution Policy. *Sexuality Research and Social Policy*, 9: 279–297.

Wagenaar, H., Altink, S., and Amesberger, H. 2013. *Final Report of the International Comparative Study of Prostitution Policy: Austria and the Netherlands*. The Hague: Platform 31.

Wagenaar, H., Amesberger, H., and Altink, S. 2017. *Designing Prostitution Policy: Intention and Reality in the Sex Trade*. Bristol, UK: Policy Press.

Walkowitz, J.R. 1982. *Prostitution and Victorian Society: Women, Class and the State*. Cambridge: Cambridge University Press.

Weitzer, R. 2015. Human Trafficking and Contemporary Slavery. *Annual Review of Sociology*, 41: 223–242.

12

Red-light districts in three Belgian cities

Ronald Weitzer

Introduction

It has long been assumed that red-light districts generate a host of social problems, including crime, antisocial behavior, public health risks, and neighborhood deterioration. It is also taken for granted that sexual commerce in such zones clashes with the surrounding community's moral values. Yet studies find that some such businesses have few or no negative environmental effects and that nearby residents do not necessarily disapprove of them (e.g., Künkel 2012; Linz 2004; Paul et al. 2001). It appears that social disorder, physical decay, and other problems are not necessarily inherent in places where erotic businesses operate and that much depends on the ways in which participants organize their activities and how external stakeholders engage with these individuals and businesses.

The chapter examines red-light districts in three Belgian cities, with a focus on internal arrangements and actors (i.e., physical conditions, social organization, behavior patterns) and external forces (police, city government, nearby residents) that have, or seek to have, an impact on the physical and social conditions in the red-light district. I assess the extent to which each district fits the conventional image of being dilapidated, socially disorganized, and crimino-genic. We will see that one of them fits this traditional model fairly well; one contrasts with it sharply; and the other falls between the two extremes. The differences are largely explained by two related factors: the amount and nature of local government engagement in the red-light district and the socio-economic status and political influence of the population residing within or adjacent to each district.

Indoor red-light districts

Indoor red-light districts are geographically distinct zones with a cluster of visible erotic busi-nesses, which may include brothels, strip clubs, porn shops, erotic bars, peep shows, and massage parlors. Studies have examined different aspects of such districts: their physical layout and social organization; how they are managed by actors inside the zone and by the authorities; sex work-ers' work styles and experiences; local residents' perceptions and engagement with the district; the zone's impact on conditions in the surrounding community, such as disorder and crime;

and the ways in which red-light district can become politicized (e.g., Aalbers and Deinema 2012; Cooper 2018; Ellison and Weitzer 2017; Hubbard et al. 2013; Kelly 2008; Künkel 2012; Remick 2014; Weitzer 2012).

Some red-light districts are multi-use: erotic businesses are mixed in with residences or other businesses and may cater to tourists as well as locals. Red-light zones in Amsterdam and Bangkok are good examples of this type of multi-use. Others are single-use, largely confined to sexual commerce. Such homogeneous zones are usually remote from the city's central core and cater mostly to local clients. The red-light districts analyzed in this chapter are largely single-use and consist of window prostitution where the sellers remain indoors yet are visible from outside through their windows or glass doors.

Study sites and research methods

This chapter replicates, updates, and synthesizes my previous studies of the three sites, and does so comparatively (Weitzer 2014; Weitzer and Boels 2015). Field observations were conducted in each red-light district during the day and night at various times of the year in Antwerp and Brussels (2008–2017) and Ghent (2014–2017). Fieldnotes consisted of diagrams and descriptions of physical arrangements and observations of individual behavior and social interaction.[1] In addition, in-depth interviews were conducted with some health workers, police, social workers, and city government officials. These two main data sources were supplemented with other available material.[2]

Commonalities across red-light districts

The legal order

A 1948 law outlawed all third-party participation in prostitution, leaving independent operators free to sell sexual services. Some local governments responded by actively eliminating brothels and other types of third-party involvement, while others tolerated or imposed certain regulations on the actors. The latter approach is known as *de facto legalization* (i.e., illegal but officially regulated). As in the Netherlands prior to *de jure* legalization in 2000, the *de facto* approach is a way of managing third-party involvement when technically prohibited by national law (Brants 1998). With the national government in Belgium taking a hands-off approach, local prostitution policy became "dependent on the whims of municipal authorities," yet these policies are somewhat precarious insofar as they depart from what is legally stipulated at the national level (David and Loopmans 2018, 86). City authorities certainly recognize that the regulations they impose may violate the law against third-party involvement, but nevertheless manage their red-light district in ingenious ways.

Ghent's authorities circumvent national law by applying to window prostitution the regulations that govern the hotel and restaurant industry (*horeca*). The buildings where prostitution takes place are officially designated as bars or cafés (with drinks available) and the women working in these premises are classified as waitresses and their managers as barkeepers. Few customers purchase a drink, however, and instead proceed directly to sexual activity.

In Brussels, municipal regulations outlaw beds in window-prostitution rooms, because a bed would suggest that sex was taking place; proprietors provide couches instead to give the appearance of a lounge (Seinpost 2008, 33).[3] Showers are lacking for the same reason. Like Ghent, window rooms have been rebranded as bars where drinks can be purchased. Each unit has a price list for drinks on the window and a small bar inside. The norms are violated in some buildings (where there is a bed or floor mattress) and these violations are generally ignored by officials (Seinpost 2008, 33). Interestingly, the non-sexual branding in Brussels and Ghent is belied by the signage on some of the window buildings, with names like Venus, Babylon, Salon de Cupido, and La Seduction.

None of these euphemisms are evident in Antwerp. Window workers simply rent rooms from building owners; drinks are not available; and there is no pretense that these places are anything but sexually oriented. The lack of overt management by third parties, in contrast to Brussels and Ghent, allows window workers in Antwerp to assume the role of lawful independent operators. Building owners who rent rooms are not considered illicit managers under a 1995 national law as long as they do not make an "abnormal profit" from doing so (David and Loopmans 2018).

Location

Each city has a single window-prostitution district that has existed in its current location for many decades. Within each red-light district proper, there are either few or no other businesses or amenities, unlike the multi-purpose and tourist-oriented districts in Amsterdam and Bangkok. Each is remote from the city center and unknown to most tourists. Brussels' district is parallel to the north train station and a few nearby streets in a district that is largely populated by working-class immigrants. Antwerp and Ghent's are about a 20-minute walk from the city center in enclaves surrounded by commercial properties and residents who are largely white and middle class.

Interactional styles

Window workers sit or stand in their rooms and are quite visible to visitors. Waiting for customers for hours, they break the monotony by "performing" in some way. When men walk by the women knock on their windows, dance, assume suggestive poses, smile, throw kisses, and call out to the men. When they tire of such promotional rituals, they read magazines, chat on the phone, stare into space, apply makeup, and take breaks out of sight (cf. Aalbers 2005).

Most visitors to the red-light districts are male voyeurs rather than prospective customers. Some are loud, obnoxious, or drunk, and some engage in micro-aggression, such as blocking a door, spitting on a window, or yelling obscenities. I have overheard men asking for sex without a condom, haggling over price, time, or services, and arguing with sex workers. By contrast, other men engage in pleasant or jovial chats with the women, wave or blow kisses at them, and interact with them in other endearing ways. I have heard men compliment a particular woman, saying "you're so beautiful" or "hello gorgeous" or "you're too hot for me!" But most of the visitors simply walk through the area silently looking at the sights (cf. Aalbers 2005). The client stigma makes most men wary of drawing attention to themselves, even in a red-light district (Aalbers 2005).

For men interested in sex, the window district may be preferred over other venues because one can view and converse with multiple sellers before making a decision. Apart from those men who seek out a certain provider because they have visited her before, many prospective customers traverse the entire red-light district several times before selecting someone because, as one man exclaimed on a discussion board, "the joy of walking around picking your favorite is immense fun," and another stated that "walking around and seeing who's still smiling or available [after several rounds] is key to an excellent punter experience." For at least some customers, extensive cruising is necessary before they can decide which sex worker appeals to them most.

Figure 12.1 Brussels' red-light district.

Figure 12.2 Antwerp's red-light district.

Figure 12.3 Ghent's red-light district.

Key differences across the three districts

Despite the above similarities in basic structure and interactional patterns, the three districts vary significantly in many other ways. One difference is the cost of renting a window room: for one day or night shift, the prices are €70–100 in Antwerp, €120 in Ghent, and €200 in Brussels.[4] Assuming €40–50 per transaction, it takes takes more clients to break even during a shift in Brussels than in Antwerp or Ghent.[5] Because of differences in capacity, noted below, the number of annual transactions and aggregate income differs considerably across the three districts.[6]

Brussels red-light district is split geographically and ethnically. The core is Aarschot Street, with 58 window buildings, each containing 1–4 sex workers, mostly Bulgarian and Romanian migrants. The periphery on some nearby streets is staffed by workers of African descent. A few bars and cafés dot Aarschot Street, but window prostitution predominates. The neighborhood surrounding this district is largely composed of working-class and poor Moroccan and Turkish residents with high unemployment and low medium income.[7]

Antwerp's red-light district is located in the historic harbor area, frequented by sailors in the distant past. Today it contains a tattoo parlor, nightclub, restaurant, and pornography shop, but no other businesses apart from its 300 window units. The district is nestled within a fully gentrified neighborhood hosting trendy restaurants, bars, and residences occupied largely by middle-class whites.

The first window-prostitution building appeared in Ghent in 1948 in an area then filled with bars and cabarets. The area thus has a long history as an entertainment district. Today, the red-light district consists of three main streets and a glass-covered arcade, the Glazen Straatje, with a total of 101 window units. Like Brussels and Antwerp, Ghent's district is mostly single-use, revolving around window prostitution, although some residents live inside the zone itself. Just outside the RLD there are many shops, bars, restaurants, and apartments. This red-light district is therefore largely single-use internally but surrounded by a mixed-use and increasingly gentrified neighborhood.

Physical disorder

Brussels' red-light district and the neighborhood surrounding it have long been in decay. Several window-prostitution buildings are in disrepair, a few are boarded up, and graffiti taints most of them. Litter is abundant and includes beer cans and broken bottles; the street has only a few garbage bins, thus encouraging littering. Brussels' physical disorder score is the inverse of Antwerp's, which is entirely free of litter and grafitti and its buildings and walkways are clean and tidy.

Physical conditions in Ghent have improved recently. My observations in 2014 noted that some buildings and walkways were in poor condition, but municipal regulations passed in March 2015 have had the effect of substantially enhancing the red-light district's physical appearance (Stad Gent 2015). Graffiti is entirely absent, and some buildings were freshly painted by the time of my visit in 2017. Likewise, conditions inside the buildings have improved since 2015. Building owners are now required to install internal alarm buttons, a security camera outside the door, and greater amenities for hygiene or comfort: showers, smoke detectors, lockers, first-aid supplies, safe-sex posters (Stad Gent 2015).[8] These innovations were inspired by Antwerp's regulations, which Ghent's authorities had studied.

Social disorder

Aarshot Street in Brussels has a single congested traffic lane with abundant car noise, honking, and exhaust fumes. Some cars stop in the road so the occupants can gaze at a particular woman, blocking all vehicles behind them. The constant presence of cars thus produces one type of social disorder. In addition, there are individuals who post comments on client-based online forums mention seeing drunks, drug users, beggars, and gang members, and describe the entire red-light district as "seedy," "shabby," "rough," and "intimidating." These descriptions are largely consistent with my field observations. I witnessed verbal altercations between male visitors and sex workers and occasionally among the men themselves. Many are drinking alcohol or quite drunk as they wander through the district. During my visit in 2017, I saw a few homeless individuals encamped on Aarschot Street and several Roma women panhandling with young children in tow, neither of which was observed on previous visits and indicating that social order has deteriorated to an even greater extent recently. Such actors are entirely absent from Antwerp and Ghent's red-light districts.

Social disorder in Antwerp is rare in comparison with Brussels. Antwerp's red-light district is the only car-free pedestrian zone, which contributes to its tranquil atmosphere. In online discussion boards, posters describe this district as "modern and clean"; "very laid back and well policed"; "no gangs hanging around or any noticeable pimps"; and "a gem, fantastic place, clean, safe." These descriptions are consistent with my observations. While the overall tranquility of the zone is sometimes disrupted by disorderly individuals and the occasional fight, most visitors are quiet and well behaved.

Social disorder in Ghent is manifested in vehicle traffic that slowly cruises the area, creating noise, exhaust fumes, and encroaching on pedestrians who walk on the streets (because the sidewalks are extremely narrow). Disorderly behavior is rare during the day according to my observations, officials' accounts, and postings on online discussion forums. It is more common at night, and especially weekend nights. I occasionally saw men who were drunk and obnoxious, arguing with a window woman, pushing at an open door, or spitting on a window. Police are called approximately once a week by a sex worker or a manager to deal with a problem visitor.[9]

Until recently, Ghent's red-light district lacked security cameras, but that changed in 2015 when cameras were installed per new municipal regulations (Stad Gent 2015). Security cameras are also visible in Antwerp but absent in Brussels, where they are most needed. As in Antwerp, Ghent's rooms are now equipped with internal alarm buttons. Comparing the three cases on the social-disorder variable, Ghent would score moderate, Antwerp low, and Brussels high.

State involvement

The involvement of the local state is much more extensive in Antwerp and Ghent than in Brussels. The authorities in Brussels have implemented virtually none of the regulations and little of the oversight that exist in Antwerp and Ghent, and its approach can best be described as laissez-faire.

In the early 2000s, Antwerp launched a major initiative against organized crime in prostitution—investigating sources of income, tax payments, and possible trafficking. Several individuals were convicted in court. Today, organized crime has been greatly reduced according to my sources and another study (Loopmans and van den Broeck 2011). Owners of Antwerp's window-prostitution buildings are required to apply for a permit; there is a specific building code for these buildings (for sanitation, comfort, exterior conditions); compliance is monitored by city officials; and premises may not be rented to minors and undocumented immigrants, neither of which operate in the district today.[10] Partly because of mandatory building renovation since 2000, "the working conditions for prostitutes thereby improved drastically" (Willems 2009, 5). City officials meet with all window owners twice a year, informing them of any new policies and discussing other issues.

As noted above, window workers in Ghent are officially registered as "waitresses," managers are designated as "barkeepers," and their workplaces are governed by *horeca* (hotel, restaurant) regulations. Prostitution windows are licenced and all *horeca* regulations, including hygiene, are applicable to them. Barkeeper-managers are required to enter into a written contract with each newly hired waitress and register her with the national social security office and the municipal police within 48 hours of her employment. The registration process records passport information, the woman's real and work names, her residence address, and the window unit she occupies. Access to this information is restricted to a designated police unit. Subsequently, social workers visit each new waitress *in situ* to confirm that she is indeed the person who was registered by the manager. Violation of this regulation results in a €1,000 fine, and the authorities almost never encounter a woman without a valid contract.[11] Under the contract system, waitresses are technically employees of the café, not independent operators as in Antwerp, yet they are paid not by managers but instead directly by clients and this income is entirely theirs.

The net effect of these regulations is that Ghent's authorities exert more control over both workers and managers than their counterparts in Antwerp or Brussels. Yet by applying the same regulations and nomenclature to window prostitution as to bars and cafés, the authorities have found a way to circumvent the national prohibition on third-party involvement in prostitution. As one official described it, "It is officially not prostitution. They are servers in a bar, a café. They are cafés that have women behind a window to attract customers and drink with the customers."[12] Despite such subterfuge, there are two advantages to Ghent's system: being registered as waitresses shields the women from the stigma of having to register as sex workers and registration entitles them to social security and health benefits.

Differences in state involvement in the three red-light districts are also reflected in policing. In Brussels, the municipal police play a minor role, mainly responding to problems after the fact, and minimally regulating third parties or protecting the participants (Seinpost 2008; Sivri 2008).

Federal police, however, conduct occasional site visits to the window rooms in order to inquire about the workers' circumstances and potential coercion. Not only do the police visit window workers infrequently, they are also rarely present on the street. Indeed, I have never seen a uniformed police officer during any of my observations in these red-light districts. It is thus not surprising that window workers complain about a "lack of police surveillance in the street, especially on weekends" (Seinpost 2008, 32).

By contrast, a mini police station sits in the heart of Antwerp's red-light district and police routinely patrol the area in uniform and undercover. I have seen officers stop and question certain men, and they periodically seal off the district to check all visitors' identity documents and search for weapons or drugs; these operations yield fairly low hit rates according to official sources, but play a proactive role in deterring potential offenders.[13] In addition, police officers routinely visit window workers to confirm that they are adults and are either citizens or possess documents allowing them to work in Belgium.

Official monitoring is even more extensive in Ghent. Officials from the city's Meprosch unit routinely visit the red-light district and speak to window workers. Formed in 1993, Meprosch is staffed by social workers and police officers and is responsible for cases involving prostitution, trafficking, and fake marriages. On two occasions I accompanied Meprosch social workers on their window visit rounds. They question every newly arrived waitress about her motives for engaging in prostitution, whether she sold sex in her home country (if she is not from Belgium), her private life (e.g., residence, intimate partner, children), and whether she has any problems or complaints. The Meprosch team also provides information about rights and duties, safe sex and support services, and ways to avoid victimization. When I accompanied the team on site visits, they interacted with sex workers in a consistently supportive and friendly manner.

There is no police station in Ghent's red-light zone, but uniformed officers occasionally drive through the area in cars and undercover officers monitor the area on foot. The Meprosch team of police officers and social workers has primary responsibility for the district. According to a manager I interviewed, managers and building owners have a "generally positive" relationship with the police who work in the district.[14]

Unique to Ghent, in 2012 the authorities imposed a code of conduct in the red-light district. The code mandates that sex workers wear clothing that is not revealing—banning lingerie, bikinis, or transparent clothes—and avoid behaving aggressively by knocking on the window, dancing, calling out to persons on the street, or assuming a provocative pose. A police official told me that "they cannot do anything to attract clients. The only thing they can do is sit and wait."[15] Violators are subject to a €120 fine. When asked about the logic of the conduct code, another official stated that allowing women to dress scantily would be tantamount to a "free movie" for onlookers: "We say, if a client wants to see the body, he has to pay for it."[16] And a member of the team of city government officials responsible for prostitution policy elaborated:

> If we don't have the rules, maybe they will sit there naked! And it will create more nuisance, because more people will go there just to have a look and this [influx] may even increase the amount of aggression toward the ladies. So, the rule is a kind of protection for them.

Another member of that team argued that, since the area is so close to residents and not in a restricted area, the conduct and attire rules make sense: "This is a living place, not an isolated red-light district."[17]

Providing direct health services is another type of intervention. In Brussels, the sex worker rights organization Espace P provides free and anonymous health care, drug and other counseling, legal advice, and self-defense training. Antwerp installed a health clinic, Ghapro, in the heart of its red-light district in 2002. Ghapro's mission is to promote "safer sex work and empowered sex workers," and it offers free, anonymous psychological counseling, tests and treatment for sexually transmitted infections, and assistance for those who wish to leave the trade.[18] Ghapro sees a large number of sex workers every year: 4,133 medical and social service consultations were provided to sex workers throughout the entire province of Antwerp in 2016, which includes 474 consultations with window workers in the city (Ghapro 2016, 26, 34). A recent innovation is that all of the windows now have green stickers that announce "Only Safe Sex."

Since 1990, Ghent's red-light district has hosted a health center, Pasop, funded by the government but independently operated. Pasop offers advice regarding health, safe sex practices, health insurance, temporary housing, and psycho-social counseling, and staff members conduct regular outreach visits to women working in the district and elsewhere in the vicinity of Ghent. In 2016, for example, the center had a total of 2,441 consultations with 449 sex workers, some of whom were repeat visitors.[19] In these consultations, staff members inquire about the worker's consent in doing this work, their social relationships outside work, and whether they are required to give their earnings to someone else, but these issues are raised only after establishing some degree of rapport. Pasop staff make it clear to everyone that they are strictly independent of the police and other authorities, and the center has a good reputation among the sex workers.[20]

An official in the Meprosch unit praised Ghent's system:

> I prefer our system because we really have good control over who is working here, and she has rights. If you only rent a room [e.g., Antwerp, Brussels], you don't have any rights. If a girl in Antwerp rents a room and a customer beats her, it is her problem. In Ghent, if a customer beats her, it is a problem for the barkeeper because she is working for him . . . And women know there is a lot of control here by the police, and we know a lot of them. So it is safer for the girls who work in Ghent than in Antwerp or Brussels.[21]

Antwerp's officials, however, regard *their* system as a model, and they have actively *promoted* their system outside Antwerp. Indeed, a Belgian association awarded Antwerp a prize in 2006 for the innovative renovation of its red-light district, which began in the late 1990s.[22] Today, the general lack of physical and social disorder helps to explain why Antwerp's red-light zone is uncontroversial. The authorities actively monitor visitors, workers, building owners, and physical conditions in the zone; working conditions have improved significantly over the past 15 years; clients consider it clean and safe; and local residents rarely complain about it (Loopmans and van den Broeck 2011; Willems 2009).

Managers

Window workers are not formally managed in Antwerp. Their work agreement is negotiated with a building owner who initially screens their eligibility (e.g., age, legal work status) and instructs them on general operational norms, but does not manage them on a daily basis. In Brussels and Ghent, however, managers are involved in two very different kinds of relationships with their respective workers.

Window prostitution in Brussels is largely controlled by networks of procurers, pimps, and madams who enter into agreements with the women, keep half of the earnings, and exercise tight control over them at work (Petrunov 2010; Sivri 2008). Unique to this red-light district is the presence of a madam in each window building. Most madams are Bulgarian and part of a network connected to pimps who reside in Bulgaria (Petrunov 2010; Seinpost 2008). They serve a number of functions: renting the room from a building owner and placing sex workers in specific rooms; taking the customer's payment; informing the sex worker when her time with a customer is finished; intervening on the worker's behalf in the event of an altercation; and supervising and otherwise controlling the workers. In these roles madams are fully managing the sex workers and thus clearly violating the national law against third-party involvement in prostitution.

In Ghent, barkeeper-managers rent space from the building owner, and sex workers enter into written contracts with managers to occupy the space for a specific period of time. Police conduct a criminal-background check on new managers, who are then licenced by the city. Unlike the madams working in Brussels, managers in Ghent are rarely present in their window buildings. They visit them periodically to arrange work schedules, pick up rent money, and stock the bar with drinks. Managers instruct the workers on rules regarding hygiene or other practices, but they do not routinely monitor or supervise them.

Sex workers

In all three cities the majority of window workers are of Eastern European background: Romanian and Bulgarian in Antwerp and Brussels and Hungarian in Ghent. They live outside the red-light districts in apartments or hotels.

Little is known about the ways sex workers themselves view the window districts in which they work. A survey conducted in 2013 of 121 window workers in Ghent provides unique data relevant to this question (Politie Gent 2013).[23] When asked how frequently they are bothered by nuisances in the district, only a minority of survey respondents were often bothered by litter (33%), voyeurs staring at them (28%), noise (22%), drug use (22%), and public urination (21%). Only one-eighth said they were often bothered by vandalism, theft, or violence. Those responsible for most of the nuisances were identified as drunks, drug users and dealers, and young Middle-Eastern men who visit from French border towns. One-sixth said they often or always avoid certain places in the red-light district because they do not feel safe there, whereas 60% said they seldom or never do this. For those who feel unsafe, it is largely because of people who loiter in the area.

A major problem involves the recent arrival of Hungarian migrants.[24] The number of Hungarian sex workers in the red-light district skyrocketed from 4 in 2009 to 283 in 2013, while the number of established Belgian and French workers dropped by half during this time period. As the survey was being administered, interviewers heard "a lot of complaints about other prostitutes, mainly those of Hungarian descent" (Politie Gent 2013, 21). The Hungarians are accused of charging below the standard €50 rate and offering condom-less sex—which other workers consider unfair competition. According to my interviewees, some Hungarians indeed engage in these practices, and there is also a severe communication problem, given that so few other participants speak Hungarian. It is not unusual for sex workers of different ethnic or nationality backgrounds, working in the same vicinity, to harbor prejudices toward, compete with, and shun each other. Such antagonism has become quite acute in Ghent over the past few years.

Another serious problem is the fairly recent arrival of visiting French youths of Algerian and Tunisian descent, beginning approximately four years ago. Ghent is a 40-minute drive from the French border, thus quite accessible for a brief excursion. Many of these youths are intoxicated when they enter the red-light district, and sex workers generally avoid them because of bad experiences in the past. The authorities periodically launch "actions" that consist of stopping and searching all cars with French licence plates entering the city from a certain highway. Police officers search for drugs, pepper spray, knives, and guns, and find these items during each stop-and-search action. My observation of one such operation concluded that about one-third of the cars stopped had some contraband or weapon. A €250 fine is imposed on the spot for each illicit item discovered, and the culprits are then escorted out of Ghent by a police car. Inability to pay the fine results in a night in jail.

While the sex workers generally support police search operations, they dislike the code of conduct governing their behavior, mentioned above. The survey found "much displeasure" about the clothing and behavior rules (Politie Gent 2013, 22). The women find it ridiculous to be required to sit quietly and cover up in a context where public display is intrinsic to this type of prostitution. Yet another kind of complaint comes from workers who obey the rules and believe that those who violate them get more customers because they are more animated or appear sexier. Despite being subject to a €120 fine, many window women disregard the rules according to both my observations and postings in online discussion forums.[25] I observed women in scanty attire, knocking on their windows, calling out to men, dancing, assuming provocative poses, and sometimes baring their breasts. Indeed, the majority of window women were sometimes observed violating at least one of the conduct norms.

Antwerp and Brussels have no such code of conduct, eliminating one source of grievance among the workers. They are free to dress and act as they please as long as they remain inside their window rooms. We lack survey or interview data, comparable to Ghent's, on the women working in Antwerp and Brussels, but their views of working conditions, visitors, and social order are likely closely linked to objective conditions in their respective red-light districts. Job satisfaction, in the aggregate, should therefore be considerably higher in Antwerp than Brussels.

Residents

It should not be assumed that residents who live near a red-light district are necessarily opposed to it for moral reasons or associate it with nuisances (Cooper 2018; Hubbard et al. 2013; Künkel 2012). In Antwerp, for example, the effect of strict controls in its red-light zone is that local residents' "complaints related to prostitution have stopped almost completely," according to a government report (Willems 2009, 5).

In Brussels, the surrounding community is culturally a parallel universe to the red-light district's moral economy. In the past, the local Moroccan and Turkish residents and merchants have complained about nuisances spilling over from the red-light district, building owners whose properties are deteriorating, and the very existence of an erotic zone near conservative Muslim families (Seinpost 2008). Their complaints about these issues have rarely been addressed by the authorities (Seinpost 2008) because of the latter's basic laissez-faire approach to this red-light district coupled with the marginalized socio-political status of the residents. Indeed, relations between the predominantly Muslim residents of this district (Schaerbeek) and the local state were described in one study as "hostile" until recently, and Schaerbeek's communal government had the distinction of being "the Brussels borough with the most explicit Islamophobic tendencies" (Manço and Kanmaz 2005, 1120). After the mid-1990s, local Muslim representatives gained somewhat greater incorporation into Schaerbeek's policymaking circle (Manço and Kanmaz 2005), but this has not translated into clout regarding the status of the red-light district (Seinpost 2008).

In Ghent, a segment of the surrounding population has been quite vocal in recent years, complaining that disorder from the red-light district is spilling over into their gentrifying neighborhood and degrading their quality of life. Litter, car traffic, public urination, and unruly visitors are the main complaints (Maesschalck 2014). A residents' association, formed in 2012, now meets with city officials every few months to discuss problems and ideas for reform. The residents and local merchants are not unified, however: some advocate changes that would reduce nuisances and disorder, while others want the district closed and relocated to another area of town (Maesschalck 2014). In response to the residents' association, a window-owners' association, Glastra, was formed in 2017. Its mission is to advocate for the rights of the owners and to communicate their positions to residents, local merchants, the media, and the authorities. The group contests some community residents' negative depiction of the district: a Glastra member who owns two window buildings told me that "their claims are all exaggerated; I come here every day, and the red-light district is the *safest* location, because there are always some people around."[26] At the same time, Glastra has taken "a positive approach to the regulations imposed by Ghent's government" since 2015, even though these measures (hygiene, amenities, security) have cost owners significant money.[27] Almost all of the owners have accepted and implemented the new regulations.

At the meetings, the authorities and some residents have, perhaps surprisingly, advocated on behalf of the sex workers. As one official told me,

> We [city government] want quality of life in this place, and also quality of life for the girls. We say this at every meeting: we are not working only for neighborhood residents, but also for the girls' quality of life.[28]

The official defined "quality of life" for sex workers as safety, good working conditions, and the rights enshrined in their contracts with managers.

Conclusion

One of my main research questions is the extent to which the cities' red-light districts fit the conventional image of such zones as dilapidated, anomic, and criminogenic. I have shown that the three sites differ substantially in physical appearance and social organization. Antwerp's has been thoroughly modernized; disorder and decay are prominent in Brussels; and Ghent is intermediate between the other two cases. Physical disorder is fairly low in Ghent, but social disorder fluctuates between low to moderate depending on the day and time. Ghent's red-light district is in more flux than the other two: the recent ascendancy of Hungarian sex workers in the red-light district; the influx of disorderly youths on weekend nights; mobilization of a residents' association, reflecting the growing gentrification of the surrounding area; and the efforts of state officials to remedy problems and assert greater social control.

Brussels is unique in that madams operate as "assistant pimps" who front for bosses who reside in Eastern Europe. They dictate working conditions, take half the earnings, and exercise tight control over the window workers. In this role, madams clearly violate the law against third-party control of sex workers. They are allowed to operate largely unfettered because of the local state's laissez-faire approach to this red-light district. In Antwerp, by contrast, exploitation is limited due to the combined effect of independent entrepreneurship (with no madams or other managers overtly involved) and comprehensive government oversight—both of which facilitate some measure of sex worker control over their working conditions. City officials monitor owners and building conditions and police conduct foot patrols, staff an on-site mini police station, and routinely visit window workers to assess their situation and build trust with them. Ghent has recently made signficant progress in implementing reforms similar to Antwerp's.

The stark differences between the three red-light districts is explained by the confluence of radically different governance orientations of each local state and the nature of the local population. The two factors are related. The role of the local government is partly a function of residents' capacity to influence the authorities, which in turn depends on residents' class status and ethnic background, as confirmed in related studies (Aalbers and Deinema 2012; Hubbard 1998; Kingston 2014; Larsen 1992; Mathieu 2011; Weitzer 2012). Brussels' district is located in one of the city's most disadvantaged districts with a population that is mostly Moroccan and Turkish. The low socio-economic status and ethnic complexion of the community translates into a lack of influence over the authorities and results in a state of affairs best described as inertia. The neighborhoods surrounding Ghent and Antwerp's red-light zones, by contrast, have been gentrified and consist of trendy businesses and housing occupied by largely white, middle-class residents. In the late 1990s and early 2000s, Antwerp's residents successfully lobbied city officials to address a host of problems associated with this zone, which resulted in "a totally segregated, highly regulated, and fashionably renovated sex work district" (Loopmans and van den Broeck 2011, 558). Residents living near Ghent's red-light district are currently pressing for reforms as well and they have met with some success to date, as reflected in new regulations in March 2015.

A strong sex workers' rights association can also help to shape policies regarding erotic zones. But this kind of advocacy is the exception to the rule in our three cities, with only one such group playing any role: Payoke in Antwerp. After its creation in 1988, Payoke "rapidly gained political strength and leverage, and was integrated into local policy networks" (Loopmans and van den Broeck 2011, 554). One of Payoke's two founders was elected to the city council and played a direct role in the reconstruction of the red-light district in the early 2000s. The counterpart organization in Brussels (Espace P) has a long and respected history but has been much less politically involved. Ghent lacks a sex workers' association entirely. Strong sex workers' rights organizations in Brussels and Ghent could have some success in advocating for the rights of sex workers and for improved working conditions in their window-prostitution districts.

My comparison of the three red-light zones points to some important conclusions. First, national legal norms have little effect on local prostitution policies in Belgium. Third-party facilitation of prostitution is outlawed throughout the country, yet Brussels and Ghent allow management by madams and barkeepers. Moreover, all three cities exercise at least some official governance of window prostitution. This is known as *de facto* legalization—a regulatory model that departs from what is permitted by national law. My study documents the ways in which local authorities circumvent national law: rebranding window-prostitution units as bars or cafés, banning beds or showers, or officially designating sex workers as waitresses. Such subterfuge is not needed in places where prostitution is *de jure* legal, such as Australia, Germany, and the Netherlands.

Second, it is worth repeating that red-light districts can vary tremendously in their impact on social and physical order. The cases of Ghent and especially Antwerp demonstrate that it is not inevitable that such zones will generate substantial amounts of crime, antisocial behavior, public health hazards, physical decay, or neighborhood social disorganization. Such problems are uncommon or nonexistent in Antwerp and have diminished in Ghent in the past few years. These findings are consistent with some studies in other cities (e.g., Hubbard et al. 2013; Künkel 2012; Linz 2004; Paul et al. 2001).

Third, by comparing red-light districts we can identify a set of best practices that can be used to inform public policy in places where existing arrangements are problematic or counterproductive. Policymakers in the Schaerbeek municipality in Brussels could follow Antwerp's and Ghent's lead and radically reform the commune's red-light district, with the twin goals of empowering the workers and intensifying the amount of social control in the area. These goals would be furthered by:

- routinely removing graffiti and collecting trash;
- requiring building owners to improve the external condition of their buildings, many of which are in disrepair;
- adopting minimum mandatory standards for amenities and hygiene in the window rooms;
- capping day and night shifts at 8 instead of 12 hours;
- increasing the number of site visits by government officials, in order to monitor working conditions and confirm workers' voluntary involvement;
- requiring sex workers to rent rooms directly from building owners and banning madams entirely from window units;
- installing security cameras throughout the district;
- conducting uniformed police foot patrols to deter anti-social behavior; and
- increasing the amount of police surveillance, via both security cameras and undercover officers on the ground.

That Ghent has adopted many of Antwerp's progressive policies in the past three years shows that cross-fertilization is indeed possible for Brussels as well, if the local state is prepared to devote the necessary resources to transform its red-light district into one that is less dilapidated and disorderly and genuinely committed to eliminating third-party exploitation of the sex workers who work there.

My comparative analysis shows that external forces play a major role in shaping health, safety, and working conditions in the red-light zones. As documented throughout the chapter, the interventions of local government, police, and residents have had quite different impacts on each red-light zone and the participants therein. At the same time, the participants themselves—sex workers, managers, clients, and other visitors—have a measure of agency in how they navigate the rules, deal with problems, and interact with each other. In other words, the social organization of each red-light district reflects the amount and kind of involvement by outside forces as well as the practices of those who occupy these spaces and respond to external demands. Regarding the latter, I have shown that sex workers in Brussels have much more autonomy from the local state than in Antwerp and Ghent, yet because of the state's laissez-faire approach in Brussels, they are much more vulnerable to control and exploitation by indigenous actors (i.e., madams) than their counterparts in Antwerp and Ghent. Therefore, whereas sex workers in all three window-prostitution districts are fairly comprehensively controlled, they are monitored by quite different actors, and the sex workers clearly have more rights and protections in the two cities where the local state is heavily involved than the city (Brussels) where control is largely exercised by non-state actors. The study thus documents serious flaws where window prostitution is left unregulated by the authorities and the need for the kind of state involvement that enforces a set of norms designed to enhance worker health and safety—ideally in collaboration with the sex workers themselves. This benign regulatory approach is applicable to other types of prostitution as well (Dölemeyer et al. 2010; Wagenaar et al. 2017; Weitzer 2012).

Notes

1 I documented signs of *physical disorder* (litter, garbage, condoms, alcohol containers, graffiti, and buildings that are vacant or in disrepair) and *social disorder* (persons loitering, consuming alcohol or drugs, being visibly intoxicated, arguing/fighting, harassing others, begging, auto congestion, and the lack of a visible police presence).

2 This included a few other academic studies; a review of five years of postings regarding the red-light districts from two client-centered online discussion boards; a 2013 survey of 121 window workers,

sponsored by the city of Ghent; and my observation of social workers' visits to window workers and a police stop-and-search operation in Ghent.

3 In online postings, customers complain that the couches are not well suited for sexual encounters.

4 The lower cost in Antwerp is due to an agreement in 2002 between building owners and city officials, where they agreed to the €70–100 daily shift price for renting window units. The agreement was based on the 1995 law, mentioned above, that prohibited building owners from deriving "an abnormal profit" in renting window rooms.

5 The base price for 15–20 minutes of sexual contact is €50 in Antwerp and Ghent and €40 in Brussels, but some customers pay extra for more time or services. For Antwerp and Ghent the estimated average income per session was €66.59 in 2015 (Adriaenssens and Hendrickx 2017).

6 A systematic study estimated the number of annual transactions as follows: 915,370 in Antwerp, 619,249 in Brussels, and 361,814 in Ghent (Adriaenssens and Hendrickx 2010).

7 In 2015, medium income in this district (Schaerbeek) was €17,629 ($21,500). Male and female unemployment was 23.9% and 25.5%, respectively. http://statistics.brussels/figures/key-figures-per-municipality/schaerbeek#.WloqJqinGUk.

8 I observed all of these improvements when a building owner gave me a tour of his window rooms in July 2017.

9 Interview with three city government officials, May 14, 2014.

10 Interview with prostitution official, May 16, 2011.

11 Interview with police officials, May 23, 2014.

12 Interview with police officials, May 12, 2014.

13 Interview with two Antwerp prostitution officials, May 28, 2014.

14 Interview with barkeeper-manager, July 12, 2017.

15 Interview with three Meprosch officials, May 12, 2014.

16 Interview with three Meprosch officials, May 12, 2014.

17 Interview with city government officials, May 14, 2014.

18 The Antwerp Health House, www.ghapro.be.

19 Interview with Pasop staff member, July 11, 2017.

20 Interview with Pasop staff member, May 29, 2014.

21 Interview with three Meprosch officials, May 12, 2014.

22 See the website for a documentary, *Skippers Quarter*, which presents it as "Antwerp's Prize-Winning Approach to Urban Renewal in its Red-Light District." The film was commissioned by the Flemish Association for Space and Planning.

23 Dominique Boels and I collaborated in analyzing this survey.

24 Virtually no Hungarians work in Brussels or Antwerp's red-light districts.

25 For example, one posted: "Girls were sitting or standing in their doorways, being pretty pushy about trying to entice me in and [one] literally grabbed my arm and tried to pull me into her room. There was a distinct whiff of desperation in the air."

26 Interview with Glastra member, July 12, 2017.

27 Interview with Glastra member, July 12, 2017.

28 Interview with city government official, May 14, 2014.

References

Aalbers, Manuel. 2005. Big sister is watching you: Gender interaction and the unwritten rules of the Amsterdam red-light district. *Journal of Sex Research* 42: 54–62.

Aalbers, Manuel, and Michael Deinema. 2012. Placing prostitution: The spatial-sexual order of Amsterdam and its growth coalition. *City* 16: 129–145.

Adriaenssens, Stef, and Jef Hendrickx. 2010. Sex, prices, and preferences: Unsafe sexual practices in prostitution markets of the Low Countries. HUB Research Paper 2010/5. University College, Brussels.

Adriaenssens, Stef, and Jef Hendrickx. 2017. Calculating value added of prostitution with multiple data: A new approach for Belgium. *Public Finance Review* doi: 10.1177/1091142117734173.

Brants, Crisje. 1998. The fine art of regulated tolerance: Prostitution in Amsterdam. *Journal of Law and Society* 25: 621–635.

David, Marion, and Maarten Loopmans. 2018. Belgium. In S. Jahnsen and H. Wagenaar (Eds.), *Assessing prostitution policies in Europe*, 77–91. New York: Routledge.

Cooper, Emily. 2018. "It's better than daytime television": Questioning the socio-spatial impacts of massage parlors on residential communities. *Sexualities* doi: 10.1177/1363460715616949.

Dölemeyer, Anne, Rebecca Pates, and Daniel Schmidt. 2010. Deviant girls, small-scale entrepreneurs, and the regulation of German sex workers. In M. Ditmore, A. Levy, and A. Willman (Eds.), *Sex work matters*, 184–202. New York: Zed.

Ellison, Graham, and Ronald Weitzer. 2017. Young men doing business: Male bar prostitution in Berlin and Prague. *Sexualities* doi: 10.1177/1363460717708139.

Ghapro. 2016. *Jaarverslag 2016*. Antwerp: Ghapro.

Hubbard. Phil. 1998. Community action and the displacement of street prostitution: Evidence from British cities. *Geoforum* 29: 269–286.

Hubbard. Phil, Spike Boydell, Penny Crofts, Jason Prior, and Glen Searle. 2013. Noxious neighbours? Interrogating the impacts of sex premises in residential areas. *Environment and Planning A* 45: 126–141.

Kelly, Patty. 2008. *Lydia's open door: Inside Mexico's most modern brothel*. Berkeley, CA: University of California Press.

Kingston, Sarah. 2014. *Prostitution in the community*. New York: Routledge.

Künkel, Jenny. 2012. These dolls are an attraction: Othering and normalising sex work in a neoliberal city. In J. Künkel and M. Mayer (Eds.), *Neoliberal urbanism and its contestations*, 198–207. New York: Palgrave Macmillan.

Larsen, E. Nick. 1992. The politics of prostitution control: Interest group politics in four Canadian cities. *International Journal of Urban and Regional Research* 16: 169–189.

Linz, Daniel. 2004. An examination of the assumption that adult businesses are associated with crime in surrounding areas. *Law and Society Review* 38: 69–104.

Loopmans, Maarten, and Pieter van den Broeck. 2011. Global pressures, local measures: The re-regulation of sex work in the Antwerp Schipperskwartier. *Tijdschrift voor Economische en Sociale Geografie* 102: 548–561.

Maesschalck, Sarah. 2014. *Overlast in de prostitutiebuurt Gent zuid: Een beleids-en buurtperspectief*. Master's thesis, Criminological Sciences, University of Ghent.

Manço, Ural, and Meryem Kanmaz. 2005. From conflict to cooperation between Muslims and local authorities in a Brussels borough: Schaerbeek. *Journal of Ethnic and Migration Studies* 31: 1105–1123.

Mathieu, Lilian. 2011. Neighbours' anxieties against prostitutes' fears: Ambivalence and repression in the policing of street prostitution in France. *Emotion, Space, and Society* 4: 113–120.

Paul, Bryant, Daniel Linz, and Bradley Shafer. 2001. Government regulation of adult businesses through zoning and anti-nudity ordinances: Debunking the legal myth of negative secondary effects. *Communications in Law and Policy* 6: 355–392.

Petrunov, Georgi. 2010. *Sex trafficking and money laundering: The case of Bulgaria*. Sofia: Risk Monitor Foundation.

Politie Gent. 2013. *Research results on the problem of nuisances in Ghent's prostitution neighbourhood*. Ghent: Police Office.

Remick, Elizabeth. 2014. *Regulating prostitution in China*. Palo Alto, CA: Stanford University Press.

Seinpost. 2008. *Prostitution: Bruxelles en image*. Arnhem, Netherlands: Seinpost Adviesbureau.

Sivri, Salih. 2008. *Prostitution in Brussels: Export of Bulgarian prostitutes from Bulgaria*. Masters thesis, Katholieke Universiteit, Leuven, Belgium.

Stad Gent. 2015. *Politieverordening betreffende de raamprostitutie en het bekomen van een geschiktheidsverklaring bij uitbating van raamprostitutie panden*. Approved by Ghent City Council, March 23, 2015.

Wagenaar, Hendrik, Helga Amesberger, and Sietske Altink. 2017. *Designing prostitution policy*. Bristol, UK: Policy Press.

Weitzer, Ronald. 2012. *Legalising prostitution: From illicit vice to lawful business*. New York: New York University Press.

Weitzer, Ronald. 2014. The social ecology of red-light districts: A comparison of Antwerp and Brussels. *Urban Affairs Review* 50: 702–730.

Weitzer, Ronald, and Dominique Boels. 2015. Ghent's red-light district in comparative perspective. *Sexuality Research and Social Policy* 12: 248–260.

Willems, Hans. 2009. *Schipperskwartier: A seductive quarter in Antwerp*. Antwerp: Social Welfare Office.

13

Sex worker rights activism and the decriminalisation of sex work in New Zealand

Lynzi Armstrong

Introduction

Sex work laws are subject to ongoing debate globally with different countries taking divergent legislative approaches to regulating sex work. New Zealand is a unique example as the only country to have decriminalised sex work nationwide. Despite being a policy for which sex worker rights organisations around the world have campaigned for decades, which is endorsed by several international organisations such as Amnesty International and the World Health Organisation (WHO), decriminalisation remains exceptional in the context of global sex work regulation (Amnesty International 2016; Day & Ward 2004; Wojcicki 1999). Instead, the criminalisation of clients, commonly referred to as the 'Nordic Model', has been adopted in several countries such as Sweden, Norway, Iceland, Northern Ireland and France (Huschke & Ward 2017). This policy approach is based on the premise that sex work is intrinsically harmful, and proponents of this perspective conceptualise the sex industry as emblematic of gender inequality (Svanström 2017).

Countries where sex work is legal, such as Germany and the Netherlands, require invasive and often complex regulations such as mandatory registration and, in some cases, compulsory sexual health checks (Outshoorn 2012; Wagenaar, Amesberger & Altink 2017). Full criminalisation of the sale and purchase of sex has been adopted in some countries, such as most parts of the United States, in an attempt to eradicate the sex industry through a criminal justice response. In the UK, there is a system of partial criminalisation in place (Phoenix 2009). In this context, while being paid for sex is not in itself a crime, the range of offences associated with sex work make it extremely difficult for sex workers to work within the law, unless they work in isolation without the assistance of others. Considering the complexity of the range of legislative frameworks, Östergren (2017) argues for a more nuanced typology of prostitution policies. She suggests that instead of conceptualising policy approaches as 'legalised', 'decriminalised' or 'criminalised', it is more useful to conceptualise these policies in a way that truly captures what they represent. Thus, she posits that the different policy approaches can be better understood as either 'integrative', 'restrictive' or 'repressive'. New Zealand's framework, Östergren (2017) outlines, can be best understood as integrative since sex work is viewed as encompassing positive and negative elements. Thus, the approach to mitigating the negative elements is to integrate sex work into existing social and legal structures, instead of singling it out as a special case. This sets New Zealand apart from countries in which sex work is viewed as entirely negative and criminal law is used in attempt to eradicate it, what Östergren (2017) defines as a 'repressive' regime. Countries in which sex work is legalised differ, she states, in that they conceptualise sex work in negative terms but rather than attempting to repress sexual commerce through the use of criminal law, they attempt to restrict it through strict regulation of the conditions under which sex work can operate. Thus, sex work is singled out as something exceptional – it is controlled in a different way than other commercial industries, which is characteristic of a 'restrictive' approach (Östergren 2017, pp. 2–3). New Zealand is therefore a unique case in pursuing this integrative approach.

Despite the significant differences between these integrative, restrictive and repressive approaches, one consistent element in each of these contexts is that sex workers have organised and continue to organise regardless of the veracity of attempts to eradicate sex work. What differs is how sex worker-led organising has been responded to by government officials. The nature of each framework arguably reflects the status that sex workers are afforded, and repressive and restrictive regimes create barriers to the role that sex workers can play in influencing policy. Sex workers are simply not listened to when repressive and restrictive regimes are in place – if they were, the framework in place would be a version of the integrative, decriminalised model in place in New Zealand, which sex workers globally have long been calling for. However, the decriminalisation of sex work in New Zealand was a hard-won achievement that involved years of of work by New Zealand's sex worker-led organisation, the New Zealand Prostitutes' Collective (NZPC) and their allies. Why has the process and outcome of sex worker-led organising in New Zealand been so different, and what lessons does this offer for policymakers in other countries? In this chapter, I explore the process of decriminalising sex work, which enabled a shift from a restrictive to an integrative model in New Zealand, and the role that sex worker organising played in this process. The overall aim of this chapter is to showcase how the process and outcome of sex work policy change in New Zealand offers a best-practice model for other countries to follow in pursuit of evidence-based law and policy on sex work – and specifically to outline the role that sex worker rights activism played in the process of law change. This chapter begins with a brief outline of the history of sex worker organising in New Zealand, before exploring the campaign for decriminalisation and the very unique role that sex workers played in this collaborative process. The Prostitution Reform Act (PRA) that underpins New Zealand's integrative approach is then discussed in relation to how it supports sex worker rights and organising to challenge exploitation. The way in which sex work organising operates in an integrative framework is then explored before discussing potential reasons why sex worker-led campaigning in New Zealand has been successful, in a global context that is still dominated by repressive and restrictive policy approaches.

The New Zealand context

New Zealand is a small geographically isolated country, located in the South Pacific, with a total population of 4.7 million. The laws relating to sex work in New Zealand were historically based on those in place in Britain. Prior to the decriminalisation of sex work in 2003, working as a sex worker was technically not illegal but related offences made it very difficult to sell sexual services without breaking the law. Sex worker-led organising emerged from concerns among sex workers regarding the impacts of this approach to regulating sex work. Thus, the circumstances that surrounded sex worker activism are similar to other countries in which sex workers have raised concerns regarding the impacts of laws on their work. However, as this chapter will demonstrate, the process of organising and the subsequent outcome makes New Zealand a unique example. One factor that arguably makes New Zealand different is its small population size, which is more conducive to lobbying for change. Another is that New Zealand is home to one national sex worker-led organisation – the NZPC – which was instrumental in the process of law change. While sex worker-led organisations exist around the world, the presence of one national, sustainably funded organisation instead of several smaller organisations arguably meant that it was easier for sex worker voices to be heard by government officials. However, to better understand how sex worker-led activism influenced changes to sex work laws, and the unique process that has taken place in New Zealand, it is important to first outline in more detail how sex worker-led activism developed in this context.

Sex worker organising in New Zealand

Sex worker organising in New Zealand began in 1987 when a small group of sex workers met to discuss forming an organisation. The group, which established the NZPC, quickly expanded to include indoor and outdoor sex workers, and focused on the problems of existing law, stigma, and the issue of sexual health (Healy, Bennachie & Reed 2010). The laws in place at the time prohibited most activities that were related to sex work. The police played an active role in the repression and restriction of sex work through 'sting' operations in which they would pose as clients and proposition sex workers before arresting them for soliciting. Police also maintained a register of sex workers' names (Healy et al. 2010). The significant impact of this legislative regime was a key motivation for sex workers coming together to organise.

While responding to the harms caused by criminalisation is a common rationale for sex worker activism globally, New Zealand is a unique example of sex worker-led organising in terms of how this activism has been responded to by government officials, and the impact that it has had. In 1988, a year after a small group of sex workers had initially met to discuss forming an organisation, the NZPC secured a contract with the Department of Health to deliver HIV prevention services and has retained government funding to support the organisation ever since. Funding a sex worker-led organisation to deliver sexual health services to sex workers may appear a common-sense approach but is, unfortunately, very unique in a global context in which sex worker-led organisations are visible and vocal but are more often than not unheard and under-resourced. The NZPC was recognised by government officials as offering valuable expertise that could not be provided by people without sex work experience. Thus, owing to the NZPCs unique story, Radačić (2017, p. 1) argues that organisation can be considered illustrative of a 'successful policy actor'.

The NZPC rapidly expanded after its initial establishment, growing from one community base in Wellington to several community bases around the country. The NZPC has performed multiple roles – including offering confidential sexual health services to sex workers, support to sex workers who have had negative experiences, educational resources and a space that fosters camaraderie between sex workers in which they can organise and strategise. While the NZPC was contracted by the Department of Health to provide HIV prevention services and this was a key focus of their work, they also remained true to the rationale for establishing the organisation – to address the issue of negative laws that impacted sex workers in a multitude of ways. Thus, concurrent to providing community-based services and outreach, a focus of NZPCs work from inception was to work towards changing the laws in place to create a framework that recognised sex workers' rights (Healy et al. 2010).

The campaign for decriminalisation

Although the NZPC was established in 1987, it was not until 2003 that the PRA was passed, which decriminalised sex work. The campaign for decriminalisation was therefore a long process that the NZPC, along with allies, strategically worked towards for over 15 years. The NZPC essentially provided a national voice for sex workers, a space through which sex workers could raise awareness of the issues presented by the law – not only within the sex industry but also more broadly in the media and across a range of organisations (Barnett, Healy, Bennachie & Reed 2010).

The NZPC played a number of roles in the campaign for decriminalisation. First and foremost, they were the organisation that provided the impetus for change. While a range of people from diverse organisations supported the decriminalisation of sex work, and a Labour MP, Tim Barnett, sponsored the Bill – it is fair to say that decriminalisation would not have been achieved without the NZPC. Sex workers were, undoubtedly, the driving force behind the law change and the NZPC was involved at all stages – including the initial process of researching legislative options and drafting the initial Bill (Barnett et al. 2010.

Arguably one of the most important roles played by sex workers in the campaign for decriminalisation was the process of lobbying. The NZPC built relationships with a diverse range of individuals and organisations who became part of the movement calling for decriminalisation. Organisations such as the New Zealand AIDS Foundation, the Young Women's Christian Association, the New Zealand Council of Women, in addition to several churches and some Catholic nuns also came out in support of decriminalisation (Barnett et al. 2010). This relationship building meant that sex workers' voices were not isolated voices in the call for decriminalisation – they were surrounded by a diverse range of allies, which strengthened the campaign. In the law reform process, personal testimony was also a key contribution made by sex workers that led to the eventual passing of the law. As part of the process that resulted in decriminalisation, sex workers provided submissions and spoke directly to decision makers about their experiences, and personal approaches by sex workers to politicians who had initially opposed decriminalisation were said to be effective (Barnett et al. 2010). This meant that politicians, who may have little understanding of the sex industry, could connect with people who were involved in it and have an appreciation of the direct impacts of harmful laws in sex workers lives. Indeed, one politician who was in parliament at that time, Georgina Beyer, was a former sex worker, who spoke about her own experiences of being arrested. Beyer also gave an impassioned speech in Parliament on the night of the vote, sharing her experience of being raped at knife point while working on the street, and feeling unable to report the experience to the police at the time, which silenced the public gallery (Crampton 2003). Hearing a colleague describe their lived experience of violence under a criminalised framework arguably enabled other politicians involved in the debate to better understand the impacts of the law and the potential benefits of decriminalisation. New Zealand is a small country and a possible implication of this is that closer and more personal connections can be made between government officials. Thus, while in larger countries the personal testimony made by Beyer may have had a lesser impact, the small population in New Zealand arguably meant that others could better understand the issues at stake on a more personal level.

Thus, the tactics used by the sex workers in campaign for change in New Zealand were focused on garnering support for change by connecting with a diverse range of people rather than agitating for change via protests and marches. While deeply entrenched stigma meant building a large public movement was not possible, politically shrewd and strategic lobbying meant that sex workers were surrounded by diverse and influential individuals and organisations in the campaign for change (Barnett et al. 2010).

The collaborative nature of this campaign for legal change really sets New Zealand apart in a global context in which sex workers' voices on law reform remain marginalised. Sex worker activism exists throughout the world, but New Zealand remains the only country where sex workers have been joined by such a diverse range of other actors in calling for decriminalisation. The experience in New Zealand therefore emphasises the importance of other voices joining sex workers and developing a strong and diverse movement led by, but not solely comprised of sex workers. For this to occur, however, it is essential that there is a willingness to listen among organisations outside of sex work, and a respect for sex workers as the experts on their own lives.

The Prostitution Reform Act

The Prostitution Reform Act (PRA) passed on 25 June 2003 by one vote, decriminalising sex work. Thus, although the law change was contentious, the sex worker-led campaign for change was clearly effective since the law successfully passed. However, to fully understand the extent to which the campaign was successful it is important to consider the extent to which the law that was passed reflects what sex workers had requested.

The motivation for change among sex workers was a desire to realise sex worker rights and address the harms of criminalisation (Armstrong 2018). In an ideal world, law reform would be possible for sex workers simply on the basis that they deserve access to the same rights as other citizens. However, sex work is a controversial issue for some people, which necessitated framing the law in such a way that it would appeal to a diverse range of people. As such, Abel (2017) notes that while initially the law was framed as being in the interests of fairness and freedom – couched in the language of human rights – in the latter stages the discourse shifted to focus on harm minimisation. The need to minimise harm in sex work was considered to represent a more marketable message in the context of arguments against decriminalisation, which were largely based on moral discourses and beliefs that sex work is intrinsically harmful. Such arguments could be more easily countered with the language of harm minimisation than by drawing on human rights-based reasoning (Abel 2017).

The wording of the PRA reflects this focus on harm minimisation, though still retains a strong focus on human rights. As stated in Section three of the PRA:

> The purpose of this Act is to decriminalise prostitution (while not endorsing or morally sanctioning prostitution or its use) and to create a framework that –
>
> (a) safeguards the human rights of sex workers and protects them from exploitation;
> (b) promotes the welfare and occupational health and safety of sex workers;
> (c) is conducive to public health;
> (d) prohibits the use in prostitution of persons under 18 years of age;
> (e) implements certain other related reforms.
>
> *(Parliamentary Council Office 2003)*

A shift to the language of harm reduction therefore did not move the focus away from sex workers' rights and addressing the harms of criminalisation – it simply framed it in a way that could appeal to a wider range of people who may not initially recognise the importance of sex workers' rights. A critical point is the way in which the law was implemented – the means through which harm minimisation is pursued and *how* sex workers' human rights are safeguarded through the PRA. The mode of implementation is critical, as well-intentioned laws can still have negative consequences. For example, in Germany the 2017 Prostitutes Protection

Act (ProstSchG) was ostensibly introduced to better protect sex workers from harm. However, the way this was pursued was through the introduction of increasingly complex regulation that sex workers argued would in fact create more risks rather than greater protection from harm (Herter, Fem & Lehmann 2017) Similarly, while anti-trafficking policies globally are positioned as offering greater protection against exploitation in sex work, it has been noted that these policies are often opposed by sex workers because they increase risks and harm, often through aggressive policing (GAATW 2006). Thus, simply introducing laws that aim to protect sex workers is not enough – it must be pursued in a way that can actually achieve this. What other countries can learn from the experience in New Zealand is the importance of sex workers themselves shaping the content of these laws and how they are implemented – since they are better placed to advised on what would help than policymakers with no experience of sex work.

The PRA had two significant impacts for sex workers in terms of strengthening their rights and safeguarding their occupational health and safety – it removed previous laws that criminalised their work and it afforded specific rights to sex workers to challenge exploitation. In contrast to contexts in which sex work is legalised, such as Germany and the Netherlands, sex workers in New Zealand are not subject to multiple sex work specific regulations. Sex workers are protected by labour laws and have access to social services in the same way as other citizens. It is for this reason that Östergren (2017) argues the New Zealand framework can be considered an integrative framework, and this is precisely what sets the New Zealand model apart from frameworks in place in other jurisdictions.

Sex workers in New Zealand were not seeking a perfect society when they began organising and calling for change – what they wanted was a context in which they would not be criminalised, where they had rights to undertake their work like individuals in other commercial businesses, and where they could more easily report adverse experiences to police and access justice if they experience exploitation and/or violence. Reflecting this aim, the PRA afforded sex workers with rights to challenge exploitation in their work. For example, it is an offence to induce or compel a person to provide or continue to provide commercial sexual services, and a sex worker may refuse at any point for any reason to provide commercial sexual services (Armstrong 2010). Research conducted after the passing of the PRA indicates that the law has been successful in strengthening sex workers' rights and their ability to report adverse experiences. In a study carried out to evaluate the impact of the PRA, 95% of respondents reported feeling as though they had rights under the Act, while approximately 60% of sex workers reported feeling more able to refuse to see certain clients following the law change (Abel, Fitzgerald & Brunton 2007). The law change has also improved relationships between police and sex workers, particularly street-based sex workers, who were most likely to be criminalised prior to the law change (Armstrong 2017).

Decriminalisation has resulted in a shift in power that works in sex workers' favour and is well illustrated by a 2014 case in which an indoor sex worker, with the support of the NZPC, complained to the Human Rights Commission regarding sexual harassment by the owner of a brothel where she had been working. She won the case and was awarded $25,000 NZD in compensation (Duff 2014). This case sent a clear message that sex workers in New Zealand are entitled to the same rights in the workplace as other citizens. This example clearly illustrates what is possible for sex workers in a context in which sex work is decriminalised and offers a vision for other countries in which policymakers truly aspire to protect sex workers from exploitation and harm.

The PRA has therefore been successful in creating a context in which sex workers have access to rights to challenge exploitation and no longer live with the risk of arrest, regardless of whether they work indoors or on the street. However, New Zealand's framework is not perfect, and a limitation is that temporary migrants are prohibited from engaging in sex work. As such they do not have access to the same rights and protections as other sex workers in New Zealand (Roguski 2013). Thus, while sex workers were successful in achieving a change in law that means they are in in a better position than they were when sex work was criminalised, this is not the end of the story. It is therefore important to consider the extent to which an integrative framework strengthens and supports sex worker-led organising to enable further change.

Sex worker organising in a decriminalised context

Given that New Zealand is the only full country in which sex work is decriminalised, it also provides a particularly interesting context to explore sex worker organising, and the extent to which an integrative framework may help to strengthen and support sex workers organising. Indeed, while a fundamental goal of the NZPC's founders was to change harmful laws, the achievement of decriminalisation does not mean that sex worker activism is now less important.

Under decriminalisation, the NZPC continues to play a significant role in defending sex workers' rights. The decriminalisation of sex work has arguably strengthened their power to defend sex workers' rights in two fundamental ways. First, the provision of rights to sex workers has extended the options that the NZPC have available to them to support sex workers who are treated poorly by those they work for, or by their clients. The rights afforded by the PRA have empowered sex workers both collectively and individually. In research with the NZPC, Radačić (2017) found that representatives of the organisation see the law as a very important tool for the advancement of sex workers' rights, which they can use in their work supporting sex workers. Their role has arguably shifted from one where they were primarily focused on challenging harmful laws and assisting sex workers struggling with such laws, to one where they are focused on supporting sex workers to use *helpful* laws to exercise their rights to challenge those who seek to harm and exploit them.

Second, the change in law has arguably strengthened the NZPCs relationships with other organisations that have an interest in the safety and well-being of sex workers. The NZPC have strong relationships with individuals within organisations such as the New Zealand Police, and have fostered sex worker rights 'champions' – individuals they have worked with in the past – who they can trust to model good practice within their own organisation (Armstrong 2018). While productive relationships between police and sex workers may be possible when sex workers are criminalised, it is reasonable to conclude that this is more difficult and fraught with tension when when police are tasked with controlling and disciplining sex workers. The change in law has therefore meant more productive relationships between sex workers and police, which is more conducive to collective organising and individual safety and well-being.

NZPC is unique case in that the organisation had secured government funding prior to decriminalisation to provide sexual health services to sex workers, which meant that the organisation already had status that many sex worker-led organisations in other countries are not afforded. Thus, prior to decriminalisation the NZPC was already recognised as a valid and important organisation that had something valuable to offer. The decriminalisation of sex work arguably strengthened this even further and has extended the NZPC's role in that they are now considered an authority on sex work issues at a local and global level. While they continue to support sex workers in the New Zealand context, representatives of the organisation also play a significant role in the global movement for sex workers' rights by sharing their experiences and expertise with sex worker-led organisations and governments of other countries and contributing to media commentary (Radačić 2017).

Although sex work is now decriminalised, several examples demonstrate that the NZPC continue to negotiate challenges in the New Zealand context. An ongoing challenge is stigma and discrimination, which continues to manifest in the context of decriminalisation, and as noted earlier in this chapter, particularly the discriminatory policy that prohibits temporary migrants from engaging in sex work or investing in or operating a sex work business. Drawing attention to the impacts of this aspect of the law on the vulnerability of migrant sex workers and strengthening the rights of all sex workers is therefore important to the organisation going forward (Armstrong 2018; Barnett et al. 2010; Roguski 2013). As such, the NZPC has recently recommended the establishment of an Inter-Departmental Committee to consider the impacts of the current law on migrant sex work with a view to changing this policy, and a formal firewall between immigration officials and people who have a responsibility to protect sex workers (such as police), to ensure that migrant sex workers who are harmed can report crimes without fear of repercussions (Armstrong 2018).

The current situation in New Zealand emphasises the importance of affording protection to *all* sex workers, since prohibiting migrant sex work within the decriminalised framework has had no positive impacts – it has created a population of sex workers who are more vulnerable to exploitation. Migrants will engage in sex work regardless of their immigration status and any country that truly aspires and prioritises the safety of sex workers must guarantee protection for migrants who report violence, and specifically protection from state violence of deportation. Creating a context in which all sex workers can contact authorities when they need help is the only way to protect migrant workers in a meaningful way and ensure they can collectively organise against exploitation in sex work.

The NZPC have also continued to manage intermittent (though ultimately unsuccessful) attempts by territorial authorities to pass bylaws to restrict sex work, specifically street-based sex work, which continues to be subject to tensions in some areas, due to complaints largely regarding noise and litter (Law 2017). In the context of ongoing challenges, the decriminalisation of sex work arguably strengthens the NZPC's position to push back against attempts to repress and restrict sex work but there is also arguably an enduring tension. While the realisation of rights for sex workers is a significant achievement, the vital importance of these rights means that it would be devastating if they were taken away. While sex worker organising in a decriminalised context is arguably better supported, having rights also means that there is also a lot to potentially lose if the boat is rocked too much. While the power of sex workers to influence policy and practice in a decriminalised context is unquestionably stronger than it is under repressive and restrictive regimes, the exceptional nature of the New Zealand framework arguably means that sex workers' rights remain vulnerable. Until the decriminalisation of sex work is adopted by more countries, integrative frameworks like New Zealand's become the norm and there is a better understanding of sex work throughout society, the rights of sex workers will continue to be tenuous even in a decriminalised context and challenging policies will continue to carry degree of risk.

Why is New Zealand different?

The unique situation in New Zealand with regards to the status of the NZPC and the relationship between sex worker organising and the legal framework in place begs the question of why and how this has been achieved. And why similar change has not occurred in other countries, despite there being a large and active sex worker rights movement throughout the world calling for the decriminalisation of sex work. The answer may lie in how sex work is conceptualised, and how sex workers and sex worker-led organisations are perceived as a result.

For example, in Sweden sex work is conceptualised as a form of violence against women with sex workers defined as passive victims who need the state to make decisions on their behalf. As a consequence, sex worker-led organisations such as the Rose Alliance are not listened to by government officials, and a flow-on effect of this is that realising sex workers' rights through full decriminalisation becomes very unlikely.

In Europe and North America, concerns regarding trafficking combined with moral discourses that construct sex work as a social ill dominate popular perceptions. This means that sex workers are not positioned as equal citizens and those who do speak out are also frequently dismissed by anti-sex work campaigners who endorse an abolitionist perspective as 'unrepresentative' and therefore not worth listening to (Phipps 2016). The outcome in both of these contexts is that no matter how strong sex worker-led organisations are, and regardless of how loudly they campaign for rights, they are not heard. A crucial difference in New Zealand is then simply, perhaps, that there was a willingness to listen to sex workers among people in positions of power and influence. Thus, while New Zealand is different it is not necessarily exceptional – decriminalisation could easily be achieved in other countries if there is political will to listen to sex workers and recognise the value of their expertise.

Conclusion

The decriminalisation of sex work in New Zealand was a unique change in a global context in which sex work law is subject to significant debate and sex work remains at least partially criminalised in most parts of the world. The law in place in New Zealand is not the only unique factor, however, what also differentiates New Zealand to other countries is the influence that sex worker organising has had on sex work policy and law, and the process of law change. The success of the law in New Zealand in strengthening sex workers' rights and better protecting them from harms is a consequence of the direct role that sex workers played in drafting the law. Achieving a similar outcome in other countries necessitates that those in positions of power listen to sex workers, value their expertise and provide funding so that sex worker-led organisations are sustainable. The lessons from New Zealand show how powerful sex worker-led organising can be when sex workers are listened to, sustainably resourced to work with their own communities and surrounded by solid and respectful allies. If policymakers in other countries are truly committed to prioritising the safety and well-being of sex workers, then they must learn from the collaborative process that has taken place in New Zealand and move towards an integrative framework that affords rights to all sex workers.

References

Abel, G. 2017. In search of a free and fair society: The regulation of sex work in New Zealand. In Ellis Ward and Gillian Wylie, eds., *Feminism, Prostitution and the State*, 140–154. Abingdon, UK: Routledge.

Abel, G., L. Fitzgerald, and C. Brunton. 2007. *The Impact of the Prostitution Reform Act on the Health and Safety Practices of Sex Workers*. Christchurch, NZ: Department of Public Health and General Practice, University of Otago.

Amnesty International. 2016. *Amnesty International Policy on State Obligations to Respect, Protect, and Fulfil the Human Rights of Sex Workers*, www.amnesty.org/en/documents/pol30/4062/2016/en/.

Armstrong, Lynzi. 2010. Out of the shadows (and into a bit of light): Decriminalisation, human rights and street-based sex work in New Zealand. In Kate Hardy, Sarah Kingston and Teela Sanders, eds., *New Sociologies of Sex Work*, 39–59. Farnham, UK: Ashgate.

Armstrong, Lynzi. 2017. From law enforcement to protection? Interactions between sex workers and police in a decriminalised street-based sex industry. *British Journal of Criminology*, 57: 570–588.

Armstrong, Lynzi. 2018. New Zealand. In Global Alliance Against Traffic in Women, ed., *Sex Workers Organising for Change: Self-Representation, Community Mobilisation and Working Conditions*, 73–108. Bangkok: Global Alliance Against Traffic in Women.

Barnett, T., C. Healy, A. Reed, and C. Bennachie. 2010. Lobbying for decriminalisation. In G. Abel, L. Fitzgerald, C. Healy and A. Taylor eds., *Taking the Crime Out of Sex Work: New Zealand Sex Workers Fight for Decriminalisation*, 57–75. Bristol, UK: Policy Press.

Crampton, D. 2003. Prostitution Bill passes by one vote. *Scoop Media*, 26 June, www.scoop.co.nz/stories/HL0306/S00192.htm.

Day, Sophie and Ward, Helen. 2004. *Sex work, Mobility and Health in Europe*. London: Kegan Paul.

Duff, M. 2014. Sex worker gets $25,000 over harassment. *Dominion Post*, 28 February, www.stuff.co.nz/business/industries/9777879/Sex-worker-gets-25-000-over-harassment.

Global Alliance Against Traffic in Women. 2006. *Collateral Damage: The Impact of Anti-Trafficking Measures on Human Rights Around the World*. Bangkok: Global Alliance Against Traffic in Women.

Healy, C., Bennachie, C. and Reed, A. 2010. History of the New Zealand Prostitutes' Collective. In G. Abel, L. Fitzgerald, C. Healy and A. Taylor, eds., *Taking the Crime Out of Sex Work: New Zealand Sex Workers Fight for Decriminalisation*, 57–75. Bristol, UK: Policy Press.

Herter, A., Fem, E. and Lehmann, M. 2017. Professed protection, pointless provisions: Overview of the German Prostitutes Protection Act, www.sexworkeurope.org/news/general-news/germany-sex-workers-rights-day-icrse-launches-briefing-paper-germanys-new.

Huschke, Susanne and Ward, Ellis. 2017. Stopping the traffick? The problem of evidence and legislating for the 'Swedish model' in Northern Ireland. *Anti-Trafficking Review* 8: 16–33.

Law, T. 2017. Residents and advocates clash over ways to prevent prostitutes working in suburbia. *The Press*, 2 June, www.stuff.co.nz/the-press/news/93084710/Residents-and-advocates-clash-over-ways-to-prevent-prostitutes-working-in-suburbia.

Östergren, Petra. 2017. From zero tolerance to full integration. Rethinking prostitution policies. DemandAT Working Paper, www.demandat.eu/publications/zero-tolerance-full-integration-rethinking-prostitution-policies.

Outshoorn, Joyce. 2012. Policy change in prostitution in the Netherlands: From legalization to strict control. *Sexuality Research and Social Policy* 9: 233–243.

Parliamentary Council Office. 2003. Prostitution Reform Act, www.legislation.govt.nz/act/public/2003/0028/latest/DLM197815.html.

Phipps, Alison. 2016. Whose personal is more political? Experience in contemporary feminist politics. *Feminist Theory* 17: 303–321.

Phoenix, Joanna. 2009. *Regulating sex for sale: Prostitution policy reform in the UK*. Bristol, UK: Policy Press.

Radačić, Ivana. 2017. New Zealand Prostitutes' Collective: Example of a successful policy actor. *Social Sciences* 6: 46.

Roguski, Michael. 2013. *Occupational Health and Safety of Migrant Sex Workers in New Zealand*. Wellington, NZ: Kaitiaki Research and Evaluation.

Svanström, Yvonne. 2017. From Contested to Consensus: Swedish Politics on Prostitution and Trafficking. In Ellis Ward and Gillian Wylie, eds., *Feminism, Prostitution and the State*, 29–45. Abingdon, UK: Routledge.

Wagenaar, Hendrik, Amesberger, Helga and Altink, Sietske. 2017. *Designing Prostitution Policy: Intention and Reality in Regulating the Sex Trade*. Bristol, UK: Policy Press.

Wojcicki, Janet. 1999. Race, class and sex: The politics of the decriminalisation of sex work. *Agenda* 42: 94–105.

14

Sex work and the socio-legal space in Nigeria

An update

Mfon Umoren Ekpootu

Introduction

Research on the dynamics of, and efforts to regulate, the sex industry continues to grow. Attention has focused on the social production of prostitution and the geographies of sexuality by national and international socio-legal practices (Gibson, 2003; Howell, 2004; Hubbard, 2015). Other studies have explored the complex implications of different prostitution regulatory strategies (Abel et. al., 2009). This chapter explores the prostitution space in Nigeria, highlighting the historical socio-legal issues surrounding it in the country. While male sex workers exist in Nigeria, I have chosen to limit the current chapter to women who sell sex.

This chapter draws on qualitative fieldwork conducted between 2004 and 2006 in the Nigerian cities of Port Harcourt, Calabar, Lagos, and Benin as well as additional research on sex work, sexuality, and the Nigerian state in 2013 (Ekpootu, 2017). I have complemented my primary data with information from existing research and other publications, including media reports and relevant government papers and documents. In what follows, I provide an overview of sex work in colonial Nigeria, setting the background for understanding the dynamics of sexual labour and their interplay with policies and laws of the Nigerian state. The next section addresses regulatory strategies of the colonial Nigerian state and how they shaped the dynamics of sex work. I then show how the anti-prostitution stance of the colonial government was contested by sex workers and local communities. The rest of the chapter addresses sex work in contemporary Nigeria in the context of new laws, technologies, spaces, and sexual economies. I conclude with a brief reflection on the future of the sex industry in Nigeria.

The colonial roots of sex work in Nigeria

In many precolonial Nigerian societies, sexual relationships took a variety of forms. While few of these relations would qualify as sex work, exchange of sex for financial or material gains also possibly happened in some precolonial Nigerian societies. However, there is little evidence that in pre-colonial Nigeria sex work was a professional identity that people chose or used to describe themselves. Historical research indicates that prostitution in contemporary Nigeria is a product of colonialism. Colonial economic and structural transformations initiated the institutionalization of prostitution and the problematization of women who sold sex.

Migration of young women to urban centres in Nigeria and West Africa was a common feature of colonialism. In Lagos, Nigeria, for instance, the high incidence of commercial sex occupied colonial government attention, exemplified in copious documentations on prostitution in Lagos (Ekpootu, 2013). In colonial West Africa, the Gold Coast (now Ghana), Equatorial Guinea, and Cameroon witnessed a large influx of female sex workers from Nigeria. By the 1930s, a distinctive pattern of transnational migration of sex workers into different parts of West African sex industry had emerged. Aderinto notes that by 1938, about 400 women from Calabar Province in Nigeria were engaged in prostitution in Accra, Gold Coast. A 1939 census of Nigerian prostitutes in the Gold Coast recorded 1,206 women (Aderinto, 2015: 105). In Obubra division, in present Northern Cross River State, transnational prostitutes were among the wealthiest persons. Total income derived from public revenue in 1937–1938 was £3,325 in Obubra. On the other hand, remittances from migrant Obubra prostitutes in 1942 totaled £6,791 and in Ogoja Province, by the next year, these remittances stood at £4,534 (Ekpootu, 2013: 76). Because of their enormous wealth and spending power, transnational prostitutes in this region were referred to as 'itinerant gold mines' (Naanen, 1991). Income from sexual transactions ranged from £72 to £108 per annum and could go as high as £120 for young girls. During the period, the colonial government in Lagos paid an annual minimum wage of £36, indicating that sex workers earned substantially higher than government employees (Aderinto, 2015: 57–58). Prostitutes used their wealth to avoid punitive measures. In February 1947, one female welfare officer was sentenced to six months in prison for receiving a bribe from two prostitutes and supporting them to evade repatriation from a brothel in Lagos (Aderinto, 2010: 1).

The period was also characterized by the active and large-scale recruitment, by old or retired prostitutes as well as other agents, of women and girls in local communities into the trade. Organizations for the management of sex work sprang up in some Nigerian communities with branches in other West African countries. As women travelled, they had to register with the international branches of their ethnic organizations before joining the sex trade. The local communities in Nigeria sometimes also loaned money to new recruits for their travel to, and registration in branch offices of the receiving countries. Such loans were to be repaid within a stipulated time.

Transnational prostitutes in colonial Nigeria regularly deployed their kinship networks to facilitate their work. A letter written in 1941 by the District Officer Obubra to the Colonial Resident of Ogoja Province on the problem of 'Cross River harlots' showed that women selling sex on the Gold Coast lived with members of their ethnic groups in the 'strangers' quarters'. Established transnational sex workers also recruited boys from their communities to support their trade in the Gold Coast. Such boys helped to solicit clients and keep financial books for the sex workers. They also provided security to the sex workers.

In colonial Nigeria, sexual commerce flourished in the local urban centres. Of these, Lagos, then Nigeria's most urbanized city and biggest employer of labour, drew many male and female migrants. The latter included young single, divorced, and married women (Ekpootu, 2017). Many of the married women were runaway wives from other parts of Nigeria who saw Lagos as a haven from spousal neglect, marginalization, and a life of drudgery. Further, the colonial labour system created a pool of unattached city men who became ready buyers of female sexual services. Sailors and soldiers were a prominent group of buyers of sexual services in colonial Lagos. Aderinto (2007: 18–19) writes that in Lagos areas such as Ikoyi, Ijora, Surulere, Cumberland, and Yaba, which had military barracks, the sale of sex thrived. The popularity of the relationships between prostitutes and soldiers in Lagos during the period earned the women the title 'ammunition wives' (Aderinto, 2007). In Enugu, miners and other migrant male workers also constituted a pool of consumers of sexual services of sex workers (Ekpootu, 2008).

From the turn of the twentieth century, venereal disease increased in military camps, causing commercial sex work to come under intense policy focus and surveillance. During the period, the public health discourse of the prostitute as a diseased and contagious body took roots in Nigeria (Aderinto, 2015; Ekpootu, 2008). Such characterizations positioned sex workers as undesirable elements, facilitating their stigmatization and criminalization. Sex workers in colonial Nigeria challenged the image of a pristine womanhood defined by Victorian ideals. They were thus positioned in colonial discourse as a threat to the moral order. The centrality of gender and sexuality as markers of female identity in the colonial state had an important bearing on the social construction of the prostitute (Aderinto, 2015; Levine, 2003; Stoler, 2006).

Regulation of sex work in colonial Nigeria

Commercial sex in colonial Nigeria was controlled through both civil and criminal legislations. Sections 222A, 223, 224, 225A, and 227 of the 1916 Criminal Code addressed commodified sex. In section 222A, anyone found to cause or encourage the seduction, unlawful carnal knowledge or prostitution of, or the commission of an indecent assault upon a girl (under the age of 16) was liable to imprisonment for two years. Section 223 punished the procurement of 'a girl or woman under 18 years' for purposes of prostitution in Nigeria or elsewhere with an imprisonment term of two years. However, people could not be convicted with the 'uncorroborated testimony of one witness'. Section 225 penalized men who lived on the earnings of or solicited for prostitution. First time offenders under this law risked a two-year imprisonment. Subsequent offences attracted caning in addition to a prison term. Sections 275, 278, and 281 of the Penal Code law of 1959 stipulated more stringent punishment for offenders. Section 275 criminalized any third party who 'induces a girl under the age of 18' to engage in 'illicit intercourse'. Such offenders were liable to 10 years imprisonment.

The same punishment was prescribed under section 278 for anyone 'who buys, sells, hires, lets to hire or otherwise obtains possession or disposes of any person below 18 years' for purposes of prostitution or other immoral purposes. The Native Children (Custody and Reformation) Ordinance was also promulgated to address the growing problem of child prostitution in the 1940s. In 1920, prior to this law, local elite women in Lagos had drawn the government's attention to street hawking by girls as a risk factor for prostitution, sexual molestation, and 'moral danger' (Abosede, 2011; Aderinto, 2015). Sex work was also regulated through laws such as the Undesirable Advertisement Ordinance of 1932, the Unlicensed (Prohibition) Act of 1941, and the Venereal Disease Ordinance of 1943 (Aderinto, 2015).

In colonial cities, sexual management was pivotal to colonial constructions of difference and dominance (Levine, 2003; Stoler, 2006). In colonial Nigeria, efforts to regulate perceived sexual others, particularly sex workers, also took spatial dimensions. Colonial slum clearance activities ensured that sex workers and other socially defamed groups operated at the margins of the city (Fourchard, 2005). Raids on red-light districts were also regularly conducted by the anti-vice squad of the colonial police force (Aderinto, 2016). Colonial authorities also required native authorities (local governments) to identify and report prostitutes and persons facilitating sex work and to bring the government's attention to earnings that were derived immorally. This law was, however, particularly difficult to implement as demonstrated in a letter written by the District Officer of Obubra division in the old Calabar region to the colonial office in Ogoja province, stating that 'the police have no way of ascertaining whether the woman is going for purposes of prostitution or not' (Ekpootu, 2008: 136).

The colonial media participated in the regulation of sex work, linking prostitution to crime and other social problems including corruption. On 29 November 1950, the *Southern Nigeria Defender* published an editorial on 'Prostitutes and Criminals' (Aderinto, 2015). The author argued that: 'It is a plain truth and well-known fact that prostitutes and criminals go together . . . the two are a disgraceful pair and in order to clear any community of one menace, the other also must be given similar attention.' Colonial regulation of sex work in Nigeria also had a transnational dimension. In a bilateral agreement between Nigeria and the Gold Coast in the 1940s, Nigerian females were to be refused entry into the Gold Coast 'without good reason'. Nigerian women engaged in prostitution in the Gold Coast were also to be repatriated to Nigeria. In Nigeria, travellers were required to purchase a travel certificate and an exit permit from the local superintendent of police and the Nigerian Police (Ekpootu, 2013). The implementation of this policy was, however, marred by insufficient staff and lack of funds (Nigeria had to bear the cost of repatriation). Many repatriated women were known to have either slipped back to the Gold Coast and other West African countries or merely continued sex work in the local Nigerian ports of Lagos, Calabar, and Port Harcourt. If anything, colonial efforts to regulate transnational sex work resulted in new strategies of evasion such as illicit 'canoe traffic' through which several women were ferried from Nigeria to the Gold Coast and other parts of West Africa (Tapela, 1985).

The desperation of the colonial government to end prostitution is also demonstrated in their enlistment of the help of Native authorities and urban ethnic unions. In 1942, the Colonial Welfare Office mandated ethnic unions to address the problem of girl trafficking within a month. Urban ethnic unions responded by including clauses relating to proper and improper sexual relations in their constitutions. They also began providing the colonial state with information on women suspected to be involved in sex work. Chapter 51 of the Constitution of the Owerri Union in Lagos stipulated repatriation of any of its members who participated in sex work. The Efik Ladies' Union in Lagos opted to dismiss members found guilty of prostitution while the Lagos branch of the Warri Women's Society required offenders to pay a fine of £2 (Aderinto, 2015: 131). However, evidence of the success of these efforts is scarce. These unions often drew their membership from elite urban women, most of whom were married. Sex workers generally avoided joining them.

Mann and Roberts (1991) have argued that colonial laws were often resisted by natives. Financial accumulation by women selling sex facilitated their navigation of the repressive colonial laws and activities. With economic independence, many sex workers could access health care outside the public health system, helping them to evade the stipulations of the Venereal Disease Ordinance of 1943, among other laws. In the Cross River region, high income afforded prostitutes a voice in communal affairs. They mobilized local authorities to thwart official efforts to identify and punish participants in and promoters of the trade.

Sex work in contemporary Nigeria

The organization of sex work in contemporary Nigeria is shaped by a combination of different factors, including the law, religious morality, economics, new media, and local and global social movements, among others. Legal regulation of commercial sex work in contemporary Nigeria draws largely from the colonial Criminal and Penal Code. The Trafficking in Persons (Prohibition) Law Enforcement and Administration Act (TIP) established in 2003 and amended in 2005 is the major legal instrument for regulating sex work in Nigeria. The Act, enforced by the National Agency for the Prohibition of Trafficking in Persons (NAPTIP), prescribes a ten-year jail term for 'anyone who enables the prostitution, or procurement into the sex industry within or outside Nigeria, of any person below the age of 18 years'. Brothel-keeping or use of persons below 18 years for pornography attracts a heavier punishment of 14 years without the option of fine. Adult prostitution except when conducted within a brothel is, however, not included and therefore legal in contemporary Nigeria.

Nigeria's Trafficking in Persons (Prohibition) Law Enforcement and Administration Act (TIP) is, however, poorly implemented and selectively enforced. In November 2009, the Lagos State Environmental Task Force shut down four strip clubs. However, the clubs were reopened months later after the Lagos state legislative council ruled that the action of the Task Force was illegal (Ekpootu, 2017). In some of the strip clubs, sex is regularly sold and bought by dancers and patrons respectively (Ekpootu, 2017). And club owners also often bribe the police to avoid harassment.

The most stigmatized and policed form of sex work in contemporary Nigeria is perhaps street and brothel-based prostitution, both of which continue to flourish despite different forms of state regulation and surveillance. In most major Nigerian cities today, several streets and city sections are notorious for prostitution. For instance, in the 1990s, Ayilara bustled as a notorious red-light Lagos district. Several private homes in the area were redesigned into pubs and brothels while indoor cafes were extended to accommodate rooms for rental. Lekki, an affluent neighbourhood in Lagos, is also widely known for its thriving prostitute community (Tayo, 2017) who operate from their own homes or rented rooms. Buyers and sellers of sex in street and brothel-based prostitution in Nigeria are heterogenous in their social and demographic backgrounds. The Nigerian police also regularly conduct raids in these streets and locations, creating the impression that adult sex work is illegal.

A booming transnational sex trade, involving mainly girls from Edo state in Nigeria's south-south region, continues in contemporary Nigeria. Italy, France, and Spain are popular destinations for sex work among for these women. Other interesting forms of sex work exist in Nigeria. In one form, dominated by tertiary school female students, sexual relationships are entered with rich patrons, often politicians and business executives also called 'sugar daddies', who keep and support the girls as mistresses. Social events such as marriages, funerals, and parties, and the newly emerging fancy shopping malls in Nigerian cities are also popular and have become sites for sex work and the solicitation of clients. New media, in the form of the Internet and other communication technologies, have added to the complexity of sex work in Nigeria, permitting online adverts, chatrooms, and other forms of discreet sexual solicitations. Following these media technologies is the growing business of 'commercial sexual apprenticeship' whereby young girls work with high-class escort/call girls to learn the ropes, including the art of seductive dressing, client manipulation, and grooming for sexual appeal. These forms of sex work have continued to defy state regulation.

The persistence and dynamism of prostitution in the face of prohibitive laws have provided momentum for calls to legalize it in Nigeria. This is despite conservative movements spearheaded by Nigeria's religious and other culture-based groups for harsher measures on sex workers and for the continued criminalization of the prostitution. In 2011, David Mark, then president of the Nigerian senate, and his deputy Ike Ekweremadu initiated a bill for the legalization of sex work (Sessou, 2011). Further, egged on by the women's rights movement, sex workers in Nigeria have begun to organize and agitate openly for their rights as workers and Nigerian citizens. In August 2014, prostitutes protested openly in the streets of Lagos demanding for the recognition of their rights and 'sex work as work' (Orenuga, 2014). Currently, sex worker organizations exist in many parts of the country, some with affiliations to major global and regional networks and institutions. For instance, the Nigeria Sex Workers Association in Abuja (Precious Jewels) has been engaged in efforts to make PrEP, a HIV preventive drug, available to sex workers. In collaboration with USAID and other partners, Precious Jewels has opened a drop-in clinic for sex workers, where services such as HIV screening and treatment and distribution of condoms and lubricants are offered.

Conclusion

This chapter has addressed the historical dynamics of sex work in Nigeria. Colonial and post-colonial governments in Nigeria have criminalized sex work, constituting it as immoral and a source of public health risks. Laws, community engagement activities, and public education programs are the key official strategies that have been used to regulate sex work in the country. Government efforts are supported by religious bodies that continue to frame prostitution in terms of irreligiosity, sin, depravity, greed, and lack of respect for local cultures of femininity. Very little effort has been made by successive governments in the country to focus on the socio-economic and inequality issues that have historically driven women into sex work in Nigeria. As a result, prostitution continues to thrive in the country, even assuming newer dimensions that have not been anticipated by existing laws.

A bourgeoning rights-based movement, spearheaded by both sex workers and their local and global allies, is currently underway in Nigeria. The 2011 call by leading Nigerian lawmakers for the legalization of prostitution in the country indicates high-level interests in moving away from dominant narratives related to sex work. The proliferation of civil rights organizations with a focus on the protection of sexual minorities and marginalized groups in Nigeria also heralds improved safety prospects for sex workers. The involvement of sex workers in programming efforts by international and local development organizations is an important step towards ensuring that sex workers are part of efforts to support them to enjoy their basic rights as citizens in a context of elevated anti-prostitution sentiments. The growing capacity of sex workers in Nigeria to organize and demand for their basic rights also portends a significant shift that could increase their impact on policymaking in Nigeria. However, the future of sex work in Nigeria will depend, to a large extent, on the future strides of the global rights-based sex workers' movement.

References

Abel, G.M., Fitzgerald. L.G., and Brunton, C. 2009. The impact of decriminalisation on the number of sex workers in New Zealand. *Journal of Social Policy* 38(3): 515–531.

Abosede, George. 2011. Within salvation: girl hawkers and the colonial state in development era Lagos. *Journal of Social History* 44: 837–859.

Aderinto, Saheed. 2007. The girls in moral danger: child prostitution and sexuality in Colonial Lagos, Nigeria 1930s–1950. *Journal of Humanities and Social Sciences* 1: 1–22.

Aderinto, Saheed. 2010. Sexualized nationalism: Lagos and the politics of illicit sexuality. PhD dissertation, University of Austin at Texas, Austin.

Aderinto, Saheed. 2015. *When sex threatened the state: illicit sexuality, nationalism and politics in Colonial Nigeria, 1900–1958*. Urbana, Chicago and Springfield: University of Illinois Press.

Aderinto, Saheed. 2016. Pleasure for sale: prostitution in Colonial Africa, 1880s–1960s. In Frank Jacob, ed., *Prostitution: a companion to mankind*, 469–480. Frankfurt am Main: Peter Lang.

Ekpootu, Mfon. 2008. Prostitution and child labour in the Cross River region from 1990. PhD dissertation, University of Calabar, Calabar.

Ekpootu, Mfon. 2013. Contestation of identity: colonial policing of female sexuality in the Cross River region of Southern Nigeria. *Inkanyiso, Journal of Humanities and Social Sciences* 5: 72–80.

Ekpootu, Mfon. 2017. Sexualizing the city: female prostitution in Nigeria's urban centres in a historical perspective. In Magaly R. Garcia, Lex H. Van Voss, and Elise Meerkerk, eds, *Selling sex in the city: a global history of prostitution*, 306–328. Leiden, Boston: Brill.

Fourchard, Laurent. 2005. Urban poverty, urban crime, and crime control: the Lagos and Ibadan cases, 1929–45, In Steven J. Salim and Toyin Falola eds, *African urban spaces in historical perspective*, 291–319. Rochester: University of Rochester Press.

Gibson, Lisa. 2003. Innocence and purity vs. deviance and immorality: the spaces of prostitution in Nepal and Canada. MA thesis, Institute of Development Studies, University of Sussex, Brighton.

Howell, Philip. 2004. Sexuality, sovereignty and space: law, government and the geography of prostitution in Colonial Gibraltar. *Social History* 29: 444–464. www.jstor.org/stable/4100794.

Hubbard, Philip. 2015. Law, sex and the city: regulating sexual entertainment venues in England and Wales. *International Journal of Law in the Built Environment* 7: 5–20.

Levine, Philippa. 2003. *Prostitution, race, and politics: policing venereal disease in the British Empire*. New York: Routledge.

Mann, Kristen and Richard Roberts, eds, 1991. *Law in colonial Africa*. London: James Currey.

Naanen, Ben.1991 'Itinerant gold mines': prostitution in the Cross River Basin of Nigeria, 1930–1950. *African Studies Review* 34: 57–79.

Orenuga, Adenike. 2014. 'Sex is work too': Nigerian prostitutes protest on the streets of Lagos. *Daily Post*. http://dailypost.ng/2014/08/04/sex-work-nigerian-prostitutes-protest-streets-lagos-photos. Accessed 3 February 2018.

Sessou, Ebun. 2011. Legalising prostitution: women give Ekwereamadu hard knocks. *The Vanguard*. www. vanguardngr.com/2011/10/legalising-prostitution-women-give-ekweremadu-hard-knocks. Accessed 7 February 2018.

Stoler, Ann Laura, ed., 2006. *Geographies of intimacy in North American history*. Durham and London: Duke University Press.

Tayo, O. Ayomide, 2017. The economy of sex in Lagos city. *Pulse NG*. www.pulse.ng/gist/prostitution-the-economy-of-sex-in-lagos-city-id6101016.html. Accessed 20 April 2018.

Tapela, Henderson. 1985. Nigerian labour for Fernando Po (part 1). *Calabar Historical Journal* 3: 36–56.

15

"Bridge over troubled water"

What sex workers face while embarking on new paths and what helps them leave prostitution in Germany

Tzvetina Arsova Netzelmann, Elfriede Steffan,
and Barbara Kavemann

Introduction

No recent studies derived from statistical methods of data collection offer reliable estimates on the size of the sex worker community in Germany, although empirical research conducted over two decades ago suggested that the number of people engaged in sex work in Germany at that time was close to 200,000 (Leopold and Steffan 1994). As is the case in many countries throughout the world, the German sex industry encompasses many diverse types of indoor and outdoor workplaces. The largest part is represented by indoor sex work scenes, including those in apartments, brothels and escorting, with outdoor forms of sex work occupying not more than 20% of the sex industry (Destatis 2017) and taking place in street areas zoned for that purpose, such as Geestemünder Street in Cologne, or in mobile campervans.

Notwithstanding widespread public debates on sex work in Germany that have taken place within the last several years (Czarnecki et al. 2014), there is still evident lack of comprehensive data and empirical studies that examine the multidimensional aspects of the sex industry, the working conditions and the lived realities of sex workers. Moreover, most of the studies in Germany are of limited scope and not widely shared with the general public or the international research community (Döring 2014); even less is known about sex workers who seek to leave prostitution and embark on new paths. In order to examine this heterogeneous group with diverse types of support needs and to assess factors that facilitate or hinder the exit process, a five-year model support project and evaluation study were conducted in Germany (BMFSFJ 2015).

Three exit programmes operated in the frame of the model project from 2009 to 2014, funded by the national government in four country regions: DIWA in Berlin, OPERA in Nuremberg and PINK in Freiburg and Kehl.[1] The exit-support programmes were located at specialised counselling services for sex workers that were open to anyone with direct experience in sex work. Individuals did not have to be leaving sex work in order to attend the services. The participants were reached through publicity or low-threshold outreach. The exit support encompassed basic offers such as stabilisation through psychosocial, social, legal and health counselling plus accompaniment to institutions and government agencies. An important part

155

of the programmes was to develop and adapt support for job orientation and job referral. The exit programmes implemented individual trainings and group courses covering skills assessment, language courses, occupational orientation and coaching, application assistance, occupational training and organisation of internships. The occupational trainings were implemented in cooperation with further specialised training institutions. After the end of the model project the three exit programmes received funding for continuation of their support services on a regional or local level. Alongside a handful of other sex work exit programmes has been established across Germany, partly run by sex work activist organisations, partly by prostitution counselling centres and partly by faith-based projects.

This chapter presents the results of the evaluation study within the broader global context of what is known about the circumstances and characteristics of those who seek to end their sex industry involvement and the actors, support structures and other factors that assist or inhibit them from doing so.

Framing data and research on exiting prostitution

The process of exiting prostitution remains an understudied topic internationally, with limited examinations of the various factors that influence exiting and embarking on new pathways. In a longitudinal study that stretched over 15 years Ward and Day (2006) studied the occupational mobility of sex workers across various segments of the sex industry and during the exit process. They provided insights into the exit motives and associated opportunities, both used and unused, for 130 sex workers in London. The authors found out at the follow-up study that the majority of study respondents had still worked in or had re-entered the sex industry. Nevertheless most of the women combined their engagement with sex work with other types of work, education and training outside the sex industry (Ward and Day 2006, 416). Leopold and Steffan (1997) analysed the social and psychological situations of 260 sex workers in Germany during the exit process, demonstrating high levels of social and psychological stress, frequent exposure to violence during childhood and adolescence and a strong need for support. Accordingly the authors stressed that social stigmatisation, economic and health problems as well as bad working conditions increase the exit pressure. Baker et al. (2010) examined four different exit models from street-level prostitution, identifying a set of barriers and outlined a six-stage exit model. Bilardi et al. (2011) focused on sex workers' level of satisfaction with their work outlining working time and flexibility as positive aspects that influence the motivation for leaving, or remaining in, the sex industry. Dodsworth (2012) and Mayhew and Mossman (2007) emphasised that the interaction of push and pull factors is key to the process of both entering and exiting prostitution. Positive motives for entering sex work included examples set by other sex workers and above all the expectation of greater income than from other low-qualified jobs. The study results corroborate that exiting sex work is difficult and rarely succeeds at first attempt, five to six exit trials are described to be the usual case while leaving prostitution. A decisive role thereby is played by factors such as "resilience" and "risks" (Dodsworth 2012), named by other authors explicitly as "push" and "pull" factors (Bindel at al. 2012). The strength of these factors affects sex workers' agency and vulnerability (Dodsworth 2012) in different stages of their lives and work, and also influences the success of their decision to leave sex work. Motives for leaving prostitution are extremely heterogeneous and complex, and exit programmes can only be effective if they adequately meet these different needs (Leopold and Steffan 1997; Hester and Westmarland 2004; Steffan and Kerschl 2004; Kavemann and Fischer 2006; BMFSFJ 2007; Mayhew and Mossman 2007). Various authors underlined the importance of individual, comprehensive exit-support programmes that tackle social marginalisation as well as stabilisation and support mechanisms for those particularly vulnerable such as street-based sex workers (Bury 2011; Oselin 2014).

Both German and international literature points largely to economic motives for both entering and leaving prostitution (Leopold and Steffan 1997; Gangoli and Westmarland 2006; Svanström 2006). For many women, however, the primary reason for wanting to leave prostitution seems to derive from mental, physical and/or economic burnout (Leopold und Steffan 1997). Stigmatisation of sex work – the "whore stigma" (*Hurenstigma*, Macioti 2014) informs pervasive cultural judgments of "moral incompetence" among sex workers that likewise prevents them from accessing support services (Sanders 2007; Macioti 2014; Shdaimah and Leon 2016).

Methodology and study sample

The evaluation and research study was commissioned by the the German Federal Ministry for Family Affairs, Senior Citizens, Women and Youth (BMFSFJ), the primary German government agency tasking with the well-being of children, the elderly and women. We conducted our research between November 2011 and May 2015 in four different areas with very different sex industry sectors and dynamics: Berlin, a major metropolitan area with a widely distributed prostitution scene and diversified support structures, and three less-populated areas with clear and manageable service provision infrastructures including a semi-rural area in the town of Kehl, located on the French border near Strasbourg, a medium-sized city (Nuremberg) and smaller city (Freiburg). A mixed-method approach combined quantitative analysis of data from the participants' case files documented at the exit programmes (N = 256) and qualitative semi-narrative interviews (N = 29, two points of time) with 20 former sex workers, 5 of whom had independently left prostitution without support from an exit programme. All contacts to study participants were made via the specialised exit-support programmes set up in the regions. Our findings therefore reflect the views and circumstance only of those seeking to leave sex work, and as such make no statements about this work or the community of sex workers in general.

Findings: the process of leaving prostitution

A profile of exit-support programme clients

Most of the sex workers whose case files we documented at the exit programmes were female (N = 241), with nine males and four trans persons. They ranged in age from 18 to 59, with an average age of 30, with the 25–34 age group most frequently represented. Most of the sex workers were German (37.5%) or citizens of another EU country (43.4%); of the non-German citizens, more than half had arrived in Germany since the last enlargements of the EU (2004 and 2007). Around 55% of the sex workers were single or separated and 33% had children, many of them under 18 years of age. Around 27% – mainly migrant sex workers – did not have health insurance. At their first contact with the exit-support programmes 60% of the participants were active as sex workers, nearly 30% had already exited prostitution, and the rest did not provide information. Almost 46% expressed the wish to exit at either the initial or subsequent counselling sessions. The most frequently reported motives for leaving sex work were: a desire for career reorientation and a new occupation, lack of satisfaction with the work ("don't like it anymore"), worsening work conditions and extremely high stress levels ("can't stand it anymore").

Support needs and obstacles

Our results indicate that sex workers who seek help in their transition out of prostitution shoulder the burden of complex problems and diverse assistance needs. A large number of study participants entered the support programme at a point when they were in poor physical and mental shape and without sufficient resources of their own to make a new start. Stress and stigmatisation play a decisive role that often leads to time-consuming assistance processes, such that the relationships of the sex workers to the exit-programme counsellors were of high intensity and long duration. In many cases the desired change process took longer than initially expected and was marked by fluctuations, indecision or even stagnation. The average length of contact with exit programme was 12 months, with 35% of the clients attending counselling for more than a year.

S, a 35-year-old German sex worker, took the decision and left sex work on her first attempt after she had spent more than 15 years in the sex industry. Nevertheless she described the exit process as fraught with indecision:

> Well, I have been considering this for quite a while, I wasn't happy [. . .] there. I was not satisfied, no longer contented. I had struggled with myself already half a year before that: Would I search for something new? Would I search for something else? But I could not pick myself up . . . Maybe I was too long in it [sex work] or I just did not have the guts to say "Stop, full stop, finish," I don't know. Then I visited Hydra [specialised sex work counselling with exit-support services] because I had problems with the health insurance. This turned out to be rather complicated, but the counsellor told me about the other offers of the programme, about the job centre and the school graduation possibility and then I made up my mind. Lastly I took the decision overnight; there were no creeping thoughts any longer. Because previously I had never had the idea that women like me would have a chance to leave.

Over a period of five years 3,817 individual counselling sessions with 256 sex workers were documented in the participant files of the exit programmes, an average of 15 sessions per participant. One session often covered multiple topics and a total of 6,494 topics were handled. Counselling focused primarily on the participants' progress toward and struggles with securing a job, unemployment, social assistance, housing, as well as psychosocial support, residence status, family situation, health insurance and other health issues. Many participants were in such precarious situations, such as on the verge of homelessness, that crisis intervention or first aid was required just to ensure subsistence. B, a 30-year-old migrant from south-east Europe who had worked more than 10 years in the sex industry in Germany opted for exit due to the increasingly stressful working conditions. She had participated in the exit programme over two and half years putting untiring efforts to overcome multiple hurdles on the way out of sex work. It took almost one year and 26 counselling sessions for the support services to secure her residence status, to obtain state social assistance and to recover her health insurance rights. Due to the lack of other livelihood sources she kept working in the sex industry throughout the whole period. Only after she could start a part-time cleaning job and received additional social welfare could she stop with the sex work. Only then the exit support process could focus on further steps like a language course, job orientation and qualification training.

Income was a major issue in considering whether to leave sex work, especially but not only for migrant sex workers. Sex work was seen as the only way to earn a living – very often for the family in the home country as well. For some study participants, the exit hurdles were too high and they opted to remain in the sex industry longer than they desired.

Case study

"I'm stuck in a vicious circle"

One interview partner, a migrant, had a sense of limited opportunities and hopelessness after her first attempt to leave sex work. She had worked for 15 years as sex worker, the last 8 in Germany.

"It has been no fun in the last years, it was really only [. . .] fight for money!"

Multiple structural and individual factors posed insurmountable barriers. She lived at the brothel and could not find her own flat. Because she could not show "proper" residence documents, she had not yet been able to register at a job centre[2] and also did not have health insurance in Germany. Despite this she attempted to make a living outside sex work with a low-paying job in her originally learned vocation. But she was "outed" as a sex worker, and lost the job as a consequence. Her family was also informed anonymously, and withdrew their support. Mounting health problems made it difficult to pursue her original profession, which was physically demanding. Her situation worsened in the year between the two interviews, despite her untiring efforts to initiate actions and seek other job opportunities.

I said it's a vicious circle. First of course, the place to live, and then the work. And if I don't get a flat then of course I can't get work, which like I said is a vicious circle [. . .] I don't say that I regret it, but this is of course difficult now to quit the [sex] work and at the moment I have no idea how can it go further.

Stigmatisation: a key obstacle to exiting prostitution

Our findings confirm that most important factor in sex workers' successful exit involves being accompanied from the world of sex work to the other or "conventional world" (*bürgerliche Welt*). The distance between these two worlds may seem insurmountable, and the bridge over them can be filled with troubled water. Sex workers' life histories and their social environments also play a significant role in the process of exit. The study participants' narratives provided plentiful insights into their biographical contexts and the types of problems for which sex workers sought solutions in counselling. The findings highlighted how experienced and anticipated stigmatisation influences not only sex workers' identities and attitudes towards their work, but also decision-making processes with respect to leaving prostitution, the management of the exit and its consequences for their current life situations. Many interview partners were convinced that most people view prostitution as "reprehensible" or "disgraceful". They stated that prostitutes are looked down upon, "branded" and "condemned" by "normal" or "respectable" people. "For ordinary people I'm just the dregs," one said. Many already feared and anticipated social stigma, and even expressed surprise when workers at government agencies such as public health offices or job centres treated them with courtesy and respect.

Even sex workers who did not consider their own work reprehensible suffered stigmatisation in their social environments, causing one participant to note, "in fact everybody who knows me knows that I used to work as a prostitute, many judged me and broke our contact [. . .] I stand by it, I had been doing this, it is a service and nothing reprehensible." Other interview partners internalised stigma, felt ashamed, self-alienated and, as one participant put it, "could not recognise" themselves. They had internalised the societal perspective, thereby converting public stigma into self-stigma (Deitz et al. 2015). Subjective correlates of social stigmatisation include shame and a lack of self-esteem, yet a professional attitude to prostitution appeared to enable some individuals to resist stigmatisation. When counsellors accompanied them to public institutions such as health insurance offices, welfare agencies or foreigners' registration offices, study participants were over time able to reflect on stigma and handle it better. N referred to the important role counselling played in the way she revisited her own attitudes: "things became different over time, and I could also talk about it more easily, and . . . I could also take a different attitude toward it."

Shifting the focus to the experiences with governmental agencies we did not obtain data on how many sex workers had avoided contact with them due to fear of stigmatisation. However, statements by interview partners and counsellors suggest that many do not even consider the possibility of contacting agencies because they anticipate stigmatisation. In the course of leaving prostitution, some study participants had to visit a number of agencies, including the tax office, health insurance companies, residents' registration offices, job centres and immigration authorities. Counsellors set up many of these appointments and/or accompanied the sex workers. Agency employees were some of the projects' close cooperation partners or had at least been informed about issues facing the target group. Despite this, some of the interview partners expressly emphasised that they had not expected a positive reception or a helping hand, as P put it, "this is definitely a rare thing, that they helped me".

Two study participants had explicitly negative records from job centre visits. Within sight and sound of other job seekers, employees had described them as prostitutes. This was an utterly humiliating experience for Z, a migrant sex worker in her late twenties, who exited sex work after five years in the job. Along with psychosocial support and counselling the exit programme provided skills assessment, occupational orientation and coaching. Z had clear goals and precise job aspirations she needed training for. With a counsellor's support she applied for a qualification course that had to be approved and financed by the respective job agency:

> The job officer asked loud before all others in the line: "Aha, you are a prostitute?" In that moment all turned their heads to look at us of course [. . .] and how they looked at me [.] These felt like thunder flashes. Then I thought to myself "You can't fall deeper than that" and still, I fell three steps deeper than that: "Please, let this be [only] a nightmare" . . . Then I'd rather be left to my own devices, and never go back to that person, because I have no words to describe that moment.

Similar feelings about confrontations of this type were vastly shared by other sex workers who described the experience as: "extremely embarrassing", "totally unacceptable", "tough", "really bad".

Diverse experiences with stigmatisation with new colleagues, acquaintances and partners were reported as well. That demonstrates that stigma bears its weight on sex workers beyond the exit as fear of stigmatisation does not end when a new job has been found. The double life led during the time in sex work turns into avoidance behaviour, secrecy, split identity, as one participant put it she "has become another person". Evident gaps in the curriculum vitae for job applications had to be disguised through more "decent" occupations e.g., dancer, model, masseur, translator or socially valued tasks, such as care for a parent.

Speaking openly about their past in sex work was not an option, it could only bring more harm, but no reconciliation, as R noted: "I can't tell [about it] – it destroyed me and it is already behind me."

Several interview partners were convinced that they would lose their new jobs if their past became known. Even after leaving sex work, a sense of insecurity remained along with stress in the form of enormous pressure to strictly conceal their previous activity. The book on sex work was not completely closed and the past could catch up with them any time, an anticipation that felt like tightrope walking.

N's narrative, a migrant former sex worker, confirms that. After her exit from sex work she started a rotating shift job while sorting out what the most suitable qualification training would be for her. Even though her new colleagues knew nothing about her past she was very careful not to reveal anything, as she feared losing the job: "If I would admit it [the sex work], all colleagues would be totally knocked over, nope, then I'd rather go right away. So, of course I would not admit it." N had to be particularly alert when sex was the topic of conversation, since she was afraid she could reveal herself easily because she was so used to talking about sex in a confident manner, due to her long time working in the sex industry. That had already made her new colleagues curious about her previous experiences. These moments could be unexpected. They were accompanied by a growing realisation that the transition from one world to the other required much more change and self-control than previously imagined, and that this would continue to be the case for a long time.

> They [the colleagues] are still not quite sure, but they suspect it. I wear pumps and this is for some of them already a reason to label me. Sometimes I act extremely dominating and they can feel it. And my colleague told me the other day: "When a woman talks about sex in such a convincing manner, then she must be a [. . .]". So you see that is not at all easy to enter the world outside – to me this is already normality, but I still keep in my mind who I was before and who am I now.

One condition for successful "retirement" from sex work and safer steering of the post-sex work period is the ability to establish or maintain stable emotional relationships and ensure backup from the social environment. Here too, the stigma of sex work poses an obstacle, with respect to keeping the contact to old friends or making new ones. L, a 55-year-old mother of four sons and a qualified nursery school teacher, came from a well-situated family and entered sex work in her mid-forties after separation from her partner that caused great financial losses. After exiting she hoped to be able to recover her economic and social status. In the post-sex work time she suffered from her precarious financial situation, the lost ties to former friends and the growing isolation.

> At the moment I experience great problems in getting back to the [conventional] society. When you are on the dole, you have plenty of time and no money, which means you don't really have a friends' circle. Because they go out dining, go to movies. I can't afford all this, so I am very often alone [. . .] That's badly hurting. It was clear to me: no work, no money, and no friends. Either they have to ask you out and pay your bill, or you would have to drink only orange juice. Then it gets quite risky that you eventually go back to sex work.

Prostitution is a real taboo vis-à-vis one's children, and self-stigmatisation can be especially intense if sex workers develop feelings of guilt. Some interview partners maintained the same secrecy to their families and to their partner and children. One 30-year-old participant who had left sex work when she got pregnant, suffered depression one year after the birth of her son. For a long time she was tormented by the thought of what she would tell her child one day. Similar feelings were shared by T, a migrant former sex worker, mother of five children:

> I feel ashamed now, I cannot image going out into the town with my children. I am afraid I could meet someone who recognises me [. . .] I am afraid they could learn what I had been doing, because they would then disrespect me as mother.

This too is a fraught situation, because revealing a history of sex work can lead to great personal loss and can also transfer that stigma to others.

Stigma management and the exit process

Individuals who face stigmatisation have to organise their lives such that they do not constantly encounter these stressful situations, or such that the people close to them also face the stigma. This requires stigma management (Goffman 1963) for all parts of daily life. For sex workers it means having to present different versions of their identity and employment in different contexts or everyday parts of their lives. Discrimination and disadvantages arise when the past activity becomes known. The study participants internalised devaluation, did not expect help or support, lacked self-confidence, felt increasingly inferior, thereby reproducing the narratives of stigmatised identities. Many interview partners referred to the dilemmas they were facing. Upholding a professional attitude toward prostitution could strengthen their self-confidence and coping resources, but it requires identifying with the stigmatised activity. Likewise it was important to them to be viewed as people instead of being reduced to the status of prostitutes. This could be achieved when relationships develop, but for that they had to be open about themselves and risk losing the relationship.

There is not yet sufficient evidence on what successful "retirement" from sex work looks like. Considering the long-lasting impact of stigma it would likely require a successful integration of a new identity. The end of an exit process is marked by resolute actions to leave sex work behind forever, to establish an income and livelihood as well as new social ties. The road towards this target is however not straightforward, there are several "stages of change" (Bindel et al. 2012), which do not follow one another, but often overlap. The transition process is a complex mixture of motives and events, "push and pull" factors that lead to this decision – often provisionally at first, then final – and then putting it into practice. Understanding how enmeshed the push and pulls can be helps in understanding why the process of leaving is not easy to manage (Mayhew and Mossman 2007). This also helps to show that the obstacles to exit do not consist solely of negative push factors (i.e. stigmatisation, stress). Often the positively perceived pull factors (i.e. incentives, such as a high degree of flexibility and freedom) play an inhibiting role. Then the exit process can be "on hold" due to fluctuations or stagnation of the decisions to act or even experience relapses.

Entering prostitution means travelling from the "conventional" world to the world of sex work, and new arrivals often do not realise how far-reaching this decision can be, and that they risk becoming a "discreditable" person (Goffman 1963). When exit-support programme participants start considering a way out of prostitution, they realise how difficult the road ahead is. Even if they are not yet fully aware of the extent of the changes to be made they anticipate that it is not at all easy to come into the "world outside".

The new identity that comes to substitute the sex worker's old one has to suit the "conventional" world while at the same time somehow integrating the past. Just like the decision to enter prostitution was not arbitrary and different paths to a goal were considered, the same is true for leaving and available alternatives are examined (except when the need to leave is so urgent that the question of alternatives does not arise). Step by step, the conditions for leaving prostitution change: (1) contacting a counselling centre brings information and access to ways of ensuring a livelihood; (2) financial support and a place to live make it possible to think about the next steps; (3) positive experiences with agencies or in social settings build self-confidence whereas negative experiences set the process back. Each next step not only has to be imagined and deemed possible; it also has to be objectively feasible. Motivation needs to turn into the willingness to act, and the willingness to act must turn into successful action. A key component of success lies in a new identity – which in the case of sex work means an "ex-identity" (Fuchs Ebaugh 1988).

For the study participants who successfully completed the exit process, this often meant an abrupt break with their past. They viewed that part of their lives as wrong, unwanted and finished, as something that must not encroach upon the present. Whether or not they managed to leave prostitution completely behind, our analysis showed a decisional and developmental process in which a new identity is forged vis-à-vis the past that could be considered as an account of successful retirement of sex work. Many former sex workers need a new identity simply because they cannot draw on an earlier one. Many parts of their identity have been altered or damaged either by sex work as such or by the associated stigma. A particularly destructive effect on their mental health and prospects for transition consists of internalising social stigmatisation that creates self-stigmatisation.

Contrastingly, self-confidence and optimism were important agency factors and predictors for a successful retirement of sex work. These include the ability to develop an open and positive view of the future, social and communication skills, clear job goals, and a realistic assessment of one's resources and weaknesses, as one study participant described it: "You have to look forward, not back, because our future is in front of us, not behind us. You have to look ahead." The study participants who expected to be self-efficient took more initiative and acted more resolutely. A positive approach to their own abilities to act, which was one of the key achievements of the resources-oriented counseling, strengthened participants' independence from the counsellors and increased their sense of control and responsibility for their new course. Exit-support services like skill assessments and coaching opened new avenues for their self-image and self-esteem. One sex worker who learned to trust her abilities was convinced of the positive outcome of the exit process: "It's going to work because I want it to. I'm going to school now and you know how it works: just keep moving ahead and everything will work out."

An absence or limited degree of these personality resources had an enduring negative effect on sex workers' agency, and was a push factor back into sex work. The study participants needed first to gain or restore their self-confidence before they could manage the next steps of changing their personal and professional lives.

Discussion

The study's findings clearly show that sex workers in Germany face stigmatisation and exclusion. As long as that remains the case, prostitution-specific counselling and support programmes will be needed to reach these heterogeneous groups and work with them in open and non-judgmental ways. Despite the local evidence compiled by our data the findings have broader implications informing how to tailor effectively sex work exit-support programmes in other settings. The processes of leaving prostitution can succeed by means of needs-informed individual support and assistance for sex workers and close cooperation among specialised sex work counselling centres, exit programmes and training institutes including employment agencies.

Two important conditions for overcoming individual and societal obstacles on the way to new occupation and employment, namely reducing social stigmatisation and striving for social inclusion have global relevance.

Therefore sex workers should be entitled to receive support by the services regardless of whether they seek to leave prostitution or not, which in many contexts is often not the case.

Our findings demonstrate that not all sex workers require specific support to exit. However, the proportion of these who in frequent cases need prolonged and intense counselling and support to leave prostitution is not marginal. Therefore understanding the effects of stigmatisation can help support providers not only better understand the difficulties and setbacks in the exit process, but also enable them to reflect on and better attend to the prostitutes' complex problems and needs.

The assistance and support needs of sex workers can then be adequately met when access barriers are reduced and counselling service uptake is not associated with embarrassment or defamation of their personalities. Conjunction of the exit-support programmes with basic legal, occupational, health and psychosocial counselling is indispensable. Therefore prostitution-specific counselling centres are needed for exit-support programmes to work. They offer basic needs-oriented services supplemented by additional counselling and occupational training. Their goal should be to promote equal opportunities, advocacy and social inclusion.

Our findings demonstrate that this approach is also transferable to other regions internationally, where a specialised prostitute counselling centre can act at the core of the local and regional support networks. Alongside this, professionals from other institutions, e.g. employment agencies, occupational training organisations, health insurance companies as well as potential employers, need still to gain awareness of the life circumstances and barriers that sex workers encounter.

All assistance agencies and service offers for sex workers, regardless of whether they favour the abolition of prostitution or endorse its full legalisation should discern between political views on the one hand and the professional position on the other. Our findings advise further that in societal contexts marked by stigmatisation of sex workers it is all the more important to attend them with acceptance and non-judgment in order to allow for an open and unbiased counselling and exit assistance, guided by professional codes of conduct and respect towards the decisions and life planning of the persons whose living and working situations are affected.

Acknowledgements

The authors would like to thank all interview partners for their willingness to share their stories and experiences of their way out of sex work, the staff members of the exit-support programmes and their partner organisations for their cooperation, our partner research fellow Professor Cornelia Helfferich from the Women's Research Institute in Freiburg for her valuable advice and the Federal Ministry for Family Affairs, Senior Citizens, Women and Youth (BMFSFJ) for entrusting us with carrying out this study.

Notes

1 For more information on the three exit-support programmes visit DIWA (www.hydra-berlin.de), OPERA (currently operating a under new name – START) http://kassandra-nbg.de) and PINK (www. pink-baden.de).
2 In Germany, under particular preconditions, sex workers (including non-German citizens coming from EU countries) are entitled to receive unemployment allowances, training and employment offers when they register as unemployed, because sex work is formally recognised as an occupation activity. Employment placement in the sex work is, however legally, impossible.

References

Baker, L.M., R.L. Dalla and C. Williamson, C. 2010. Exiting prostitution: an integrated model. *Violence Against Women* 16 (5), 579–600.

Bilardi, J. E., A. Miller, J.S. Hocking, L. Keogh, R. Cummings, M.Y. Chen, C.S. Bradshaw and C.K. Fairley. 2011. The job satisfaction of female sex workers working in licensed brothels in Victoria, Australia. *Journal of Sexual Medicine* 8 (1), 116–122.

Bindel, J., L. Brown, H. Easton, R. Matthews and L. Reynolds. 2012. *Breaking down the barriers: A study of how women exit prostitution*. London: Eaves and London South Bank University.

Bundesministerium für Familie, Senioren, Frauen und Jugend (BMFSFJ). 2007. *Bericht der Bundesregierung zu den Auswirkungen des Gesetzes zur Regelung der Rechtsverhältnisse der Prostituierten (Prostitutionsgesetz – ProstG)*. Berlin: BMFSFJ.

Bundesministerium für Familie, Senioren, Frauen und Jugend (BMFSFJ). 2015. *Abschlussbericht der wissenschaftlichen Begleitung zum Bundesmodellprojekt Unterstützung des Ausstiegs aus der Prostitution*. Berlin: BMFSFJ.

Bury, I. 2011. *Men in the shadows: Reaching the need of male partners of street based sex workers – Evaluation Report. Open Doors Male Partners Project*. London: Open Doors, City and Hackney Primary Care Trust.

Czarnecki, D., H. Engels, B. Kavemann, E. Steffan, W. Schenk and D. Türnau. 2014. *Prostitution in Germany: A comprehensive analysis of complex challenges*. Berlin: SPI Forschung.

Deitz, M.F., S.L. Williams, S.C. Rife and P. Cantrell, P. 2015. Examining cultural, social, and self-related aspects of stigma in relation to sexual assault and trauma symptoms. *Violence Against Women* 21 (5), 598–615.

Destatis. 2017. *Statistisches Bundesamt. Verordnung über die Führung einer Bundesstatistik nach dem Prostituiertenschutzgesetz (Prostitutions-Statistikverordnung – ProstStatV)*. www.destatis.de/DE/Methoden/Rechtsgrundlagen/Statistikbereiche/Inhalte/1069_ProstStatV.pdf?__blob=publicationFile.

Dodsworth, J. 2012. Pathways through sex work: childhood experiences and adult identities. *British Journal of Social Work* 42 (3), 519–536.

Döring, N. 2014. Prostitution in Deutschland: Eckdaten und die Veränderung durch das Internet. *Zeitschrift für Sexualforschung* 27 (2), 99–137.

Fuchs Ebaugh, H.R. (ed.). 1988. *Becoming an ex: The process of role exit*. Chicago: University of Chicago Press.

Gangoli, G. and N. Westmarland. 2006. *International approaches to prostitution: Law and policy in Europe and Asia*. Bristol, UK: Policy Press.

Goffman, E. 1963. *Stigma: Notes on the management of spoiled identity*. Englewood Cliffs, NJ: Prentice Hall.

Hester, M. and N. Westmarland. 2004. *Tackling street prostitution: Towards an holistic approach*. Home Office Research Study 279. Bristol, UK: University of Bristol.

Kavemann, B. and C. Fischer. 2006. *Vertiefung spezifischer Fragestellungen zu den Auswirkungen des Prostitutionsgesetzes: Ausstieg aus der Prostitution. Kriminalitätsbekämpfung und Prostitutionsgesetz*. Berlin: BMFSFJ.

Leopold, B. and E. Steffan. 1994. *Dokumentation zur rechtlichen und sozialen Situation von Prostituierten in der Bundesrepublik Deutschland*. Stuttgart, Berlin. Köln, Kohlhammer: Schriftreihe des Bundesministeriums für Frauen und Jugend.

Leopold, B. and E. Steffan. 1997. *EVA – Projekt: Evaluierung unterstützender Maßnahmen beim Ausstieg aus der Prostitution*. Berlin: SPI Forschung.

Macioti, P.G. 2014. Liberal zu sein reicht nicht aus. Eine progressive Prostitutionspolitik muss das "Hurenstigma" ebenso bekämpfen wie die Kriminalisierung von Sexarbeit. *Standpunkte 7/2014*. Berlin: Rosa-Luxemburg-Stiftung.

Mayhew, P. and E. Mossman. 2007. *Exiting prostitution: Models of best practice*. Wellington, NZ: Victoria University of Wellington.

Oselin, S. 2014. *Leaving prostitution: Getting out and staying out of sex work*. New York: New York University Press.

Sanders, T. 2007. Becoming an ex-sex worker: making transitions out of a deviant career. *Feminist Criminology*, 2 (1), 74–95.

Shdaimah, C. and C.S. Leon. 2016. Relationships among stigmatized women engaged in street-level prostitution: coping with stigma and stigma management. *Special Issue: Problematizing Prostitution: Critical Research and Scholarship (Studies in Law, Politics and Society)*, 71, 43–62.

Steffan, E. and A.V. Kerschl. 2004. *Die Verlagerung des Straßenstriches der Stadt Köln. Abschlussbericht der wissenschaftlichen Begleitung.* Berlin: SPI Forschung.

Svanström, Y. 2006. Prostitution in Sweden: debates and policies 1980–2004. In Gangoli, G. and N. Westmarland, eds, *International approaches to prostitution: Law and policy in Europe and Asia*, 67–90. Bristol, UK: Policy Press.

Ward, H. and S. Day. 2006. What happens to women who sell sex? Report of a unique occupational cohort. *Sexually Transmitted Infections* 82 (5), 413–417.

16

Exploring resilience among female sex workers in Johannesburg

Lawrence Lekau Mamabolo and Khonzi Mbatha[1]

Introduction

As is the case throughout virtually all of Africa, sex work is criminalized in South Africa under the Sexual Offences Act (23 of 1957, amended in 2007);[2] this criminalization means that all forms of sex work, including the purchasing of sexual services and living off the proceeds of sex work, are illegal. Criminalization and the intense stigma attached to sex work shapes interactions between sex workers and their clients, family, fellow community members, and societal structures such as the police and social services (Scorgie et al. 2013). Despite the criminalized legal status of sex work in Johannesburg, agents of the criminal justice system seldom detain street-based sex workers under anti-prostitution laws because of difficulties associated with gathering sufficient evidence to successfully prosecute prostitution-related cases (Manoek & Shackleton 2011). The Women's Legal Centre (WLC 2011), a nonprofit organization that provides legal advocacy to marginalized women in South Africa, observes that police invoke municipal by-laws or vague non-criminal legislation to arrest and detain, but do not charge sex workers on charges of loitering, indecent exposure, public nuisance, or offences that do not warrant arrest, such as blocking the pavement.

High levels of poverty, unemployment, and inequality in South Africa often force women to migrate to cities such as Johannesburg to look for work opportunities (Borel-Saladin 2013). When they do not find employment, some women start engaging in commercial sex in order to support themselves, their families, and children (Bujra 1975; Busza 2004; Vanwesenbeeck 2001). Sex work is an important source of income in the informal sector and sex workers often provide financially for extended families because of high unemployment rates in South Africa (Gould 2011). Commercial sex work is a more viable option for some people because it pays better than the other types of service work generally open to rural migrant women, including cleaning, cooking, cashier, and security services. Sex work also provides flexible working hours and self-employment with no requirements for formal qualifications, documentation, or sizable initial capital outlay (Oliviera 2011).

Anti-prostitution activists argue that the act of prostitution is not by definition a fully consensual act because all prostitutes, as they would refer to them, are in some capacity forced to sell sex, either by somebody else or due to the unfortunate circumstances of their lives such as poverty, lack of opportunity, drug addiction, and history of childhood abuse or neglect (Burnette et al. 2008). Irrespective of the position one takes on the sex industry, it must be acknowledged that poverty, marginalization, and sexism are very real issues facing women across the globe and especially in Africa. Many sex workers do yearn for alternative or additional forms of employment and yet they usually do not wish to be rescued from their profession; instead, they would prefer to see their profession and their rights recognized (Konstant et al. 2015). Failure to recognize sex work as a legitimate form of labor has very real consequences for sex workers' health and safety, and the South African National AIDS Council (SANAC 2013) acknowledges that criminalization compounds and legitimates the stigma attached to sex work, limits sex worker resiliency, and increases their risk of contractng sexually transmitted infections including the Human Immunodeficiency Virus (HIV). Researchers and activists in the fields of health and HIV have long argued for a rights-based approach to sex work interventions, including decriminalization of all forms of sex work (Scorgie et al. 2013), an approach further supported by SANAC's Strategic Plan for HIV Prevention, Care and Treatment of Sex Workers (SANAC 2013, 9).

The psychological and physical scars of apartheid are still felt two decades into democracy; hence, it would be unreasonable to suggest that decriminalization alone would erase the deeply rooted stigmatization and marginalization associated with sex work. Activists, service providers, and others who hope to provide meaningful services to—or otherwise support—sex workers, need to understand the coping mechanisms of sex workers so that they might not only support them with physical resources but also with psychological tools to cope with their present situation. This chapter accordingly attends to the subject of resilience in sex work, which has received limited scholarly attention in comparison with heated debates about the negative and positive effects of sex work, legal and regulatory approaches, and public health-related issues such as addiction and sexual health. The authors are aware of only two resilience-based research studies in a South African context that specifically investigated sex work, conducted in 2005 by the South African organization Sex Workers Education and Advocacy Taskforce (SWEAT)[3] (Burnes et al. 2012) and the other by Scorgie et al. in 2013.

A predominant approach in psychology adopts a psychopathology-based perspective that focuses on understanding human behavior from a model of mental illness, stress, and abnormal or maladaptive behavior (Maddux et al. 2008). When using the lens of psychopathology in practice, psychologists and other mental health professionals may fail to assess and support sex workers' coping skills holistically. Using such a model creates an understanding of sex work as inherently exploitative and harmful, and the resulting perspective is one in which sex workers are mentally ill, unable to keep other jobs due to character defects, and otherwise pathologized in ways that contribute to adversarial relationships between sex workers, governments, and legal bodies, mandating that sex work should be illegal because of its perceived detriments to society.

A resilience-based model of sex work can accordingly provide alternative ways for researchers, advocates, and clinical practitioners to more holistically and accurately conceptualize the challenges that sex workers face (Burnes et al. 2012). Like many other kinds of work, sex work can be a stressful job and it is important to understand how sex workers cope with the types of stresses they experience in order to promote positive coping mechanisms and design interventions that facilitate effective problem-solving among sex workers to help them cope with the difficult situations they encounter (Fick 2005). This chapter derives from a study that, with these goals in mind, explored heterosexual street-based female sex workers' abilities to cope with challenges they encounter in the sex industry and to explore factors that promote active coping mechanisms.

Resilience in sex work

When individuals are exposed to traumatic or stressful situations, as street-based sex workers often are, some may display psychological distress while others may have the ability to positively adapt to adversity and function competently; such positive adjustments are referred to as resilience (Yuen et al. 2013). The task of predicting an individual's ability to practice resilience is complicated because there is no universally defined concept of what constitutes resilient behavior. In some cases, resiliency is defined by the absence of psychopathology, prolonged stress response patterns, or maladaptive coping, and in other cases resilience is defined by having superior coping mechanisms, on average, over a longitudinal course of life-span development (Southwick et al. 2014). Braverman (2001, 2), defines resilience as "a concept that incorporates two components: (a) exposure to significant stressors or risks, and (b) demonstration of competence and successful adaptation." Resilience is a set of processes rather than a fixed characteristic and can account for the ways that individuals have adapted to numerous challenges within sex work for millennia (McNeil 2010).

It is key for services providers, advocates, and others who wish to meaningfully support sex workers to understand how they develop their abilities to adapt and survive in the face of poverty, unemployment, sexism, racism, and numerous other structural vulnerabilities that often inform their decision to sell sex. Despite sex workers' experiences with marginalization, stigmatization, violence, and many other human rights abuses, the fact that the sex industry continues to thrive is an indication of sex workers' resilience.[4] This chapter analyzes some of the many different techniques sex workers use to cope with challenges they face as they go about earning a living.

Challenges faced by Johannesburg sex workers

Participants in the study that informs this chapter reported numerous challenges related to their engagement in commercial sex, including physical and emotional abuse by clients, verbal abuse by the public, and secondary victimization by health professionals and law enforcement. Sex workers are vulnerable to clients who abuse them with impunity because sex workers are not protected by law in South Africa and indeed are criminalized under existing legislation. Lorraine, an emigrant from Zimbabwe, and Mbalenhle, an internal migrant from Kwa-Zulu Natal, indicate the following when it comes to abuse by clients:

> Someone just comes and say hey you I gave you my money or say hey, let's have sex without a condom and when you disagree they just assault you. Some clients say I gave you my money but you don't want to give me the way I want, then they assault you and leave.
>
> *(Lorraine)*

> Sometimes when they come they come with guns and say open the whole vagina, open your legs wide. There are many things we go through here even death.
>
> *(Mbalenhle)*

This abuse often leaves physical scars on sex workers that remind them about the dangers associated with it. Indeed, 32-year-old Nomusa showed me lifelong scars inflicted by clients and alluded to what transpired when she was a novice sex worker: "Since I joined sex work you see here (pointing at scar on the head) I was assaulted by a client" (Nomusa). Some participants noted that those scars act as a reminder for sex workers to take precautionary measures where necessary in order to save their lives. Clients also sometimes take advantage of sex workers' vulnerability, especially when they are aware that business is not going well, especially by requesting condom-less penetrative sex in return for extra cash, potentially exposing both parties to the risk of contracting HIV and other sexually transmitted infections as concerned Mbalenhle indicates: "Eish, sometimes you enter with a client and they will tell you they do not want to use a condom and it is up to you if you want to give me or not" (Mbalenhle). Prejudice resulting from stigma attached to prostitution by the public often leads to discrimination and verbal abuse on the basis of one's working in the sex industry.

> People will pass by, sometimes during the day insulting us and everyone would be listening, you understand especially men like to call us *magosha*[5] things like that.
>
> *(Koketso)*

> Like us here in Johannesburg we do not enter other clinics because we do not want to be undermined.
>
> *(Daphney)*

Such widespread negative public perceptions result in secondary victimization by biased health professionals and law enforcers in the form of poor treatment, fear of being ridiculed, and verbal abuse as alluded above by Koketso, who has primary school education, and Daphney who joined sex work in 2006.

Participants reported that harassment from the police had decreased since they organized a protest march through SISONKE,[6] a sex worker rights movement, but because sex work is illegal, there is still victimization by law enforcers in some instances. "We work on the streets not hotels so wherever we go police or metro police just close the place if someone complains even if that person is a sex worker complaining about a client" (Zanele).

When sex workers report incidents, the police fail to assist them, thus contributing to their secondary victimization by not providing any assistance or redress. Zanele, a divorcee who has ailing parents, alluded for example that law enforcers often choose to close down the sex work venue that employs the sex worker complainant, rather than addressing a reported incident whether reported by the client, the public, or sometimes sex workers themselves.

Factors contributing to sex workers' resilience

The majority of female sex workers interviewed believe that they are eking out a living to support their children and families, because sex work is an important livelihood for some unemployed women in South Africa, as Koketso, Lorraine, and Mbalenhle allude to below:

> To tell you the truth in this business of sex work I'm a long time, I raised my son alone as a single mother now he is old enough and I'm still raising him to be a big man so that he can take care of himself.
>
> *(Koketso)*

> I just tell myself that my life is here in Johannesburg, I'm a sex worker. I'm a sex worker and it won't change, this is my work.
>
> *(Lorraine)*

There is no other way to survive except sex work for me.

(Mbalenhle)

The women regard commercial sex as a business transaction, simply a means to generate money through offering some form of service (McNeil 2010), for example: "[T]hey must know that we do this thing to help each other, I'm helping him with a service as a client and he is also helping me with money you see" (Mbalenhle).

Research shows that resilient people have a purpose in life and most of their activities are guided by that purpose (Bronk et al. 2010). Interviewed sex workers had a purpose because they were "pushed" by some force, economic or otherwise, to become sex workers and accordingly had a broader goal to improve their lives. "I was supporting my family with the money I was getting at my previous work, I was working then I came here to Johannesburg after I lost my work to be a sex worker" (Nomusa).

Nomusa, who is a regular internal migrant, indicates that she was a bread winner working as a clerk, meaning that she provided for her family, and when she lost her employment and still believed it was her duty to provide for her family as a nurturer she relocated from Eastern Cape province to Gauteng province to be a sex worker. Bronk et al. (2010) indicate that purpose as a motivator orients life goals and daily decisions by directing the use of personal resources such as time, energy, and effort toward pro-social aims, like earning a living to support one's family or otherwise to advance in life.

Sex workers also reported a purpose and sense of obligation to raise their children and support their families. SISONKE's mobilizer and Mothers for the Future's founder Duduzile Dlamini is quoted as saying, "Children of sex workers deserve the right to education, health and safety. The South African government should respect my job and decriminalize sex work for my children's future" (Lakhani & Dlamini 2016, 17). This does not only display purpose but also an obligation from sex workers as mothers, nurturers, and breadwinners to provide a better future for their children through sex work. It also indicates the lengths they are willing to go in order to support themselves, their children, and their families, even though there is a risk of being ridiculed, humiliated, arrested, abused, and even killed by clients (Lakhami & Dlamini 2016).

Some sex workers entered the sex industry because it pays better than other service jobs, such as being a cashier. This is the case for Zama, who was a domestic worker and believes that the South African government does not care about sex workers:

I saw that there is plenty of work and money here in sex work so I decided to quit my cleaning job and be a sex worker full-time because to wake up and go to work and at the end of the month you get little money and I saw that what I get at the cleaning job I can make it within two days or in a day if it is busy like this on month end.

(Zama)

Mental health has an impact on a very wide range of outcomes for individuals, including whether one will live a healthy lifestyle and be able to gain high earnings. These outcomes are not just a consequence of the absence of mental illness but are associated with the presence of positive mental health (Friedli 2009). The literature on resilience and capability is centrally concerned with positive adaptation, protective factors and assets like earnings that moderate risk factors and therefore reduce the impact of risk on outcomes (Friedli 2009). Interviewed sex workers also indicated that sex work reduced their financial stress and this in turn could have improved their quality of life.

Sex workers also showed resilience by indicating that they support each other, work together, and share personal experiences and emotions related to sex work, as Lorraine and Refilwe mention:

I speak with other friends of mine who are also sex workers and we guide each other regarding work issues.

(Lorraine)

Yes, we support each other, we talk and we are free here. Even when they say we do not agree we do not show it and we do not want people to stick their noses into our business, especially abusive men [. . .] when we see that things are not well and getting tough, we hold each other.

(Refilwe)

The development and strengthening of relationships among community members, including sex workers, fosters resilience through feelings of connectedness, cohesion, and the development of social capital (Arewasikporn et al. 2013). Social support is an important and valuable resource in the social environment and the availability of social support plays and important role in resilience (Herrick et al. 2013). Sex workers discuss their challenges among themselves and encourage each other where needed, even if they sometimes have conflicts of their own. Kwon (2013) further states that when key populations such as sex workers share challenges among themselves, they tend to accept their reality and situation, and tend to be less burdened emotionally; this assists in dealing with issues such as stigma and discrimination, therefore increasing their resilience.

When sex workers work together as a community, they are able to achieve success even with goals that may initially seem impossible to achieve. Interviewed sex workers were all aware of the existence of the sex worker rights group SISONKE even though some are not contributing members, and SISONKE assisted them by offering supportive services including legal assistance through the Women's Legal Centre.

You see with SISONKE, if we are arrested we call SISONKE and they help us, if the police harass us and you call SISONKE they help us.

(Koketso)

We have SISONKE that fights for sex workers' rights.

(Lorraine)

Koketso and Lorraine indicated that SISONKE is a pillar of strength for them and other interviewed sex workers mentioned that abuse by police and other public officials has decreased since SISONKE started to assist them.

Sex workers also reported engaging in flight, fight, or freeze responses to stress, which are also known as survival reflexes, when faced with a stressful event (Rothschild 1997). During the interviews with participants, it appeared that these survival reflexes are used depending on the situation the female sex workers find themselves in. A situation where a freeze response might be useful is, for example, where there is nowhere to run or where danger cannot be avoided, such as being threatened with a weapon. The flight response is more useful for a sex worker who has analyzed the situation carefully and seen that she can out-run the perpetrator, and the fight response is more suitable when a sex worker realizes that she can overpower the perpetrator, or when a flight or freeze response will not yield positive results:

The girl said she was helped by a car it was a distance but she said that she was alone and she was naked because the client made her take off her clothes she said she ran and ran, they were outside and she ran God gave her strength she said.

(Rudzani)

We entered a car wash nicely and he pulled out the gun and removed the condom. And there was no way I could scream.

(Tanya)

You will find that you are fighting with this client because they want their money back.

(Tshidi)

Rudzani above eluded her attacker by out running him, which is an example of a flight response, while Tanya used a freeze response to save her life, and Tshidi indicates that at times they fight if the situation permits in order to keep their earnings, an example of fight response.

Sex workers also described the safety precautions they take in their work, which exemplifies the strengthening effects associated with resilience (Rutter 2012). This means that services providers, advocates, and others must examine how sex workers' responses to different situations strengthen them and their communities, rather than solely assessing their negative reactions. Resilient, experienced female sex workers can assess the likelihood of danger accurately and take the necessary steps to avoid harm, sometimes even giving clients their money back if they become aggressive. The examples below show how experienced sex workers who have been in the industry for more than a decade (Daphney and Mbalenhle) act in case of danger:

I give them their money back because I do not want to be assaulted (laughing).

(Daphney)

You must be obedient and think about your life, you see, you need to avoid, these people you must give them their money and you will not die.

(Mbalenhle)

Safety mechanisms such as recording a vehicle number plate has shown to be a success because some clients have been successfully prosecuted through the assistance of SISONKE and the Women's Legal Centre. Sex workers have learnt from experience that for their safety they must go to a neutral place or somewhere where the client will have a lesser chance of causing harm to them.

We always take vehicle number plates even if you say we are just going nearer, we take it. If I say my friend: take the vehicle number plate, they do, in case I do not come back because they abuse us.

(Refilwe)

Refilwe, who at first hesitated to become a sex worker but did so in order to improve her living conditions, said that safety is of paramount importance and as sex workers they always share safety techniques to minimize harm or even evade death at times.

Resilient people are optimistic about their future and will always look at how things can turn out for the better if certain practices are outlawed, improved, or totally eradicated. Most of the time they will play an active role in contributing to the betterment of the situation and have a strong belief in the future (Coutu 2002; Everall et al. 2006; Luthans et al. 2005). Even though these interviewed sex workers experienced challenges on the streets, they were still optimistic about their future and their children's future and contribute actively to the improvement of sex workers' lives and recognition—all of which are some of the key characteristics of resilient people (Connor & Davidson 2003; Kwon 2013).

> I think in South Africa, people should start understanding the sex industry. Like, we should have rights.
>
> *(Rudzani)*

> At least if they tell us what to do so that our places of work cannot be closed and that they (places) become legal and we girls on the streets become legal.
>
> *(Zanele)*

The interviewed sex workers above not only show hope, but they are also aware of what needs to be done so that their situation can be better. Moreover, as this section has shown, through experience, female sex workers learn survival techniques that are useful to keep them alive on the streets (Fick 2005).

Coutu (2002) contends that resilient people use effective survival strategies according to the situation they find themselves in, have a firm understanding of reality and fiction, and the ability to improvise when necessary. However, even though sex workers in this chapter showed some form of resilience and how they coped with situations they find themselves in, these techniques have limits as sometimes the incidents are so severe that they need more sophisticated interventions to deal with the physical and mental trauma involved. There might be a level of fear of the unknown because of the criminalized environment sex workers operate in. At times when individuals are exposed to challenging environments for a prolonged time they might show signs of mental problems like post-traumatic stress disorder (PTSD), which might hamper an individual in fully realizing their potential.

Building on sex workers' strengths to foster resilience

Resilience and positive psychology are highly significant in sex work research, especially taking into account that resilience studies emerged from this branch of psychology (Park 2012). Positive psychologists have shown that a variety of brief interventions can, in the short term, increase well-being and reduce problems such as depression. These interventions have a role not only in remedying distress following experience with adversity but also in building resources that reduce the negative effects of suffering (Park 2012). The strength-based perspective is an intervention technique employed by positive psychologists who believe that individuals and their families have strengths, resources, and the ability to recover from adversity (Hammond & Zimmerman 2010).

Based on the strength-based perspective, the following principles serve as the foundation for guiding and implementing strength-based practice and programmes as adapted to sex work:

1. *Given the right conditions and resources, sex workers' capacity to learn and grow can be nurtured and realized.*

    The South African National HIV Sex Worker Plan 2016–2019 (SANAC 2016) stresses the need for sex workers to be personally developed in order to increase their resilience. It also emphasizes the need for sex work laws to be reformed so that the conditions of sex workers can be improved and resources can be freely available to sex workers without fear of stigma of discrimination. SISONKE has made strides in assisting sex workers to fend for themselves, their families, and their children. It has decreased the level of stigma and discrimination among communities, law enforcement agencies, and health professionals using a variety of interventions. By doing that sex workers are starting to be more vocal than ever and at times individually challenge injustices associated with being a sex worker. Furthermore this has increased their resilience.

2. *Sex workers change and grow through their strengths and capacities.*

Depending on their level of skills, female sex workers indicated that they adapt to constant change using different coping techniques and safety precautions. They are in charge of their lives and do not need society to feel pity for them but to understand them and the reasons why they became sex workers.

3. *Sex workers are experts of their own situation.*

The results indicated that sex workers are the experts of their situation and understand it better than people who are not in the sex industry. They showed resilience by adapting to the many challenges they face daily, using safety precautions and techniques demanded by the situation they find themselves in. They understand that clients are two sides of the same coin; they are often abusive but also good in that they help them make a living to support their families. Furthermore, they are aware of what law enforcers could do to assist them. Training programmes must be guided by sex workers as they know what they need and how those programmes could assist them.

4. *Criminalization of sex work is the problem, not sex work.*

The results of this study alluded to problems inherent in the criminalization of sex work. Criminalization is a stumbling block and an insult to efforts by the South African government to reduce epidemics like HIV through the National Strategic Plan on HIV, TB, and STIs (2017–2022), the National Sex Worker HIV Plan (2016–2019), and hate-speech criminalization through the Prevention and Combating of Hate Crimes and Hate Speech Bill.

5. *Criminalization "blinds" sex workers and prevents them from noticing and appreciating their strengths and capacity to find their own meaningful solutions.*

Sex workers are often stigmatized and have a lesser chance of gaining the necessary psychological resources to be able to build their resilience and strength. As results indicated, sex workers felt a need to be empowered, but this very process can be greatly undermined by the criminalization of sex work. Under criminalization, the abuse of sex workers by clients and the general public is evident from their narratives. The abuse also makes it difficult for sex workers to find meaningful solutions to the challenges they face.

6. *Sex workers are doing the best they can in light of their experiences to date.*

The results of the study indicate that sex workers are resilient and tap into many resources such as cohesion among themselves in order to survive the sex industry. They "choose" sex work because of the economic challenges they experience. The earnings made from sex work are used to upgrade their economic status and to help support their families and children.

Furthermore, they indicated that the public should be sensitive to the appalling conditions they work under and the reasons they became sex workers. They were of the opinion that they are doing the best they could under harsh South African economic conditions.

7. *The ability to change is within sex workers.*

Some sex workers indicated that if an opportunity arose, they could leave the sex industry, others indicated that they need to be empowered and continue working in the sex industry, and others indicated that if they could be empowered, they would work as sex workers on a part-time basis. The general public cannot decide on their behalf what is good, rather, they are urged to respect sex workers' choices and support them.

8. *Sex workers want good things for themselves and have good intentions.*

The participants in this inquiry indicated that by offering sexual services, they have good intentions, and contrary to popular belief, they take all necessary safety precautions to protect themselves and their clientele. According to them, commercial sex is work and it is also a way of earning a living in order to support themselves, their families and their children.

Conclusion

Decriminalization of sex work in South Africa might be coming, but not soon, and in fact change in this direction is moving at a tortoise pace. We therefore need to support sex workers with psycho-social resources that will assist them in dealing as best they can with the challenges they are facing currently. Organizations such as SWEAT and sex worker movements like SISONKE should continue to holistically support sex workers. Moreover, psychological research on resilience should also examine the role of resilience in marginalized groups such as sex workers instead of focusing on a psychopathological lens. Too little has been reported within this body of work on functioning individuals and groups such as sex workers that operate optimally under appalling conditions (Luthans et al. 2007). Resilience is based on many factors and also depends on context and time. More research needs to be conducted to understand how sex workers cope in order to provide better-targeted help by organizations that support them.

Notes

1 Khonzi Mbatha is a Senior Lecturer at the University of South Africa (Department of Psychology) who supervised me (Lawrence Lekau Mamabolo) during my MA studies when producing this chapter.
2 In 1988 the apartheid government renamed the Immorality Act that criminalized sexual relations between different racial groups to Sexual Offences Act.
3 Sex Worker Education and Advocacy Taskforce (SWEAT) was founded in the early 1990s by Shane Petzer, a male sex worker, and Ilse Pauw, a clinical psychologist. SWEAT advocates for the decriminalization of adult sex work and has an advocacy programme reaching sex workers nationally to engage in issues related to health and legal reform.
4 This does not mean that factors such as inequality, poverty, low levels of education, and lack of employment should be overlooked, as they may also be at play.
5 *Magosha* is a degrading term or name used to call sex workers. The term also refers to easy woman, whore, etc.
6 In 2003 SWEAT supported the launch of SISONKE, a sex workers' movement that was initiated in order to gather credible information on sex work and the sex work industry.

References

Arewasikporn, A., M.C. Davis, and A. Zautra. 2013. Resilience: A framework for understanding the dynamic relationship between social relations and health. In M.L. Mathews and N.A. Roberts (Eds.), *Health and social relationships: The good, the bad, and the complicated.* Washington, DC: APA.

Borel-Saladin, J. 2013. *Social polarisation and migration to Johannesburg.* Sussex, UK: University of Sussex.

Braverman, M.T. 2001. *Applying resilience theory to the prevention of adolescent substance abuse.* Berkeley, CA: University of California, Center for Youth Development.

Bronk, K.C., W.H. Finch, and T.L. Talib. 2010. Purpose in life among high ability adolescents. *High Ability Studies, 21,* 133–145.

Bujra, J.M. 1975. Women entrepreneurs of early Nairobi. *Canadian Journal of African Studies, 9*, 213–234.

Burnette, M.L., E. Lucas, M. Ilgen, S.M. Frayne, J. Mayo, and J.C. Weitlauf. 2008. Prevalence and health correlates of prostitution among patients entering treatment for substance use disorders. *Archive of General Psychiatry, 65*, 337–344. doi: 10.1001/archpsyc.65.3.337.

Burnes, T.R., R. Schept, and S.L. Long. 2012. A resilience-based lens of sex work: Implications for professional psychologists. *Professional Psychology: Research and Practice, 43*(2), 137–144. doi: 10.1037/a0026205.

Busza, J. 2004. Sex work and migration: The dangers of oversimplification. A case study of Vietnamese women in Cambodia. *Health and Human Rights, 7*(2), 213–249. doi: 10.2307/4065357.

Coutu, D. 2002. How resilience works. *Harvard Business Review, 80*(2), 46–55.

Connor, K.M. and J.R.T. Davidson. 2003. Development of a new resilience scale: The Connor-Davidson resilience scale (CD-RISC). *Depression and Anxiety, 18*, 76–82.

Department of Justice and Constitutional Development. (Act No. 32 December, 2007). *Criminal Law (Sexual Offences and Related Matters) Amendment Act.*

Everall, R., J. Altrows, and B. Paulson. 2006. Creating a future: A study of resilience in suicidal female adolescents. *Journal of Counselling and Development, 84*, 461–470.

Fick, N. 2005. *Coping with stigma, discrimination and violence: Sex workers talk about their experiences.* Cape Town: SWEAT.

Friedli, N. 2009. *Mental health, resilience and inequalities. World Health Organisation.* www.euro.who.int. Retrieved from /__data/assets/pdf_file/0012/100821/E92227.pdf.

Gould, C. 2011. Trafficking? Exploring the relevance of the notion of human trafficking to describe the lived experience of sex workers in Cape Town, South Africa. *Crime, Law & Social Change, 56*, 529–546.

Hammond, W., and R. Zimmerman. 2010. *A strength-based perspective.* Retrieved from www.resil.ca.

Herrick, A.L., M.S. Friedman, and R. Stall. 2013. Gay men's health and the theory of cultural resilience. In C.J. Patterson and A.R. D'Augelli (Eds.), *Handbook of psychology and sexual orientation* (pp. 191–203). New York: Oxford University Press.

Konstant, T., J. Rangasami, M. Stacey, M. Stewart, and C. Nogoduka. 2015. *Estimating the number of sex workers in South Africa: Rapid population size estimation.* New York: Springer Media. doi: 10.1007/s10461-014-0981-y.

Kwon, P. 2013. Resilience in lesbian, gay, and bisexual individuals. *Personality and Social Psychology Review, 17*, 371–383. doi: org/10.1177/1088868313490248.

Lakhani, I. and D. Dlamini. 2016. The mother of the child holds the knife on the sharper edge. *Research for Sex Workers, 15*, 16.

Luthans, F., B. Avolio, F. Walumbwa, and W. Li. 2005. The psychological capital of chinese workers: Exploring the relationship with performance. *Management and Organizational Review, 1*(2), 249–271.

Luthans, F., C. Youssef, and B. Avolio. 2007. *Psychological capital: Developing the human competitive edge.* New York: Oxford University Press.

McNeill, M. 2010. *An older profession than you may have thought.* New York: The Honest Courtesan.

Maddux, J.E., G. Mason, J.T. Gosselin, and A. Barbara. 2008. *Winstead conceptions of psychopathology: A social constructionist perspective.* Malibu, CA: Pepperdine University.

Manoek, S., and S, Shackleton. 2011. *SWEAT condemns NPA guidelines on prosecution of sex workers.* Cape Town: SWEAT.

Oliviera, E. 2011. *Migrant women in sex work: Does urban space impact on self-(re)presentation in Hillbrow, Johannesburg?* (Unpublished MA degree thesis). Johannesburg: University of the Witwatersrand.

Park, N. 2012. Adversity, resilience, and thriving: A positive psychology perspective on research and practices. In R.A. McMackin, E. Newman, J.M. Fogler, and T. M. Keane (Eds.), *Trauma therapy in context: The science and craft of evidence-based practice* (pp. 121–140). doi.org/10.1037/13746-006.

Rothschild, B. 1997. Post-traumatic stress disorder: Identification and diagnosis. *Swiss Journal of Social Work.* www.healing-arts.org/tir/n-r-rothschild.htm.

Rutter, M. 2012. Resilience as a dynamic concept. *Development and Psychopathology, 24*, 335–344. doi: 10.1017/S0954579412000028.

SANAC. 2013. *National strategic plan for HIV Prevention, care and treatment for sex workers.* South Africa, Pretoria: SANAC.

SANAC. 2016. *The South African national sex worker HIV plan 2016–2019.* South Africa, Pretoria: SANAC.

Scorgie, F., K. Vasey, E. Harper, M. Richter, P. Nare, S. Maseko, and M. Chersich. 2013. Human rights abuses and collective resilience among sex workers in four African countries: A qualitative study. *Global Health, 9*(1), 33. doi: 10.1186/1744-8603-9-33.

Southwick, S., G. Bonanno, A. Masten, C. Panter-Brick, and R. Yehuda. 2014. Resilience definitions, theory, and challenges: Interdisciplinary perspectives. *European Journal of Psychotraumatology, 5*(25338), 1–14. doi: org10.3402/ejpt.v5.25338.

Vanwesenbeeck, I. 2001. Another decade of social scientific work on sex work: A review of research 1990–2000. *Annual Review of Sex Research, 12,* 242–289.

Women's Legal Centre. 2011. *Every sex worker, human rights defender.* Cape Town: WLC.

Yuen, W., W. Wong, C. Tang, E. Holroyd, A. Tiwari, D. Fong, and W. Chin. 2013. Evaluating the effectiveness of personal resilience and enrichment programme (PREP) for HIV prevention among female sex workers: A randomised controlled trial. *Bio Med Central Public Health, 13,* 683–692. doi: 10.1186/1471-2458-13-683.

Part III
Global knowledge flows

17

Global knowledge flows

An introduction

Susan Dewey, Isabel Crowhurst, and Chimaraoke Izugbara

Introduction

The development and global circulation of "best practices" for sex industry knowledge production, regulatory measures, and legislation reflects the existence of complex circuits of communication among scholars, policymakers, activists, and others concerned with issues in this field. Key themes in existing literature include connections between this field and global movements that variously coalesce around anti-trafficking, social inequalities, feminisms, queer/LGBTQ rights movements, and how these dominant concerns influence available funding for research and activism. Chapters in this section engage with these ongoing challenges while offering clear directions for future research.

Key themes in existing literature

The trafficking paradigm regards all commercial sex as the product of force, fraud, and coercion and accordingly advocates for sex workers' rescue and rehabilitation. This globally prevalent paradigm informs a heteronormative master narrative in which unscrupulous third parties trick vulnerable, naïve young women into the sex industry, where they face abuse and various forms of denigration (Snajdr, 2013). Closely resembling "white slavery" panics in Progressive Era (1880–1920) North America and Western Europe by focusing on lighter-skinned, native-born women as victims and racialized, migrant men as violent perpetrators, this master narrative has been actively promulgated by international organizations, national governments, and municipalities (Doezema, 2010; Kempadoo, 2015). This close resemblance has led numerous scholars to critique globally prevalent anti-trafficking approaches as a moral panic that inflates or otherwise skews statistical evidence and eschews contradictory points of view as the product of an immoral agenda (Weitzer, 2007; Blanchette & da Silva, 2012).

Intersections between the sex industry and sexism, racism, classism, citizenship status, and xenophobia give rise to questions regarding how this labor sector replicates or reinforces these global inequalities. These inequalities have deep historical roots; for instance, pervasively held European colonial beliefs about the supposedly inferior moral character and sexualities of colonized people served to justify oppressive policing of women in sex work under the guise of maintaining public health and order (Levine, 2003). Today these inequalities are most apparent in how the sex industry's most disadvantaged participants face intensified policing measures because of their status as rural-to-urban migrants (Shah, 2014) or cross-border workers (Chin, 2013) seeking to improve their lives. Often such measures derive their justification from the ostensible need to protect migrants from sexual exploitation, even though many migrants enter the sex industry precisely because xenophobia or irregular citizenship status excludes them from other forms of work (Sharma, 2005).

Feminist movements have historically been at the forefront of advocacy efforts that variously promote approaches that span a continuum from sex-as-labour to prostitution as the ultimate form of oppressive male domination. The prevailing anti-trafficking paradigm emphasizes a need to protect women's bodily borders from invasion in ways that reflect broader global concerns regarding securitization (Szorenyi, 2014). This paradigm also reflects solidarity with the United States and other global criminal justice systems among second-wave feminists who oppose prostitution as a form of violence against women and regard police and other state agents as allies in their efforts to abolish it (Bernstein, 2010). In their focus on the act of prostitution and the meanings ascribed to it, such framings ignore how social class, poverty, and related factors are driving forces in many individuals' decisions to engage in commercial sex (Beloso, 2012). Sex worker rights activism typically engages with feminist perspectives by focusing on women's agency and rights to bodily autonomy while also considering the feminization of poverty, albeit in ways that have faced significant global challenges to reducing prostitution-related stigma (Sultana, 2015).

Queer/LGBTQ rights movements have, in many ways, engaged with and built upon the work of feminist theorists and activists in this field, particularly by questioning heteronormative assumptions about sexualities, associated gender norms, and the political economy underlying both (Laing, Pilcher, & Smith, 2015). Queer theory opens analytical vistas through critical engagement with core assumptions that underpin many globally prevalent assumptions about the sex industry, including the notion that objectification is always inherently harmful (Cahill, 2014). By drawing on successful rights-based movements to contest heteronormativity, queer theorists have been able to propose the mobilization of similar strategies to promote sex workers' human and labour rights (Kallock, 2017). Work in this theoretical field likewise emphasizes the inadequacy of dominant (and typically heteronormative) approaches—particularly those that mandate government agents to rescue and rehabilitate individuals from their workplaces in the sex industry—to address the totality of intersectional forces confronting poor sex workers of colour (Mitchell, 2016).

Available funding for research and activism emerges from dominant cultural concerns regarding the sex industry (Clancey, Khushrushahi, & Ham, 2014). Mass media attention through salacious accounts of extreme exploitation and celebrity endorsement of prevailing anti-trafficking approaches that regard prostitution as a form of "modern-day slavery" are the primary means by which the general public in any country in the world learns about related issues (Haynes, 2014). Media coverage of global sporting events often emphasize the threat of sexual exploitation thought to accompany a large number of temporary male visitors and, in so doing, reflect underlying issues of concern regarding simmering crises (Isgro, Stehle, & Weber, 2013). Such crises can include national security, fears about crime, and xenophobia, but all produce the same panicked results when presented by mass media in ways that rarely depict the central concerns facing those in the sex industry, including the need to earn a living (Soderlund, 2005).

Chapter overview

Dewey, Crowhurst, and Izugbara (Chapter 18) juxtapose global discourses on the sex industry from the Americas, Europe, and Africa to demonstrate the complexity inherent to prostitution and its regulation within particular contexts while remaining attuned to how such discourses circulate among and within these contexts in ways that directly impact sex workers' lives. Varela (Chapter 19) examines how these global knowledge flows adhere to particular cultural scripts and political rhetoric that, in turn, provide them with performative powers. Adhikari (Chapter 20) identifies gaps between dominant anti-trafficking discourses of rescue/reintegration and the realities faced "on the ground" by third-sector and government workers tasked with the policing or management of commercial sex.

Schuler and Oliveira (Chapter 21) analyze the challenges and benefits of a participatory arts-based project with sex workers that facilitated creative self-expression and capacity-building to assist sex workers in producing a newsletter to help them advocate for their rights. Phoenix (Chapter 22) argues that an informed analysis of how, where, and why the boundaries get drawn between prostitution and child abuse tells us much about state, official, and hegemonic ideals of childhood, girlhood, sex, and victimhood. Mitchell (Chapter 23) explores how critical examination of the portrayal of migrant men as rational actors functioning in the classical *homo economicus* form reveals how migrant women are denied that same status and treated as vulnerable creatures incapable of reason and self-determination when faced with difficult conditions. Zhaivoronok and Kondakov (Chapter 24) analyze the specific forms that the global feminist "sex wars" have taken in Russia to suggest alternatives to these enduringly dichotomous ways of thinking about the sex industry.

Future directions

It is now well established that global discourses on the sex industry circulate through complex political networks, yet no systematic documentation or analysis exists regarding the funding streams that facilitate particular types of research, intervention, and activism. Sex industry researchers routinely accept the economic realities that shape decision-making processes vis-à-vis commercial sex but have yet to systematically analyze the political economy that suffuses funded work in this field or in activism related to it. Such a systematic analysis would likely illuminate the array of interests/actors that coalesce around the sex industry as a social issue and a material reality, thus facilitating further empirical inquiry into what the sex industry (or casting participation in it as "sex trafficking") symbolizes for these interests/actors. Fully understanding these motivations and corresponding actions by "following the money" will likely result in suggestions for engaging in meaningful dialogue with these interests/actors rather than an ongoing echo chamber within ideological silos.

A related area for further engagement might involve the "street-level bureaucrats" tasked with the everyday implementation of the socio-legal practices that govern the sex industry and/or anti-trafficking initiatives. Sex industry researchers have by now recognized that significant disconnections exist between anti-trafficking rhetoric and on-the-ground realities, with even those who self-identify as neo-abolitionists recognizing the low numbers of arrests made of "traffickers" or assistance measures provided to their "victims." While some neo-abolitionists might argue that such low numbers result from the sex industry's clandestine nature, most law enforcement professionals would certainly not make the same claims with respect to the equally clandestine and stigmatized illicit drug economy. Researchers would do well to respectfully engage with criminal justice professionals, social services providers, and other "stakeholders" as a means to understand the difficulties inherent in enforcing legislation and policy that is, in the vast majority of cases, derived from dominant cultural values regarding morality than it is from the realities at work within the sex industry. Doing so might help to facilitate the kind of collaborative governance among divergent stakeholders that has successfully been implemented in some locales through inclusion of sex workers' perspectives (Wagenaar, Altink, & Amesberger, 2017).

Future research will likely continue to recast sex industry involvement as generally coupled with other means of earning a living in the informal economic sector. Sex industry researchers generally recognize that sexual labor is disproportionately performed by those who are marginalized by economic need, undocumented status, and other historical inequalities. A vibrant global literature on informal economies exists, yet this research has remained underexplored by sex industry researchers, who tend to focus on commercial sexual exchanges to the exclusion of other ways that participants in their work also earn a living. Uniting these literatures, and the perspectives that undergird them, offers great potential to engage with broader global initiatives to improve socio-economic well-being by recasting commercial sex work as another aspect of activities such as market trade, street vending, and other activities undertaken by a significant proportion of the people struggling with economic disenfranchisement worldwide.

References

Beloso, Brooke. 2012. Sex, Work, and the Feminist Erasure of Class. *Signs: Journal of Women in Culture and Society* 38(1): 47–70.

Bernstein, Elizabeth. 2010. Militarized Humanitarianism Meets Carceral Feminism: The Politics of Sex, Rights, and Freedom in Contemporary Antitrafficking Campaigns. *Signs: Journal of Women in Culture and Society* 36(1): 45–71.

Blanchette, Thaddeus and da Silva, Ana Paula. 2012. On Bullshit and the Trafficking of Women: Moral Entrepreneurs and the Invention of Trafficking in Persons in Brazil. *Dialectical Anthropology* 36(1/2): 1–19.

Cahill, Ann. 2014. The Difference Sameness Makes: Objectification, Sex Work, and Queerness. *Hypatia* 29(4): 840–856.

Chin, Christine. 2013. *Cosmopolitan Sex Workers: Women and Migration in a Global City.* Oxford: Oxford University Press.

Clancey, Alison, Khushrushahi, Noushin, and Ham, Julie. 2014. Do Evidence-Based Approaches Alienate Canadian Anti-Trafficking Funders? *Anti-Trafficking Review* 3: 87–108.

Doezema, Jo. 2010. *Sex Slaves and Discourse Masters: The Construction of Trafficking.* London: Zed.

Haynes, Dina Francesca. 2014. The Celebritization of Human Trafficking. *Annals of the American Academy of Political and Social Science* 653: 25–45.

Isgro, Kirsten, Stehle, Maria, and Weber, Beverly, 2013. From Sex Shacks to Mega-Brothels: The Politics of Anti-Trafficking and the 2006 Soccer World Cup. *European Journal of Cultural Studies* 16(2): 171–193.

Kallock, Sara. 2017. Livability: A Politics for Abnormative Lives. *Sexualities* 20. https://doi.org/10.1177/1363460717731929

Kempadoo, Kamala. 2015. The Modern-Day White (Wo)Man's Burden: Trends in Anti-Trafficking and Anti-Slavery Campaigns. *Journal of Human Trafficking* 1(1): 8–20.

Laing, Mary, Pilcher, Katy, and Smith, Nicola, Eds. 2015. *Queer Sex Work.* London: Routledge.

Levine, Philippa. 2003. *Prostitution, Race, and Politics: Policing Venereal Disease in the British Empire.* London: Routledge.

Mitchell, Gregory. 2016. Evangelical Ecstasy Meets Feminist Fury: Sex Trafficking, Moral Panics, and Homonationalism During Global Sporting Events. *GLQ* 22(3): 325–357.

Sharma, Nandita. 2005. Anti-Trafficking Rhetoric and the Making of a Global Apartheid. *NWSA Journal* 17(3): 88–111.

Shah, Swati. 2014. *Street Corner Secrets: Sex, Work, and Migration in the City of Mumbai.* Durham, NC: Duke University Press.

Snajdr, Edward. 2013. Beneath the Master Narrative: Human Trafficking, Myths of Sexual Slavery, and Ethnographic Realities. *Dialectical Anthropology* 37: 14–37.

Soderlund, Gretchen. 2005. Running from the Rescuers: New U.S. Crusades Against Sex Trafficking and the Rhetoric of Abolition. *NWSA Journal* 17(3): 64–87.

Sultana, Habiba. 2015. Sex Worker Activism: Feminist Discourse and HIV in Bangladesh. *Culture, Health & Sexuality* 17(6): 777–788.

Szorenyi, Anna. 2014. Rethinking the Boundaries: Towards a Butlerian Ethics of Vulnerability in Sex Trafficking Debates. *Feminist Review* 107(1): 20–36.

Wagenaar, Hendrik, Altink, Sietske, and Amesberger, Helga. 2017. *Designing Prostitution Policy: Intention and Reality in Regulating the Sex Trade*. Bristol, UK: Policy Press.

Weitzer, Ronald. 2007. The Social Construction of Sex Trafficking: Ideology and Institutionalization of a Moral Crusade. *Politics & Society* 35: 447–475.

18

Globally circulating discourses on the sex industry

A focus on three world regions

Susan Dewey, Isabel Crowhurst, and Chimaraoke Izugbara

Introduction

Chapters in this Handbook affirm the importance of considering context while simultaneously emphasizing cross-cultural similarities in knowledge production about the sex industry, associated legal and regulatory practices, and the impact of both on sex industry participants and the communities in which they live and work. These chapters and the rich bodies of multidisciplinary literature and activism they represent clearly demonstrate the complex contextual dynamics prevalent in each of these areas. Yet, they also link these dynamics to the global circulation of discourse related to governance, research, and the lived experiences of those who make their living within the sex industry. In this chapter, we argue that exercises like the one we undertake in this chapter are essential both to critical engagement with cultural and labor practices in the sex industry and to designing alternatives that respect the core principles of human rights and socio-economic justice enshrined in international law.

Globally, regulations designed to govern the sex industry derive from ideological stances that reflect dominant cultural values and social concerns, including those regarding sexual behaviours, public health, labor, and human rights. These dominant values and concerns directly impact knowledge production by disproportionately allocating government funds, endorsement, or other forms of support to research and initiatives that align with prevailing public sentiments, hence the enormous numbers of research studies and state-funded initiatives that focus on sex trafficking, public health, and the maintenance of social order through the justice system. Dominant values and concerns also reinforce the significant stigma associated with commercial sex irrespective of its legal status, which in turn directly impacts sex workers' relationships with their work, loved ones, and themselves. Stigma likewise harms sex workers by contributing to the conditions that enable violence, isolation/marginalization to unsafe work areas, and exploitative labor practices, even in legal or decriminalized settings. Such stigma impacts other sex industry participants, including third parties and clients, who criminal and civil measures increasingly target as perpetrators of oppressive harms. Sex work-related stigma is also frequently extended to researchers, civil society organizations, and advocates who call for the recognition of the rights of sex workers.

Like the socio-economic, cultural, and political economic forces that produce them, these regulations and their real-world consequences mesh with globally circulating discourses that achieve predominance through endorsement by powerful actors. In this chapter, we accordingly summarize some of the prevailing discourses on the sex industry in the Americas, Europe, and Africa, the regions in which we have each worked for many years. Detailed analyses of particular sex industry venues and contexts are essential for a nuanced understanding of the interactions that take place within them as a means to develop evidence-based law, policy, and interventions. Yet, juxtaposing the predominant discourses surrounding the sex industry within and across world regions is an essential task for those concerned with the impacts of law and policy, the socio-legal and economic forces that drive them, and the political economy that facilitates their global circulation.

The Americas

Comprising a vast geographical region of 46 countries, the Americas span distinctly different hemispheres, cultures, ecosystems, and languages. The boundaries of the Americas encompass the North Pole of the Canadian Arctic, Tierra del Fuego near the southern Antarctic Peninsula, and the easternmost Caribbean island of Barbados, with the western US state of Alaska bordering Russia. The Americas include the 12 countries of South America, 7 Central American nations, 25 independent Caribbean states, and the United States and Canada. These nations have tremendous socio-economic differences; for instance, Haiti struggles with endemic poverty and violence while Costa Rica's excellent and low-cost medical care has fostered a popular medical tourism industry that provides North Americans and Western Europeans with cosmetic surgical procedures they cannot afford in their home countries. Such striking differences are also apparent between countries that share a border, as is the case with the United States and Mexico, whose historically fraught borderlands prompted former Mexican President Sebastián Lerdo de Tejada's oft-quoted observation, "between the weak and the strong there must be a desert" (Creelman, 1911, p. 328).

All countries of the Americas are united by a shared "New World" legacy of colonial conquest, genocide, and slavery created by European conquest, capitalist accumulation, natural resource exploitation, and quest for agricultural lands. Contemporary consequences of these practices are evident in many aspects of the sex industry, including sexual exoticization of women of African descent (Miller-Young, 2015), higher pay and status for white sex workers relative to their peers of color (Brooks, 2010), the Caribbean replacement of "King Sugar" with "King Tourism" reliant on labor performed by people of color for whites (Padilla, 2007), and disproportionately high rates of incarceration among African American women and Latinas for prostitution-related criminal offences (Dewey & St. Germain, 2017). Dominant discourses on the sex industry are as complex as the cultural-historical terrain that characterizes the Americas, but generally take four primary forms: neo-abolitionism, sex worker rights, criminal-justice social services alliances, and harm reduction. In many of these approaches, dominant popular cultural and institutional attention to the sex industry reflects public anxieties about sexual and gender norms.

Neo-abolitionists in the Americas regard all aspects of the sex industry as morally reprehensible either because of its perceived violation of religious-moral principles (Bernstein, 2007) or because it is seen as a form of violence against women (Bernstein, 2010); all support criminalizing the purchase and/or sale of sex as the most effective means to eradicate the practice.

Neo-abolitionists have considerable support from powerful governments, especially the United States, which imposes significant economic sanctions on those countries that do not comply with US recommended methods of prosecuting traffickers, preventing human trafficking, and protecting victims and survivors of trafficking (DeStefano, 2008). The widespread endorsement of such legislation by powerful figures has direct implications for migrants, with prevailing anti-trafficking efforts critiqued as a control mechanism that justifies tightening borders against unwanted migrants in the name of reducing trafficking in both historical and contemporary eras (Doezema, 2010). Critics also note that the neo-abolitionists' focus on the sale and purchase of sex decontextualizes the sex industry from its broader context, thereby negating the agency women demonstrate through the practice of "tactical sex" in otherwise highly constrained socio-economic circumstances (Cabezas, 2009).

Sex worker rights supporters regard transactional sex as a form of feminized labor interconnected with other aspects of the economic processes that disproportionately negatively impact the working poor. Sex worker rights groups first emerged in the United States in conjunction with other rights-based movements in the late 1970s (Leigh, 1997) but now exist in nearly all countries in the Americas with varying degrees of political power and support; in Brazil, where prostitution is decriminalized, sex workers are active partners in public health efforts (Blanchette & da Silva, 2011) whereas sex worker rights activists in the United States routinely lament the impact that prostitution's criminalization has on their abilities to organize. Sex worker rights activist Annie Oakley, for example, conveys the plight of sex workers vulnerable to a host of social and legal sanctions in noting, "When you refuse to recognize someone's humanity, you don't have to worry about their working conditions, their safety, their health, their ability to make a decent living" (Oakley, 2007, p. 10). Proponents of sex worker rights often support prostitution's decriminalization because, as happens in the Mexican border city of Tijuana, legalization creates "a bifurcated industry with both a formal and legal sector and an informal and illegal sector" (Katsulis, 2009, p. 64).

Criminal justice–social services alliances regard the sex industry, and street prostitution in particular, as the product of addiction, compromised mental health, and trauma in ways that justify state intervention in sex workers' lives in the form of arrest, incarceration, court-mandated drug and other therapeutic treatment. This approach, while most prevalent in the United States due to the unparalleled size and scope of that country's criminal justice system, is evident throughout the Americas in forms of policing that target particularly marginalized sex worker communities, especially those working in public spaces, as part of a totalizing pathology that focuses particularly on queer-identified people as well as those struggling with addiction (Pettiway, 1997). Male sex workers, who face all the same challenges as their female peers with the added burden of pervasive cultural homophobia, face particular challenges with respect to these alliances, often dismissing them as particularly irrelevant to their lives (Dorais, 2005; Mitchell, 2015).

Harm reduction emerged from the field of public health and relies on the core "do no harm" principles of the Hippocratic Oath while prioritizing the health and safety of individuals who do not wish to cease their involvement in illicit drug use, sex trading, or other stigmatized behaviors. Harm reduction emphasizes the need for services providers to work with those most affected by a potentially health-damaging practice to develop measures and practices that can minimize the likelihood of facing violence, contracting sexually transmitted infections, overdosing, and experiencing other negative outcomes. Its commitment to "meeting people where they are at" is prevalent in Canada and Brazil and is practiced in almost all countries of the Americas despite the controversy it still generates due to the belief that harm reduction enables illicit drug use, transactional sex, and other behaviors that the dominant culture generally regards as morally problematic or unacceptable (Rekart, 2005).

These dominant discourses on the sex industry also occur in other world regions but take on unique forms in the Americas, particularly with respect to the notion of the frontier. Historical research indicates that many sex workers in settler colonial societies in the Americas were women migrants whose regulation was of prime interest to newly formed states (Butler, 1987; Goldman, 1981). Migrant men likewise played a significant role as sex industry third parties due to their xenophobic exclusion from well-established economic networks (Guy, 1991; Ross, 2009). Throughout the Americas, complex and diverse labor practices both inform and co-constitute the sex industry by reflecting myriad socio-economic inequalities surrounding social class, race, citizenship, and gender.

Europe

As a geographical entity, Europe is the smallest of the continents, although its political boundaries and borders remain contested around divergent notions of what constitutes a modern and unitary European identity and what might be its core values. After the two devastating World Wars of the twentieth century, some European countries formed an economic community aimed at avoiding any further conflict. This community progressively grew and evolved into the current European Union (EU), comprising 28 countries with more than 340 million EU citizens, which establishes joint rules on policy areas such as security, migration, justice, and the environment. Prostitution remains a matter of national policy, and therefore the European landscape of laws and policies on this matter varies from country to country, and oftentimes also regionally and locally within each nation state. This diversity in prostitution policy approaches also reflects rapidly changing developments and structures of European sex industries as a result of broader political and socio-economic changes both in the region and across the globe, for example the fall of communist regimes in the 1990s and progressive EU enlargement in the past three decades.

In the context of these changes, and in light of its historical construction as a problematic infringement of gendered norms of appropriate sexual behavior, prostitution and its regulation in Europe remain to this day the subject of highly contentious debates. The latter, framed around both old and new divergent conceptualizations and discourses of commercial sex, are in turn reflected in shifting and often antithetic politics and policies across the region. In order to explore recent developments in this complex landscape, we take as our cue the following claim, written in 1999 by historian Mary Gibson:

> While prostitution legislation in Europe and the United States has failed on its own terms, lawmakers have been unable, or unwilling, to develop innovative alternatives. It is prostitutes themselves, rather than governmental officials, who are now beginning to speak up and out their plight on the political agenda.
>
> *(Gibson, 1999: 9)*

As we explain below, a lot has changed since the above point was made, but significant is the identification of the increasing prominence of prostitutes' movements. Here Gibson is referring to the second wave of sex workers' mobilization. This, after the first ephemeral and localized mobilizations of the eighteenth and nineteenth centuries (Stevenson and Dziuban, 2017), developed in the 1970s, in and beyond Europe, with the formation of the first collectives of prostitutes that demanded the decriminalization of sex work and its recognition as legitimate labor. This mobilization has expanded since those early beginnings, and currently there are approximately 40 sex worker-led collectives in Europe giving voice to a strong and diversified sex work discourse. Today, what Stevenson and Dziuban (2017) identify as the third wave of sex workers' collectivization in Europe is characterized by a new form of political engagements with broader social justice struggles that "has resulted in both the revitalization of the sex workers' movement and the dynamic hybridization of its involvements" (Stevenson and Dziuban, 2017: 381). This is partly the result of a commitment to represent the diversity of gender identities and sexual orientations of sex workers and of the need to take into account the diversification of European sex industries, which see now an ever-increasing number of, often undocumented, migrant sex workers. Involved in both localized and grassroots campaigns and, through its expanding transnational and regional sex workers' networks, also in national and supra-national policy developments, sex workers' mobilization in Europe and the sex work discourse it promotes is vibrant and active, yet still facing notable challenges (Stevenson and Dziuban, 2017).

To make sense of such challenges, it is useful to get back to Gibson's earlier statement about the failure and/or unwillingness (as of the late 1990s) to develop "innovative alternatives" in prostitution legislation. This does not mean that prostitution had not been the subject of state intervention in Europe—quite the contrary, it has historically been dealt with by either regulating or criminalizing women and their bodies. But as a case of "morality politics" ruled by ideology (Wagenaar and Altink, 2012) and concerned with the sensitive realms of gender and sexuality, it has often proven difficult, and therefore not politically appealing, to pass new legislation and national policies on prostitution, especially if these were deemed "innovative." In the last two decades, however, Europe has witnessed the ascendance and increasing dominance of the neo-abolitionist discourse and agenda, which are contributing to changing significantly the picture drawn by Gibson. During this time, "a coalition of radical feminists and Christian and Social-Democratic politicians has captured the moral high ground in the debate about prostitution" (Wagenaar, 2017: 7) and has succeeded in implementing, across some European countries, legal and policy changes that are in antithesis to the demands of sex worker-led organizations. Neo-abolitionists argue that states should intervene to abolish prostitution. Unlike prohibitionists they move away from the belief that prostitution is an immoral act for which the prostitute should be punished, and focus instead on the male client whose act of "buying women's bodies" is viewed as violence against women and therefore needs to be criminalized. Neo-abolitionism also "conceives prostitution and sex-trafficking as inseparable both conceptually (how we think of them) and in terms of policy fields (how states respond to them)" (Ward and Wylie, 2017: 2). Prostitution, within this perspective, is a modern form of sexual slavery, thus marking a significant reversal in previously dominant approaches which targeted prostitutes as "fallen women" to be strictly controlled via regulation or criminalization. Within a neo-abolitionist framework, the new targets of state interventions are clients, third parties, and traffickers "because of the threats of abuse and exploitation that they pose to 'society,' 'the vulnerable,' and 'the victimised'" (Phoenix, 2017: 694).

This perspective found concrete application in the Swedish Prohibition of the Purchase of Sexual Services Act 1998, which implemented a highly innovative approach by criminalizing, for the first time in history, only the purchase of sexual services and not its supply. Soon after its application, what became known as the "Swedish model" has been hailed as exemplary and implemented, with variations, in Finland (2006), Norway (2009), Iceland (2009), Northern Ireland (2015), France (2016), and the Republic of Ireland (2017).

The clearly influential character of this "model" can partly be explained by the financial and political efforts put by Sweden to promote it "as part of its own identity-shaping in the international realm" (Ward and Wylie, 2017: 4). But the success of the neo-abolitionist discourse in Europe also needs to be understood in the context of diffused and hyperbolic messages reproduced by political groups and the media about the explosive increase in sex trafficking and exploitative sex industries, accompanied by often exaggerated and unsubstantiated numbers about the scale of the phenomenon (Scoular, 2015). The sensationalistic campaigns about the expected rise in sex trafficking victims during the sports mega-events that took place in Europe between 2006 and 2012, and representations of male tourists as drunken hordes coming to Europe to buy sex from exploited women helped strengthen the support for clients' criminalization (Darley et al., 2017; Goodey, 2008; Hubbard and Wilkinson, 2014). The Swedish "model" was promoted as a progressive solution to these problems: it would eliminate sex trafficking and prostitution, and in so doing promote gender equality. It is worth noting that less advertised have been the more critical views and studies on the negative effects of this policy approach, especially on migrant sex workers who, far from being treated as "victims" have found themselves highly penalized by the sex purchase ban (Skilbrei and Holmström, 2013).

But the reach of the Swedish "model" has also gone beyond other European countries, and has recently been endorsed by European supra-national institutions. In her review of the European Union's (EU) shifting approaches to prostitution policy (a realm that falls under the jurisdiction of individual member states), Outshoorn (2017, p. 17) explains that until the 2000s, the EU's approach to trafficking included references to "forced prostitution," "implying there was such a thing as 'voluntary' prostitution," and in its official documentation "the tie between trafficking and prostitution remained severed." For abolitionists re-establishing this link was instrumental in setting an EU agenda that would oppose the sex work discourse. After a number of failed attempts, and now strengthened by the strong support of Swedish female members of the European Parliament, in 2014 the neo-abolitionists' approach was submitted to a vote to the European Parliament in a non-binding resolution. In it, prostitution is equalled to sex trafficking and the (failing) regulationist approach exemplified by the Netherlands is contrasted to the (successful) neo-abolitionist "Nordic model" exemplified by Sweden. European states were called upon to change their legislations in favor of the latter "model." Despite large opposition to the resolution, and a campaign against it coordinated by the International Committee on the Rights of Sex Workers in Europe, the resolution was passed with a majority of votes in favor. Albeit non-binding, "it does carry symbolic and political weight" (Scoular, 2015, p. 10) and has provided strong momentum in the neo-abolitionists' campaigning in and beyond Europe (Outshoorn, 2017). However, as Outshoorn (2017) also points out, resurgent anti-EU sentiments and nationalism in Europe might play a role in the future in possibly rejecting a harmonized and super-imposed European neo-abolitionist approach to prostitution.

The centrality given to national "models" emerging from the European Parliament resolution is an aspect worth pointing out, as it reveals a discourse in prostitution policy debates framed around one-size-fits all "models." As Munro and Della Giusta (2008) claim, such concern for a "best model" has reduced the scope of debate in the field, trivializing the peculiarities and specificities of European sex industries across and within countries and disregarding the importance of context to how policies work in practice.

While the discussion above shows the extent of the reach of the neo-abolitionist discourse in Europe, its critics, including sex worker-led organizations and others, among which it is worth mentioning the expanding field of critical sex work studies in Europe, have not been silent against the harms of criminalization. Amnesty International's and other organizations' support of decriminalization have bolstered this "position," but, despite extensive evidence gathered in support of this approach, New Zealand remains the only country to have adopted it.

To conclude this section, it is worth reciting the suggestion by Phoenix (2017) that all the changes and developments cited above merely represent a change in discourse, rather than in the actual practice of the regulation of prostitution. "The justification for making this argument is the recognition that little has actually changed," women who sell sex are still the subjects of heavy state interventions that "are often experienced as punishment and sex workers remain under-protected in terms of the crimes committed against them" (Phoenix, 2017, p. 698).

Africa

Africa, the largest and second most populous continent, comprises 54 fully recognized sovereign states. The region is characterized by rich socio-political and economic diversity. For instance, Nigeria, on the continent's west coast, was a British colony. Currently the region's largest economy, Nigeria's population is estimated at over 190 million people. The country has about 340 distinct languages and ethnicities, and until two decades ago was a military dictatorship. On the other hand, Namibia on the southern end of the continent was first colonized by Germany and later by South Africa. With only about 12 ethnic groups and an estimated 2.1 million people, Namibia has enjoyed a stable electoral democracy since its independence in 1990. Africa's economic diversity is also striking. The region hosts some of the world's richest countries by commodity wealth as well as the majority of the world's poorest countries. The Democratic Republic of Congo (DRC) has an estimated worth of $54 trillion in unexploited mineral deposits, and South Africa more than $2.5 trillion in mineral reserves. On the other hand, 21 of the world's 25 poorest countries are African (Chandy, 2015).

Despite the extensive diversities that characterize Africa, a majority of the region's countries share a few common features: the legacy of colonialism, weak democratic structures, political instability, rapid urbanization, heavy reliance on development aids, the strong role of religion in everyday life, the dominance of received laws, and a persistent crisis of basic civil liberties and human rights (Elias, 2018). Across the region exploitative colonial policies dispossessed and displaced local people and communities, underdeveloped indigenous productive capacities, and destroyed critical local social institutions (Lonsdale, 2016). Post-colonial African countries also generally depend on Western aid for development, resulting in policies and programs that exacerbate poverty and impoverish citizens (Asongu and Nwachukwu, 2016).

While each sex worker in Africa may be unique, evidence points to the critical role of socio-economic stressors as a key driver of sex work in Africa. Sex workers in the region also generally experience deep societal stigma and discrimination, violence, and denial of services (Izugbara, 2012; Scorgie et al., 2012; Stoebenau et al., 2016). Currently, there is no African country where sex work is entirely licit. In Senegal, the only African country where prostitution is legal, some regulations still apply. Two main sex work-related frameworks have been identified in Africa (Mgbako and Smith, 2009; Ngugi et al., 2012). In the first, sex work itself, and sex work-related activities are illicit as is the case in Angola, Equatorial Guinea, Eritrea, Gabon, Ghana, Guinea, Kenya, Liberia, Mozambique, Namibia, Rwanda, Somalia, South Africa, Tanzania, Uganda, and Zambia. In the second, sex work is not proscribed, but the procurement and solicitation of sex in public places are prohibited. This is currently the case in Burkina Faso, Cape Verde, the Central African Republic, Côte d'Ivoire, Ethiopia, Lesotho, Madagascar, Malawi, Sierra Leone, Swaziland, and Zimbabwe. As in other parts of the world, fierce debates surround sex work in Africa. Below, we summarize some of the key discursive practices related to sex work in Africa.

The anti-prostitution movement, perhaps, the dominant voice on sex work in Africa, rejects sex work as a viable means of livelihood or economic survival. The movement constitutes sex work as both a form of and the result of violence against women and takes the view that sex workers are often women and girls exposed to poverty, coercion, and unequal gender relations. The anti-prostitution movement's response to sex work in Africa takes the form of: campaigns to prevent women from entering the profession, activities to "rescue" women involved in sex work, and high-level advocacy for the recognition and prohibition of sex work as a form of sexual exploitation. In Africa, anti-prostitution has historically enjoyed high-profile support from a range of actors, including politicians, women's right activists, and religious leaders. Rising global interest in human trafficking and commercial sexual exploitation has also continued to yield higher visibility for the anti-prostitution discourse in Africa. Asserting the mind of the anti-prostitution movement in Africa, Fatoumata Diakite of the Association for the Progress and Defense of Malian Women and the Coalition against Trafficking in Women noted in the early 1990s that prostitution is a violation of human rights and a form of violence and slavery. Similar sentiments have been and continue to be expressed by political leaders in Gambia, Sierra Leone, Uganda, and Zimbabwe. African anti-prostitution supporters also often justify their position by depicting prostitution as un-African, irreligious, and immoral. President Kagame of Rwanda in his speech at the 2015 International Women's Day constituted prostitution as un-African and advised sex workers in Rwanda "to go to other countries where the vice is accepted" (Mgbako and Smith, 2009).

The pro-sex workers' rights discourse in Africa has been advanced largely by social science researchers, human rights activists, and a handful of "radical" politicians. Rather than focus on the ethical, religious, or personal attitudes towards sex work, the pro-sex workers' rights movement in Africa has championed sex work as a legitimate profession. The movement identifies sex workers to be at high risk for sexual, physical, and other forms of abuse from clients. Consequently, advocacy and activism for the legalization and decriminalization of sex work lie at the heart of the sex workers' rights movement in the region. The movement has also been at the forefront of supporting the organizing of sex workers in Africa and the mainstreaming of sex workers' rights within the larger agenda of African women's rights movement. Despite significant opposition, the sex workers' rights movement in Africa is growing. For instance, in South Africa, Zambia, Cameroon, Kenya, and Uganda, sex workers and supporters of sex workers often protest and march openly for the legalization and decriminalization of sex work.

Mgbako and Smith (2009) have noted that the sex workers' right movement in Africa has particularly enjoyed the support of key multinational organizations such as the UNFPA and WHO, who continue to call for an end to violence, stigma, and discrimination against sex workers; the strengthening of legal and health support systems for sex workers; and the creation of partnerships for sex workers' rights. High-level political support for the movement has been recorded in countries such as Mozambique, Namibia, South Africa, and more recently Nigeria, where a top political leader tabled a national bill for the decriminalization and legalization of sex work. Backlash against the sex workers' rights movement is also pervasive in Africa. Uganda's Minister of Ethics and Integrity, James Buturo, noted in 2008 that: "We don't take any delight at all in the idea that prostitutes are coming together to devise ways of spreading their vice."

Currently, criminal justice–social services alliances are a poorly developed response to sex work in Africa. In the few countries where they are beginning to emerge, these alliances have been driven largely by a belief that sex workers who want to exit the profession can do so if they are provided alternative livelihood skills. At the heart of these alliances in Africa is a belief that many sex workers want to leave the trade and can be supported to do so through quality counselling and livelihood opportunities. Criminal justice–social services alliances in Africa are generally NGO-led and take the form of mediations by NGOs with criminal and justice system institutions on behalf of arrested and convicted sex workers. Often not supported by any nationally recognized legal frameworks, these efforts have primarily sought to support the rehabilitation of arrested or convicted sex workers. In Nigeria, for example, the Rufai Foundation works with the police to secure the release of arrested sex workers and to give them alternative livelihoods, training, and skills. Hope for Future Generations, a Ghanaian NGO, also uses retired and rehabilitated sex workers to train and provide alternative livelihood skills to sex workers released to them by the police.

The public health discourse on sex work in Africa identifies sex workers to be at critical risk for major health problems, a source of infections and harm to the larger population, and an important population health group for support and engagement. As in many regions of the world, harm reduction is at the heart of public health discourse on sex work in Africa. Consequently, sex workers in Africa have been common targets of programs seeking to improve their use of condoms, enhance their capacity to negotiate safe sex with clients, and increase their utilization of formal health care systems (Ngugi et al., 2012). In many parts of Africa, clients of sex workers have also been targeted with interventions and programs that emphasize sex workers as a risky group, the need for regular use of condoms with sex workers, and the importance of the use of formal health facilities in the early identification and prevention of sexually transmitted infections among clients of sex workers.

Concluding thoughts

Even within the tremendous geographic and cultural diversity that constitutes the three major world regions described, this chapter sheds light on significant similarities and contestations that exist across, and possibly beyond them, more globally. First, historically marginalized groups remain overrepresented in the lowest paid sex industry sectors where individuals are more likely to suffer from violence and exploitation compounded by punitive laws and policies. Second, ideological stances that regard the sex industry as morally reprehensible and harmful to assumed gender and sexuality norms have not wavered through time, and, if anything, they become stronger at historical moments when these norms appear to be especially in flux. Their recrudescence in recent times, for example, is closely linked to popular and populist discourses framed around incumbent threats of invasion: invasion of unwanted migrant sex workers from the South to the Global North, and invasion of immorality and corrupted/ing sexual practices from the North to the Global South.

Third, alongside the persistence of historical constructions of prostitution as immoral and deviant, the discussion of the three regions presented in this chapter also reveals changes in dominant discourses on the sex industry. Among these is the increasingly vocal and politically (and financially) strong abolitionist perspective that views prostitution as violence against women, and, what is new, aims to eradicate it by rescuing "prostituted women" and punishing and/or educating clients—who had previously been largely ignored in laws and policy interventions. Also, a relatively recent development in the three regions is the growth and internationalization of sex worker rights groups and therefore of the strengthening and increased visibility of the sex work discourse. Many of these groups operate at the very localized level, often with little funds and limited resources. However, they have become part of larger umbrella organizations that continue to politically engage with broader movements for socio-economic justice and human rights, with varying (mostly limited) levels of access to participation in policymaking or other initiatives that directly impact their everyday lives and working conditions.

Finally, a great deal of contemporary academic and activist literature attributes the increased popular cultural, criminal justice, and social services attention prostitution has received in recent decades to global shifts toward securitization and the associated legislative, policy, and activist focus on sex trafficking. This attribution, while not incorrect, risks de-historicizing the stigma, limited or nonexistent labor rights, prevalence of exploitative practices, and other forms of abuse enabled by widespread socio-legal condemnation of the sex industry. These similarities notwithstanding, some differences exist in the response to sex work in these three continents.

For instance, the discourses surrounding buyers of sex appear dissimilar in the three regions. In much of Europe clients are often blamed for prostitution. They are to be eradicated or their behaviors fully regulated for sex work to stop or become safer. In Africa, clients of sex workers are considered a critical public health group who need to adopt safer sexual practices with sex workers. Clients are rarely criminalized in Africa. In the Americas, clients have hardly featured in policies and interventions related to sex work. Rather, attention has largely resided on addressing the social inequities that drive prostitution and the structural factors that expose sex workers to harm.

Indeed, nearly all proponents of particular discourses on the sex industry will concur that status quo approaches to its regulation are failing worldwide. Criminalization has universally failed to eradicate or abate prostitution and instead relegates it and other criminalized forms of commercial sex to neighborhoods and social actors that facilitate harm in various forms, often while incurring significant financial and social costs to the state. Legalization continues to endorse regulated sex industry venues, but these are often managed and owned by third parties who demand very high percentages of earnings and are only open to those sex workers who have citizenship or a work permit and can pass mandatory health tests. Decriminalization, while preferred by the vast majority of sex worker rights advocates and many researchers, does not appear to reduce the stigma attached to prostitution.

As the analysis of the three regions reveals, new and old social constructions on prostitution and on those who are involved in it as sellers, buyers, or in other roles, abound and feed discourses that are often antithetical. A much needed investigation in this field should focus on the political economy of such globally flowing discourses, of the economic, political, and ideological interests they subtend determining their strength or weakness. This is especially the case in light of the fact that the substance of the issues facing sex workers have not fundamentally changed since the dawn of human history, and still revolves around poverty, inequality, and social exclusion. Discursively constructed myths about prostitution often contribute to obscuring such pervasive realities, and resources need to be mobilized to give voice and to listen to sex workers, individually and collectively, as rights-bearing subjects.

References

Asongu, Simplice and Nwachukwu, Jacinta. 2016. Foreign aid and governance in Africa. *International Review of Applied Economics* 30: 69–88.

Bernstein, Elizabeth. 2007. The sexual politics of the "new abolitionism." *Differences: A Journal of Feminist Cultural Studies* 18(3): 128–151.

Bernstein, Elizabeth. 2010. Militarized humanitarianism meets carceral feminism: The politics of sex, rights, and freedom in contemporary antitrafficking campaigns. *Signs: Journal of Women in Culture & Society* 36(1): 45–72.

Blanchette, Thaddeus and da Silva, Ana Paula. 2011. Prostitution in contemporary Rio de Janeiro. In S. Dewey and P. Kelly (Eds.), *Policing Pleasure: Sex Work, Policy, and the State in Global Perspective* (pp. 130–145). New York: New York University Press.

Brooks, Siobhan. 2010. *Unequal Desires: Race and Erotic Capital in the Stripping Industry*. Albany, NY: SUNY Press.

Butler, Anne. 1987. *Daughters of Joy, Sisters of Misery: Prostitutes of the American West, 1865–90*. Champaign, IL: University of Illinois Press.

Cabezas, Amalia. 2009. *Economies of Desire: Sex and Tourism in Cuba and the Dominican Republic*. Philadelphia, PA: Temple University Press.

Chandy, Laurence (2015). Why is the number of poor people in Africa increasing when Africa's economies are growing? Available from www.brookings.edu/blog/africa-in-focus/2015/05/04/why-is-the-number-of-poor-people-in-africa-increasing-when-africas-economies-are- growing.

Creelman, James. 1911. *Diaz: Master of Mexico*. New York: D. Appleton & Company.

Darley, M., David, M., Guienne, V., Mainsant, G., and Mathieu, L. 2017. "France." In S.O. Jahnsen and H. Wagenaar (Eds.) *Assessing Prostitution Policies in Europe* (pp. 27–39). Abingdon, UK: Routledge.

DeStefano, Anthony. 2008. *The War on Human Trafficking: U.S. Policy Assessed*. Camden, NJ: Rutgers University Press.

Dewey, Susan and Tonia St. Germain. 2017. *Women of the Street: How the Criminal Justice–Social Services Alliance Fails Women in Prostitution*. New York: New York University Press.

Doezema, Jo. 2010. *Sex Slaves and Discourse Masters: The Construction of Trafficking*. London: Zed Books.

Dorais, Michel. 2005. *Rent Boys: The World of Male Sex Trade Workers*. Montreal: McGill-Queen's University Press.

Elias, P. 2018. *African Development Initiatives: The Development of Africa*. New York: Springer.

Gibson, M. 1999. *Prostitution and the State in Italy*. Columbus, OH: Ohio State University Press.

Goldman, Marion. 1981. *Gold Diggers and Silver Miners: Prostitution and Social Life on Comstock Lode*. Ann Arbor, MI: University of Michigan Press.

Goodey, J. 2008. Human trafficking: Sketchy data and policy responses. *Criminology and Criminal Justice* 8(4): 421–442

Guy, Donna. 1991. *Sex and Danger in Buenos Aires: Prostitution, Family, and Nation in Argentina*. Lincoln, NE: University of Nebraska Press.

Hubbard, P. and Wilkinson, E. 2014. Welcoming the world? Hospitality, homonationalism, and the London 2012 Olympics. *Antipode* 47(3): 598–615

Izugbara, Chimaraoke. 2012. Client retention and health among sex workers in Nairobi, Kenya. *Archives of Sexual Behavior* 41: 1345–1352.

Katsulis, Yasmina. 2009. *Sex Work and the City: The Social Geography of Health and Safety in Tijuana, Mexico*. Austin, TX: University of Texas Press.

Leigh, Carol. 1997. Inventing sex work. In J. Nagle, *Whores & Other Feminists*, pp. 225–231. New York: Routledge.

Lonsdale, J. 2016. State and peasantry in colonial Africa. In R. Samuel (Ed.) *People's History and Socialist Theory (Routledge Revivals)* (pp. 106–118). Abingdon, UK: Routledge.

Mgbako, C. and Smith, L.A. 2009. Sex work and human rights in Africa. *Fordham International Law Journal* 33, 1178.

Miller-Young, Mireille. 2015. *A Taste for Brown Sugar: Black Women in Pornography*. Durham, NC: Duke University Press.

Mitchell, Gregory. 2015. *Tourist Attractions: Performing Race and Masculinity in Brazil's Sexual Economy*. Chicago, IL: University of Chicago Press.

Munro, V. and Della Giusta, M. 2008. *Demanding Sex: Critical Reflections on the Regulation of Prostitution*. Farnham, UK: Ashgate.

Ngugi, E.N., Roth, E., Mastin, T., Nderitu, M.G., and Yasmin, S. 2012. Female sex workers in Africa: Epidemiology overview, data gaps, ways forward. *Journal of Social Aspects of HIV/AIDS Research Alliance/ SAHARA, Human Sciences Research Council* 9, 148–153.

Oakley, Annie, Ed. 2007. *Working Sex: Sex Workers Write About a Changing Industry*. Berkeley, CA: Seal Press.

Outshoorn, Joyce. 2017. European Union and prostitution policy. In S.O. Jahnsen and H. Wagenaar (Eds.) *Assessing Prostitution Policies in Europe* (pp. 15–27). Abingdon, UK: Routledge.

Padilla, Mark. 2007. *Caribbean Pleasure Industry: Tourism, Sexuality, and AIDS in the Dominican Republic*. Chicago, IL: University of Chicago Press.

Pettiway, Leon. 1997. *Honey, Honey, Miss Thang: Being Black, Gay, and On the Streets*. Philadelphia, PA: Temple University Press.

Phoenix, J. 2017. Prostitution and sex work. In A. Liebling, S. Maruna, and L. McAra (Eds.) *The Oxford Handbook of Criminology*. Oxford: Oxford University Press.

Rekart, M. 2005. Sex-work harm reduction. *Lancet* 366(9503): 2123–2134.

Ross, Becki. 2009. *Burlesque West: Showgirls, Sex, and Sin in Postwar Vancouver*. Toronto, ON: University of Toronto Press.

Scorgie, F., Chersich, M.F., Ntaganira, I., Gerbase, A., Lule, F., and Lo, Y.-R. 2012. Socio-demographic characteristics and behavioral risk factors of female sex workers in sub-Saharan Africa: A systematic review. *AIDS and Behavior* 16: 920–933.

Scoular, J. 2015. *The Subject of Prostitution*. Abingdon, UK: Routledge.

Skilbrei, M.-L. and Holmström, C. 2013. *Prostitution Policy in the Nordic Region*. Abingdon, UK: Routledge.

Stevenson, L. and Dziuban, A. 2017. Sex workers' self-organizing in Europe. In S.O. Jahnsen and H. Wagenaar (Eds.) *Assessing Prostitution Policies in Europe*. Abingdon, UK: Routledge.

Stoebenau, K., Heise, L., Wamoyi, J., and Bobrova, N. 2016. Revisiting the understanding of "transactional sex" in sub-Saharan Africa: A review and synthesis of the literature. *Social Science & Medicine* 168: 186–197.

Ward, E. and Wylie, G. 2017. *Feminism, Prostitution and the State*. Abingdon, UK: Routledge.

Wagenaar, H. 2017. Introduction. Prostitution policy in Europe: An overview. In S.O Jahnsen and H. Wagenaar (Eds.) *Assessing Prostitution Policies in Europe*. Abingdon, UK: Routledge.

Wagenaar, H. and Altink, S. 2012. Prostitution as morality politics or why it is exceedingly difficult to design and sustain effective prostitution policy. *Sexuality Research and Social Policy* 9: 279–292.

19

Sex trafficking as *desaparición* [disappearance]

Vernacularised human rights discourses in the Argentine anti-trafficking campaign

Cecilia Varela

Introduction

In this way, in the name of national security, thousands and thousands of human beings, generally young and even adolescents, became part of a gloomy and ghostly category: that of the *Desaparecidos* [the disappeared]. A word . . . that today is written . . . in all the press of the world.

(Comisión Nacional sobre la Desaparición de Personas 1984)

Many of the disappeared who are presumed to have been victims of trafficking are adults. Where are they? There is no other name for them than that, *desaparecidas* [disappeared women], and their very mention echoes an experience: the experience of relatives of state terrorism reflected in those who search for, wait for, or mourn in absentia those women disappeared in democracy. And also in the experience of the victims, in the torture and rape . . . the loss of identity, even the appropriation of their children.

(Dillon 2014)

The two quoted texts juxtaposed above reflect two very different social movements at two equally unique periods in Argentine history yet employ the same term as a means to mobilise support around the cause of human rights: the disappeared. The first, from 1984, belongs to the prologue of the final report of the Comisión Nacional sobre la Desaparición de Personas [National Commission on the Disappearance of Persons] that reconstructed the kidnappings, forced disappearances, and torture of thousands of political dissidents during the 1976–1983 military dictatorship. The second, from 2014, uses the same language to refer to women victims of trafficking as "disappeared in democracy". This chapter engages with the seeming effortlessness with which activists mobilise "the disappeared" as a political cause, albeit for very different reasons and to very different ends.

The campaign against human trafficking went global at the start of the twenty-first century, as transnational activism expanded the reach of this campaign across national and supranational spheres.

Within a broader agenda targeting transnational organised crime, the United Nations produced an official definition of the crime of "trafficking in persons" in the 2001 Palermo Protocol. The United States, in turn, played an important role in disseminating anti-trafficking discourse by passing legislation to monitor other countries' policies in the fight against so-called "twenty-first-century slavery". Various commentators have pointed out that the Palermo Protocol, adopted as part of the Convention Against Transnational Organised Crime, lacked a human rights perspective (Ditmore and Wijers 2003; Anderson and Andrijasevic 2008). However, a campaign against sex trafficking expressed in human rights language rapidly spread through different national contexts.

Argentina was part of this wave and from 2008 a cluster of organisations successfully forced through various legal reforms that broadened the definition of "human trafficking" and "sexual exploitation". The Argentine movement sought the abolition of prostitution and its message quickly found support outside of the initial community of campaigners. While the feminist movement's long-standing demands, such as the decriminalisation of abortion, made little progress in the last decade, the fight against human trafficking became a matter of utmost priority, evidence of an emerging "gender perspective" in public policies, and an area in which politicians of all stripes could come together.

In this chapter, I address some aspects of the campaign against sex trafficking in Argentina. Since the campaign's discourse originally coalesced in transnational and supranational spaces, I examine the processes through which the campaign was appropriated and recreated in Argentina. These processes of *vernacularisation* of international law, as Merry (2006) calls them, require the production of interpretative frameworks capable of mobilising resources and appealing to subjects in specific cultural contexts outside of the original community of activists committed to the issue (Merry 2006: 266). I employ this theoretical approach to critically examine the interpretative frameworks of "sex trafficking" produced by the domestic neo-abolitionist movement, the repertoire of historical and contemporary symbols deployed to frame it as a human rights issue and the conceptions of gender and sexuality mobilised in these processes.

Doezema (2010) points out that successive attempts to separate truth from fiction in the "white slavery" panic reveals the extent to which we are taken in by it. She therefore proposes approaching the narratives of "white slavery" of the late nineteenth century and early twentieth century and "sex trafficking" in the present day as cultural myths that construct meanings around sex work and gender. In turn, Bernstein (2010, 2016) and Cheng (2011) have focused on the emergence of anti-trafficking activism in their connection with state transformations in a neoliberal context, and the construction of national hegemony in postcolonial contexts. In Latin America, Piscitelli (2015) has drawn attention to the capillarisation of anti-trafficking discourses, like the networks formed by capillary blood vessels in the body, to include issues and problems that the writers of the Protocol did not foresee (such as child sexual abuse and commercial sexual exploitation of children).

Based on these critical reflections, I seek here to analyse sex trafficking as a powerful social narrative. In this regard, any reflection on the form that the anti-trafficking campaign in Argentina has taken needs to question the symbols and repertoire of contention deployed, a large part of which stems from the Argentine human rights movement. This movement emerged during the last military dictatorship (1976–1983) from protests about illegal detentions and forced disappearances of political militants and was consolidated in the 1980s in the process of transition to democracy. Since the 1990s, the human rights movement has served as a cultural substrate for the development of social and women's movements in Argentina (Schuster and Pereyra 2001; Sutton 2010; Di Marco 2011). In this chapter I suggest that one of the singularities of the Argentine anti-trafficking campaign has been its appeal to the political rhetoric and symbols used by human rights organisations in their long-standing demands of "memory, truth and justice" for the crimes committed in the context of the state terrorism of the 1970s. Thus, trafficking as *desaparición* [disappearance] is the cornerstone of translation into the language of vernacular human rights.

While Merry (2006) is optimistic about the potential of these processes of translation of human rights regimes, Cheng (2011) is more cautious in her analysis of the anti-trafficking campaign in South Korea. She believes it is not self-evident which policies and initiatives would protect women in sexual commerce, while there are differing views about what constitutes a violation of their human rights and how these should be protected. In this regard, I am interested in taking from her criticism the focus on the power relations within which these processes of vernacularisation are produced. In the case of Argentina, I am interested in looking into the silencing and effacement produced by trafficking understood as *desaparición*.

Accumulated research in the field has shown the link between anti-trafficking policies and the restriction of transnational mobilities (Aradau 2014; Fitzgerald 2012; Piscitelli and Lowenkron 2015) and the dissemination of neoliberal political rationalities (Bernstein 2010, 2016). These connections might not be so clear in the case examined here. Unlike the global trend aiming to strengthen transnational borders, no efforts to restrict immigration can be identified in Argentina during this period. On the contrary, the immigration law passed in 2004 recognised migration as a human right and guaranteed access to rights for all the foreign populations regardless of their migratory situation. Between 2004 and 2014, this law allowed more than 1 million citizens from South American countries to apply for residency and regularise their situation. On the other hand, during this period the neoliberal discourses that had prevailed in the 1990s were politically discussed and contested. Thus, the new centre-left government cultivated the language of political mediations and a discourse of rights was expanded through policies of social inclusion and recognition of minorities (egalitarian marriage, transgender rights). However, the expansion of this language of social justice and rights coexisted with a gender agenda that, as it was defined predominantly through the lens of the criminal justice system, reinstated sexual victimisation as a condition for fundamental legibility.

Merry (2006) argues that transnationalised human rights language needs to be translated into networks of local meaning in order to be both attractive and legitimate. In this sense, another of the particularities of Argentina is that after the transition to democracy in the 1980s, human rights discourse had already formed a local cultural narrative with deep historical resonances. The idea of "Nunca más" [Never Again][1] has functioned as a fundamental myth of democratic Argentina (Tonkonoff 2014) that rejects the idea that the guerrilla violence of the 1970s was the cause of the excessive military reaction, presents the *desaparecidos* as innocents and holds the high military command responsible for their disappearance (Crenzel 2010). The creation of the category of "forced disappearance" in supranational legislation was to a large extent the result of the involvement of Argentine lawyers in transnational human rights networks. Subject to an intense work of legal translation, the "original disappeared" of the Argentine historical experience gave rise to the universal and legal type of the "transnational disappeared" (Gatti 2017). In a third movement, the category expanded, seeking to make human rights violations intelligible across different contexts (victims of drugs trafficking in Mexico, victims of the civil war in Spain, among others). Argentina is then a country in the Global South that has both received and produced human rights regimes that circulate globally (Sikkink 2008). Therefore, in analysing the anti-trafficking campaign's translation operations it is necessary to keep in mind this availability of a human rights language with a firmly rooted vernacular tradition, deeply politicised and connected to the memory policies of the recent past.

The methodological strategy combined participatory observation at anti-trafficking events, interviews with activists, and an analysis of documentation from 2007 to 2011. This period corresponds to the initial stage of vernacularisation of the campaign, when civil society organisations maintained ownership of the public problem, that is, they retained "the capacity to create the public definition of a problem and have an influence on it" (Gusfield 2014: 76).[2] First, I will show the repertoire of contention and language that the *trafficking-disappearance* narrative mobilised as well as the pedagogy that it deployed. Second, I will analyse the resonances of the symbols mobilised, the circumstances in which they were deployed and the political responsibilities that were remodelled in this process. Finally, I intend to draw some reflections from feminism's uses of human rights languages seeking to grasp their potentialities, limits and ambivalences.

The anti-trafficking movement in Argentina: competing symbols and narratives

Argentina underwent a profound socio-economic and political crisis in 2001, after which the centre-left politician Néstor Kirchner was elected president. In a context of post-crash economic recovery, anti-trafficking discourse made inroads as both a human rights matter and as part of an emerging "gender perspective" in public policies. Gender violence and sex trafficking became fundamental issues in the gender agenda in a period characterised as post-neo-liberal (Pecheny 2013).

Between 2007 and 2008, concurrently with US State Department demands for a new anti-trafficking law, a group of anti-trafficking organisations came into the public eye. Professionalised feminist NGOs, autonomous feminist collectives and organisations with ties to the Catholic Church – accompanied by left-wing Trotskyite parties – made up a heterogeneous coalition that alleged an increase in human trafficking and demanded immediate legal reform. These organisations strongly criticised the bill, which defined the crime of trafficking according to the Palermo Protocol. They instead proposed a definition that would erase any possible distinction between forced prostitution and voluntary prostitution. As soon as the first anti-trafficking law was passed in 2008, the movement embarked on a strong campaign to reform it. The central demand was to remove any reference to the possibility of a person consenting to offer sexual services.

In this initial period, the organisations developed different strategies to frame an interpretation of trafficking and sexual commerce and fought for modifications to the law. Although the organisations all stuck to the principles of abolitionism and called for the same legal reform, the names they chose to mobilise in their campaigns and respective public discourses revealed nuances and were tied to their own formative backgrounds. Those organisations that came from historic abolitionism positioned themselves around an autonomous campaign that they called "Ni una mujer más víctima de las redes de prostitución" ["Not one more woman victim of prostitution networks] (from here on, the "Campaign")]. They sought to have a bearing on the emerging anti-trafficking agenda with a perspective that remained loyal to its concerns about prostitution as a form of gender violence and portrayed women in sexual commerce as "victims" of patriarchal domination.

The feminist NGO "Casa del Encuentro" [Meeting House] developed and disseminated a second narrative that quickly resonated with the general public and associated trafficking with kidnapping and torture by imagining prostitutes as *desaparecidas en democracia* [women disappeared in democracy]. Both the Campaign and Casa del Encuentro defined themselves as feminist abolitionist organisations fighting for women's human rights. However, they used different languages and symbols to classify prostitution as a violation of human rights.

The trafficking-disappearance narrative was very successful and was rapidly capillarised among feminist activists and the wider public as a way of focussing attention on sex trafficking and, ultimately, any form of sexual commerce. The narrative was also unexpectedly extended as a way of understanding the trajectory of young women who ran away from home, while the brothel was indicated as the destination of all the young women who had been *desaparecidas*. Slogans such as "They are being disappeared to be your whore" sprang up in street graffiti and on social media, producing automatic associations between *desaparición* and prostitution.

The trafficking-disappearance narrative: the *"desaparecidas en democracia"*

The first cases of "sex trafficking" in Argentina to gain attention from the general public were that of Dominican migrant women, whose stories offered some elements for a reading in that area and even created a minor flurry of media and institutional interest in 2001. However, the high visibility that the issue gained was mainly due to one particular case not related to the Dominican women: the disappearance of María de los Ángeles ("Marita") Verón in 2002 and her mother Susana Trimarco's fight to find her.

At the time when Marita went missing the category of "sex trafficking" was not yet used and the case was reported as a kidnap connected to a network of brothels operating in northern Argentina. The legal investigation made scarce progress, while Susana Trimarco publicly denounced the complicity of politicians and urged the government to support her in her search for her daughter. Eventually, when it seemed the case would be forgotten, the attention of the US State Department was drawn to the story of Susana and Marita. On 8 March 2007, Susana travelled to the United States to receive the Mothers of Courage Award for her fight against human trafficking. Her nomination had been raised by the Argentine Embassy over other local candidates because human trafficking was a priority issue for the US government (Vallejos 2013).

Trimarco's recognition had immediate consequences in Argentina. A few days after the ceremony, Casa del Encuentro – on the occasion of the fifth anniversary of Marita Verón's disappearance – called for the first public demonstration at the National Congress under the slogan *"Aparición con vida de las mujeres desaparecidas en democracia y castigo a los responsables"* [May the women disappeared in democracy appear alive and may those responsible be punished]. The slogan merged the rhetoric of the Argentine human rights movement with feminist activism and sought to call on a government that at the time endorsed the long-standing demands for "memory, truth and justice" for the crimes against humanity committed during the period of state terrorism. The repeal of the Obediencia Debida [Law of Due Obedience] and Punto Final [Full Stop Law] in 2003,[3] put forward by the government and then passed by the Supreme Court, had reopened hundreds of legal cases against those figures involved in the repression between 1976 and 1983, 20 years after the fact. The creation of the Museo de la Memoria [Museum of Memory] at the former Escuela de Mecánica de la Armada [Navy School of Mechanics] in 2004 symbolised the opening up of a new political process that announced historic reparations for the impunity of the preceding years. These initiatives earned the government growing support among human rights organisations and progressive sectors. In this context, Susana Trimarco supported the demonstration and targeted the government in the media: "The Government talks about the disappeared of the 1970s, but they don't say anything about those disappeared in democracy. There needs to be a political commitment to this issue" (Carbajal, 2007). In turn, the figure of Trimarco represented a paradigmatic political subject in democratic Argentina as motherhood has been legitimised – from the Madres de Plaza de Mayo to social movements emerging in the 1990s – as a source of political commitment. Mothers who go through a personal ordeal, combining politics, kinship and family values, represent a recurrent form of maternal politics in the Argentine context.

The demonstrations for the *desaparecidas en democracia* became a monthly ritual for the emerging anti-trafficking movement. The protests gradually incorporated the names of other young women who had gone missing under mysterious circumstances, whose absence was now reported as resulting from the actions of "trafficking networks". In the early years, the cases of Marita Verón, Fernanda Aguirre and Florencia Penacchi formed the most visible trio.[4] These cases whose "very mention" – according to the country's most popular feminist supplement – "describes an experience: that of the families of the victims of State terrorism" (Dillon 2014) shared some basic characteristics: the three victims were presented as young women with "normal" lives, mothers or students, abruptly snatched from the heart of a family that demanded their return. These were "perfect victims" who fit a number of traditional gender stereotypes in which sexual innocence and passivity are central characteristics (Doezema 2004; Vance 2004). The visibility that these cases acquired contrasted with the way that the initial concern for the Dominican women was quickly forgotten, even though their migration had been clearly documented in its link to sexual commerce and in the forms of precariousness that these women experienced (IOM 2003).

Another common element in these cases was that the reasons for the disappearances could never be clarified completely and the bodies were never found, despite the incessant efforts of the victims' families. With the passing of time, the lack of clues and scarce progress in the investigations seemed to confirm the activists' and families' suspicions of trafficking. As a result, these cases were framed as trafficking not so much because of the evidence or firm clues that would suggest sexual commerce, but because of the mysteries surrounding the cases. The issues perceived as "trafficking" gradually shifted from the migratory trajectories of black women related to sexual commerce to the mysterious cases of missing young white women who embodied sexual respectability. Consequently, in Argentina the term "trafficking" gradually lost its connotation with migratory processes and was far more associated with the *desapariciones* of women. Casa del Encuentro successfully developed a "pedagogy of fear" (Lowenkron 2012) that classed any absence of a young woman from her home as a *desaparición* under the hypothesis of a "sex trafficking" crime. The capillarisation and activation of this paradigm gradually undermined other explanations such as young women leaving home willingly, homicide, femicide, sexual violence and accidents[5] and ultimately has had an effect on the perceptions of danger for young women in large urban centres. Old urban legends about a white van kidnapping people made a return, in this case supposedly kidnapping young women in broad daylight to force them into prostitution. The proliferation of this rumour succeeded in sowing panic among young women in working-class neighbourhoods and also in the university environment.

The demonstrations organised by Casa del Encuentro mobilised repertoires of contention, as well as rituals and languages that originated in the human rights movement in Argentina. Demonstrators carried banners with the photo and name of each of the *desaparecidas* while walking in a circle around the National Congress. In this way, they emulated the demonstrations of the Madres de Plaza de Mayo who in carrying images of their children positively affirmed their particular existence as the repressors denied (Longoni 2010). The organisation made up a banner featuring its fundamental demand "*Por las mujeres desaparecidas. Aparición con vida de las víctimas de la trata secuestradas para la prostitución. Castigo a los responsables y a sus cómplices*" [For the disappeared women. May the victims of trafficking kidnapped into prostitution appear alive. Punishment for those responsible and their accomplices]." This slogan placed the sex trade at the core of the repressive circuits of the military dictatorship, thus evoking images and strengthening associations between torture and sex work, between clandestine detention centres and brothels. The anti-trafficking movement also recuperated both the language and the rituals of the commemoration of the militants disappeared during the last military dictatorship. For example, at the end of each protest, the speaker declaimed the names of the *desaparecidas* and the public responded to each one of them with "present!" and finally "now and forever!" In 2009, activists started to demand that human trafficking be considered a "crime against humanity", like crimes committed during state terrorism, and therefore defined as an imprescriptible offence.

Casa del Encuentro also sought to provide a quantitative representation to show the scope of the problem. In the national media and their own publications, the main spokeswomen of the organisation claimed that 700 women had been *desaparecidas* into the hands of trafficking networks. The possibility of circulating a figure, regardless of whether this number corresponds to a strategy that might presume any kind of methodology, is vital in the process of constructing trafficking as a public problem, as has been widely documented in different contexts (Silva et al 2005; Feingold 2010; Jordan 2011; Blanchette and Da Silva 2012). Casa del Encuentro's figure was an "invention" produced, at least in part, from the transmutation of other figures circulating previously. By 2007, the figure of 476 women *desaparecidas* into the hands of trafficking networks was appearing in journalistic sources and NGO reports citing the International Organization for Migration (IOM) as the source of the information (Clarin 2007; Fundación El Otro 2007; Las Juanas 2009; Infobae 2010). However, what the IOM was registering were persons assisted in the context of their programmes for victims of trafficking. Thus, in a double operation, the figure of 476 *victims assisted* by the IOM (men and women for sexual and labour exploitation) became a figure that referred to *disappeared women* in the hands of sexual slavery networks. On this basis, Casa del Encuentro introduced the figure of "700 women disappeared" at the hands of sex trafficking networks, which was quickly echoed in the media (Clarin 2008; Carabajal 2010; La Nación 2010) and went on to inform the activist practices of many other organisations.

I have addressed elsewhere the logic behind the construction and circulation of these strategic figures (Varela and González 2015). Although "the politics of numbers" (Andreas and Greenhill 2010) is a fundamental tool in the processes of constructing many public problems, in this case it also echoed the human rights vernacular. During the transitional justice process the human rights movement drew up the number of 30,000 disappeared during the civic-military dictatorship as a way of giving a quantitative representation of the scope of the brutal repression unleashed and to dispute the negationist perspectives of the crimes that had occurred.[6] The anti-trafficking movement, in turn, submitted its own number of *desaparecidas* as a way of positioning its demands and calling on the state to deal with the issue.[7] But the number of 30,000 vindicated by the human rights organisations is not just a quantitative representation, but forms a "site of memory" (Nora 1992) that condenses meanings around the recent past.[8] Any attempt to call that number into question in democratic Argentina implies a challenge to the wider memorial heritage and is frequently perceived as an attempt to deny the crimes of the last military dictatorship.

So it was that although the figure put in circulation by Casa del Encuentro was "invented", it was hard to question for two main reasons. First, at that time there was no knowledge available that could contravene that figure, as sex trafficking statistics and records of missing adult women were not yet available. Second, and fundamentally, because *desaparición* is the political symbol that – through the struggle of the human rights movement for over three decades – has served to signal that precisely *even* in the absence of material evidence (fundamentally because the bodies are absent) the state must recognise the existence of a citizen and take responsibility for the crimes that could have been committed against him or her. Then, how to relativise or reframe within this political field, the existence of a *desaparecido*?

"Disappearance" and the trafficking of innocence

What were the main effects of the capillarisation of the trafficking-disappearance paradigm? This frame, as proposed by Casa del Encuentro, was a twofold simplification: on the one hand, every young woman being searched for by her relatives became a *desaparecida* at the hands of a trafficking network; and on the other hand, every woman involved in sexual commerce ended up being imagined as a *desaparecida*. In this way, prostitution was equated with *desaparición*. In presenting kidnapping as the predominant form of insertion into sexual commerce, the paradigm reinforced discursively the idea that no woman would undertake sex work unless some extreme forms of violence were present. Second, presenting any absence of a young woman as a *desaparecida* under the hypothesis of a crime of "trafficking" ruled out the possibility of a young woman voluntarily leaving home, while reaffirming the nuclear family as the safest and most natural space. As Gusfield (2014) points out, the symbolic categories rolled out to construct the public problem are tied to the types of political responsibilities assigned. Thus, via both paths, the legal system emerged as the most suitable tool for intervening in the lives of women and as the prospect of justice.

But the term *desaparición* contains a unique connotation in the Argentine political field. Not only does it refer to the absence of traces and clues as to the whereabouts of the person (as in the English word "missing"), but it is also a signifier that condenses the historic experience of state terrorism and the demands of "memory, truth and justice" for the crimes committed in those years. The figure of the *desaparecido* appeared in the 1970s as a way for the emergent human rights movement to stand up to the civic-military dictatorship; *desaparición* was a symbol that had made it possible to hold the state responsible even when the bodies were absent. The figure is also closely tied in its historical genealogy to the idea of the innocent victim. That is, it constitutes a form of rejecting the responsibilities that militants might have had – in the form of their political commitment – for the events in which they were involved. This representation of the *desaparecidos* was a response to the stigmatisation of the political identities of militants by the military dictatorship, while introducing the marks of humanitarian discourses that arrived with the incorporation of denouncers to transnational networks (Crenzel 2008a).

Thus, as a symbolic category arising from a historic experience of enormous impact in the forms of political practice in democratic Argentina, the symbol of the *desaparición* made it possible 30 years later to project a new set of innocents. The old discourse that made women responsible for the violence to which they had been subjected – habitual in judiciary bureaucracies and the media – was contested through this powerful symbol. This enabled a place where women engaged in sexual commerce – whose reputation was always questioned[9] – could be thought of as victims of crimes without any moral censure being imposed on their access to justice. The same applied for young women: their frequent stigmatisation as "sluts", especially when they belonged to subaltern sectors and escaped from the mandate of domesticity did not free the state from its responsibility to protect them. While the choice of the category by those who put it into circulation could have been strictly tactical and in connection with the situation in which it was deployed, its resonances were always broader. The trafficking-disappearance narrative, aside from the simplifications and binarisms that it involved, also constituted a tool to reconstruct political responsibilities and demand that the state listen and attend to violence against women more sensitively.

Final reflections

The Argentine case helps to illustrate how flexible and malleable anti-trafficking discourses can be. Cheng shows how the vernacularisation was connected in South Korea to the defense of nationalist culture as well as to the desire to guarantee South Korea's entry into the world of modern nations. In Argentina the campaign constructed a "hyper-local" narrative deeply linked to the transitional justice process and the politics of memory of the recent past. In doing so, the campaign lost its original references to supranational and transnational spaces and established itself within a local tradition of political struggle.[10]

The support garnered by the Argentine anti-trafficking campaign and the rapid institution-alisation of its demands did not result directly from the state's interests in restricting migration or from the rise of a neoliberal regime, although components of a neoliberal political rationality can be identified within it.[11] While pressures from the US State Department were key in the initial impetus, the campaign soon succeeded in delineating an agenda and course of its own, in which even an anti-imperialist rhetoric could quickly be mobilised. In this chapter I have sought to highlight the labourious work on the part of activists who produced interpretative frameworks that modeled a local version of trafficking as a public problem.

In the early years of the campaign, the idea of *mujeres desaparecidas en democracia* [women disap-peared in democracy] constituted an indisputable political symbol, both because of its resonances in Argentine history and because of the "structure of the conjuncture" (Sahlins 2008) in which it was put into circulation, that is, in a context in which the government endorsed the human rights movement's historic demands for "memory, truth and justice" and inscribed itself in the geneal-ogy of the militants of the 1970s.[12] While evoking the figure of the *desaparecido* in the years of democratic transition had been a way of disputing the negationist perspectives of crimes commit-ted during state terrorism, three decades later it constituted a now-consolidated political symbol that allowed anti-trafficking activists to model a familiar framework for a broader audience than the initial community of committed activists.

In observing the effects of this strategy, its consequences seem ambivalent, and the issue opens up a number of questions: Did these new innocents – projected through the vernacular language of human rights – effectively succeed in displacing the moral censure over women's sexual conduct and in reconstructing new responsibilities? What were the potentialities of the rhetoric of *desaparición* for questioning the justice systems and the media's dissimilar treatment of women based on their reputation? What were the limits of this rhetoric? In posing these questions I put forward an approach to the uses by local feminisms of the vernacular language of human rights, and seek to grasp their potentialities as well as their limits, and ambivalences.

Vance (2012) has argued that describing violations of human rights in the area of sex trafficking confronts us with the specific problems of representing sexuality. The trafficking-disappearance metaphor provided a powerful and indisputable symbol that allowed feminist activists to access areas that had previously been hostile to their demands, but also suppressed heterogeneities and portrayed victims according to traditional gender models. On the one hand, it imposed a stereotyped representation of sex work that left no room for the desires, projects and experiences of sex workers when they placed themselves outside of victimisation. On the other hand, it undermined the agency of young women and their sexual-affective experimentation, as they were presented as subjects who were no longer "corruptible" but sexually "vulnerable" in their movement outside of domesticity. The new paradigm thus radically inverted the feminist perspectives that had placed the greatest dangers to women within the domestic/private sphere.

The idea that "women's rights are human rights" has a long history since the 1993 Vienna Conference, and was embraced by local feminists in Argentina from an early stage. But human rights, from an anthropological perspective, are not just instrumental mechanisms but also expres-sive tools: they construct identities, class subjects and legitimise claims in the context of power relations (Vance 2012; Vianna 2013). In the case here analysed, a human rights perspective constructed through a rhetoric based on the "innocence" of women raises a number of problematic questions. If the figure of the *desaparecido* omitted militants' political commitment, the representation of the victim of trafficking – or the young woman who leaves home – as *desaparecida* was premised on the effacement of the sexual experience. As Pecheny (2013) has pointed out, depoliticisation and desexualisation are coordinated movements. In some way, the cost of shifting moral censure towards those women suspected of crossing the limits of gender norms was the effacement of their sexual experience. Along this path, the human rights rhetoric in Argentina was quickly articulated with traditional ideals of femininity and sexual respectability and the language of the struggle between good and evil. Lastly, by filtering the human rights perspective of women who sell sex through the trafficking-disappearance paradigm, we paradoxically run the risk of "disappearing" sex workers and their voices from the debate. Their perspectives are urgently required to outline interventions that will make it possible to expand their capacity to not only exercise rights but also to imagine them.

Notes

1 "Never again" was the name used by the Comisión Nacional sobre la Desaparición de Personas (CONADEP) to title the final report on their investigation. By extension, it is an expression frequently used in Argentina to repudiate state terrorism.

2 Following Gusfield (2003: 71), the idea of a "public problem" allows us to designate "the process through which a state of affairs becomes an object of public reflection and protest as well as a target and resources for public action".

3 The Full Stop Law, passed in 1986, set a deadline for criminal action against those charged with the crime of forced disappearance during the civic-military dictatorship. The Law of Due Obedience, passed in 1987, established the assumption that the crimes committed by members of the armed forces ranked below colonel were not punishable, as they acted in virtue of so-called "due obedience" to their superiors. Both laws were opposed by the human rights movement and, together with the pardons for the heads of the armed forces in 1989 and 1990 were known as the "laws of impunity".

4 The Argentine courts have verified the kidnapping of Fernanda Aguirre in 2004 – for which her parents paid a ransom – and have condemned a responsible party for the crime. The case contains numerous mysteries, as Fernanda's body was never found. Florencia Penacchi was a young middle-class woman, an economic science student, who disappeared in 2005 in a neighbourhood in central Buenos Aires.

5 In particular, the Registro Nacional de Información de Personas Menores Extraviadas [National Registry of Missing Children] (2011 2012, 2013) documented extensively the "feminisation of runaways". But the reports put this disparity down to many issues far-removed from the trafficking-disappearance paradigm: gender-based violence, excess of domestic duties, teenage pregnancy, oppressive limits on the use of free time and restrictions on sexual-affective relationships. This perspective was excluded in the construction of the public problem as the trafficking-disappearance paradigm gradually became institutionalised in the following years (Varela and González 2015).

6 In 1984 the CONADEP registered 8,960 disappeared. Argentine human rights organisations claim the existence of 30,000 cases of disappeared persons.

7 In other aspects, the politics of numbers are incomparable. From the late 1970s, human rights organisations constructed a solid repertoire of strategies through which information was documented on kidnappings, places of detention, names of victims and perpetrators (Basualdo 2011). The anti-trafficking movement, in contrast, submitted figures bearing no relation to the few real persons reported "disappeared" publicly (Varela and González 2015).

8 According to Nora (1992: 20), a *lieu de memoire* is "any significant entity, whether material or immaterial, which by dint of human will or the work of time has become a symbolic element of the memorial heritage of any community". It is a notion that aims at the commemorative capacity of objects, whether material or immaterial.

9 Sexual reputations are constituted from gender normativities that value differentially the sexual experiences of young men and women. The "slut" stigma is the main stereotype of feminine sexuality in the region and functions as a regulating perspective of young women's sexuality, producing a hierarchy based on traditional gender models (Jones 2010)

10 In fact, the ideas of "being part of the world" or "modern" are self-definitions of the new right-wing government that started in 2015, in opposition to the Kirchnerist past, perceived as isolated from the free market economy.

11 For example, in the growing identification between criminal justice and social justice (Bernstein 2010). What deserves more attention in the Argentine case is how anti-trafficking rhetoric, while maintaining a neoliberal logic, coexisted with an expanding language of rights and mobilised anti-capitalist imaginaries.

12 Sahlins (2008: XIV) defines the "structure of the conjuncture" as "the practical realisation of the cultural categories in a specific historical context, as expressed in the interested action of the historic actors, including the microsociology of their interaction".

References

Anderson, B. and Andrijasevic, R. (2008). Sex, slaves and citizens: the politics of anti-trafficking. *Soundings*, 40(40), pp. 135–145.

Andreas, P. and Greenhill, K. (2010). *Sex, drugs, and body counts*. Ithaca, NY: Cornell University Press.

Aradau, C. (2014). *Rethinking trafficking in women*. New York: Palgrave Macmillan.

Basualdo, G. (2011). Las estrategias políticas y jurídicas del Centro de estudios Legales y Sociales en la movilización legal internacional durante la última dictadura militar (1976–1983). Licenciatura: UBA.

Bernstein, E. (2010). Militarized humanitarianism meets carceral feminism: the politics of sex, rights, and freedom in contemporary antitrafficking campaigns. *Signs: Journal of Women in Culture and Society*, 36(1), pp. 45–71.

Bernstein, E. (2016). Redemptive capitalism and sexual investability. Perverse Politics? Feminism, Anti-Imperialism, Multiplicity. Political Power and Social Theory, 30, pp. 45–80.

Blanchette, T. and da Silva, A.P. (2012). On bullshit and the trafficking of women: moral entrepreneurs and the invention of trafficking of persons in Brazil. *Dialectical Anthropology*, 36(1–2), pp. 107–125.

Carbajal, M. (2007). Son las desaparecidas de la democracia. *Página 12* [online]. Available at: www.pagina12.com.ar/diario/sociedad/3-82768-2007-04-04.html [Accessed 8 February 2018].

Carabajal, G. (2010). Trata de personas, un delito que crece. *La Nación* [online]. Available at: www.lanacion.com.ar/1248140-trata-de-personas-un-delito-que-crece [Accessed 8 February 2018].

Cheng, S. (2011). The paradox of vernacularization: women's human rights and the gendering of nation-hood. *Anthropological Quarterly*, 84(2), pp. 475–505.

Clarin (2007). Susana Trimarco: "No le tengo miedo a nada" [online]. Available at: http://edant.clarin.com/suplementos/mujer/2007/06/05/m-01432083.htm [Accessed 8 February 2018].

Clarin (2008). Explotación sexual: desde 2007 desaparecieron 550 mujeres [online]. Available at: www.clarin.com/sociedad/explotacion-sexual-2007-desaparecieron-550-mujeres_0_BkclW-TRTFl.html [Accessed 8 February 2018].

Comisión Nacional sobre la Desaparición de Personas (1984) *Nunca Más*. Buenos Aires: Eudeba.

Crenzel, E. (2008a). *La historia política del Nunca más*. Buenos Aires: Siglo Veintiuno Editores.

Crenzel, E. (2008b). Memorias y representaciones de los desaparecidos en la Argentina 1983–2008. In: E. Crenzel, ed., *Los desaparecidos en la Argentina. Memorias, representaciones e ideas (1983–2008)*. Buenos Aires: Biblos, pp. 11–23.

Crenzel, E. (2010). *Los desaparecidos en la Argentina. Memorias, representaciones e ideas. 1983–2008*. Buenos Aires: Editorial Biblos.

Dillon, M. (2014). Mover cielo y tierra. *Página 12* [online]. Available at: www.pagina12.com.ar/diario/suplementos/las12/13-8790-2014-04-19.html [Accessed 8 February 2018].

Di Marco, G. (2011). *El pueblo feminista*. Buenos Aires: Editorial Biblos.

Ditmore, M. and Wijers, M. (2003). The negotiations on the UN Protocol to trafficking in persons. *NEMESIS*, 4, pp. 79–88.

Doezema, J. (2004). A crecer! La infantilización de las mujeres en los debates sobre "tráfico de mujeres". In: R. Osborne, ed., *Trabajador@s del sexo. Derechos, migraciones y tráfico en el siglo XXI*. Madrid: Belaterra, pp. 151–163.

Doezema, J. (2010). *Sex slaves and discourse masters*. Zed Books.

Feingold, D. (2010). Trafficking in numbers: the social construction of human trafficking data. In: P. Andreas and K. Greenhill, ed., *Sex, drugs, and body counts: the politics of number in global crime and conflict*. Ithacca: Cornell University, pp. 46–51.

Fitzgerald, S. (2012). Vulnerable bodies, vulnerable borders: extraterritoriality and human trafficking. *Feminist Legal Studies*, 20(3), pp. 227–244.

Fundación El Otro (2007). *Informe: La trata de personas en Argentina* [online]. Available at: https://filatina. wordpress.com/2009/03/23/fundacion-el-otro-para-evitar-la-esclavitud-wwwelotroorgar/ [Accessed 8 February 2018].

Gatti, G. (2017). Prolegómeno. Para un concepto científico de desaparición. In: G. Gatti, ed., *Desapariciones. Usos locales, circulaciones globales*. Bogotá: Siglo del Hombre editores. Universidad de los Andes, pp. 15–30.

Gusfield, J. (2003). "Action collective et problèmes publics". In D. Cefai and D. Pasquier, ed., *Le sens du public. Publics politiques, publiques médiatiques* Paris: Presses Universitaires de France, pp. 63–78.

Gusfield, J. (2014). *La cultura de los problemas públicos*. CABA: Siglo XXI.

Infobae (2010). Las desaparecidas de la Argentina [online]. Available at: www.infobae.com/2010/09/24/538242-las-desaparecidas-la-argentina/ [Accessed 9 February 2018].

Jones, D. (2010). *Sexualidades adolescentes*. Buenos Aires: CLACSO.

Jordan, A. (2011). *Fact or fiction: what do we really know about human trafficking?* Issue Paper 3. Washington, DC: Center for Human Rights and Humanitarian Law, American University Washington College of Law.

La Nación (2010). 700 mujeres secuestradas en Argentina en 18 meses [online]. Available at: www.nacion. com/el-mundo/700-mujeres-secuestradas-en-argentina-en-18-meses/5VPOB42WVRGMLIAUC X5PDNWOCE/story/ [Accessed 8 February 2018].

Las Juanas (2009). *Construyendo prevención. Se trata de nosotras* [online]. Las Juanas. Available at: https:// es.scribd.com/doc/23303652/cuadernillo-trata [Accessed 8 February 2018].

Longoni, A. (2010). Fotos y siluetas: dos estrategias en la representación de los desaparecidos. In Crenzel, E. (ed.). *Los desaparecidos en la Argentina. Memorias, representaciones e ideas (1983–2008)*. Buenos Aires: Biblos, pp. 43–63.

Lowenkron, L. (2012). O monstro contemporâneo: a construção social da pedofilia em múltiplos planos. Rio de Janeiro: EdUERJ.

Merry, S.E. (2006). Human rights and gender violence: translating international law into local justice. Chicago, IL: University of Chicago Press.

Nora, P. (1992). Comment écrire l'histoire de France. In: P. Nora, ed., *Les lieux de mémoire, Les France*. Paris: Gallimard, pp. 12–32.

Organización Internacional para las Migraciones [International Organization for Migration] (2003). *Migración, prostitución y trata de mujeres dominicanas en Argentina*. Buenos Aires: IOM.

Pecheny, M. (2013). Sexual politics and post-neoliberalism in Latin America. *Scholar & Feminist Online* [online] (11.1–11.2). Available at: http://sfonline.barnard.edu/gender-justice-and-neoliberal-transfor mations/sexual-politics-and-post-neoliberalism-in-latin-america [Accessed 31 January 2018].

Piscitelli, A. (2015). Riesgos: la capilarización del enfrentamiento a la trata de personas en las tensiones entre planos supranacionales, nacionales y locales. Paper presented to 4th Latin American Congress on Human trafficking, La Paz.

Piscitelli, A. and Lowenkron, L. (2015). Trabajadoras sexuales, policía, migración y trata internacional de seres humanos en Brasil y España. In: D. Daich and M. Sirimarco, ed., *Género y Violencia en el mercado del sexo*. Buenos Aires: Biblos, pp. 173–203.

Rabotnikof, N. (2018). Memoria y política a treinta años del golpe. In: C. Lida, H. Gutierrez Crespo and P. Yankelevich, ed., *Argentina, 1976. Estudios en torno al golpe de estado*. Mexico DF: Centro de estudios históricos del Colegio de México, pp. 259–284.

Registro Nacional de Información de Personas Menores Extraviadas. (2011). *Informe de gestión 2010*. Aguilar: CABA.

Registro Nacional de Información de Personas Menores Extraviadas. (2012). *Informe de gestión 2011*. Aguilar: CABA.

Registro Nacional de Información de Personas Menores Extraviadas. (2013). *Informe de gestión 2012*. Aguilar: CABA.

Sahlins, Marshall. (2008). *Islas de historia*. Barcelona: Gedisa.

Schuster, F. and Pereyra, S. (2001). Transformaciones de la protesta social en Argentina: balance y perspectivas de una forma de acción política. In: N. Giarraca, ed., *Protesta social en Argentina. Transformaciones económicas y crisis social en el interior del país*. Buenos Aires: Alianza, pp. 42–63.

Sikkink, K. (2008). From pariah state to global protagonist: Argentina and the struggle for international human rights. *Latin American Politics and Society*, 50(1), pp. 1–29.

Silva, A., Blanchette, T., Pinho, A., Pinheiro, B. and Leite, G. (2005). Prostitutas, "traficadas" e pânicos morais: uma análise da produção de fatos em pesquisas sobre o "tráfico de seres humanos". *Cadernos Pagu*, 25, pp. 153–184.

Sutton, B. (2010). *Bodies in crisis*. New Brunswick, NJ: Rutgers University Press.

Tonkonoff, S. (2014). Violencia, política y cultura. Una aproximación teórica. In: S. Tonkonoff, ed., *Violencia y Cultura. Reflexiones contemporáneas sobre Argentina*. Buenos Aires: CLACSO, pp. 15–30.

Vallejos, S. (2013). Trimarco. *La mujer que lucha por todas las mujeres*. Aguilar: CABA.

Vance, C. (2012). Innocence and experience: melodramatic narratives of sex trafficking and their consequences for law and policy. *History of the Present*, 2(2), pp. 200–218.

Varela, C. and González, F. (2015). Tráfico de cifras: "Desaparecidas" y "rescatadas" en la construcción de la trata como problema público en la Argentina. *Apuntes de investigación del CECYP*, 26, pp. 74–99.

Vianna, A. (2013). Apresentacao. In: A. Vianna, ed., O fazer e o desfazer dos direitos: Experiências etnográficas sobre política, administração e moralidades. Rio de Janeiro: E-papers.

20

Beyond dichotomies

Exploring responses to tackling the sex industry in Nepal

Shovita Dhakal Adhikari

Introduction

> If a girl would like to work as a dancer or a sex worker, it is fine – she has the right do so. However, she should be able to perform in an environment free from exploitation, and there should be no compromise when it comes to issues relating to her health and safety. We run awareness programmes: we tell them it is a highly risky job; we tell them: 'be safe'; and [we] talk about their rights.
>
> *(Interview with Ravina, NGO officer working with sex workers, April 2014)*

This statement articulates the concern that inadequate protection of women and girls working in the sex industry has led to the violation of their rights to work and obtain necessary health care and social respect. Regulation of the sex industry[1] is envisaged as a way forward in several countries (Armstrong 2010; Chapkis 2000). The organisation and regulation of the sex industry is a highly debated issue in contemporary Nepal and is frequently featured in the national media, often with sensationalistic headlines. The sex industry in Nepal has witnessed a massive resurgence, largely due to the expansion of the entertainment sector in the last decade. This has resulted in an unprecedented rise in a number of non-governmental organisations (NGOs) and international NGOs (INGOs)[2] focused on the sex industry with a range of programmes and intervention strategies. The government's attempts at addressing the issues facing the entertainment sector have led to the enactment of several regulations in recent years. In particular, two documents are worth mentioning (both of which are meant to regulate and protect the rights of women and girls in entertainment sector): the *Guidelines for the Control of Sexual Exploitation among Female Workers in Dance and Bar Restaurants and the Like Business* (2008) and the *Code of Conduct for the Night-Time Entertainment Industry* (2009) (NHRC 2010).[3] However, there is little evidence to indicate the extent to which these regulations have been put into practice. Such uncertainties in tackling the sex industry in practice are also experienced in other countries. For instance, Gangoli and Westmarland (2006) note the problems of enforcing sex industry regulations in countries such as India, Pakistan, and Moldova. In the context of Nepal, this problem has been further complicated due to the fact that the sex industry overlaps with certain trafficking phenomena. In this chapter, I show how this situation has led to tensions and dilemmas when addressing the vulnerabilities of sex workers and identifying trafficked victims in the sex industry. The remainder of the chapter is organised as follows. At the outset, I briefly discuss the existing literature on regulating sex work. This is followed by an overview of sex work in Nepal, including the historical development of sex work, the connection between the sex industry and trafficking, urbanisation in the 1980s and the 1990s, and the expansion of the sex industry. The empirical analysis – which is based on semi-structured interviews conducted between 2014 and 2015, with 58 interviewees representing donor agencies, government offices, I/NGOs, and other anti-trafficking networks – focuses on the approaches taken by different agencies to intervening in the sex industry. Despite attempts to regulate the sex industry, the practices employed by support organisations are often limited to controlling measures (rescue, rehabilitation, and reintegration model). Such measures often bound up in the choice/coercion and innocent/savvy dichotomies. Discussing the key factors at play in shaping the experiences of women and girls (for instance, the process of entry into the sex industry, working conditions, and the reasons for remaining in the industry), I argue that responses to the sex industry have been largely inadequate. I conclude by noting the importance of looking beyond the dichotomies and addressing the labour exploitation and other human rights violations that women and girls are facing in the Nepalese sex industry.

Regulating sex work

Much of the prior work in this area explores the interactions between sex workers, police, and support agencies in street-based sex work in developed nations (Armstrong 2017; Dalla 2006; Dewey and Germain 2017; Weitzer 2014). For instance, Armstrong (2017) argues that the relationship between police and sex workers takes place in a criminalised context and therefore is fraught with tensions. Consequently, sex workers are often isolated from available legal, health, and social services (Dewey and Germain 2017). Research conducted on street-based sex work in the United States shows that the responses from the criminal justice system and social services are problematic since they penalise women for the choices and decisions they have undertaken in very restricted circumstances (Dewey and Germain 2017). It has been pointed out that the decriminalisation of prostitution would likely improve in the relationship between police and street-based sex workers (Armstrong 2017).

However, there is only limited research available on the perceptions of support agencies' efforts in dealing with the indoor commercial sex venues in developing countries (particularly in a context where there is a strong link between sex work and sex trafficking). Weitzer (2014) argues that an understanding of the geographical contexts plays an important role in this regard as sex work differs significantly from one context to another. Presenting the case of Nepal, this study adds to the existing debate on sex work. There are no specific laws that define or penalise sex workers or prostitution in Nepal (Godwin 2012).[4] As I discuss later, some legal provisions have actually codified prostitution as a form of exploitation. Given these ambiguities in the legal framework, and considering the historical trajectories of sex work, the case of Nepal provides a unique setting to provide a nuanced understanding of the responses to the sex industry in developing countries.

Sex work in Nepal

Historical overview

To understand the responses to the sex industry, it is useful to first explore the historical roots of prostitution in Nepal. The historical roots of prostitution in Nepal are, as stated by

Richardson et al. (2009), cemented by the dominant Hindu value system. This system has reinforced the country's traditional patriarchal society and contributed to institutionalised prostitution in the country. Historically, the sex trade in Nepal has been confined to particular caste groups – *Badi* and *Deuki* – which are at the bottom of the caste hierarchy. For instance, in the *Badi* caste (untouchable Hindu caste), children are forced to work as prostitutes from early puberty by their parents to generate income (Ghimire 1994). In the nineteenth and early twentieth centuries, *Badi* women and girls were often recruited as professional dancers, singers, and *Keti syams* (housemaids) to offer entertainment and sexual services to the Rana rulers,[5] religious leaders, and landlords (Cox 1992; Kara 2012; Sangroula 2001). As a consequence, prostitution eventually became a means of survival for the *Badi* community, especially after the demand for singing and dancing declined in later years. Cox (1992) states that the market of *Badi* prostitution witnessed a significant rise after the fall of the Ranas in the 1950s. In the *Deuki* tradition, young girls from very poor and socially disadvantaged families, mainly from south-west Nepal, were offered to temples by their parents so as to fulfil their religious obligations (Ghimire 1994). Having been offered to serve in the temple, these girls were deprived the right of getting married or obtaining education. Many of these girls embraced prostitution as a profession since they had few alternatives for survival in the transition from childhood to adolescence. Although the practice of the *Deuki* was abolished later in the 1990s, *Deuki* women and girls continued to be deprived of many rights, including the right to education and marriage, all of which made it much harder to abandon prostitution and return to normal living (personal interviews).

Historically established connection between the sex industry and trafficking

The sex industry in Nepal differs from many other developing countries in that there is a close connection to cross-border trafficking (Cox 1992). In the aftermath of the Rana regime, young girls who were once recruited to entertain the rulers were trafficked to various Indian brothels (ILO-IPEC 2002; Samarasinghe 2008; Sangroula 2001). In fact, by the 1960s there was already a high demand for Nepalese girls in Indian brothels. The sex trade evolved into a lucrative business and a large number of brokers were involved in trafficking illiterate girls and women from villages and marginalised caste groups to brothels, luring them with the promise of opportunities for a better life and employment in big Indian cities. Young women and girls who had been involved in the *Badini* and *Deuki*, and girls from marginalised caste groups in western Nepal (including Tamang, Magar, Sherpa, Kami, and Majhi), were particularly victimised by sex trafficking (Samarasinghe 2008). The sex trade flourished further in the 1970s with the establishment of large criminal gangs and well-established links connecting the Indian sex industry and Nepalese recruiters (Ghimire 1994; NHRC 2008; Sangroula 2001; Terre des Hommes 2003). As a result, discourses on trafficking in Nepal were constructed, predicated on the assumption that it is primarily an issue of 'buying and selling of girls in the sex industry' (Samarasinghe 2008; Sanghera 2005). Such historical trajectories have influenced the responses to the sex industry, which makes the case of Nepal stand out in comparison to other developing countries.

Urbanisation of the sex industry in the 1980s and 1990s

Since the 1980s, so-called 'urban prostitution' (Worthen 2011) has become distinct in Nepal. The emergence of this form of prostitution is directly related to the expansion of the entertainment sector in the country and the promotion of commercial sex-based industries such as dance bars, *Dohori* restaurants,[6] cabin restaurants,[7] and massage parlours. Such an expansion of sex-based activities has further contributed both to the domestication and expansion of the sex trade in Nepal. The country experienced a wave of rural–urban migration in the 1990s due to the escalating Maoist armed conflict, which culminated in 2005 after the monarchy was abolished and the country became a federal state. The 1990s was also marked by the country's falling international trade (mainly the decline of carpet and garment exports to the West), thereby accumulating huge budget deficits and stifling economic growth (IIDS and UNIFEM 2004; NHRC 2008, 2010). A large number of workers once employed in the garment and carpets industries shifted to the entertainment sector as it was the only alternative left to them. Various studies (Malik et al. 2009 and personal interviews) show that, in the process of adjusting themselves to the entertainment sector, many of these workers were eventually plunged into the sex industry.

Further expansion of the sex industry

Today, the domestic sex industry has expanded in various forms – ranging from bars and guest houses to tea shops and different types of restaurants (including cabin restaurants), both in urban and semi-urban areas.[8] Prior studies claim that workers engaged in the entertainment sector are subject to increasing sexual and labour exploitation (Frederick 2012; NHRC 2008). The structure of the Nepalese entertainment sector is constructed in such a way that once the young girls and women enter this sector, most of them end up being engaged in sex work (as discussed later in the chapter).[9] These workers face widespread sexual abuse (which is institutionalised in the entertainment sector), stigma associated with the entertainment sector, and meagre salaries for the hard and exploitative work. Without clear regulations to protect against these problems, it is unsurprising that women and girls end up in street-based sex work, which is arguably more dangerous (Armstrong 2017; Dalla 2006). The expansion of the sex industry provides a useful context for the analysis of empirical findings. Before moving on to explore the key factors that have shaped workers' experiences in the sex industry, I provide an overview of the contextual background and the approaches taken by different organisations to tackle the sex industry in Nepal. This will contribute to an understanding of why the responses to the sex industry in Nepal have remained problematic.

Findings

Approaches to intervening in the sex industry: the 'rescue, rehabilitation, and reintegration' model

As mentioned earlier, sex trafficking and the sex trade are so closely intertwined in Nepal that national policies and programmes relating to the sex industry have been developed with a view to deterring trafficking activities rather than addressing the violence, exploitation, and other harms associated with the sex industry. The approaches used by different organisations to intervene in the sex industry focus on control measures informed by abolitionist discourses. This can be observed in several enactments, for instance the National Code of the 1980s, and the 1986 Human Trafficking (Control) Act including its revised version, which was issued in 2007 with a view to prohibiting the slave trade and human trafficking (FWLD 2014; IIDS and UNIFEM 2004). These legislations have in fact codified prostitution as a form of exploitation.

The issue of trafficking for the purpose of prostitution in Nepal came to international attention in the mid-1990s, after 128 Nepalese girls were rescued from brothels in India. This rescue mission was a joint effort of the Indian Government and Nepalese NGOs (Pradhan 1996).

This rescue mission also impacted the way local NGOs were dealing with those who were assumed to be victims of the sex trade. Given that they had to prioritise immediate shelter and relief to these victims, many of these NGOs started looking at international resources. Some NGOs even made an appeal for international support at the Stockholm World Congress Against Commercial Sexual Exploitation of Children in 1996 (Pradhan 1996). Such an attempt at internationalising sex trafficking resulted in a proliferation of anti-trafficking organisations in the country supported by international donors (Crawford 2010). The 'Three Rs' – rescue, rehabilitation, and reintegration[10] – has been one of the most important areas of interventions since then.

At present, more than 100 NGOs work in collaboration with government agencies and donors in order to combat trafficking to the sex industry in Nepal (as well as cross-border and international trafficking) (IIDS and UNIFEM 2004).[11] There are 19 UN agencies, INGOs, and other international agencies (e.g. UNDP, UNICEF, ILO-IPEC, PLAN International, Save the Children Alliance, Asia Foundation, and World Education) offering financial and technical support to facilitate interventions in the sex trade, including projects to rescue/rehabilitate the victims (IIDS and UNIFEM 2004). However, very little is known about how the financial support is being used (Crawford 2010). A study by the Institute for Integrated Development Studies (IIDS) and the United Nations Development Fund for Women (UNIFEM) (2004) states that money spent on anti-trafficking initiatives in Nepal in 2001 (including controlling the sex trade) exceeded US $2.5 million. It is unclear, however, whether the money has been spent on the 'target group' or has been used for other purposes.

Police raids at the behest of local and international organisations engaged in the rescue and rehabilitation of sex workers are quite common across countries (Ahmed and Seshu 2012). The effectiveness of rescue and raid programmes targeted particularly on women and girls working in the entertainment sector has been widely debated in Nepal. Some of the rescue workers representing I/NGOs that I interviewed seemed to be convinced of the positive impact that police raids could have in protecting sex workers. For instance, an INGO officer I interviewed remarked: 'police raids have certainly helped regulate the closing time of restaurants/bars and control sex activities' (Manu, April 2014). However, most of the rescue operators, mainly those involved in developing programmes in the entertainment sector have questioned the significance of such raids, as they tend to take little consideration of the impact that such interventions could have on women and girls. This has been well documented in several other countries (e.g. Ahmed and Seshu 2012; Segrave et al. 2009), and is also evident in the case of Nepal, where police raids have resulted in more harm to women and girls in the sex industry. For instance, an NGO officer stated:

> Police raids have led to more negative consequences in the sex industry. I am aware of many cases in which the police officers who rescued the girls and women through raids have brought them back to the same place [a bar or restaurant]. Most of the police officers are already bribed and they undertake raids in the sex industry just to show the public that they are doing something to control sex activities.
>
> *(Gita, August 2015)*

The adoption of the 'abolitionist' approach – as seen in the practice of police raids, for instance – has contributed to concealing sex work in Nepal.[12] The failure of rescue and reintegration programmes was highlighted during the interviews. For instance, an NGO officer noted: 'Out of 100 girls who were reintegrated after the raids, two have returned to their families and the others are back in the same sector [entertainment]' (Ravina, April 2014). The programmes being offered in Nepal have therefore appeared inadequate in terms of mitigating the risk of sexual and physical violence against women and girls working in the sex industry. Mentions are made that the programmes designed to help women and girls working in the sex industry should therefore carefully assess the factors – such as the process of entry, working conditions, economic conditions, and stigma – contributing to such exploitation and vulnerabilities. Some of these factors are explored below.

Process of entry and working conditions

The process of entry into the entertainment sector is subtle. Initially women and girls are recruited in the entertainment sector as waitresses, dancers, and singers. The actual intention of preparing them for sexual services is never disclosed. The transition into sex work is, however, not straightforward and may take a considerable amount of time. In many instances, the process starts in rural areas where women and girls are approached by an agent or a middle man (*dalal*). For example, women and girls and their families are promised employment and better education opportunities. An element of 'deception' is usually involved in this process. A police officer during an interview shared with me a job advert in which women and girls are encouraged to apply for 'a lucrative employment in a dance bar in the city with a good salary and an opportunity of getting an education' (Ram, August 2015). Once trained, some of them are given the opportunity to go to Middle Eastern countries and continue performing similar activities, but with higher salary and in better living conditions.

Chapkis (2000, 184) argues that whether legal or illegal, those employed in third-party controlled sex work encounter 'special challenges in their efforts to exercise control over their work'. Such is also evident in the case of Nepal, where workers in the entertainment sector are often exposed to various other forms of exploitation. For instance, they are forced to work long hours, usually at night, with low wages, and adverse working conditions. Moreover, they are victimised by both exploitative working conditions and frequent arrests and abuse they are subject to by the police (Maiti Nepal 2010). Some minors are even given hormonal medicines so as to make them look mature (older) and avoid questions about their age. Women and girls are often forced to maintain their physical appearance because their wages are determined by how they look. A government officer stated: 'the lighter the colour, the more the wages – this is a simple fact' (Prem, August 2015). There are also cases in which women and girls working in the entertainment sector have been indebted in the process of maintaining their living standards. These women and girls are not allowed to abandon the sector without paying their debts, thus leaving them with few alternatives other than to accept foreign employment. The way Nepal's sex industry operates is therefore rather unique.

These women and girls working in the entertainment sector are the most at risk of being victims of exploitation, but are the least protected due to the conflation of sex trafficking and sex work. Some of those I interviewed from the government and I/NGOs strongly believed that these workers should be considered victims of sex trafficking since they are subject to deception and exploitation. Others were of the opinion that 'freedom' is a key factor and that this is a sufficient criterion to determine the status of a woman or girl as trafficked or not. An NGO officer summarised her view about 'choice' stating: 'the girls working in dance bars have flexible working hours and are not concerned by the bar owners. They are free to roam during the daytime with friends' (Ravina, April 2014). It was revealed during interviews with government officers that law enforcement authorities often believe women and girls working in the entertainment sector enter into sex work by their own 'choice' and should not be seen as sex trafficking victims. Such complexities in defining and understanding sex workers are also evident in developed nations. In the case of the United States, Farrell and Cronin (2015, 211) argue that, despite law enforcement officers receiving training on how to identify human trafficking cases, there is still confusion about human trafficking and prostitution, and therefore it requires different types of law enforcement responses. Delivering support in Nepal has thus been marred by conflicting practices and tensions between different perspectives. In such circumstances, clear categories of who are innocent (if they are duped) or savvy (eager to try their luck) are constructed that facilitate an implementation of the protection of certain women and girls in the entertainment sector. This corresponds to the work of O'Brien et al. (2013, 71) stating that 'in attempting to create a blameless Madonna, these depictions have created a narrative that ignores women who choose to work in the sex industry (but who are also exploited or trafficked)'. As I show below, reasons to stay in the sex industry have, in many situations, been determined by factors such as self-stigma and money. The next section discusses the impact of these factors on women and girls in the sex industry.

Reasons to stay: self-stigma and money

There appear to be at least two underlying reasons for women and girls to continue in the sex industry: self-stigma and money. These women and girls often hold the perception that once they enter this profession, they cannot get out of it or work anywhere else. This further encourages them to stay and accept the kind of work they do. They tend to develop self-stigma, which hinders them from considering returning to the community and having a normal life. Some interviewees told me that it takes a considerable amount of time for these women and girls to realise that they have been trapped and that they are bonded.[13] In addition, by the time they realise that they have been trapped, they have become accustomed to an extravagant lifestyle, which they find rather difficult to surrender. Self-stigma and money (as well as other material gains) have therefore become dominant factors in encouraging victims to continue as sex workers. Women and girls face various structural constraints that contribute to their decision to be involved with in sex work, namely poverty and unemployment. This is also echoed in other countries (see Gangoli and Westmarland 2006), with Maiti Nepal (2010) arguing that structural and individual limitations provide the impetus for the entry of women and girls into the sex industry. Employment opportunities for women and girls are in fact limited in Nepal. According to the *Economist* (2011), income inequality in Nepal is the highest in Asia, overtaking countries such as China and the Philippines. Limited employment opportunities have forced many women and girls to undertake whatever jobs are available to them. A large number of women and girls have selected the entertainment sector since it appears to the best available option. O'Neill (2001, 160) states: 'Because there are limited resources in these villages and no employment opportunities, illiteracy, social unconsciousness, and social acceptance of multi-partner sexual behaviour have all contributed to the migration of girls into prostitution, though unknowingly and reluctantly.' An NGO officer during an interview expressed the dilemma in addressing the economic circumstances of sex workers:

> For example, [sex workers] stay with a guest [and they] get Rs.250 in one day; they might have 5–6 customers. Therefore, once in this business, they are used to generating money in a rather easy manner. It is really challenging to motivate them to withdraw from their work.

> *(Sushma, April 2014)*

On the whole, the realities of sex workers in practice are extremely complicated since there are several factors that explain why women and girls remain in the sex industry (Busza 2004). It is important to understand not only the underlying causes that encourage women and girls to choose the sex industry, but also their lack of awareness of the consequences of being sex workers. In fact, the way the government and I/NGOs have emphasised rescue and rehabilitation missions has, in some ways, reproduced the narrative of 'innocent victim'– which is counter to the very essence of the principles of human rights.

There are, however, a small group of support organisations I interviewed that outlined an alternative, by suggesting the importance of adopting a 'regulatory' approach (to promote and protect the rights of workers in the entertainment sector), as opposed to an 'abolitionist' approach. But, despite the fact that the guidelines on the operation of the entertainment sector (mentioned at the beginning of this chapter) are in place, the agencies assigned to implement them are unable to do so due to limited resources. Therefore, they are unable to identify those vulnerable to violence and exploitation in a timely manner.

Conclusion

The analysis of the responses to the sex industry in Nepal reveals a perceived overlap between the sex industry and sex trafficking, as seen in various countries. The rights of women and girls to work in a safe and healthy environment have been largely neglected due to several factors: the historical trajectories of sex work, conflicting laws and regulations, and the adoption of practices based on the 'abolitionist' approach. The programmes being offered in Nepal have appeared inadequate in terms of mitigating the risk of sexual and physical violence against women and girls working in the sex industry. Responses to tackling the sex industry become more productive when efforts are made to move beyond dichotomies like choice versus coercion and innocent versus savvy. Careful consideration should be given to such tensions while developing and executing programmes for regulating the sex industry and protecting the rights of sex workers. The support agencies involved in developing responses need to listen to the women and girls working in the sex industry. Those wanting to promote the well-being of sex industry workers should focus on the socio-cultural and historical dimensions that have driven women and girls into the sex industry and increased their vulnerabilities. Armstrong (2017, 571) argues that 'the provisions of rights can afford sex workers greater agency and control in a context in which they are typically understood as inherently disempowered'. There is also a need for further research demonstrating the effectiveness of 'regulatory' approaches to protecting women who are already in the sex industry. In many South Asian countries, including Nepal, there is an ongoing debate about the need for decriminalising prostitution/sex work to ensure that sex workers 'fully enjoy legal rights to health and safety at work' (Godwin 2012, 7). For instance, a recent study on the assessment of the vulnerability of young women working in the entertainment sector concluded that 'there should be a policy in place to decriminalise employees in this sector' (Maiti Nepal 2010, 60). If this is the case, Nepal may also follow the model of decriminalisation in New Zealand, which, according to Armstrong (Chapter 13 in this volume), 'could easily be achieved in other countries if there is a political will to listen to sex workers and recognise the value of their expertise'. It should be noted, however, that this may face specific difficulties in Nepal as the country is not 'equipped to effectively regulate the industry or to address the violence, health and labour problems that accompany a sex industry' (Frederick et al. 2010, 62).

Notes

1 The terms 'sex industry' and 'sex work' are not 'limited to the act of "sex", but also [refer] to various forms of direct and indirect sexual activities' (Hardy et al. 2010, 3).
2 I also refer to both types of organisation with the acronym I/NGOs.
3 The Guidelines require all businesses belonging to the entertainment sector to register in the District Administration Offices (DAO). Furthermore, the Guidelines have prohibited sexual exploitation of workers and other forms or harassment. The Code of Conduct emphasises the provision of an identity card and a work contract, as well as declaring minimum wages for workers in the entertainment sector. To implement these regulations, a Monitoring and Action Committee (MAC) has been established by including representatives from various government offices such as: the Chief District Officer (CDO), police officers, officers from the Nepal Women's Commission, and the Women's Welfare Officer (NHRC 2010).
4 The constitution of Nepal 2015 has ensured the rights of citizens to practice the profession they wish to engage in. Sex work therefore, as an act itself, is not a criminal activity in Nepal. However, very often, sex workers are arrested and prosecuted using the Public Offences and Penalties Act of 1970 (Godwin 2012).
5 The Ranas were a feudal family who called themselves 'the Kings' and their regime lasted from 1846–1951 (Sangroula 2001).
6 *Dohori* restaurants offer live performance of duet songs (Maiti Nepal 2010).
7 These are restaurants that offer food and drinks, as well as sexual services, and that include an eating space as well as some cabins separated by wooden frames or a curtain where sexual services are provided (NHRC 2010).
8 In 2010, it was estimated that approximately 2,600 female sex workers are working in Nepal. Approximately 20% of the sex workers are street-based and 40% were associated with the entertainment sector (mainly cabin restaurants, dance bars, and massage parlours) (HSCB/NCASC 2011).
9 It should be noted that this structure may well also be found in other countries – thus Nepal would not necessarily be unique in this regard.
10 Rescue and rehabilitation refers 'to a process by which brothels are raided by the police or NGO workers, women are removed from brothels (rescued), and then placed in a rehabilitation facility' (Ahmed and Seshu 2012, 154). Reintegration refers to a process through which the women and girls are re-united with their life, family, community, and even to create a new life in another place in society (Sangroula 2001).
11 Some of the major NGOs include: ABC Nepal, Maiti Nepal, Child Workers in Nepal (CWIN), Shanti Rehabilitation Center, the Women Rehabilitation Center (WOREC), SAATHI, HimRights (Himalayan Human Rights Monitors), the Center for Legal Research and Resource Development (CeLRRD), Shakti Samuha (the only survivors' organisation), and the Legal Aid and Consultancy Center (LACC), among others (IIDS and UNIFEM 2004).
12 Prior studies have delineated the implication of street-based prostitution on women's health. For instance, HIV is common among street-based sex workers in Kathmandu valley. Almost 4% of street-based sex workers suffer from HIV (NCASC 2015).
13 The term bondage is 'the condition of any person whose liberty is unlawfully restricted while the person is coerced through any means to render labor or services [...] including those who enter the condition because of the lack of reasonable alternative' (Kara 2012, 31). The term 'debt bondage' is commonly used by counter-trafficking organisations and means that the women owe money to the trafficker for travel, producing authentic or fraudulent documents, or helping them find jobs (Dewey 2008). However, Dewey (2008, 132), argues that 'debt bondage does not necessarily indicate a lack of agency or even a woman's perception that she has been unfairly treated by the individual who keeps her earnings'.

References

Armstrong, Lynzi. 2010. Out of the shadows (and into a bit of light): Decriminalisation, human rights and street-based sex work in New Zealand. In Hardy, K., Kingston, S., and Sanders, T., eds, *New Sociologies of Sex Work*, 39–58. Farnham, UK: Ashgate.

Armstrong, Lynzi. 2017. From law enforcement to protection? Interactions between sex workers and police in a decriminalized street-based sex industry. *British Journal of Criminology*, 57(3): 570–588.

Ahmed, Aziza and Seshu, Meena. 2012. We have the right not to be 'rescued': When anti-trafficking programmes undermine the health and well-being of sex workers. *Anti-Trafficking Review*, 1: 149–165.

Busza, Joanna. 2004. Sex work and migration: The dangers of oversimplification – a case study of Vietnamese women in Cambodia. *Health and Human Rights*, 7(2): 231–249.

Chapkis, Wendy. 2000. Power and control in the commercial sex trade. In Weitzer R., ed., *Prostitution, Pornography and the Sex Industry: Sex for Sale*, 160–181. London: Routledge.

Cox, Thomas. 1992. The Badi: Prostitution as a social norm among an untouchable caste of west Nepal. *Contributions to Nepalese Studies*, 19(1): 51–71.

Crawford, Mary. 2010. *Sex Trafficking in South Asia: Telling Maya's Story*. New York: Routledge.

Dalla, L. Rochelle. 2006. 'You can't hustle all your life': An exploratory investigation of the exit process among street-level prostituted women. *Psychology of Women Quarterly*, 30: 276–290.

Dewey, Susan. 2008. *Hollow Bodies: Institutional Responses to Sex Trafficking in Armenia, Bosnia, and India*. Sterling: Kumarian Press.

Dewey, Susan and Germain St. Tonia. 2017. *Women of the Street: How the Criminal Justice-Social Services Alliance Fails Women in Prostitution*: New York: New York University Press.

Farrell, Amy and Cronin, Shea. 2015. Policing prostitution in an era of human trafficking enforcement. *Crime, Law and Social Change*, 64(4–5): 211–228.

Forum for Women, Law, and Development (FWLD). 2014. *Human Trafficking and Transportation (Control) Act, 2007: Its Implementation*. Kathmandu: Forum for Women, Law and Development.

Frederick, John. 2012. The myth of Nepal-to-India sex trafficking. In Kempadoo, K., Sanghera, J., and Pattanaik, B., eds, *Trafficking and Prostitution Reconsidered: New Perspectives on Migration, Sex Work and Human Rights*, 127–147. London: Paradigm.

Frederick, John, Basnyat, Muna, and Aguettant, L. Joseph. 2010. *Trafficking and Exploitation in the Entertainment and Sex Industries in Nepal: A Handbook for Decision-Makers*. Kathmandu: Terre des Hommes Foundation.

Gangoli, Geetanjali and Westmarland, Nicole, eds. 2006. *International Approaches to Prostitution: Law and Policy in Europe and Asia*. Bristol, UK: Policy Press.

Ghimire, Durga. 1994. *Red-Light Traffic: The Trade in Nepali Girls*. Nepal: ABC Nepal.

Godwin, John. 2012. *Sex Work and the Law in Asia and the Pacific*. Thailand: UNDP, UNFPA, and UNAIDS.

Hardy, K., Kingston, S., and Sanders, T., eds. 2010. *New Sociologies of Sex Work*. Farnham, UK: Ashgate.

HIV/AIDS and STI Control Board (HSCB)/National Centre for AIDS and STD Control (NCASC). 2011. *Mapping and Size Estimation of Most At Risk Population in Nepal Female Sex Workers*. New York: HSBC/NCASC.

Institute for Integrated Development Studies (IIDS) and the United Nations Development Fund for Women (UNIFEM). 2004. *Status and Dimensions of Trafficking within Nepalese Context*. Kathmandu: IIDS and UNIFEM.

International Labour Organisation (ILO) and the International Programme on the Elimination of Child Labour (IPEC). 2002. *Unbearable to the Human Heart: Child Trafficking and Action to Eliminate It*. Geneva: ILO-IPEC.

Kara, Siddharth. 2012. *Bonded Labor: Tackling the Sytem of Slavery in South Asia*. Columbia: University Press.

Malik, K. Yogendra, Kennedy, H. Charles, Oberst, C. Robert, Kapur, Ashok, Luwoti, Mahendra, and Rahman, Syedur, eds. 2009. *Government and Politics in South Asia*. Philadelphia: Westview Press.

Maiti Nepal. 2010. *Youth-Led Study on the Vulnerability of Young Girls Working in Restaurants, Bars and Massage Parlours in Kathmandu*. Kathmandu: Maiti Nepal.

National Centre for AIDS and STD Control (NCASC). 2015. *Integrated Biological and Behavioural Surveillance (IBBS) Surveys Among Female Sex Workers in Kathmandu Valley*. Kathmandu: Ministry of Health and Population. Available at: www.google.co.uk/url?sa=t&rct=j&q=&esrc=s&source=web&cd=1&ved =0ahUKEwjSuvK1d_ZAhUP26QKHROADVUQFggnMAA&url=http%3A%2F%2Fwww.aidsda tahub.org%2Fsites%2Fdefault%2Ffiles%2Fpublication%2FNepal_IBBS_Full_Report_PWID_KTM_ Rd6_2015.pdf&usg=AOvVaw060u-isSKZtzBPbLZBz6iK [Accessed 10 July 2017].

National Human Rights Commission (NHRC). 2008. *Trafficking in Persons, Especially on Women and Children in Nepal. National Report 2006–7*. Lalitpur: National Human Rights Commission Nepal.

National Human Rights Commission (NHRC). 2010. *Trafficking in Persons, Especially on Women and Children in Nepal. National Report 2008–9*. Lalitpur: National Human Rights Commission Nepal.

O'Brien, Erin, Hayes, Sharon, and Carpenter, Belinda. 2013. *The Politics of Sex Trafficking: A Moral Geography*. New York: Palgrave Macmillan.

O'Neill, Tom. 2001. 'Selling girls in Kuwait': Domestic labour migration and trafficking discourse in Nepal. *Anthopologica*, 43(2): 153–164.

Pradhan, Gauri. 1996. *Back Home from Brothels*. Kathmandu: Child Workers in Nepal Concerned Center.

Richardson, Diane, Poudel, Meena, and Laurie, Nina. 2009. Sexual trafficking in Nepal: Constructing citizenship and livelihoods. *Gender Place & Culture*, 16(3): 259–278.

Segrave, Marie, Milivojevic, Sanja, and Pickering Sharon. 2009. *Sex Trafficking: International Context and Response*. New York: Willan.

Samarasinghe, Vidyamali. 2008. *Female Sex Traffickuing in Asia: The Resilience of Patriarchy in a Changing World*. New York: Taylor & Francis.

Sanghera, Jyoti. 2005. Unpacking the Trafficking Discourse. In Kempadoo, K., Sanghera, J., and Pattanaik, B. eds, *Trafficking and Prostitution Reconsidered: New Perspectives on Migration, Sex Work, and Human Rights*, 3–24. Boulder, CO: Paradigm.

Sangroula, Yubraj. 2001. *Condemned to Exploitation: Trafficking of Girls and Women in Nepal: Building a Community Surveillance for Prevention*. Kathmandu: Kathmandu School of Law.

Terre des Hommes (TDH). 2003. *Child Trafficking in Nepal: An Assessment of the Present Situation*. Kathmandu: TDH.

The Economist. 2011. Aid and corruption in Nepal: Low road through the Himalayas (2011, 31 May). Available at: www.economist.com/blogs/banyan/2011/05/aid-and-corruption-nepal [Accessed 10.05.16].

Weitzer, Ronald. 2014. Sex work, gender, and criminal justice. In Gartner, R. and McCathy, B. eds, *The Oxford Handbook of Gender, Sex and Crime*, 508–526. Oxford: Oxford University Press.

Worthen, E. Miranda. 2011. Sex trafficking or sex work: Conceptions of trafficking among anti-trafficking organizations in Nepal. *Refugee Survey Quarterly*, 30(3): 87–106.

21

"Something about us for us"

Exploring ways of making research with sex workers in South Africa

Greta Schuler and Elsa Oliveira

Introduction

Selling sex is an important livelihood strategy for many people across the world. This is no different in South Africa, a country associated with high levels of unemployment and increasingly restrictive immigration policies (Scheibe, Richter, and Vearey, 2016). While insights into the challenges facing migrants and sex workers in South Africa continue to emerge, much of the knowledge that is circulated about migrant sex workers is the result of research undertaken on rather than with them and is considered by some sex workers and their scholar and activist allies to be the "(re) production of often superficial, sometimes inaccurate, and potentially unethical portrayals of the lives of migrants who sell sex" (Oliveira and Vearey, 2017: 266).

Building on a history of working with the Sisonke National Sex Worker Movement, an activist organization in South Africa, researchers at the African Centre for Migration and Society (ACMS) at the University of the Witwatersrand embarked on a project in 2015 to better understand the diverse needs, experiences, and aspirations of migrant sex workers in South Africa and the ways participatory research approaches might be used to support what Nigerian novelist, poet, and critic Chinua Achebe (2001) described as the need for a "balance of stories," meaning that those who are often written about are also able to contribute to the making of their own stories, to definitions of themselves and of their worlds. The direct involvement of sex workers in research and the opportunity for those engaged to produce their own stories for public dissemination is especially critical in the context of increasingly fraught and contentious debates surrounding sex worker research (Dewey and Zheng, 2014; Dutta, 2016; Mgbako, 2016; Palmary, 2016).

The *Izwi Lethu: Our Voice* project documents the lived experiences of sex workers in South Africa, focusing on topics of interest to them. The array of stories and images produced by the sex worker participants provide a picture of the varied social, cultural, political, and economic realities of doing sex work in a Global South context, offering insights that are often missing from contemporary research on sex work that predominantly focuses on health concerns, with increased attention to HIV (Murray, Oliveira, and Dutta, in press; Nyangairi and Palmary, 2014; Shah, 2014).

Unlike more conventional research approaches, participatory research strives to gain knowledge using a "bottom-up" approach, positioning those who are often the objects of the research process as experts of their own lives (Cornwall and Jewkes, 1995). It aims to generate knowledge in ways that will contribute towards positive social change and is often guided by a strong social justice agenda (Oliveira and Vearey, 2017). Sex worker insights revealed in *Izwi Lethu* can be used by Sisonke activists to fight stigma and build solidarity while also offering ACMS researchers the opportunity to learn more about the "complex personhoods" (Gordon, 1997) of this unfairly marginalized and criminalized population group whose voices are often missing from academic literature, public debates, and political discourses on issues pertaining directly to their livelihoods, movements, and well-being (Schuler, Oliveira, and Vearey, 2016).

Although the *Izwi Lethu* newsletter project began in 2015, the ACMS and Sisonke have a longer history of partnerships using participatory approaches. Much of this work is part of the MoVE: methods:visual:explore project housed at the ACMS. The second author and Dr. Jo Vearey developed MoVE to explore ways of doing research differently, including finding "platforms for public dissemination and engagement that extend outside traditional research outlets" (Oliveira, 2016: 261). Moreover, the idea for *Izwi Lethu* arose out of other MoVE projects involving partnership with Sisonke and builds on earlier attempts "to tackle normative depictions of migrant sex workers by making 'visible' their own visual and narrative representations" (Oliveira, 2016: 261–262). Some of these projects include the adapted photo-voice projects Working the City (2010–2011) and Volume 44 (2013–2014) and the narrative writing project "At Your Own Risk" (2013) facilitated by the first author (MoVe, 2017). While most of these collaborations included a public engagement component—such as publications and public exhibitions—the cost of printing and curating a space to hang the materials often made them expensive to replicate, especially for an organization with a limited budget (Oliveira, 2016). As Susan Finely (2008: 74) notes, "[s]ocially responsible research for and by the people cannot reside inside the lonely walls of academic institutions." The ACMS researchers envisioned the newsletter as a product that could be cheaply printed and easily distributed—a form of public engagement that an organization like Sisonke could sustainably fund and circulate. All issues of the newsletter are available on the MoVE Issuu website and can be downloaded and printed (MoVE, 2017).

Evolution of *Izwi Lethu*

Though ACMS researchers brought the idea of the newsletter to Sisonke, we worked together to plan the project. Sisonke's Provincial Coordinator of the Gauteng Province (based in Johannesburg) would participate in each workshop and help recruit other participants from Sisonke members, all of whom identify as active sex workers. The four-day workshop would take place in Sisonke's office in Johannesburg for the first year, facilitated by the first author with the assistance of the Provincial Coordinator.

While still in the planning phase of the project, the first author attended a Sisonke Creative Space, a monthly meeting for Sisonke members, to present what the ACMS and Sisonke leaders were discussing. This Creative Space in February 2015 was held at the former Women's Jail on Constitution Hill—where South Africa's new Constitutional Court was built on an old prison complex after the end of Apartheid. Dozens of sex workers crowded the jail cell and brainstormed ideas for titles and then voted—*Izwi Lethu: Our Voice* was the winner. But an important sub-heading also arose out of the discussion: "A Newsletter by Sex Workers for Sex Workers." We did not realize at the time how important or controversial this subheading would become. This idea was the force behind the group's support for *Izwi Lethu*, which means "our voice" in Zulu. Finally, something "written about us for us," as a participant later said. This emphasis was important to the group of women, men, and transgender people in that former cell because few of them publicly speak about sex work for fear of the stigma sex workers face in a country where sex work is criminalized. However, as *Izwi Lethu* has grown, its subtitle has fallen under the scrutiny of activist and academic partners. Some members of Sisonke and some members of the ACMS pointed out that the newsletter is meant for a broad audience. Sisonke and other activist groups bring *Izwi Lethu* to meetings with stakeholders; the ACMS shares *Izwi Lethu* at academic conferences. While reporters know this and sometimes even directly address readers who are not sex workers, the first author begins each workshop by introducing the idea of audience and stressing that *Izwi Lethu* is by sex workers for sex workers. Building on that concept, participants discuss what kinds of stories they would like to read. Not only is audience an important consideration for any writer, but it is also important to stress that the newsletter is meant to be something that participants should want to read and share with other sex workers. The subtitle "A Newsletter by Sex Workers for Sex Workers" does not necessarily exclude policymakers and academics but highlights that sex workers can form a community and engage in activities other than sex work (which seems like an obvious observation but an important point in countering stigma). In discussing motivation for starting the sex worker magazine *Spread* in 2004 in the United States, Rachel Aimee, Eliyaana Kaiser, and Audacia Ray (2015: 17–18) explain that available sex worker narratives written by sex workers were "academic essays written for a college-educated readership" and could not counter the polarized mass media presentation of sex workers as "glamorous, highly paid call girls or drug-addicted victims without agency"; furthermore, they "thought that the simple act of holding a magazine in their hands and knowing that sex workers made this would encourage sex workers to feel like part of a community." While participants discuss the wide variety of potential readers who may engage with *Izwi Lethu*, especially since it is available online, the target audience is sex workers.

The workshops run for four days. After an initial discussion of story, the workshop process moves from writing to sharing to discussing to rewriting to sharing to discussing to revising and sharing again (Schuler et al., 2016). Participants learn to become better storytellers as they listen to and then critique their peers' work during discussions. The first author guides the conversations and refocuses when needed, but for the most part, participants lead the discussion. After rewriting and revising, participants type their stories on laptops. The first author assists with light editing, using repeated errors as opportunities to go over questions of grammar. While this part of the process can be time consuming, it is a valuable aspect of the workshop. Sisonke staff member and *Izwi Lethu* participant (editor and reporter) Kagee highlighted the importance of using computers in the workshop, observing in his reflection on the project:

> I also liked the story typing sessions. As one specific participant said, "I cannot believe that I am sitting with the laptop typing my own story. Can you take me a photo? I want my family to see that I can now type." It was her first time touching a laptop in her life.
>
> *(Schuler et al., 2016: 45)*

Most participants have not had much experience using computers and word-processing applications. They consider the practice valuable for their personal growth, and Sisonke believes this aspect of the workshop helps build capacity in the organization.

Over the course of three years, the *Izwi Lethu* newsletter has kept the same basic format. Sisonke members chose a template from Microsoft Word, a program accessible to a small organization and fairly straightforward to use. The ACMS and Sisonke considered the sustainability of the design of the product. The template for standard printer-sized paper would be easy to replicate. Sisonke members chose a template that had an orange theme similar to Sisonke's logo's color. Each issue has an editor's note, at least three feature stories, an advice column by the wise old (and fictional) sex worker, Mastoep, and a guest column, which is the only story not written by a sex worker. Guest columnists have included a pastor who welcomes sex workers into his congregation and a self-defense trainer who offered safety tips. Two additional features were added to the newsletter the first year: a legal fact and a health tip. Depending on the participants at the time, other *Izwi Lethu* columns have been introduced, including recipes with cooking tips and a beauty advice column.

In the first year of the project, 2012, *Izwi Lethu* ran every month from March to December—with the exception of double month issues for June/July and November/December. In August, we traveled to the northern province of Limpopo to conduct an *Izwi Lethu* workshop with participants from the Volume 44 project. This was the largest workshop with 11 participants. All of the other workshops in 2015 were held in the boardroom of the office Sisonke shared with several other organizations. With the exception of the Limpopo workshop, participants were selected through a process that began with Creative Space. The Provincial Coordinator or the first author would hand out strips of paper at Sisonke's monthly meeting and ask for those willing to participate to submit story pitches for the newsletter. Everyone interested would write their story pitch on one side of the paper and their name and phone number on the other side. A group of Sisonke staff members and the first author would then select the best story ideas and contact the top four to participate. The fifth participant was the Provincial Coordinator for Gauteng who also acted as editor in chief, writing the editor's note and helping to organize the workshops. While the variety of stories was vast from new people attending each workshop, the first author began to see that participants were eager to return to another workshop and that both they and the newsletter could benefit from having participants repeat the process. Several dedicated participants were invited back; they had not only shown particular talent in their writing but they had also gone out of their way to report on and write stories outside of the workshop. As their workshop experience grew so did their editing skills, and they became important leaders of group discussions. Their computer skills also improved, so they were able to help new participants learn to type and edit their stories. While having different sex workers take part in each edition offered a more diverse range of perspectives and stories, the first author realized that in order to support Sisonke in taking over the newsletter (an intention set forth at the onset of the project) a dedicated team of reporters was needed, reporters who would not only improve their writing and editing skills but would also learn how to run a workshop themselves. Sisonke and the ACMS began to plan the second year of *Izwi Lethu* with this goal in mind.

The second year of the project, 2016, was originally envisioned as a year of transitioning the project from mainly ACMS-led (through funding and organizing) to mainly Sisonke-led so that the third year of the project could be completely Sisonke-led. Part of this process was building capacity among a dedicated team of *Izwi Lethu* reporters. The ACMS and Sisonke selected a team of three participants based on how they demonstrated their commitment to the project and their writing skills in 2015 workshops. Sisonke's Gauteng Provincial Coordinator and its Media Liaison also participated in each workshop. While the first author held only three workshops in 2016, producing three newsletters, she kept in touch with the three reporters and even accompanied some of them to events on which they would report.

One of these reporters, Linda, noted in a written reflection on the project:

> Being an *Izwi Lethu* newsletter writer, I have learned a lot of things like using a computer and improving my writing and English speaking skills. I have also learned to communicate with different people, especially when doing interviews. I have travelled to different provinces, doing the *Izwi Lethu* newsletter, and I have written a lot of stories.
>
> (Schuler et al., 2016: 48)

These skills were so valuable that the three participants found jobs outside of *Izwi Lethu* and sex work and were unavailable to participate the following year.

In addition to publishing the three newsletters (Issues 10, 11, and 12) in 2016, MoVE at the ACMS published a book about the process of making *Izwi Lethu* (Schuler et al., 2016). Five participants and several stakeholders wrote reflections on their experiences that were valuable for the ACMS and Sisonke in shaping the third year of the project. One example of this influence comes from Kagee's reflection:

> I am thinking for future recommendations, it will be nice to have field reporters that will interview and interact in story writing with sex workers at their safe spaces. As at times board rooms and offices can be very intimidating to sex workers that have never worked in an office space.
>
> *(Schuler et al., 2016: 45)*

After reading this suggestion and reflecting on the experience of hosting the workshops at the University of the Witwatersrand during the second year of the project, the first author agreed to move the workshop to the more neutral space of the Workers' Museum in Johannesburg. However, Kagee's suggestion was to go even further, and he took the matter into his own hands.

When the Provincial Coordinator left Sisonke in 2016, Kagee stepped into the role of editor in chief. He also went looking for stories outside of his own experience. Since the workshops were no longer accepting new participants but training reporters, Kagee wanted to still give other sex workers a voice in the newsletter. In a story for Issue 12, "The Impact of Criminalisation on Sex Workers in South Africa," Kagee recounts the stories of three women with whom he conducted a small workshop in his own time. They wanted their stories to appear in *Izwi Lethu*, so Kagee gave them paper and pens and asked them to write. He went over their stories with them and helped them revise their stories. While the *Izwi Lethu* team still had more questions in our *Izwi Lethu* discussion for Kagee and the friends who shared their stories with him, we were thrilled that participants were conducting their own workshops (however informal) as we had hoped that they someday would.

One of the limitations of the project has been that the first author can only facilitate the workshops in English. As multilingual participants gain workshop experience, they will be able to conduct workshops, lead discussions, and edit stories in other languages, making the newsletter accessible to more sex workers.

In the third year of the project, 2017, Sisonke has taken the lead in organizing workshops though the first author is still facilitating them. At the beginning of the year, Sisonke put out a call for reporters and offered a small stipend. The ACMS and Sisonke agreed on a contract that would require reporters to attend three workshops and submit drafts of at least two stories at an additional pre-meeting, which would allow for more discussion of the stories and the shape of each issue as a whole. After reviewing writing samples and conducting interviews, a team of researchers from the ACMS and staff members of Sisonke selected the participants for 2017.

Sisonke's ownership of the newsletter has already had an impact. By offering a stipend (albeit small), Sisonke has given the reporters an important position in their communities and has allowed reporters more time to focus on reporting and writing. Whereas in the first year participants would write their stories during the workshop hours—sometimes completing them in the evenings at home between workshop days—reporters can now put more time into their stories, conduct interviews, and take relevant photographs. Some reporters have said that other sex workers now approach them with stories that they think should be in the newsletter. Writing stories outside of the workshop has also allowed for more time not only to edit and revise but also for the first author to spend more time focusing on teaching revision and editing skills. Participants now can discuss one another's stories in more depth and glean greater insights from those discussions.

The team of reporters prepared to write stories outside of the workshop also allows for Sisonke to direct some articles, paying for reporters to attend certain events and report on them for the Sisonke community. Reporters are encouraged to come to Sisonke's office in Johannesburg to use the computer and telephone for research and interviews. Sisonke can use *Izwi Lethu* as a tool for activism, highlighting certain stories, but can also use the newsletter to simply reach out to the sex workers themselves.

Ethical considerations

While the editor in chief is still a Sisonke staff member and at times pushes for articles to support Sisonke's agenda, the reporters bring their own ideas and stories to each workshop and as a group they discuss what should be included in each issue. Another ethical consideration in every issue and in presenting *Izwi Lethu* in conferences or academic papers or books (including this one) is that of participants' identities. Anonymity is important for projects involving active sex workers. Since sex work is criminalized and stigmatized in South Africa, and much of the world, many sex worker participants do not want to disclose their identities (Radačić, 2017). Some have not told family or friends about their engagement in sex work and do not want their names to appear in association with sex work material. However, involvement with MoVE Projects, including *Izwi Lethu*, can be prestigious (Oliveira, 2018). At the beginning of each workshop, the first author encourages new participants to select a pseudonym to use for the project. Anonymity cannot be guaranteed since it is a group project, but as a group we discuss respecting one another's privacy. Some participants choose the same pseudonym that they use when engaging in sex work. One participant chose a pseudonym very different from her real name for her first workshop, then in her second workshop she changed to a name very similar to her real name. When the first author asked her why, she said that her friends did not believe that she had written the *Izwi Lethu* story that she had claimed to write because the name was not hers. She wanted a name close enough to her real name that she could show off her work. She took pride in her stories. Other participants have also expressed uncertainty over what name to use and how they can still share their accomplishments making *Izwi Lethu* and gaining new skills with friends and family who do not know that they are sex workers.

Participants, who are also partners in this process, have presented the *Izwi Lethu* project with the ACMS researchers at academic events. Speaking in front of a large group is significant, and participants want to share their accomplishment with friends and family but do not necessarily want to reveal their association with sex work. However, if they are named as participants in a sex worker project or as Sisonke members, then they are "out-ed" as sex workers. Kagee's observation about the participant who wanted a picture of herself typing on a computer also alludes to this tension: the participant wishes to remain anonymous as a sex worker yet takes pride in experiences attained through association with sex worker projects.

Though a program at a symposium might circulate among the limited audience present, often attendees use social media to share information about and pictures from the symposium—including pictures of speakers. If participants share photographs of themselves in certain spaces, it would be clear that they were at a particular event. Social media complicates issues of anonymity in a project that is meant to reach a wide audience outside of academia. Writing under a name similar to ones own and sharing personal stories in a print newsletter distributed locally to other sex workers is one thing; however, all issues of *Izwi Lethu* are freely available online. The ACMS and Sisonke share links to these issues on various social media platforms and often tag colleagues. Sex worker participants are also colleagues in this work, but social media platforms like Facebook connect networks of people a participant might want to keep separate. In working on the *Izwi Lethu* project, the ACMS researchers are constantly negotiating how to help amplify sex worker voices while protecting the anonymity of sex worker writers.

Conclusion

Patricia Leavy (2018: 10) argues that arts-based research is "used often in social justice work because it can be configured inclusively and has the potential to jar people into seeing and thinking differently (critical to challenging stereotypes and the ideologies they promote)." Not only do ACMS researchers learn about the lives of sex workers through the newsletter and Sisonke activists have a product to disseminate, but also sex worker participants have made something that they can be proud of and can share. They have a tool to share their stories and raise their voices. One *Izwi Lethu* story struck the first author as demonstrating the power of the newsletter and the power of one voice. The following is Clara's story, "Who Is a Sex Worker?" from Issue 9 (November/December 2015):

> The other day I went to a hair salon to distribute *Izwi Lethu* copies. I wanted them to read the newsletter, so I promised them that after I distributed my newsletters I would come back for a hairdo.
>
> As promised, I returned to the salon after an hour. While I was sitting drying my hair in their dryer, I overheard two ladies discussing the newsletter. One said she didn't like sex workers. The friend asked why she despised sex workers like that. Then I joined the conversation, and I asked her how many boyfriends does she have. She told me she has got three boyfriends, one to buy lunch, one to pay for rent, and the last one is the one she loves. I told the lady that if she is sleeping with men in exchange of anything then she is doing sex work.
>
> Sex workers who stand in the streets are despised because it's pay as you go, but we have many sex workers who hide themselves, hairdressers, secretaries, street vendors, waitresses. At universities, some girls do sex work to make ends meet. How many men do women sleep with before settling down for marriage? Women lie to their men about their birthdays in order to get presents that will later be exchanged for sex.
>
> Every woman is a sex worker. For some it is pay as you go. Women get married for sex in exchange the husband buys food for the house and pays bills. That's sex work.
>
> Most women hate those who charge pay as you go because they sleep with their husbands. Sex workers do not chase husbands; husbands choose to be clients. If there were no clients, there wouldn't be sex workers.

This story about a reporter's experience distributing the newsletter is at the heart of the project: starting conversations about sex workers' lives. In *Ethical Research with Sex Workers*, Tiantian Zheng writes, "We as researchers have obligations toward individuals who participate in our research and put our obligations into action through practice of reciprocity with those who help us with our research" (Dewey and Zheng, 2013: 52). Using arts-based participatory methods, such as the creation of a newsletter, can empower participants, helping them learn new skills to create a product of which they can be proud. By structuring this ongoing project to become a sustainable newsletter for a sex worker rights activist group, the ACMS researchers have attempted to help sex workers and an activist organization that assists us while learning about the lived experiences of sex workers and their self-representations. But more importantly, by training sex worker reporters to write and type and distribute their stories and stories from their communities, the *Izwi Lethu* project is helping share sex worker voices and perhaps change perceptions.

References

Achebe, Chinua. 2001. *Home and Exile*. New York: Anchor Books.

Aimee, R., E. Kaiser, and A. Ray, Eds. 2015. *$pread: The Best of the Magazine that Illuminated the Sex Industry and Started a Media Revolution*. New York: The Feminist Press at the City University of New York.

Cornwall, A. and Jewkes, R. 1995. What is Participatory Research? *Social Science and Medicine*, *41*(12): 1667–1676.

Dewey, S. and T. Zheng. 2013. *Ethical Research with Sex Workers: Anthropological Approaches*. New York: Springer.

Dutta, D. 2016. Rethinking Care and Economic Justice with Third-World Sex Workers. In W. Harcourt (Ed.), *The Palgrave Handbook of Gender Development* (pp. 186–200). London: Palgrave Macmillan.

Finely, S. 2008. "Arts-Based Research." In J. Gary Knowles and Ardra L. Cole (Eds.), *Handbook of the Arts in Qualitative Research*. Los Angeles, CA: Sage.

Gordon, Avery. 1997. *Ghostly Matters: Haunting and the Sociological Imagination*. Minneapolis, MN: University of Minnesota Press.

Leavy, P., Ed. 2018. *Handbook of Arts-Based Research*. New York: Guilford Press.

Mgbako, C.A. 2016. *To Live Freely in This World: Sex Worker Activism in Africa*. New York: New York University Press.

MoVE methods:visual:explore. 2017. "*Izwi Lethu: Our Voice* Newsletter." https://issuu.com/move.methods.visual.explore/stacks/f370165798154ee69cd94a901d957922.

Murray, L., E. Oliveira, and D. Dutta (In press). Sex Work, Academic Research and Power in the Fields of HIV/AIDS and Global Public Health. In R. Parker and G. Garcia (Eds.), *The Routledge Handbook on the Politics of Global Public Health*. New York: Routledge.

Nyangairi, B. and I. Palmary. 2014. Watching Each Others' Back, Coping with Precarity. In I. Palmary, B. Hamber, and Núñez, L. (Eds.), *Healing and Change in the City of Gold* (pp. 122–134). New York: Springer International.

Oliveira, E. 2016. "Empowering, Invasive or a Little Bit of Both? A Reflection on the Use of Visual and Narrative Methods in Research with Migrant Sex Workers in South Africa." *Visual Studies*, *31*(3): 260–278.

Oliveira, E. 2018. Volume 44: Research with Migrants Who Sell Sex in South Africa. *Agenda*. https://doi.org/10.1080/10130950.2018.1438974

Oliveira, E. and J. Vearey. 2017. Making Research and Building Knowledge with Communities: Examining Three Participatory Visual and Narrative Projects with Migrants Who Sell Sex in South Africa. In M. Capous-Desyllas and K. Morgaine, *Creating Social Change Through Creativity* (pp. 265–289). New York: Palgrave.

Palmary, I. 2016. *Gender, Sexuality and Migration in South Africa: Governing morality*. Switzerland: Palgrave Macmillan.

Radačić, Ivana. 2017. Doing Feminist, Human Rights-Based, Socio-Legal Research on Prostitution: Challenges and Potential. *feminists@law*, *6*(2): unpaginated. Available at: http://journals.kent.ac.uk/index.php/feministsatlaw/article/view/287/944.

Scheibe, A., M. Richter, and J. Vearey. 2016. Sex Work and South Africa's Health System: Addressing the Needs of the Underserved. *South African Health Review*, 165–178.

Schuler, G., E. Oliveira, and J. Vearey, Eds. 2016. *Izwi Lethu: A Participatory Arts-Based Project*. South Africa: The MoVE Project. https://issuu.com/move.methods.visual.explore/docs/izwi_lethu-_our_voice_ebook.

Shah, S. 2014. *Street Corner Secrets: Sex, Work, and Migration in the City of Mumbai*. Durham, NC: Duke University Press.

22

We need to talk about youth prostitution
A story about the demise of youth prostitution in England and Wales

Jo Phoenix

Introduction

> Although not always prominent or visible, children are involved in prostitution across England and Wales. It is a tragedy for any child to become involved in prostitution . . . Children involved in prostitution should be treated primarily as the victims of abuse and their needs require careful assessment . . . Whilst there is no single route through which children become involved in prostitution, we know that the most common factors are vulnerability and low self-esteem. Vulnerable children are identified and targeted by those who abuse children through prostitution irrespective of whether a child is living with their own family, looked after away from home or has run away.
>
> *(Department of Health and Home Office 2000: 3)*

> We use the term child sexual exploitation to describe a form of child sexual abuse where an individual or group takes advantage of an imbalance of power to coerce, manipulate or deceive a child or young person under the age of 18 into sexual activity (a) in exchange for something the victim needs or want, and/or (b) for the financial advantage or increased status of the perpetrator or facilitator.
>
> *(Cabinet Office 2017: 10)*

Prostitution is a hot political topic in the twenty-first century. Various international policy frameworks, including the United Nations Conventions on Human Rights and the Rights of the Child, as well various European Council treatises, place upon each signatory country an obligation to 'see' and 'understand' prostitution's problematic links with trafficking, slavery, organised crime and child exploitation. The same conventions require signatory countries to take action to ameliorate those problems. Recent history has demonstrated, particularly across Europe, Canada, Australia and New Zealand, that there are global flows of knowledge about the problems of prostitution and that policies developed in one national context have the potential to migrate to others (Skilbrei and Holmström 2016). There is no doubt, therefore, that global 'meta-narratives' exist about prostitution and what ought to be done about it. But, what is the relationship between these international level discussions and policy frameworks and national policy and local-level practice change?

At the level of theory, this chapter argues that while many of the problems of prostitution are indeed global in reach and character, the necessary and the sufficient conditions for change (to prostitution and/or its regulation) come from the ground up. In other words, while constructions of 'the problems' of prostitution and proposals for ways of dealing with it may well circulate internationally and globally, change is dependent on local and national institutional and organisational arrangements, in specific countries, within specific economic and political conditions and at specific moments in history.

At the empirical level, this chapter gives an account of youth prostitution policy and practice reform in England and Wales in the last few decades. The question the chapter addresses is a relatively simple one: how was it possible that over a short period youth or juvenile prostitution 'disappeared' as a subject and object of governance? For, as the quotations opening this chapter indicate, the twenty-first century opened with a recognition that prostitution was no place for children and thus action needed to be taken to address youth prostitution. Within a relatively short period, commodified commercial sexual activities involving young people were re-constituted as a particular type of child sexual abuse. Along the way, in 2009, 'youth prostitution' was officially defined out of existence. By 2017, it became the unspeakable.

Before moving on, a note of clarification may be helpful: this chapter is not about young women's experiences of prostitution. It is not about the violence, abuse (emotional, physical or otherwise) and exploitation that often accompanies involvement in prostitution. Likewise, this chapter is not about whether, or to what extent young women are coerced into prostitution, consent to it or are abused through it or whether youth prostitution is or is not child sexual abuse. In any case, these debates have been going on in England for at least a century and are likely to continue into the future (see Walkowitz 1982).

This chapter is divided into three sections. The first section sets the scene and describes how, in England and Wales, official constructions shifted in the twentieth century towards seeing the primary problems of prostitution as being the victimisation and vulnerability of women. This section also highlights the role played in this shift by the knowledge and practices of sexual health outreach projects. The second section provides a more detailed look at the development of a national policy framework to deal with youth prostitution and how the definition of what sort of problem it is has shifted, partly as a result of the development of practice in the area. The third section examines the role played by two sexual abuse scandals that prompted a crisis of legitimacy in the capacity of public institutions to protect children from sexual exploitation and abuse and the demise of youth prostitution as a speakable discourse.

Setting the scene: from the nuisance of visibility to concerns about vulnerability and victimisation

This section argues that to create the sort of policy changes regarding 'youth prostitution' described in the introduction to this chapter, it first had to be distinguished from adult prostitution. In the context of England and Wales, this occurred as a result of a shift in the official discourses about the nature and types of problems that prostitution presented, which was, in part, an unintended result of government attempts to manage the threat that prostitution posed regarding the spread of HIV/AIDS.

Regulating public nuisance and visible prostitution through the targeting of publicly visible women

Throughout most of the twentieth century, the official constructions of the problem of prostitution, and the approach to policing and regulating it was shaped by the recommendations of the Report of the Committee on Homosexual Offences and Prostitution (Wolfenden 1957), which subsequently formed the basis of the Street Offences Act 1959 in England and Wales. The Wolfenden Report, as it came to be known, drew a sharp line of distinction between matters of sexual morality and the role of criminal law in 'preserving public order and decency' and protecting individuals from the 'injurious' or 'offensive' behaviours of others. In short, consenting adults could do what they wanted with each other no matter how immoral other people may think it is as long as they did it in private. The criminal law had no role in regulating sexual morality. Hence, the Wolfenden Committee recommended the partial decriminalisation of homosexual sex. Applying the same logic to prostitution, the committee recommended that the extant piecemeal legislation on prostitution be consolidated within a new framework of laws in which the exchange of sex for money was not made illegal and where it became (or continued to be) illegal to loiter or solicit in a public place for the purposes of prostitution; to keep a brothel; to cause or incite a person into prostitution; or to live off the immoral earnings of a prostitute. The committee was very clear in constituting that the critical problem, which required criminal justice intervention, was the nuisance and offence caused by *the visibility* of street prostitution. They wrote: 'those ordinary citizens who live in these areas . . . cannot in going about their daily business, avoid the sight of a state of affairs which seems to them to be an affront to public order and decency' (Wolfenden 1957: 82). With that, Wolfenden inaugurated an approach to dealing with the problems of prostitution that focused almost exclusively on arresting, prosecuting and convicting women working from the streets and tolerance towards less visible forms of prostitution (such as indoor sex work).

Of relevance to this chapter, the Wolfenden Committee codified and enshrined in the legal statute made no distinction between children, young people and adults in prostitution. It is (albeit perversely) legal to prosecute children below the age of sexual consent (aged 16 years old) for prostitution-related offences. It continues to be despite the plethora of policy changes that claim that any child's (aged under 18 years old) involvement in prostitution is a form of abuse on the grounds that to decriminalise child and youth prostitution would indicate to young people that it is permissible to engage in commercial sexual exchanges (DCSF 2009).

Public health, the growth of multi-agency welfare provision and new knowledge about 'the problems' of prostitution

For the most part, little changed in official understandings about the problems of prostitution – or its policing and regulation, from Wolfenden until the early 1990s. Prosecutions and convictions for soliciting and loitering numbered in the thousands every year and courts routinely and regularly fined those they convicted.

Throughout the 1980s and 1990s, fears about a HIV/AIDS pandemic raised governmental concerns about the impact of prostitution on the sexual health of the general populace. Within popular discourse, prostitution had long since been identified as a bridge between the undeserving and diseased few and the healthy, moral many.[1] The tone of the public discussion was comparatively harsh (calls were made, for instance, to segregate sex workers). Yet, there was burgeoning public health and medical research literature linking risky behaviours and lifestyles (promiscuity, intravenous drug use, anal sex) to the spread of HIV/AIDS. Primarily as a result of this expanding epidemiological research, a plethora of new services started to develop across the UK with the aim of minimising the potential health risks to sex workers who engaged in many of the risky behaviours. This 'harm minimisation' approach to prostitution was new to the UK (see Kinnell 2013). The aim of intervention was not to reduce or abolish prostitution or compel or convince women to leave it. Instead the aim was merely to minimise the sexual health risks sex workers faced and the harms they encountered. Throughout the 1990s, the Department of Health put considerable financial resources into developing these services via genito-urinary clinics and sexual health outreach projects. These new local sexual health and drugs outreach projects were pragmatic and adopted a broad definition of harm in which everything from general and sexual health concerns (most often, the sexual health outreach services provided free condoms to sex workers), drugs and alcohol abuse, housing and homelessness and domestic violence were addressed. Involvement by sex workers with the agencies was purely voluntary. That same pragmatism also marked the relationships that many of these services developed with the local police constabularies. Projects such as the SAFE project in Birmingham, POW in Nottingham and the Praed Street Project in London began to identify violence from clients as being a critical threat to the health of sex workers and pressed their local police forces to do something about violent clients and other local men who were exploiting and abusing the women they worked with. The Ugly Mugs scheme was pioneered at the SAFE project in Birmingham in the 1990s as a means of sharing and disseminating information between sex workers about potentially violent clients, but it also highlighted the woeful lack of protection accorded to female sex workers by the police. So, by the end of the 1990s, many of the UK urban centres approached the issue of prostitution through a complex combination of traditional criminal justice mechanisms (targeting women working on the streets) and statutory and voluntary, non-governmental service provision. The general orientation of policing began to shift to what might broadly be called welfarist in that police and other agencies were providing services that could better meet the welfare needs of the (mostly) street-based sex workers.

It is difficult to overstate the enormous wealth of information that was generated during this period about the working lives, welfare issues, backgrounds and struggles of the women that came into the view of these sexual health outreach projects. It described the links between poverty, homelessness, growing up in local authority care, domestic violence and abuse and prostitution, along with high levels of drug and alcohol problems that street-based sex workers experienced, the endemic levels of violence and harassment to which they were exposed (see McKeganey and Barnard 1996; Church et al. 2001; O'Neill 2001; Phoenix 2001; see also Balfour and Allen 2014). By the end of the turn of the century, this new wealth of information – along with the birth of what some have called 'sex work studies' or the new sociologies of sex work (Hardy and Kingston 2016) – found its way into central governmental debates about what 'the problems' of prostitution were and what ought to be done about them.

From nuisance to vulnerability and victimisation

The first decade of the twenty-first century was a period of dramatic prostitution policy reform. Following a 'modernising' agenda, the New Labour government reviewed and overhauled almost all aspects of sexual offences in the UK. It drew on much of the research discussed above and produced a variety of consultation documents and new guidance. It created policies that would be in line with the UK's obligations to review legislation and practice concerning the sexual exploitation, trafficking and involvement in pornography and prostitution of children and young people as per the UN Convention on the Rights of the Child and the Council of Europe's Convention on the Protection of Children – both of which were ratified in the previous decade.

The Department of Health and the Home Office jointly issued *Safeguarding Children Involved in Prostitution* early in 2000, which was rapidly followed by a *National Plan for Safeguarding Children Involved in Commercial Exploitation*. Shortly afterwards, the Sexual Offences Act 2003, introduced a raft of new crimes – including criminalising 'commercial sexual exploitation' of a child (i.e. someone under the age of 18 years old), facilitating or purchasing sex from someone under the age of 16 years old and all sexual activities or conduct between or with someone under the age of 16 years old. In 2004, the Home Office published *Paying the Price* as a public consultation on prostitution and *Tackling Street Prostitution* in 2006, which evaluated policing strategies. In 2006, it further published *A Coordinated Strategy on Prostitution*, which inaugurated a new system for dealing with prostitution that became known as 'enforcement plus support'. In 2007, the government published its first *UK National Action Plan on Tackling Human Trafficking*. By 2010, the government had passed the *Criminal Justice and Immigration Bill 2008*, which refined the definitions of what a 'photograph' is in relation to child pornography (to include digitised and pseudo-photographic) images and the *Policing and Crime Act 2009*, which criminalised (on a strict liability basis) purchasing sexual services from someone subjected to force. In ten years, England's approach to policing prostitution shifted from one that focused almost exclusively on the visibility of prostitution to one whose rationale was to protect the victims and the vulnerable from those that would exploit them. The Foreword to the Home Office report *Paying the Price* best summarised that shift:

> Prostitution can have devastating consequences for the individuals involved and for the wider community. It involves the abuse of children and the serious exploitation of adults – many of whom are trafficked into and around the UK for this purpose. It has close links with problematic drug use and, increasingly, with transnational and organised crime . . . Many of the laws relating to prostitution are outdated, confusing and ineffective. The Sexual Offences Act 2003 began the process of reform by addressing concerns about the growing level of trafficking. New offences and penalties were introduced for those who exploit anyone for the purposes of prostitution or pornography . . . Research shows that as many as 70 per cent of those involved in prostitution started out as children or young teenagers. Their vulnerability and need for affection mean that they can be easy prey for those determined to exploit them. Often they become trapped in a web of fear and deceit in which drug addiction, prostitution and responding to the demand of pimps becomes a way of life . . . While street prostitution is the most obvious cause of danger both to those involved and to the wider community, there is a growing trade in selling sexual services in premises licensed for other activity, including massage and also video and film. Prostitution must not be concealed behind the façade of legitimate business.
>
> *(HO 2004: 5)*

Constructing the problem of childhood sexual exploitation

This section argues that shifts in official discourses about 'the problems' of prostitution ultimately split services for young people involved in commercial sexual exchanges from those for adults, which in turn created the necessary organisational and institutional conditions for the social construction of the problem of childhood sexual exploitation.

In an earlier publication, I commented that any number of social problems can become categorically and metonymically attached to the discourse of prostitution and can thereby 'stand-in for' the problems of prostitution:

> I use the term 'categorical and metonymic association' to describe the discursive process by which 'prostitution' becomes categorically associated with other social phenomena in ways that make it possible for those other phenomena to act as a proxy. It is *categorical* because the process involves assigning the exchange of sex to a *category* of social problems in relation to both seriousness and type. It is *metonymic* because the two social phenomena become associated in a way that means that one can stand for the other.
>
> *(Phoenix 2009: 6)*

Yet, as time was to tell, in England and Wales this does not apply to the discourse of youth prostitution. In the late twentieth century, while youth prostitution became *categorically* associated with youthful vulnerability, victimisation and abuse, by the early twenty-first century child sexual exploitation and youth prostitution were not metonymically associated. Instead, the discourse of child abuse proved to be so dominant that it erased any traces of its earlier association with prostitution. Thus, in contemporary policy and practice, one has to look very closely to see that the phenomenon of 'childhood sexual exploitation' was ever discursively linked to prostitution. This section focuses on how that happened. It is divided into two subsections. The first details the discursive, practice and organisational changes that occurred as a result of government redefining youth prostitution as a form of abuse. The second describes how 'childhood sexual exploitation' took on new meanings and created new subjects of intervention.

Renaming youth prostitution as sexual exploitation

As mentioned in the first section, at the turn of the twenty-first century, the Department of Health and the Home Office issued a joint guidance (*Safeguarding Children Involved in Prostitution* – hereafter SCIP) that redirected the efforts of criminal justice and social welfare organisations to treat anyone involved in prostitution but under the age of 18 years as, in the first instance, a victim of child abuse. The guidance drew directly on two high-profile reports from two of the large UK children's charities. Together, these reports described the problems young people in prostitution experience, the woeful lack of social welfare provision for them and the (at best) inappropriate policing response to them (Lee and O'Brien 1995; Barnardos 1998) – areas of concern that had been exposed as a result of the expansion of sexual health outreach and drugs projects and their links with statutory social services and police constabularies.

SCIP instructed criminal justice, welfare, health and educational authorities to: work together to provide an integrated approach to the problem of children in prostitution; treat young people in prostitution as being, primarily, victims of abuse; work together to help children and young people 'exit' prostitution (i.e. to stop selling sex); and, investigate and prosecute those who coerced, exploited and abused young people in the course of their prostitution – including those that purchase sex from them. The guidance provided no new resources. It simply redefined 'the problem'. The 'real' problem that needed addressing was the presence of *criminal* men who enticed, threatened, intimidated and preyed on the vulnerability of girls and young women and then profited from that involvement or purchased sex. These men were no longer to be understood as boyfriends, partners or clients but as exploiters and child abusers and thus to be treated as such. The 'real' problem of youth prostitution was that the young women involved, being under the age of 18 years old could not consent to their own exploitation or abuse and thus, by definition, were 'children in need' or 'at risk of significant harm' (both of these being the threshold into statutory child protection and social services).

There are a couple of important points to make about SCIP. The first important note: SCIP did not decriminalise young people's involvement in prostitution. It (and all subsequent guidance) did not instruct criminal justice agencies to *never* prosecute. SCIP instructed that where a young person persistently and voluntarily returns to prostitution, criminal justice sanction is a possibility. At the risk of labouring the point, SCIP created a policy landscape in which what determines whether a young person is treated as a victim of abuse or an offender is a judgement about whether she has consented and acted voluntarily or not. The second, and related, important note: in renaming the problem of youth prostitution as a problem of child abuse, it foreclosed the possibility of recognising that what drives many young women into prostitution are the same social, economic and material conditions that drive adult women into – and then justify their involvement in – prostitution. To put it another way, SCIP dematerialised young women's involvement in prostitution by constituting such involvement as *nothing other than child abuse*. It did this despite the plethora of empirical research that demonstrated that young women's involvement in prostitution takes place in relation to the fracturing and aggregate effects of poverty, growing up in local authority care, having few opportunities for economic or social security and that often such involvement can also be a form of survivalism (see esp. Phoenix 2001).

Elsewhere I argued that SCIP relied on two of the standard troupes in prostitution discourse, found all over the world: criminal and toxic masculinity and childhood and girlhood sexual purity and innocence (Phoenix 2002a). Most importantly for the English context, it also relied on a fundamentally asocial understanding of 'consent' as being the capacity to freely act and 'coercion' as the forceful actions of others to inhibit that capacity. SCIP does not permit recognition of the force of necessity or indeed how social conditions often act to constrain the choices young women can and do make (Phoenix 2002b).

Creating new services and new knowledges about the 'problems' of sexual exploitation

By the end of 2004, SCIP and the Sexual Offences Act 2003 impacted both the organisation of services at the local level and the types of services available to young women. In the immediate years following, many of the sexual health outreach services stopped working with young women under 18 years old because if they did not they would automatically become subject to the statutory powers (and responsibilities) of child protection legislation and agencies. In practice, this meant they could not guarantee anonymity and confidentiality to the young people they worked with, or indeed to adopt the same harm minimisation approach they had with adults. Where new specialist services were developed, these services had to establish ways of working with the young people that prioritised the statutory child protection concerns of social services and the police (including the desire to place young people in secure accommodation in the name of protection) (see Phoenix 2002b). Many new services were developed through two children's charities (Barnardo's and the National Society for the Prevention of Cruelty to Children (NSPCC)) and worked with police, local statutory children's services and a host of other interested parties. Barnardo's pioneered this work with organisations like SECOS in Middlesbrough or BASE in Bristol. The National Working Group was established, partly through the NSPCC. This was a network of agencies, organisations and professionals – including academics – interested in the area. By September 2004, there were 42 specialist agencies in the

UK, most of which worked closely with statutory social services and local police child protection teams to 'exit' young people from prostitution (Phoenix 2005).

The effect of this expansion of new services was the creation of new 'professional' knowledges. Many agencies reported that the realities of young people's experiences and what agencies could do simply did not fit into the new policy framework. Young people's experiences of exchanging sex for economic reward were far more complex, varied and informal than SCIP allowed for. So for instance, many agencies reported that the young people were swapping sex for (loosely defined) economic rewards, like drugs, alcohol or accommodation (Galvin et al. 2003) and that there were complex issues around consent, coercion (Melrose 2002; Melrose and Barret 2004), force of necessity (Phoenix 2002b), resilience and risk (Thom et al. 2007) and violence and sexual exploitation in relation to gangs (Firmin 2011). Much of this was channelled through and disseminated by the National Working Group.

A decisive moment in the story came in 2009 with the Department of Children, School and Families' *Safeguarding Children and Young People from Sexual Exploitation: Supplementary Guidance.* Taken directly from the National Working Group, this guidance defined sexual exploitation in the following way:

> Sexual exploitation of children and young people under 18 involves exploitative situations, contexts and relationships where young people (or a third person or persons) receive 'something' (e.g. food, accommodation, drugs, alcohol, cigarettes, affection, gifts, money) as a result of them performing, and/or another or others performing on them, sexual activities . . . In all cases, those exploiting the child/young person have power over them by virtue of their age, gender, intellect, physical strength and/or economic or other resources. Violence, coercion and intimidation are common, involvement in exploitative relationships being characterised in the main by the child or young person's limited availability of choice resulting from their social/economic and/or emotional vulnerability.
>
> *(DCSF 2009: 10)*

With that, 'the problem' that policy and agencies addressed was not young people's involvement in prostitution but rather abusive, exploitation sexual relationships and behaviours involving young people. The ideological conditions were now in place. Sexual exploitation was not prostitution. It was its own phenomenon and was a particular type of abusive sexual activity that involved young people.

Since the publication of the DCSF guidance much has changed. Sexual exploitation became a cause célèbre and was taken on as a campaigning issue by a wide range of social actors and agencies, including, for instance, a two-year inquiry conducted by the Office of the Children's Commission (Berelowitz et al. 2012) and the Howard League for Penal Reform (Phoenix 2012). On the ground, by 2012, most of the 42 specialist services dealing with sexual exploitation had closed (see Phoenix 2012). By 2017, two third-sector organisations (NSPCC and Barnardos) dominate most of the nation's services for sexually exploited young people. They do this in a political context of 'austerity' and the massive reduction of the public sector. In practice, this means that local governmental authorities commission services and third-sector organisations 'bid' to 'win' the tender. The point here is that within only one decade, the infrastructure of services and the practitioners and professionals who deal with 'the problem' of sexual exploitation could not be more different than those that were tackling the issue at the turn of the twenty-first century. Sexual exploitation is now dealt with almost exclusively via statutory social services – even if the actual service provision is commissioned by outside agencies. As a social problem, sexual exploitation is now fully incorporated into social work child abuse discourse. With that, youth prostitution has been officially defined out of existence and the targets of intervention are the sexual relationships and behaviours of young women defined as 'vulnerable' or 'at risk' (i.e. transgressive, poor, working class, educationally excluded). Those critical of this turn of events have linked the discourse of sexual exploitation and 'vulnerability' to the increase in gendered surveillance and the creation of new modes of social control targeting young working-class women especially (see Phoenix 2010; Melrose 2013; Brown 2016).

Rendering youth prostitution unspeakable: a crisis of legitimacy in public institutions and child abuse

It cuts to the heart of this chapter to speculate on the necessary and sufficient conditions that rendered youth prostitution an unspeakable discourse. It would be tempting to argue that the broad definition adopted in DCSF guidance was responsible, if only because it shifted the object of concern to young people's sexual relationships more generally. However, although the DCSF (2009) provided the necessary ideological conditions, it did not provide the necessary *political* conditions that would drive local authorities and the police to invest money and resources in addressing this 'new' social problem.

In 2011 and 2012 two high-profile stories broke about the failure of the police and social services to appropriately deal with sexual exploitation and sexual abuse of children. The first was a set of stories written between 2011 and 2014 by Andrew Norfolk for the *Times*, and made claims that girls in local authority care homes in Rotherham in England were, since the late 1980s, routinely sexually exploited, raped, beaten and abused by organised groups of local British Pakistani men. The scandal was that police and social services had been aware for many years of what was happening, that complaints had been made, but they did not act. It was alleged that the authorities were worried about being seen as racist and because the girls did not fit into the stereotype of 'girlhood innocence' the authorities believed them to be voluntarily involved in prostitution. By 2012, however, the media scandal had reached such proportions that Rotherham Council commissioned an independent inquiry into the issue. The report of that inquiry was published in 2014 and concluded that an estimated 1,400 children had been sexual abused and sexually exploited since 1993 in Rotherham (Jay 2014). The second scandal broke in 2012 when stories began circulating about the prolific sexual abuse of children by the then recently deceased celebrity Jimmy Savile. Such was the scale of allegations that the Metropolitan Police launched a formal criminal investigation into historic sexual abuse. This became a scandal because of the unprecedented numbers of alleged victims (the total number fell just short of 600) and the fact the public institutions, including the British Broadcasting Corporation (BBC), failed to act on suspicions and allegations.

Together these two scandals fed newly forming social anxieties about the changing nature of sexual dangers (that abuse of children can happen 'in plain sight' and that the new sexual predators could be anyone, even people in trusted institutions) and the failure of the police and social services to act. To aggravate matters, there were increasing reports from across the globe about sexual abuse and exploitation happening within a variety of trusted public institutions (care homes, churches, educations, sporting organisations and medical establishments), which had all been previously seen as trustworthy guardians of, rather than threats to childhood innocence. By 2013, it appeared that the sexual abuse and exploitation of children and young people was everywhere, that no child was safe and that no institution was to be trusted. Worse still, modern modes of communication, particularly the Internet and smartphones, provided novel opportunities for sexual predators to exploit and abuse children. These new fears generated new calls for inquiries, justice and for institutions to be held to account. In short, the government and public institutions were facing a crisis of legitimacy and this created the necessary political conditions for change to happen. Resources were put into policing and regulating the 'new' social problem of sexual exploitation in order to shore up the legitimacy crisis.

In July 2014, the Home Secretary established the Independent Inquiry into Child Sexual Abuse and gave it wide-ranging power to investigate – historically and contemporaneously – how British institutions handle their duty of care to protect children from sexual abuse. In March 2015, the government published its plans for tackling child sexual exploitation, which included giving child sexual abuse the status of a 'national threat' and that, inter alia, created tougher means of holding local authorities (and the professionals working in them) to account for failures to adequately deal with sexual exploitation. One of the main targets of central government's plans was to 'eradicate the culture of denial' (Cabinet Office 2015: 1) for 'victims must be believed, no matter how they behave' (ibid.: 4). In other words, regardless of the empirical realities, 'the problem' of sexual exploitation is constituted such that all young women involved in any exchange of sex for money are always and already understood as being only and ever victims of child sexual abuse. All agency is eradicated and the force of necessity or constrained choices is rendered not relevant.

Hence, because of the dominance of the discourse of child sexual abuse, we no longer have a practice or policy framework that can provide support for these young women – no matter how few they may number. Instead, in England, we have created a form of regulation that: widened the net of surveillance and policing targeting working-class girls' and young women's sexual lives; generated greater levels of criminalisation and incarceration 'in the name of protection' (Phoenix 2002b; Brown 2016); increased targeting policing of girls' and young women's use of public space and their criminalisation for public order offences (Phoenix 2012); and when girls and young women do make complaints that are taken forward by the police, exposes them to profoundly unjust forms of justice perpetrated by a legal system that still relies on sexist ideologies of girlhood sexual innocence and perceives that any voluntarism in exchanging sex for money is, *ipso facto*, proof that no abuse took place (Cockbain and Brayley 2012; Phoenix 2012; Starmer 2014).

Conclusion

At the beginning of this chapter, I suggested that knowledge about the problematic nature of young people in prostitution is global in its nature and reach, if for no other reason than many international policy agreements place an obligation on countries to do something about it. I also suggested that despite these global flows of knowledges and the migration of regulatory regimes or policy models purporting to address what is constituted as the problems that must be solved, what actually happens vis-à-vis policy implementation and the sorts of regulatory frameworks that develop is dependent on institutional, organisational, political, economic, social and ideological conditions in specific countries at specific moments in history. The rest of the chapter then set about demonstrating this in the context of youth prostitution policy reform in England and Wales in the twenty-first century. The story told in this chapter is paradoxical: in trying to 'do something' about children in prostitution, policymakers and practitioners in England and Wales ended up erasing the possibility of it as a social phenomenon. In what preceded, I gave an account of some of the twists and turns that made that paradox possible.

By way of conclusion, I will end with the following thought. One of the key effects of erasing 'youth prostitution' is that it is no longer possible to talk about how economic necessity and poverty may shape the sorts of choices girls and young women make in relation to sex. Yet, we also know that sex is nevertheless an economic commodity. Creating a policy and regulatory framework based on notions of child abuse does not and has not altered that empirical reality. Thus prostitution remains a plausible option as it always has done for young women with few other means of economically resourcing themselves. This is particularly true in the context of austerity Britain where services and support for young people have been dramatically cut and their social and economic precarity has dramatically increased (Antonucci et al. 2014; Antonucci 2016). Added to this, globalisation and new technologies have altered and multiplied sex 'markets', old and new. Internet and smartphone technologies has made possible new and different commercial sexual experiences and products (take cybersex for instance) as well as novel ways to organise the sale and purchase of sex that are superseding the older, more visible, localised and geographically bounded prostitution markets (Cunningham et al. 2017; Sanders et al. 2018). Many of these newer sex markets are less visible than traditional sex markets and being so are less easily regulated and policed – both of which create the conditions for young women, especially those between the ages of 15–17 years old, to be involved without coming to the attention of authorities. Yet, if we do not retain the notion of 'youth prostitution' as something *connected to the social institution of prostitution* or to use common parlance, the sex industry, we can do nothing about it. We end up assuming that the 'sex industry' is capable of regulating itself in such a way that no one under the age of 18 years old is involved and we end up abandoning such girls and young women to their own fate. This is a position that is as naive as it is logically incorrect.

Note

1 Please also see the Contagious Diseases Acts 1984, 1866 and 1869 and the Defence of the Realm Act 1914 (section 40D) in England and Wales (see Walkowitz 1982).

References

Antonucci, L. 2016. *Student lives in crisis: Deepening inequality in times of austerity*. Bristol, UK: Policy Press.

Antonucci, L., M. Hamilton and S. Roberts eds. 2014. *Young people and social policy in Europe: Dealing with risk, inequality and precarity in times of crisis. Work and Welfare Series*. Basingstoke, UK. Palgrave.

Balfour, R. and Allen, J. 2014. *A review of the literature on sex workers and social exclusion*. London: UCL Institute of Health Equity.

Barnado's. 1998. *Whose daughter next?* Available at www.barnardos. org.uk/research/documents/WHODAUGT.PDF [accessed December 2011].

Berelowitz, S., C. Firmin, G. Edwards and S. Gulvurtlu. 2012. 'I thought I was the only one. The only one in the world'. *The Office of the Children's Commissioner's Inquiry into Child Sexual Exploitation In Gangs and Groups: Interim Report*. London: Office of the Children's Commissioner.

Brown, K. 2016. *Vulnerability and young people: Care and social control in policy and practice*. Bristol, UK: Policy Press.

Cabinet Office. 2015. *Tackling child sexual exploitation*. London: HM Government.

Cabinet Office. 2017. *Tackling child sexual exploitation: A progress report*. London: HM Government.

Church, S., M. Henderson, M. Barnard and G. Hart. 2001. Violence by clients towards female prostitutes in different work setting: Questionnaire survey. *British Medical Journal* 322: 524–525.

Cockbain, E. and H. Brayley. 2012. Child sexual exploitation and youth offending: A research note. *European Journal of Criminology* 96: 689–700.

Cunningham, S., T. Sanders, J. Scoular, R. Campbell, J. Pitcher, K. Hill, K. M. Valentine-Chase, C. Melissa, Y. Aydin and R. Hamer. 2017. Behind the screen: Commercial sex, digital spaces and working online. *Technology in Society*. https://doi.org/10.1016/j.techsoc.2017.11.004.

Department for Children, Schools and Families. 2009. *Safeguarding children and young people from sexual exploitation*. London: HM Government.

Department of Health and Home Office. 2000. *Safeguarding children involved in prostitution: Supplementary guidance to working together to safeguard children*. London: HM Government.

Firmin, C. 2011. *This is it: This is my life*. London. ROTA.

Galvin, C., J.J. Pearce and M. Williams. 2003. *It's someone taking a part of you: A study of young women and sexual exploitation*. London: Jessica Kingsley Publishers.

Hardy, K. and Kingston, S. 2016. *New sociologies of sex work*. London. Routledge.

Home Office. 2000. *Setting boundaries: Reforming the law on sex offences*. London: Home Office.

Home Office. 2004. *Paying the price*. London: The Home Office.

Home Office. 2006a. A coordinated strategy for prostitution. Available at ncapuk.org/documents/ProstitutionStrategy.pdf [accessed December 2011].

Home Office. 2006b. *Tackling street prostitution*. London: Home Office.

Home Office. 2007. *UK National action plan on tackling human trafficking*. London: Home Office.

Jay, A. 2014. *Independent inquiry into child sexual exploitation in Rotherham 1997–2013*. Rotherham, UK: Rotherham Metropolitan Borough Council.

Kinnell, H. 2013. *Violence and sex work in Britain*. London: Routledge.

Lee, M. and R. O'Brien. 1995. *The game's up: Redefining child prostitution*. London: The Children's Society.

McKeganey, N.P. and M. Barnard, M. 1996. *Sex work on the streets: Prostitutes and their clients*. Buckingham, UK. Open University Press.

Melrose, M. 2002. Labour pains: Some considerations of the difficulties in researching juvenile prostitution. *International Journal of Social Research Theory, Methodology and Practice* 54: 333–352.

Melrose, M. 2013. Twenty-first century party people: Young people and sexual exploitation in the new millennium. *Child Abuse Review* 223: 155–168.

Melrose, M. and Barrett, D. 2004. *Anchors in floating lives: Interventions with young people sexually abused through prostitution*. Dorset, UK: Russell House.

O'Neill, M. 2001. *Prostitution and feminism: Towards a politics of feeling*. London: John Wiley & Sons.

Phoenix, J. 2001. *Making sense of prostitution*. London: Palgrave Macmillan.

Phoenix, J. 2002a. In the name of protection: Youth prostitution policy reforms in England and Wales. *Critical Social Policy* 222: 353–375.

Phoenix, J. 2002b. Youth prostitution policy reform: New discourses, same old story, in Carlen, P. ed. *Women and punishment: The struggle for justice*. Devon, UK: Willan Publishing.

Phoenix, J. 2005. *Full report of research activities and results to the Economic and Social Research Council: Working with youth prostitution. A database*. Available at www.esrc.ac.uk/my-esrc/grants/R000223916/read [accessed March 2012].

Phoenix, J. ed. 2009. *Regulating sex for sale: Prostitution policy reform in the UK*. Bristol, UK: Policy Press.

Phoenix, J. 2010. Living and working on the cusp of contradictions. *Youth and Policy* 104: 37–47.

Phoenix, J. 2012. *Out of place: The policing and criminalisation of sexually exploited girls*. London: Howard League For Penal Reform.

Sanders, T.J., Scoular, R. Campbell, J. Pitcher, J. and S. Cunningham. 2018. *Internet sex work: Beyond the gaze*. London: Springer.

Skilbrei, M.L. and C. Holmström. 2016. *Prostitution policy in the Nordic region: Ambiguous sympathies*. London: Routledge.

Starmer, K. 2014. Britain's criminal justice system fails the vulnerable: We need a victims' law. *Guardian*. 3 February. Available at www.theguardian.com/commentisfree/2014/feb/03/britain-criminal-justice-system-victims-law-public-prosecutions [accessed 17 April 2018].

Thom, B.R. Sales and J.J. Pearce. eds. 2007. *Growing up with risk*. Bristol, UK: Policy Press.

Walkowitz, J.R. 1982. *Prostitution and Victorian society: Women, class, and the state*. Cambridge, UK: Cambridge University Press.

Wolfenden, J. 1957. *Report of the Committee on Homosexual Offences and Prostitution*. London: Her Majesty's Stationary Office.

23

The *garotos* from Brazil

Xenophobia and the sex trafficking of men

Gregory Mitchell

Introduction

While news media, television shows, movies, governments, and NGOs spend a great deal of time depicting the "sex trafficking" and "sexual slavery" of women, there has been very little discussion of the sexual exploitation of men. Although there are sometimes references to rings of pedophiles who abuse underage boys, the idea that adult men – even heterosexually identified ones – could be vulnerable to sex trafficking is not one commonly considered even by media or entities that devote time and energy to the subject. This is remarkable because campaigns targeting sex trafficking frequently claim that it is so ubiquitous as to be hidden in plain sight. This chapter contends that the strategic elimination of men from the discourses of sex trafficking reveals suppositions, biases, and problematic positions within that discourse regarding the agency of women. That is, when we examine the ways that migrant men are portrayed simply as rational actors – as always functioning in classical *homo economicus* form – we can actually see how migrant women are denied that same status and treated as vulnerable creatures incapable of reason and self-determination when faced with difficult conditions.

And yet, male migrant sex workers are plentiful. As I document in this chapter, tens of thousands of male sex workers known as *garotos* or *garotos de programa* (meaning "boys" or "rent boys") have come from Brazil to Spain. Yet the media has almost no depictions of the lived experiences of such men. Below I examine an exception to this oversight. In 2010, there was a major international news story covering the first sex trafficking ring to focus on male sex workers. I describe the coverage of this case and assess the public reactions to it. I also position this case within a broader political economic context and argue that close attention to the details of the case can reveal how xenophobia courses through various aspects of the raid and the treatment of the men. Ultimately, examining this case of male sex trafficking reveals how knowledge about men, migration, and sexuality circulate. Better attention to such subjects and to the media's reaction to such subjects could go a long way to developing better standards and practices. Among these outcomes would be a reformation of immigration policy so that sex workers (such as the men examined in the Spanish case below) are not arrested and charged criminally while simultaneously being described as sexually exploited. That is, how can one state agency maintain that someone is a slave while another agent of the same state charges them for working illegally? The case also shows how migrant sex workers are forced to perform narratives of victimization to avoid deportation, which is in and of itself another forced movement tantamount to trafficking. And my appraisal of the news coverage and video footage released by authorities shows how immigration authorities work hand in hand with the media to create sexually titillating and harmful depictions of migrants' sexuality. Better delineation in the execution of duties among immigration authorities, branches of the police, and the news media is essential for more ethical regulatory instruments.

The case at hand

In August of 2010, BBC, CNN, MSNBC, ABC, and other networks briefly, but prominently featured the busting of Spain's first sex trafficking ring to specialize in men. One version of the two-minute video that accompanied the story begins with a rear view of well-muscled, brown, mostly shirtless Brazilian men standing inside a kitchen and living room area all facing away from the camera. An Englishman opines in voiceover:

> Spanish police say these are just some of the men they have found living as sex slaves in brothels across the country. They're all Brazilian. Police say most were lured to Spain with the promise of modeling or dancing work, but were then kept in small apartments like this one, sleeping six to a room and they were forced into prostitution.
>
> *(CNN Wire Staff 2010)*

The camera pans left past a police officer to show some laundry drying in a bedroom to the side. Cut to a policeman, Chief Inspector Jose Nieto, seated behind a cluster of ten microphones at a press conference, who says: "The rooms where they spent twenty-four hours a day were like submarines – small rooms and they had to be on duty and permanently in service." The camera cuts to a shelf with bottles of liquor and cava. Spanish immigration police mill about the crime scene wearing yellow reflective vests. As the Englishman resumes, we briefly see an unmade bed and crumpled pillow.

> To ensure they worked around the clock, police say the men were given drugs, including Viagra and cocaine. The customers were always men. This alleged brothel was on the island of Mallorca, the suspected center of a criminal network responsible for trafficking between 60 and 80 Brazilians into and across Spain. [A map appears showing locations as red dots; the camera zooms in and out.] Eight people were arrested in Mallorca including the accused ringleader. Raids were also carried out in Leon. Police arrested three there, and three others in Barcelona, Alicante and Madrid. Police believe the men were routinely moved between these areas to meet local demand.
>
> *(CNN Wire Staff 2010)*

The video shifts to a press conference, now showing an impossibly handsome young policeman named Chief Inspector Pedro Bernardo. "Some of the victims said that after being moved," the narrator says, "if they wanted to stop working they were told they would be killed."

The voiceover goes on, but now viewers see some more brothel rooms. Another unmade bed, this one with a mirror over the headboard a red lampshade that gives a soft pink glow. It seems there may be condoms and lubricant. There is a shower in the bedroom.

Investigators say the men were forced to pay back their air ticket at the inflated price of more than 5,000 dollars. They also had to give up half their earnings, and pay weekly rent of 250 dollars. Police say the ring trafficked some women as well, but is unique for being the first they're aware to concentrate on smuggling and exploiting men.

(CNN Wire Staff 2010)

The video concludes by returning to the image of the shirtless young men standing, all displayed in rows with their backs turned to the camera. It is unclear why the police have made them stand like this, as if they were naughty children put into "time out." The men do not look around, but mostly look down. In truth, the police are from the Immigration Networks and Falsified Documents Unit of the National Police and these men are not being legally treated as rape victims or liberated slaves but as illegal aliens who are eligible for deportation (CNN Wire Staff 2010). Some of the trafficking victims were then arrested for "working illegally in Spain" because they were selling sex (Minder 2010). Thus, the men were caught in the paradox of being declared criminals because they failed to stop their own victimization.

When the story broke, my inbox was flooded with links by people who knew of my research on Brazilian male sex workers known as *garotos de programa* (rent boys, *garotos* for short) – research that later became my book *Tourist Attractions: Performing Race and Masculinity in Brazil's Sexual Economy* (Mitchell 2016). That book includes interviews with more than 40 male sex workers in Brazil, many of whom identify as heterosexual despite selling sex to gay clients and many of whom have traveled as migrants to sell sex abroad, sometimes taking out loans, sometimes using third-party clients, lenders, and others who facilitate their international movement within the sex trade though no one actually involved in these interactions would ever even think to use words like sex trafficker or pimp.

Having had first-hand experience with migrant male sex workers from Brazil, I could not help but be skeptical of this first ever "sex slave" ring concentrating on men. And when I compared the media's editing, omissions, and decontextualizations to the details released in police reports, my skepticism gave way to disgust. What I offer in this brief chapter is a rehearsal of that skepticism as an illustration of the ways that discourses about sex trafficking combine with assumptions about male sexuality and masculinity to erase the "complex personhood" of male sex workers (see Gordon 1997). This global case is unique in some of its details, but is an important case study for what it reveals about the portrayals and construction of narratives about male sex workers and their purported exceptionalism.

To begin with, it was immigration police and not journalists or regular police who released the video footage. Versions of the video and story were broadcast in Spanish, Portuguese, and English, each with slight variation. I maintain that this case study represents a sensationalized attempt to make it look like sex trafficking is getting worse, the message being that not even men are safe anymore. In fact, it follows what Adriana Piscitelli (2006) clearly demonstrated in heterosexual cases of Brazilian women supposedly trafficked in Spain, one implication of which is that it bolsters anti-immigrant sentiments while regimenting the bodies and sexuality of sex workers. Thus, it is important for scholars to challenge this media narrative and expose its anti-immigrant qualities while also noting its implications for theories of circulation and diaspora.

This case received an unusual amount of attention because of the additional titillation factor: *men – and ostensibly straight men at that – can be trafficked, too?* As I collected reactions in my notes, I realized that readers of the news stories did not all take it so seriously. So in addition to many comments indicating how horrifying sex trafficking is becoming these days, I jotted down quite a few jokes from the comments sections. "Viagra, cocaine, and marijuana? Where do I sign up???" read one. A commenter with a woman's name wrote on CNN, "Dam! Brasilians servicing [people] . . . Why didnt I know this last time I was in Spain! Grrrrr." And male and female readers on a site that had only text and no video or other images complained, saying they had clicked on the story about sex trafficking because they hoped to see pictures of the "hot Brazilian" men. A number of the commenters came for the hot Brazilians, but instead fixated on the Spanish policeman mentioned above and talked about how "hot" he was. Another opined that unlike women "these grown men" couldn't have been "duped into prostitution" and could have left. Not a single commenter applied this sort of skepticism to "trafficking" stories in general or those about female sex trafficking victims, who they presume to be incapable of being anything other than sex slaves.

I maintain that skepticism here is good, but their basis is faulty. To be clear, my shared skepticism isn't based on the wrongheaded notion that men cannot be raped, coerced, or held in sexual debt bondage. The readers' sexist double standards about consent are problematic, but their skepticism is nevertheless useful, if misdirected, because from a skeptic's vantage they might begin to see other things in this case that don't add up and then be inclined to see similarities in this case and the many more cases that involve women, who are far more easily cast as unagentive victims.

Seeing trafficking

So what do the videos actually show? That is, what do we really *see* when we "see sex trafficking?" Here in these videos we see condoms, lube, red lighting, a mirror at the headboard, a shower, and one video shows a copy of Spartacus, a gay tourist guidebook. It's unclear why the rent boys would need that. Perhaps it's there for the edification of clients if they want some reading to go along with their post-coital pillow talk. Maybe a client forgot it. Maybe the *garotos* study it to find clients or decide where to go out dancing or cruising. News outlets highlighted the presence of the supply of Viagra, cocaine, and vasodilators or "poppers" that induce euphoria, cause sexual arousal, and relax the sphincter (e.g., Woolls 2010). There's the image of the overcrowded dormitory-style conditions, described in military terms as "like a submarine." For some viewers who have never been to a *sauna* or bath house in Brazil where male prostitution occurs legally, this brothel scene might be shocking, but it's actually pretty standard or even better than some of the *saunas* in Brazil I've done research in.

And the housing here offers far better conditions than one finds in the desperately poor state of Maranhão, where it turns out *all* of the men are from (Seco 2010). The ringleader, known as "Lucas," arranged their air travel using cloned credit cards, flew them into France and Luxembourg, and then drove them to the Spanish cities, with the largest operation being in the gay tourist mecca of Mallorca, where 8 foremen oversaw 40 men. The operation in Leon had 3 foremen for 15 men, while Barcelona, Alicante, and Madrid had 1 foreman for 6 men (Agencia Brasil 2010). Nine of those arrested were Brazilian, but there were also four Spaniards and one Venezuelan (Dias 2010). We also know that migration routes for male sex workers from Brazil to Spain are very well established. The Spanish Ministry of Health surveyed 7,000 men in its report on male sex work in 2005 and discovered that an incredible 70% of men selling sex in Spain were Brazilian migrant men, but notes that instances of force and coercion were incredibly rare (Infante 2008).

For readers wondering how a single foreman running a house around the clock could manage to keep a half dozen unwilling, physically strong, and capable male sex workers from rebelling, it might help to know that according to the police reports, the men were already sex workers or knew they were coming to be sex workers. Police did point out that "a few" of the men said they thought they would be go-go dancers or models, although in my own experience in Brazil the imported English term *"go-go boy"* and the word *"modelo"* are euphemisms for sex worker and one also finds the terms used in the male brothels and by gay porn studios (Woolls 2010). In 12 years of researching sex work in Rio, I've never met any male sex workers with any confusion about this terminology. Around a quarter of the men in this case were "illegal" immigrants. Police said that undocumented men who cooperated with the investigation and prosecution of ringleaders might be permitted to stay, while those who would not cooperate and testify would be charged by police and deported (Chaves 2010). It remains unclear whether the men were able to stay or not. (In 2014, my research assistant, Chienfa Wong, went to the government officials in Madrid seeking records and information, but was denied.) It is important to remember that the condition of agreeing to testify in a sex trafficking trial in exchange for not being deported or charged criminally means there's an incentive to tell police and social workers trafficking horror stories. Since the initial report, five more men were charged in the case, but it is unclear whether these five are newly found ringleaders or merely uncooperative "victims" (CNN Wire Staff 2010).

Here's what we actually know from the various Spanish reports described above: The prostitution operation began in June of 2009 and the police began investigating in February of 2010, but did not intervene until August. The operation involved 64 Brazilian men, and 16 Brazilian women (mostly *travestis* or trans women). The sex workers were between 22 and 29, except for one 16-year-old male (which is above Spain's age of consent) who worked for only three weeks, but whose presence allowed media to report this as a ring that was trafficking "men and boys," implying this was a child sex ring. This assertion that the adult migrant sex workers' clients were also seeking children is also a homophobic and inaccurate way of conflating gays with pedophiles. Of the 16 foremen, 10 were Brazilian. The operation was financed by ringleaders who were already in prison and most of those Brazilian foremen were former prostitutes, suggesting these purported "traffickers" were simply sex workers who had been promoted to captains of the squad or "den mothers" of a sort. Regardless, they weren't high up enough in the organization that their arrests have much if any impact on the organized crime rings.

In response to the story, Brazil's largest newspaper, *O Globo*, interviewed Brazilian male sex workers living in Spain (Redação Correio 2010). One said he makes between $200 and $400 per trick, making his career move to Spain very lucrative. He said he had heard of this story, but that he doesn't believe the men would have needed to be forced to take drugs. "I don't know anyone who would force someone to use cocaine and Viagra, [because] everybody in our world already takes these" (Author's translation). Again, as current male sex workers working in Brazil prior to leaving, this would not have been a new addition to their repertoire. Another man, a 30-year-old *garoto* originally from Rio explained:

> You earn more [when you take those], and whoever uses the drugs receives more money because you can be active longer. Everyone knows what they're going to do here [in Spain and they know that] in order to send money to their family and free themselves from the *cafetões* [pimps] they need to always be ready for a *programa* [trick]. (Author's translation)

So the men probably weren't being force fed drugs. In fact, the flow of coke, poppers, and Viagra (or knockoffs of it) are very common among the men I know in Brazil. Not only sex workers, but for gay men. Given the rise of homonormativity and gay rights messaging that has sought to normalize and asexualize gay men by promoting conservative notions of gay marriage and assimilation, it may come as a shock that poppers, Viagra, alcohol, recreational drugs, and open bottles of lube are constitutive parts of the gay sexual landscape. Indeed, the insistence that such things are aberrant is a refusal of queerness and a neutering of gay men into anodyne and easily assimilated creatures that is homophobic in its own right (see Duggan 2004).

As for sleeping six people to a room, concerned readers might first check out the living conditions among the poor back in Maranhão, where they will find large families sleeping many more people than that to a room and not necessarily in beds at all. The dormitory style bunk beds in these brothels might be more akin to a squalid youth hostel than a Four Seasons Resort, but they're likely better than home. It is only through a condescending Western middle-class gaze that this "squalor" is rendered pitiable rather than desirable.

Basic economics

The conditions were exploitative financially. That part is clear. According to El Pais, the men made a fixed rate of $78 USD (by 2010 exchange rates) per 30-minute *programa* (Seco 2010). The house takes half, leaving them with $39 per *programa*. Incidentally, $39 was around the going rate for a programa in Rio de Janeiro for men. But this *is* still a pretty bad deal. However, 50% is also the standard for female brothels in Brazil where half the profit going to the house is considered normal. Anything more and women will protest, but they see up to 50% as within reason for the benefits third parties can provide in terms of security, supplying clients, screening clients, and so on. So while the managers in this case are being financially exploitative, this part of the financial arrangement is also consistent with what legal sex work practices back home look like.

After this deduction, they then must pay back the inflated price of $5,000 for an air ticket when a flight from São Luis to Madrid costs closer to $2,000. The traffickers therefore make a significant profit on the "loan" for the ticket. So put another way: the *garotos* owe the house 133 tricks, or 67 hours of sexual labor. So if a man wanted to discharge his entire debt in a single year, that would be 2.5 *programas* per week owed to the house. The rest would be his. But there's more: The English reports says they were charged $250 a week for rent and food (CNN Wire 2010). However, Lusophone reports from *Estadão* suggest it may actually have been per month, not per week. If that is the case, this room and board would have been about seven programas or 3.5 hours a week owed to the house. That means a man wanting financial independence in a year starts out each week ten tricks in debt. To be sure, it's not a great deal. But calling it "sexual slavery" also doesn't feel apt. Rather, the exploitation here would seem to be just enough incentive for a migrant male sex worker arriving in Spain to want to become a free agent.

In fact, if he turns just two tricks a day – even adjusted for all that he owes the house under this supposed situation of sexual slavery – he would *still* make 33% more than the average resident of his home state's capital (i.e., his $7,500 per year compared to their $5,000) (World Data Atlas 2009). If he worked in this situation in Spain a second year (assuming he wasn't saddled with more bogus debts) even continuing to lose 50% to the house, he would make $20,000 a year, which is four times the average back home. (So even if the contradictory reporting was correct that he was paying 200 euros per week and not per month, he would still come out considerably ahead.) Put another way, even a fraction of his salary remitted to his family back home could make them the richest people in their neighborhood. If he actually left the ringleader Lucas and his henchmen, the *garoto* could be wealthier than most Spaniards, including some clients. Thus, it's not hard to see why so many thousands of Brazilian male sex workers have moved to Spain. So while the situation is exploitative, the men *are* making a rational choice to come to Spain to sell sex, and while they may not "like" the work, they don't need to be held padlocked into their room or held at gunpoint. The foremen don't need to force them to do anything because the economics are so cleanly calibrated. In this sense, the sexist commenters on the news websites are correct. The men could easily muscle their way out of the situation. But the exploitation here isn't "sexual slavery" as CNN and the Western news outlets so salaciously labeled it so much as it is run-of-the-mill exploitation of basic capitalism and waged labor.

Ambulation and prostitution

But what does this teach us about the state of sex work and male "sex trafficking" today? What broader theoretical import does this have? I argue that this case presents us with an opportunity to reconceptualize the idea of circulation. This case extends our thinking about diaspora. As *morenos* or mixed-race brown-skinned men from Maranhão, the men are descendents of African slaves, indigenous populations, and Portuguese colonists who have now – in some sense – "returned" to Iberia. Their diasporic flow is halted by (debt) bondage – by a moment of partial stasis in their journey as migrants, although more accurately they are not static but caught in a closed pattern of ambulation as foremen shuttle them between a handful of cities.

The first person to write a book-length study of *michês*, or male hustlers in Brazil, was an Argentine expatriate named Nestor Perlongher who studied street hustlers in the 1980s in Sao Paulo (Perlongher 2008). He was a peculiar figure. A heavy drug user, a poet, and someone who regularly had sex with his informants. He was fanatical in his love of Gilles Deleuze, the philosopher, and Antonin Artaud, the founder of the Theater of Cruelty movement. For Perlongher, *michês* are nomads, circulating along customary paths from point to point, client to client, always reaching the point in order to leave it behind rather than to dwell. It is in the state of cruising – when betwixt and between points – that he feels the *michê* is best understood. This instability allows the *michê* to remain a mercurial and romantic figure for Perlongher, and so it is difficult to say how the famed poet-anthropologist would have theorized the great migration of *michês* indoors, where they have become increasingly static and non-nomadic. But here in this case, the *michês* are once again on the move. This time, unlike during the last years of the military dictatorship of the 1980s in Brazil, they are able to come to Europe.

And then, in order not to be ejected from Iberia and sent back "home," they must properly perform a citizenship predicated on victimhood. As Brazilian immigrants, they cannot be dignified subjects. The path to proper European subjectivity requires that the only worthy Brazilian entrant in this case is a trafficked one, stripped of rational choice and cleansed of the stigma of willful whoring, and in this case, attesting to being a trafficking victim also means confessing and receiving absolution for sodomy and the attendant taint of heterosexuality. Spain demands that proper hegemonic masculinity be restored if the men wish to stay. This is the paradox of masculinity that the state asks the men to perform. They must be hegemonically masculine and also victims. Spain insists that before giving its blessing and legitimacy to the migrant men that any feeling they have of their own agency be sacrificed on the altar of the nation-state. In circulating this narrative from Spanish immigration police to Brazilian media, the message to colonial corners of the diaspora is that sexuality is relegated to the authority of the state as the price of re-entering the diasporic flow. And this neocolonialism masks the latent xenophobia and anti-immigrant policies of Europe. Theirs is a demand that evacuates agency and voids any possibility of reconfiguring the diaspora as a place where willful circulation – rather than only abject exile – could be a possible ontological category. This collusion by immigration police, Spanish politicians, and global media reifies gender in order to constrain racialized diasporic subjects, thereby curtailing freedom and withholding opportunity – all in the name of stopping so-called sex trafficking.

References

Agencia Brasil. "Redes de prostituição que ligam Brasil e Espanha podem envolver outros crimes." August 31, 2010. *Folha.* https://noticias.uol.com.br/internacional/ultimas- noticias/2010/08/31/redes-de-prostituicao-que-ligam-brasil-e-espanha-envolvem-outros- crimes.htm.

Chaves, Érica. "Vítimas de rede espanhola sabiam que iam se prostituir, diz polícia." 2010. *O Globo.* August 31, 2010. http://g1.globo.com/mundo/noticia/2010/08/vitimas-de-rede-espanhola-sabiam-que-iam-se- prostituir-diz-policia.html.

CNN Wire Staff. "5 arrested in Spain for male prostitution ring." September 7, 2010. *CNN World.* www.cnn.com/2010/WORLD/europe/09/07/spain.male.prostitutes/index.html.

Dias, Roberto. "Espanha mira anúncio de sexo após flagrar esquema de prostituição com brasileiros." January 9, 2010. *Folha.* www.folha.uol.com.br/cotidiano/792123- espanha-mira-anuncio-de-sexo-apos-flagrar-esquema-de-prostituicao-com- brasileiros.shtml.

Duggan, Lisa. *The Twilight of Equality: Neoliberalism, Cultural Politics, and the Attack on Democracy.* Boston, MA: Beacon Press, 2004.

Infante, Anelise. "70% dos homens que se prostituem na Espanha são brasileiros, dis estudo." January 11, 2008. *BBC Brasil.com.* www.bbc.com/portuguese/reporterbbc/story/2008/01/080111_prostituicao espanha.s html.

Gordon, Avery. *Ghostly Matters: Haunting and the Sociological Imagination.* Minneapolis, MN: University of Minnesota Press, 1997.

Minder, Raphael. "Spain breaks up a trafficking ring for male prostitution." August 31, 2010. *New York Times.* www.nytimes.com/2010/09/01/world/europe/01iht- spain.html.

Mitchell, Gregory. *Tourist Attractions: Performing Race and Masculinity in Brazil's Sexual Economy.* Chicago, IL: University of Chicago Press, 2016.

Perlongher, Néstor. *O Negócio do Michê – Prostituição Viril em São Paulo.* São Paula, Brazil: Editora Fundação Perseu Abramo, 2008.

Piscitelli, A. "Sujeição ou subversão: migrantes brasileiras na indústria do sexo na Espanha." *Revista História & Perspectivas,* 1, 35 (2006).

Redação Correio. "Brasileiros oferecem sexo '24 horas' em sites de prostituição espanhóis." August 31, 2010. *Correio.* www.correio24horas.com.br/noticia/nid/brasileiros- oferecem-sexo-24-horas-em-sites-de-prostituicao-espanhois.

Seco, Raquel. "La primera red sexual masculine desarticulada en España explotó a decease de vítimas." August 31, 2010. *El Pais.* https://elpais.com/sociedad/2010/08/31/actualidad/1283205601_850215.html.

Woolls, Daniel. "Spain breaks up male-prostitute trafficking gang." August 31, 2010. *Associated Press.* www.washingtontimes.com/news/2010/aug/31/spain-breaks-male- prostitute-trafficking-gang.

World Data Atlas. *Maranhão: Average Monthly Income.* 2009. https://knoema.com/atlas/Brazil/Maranh %C3%A3o/Average-monthly-income.

24

Re-assembling the feminist war machine

State, feminisms and sex workers in Russia

Alexander Kondakov and Daniil Zhaivoronok

> Why do we always fight with homosexuality or smoking or sexual industry or what else? Because this doesn't require any investments from the state. Because if we start to resolve real serious social issues – like pensions, for example, or healthcare, education and so on – this will require money, billions of investments. [. . .] It is just to draw away the attention of people from real economic issues by finding an internal enemy.
>
> *(Woman, born 1975, provider of heterosexual services)*

Introduction

This chapter deals with a variety of representations associated with debates around sex work in Russia. Just like in many other parts of the world, these debates are structured by the feminist 'sex wars' (Rubin 1984) that, having developed in the 1970s, continue to have a profound impact on the epistemology, imagination, organization and political trajectories of feminist projects locally and globally. Our aim is to analyse how the oppositional approaches to commercial sex that have emerged out of these feminist confrontations take shape in Russia, and we also suggest more general implications for sexual politics from our analysis. Thus, we offer a theoretically and empirically informed reflection of these debates as a transcultural phenomenon that is locally enacted in various forms.

Though we still plan to employ the broader framework of feminist 'sex wars' and to apply militarist conceptions developed by Gilles Deleuze and Felix Guattari (1987), we also consider overcoming the binary division that splits the approaches towards sex work in two opposite 'camps'. In this endeavour, our main concern is to propose a more nuanced understanding of the politics in sex work through an analysis of the claims of representations that are made by various political groups in Russia. More specifically, we analyse which subjects are claimed to be represented by neo-abolitionist and pro-sex work feminists in order to seek more elusive and less absolute political solutions. This approach, we believe, gives ground for possible connections beyond representational politics. Judith Butler (2015: 4), for example, offers to understand political representation as always exclusionary: any representation of a group necessarily excludes some bodies from the group currently represented. Her proposal is to pursue a politics of alliances that would unite people in a political grassroots network by shared grounds (see also Kondakov 2017). Drawing on these insights, in our analysis we look more closely at some of the possible connections that may give rise to a new type of political action beyond ontological and epistemological 'wars' and dichotomous positions. Thus, we will employ concepts – even those presumably marking a conflict such as 'war machine', as applied by Johannes Ungelenk (2014) – in a way that will help to convey not only disengagements, but also moments of co-constituting interactions and common challenges.

Our analysis is based on two different depositories of ideas. For the first one, we shall turn to written debates that have emerged from Russian social networks and new media. The current composition of feminist movements in Russia is not imaginable without the Internet and digital technologies: feminist groups and pages on *VKontakte, Facebook* and *Livejournal* account for dozens of thousands of participants. The wave of online feminism in Russia emerged in the mid-2000s and social media should now be viewed as a highly significant location of production, dissemination and management of feminist knowledge, identities and affections. Therefore, for the analysis of feminist positions on commercial sex we mostly rely on texts from online sources. These texts are complemented by a literature review of scholarship on commercial sex in Russia published in local academic journals. The second set of 'data' for this analysis is interviews with sex workers from St. Petersburg, Russia's second largest city. The interviews were collected in the course of a research project conducted by the Centre for Independent Social Research and the Union of Artists and Sex Workers 'Therese' in 2015. In this project, we used participatory methods, which entailed 7 trained sex workers interviewing a very diverse cohort of 41 sex worker peers (for a more detailed discussion of the methodology, see Kondakov 2018).

War machine and the state feminism

For better or for worse, the metaphor of feminist 'war' has stuck to debates about sex work. Recognizing its militaristic character, we will use it in light of Mikhail Bakunin's assertion that 'the passion for destruction is a creative passion' (1971 [1842]: n.p.). In this sense, Deleuze and Guattari (1987) offer a productive interpretation of war as an ideological process. In their reading, 'war machines' as ideologies draw 'a creative line of flight, the composition of a smooth space and of the movement of people in that space' (Deleuze and Guattari 1987: 422). They talk about power relations and the ways in which configuration of power is reconstituted. Their concept of the war machine refers to strategies and tactics that are employed to challenge established modes of the distribution of power through creation of new collectivities (Ranciere 1999: ix). Hence, 'war machines' are processes of transforming existing political imagination beyond dominant representations by subverting existent configurations of power relations.

As Deleuze and Guattari (1987: 351) see it, war machines are oppositional to the state apparatuses. This understanding is drawn by Ungelenk (2014: 96) in his analysis of feminism:

> Feminism is a war machine, and as a war machine, it is not to be defined solely by its supplementary objects, war against blockages, war against *states*, but also by, and foremost by, its 'sole and veritable positive object', the creation of new collectivities.

A fuller picture of the war machine should also include Brent Adkins' (2015: 191) observation:

[C]aution is needed to avoid turning Deleuze and Guattari's claims about the war machine into moral claims. It is not the case that politically there are two kinds of objects, states and war machines, and that states are 'bad' and war machines are 'good'. No, the opposition here, as with all of the oppositions in *A Thousand Plateaus*, is the opposition between the two tendencies found in any assemblage.

In this way, a feminist project as a war machine is not defined by its position vis-à-vis the state, but as an assemblage of multiple ideological grounds, including those that prioritize the state. In other words, the tension between the state and a war machine is a process of their mutual co-constitution and transformation. Following this line of thought, the state is also not a definite institution. Rather, it is an assemblage of some sort. The state appropriates elements of the war machines and turns them into mechanisms of control (see Adkins 2015). Therefore, the boundary between these two projects constantly shifts and lies not only between them, but within both fields.

Current debates on sex work fit these theoretical considerations. There are two clear-cut camps. One of them is neo-abolitionist feminism that argues that prostitution should be considered a form of violence against women. Within this approach, sex and sexuality are seen as inevitably traumatic manifestations of patriarchy (Dworkin 1987), and prostitution as an institutionalized form of male domination over women (Barry 1995). Using universalist claims of representation, neo-abolitionists propose to save all women from prostitution and portray 'prostituted women', as they call women doing sex work, as passive and helpless victims. Rescue endeavours result from state-led initiatives via its policing, carceral and caring apparatuses. The so-called Swedish or Nordic 'model' of client criminalization is promoted as exemplary by feminist neo-abolitionists (Skilbrei and Holmström 2011).

Another camp – one to which we would like to ally ourselves – is pro-sex work feminism, which argues that sex work should not be reduced to any single experience or situation (Agustín 1998; Kontula 2008; Sanders 2004). Violence is rather understood as contextualized within social, historical and political circumstances: legal and social marginalization and exclusion experienced by sex workers, and the emergence of the new forms of governance or reconfiguration of patriarchal control apparatuses (Bernstein 2012; Doezema 2001; Kulick 2003). This feminist political project stands for the decriminalization of sex work and for lowering of state/police intervention, which is often seen as the main source of violence against sex workers.

While, as presented here, these two feminist projects are opposed and confrontational, we look for overlaps between them. For example, there is good reason to consider earlier 'second-wave' feminism associated with neo-abolitionism as the catalyst for the creation of the line of flight. In Deleuze and Guattari's terms, this line of flight is the crucial condition of emancipation, of challenging power hierarchies and of constitution of new political collectives (see Fournier 2014). Thus, other feminist projects would be less grounded and intelligible without this version of feminism that contested patriarchal hierarchies in the first place. However, '[a] complex new constellation has emerged in which [. . .] the feminist project has also increasingly been linked with non-emancipatory agendas' (Farris and Rottenberg 2017: 6). In later stages, this version of feminism was absorbed by the state to a great degree and transformed into a technique of power and administration. This is reflected in the analysis of 'state feminism' or 'market feminism' (Kantola and Squires 2012), 'carceral feminism' (Bernstein 2012), 'white feminism' (Whalley and Hackett 2017) and 'governance feminism' (Halley et al. 2006). In what follows, we apply these conceptions of the war machine and the state to analyse feminist projects in Russia.

The neo-abolitionist project and its bedfellow

In this section, we analyse articulations of feminist positions to sex work in Russia mostly published in online sources. It is important to underline from the outset that both pro-sex work and neo-abolitionist feminist groups are rather sceptical of the state. They embrace a left grassroots politics stand that in one way or another challenges current state policies. For example, the leader of the Sex Workers' Trade Union 'Silver Rose' puts it boldly: 'Why on earth does the state get into its citizens' beds, instead of defending their rights?'[1] (Maslova 2013). As for neo-abolitionists, they are more ambiguous as further discussed below. They also criticize state institutions, and most importantly the police, whose officers are seen as one of the major sources of violence against sex workers: 'It is not clear if someone in front of you is a criminal or from the police, you can only find out if the police show their paper' (on VKontakte 2016).[2] Generally, Russian neo-abolitionists situate themselves in opposition to the current political regime in Russia, because it is considered – with good reason – as patriarchal and anti-feminist.

The following case is indicative of this position. In the Russian translation of the eighth chapter of *The State as Pimp* by Sheila Jeffreys published on one of the oldest and most popular sites of trans-exclusive neo-abolitionists, Womenation.org, one can read: 'From a feminist perspective, *prostitution* can be understood as the policy of patriarchal states acting in the interests of male citizens' (Womenation 2016, emphasis added). Yet, Jeffreys' original text reads: '*Legalization* can, from a critical feminist perspective, be understood as the behaviour of patriarchal governments acting in the interests of male citizens' (2008: 177, emphasis added). The difference between the translation and the original text is indicative: while the original critique moved by Jeffreys touches only upon the patriarchal nature of governments that legalize commercial sex, the translator re-assembled the text to point to the patriarchal nature of the state as such, regardless of the legal status of prostitution. The original wording would make little sense in Russia, where despite the fact that prostitution is criminalized, the state is still not perceived as any less patriarchal. This amendment in the translation leads to a significant radicalization of the statement, turning it from a critique of a particular kind of state, to the critique of all states in general.

Nevertheless, as indicated earlier, Russian neo-abolitionists are rather ambiguous about the state. Natalia Khodyreva, a prominent neo-abolitionist and author of the seminal *Contemporary Debates on Prostitution: Gender Studies Approach* (2006), introduced on Facebook a quick-fix solution to deal with prostitution, i.e. to implement the Swedish 'model'. She commented on Facebook in 2014:

> Those who make a living out of prostitution and sell themselves must be completely decriminalized . . . This is not to be confused with legalization! But those who exploit and promote the system of prostitution and use it must be criminalized.

As a political recipe this commentary includes a profound controversy: while recognizing that the state is a suspicious ally in pursuing an emancipatory feminist agenda, it also approaches the state as the main agent of positive feminist transformation in the project of combating prostitution, since legislative and executive powers are supposed to implement and enforce the law.

This controversial position that views the state as patriarchal yet also asks the state itself to intervene to get rid of patriarchal institutions is a ground for connectedness between the neo-abolitionist feminist project and conservative groups. For example, there are pro-governmental experts who are also highly favourable of the Swedish client-criminalization. However, their idea is that clients should be criminalized alongside sex workers, thus substantially deviating from the original feminist idea underpinning the Swedish 'model'. Nevertheless, conservative experts directly refer to and praise such 'models', as can be seen in the words of the director of the Police Academy in Nizhny Novgorod:

> In Sweden, it is believed 'that by prohibiting the purchase of sexual services, prostitution and its destructive effects can be counteracted more effectively than before'.[3] Moreover, this law clearly indicates that 'prostitution is an undesirable social phenomenon' and 'an obstacle to the development of equality between men and women'. This legal tool could and should be applied in Russia.
>
> *(Konev 2011: 206)*

Compare this statement with Khodyreva's (2006: 211) feminist argument from *Contemporary Debates on Prostitution*: 'The use of women in prostitution is an obstacle on the way to equal opportunities for women and to improvement of their status in society'. Here, Khodyreva also takes a legalist position towards gender equality to argue against prostitution and for the Swedish 'model'. Her style of writing is different as she does not refer to heavily charged conceptions such as 'undesirable social phenomenon'. Yet, the logic of conveying gender equality with a formal application of criminal law targeting clients is clearly there.

The same Police Academy director criticizes the possibility of legalizing sex work in Russia because: 'The majority of the country's population is formed of religious people or sympathizers, and fornication is a sin. The legalization of prostitution will create an illusion of admissibility of the sin' (Konev 2011: 204). This argument is close to the Russian Orthodox Church official views that are also supportive of the Swedish 'model'. Indeed, the head of the Russian Synodic Department for Relations between the Church, Society and Mass Media stated that in supporting the criminalization of clients introduced in France in 2016 'there is no difference between the seller and the buyer of human dignity. Both sides, degrading and degraded, are equally distancing themselves from happiness, from family happiness, from love, from God' (Legoida 2016).

The dangers of prostitution are best summarized by another police academy scholar, Olga Petryanina (2014: 335–336) who lists them as: 'degradation of national culture', 'agony and destruction of the family institution', the threat to the 'development of moral foundations of the younger generation' and, finally, the treatment of all women as 'second-class beings'. Not surprisingly, the optimal political solution to these perils is the Swedish 'model', which, she claims, 'immediately leads to decline in the demand of prostitution' (Petryanina 2014: 336). Petryanina was also very supportive of the implementation of a client criminalization policy in Belgorod, a region in Russia where in 2012 the local parliament introduced administrative penalties (~70 EUR) for the purchase of sexual services. The Belgorod parliament justified this legal initiative by crediting Sweden as a positive example (Belduma 2013). Yet, neo-abolitionists in Russia prefer to pay no attention to the appreciation of the Swedish 'model' by conservative politicians and experts like Petryanina. Instead they continue to uncritically reproduce narratives of the need to 'turn attention to clients' and 'criminalize the purchase of sex', regardless of the use of the same rhetorical devices mixed with family values, moral panic and Orthodox beliefs in the dominant Russian state politics.

There are exceptions from the general trend in Russian academic 'sex wars' (see Krupets and Nartova 2010; Zhaivoronok 2017). However, this discussion shows that Russian neo-abolitionists and conservatives share a great deal of reliance on the state and its monopoly on legal violence. The very idea of eradicating prostitution through the criminalization of clients implies a legitimate interference of the state on the lives of its citizens through the employment of various forms of coercion. Conservatives and neo-abolitionists alike have an 'obsessional neurotic belief in the power of the law' (Carline 2011: 70). Consequently, within both approaches, the state plays a role as the ultimate moral arbiter. An illustrative statement of a Russian neo-abolitionist posted on Facebook in 2015 indicates the recognition of the state as an apparatus that legitimately imposes moral norms on its subjects: 'I didn't say that the criminalization of clients will solve the problem of prostitution. I said that the criminalization of clients is good, because the client behaviour is bad.' Moreover, state power is understood in instrumental and selective terms:

> I'm looking at the homophobic law [propaganda of homosexuality ban [. . .], which inten-
> sified homophobic sentiments in society, attracted additional negative attention to LGBT
> people, created more problems for community representatives, conflicts at work and with
> close friends, caused many to be ashamed of their identity, persuaded both hetero and many
> LGBT that LGBT people are unequivocally bad. I look at this law and I'm thinking: if
> only all this negativity could be shifted to target those who buy sex from people who do
> not want to sell sex!
>
> *(Facebook 2016)*

This quotation shows that neo-abolitionists are able to problematize the stigmatization of certain groups by law, but do not consider the very mechanism of stigmatization as problematic in itself. On the contrary, repressive techniques are seen as positive tools if directed to the 'bad people'. Hence, while capable of criticizing actual state policies, the political imagination of this feminist neo-abolitionist project heavily relies on the state's normative and moral authority.

In terms of claims of political representation, we argue that neo-abolitionist feminists in Russia are claiming to represent a 'majoritarian subject' that needs to be protected from commercial sex. For Deleuze and Guattari (1987: 291), 'majoritarian subject' does not refer to 'greater relative quantity but to the determination of a state or standard'. This subject legitimizes the working of the state that always acts in the service of a majority. In the case of neo-abolitionists, the majoritarian subject is presented in two forms. The first is the figure of 'the majority of women involved in prostitution' exposed to exploitation and violence. This figure is evoked to legitimize the abolition of sex work for the interests of the suffering majority, regardless of any dissenting voices that are referred to as 'a very small percentage in this powerful industry' (Facebook 2014): 'even if someone really enjoys prostitution, perhaps she should think again and quit it because of the majority of women who suffer from prostitution' (Facebook 2014). The majoritarian subject is reinforced through reference to the second figure: women in general, all women, abstract and universal women who always risk being 'prostituted' for the very fact of being women. Even if they are not prostituted, they are still under constant threat of other forms of violence 'promoted' by prostitution: 'prostitution leads to an increase in the number of rapes, and not to a decrease' since through the access to commercial sexual services 'men are becoming more confident that a woman is a resource, not a person' (Facebook 2014). Compare this representation policy with the Russian conservatives who refer to public opinion (representing the population, nation or citizens) when they attempt to justify criminalization of sex work. Within this conservative discourse, the issue of sex workers' interests, experiences and voices is of no importance:

> Regardless of results of surveys that show that the majority of prostitutes come to the sphere
> of commercial sexual services voluntarily, their answers cannot be 100% trusted [. . .] pros-
> titutes are intimidated and subject to constant violence from employers [. . .]. Like women
> who have been subjected to domestic violence, prostitutes reject these facts.
>
> *(Petryanina 2014: 336)*

Thus, sex workers are treated by both neo-abolitionists and conservatives as subjects unable to produce the 'true' account of themselves due to either 'moral degradation', or due to experience of victimization. Therefore, their views are irrelevant to the process of making decisions about themselves.

This approach implies that those who do not advocate the abolition of prostitution indirectly support patriarchy even if they themselves are subjects to be 'rescued'. Eventually, the neo-abolitionist project does not need any sex workers' voices since the ultimate foundation of its politics is guaranteed by an abstract notion of universal womanhood: 'Women as a class are affected by the fact of sex work' (Womenation 2014). Since this majoritarian subject in the form of 'women as a class' is endangered by commercial sex, then dissenting voices of sex workers and other feminists could be justifiably ignored. Hence, despite the fact that neo-abolitionists in Russia situate themselves in opposition to the state – as an emancipatory 'war machine' – there are reasons to believe that their project does not undermine, but rather supports the existing conservative and, what they themselves define as the patriarchal and anti-feminist state. Neo-abolitionism finds itself in a political impasse, legitimizing and reproducing the very relations of power that it aims to overcome.

Multitude of sex workers

We have so far offered little analysis of the pro-sex work feminist position. One of its major principles is to give voice to sex workers themselves. Hence, in this section we go back to the question of political representation of sex workers, but instead of reviewing feminist discussions, we refer to the interviews carried out with sex workers. Our aim is to track the great variety of political opinions that were voiced during these interviews, and we present our analysis here by looking at three key themes emerging from the transcripts: political views, opinions on sex as work and thoughts about legalization. We ask, what assemblages of ideas are enacted in these accounts?

Let us start with the general political inclinations of our interviewees. Many did not reveal any political views or claimed indifference to politics. Yet, they highlighted various issues of political importance. Few of the interviewees showed any interest in politics but expressed a variety of different emotional attachments towards current political events and public persons. For example, consider this interview fragment:

> In principle, it is logical that this United Russia even has the right to pay for votes because [. . .] well, while Putin is alive we can rely on it [the party], we can hope that Russia will stay. But when Putin dies, he is not immortal, what is going to happen is unknown. And this is terrifying actually. Because [. . .] now we have devastation, kind of.
>
> *(Woman, born 1994, provider of heterosexual services)*

Here the interviewee argues that the current conservative party in power, United Russia, should be supported because they are backed by the current president Putin. The Party, as the sex worker assures, may even engage in corruption and pay voters to win elections as this is justified by its greater achievements. This suggests that the interviewee is satisfied with the current status quo, yet she also describes the current situation with the strong negative emotional term 'devastation'. Her fear is that a future without Putin might be even worse and uncertain. This fear of future uncertainty is a dominant message of conservative ideology, although the same sex worker does not embrace conservatism in its entirety and is supportive of same-sex marriages, for example, which have been the cornerstone of many political battles between progressive and conservative politicians in Russia recently (Kondakov 2014).

LGBT rights, the war in Ukraine and international relations between Russia and the West were the most common topics of political discussions in the interviews, which is not surprising given the current direction of Russian's national and foreign politics. The following excerpt shows how the speaker is not supportive of the Russian government's social policy (he previously argued for a more socialist approach and claimed he was a communist), but is satisfied with its attempt to combat US global hegemony:

I do not support current policies entirely, but only in the social, or at least in the social sphere I do not support current policies [. . .]. I support it with its strategic military development though, that our president fights these sanctions and holds back the crisis [that] has already resulted in these sanctions [. . .]. Our American puppeteers, so to speak, who guide [. . .] I think they guide Ukraine which is divided in two parts, the Russian part and Western Ukraine which hates the Russian population.

(Man, born 1984, submissive in BDSM services)

This interviewee also objects to same-sex marriages and the legalization of sex work. In this sense, he is a communist in a 'USSR style' whereby anti-Westernism justifies moral conservatism and poor social policies. What he expresses as real matters of concern (Western influence, LGBT 'invasion' and legalization of sex work), some others call a 'smokescreen' to draw attention away from economic troubles (see the quote at the outset of this chapter). What is important to observe here is that on a political ideological map, the sex workers interviewed in our project maintain a variety of different, sometimes contradictory, political perspectives that might be understood as a rejection of any clear positionality in collective terms. Their expressions of political views refuse clear-cut classification, and simultaneously fall under different and opposed rubrics. We are not suggesting this is true for only sex workers, yet it is worth bearing in mind when thinking about political representation of this 'group'.

As far as sex work is considered, the positions expressed by our interviewees are varied and not easy to locate in one of the two 'camps' previously outlined in relation to feminism. All interviewees spoke of their activity in labour market terms, using terms such as: shifts, vacation, cadres, manager, job instruction, salary, honorary, time schedule, day off and so on. However, when they addressed the debate on whether prostitution is work or not, they split in three positions: some claimed that sex work is not work, others that it is work, and yet others claimed that sex work is more than work.

Those who did not consider prostitution as work proposed various arguments to support this perspective. First, they explained that they engaged in commercial sex out of economic necessity. In the words of a transgender person, she had no choice but to become a prostitute because her gender expression did not match her identity documents and employers outside of the sexual industry saw this as an obstacle in her employment. Second, they viewed prostitution as a way to generate income, but not as a legitimate and 'normal' job. For example, a gay male escort said he officially works as a waiter and escorting is just an occasional activity. Lastly, there were those who emotionally opposed the idea of calling prostitution sex work because, in line with conservative ideas, sex workers disseminate diseases, ruin families and engage in criminal activity.

Interviewees, for whom sex work is work, offered a variety of parallels with other occupations: 'I can say this about the work of electricians or plumbers, it's everywhere the same', 'You get money for this, so it's a job.' Nonetheless, sex work is also seen as a vocation with a somewhat grandiose humanitarian mission: 'sex workers rescue the world from violence. [A client] could force his wife to do this [a certain sexual fantasy], but this would be domestic violence.' Finally, the measure of skills and techniques applied serves as another argument to consider sex work as work:

> I do my job good, with quality, with love, I don't juggle, I don't abuse anyone, I try to deliver to the person who comes to me and brings money the maximum pleasure so that he comes again [. . .] Just like any other job, our work should be paid. After forty minutes or an hour of work with a client I sweat [. . .] my makeup falls down, hairs go up – this is how I work, believe me or not. So this all should be paid.
>
> *(Woman, born 1965, dominant in BDSM services)*

Some of the sex workers who participated in the project also argued that their occupation is not simply work, but something more than that. This idea took different forms. For example, a woman saw sex work as a way of gaining psychological satisfaction and discovering herself as a sexually attractive person: 'I raised my self-esteem when I succeeded [in bed] and also got money for this.' Exploring sexuality is important for some of the interviewees, and sex work can offer this possibility, as in the case of a lesbian sex worker:

> The thing is that I [. . .] I extremely like women. One woman is not enough. I don't like long relationships, I'd say I hate them. I incredibly love women's bodies. This is what has been the reason for this [decision to start sex work], these thoughts have been. So this is why I came to this sphere and why I could be called a prostitute [. . .] Well, I have a profile and I get girls, many girls, enough for me. I am satisfied, not sexually, but my desires are satisfied, I get what I want, the possibilities [. . .] I want to have three or four girls each night, I can have it: my spirit, craziness, energy, power and capabilities are enough for this. But [if you go clubbing], you can't get four girls and have sex with them. This is a different situation. That's why I am in this sector, I even work more for pleasure than for money.
>
> *(Woman, born 1992, provider of lesbian services)*

Overall our interviewees described sex work as a hobby, a way of life, leisure activities, sexual realization, pleasure and in many other different ways beyond the work/not work dichotomy. How does this multitude of ideas and feelings translate into advocated regulatory approaches to sex work? Sex workers in our study did not show a clear priority in the way they would deal with sex work legally. Moreover, the proposed solutions often do not correspond to the feminist arguments presented above, and often regardless of political views and position vis-à-vis sex work had a variety of views on the regulation of prostitution. Some suggested leaving sex workers alone, along the lines of decriminalization, to 'create a law that says prostitution is free. Prostitution freely existed, it will exist and [. . .] it already exists'. Others argued for legalization, 'just like many civilized countries have actually done', as a modernizing approach that will allow Russia to join the West culturally and politically, whilst also protecting sex workers:

> Legalization of the work is a very simple thing: we will start to pay taxes, we will know we are protected, not simply secured, but protected by rights, yes, so that we could go to the police as other people do and submit a report on our, let's say, not so very polite clients, yes, who threatened us. Now, you see, even if we go to police with a report, we will be jailed instead.
>
> *(Woman, born 1965, dominant in BDSM services)*

Others saw legalization as a way to protect sex workers from the police: 'If we legalize it, then it would bring good tax return: the police would have their bread taken away, so to say, they would stop taking bribes and would become more honest, maybe.' Legalization for others is a way to make sex work less dangerous for society by increasing control over those involved in it:

> If it is official, then doctors would check everyone, so girls would be clean. And men [. . .] they should bring a medical certificate, doctor should check them if they have gonorrhoea or syphilis or anything, so that there would be no disease. Then, please, come and go, you've done your business, he's done his, paid money, paid taxes – everything is official, good, she's good, he's good, and everything is good: no disease, no filth.
>
> *(Woman, born 1985, provider of heterosexual services)*

Apart from an interviewee who viewed legalization as a 'threat to families', most other interviewees supported legalization either as a system of control, or as an opportunity to gain more freedom claiming that they are entitled to advance their own sexual and other kinds of desires without constant surveillance. One interviewee even claimed that she had political aspirations and would pursue a career in politics to fight for the legalization of prostitution.

Overall, debates around legalization bore multiple meanings and revealed varying political affiliations. On the one hand, some views were closer to either one of the two feminist positions presented earlier. On the other hand, some sex workers wanted to create their own political agenda and programme to improve sex workers' lives.

Conclusion

Neo-abolitionists and conservatives in Russia embrace the Swedish 'model' as a desirable political solution and share the goal of a world without prostitution, however, important differences in the ways they conceive of this model are widespread. Both neo-abolitionists and conservatives centre their strategies on the power of the state. This is the result of representational politics whereby political groups claim to represent a majority: in this case, the population in its entirety or the universalized notion of womanhood. Ultimately, this majoritarian representation makes the neo-abolitionist feminist project less emancipatory and more conservative. Yet, it is worth noting that it is not only neo-abolitionist feminism that embraces conservative arguments, but also conservative discourses are significantly reconfigured with the embracement and enactment of some aspects of feminist narratives.

At the same time, the sex workers movement and pro-sex work feminists claim to represent the interests of all sex workers arguing for decriminalization of commercial sex in Russia. However, 'sex workers' is not a homogeneous group who clearly define their common interests. Rather, they share a variety of political affiliations, views on their occupation, moral concerns and arguments regarding legalization of sex work. In this situation, the pro-sex work position is not a representation of sex workers' voices, but a fraction of feminist debates against the state solutions of issues within the sex industry. In its current condition, this feminist project becomes an emancipatory agenda that corresponds to Deleuze and Guattari's (1987) notion of 'war machine'. Hence, it assumes the role of resistance to apparatuses of the state to redefine existent configuration of power relations. Yet, it is at the same time exclusionary for some sex workers who oppose a stand-off with the state and its institutions.

This complexity poses new questions to the politics of sex work. We started with an understanding of feminist arguments about sex work as falling into two distinct camps: neo-abolitionist and pro-sex work positions. Our analysis showed that neo-abolitionists share a great deal of respect for the state institutions just like political conservatives in Russia. At the same time, we concluded that sex workers may also favour conservative arguments and even contribute to the stigmatization of their occupation on moral grounds. This aspect of the debates challenges pro-sex work feminism attempting to build emancipatory politics through representation of sex workers' voices. Nonetheless, emancipation is not a necessary concern for all sex workers. Political commitments of sex workers are not automatically determined by their everyday experience: they are contingent, changeable, fluid; they are performed and re-assembled through interactions with multiple other actors.

Still, the politics of representation seems to be a common battlefield on which feminist sex wars are waged. Though strategies of representation used by neo-abolitionist and pro-sex work feminists are different, the very engagement in the politics of representation is understood by them as unproblematic. However, despite many gains of the politics of representation, this politics also has its limits, most importantly the principal impossibility of representation and invitation of discipline and control over the group claimed to be represented. In this regard, we call for the creation of material and discursive spaces, where more active forms of interaction than listening to voices would be possible. In this way, it would be possible to build trust between researchers, activists and sex workers through discussions, disputes and collective experimentation. For example, the sex workers' argument of not being seen could be considered important in grassroots politics. Given the ever-decreasing opportunities for building political initiatives and spaces in Russia, it could enrich strategies of resistance to patriarchy. We suggest that is important to remember that sex work policies are always more than just about sex work. The line of flight from the repressive and conservative state is often drawn not from just one point, but from a multitude of positions that offer possibilities of creative alliances or coalitions.

Notes

1 All quotations in Russian are translated by the authors.
2 Due to respect of privacy, we do not give direct links to personal pages on social networks, but all analysed materials are stored and can be accessed from one the authors.
3 Quotation marks in the original.

References

Adkins, B. 2015. *Deleuze and Guattari's A Thousand Plateaus: A Critical Introduction and Guide*. Edinburgh: Edinburgh University Press.
Agustín, L. 1998. *Sex at the Margins: Migration, Labour Markets and the Rescue Industry*. New York: Zed Books.
Bakunin, M. 1971 [1842]. *The Reaction in Germany: From the Notebooks of a Frenchman*. Available at: www.marxists.org/reference/archive/bakunin/works/1842/reaction-germany.htm (accessed 19 March 2018).
Barry, K. 1995. *The Prostitution of Sexuality*. New York: New York University Press.
Belduma. 2013. *Rezul'taty monitoringa pravoprimeneniya statei 6.24 i 6.25 zakona Belgorodskoi oblasti ot 4 iyulya 2002 goda № 35 'Ob administrativnykh pravonarusheniyakh na territorii Belgorodskoi oblasti'* [*The Results of Monitoring the Enforcement of Articles 6.24 and 6.25 of the Belgorod Region Law No. 35 of July 4, 2002 'On Administrative Offenses in the Territory of the Belgorod Region'*]. Accessible at: http://belduma.ru/monprav/rezmon.pdf (accessed 10 January 2018).
Bernstein, E. 2012. Carceral Politics as Gender Justice? The 'Traffic in Women' and Neoliberal Circuits of Crime, Sex, and Rights. *Theory and Society*, 41(3): 233–259.
Butler, J. 2015. *Notes Toward a Performative Theory of Assembly*. Cambridge, MA: Harvard University Press.

Carline, A. 2011. Constructing the Subject of Prostitution: A Butlerian Reading of the Regulation of Sex Work. *International Journal for the Semiotics of Law*, 24(1): 61–78.

Deleuze, G. and F. Guattari. 1987. *A Thousand Plateaus: Capitalism and Schizophrenia*. Minneapolis: University of Minnesota Press.

Doezema, J. 2001. Western Feminists' 'Wounded Attachment' to the 'Third World Prostitute'. *Feminist Review*, 67: 16–38.

Dworkin, A. 1987. *Intercourse*. New York: Free Press.

Farris, S. and C. Rottenberg. 2017. Introduction: Righting Feminism. *New Formations: A Journal of Culture/ Theory/Politics*, 91: 5–15.

Fournier, M. 2014. Lines of Flight. *TSQ: Transgender Studies Quarterly*, 1(1–2): 121–123.

Halley, J., P. Kotsiwaran, H. Shamir and C. Thomas. 2006. From the International to the Local in Feminist Legal Responses to Rape, Prostitution/Sex Work, and Sex Trafficking: Four Studies in Contemporary Governance Feminism. *Harvard Journal of Law & Gender*, 29: 335–423.

Jeffreys, S. 2008. *The Industrial Vagina: The Political Economy of the Global Sex Trade*. London: Routledge.

Kantola, J. and J. Squires. 2012. From State Feminism to Market Feminism? *International Political Science Review*, 33(4): 382–400.

Khodyreva, N. 2006. *Sovremenniedebaty o prostitucii: gendernii podhod* [*Contemporary Debates About Prostitution: Gender Studies Approach*]. St. Petersburg: Alletia.

Kondakov, A. 2014. The Silenced Citizens of Russia: Exclusion of Non-heterosexual Subjects from Rights-Based Citizenship. *Social & Legal Studies*, 23(2): 151–174.

Kondakov, A. 2017. Queer Coalitions: An Examination of Political Resistance to the Russian Migration Law. *Europe-Asia Studies*, 69(8): 1222–1241.

Kondakov, A. 2018. Spatial Justice: How the Police Craft the City by Enforcing Law on Prostitution. In: M.-L. Skilbrei and M. Spanger, eds. *Understanding Sex for Sale: Meanings and Moralities of Sexual Commerce*. London: Routledge.

Konev, A. 2011. O sotsialno-politicheskoy, kulturno-vospitatelnoy, imoralno-pravovoy nedopustimosti legalizatsii prostitutsii v Rossii [On Social-Political, Cultural-Educational and Moral-Juridical Impermissibility of Legalisation of Prostitution in Russia]. *Juridicheskaya nauka i praktika* [*Legal Science and Practice*], 1(14): 200–207.

Kontula, A. 2008. The Sex Worker and Her Pleasure. *Current Sociology*, 56: 605–620.

Krupets, Y. and N. Nartova. 2010. Pereopredelenie granits mezhdu trudom, udovol'stviem i nasiliem: Seks-rabota kak osobyy vid neformal'noy zanyatosti [Revising the Borders Between Labour, Pleasure and Violence: Sex-Work as a Specific Kind of Informal Employment]. *Journal of Social Policy Studies*, 8(4): 537–550.

Kulick, D. 2003. Sex in the New Europe: The Criminalization of Clients and Swedish Fear of Penetration. *Anthropological Theory*, 3(2): 199–218.

Maslova, I. 2013. *Professiya seks-rabotnika v Rossii ne prosto est', eta odna iz samykh massovykh professii v strane* [The Profession of a Sex Worker in Russia Is Not Just There, This Is One of the Most Massive Professions in the Country]. Available at: http://zrpress.ru/society/v-rossii_23.07.2013_61826_irina-maslova-pro fessija-seks-rabotnika-v-rossii-ne-prosto-est-eta-odna-iz-samykh-massovykh-professij-v-strane.html (accessed 20 March 2018).

Legoida, V. 2016. *Osuzhdaya 'zhrits lyubvi', nel'zya opravdyvat' ikh klientov* [Condemning the 'Priestesses of Love', One Cannot Justify Their Clients]. Available at: www.spb.kp.ru/daily/26515.5/3532253/ (accessed 8 January 2018).

Petryanina, O. 2014. Nuzhna ly legalizatsiya prostitucii v ramkakh realizacii principov democratizacii? [Is Legalisation of Prostitution Necessary for the Implementation of the Principles of Democratisation?]. *Uridicheskaya technika* [*Legal Technique*], 8: 334–337.

Ranciere, J. 1999. *Disagreement: Politics and Philosophy*. Minneapolis: University of Minnesota Press.

Rubin, G. 1984. Thinking Sex: Notes for a Radical Theory of the Politics of Sexuality. In C. Vance, ed. *Pleasure and Danger: Exploring Female Sexuality*. London: Routledge and Kegan Paul, pp. 143–178.

Sanders, T. 2004. Controllable Laughter: Managing Sex Work through Humour. *Sociology*, 38(2): 273–291.

Skilbrei, M.-L. and C. Holmström. 2011. Is There a Nordic Prostitution Regime? *Crime and Justice* 40(1): 479–517.

Ungelenk, J. 2014. *Sexes of Winds and Packs: Rethinking Feminism with Deleuze and Guattari*. Hamburg: Marta Press.

Whalley, E. and C. Hackett. 2017. Carceral Feminisms: The Abolitionist Project and Undoing Dominant Feminisms. *Contemporary Justice Review*, 20(4): 456–473.

Womenation. 2014. *Who Are You Listening To? About What It Means to 'Listen to Sex Workers'*. Available at: http://womenation.org/кого-вы-слушаете-о-том-что-такое-слуша/ (accessed 20 March 2018).

Womenation. 2016. *Pimp State: Legalization of Prostitution*. Available at: http://womenation.org/state-as-a-pimp-legalizing-prostitution (accessed 20 March 2018).

Zhaivoronok D. 2017. 'Chto ne tak s prostituciej?' diskurs pechatnyh SMI jepohi Perestrojki ['What's Wrong with Prostitution?': The Discourse of the Print Media in the Perestroika Era]. *Zhurnal sotsiologii i sotsialnoy antropologii* [*Journal of Sociology and Social Anthropology*], 5: 75–94.

Part IV

Families and intimate relationships

25

Families and intimate relationships

An introduction

Susan Dewey, Isabel Crowhurst, and Chimaraoke Izugbara

Introduction

People in the sex industry financially and emotionally support their children, family members, and intimate partners in ways that legal, policy, and available support structures directly inform or even co-constitute. Key themes in existing literature include affective relationships, families of origin, supporting family through sex work, stigmatization of sex workers' motherhood, and relationships with intimate partners. Chapters in this section engage with these ongoing challenges while offering clear directions for future research.

Key themes in existing literature

Affective relationships almost always have a transactional aspect through the sharing of money, resources, housing, or other needs. For people in the sex industry, affective relationships are an important aspect of how they earn a living even as income generated through commercial sex provides an important or essential form of economic support. Women in sex work may experience shifting boundaries with respect to their clients as they attempt to discursively and otherwise manage the relationships they engage in for pay (Smith, 2017). These separations tend to revolve around the concept of "authenticity" as distinguished from intimate labor (Carbonero & Garrido, 2017). Others who accept money from sexual partners may not identify as sex workers, instead self-identifying as "professional girlfriends" or by using other less stigmatized terminology (Hoefinger, 2014).

Families of origin often feature in research as an explanatory mechanism within life-course analysis, such that childhood abuse creates a cycle of instability and substance abuse that functions as a strong predictor of sex industry involvement (McCarthy, Benoit, & Jansson, 2014). The need to conform to dominant social norms and protect personal and family reputations also features predominantly in sex workers' decision-making, including the need to hide their source of earnings and, in some societies, physical manifestations of sexual expression, such as pregnancy (Katz et al., 2016). Dominant cultural expectations in some societies that daughters in particular will financially support parents and other family members is both a powerful motivator, and a justification, for sex industry involvement (Koch, 2016).

Motherhood is likewise a common justification for doing commercial sex, particularly in highly constrained socio-economic situations that force women to make difficult choices due to food insecurity and other immediate economic needs (Beckham et al., 2015; Tsai et al., 2013). Responsibilities to children can also be a powerful motivator for women in sex work to engage in safer sex practices, particularly in regions where HIV/AIDS is especially endemic and accordingly a major concern for sex workers (Basu & Dutta, 2011). Yet, women in sex work remain heavily stigmatized as mothers, as is reflected in a focus among both researchers and practitioners on the negative impacts that mothers' sex industry involvement is thought to have on children (Willis et al., 2016).

Mothering is as diverse an experience for sex workers as it is for their peers who earn income in other ways (Bromwich & DeJong, 2015). The experiences of mothers involved in lower-status, more public sex industry forms, such as street prostitution and its association with addiction in many countries, tend to focus on negative outcomes, including custody loss, social services involvement, and difficulties accessing health care (Duff et al., 2015; McClelland & Newell, 2008). As is the case with other family members and loved ones, the pervasive stigma associated with sex work forces mothers to manage their respective identities in ways that can create conflict (Dodworth, 2014; Rivers-Moore, 2010).

Sex workers' relationships with intimate partners can influence decision-making regarding whether to stay within or leave the sex industry because of the challenges that stigma and the sex industry's unique dynamics pose to relationships (Slezak, 2015), including potentially negative impacts on mental health for both partners. These challenges can result in boundary management such as not using condoms with intimate partners (Maher et al., 2013) and particular types of decision-making regarding pregnancy, particularly in societies that place an extremely high value on children as a measure of personal worth (Yam et al., 2017).

Chapter overview

Capous-Desyllas and colleagues (Chapter 26) use work–life border theory to discuss how sex workers balance their work and personal lives through negotiation of sex worker identity, intentionality in addressing challenges within relationships, controlling disclosure of sex work, giving and receiving support; and using various institutions as a platform for legitimacy. Piscitelli (Chapter 27) analyzes the characteristics of economic, sexual, and emotional exchanges between Brazil and Spain in light of the latter's economic crisis to argue that sex workers' relatives regard their labor as tolerable or even desirable when it generates a redistribution of material resources. Morcillo (Chapter 28) explores the micro-political dimensions of secrecy and its links to money, gender, and kinship by examining the regulation of secret-keeping, disclosure, and communication among sex workers and their families.

Spanger (Chapter 29) examines how female migrants selling sexual services organize their mothering and the various ways in which their identities as single mothers, migrants, and sex workers intersect. Yang (Chapter 30) analyzes power dynamics between men who purchase and provide erotic massage within the context of sex tourism-related encounters, including perceived authenticity of desire, cultivation of self-esteem, and provision of intimacy to those who lack it in their daily lives.

Future directions

Families and intimate bonds remain a relatively unexplored avenue of inquiry in this area of research, as prevailing approaches tend to emphasize the dynamics surrounding sex industry involvement to the exclusion of these important social relationships. Hence little is known about how resource-sharing occurs in households or other family structures where one or more people engage in commercial sex. Studying such sharing arrangements is important because they could potentially lead to at least some redefinition of gender roles and other aspects of what being a person in a particular gendered body "means" through significant changes to household division of labor in terms of childcare, cooking, or other reproductive labor.

Future research is also likely to explore how affective relationships with intimate partners, children, or other loved ones change when a person is involved in the sex industry, particularly when the sex industry participant is male or transgender. Such explorations would likely examine how individuals in such relationships express and differentiate between particular types of affection, intimacy, "real love," and other emotional overtures expressed with intimate partners who pay them for sex and those who do not. Critical engagement with how individuals use resources or income-sharing to mitigate the stigma associated with the sex industry, as well as how their decisions impact long-term relationships once they leave the profession, will provide insights that the field currently lacks.

References

Basu, Ambar and Dutta, Mohan. 2011. "We Are Mothers First": Localocentric Articulation of Sex Worker Identity as a Key in HIV/AIDS Communication. *Women & Health* 51(2): 106–123.

Beckham, Sarah, Shembilu, Catherine, Winch, Peter, Beyrer, Chris, and Kerrigan, Deanna. 2015. "If You Have Children, You Have Responsibilities": Motherhood, Sex Work and HIV in Southern Tanzania. *Culture, Health & Sexuality* 17(2): 165–179.

Bellhouse, Clare, Crebbin, Susan, Fairley, Christopher, and Bilardi, Jade. 2015. The Impact of Sex Work on Women's Personal Romantic Relationships and the Mental Separation of Their Work and Personal Lives. *PLoS One* 10(1): 1–20.

Bromwich, Rebecca and DeJong, Monique. 2015. *Mothers, Mothering and Sex Work*. Bradford, ON: Demeter Press.

Carbonero, Antonia and Garrido, Maria. 2017. Being Like Your Girlfriend: Authenticity and the Shifting Borders of Intimacy in Sex Work. *Sociology* 52(2): 384–399. https://doi.org/10.1177/0038038516688609.

Dodworth, Jane. 2014. Sex Worker and Mother: Managing Dual and Threatened Identities. *Child & Family Social Work* 19(1): 99–108.

Duff, Putu, Jean Shoveller, Jill Chettiar, Patricia Feng, Rachel Nicoletti, and Kate Shannon. 2015. Sex Work and Motherhood: Social and Structural Barriers to Health and Social Services for Pregnant and Parenting Street and Off-Street Sex Workers. *Health Care for Women International* 36: 1039–1055.

Hoefinger, Heidi. 2014. Gendered Motivations, Sociocultural Constraints, and Psychobehavioral Consequences of Transnational Partnerships in Cambodia. *Studies in Gender and Sexuality* 15(1): 54–72.

Katz, Karen, McDowell, Misti, Johnson, Laura, and Aziz, Sultana. 2016. "I Won't Be Able to Go Home Being Pregnant": Sex Work and Pregnancy in Dhaka, Bangladesh. *Culture, Health & Sexuality* 18(7): 756–769.

Koch, Gabriele. 2016. Willing Daughters: The Moral Rhetoric of Filial Sacrifice and Financial Autonomy in Tokyo's Sex Industry. *Critical Asian Studies* 48: 215–234.

McCarthy, Bill, Benoit, Cecila, and Jansson, Mikael. 2014. Sex Work: A Comparative Study. *Archives of Sexual Behavior* 43(7): 1379–1390.

McClelland, Gabrielle and Robert Newell. 2008. A Qualitative Study of the Experiences of Mothers Involved in Street-Based Prostitution and Problematic Substance Use. *Journal of Research in Nursing* 13(5): 437–447.

Maher, Lisa, Mooney-Somers, Julie, Phlong, Pisith, Couture, Marie-Claude, Kien, Serey, Stein, Ellen, Bates, Anna, Sansothy, Neth, and Kimberly Page, on behalf of the Young Women's Health Study Collaborative. 2013. Condom Negotiation Across Different Relationship Types by Young Women Engaged in Sex Work in Phnom Penh, Cambodia. *Global Public Health* 8(3): 270–283.

Orchard, Treena. 2014. Expanding the Scope of Inquiry: Exploring Accounts of Childhood and Family Life Among Sex Workers in London, Ontario. *Canadian Journal of Human Sexuality* 23(1): 9–18.

Rivers-Moore, Megan. 2010. But the Kids Are Okay: Motherhood, Consumption and Sex Work in Neo-Liberal Latin America. *British Journal of Sociology* 61(4): 716–736.

Slezak, Izabela. 2015. The Influence of Significant Others on the Course of the Process of Leaving Sex Work. *Przegląd Socjologii Jakościowej* 11(3): 132–153.

Smith, Elizabeth Megan. 2017. "It Gets Very Intimate for Me": Discursive Boundaries of Pleasure and Performance in Sex Work. *Sexualities* 20(3): 344–363.

Tsai, Laura, Witte, Susan, Aira, Toivgoo, Riedel, Marion, Hwang, Hyesung, and Ssewamala, Fred. 2013. "There is No Other Option; We Have to Feed Our Families . . . Who Else Would Do It?" The Financial Lives of Women Engaging in Sex Work in Ulaanbaatar, Mongolia. *Global Journal of Health Science* 5(5): 41–50.

Yam, Eileen, Kidanu, Akililu, Burnett-Zieman, Brady, Pilgrim, Nanlesta, Okal, Jerry, Bekele, Assefa, Gudeta, Daniel, and Caswell, Georgina. 2017. Pregnancy Experiences of Female Sex Workers in Adama City, Ethiopia: Complexity of Partner Relationships and Pregnancy Intentions. *Studies in Family Planning* 48(2): 107–119.

Willis, Brian, Vines, Diane, Bubar, Sara, and Suchard, Maria. 2016. The Health of Children Whose Mothers Are Trafficked or in Sex Work in the US: An Exploratory Study. *Vulnerable Children and Youth Studies* 11(2): 127–135.

26

Understanding the strengths, challenges, and strategies of navigating work life and personal life among sex workers

Moshoula Capous-Desyllas, Denice Palacios, Patricia Rivas, and Jessica Hernandez

Introduction

This chapter explores the intersections of work life and personal life among female, male, and trans sex workers, and the strategies they use to manage work/life balance as they navigate their intersecting identities, self-representation, relationships with others, and membership in various institutions and groups. Moving beyond the notion of maintaining a distinct separation between the public and private sphere advanced by work–family border theory, we illustrate how sex workers' acts of intentionality as they create, blur, and manage the fluidity of these boundaries within particular positionalities and the social, cultural, and institutional contexts of family, school, child welfare, and the criminal justice system.

Beyond work–family border theory

Work–family border theory, also conceptualized as work/life balance, maintains that people are border-crossers who make daily transitions between two worlds —the world of work and the world of family (Clark, 2000). According to work–family border theory, borders are lines of segregation between private and public domains that define acceptable limits for a person's behavior. This theory distinguishes between the public sphere (work) and the private sphere (family), and maintains that individuals must navigate their respective roles within and responsibilities to each by creating distinct boundaries between these spheres (Gill, 2006; Jorgenson, 2000; Nippert-Eng, 1996; Wieland, 2001). These borders comprise three components: "physical (where the behavior takes place), temporal (when the behavior takes place), and psychological (defined by the individual, dictating when behaviors, thinking patterns and emotions are appropriate for each)" (Clark, 2000).

Central to work–family border theory is the idea that work and family constitute different and distinct spheres that influence one another with competing expectations and desires, with the ideal scenario being the achievement of "balance" between the two in order to minimize conflict (Blithe & Wolfe, 2017). This theory attempts to explain the interaction between the ways in which individuals cross the borders between their work and family lives, to predict when conflict will occur, and to gain a framework for achieving balance (Clark, 2000). Achieving this balance implies high levels of satisfaction and role functioning as well as low levels of work–family conflict (Schieman & Glavin, 2008), with family defined broadly in terms of co-existence. Scholarship on work–life management originated from the ideology of separate spheres (Gill, 2006; Jorgenson, 2000; Nippert-End, 1996; Wieland, 2001), with some researchers describing the way people address the differences between these domains as part of a continuum spanning from "integration" to "segmentation," with "separate with integration" being the equivalent of achieving balance between these two extremes (Nippert-Eng, 1996).

However, while acknowledging that this dichotomy has been useful to illustrate competing expectations between organizations and home concerns, Blithe and Wolfe (2017) point out that this theory does not accurately capture many individuals' experiences. Other critics argue that undisturbed harmony is not always the result of equal weight given to work and family since the two are not necessarily opposing ways of existing (Kirby, 2006). Blithe and Wolfe (2017) build on these critiques by problematizing the assumption that work and family balance is an attainable possibility given the pressure both place on individuals. These scholars also offer the term "work–life management" (Golden & Geisler, 2007) as a more useful way to describe how individuals make decisions about how to allocate their time and resources between competing responsibilities in the work arena and in other aspects of their lives. This nuanced understanding maintains a more inclusive definition of work that also comprises family life by focusing on an active process of *management* rather than a static condition of *balance*.

Work–life boundaries in the sex industry

Some scholars argue that a desire to manage conflict between work personae and personal identities drives individuals to manage both their work and life in particular ways (Blithe, 2015; Kuhn, 2006; Trethewey, Tracy, & Alberts, 2006). We explore this concept with regard to the experiences of individuals working in the sex industry as a means to highlight the ways in which they separate their work from their personal lives with respect to stigma management, an intentional mode of interaction that reduces the negative effects of stigma on one's social status (Goffman, 1963). Given the stigma attached to sex work, Blithe and Wolfe (2017) illustrate the ways in which "dirty workers" engage in stigma management as a work–life issue to manage conflicts between their personal and work identities. One way that sex workers achieve this goal is by building sex worker-friendly networks where they conduct all worker-related business, such as dealing with specific financial institutions where they do not experience stigma and can take out a loan, if eligible and conduct financial planning (give their marginalized social status), without judgment. Other ways that sex workers manage stigma associated with their work and regain control over the boundaries between their public and private lives include distancing techniques, such as joking about clients, classifying types of sexual encounters (i.e. romantic versus work), and/or using drugs (Brewis & Linstead, 2000; Sanders 2004). Much of this research suggests that sex workers cope with the stigma of their work by compartmentalizing their work and personal lives (Blithe & Wolfe, 2017). Sex workers also use this strategy in their personal romantic relationships through mental separation as a coping mechanism to navigate the two aspects of their lives (Bellhouse, Crebbin, Fairley, & Bilardi, 2015).

Researchers who explored stigma management techniques among male sex workers in Vietnam found that the men concealed their involvement in sex work by restricting sexual communication with non-paying sex partners, thus limiting their ability to seek social support from family and friends (Closson et al., 2015). Social and structural factors, such as social stigma, techniques to minimize exposure to stigma, economic imperatives, and familial responsibilities all shaped their decisions to disclose sex industry involvement. Another study with male sex workers found that subtle or indirect forms of communication with family members and partners facilitated tacit acknowledgment of a certain shared understanding without disrupting the relationship through forthright sexual disclosures (Padilla et al., 2008). These dynamics permit both sex workers and their families to maintain a comfortable ambiguity, since the elaborate techniques used to manage stigma allowed for alternative explanations for "suspicious" activities or associations. Warr and Pyett (1999) found that it was common for sex workers to maintain a distinction between their work and their personal life, using separation as a coping mechanism to manage the two spheres of their lives. This separation included not socializing with other sex workers and using condoms with clients but not with romantic partners; acts that create a symbolic barrier between sex at work and sex at home (Clark, 2000; Warr & Pyett, 1999).

Methodology

This analysis draws upon data from in-depth interviews and a subsequent life timeline approach to research with 16 individuals working in the sex industry. Our interviews were interactive and collaborative, with a focus on individual stories as well as the combined stories that arose from the interview interaction (Ellis, 2004). This approach provided the opportunity for developing relationships that value the shared space of the interaction. A life timeline approach, in which participants mapped out important life events—from geographical locations and physical moves, to tragedies and deaths, births, unions, and separations, special events, and significant issues that occurred throughout their life—to augment the interview data. This process assisted with creating an awareness of how earlier life events played out in each of the participants' lives.

An intersectional lens (Crenshaw, 1991) suggests that sex workers' unique lived experiences are informed by the intersections of their multiple identities and social locations. Educational levels, sub-culture, age, lifestyle, personality, citizenship status, and roles in life inform the participants' diverse identities and influence their experiences in the sex industry. Some of the life circumstances relevant to the participants in this study include working conditions, family situation, living and working in Southern California, and involvement in various institutions, such as family, education, child welfare, and the criminal justice system. The findings presented are informed by diverse women, men, and trans sex workers involved in various aspects of the sex industry including, but not limited to BDSM (dominatrix) work, web-camming, phone sex, in-call and out-call escorting, dancing/stripping, street work, nude modeling, erotic massage, pornography/adult film, as well as forms of labor not always associated with the sex industry, including sugar baby relationships, in which a wealthier (and usually older) partner supports a less established (and usually younger) sexual partner.

Managing work–life boundaries

Expanding on work–family border theory as an analytic framework and challenging the separation of the public/private spheres, our findings highlight the multi-layered ways in which individuals working in various sex industry sectors manage and negotiate their work–life boundaries. Sex workers in this study were intentional in their creation, blurring, and management of boundaries between work and personal life. Thematic analysis, in which we segmented, categorized, summarized, and reconstructed interview transcripts in a way that captured the important concepts (Ayres, 2008), revealed five themes related to the management of work and personal life in fluid yet distinct ways: negotiating sex worker identity, intentionality in addressing relationship challenges, controlling disclosure, practicing reciprocity, and attaining legitimacy through particular types of institutional connections.

Negotiating sex worker identity

Participants in this study actively negotiated their sex worker identity in various social and physical spaces, with some sex workers being open about their occupation as a way of resisting dominant narratives about their work. This was the case for Domino, a 36-year-old white trans female involved in BDSM work, who noted:

> I found that just within my own academic department of social work I've gotten, not only pushback, but judgment. I've gotten shamed. There is a misunderstanding and this rigid idea that unless I stick to a narrative of victimhood, then there must be something wrong with me. Somehow people like me need to be saved, and need to be helped and coddled.

Reconciling her intersecting identities and roles served to blur the boundaries of her work and personal life. Other participants struggled with negotiating the tensions between work and family responsibility, especially when there were cultural expectations of certain roles that family members are obligated to fulfill. Krystal, a 33-year-old Mexican trans female involved in escorting, BDSM, and street work described the consequences of being "outed" on-line:

> My family knew. I had ads in the paper, on the Internet. They would find me and see the ads. My whole family knew the whole struggle. My mom, my grandma, my sister, they all know. But my younger brother resents me and tells me, "I needed a brother growing up." He was molested by a babysitter's son while I was gone working on the streets, but I can't tell him everything. I just let him know, "I love you and it wasn't my choice to be out there" . . . I had my own demons I had to deal with.

Feelings of tension and guilt for not being able to protect her little brother from harm, her own struggles in life related to her gender transition, and family expectations that she serve as a traditional male role model within the family, were also informed by her intersecting identities as a Latina trans sex worker.

Cultural expectations of gender roles also played a role for Fernanda, a 29-year-old migrant from Mexico who provides erotic massage and a single mother who saw her work in the sex industry as a means to supporting her children. Fernanda shared:

> I posted my announcement and sometimes when I would get calls I would not answer them when I was at home with my kids. When I received a text or a call, I always had my cell phone in another place, not near my kids . . . I would go to my room and answer, but let's say my priority was always my kids, not my work.

Like other sex workers, she used separation as a coping mechanism to manage the tensions between sex work and her personal relationships and roles within them (Bellhouse, et al., 2015). Various factors determined how participants chose to reconcile their identity as a sex worker with their other intersecting identities, including their gender identity, ethnicity, social roles, and the various circumstances they faced. Maintaining the fluidity of their shifting identities at the forefront of their interactions with others, depending on the context, was frequently used as a strategy to manage their personal and professional lives.

Being intentional when addressing challenges within relationships

Sex workers were intentional in addressing various challenges in their personal, romantic, and professional relationships. Participants shared a range of emotions and lived experiences with respect to the influence of sex work on their romantic relationships, with many intimate partners expressing unhappiness with their work by using it against them or insisting they exit the sex industry. Megan, a 21-year-old bi-racial woman working as a sugar baby and stripper, stated: "My boyfriend, we've been together for four years, and he's known me my whole life and for the first time, he called me a whore a few weeks ago . . . just because I stripped." Sophia, a 19-year-old Latina female involved in escorting, likewise expressed:

> One guy told me that he couldn't love me because I was a stripper and an escort. I'm just like, "Why? Why can't you love me? Am I not lovable? Like, what do you mean? I have a heart, too. I have feelings, you know?"

30-year-old South Asian gay male escort Skyler's boyfriend knew that he was an escort yet responded negatively when he crossed paths with a client:

> When he [my boyfriend] got here, the client was still here, so he had to drive around. He was driving around for like 30 minutes, and he got really, really pissed. Then we started talking about it and he was like, he doesn't want me to do it anymore.

Skyler meets clients in his home and, unable to create a physical separation between his work and personal life, negotiated the tensions in his relationship by acknowledging his partner's frustration and resolving to be more mindful about scheduling future client appointments.

While sex work can negatively impact romantic relationships due to issues stemming from trust, guilt, and jealousy (Bellhouse, et al., 2015), participants in this study shared how strategy, intent, and caution informed their desire to avoid conflict and tensions. Some participants were very careful in their selection of romantic partners, as they did not want to be judged or to sacrifice their work for a romantic relationship. Tiff, a 25-year-old Mexican female who was working as a sugar baby and dancer, engaged in such stigma management:

> The guys I meet here [at the strip club], they're cool with it, but the guys I meet out, they don't like it. I usually date the ones I meet here because they are more open-minded and they know what's up with everything. My ex-boyfriend knew I had a sugar daddy and he didn't like it.

Rather than separating her personal life and work life, Tiff was intentional in selecting romantic partners who allowed her to integrate these two spheres of her life. Similarly, Strawberry a 37-year-old white immigrant woman involved in nude modeling, pornography, dancing, webcamming, and phone sex, shared how many potential partners did not approve of her work:

> When you are dating someone or when you are in a relationship, it's usually very difficult for that other person to understand what's going on and not feel threatened by it. I've never had an experience where the other person was super open with it. There are people who will not date me no matter what, even if I quit the business, because they don't want that stigma. But there are a lot of people that are open and they embrace that, but they still don't want me to go and do [porn] movies and see clients. So, when I was getting in relationships, it was always not just, "Am I in love with this person?" It was always, "Is that worth it for me to give up my job?"

Like Strawberry, participants who viewed sex work as part of their personal life were more likely to be in a position to freely discuss their work with their romantic partners, most of whom accepted it and often had a greater understanding of the industry (Bellhouse, et al., 2015). Disclosing sex work to an intimate partner has the potential to allow sex workers to develop trust and honesty within their relationships while also serving to cultivate feelings of support and acceptance (Murphy, Dunk-West, & Chonody, 2015).

Some sex workers experienced difficulty compartmentalizing their work and personal relationships, including their romantic and sexual desires. A few participants expressed how they struggled with relationships because of their work in the sex industry and its influence on how they viewed sexual relations. Finding it hard to mentally separate and compartmentalize sex work, romantic partnerships, and sexual desires, Mykal, a 28-year-old black gay male escort and street worker, shared how he felt "cursed" because of his work:

> I can't find anyone that I really want to be in a relationship with for the simple fact that I like older white guys, probably from hoeing all these years as a black man . . . that's usually who you get . . . so I recently I met this white guy and he took an interest in me, but it just kept coming up in my head, "Okay, when am I gonna to get paid? When am I gonna get paid? Should I ask him for money? Should I ask him to buy me something?" When I started to see him as an older white guy with a lot of money, I broke it off with him . . . I want to get out of the habit of being in a relationship like that.

Krystal had a similarly difficult time separating sex with clients from sex with romantic partners:

> I'll meet guys though apps, like Tinder, and it's like, quick sex and then you're done and alone, by yourself again with emptiness . . . it still bugs me, affects me at times. I don't know how to be normal. Trying to get there. Like sex and relationships, it's hard. Especially doing that [sex work] for so long. It's really hard to find balance.

For Krystal, the concept of balance was defined as an aspiration that was conflated with normalcy; something that she aimed to achieve while trying to negotiate the internalized stigma of identifying as a sex worker.

Maintaining the power of self-representation and disclosure of sex work

Rather than choosing to keep their personal life separate from their work life, sex workers may merge their personal and professional identities. Various factors informed each participant's decision-making process around if, when, and how they would disclose their involvement in sex work. Oftentimes, this was a process based on social acceptance or rejection, taking into account the implications of their decision. Some participants had to negotiate whether they would share their work with classmates. For Strawberry the decision to disclose her personal life with her classmates came from a sense of embodying privileged identities:

> I'm privileged because my family lives in Europe and they are not religious and they have a sex-positive attitude. Even though my mom doesn't know everything about my personal sex life, which would be creepy, she knows I do movies, she knows I escort, she knows all of that stuff. My siblings know, my friends know. Even now in my graduate program, everyone knows, because at some point I'm like . . . people started talking and I was like, "Okay, I'm just going to tell everyone."

Unlike Strawberry, Moon, a 28-year-old white, pan-sexual trans woman engaged in escorting was very intentional in keeping her work life separate from her school life. She was enrolled in a doctoral program and did not want the stigma of sex work to affect her "rise on the career ladder." Moon went on to express:

> I just don't tell people about it. I only tell really close friends because I am in a very academic, professional field now. I have friends in school who, if I told them, they'd probably flip out because there is the negative connotations against it—being a whore or a slut or just dirty. The reason why I share with my friends is because they are also in sex work, too, so it's ok. We talk about it all the time.

This was common among trans sex workers who cope with the stigma of their work by compartmentalizing their work and their personal life (Blithe & Wolfe, 2017); however, for Moon, her intersecting identities as a trans woman and sex worker were integrated and shared her close friendships.

Conversely, many participants were open about their involvement in sex work and based their decision to disclose their work on wanting to be open about their livelihood. These participants were not afraid of being rejected, but rather, wanted to be accepted for identifying as a sex worker, thus blurring the boundaries of the public and private sphere. Oftentimes, their decision to merge their identities and roles were informed by their positionality and level of privilege. Skyler shared that he was very intentional in disclosing his identity as a sex worker when it came to relationships; being transparent was important to him and a strategy for avoiding heartache and potential distress. When talking about his romantic partnerships, Skyler stated:

> My involvement in sex work is definitely one of the first conversations I try to have. Because sometimes it goes south after that . . . not always . . . but everyone that's really close to me knows what I do, they don't feel like that at all. They are very supportive of what I do.

For some sex workers, claiming the power to self-represent and merge their private and public identities was a source of empowerment and a way to be transparent, open and forthright.

For some participants, disclosing their work was a way to connect with others and integrate their identities in a way that felt authentic as well as opportunistic. Mykal was very open about his work and saw his disclosure as a way to potentially meet new clients:

> I'm very open about it, I mean, I don't just go around saying, "oh, hey, yeah, I'm a prostitute," or "I'm an escort." But because I don't mind escorting, I always look for opportunities. I've met a couple of clients here working at Dunkin' Donuts. As far as partners go, I told my boyfriend that I escort and he wasn't judgmental. He understood it. Most people that I tell are very understanding. They understand the hustle's real, the struggle's real.

Embodying a mentality of having "nothing to lose" by disclosing sex work and creating empathy around "the hustle," serves to create a connection for understanding survival. This also places the power of representation in the hands of the sex workers themselves, while simultaneously removing the need to compartmentalize identities in order to manage stigma; for Mykal, disclosure of sex work opened up opportunities to gain new clients.

In contrast, others were very intentional in keeping their work a secret from family members and loved ones, due to the judgment and stigma associated with sex work. This was often a theme found among newly arrived migrant sex workers from more collectivist cultures, creating a distinct divide between the work and family domains. Fernanda decided not to disclose her involvement in sex work to all of her family members:

> I still fear that my mom or my dad or my brothers will find out, and I am afraid of their reaction . . . but I feel a weight has been lifted because at least I have the support of my sister, but she obviously isn't happy with what I am doing.

Roxanne, a 26-year-old mixed race female dancer does not reveal her work to loved ones: "I have to hide it from everybody . . . keeping it a secret from my family. With boyfriends, I have to tell them that I am bartending, because they will try to make me stop [dancing]."

For some, disclosure of their involvement in sex work was not a choice, as various external circumstances beyond their control led to their family members finding out about their involvement in sex work. Princess, a 22-year-old black female engaged in street work and escorting, shared how she didn't have a choice in the matter. She stated: "I went to jail. That's when my mom found out because I finally wanted her to be in court with me, so that's how she found out." Sophia experienced being "outed" by a friend of her father who sought out her sexual services:

> My dad's friend came to see me and I was like, "What are you doing here? Is my family coming?" Like OMG! I've known him since I was 15! He was like, "I have money," but I was like, "No you need to leave!" He went and told my dad's whole family what I was doing. And my dad's side of the family are really Latino so they really judged me.

Sex workers often experience "whore" stigma from the wider community, attributing blame and shame due to their work in the sex industry, which can result in them being unwilling to disclose their work to friends and family (Scrambler, 2007). The shame associated with doing sex work can contribute to individuals not disclosing the nature of their work for fear of being judged or rejected (Fick, 2005; Sanders, 2005). While some of the participants decided not to disclose their work to friends, family, and loved ones because of the social stigma associated with sex work, others had no choice in the matter, particularly when they encountered the criminal justice system.

Engaging in the interplay of giving and receiving support

The participants varied in the ways in which they exchanged financial and emotional support from family, friends, and loved ones. There were many participants who were responsible for financially supporting their parents, partners, and extended family members, creating fluid boundaries between work and personal life. Specifically, a few participants discussed how their mothers were dependent on them for financial assistance and support. Oftentimes, when parents were acquiring monetary benefits from their adult child's sex work, they did not discourage sex work, but rather accepted it or ignored any undesirable information or truths about the work. Mykal shared:

> Even with my mom, when I first had an adult conversation with my mom, "Yeah I'm prostituting, I'm dressing in drag, and all that." She didn't know how to accept it and I told her though, I would give her money, I would drop off money to her. Every time she seen me, I always was clean, I always had my own place to stay, whether it was a hotel or an apartment or whatever, and it gradually got to a point where she was like, "Well, you know, I mean, he's not doing that bad."

This was also Skyler's experience with his mother, who he supported through escorting. Sex workers often provided their parents, especially their mothers, extended family, and loved ones with monetary support as a way to manage the stigma around their work. Family members and romantic partners who benefited from the participants' sex work chose to overlook where the money was coming from. Decisions to reveal involvement in sex work were found to be shaped by social, cultural, and structural factors, such as social stigma, techniques to minimize exposure to stigma, economic imperatives, and familial responsibilities. These dynamics of financial support allow sex workers and their families to maintain a comfortable ambiguity about the stigma of sex work itself (Padilla et al., 2008).

Similarly, another participant earned a great deal from a client and gave it all to her mother to invest in a small business venture. Krystal said:

> I was dealing with [well-known actor]. He gave me some money. He's been known to be a freak and he would cruise [XX] Boulevard . . . I never had sex with him. I've only grabbed his penis and played with him. Each time I saw him I got over $10,000. And I'm a street tweaker prostitute; I didn't know what to do with it. One time he's like, "What do you want?" He gave me $28,000 one-time to get breasts done. "Here, you want boobs?" And he gave me the money for it . . . I called my mom because I was so freaked out and paranoid that I would get robbed or killed . . . $28,000, I gave her one time.

It was interesting to see that many of the participants supported their mothers financially, including Skyler who expressed that he would

> pay for her [mom's] vacation to visit me [from the Caribbean]. Because, I mean, usually, when she wants any kind of money, I give it to her. When she visits me, I buy her whatever she wants. I take her wherever she wants. I couldn't let her know that things have changed, because then she would start to worry.

For him, being able to support his mother financially and provide her with a certain standard of living was incredibly important. This was also the situation for Moon, who also supported her mother financially and emotionally:

> I don't have children . . . I have supported my mom before in the past because she's been homeless a couple times, actually. I've had to find a place for her to stay, which was really difficult. I was going through different social work services to try to find a place that would accept her and her husband. That was really tricky because they were both homeless.

Similarly, Fernanda shared:

> With the little bit of savings that I had, I sent money [to my mom] because she separated . . . well actually her husband left her with five kids so then I was the one that was helping her economically for my siblings and for my mom. I knew my dad would send them money, but obviously we know the situation in Mexico and it was not a lot what my dad would send so them, so I would help them a lot.

Some participants shared that they were the recipients of financial and emotional support from parents, partners, and other important people in their life. The types of support varied and depended on the circumstances and need. For example, Domino was part of a polyamorous family where there was reciprocal support. She shared:

When I first entered the industry, I was a budding, freshly transitioning trans woman who very much relied on the financial support of my partners, because I was going to school full time. So not only have I been able to end that but I've been able to now be a contributing member of our family.

Her family members helped her financially and emotionally when she was transitioning and attending graduate school. Similarly, Krystal relied on her boyfriend for support when she was attending school. She expressed:

I met my ex-boyfriend online and we hooked up and he owned a salon and he helped me get a car, helped me get my credit together, helped me get involved more in school, started paying for my schooling a little bit more. He helped a lot. He was a lot older too. I was 25 and he was 52 or 53. It was kind of a sugar daddy situation in a way, but I stayed with him for about four and a half years.

Sex workers who relied on others for support tended to blur the boundaries between work and personal life, often integrating the two. This was evidenced with Ambrosia, a 25-year-old bisexual Latina female engaged in pornography, exotic dancing, webcam work, and phone sex. She shared that she received support from her mom in the form of driving:

Actually, my mom still kind of helps me out in a sense, she'll like, Uber me places. I don't have a car. I don't like driving, I won't do it. It's just not something for me, so she kind of is my car, in some sense. Like, she drives me around everywhere with her Uber account.

This mother and daughter relied on one another for emotional and financial support, representing another example of integrated domains.

When talking about the sex work-related struggles, Mykal communicated the power of friendships. He expressed: "I'll do what I have to do, but as long as I know I can pick up a phone and call somebody, I feel like that is all the support that I really need." Domino shared the importance of having her chosen family for support:

Having that nest where I feel comfortable, where I can recharge, like my poly family and my collared submissive are the most important people in my life. I fiercely protect them and I fiercely protect my space. Communication, ultimately, is so desperately important with my family.

Skyler noted how having acceptance from friends was an important source of emotional support: "everyone that's really close to me knows about what I do . . . they're very supportive of what I do." Being able to integrate personal life with work life was a way to cope with the challenges of sex work and served as space to process experiences, thoughts and emotions.

Interacting with various institutions as a platform for legitimacy

Some participants discussed their engagement with various institutions and how this engagement informed and shaped their social relationships. Their interactions with diverse institutions often served to legitimize and validate their sex worker identity as it intersected with other identities and roles in life. The most common institutions that the participants were involved with included the educational system and entertainment industry, such as the adult print and film industry (for those who held more privileged intersecting identities) and the child welfare and criminal justice system (for those participants who were most marginalized). Both Strawberry and Domino shared how they revealed their identities as sex workers in graduate school as a form of resistance to stereotypes and assumptions about sex workers. Strawberry, who was "out" to her classmates, said:

> I tell my classmates all of the time that not every sex worker is a victim, and not every sex worker was forced to do what they're doing, and that a lot of sex workers, they want to be in that exact spot. They don't want to be rescued or saved.

Both Strawberry and Domino felt empowered by sex work and used school as a platform for activism and challenging stereotypes. They used their role as graduate students to cultivate legitimacy as smart, empowered sex workers. In particular, Strawberry, who has featured in various well-known pornography films, used her fame in films to legitimize her career and identity as a successful sex worker. Within these institutions, sex workers merged their personal and work identities and used institutions as a platform for validating their work.

For Krystal, who often faces arrest for engaging in street work as a trans woman, her friends in jail and prison served as a community that legitimized her sex worker and trans identity:

> Jail for me was like a reunion. I'd go in and hear, "Krystal, Krystal!" Everyone knew I was coming up before I even got in there through the trustees and the workers talking and before I went up there I already had—it was like a reunion. "Ah, she's here," and I'd get there and like, crazy. It was like coming back to my family. So that, to me, even got comfortable. I'd look forward to it sometimes. When I was going through shit on the streets so bad I'm like, "Fuck, I can't wait to get busted."

During the low points in her life, the criminal justice system also served as a place for Krystal to feel safe, accepted, and recognized in comparison to working the streets where she often struggled to gain legitimacy as a trans female sex worker.

Neaveh, a 40-year-old white, bisexual street worker and escort, shared that she had eight children in the child welfare system. As a street-based sex worker, she disclosed her drug addiction and was very transparent with sharing that she was not able to achieve her professional goals because of her criminal record:

> I am already 40 years old. I have been a prostitute since I was 12 years old. I always said I wanted to do things in my life . . . I wanted to work with kids, but because of my [prostitution] charges, and my first charge of failure to protect my minor, I cannot work with children. Nobody under the age of 18.

The manner in which she talked about her interactions with the child welfare system through her identity as a sex worker at such a young age served to legitimize her intersecting identities while highlighting her internalized stigma and regret. To cope with this regret, she had compartmentalized her role as a mother and talked about her lost opportunities. For sex workers in this study, these various institutions also functioned as a platform to re-story their narrative and engage in image, identity, and impression management (Blithe & Wolfe, 2017).

Concluding thoughts

Rather than always maintaining distinct physical, emotional, and social separations between their work and personal life, sex workers are intentional in the ways in which they create, blur, and manage the fluidity of these boundaries, depending on their positionality and informed by social, cultural, and institutional contexts. Bellhouse, et al. (2015) and Clark (2000) highlight work–family border theory and argue that the domains of work and family influence one another. While these two domains are mediated by purpose, culture, attitudes, and behavior, they differ for individuals depending on their social location, and for some these domains are integrated, rather than separated. Integration of the work and family domain is evident among sex workers whose home is also their place of work, like Skyler and Neveah. For sex workers who cannot physically separate their place of work from their personal life, these spheres are integrated, fluid, and negotiated as needed.

Explicit separation of domains as a form of coping, self-protection, or stigma management can be observed among trans sex workers (negotiating identities and stigma), migrant sex workers (experiencing cultural pressures, immigrant status, and stigma), and individuals working in sex industry establishments where places of work are physically separated from home. The need to negotiate their sex worker identity with other intersecting identities, such as gender, migrant status, and their roles within family or school, can lead to a range of feelings, including pride, embarrassment, and conflicted emotions. While many sex workers choose to reconcile their identities within the personal and professional domain, others are very intentional in keeping their identities separate in order to manage work life balance through separation. This aligns with other research by Sanders (2005) that highlights how sex workers commonly adopt behaviors to separate their work and personal life.

While sex workers perform different roles in the work and family domains, their navigation process varies and depends on their level of comfort with their sex worker identity, ethnic/cultural background, and socio-economic status. Financial interdependency between family, friends, and romantic partners mediates the blurring of boundaries between work and personal life. Sex workers who are financially independent have the option of creating more distinct boundaries and separations between work and personal life. In addition, personal relationships are always negotiated and selective disclosure about sex work is an intentional and thoughtful process. Sex workers who have the privilege of discretion are careful about who to trust when disclosing their involvement in the sex industry because of stereotypes and judgment, particularly those who have educational privilege.

Sex workers who experience "whore" stigma are often unwilling to disclose their work to family and friends, thus engaging in stigma management practices (Scrambler, 2007). However, due to increased access to technology and the Internet, oftentimes sex workers do have the option of hiding their work in the sex industry from family members, friends, lovers, and acquaintances. The decision-making process around disclosure of sex worker identity is mediated by various factors, including the implications involved by telling others, the need to reveal their sex worker identity as a way to challenge stereotypes and assumptions, the potential future repercussions of when changing careers, the opportunity to gain new clientele as a result of disclosure, and the fear of rejection from family members and romantic partners.

With respect to romantic relationships, sex workers decide whether to disclose their work with romantic partners by assessing the level of judgment, stereotyping, and rejection. Sex workers are intentional in their selection of romantic partners and contemplate the monetary and emotional benefits of choosing romance over sex work. Oftentimes sex workers who tell their romantic partners about their work in the sex industry experience negative impacts around jealousy and misunderstanding due to the stigma associated with sex work (Bellhouse, et al, 2015; Murphy & Venkatesh, 2006). Sex workers who struggle with tensions between sex work and their personal romantic relationships use mental separation as a coping mechanism to balance the two aspects of their lives (Bilardi et al., 2011). The degree and level of stigma often informs sex workers' separation, integration, and management of work and personal life.

This research challenges the unconditional separation of work and personal life, since factors exist that are beyond control, such as technology that results in increased access to personal lives and the policing of sex workers' bodies through social stigma and the criminalization of sex workers. Sex workers' attempts to mitigate stigma and stereotypes must be viewed in relation to the conditions of inequality and structural violence that they routinely confront. The stigmas of sex work and other intersecting marginalized identities function in synergy with social inequalities to raise the stakes of sex workers' marginalization within various institutions. However, this marginalized status can also serve as a platform from which sex workers routinely challenge stigma and stereotypes within various institutions and within their interpersonal relationships. Sex workers embody strength, agency, power, and resilience in the ways in which they navigate their personal and interpersonal relationships. They also use their role as sex workers to resist oppressive factors within various institutions. By reclaiming their sex worker identity in various ways within different institutions, they cultivate a sense of legitimacy that serves to assist them in anchoring and navigating the various arenas of their life.

References

Ayres, L. 2008. "Thematic coding and analysis." In L. Given (Ed.), *The SAGE encyclopedia of qualitative research methods*. Los Angeles, CA: Sage.

Bellhouse, C., Crebbin S., Fairley C., and Bilardi J. 2015. The impact of sex work on women's personal romantic relationship and the mental separation of their work and personal lives: A mixed methods study. *PLoS ONE*, 10(10): e0141575. https://doi.org/10.1371/journal.pone.0141575.

Bilardi, J.E., Miller, A., Hocking, J.S., Keogh, L., Cummings, R., and Chen, M.Y. 2011. The job satisfaction of female sex workers in licensed brothels in Victoria Australia. *Journal of Sexual Medicine*, 8: 116–122.

Blithe, S.J. 2015. *Gender equality and work-life balance: Glass handcuffs and working men in the U.S.* New York, NY: Routledge.

Blithe, S.J. and Wolfe, A.W. 2017. Work–life management in legal prostitution: Stigma and lockdown in Nevada's brothels. *Human Relations*, 70(6): 725–750.

Brewis, J. and Linstead, S. 2000. "The worst thing is the screwing"(1): Consumption and the management of identity in sex work. *Gender, Work and Organization*, 7(2): 84–97.

Clark, S. C. 2000. Work/family border theory: A new theory of work/family balance. *Human Relations*, 53(6): 747–770.

Closson, E., Colby, D., Nguyen, T., Cohen, S., Biello, K., and Mimiaga, M. 2015. The balancing act: Exploring stigma, economic need and disclosure among male sex workers in Ho Chi Minh City, Vietnam Global Public Health. *An International Journal for Research, Policy and Practice*, 10(4): 520–531.

Crenshaw, Kimberle. 1991. Mapping the margins: Intersectionality, identity politics, and violence against women of color. *Stanford Law Review*, 43(6): 1241–1299.

Ellis, C. 2004. *The ethnographic I: A methodological novel about autoethnography*. Walnut Creek, CA: AltaMira Press.

Fick, N. 2005. *Coping with stigma, discrimination and violence: Sex workers talk about their experiences*. Cape Town: SWEAT.

Gill, R. 2006. The work-life relationship for "people with choices": Women entrepreneurs as crystallized selves. *Electronic Journal of Communication*, 16(3): n.p.

Golden, A.G. and Geisler, C. 2007. Work-life boundary management and the personal digital assistant. *Human Relations*, 60(3): 519–551.

Goffman, E. 1963. *Stigma: Notes on the management of spoiled identity*. New York, NY: Simon & Schuster.

Jorgenson, J. 2000. Interpreting the intersections of work and family: Frame conflicts in women's work. *Electronic Journal of Communication*, 10(3–4): n.p.

Kirby, E.L. 2006. "Helping you make room in your life for your needs": When organizations appropriate family roles. *Communication Monographs*, 73(4): 474–480.

Kuhn, T. 2006. A "demented work ethic" and a "lifestyle firm": Discourse, identity, and workplace time commitments. *Organization Studies*, 27(9): 1339–1358.

Murphy, A.K. and Venkatesh, S.A. 2006. Vice careers: The changing contours of sex work in New York City. *Qualitative Sociology*, 29: 129–154.

Murphy, H., Dunk-West, P., and Chonody, J. 2015. Emotion work and the management of stigma in female sex workers' long-term intimate relationships. *Journal of Sociology*, 51(4): 1103–1116.

Nippert-Eng, C.E. 1996. *Home and work*. Chicago, IL: University of Chicago Press.

Padilla, M., Castellanos, D., Guilamo-Ramos, V., Reyes, A., Marte, L., and Sorianod, M. 2008. Stigma, social inequality, and HIV risk disclosure among Dominican male sex workers. *Social Science Medicine*, 67(3): 380–388.

Sanders, T. 2004. Controllable laughter: Managing sex work through humour. *Sociology*, 38(2): 273–291.

Sanders, T. 2005. "It's just acting": Sex workers' strategies for capitalizing on sexuality. *Gender, Work and Organisation*, 12(4): 319–341.

Scrambler, G. 2007. Sex work stigma: Opportunist migrants in London. *Sociology*, 41(6): 1079–1096.

Schieman, S. and Glavin, P. 2008. Trouble at the border? Gender flexibility at work, and the work-home interface. *Social Problems*, 55(4): 590–611.

Trethewey, A., Tracy, S.J., and Alberts, J.K. 2006. Crystallizing frames for work-life. *Electronic Journal of Communication*, 16(3–4): n.p.

Warr, D.J. and Pyett, P.M. 1999. Difficult relations: Sex work, love and intimacy. *Sociology of Health & Illness*, 21(3): 290–309.

Wieland, S.M.B. 2001. Struggling to manage work as a part of everyday life: Complicating control, rethinking resistance, and contextualizing work/life studies. *Communication Monographs*, 78(2): 162–184.

27

From clients to "friends" or "lovers"

Latin American sex workers coping with the economic crisis in Spain

Adriana Piscitelli

Introduction

In this chapter I address forms of support offered between sex industry workers, their family members, and intimate partners, considering how Latin American sex workers, mainly Brazilians, have coped with Spain's economic crisis. I reflect on the connections between sex work, intimacy, and kinship relationships drawing on studies that have analyzed the modalities of intimacy in which sex workers are engaged and on scholarship on migration that considers kinship relationships as central aspects of sex work and gendered migration (Fonseca 2004; Olivar 2013; Parreñas 2001; Piscitelli 2014; Tavori and Poulin 2012). Both lines of thought pay attention to the interconnections between exchange and intimacy (Zelizer 2005).

In terms of intimacy, since the pioneer studies in the field (Bacelar 1982), socio-anthropological production concerning sex workers in Brazil has analyzed the relevance of kinship to the organization of the dynamics of sex work and to the motivations for undertaking this activity (Fonseca 2004; Olivar 2013; Piscitelli 2014). The studies that analyze conjugal and romantic relations of women, men, and *travesti* in Brazilian and transnational sex markets have shown the importance of the emotions that permeate these relations to sex workers and the particularities of the delicate relational work (Zelizer 2005) performed to differentiate commercial sex from loving relationships (França 2011; Maia 2011; Mitchell 2011; Piscitelli 2007, 2014; Teixeira 2008, 2011).

In terms of kinship, these studies firmly establish relationships between sexual and affective aspects in the transnationalization of sexual economies[1] by mostly considering transactional sex[2] (Groes-Green 2013) and transactional marriages (Cole 2009, 2014) to show how these economies are tied to broader moral economies of exchange (Piscitelli forthcoming). The operation of these economies across borders—in which migrant work marked by gender supports the provision of care at a distance for children, mothers and siblings (Parreñas 2001)—allows perceiving the analogies between migrations linked to sex markets and other sectors of activity (Piscitelli 2014).

In this text I expand on these lines of discussion, considering how the connections between increased precariousness and intimacy offer elements to deepen the understanding of how reciprocity operates in these moral economies, in the case of sex workers. This analysis, in which I consider how economic, sexual, and emotional exchanges operate at a time of changing migratory flows between Spain and Brazil, is part of a broader multi-sited ethnography (Marcus 1995) conducted since 2004.[3]

During 2005–2010, Brazilian migration, although it was numerically reduced in relation to that of other Latin American countries, acquired high visibility in Spain's sex and marriage markets. But in the years 2000–2005, the direction of the migratory flows changed. For a few years, Brazil became one of the main destinations of Spanish emigrants in Latin America. At that time, many Latin American emigrants in Spain began to return, although many others, like several of my interviewees, made great efforts to remain in Spain.

Here I consider the period between 2011 and 2015 when the narratives about the economic opportunities in Brazil appeared to identify a situation that was opposite to the crisis afflicting Spain. In this context, I asked how the economic, sexual, and affective exchanges that acquired significant importance in the flows of Brazilian migrants to this country were "participating" in these mobilities and permanences in times of crisis. I worked mostly on the trajectories of lower middle-class Brazilians resident in Spain, who struggled to remain in this country and who I have accompanied for almost ten years. In that period they already had a regular migratory status. Some offered sexual services and others worked cleaning homes and taking care of elderly people or children. The economic crisis affected them all, but mostly the sex workers, who faced a severely declining income, of as much as 60% of their earnings.

My main argument is that economic re-configurations related to Spain's crisis influence changes in sexual economies and intimate dimensions of life. My interviewees' involvement in these economies changed and so did the styles of affection that were predominant in the intimate relations. The flows of re-distribution of resources in the realm of kinship were also modified, affecting these relationships and revealing the particularities that reciprocity assumes in these flows.

Sex work and economic crises

I will consider the narratives of two Brazilian women who worked in the sex industry in Barcelona and that of Shirley, a *travesti* from Uruguay, who also offered sexual services in that city and whose stories have significant relations with the narratives of the Brazilian women. Shirley is in her fifties. She is a tall, strong, and very sweet person, with long grey hair. Having lived for almost 30 years in Spain, she had recently lost her job at an NGO in Barcelona, and almost no longer performed "*programas*"—the word used in Brazil for "tricks." In 2013, when the economic crisis was one of the main themes in the public debate in Spain, Shirley told me: "Look, this is the crisis. There are few clients. But you know what, I am not thinking of leaving. We, in Latin America, have always been in crisis."

This comment on the crisis evokes the reflections of Susana Narotsky and Niko Besnier (2014: 57, 58). According to these authors, the idea of crisis contrasts with the forms of stability that allow the elaboration of projects that provide confidence in the possibility of conducting these projects. The crisis expresses a break with normality, emerges as a threat, and at the same time, requires a certain creativity. The authors observe that there is a tradition of thought that considers these ruptures limited moments in time, which give way to stability. Nevertheless, there is evidence that instability and insecurity have been the norm in most contexts. And while in Southern Europe the crisis was presented as an exceptional situation, many people around the world are required to act in the realm of a permanent experience of chaos and insecurity. Alluding to the constant Latin American crisis, Shirley refered to the precariousness in which she lived before migrating, in which her family was also immersed and that she was facing again in Spain.

At that time, the news in Spain recurrently called attention to the fact that due to the economic crisis, women who had not been prostitutes before, particularly Spanish women, were entering the sex industry. Several reports observed that persons who had left prostitution were returning to it due to the lack of employment during the crisis (Cáritas 2016; Médicos del Mundo 2011). In this frame of narratives, sex workers who offered their services in the street complained about the decreasing earnings. Tricks that had been 50 or 60 euros[4] had dropped below 30 euros, in competition with young girls from Romania and China who charged even less. NGO agents state that during the crisis the working conditions in sex clubs or apartments were worse. Since there were fewer clients, they had to work longer hours and had to pay for things that were previously free of charge, such as toilet paper or soda. They also said that an increased number of sex workers were leaving venues where they were economically exploited and some opened their own working places, administrated as cooperatives.[5] And academic studies called attention to other sex workers' strategies in terms of mobilities, intensifying their circulation inside and outside the country, offering sexual services in cities of France, Italy, and Germany (López-Riopedre, 2013). And others moved between different occupations, alternating between sex work and other paid occupations (Martinez, 2016).

During the first years of the crisis in 2008–2009, some of my Brazilian interviewees lost their jobs taking care of children and began to work as prostitutes. But the lack of clients led them to return to Brazil. The ones who remained in Spain, who considered themselves professional sex workers, diversified their activities in and outside the sex industry in efforts to avoid a "return" to the precariousness they experienced in their home country. And they gradually abandoned prostitution, which suggests that in their cases perhaps the "crisis" has had more significant effects on this activity than policies to criminalize the practice. Two of these interviewees were in their late forties and fifies. In their trajectories, the economic crisis coincided with aging processes. Yet, it is important to state that until that moment some of these elder sex workers in Spain had a regular number of clients—which declined with the crisis. Precisely the possibility offered by the Spanish sex market for older women was a crucial factor in Olympia's decision to migrate. In Brazil, in her forties, she had scarce clients, but once she arrived in Spain she realized there was a demand for her work, not in clubs, but in the streets where until that time she was able to earn between 4,000 and 5,000 euros per month.

Olympia was a woman with blond hair, light eyes, wide hips, and was very warm. She offered sexual services in the El Raval neighborhood in Barcelona and had expanded her range of activities in the sex industry. She continued to look for clients, but with little success, despite having lowered the price of her sexual services to 20 euros. She attributed the lack of demand to a combination of factors in which the economic crisis was related to new regulations on commercial sex, manifest in the intensification of government efforts to repress it, particularly in the streets of the Old City of Barcelona, which is undergoing an intense gentrification process.

Since 2006, in various cities, including Barcelona, street prostitution was fought with municipal laws about activities in public places.[6] They included fines not only for clients but also for the supposed victims, the sex workers, as well as controls by the police.[7] Despite support from various NGOs that challenged the fines, they still influenced the daily life of sex workers, because the fines could be as high as 30,000 euros and prevented them from having bank accounts or obtaining credit or support from the municipality. In 2015, the situation decayed with the passage of a national citizen protection law known as the Gag Law,[8] which made it a grave crime to solicit or accept sexual services for money in public places. In this sense, the "crisis" was related to changes in sexual economies, considering this concept as going beyond the exchange of sex for money in the more literal sense, and to be related to ways in which sexual circulations are critical to other economic projects, including humanitarianism, policing, and gentrification (Bernstein 2014).

In Olympia's opinion, the municipal government was also responsible for the scarcity of clients, because it was buying the few remaining *"mueblés"*—old buildings that served as hourly hotels where sex workers who offer sexual services in the street perform their *"programas."* She also blamed the police, who harassed clients and issued heavy fines. Her husband had worked in a restaurant but was unemployed and his unemployment assistance covered only part of the rent for the apartment that they shared. Olympia thus had to find ways to survive this situation that acquired serious connotations for her. Her response was political and economic. She began to participate in the Indignant Prostitutes collective, which demanded the right to conduct sexual work. She expanded her activities in the sex industry, and in her intervals between clients cleaned rooms in a *"mueblé"* and changed sheets. This service paid 50 euros per day and was exhausting, she preferred prostitution, but this was the opportunity she found given the scarcity of clients.

Olympia, like my *travesti* interviewee Shirley, had a nostalgia for the "golden years" in the European sex industry, the decades of 1990 and 2000. They both believe that these were their best years. They were younger and, at that time of relative economic "well-being" in the countries of southern Europe there were many clients and both had intense demand for their sexual services. But later, Shirley got work in an organization that fought AIDS and that supported migrant sexual workers and she was extremely active. She began a stable loving relationship with an Andalusian man, who lived in a town close to Barcelona who she called her "husband" and spent weekends with her. This relationship, which was highly valued by Shirley, provided her emotional security and the pleasure of having someone to look after and not offer economic resources. In parallel, she had various clients.

With the crisis, the organization that employed her twice lowered her work hours and finally laid her off. The regular clients had disappeared, only one remained who had been with her for 20 years. In a highly competitive market, due to the scarcity of clients, this aging *travesti* moved to an apartment with a considerably lower rent.

And, unlike Olympia, Shirley, diversified her work to activities outside the sex industry. To survive, she sought work in other roles traditionally considered to be within the female domain and began to clean homes three times a week; cooking for a family once a week, and working in the kitchen of a cafe one day a week. She earned extra resources by selling embroideries she made. She made a little more by doing the weekly shopping for an old Brazilian prostitute who could barely walk.

Changes in intimate relations

Shirley's only relationship based on exchanging sex for money was now that with the long-term client. For many years Shirley received him once a month and charged 50 euros. But this relationship began to change. In past years she referred to this man with a certain disdain that was related to his sexual preferences: Shirley particularly appreciated the few virile clients who penetrated her but was also comfortable with those who requested to be penetrated. She said that this client was a married man, with children, and strange: he had pleasure taking his clothes off and exhibiting himself, but there was no penetration. However, during the crisis, he spontaneously increased his visits and his payment, placing 75 euros on the table each time. Shirley began to see these visits, which now accounted for one-third of her rent, as "help." And alluding to their shared aging process, she began to refer to him with a certain kindness. She told me:

> It's not that I love him, but when I don't see him, I miss him. I feel his absence, because . . . he has become a friend. When he began he was 20 years old. Now he is fat, but, ok, I also got heavy!

The notion of "help," accompanied by a certain style of affection, is common in the sexual and economic exchanges involving Brazilians that, going beyond commercial sex, have similarities with the notion of "transactional sex" (Cabezas, 2009; Hunter 2010; Kempadoo 2004). Help is a style of exchange widely disseminated in Brazil, which was recreated by Brazilian migrants abroad. The concept refers to economic contributions frequently exchanged for sex, which although important, do not constitute the main source of resources for subsistence.

In contrast to prostitution, which involves a contract for sexual services while ideally avoiding love and pleasure in relationships with clients, "help" is a notion that evokes relationships of reciprocity, inserted in a tradition of hierarchical exchanges, and is related to notions of support, care, and affection. In Brazil it tends to involve agents in unequal positions, in terms of class or at least of access to economic resources, and often also of age, skin color, and nationality. In exchange for "help," older subjects, mostly men, receive sex, company, and at times domestic care. In the migratory contexts in Spain, "help" took on different connotations. Those who provided "help" were not necessarily older, nor did they have higher monthly incomes. But they could provide resources needed by my interviewees to establish themselves in these contexts. And it could involve marriages that allowed the regularization of their migratory status.

The Brazilian women I interviewed who offered sexual services in Spain, like Shirley, did not abandon the sexual economies, but moved between modalities of sexual and economic exchanges. These interviewees preferred "*programas*" to relationships of "help." Intimate relations in the realm of sex work offered them resources to survive with a higher income, first in Brazil and later in Spain, which allowed them to "improve their lives" and redistribute resources among different generations by sending money to Brazil in movements that produced and consolidated kinship ties. In relation to feelings, these women tend to give value to an extreme form of "love" and "passion," which they reserved for their romantic relationships that do not involve commercial sex and that are made possible by the autonomy acquired through sex work.

Like Shirley, in the context of the economic crisis, they began to choose economic and sexual exchanges that they could establish with men who "help" them rather than those clients who were increasingly poor and scarce. They began to rely on "help" from friends, lovers, or boyfriends, and at times "help" became a primary source of income. And while it is possible to think that the combination of the economic crisis and the aging process experienced by Shirley and Olympia was relevant in this choice, this option also appeared in the case of younger inteviewees, like Veronica, a Brazilian woman in her early thirties. I first met her in Barcelona eight years ago when she was an irregular migrant sex worker struggling to secure her "papers" and hoping to find "love." Slim, with perfect light skin, she was seen as highly attractive in the Spanish sex industry.

In the past, her work as a prostitute in Barcelona allowed her to make enough money to buy an apartment in Brazil for her mother and sisters. The beginning of the crisis converged with a traumatic experience she had when a client tried to kill her and she decided to abandon sex work. But she only obtained low paying jobs and started to rely exclusively on "help" relationships. With the mediation of an NGO she was able to regularize her migratory status. With the "help" of a Finnish boyfriend, Veronica moved to Madrid and fulfilled her dream of continuing her studies and taking a technical course. But at a certain point this man became violent. When she left him, she perceived the risks of depending entirely on a relationship of "help." She found herself without a home, work, or money in a city where she knew few people.

A few months later, she was living with another man, a Spanish teacher from her new school, who had left his wife and children, and was "helping" her. She thought she would just be his lover and accepted this. But this man rented an apartment so he could live with Veronica. He paid the rent, her school fees, and most of her expenses. When he returned home in the evenings, he helped her with her lessons. He was also supervising her final essay and promised to "help" her to find what she most wanted at the time: a job as a highly qualified electrician in the construction sector.

Without mentioning "love," Veronica said that she liked this man, a feeling fed by her gratefulness for his support. This feeling is not surprising considering that if what various authors consider to be expressions of "romantic love"—such as spontaneous and irrational feelings—(hooks 2000; Illouz 2007) are sometimes present in the realm of "help," the affection linked to this modality of exchange is frequently expressed in other terms, particularly respect and *consideration*, terms that allude to social obligations and can be given priority in relation to pleasure.

To stay with a man who she only "liked" had been unthinkable for her a few years ago when, supported by the economic autonomy acquired through sex work, she hoped to find "love" and "passion." She did not succeed. At some point in the relationships the boyfriends brought up the issue of sex work. Later on, when she abandoned sex work, she gradually discarded the struggle to find a relationship based on love. As if "love" and "passion" became out of her reach when she began to rely on "help" relationships. And at that moment she depended almost entirely on this man. The affection between her and her teacher was tenuous, but involved care and support and was the only connection that provided her some degree of economic and social security at this time of "crisis." Perceiving the fragility of this tie she invested her energy in the continued sexual seduction of this man as well as in her studies, with the hope of finding a job. In this situation, she would not take the risk of asking him for money to send to her family, out of fear that if he felt he was being exploited, this would weaken their relationship.

In terms of loving intimacy, the shift in the forms of involvement in the sexual economies, with the re-activation and displacement of "help" relationships, has implications. The shift of this exchange from the place of a support strategy to the central means of survival shows the risks of an interlinking between economics, intimacy, and affection when one member of the couple is in a dependent and thus unequal situation. And these effects are expressed in the language of emotions.

Fractures in kinship relationships

Analyzing love, in contexts of poverty, Hunter (2010) makes an important observation about the relationship between material and emotional aspects. According to Hunter, emotional and material practices are always related. Therefore, in these contexts, sex and love are always material and love can rarely be separated from a world of dependencies, involving reciprocity, inequalities, and even violence. Hunter (2010) refers to love in the realm of economic, sexual, and romantic exchanges. However, this materiality of love is also present in kinship relations.

Groes-Green (2014) provides an idea of this materiality by analyzing how moralities of exchange operate in young Mozambican women's migratory trajectories towards Europe, which are shaped by sexual relationships with older white men and obligations towards female kin. Groes-Green (2014) understands these relationships through theories of patronage and moralities of exchange. Placing the concept of patronage within a broader moral economy of exchange that encompasses not only economic and social bonds but also sexual favors, care, love, and gender and kinship obligations, he considers that patronage applies to young women's exchanges with partners and to exchanges with kin, although it is guided by different moralities.

Something analogous takes place among the Brazilian migrants with whom I have worked. For some of them, their families' expectations of receiving remittances caused tensions in the familial relations if the women refused to support the family. But most of my interviewees, whether sex workers or not, acknowledged and took care of their parental obligations. This applied to transnational[9] heads of families (Parreñas 2001), whose children remained in Brazil, under the custody of a sister or grandmother, however, it was not restricted to them. The concept of family and familial obligations may include not only children, but also mothers, younger brothers, and even nephews and nieces in Brazil. The familial obligations involved the purchase or repair of homes in Brazil, the monthly remittances they never failed to make and occasional remittances in special circumstances, such as for medical treatments, school material or trousseaus. As a 27-year-old sex worker from the northeast of Brazil told me, before the "crisis" in Spain:

> My mother used to live in a mud house in Natal. I had the house rebuilt; five rooms and a tiled patio. I bought a fridge, cupboards, everything, even the tableware and dishes. I wanted to give my brothers and sisters all those things I hadn't had. I bought one bike for each of them. I send 100 euros a month, maybe more if there is an urgent need.

In these interviewees' narratives, remittances and presents are part of the circulation of economic and symbolic goods that feed transnational bonds of kinship across borders. In the past, in some cases, this circulation was the main source of economic support for those who remained and contributed to support the emotional life of those women who departed, by offering them affective resources and emotional references.

In the articulation between sexual economies and a broader moral economy of exchange—that involves kinship obligations—with the income from sex work, Shirley sent money and airplane tickets to her mother. And through this material expression of love she gained acceptance of her condition as a *travesti* daughter, sister and sex worker, which she did not have when she lived in Uruguay. Olympia's affection was expressed in the money she sent to Brazil that paid for the university studies of her two daughters and land and a house on a small farm and dairy cattle that her son cared for and depended on. Now, during the crisis, she expected to benefit from a reversal, and to receive a monthly allowance from her son. However, she did not tell her son about this plan, not wanting to express it by telephone, and waited for her next trip to Brazil to do so.

Veronica, meanwhile, thought that at this time of "crisis," the flux of kinship solidarity should change direction. She felt that she had done a lot for her family. But when she needed money, and after the death of her mother wanted to sell the apartment that she had bought in Brazil, her family was against the sale. She affirmed that her family wound up being the worst of the pimps. And she feared that Olympia, who she knew, would have a similar deception, in terms of receiving a return from the investments she made in her son's business. She told me that when her mother was alive she sent money home for ten years. She bought the apartment in which her mother and sisters lived and sent money each month. She paid for her middle sister's college expenses. This sister had lived for some time in England and spent three months in Barcelona working as a prostitute. But she did not like it. Veronica said that her sister was repulsed by the clients and returned to Brazil, did not work and her mother supported her because Veronica continued to send money. A time came when Veronica perceived that she was being exploited and said she wanted to sell the apartment and take the money back to Barcelona because she has nothing.

When Veronica had economic problems she wound up in a shelter. And when she attended college her sister did not help. Veronica helped her sister, but no one helped Veronica. She told me: "deep down you expect reciprocity." She also said that she would go home for Christmas but was concerned because in the past she was very well received when she came with lots of presents. But at the time she had no money and could not bring anything.

These accounts indicate that one of the most outstanding and painful effects of the crisis is the uncertainty it creates in kinship ties, given the lack of material resources to support them. This problem affects migrants in various sectors of activity. But in the case of these Brazilians engaged in sexual economies, the interruption of the flow of resources seems to cause a particular rupture in the broad morality of exchanges. In this morality, participation in sexual economies is tolerable and sometimes even desirable, whenever it generates a redistribution of material resources among relatives. The reciprocity here is manifest in terms of affection from those who receive material resources. But the flow of material goods is necessarily unilateral.

Concluding thoughts

The narratives of the crisis among these Brazilian migrants highlight two central factors, which refer to changes regarding the support of partners and relatives in the realms of loving intimacy and kinship. Considering these aspects expands the existing sex work scholarship focused on analyses about the relations between prostitution and crisis in Spain and on the connections between affections and moralities of exchange.

Following the lines drawn by Brennan (2004), Bernstein (2007), and Cheng (2010) and by paying attention to how affections operate, and in particular "love," in the relationships established by sexual workers, reveals how in times of crisis there is an expansion in the range of sexual and economic exchanges, accompanied by different styles of affection. Moving on to old clients, transforming them into "friends" and seeking love-based relationships are some of the tactics used by the people I interviewed, expanding the range of strategies registered by other researchers who analyze the responses of sexual workers to the crisis in Spain (Ballester, Orte, and Oliver 2013; López-Riopedre 2013; Martinez 2016)

In this movement, the option for relations of "help" also expresses a choice for styles of affection that are less valued. The tenuous affections associated with the re-activation of "help" relationships differed from the intense emotions associated with loving intimacies mentioned in the narratives of my interviewees at the time they performed sex work. In those days, they made distinctions between commercial sexual intimacy, associated with performances of care, and loving intimacy. The latter was the place of intense emotions, of "true love" and "passion," which were associated with "native" notions of choice and autonomy. Indicating an apparently paradoxical aspect of the sexual economies, sex work allowed them to envision something that resembles an emancipatory ideal, which although not necessarily fulfilled, helped them to imagine and plan for a future deemed to be worth living. Nevertheless, in times of crisis, the option for more tenuous feelings, accompanying a certain economic security, was part of the strategies used by these migrants.

The attention given to feelings, and in parallel to the range of sexual and economic exchanges in which the people I interviewed are involved over these years, expands the reflections about the moralities articulated to sexual and economic exchanges. These reflections have yielded excellent analyses that show how these exchanges are intimately interlinked to other dimensions of the social and permeated by feelings. Nevertheless, they tend to be focused on modalities of transactional sex (Groes-Green 2013; Cole 2009, 2014), provoking the impression that the borders that are delineated between these exchanges and sex work are related to separate universes of study. The trajectories of the women I interviewed show their movements between modalities of exchanges and showed how these moralities involving kinship permeate their participation in all these exchanges, including prostitution.

In terms of kinship, the "crisis" illuminates the differentiated distributions of the circulation of goods and affections in the circuits of kinship relations. This circulation, according to hierarchies internal to kinship, is analogous to the cases of migrants occupied in various sectors of activity. Nevertheless, in the case of sex workers, these hierarchies seemed to be sharply exacerbated, certainly due to the stigma that marks commercial sex, which interfered in the flows of affection when the material provision they offer is interrupted and in the possibility of sex workers receiving economic support. The fact that these migrants had moved within the realm of sexual economies, even abandoning work in the sex industry, does not seem to alter the assymetry of those flows.

Notes

1 Including transactional sex in which the economic and sexual exchanges are distant from prostitution (Cabezas 2009; Hunter 2002, 2010; Kempadoo 2004).
2 Exchanges of material and symbolic goods, sometimes including affection, and sex that are differentiated from "tricks" and are not considered as prostitution by those involved (Hunter 2010)
3 This research gives continuity to an ethnographic study conducted for a total of 20 months since 2004 in the Spanish cities of Madrid, Granada, Bilbao and mainly Barcelona, at a time when this country attracted a significant flow of Brazilian immigration. I worked with women, *travestis*, and men from various social classes in Brazil and who had ties to various sectors of activity in Spain, paying particular attention to the sex industry. The study focused on understanding how the intersection between gender and other categories of differentiation permeate the insertion of Brazilians in Spain's sex and marriage markets. The fieldwork included interviews with 57 people: Brazilian women and transvestites who offer sexual services, clients, owners of prostitution establishments and agents linked to various support entities for migrants and or sex workers. It also included interviews with 14 Brazilian migrants occupied in other sectors of activity, mainly in services of care aimed at children and the elderly and in domestic service.
4 Interview with a Brazilian sex worker, Barcelona, 2013.
5 Interview with Hetaira's coordinator in Barcelona, April 2013.
6 "EU alega contra la ordenanza que multa em Valencia a las prostitutas," *El País*, 01/03/2006; "Barcelona multa por primera vez a prostitutas en aplicación de la nueva ordenanza cívica." *El País*, 01/02/2006.
7 "Barcelona impone multas de hasta 3,000 euros a las prostitutas." *El País*, 11/02/2006; Plataforma comunitária: treball sexual i convivència, *Comunicado de prensa: las entidades que conformamos la Plataforma Trabajo Sexual y Convivència denunciamos*, 2006; "La mitad de las multas de la ordenanza cívica se imponen por pintadas y por beber en la calle," *El País*, 18/02/2006.
8 Ley Orgánica 4/2015, 30/03/2015 de protección de la seguridad ciudadana.
9 I consider "transnational family" as a domestic nucleus whose members live in, at least, two different national states. A transnational head of the family refers to, in this case, a family in which the mother lives and works abroad whereas some or all of the other members of the family that depend on her remain at home (Parreñas 2001: 361).

References

Bacelar, Jeferson Afonso. 1982. *A família da prostituta*. São Paulo: Editora Ática, 1982.
Ballester, L., Orte, C., and Oliver, J.L. 2013. La casi-prostitución como consecuencia de la crisis para mujeres jóvenes en situaciones de grave precariedad. En S. Torio, O. García-Pérez, J.V. Peña, and M.C. Fernández (Eds.), *Crisis social y el estado del bienestar: las respuestas desde la pedagogia social*, 222–227. Oviedo: Universidad de Oviedo.
Bernstein, Elizabeth. 2007. *Temporarily yours: Intimacy, authenticity, and the commerce of sex*. Chicago: University of Chicago Press.
Bernstein, Elizabeth. 2014. Introduction: Sexual economies and new regimes of governance. *Social Politics: International Studies in Gender, State & Society* 21(3): 345–354.
Brennan, Denise. 2004. *What's love got to do with it? Transnational desires and sex tourism in the Dominican Republic*. Durham: Duke University Press.
Cabezas, Amalia. 2009. *Economies of desire: Sex and tourism in Cuba and the Dominican Republic*. Philadelphia: Temple University Press.
Cáritas. 2016. *La prostitución desde la experiencia y la Mirada de Cáritas*. Madrid: Cáritas Española Editores.
Cheng, Sealing. 2010. *On the move for love: Migrant entertainers and the U.S. military in South Korea*. Philadelphia: University of Pennsylvania Press.

Cole, Jennifer. 2014. Producing value among Malagasy Marriage migrants in France: Managing horizons of expectation. *Current Anthropology*, 55(9): S85.

Cole, Jennifer and Thomas, Lynn. 2009. *Love in Africa*. Chicago: University of Chicago Press.

Fonseca, Claudia. 2004. A morte de um gigolô: fronteiras da transgressão e sexualidade nos dias atuais. In Adriana Piscitelli, Maria Filomena Gregori, and Sérgio Carrar (Eds.), *Sexualidade e Saberes: Convenções e Fronteiras*, 257–281. Rio de Janeiro: Garamond.

França, Marina Veiga. 2011. Dentro e fora do programa: interações afetivo-sexuais de prostitutas da zona boêmia de Belo Horizonte. Paper presented at the 35º Encontro Anual da ANPOCS, Caxambu-MG.

Groes-Green Christian. 2013. "To put men in a bottle": Eroticism, kinship, female power, and transactional sex in Maputo, Mozambique. *American Ethnologist* 40(1): 102–117.

Groes-Green Christian. 2014. Journeys of patronage: Moral economies of transactional sex, kinship, and female migration from Mozambique to Europe. *Journal of the Royal Anthropological Institute* 20: 237–255.

hooks, Bell. 2000. *All about love: New visions*. New York: William Morrow.

Hunter, Mark. 2010, *Love in the time of Aids: Inequality, gender and rights in South Africa*, Bloomington: Indiana University Press.

Illouz, Eva. 2007. *Consuming the romantic utopia, love and the cultural contradictions of capitalism*. Berkeley: University of California Press.

Kempadoo, Kamala. 2004. *Sexing the Caribbean: Gender, race and sexual labour*. Abingdon: Routledge.

López-Riopedre, J. 2013. Trabajo sexual transnacional: consecuencias de las políticas criminalizantes de la prostitución y de la crisis económica española sobre las trabajadoras sexuales migrantes. Paper presented at the XI Congreso Español de Sociología. Madrid.

Maia, Suzana. 2011. Cosmopolitismo, desejo e afetos: sobre mulheres brasileiras e os seus amigos transnacionais. In Adriana Piscitelli, Glaucia de Oliveira Assis, and José Miguel Nieto Olivar (Eds.), *Gênero, sexo, amor e dinheiro: mobilidades transnacionais envolvendo o Brasil*, 363–385. Campinas: Unicamp.

Marcus, George. 1995. Ethnography in/of the world system: The emergence of multi-sited ethnography. *Annual Review of Anthropology* 24: 95–117.

Martinez, Francisco Majuelos. 2016. Dinámicas de movilidad de las trabajadores sexuales como estrategias ante la crisis. Una aproximación desde la etnografia. *Revista internacional de estudios migratorios*, 6–2: 170–190.

Médicos del Mundo. *Programas para personas en situación de prostitución. Memória 2011*. www.medicosdelmundo.es/memorias/2011/nuestra-intervencion/inclusion-social/prostitucion/.

Mitchell, Gregory. 2011. Padrinhos gringos: turismo sexual, parentesco queer e as famílias do futuro In Adriana Piscitelli, Glaucia de Oliveira Assis, and José Miguel Nieto Olivar (Eds.), *Gênero, sexo, amor e dinheiro: mobilidades transnacionais envolvendo o Brasil*, 31–57. Campinas: Unicamp.

Narotsky, Susana and Besnier, Niko. 2014. Crisis, value, and hope: Rethinking the economy: An introduction to supplement. *Current Anthropology* 55(9): S4.

Olivar, José Miguel Nieto. 2013. *Devir puta: políticas da prostituição na experiências de quatro mulheres militantes*. Rio de Janeiro: Eduerj.

Parreñas, Rhacel Salazar. 2001. Mothering from a distance: Emotions, gender, and intergenerational relations in Filipino transnational families. *Feminist Studies* 2(2): 361–390.

Piscitelli, Adriana. 2007. Shifting boundaries: Sex and money in the northeast of Brazil, *Sexualities* 10(4): 489–500.

Piscitelli, Adriana. 2014. Violências e afetos: intercâmbios sexuais e econômicos na (recente) produção antropológica realizada no Brasil. *Cadernos Pagu* 42: 159–199. https://dx.doi.org/10.1590/0104-83 33201400420159.

Piscitelli, Adriana. Forthcoming. From *programas* to help and marriage: Sexual, economic and affective exchanges among Brazilian women in Fortaleza, Brazil and southern Europe. In Christian Groess Gren and Nadine Fernandes, *Intimate mobilities: Sexual economies, marriage and migration*. Berghahn Books.

Tavory Iddo and Poulin Michelle. 2012. Sex work and the construction of intimacies: Meanings and work pragmatics in rural Malawi. *Theory and Society* 41(3): 211–231.

Teixeira, Flávia do Bonsucesso. 2008. L'Italia dei Divieti: entre o sonho de ser *européia* e o *babado* da prostituição. *Cadernos Pagu* 31: 275–308.

Teixeira, Flávia do Bonsucesso. 2011. Juízo e Sorte: enredando maridos e clientes nas narrativas sobre o projeto migratório das travestis brasileiras para a Itália. In Adriana Piscitelli, Glaucia de Oliveira Assis, and José Miguel Nieto Olivar (Eds.), *Gênero, sexo, amor e dinheiro: mobilidades transnacionais envolvendo o Brasil*, 225–262. Campinas: Unicamp.

Zelizer, Viviana. 2005. *The purchase of intimacy*. Princeton: Princeton University Press.

28

Money talks?

Secrecy and money management in the family affective bonds of women who perform sex commerce in Argentina

Santiago Morcillo

Introduction

Research and public discourses on prostitution usually spotlight life in the sex market, while prostitutes' family and affective relationships remain in the shadows. Family, even with its historical transformations, has been in charge of controlling and administering domesticity, sexualities, and finances (Jelin 1995), making family bonds a key dimension to consider in the discourses of women who engage in sex commerce. Secrecy emerges as a key feature in the complex family ties of these women, who are in a position that is marked both by the displacement of their legitimized roles in the family and by the "whore stigma" (Pheterson 2000). In this chapter I use the tension stemming from secrecy and its links with money, gender, and kinship to analyze sex workers' family and affective relationships focusing on its micropolitical dimensions.[1]

Secrecy expresses social relations and therefore constitutes a vector for sociological analysis that is just as important as analyses of open communication. Georg Simmel (1906) had already raised this point. His approach links economies of money and secrecy, since both are related to the social transformations brought on by modernity, namely increased individual autonomy accompanied by impersonal relations that require greater trust. In such transformations, transparency had a democratizing effect, accordingly to Simmel, who nonetheless recommended that some aspects of marriage should remain private to avoid routinization and thus maintain continued sexual attraction between marriage partners. He also warned that romantic or erotic bonds conspire against secrecy and invite couples to abandon all privacy, and speculated (but did not explain why) that women are more inclined to do so than men. Also family secrets have typically been studied from a psychological perspective (Brown-Smith 1998; Orgad 2015). These investigations have highlighted the prominence of sexual secrets in the family and the role of secrets in sustaining family ideals, which in this case are linked to gender roles.

Gender and sexuality studies illuminate more clearly how these secrets generate power relations, as what we reveal and what we withhold are sites of negotiation, integral to the ways in which we inhabit the social world . . . to have no capacity for secrecy is to lose control over how others see you—it leaves one open to coercion.

(Hardon and Posel 2012, 4)

On the one hand, those who share a secret (or a "closet") can develop a bond—particularly outside family—and even a common perspective (Sedgwick 1990), while on the other hand, sexual gossip can be a form of control, especially among relatives and in small cities or rural areas (see for example Jones 2010). In addition to its symbolic and psycho-affective dimension, there is a political economy of secrecy that is crucial for stigmatized subjects, including sex workers, to maintain. Silence can be a tool of oppression as well as a strategic response to oppression. Paying attention to oppressive contexts, the costs of speaking out, and gradual transformations in power asymmetries are key aspects for understanding the meanings of silences (Gill and Ryan-Flood 2009; Parpart and Kabeer 2010).

In order to analyze sex workers' family relationships and the role of secrecy within them, it is critical to challenge the dichotomy between silence and voice, and to conceptualize the circulation of information in a more nuanced way. Zempleni (1976) conceptualized in three forms the tension and separation between who owns the secret and from whom it is hidden (its "recipient"): revelation, communication, and secretion. Revelation implies a sudden relief of the tension, which cancels the separation and therefore the secret. Communication, instead of abolishing separation, preserves secrecy but alleviates its tension. Unlike revelation, secrecy is communicated to chosen confidantes—friends, intimates, peers—who become "depositaries." What is interesting, according to Zempleni, is that, contrary to belief, the social proximity of the depositaries and the recipients is (in many cases) one of the common conditions of the communication of secrets. Finally, secretion is the most common form of regulation and preservation of secrecy tension and constitutes its "most remarkable and paradoxical property" (Zempleni, quoted in Pecheny 2003, 138–139). The secret seems to be unable to subsist as such without showing itself in some way to its recipients, through fragments or signs.

Secrecy is a key issue to understanding experiences of women who perform commercial sex because it marks their daily lives and is their main tactic for avoiding stigmatization. I have addressed elsewhere the potential and limitations that secrecy and the tactic of covering/splitting— through performance of an alternative identity or character, who often has a different name—hold for sex workers' relationships and political organization (Morcillo 2014, 2017). Here I focus on relationships that exist outside the "scene," namely outside the sex market. Through the lens of secrecy, I approach different dimensions of affective bonds: ties with family and friends, the role of money, relationships within a couple, and vis-à-vis children. My main argument is that the three forms in which the tension of secrecy circulates—secretion, revelation, and communication—are regulated by and through three factors: monetary exchanges, gender relations, and kinship relations.

The analysis presented here is based on fieldwork carried out over a period of four years, from 2008 to 2012. Fieldwork comprised interviews and observation in different modalities or strata of sexual commerce, including streets, cabarets, flats, and escorts. Participants were women between the ages of 21 and 53 who had varying degrees of contact with abolitionist or sex worker rights organizations, both of which I included in my study. Conducting fieldwork in Buenos Aires, Rosario, and San Juan, three Argentine cities of different size and dissimilar characteristics, highlighted different realities for sex workers with respect to visibility or possibility of anonymity, socio-cultural norms, sexual morality, and the presence of sex workers' organizations.

All in the family: sex and silence

Examination of sex commerce's complex impacts on family bonds shows tensions between what is known and what can be spoken, as Marisol,[2] a 45-year-old sex worker from Rosario, explained:

> All my family knows [. . .] they knew it, they've always known it because I helped out with expenses at home, and went out at night until dawn. Now, because I'm older and I speak out without shame, I tell them what I feel, but when I was younger and I wanted to talk about it, only a few people listened to me. When I was distressed, when I had problems, my comrades were there on the corner, I could not tell my family.

Discrimination and the potential reactions of interlocutors may make talking about sex commerce difficult, but this also depends on the type of bond that the person has with their interlocutor. Marisol initially felt too ashamed to talk with her family and only communicated with other sex workers who she felt could understand her. Most interviewees viewed relatives simultaneously as interlocutors to elude with respect to discussions of sex work and as persons in front of whom it was more difficult to hide their secret. While it is not always easy to communicate this secret to friends, many interviewees found that it was simpler than talking to their families. Friends were viewed as more empathic listeners because the women regarded them as more open-minded toward sexuality and holding less rigid gender role expectations than their relatives. Friendships may allow a partial recovery of the support network, and associated social capital, that can disappear or be eclipsed within the family.

Another factor that marks communications is the gender of interlocutors.[3] As sex work is a sexualized secret, patriarchal bias became evident in interviewees' perceptions of communication with men as riskier or more difficult, especially with male relatives. If trustworthy friends were not within reach, sisters, female cousins, or even mothers could be depositaries, but brothers, fathers, or sons stirred the greatest fears of revelation. Nelly, 43 and engaged in commercial sex in Buenos Aires, commented:

> I would tell my mother that I had been working in a bar, cleaning glasses until late, but I couldn't fool her, she didn't believe it. I figured that out two days before she died. She never said anything during five months of agony, but two days before she died, she said, "Do you know what I'm hearing from neighbors?" "What?" I said, and she said, "No, that you work . . . eh . . . as . . ." [silence].

Information linked to the "scene" can remain completely hidden from the families of women who have not been on the sex market for a long time. As women spent more time on the sex market, however, the resulting tension begins to generate leaks, as it did for Nelly. Secretions could begin with absences from home, a space normatively assigned by families to women. A nocturnal work schedule prompts some women, such as Nelly, to pretend to work in a less-stigmatized entertainment venue, such as a bar. Having more money can also be a cause of leaks. Women who had been working for several years said that their families all knew about their sex trade involvement, even if they had not told them about it. Marisol assumed that her family always knew because she "helped out with expenses at home." Abril, 24, assumed that her family and friends in San Juan knew because: "money doesn't appear magically. I think there are people who must figure it out but don't want to know specifically, then you do not talk." When information is filtered through money, this usually generates a greater silence, because there is something that is intuited and denied at the same time.

How much does it cost to keep a secret?

Money establishes silences within the family when it is received as "*ayuda*" (assistance). Yet if money is not shared with family members, money often sparks questions, moral condemnation, and, in the case of the in-laws, envy and resentment. This occurred in the case of Irene, a 49-year-old who entered the trade after her husband's death in Buenos Aires, on the occasion of her daughter's fifteenth birthday party. This celebration entailed a significant expense for Irene, along with the sacrifice of a central project: finishing the construction of her house. Yet, on the day that her daughter "became a woman" according to dominant Latin American cultural norms, Irene's maternal sacrifice was challenged by the relatives who did not receive financial assistance from her. These relatives, specifically those from her deceased husband's side of the family, used the whore stigma to question the sanctity of the money spent on the party. Consider how Irene's account of the event crystallizes symbolic and material positions around money, gender, and kinship:

> Well, [doing sex work] cost me a lot because it was a way to help my family, my brothers . . . not because they forced me, but I felt the need to help them because it is a way of escape for me, to say . . . like justifying . . . until today, they never asked me what my work is . . . I never asked them for anything, never, not my family, or the family of . . . my daughters [in-laws] or uncles, or grandparents. They did question me a lot and said many things about me, like, for example, that I was a prostitute. A whore. They didn't use the word "prostitute," but they said "a whore: . . . they questioned, but they never helped me at all. Later, when my youngest daughter turned 15, she told me: "Mom, I'm going to invite my grandparents and my uncles." And I don't even want to see those people, but hey, it's her blood. Her decision was respected. They came. All of them. I thought they were not coming, but they came. I felt . . . I was very nervous because, well, I wanted the party, for everything, to go well. Well, everything went well. But even so, one of them came out saying . . . "She must have sold out [lowering her voice] her pussy to pay for this party."

When money is given as "*ayuda*," even parents and siblings can turn a blind eye, but that does not constitute an affirmative "coming out of the closet." The meanings of money can vary across relationships and according to the forms in which it is delivered (Zelizer 2008). Adriana Piscitelli (2011, 13) argues that "*ayuda*" can be understood, in a broad sense, as "exchanges, generally asymmetrical, involving money and/or other benefits and that tend to create obligations and often affective bonds." Interviewees' testimonies reveal a tension between how money is delivered (as "*ayuda*") and its symbolic devaluation as "dirty money," as it is morally and even legally questionable since the current legal frame defines those who benefit from this money as exploitative third parties.[4] This "dirty money" is difficult to recount, both in the sense of talking about it and accounting for it[5] because it functions as "*ayuda*" but also as the payment of a tribute towards families in compensation for the rupture of gender expectations.[6] María, age 30, was raised in a conservative family in San Juan, yet her parents did not complain about her behavior:

> In this world if you have money, you have a lot of friends, always. Even your family accepts everything. For money they accept that you use coke, you come home fucked up, a lot of things that they wouldn't put up with if you didn't have money. Then, as you sometimes pay for "jewels" or other things, they accept, you see? It's depressing for me, it's like I've already accepted it, but sometimes I have been shocked by my own family.

In "open secret" mode, the origin of the money is silenced. This silence may lessen tension among family members but does not grant recognition for women and a negative assessment tacitly persists. Thus, secrecy often exacts strong emotional and economic costs to prostitutes because it forecloses any discussion of hegemonic moral judgments and sets up a relationship fraught with hypocrisy. Even when helping was a source of pride, such pride is compromised when the origin of the money cannot be disclosed. This was the case for 46-year-old Carina, who was moved to tears in remembering how she helped her parents out of poverty by sending them money from Buenos Aires.

Unexpected revelation can also turn into silence about sex commerce. The sudden release of the tension associated with secrecy can generate a quick chain reaction, but this explosion does not create a space for dialogue. Daniela was 26 and had just begun to do sex commerce in San Juan when her coworkers "outed" her by informing her husband who, in turn, told her family. After this episode, the whole family knew about her work, but they never talk about it. She said, "it's like . . . they know and don't know . . . it's like they do and don't want to ask me at the same time . . . nobody talks about that."

Pillow talk?

The tensions associated with secrecy were more unstable within couple bonds, which were in almost all cases heterosexual. Couple relationships were seen as difficult and many interviewees said that it was impossible to sustain an intimate relationship while working in the sex market. Covering tactics can become an obstacle in building shared intimacy because they collide with romantic feelings of amorous fusion and the desire to share everything with one another. When Sabrina, who was 21 and from Buenos Aires, was in love with a man, she experienced all of these contradictions:

> I supposed he didn't lie to me at all. Then I felt bad . . . Because he would say to me, "Oh, I love you," and all these things . . . And I thought "No, I'm lying. What if I tell him?" Sometimes I wanted to say "Look, this is what I do this" But I thought, "If I ever told him, he would kill me."

The interviewees regarded disclosure of sex work involvement to their partners as an intractable problem, with the very idea that these partners could find out raising great concern. In turn, the stigmatizing content of this secret hindered the supposedly positive functions that Simmel (1906) ascribed to privacy within the couple, and the risk was being labeled as "whore." Fear of introducing stigma in the couple's intimate environment leads women to act with caution, both in the handling of information and in the selection of intimate partnerships. The widespread but transgressed rule forbidding falling in love with clients aims in part to maintain some control of information and avoid being judged and/or surveilled by boyfriends or husbands. Even if this information is not used to stigmatize, communication does not solve the problem because it is still difficult to know what to tell, how far to go, and how to prevent their partners from becoming overcome with jealousy. The fact that many male intimate partners can't understand sex commerce as work and feel threatened by losing monopoly on their female partner's sexuality, adds to the reasons for secrecy.

Some women "paid for" secrecy within a couple by undertaking additional domestic responsibilities, for example, housework. Nelly balanced her relative independence and autonomous schedules by being obliging at home:

> I have always had a . . . strong personality, I do what I want, I don't take orders, you don't ask me at what time I leave, at what time I come home, if you have your house, your food cooked, your clothes clean, all on time.

Yet unlike other family ties, using money to maintain silence in a couple proved unbearable for most interviewees. That dynamic carried the risk of supporting a husband who became a sort of "pimp." Some interviewees, mostly those over 40, had previously been in this type of relationship and ended up emancipating themselves from it as they got older and developed more experience.[7] Beatriz, 51 and from Buenos Aires, said that while she had never enjoyed doing sex commerce, doing so allowed her to eventually gain independence by abandoning her husband-pimp and then handling her own money:

> I felt different, I could buy what I wanted, I could enjoy myself, manage money by myself, buy things for my daughter, go out and have a good time, be with my family. You see? It's very different to be able to manage your money, not having to ask anyone, "I need a pair of pants" or "I want a pair of pants."

Beatriz described this change to handling her own money as "no longer being a little girl" who was infantilized by her husband. Gender role transformations with respect to responsibilities for money management within the couple provides some women who perform sex commerce with an opportunity to question some patriarchal structures. Yet such repositioning appears to be much more difficult in relationships with their children.

(Ab)negation and guilt: all for them (but secretly)

When asked if she worked for a third party, 38-year-old Juana from San Juan first responded negatively before adding, with laughter that she had a "pimp that is 18 months old, because diapers, milk." in reference to her infant. María likewise described her desire to "invest in my son—giving him love, affection, money, whatever—but not in a husband."

For all the interviewees who were mothers, children were the most feared recipients of the secret, and revelation in front of them was their worst nightmare. Within the mother–child relationship, money management appeared as diametrically opposed to that described for couples, as María explained. Spending money on children was seen as good and unproblematic, allowing Juana to joke about her son being her pimp. We can analyze how women in sex commerce relate with their children by considering how they manage the money they earn: how much, and where, do they spend their earnings on their children?

Mothers who cater to their children's whims are quite common, yet this dynamic took on particular characteristics in interviewees. Almost all those who had children said, without regrets, that they bought their children all kinds of things, with many women proudly declaring their luxury spending. Deby, age 21, had not completed primary school and worked the streets near San Juan's bus terminal, told me she lavishly spent much of her income on her son. "He can't wear fakes," she said, so she purchased him costly imported athletic shoes and even traveled to other cities or placed orders from Buenos Aires to get him more exclusive models. This type of consumer spending sharply contrasted with the women's socio-economic position, as exemplified by 36-year-old Valeria, who lived in a Buenos Aires informal housing settlement: "I dressed my oldest son in the best clothes. He never had cheap shoes, always the most expensive. And had a computer, had Internet, had everything, in my complete house, in the *casilla* [shanty]."

Financially supporting children can delay women's decision to leave the sex industry. Irene aimed to leave the sex market once she had finished building her house but, as mentioned above, when she was about to finish she had to choose between that and celebrating her daughter's fifteenth birthday. She chose the latter for her daughter's sake because "her happiness was the *quince*. And, so, I chose to give her the birthday party." Although 49-year-old Susy from Buenos Aires already had a house and a widow's pension she said she was unable to exit the sex market because she felt obligated to keep working to buy things for her adult children:

> I earn so little with the pension . . . [slight laughter] I don't retire because always . . . You always have family . . . you want to help. Because you get used to always producing, to producing for others . . . For example, now I'm older and I have a small pension . . . But . . . you get used to, with the children . . . giving them things to make them happy . . . you can't quit doing that, you must always give them things. Because you feel happy . . . and make others happy. So . . . it's a reward for . . . for oneself.

In endless gifts to children, luxury expenses, overprotection, and the everlasting need to "produce for others," some sex workers obtain the "reward for oneself" that Susy mentions. The circular dynamic of gift-giving may derive from feelings of guilt. María explicitly said that every time she bought something for herself she also bought something for her daughter so as not to feel guilty. This guilt appeared most strongly in those who had internalized the most stigmatized conceptions of prostitution as dirty, immoral, or anti-social behavior. By framing consumption as a contemporary ritual (Douglas and Isherwood 1990; Garcia Canclini 1995) these expenditures can be understood as a sophisticated ritual of purification whereby "dirty money" can be cleansed by becoming gifts for children. Since this purification ritual is linked to consumption, moral condemnation itself leads women who have children to continue doing sex commerce "for them." Only one respondent consciously opposed this pattern: 25-year-old Luli, who earned more than her Buenos Aires counterparts yet limited her spending on gifts and only gave her son rewards in exchange for completing household tasks. She tried to prepare for her retirement because "I'm not always going to earn the same money . . . I can't let him get used to it."

Relationships with children were not exclusively centered on this dynamic of guilty consumption. Education was another frequently declared expense associated with children, and linked to a wish for upward social mobility, as others researchers have also found in Latin America (Rivers-Moore 2010). Caring for children in general was often mentioned, as it serves both as a way to neutralize stigma and as a motivation for much of the interviewees' actions ("I do it for my children"). But this care was also often associated with keeping it secret from children. Within family care bonds, the fear of disclosure meant that the need to protect secrecy from children became a priority and interviewees' mothers became privileged depositaries of communications. The feminization of care work and frequently absent fathers made grandmothers into caregivers for children while their daughters worked. Just as some colleagues helped with alibis in front of children, grandmothers also collaborated with cover-ups. Nelly's daughter Sabrina recalled her grandmother's complicity with her mother: "I asked my grandmother, 'Why isn't my mother coming?' and she would say, 'No, she still washing glasses' because she said she worked as a dishwasher in a restaurant." Gender solidarity and maternal bonds allow for communication of the secret under the broader crucial mission of hiding it from children or grandchildren.

The mere idea of having to disclose their secret to their children (especially their sons) was frightening to most interviewees. Only a few of them had thought of this, especially those participating in the sex workers' organization Asociación de Mujeres Meretrices de Argentina (Association of Harlot Women of Argentina, AMMAR), where dialogue and reflection among peers began to deconstruct stigmatizing discourses. Ursula, 42 years old and from San Juan, described her anticipation of this disclosure as "asking for forgiveness" from her children and as a way for them to understand her and know how to combat discrimination, yet she still had to prepare herself:

> asking my children for forgiveness . . . though I gave them education so that tomorrow they can be somebody . . . without anyone reproaching them anything. With them I would have to try a good . . . like a speech to give them, someday.

For many interviewees, the years of concealment from their children became a heavy burden that is difficult both to carry and to put down. The weight of this burden is linked to the emotional work (Hochschild 2008) of maintaining concealment in a bond so charged with affection. Doris, after years of activism with other sex workers in AMMAR, gathered enough courage to get rid of that burden, prompting her colleagues to comment in surprise: "I don't know how she did it!" She thought she was going to lose her children, but received silent acceptance from her son and some understanding and appreciation from her daughter.

Yet most of the interviewees found it impossible to talk to their children about their secret. This fear sometimes stemmed from their own appraisal of sex commerce, or how they imagined the children's reaction. According to María, "children are always their parents' judges," with the children's gaze representing negative social views and moral judgments. Since supporting and providing well-being for their children is often the reason women invoke for doing sex commerce, children's judgment is also the most feared. Although many of these women may put aside some moral conceptions, the pervasive cultural ideals regarding women's sexuality that marks them as impure women seeps in through their children. The effects of this are doubly difficult to bear because the children themselves seem to question—albeit typically only in imagined fears regarding revelation—the women's appeal to their motherhood to justify their actions and neutralize stigma, as noted by 39-year-old Pia from Buenos Aires:

> I'm ashamed to say to my children: "Yes, your mom was working the streets to support you." I wish I had a better job . . . but it doesn't happen . . . I could do . . . better than this. Obviously, with my work, my children don't lack anything. They live like kings . . . But I'd like something else . . . like studying, because I have the chance to study . . . and . . . graduate at something, well, I'll think about myself then, now I can't. My children come first.

Pia's narrative alluded to how a mechanism of circular persecution sets in where children embody, first, the reason why women begin to do sex commerce and keep it secret; then, the fear of revelation, the stigmatization that places women at the crossroads between communicating their secret or quitting; and, when they do not solve this tension, because they do not find alternative work to support the children's living standard (fundamentally, their education), then finally, for them, the decision to continue doing sex commerce. Whether this decision would be accompanied by a "coming out" to children depends not only on tactical or emotional needs—as may happen with parents—but also on a subjective repositioning and deconstructing of stigmatizing discourses, whether condemnatory or victimizing.

Concluding thoughts

In analyzing the affective relationships maintained by sex workers outside the sex industry, we have observed the key role of secrecy. The stigmatization and clandestine conditions of sex commerce make the management of information crucial in these relationships and especially within the family. Adverse conditions for stigmatized subaltern subjects mean that their success in hiding their secret is very irregular over time, which generates ways of coping with affective and family bonds. By adopting a more nuanced approach towards secrecy, we have seen how the regulation between revelation, secretion, or communication is linked to three factors: gender, monetary exchanges, and kinship forms. Compared to the more fluid dynamic at work with friends, both covering and communication prove to be more difficult within the family. Keeping involvement in the sex market hidden is related not only to norms governing sexuality but also to income. Money, an issue as intimate as sexuality, is the main means of filtering and silently translating that aspect of the women's sexualities that the family cannot bear to speak about. Secretion expresses the tension between the positive valuation of monetary "*ayudas*" that women provide to their families and the silence about the origin of that money, which is "dirty" and difficult to (re)count.

The functioning of this mechanism is more difficult in couple relationships. As marriage is a sex-economic arrangement, it is difficult to combine it with the sale of sex. On the one hand, the romantic framework makes it difficult to maintain concealment. Here, the secret of prostitution sheds light on other sex-economic relationships because, if secrecy is a mode of visibility, prostitution's counterpart is the monogamy-romantic-love complex that operates as a regime of regulatory visibility. On the other hand, a pragmatic view indicates the risk of ending up as the sole breadwinner. Not having a pimp-husband or abandoning him generates a crack in the patriarchal traditions that structure kinship and sex-economic relationships—perhaps more forcefully than if the sex commerce were done secretly.

Marriage as a sexual-economic bond seems in opposition to maternal, asexual, and disinterested love. The covering tactic is more deeply disturbed by the interpellation of the filial gaze than in other relationships. When it is possible to communicate the secret within the family, other women are preferred and men dismissed, especially sons.

Often the main depositaries will be the women's mothers, who have the crucial mission of collaborating to avoid revelation in front of the most dreaded recipients. Relationships with children appear overloaded with contradictory meanings. On the one hand, a "gift-giving" dynamic functions as a purifying ritual consuming important sums of "dirty money." On the other hand, various forms of care constitute attempts to keep children segregated from the secret.

Maternal relationships also expose the difficulties for sustaining both material and symbolic reproduction, where the second squanders the resources of the first. Secrecy tries to mitigate these effects, but as we saw, it can be a double-edged sword. The stigmatization that motivates secrecy launches a perverse mechanism that situates the main source of guilt and worst fears in the eyes of the children, who are the most beloved and the main form of symbolic legitimation. While motherhood represent the best "moral shield" in the eyes of those who know the secret, staying "in the closet" makes motherhood challenging and enables the whore stigma women to be felt from the gaze of their own children.

Analyzing these dynamics allows us to see that conflicts and confrontations are not confined to the sex market, as they also arise within the family home—a fact often overlooked in the criticisms of some neo-abolitionist feminisms. Secrecy in the family is a precarious form of protection that does not allow for the deactivation of stigmatization as a mechanism for the reproduction of asymmetries. Lower-class women, with less material and symbolic capital, end up paying the emotional, social, and economic costs of such arrangements. In this oppressive context, processes of stigma deconstruction undertaken by women who organize themselves as sex workers open up questions about the scope, and possibilities, for their experiences of empowerment.

Notes

1 This chapter was reworked from an earlier version: "Las joyas de la familia. Secretos, género y dineros en los vínculos afectivo familiares de mujeres que hacen comercio sexual." *Apuntes de Investigación del CECYP*, 29, 48–67.
2 All names and identifiable elements have been replaced to protect anonymity. I am very grateful to all those interviewed for trusting me with their secret.
3 The interviewees did not mention transgender people.
4 Although prostitution in Argentina is not illegal, the exploitation of prostitution has been criminalized since 1921. In addition, as part of the current campaign against human trafficking, several changes have been made to the legal regulations, expanding the spectrum of cases that can be considered as "trafficking" (Varela 2015).
5 Several interviewees commented that they found it difficult to keep track of how much they earned, some even felt too disgusted to count that money. Accounting problems seem to be frequent for sex workers (Weldon 2010).
6 This hypothesis is also suggested to understand how migrant *travestis* help their relatives, which does not always guarantee them a place to return home (see Goulart in Piscitelli, Oliveira Assis, and Olivar, 2011).
7 It is interesting to contrast with forms of prostitution where the family framework husband/pimp/wife/ prostitute functions as a productive unit. José Miguel Nieto Olivar (2013) has analyzed this type of prostitution, frequent in the 1980s in Porto Alegre (Brazil), as a form of "familiar predation."

References

Brown-Smith, Naima. 1998. "Family secrets." *Journal of Family Issues* 19 (1): 20–42. doi:10.1177/019251398019001003.
Douglas, Mary, and Baron Isherwood. 1990. *El mundo de los bienes: Hacia una antropología del consumo*. México: Grijalbo-CNCA.
Garcia Canclini, Nestor. 1995. "El consumo sirve para pensar." In *Consumidores y ciudadanos: Conflictos multiculturales de la globalización*, 41–55. México: Grijalbo.
Gill, Rosalind, and Róisín Ryan-Flood. 2009. *Secrecy and silence in the research process: Feminist reflections*. New York: Routledge.
Hardon, Anita, and Deborah Posel. 2012. "Secrecy as embodied practice: Beyond the confessional imperative." *Culture, Health & Sexuality* 14 (suppl. 1): S1–S13. doi: 10.1080/13691058.2012.726376.
Hochschild, Arlie Russell. 2008. *La Mercantilización de la vida Íntima: apuntes de la casa y el trabajo*. Buenos Aires; Madrid: Katz.
Jelin, Elizabeth. 1995. "Familia y género: Notas para el debate." *Estudos Feministas* 3 (2): 394–413.
Jones, Daniel. 2010. *Sexualidades adolescentes. Amor, placer y control en la Argentina contemporánea*. Buenos Aires: CICCUS/CLACSO.
Morcillo, Santiago. 2014. "'Como un trabajo.' Tensiones entre sentidos de lo laboral y la sexualidad en mujeres que hacen sexo comercial en Argentina." *Sexualidad, Salud y Sociedad (Rio de Janeiro)* 18: 12–40. doi: http://dx.doi.org/10.1590/1984-6487.sess.2014.18.04.a.
Morcillo, Santiago. 2017. "Mujeres invisibles: Políticas del ocultamiento entre mujeres que hacen sexo comercial." *Trabajo y sociedad* (en prensa).
Olivar, José Miguel Nieto. 2013. *Devir puta: políticas da prostituição na experiências de quatro mulheres militantes*. Rio de Janeiro: EDUERJ.
Orgad, Yariv. 2015. "The culture of family secrets." *Culture & Psychology* 21 (1): 59–80. doi: doi:10.1177/1354067X15568979.
Parpart, Jane L., and Naila Kabeer. 2010. *Choosing silence: Rethinking voice, agency, and women's empowerment*. East Lansing, MI: Michigan State University. Center for Gender in Global Context. Gender, Development, and Globalization Program.
Pecheny, Mario. 2003. "Identidades discretas." In *Identidades, sujetos y subjetividades: Narrativas de la diferencia*, edited by Leonor Arfuch, 15–30. Buenos Aires: Prometeo.
Pheterson, Gail. 2000. *El prisma de la prostitución, Hablan las mujeres, 19*. Madrid: Talasa Ediciones.
Piscitelli, Adriana, Glaucia de Oliveira Assis, and José Miguel Nieto Olivar. 2011. *Gênero, sexo, amor e dinheiro: Mobilidades transnacionais envolvendo o Brasil*. Campinas, SP: Unicamp/PAGU.

Rivers-Moore, Megan. 2010. "But the kids are okay: Motherhood, consumption and sex work in neo-liberal Latin America." *British Journal of Sociology* 61 (4): 716–736. doi: 10.1111/j.1468-4446.2010.01338.x.

Sedgwick, Eve Kosofsky. 1990. *Epistemology of the closet*. Berkeley: University of California Press.

Simmel, Georg. 1906. "The sociology of secrecy and of secret societies." *American Journal of Sociology* 11 (4): 441–498.

Varela, Cecilia. 2015. "La campaña anti-trata en la Argentina y la agenda supranacional." In *Género y violencia en el mercado del sexo: Política, policía y prostitución*, edited by D. Daich and M. Sirimarco. Buenos Aires: Biblos.

Weldon, Jo. 2010. "Show me the money: A sex worker reflects on research into the sex industry." In *Sex work matters: Exploring money, power, and intimacy in the sex industry*, edited by Melissa Hope Ditmore, Antonia Levy, and Alys Willman, 26–38. London and New York: Zed Books.

Zelizer, Viviana A. 2008. "Pagos y lazos sociales." *Crítica en desarrollo* 2: 43–63.

Zempleni, Andras. 1976. "La chaîne du secret." *Nouvelle revue de psychanalyse* 14: 313–324.

29

The presence and absence of sex workers' mothering

Marlene Spanger

Introduction

In recent decades, dichotomous thinking has dominated research into sex for sale. When it comes to agency, for example, sex workers tend to be understood as either victims or empowered subjects (Spanger, 2010; Skilbrei and Spanger, 2018). In this chapter, I argue that the understanding of the intersection of motherhood and sex work is informed by this very logic of dichotomy. This means that the entanglement of familial, intimate relationships with the organisation of female sex work is often neglected in the literature of sex for sale. If the question of how mothering and the identities of motherhood relate to sex worker identities is rarely addressed, this is because mothering and sex work are understood as each other's opposites. Motherhood connotes ideal femininity, while sex work is often subject to shame.[1]

This logic is confirmed by studies (e.g. Ruenkaew, 2003; Brennan, 2004; Casas, 2017) that explore how migrants sell sexual services as a survival strategy to provide for their children and for the family they have left behind. Such studies articulate sex work as a means of survival, but they leave out other reasons for selling sex. I do not wish to reject this highly relevant focus on engagement into sex work to support children and dependants. However, these approaches do not transcend the dichotomy previously outlined, and thus preclude new ways of understanding how sex workers relate their selling sex to other crucial dimensions of their everyday lives such as marriage, motherhood, etc. Other sex work studies that focus on the engagement of social service providers with sex workers engage with the entanglement of mothering and sex work. These studies examine the negotiation of ideal mothering between sex workers and social service providers, reflecting, for instance, on how the state or NGOs try to control or guide female sex sellers and how they should perform mothering (Spanger, 2012; Bjønness, 2015; Brown et al., 2018). Taking a slightly different direction, this chapter addresses the different ways in which single mothering, migration and sex work intersect.

Drawing on an earlier ethnographic study,[2] I ground my analysis in two stories of female Thai migrants selling sex and living in Denmark: Khem and Nee.[3] Khem is an absent mother whose two children are taken care of in Thailand by their grandmother and Khem's ex-husband. Nee is a mother who has brought her daughter to live with her in Denmark. The stories told by Khem and Nee reveal how sex work and motherhood interact to constitute different migratory trajectories. This chapter investigates the different ways in which mother-hood is framed when children are left behind and when a child is brought to the receiving society. The ways in which female Thai migrant sex workers do mothering and give familial care cannot exclusively be defined within what Nina Glick Schiller and Noel B. Salazar (2013) have termed a nation-state methodology. In other words, female Thai migrants who sell sex cannot be confined by the boundaries of the nation-state because they can participate simultaneously in local, national and transnational communities. I examine how female Thai migrants selling sex create local and transnational mothering through telephone calls, Skype, e-mails and financial remittances, thus maintaining social, emotional and economic relations with their children in either the sending society, Thailand, or in the receiving society, Denmark. In many cases, it is the mother who has sole responsibility for her children and their care. This includes Thai migrant single mothers selling sexual services in Denmark.[4] Inspired by the literature on transnational mothering (e.g. Avila and Hondagneu-Sotelo, 1997; Parreñas, 2001; Sørensen, 2002; Lutz and Palenga-Möllenbeck, 2009; Baldassar and Merla, 2014) and in particular by Madianou and Miller's (2012) and Baldassar's (2008) link between transnational mothering and technology, I pay special attention to how single mothering is re-organised in the process of migration and the organisation of sex for sale within Danish migration and prostitution regimes. Stressing the agency of female migrants in performing single mothering in ways that are constrained by the local sex work industry, a national migration regime and technological opportunities, I analyse the ways in which proximity and social cohesion are established in transnational families through different constellations of absence and presence intersecting, respectively, with virtual and physical space.

In what follows, the chapter briefly introduces the analytical framework of transnational mothering and transnational familial care. The Danish migration regime is then outlined. Two sections analyse the stories of Khem and Nee before the conclusion is presented.

Transnational mothering and familial care

Ernestine Avila and Pierrette Hondagneu-Sotelo (1997) introduce the concept of transnational motherhood in studying female labour migration from poor countries to rich countries. They show that strategies for mothering change in transnational families and that female migrants construct new definitions of good mothering in transforming mothering practices to stay in contact with their children. Rhacel Parreñas (2001) refines the concept of transnational motherhood, reminding us that the relationship between these mothers and their children is affected by the paradox that the financial security gained by migration often entails the emotional insecurity caused by the mother's absence.

A more recent branch of the literature investigates how different kinds of technologies establish multiple familial relations in a transnational setting (Baldassar, 2008; Lutz and Palenga-Möllenbeck, 2009; Madianou and Miller, 2012). In relating technologies to migration, Madianou and Miller (2012) break with globalised ideas about naturalised motherhood that derive from a normative and universal concept of biological motherhood performed in a situation of physical co-presence (of the mother living together with her child/children). They introduce the concept 'polymedia' as: 'a plurality of media which supplement each other and help overcome the shortcomings of a particular medium' (ibid.: 8). This concept describes an emerging environment of proliferating technological communicative opportunities in which families do not just stick to one medium (ibid.: 104). The new media are not just media for communication between family members – the media themselves carry meaning in a given situation (ibid.: 126).

For instance, family members interpret texting 50 times a day or expensive mobile phone calls as expressions of affection and love.

Taking this work as my starting point, my investigation looks at how the mothering practices of migrant sex workers are established in terms of closeness and intensity through different forms of care where there is limited physical face-to-face interaction – or none at all. Here, different constellations of temporality and geographical distance affect relations between migrants and children who have been left behind or brought along, in this case to Denmark. These relations are defined by *presence* or *absence*, which are not bound to distance but to the means of communication. In the case of these female migrants, I argue that the way in which their sex work is organised and the Danish migration regime combine to condition the way in which they give care to their children. This perspective allows new contours of family lives to emerge: while it also allows us to look at the lives of female migrants as contradictory and complex, it also recognises their agency. In this way it is possible to both capture the complexities and ambiguities of how sex work and mothering interact and to question the dichotomous approach to sex work and motherhood that permeates research into sex for sale.

The Danish migration and prostitution regimes

Fiona Williams (2011: 50) suggests that the definition of a regime points beyond policies, seeing a regime as a 'cluster of relevant policies as well as practices, discourses, social relations and forms of contestation'.[5] In this chapter, I only investigate the policies of migration and prostitution in a broad sense, including policies on family unification and anti-trafficking. I will briefly introduce the way in which these policies regulate the citizenship of female Thais in Denmark and how this relates to their sale of sex and to their parental obligations and rights. In addition, I briefly describe the organisation of their work.

Marrying a Danish male citizen is the only way for female Thai migrants to overcome the strict Danish migration policy on residence permits.[6] All of the migrants who figure in my empirical material have obtained a residence permit in this way. They establish contacts in Denmark, obtain jobs and/or are introduced to their future Danish husbands through informal networks. Some have children from former relationships in Thailand, others sometimes with the same man they married. As in the case of Nee, some migrants bring their children to Denmark. In some cases, the children return to Thailand after staying for a period of time. Other children remain in Thailand, as in the case of Khem.

The way in which the women are able to 'do' local and transnational motherhood depends not only on other family members, but also on how they organise their sex work. Their mothering practices are conditioned by migration and prostitution regimes. Compared to other European states, Denmark has one of the most restrictive policies on residence permits for non-EU citizens. For migrants from non-EU nation states who apply for a residence permit through marriage,[7] the Danish government stipulates a number of demands and obligations, such as age, the size of the residence, self-support of the married couple and language training (New to Denmark, 2017a). Since 2010, it has been possible to gain a permanent residence permit after five years of marriage to a Danish citizen. If the marriage breaks down before the five years have passed, the residence permit is automatically suspended and the migrant has to apply for a new permit (New to Denmark, 2017a).[8] According to the Danish legislation on family reunification, Thais have a right to bring along their children if they are under 15.[9] When children are granted a residence permit, they have the right to receive care in public crèches or kindergartens and the right to free education. In order to bring their children to Denmark, migrants and their Danish partners must meet a number of obligations.[10] Since 2007, minor adjustments of the criteria for applying for permanent residence permit have been introduced. However, the immigration regime remains strict. According to the Danish government (New to Denmark, 2017b), the social and economic obligations of the parent and the Danish partner are supposed to serve the child's best interest. The obligations encompass, for example, housing requirements (size of the residence) and that neither the migrant nor their partner is allowed to receive public assistance.[11]

The legislation regulating the sale of sex in Denmark is ambiguous, since persons over 18 years of age are not forbidden to sell or buy sexual services. Since the 1970s, the Danish authorities have perceived sex work as a social problem, and a number of social and health programmes offer counselling and help, and often so-called 'exit routes' (Spanger, 2008; Bjønness and Spanger, 2017). Regardless of whether they are undocumented or documented migrants in Denmark, the majority of female migrants who sell sex are seen as potential victims of human trafficking by social authorities (Spanger, 2008). The Danish anti-trafficking policy reflected in the government's action plan for combatting human trafficking are of great importance for female Thai migrant sex workers who have been granted a temporary residence permit. One of the purposes of the action plan is to implement a repatriation programme and to offer health and social counselling to migrant sex workers. Nonetheless, few migrant sex workers have agreed to be part of the repatriation programme nor be enrolled in an exit programme for sex workers.

The forms of help the Danish migration and prostitution regimes offer the Thai migrant as well as the way in which the state regulate the migrants do not align with how the women wish to live their lives as we will see in the following section. Rather, the Thai migrants, as in the case of Nee and Khem and their children (if they live in Denmark) are placed in a vulnerable position. For instance, in order to keep their residence permits within the first seven years[12] they are dependent on their marriage to a Danish citizen. Likewise, they are often dependent on their Danish husbands regarding housing, since the female Thais move to their Danish spouses' place when they arrive to Denmark. In addition, the Danish state does not perceive their sex work as labour, and therefore they do not have any labour rights. In the following, I analyse the two case studies of Khem and Nee to investigate how transnational and local mothering interacts with sex work using a framework of constellations of absence/presence and the virtual/physical.

Khem: physical distance and emotional presence

I first made contact with Khem through an outreach social work programme targeting migrants selling sexual services, and I first met her at her work place, a massage parlour where she performs traditional massage and some sexual services. She is 36 years old and had migrated to Denmark in 1999. It was through her second husband, an Israeli man who lived in Denmark, that she became familiar with the country. Khem holds a permanent residence permit and she has just separated from her Israeli husband. When they lived together, she worked at his clothing company, importing and exporting clothes. Khem tells me that he represented her family in Denmark when they were married. Currently, she mostly resides at the massage parlour since she has no home of her own due to her recent divorce. Khem is a single mother, and her two daughters from her first marriage, aged 14 and 15, live in Thailand. After she migrated to Denmark both daughters moved to live with their grandmother, and later one of them moved in with her father – a decision that was taken by Khem's mother. Thus, Khem's transnational family relations involve her mother and her ex-husband, both of whom take care of her children in Thailand. The quote below reflects her ex-husband's view on where her children should live:

Marlene:	Have you considered bringing your children to Denmark?
Khem:	Of course! But [sighs heavily] some families [other female Thai migrants] here in Denmark are lucky because their husbands accept that they have their children here. But my [ex-] husband does not want . . . it is not because he does not want to accept them. But he told me that it is better for Thais [she probably means the children] to stay in their country. I think he is selfish, because I want my children close to me. My ex-husband, I do not think he accepts it and he talks in another way because he has two sons. They are adults now, 30 and 27 years old.

When Khem lived with her Israeli husband, her economic obligations towards her children and mother in Thailand caused problems between them because he did not approve of her bread-winner role. In marriages between female Thais and Danish men, the husbands sometimes find it difficult to accept that their wives have economic obligations to family in Thailand. As in the case of Khem, Thai migrants and their spouses often disagree about the size of the remittance. It was not just the prospect of a better income that motivated her to migrate, but also the opportunity to prioritize herself:

> I have my mother and my family and my two daughters that I have to take care of and I decided [to go abroad]. Before, I did not work with that kind of job [massage]. I chose Denmark because I wanted some kind of freedom.

The way she 'does' transnational mothering has changed during the migration process. Khem first migrated to Denmark as a single mother, leaving her children behind. After she married her second husband she visited Thailand and her daughters from Denmark quite frequently thanks to her husband's business links with Thailand. Khem narrates: 'Every second week I went to Thailand with my husband. I was helping him buy clothes. Every time I was in Thailand I booked a hotel room for my daughters and my mother. Every day we stayed over together.' During this time, her mothering was based on a combination of physical and virtual presence (via telephone calls) that created an emotional and a social proximity. After the divorce, however, she has no longer been able to afford regular trips to Thailand and has used daily telephone conversations to keep abreast of her children's daily lives and to discuss solutions to any problems they might experience. In this way, her mothering practices performed in local physical spaces (hotels in Bangkok) was transformed into transnational mothering practices constituted through the virtual space:

Marlene:	How often do you contact your daughters?
Khem:	I call them every day. I buy these cards [prepaid cell phone cards]. I call my mother. I have her phone number and my daughter's number. And then I call my other daughter in Bangkok.
Marlene:	What do you talk about when you talk with your daughters?
Khem:	About her life . . . if she has any problems then we take care of them together. My mother, she is a little bit difficult because she is just like old people are towards children. I tell my mother that she should not yell or scream at her, but instead she has to listen and talk to my daughter's teacher if something happens. I tell her that she has to listen to what she [her daughter] says and what the teacher says. And then I ask my child what is going on. I try to explain so she [her mother] understands. If they hit my child I get sad and cry and the child cries, too.

Both physical distance and virtual proximity condition Khem's transnational mothering. This new emerging form of mothering is what Lutz and Palenga-Möllenbeck (2009) call 'Skype mothering' and it allows Khem to see herself as a caring mother and to inscribe herself in a discourse of motherhood that stresses emotional closeness. She is a physically absent though emotionally present mother who shares feelings with her children and discusses their problems on the phone. She obviously misses her children, but for different reasons she has not brought them to Denmark. When they were still married, her Israeli husband opposed the idea, and her right to bring her children to Denmark relied on his consent, given that both Khem and her children were dependent on him with regard to housing and economic matters. Once she had been granted a permanent residence permit, she did not need her ex-husband's consent. However, at that point, had Khem brought her children to Denmark, she would have faced challenges in meeting the social and financial obligations required by Danish authorities due to her long working hours at the massage parlour and due to not having her own apartment.

The combination of both virtual and physical social and emotional presence(s) as well as economic responsibilities define Khem's mothering practices. Being a caring transnational mother, she experiences the clash between two different ideals of care: the traditional one performed by her mother who is physically present, but also very authoritarian towards Khems' daughters, and her own ideal of care as based on dialogue and trust. Khem accepts that her mother should take important decisions on her behalf, for example on where one of the daughters should live. But she also interferes with how her mother, with a more traditional approach, brings up the children, for example by taking an active role on how her children should be educated in Thailand. Despite the fact that she misses being with them, she stresses that living in Denmark and being able to be herself has given her the independence to structure her working life as the owner of the massage parlour and to manage her leisure time. My interlocutors gave the impression that the massage parlours they work at function as social meeting points for the sex workers and their friends, including other Thai women, and sometimes their Danish husbands as well as clients. The boundaries between clients, husband and friends are sometimes blurred. For example, at the massage parlour they might eat together, watch television and play cards. When I met Khem, the massage parlour functioned both as her home and her workplace, allowing her opportunity to perform 'skype mothering' based on the virtual space and emotional proximity with her children.'

Khem has maintained emotional and social relations to her children in different ways since she migrated. When Khem worked together with her ex-husband she was partly physically present through her regular trips to Thailand. When she was divorced and started working at the massage parlour she was physically absent but virtually present through frequent telephone calls. This changeable mothering challenges Western ideals of motherhood based solely on physical local proximity.

Khem's transnational mothering, engaging and going into a dialogical and freedom-oriented form, depends on the means of technology. This emerging form of mothering questions the form of motherhood that solely derives from the physical space. As Baldassar and Merla's (2014) definition of family caregiving suggests, care is not necessarily face-to-face. They stress that 'caring about' through emotional support need not necessarily require physical presence, as we see in the story of Khem. Similarly, Madianou and Miller (2012) bring technology to the fore, arguing that it can maintain intensive and close familial relations. Despite, the close familial relations, as we have seen in the case of Khem, they argue that both absence and presence can play a role in mothering. The social media, webcams and chat add 'considerable naturalism to the encounter . . . the more effective the new media, the more they can still be an unbearable reminder of an actual absence, which becomes the main consequence of the realism of "connected presence"' (ibid.: 119). Taking this perspective, we can identify an emerging form of mothering, as we have seen in the story of Khem. Other women choose to bring their children to the sending society as a way to ensure a physical proximity. Nonetheless, even if they overcome the geographical distances, physical and emotional presence are not a guarantee. We will meet Nee below and her challenging practices with mothering practices.

Nee: physical presence and emotional absence

I followed 35-year-old Nee through a social outreach programme targeting migrants selling sexual services at massage parlours, which involved weekly contact with the social worker from the programme. This meant that I met Nee in a variety of situations and settings, sometimes with her daughter. Nee's story reveals some of the complications related to mothering that arise when migrant sex workers bring their children to Denmark. Her familial network informed the trajectory of her transnational migration. Her sisters, who already lived in Denmark, helped her settle in the new country where, shortly after her arrival in 2001, also through one of her sisters, she met and then married a Danish man. Initially Nee worked for one of her sisters as a cleaner and later found a job at a massage parlour and as a kitchen assistant in a Thai restaurant, again helped by her sisters, who were already working in massage parlours.

Nee has one daughter, Sank, from a previous relationship in Thailand. As in the case of Khem, Nee's motherhood has changed from transnational to local mothering. Her aunt and uncle, and to a certain extent her ex-mother-in-law, took care of Sank who stayed in Thailand after Nee's departure. Nee and her Danish husband visited her daughter once a year. Nee did not mention close everyday contact through telephone calls during the years when she was physically separated from her daughter, but she emphasises that she missed her daughter and wanted to bring her to Denmark. Every time she left her daughter after a visit in Thailand, her daughter would not let her go and it was very difficult separating each time. Nee's transnational mothering during these times was characterised by emotional proximity and physical absence.

In 2004, Nee brought Sank, who was 12 by then, over to Denmark. This was made possible by the Danish migration policy on family reunification. Nee's application for a residence permit for Sank, however, depended on the consent of her Danish husband with regard to housing and economy, which placed Nee in a vulnerable position. In 2005 she filed for divorce from her Danish husband and applied for a permanent residence permit. Like Khem, when Nee filed for divorce, she faced a housing problem, but she solved it by finding a rented flat through the social programme. Currently Nee no longer depends on her Danish ex-husband for her social rights and she receives various social benefits, enabling her to meet her financial and social obligations with regard to Sank. The social programme targeting migrants selling sex has supported and guided Nee during this process. However the same programme has established that Nee is having difficulty in meeting her emotional and social obligations to Sank.

Since she brought her child to Denmark, Nee's local mothering has been characterised by physical presence but emotional absence. Sank's move to Denmark was difficult for both Nee and Sank. Nee works during the day as a kitchen assistant or in a massage parlour, and she sometimes keeps her older sister company at the massage parlour at night. The Thais in this study work primarily in the sex industry, in massage parlours or bars. Long nights and evening shifts characterise their work in the sex industry. Some of them supplement their income from sex work with low-skilled temporary jobs as kitchen assistants, cleaners, masseuses or factory workers, for which the turnover is high as in the case of Nee. Others only ever work in the sex industry. Such working conditions leave Nee hardly any time to take care of her daughter.

Moreover, Nee has a new boyfriend who she met at the massage parlour and with whom she often spends the night. This means that Sank is alone all night and in the morning. Every afternoon, Nee sees Sank and gives her some money for food. As was the case for Khem, the massage parlour has become both a workplace and a leisure space, so the borders between work and spare time are blurred, often making it difficult for sex workers to take care of their children during the evening. This sometimes causes problems if the migrants have their children in Denmark, as in Nee's case, leaving her little time to engage in her daughter's everyday life. These dynamics have led to a troubled relationship between Nee and Sank. Quite often, Sank plays truant with another Thai girl who is in a similar situation. The following extract from my field notes reveal the complexity of the situation, during a visit I made to Nee with a social worker:

> With an insisting voice, the social worker underscores to Nee that it is important she is at home in the morning, afternoon and evening so Sank is not alone. Likewise, the social worker tells Nee that it is important that they eat together, that she talks to her daughter, does things together with her, holds her and gives her a hug. Nee does not say anything, she just nods. The social worker continues, asking: 'Why do you choose living with your boyfriend rather than living with your daughter? You cannot just dump her!' Nee's only answer is 'Sank cannot change. She looks like her father too much. She does not behave as I tell her to and she pulls faces in front of me.' Nee emphasises to me and the social worker that she just wants her daughter to go to school and get an education so she can take care of herself. Nee continues: 'It is like that I cannot focus on the job when I have problems with Sank, when she does not listen to me.' At the same time Nee says that she cannot afford to take care of her daughter. This reply is not acceptable to the social worker, who says: 'You need to have close [gesticulating with her arms that she has to hug her] contact to your child and you are obliged to pay maintenance for your child.' Nee is considering sending Sank back to Thailand to her father. Her younger sister suggested that the Danish state could assume responsibility for Sank as an alternative to sending Sank back to Thailand. To the social worker, Nee stresses that she did a lot for Sank when she brought her to Denmark. This, she repeats several times during the meeting.

Nee is confronted with the dominant discourse of motherhood that permeates Danish social outreach programmes for sex workers; this discourse constructs local motherhood in terms of a female subject who is emotionally present and who takes an active, involved part in the everyday life of the child(ren). Intersecting with this, is the notion of the ideal 'prostitute' who is forced into the sex industry due to poverty and/or abuse and therefore is striving for a 'proper' job through exit strategies, self-discipline and self-support (Spanger, 2012; Bjønness, 2015). However, these ideals of good motherhood are quite different from Nee's way of mothering, which is less about emotional attachment and more centred around the provision of material support through housing, food and access to education. Moreover, Nee expects gratitude from Sank, given that her daughter has the opportunity to go to school. However, since her way of doing local mothering involves being physically absent and spending her leisure time at the massage parlours or with her boyfriend, it is non-intelligible to the local social programme targeting migrants who sell sex. The encounter between the social worker and Nee reflects how the social worker tries to discipline Nee so that she conforms to the ideal of the good mother.

During the transition from transnational mothering to local mothering, Nee's practices have changed from 'Skype motherhood' to local, physically present mothering. Despite the change, emotional insecurity and financial security are still characteristic of Nee's situation.

Conclusion

Drawing on the empirical example of Thai migrant sex workers in Denmark, this chapter has investigated how single mothering as practised by migrant sex workers can be constituted by how the complex combination of physical presence/emotional absence and physical absence/emotional absence plays out in relation to (Danish) ideals of good motherhood and how technology can mediate and facilitate these intersections. In the case of Khem, we have seen how her mothering has changed from emotional and physical presence to physical absence but virtual presence. In the case of Nee, we have seen a change from transnational mothering to local mothering in which physical and virtual absence are replaced by emotional and physical absence, despite Nee's geographical proximity to her daughter. The two women perform single mothering in different ways.

The examples of Nee and Khem show the need for a broader discussion of how the intertwinement of sex work and migration both complicates the mothering practices of migrant sex workers and creates new ways for them to engage in their children's everyday lives using technological means such as webcams and smart phones. On the one hand, technologies offer new opportunities for doing motherhood, since social and emotional proximity can be created in virtual space, as we see in the case of Khem. On the other hand, they still remind us of loss and physical absence (Madianou and Miller, 2012).

The life of female Thai migrant sex workers who work in massage parlours can make it difficult for them to take care of their children as physically present mothers, as we have seen in the case of Nee and Khem. With no education or professional experience, both Nee and Khem find sex work an attractive alternative to poorly paid jobs as cleaners or kitchen assistants. This means, however, that their working life conflicts with local physical mothering. Nee brought her daughter to Denmark, but Sank's physical presence has not involved emotional care, and thus the emotional insecurity and financial security that characterised their relationship when Sank was in Thailand is still present, even after Sank moved to Denmark. Frustrations dominate their relationship. Also at play is the confrontation between Nee's understanding of good motherhood and the understanding represented by the Danish social service provider. On the one hand, the social programme helps Nee with her housing situation, with her divorce and with her application for a government subsidy. On the other hand, the social programme tries to change her way of practising single motherhood. Such attempts ultimately derive from the social policy discourse that suffuses the Danish policy field of prostitution (Spanger, 2011). In particular, notions about mothering represented by the social programme reflect a gendered morality, which deems selling sex and motherhood as incompatible, since the sale of sex is defined as a social problem and ('proper') motherhood connotes accepted femininity. Khem has rejected help offered by the social programme. Thus, she has avoided a confrontation with the predominating local mothering discourse, which expects physical, social and emotional presence. Instead, her ways of doing mothering reflect the emergence of a new form of motherhood. It transcends physical presence by means of technology and questions the mothering discourse represented by the social service providers, which constructs physically present motherhood as natural.

Together, the examples of Khem and Nee illustrate different varieties of intertwinement of migration, mothering and sex work at massage parlours. They challenge traditional and local understandings of the 'good mother' as physically present and reflect a new form of mothering built on emotional and social proximity established through virtual spaces in the face of new possibilities for sex workers to maintain their mothering, but also open up for array of challenges.

Few studies like Brown et al. (2018) and Bjønness (2015) show the way in which sex workers negotiate how to perform motherhood with social workers in local contexts. Bringing in the aspect of migration the contexualised stories of Khem and Nee are examples that help us to further shed light on sex work on a more general level. These stories reveal how the dimension of migration plays a role in the societal understandings of 'good/bad' morality. In particular, this chapter has demonstrated how the body of transnational motherhood and technology literature (Baldassar, 2008; Madianou and Miller, 2012; Baldassar and Merla, 2014) enriches the literature on migrant sex workers' mothering practices by offering the analytical perspective of emotional absence/presence in virtual and physical spaces. In future research this perspective will help to reveal new understandings of mothering and intimate relationships in sex work where physical, emotional and social mobility to a greater extent condition sex workers' everyday lives.

Notes

1 According to Pheterson (1996), morality and stigmatisation permeate the research field of sex for sale. For instance, the fear of being stigmatised as 'a whore' afflicts not just women selling sex, but all women in general, thus contributing to demarcations between ideal and improper femininity.
2 The fieldwork consisted of observations and interviews with Thai female migrant sex workers in Denmark who are also mothers. I conducted 18 in-depth interviews with female Thais working in the sex industry and key persons in the Thai community in Denmark from 2005–2006. In order to gain access to this highly sensitive field, I conducted fieldwork at a programme targeting migrant sex workers. The objective of the outreach programme was to inform them about safe sex, offer support and counselling about social and health problems and communicate contact to relevant public offices such as housing offices and social services. I joined a social worker in her work with the migrants for a period of four months. I met the sex workers in different places and later interviewed some of them about their everyday lives. The two stories of Khem and Nee are representative of the narratives told by these single mothers.
3 This chapter is a revised version of a former chapter authored by Hanne Marlene Dahl and Marlene Spanger (2010) and the ethnographic material from Spanger's PhD dissertation.
4 In this chapter I draw on Joan Tronto's (1993, 2011) definition of care: 'Care is what makes us human – relating us as individuals to the community interweaving us into a net of obligations and/or rights at various levels. It includes being attentive to human needs, taking responsibility to meet them, getting the concrete work done as well as awaiting the response by the person we give care.' Her concept encompasses both bodily practices, face-to-face interaction, emotions, obligated (forced to give) care, formal and informal, spontaneous or taking place as a long-run commitment by the state, the community or the family. These multiple settings and conditions create different power relations as well as complex social and emotional relations.
5 Williams (2011, 50–51) specifically defines the three regimes of care, migration and employment. Applying the concept of regime, Williams (2011 and 2012) compares how different receiving states condition and enable migrant care work. Variation is understood as emerging in the ways the three regimes intersect within a nation-state.
6 In the article 'Doing Marriage and Love in the Borderland of Transnational Sex Work: Female Thai Migrants in Denmark' (2013) I demonstrated how the subject positions of wife, sex worker and female migrant intersect in the narratives of love of female Thai migrants selling sex in Denmark. I argue that such narratives of love are highly relevant in studies of transnational sex work if we want to grasp the complexity involved when female migrants sell sexual services.
7 www.nyidanmark.dk/da-dk/Ophold/familiesammenfoering/aegtefaeller/betingelser-permanent-ophold.htm (accessed 3 November 2017). See also Law on Foreigners §§7–9.
8 The length of the stay and the criteria to be met before the migrant can apply for permanent residence permit have varied during the last two decades. For instance, in 2018 a non-EU citizen can apply for a permanent residence permit in Denmark when they have had a temporary residence permit for eight years (New to Denmark 2018).
9 However, whether a residence permit is granted for their children depends on the connection between the parent(s) and the child(ren), the length of separation and the child's belonging to the sending society.

10 None of the interviewees had children over 15 years old when they applied for a residence permit for their children.

11 In addition, the Danish social authorities also 'consider whether the child is vulnerable to serious social problems in Denmark by identifying whether the family in Denmark has social problems' (New to Denmark 2010). '[I]f one of the child's parents continues to reside in the country of origin [...], and if the application for family reunification is submitted more than two years after the parent residing in Denmark meets the requirements for family reunification with a child, a special attachment requirement applies. This requirement stipulates that a residence permit will only be granted if the child has [...] an attachment to Denmark sufficient to form the basis for successful integration in Denmark' (ibid.). This means that the other parent, who lives in the sending society, plays a central role regarding the rights of the migrant to bring the child(ren).

12 As already mentioned, the time span before the migrants are able to apply for a permanent residence permit differs due to the migration policy of the government.

References

Avila, E. and Hondagneu-Sotelo, P. (1997). I'm Here, But I'm There: The Meanings of Latina Transnational Motherhood. *Gender & Society* 11(5), pp. 548–571.

Baldassar, L. (2008). Missing Kin and Longing to be Together: Emotions and the Construction of Co-Presence in Transnational Relationships. *Journal of Intercultural Studies* 29(3), pp. 247–266.

Baldassar, L. and Merla, L. (eds) (2014). *Transnational Families, Migration and the Circulation of Care: Understanding Mobility and Absence in Family Life*. Abingdon: Routledge.

Bjønness, J. (2015). Narratives About Necessity: Constructions of Motherhood Among Drug Using Sex-Sellers in Denmark. *Substance Use & Misuse* 50(6), pp. 783–793.

Bjønness, J. and Spanger, M. (2017). Danish Prostitution Policy. In H. Wagner and S. Jahnsen, eds, *Country Studies in Prostitution*. Abingdon: Routledge.

Brennan, D. (2004). *What's Love Got to Do with It? Transnational Desires and Sex Tourism in the Dominican Republic*. Durham: Duke University Press.

Brown, K., Dewey, S. and Orchard, T (2018). Intensive Mothering as Cultural Script: Boundary Setting Among Street-Involved Women. In M.-L. Skilbrei and M. Spanger, eds, *Understanding Sex for Sale: Meanings and Moralities of Sexual Commerce*. Abingdon: Routledge.

Dahl, H.M. and Spanger, M. (2010). Sex Workers transnational And Local Motherhood: Presence and/or Absence. In A.L.W. Isaksen, ed., *Global Care Work: Gender and Migration in Nordic Societies*. Lund: Nordic Academic Press.

Casas, O.L. (2017). Survival within a Multi-Circuited Maze: Latin American Sex Workers in Spain. In Christian Groes and Nadine T. Fernandez, eds, *Intimate Mobilities: Sexual Economies, Marriage and Migration in a Disparate World*. New York and Oxford: Berghahn.

Lutz, H. and Palenga-Möllenbeck, E. (2009). The Care Chain Concept Under Scrutinity: Female Ukrainian/Polish Care Migrants and Their Families Left Behind. Unpublished paper for conference: 'Care and Migration', Frankfurt, April 22–23.

Madianou, M. and Miller, D. (2012). *Migration and New Media: Transnational Families and Polymedia*. Abingdon: Routledge.

New to Denmark. (2010). Children Under the Age of 15. [Online] Ministry for Refugee, Immigration and Integration Affairs. www.nyidanmark.dk/en-us/coming_to_dk/familyreunification/children.htm [accessed 11 March 2010].

New to Denmark. (2017a). Spouses and Cohabiting Partners. [Online] Ministry for Refugee, Immigration and Integration Affairs. www.nyidanmark.dk/en-us/coming_to_dk/familyreunification/spouses/spouses.htm [accessed 2 November 2017].

New to Denmark. (2017b). Children Under the Age of 15. [Online] Ministry for Refugee, Immigration and Integration Affairs. www.nyidanmark.dk/en-us/coming_to_dk/familyreunification/children/ [accessed 3 November 2017].

New to Denmark. (2018). Spouses and Cohabiting Partners. [Online] Ministry for Refugee, Immigration and Integration Affairs. www.nyidanmark.dk/en-GB/You-want-to-apply/Permanent-residence-permit/Permanent-residence [accessed 8 February 2018].

Parreñas, R. (2001). Mothering from a Distance: Emotions, Gender, and Intergenerational Relations in Filipino Transnational Families. *Feminist Studies* 27(2), pp. 361–390.

Pheterson, G. (1996). *The Prostitution Prism*. Amsterdam: Amsterdam University Press.

Ruenkaew, P. (2003). The Transnational Prostitution of Thai Women to Germany: A Variety of Transnational Labour Migration? In S. Thorbek and P. Pattanaik, eds, *Transnational Prostitution: Changing Patterns in a Global Context*. London: Zed books.

Schiller, N.G. and Salazar, N.B. (2013). Regimes of Mobility Across the Globe. *Journal of Ethnic and Migration Studies* 39(2), pp. 183–200.

Skilbrei, M.-L. and Spanger, M. (2018). *Understanding Sex for Sale: Meanings and Moralities of Sexual Commerce*. Abingdon: Routledge.

Spanger, M. (2008). Socialpolitiske tiltag og feministisk gennemslagskraft? Trafficking som policyfelt i Danmark. In C. Holmström and M.-L. Skilbrei, eds, *Prostitution i Norden*. Copenhagen: Nordisk Ministerråd, TemaNord nr 604.

Spanger, M. (2010). *Destabilising Sex Work & Intimacy? Gender Performances of Female Thai migrants Selling Sex in Denmark*. Unpublished PhD thesis. Roskilde University, Denmark.

Spanger, M. (2011). Human Trafficking a Lever for Feminist Voices? Transformations of the Danish Policy Field of Prostitution. *Critical Social Policy* 33(1), pp. 140–159.

Spanger, M. (2012). Gender Performances as Spatial Acts: (Fe)male Thai Migrant Sex Workers in Denmark. *Gender, Place & Culture* 20(1), pp. 37–52.

Spanger, M. (2013). Doing Love in the Borderland of Transnational Sex Work: Female Thai Migrants in Denmark. *NORA (Nordic Journal of Feminist and Gender Research)* 21(2), pp. 92–107.

Sørensen, N.N. (2002). Transnationaliseringen af husmoderlige pligter. *Kvinder, Køn & Forskning* 11(2), pp. 9–19.

Tronto, J. (1993). *Moral Boundaries: A Political Argument for an Ethic of Care*. New York: Routledge.

Tronto, J. (2011). Privatizing Neo-Colonialism: Migrant Domestic Care Workers, Partial Citizenship and Responsibility. In H.M. Dahl, M. Keränen and A. Kovalainen, eds, *Europeanization, Care and Gender: Global Complexities*. Basingstoke: Palgrave Macmillan.

Williams, F. (2011). Care, Migration and Citizenship: Migration and Home-Based Care in Europe. In H.M. Dahl, M. Keränen and A. Kovalainen, eds, *Europeanization, Care and Gender: Global Complexities*. Basingstoke: Palgrave Macmillan.

Williams, F. (2012). Converging Variations in Migrant Care Work in Europe, *Journal of European Social Policy* 22(4), pp. 363–376.

30

Bridging tourism and prostitution through intimacy

Gay men's sex tourism in Bangkok

Yo-Hsin Yang

Introduction

Gay East Asian men travelling to Bangkok has been one of the most notable transnational tourism flows on a global scale. This transnational flow represents not just a typical form of gay tourism, but also sex tourism since gay men's itineraries in Bangkok generally involve intensive engagements of sexual activities, especially commercially provided ones. Gay male tourists' transnational engagements in prostitution when they travelled to Bangkok closely relate to the city's prosperous domestic sex industry, which as Jackson, the author of *Queer Bangkok* claims, leads the city to become one of the most celebrated sites where 'increasingly well-off Asian gay men' gather (Jackson 2011, 25). Through interviewing gay Taiwanese men about their experiences of buying sex in Bangkok, it is evident that their relationships with local male sex workers or "money boys" as they are commonly known in local parlance, are more than just sexual transactions, with numerous forms of intimacy also being involved. However, as the issue of intimacy between sex workers and their clients is broadly discussed and accumulated into considerable literature in sex work and sex tourism studies, it is still underrepresented in the research field of gay tourism.

Thus, the first aim of this chapter is to fill this unexplored research gap by appropriating the theoretical framework of intimacy from sex work/tourism studies to investigate relationships between gay Taiwanese men and Thai money boys. Second, since current debates on intimacy within prostitution are mostly on the basis of sex tourists and clients being Western and White, by focusing on gay Taiwanese men's experiences of engaging in commercial sex in Bangkok, this chapter represents a long-absent voice from the Global South in both gay and sex tourism studies, which constitutes one of its most important global implications. Third, this chapter also aims to shed new light on existing discussions of intimacy in prostitution by highlighting the multiple meanings and functions of intimacy with the local prostitute for sex tourists, due to the duality of their roles as both tourists and clients.

To critically rethink the meanings and functions of intimacy within prostitution for clients in the context of gay Taiwanese men travelling to Bangkok, the chapter will start with a brief review of the genealogy of gay tourism studies and trace its ties between sex tourism and domestic prostitution. The chapter then moves on to compare the literature on sex tourism to studies of domestic prostitution from the perspective of intimacy within prostitution. This comparison unpacks the meanings and functions of intimacy in prostitution for sex tourists/clients and also highlights their desire for an 'authentic intimacy'. The chapter then sets this desire in the context of another body of work on tourism that centres on tourists' desire for the authenticity of places they visit in general, a body of work that has rarely been used in terms of thinking about desire for intimacy in sex tourism. Lastly, this chapter will explore how these two different types of desire for authenticity intersect in the context of gay sex tourism, using two empirical examples of Taiwanese men travelling to Bangkok.

The empirical material of this chapter is collected from a broad project that investigates the meanings of gay Taiwanese men's sexual engagements when they travel to Bangkok. The project involved a six-month ethnographic study, where the research followed a total of 64 Taiwanese gay men who travelled to Bangkok during December 2015 to May 2016 and talked to 35 of them in follow-up interviews after their trips from June 2016 to August 2016. These interviews focused on participants' experiences of engaging in varying forms of sexual activities in different sexualised spaces such as gay clubs, saunas, erotic massage parlours and go-go boy bars in Bangkok.

The genealogy of gay men's sex tourism

Gay tourism first drew attention in academia some decades ago and brought in a great body of literature discussing this rapidly developing transnational mobility from varying perspectives. One focus of academic studies has been on the connection between sexual identity and tourism, which exemplifies that for gay tourists, travelling to somewhere far away works as a metaphorical process of 'coming out' that enables them to experiment with and construct their sexual identities (Pritchard et al. 2000; Howe 2001; Waitt & Markwell 2006). Some studies tease out the economic implications of gay tourism and present its contributions to both extend social tolerance toward homosexuality and create a niche market in the tourism industry (Visser 2003; Hughes 2006; Coon 2012). Another body of research explores gay tourists, especially gay men's intensive engagements in sex activities when they travel, and further investigates the entanglement between their sexual behaviours and liminality in gay spaces and circulations of STDs (Clift & Forrest 1999; Clift et al. 2002; Hughes 2002; Johnston 2007; Casey 2009), which intersects with many existing debates in sex tourism (Padilla et al. 2010; Vivancos et al. 2010; Tutenges 2012).

Indeed, to a large extent, gay men's tourism is similar to a branch of sex tourism since as Hughes (2002, 65) asserts, gay male tourists may travel abroad 'with the primary purpose of having sexual encounters', especially when it comes to specific destinations. Although the meaning of the term 'sex tourism' is complex and may also refer to non-commercial sex that occurs with other tourists or even between couples (Ryan 2000; Bauer & McKercher 2003), according to numerous research, prostitution between foreign tourists and local sex workers is still the most notable component of sex tourism (O'Connell Davidson 2001; Nyanzi et al. 2005; Katsulis 2010; Frohlick 2013). In this sense, sex tourism can also be counted as being part of the sex industry but in a specific transnational context. On the basis of these genealogical ties between gay men's tourism, sex tourism and the sex industry, while the intimacy between gay male tourists and local sex workers is apparently absent from current research, the relevant theoretical framework of intimacy that has developed in sex tourism and prostitution studies is an area that warrants further exploration in terms of gay tourism.

The 'authentic intimacy' in sex work/tourism

With respect to intimacy in sex tourism, a series of studies focusing on 'romantic tourism' (Pruitt & LaFont 1995; Herold et al. 2001; Jacobs 2009; Törnqvist 2012) demonstrate that even sexual encounters between tourists and locals are based on the settings of prostitution even though they may not be circumscribed into temporary and monetary transactions but can be 'ongoing, and long-lasting romantic/loving relationships' (Bauer & McKercher 2003, 8). This finding resonates with a great body of literature on prostitution in the domestic context. On studying clients of prostitution, Sanders (2008, 96) argues that there are notable urges for intimacy among these clients who 'give lower priority to sex and high status to emotional connectivity' in sexual transactions. To depict this intimacy-centred demand of clients, Bernstein (2007a) develops the concept of 'girlfriend experience' to indicate that numerous forms of physical, verbal and emotional intimacy that are normally reserved for non-commercial partnership have become one of the services that the sexual industry sells and its clients expect to experience. Subsequently, Bernstein (2007b) goes on to claim that in response to clients' expectation for 'girlfriend experiences', sex workers tend to manipulate a series of intimate labours to convince clients that the desires and pleasures in their sexual services are on a mutual basis and are therefore 'authentic'.

Sex tourism research also highlights a rising concern with the production of intimacy in transnational contexts and contributes different perspectives to explain why the authenticity of intimacy matters in sexual transactions for clients (and sometimes providers, see Yea 2005). For instance, many scholars suggest that feelings of 'authentic intimacy' within transnational prostitution enable sex tourists to rebuild their self-esteem (Dorfman 2011; Mitchell 2011; Rivers-Moore 2013) since it makes them believe that the apparent mutual desire with sex workers is genuine rather than just a business transaction (O'Connell Davidson 1998, 50–51). Additionally, other research also suggests that sex tourists' utilise the feeling of authentic intimacy to lessen their sense of guilt in engaging in prostitution and escape the stigma attached to sex tourism, exacerbated by the significant economic gap between locals and foreign tourists (Cabezas 2011; Rivers-Moore 2012). As Padilla (2007) exemplifies, by developing intimate relationships with local prostitutes, sex tourists 'reconfigure their payments as a kind of humanitarian assistance' and thus transform themselves into 'an empathic benefactor rather than a sex tourist' (Padilla 2007, 265). On the other hand, for local prostitutes, knowing tourists' urges for intimacy also motivates them to manipulate a series of tactics to perform both sexual and psychological intimacy in order to extract more economic benefits (Cohen 1986; Mitchell 2011)

Intersecting desire for authenticity of intimacy/place

The involvement of intimacy in prostitution, which blurs the boundary between commercial and non-commercial relations, makes sexual encounters with locals appealing but also dangerous for tourists. On the one hand, this intimacy decreases tourists' sense of the mercenary nature of prostitution while, on the other hand, it also creates their vulnerability to financial exploitation by sex workers, which is extensively documented in the literature that explores transnational relationships arising from commercial sex (Bernstein 2007a; Cheng 2007; Peng 2007). One of the most influential studies is from Cohen (1986), in which he carefully elucidates how the transnational context entangles with the commercial nature of prostitution and results in ambiguous and suspicious intimate relationships between farangs and Thai girls who work in the sex industry. Through analysing the love letters between lovelorn farangs and their Thai girlfriends, Cohen argues that this kind of intimate relationship is indeed superficial because not only does its transnational nature limit the frequency and length of interactions, but also creates barriers of communication due to both 'cultural differences' and 'language difficulties' (Cohen 1986, 121). However, this superficial relationship is still appealing for farangs since as Wilson (2004) suggests, the open-ended character of prostitution in Thailand leaves much space for Thai girls to perform 'girlfriend experiences' such as telling 'sweet words' or pretending that they have no interest in money, which leads farangs to believe their relationship is authentic and that these interactions are based on mutual desires instead of being purely commercial transactions (Wilson 2004) and thereby motivates farangs to continue to provide financial support to their Thai 'lovers'.

Cohen (1986) argues that intimacy can be utilised by Thai girls to reverse their power relationships with farangs and states that, 'sex-tourism may indeed engender sexual exploitation of local women on the macro-social level; but on the micro-level of interpersonal relationships, the state of affairs may often be inverted – the local women actually exploiting the foreigners (Cohen 1986, 124). Furthermore, Cohen (1986) also notices that the power reversal within this form of transnational prostitution is not only embodied in farangs' considerable financial expenditures but also emotional suffering as they usually feel guilt, longing, doubt, anxiety and uncertainty in their relationship with their Thai girlfriends and thus seek further evidence that demonstrates the authenticity of the intimacy between them.

This quest for 'authentic' and meaningful contact with people of another culture, a contact and exchange that transcends pecuniary motivations and paid performance, has often been said to lie at the heart of more elite forms of tourism generally. The structure of the quest for authenticity as an experience or form of contact hidden behind paid for and staged encounters in tourism, was first proposed by MacCannell (1973). His thesis was that growing tourism was symptomatic of a rising demand for genuine experiences in a postmodern society; a demand that motivated people to go travelling to collect the 'authentic' cultural experiences unavailable to them at home (MacCannell 1973, 590). Following this trend, MacCannell (1973) suggested that people in host countries have rapidly learnt to perform particular features that represent 'authentic' local culture to attract tourists in what he terms 'staged authenticity'. However, while tourists may realise the performative nature of this staged authenticity, some may start to pursue the uncontaminated 'authentic' experiences in their trips by means of entering 'to the back regions of the places they visit' since these areas are normally associated with ultimate truth and intimacy of locals' private lives (MacCannell 1973, 589). In turn, the 'back regions' themselves becoming spectacularised and staged.

This authenticity-seeking understanding of tourism has some clear parallels with the case of sex tourism outlined here. Specifically, the staged authenticity of local culture performed by local people in the host country is equivalent to Thai girls' work to perform a submissive sexual identity while 'authentic', backstage cultural experiences that tourists desire are akin to farangs' desires for authentic emotional intimacy with Thai girls. Despite the striking parallels, the theoretical frameworks around desires for authenticity in tourism have rarely been applied in sex tourism research. One of the exceptions is Padilla's (2007, 269) work in which he discusses tourists' desires for seeking the authenticity of masculinity, namely, that looking for 'macho' and 'real' men to hook up in certain places with has become a principle motivation for gay men from the West to engage in sex tourism.

The intersection of desire for authenticity of local culture and intimacy with locals is documented in Stout's research (2015) on North American and European gay men's sex tourism in Cuba, in which he identifies that a common practice of Cuban male prostitutes is to bring foreign clients to their homes and introduce them to their families. For Cuban prostitutes, this practice may derive from both their sentimental attachments to clients and equally their pecuniary interests of seeking these clients' continued financial support. Some tourists interpret this practice as a 'turning point' of their relationship with local prostitutes since it affirms the romantic love between them is authentic because it establishes an imaginary kinship due to the Cuban families' wholehearted acceptance (Stout 2015, 677). Moreover, Stout also indicates that local prostitutes' practice of introducing foreign clients to their families offers more than an endorsement of their sexual relationship, it offers their clients a bridge to approach authentic Cuban life more generally, which ordinary tourists have no chance to experience (Stout 2015, 679). The practice of taking clients home may be a tactic that Cuban male prostitutes manipulate to create a sense of authentic intimacy with their clients for the sake of further extracting their economic resources, reflecting Cohen's (1986) theorising on the embodiment of 'the power of the weak' in transnational female prostitution. Moreover, it also offers tourists the experience of authentic intimacy and local culture at the same time. In the following section, two cases from the context of gay Taiwanese men travelling to Bangkok reveal that the practice of taking foreign clients back to their hometown is also carried out by local prostitutes on the other side of globe, which proposes an alternative way of rethinking the meanings and functions of intimacy in the context of transnational prostitution.

Going back to the hometown: misinterpreting intimacy

In interviews, when participants recalled their romances in Bangkok, stories of how they fell in love with local money boys but ended up with pecuniary loss and emotional suffering were repeatedly mentioned. In reflecting these heartbroken experiences, many participants emphasise that their misinterpretation of regarding these relationships as 'true love' was mainly due to the money boy's act of taking them to his hometown. For example, Joe described his five-year relationship with his Thai ex-boyfriend as a fraud since it involved not only discovering and forgiving the boy's infidelity but also endless requests for financial support. Nevertheless, at that time, he still believed their love was authentic because:

> He (the Thai ex-boyfriend) brought me to his hometown to visit his parents and introduced me as his boyfriend. He also brought me to other private events such as his friend's wedding ceremony, which touched me so much. You know, it's just like I was affirmed as his 'real partner'.
>
> *(Joe, 51 years old, interview)*

Following this account, Joe further stressed that his Thai ex-boyfriend taking him to his hometown in Thailand's countryside resulted in his blindness to notice that the boy just counted him as a sugar daddy. This case resonates with Stout's (2015, 677) insight in recognising 'going home with locals' as a turning point for gay foreign tourists to redefine their relationships with local prostitutes and feeling that they are 'more than just a client'.

However, the transnational intimacies between gay tourists and local prostitutes that derive from the act of 'going back to the prostitute's hometown' in Cuba and Bangkok differ in respect of both their pattern and origins. In the case of Cuba, it is through the movement of going back to Cuban prostitutes' hometown that gay tourists had the chances to receive hospitality and acceptance from Cuban families and thus establish a kind of intimacy in the form of kinship with the prostitute and his family. On the other hand, in the case of gay Taiwanese tourists in Bangkok, it is especially powerful because in Taiwanese society, bringing someone back to the hometown and introducing him/her to parents signifies the person may be a potential candidate for marriage or at least represents this is a serious relationship. In this sense, taking a partner to the hometown is normally interpreted as an implicit symbol to confirm and express the authenticity of a given intimacy of partnership. But, conversely, in Thai society, taking someone back to the hometown or social events such as a friend's wedding feast are just ordinary practices that are not usually freighted with such heavy symbolic meaning.

Therefore it is the cultural difference between Taiwanese and Thai society in interpreting the act of taking someone back to the hometown that leads gay Taiwanese tourists to misinterpret their relationship with Thai money boys as being serious and 'authentic' rather than just commercial. Therefore, many of them fall into a vulnerable position to be both monetarily and emotionally exploited by their Thai ex-boyfriends, which subverts the oversimplified victim–exploiter dichotomy between local prostitutes and foreign tourists that current sex tourism literature stresses, and also exemplifies Cohen's (1986) insight that intimacy can sometimes be manipulated by sex workers to reverse power relations between them and their clients.

Instrumentalising intimacy to approach the authenticity of the place

However, some other gay Taiwanese men's cases illustrate that their transnational intimacy with Thai money boys initiated from the act of going back to their hometown also brings them some other additional benefits. For example, many participants highlighted the cultural perspective of their experiences in visiting Thai money boys' hometowns while stressing that the advantages of developing intimacy from sexual transactions were a springboard that enabled them to discover 'the real' Thailand, which as participant Gary, 27 years old and a big fan of Thai pop culture who enjoys watching Thai series and films claimed,

> In his (Thai money boy's) hometown, I saw the everyday lives of his family such as the market they buy food or the way they hang out with friends . . . just sit on the floor and drink (alcohol), it's so authentic! I guess all of this is what other tourists have never had the chance to see.

This narrative to some extent echoes Stouts's (2015) work in Cuba in which he finds that the intimate act of going back to a prostitute's hometown serves as a bridge for gay tourists to access the usually unreachable local culture. However, what makes intimacy in transnational prostitution between gay Taiwanese tourists and local money boys unique is that it develops not only out of gay Taiwanese men's instinctive affections but also practical considerations. To be more specific, some gay Taiwanese tourists realised that this transnational intimacy would bring them not just a temporary lover but also a personal guide with multiple functions include delivering cultural knowledge about authentic lives of locals through taking them to specific places such as their hometown. To reiterate, gay Taiwanese tourists like Gary somehow instrumentalised their sexual intimacy with Thai money boys by consciously manipulating this relationship to experience the authenticity of Thailand.

Apart from these gay Taiwanese tourists' inherent interests in Thai culture, the access to authentic local culture that is afforded by sexual intimacy offered the advantage, as in Gary's account, of fostering a sense of superiority over other cultural tourists. So for these tourists, their sexual interactions provided them with a privileged and exclusive approach to experience the real Thailand and non-sexual cultural experiences and exchanges that other tourists who are not involved in commercial sex will not have the chance to experience. Second, the cultural intention of experiencing authentic Thailand derived from the act of going to the money boy's hometown, also enables gay Taiwanese tourists to be distinct from other sex tourists or clients who engage in prostitution. As many of them emphasised, they bought sex in Bangkok not only for sexual release but also a chance to access local culture through being involved in the money boy's everyday life such as going back to his hometown. In this sense, the intimate act of going to a prostitute's hometown enriches the experience and blurs the boundary between sex tourism and cultural tourism since this practice demonstrates that buying sex abroad can be an alternative approach to experience local lives.

Conclusion

Taiwanese gay men's experiences of developing intimate relationships with local money boys in Bangkok shows that the transnational context of sex tourism trades on cultural differences that result in certain impacts on intimacy between sex tourists and local prostitutes. In Joe's case, cultural differences between Thai and Taiwanese society in interpreting the act of taking someone home, or to be more specific, different perceptions of the line of public/private space made him misinterpret the authenticity of intimacy with his Thai ex-boyfriend and thus in the end led to his feeling of being economically and emotionally exploited. However, in Gary's experience, it is the transnational context that arouses his curiosity about cultural differences and so that leads him to instrumentalise the relationship with the Thai prostitute as a means of approaching generally unreachable local lives and allows him to experience authentic Thailand. In this sense, gay men like Gary situate themselves in a position where they are superior to ordinary tourists since they possess privileged accesses to the backstage regions of Thai locals' everyday lives. Also, they distinguish themselves from other sex tourists while emphasising their cultural immersions of authenticity in the places they visit. So, Taiwanese gay men's instrumentalisation of their intimacy with Thai money boys seems to make sex tourism an alternative way to carry out cultural tourism, which blurs the fixed conceptual dichotomy between them and the desires and practices of sex tourism as part of the sex industry.

To sum up, according to the two empirical cases discussed above, this chapter aims to provide an alternative perspective to rethink meanings and functions of intimacy for clients in prostitution. First, other than viewing intimacy as an illusion that is created by prostitutes' conscious performance of a 'girlfriend experience' for the sake of extracting more economic resources from sex tourists as presumed in much current research (Cohen 1986; Stout 2015). This chapter argues that while in the transnational context, this intimate illusion may also result from the cultural difference in interpreting specific practices such as taking sex tourists back to their hometown that local prostitutes unconsciously carry out without any specific purpose. Second, this transnational context also appears to make sex tourists' pursuits of authenticity in sex tourism range from sexual intimacy to local culture. In this sense, for some sex tourists, the function of intimacy in prostitution may be transformed as an alternative way to seek authenticity of local cultures and places. Following this, what is being traded in transnational prostitution with local prostitutes is more than just money and intimacy but also the experiences of entering into the locals' 'backstage', reflecting the dual roles of sex tourists as they are simultaneously both tourists and clients of prostitution. This duality makes sex tourism indistinct from tourism more generally, with sex tourists not only travelling for prostitution but also buying sex for tourism.

References

Bauer, T.G. & McKercher, B., 2003. *Sex and tourism: journeys of romance, love, and lust*. New York: Haworth Hospitality Press.

Bernstein, E., 2007a. Buying and selling the 'girlfriend experience': the social and subjective contours of market intimacy. In M.B. Padilla, J.S. Hirsch, M. Munoz-Laboy, R. Sember & R.G. Parker, eds. *Love and globalization*. Nashville: Vanderbilt University Press, pp. 186–202.

Bernstein, E., 2007b. Sex work for the middle classes. *Sexualities*, 10(4), pp. 473–488.

Cabezas, A., 2011. Intimate encounters: affective economies in Cuba and the Dominican Republic. *European Review of Latin American and Caribbean studies*, 91, pp. 3–14.

Casey, M.E., 2009. The queer unwanted and their undesirable 'otherness'. In G. Browne, Kath Lim & Jason Brown, ed. *Geographies of sexualities: theory, practices, and politics*. Farnham, UK: Ashgate, pp. 125–135.

Cheng, S., 2007. Romancing the club: love dynamics between Filipina entertainers and GIs in US military camp towns in South Korea. In M.B. Padilla, J.S. Hirsch, M. Munoz-Laboy, R. Sember & R.G. Parker, eds. *Love and globalization*. Nashville: Vanderbilt University Press, pp. 226–251.

Clift, S.M. & Forrest, S.P., 1999. Factors associated with gay men's sexual behaviours and risk on holiday. *AIDS Care*, 11(3), pp. 281–295.

Clift, S.M., Luongo, M. & Callister, C., 2002. *Gay tourism: culture, identity and sex*. London: Continuum.

Cohen, E., 1986. Lovelorn farangs: the correspondence between foreign men and Thai girls. *Anthropological Quarterly*, 59(3), pp. 115–127.

Coon, D.R., 2012. Sun, sand, and citizenship: the marketing of gay tourism. *Journal of Homosexuality*, 59(4), pp. 511–534.

Frohlick, S., 2013. Intimate tourism markets: money, gender, and the complexity of erotic exchange in a Costa Rican Caribbean town. *Anthropological Quarterly*, 86(1), pp. 133–162.

Herold, E., Garcia, R. & DeMoya, T., 2001. Female tourists and beach boys, romance or sex tourism? *Annals of Tourism Research*, 28(4), pp. 978–997.

Howe, A.C., 2001. Queer pilgrimage: the San Francisco homeland and identity tourism. *Cultural Anthropology*, 16(1), pp. 35–61.

Hughes, H., 2002. Gay men's holiday destination choice: a case of risk and avoidance. *International Journal of Tourism Research*, 4(4), pp. 299–312.

Hughes, H., 2006. *Pink tourism: holidays of gay men and lesbians*. London: CABI.

Jackson, Peter, 2011. *Queer Bangkok: 21st-century markets, media, and rights*. Hong Kong: Hong Kong University Press.

Jacobs, J., 2009. Have sex will travel: romantic 'sex tourism' and women negotiating modernity in the Sinai. *Gender, Place and Culture*, 16(1), pp. 43–61.

Johnston, L., 2007. *Queering tourism: paradoxical performances of gay pride parades*. New York: Routledge.

Katsulis, Y., 2010. Living like a king: conspicuous consumption, virtual communities, and the social construction of paid sexual encounters by U.S. sex tourists. *Men and Masculinities*, 13(2), pp. 210–230.

MacCannell, D., 1973. Staged authenticity: arrangements of social space in tourist settings. *American Journal of Sociology*, 79(3), pp. 589–603.

Mitchell, G., 2011. TurboConsumers™ in paradise: tourism, civil rights, and Brazil's gay sex industry. *American Ethnologist*, 38(4), pp. 666–682.

Nyanzi, S. et al., 2005. Bumsters, big black organs and old white gold: embodied racial myths in sexual relationships of Gambian beach boys. *Culture, Health & Sexuality*, 7(6), pp. 557–569.

O'Connell Davidson, J., 1998. *Power, prostitution, and freedom*. Cambridge: Polity.

O'Connell Davidson, J., 2001. The sex tourist, the expatriate, his ex-wife and her 'other': the politics of loss, difference and desire. *Sexualities*, 4(1), pp. 5–24.

Padilla, M.B., 2007. 'Western union daddies' and their quest for authenticity: an ethnographic study of the Dominican gay sex tourism industry. *Journal of Homosexuality*, 53(1–2), pp. 241–275.

Padilla, M.B. et al., 2010. HIV/AIDS and tourism in the Caribbean: an ecological systems perspective. *American Journal of Public Health*, 100(1), pp. 70–77.

Peng, Y.-W., 2007. Buying sex: domination and difference in the discourses of Taiwanese Piao-ke. *Men and Masculinities*, 9(3), pp. 315–336.

Pritchard, A., Morgan, N.J., Sedgley, D., Khan, E. & Jenkins, A., 2000. Sexuality and holiday choices: conversations with gay and lesbian tourists. *Leisure Studies*, 19(4), pp. 267–282.

Pruitt, D. & LaFont, S., 1995. For love and money: romance tourism in Jamaica. *Annals of Tourism Research*, 22(2), pp. 422–440.

Rivers-Moore, M., 2012. Almighty gringos: masculinity and value in sex tourism. *Sexualities*, 15, pp. 850–870.

Rivers-Moore, M., 2013. Affective sex: beauty, race and nation in the sex industry. *Feminist Theory*, 14(2), pp. 153–169.

Ryan, C., 2000. Sex tourism: paradigms of confusion? In S. Clift & S. Carter, eds. *Tourism and sex: culture, commerce and coercion*. New York: Pinter, pp. 23–40.

Stout, N., 2015. When a yuma meets mama: commodified kin and the affective economies of queer tourism in Cuba. *Anthropological Quarterly*, 88(3), pp. 665–691.

Sylvia Dorfman, R., 2011. A Foucauldian analysis of power and prostitution: comparing sex tourism and sex work migration. *POLIS Journal*, 5, pp. 1–23.

Sanders, Teela, 2008. *Paying for pleasure: men who buy sex*. Devon, UK: Willan Publishing.

Törnqvist, M., 2012. Troubling romance tourism: sex, gender and class inside the Argentinean tango clubs. *Feminist Review*, 102(1), pp. 21–40.

Tutenges, S., 2012. Nightlife tourism: a mixed methods study of young tourists at an international nightlife resort. *Tourist Studies*, 12(2), pp. 131–150.

Visser, G., 2003. Gay men, tourism and urban space: reflections on Africa's 'gay capital.' *Tourism Geographies*, 5(2), pp. 168–189.

Vivancos, R., Abubakar, I. & Hunter, P.R., 2010. Foreign travel associated with increased sexual risk-taking, alcohol and drug use among UK university students: a cohort study. *International Journal of STD & AIDS*, 21(1), pp. 46–51.

Waitt, G. & Markwell, K., 2006. *Gay tourism: culture and context*. New York: Haworth Hospitality Press.

Wilson, A., 2004. *The intimate economies of Bangkok: tomboys, tycoons, and Avon ladies in the global city*. Berkeley, CA: University of California Press.

Yea, S., 2005. Labour of love: Filipina entertainer's narratives of romance and relationships with GIs in US military camp towns in Korea. *Women's Studies International Forum*, 28(6), pp. 456–472.

Part V
Clients

31

Clients

An introduction

Susan Dewey, Isabel Crowhurst, and Chimaraoke Izugbara

Introduction

Cultural, interpersonal, and socio-legal factors all variously have implications for sex industry patronage as well as the ways in which sex workers select their clients and cultivate various forms of relationships with them. Key themes in existing literature include characteristics of persons who buy sex, strategies for buying sex, forms of sexual services clients buy, different types of relationships with/to sex workers, clients' perspectives on sex work, client-perpetrated violence against sex workers, and the criminalization of clients. Chapters in this section engage with these ongoing challenges while offering clear directions for future research.

Key themes in existing literature

The vast majority of literature focuses on providers of sexual services, who are almost always of lower socio-economic status than their clients. A relative lack of analytical attention devoted to clients also reflects deeply entrenched discomfort across a wide variety of cultural contexts with respect to boundaries between intimacy and paid work. Financial exchange cements many forms of affective and sexual bonds, including marriage, and discomfort with the idea of prostitution is particularly indicative of the culturally conflicted distinctions between intimacy and money (Zelizer, 2005). Such cultural conflicts are also apparent in studies that document clients' characteristics in comparison to men who do not buy sex, raising the question of whether clients differ profoundly from men who do not (Groom & Nandwani, 2006; Monto, 2013). Prevailing approaches to studying clients' characteristics regard them as a "risky" population who engage in sexual practices, such as condom-less sex with multiple partners, and violent behaviors that cause harm to sex workers and society as a whole (Joseph & Black, 2012; Ompad et al., 2013).

Clients have different types of relationships with and to sex workers and, like sex workers, must psychologically manage the stigma of their sex industry involvement and associated deviant identity (Sanders, 2008). Studies of female sex tourists' deployment of racist ideas and gendered notions of intimacy to justify their "holiday romances" add another layer of complexity to the study of clients (Nyanzi, Rosenberg-Jallow, Bah & Nyanzi, 2005; Sanchez Taylor, 2006).

The sex industry is globally stratified by social class in ways that mirror other forms of economic exchange, so that the highest-earning sex workers almost always have more autonomy, education, and resources than the lowest-paying clients (Hoang, 2011). Clients' relationships with sex workers can include both regular and non-regular arrangements, long-term financial providers, and may also be indistinguishable from other affective relationships (Milrod & Monto, 2016; Robertson et al., 2014). These relationships take place within a global political economy in which sex workers sometimes strategically mobilize the socio-economic inequalities between themselves and their clients to encourage their benevolence in the form of additional or extended financial support or international migration (Choo, 2016).

Clients' perspectives on the sex industry derive from dominant cultural perspectives on sexuality and gender norms as well as individual orientations, with paying for sex sometimes seen as an act of rebellion in sex-negative societies (Huschke & Schubotz, 2016). Online fora create community among clients as they anonymously share information about their experiences and advise one another on topics such as how to evade arrest and negotiate rates with sex workers (Blevins & Holt, 2009). In public health parlance, clients are a "bridge population" whose sexual encounters with long-term partners and sex workers make them a disease-bearing conduit between these two groups (Patterson et al., 2012).

Client violence against sex workers appears to be strongly associated with patriarchal gender norms that encourage men to assume ownership over women's labour and autonomy (Karandikar & Gezinski, 2012), with men who have sex with men for pay reporting much lower incidents of violence than their female peers (Jamela, 2011). The globally expanding neo-abolitionist approach originated in Sweden, based on the criminalization of the purchase (but not the sale) of sex, has resulted in the emergence of court-mandated pedagogical programs in North America and elsewhere that instruct men on the social and interpersonal harms that accompany buying sexual services (Cook, 2015; Majic, 2014). Taken together, this literature on clients leaves significant room for critical and analytical expansion in a wide variety of areas.

Chapter overview

Blanchette and da Silva (Chapter 32) argue that "objectification" and "male domination" incorrectly assess the behavior of men in brothels, which instead can more effectively be characterized as an inversion of the heteronormative socio-sexual order that requires men's sexual pursuit of women. Caldwell and deWit's important contribution to the field (Chapter 33), mostly focused on male clients, is that women sex buyers' descriptions of the exchange are largely therapeutic and positive yet also constrained by stigma, fear, and cost. Mosley (Chapter 34) contends that dominant cultural stereotypes regarding clients as victimizers do not reflect reality and that "End Demand" initiatives that target clients for arrest and punitive sanctions are detrimental to public policy and law enforcement.

Ezeh and colleagues (Chapter 35) examine cultural configurations of masculinity and modernity that encourage men to purchase sexual labor from women who are cultural "rebels" through unique client–sex worker relationships centered on intimacy, friendship, trust, emotional exchange, love, care, and money. Zheng (Chapter 36) contends that clients' "consumption" of hostesses becomes the criterion by which clients evaluate each other's moral quality and business competence in Chinese state-clientelism that requires the cultivation of intense trust bonds in the context of highly competitive and relatively unregulated rapid capitalist expansion.

Future directions

Research clearly demonstrates the wide array of relationships that exist between clients and sex workers with diverse characteristics and the justifications that both parties provide for their sex industry involvement. Nevertheless, little is known about the dynamics within relationships that are not clearly defined as sex work, yet involve forms of intimate and economic exchange that closely resemble prostitution. Future research will likely explore how individuals in such relationships set particular boundaries that distinguish them from commercial sex, both in cultural contexts and globally. Research is also needed to understand the social ecologies and geographies of buying particular forms of sex. For instance, Nigeria and Senegal have similar laws with regards to gay sex. But Senegal remains a more popular destination for gay sex tourism. Despite the significant body of literature depicting clients as violent abusers or victimizers, little to nothing is known about the negative experiences of sex workers' clients, including those robbed, harmed, or even killed by sex workers or their associates. These issues could potentially be very interesting areas to explore in sex tourism scenarios, where clients can be less familiar with local norms, practices, and rules.

The increasing frequency with which clients are criminalized and targeted by the criminal justice system presents rich opportunities for analytical engagement, particularly with respect to men's gendered experiences as they face court, incarceration, pay bribes, or otherwise navigate their status as perpetrators of a crime. It may likewise be worthwhile to explore whether particular legal and other regulatory approaches to the sex industry change how clients approach commercial sex. For instance, clients may avoid legalized sex industry forms because these are less "exciting" due to regulations removing or diminishing the sex industry's transgressive allure, or because regulatory forms often make sex industry participation visible through registration and other forms of recording.

References

Blevins, Kristine and Holt, Thomas. 2009. Examining the Virtual Subculture of Johns. *Journal of Contemporary Ethnography* 38: 619–648.

Choo, Hae Yeon. 2016. Selling Fantasies of Rescue: Intimate Labor, Filipina Migrant Hostesses, and US GIs in a Shifting Global Order. *Positions: East Asia Cultures Critique* 24(1): 179– 203.

Cook, Ian. 2015. Making Links Between Sex Work, Gender and Victimization: The Politics and Pedagogies of John Schools. *Gender, Place & Culture* 22(6): 817–832.

Groom, T. and Nandwani, R. 2006. Characteristics of Men Who Pay for Sex: A UK Sexual Health Clinic Survey. *Sexually Transmitted Infections* 82(5): 364–367.

Hoang, Kimberley Kay. 2011. "She's Not a Low-Class Dirty Girl!": Sex Work in Ho Chi Minh City, Vietnam. *Journal of Contemporary Ethnography* 40(4): 367–396.

Huschke, Susann and Schubotz, Dirk. 2016. Commercial Sex, Clients, and Christian Morals: Paying for Sex in Ireland. *Sexualities* 19(7): 869–887.

Jamela, Joanna. 2011. An Investigation of the Incidence of Client-Perpetrated Sexual Violence Against Male Sex Workers. *International Journal of Sexual Health* 23(1): 63–78.

Joseph, Lauren and Black, Pamela. 2012. Who's the Man? Fragile Masculinities, Consumer Masculinities, and the Profiles of Sex Work Clients. *Men and Masculinities* 15(5): 486–506.

Karandikar, Sharvari and Gezinski, Lindsay. 2012. "Without Us, Sex Workers will Die Like Weeds": Sex Work and Client Violence in Kamathipur. *Indian Journal of Gender Studies* 19(3): 351–371.

Majic, Samantha. 2014. Teaching Equality? "John Schools," Gender, and Institutional Reform. *Polity* 46(1): 5–30.

Milrod, Christine and Monto, Martin. 2016. Older Male Clients of Female Sex Workers in the United States. *Archives of Sexual Behavior* 46(6): 1867–1876.

Monto, Martin. 2013. Ordinary or Peculiar Men? Comparing the Customers of Prostitutes with a Nationally Representative Sample of Men. *International Journal of Offender Therapy and Comparative Criminology* 58(7): 802–820.

Nyanzi, Stella, Rosenberg-Jallow, Bah, Ousman, and Nyanzi, Susan. 2005. Bumsters, Big Black Organs and Old White Gold: Embodied Racial Myths in Sexual Relationships of Gambian Beach Boys. *Culture, Health & Sexuality* 7(6): 557–569.

Ompad, Danielle, Bell, David, Amesty, Silvia, Nyitray, Alan, Papenfuss, Mary, Lazcano-Ponce, Eduardo, Villa, Luisa, and Giuliano, Anna. 2013. Men Who Purchase Sex, Who Are They? An Interurban Comparison. *Journal of Urban Health* 90(6): 1166–1180.

Patterson, Thomas, Volkmann, Tyson, Goldenberg, Shira, Lozada, Remedios, Semple, Shirley, Anderson, Christy, and Strathdee, Steffanie. 2012. Identifying the HIV Transmission Bridge: Which Men Are Having Unprotected Sex with Female Sex Workers and Their Own Wives or Steady Partners? *Journal of Acquired Immune Deficiency Syndromes* 60: 414–420.

Robertson, Angela, Syvertsen, Jennifer, Amaro, Hortensia, Martinez, Gustavo, Rangel, Gudelia, Patterson, Thomas, and Strathdee, Steffanie. 2014. Can't Buy My Love: A Typology of Female Sex Workers' Commercial Relationships in the Mexico-US Border Region. *Journal of Sex Research* 51(6): 711–720.

Sanchez Taylor, Jaqueline (2006). Female Sex Tourism: A Contradiction in Terms? *Feminist Review* 83: 42–59.

Sanders, Teela. 2008. *Paying for Pleasure: Men Who Buy Sex*. Cullompton, UK: Willan.

Zelizer, Viviana. 2005. *The Purchase of Intimacy*. Princeton: Princeton University Press.

32

Men in brothels

(Homo)sexuality in Rio de Janeiro's commercial sexual venues

Thaddeus Blanchette and Ana Paula da Silva[1]

Introduction

> If there is such a thing – still – as feminine pleasure, then, it is because men need it in order to maintain themselves in their own existence. It is *useful* to them: it helps them bear what is intolerable in their world as speaking beings, to have a soul foreign to that world: a fantasmatic one . . . It is quite obvious who has to assume the responsibility for preserving this fantasy. Women do not have a soul: they serve as a guarantee for man's.
>
> *(Irigaray, 1973: 96, emphasis in original)*

Little research has been done regarding male clients of female prostitutes.[2] What exists tends to come from the fields of public health, law enforcement, and psychology. It is generally statistical in nature and focused on whether or not said men are "normal" (Brewer et al., 2008; Brewer & Roberts, 2006; Gibbens & Silberman, 1960; Monto & McRee, 2005; Monto & Milrod, 2013), their motivations (Kern, 2000; Winick, 1962), their contributions to violence against women (Farley et al., 2015; Monto, 2000), and their criminal profile (Diana, 1985). Feminist theorists also talk about clients (Farley, Bindel, & Golding, 2009; Jeffreys, 1997), but do not seem to spend time observing them. Even Melissa Farley (2017), who has interviewed hundreds of clients, does not do more than talk to them from outside the context of sex work. Few feminists and fewer of today's neo-abolitionists have spent time in brothels, watching sex workers and clients interact. Researchers seem more comfortable applying questionnaires to clients than "sharing time" with them (Fabian, 1983). We cannot say why this blind spot has developed, but we suggest that part of the answer lies in a persistent view of prostitution as a relationship made up of male victimizers and female victims. This view draws heavily on a priori assumptions about men and women, sex and work.

Our first visits to sex work venues showed us how problematic this dichotomy is. It is not that the relations we observed did not reflect men's significant and persistent social, political, and economic advantages: it was that these relations were not more (or less) reflective of patriarchy, objectification, or domination than those in marriages, jobs, the dating scene, etc. Our ethnographic research has brought to light how variable and changing relations between clients and sex workers can be. This is something that is not easily captured by questionnaires and surveys.

Watching men and women interact in brothels, it is hard for us to affirm the feminist *koan*[3] that these are spaces where women are the most objectified. As is the role of all good *koans*, this has provoked doubts for us. Brothels are spaces of gender domination – as are almost all social spaces. However, is this domination mostly expressed through *objectification*? Is it more present in brothels than in, say, bars? Are men in brothels primarily there to exercise domination over women? How does said domination play out?

These are some of the questions that surveys cannot answer, but ethnography can. This chapter evaluates clients in brothels, based on 13 years of ethnographic work in Rio de Janeiro. As such, it needs to be accompanied by a caveat: the sale and purchase of sex are not (yet) criminalized in Brazil. Many things surrounding sex work are, however: running a brothel in particular. Nonetheless, Rio has some 300 sex work venues. This is the result of the "unofficially official regulation" of prostitution, where brothels are tolerated by authorities as long as kickbacks are paid (Blanchette, Murray, & Mitchell, forthcoming), and that allows the commercial sex venues of Rio to operate more or less openly. The men who frequent these brothels do not do so furtively, while watching for police. We thus warn readers that the type of men who frequent carioca[4] brothels and the relations observed there may not apply to other sorts of legal/sexual regimes.

Another caveat is that what we describe below does not apply to all men in brothels, even in Rio. In spite of what neo-abolitionists claim, men frequent brothels for a wide variety of reasons (Blanchette & da Silva, 2005). What we describe below is "normative" in the Durkheimian sense (Durkheim, 1998), however, in that it is observable in pretty much any brothel in Rio. We believe that what we discuss below is a much better understanding of what men do in brothels than the commonly attributed notion that they buy women's bodies or – even more extreme – that they rape women (Farley, 2017).

We also feel that our observations of men in brothels in Rio have applications that are not restricted to this city or to Brazil. In the past 15 years, we have gone to many brothels and strip clubs outside of our country and the dynamics we have observed are not radically different. To put it bluntly, we feel that much of today's analysis of men in brothels relies on ideological a priori affirmations and not on empirical observation. In 2011, for example, we conducted fieldwork in New Orleans strip clubs and noticed that many of the same things that happen in Rio also go on there. One couple in particular stands out in our memory: a young man who placed a ten-dollar bill on the floor next to a stripper and was "rewarded" by having her drape her legs over his shoulders while ramming her pelvis into his face with enough force to almost give him whiplash. Who is the "object" of desire in this interaction? Who is the dominated? We would stipulate that – as Katherine Frank (2002) and Susan Dewey (2011) pointed out in the context of US strip clubs – these questions do not have easy, "just so" answers.

Our experiences lead us to believe that existing studies rely too much on the concepts of "objectification of women" and a simplistic view of "male domination" in understanding what goes on in brothels. Borrowing the concept of *hommo-sexualité* (translated as (homo)sexuality) from Luce Irigaray (1973), we argue that these spaces are better understood as stages upon which men enact and renew performances of masculine sexuality for a primarily male audience. Women *act* in these mini-dramas: their immanence as agents is a necessary part of the *mise-en-scène*. Women's actions and consent are crucial as they reaffirm the centrality – the very indifference – of masculine sexuality.

Although there are many different men in brothels and many different fantasies being portrayed, the performances we most commonly observe evoke female aggression and male passivity. However, as we shall see, this should not necessarily be understood as female empowerment. Ironically, in brothels – different from supposedly normative[5] (homo)sexual relationships – commerce with women is necessary, even though the main fantasy being sold is the centrality of male sexual indifference. We suspect that this is a reason why brothels are simultaneously liminal and traditional environments: they promise escape from normative gender relations without threatening male domination, constantly containing (in both senses of the word) the immanence of women as sexual agents even as they highlight this. This very liminality, in fact, may be key to understanding male violence against sex workers. That, however, is a subject for a future article.

Scenes from the field

We would like to begin with a discussion of who we are and what brothels look like in Rio de Janeiro, before passing on to descriptions of incidents we have encountered in fieldwork and that have provoked the present article. We have worked as ethnographers associated with the Davida prostitutes' rights collective for 13 years. Thaddeus is a white male immigrant and has lived for 26 years in Brazil. Ana Paula is a black female and native-born carioca. We are sexual/affective partners as well as co-researchers. Because we are a binational, biracial, heterosexual couple, we are constantly presumed to be a sex worker and a client. This aids our research, because even though we identify ourselves as anthropologists, we are rarely perceived as such.

Originally, our research began in the sex tourism venues of the Copacabana neighborhood of Rio de Janeiro (Blanchette & da Silva, 2005). This expanded to downtown, Rio's largest concentration of commercial sexual venues (Blanchette & da Silva, 2011), and finally to Vila Mimosa, the city's only "red light district"[6] (see Murray et al., Chapter 45 this volume). In the course of this work, we have mapped close to 300 commercial sexual venues, conducting research in over half of them and persistent fieldwork in the 20 most popular. There are a variety of commercial sexual venues in Rio that we have described elsewhere (Blanchette & da Silva 2011; Blanchette & Schettini, 2017). Nevertheless, the outlines of the city's "closed"[7] sexual venues (brothels) follow a general pattern. There is an entryway, which may be a simple corridor. Bouncers are stationed here and, in more upscale brothels, here is where the cash registers are located. Entering, one receives a *comanda*, which is a piece of paper[8] listing consumption of goods and services. This space opens to a lounge, containing a dance floor, a bar, and maybe a small stage and pole. Music booms in this space, forcing conversations into intimate distance. Clients and sex workers congregate and socialize here. There is a door leading to a segregated space where rooms (or *cabines*[9]) can be rented.

Prices are established by a common table according to time and clients and sex workers negotiate a set amount of time for a *programa*,[10] typically ranging from ten minutes to an hour. Before going to the rooms, a couple stops at the cash register and notes the *programa*, receiving a condom, which the man pays for, one condom per *programa*. The dodge that allows brothels to function in Brazil is that the house has nothing to do with prostitution: it just rents rooms and sells food and drink. Technically, this is true as the woman's fee for the *programa* is not touched by the house. In reality, the *programa* and the room fee go on the man's *comanda* and *programas* all cost the same, per hour,[11] in order to avoid competition among the women. Women can charge clients for "special services," such as anal sex, condom-free oral sex, etc., and receive tips, however. Room rental fees run from 25–40% of the total paid by the client. When the client leaves, expenditures are calculated on the same bill. The women receive their money on a daily, weekly, or biweekly basis.[12]

Some houses are more elaborate. *Termas* (heterosexual saunas), for example, have clients change into robes before entering the lounge. They might have pools, saunas, smoking rooms, and quiet areas. But the above is a bare bones description of how almost all closed prostitution venues in Rio operate. The first thing to note is that the women do not "line up" for the men.

In our fieldwork to date, we have seen women passively display themselves for men once. On all other occasions, initial contact between men and women took place in the common room. Aside from female dress,[13] this space resembles a regular bar. The men come in alone, in pairs, or groups, buy drinks, and occupy seats. They talk among themselves. They generally ignore the women. It is the women who move towards the men, often in such a decisive manner that it can alarm first-time visitors.

One evening during the 2014 World Cup, we followed a group of Chileans who were searching for a bar to celebrate their team's victory. We came upon them in Praça da República, just as they spied the neon sign of a small *fast foda*.[14] They made a beeline towards the establishment and climbed the stairs of its entry corridor. The Chileans debouched into the brothel's lounge and came face-to-face with the female manager and eight sex workers, who were filing their nails and surfing the Internet on their phones. Both groups stared at each other for an instant. Then the women flew off their chairs and swarmed the men, forcibly pulling the group apart while shooting questions at the Chileans and shouting orders to the manager: "Hello, honey! Where are you from? Do you want a beer? Do you want company? Priscila, put on Bob Marley! Bring us beer!" Before the men could stammer out an answer, they were led off to separate tables, a cold beer in front of each of them and a woman on either side. The women chattered away at them, running their hands over the men's crotches and chests. Reggae boomed out in the club. It took more than a half hour of beers and increasingly strenuous refusals on the part of the Chileans before they were able to extract themselves from the tables, pay a substantial bar tab, and tumble down the stairs and into the night.

A pejorative term for prostitutes in Brazil is *piranha* and situations like the one described above show how this may have come about. The night in question had been slow and that contributed to the almost caricaturized scene that had unfolded before us. In our experience, however, female aggression and male passivity are the norm in carioca brothels. In fact, the process of convincing a client to pay for sex is often called "seduction" by carioca sex workers. The women spend enormous amounts of (unpaid) time and energy trying to get a man pay for a *programa*.

We tell our male student researchers that if they want to see how it feels to be a woman in a typical bar or disco, they should go into a brothel. They will be groped, pinched, pummelled, and (wo)manhandled. The students laugh, but often betray signs of panic when it starts happening to them. Macho ideology aside, it is not an agreeable experience for many men.

As a male,[15] Thaddeus is often on the receiving end of this behavior. As common, however, is verbal seduction. This often feels as if the woman in question is trying to "tune in" on the man, fishing for an indication of what role she is to play in his fantasy. An example of this happened to Thaddeus one night in a Copacabana *boate*. Upon discovering that he was a professor, his seductress presented herself as a "communications major" making a film about a professor falling in love with a prostitute. When that did not move Thaddeus to pay for a *programa*, she started showing him pictures of her children, remarking how she missed them. When Thaddeus repeated that he wasn't interested in a *programa*, the woman switched gears again, becoming extremely lascivious, trying to sit on his lap and slipping her hand in his shirt to grab at his nipples. All this occurred in less than 15 minutes. On another occasion, a woman approached Thaddeus and asked "Do you want to see pictures of my pussy?" When he declined the offer, she immediately changed tack: "Do you want to see pictures of my children, then?"

Such mood whiplash is common in Rio's brothels. Stoicism and passivity seem to be the rule for males in these interchanges. The women do the work of seducing, deploying story elements drawn from their lives or invented, while the men – more often than not – ignore the women. As one of our sex worker informants, Pamela,[16] a 38-year-old white woman, remarked: "People think it's just saying, 'I have pussy for sale!' I wish! Girl, you have to *work* to get fucked in this city!" Pamela's point is often repeated by sex workers. According to these women, what men want in brothels is "to feel like a big shot."[17] Time and again, we have heard that "the guys are mostly here to drink with their buddies, not pay for *programas*." This is one of the greatest frustrations carioca sex workers express to us. They perform emotional labor seducing men and "making them feel like big shots," but only earn if a man pays for sex. The sex workers of Copacabana have a term for the man who never pays: *fariseu*.[18] The anger this sort of behavior causes should not be underestimated: the only incident we have heard of involving a public act of serious violence by a sex worker against a client[19] occurred against a *fariseu* who got bashed on the head with a barstool by a frustrated sex worker.

As a black carioca woman, Ana Paula experiences seduction from another angle. Friends remark that she is courageous to walk into brothels: Ana replies that it does not take courage as she is ignored. With half naked women doing their best to attract men's attention, a fully dressed woman who is minding her own business is generally left alone. It was Ana Paula who noticed the most interesting thing about men in brothels: they generally pay attention to other men. In fact, it often seems that women are purely decorative, so little attention do they receive from the male clientele. Brothels are male dominated, not in the sense that women are cowed or treated like objects, but in the sense that women are often treated as if they simply do not exist.

In smaller downscale venues there will be less male–male socialization than in larger upscale venues such as *termas*. Still, the male gaze tends to fall predominantly on other men. Women get ogled and manhandled, but as part of negotiation for a *programa*. Men who do not want to pay generally keep their attention on other men. Ana never feels so invisible, as a woman, than when she walks through a brothel.

Vila Mimosa (VM) is Rio's only red-light district, a remnant of early twentieth-century containment policies (Blanchette & Schettini, 2017). Some 70 small *cabarés* line its one street. It is frequented by working and lower middle-class men who pay around 20 USD for 20 minutes of sex in its cramped *cabines*. VM is also the only brothel space where Ana Paula has received male sexual attention: only once and very politely. An older man came up to her while she was interviewing a sex worker and asked, "Excuse me, but are you working here?"

"Yes," Ana replied. "As an anthropologist, collecting interviews."

"What a pity," the man said, smiling. "Excuse me for having bothered you." And he walked away.

During the 2017 Olympic Games Ana had another experience in VM, along with a black female colleague. The pair spent close to six hours in the Vila, interviewing sex workers and watching the Games on TV and were ignored or politely acknowledged by the clientele. At no time did the women feel pressured, threatened, or unwelcome.[20] Ana and her colleague then walked to a rock bar for a hamburger and a beer. The male clients of the bar refused to leave them alone. Eventually, the harassment became too annoying and Ana and her colleague left the bar.

With women being more aggressive in brothels and men more passive, the body language of the two genders is often reversed. Men – especially men alone – will sit hunched, arms drawn in and hands on their laps while women will spread out while seated, arms splayed, legs rubbing up against those of the men. When men agree to a *programa*, it is generally the woman who takes them by the hand and leads them to the back rooms, as if the men were children. Of course, some men reciprocate women's advances and do not pay for sex. If this happens too often, the women stop paying attention to them.

Female aggression is driven by the laws of the market, not by the house. On only two occasions have we seen management call for sex workers to "get active on the floor" and start talking to clients. Both cases occurred in small *privés* downtown while the women were finishing lunch breaks. In both the cases, the women simply did not go until they felt they were ready.

Female aggression extends to violence. Although we have only heard of one act of serious public female on male violence, female on female violence often occurs in brothels. Almost always, the fight is because one woman feels that another is moving in on "her" client. Our male informants agree that the women try to "lay claim" to them. One 45-year-old African American says,

> You do not want to go with the same girl too many times or you'll have a girlfriend. No other girl in the brothel will come up to you unless she allows it. If you want to go with someone else, she will introduce you to her friends. You are now her property. If you go to another brothel, the next time you come back, she'll be there saying, "So I heard you went to X?" I'm telling you: *putanet* is faster than the Internet.

Women who encroach on other women's clients can meet violence, from thrown drinks to murder. At one bar in Copacabana, a serial encroacher was supposedly sold a packet of cocaine cut with ground glass. She died from a lung haemorrhage.

Pamela describes the economic logic behind aggressive behavior:

> There are usually more women than men. Only some men are going to pay for a *programa*. If you hang back, you are going to be ignored. Men do not want to hunt women: they want to feel hunted. If you want to make money, you need to go and seduce them.

Our male informants confirm Pamela's words. When we ask them why they come into brothels, their most common answer is "to relax." One evening, we chatted with Alex, a 38-year-old medium-brown carioca man in a downtown *boate*. Alex was extremely fit and handsome, wearing flip-flops, sweatpants, and a t-shirt. He was folded into a corner sofa in the back of the common room, drinking a *caipirinha*. Because of his build and demeanour, we thought he might be an Olympic athlete. When we told him this, he smiled:

> No, I am a military policeman.[21] Off-duty, of course. I come here to relax after a bad day.[22] I talk with friends and take the edge off before I go home. No one bothers me here. No one makes demands. The girls come up to me and if I want to pay for a *programa*, I do. Mostly, however, I just enjoy the attention.

Other men who pay for sex talk about the experience in terms of convenience and economy. Fernando, a 40-year-old white carioca lawyer says:

> This is the best use of money for sex. If you take a woman out, you will spend 300 reais [91 USD]? Maybe you'll have sex. But you have to talk, seduce . . . Here [a Copacabana *boate*], you can drink with your friends and sex is guaranteed for 300 reais. You do not have to do anything: the women come after you. You can feel like a rock star. And they do not bother you after.

This "day after" factor is also a reason why men say they frequent brothels. On many occasions, we have heard men repeat the old adage that "you do not pay for sex; you pay for them to go away afterwards." This is particularly true for husbands. A 55-year-old white English banker describes frequenting brothels in the following way:

Let's say I have a lover. People may see us. She may call me up when my wife is home. She will say she will not get romantically involved, but that's a lie. It will become a scandal. But here [a Copacabana *boate*] no one is the wiser. I'm happy to have sex and maintain my marriage. The girls are happy to get money. My wife's happy because there is no scandal.

Brothels know that many clients are married. In upscale *termas*, a TV in the sauna will often be tuned to the traffic news, providing men with the means to craft an excuse for a late arrival home. The house is also generally registered under an innocuous name – "C. Carlos Food & Beverages," for example – so that credit card bills do not alarm.

(Homo)sexuality

But why is the need for – or possibility of – sex without commitment important for these men to "relax"? Many reasons have been offered but we heard the most succinct during our original research on Copacabana: "Why does a dog lick his balls? Because he can." Certainly, the appeal of "a zipless fuck" (Jong, 1973/1994) transcends gender. After seeing carioca brothels, many of our female colleagues (especially those above 40) remark that if such places existed for women, they'd be tempted to use them. But this does not explain why such places do not exist, nor why so many men say their brothel visits meet a "need."

One of the most common explanations we hear is that, unlike women, men have a "biological drive" to have sex with many partners. According to this view – traditional in Western sexual philosophy – brothels permit men to maintain social monogamy while exercising their biological imperative. This explanation is not sustained by our observations, for the men who most often frequent brothels are also often avid consumers of erectile dysfunction medication, which can be purchased directly in most upscale brothels in Rio. This behavior is so normative that many Anglophone informants call Viagra "Vitamin V." If these men's need for paid sex is predominantly biologically driven, why the consumption of little blue pills? It seems to us that this behavior only underlines how masculine "needs" are, in fact, socially constructed.

Another hypothesis is that men who frequent brothels feel entitled to sex. Certainly, there are men who feel this way and they can be found in brothels as often as they can be found in bars, churches, or on college campuses. But again, this is not the reason most clients seem to go to brothels. As incredible as it may sound to some, there is good evidence that consent is important to these men. Both clients and sex workers are adamant about drawing a line between rape and the consensual sale of sex. Many prostitutes do not like sex work, but they insist on the primacy of women's control and consent. "I decide what happens, when, and with whom," says Simone, a 20-year-old light-brown carioca sex worker.

I talk to the client and find out what he wants. We agree on a time. He has that long. If he cums first, done. If he cannot get it up, done. If he wants longer, he pays. But if I say no, he does not get a say. He's not buying me.

Although sex workers might rhetorically refer to prostitution as "selling one's body," they are clear that their bodies are not alienated in the *programa*. Selling sex is not "selling the body." This should be obvious when one reflects that a true "sale" of the body would logically mean that the purchaser could resell it, something that never occurs in carioca brothels.[23] As sex worker activist Indianara Siqueira puts it, "Honey, if I 'sold my body' there'd be nothing left here to talk with you."

Negotiation establishes what is to take place. Moving beyond what has been agreed is considered rape by all of the sex workers and most of the clients we have talked to. This is, of course, an idealization – just as is the notion of consent outside of brothels.[24] However, rape is not considered to be a normative state of affairs by sex workers or their clients. Once, in a discussion on a client website, a man admitted to raping a sex worker. He claimed that he had negotiated for anal sex, but the woman decided that she did not want to do it. He forced her. Of the nine men who responded to the story, only one took the rapist's side and was quickly shouted down. The other eight called the man a rapist. Some called for his removal from the site; others wanted to report him to the police;[25] others threatened to beat him. One employed a common feminist slogan: "Yes means yes; no means no." This man elaborated on his sentiments: "First and foremost, these women are human beings. To be clear, I am not saying paying for sex is 'rape': I am saying that you forcing anyone, prostitute or not, to do anything against her will is rape." Whatever else may be said about clients, the majority we have talked to do not feel entitled to sex. As Daniel, a 42-year old African American succinctly put it, "If I felt 'entitled' to sex, I certainly wouldn't be paying for it."

A third hypothesis is that men go to brothels to objectify women. But what is objectification and is it necessarily bad? Feminist scholar Martha Nussbaum (1995: 256–257) points out that "not all types of objectification are equally objectionable." Nussbaum invites us to carefully evaluate context and circumstance when looking at objectification and provides a list of "seven ways to treat a person as a thing": instrumentality, denial of autonomy, inertness, fungibility, violability, ownership, and denial of subjectivity. Rae Langton (2009: 228–229 adds three more characteristics: reduction to body, reduction to appearance, and silencing.

In carioca brothels, instrumentality, denial of subjectivity, reduction to body, reduction to appearance, and silencing seem to apply. Although Nussbaum points out that the presence of even one of these can create objectification, comparatively speaking, it is certainly clear that objectification is generally as or more present in other forms of interaction in Rio. As we have pointed out (Blanchette, da Silva, & Camargo, 2014), labor in a restaurant or as a maid invokes instrumentality, denial of autonomy, fungibility, denial of subjectivity, inertness, and silencing, and often reduction to appearance. "Normative" sexual/affective courting may involve all ten characteristics. Certainly, traditional marriage can be as or more objectifying than prostitution. It is hard to believe, then, that men go to brothels to objectify women, given so many other, more intense, opportunities to do this in their daily lives,

We may be on firmer ground if we presume that men come into brothels to sexually objectify women. But how, then, does one conflate this presumption with the manifest indifference with which so many men treat sex workers in brothels? If the primary drive is to sexually objectify women, why do men spend so much time in brothels doing anything but? We believe that Belgian feminist Luce Irigaray may offer a fresh perspective.

In her critique of Freud and Lacan, Irigaray (1973) postulates that a basic indifference (indifference and a denial of women's sexuality as different from men's) exists towards the feminine. She terms this *hommo-sexualité*, equating the sexuality of men with a sexuality that does not contemplate women as separate sexual beings. As the epigraph with which we began this chapter points out, within this view of the world, men need women – and, indeed, women's desire and pleasure, as long as these are a reflection of the phallus – in order to (re)create themselves. This (male) desire and pleasure must be performatively reflected by women. It calls upon women not as objects, but as agents within a horizon of possibilities bounded by the masculine.

The main fantasy that men consume in a brothel is one of their centrality. The brothel is an inversion of normal courting behavior. Men become the center of attention, the hunted, and women the hunters (Olivar Nieto, 2013). Men are desired and women desiring. It is significant, in this context, that the Indo-European root of "whore" is *horaz*: "one who desires" (Raccioppi, 2009). Men in brothels are seeking a conditional, temporary, sexual objectification of themselves as men – an objectification that they can always escape by leaving the brothel.

Irigaray's analysis, however, is based upon "normative" sexual exchange and not prostitution. Irigaray herself admits that she hasn't thought about prostitution in the context of her theory, but she seems to presume that it is a simple dynamic of men selling women to other men (Irigaray, 1978). Women, however, are not "owned" by brothels in Rio. In all our years of research, we have never met a woman who has a pimp – if by "pimp" one means a man who controls the woman and "owns" her sexuality. It is thus difficult to understand the commercial dynamics of brothels as men selling women to men, even in symbolic fashion, especially as carioca brothels symbolically distance themselves from this wherever possible.

So, what do brothels in Rio ultimately sell, aside from drinks and a "men's club" atmosphere? The answer seems to be security, for both the sex worker and the client. Taking up Irigaray's analysis again, they provide a "circuit breaker" that cuts the underlying presumption of (hommo)sexuality: that women are exchanged between men as property. The underlying arrangement of patriarchal sexual exchange is that the woman trades sex for sustenance and this gives the man permanent authority over her. The normative "permanency" of relationships that clients fear also exists for the woman as fear of violence, robbery, possession. A prostitute, working alone, has to negotiate this fraught social-psychological exchange that is notoriously dangerous for, as Irigaray points out, "Men make commerce *of* [women], but do not enter into any exchanges *with* them" (Irigaray, 1978: 172). Women who presume to negotiate sex *with* men do so at their own peril.

A brothel, however, provides a structure within which these negotiations can be relatively easily accomplished. It provides a stage and props for the dearest male fantasy – centrality and sexual indifference – while securing the conditions for female negotiation.

The key to the application of this fantasy within carioca brothels is domination, in the sense attributed by Max Weber: the probability that commands will be obeyed (1999). These "commands," however – which make men in brothels feel like "big shots" – have only conditional and temporally bound legitimacy. They are not backed by legal, traditional, or charismatic authority. They are obeyed only to the degree that they have been previously negotiated *with women* and are paid for. The "command," in other words, must be inscribed on the *comanda* and, for that to occur in carioca brothels, negotiation with women – and women's consent – is absolutely essential.

Notes

1 The authors would like to thank Christine Sardina for her preliminary reading and suggestions.
2 We will use "prostitute" and "sex worker" interchangeably in reference to women who sell sex.
3 A statement, used in Zen practice, to provoke doubts.
4 An adjective for things and people from Rio de Janeiro.
5 By "supposedly normative" we mean sexual/affective relationships that are understood to be based on mutual pleasure, affection, and reciprocity. However, as José Miguel Olivar Nieto points out (2013) and our experiences confirm, economic, affective, and status concerns permeate all sexual/affective markets (Piscitelli, 2004), blurring the line between "prostitution" and "normative" relations.
6 In the sense that it is a distinctly separate geographic/moral zone that specializes in sexual commerce (Park & Burgess, 1925/1984).
7 "Closed" venues are areas specifically given over to sexual commerce out of view of the general public. In Rio, this includes *termas* (heterosexual saunas), *privés* and *massagens* (small apartments), *boates* (nightclubs or stripclubs), and also simple brothels (generally called *casas, cabarés, clubes recreativos*, or *relax*).
8 Occasionally a computerized card, key, or chit.
9 *Cabines*, or cabins, are rooms generally walled off by thin plywood dividers and measuring 3 x 2 meters. HBO's *The Deuce* shows a brothel of this sort, complete with *cabines*.

10 The *programa*, or "program," is the name for a single act of commercial sex.
11 Or per minute in the downscale *fast fodas* (i.e. cheap knocking shops).
12 Typically, Brazilians are paid once a month and being paid daily or weekly is considered to be one of the "perks" of prostitution by most women we have talked to.
13 Typically underwear, bikinis, or (rarely) topless or full nudity. In *termas* the men also change into bathrobes.
14 See note 7.
15 As well as being white, older, and foreign and thus perceived as a potential high-paying client.
16 All interlocutors' names have been changed to protect their identities.
17 "Sentir-se o cara."
18 "Pharisee." From Jesus' statement that prostitutes will enter into the kingdom of heaven before Pharisees and publicans. Sex workers have defined the term for us as "a man who thinks he is better than a prostitute and wastes their time."
19 Symbolic violence against clients (insults, etc.), less serious physical violence (throwing drinks in a client's face), and non-public serious violence (killing clients during a *programa*, spiking their drinks with roofies, robbing clients) are relatively common occurrences in Rio de Janeiro.
20 The perception of these spaces is not specific to Ana Paula's. Carioca abolitionist and lesbian activist Heloisa Samy Santiago claims that she also frequents VM (comment made during a debate with Ana in 2016). It should be noted that many of the brothel managers in Rio identify as lesbian.
21 Military police are Rio de Janeiro's principal armed police force, used to deal with social disturbances of every kind. They are also notoriously deadly.
22 Military policemen's "bad days" in Rio often involve firefights and death.
23 Neither does the brothel "own" the sex worker's body. We have never encountered an enslaved prostitute.
24 What "consent" means in patriarchal capitalism is something we discuss elsewhere (Blanchette, da Silva, & Camargo, 2014; da Silva & Blanchette, 2017).
25 Difficult, given that everyone posting on the site did so under an assumed name.

References

Blanchette, T., and A.P. da Silva. 2005. "Nossa Senhora da Help": Sexo, turismo e deslocamento transnacional em Copacabana. *Cadernos Pagu* 25: 249–280.
Blanchette, T., and A.P. da Silva. 2011. Amor aum real por minuto – a prostituição como atividade econômica no Brasil urbano. In Sexual Policies Watch, Ed., *Sexualidade e política na America Latina: histórias, intersecções, paradoxos*, 192–233. Rio de Janeiro: Sexual Policies Watch.
Blanchette, T., A.P. da Silva, and G. Camargo. 2014. Idealismo alemão e o corpo alienável: repensando a "objetificação" no contexto do trabalho sexual. In S. Simões, Ed., *Prostituição e Outras Histórias de Amor*, 101–121. Niterói: Editora da UFF.
Blanchette, T., L. Murray, and G. Mitchell. Forthcoming. Discretionary policing, or the lesser part of valor: prostitution, law enforcement, and unregulated regulation in Rio de Janeiro's sexual economy. *Criminal Justice and Law Enforcement Annual: Global Perspectives* 1: 21–40.
Blanchette, T., and C. Schettini. 2017. Sex work in Rio de Janeiro: police management without regulation. In E. van Meerkerk, M. RodríguezGarcía , and L. Heerma van Voss, Eds., *Sex sold in world cities: 1600s– 2000s.* Leiden, Holland: Brill.
Brewer, D., and J. Roberts Jr. 2006. Estimating the prevalence of male clients of prostitute women in Vancouver with a simple capture–recapture method. *Journal of the Royal Statistical Society: Series A (Statistics in Society)*, 169(4): 745–756.
Brewer, D, J. Roberts Jr., S. Muth, and J. Potterat. 2008. Prevalence of male clients of street prostitute women in the United States. *Human Organization*, 67(3): 346–356.
da Silva, A.P., and T.G. Blanchette. 2017. Por amor, por dinheiro? Trabalho (re)produtivo, trabalho sexual e a transformação da mão-de-obra feminina. *Cadernos Pagú*, 50.
Dewey, S. 2011. *Neon wasteland: on love, motherhood, and sex work in a rust belt town.* Berkeley, CA: University of California Press.
Diana, L. 1985. *The prostitute and her clients: her business is your pleasure.* Springfield, IL: Charles C Thomas.
Durkheim, E. 1998. *Durkheim sociologia.* Org. José Albertino Rodrigues. SP: Editora Ática.

Fabian, Johannes. 1983. *Time and the other: how anthropology makes its object.* New York: Columbia University Press.

Farley, M. (2017) Very inconvenient truths: sex buyers, sexual coercion, and prostitution: harm-denial. *Logos: A Journal of Modern Culture and Society.* http://logosjournal.com/2016/farley-2 (accessed October 23, 2017).

Farley, M., Bindel, J., and J.M. Golding. 2009. *Men who buy sex: who they buy and what they know.* San Francisco, CA: Prostitution Research & Education.

Farley, M., J.M. Golding, E. Schuckman Matthews, N. Malamuth, and L. Jarrett. 2015. Comparing sex buyers with men who do not buy sex: new data on prostitution and trafficking. *Journal of Interpersonal Violence,* 32(23): 3601–3625.

Frank, C. 2002. *G-strings and sympathy: strip club regulars and male desire.* Durham, NC: Duke University Press.

Gibbens, T.C.N., and M. Silberman. 1960. The clients of prostitutes. *British Journal of Venereal Diseases,* 26(2): 113–117.

Irigaray, L. 1973. Cosi fan tutti. In L. Irigaray, *This sex which is not one,* 86–105. Ithaca, NY: Cornell University Press.

Irigaray, L. 1978. Women on the market. In L. Irigaray, *This sex which is not one,* 170–191. Ithaca, NY: Cornell University Press.

Jeffreys, S. 1997. *The idea of prostitution.* North Melbourne: Spinifex Press.

Kern, R.M. 2000. Where's the action? Criminal motivations among prostitute clients. PhD thesis, Vanderbilt University, Nashville, Tennesse.

Langton, R. 2009. *Sexual solipsism: philosophical essays on pornography and objectification.* Oxford: Oxford University Press.

Monto, M.A. 2000. "Why men seek out prostitutes." In R. Weitzer (Ed.), *Sex for sale: prostitution, pornography, and the sex industry,* 67–83. New York: Routledge.

Monto, M.A., and N. McRee. 2005. A comparison of the male customers of female street prostitutes with national samples of men. *International Journal of Offender Therapy and Comparative Criminology,* 49(5): 505–529.

Monto, M.A., and C. Milrod. 2013. Ordinary or peculiar men? Comparing the customers of prostitutes with a nationally representative sample of men. *International Journal of Offender Therapy and Comparative Criminology,* 58(7): 802–820.

Nussbaum, M. 1995. Objectification. *Philosophy and Public Affairs,* 24(4): 249–291.

Olivar Nieto, J.M. 2013. *Devir Puta: políticas da prostituição nas experiências de quatro mulheres militantes.* Rio de Janeiro: EdUERJ.

Park, R., and E. Burgess. 1984 [1925]. *The city: suggestions for the investigation of human behavior in the urban environment.* Chicago, IL: University of Chicago Press.

Piscitelli, Adriana. 2004. On gringos and natives, gender and sexuality in the context of international sex tourism. *Vibrant – Virtual Brazilian Anthropology,* 1(1): 1–27.

Raccioppi, K. 2009. From "friend'" to "whore." *Living Language: Politics, Philology, Theory.* www.livingwithlanguage.wordpress.com/2009/03/02/from-friend- to-whore (accessed June 8, 2017).

Weber, M. 1999 [1922]. The three types of legitimate domination. In M. Weber, *Essays in economic sociology,* 99–108. Princeton, NJ: Princeton University Press.

Winick, C. 1962. Prostitutes' clients' perception of the prostitutes and of themselves. *International Journal of Social Psychiatry,* 8(4): 289–297.

33

The characteristics and motivations of women who buy sex in Australia

Hilary Caldwell and John de Wit

Introduction

Women buying sex are often portrayed in the media as humorous or extraordinary, although we know little about them. They have not come to the attention of scholarly researchers because they are generally perceived as exceptional or not problematic. General and scholarly perceptions of the low prevalence of women buying sex are, however, unfounded, due to an absence of research. Despite this lack of evidence, social debates about the possibility of women buying sex continues, often relying on gendered stereotypes of female sexuality, notably 'women just do not do that', while positioning men who buy sex as the 'problem' (Jeffreys 2003). Rigid gendering of clients of the sex industry as only male biases academic, social, and political debate. The consequences of erroneous gendering of the sex industry are felt by individuals socially, through stigmatisation, and politically, in terms of policy and legal regulation. This chapter aims to challenge the gendering and stereotyping of sex industry clients by presenting empirical evidence of women buying sex in Australia.

Scholarly perception of a low prevalence of women buying sex is reflected in survey data. The Australian longitudinal study of health and relationships (ASHR) found that very few women reported they had ever paid for sex. The ASHR1 surveyed 9,134 women in 2004/2005 finding 0.1% and ASHR2 surveyed 10,038 women in 2012/2013 finding 0.3%, reported ever paying for sex (Rissel et al. 2005; Richters et al. 2014). In part, this may be due to women not framing their sexual service use as buying 'sex'. Sexual services are diverse; Harcourt and Donovan (2005) found over 25 different types of sexual services sold in Australia. Many of these services may not be conceptualised as paying for sex by all genders. For instance, Taylor (2006) found that 60% of her sample of female tourists in the Caribbean, who denied commercial sex with locals, later reported transactional relationships when questioned further. The women in Taylor's sample deny participation through defining commercial sex as a singular overtly negotiated cash exchange for fully negotiated penetrative sex devoid of emotional involvement, a stereotypical definition that does not correspond to most commercial sex transactions. Commercial sex often involves ongoing emotional attachment (Sanders 2008; Caldwell 2012). Although a larger percentage of men reported buying sex, 16% in 2004/2005 and 17% in 2012/2013 in the ASHR surveys, women, as Taylor found, may need more explanation about what is defined by 'buying' and 'sex' in surveys. As a consequence, low rates of women buying sex found in large surveys should be viewed cautiously.

Another reason why survey data may not adequately reflect female commercial sex use is because women do not have a tradition of buying sex and are often excluded from survey questions about buying sex when traditional views about female sexuality inform study design. Examples of how gender ideology influences research include the British National Survey of Sexual Attitudes and lifestyles (NATSAL) 2000 survey, a large population-based survey that only asked men if they had bought sex (Brooks-Gordon 2010). Natsal-3, in 2010, asked all genders if they had bought sex from an opposite-sex provider and asked only men if they had bought sex from a same-sex provider. Analysis of data may also be influenced by researcher bias. For instance, a study of Danish tourists returning home found that 8% of women had attended strip clubs and 1% reported paying for sex abroad. However, these figures appeared 'unserious' to researchers and were discounted (Hesse and Tutenges 2011). Studies intended to assess commercial sexual practices need an inclusive approach and we may need to find out more about how women construct their sexual purchases to know the best way of asking them about it.

The current research gap regarding women buying sex contributes to perpetuating a dominant, one-sided debate about gender, sexuality and power relationships between men and women in the sex industry. As journalistic and anecdotal evidence of women buying sex proliferates (Lipkin and Burson 2009; Tankard Reist 2010; Cynthiavankleeck 2011; Grieco and Walker 2011; Robinson 2013; Silver 2013a; Silver 2013b; Law 2014; Ninemsm 2014; Sebag-Montefiore 2014; White 2015; Goldstein 2016; Law 2016; Silver 2017), this questions notions of the low prevalence of women buying sex that inform academic debate. Until now, there has however been no academic empirical research to support or critique arguments regarding the low prevalence of women buying sex. This is despite several researchers indicating a need for research on issues relevant to increasing knowledge of women buying sex (Weitzer 2000; Taylor 2006; Brooks-Gordon 2010; Scott and Minichiello 2014; Aggleton and Parker 2015).

This chapter is based on a research project undertaken at UNSW Sydney with the experiential experts in this topic, women who buy sex. This exploratory study used a qualitative, post-structural design. Advertisements were placed online on Facebook, to which self-selecting volunteers who identified as women who had bought sex responded and were interviewed via Skype. Interview transcriptions formed the data for interpretative phenomenological analysis. Each interviewee was asked to tell their story about buying sex, and women recounted their stories largely un-interrupted. Following this, questions regarding socio-demographic characteristics such as age, relationship status, educational level, ethnicity and income were asked to provide background on the sample.

The sample of interviewees comprises 21 female identifying people, including one trans-identified woman. The women's age at the first time they bought sex ranged from 18–69, with 12 women under 45 and 9 over 45. Interviewees lived in most Australian States and Territories. Interviewees were generally well-educated women, 4 were graduates and 11 had post-graduate qualifications, although 3 did not comment about their education and 3 had secondary schooling. All interviewees were Caucasian, which might reflect recruitment methods, sampling, or the phenomenon. Regarding incomes, 3 said they had low incomes and saved for longer periods to buy sex, and 14 described their incomes as high or medium-high.

In this chapter, we first define the use of the term 'buying sex' and then present findings of the types of sex interviewees bought. We next present findings from the in-depth analysis of interviews, in particular the motivations and barriers to buying sex that were experienced by the women. Lastly, we suggest opportunities for further research and make recommendations to guide future research approaches.

What is considered 'buying sex'?

Most studies of the sex industry do not clearly define what is and is not considered commercial sex. During the course of this study, notions of which type of services and which types of motivations to buy sex should be included in understandings of buying sex were challenged. In a project that is designed to broaden understandings and challenge common gendering of the sex industry, clarity of what constitutes buying sex is of utmost importance. Should the purchase of erotic dance be included? What about sexual services that are one-directional, meaning the client experiences sexual or sensual pleasure and the provider adopts a professional healer persona? And how should services such as dilator application for vaginismus without sexual pleasure be considered? Also, calls to treat motivations to buy therapeutic sex as separate from entertainment sex were considered and rejected due to a risk of suggesting that a hierarchy of commercial sexual services exists, or should exist, in Australia. Although each State and Territory has different regulations and laws regulating the sex industry, for the purpose of this project we chose to use the definition common to by all State and Territory law, which considers sex workers as people who sell erotic or direct sexual services. Therefore, the interviewees in this study had bought sex in the sense that they had procured services from people who are defined by the law in their jurisdictions as sex workers.

Services procured

Almost all the women in the sample had bought sex multiple times. The services they sought included heterosexual sex (13), same-sex attracted sex (7), threesomes with all genders (6), bondage and discipline (BDSM) (4), and body-work therapy (2). Although the sample was almost equally divided into heterosexual women and women of diverse orientations, there did not appear to be any significant difference in demographics between the two groups, except with respect to age. The average age of the women who only sought heterosexual services was 44 and the average age of the women who were flexible in their sexual choices was 35. Of the women seeking same-sex attracted services (7), about half indicated that they were exploring their orientation and only two identified as lesbian. Of the interviewees who bought sex with a partner or friend as a threesome (6), three did so as a result of a male partner's wish, of which two went on to buying sex independently.

Motivations to buy sex

All of the interviewees embedded the reasons why they bought sex into their stories without prompting. Most provided multiple reasons to explain behaviour they perceived to be socially deviant or at least unexpected.

Therapy

The most common reason for buying sex in this sample (10 of 21 interviewees) was referred to as therapy. Underlying conditions indicating a need for therapy were vaginismus (3), healing from intimate partner violence (3), healing from childhood sexual abuse (2), 'trans issues' (1) and depression and stress (1). The various goals of therapy were to achieve physical penetration, to learn about bodies and sexuality and to practise good sexual communication around boundaries and consent. Two interviewees indicated that sex was not important to them, but relationships were and they wanted to increase their sexual confidence before engaging in a relationship.

For example, 'I can't have a relationship because I can't fuck. You know?' (Interviewee 16). Several interviewees who bought sex as therapy felt sexual services should be rebatable from Medicare. Two interviewees recalled buying somatic (hands-on) sex therapy in the past through being interviewed about current commercial sex activity. Three interviewees who had bought sex for therapy objected to the idea that they were buying sex, and one separated all fun and pleasure from her therapeutic experience. As if speaking to a sex worker, Interviewee 12 said, 'Look, I am here for physio'. Four interviewees were under psychological care at the time of buying sex and all had the positive regard of their psychological care provider and all cited their motivations to buy sex to be for therapy. In addition, a desire to learn more about sex was a primary motivation to buy sex by several interviewees. Interviewees wanted to learn about their sexual function (4), sexual orientations (3), and particular sexual acts (3). Three of these complained about their lack of sex education from parents and school, and considered learning about sex to be an investment. Some interviewees spoke about paying for sex as a rebellion against perceived restrictions and shaming of female sexuality. Some therapeutically motivated interviewees said they wanted to be able to have sex and Interviewee 15 said she wanted to learn to be a good lover.

Entertainment

The major motivation to buy sex for eight interviewees was to have fun and experience sexual pleasure. For example, 'it was based around my wanting to get off' (Interviewee 2), and 'I don't need to be massaged. I don't need gently. I don't want to be romanticised. I am paying for sex because I want sex' (Interviewee 9). Some women described their desires for sex as selfish, such as, 'with the sex worker, maybe it sounds slightly weird to say this, but you can be a bit more selfish' (Interviewee 7), 'you don't really have to put any effort in' (Interviewee 1), 'this is all about me' (Interviewee 11), 'you just want to be totally indulged, that is what you get' (Interviewee 8) and, 'you can be completely selfish' (Interviewee 16).

Safety

Most women interviewed referred to their physical and emotional safety as important issues. Some felt that 'safety' is part of what you pay for, and Interviewee 10 used the word 'safe' nine times in her one-hour interview. Some interviewees explicitly said buying sex was safer than picking up, for example, 'I can make the choice to go out to a bar and pick someone up, which is certainly less safe' (Interviewee 15). Three interviewees also used a friend to call for security backup upon arrival and departure from the sex worker premises. Other interviewees were more specific about what they considered safe by saying that a sex worker would not pressure you into doing anything, will not stalk you afterwards and will respect boundaries and consent. To illustrate, 'and it's like a security thing, like, I never feel kind of pressured into doing anything that I don't want to' (Interviewee 1), and 'it didn't occur to me in that circumstance that I wouldn't have been safe . . . Any guy you meet in the bar can turn out to be a nutter' (Interviewee 11). Interviewee 13 considered the behaviour of male sex workers she had engaged as more caring and supportive than previous abusive intimate partners. Interviewee 1 mentioned that specialist BDSM practices require training for safety purposes, and that a sex worker felt more experienced in this regard. Interestingly, Interviewee 12 said, 'seeing a sex worker who is accredited, who is tested, who is professional gives me the reassurance that I am safe'. This statement needs clarification because there are no accrediting bodies for sex workers, which is not the same as registration required in some states. Mandatory testing for STIs does occur in Victoria, but does not ensure that a sex worker does not have an STI. Interviewee 12 may have a sense of safety in these matters based on a sex worker's professional standing.

Emotional safety was valued by women who bought sex and mentioned as an important factor in their decision to buy it. Interviewees said they enjoyed being able to decide when, where, how and with whom to have sex. Women said they felt safe from rejection as a 'sex worker won't belittle you, or be hurt, if you are unattractive or bad at sex' (Interviewee 12). One Interviewee said she had the freedom to explore her sexuality without jeopardising current relationships. For example, 'and in the future for me to have other kinds of relationships with women, this would be sort of a safer way of doing it. Um, without compromising our relationship and our family' (Interviewee 20). And Interviewee 4 said that paying a sex worker ensured emotional safety to be treated and respected as her preferred gender. In a similar way, Interviewee 7 valued being authentic and not having to try hard to be sexy or desirable. The women interviewed said they assessed sex workers by the way they communicated the concept of safety in their online presence, through their reputations and by demonstrating good verbal communication. The women interviewed were not impressed by sex workers who advertised as being 'sex gods'. For example,

> but I think that men just promote themselves in a fashion that is completely over the top ... They are all very good looking and they are all Valentino, and they are all studs in bed, and all the rest of it. And the reality is very far removed from that.
>
> *(Interviewee 8)*

Intimacy

Most interviewees expressed a desire for intimacy when buying sex. For some, the word intimacy may have been used as a euphemism for sex, possibly to disguise their desire for sex as a physical act. Others explicitly separated intimacy and sex, and expressed a desire for intimacy alone, describing intimate acts such as hair stroking and affirmations. Seven interviewees valued authenticity of the sex worker as important for real intimacy. They said they did not want fake, forced or awkward communication. For example, Interviewee 8 was scathing of insincere flattery and wanted only genuine exchange and Interviewee 21 said it was difficult to find a worker who is '100% into it'.

Barriers to buying sex

Women were asked if they felt there were any barriers to buying sex. The women who had knowledge of the sex industry noted a gendered difference in services available such as no quickie services or brothels for women. They did not, however, say they would buy these services if available. Women who bought heterosexual services complained that there were not enough straight male sex workers to choose from. Common themes that emerged from data analysis included feeling nervous and scared about buying sex, the price, experiences of stigma and navigating laws.

Nerves

As expected, being nervous or fearful about buying sex was a common theme throughout the interviews. However, women who had contact with the sex industry prior to buying sex said they did not suffer nervous feelings and the key was knowing what to expect (Interviewee 5), and having a gradual introduction to the idea (Interviewees 3 and 4). The most affected were women who bought heterosexual services. Some examples include, 'I nearly called the whole thing off' (Interviewee 11), 'I was so scared I didn't even want to ring the doorbell. Literally scared out of my mind' (Interviewee 12), 'I was freaking out' (Interviewees 6 and 13), 'for me it was huge, I was beside myself. I have never had so much adrenaline and nerves in my life' (Interviewee 14), 'I was incredibly nervous beforehand' (Interviewee 7), 'I don't think I have ever been so nervous about anything' (Interviewee 17), 'I was fucking scared' (Interviewee 19), 'I don't think I have ever been so nervous in my whole life. I wanted to run away' (Interviewee 20), 'I was very nervous' (Interviewee 15) and 'the first time you are going through this huge turmoil' (Interviewee 16). As demonstrated, women graphically described the fear they felt before buying sex but were mostly unspecific about the exact source of fear. The most likely reasons, considering most fear was felt by the heterosexual women we interviewed, are fear of male violence and the effect of being socialised to be fearful. Their fear may be rational. Most of the heterosexual women interviewed who framed their sexual services as therapeutic also voiced a history of male violence and/or anxiety issues.

Cost

The cost of buying sex was mentioned as a barrier by most interviewees. Some specifically noted a gendered difference between the cost for male or female clients. For example, 'I have a perception that fewer women just go and pay for a half-hour session like men for just a blow job or whatever' (Interviewee 19), and 'for good experiences women buying sex need a nice hotel and an expensive escort. But men can go to brothels' (Interviewee 7). Alternatively, Interviewee 1 said,

> [T]he first girl was really expensive. Then, the dungeon was a lot cheaper. When you are a woman you don't care if you can't stick your penis into their vagina because you don't have one, so it's like, I was getting the same service and it cost less. Sex is the thing that is expensive.

However sex is defined, rates for various sexual services and providers can be extremely variable, some being gender dependent.

Women described buying sex less often due to the expense. Interviewees said, 'So, I can't afford it all the time. Because it is expensive' (Interviewee 10), 'Price is a massive barrier for a lot of people' (Interview 17), 'we have to keep saving up because it is expensive' (Interview 20), and 'I've been reluctant to try again due to financial stress' (Interviewee 21). Interviewee 4 said she had bought sex 'only once. The only reason for that is money, unfortunately.' For some women, buying sex may have adjunct expenses, such as Interviewee 16 who said,

> I have to get a carer for [partner with dementia] so it is an expensive business. It [commercial sex] is frighteningly expensive. If it is an agency they certainly take their cut. I hope that the escort still gets the lion's share, as it were, but God it is expensive. It is shockingly expensive.

However, money was not an issue for all women. Interviewee 8 said, 'I've had experiences with really high-end sort of female providers, in the sort of $800/hr plus category'. And, Interviewee 9 chooses 'lower-end' escorts because they come to her place, saying, 'I am an independent woman. I make money. I am allowed to spend it however I want to.' While the cost of paying for sex may be a barrier for some women, Interviewee 8 made an important point in saying that many women 'believe in their entitlement to free sex', effectively preventing their purchase of it.

Women interviewed who framed their sexual services as primarily therapeutic were more likely to rationalise the expense as an investment. For example, 'he is not the cheapest obviously, but I looked at it as an investment that I have to do to address this situation once and all' (Interviewee 12) and, 'if I spread the money out that I spent on that over the year, it is a very good investment. It is investment in myself' (Interviewee 19). Further, 'I was willing to pay . . . my psychiatrist said to me that I had probably saved quite a bit on therapy fees' (Interviewee 15) and, 'It wasn't just that I loved sex and I wanted to have sex with him. He actually offered me a reduced rate for that, which enabled me to be able to afford to go a bit more regularly' (Interviewee 17). Therapeutic frameworks when buying sex appear to fare better than entertainment in cost/benefit analysis, which may have some relationship to social stigma related to buying sex. This relationship was specifically noted by Interviewee 5, who said that 'it is stigma that prevents women buying sex and [means that they are] missing the therapeutic benefits'.

Stigma

Interviewees were asked if they experienced any feelings of stigmatisation in relation to buying sex. This question caused some confusion. For example, Interviewee 10 only talked about sex worker stigma, not understanding that she was asked about her own, and Interviewee 14 conflated stigma with shame, saying, 'I have no shame'. Yet, the implications of stigmatisation were clear, for example Interviewee 17 said, 'the risk of being publically shamed is like, really scary'. To further explore stigma, interviewees were asked if they would recommend buying sex to a friend and how many people they told about it. The interviewees would mostly recommend it to a friend, meaning that they felt they had made the right decision. Alternatively, most interviewees told very few people, meaning that they were aware it was a stigmatised activity.

All interviewees said they would recommend a friend buy sex in some situations. For example, 'it would depend on the circumstances. But I would not, not recommend it' (Interviewee 6), 'if I think someone was not coping then yes' (Interviewee 10) and, 'if I had that sort of relationship with a friend' (Interviewee 11). Interviewee 1, 'highly recommends it', and went on to say, 'some [people] get offended and it is like . . . yeah, go home and make your own coffee then and don't buy one in a shop either'. Twelve women who had bought sex said they would unconditionally recommend it to friends. Interviewee 18 said, 'if I met [a good sex worker] I would give his business cards to all my friends'. Although Interviewee 9 and 10 denied feeling stigmatised, Interviewee 9 told 'everyone except for like, my parents and relatives, yeah. Like, about 10 people, I have told', and Interviewee 10 said that she kept her buying sex a secret from most of her friends. Other methods of managing stigma were Interviewee 2 who only associates with sex industry allies, and Interviewee 16 who told all manner of strangers and health professionals but not a single friend or family member. Exceptions were Interviewee 13 and 15 who told most people including extended family and work colleagues.

To specifically explore the relationship between motivations for buying sex and stigma, we compared, the responses to questions about stigma of women who framed their sexual service experiences as therapy and of women who framed their sexual services as entertainment and fun. These comparisons were unremarkable. Regardless of the reason for buying sex, most women who did so were reluctant to tell other people, and expressed feeling stigmatised. Interviewee 5, who had bought sexual services through both frameworks, said, 'I've talked more about the therapy than I have about the male escort'. Experiences of stigma may be gendered. Interviewees were asked if they thought men or women suffered more stigma when buying sex. The answers revealed that women who bought sex were aware of, and affected by, stigmatising notions of slut and sexuality shaming. The most obvious perceived gendered differences in the experience of stigma when buying sex regarded slut shaming. Some interviewees felt that, 'female pleasure is not regarded as important (Interviewee 5), ideas of female sexual passivity are 'unauthentic and dirty' (Interviewee 20), female sexuality 'makes people deeply uncomfortable (Interviewee 17) and the 'stigma is about women having sexual desire full stop' (Interviewee 19). Complaints regarding gender-based double standards included expressing beliefs such as, there is more stigma for women with sexual dysfunction than men with sexual dysfunction (Interviewee 12), men buy sex for entertainment and it is expected of them (Interviewee 7) and men are perceived to have a high sexual desire yet women desire love (Interviewee 9). Interestingly, Interviewees 7, 8, 9 and 12 all said they thought women are expected to get free sex and not pay for it, the stigma being as much about sex as it is about the exchange of money. This is not to say that men do not experience stigma when they buy sex, just that the basis for stigmatisation may be different for women.

Several women interviewed expressed feeling the effects of being stigmatised for the particular type of sex they bought. For example, Interviewee 2 felt stigmatised for identifying as gay and Interviewee 3 felt her interest in BDSM was stigmatising, although she said dominant females are more accepted than submissive. Interviewee 4 said she experienced such stigma around being a person who is transgender that the stigma related to buying sex seemed insignificant and Interviewee 6 said when couples bought sex, stigma was more of a concern if a man proposed and initiated buying sex as part of a couple, and not so much if a woman suggested buying sex. Interviewee 3 would like to work as a sex worker if not for the stigma and said, 'stigma steels power'. Although interviewees described their experiences of stigma as specific to individual situations, stigma of some form was almost universal in the sample of women buying sex.

Laws

Some women interviewed considered that Australian law and regulation of the sex industry influenced their experiences when buying sex. At the time of conducting the interviews, there was a surge in media attention about a New South Wales Parliamentary Inquiry considering the introduction of the Swedish model to criminalise clients, largely relying on narratives framing female sex workers as exploited. The women interviewed demonstrated they were knowledgeable about Australian laws that govern the sex industry and some women made decisions about buying sex based on their perception of the law. Interviewee 10 said that decriminalisation of the sex industry endorsed her decision to buy, and Interviewee 12 said, 'which is um, a legal activity to do. And I was very lucky that it was legal and it is still legal'. Interviewee 10 also said she was scared of being criminalised, she did not 'feel like a criminal', and felt she was being accused of raping a male sex worker.

Explicit in exploitation narratives about the sex industry is the victimisation of female sex workers and demonisation of clients, labelling them as perpetrators of violence. The women who bought sex and were interviewed for this study were adversely affected by exploitation narratives, and their experiences caused them to question the truthfulness of negative sex industry narratives. Interviewee 8 said these narratives 'make sex buyers into uncaring people' and Interviewee 11 'found the current positioning of sex work as assault to be deeply offensive to everyone engaged in it and particularly to women cast as victims'. Interviewee 11 said she, 'suspects women buying sex suffer less stigma than men' due to exploitation narratives. Interviewee 15 said she tried to advocate for women buying sex on Twitter and was publically shamed and accused of being exploited by a male sex worker. She found the conflation of childhood sexual assault and sex work to be 'deeply disturbing and disrespectful'. Interviewee 17 complained that clients of sex workers are talked about with 'no authority', and that all clients were neglected during public inquiries. She said she feels 'like a really strong feminist but there are other women out there who are going to shame me around this. They are pushing my story underground'.

Interviewees from Victoria said they were aware of the debate in New South Wales and also concerned about Victorian advertising and location laws in relation to sex work. Interviewee 3 said she was critical of the laws that 'make it particularly prohibitive for people to have these services and to find these services more openly, in locations that are safe'. Interviewee 16 complained that 'escort agencies can't actually describe what the services are'. And, Interviewee 5 said it was 'silly and illogical that you can't technically do things in your home' and several women complained about having to pay for a hotel room as well as escort services.

Conclusion

Our interviews with women who buy sex in Australia illustrate they are diverse and do not conform to any stereotype of rich, busy or older women as mentioned in many popular media reports. Also, the interviewees who participated in our study cited multiple reasons for buying sex that initially appeared as a dichotomy of therapy or pleasure. However, further analysis ascertained therapeutic and pleasurable outcomes for all interviewees. Some women considered participation in this project an action of activism and an opportunity to voice opinions about the value of commercial sex to their general well-being and to have some impact on stigma reduction and regulatory frameworks for sex workers and buyers.

All empirical research has limitations. We acknowledge that self-selecting interviewees do not represent all opinions about women buying sex or reflect all women's experiences of buying sex. Indeed, self-selecting interviewees may be highly motivated to participate and have stronger opinions than eligible but non-participating people. Although it is possible that women who had predominantly negative experiences buying sex would be motivated to participate in the study, no such women volunteered. In addition, digital advertising for recruitment or engagement with digital media does not reach the entire pool of eligible participants. Similarly, participation was only available to people with digital technology and skills and, who speak English, which may have the effect of only attracting women who identified as Caucasian. We also acknowledge that obtaining data through interviews may be affected by participant confirmation and researcher biases, which was minimised by asking women to tell their uninterrupted stories. Women buying sex are not a homogeneous population and this project is considered to be the beginning of a field of inquiry.

Women buying sex are a significant subject for research to challenge constructions of sex industry clients as male only, which has important implications academically, socially and politically. Scholarly debate informs research design and possible research bias in assessment of who buys sex and gender debates about the sex industry. Stereotypical representations of sex industry clients as violent men, or more recent media portrayals of rich, older, entitled women, are not identifiable to the women who participated in this study and possibly to women who responded in the negative to survey questions about buying sex in sexual behaviour studies. Any research about women buying sex is crucial, particularly because political activism towards the criminalisation of clients of sexual services is grounded in rigid gendering of clients and assumptions of inherent violence. Further evidence of women buying sex in any country or context will reflect the diversity of the sex industry and enrich debate.

The major finding of this project provides empirical evidence of women buying sex in Australia, compelling us to consider the sex industry more broadly than is common. All genders buy sex from all genders for a variety of services and debate about them should not be reduced to a singular view of immorality or entitlement.

References

Aggleton, Peter and Parker, Richard, eds. 2015. *Men who sell sex: Global perspectives*. New York: Routledge.

Brooks-Gordon, Belinda. 2010. Bellwether citizens: The regulation of male clients of sex workers. *Journal of Law and Society*, 37, 145–170.

Caldwell, Hilary. 2012. *Long-term clients who access commercial sexual services in Australia*. Masters thesis, University of Sydney.

Cynthiavankleeck. 2011. The boys of prositution and the women who buy sex. Human Traffic Watch. News on Modern Day Slavery [Web log post], 14 December. http://humantrafficwatch.wordpress.com/2011/12/14/the-boys-of-prostitution-and-the-women-who-buy-sex.

Goldstein, Nikki. 2016. Confessions of an Australia male escort: 'I don't just get booked for sex'. news.com.au.

Grieco, Richard and Walker, Shane (Producers). 2011. *Gigolos* (Motion picture). USA: Showtime.

Harcourt, Christine and Donovan, Basil. 2005. The many faces of sex work. *Sexually Transmitted Infections*, 81, 201–206.

Hesse, Morten and Tutenges, Sébastien 2011. Young tourists visiting strip clubs and paying for sex. *Tourism Management*, 32, 869–874.

Jeffreys, Sheila. 2003. Sex tourism: Do women do it too? *Leisure Studies*, 22, 223–238.

Law, Benjamin. 2014. The business of pleasure. *Sydney Morning Herald*, 1 February.

Law, Benjamin. 2016. The women who hire male escorts. *Sydney Morning Herald*, 21 July.

Lipkin, Dmitry and Burson, Colette (Producers), 2009. *Hung* (Television Series). HBO.

Ninemsm. 2014. Woman discovers she's victim of love scam. *9News World*, 19 February.

Richters, Juliet, O. De Visser, Richard, Badcock, Paul, Smith, Anthony, Rissel, Chris, Simpson, Judy and Grulich, Andrew 2014. Masturbation, paying for sex, and other sexual activities: The second Australian study of health and relationships. *Sexual Health*, 11, 461–471.

Rissel, Chris E., Richters, Juliet, Grulich, Andrew E., Visser, Richard O. and Smith, Anthony M.A. 2005. Sex in Australia: Experiences of commercial sex in a representative sample of adults. *Australian and New Zealand Journal of Public Health*, 27, 191–197.

Robinson, Doborah. 2013. Aussie mums open male escort agency catering exclusively to women. *Australian Women Online*, 5 March.

Sanders, Teela. 2008. Male sexual scrips: Intimacy, sexuality and pleasure in the purchase of commercial sex. *Sociology* 42(3), 400–417.

Scott, John and Minichiello, Victor. eds. 2014. *Male sex work and society*. New York: Harrington Park Press.

Sebag-Montefiore, Clarissa. 2014. *Male escorts*. Sydney, Australia: Aeon.

Silver, Matty. 2013a. Ladies, your holiday romance awaits. *Sydney Morning Herald*, 8 February.

Silver, Matty. 2013b. Why do women pay for sex? *Sydney Morning Herald*, 9 December.

Silver, Matty, 2017. If men pay for sex, why can't women? Huffingtonpost.com.au, 6 July.

Tankard Reist, Melinda. 2010. Women buying men for sex is not equality. *Sydney Morning Herald*, 22 April.

Taylor, Jacqueline Sanchez. 2006. Female sex tourism: A contradiction in terms? *Feminist Review*, 83(1), 42–59.

Weitzer, Ronald, ed. 2000. *Sex for sale: Prositution, pornography, and the sex industry*. New York: Routledge.

White, Rachel. 2015. Getting a happy ending: Buying sex as a girl. Thought Catalog. https://thoughtcatalog.com/rachel-r-white/2015/05/getting-a-happy-ending-buying-sex-as-a-girl.

34

The "john"

Our new folk devil

Jerald L. Mosley

Introduction

Seventeen years ago, Dutch sexuality researcher Ine Vanwesenbeeck (2001, 279) noted the gradual demise of the image of the prostitute as pathological deviant and its replacement by the image of prostitute as victim. That image of the victim prostitute has persisted, but with it a corollary image of the client as victimizer has increasingly gained traction. Recently, Vanwesenbeeck (2017, 1632) addressed and criticized the growing law enforcement focus on the prostitute's client and the trend to criminalize the client. Here I consider that image of the client and the trending effort to arrest, prosecute, and demonize the client, an effort known as "End Demand." I juxtapose claims and practices of End Demand ideology with real-world sex industry experiences of clients and providers. Those experiences reflect and exemplify the substantial literature challenging dominant cultural constructions of sex workers' clients as violent or otherwise pathological men, and illustrate baleful effects of client targeting as public policy.

The End Demand campaign

On his way to work, Jim, a middle-aged professional in the Seattle, Washington area, discovered he had drawn down upon himself the full wrath of his community's law enforcement. He was pulled over, arrested, handcuffed, charged with a felony, and threatened with both a three-year prison sentence and having to register as a sex offender if he did not cooperate with the prosecutor. His crime was having posted three comments about call girls on a website called "The Review Board," a site devoted to advertisements by, and mostly complimentary reviews of, prostitutes ("sex workers"). Although paying for sex is only a misdemeanor in Washington he was charged with "promoting prostitution," a felony. The threatened three-year incarceration represented 12 months of hard time for each of the reviews he had written.

A man who writes a complimentary note about a sex worker and says he enjoyed his time with her does not fit the image of a registered sex offender nor does he conform to the popular notion of what sex offender registries are for, but Jim had run into a juggernaut: a growing effort to arrest, prosecute, and demonize buyers of sex: the "End Demand" campaign.

That campaign is an effort to stop sex trafficking by ending demand for all commercial sex, and doing that by increasing enforcement and enhancing penalties for the purchasers of sexual services. It is based on a simple theory: sex workers are victims of degradation, abuse, and violence, and victims should not be punished. The buyer of sex is the real villain. If the criminal justice system re-doubles its efforts to catch and punish the buyers, society can eliminate the demand for commercial sex, and the entire sex industry will come to a grinding halt (Coalition Against Trafficking n.d.; Freedom Network n.d.; Vanwesenbeeck 2017, 1632; Weitzer 2012, 66–68; Sanders 2012, 135–138).

Internationally, variations on this theme have spread through a number of jurisdictions including Sweden, Norway, and Iceland, giving the name "Swedish" or "Nordic strategy" to the effort. Governments, political actors, and NGOs have devoted time and money to market the strategy internationally (Dodillet and Östergren 2011, 2), and four recent entrants into the field are Canada, Northern Ireland, France, and the Republic of Ireland. In the United States, where both the purchase and sale of sex are criminalized in all jurisdictions except a few Nevada counties, the targeting of buyers of sex is a growing focus of law enforcement and much public discourse. In 2005 the federal government authorized a $50 million grant to local law enforcement and social service agencies "to develop and execute programs targeted at reducing male demand and to investigate and prosecute buyers of commercial sex acts" (Berkowitz 2015, p. 293). In 2015, according to the *Congressional Quarterly Researcher*, 11 metropolitan areas pledged to reduce demand for prostitution by using Nordic strategies (Glazer 2016, p. 348).

Image and reality

Intertwined with End Demand ideology is the one-dimensional image of the client as a male predator who buys sex from a helpless woman. Author and human rights lawyer Eric Berkowitz, who has produced two detailed studies of laws regulating sexuality, finds that underlying the global effort against trafficking is the belief that all prostitution is coerced and that buyers are all potential slavers and rapists. This image of bondage has "given rise to the aggressive targeting of customers" (Berkowitz 2015, 283). Sociologist Teela Sanders (2012, 138) similarly noted that over the previous two decades the problem of prostitution had come to be constructed around "dirty and dangerous men" and "vulnerable female victims."

Sweden's criminalization of the buyer highlights this connection between image and End Demand policy. The law's aim was to target men's actions and attitudes because the seller was seen as needing help and the buyer as a deviant deserving of either punishment, therapy, or both (Holmstrom and Skilbrei 2017, 1). The Swedish approach uses an oppression model of sex work that regards commercial sex as a form of male sexual violence against women (Chu and Glass 2013, 104; Levy 2015, 30–31).

Modeling sex work and clients as essentially oppressive is a highly contentious issue characterized by political activism and adamant, competing claims. But what the point is here is the significant body of credible research that confronts the image of the client as victimizer and that is reflected and exemplified by the case studies below.

Sociologist Ronald Weitzer cautions against both ignoring the negative aspects of prostitution and exaggerating their prevalence. Weitzer criticizes what he terms the "oppression" paradigm of prostitution under which customers are "prostitute users," "batterers," and "sexual predators." He notes that most clients are not, in fact, violent misogynists (Weitzer 2009, 214, 224), and Belinda Brooks-Gordon, academic expert in psychology and public policy, points out data that suggest a great deal of the violence suffered by sex workers is committed by a small proportion of clients (Brooks-Gordon 2006, 198; see also Monto 2010, 243–244).

Other studies contrast even more sharply with the construct of the buyer as violent or coercive. A client's need for a "normal" relationship with a sex worker runs through all levels of the sex industry, where a "normal" relationship is read as one with a positive emotional dimension involving something more than brief, perfunctory sex (Bernstein 2007, 125–130; Hakim 2015, 26).

Teela Sanders' study of clients in Britain involved 134 emailed biographies and other correspondence and interviews with 50 clients. She found that "the desire for intimacy and romantic emotional connectivity are evident within the commercial setting," and concluded that a "false dichotomy is maintained between commercial and non-commercial relations" (Sanders 2012, 109). In fact, 16 of the 50 men she studied did not want to become a regular client of a sex worker "because of the potential emotional attachments with unavailable women" (ibid., 105).

Other studies confirm the prevalence of a positive emotional dimension occurring, or sought after, in paid-for relationships, especially indoor ones (Weitzer 2005, 212–213, 217, 223–226; 2012, 30–39). In fact, providing the emotional quality of a conventional relationship may be quite demanding on the sex worker who must work hard to create the right atmosphere for a client looking for more than sex (Weitzer, 2009, 226–227). As one sex worker Weitzer interviewed noted, "I have been cuddled to within an inch of my life by well-meaning chaps" (Weitzer 2012, 37–38).

Jay Levy, a freelance researcher in areas including sex work legislation, and feminist, gender, and queer theory, drew on fieldwork undertaken in Sweden over several years for his study of Swedish sex work, and his findings are consistent with these other studies' findings in arguing that clients are diverse in their motivations for purchasing sex. Some eroticize the actual purchase of sex, some buy sex out of convenience, some do so because they are not sexually satisfied otherwise, some wish to explore their sexuality, and some are lonely and isolated men (Levy 2015, 95). But through it all, Levy concludes that the "crude demonization" of clients as unconcerned with the well-being of sex workers and of exploited women was not confirmed by his findings (ibid., 206–207).

None of these studies suggest there are no predators targeting sex workers because the workers are reluctant to report victimization to the police, nor do they suggest that all commercial sex is driven by emotional needs. Yet my conversations with sex workers and their clients confirm that widespread assumptions regarding the prevalence of abuse, violence, and coercion are grossly off the mark. To give a human face to the dynamics of these commercial sexual exchanges, let us consider the experiences of Jack, Sol, Savannah, Maggie, and Norma Jean.

Jack

Jack is 65 and works in banking. He recalls that his first time with a sex worker was in 1974 when he was in the Navy. He picked her up on the shuttle bus that ran from the military base to town. Being a little nervous he let her take control after telling her what he wanted. He recalls it being a completely mechanical interaction lasting about 10 minutes. She didn't even remove all her clothes and all he remembers her saying was "Did you come yet?" In later life, Jack moved on from his initial experience to long-lasting social and sexual relationships with sex workers. He eventually married a sex worker he had originally contacted online.

Sol

Sol Finer is the media coordinator for the Seattle chapter of the Sex Workers' Outreach Project (SWOP), a national organization that advocates for the decriminalization of prostitution and advances sex worker rights. In her words, she is an "independent provider" of sexual services.

Her account of her work reflects both the risk of experiencing violence and abuse and the fallacy of understanding that danger is inherent in her work or her clients. Although she herself has not experienced violence in her work, she knows that there are risks that go along with sex work. In fact, it is her job to send out warning emails to other providers when she receives a report of a dangerous client, for example, a client who forcibly goes beyond the sexual acts agreed upon. She illustrates with the account of a provider who agreed to be tied up, but ended up choked and anally raped by the client.

Yet the idea that all clients are horrible perverts is just not true, she insists. Quite simply, she likes her clients and that's why she sees them. Sol's account illustrates Sanders' finding of a false dichotomy between commercial and non-commercial relations and the client search for something more than perfunctory sex. Sol describes her clients as ordinary men looking for a connection with another person. Half are ones she has seen over three or four times. About a quarter of the remainder she has seen two or three times. Often, they just need to find a space where they can be vulnerable, and it is not uncommon for her and a client to talk, and keep talking, and never get to any sexual activity. She sees couples once a week or two, and some of her clients are disabled, like the one who confided to her that women don't see him, they just see his wheelchair.

Sol's description of her clients offers no compelling rationale for targeting clients, and certainly no rationale for targeting them in order to protect her. To be sure, her account confirms she needs a respectful and responsive law enforcement community when crimes do occur, but it is difficult to argue that she is incapable of assessing her own safety and needs and the state must punish those ordinary men who come to her for a connection in order to put her out of business for her own good.

Savannah

Savannah Sly, a dominatrix, has 13 years of sex work experience and is the president of SWOP. Her work involves helping clients explore their own sexuality and search for intimacy and emotional connection. As do Sol's clients, Savannah's give no support to End Demand ideology. They come to her with fetishes, sometimes very nuanced and detailed fantasies that call for her to read the client's rather delicate needs. Her clients have included transgender individuals and couples, and no client has ever tried to physically harm her.

She remembers Rick, a client in his fifties who she knew for about three years before he passed away with cancer. He had a very slight build, pasty skin, and a spanking fetish. He just loved the sensation of being over her lap and spanked. He struck her as very innocent and awkward, both socially and physically. He had been married once in his early twenties but it didn't work out because, not being interested in conventional sex, he just couldn't please his wife. Savannah recalls him taking her out on dates. They would have lunch and walk down the street hand in hand. It was at one of those lunches that she learned he worked at a hotel as a dishwasher and would take the bus to see her. He saved up his money to spend time with her. Once, he asked her to call him at the hotel on his birthday so he could tell everyone his girlfriend was calling.

He had one of the most operatic singing voices Savannah had ever heard, and she ended up with a CD of his singing. He gave it to her because he had no one else to share it with.

Maggie

Sol is not unique in serving the disabled. Sex worker Maggie McNeill, who married one of her clients, blogs under the title *The Honest Courtesan*. In her October 17, 2010 blog, she describes her service to disabled men including clients shaking with cerebral palsy, her first blind client who asked if he could feel her face, and a burn victim horribly scarred and bent over who had never been with a woman before. Her clients have also included couples. For about six years she was seeing a couple on average once a week.

Maggie started selling sex as a teenager, but she considers her professional life to have begun in her early thirties when she was a stripper and would, on occasion, go home with one of the customers. She ultimately worked in New Orleans, Oklahoma and Washington, DC, but she was not always a sex worker. She was at one time a librarian, a madam, and now is an author and prolific blogger.

As with Sol, Maggie's personal account reflects both the reality of the dangers she faces and the deep mistake of ingraining those dangers into the profile of the typical client. She knows the risks of her line of work. On two occasions throughout her career a client has forcefully engaged her in a sex act to which she had not agreed and a third one attempted to. Nevertheless, reflecting Weitzer's conclusions, violence and misogyny do not characterize her clients. Despite the trauma of those criminal assaults, Maggie sees no rationale for the indiscriminate targeting of clients under an End Demand theory, she has no patience for the blindly generalized image of the abusive male buyer, and she remains, as she says, a little amused and sad at all the talk of hating men. As a madam she heard from her "girls" the same thing that she hears from other sex workers: about 5% of clients are awful, 5% are great clients who the worker would like to see again, and the rest are just clients—not good or bad. Her girls complained of one regular client who was "rough," but they never reported a violent client.

Norma Jean

Norma Jean Almodovar's 1993 expose, *Cop to Call Girl: Why I Left the LAPD to Make an Honest Living as a Beverly Hills Prostitute*, recaps her life as a traffic officer for the Los Angeles Police Department, then a sex worker, then a prison inmate. She was convicted of responding to a friend's expressed interest by trying to help her find a client. The "friend" was wired for sound and Norma Jean was convicted of pandering. To get a prison term, the prosecution had to appeal, and they proclaimed her crime worse than rape or robbery and ultimately squeezed out of the court a three-year prison term for her. Now, having recovered from the trauma of prosecution and prison, she has gone on to start the International Sex Workers Foundation for Art, Culture and Education.

Norma Jean's former career as a sex worker reflects, again, Sanders' false dichotomy and the positive emotional connections clients often enjoy with sex workers. End Demand gains no purchase on her difficult life, a life that offers no rationale for prosecuting her clients in order to protect her. She assures us that it is jail-time, not sex work, that is demeaning and degrading. Her book's uninhibited accounts of her clients make clear why she does not consider sex work itself demeaning or anything remotely answering to the image of the abusive male sex buyer. Norma Jean's former clients, she writes, were a "great bunch of guys" including one who would call between visits just to talk and another who she would have considered marrying but for her choice of another man (Almodovar 1993, 85, 101). She concludes, that "Although sex work is not for every woman, if prostitution was 'acceptable,' a lot of underpaid secretaries, file clerks, waitresses, telephone operators, and even traffic officers would leave their jobs" (ibid., 73). As she admits, she does not speak for every woman, but neither is she an outlier bent on gratuitously jarring dominant cultural sensibilities.

The image as juggernaut

Despite the plethora of studies and accounts from sex worker activists that describe the surprising ordinariness of clients, the sinister and sensationalized image of the buyer persists. That persistence has its effects.

One surprising effect is on buyers themselves. In the eyes of some sex workers, the image now appears deeply ingrained even among their own clients. Sex worker Aphrodite Phoenix (2012, 714) writes that she is "constantly astounded by the common misperception, even in men themselves, that other guys are crazies or creeps." One of the sex workers Jay Levy interviewed during his study of Sweden's End Demand strategy agreed to meet with him in part to defend her own clients and to tell him, "I just want the guys to feel what they're doing is not wrong, and that there're a lot of normal guys out there who does [sic] the same thing. They're nice guys" (Levy 2015, 91). Mirha-Soleil Ross, a transgender woman and sex worker in Toronto, sounds a similar note in her 2002 theatrical monologue "Dear John." She has to assure her "sweetest clients" that no, they are not hurting her sense of self and she does not feel exploited. She also provides an interesting twist on the notion of "objectification"—a concept bandied about frequently in the polemics of sexual interaction but never applied to male buyers as the ones objectified. Her clients, she says, force her to see that she is "not dealing with objects here but with complex and vulnerable individuals who can be stricken by as many body image problems, self-concept issues and fears of sexual inadequacy as anyone else" (Ross 2006, n.p.).

Not surprisingly, the effect that End Demand-driven public policy does and does not have on sex workers is a matter of some concern in the research literature. Despite its enduring popularity, there is substantial evidence that End Demand tactics are not effective in reducing sex trafficking and that, as a matter of fact, they make sex work more dangerous than it would otherwise be.

One of the most recent and significant developments came from Amnesty International's 2016 decision to support the full decriminalization of consensual sex work, including the buying of sexual services (Amnesty International 2016a, 2). Amnesty International found no reliable evidence suggesting that decriminalization would encourage human trafficking. On the contrary it found that criminalization could hinder the fight against trafficking. Rejecting the Nordic Model specifically, Amnesty International noted that criminalizing the client can harm the sex worker, often by forcing her to take more risks in order to protect the buyers from detection, as, e.g., when the sex worker feels pressured to visit the client at the client's own home. This new policy statement was the outcome of more than two years of work including first hand research in Argentina, Hong Kong, Norway, and Papua New Guinea, and consultations with organizations including UN agencies, sex worker groups, groups representing survivors of prostitution, and organizations promoting criminalization (Amnesty International 2016b, sections 9, 11, 14).

As to the workings of End Demand in Sweden itself, May-Len Skilbrei and Charlotta Holmstrom found that data often relied on in drawing connections between that country's End Demand law and trafficking are unreliable. We do not have "sophisticated knowledge" about those connections (Skilbrei and Holmstrom 2017, 68–76), and, overall, it is unclear whether the law has achieved its goals of reducing prostitution and preventing trafficking and what harms the law has imposed on sex workers (ibid., 1–2). After an extensive study of Sweden's law, Jay Levy (2015, 113) concluded there is no "robust empirical data" suggesting the law has resulted in a decline of trafficking in Sweden. But he did find evidence of significant harms done. Sex workers find the remaining clients are the violent and unstable ones, their negotiations with nervous clients concerned with arrest must now be rushed with little time to negotiate the type of service and to assess the risks a prospective client might pose (ibid., 184–188). Susanne Dodillet and Petra Ostergren (2011, 22) also found evidence of the law's suppressive effect on safe sex practices and safe working environments. For other similar critiques of the Swedish law see Chu and Glass (2013, 105–107), Weitzer (2011, 1363–1365), and Bass (2015, 180–182).

Yet the effect that End Demand ideology can have on the law enforcement machinery of the state is most starkly demonstrated in the United States by a program known as "Demand Abolition." The effect is troubling and suggests a need for further attention from legal and public policy scholars. Oil heiress Swanee Hunt, is the force behind this program of the Cambridge, Massachusetts-based Hunt Alternatives Foundation, which is dedicated to ending commercial sex by going after "demand."

Aside from its own advocacy, the Foundation funds media campaigns and, of great interest, provides money to public agencies in order to further its own vision of law enforcement's role. The District Attorney of Alameda County, across the bay from San Francisco, has declared that local jurisdictions should be focusing on demand. In its November 4, 2015 edition, the *East Bay Express* reported that Alameda County receives roughly $40,000 annually from Demand Abolition. The money comes with strings attached. The paper noted that when San Francisco made known its intent to focus exclusively on people who purchase sex from minors and on people who commit violence against sex workers, Demand Abolition objected and made an $80,000 grant conditional on the city's agreeing to pledge that the sex industry itself is "inherently harmful." The city withdrew from the grant.

On the other hand, Jim, the middle-aged Seattle defendant who posted reviews of sex workers, faced prosecutors who had no qualms about submitting to detailed directives from the Hunt Foundation. They did so in return for $141,667.00 pursuant to three consecutive written agreements covering the period from April 2014 to January 31, 2017. The extent to which this prosecutor, the King County Prosecutor Dan Satterberg, ceded influence, if not outright control, to an out-of-state private advocate of End Demand is striking.

In one or more of the agreements, the prosecutor agrees to espouse the Foundation's "values and assumptions" including the claim that prostitution is "inherently harmful" and the conclusion that attacking demand for prostitution is a fundamental strategy that must be adopted. In addition, the prosecutor agrees to "work with" a number of private individuals and organizations who subscribe to the End Demand strategy.

Yet the Foundation's control moves well beyond generalities into the details of prosecutorial work. For example, under the agreement covering February 2016 through January 2017, the prosecutor's strategy must include "direct buyer disruption tactics designed to achieve 20% demand reduction," and he must at least attempt the Foundation's specified number of buyer disruptions (14,800 buyer disruptions including 1,100 high frequency buyers).

In fact, the prosecutor is to go beyond the straightforward enforcement of the law, and he is tasked with shifting "cultural behavior and norms" to accord with the buyer-centered End Demand ideology. The prosecutor is accordingly obligated to develop and implement a strategy to "leverage media channels to help shift cultural norms." In essence, the prosecutor obligates himself to inculcate End Demand ideology into the very attitudes and beliefs of his constituents. Finally, to avoid any untoward independence on the part of the public prosecutor, he is obligated to submit his strategy and work plans to the Foundation. Such were the Hunt

Foundation-subsidized obligations of the prosecutor when the Review Board investigations were begun, when Jim was arrested, when he was arraigned, and when he was threatened with three years of incarceration and sex registration.

Jim was caught up in a well-publicized push to arrest and prosecute clients, an effort carried out as a campaign against sex trafficking, which, under Washington law, is commercial sex involving force or fraud or minors and has nothing necessarily to do with moving a sex worker from place to place. At a combined law enforcement/prosecutor press conference in January of 2016, preceding Jim's arrest, the King County Sheriff described the campaign as an investigation into a group of Korean sex workers working out of apartments in the Seattle area. He announced "the women were trafficked and were true victims," with the county prosecutor declaring "this is what human trafficking looks like," and the Bellevue Police Chief chiming in that these victims were exploited, coerced, or forced to sell sex. The idea of coercion was repeated by all three (News Conference 2016).

Their object was not to charge these women with prostitution but to "rescue" them. Law enforcement was working on the demand side, and the Police Chief was blunt in announcing their purpose to put "those responsible for this forced sexual servitude in jail." These pronouncements were, of course, squarely in line with the prosecutor's obligations under his agreement with the Hunt Foundation, and, no doubt, squarely in line with the thoughts of those private parties the prosecutor was obligated to "work with."

Yet despite the Police Chief's stirring call to arms, Jim was not charged with trafficking. In fact, he was among a batch of at least 20 individuals ultimately charged, and not one of them was charged with trafficking. One was charged with a misdemeanor, the rest with promoting prostitution. No evidence of coercion or abuse by any of these defendants came to light.

As for the Korean sex workers who were offered up as the centerpiece of the campaign against sexual slavery, none of them acted like grateful, rescued slaves. According to King County Senior Deputy Prosecutor Gary Ernsdorff, the police could not get much information from the women the one day they tried to talk to them, and seven months later the prosecutor had not even tried to contact them again. When they were not arrested themselves, they disappeared. There is no evidence these Korean women were not consenting adults, making money the way they chose, sighing with relief when they realized they themselves would not be arrested and getting away from law enforcement as quickly as they could.

Jim himself was never charged with any involvement with coercion or minors, and he makes clear that, not only was he never involved with coerced women or anyone who could possibly have been under 18, he never saw any Asian sex workers at all. When he did see a sex worker, his interactions reflected the literature on the ordinariness of sex work and clients. Before he saw any sex worker, he would exchange emails with her, and when he did see her it was in a pleasant atmosphere. The interaction would include conversation, maybe a drink, and nothing to indicate the woman was subject to any kind of pressure. The worst thing he has to say about any of the women is that on occasion there was "no chemistry."

That "no chemistry" remark does not evidence an idiosyncratic need or taste. Most of the men posting comments on the Review Board, the website targeted by law enforcement, were looking for what has come to be known as the "girl-friend experience": an experience with some affectionate dimension including physical intimacies such as hugging, kissing, talking, and foreplay.

One thread on the Board was begun by a sex worker who suggested that both sex work providers and clients post notes as to why their roles were important to them. Providers wrote in that they enjoyed their work, they liked their clients, and the income was good. Clients wrote extolling the experience of sexuality with no personal friction or strings attached, but more often they discussed the emotional quality of their encounters and the therapeutic need they had for providers. In describing the emotional dimension, they used words like "enthusiasm," "energy," "thrill of a kiss," "undivided attention," "caresses," and "intimate time." In their confessions of therapeutic needs, twice they mentioned that their therapists either recommended or supported their use of the Board. There is no word yet on whether the King County prosecutor will charge those therapists with felonious promotion of prostitution.

A website that came online in 2016 features accounts by and about clients of sex workers (sexworkclients.org). It is not a message board. No one is identifying a sex worker or trying to find one. The site just invites anyone to submit their own story, and the client stories submitted are deeply personal, touching, and full of praise for sex workers. Of course, neither that website nor the Board's thread are scientific samplings of all buyers of sex, but they do echo a rigorous 2012 study by Christine Milrod and Ronald Weitzer who examined 2,442 postings on another popular forum where clients review escorts. Approximately one-third of the postings contained discussions of emotional intimacy in client–escort relationships. Most of those posting their comments felt they were in a paid relationship. The evidence suggested men who become regular clients develop feelings for their escorts and value an emotional connection in addition to sex. Indeed, postings even revealed men who struggle with the appropriate way to "break up" with an escort they have been seeing (Milrod and Weitzer 2012, 447–467; see also Castle and Lee 2008; Milrod and Monto 2012).

None of these facts about online reviews or about Jim's own behavior could deaden the effect of End Demand ideology on the workings of law enforcement. Outrage and fear were mobilized to impose a vile image on customers and abettors of ordinary, adult prostitution. With that image fixed, the shaming machinery roared to life, making Jim not only an outlaw but a pariah, and the process of public denunciation began with his arrest. In fact, it began even before he was taken to the police station. As soon as he was picked up, out-of-uniform detectives went to his home ostensibly looking for him. They panicked his wife by banging on the front door, then the side door, yelling out his name to her, and presumably, to the neighbors, while broadcasting their intent to arrest him for prostitution. Print and television media gave out his name, and two stories named him even before he was arraigned, and he was publicly associated with a "busted sex-trafficking ring." He lost his job, and an offer of a new professional position was withdrawn after his arraignment. Public shaming and a felony charge with a possible three-year prison term were the price End Demand exacted for posting three comments about consenting, adult call girls.

Ted, the owner and manager of the Review Board website, was also arrested. An unmarried accountant in his sixties, Ted ran the website where sex workers advertised and clients reviewed sex workers with no fee for posting ads and no membership fees. He made no money off the site. He would screen the advertisers, and he never found any sex worker who was coerced other than as might be implied by the bare fact that she had a pimp, and having a pimp was enough for him to reject her posting. He recalled two women he did not allow on the Board because in their photos they looked underage. Later he discovered he had been overly cautious as they were in their twenties.

The advertising sex workers knew who owned the Board and they would contact him with questions about posting. One of the women had been waiting tables when she decided to try sex work through the Board. In time, she sent Ted a picture of the house she was able to buy after her stint as a sex worker. Another sex worker made enough money through the Board to go to college where she met her husband and started a family. She sent Ted an email with pictures of her baby and a message that she hoped he remembered her. He knew four women who went to law school on the income from their sex work advertised on the Board and was himself a client of one of them. Having graduated law school, one of them is now working on a master's degree.

Apart from his work on the Board, Ted recalled the simple but poignant glimpse he was once given into a sex worker–client relationship. It happened when he was with an escort socially and she answered a call from one of her clients. The only reason the client was calling her was to let her know that his cancer test had come out negative.

As was Jim, Ted was threatened that if he tried to defend himself in court the prosecutor would seek an additional three years of incarceration and registration as a sex offender. He pled guilty to writing reviews of sex workers, and, of course, his name found its way into the newspaper and there was press coverage at his arraignment.

Ted generously recounted his experiences to me on August 8, 2016. Two weeks later, on 22 August, he took his own life.

Coercion and poverty

The insistence that *all* prostitution is somehow coercive, along with the notion of sexual slavery, often accompanies efforts to target clients (Berkowitz 2015, 284; Chu and Glass 2013, 104; Hunt 2013, 8). That emotional driver merits its own individualized attention. A recorded dialogue between a King County trial judge and the county's prosecutor illuminates the surprising resilience of this investment in the notion of coercion. The exchange occurred during the term of the 2016 agreement between the prosecutor and the Hunt Foundation. The occasion was the sentencing hearing of a defendant who had posted sex worker reviews and leased an apartment that was used for prostitution. He was charged with promoting prostitution, second degree. The trial judge was adamant that prostitution must involve coercion and imposed a stiffer sentence than even the prosecutor recommended, despite the utter failure of that prosecutor, Gary Ernsdorff, to uncover any evidence of coercion. Here is the verbatim exchange:

> Judge Hollis: The number of lives that have been affected by this man, by you, Mr. [defendant's name], by your promotion of prostitution of young women who have been prostituted against their will—and I don't believe that you don't understand that—is huge.
>
> *(Transcript 2016, 8)*

> Prosecutor Ernsdorff: Trafficking requires some sort of coercive behavior usually physical coercive behavior. And believe me, we looked hard at whether we had facts or not to file trafficking and it did not meet the standard. There's also this coercive behavior that would go into Promoting 1 [in the first degree], and that simply we did not have the evidence in this case to file . . . Promoting 1 or trafficking.
>
> *(Transcript 2016, 13)*

> Judge Hollis: I find it incredible that none of your [defendant's] education and, evidently, your intelligence could not have some inkling that there was coercion involved in this. I find that incredible.
>
> *(Transcript 2016, 17)*

This apparent need to find coercion stands in contrast to many of the studies discussed above, which challenge coercion as a model for prostitution. Likewise, research that informed New Zealand's 2003 decriminalization of prostitution found clients to be "relatively benign," with most workers who participated in the research reporting at least some unpleasant experiences with clients, but, on the whole, stating they liked their clients and enjoyed contact with them (Abel 2017, 143). A Canadian study comparing work experiences among women in street-based prostitution with hospital aides and orderlies found that women on the streets had more personal control over their work environment than did the hospital workers (Shaver 2005, 313; see also Agustín 2007, 79–87; Monto 2010, 233–254; Monto and McRee 2005).

Again, personal sex worker accounts reflect those studies. Consider Sol. The compulsion to interpret any sex work as coercive at some level takes on the air of gratuitous doctrine when talking to Sol. She was 28 when she arrived in Seattle with a Harvard graduate degree in physics, intent on earning a PhD. With a modest sexual history, she wondered, as she says, what more there was to life. She talked to sex workers and was told that sex work either works for you or it doesn't. She tried it, and it worked for her. She is also a technical writer and editor for physics textbook publishers and other large corporations. She is not a woman with limited opportunities.

Coercion is also hard to imagine in connection with Savannah's introduction to sex work. She recalls her first client, an ordinary guy just off from work. The experience turned out to be "easy and sweet." She felt she was giving an experience, not that someone was taking something from her.

Maxine Doogan has a broad perspective on the lives of sex workers as she is the president of the Erotic Service Provider Legal Education and Research Project (ESPLERP), an organization that brings impact litigation on behalf of sex workers. As plaintiff, it brought the 2015 *ESPLERP v. Gascon* suit to federal court challenging the constitutionality of California's anti-prostitution statute. Maxine discloses that in her work with sex workers she has never come across one who has been coerced.

Maggie writes that often sex workers half-jokingly criticize other women for giving their sexual favors away. She describes a twitter hashtag "#banfreebies" under which sex workers from around the world lampooned the arguments of those trying to prohibit prostitution by joking that women who *don't* charge "suffer from 'false consciousness,'" are "'victims' in need of 'rescue,'" and that "unpaid sex is a form of rape" (McNeill 2013, 1).

Yet perhaps the above discussion is missing the principal "coercion" issue: poverty. Some individuals choose to do sex work, while others find sex work to be the only way of supporting themselves and their families. Consider Jasmine, who sold sex on the street for approximately two years. Her work put her in a distinct minority as only about 20% of sex workers in the United States work on the street (Law 2000, 529; Weitzer 2007, 29). But poverty is associated with street work, and Jasmine was no exception. Although she was attending a community college when she got started in sex work, she was homeless and living in a shelter at the time. She socialized with two women who were sex workers, saw how much they were making and decided to try it herself. As she puts it, one day it just happened.

It would be a bit disingenuous to say someone forced her into sex work, but she clearly did not have opportunities knocking at her door, and if poverty had not been a dominant feature of her life we can assume it would have taken a different course.

But what about the men who bought sex from Jasmine on the street? Her poverty does not tell us in what sense those men were coercers or vaguely part of some abstract system that coerced her into sex work. What Jasmine has to say is that clients are human just like everyone else: some of the men are horny, some stressed, some just want the company of a beautiful woman, and she has never found herself in real danger while working.

When interviewed, she had moved indoors and put together her own website, but one of her clients was a 33-year-old man she had started seeing as a worker on the street. He became a good friend, and they would meet once a week for dinner or lunch before the paid-for service. He took her shopping for food when she needed food. He even helped her out of an abusive relationship with a boyfriend. The boyfriend was the abuser; the client was the rescuer.

Jasmine's circumstance invites an examination of the client in situations where sex work is induced by poverty. The first time her friend saw her she was poor and he paid her for sex. It is unclear how her poverty is to figure in an argument that he was coercing or exploiting her. The campaign to paint the buyer as the new folk devil too often rests on an amorphous but very dark construct of an abstract, monolithic thing called "prostitution," and of buyers as somehow supporting that thing out there. Yet life is lived by individuals and it is lived concretely. End Demand advocates do not detail advice for the individual, middle-class male encountering an impoverished, marginalized female streetwalker who offers him sex for money. He looks at her and knows she is poor, perhaps desperately poor and without economic options. Should he walk away? Should he walk away just *because* he is her only option?

Perhaps he should walk away out of fear. After all, his community does not have the political will to lift this woman out of poverty but it does have the will to hunt down her paying clients. Yes, maybe he would do better to hurry home where he will enjoy the moral satisfaction of having hired a housekeeper fresh from a developing country, a woman who hates cleaning house, but with limited English skills and no education she finds it is her only option.

Comparing Jasmine and the housekeeper has global implications as economic need pressures them both, and the pressures of poverty are found across national borders and cultures and in migration between them. A study of New Zealand sex workers found that although a number of factors influenced entry into sex work, the predominant reasons were financial, with 73% of the survey participants entering because they needed money to pay for household expenses, and 82% reporting household expenses as at least one reason they stayed in the sex industry (Abel et al. 2007, 108, 110). An extensive study of Chinese migrant sex workers found that economic factors were a driving force behind the choices the sex workers made, socio-economic circumstances having put many of them into a vulnerable position (Finckenauer and Chin 2011, 47, 54). Through their national sex worker organization, the Empower Foundation (2016), Thai sex workers plead for understanding that for them sex work is a way out of generational poverty and that migration is their solution, not their problem. Laura Agustín, discussing labor migration for work in the sex industry, reminds readers that many migrants are fleeing "small-town prejudices, dead-end jobs, dangerous streets and suffocating families" (Agustín 2007, 45).

To the extent that a doctrinal focus on clients diverts attention or resources from addressing underlying poverty issues, that focus is a disservice to the very sex workers thought to be in need of protection from clients. Addressing the global issue of sex worker poverty, legal philosopher and ethicist Martha Nussbaum (1998, 724) notes that, "[W]e need, on balance, more studies of women's credit unions and fewer studies of prostitution." The needed restructuring of thought and policy is perhaps best expressed by Thailand's Empower Foundation (2016, n.p.): "We want to know, if society were asked to think of us, not as criminals, immoral women, or helpless victims, but as humans, mothers, workers, and family providers, what laws and systems could be imagined?"

References

Abel, Gillian. 2017. In Search of a Fair and Free Society: The Regulation of Sex Work In New Zealand. In Eilis Ward and Gillian Wylie, Eds., *Feminism, Prostitution and The State: The Politics of Neo-Abolitionism*, 140–154. London: Routledge.

Abel, Gillian, Lisa Fitzgerald, and Cheryl Brunton. November 2007. *The Impact of the Prostitution Reform Act on the Health and Safety Practices of Sex Workers. Report to the Prostitution Law Review Committee.* Christchurch, NZ: Department of Public Health and General Practice, University of Otago. www.otago.ac.nz/christchurch/otago018607.pdf.

Agustín, Laura Maria. 2007. *Sex at the Margins: Migration, Labour Markets and the Rescue Industry*. London: Zed Books.

Almodovar, Norma Jean. 1993. *Cop to Call Girl: Why I Left the LAPD to Make an Honest Living as a Beverly Hills Prostitute*. New York: Simon & Schuster.

Amnesty International. 2016a, May 26. *Policy on State Obligations to Respect, Protect and Fulfil the Human Rights of Sex Workers*. www.amnesty.org/en/documents/pol30/4062/2016/en.

Amnesty International. 2016b, May 26. *Q&A: Policy to Protect the Human Rights of Sex Workers*. www. amnesty.org/en/qa-policy-to-protect-the-human-rights-of-sex- workers.

Bass, Alison. 2015. *Getting Screwed: Sex Workers and the Law*. Lebanon, NH: University Press of New England.

Berkowitz, Eric. 2015. *The Boundaries of Desire: A Century of Bad Laws, Good Sex, and Changing Identities*. Berkeley, CA: Counterpoint.

Bernstein, Elizabeth. 2007. *Temporarily Yours: Intimacy, Authenticity, and the Commerce of Sex*. Chicago, IL: University of Chicago Press.

Brooks-Gordon, Belinda. 2006. *The Price of Sex: Prostitution, Policy and Society*. London: Routledge.

Castle, Tammy and Jennifer Lee. 2008. Ordering Sex in Cyberspace: A Content Analysis of Escort Websites. *International Journal of Cultural Studies* 11(4): 107–121.

Chu, Sandra Ka Hon and Rebecca Glass. 2013. Sex Work Law Reform in Canada: Considering Problems with the Nordic Model. *Alberta Law Review* 51(1): 101–124.

Coalition Against Trafficking in Women. n.d. "Ending the Demand." Best Practices. www.catwinterna tional.org/BestPractices/EndingDemand.

Dodillet, Susanne and Petra Östergren. 2011. The Swedish Sex Purchase Act: Claimed Success and Documented Effects. *Paper presented at the International Workshop: Decriminalizing Prostitution and Beyond: Practical Experiences and Challenges, The Hague*, March 3–4. www.plri.org/sites/plri.org/files/Impact%20 of%20Swedish%20law_0.pdf.

Empower Foundation. 2016. We Don't Do Sex Work Because We Are Poor, We Do Sex Work to End Our Poverty. *Open Democracy*. www.opendemocracy.net/beyondslavery/sws/we-don-t-do-sex-work-because-we- are-poor-we-do-sex-work-to-end-our-poverty.

Finckenauer, James O. and Ko-lin Chin. 2011. *Researching and Rethinking Sex Trafficking: The Movement of Chinese Women to Asia and The United States for Commercial Sex. Final Report to The United States Department of Justice*. www.ncjrs.gov/pdffiles1/nij/grants/233583.pdf.

Freedom Network USA. n.d. https://freedomnetworkusa.org/app/uploads/2016/12/End-Demand.pdf.

Glazer, Sarah. 2016. Seattle Shifts Sex Arrests from Sellers to Buyers. *Congressional Quarterly Researcher* 26(15): 337–360.

Hakim, Catherine. 2015. Supply and Desire: Sexuality and the Sex Industry in the 21st Century. *Discussion Paper No. 61, Institute of Economic Affairs*. https://iea.org.uk/wp- content/uploads/2016/07/DP_ Supply%20and%20Desire_61_amended_web.pdf.

Holmstrom, Charlotta and May-Len Skilbrei. 2017. The Swedish Sex Purchase Act: Where Does It Stand? *Oslo Law Review* 1: 1–16.

Hunt, Swanee. 2013. Deconstructing Demand: The Driving Force of Sex Trafficking. *Brown Journal of World Affairs* 19(2): 1–12. www.demandabolition.org/wp-content/uploads/2013/07/brown_jour nal_6_2013.pdf.

Law, Silvia A. 2000. Commercial Sex: Beyond Decriminalization. *Southern California Law Review* 73: 523–610.

Levy, Jay. 2015. *Criminalising the Purchase of Sex: Lessons from Sweden*. New York: Routledge.

McNeill, Maggie. 2013, December 26. Privileging Fantasy Over Reality. *Cato Unbound: A Journal of Debate*. www.cato-unbound.org/2013/12/26/maggie-mcneill/privileging-fantasy-over-reality.

Milrod, Christine and Martin A. Monto. 2012. The Hobbyist and The Girlfriend Experience: Behaviors and Preferences of Male Customers of Internet Sexual Service Providers. *Deviant Behavior* 33(10): 792–810.

Milrod, Christine and Ronald Weitzer. 2012. The Intimacy Prism: Emotion Management Among the Clients of Escorts. *Men & Masculinities* 15(5): 447–467.

Monto, Martin A. 2010. Prostitutes' Customers: Motives and Misconceptions. In Ronald Weitzer, Ed., *Sex for Sale: Prostitution, Pornography, and the Sex Industry*, 233–254. New York: Routledge.

Monto, Martin A. and Joseph N. McRee. 2005. A Comparison of the Male Customers of Female Street Prostitutes with National Samples of Men. *International Journal of Offender Therapy and Comparative Criminology* 49: 505–529.

News Conference—Human Trafficking Investigation. 2016, January 7. YouTube video, 51:06, posted by KingCountyTV. www.youtube.com/watch?v=ardUdF12LUw.

Nussbaum, Martha C. 1998. "Whether from Reason or Prejudice": Taking Money for Bodily Services. *Journal of Legal Studies* 27: 693–724.

Phoenix, Aphrodite. 2012. *Are They Bad Girls or Brilliant? The Truths Behind the Fight for Independent Prostitutes' Rights*. North Charleston, NC: CreateSpace Independent Publishing Platform.

Ross, Mirha-Soleil. 2006, May 29. Dear John. *Cybersolidaires*. http://cybersolidaires.typepad.com/ameriques/2006/05/dear_john.html. Excerpted from "Yapping Out Loud: Contagious Thoughts from an Unrepentant Whore," produced by Buddies in Bad Times Theatre as part of its 2004–2005 season. Published in eXXXpressions: Forum XXX Proceedings, Stella, April 2006.

Sanders, Teela. 2012. *Paying for Pleasure: Men Who Buy Sex*. 2nd ed. London: Routledge.

Shaver, Frances M. 2005. Sex Work Research: Methodological and Ethical Challenges. *Journal of Interpersonal Violence* 20: 296–319.

Skilbrei, May-Len and Charlotta Holmstrom. 2017. Linking Prostitution and Human Trafficking Policies: The Nordic Experience. In Hans Nelen and Dina Siegel, Eds., *Contemporary Organized Crime: Developments, Challenges and Responses*, 65–79. Cham, Switzerland: Springer.

Transcript of Oral Argument. 2016, July 22. State of Washington v. _____, Cause No. 16- 1-00 156-1 SEA.

Vanwesenbeeck, Ine. 2001. Another Decade of Social Scientific Work on Sex Work: A Review of Research 1990–2000. *Annual Review of Sex Research* 12(1): 242–289.

Vanwesenbeeck, Ine. 2017. Sex Work Criminalization Is Barking Up the Wrong Tree. *Archives of Sexual Behavior* 46: 1631–1640.

Weitzer, Ronald. 2005. New Directions in Research on Prostitution. *Crime, Law & Social Change* 43(4): 211–235.

Weitzer, Ronald. 2007. Prostitution: Facts and Fictions. *Contexts* 6(4): 28–33.

Weitzer, Ronald. 2009. Sociology of Sex Work. *Annual Review of Sociology* 35: 213–234.

Weitzer, Ronald. 2011. Sex Trafficking and the Sex Industry: The Need for Evidence-Based Theory and Legislation. *Journal of Criminal Law and Criminology* 101(4): 1337–1369.

Weitzer, Ronald. 2012. *Legalizing Prostitution: From Illicit Vice to Lawful Business*. New York: New York University Press.

35

Men, culture, modernity, and sex work in southeastern Nigeria

Valentine C. Ezeh, Joy I. Ugwu, and Festus E. Ngwu

Introduction

The sex industry in Enugu has become an integral part of the social environment although sex work has remained consistently controversial globally. Historically, in Enugu, a southeastern Nigerian region inhabited by the Igbos, the most common form of sex work is brothel-based with two main types: city sex workers who are based in city brothels and "junction" town sex workers who are based along highway junction towns (Ladipo et al. 2002). More recently, however, street-based sex work seems to have become very popular with the entrance of undergraduate college students. This is probably attributed to the growing stigma attached to brothel-based sex work and the freedom and income that street-based sex work offers (Abel & Fitzgerald 2012). Still few sex workers work indoors in their homes or in commercial and recreational venues.

Traditionally, the culture of Enugu people is to view sex work as a deviation from socially constructed norms. Culture and traditional religion are the custodians of sexuality that prescribe what is sexually right or wrong and the people are expected to imbibe the cultural tenets without questioning. The dominant culture does not encourage the view of sex for pleasure but rather sex for procreation and expansion of family lineage. In this regard, the culture highly mystifies sexuality in order to control and restrict its expression. The cultural prescriptions on sexuality are also more suppressive to women's sexuality than men. For example, while men enjoy a relatively more liberal sexuality, women's sexuality among other things is tied to traditional deities that control and restrict women's sexuality. In a case where a woman is found "guilty" she has to perform a traditional rite called "*Ngodo*" that requires her to confess her "sins" and burn the clothes on her at that moment as a sign of purification and also provide enough cooked food and drinks for her husband's parents and family members. But although the culture gives men more liberal sexuality than women it is still configured in such a way that men can hardly claim total control of women's sexuality or bodies.

The advent of post-colonial modernity in Africa as in many other parts of the world has impacted on the family, culture, and traditional religion at societal level and has further revolutionized sex work. Modernity is acknowledged as a contested concept but we find it a useful analytical tool to deploy here because it conveys the ongoing tension in many cultures worldwide between dominant cultural norms in relatively isolated communities and a more integrated and homogeneous global society and culture. Modernity essentially characterizes increased movement of people, capital, goods, technology, information (including sexual information), religion, interconnectedness, and social relations with its ongoing impact on human culture, institutions, and politics (Berman 2010). The interaction and integration of ideas, values, cultures, technology, and politics of people of different parts of the world further promote globalization such that there is a greater inclination to the emergence of a global unified culture and gradual collapse of dominant cultural ideals and values at the societal level and ushering in global changes in the social, ideological, economic, and religious configurations of communities.

In Africa and many other parts of the world modernity has led to a global shift in relationships and sexuality as a result of different types of contact between groups with different norms, including trade, war, colonialism, religion, and tourism. Thus in Enugu society most traditional views of sex and sexuality that are predicated on culture and traditional religion have been replaced with Christian beliefs with their attendant new mode of worship and laws. For example, the dominant cultural sexual practices that are gender discriminatory in favor of men as well as those embedded in traditional ritual control have come to be condemned by Christianity. This is a wholly new and emerging model of masculinity framed in terms of the 'responsible man' and that conflicts with the dominant social ideals and values that frame masculinity in terms of power and control over women's sexuality. The contradictions inherent in these realities play out in Enugu men's patronage of sex workers, as while patronage of sex workers enhances men's feelings of power and control over women's sexuality it also signifies and speaks to men's powerlessness in the sense that men are forced to perform their sexuality and sexual fantasies through the bodies of women who are cultural "rebels" or engage in something that is potentially much more difficult: questioning the culture of chastity among women.

Today, as a result of modernity and globalization, offering sexual services for money has been revolutionized. Sex workers can now connect with their clients and sell sex through the Internet and other social media platforms (Ibrahim & Mukhtar 2016). New patterns of sex worker–client relationships have also evolved even though sex work and ownership of brothels are criminalized in southeastern Nigeria.

This chapter derives from a qualitative study that explored dominant cultural values in southeastern Nigeria related to men, sexuality, and access to women's sexuality and the contributions of modernity to new laws, religion, and masculinity. We also examined the relationships that develop between sex workers and clients, the criminalization of sex work in southeastern Nigeria, and its impact on sex worker–client behavior. Respondents included 61 sex workers and 43 male clients drawn from eight "junction town" and three city brothels located at Obollo Afor, 9th Mile Corner, and Nsukka town, all in Enugu state of Nigeria. A face-to-face semi-structured interview was used to collect data through July and August 2017. Data were transcribed verbatim and analyzed using thematic analysis.

Cultural traits and sexuality in Igbo culture

As is true in many parts of the world if not globally, sexuality in Enugu, southeastern Nigeria is embedded in complex cultural and religious traditions that prescribe acceptable sexual practices. Traditionally, the culture typically endorses reproductive sex and procreation as the acceptable sexual practices just like in most African and Asian cultures (Okazaki 2002).

Thus, before the advent of modernity, culture and religion were the two dominant factors that determined sexuality and sexual behaviors, influencing sexual ideologies and instilling a sense of what is sexually normal behavior and what is not (Izugbara 2004). Usually, mothers gave their teenagers, especially the girls, some form of primitive sexual education in line with the traditional sexual tenets. However, mothers only made reference to the female genitals (*Ahu nwanyi*) as being sacred and to be guided with care. Girls were also cautioned on how they interact with male adults with the simple explanation that pregnancy results from male touch. Those who engage in sexual immorality are often punished by being mocked through lyrics, songs, and folk tales. Sex education is therefore habitually rooted in secrecy and also mystified with the aim of discouraging girls from thinking about and knowing their sexuality. While culturally the boys are also expected to abstain from sexual relationships, the major parental focus is on training the boys to learn how to work hard to eventually become responsible married adults.

The culture also prescribes acceptable sexual practices between married adults but the provisions were largely male-privileging and suppressive to women's ownership of their sex. For example, men were allowed to marry as many wives as they can maintain but not so for women. Furthermore, when a man's wife delivers a child, she has to abstain from sex for a period of time but the culture allows her to provide her husband with a mistress to meet his sexual needs although this arrangement ceases immediately after she can sexually relate with her husband. Also, women's sexuality is configured around ritual control such that the traditional deities worshipped were framed to punish women who have sexual relations with another man (*Itufu-uku*) by inducing insanity but still not so for men who can have multiple partners. The culture thus generally expected women to remain chaste, responsible, and respectable but gave men a more liberal sexuality. This is a source of gender inequality in sexuality (Turner 2014) that pervades the ancient culture of Enugu people. For the unmarried, dominant cultural norms regard discussion of sex and sexuality as indecent and taboo and stipulate total abstinence from sex until marriage is properly contracted. Hence, in traditional Enugu society, one can find a woman in the village stream barely covering her nakedness or during moonlight play without being lusted after by men.

Men interviewed during the course of this research were of the view that these cultural values partly drive them to patronize sex workers. Emeka, a 34-year-old civil servant made the following statements:

> You see, in our culture one is expected to treat sex as sacred or one will lose respect. As such, it is difficult for one to ask one's partner to do certain things that one sexually desires but one can make any demand with a sex worker as long as one pays.

The cultural configuration is also viewed by most male clients as not offering men the liberty to be in control of sex, something that for many Enugu men in our study might be considered a reaffirmation of their masculinity. Male power over women was based, among other things, on sexual dominance in most traditional African societies (Langa 2014). Many African men believe that masculinity should be constructed around the control of women's sexuality and supremacy over women's bodies. The sexualization of masculinity has also been reported in some other societies and the link of sexual activity to the definitions and practice of masculinity has greatly encouraged early sexual activity (Kempadoo & Dunn 2001) especially among the men.

Yet in the cultural context in which we conducted our research men seem to be challenged because while the dominant culture acknowledges their sexuality and maleness they still have limited power of control over women's sexuality. For example, some of the clients interviewed were of the opinion that women take advantage of the cultural view of sex as relating to procreation and maintenance of family linage to assert when to accept or deny sexual demand. Uchenna, a 34-year-old artisan mentioned his reason for patronizing prostitutes thus: "My wife always reminds me that sex is all about child bearing and she carries the baby. So I only have sex when she is in the mood which is not regular." Similarly, Ejiofor, a 39-year-old policeman, mentioned:

> You can't believe it but it is true that on many occasions I beg my partner for sex. Then, when she agrees she will insist on how we go about it. But when I am with a sex worker I take control of the moment to my satisfaction.

Hence although paradoxically the culture gives the men more sexual "freedom" than women, men still have a feeling of powerlessness in the actual control of women's sexuality but assume such control on the bodies of prostitutes who are deviant to the cultural prescription of sexuality. For example, a study in Hong Kong has identified themes suggesting that financial exchange gives clients the right to treat sex workers as they wish (Wong, Holroyd, & Bingham 2010, p. 56). These cultural realities have great costs for both men and women. For men, the cost is that some of them feel pressured to seek out paid sex, while women cannot express themselves sexually without being stigmatized. Yet sex workers bear the brunt of this cultural burden because of their 'cultural rebel' status.

Some men also claimed they are partly driven into seeking sexual relief elsewhere just to preserve their marriage especially since the culture places much value, respect, and expectations on marriage. The extended family system is also widely practiced and unusual sexual demands can be reported by a woman and discussed to the embarrassment of the man. Chika, 32-year-old driver mentioned,

> As a married man having a girl friend is risky. It cannot be hidden for a long time. In any case I don't want that to disrupt my marriage. So it is easier going to sex workers and getting sexual satisfaction without much noise.

Also, Kelechi, a 42-year-old policeman said: "My partner doesn't have much desire for sex. She used to complain about my demand for sex. But I love my marriage so occasionally I opt for sex workers." Although it is not normal and the culture cannot be directly implicated in the apparent lack of sexual desire among some women as reported by a respondent, the internalization of some cultural values relating to women's sexuality may be a contributing factor. For example, from early adulthood girls are restricted from overt expressions of sexuality and are made to believe that sex and sexuality are not for physical pleasure but exclusively for reproduction. Because marriage is held in high esteem and yet overt expression of sexuality contradicts the cultural and religious norms, some men prefer to express their sexuality by visiting commercial sex workers at least to remain married and retain the respect that accompanies marriage.

Modernity and emerging views on sexuality in Igbo culture

Modernity and globalization has resulted in the evolution of sex work over time in southeastern Nigeria specifically Enugu. Information and communication technology, particularly the Internet, has fast-tracked acculturation thereby radically altering traditional and cultural views of the people on sexuality. Thus, today no woman can introduce a mistress to her husband and no barely clad female can be seen at the stream or during moonlight play. Indeed moonlight play that is usually characterized in Igbo culture by folk tales, pranks, and games has been eroded by the onset of modernity. Saliently Enugu people are becoming less conservative with regard to sexual life and gradually rejecting cultural prescriptions of sexuality and embracing "new" sexual patterns.

For example, Chijioke-a 42-year-old driver opined that, "With modernity we have come to know much about sex and women. But some of these things can't be done openly. Brothels are best place to try out new sexual practices."

Indeed, modernity has impacted greatly on the sex industry although with variations across societies. Countries are now interconnected and people are massively moving from place to place and country to country with ease. This has restructured the world economy and increased unemployment rates and the associated socioeconomic precarity making sex work one of the ways poor people make ends meet (ILO 2009). Contemporary Enugu is no exception to this reality, and, as elsewhere in the world, the sex industry is thriving (Vandepitte et al. 2006; Ward et al. 2005). The Internet has also become a fashionable avenue where people, especially adolescents, learn about, explore, and develop their sexuality (Boies, Knudson, & Young 2004), coupled with the increased use of sexual images in advertising, the rapid growth of the adult entertainment industry, and the widespread availability of pornography (Ward & Aral 2006) the sex industry is experiencing a greater number of entrants. Prostitutes on their part are cognizant of the fact that people are increasingly tuning in to a more "global" view of sexuality and they have come to capitalize on that by objectifying and commodifying their bodies and increasingly working hard to appear seductive and "hot" in order to attract and retain clients.

Jane, a 30-year-old sex worker indicated: "My appearance is very important. I dress to reveal my cleavages. You know the curves around my buttocks and breast. Men are always crazy when they see these things."

Another sex worker (Ngozi, 26 years old) also mentioned: "Sometimes I wear transparent thigh-level clothes and when I sit down I adjust myself so that my pants can be seen."

Seduction seems to be an important element in attracting and retaining clients, and modernity has created opportunities for sex workers to master the art of handling clients in bed for maximum pleasure. Modern sex workers are constantly exploring and observing clients' erotic needs and continue to take advantage of such needs by making clients think of them as sex machines.

Ndidi, a 28-year-old sex worker disclosed: "I have discovered all my clients' needs. I pet them and encourage them to try any sex style of their choice. My customers believe so much in my ability for sex." Maximization of clients' sexual pleasure is one of the sure ways of retaining clients and globally many commercial sex workers have developed techniques to do so. Commercial sex workers in Laos, for example, engage in oral sex, kissing, and touching to stimulate erection and enhance sexual pleasure of clients (Keobounphanh & Toole 2008) but some sex workers display high professionalism by restricting certain relational activities and tactically make their body exclusion zones clear. Surface acting—an aspect of seduction—is also often employed by modern sex workers to keep their client. The majority of sex workers interviewed admitted that to meet with the erotic expectations of clients and the emotional requirements of the job they apply surface acting (Hochschild 1983). They also admitted that this is the most difficult aspect of the job as one has to be very good at acting or feigning "hotness" and emotions (Sanders 2005) and that the emotional labor is even more demanding when dealing with first timers and non regulars. As Stella, a 24-year-old sex worker puts it, "In most cases it is like detaching your real self from yourself."

Modernity also introduced Christianity to the people of Enugu, with a different outlook on sexuality, which conflicts with their traditional religious and cultural beliefs. The Christianization of the people of Enugu led to the abandonment of many traditions and cultural sexual practices in favor of the doctrine of the newfound religion. It is now sinful for Enugu people to worship deities and for a man to marry more than one wife or to have a relational affair with another woman and departure from this framework is punishable by eternal damnation. This is a wholly new and emerging mode of masculinity that is framed in terms of the 'responsible man' and that conflicts with the dominant social ideals and values in Igbo culture that frame masculinity in terms of power and control over women's sexuality. The contradictions inherent in these realities are evident in men's patronage of "women of easy virtue" as a means of enhancing the feeling of sexual dominance. Modernity and Christianity have also freed Igbo women from traditional ritual control, which has greatly impacted on the expression of their sexuality and also accentuated the campaign and advocacy for gender equality and changing the traditional cultural roles of women. Today, Igbo women have abandoned their traditional roles of homekeepers and are increasingly spending much time working or trading to earn money. Compared to in the past, spouses are now having less and less time for themselves and this has adversely affected partner intimacy and the sexual life of many Igbo couples, thus encouraging men to visit sex workers and "buy" affection and intimacy.

This is how Daniel, a 41-year-old civil servant, responded:

> My wife is a teacher and owns a shop as well and she leaves the house by 7am and sometimes comes home by 9pm looking tired. We don't have enough time for ourselves but since we need the money that comes from the work and business I don't quarrel with her but I visit these girls for sex and to escape the boredom.

Chidi, another 45-year-old civil servant said:

> You see I have five children and we have decided to stop having more. Today we are no longer as close as we used to be, the children are there, the job, the family, and so much responsibilities. I come here just to be close to a woman, listen to her and all that.

Indeed, all over the world, modernity and global revolution have altered traditional practices particularly in the area of sexuality making it more liberal and accommodating with regard to different sexual orientations and preferences in sex work. Prostitutes are increasingly becoming more daring and willing to engage in the specific sexual patterns and fantasies of their clients. Jideofor, an unemployed 28-year-old client responded:

> Sometimes I feel like trying anal sex but I dare not tell my girlfriend. Actually I know it is not acceptable in our culture but still I want to try it. So on some occasions I go to buy the sex I want.

Obiora, a 32-year-old driver also indicated: "These girls are sexy and can thrill you with some of the styles you dare not suggest to your wife or girlfriend without being looked at as being immoral or sexually perverted." Findings, however, revealed that the impact of modernity differs for Igbo men and women. While most men are more liberal in seeking deviations from compulsive forces of the culture and religion, many women still view sexuality from both the spiritual and cultural viewpoint. Most women, especially the married ones, may be hesitant to engage in sexual practices they regard as alien to their traditional culture. Thus, men tend to purchase sex because it is an opportunity to experience new sexual pleasure from those who are willing to try any sexual practice while at the same time leaving their partners in peace with their religio-cultural view of sexuality.

Criminalization of sex work in southeastern Nigeria

Sex work has remained one of the most controversial areas of work globally with different countries adopting different approaches to sex work regulation. In southeastern Nigeria, the culture of the Enugu people considers prostitution or sex work as taboo and the people involved, especially the prostitutes, are identified with different names like "*Ashawo*" and "*Akunna-Kunna*," as social misfits and deviants. In the Nigerian legal system, sex work and operation of brothels are criminal and punishable offenses under sections 223, 224 and 225 of the Nigerian Criminal Code.

But the eradication of sex work through criminalization has remained ineffective partly because the sex work law is vague, making its application somewhat difficult. This deficiency in law has inadvertently created opportunities for sex workers, clients, and the police. For example, despite prohibition, ownership of brothels and exchange of money for sex have continued and sex workers are even organizing to seek legislative approval for decriminalization of sex work. The police on their part take advantage of the vagueness of the law to exploit the sex workers by occasionally raiding brothels and arresting sex workers who have to then pay in order to be released. For the male clients, they seem to be absolved from the law since they are not harassed by agents of the law even though they contravene socially accepted norms by paying for sex. It seems then as if the players in the sex industry are free to play the game as they wish even in the face of criminalization. Eze, a 40-year-old client, remarked:

> The problem is the police are taking advantage of the law. They have never arrested us but the girls who they often intimidate. In some cases we help the girls get out of police net. The law can remain so long as it doesn't interfere with my sexual life.

Sex workers need protection from the police and miscreants and the ability to protect them is a strong determinant of the formation of certain special relationships between sex workers and their clients. The majority of the clients interviewed are aware of the law against the sale and purchase of sex and agreed that buying sexual services is a deviant behavior, however this has not deterred clients from visiting sex workers.

Patterns of sex worker–client relationships

Although sex work is anchored on exchange of sex for money, formation of relationships outside the initial goal of sex work has been documented (e.g. Goldenberg et al. 2011). The pattern of cultivation of several forms of relationships by sex workers is largely dependent on type and the disposition of clients. The sex workers interviewed described three types of clients that include regular clients, (clients that frequent particular sex workers for sex), non-regular clients (clients that visit once in a while), and first timers (clients coming for the first time to buy sex but who may or may not become regulars in future). Findings also indicate that sex workers develop various forms of social and emotional attachments with their clients only when they have known the client over time. Being a regular is therefore an essential element in this circumstance. Furthermore, relationships vary according to the marital status of clients.

The majority of the sex workers interviewed said they consider married clients as "special friends" because they come with unique forms of sexual demands while not forgetting their families. For this category of clients, the sex workers are aware that they are married and come only for sexual pleasure. The men are, however, caring and treat the sex workers with respect, which often leads to the development of mutual trust. They are also considered as "special friends" because they are richer, pay more, want secrecy, and attend to the personal issues of sex workers more than single men do. Grace, a 29-year-old sex worker indicated that:

> Some married men are good. They treat me like their girlfriend. Such men are special to me because they enjoy the affection I give them and they help me when I have financial problems. I like them but I make sure we don't get too close emotionally because I know they can't substitute me for their families.

To maintain the line of the relationship without being too emotional with married clients the prostitutes interviewed said they often feign emotions to take advantage of the situation and make more money. For example, 33-year-old Uzoamaka said:

> A married man once told me that he lacks intimacy and closeness in the form of touching, holding and feeling a woman. At first I just thought it is one of the old stories but this man continued to treat me like his wife. I don't actually like that but I make him believe I am comfortable with that and it is paying off.

There are other unmarried clients that are romantic partners of sex workers not because of the financial gains but the unique and genuine interpersonal intimacy and affection that develop between the clients and sex workers. For example, Rose, a 31-year-old sex worker, said:

> I have a customer that I have known for some time. He is kind to me and I always feel safe and relaxed when I am with him. We are very intimate and he makes me feel special. If I don't see him for some days I miss him. I also visit and spend nights in his home.

Again, one significant thing about this category of clients is that the sex workers unconsciously fall in love and relate to them as genuine lovers while offering them some privileges such as free sex and emotional and financial support. A 22-year-old sex worker called Ijeoma opined that:

> I have someone I won't call a customer but a boyfriend. We love each other and when I am with him I don't feel like a prostitute. We are so close he has become part of me and I can give him much of my time, free sex, and even support him with money when the need arises.

Findings showed that clients who in turn fall in love with sex workers tend to consider them as romantic partners just as those in a regular relationship, and also rationalize their socially unacceptable behavior to escape feelings of guilt. Eze, a 40-year-old client indicated:

> I really love her so much and I don't see her as a prostitute but a victim of circumstance. If the economy was good I am sure she wouldn't be here. In any case, I am comfortable with her and will do anything for her.

The sex workers are, however, mindful of the number of clients they fall in love with. This is because "Falling in love with clients interferes with the job. I am here to make money not to find lovers but I am human so I have only one customer that I am really in love with" (Helen, a 30-year-old sex worker). A considerable body of research has demonstrated that falling in love, and the accompanying emotional and social demands, is particularly challenging for sex workers (Robertson et al. 2014) and having romantic partners reduces their total number of sexual partners (Ngugi et al. 2012).

Other categories of regulars are generally considered as "friends" and findings revealed that most of them pose great problems to the sex workers as they sometimes seek greater intimacy from the sex workers. Chioma, a 30-year-old sex worker mentioned that:

> You see, every customer is a friend. If I don't treat a customer as a friend he may not come back and coming back is important to me but many want greater affection and attention which I can't give. So I try as much as possible to prevent being too close to my friends.

In this circumstance, the sex workers find ways of satisfying their "friends" while at the same time maintaining certain body exclusive zones, but for those they have fallen in love such restrictions are frequently compromised. As 32-year-old Chidinma recounts:

> It is really difficult to relate with every customer the same way. They all want attention so in most cases I try as much as possible to give them enough sexual satisfaction but I don't allow them to cross the boundary.

When asked what she meant by "crossing the boundary," she responded "No kissing and caressing but good sex." Overall, the findings revealed that the relationships between sex workers and their intimate partners center on friendship, trust, emotional intimacy, love, care, and money.

On whether relationships between sex workers and their clients sometimes end up in marriage, it was discovered that this seldom happens although there have been instances where marriage has occurred. Some sex workers have indicated that some of their customers have actually asked them to quit the job and marry them. This was reflected in a response made by Osinachi, a 25-year-old sex worker who said:

> I have two customers that have been pestering me to leave my work and marry them. They don't know each other and I can't marry two people at the same time. The best thing is to say no and concentrate on the money I make to take care of my people.

Sex workers may not be willing to quit the job because they are afraid of such demands to leave their source of livelihood while they are not sure what the outcome would be and again such requests may come from more than one client at a time.

Discussion

The global sex industry has grown over time to include people of diverse ethnic, religious, and economic groups. In earlier times, sexuality was moderated by the cultural and traditional religious dictum that dictated sexuality and sexual behavior. Sexual desire is a need that elicits motivated behavior aimed at its satisfaction and culture plays an important role in shaping this drive (McMahon & McMahon 1982, p. 135). However, when the culture restricts sexualities and limits sexual freedom it is likely to trigger a complex repression of sexual drives that eventually finds expression via the bodies of women who are "cultural rebels."

There is also the practice of patriarchal domination and gender inequality in sexuality in favor of men but this has not led men to be in total control of women's sexuality or the liberty to be in control of their sexual urges. This is because sexuality is framed around reproduction and not pleasure thus leaving men relatively powerless over women's sexuality and encouraging sex workers' patronage. Marriage in Igbo culture and religion defines and confers status, dignity, and respect to a man and woman is viewed as sacred and so divorce is seldom contemplated. Thus, even when there is instability in the marriage couples still stay as husband and wife so as not to lose public respect and be ridiculed (Asa & Nkan 2017). Partners who are experiencing relationship instability, particularly the women, often use sexual denial as a weapon against their partner and inadvertently create room for men to purchase sex while at the same time having an intact marriage. In essence, the culture gives men more freedom to express their masculinity over women's sexuality and yet restricts them from such expression. This contradiction has become a motivation for the men to seek assertion of their masculinity through payment for sex. These realities eventually encouraged and enhanced the emergence and sophistication of sex work within Enugu.

The advent of modernity has provided the Igbo culture with large amounts of sexual information and new sexual patterns that ultimately and radically altered the traditional and cultural views of sexuality and saliently promoted subversive sexuality. Most men who may wish to experience these new sexual patterns that are readily available through pornography prefer doing so with prostitutes because, modernity notwithstanding, most Igbo women still hold the traditional and conservative expectations of women's sexuality and so try hard not to be seen as sexual "deviants." Furthermore, traditionally, sexuality was embedded in secrecy, myths, and taboos and sex before marriage was ferociously condemned, but modernity has decimated these long-standing traditions and led to the growth and view of sex as a commodity with influences emanating from increased use of explicit sexual images in advertising and the adult entertainment industry (Ward & Aral 2006). With the Internet both young adolescents and adults can easily learn about, discuss, explore, and experiment with their sexuality without restraint. This has contributed in no small measure to the boom in the sex industry and sex workers' patronage. Dominant Igbo culture strongly values individualism and competition, which exposes them to a stressful way of living and encourages the exploitation of any available means of relaxation including seeking the services of sex workers. It is therefore important that the Igbos restructure their ways of life to give room for more dignified way of relaxation and more time with family and friends.

Many brothel-based sex workers value socialization with clients (Ghose, Swendeman, & George 2011) and the social bonding is also an integral part of sex work even though the intimacy that sex workers provided is often bogus. Sex workers know it is important that clients should have a feeling of being accepted and cared for even if it is "counterfeit." Sex workers thus cultivate several forms of relationships in other to keep going and this is largely dependent on type (i.e. whether a regular, first timer, or non regular) and the disposition of clients. They also consider whether the client is married or single and while preferring the development of intimate relationships with single men, they still have deep respect and trust for the married clients but are careful not to fall in love. Married clients may not also wish to be very intimate with sex workers as that may jeopardize their marriage and expose them to cultural shame. The sex workers, however, have single but regular clients that they genuinely consider as romantic partners; they fall in love, become emotionally attached to such clients and offer them extra free services. This category of clients usually provides security and protects them from being molested by touts and the police much like those in a regular relationship. On the whole, sex workers try to develop caring, friendly, and honest attitudes towards their clients such that clients feel respected, secured, and valued. This seems to be important in the sex industry as it reduces social inhibition and encourages the rationalization of sex workers' patronage as "normal" and "fun" and also encourages clients to become regulars.

In summary, findings revealed that men's motivations for purchasing sex is related to the cultural Igbo values that traditionally restrict sex and sexuality to reproductive sex and procreation. The modern view of sexuality has created a conflict between modernity and the cultural sex role expectations and the conflict may continue to sustain the sex industry especially because the lives of the Igbos are intricately related to their culture and traditions. Legislative approaches to the eradication of sex work seem to be counterproductive because there will always be people willing to buy and sell sex and criminalization of sex work contributes to the negligence of the sex industry by the authorities. Governments should reflect this reality and articulate a more proactive approach that will protect the sex workers, their clients, and the general public. Brothel owners especially those in "junction" towns should be compelled to be more hygienically conscious by creating spaces and keeping the brothel environment clean and habitable. Furthermore, medical personnel should frequently visit brothels to educate the sex workers on the health implications of sex work, how to avoid contracting HIV and other STDs, and where to seek medical help in case of infection.

The responses of those interviewed suggest that both men and women are trapped by social and cultural norms of sexuality. While sexual double standards that allow men more sexual freedom than women exist, men are still trapped in that they cannot demonstrate their masculinity through domination of women's sexuality. The women on their part are stigmatized and viewed as "sluts" when they try to express their sexuality. The sexual double standard and the powerlessness of men over women's sexuality have fostered the conditions in which sex workers live and work. Prostitutes offer men the opportunity to express their dominance over women's bodies yet they are equally stigmatized and viewed as "inferior."

In the current formation of the sex work industry, there are costs and benefits for sex workers and their male clients with the costs being higher for the sex workers. While sex work may greatly empower women financially, sex workers are socially stigmatized, which is the primary source of violence against sex workers and often there is little protection offered by authorities. They face emotional exhaustion and isolation in the absence of intimate relationships and are at a higher risk of contracting HIV and other STDs because they offer sexual services to multiple clients, many of which may be carried out without protective measures. For some married sex workers with children, sex work can have a strong negative impact on family members. Sex workers also provide sexual services in a society where sex work is criminalized. The implication is that there will be no legislation that will give them enabling working conditions and protect them from victimization and crimes such as bullying, rape, robbery, and ritual killings. For the male clients, sex workers offer an opportunity for sexual satisfaction and re-affirmation of patriarchal rights of men over women's sexuality. For example, it has been shown that in exchange for their money, clients of sex workers demand "control of sex" rather than just sex (Sanchez-Taylor 2001). Thus, with sex workers, clients seek control of women's bodies but are also vulnerable to HIV infection. Potential avenues for transforming these gender norms are sex education and legislative protection of sex workers.

References

Abel, G.M. & L.J. Fitzgerald. 2012. "The street's got its advantages": movement between sectors of the sex industry in a decriminalized environment. *Health, Risk & Society*, vol. 14, no. 1, pp. 7–23. http://dx.doi.org/10.1080/13698575.2011.640664.

Asa, U.A. & V.V. Nkan. 2017. 290 factors associated with marital instability among rural farming households in Akwa Ibom State, Nigeria. *European Scientific Journal*, vol. 13, no. 15. https://doi.org/10.19044/esj.2017.v13n15p290.

Berman, Marshall. 2010. *All that is solid melts into air: the experience of modernity.* London: Verso.

Boies, S.C., G. Knudson, & J. Young. 2004. The internet, sex, and youths: implications for sexual development. *Sex Addict Compulsivity*, vol. 11, no. 4, pp. 343–363. https://doi.org/10.1080/10720160490902630.

Ghose, T., D.T. Swendeman, & S.M. George. 2011. The role of brothels in reducing HIV risk in Sonagachi, India. *Qualitative Health Research*, vol. 21, no. 5, pp. 587–600. http://dx.doi.org/10.1177/1049732310395328.

Goldenberg, S.M., S.A. Strathdee, M. Gallardo, T. Rhodes, K.D. Wagner, & T.L. Patterson. 2011. "Over here, it's just drugs, women, and all the madness": the HIV risk environment of clients of female sex workers in Tijuana, Mexico. *Social Science and Medicine*, vol. 72, pp. 1185–1192. http://dx.doi.org/10.1016/j.socscimed.2011.02.014.

Hochschild, A. Russell. 1983. *The managed heart: commercialization of human feeling.* Berkeley, CA: University of California Press. https://doi.org/10.1093/sf/64.1.223.

Ibrahim, B. & J.I. Mukhtar. 2016. Changing pattern of prostitution: an assessment of transnational commercial sex work by Nigerian women. *European Scientific Journal*, vol. 12, no. 2. http://dx.doi.org/10.19044/esj.2016.v12n2p81.

International Labor Office Publications. 2009. *Global employment trends.* Geneva: ILO. Available at: www.ilo.org/wcmsp5/groups/public/@dgreports/@dcomm/documents/publication/wcms_101461.pdf (accessed December 18, 2017).

Izugbara, C. Otutubikey. 2004. Notions of sex, sexuality, and relationships among adolescent boys in rural southeastern Nigeria. *Sex Education*, vol. 4, no. 1, pp. 63–70. https://doi.org/10.1080/1468181042000176542.

Kempadoo, K. & L.L. Dunn 2001. *Factors that shape initiation of early sexual activity among adolescent boys & girls: a study in three communities in Jamaica.* A report to UNICEF and UNFPA. Kingston, Jamaica: University of the West Indies, Centre for Gender Development Studies.

Keobounphanh, I. & M. Toole. 2008. *Young women's sexual behavior study: Vientiene Capital Lao PDR.* Department of Health Vientiene Capital in Collaboration with the Burnett Institute & UNFPA. Available at: http://lao.unfpa.org/sites/default/files/resource-pdf/FinalReportYoungWomensSexualBehaviourStudy.pdf (accessed December 18, 2017).

Ladipo, O., A. Ankomah, Z. Akinyeni, & J. Anyanti. 2002. *A comparative analysis of brothel-based commercial sex work in cities and "junction towns" in Nigeria.* Society for Family Health, Abuja, Nigeria. Available at: www.researchgate.net/publication/267252014 (accessed August 15, 2017).

Langa, Julio. 2014. Notions of Sex, Masculinity and Manhood in African Cultures. Open Society Initiatives for Southern Africa (OSISA). Available at: file:///F:/Notions%20of%20Sex,%20Masculinity%20and%20Manhood%20in%20African%20Cultures%20_%20Open%20Society%20Initiative%20of%20Southern%20Africa%20(OSISA).htm (accessed August 15, 2017).

McMahon, F.B. & J.W. McMahon. 1982. *Psychology: the hybrid science.* Homewood, IL: Dorsey Press.

Ngugi, E., C. Benoit, H. Hallgrimsdottir, M. Jansson, & E.A. Roth. 2012. Partners and clients of female sex workers in an informal urban settlement in Nairobi, Kenya. *Culture, Health and Sexuality*, vol. 14, no 1, pp. 17–30. http://dx.doi.org/10.1080/13691058.2011.608436.

Okazaki, Shinji. 2002. Influences of culture on Asian Americans' sexuality. *Journal of Sex Research*, vol. 39, no. 1, pp. 34–41. Available at: www.jstor.org/stable/3813421 (accessed December 18, 2017).

Robertson, A.M., J.L. Syvertsen, H. Amaro, G. Martinez, M.G. Rangel, T.L. Patterson, & S.A. Strathdee. 2014. Can't buy my love: a typology of female sex workers' commercial relationships in the Mexico–U.S. border region. *Journal of Sex Research*, vol. 51, no. 6, pp. 711–720. http://dx.doi.org/10.1080/00224499.2012.757283.

Sanders, Teela. 2005. "It's just acting": sex workers' strategies for capitalizing on sexuality. *Gender, Work and Organization*, vol. 12, no. 4, pp. 319–342. http://dx.doi.org/10.1111/j.1468-0432.2005.00276.x.

Sanchez Taylor, J. 2001. Dollars are girl's best friend? Female tourists' sexual behaviour in the Caribbean. *Sociology: Identity Politics in the Workplace*, vol. 35, no. 3, pp. 749–760.

Turner, N. Daniel. 2014. Gender inequality in sexuality. Available at: https://prezi.com/k9xydi4bm-cn/gender-inequality-in-sexuality (accessed December 20, 2017).

Vandepitte, J., R. Lyerla, G. Dallabetta, F. Crabbe, M. Alary, & A. Buye. 2006. Estimates of the number of female sex workers in different regions of the world. *Sexually Transmitted Infection*, vol. 82, no. 3, pp. iii18–iii25. http://dx.doi.org/10.1136/sti.2006.020081.

Ward, H. & S.O. Aral 2006. Globalisation, the sex industry, and health. *Sexually Transmitted Infections*, vol. 82, no. 5, http://dx.doi.org/10.1136/sti.2006.023044.

Ward, H., C. Mercer, K. Wellings, K. Fenton, B. Erens, A. Copas, & A. Johnson. 2005. Who pays for sex? An analysis of the increasing prevalence of female commercial sex contacts among men in Britain. *Sexually Transmitted Infections*, vol. 81, no. 6, pp. 467–471. http://dx.doi.org/10.1136/sti.2005.014985.

Wong, W.C.W., E. Holroyd, & A. Bingham. 2010. Stigma and sex work from the perspective of female sex workers in Hong Kong. *Sociology of Health & Illness*, vol. 33, no. 1, pp. 50–65. http://dx.doi.org/10.1111/j.1467-9566.2010.01276.x.

36

Entrepreneurship, network building, and clientelism in China's hostess bars[1]

Tiantian Zheng

Introduction

Academic studies, dominant cultural beliefs, and activists variously attribute clients' patronage of sex industry venues to a host of factors, including social dysfunction, toxic masculinity, male bonding, and biology, among others. Despite such a wide range of perspectives on this subject, few have systematically examined sex industry venues' important role in fostering the political economy of clientelism that characterizes many market societies throughout the world. The exchange relationships inherent to clientelism feature the circulation of goods, services, or financial resources in return for political favors, which can include government contracts, business licenses, and other potentially lucrative benefits that may be otherwise difficult to obtain. Sex industry venues are one of the sites in which such relationships are formed, maintained, and consolidated among and between men. Yet women's sexual labor is an essential dynamic within these social relationships and critical engagement with it reveals a great deal about the cultural and economic assumptions that undergird clientelism.

China provides an excellent case study of the reciprocal dynamics at work in the complex relationships of clientelist exchange forged within and around sex industry venues. Findings presented here derive from the author's two years of intensive participant observation in hostess bars in Dalian, a northeastern city where, as elsewhere in China, state policy criminalizes and regards prostitution as an immoral, oppressive practice that degrades women and deleteriously impacts society as a whole. Hostess bars operate on the margins of the law by offering food, alcohol, and karaoke singing to groups of men who also purchase sexual services provided either within the establishment itself or off-site. The rural migrant women they employ often live together in dormitory-style accommodation and lack other work opportunities that pay comparable amounts of money and the potential for upward social mobility through long-term relationships, including marriage, offered by the hostess bar. Hostess bars vary significantly in price, services offered, and target clientele, but this chapter focuses on high-end venues patronized by wealthy men who strategically utilize the relationships developed there to enact entrepreneurial masculinities that foster and sustain lucrative forms of state–clientelism with powerful officials.

Why do men patronize hostess bars?

A global economic leader with a burgeoning consumer market, China is a relatively recent adopter of economic liberalization initiatives that have taken place within the course of a single lifetime. The transition from Maoist centralized planning to free market capitalism, guided by state endorsement of particular economic initiatives, began under the leadership of Deng Xiaoping in 1978 through the end of his tenure in 1989 and continues today. This significant socioeconomic shift sharply departed from Maoist egalitarian ideals in ways touted as beneficial to China's overall well-being, a sentiment best expressed in the state slogan "let one segment of the population get rich first and guide others along the way." Associated post-Mao socioeconomic ideology associates capitalist consumption with the concept of modernity within a broader ethos that connects the ideals of progress with the goal of a bountiful material life. "Make money and consume" is accordingly an aspirational ideal among both hostess bar patrons and the migrant women who serve them in order remit their earnings to their rural homes.

High-end hostess bars and other consumer entertainment venues proliferated in the wake of economic liberalization, which enabled middle-aged businessmen and government officials to actively engage with state-promulgated capitalist discourse and practices. Suffused with the seductive allure of both modernity and beautiful young women, hostess bars enable these men to engage in social interactions (*yingchou*) that cement the beneficial business connections (*guanxi*) with partners or government patrons whose favors are essential aspects of clientelism. As is the case among sex industry clients worldwide, hostess bar patrons generally justify their visits to sex industry establishments by citing unfulfilling intimate partnerships, biology, and social norms. Yet high-end hostess bar patrons in China additionally regard their interactions with hostesses and colleagues as liberating them from what they often regard as the significant social expectations and constraints imposed on them by Confucianist and socialist values that deprioritize individual desires in favor of community well-being.

Irrespective of the rationale offered, hostess bar patrons almost always situate their decision-making within a broader rhetoric that emphasize the restrictions of their families, dominant cultural values, and government practices that circumscribe their freedom. These clients couch their accounts of such restrictions in direct opposition to what they regard as the individualistic and entrepreneurial practices enabled and facilitated by their patronage of high-end hostess bars. Hence analytical engagement with the ways in which clients link their perceptions of restrictive dominant state/cultural forces to the relative freedom associated with hostess bars offers profound insight into the intersections between the social construction of sexuality, sex industry practices, and the state in contemporary urban China.

Clients who came of age in the 1970s and early 1980s, prior to the widespread implementation of market reforms, characterize their hostess bar patronage as compensation for the restrictions imposed on sexual expression during their youth. Relatives, friends, or other community acquaintances generally had arranged the marriages of these clients, who associate such unions with routinized obligations rather than impulsive passion, particularly when describing marriages of many years' duration. Family members' financial dependence on and cultural expectations of the men makes them disinclined to divorce and instead to maintain marriages in an unhappy yet socially acceptable state that often resembles a business partnership rather than the union of equals idealized in late consumer capitalism. For instance, hostess bar patron Wang observes,

Like all other men, I expect my wife to assume her part of internal family labor taking care of the old and young in the family so that I can work in the outside world. Otherwise, how can I compete well outside? She has to listen to me and my old parents and do whatever we order her, obediently and submissively.

Lin, who is also a hostess bar client, echoes this underlying sentiment in noting that familiarity dimmed the passion of his marriage to his wife:

Earlier, I would hug my wife so hard that I would not let her go; now I just pay her attention for a moment and leave. Touching her hands is no different from touching my own. This is how a 13-year marriage feels.

Other clients naturalize their sex industry venue patronage as an aspect of an ostensibly biological drive to seek out sexual pleasure, with many connecting this to the innately human urge to eat or stay warm. Many clients describe men's sexual desire (*wenbao er si yinyu*) as "men's nature," variously attributing their paid sexual encounters to a need to release excess energy, demonstrate dominance, or to achieve balance. For instance, hostess bar client Jo says,

sometimes I have to go to hostesses to release my pent-up energy. Man innately has the desire and impulse to possess women and achieve sexual power. Were Marilyn Monroe to come in right now, we would all stare at her and want to have her.

Client Li notes, "I visit hostesses to look for stimulation and an emotional release; stimulation from hostesses and peace with my wife forms my life cycle."

Economically privileged hostess bar clients typically visit these establishments in groups, making such patronage an important aspect of interactions with their peer group. Liang and Peng, both relatively young men, express their interpretations of the importance of involvement with hostesses with respect to meeting peer group expectations:

Liang: You just have to patronize hostesses. You've got to try it a few times. It's part of growing up and self-actualization. Otherwise, when other men are talking about it, you would look like a fool who never entered society in an experienced fashion. Nobody would respect you if you were like that. So you have to have this experience to gain others' recognition and respect. Meanwhile, you have to know when to stop and not get addicted to it.

Peng: Unlike old men in their forties and fifties who come for sex, we love to show off our beautiful hostesses before our young friends. I always get carried away when my beautiful hostess compliments my singing and my looks. [Hostesses] said I was like a Hong Kong star singer. It really gives me a lot of face [publically affirmed status] before the other guys. We want admiration and respect from beautiful hostesses. It definitely satisfies our psychological needs before our peers. We don't go for sex at all.

Within the context of high-end hostess bars where men cement lucrative contracts and other dealings with one another, clients express a desire to express their sexual power over women as a means to demonstrate their membership within a peer group. Yet such sexual expression also functions as market participation and as a means to flout state dominance, as well as family, norms regarding monogamy and prioritization of the collective above the individual. As Peng indicates, sex itself is but a minor aspect of what hostess bar patrons hope to purchase in the transactional sexual exchange.

Independent masculinities and hostess bar patronage

Hostess bars provide legal entertainment services in the form of drinking, eating, singing, and the company of women although the sale and purchase of sex remains criminalized. Participation in these illegal acts leads some clients to regard themselves as courageous, liberated, and willful scofflaws; as one client noted, hostess bar patronage "singles us out as more powerful, daring, and superior." Clients accordingly regard purchasing sex as an important aspect of capitalist consumer identities dissociated from the community obligations of socialism, dominant socio-cultural norms in China as a whole, and Confucian filial and family sensibilities (*renqing*).

Clients accordingly position their hostess bar patronage as an expression of their individual agency detached from their responsibilities to other members of society. They do so both by pointing to examples from the consumer capitalist societies of North America and Western Europe and by naturalizing such individualism as innate. Clients describe feeling "restrained" and "shackled" by an "inculcated Confucian ideal" that debilitated their spirits in a way that hostess bar patronage helps to recover. One client observes, "In China, if a man feels indebted to his wife, he will devote his whole life to her to pay off that debt, whereas the Americans by no means feel the same." Clients' juxtapositions of ostensible cultural norms often place China at a distinct disadvantage in terms of men's abilities to self-actualize in free and independent ways so valued by consumer capitalism.

Hostess bar client Huang likewise envisions himself as uniquely "free" and "liberated" by his visits to such establishments, which he regards as an outlet for honest self-expression in what he dismissively characterizes as society only superficially committed to community orientation: "Don't you think it's strange that China has so many nightclubs? This is a system with vast social stratifications. Socialism should not have hostesses. It's not allowed. China still wants to maintain a perfunctory socialism." Echoing Huang's sentiment, Yang expresses indignation about what he regards as hypocritical social standards:

> Our country needs the revenue from prostitution, but it still wants a layer of socialism to cover it up. We're fed up with it. It's by no means the natural way. Basic human nature is still forbidden, as in the Mao era. I want my basic human nature back. We don't believe in anything now. We just want to play and enjoy our life as it goes. What do we believe? Everything we were taught in school is such a huge joke and a lie. We feel cheated by the whole country. We need to enjoy what we have right now because there's simply nothing else worthwhile to do. We've been completely cheated.

Yang regards socialism as essentially counterintuitive to what he characterizes as an essentially selfish human instinct to seek out pleasure and serve one's own self-interests. Like many of his peers who patronize hostess bars, Yang naturalizes consumer capitalism as more reflective of the human spirit's desire for pleasure, wealth, and other benefits to the individual. China's replacement of the planned economic system, in which all citizens were expected to contribute based on revolutionary fervor and patriotism, with the capitalist market system and its associated opulence enjoyed by a minority of citizens, is often cited as irrefutable "proof" of this basic human instinct for self-interest.

Clients naturalize capitalism's supposed superiority to socialism in the same ways that they justify their patronage of hostess bars as part of their innate desire for sexual expression that celebrates their social status and economic success. These beliefs are in direct opposition to dominant socialist morality, which clients regard as unrealistic in viewing prostitution as a capitalist pathology. Clients are not alone in this view, as the continued existence of prostitution following the implementation of socialism in China seemed to indicate flaws within Marxist theory, failed leadership, or both. Since these conclusions are incompatible with then-prevalent political rhetoric, China took an abolitionist approach to prostitution that relaxed somewhat following Deng Xiaoping's repositioning of China along the Marxist development path. The resulting stance regarded China as still in socialism's rudimentary stage (*chuji jieduan*), during which social ills such as prostitution remain as temporary byproducts of social transition (*shehui zhuanxing*) guaranteed to disappear following the achievement of mature socialism.

Like Huang, Yang, and many of their peers who patronize hostess bars, Xu describes contemporary urban China as trapped in a "moral vacuum" (*xinyang zhenkong*) of "considerable confusion, dislocation, and disillusion." Another client notes:

> There is no future for this country! Nobody has any belief in life. Everything they consider is money and self-interest. No belief in life! What does the Chinese Communist Party promise the nation? What does socialism do for the people? No more than laid-off workers, too much corruption, unemployment, and increasing stratification between people. So we just want to numb ourselves by being addicted to something and do not want to wake up and face reality. The country has no future!

For many clients, Chinese socialism and Confucianism are two parts of the same whole: an oppressive regulatory regime that stifles and contradicts "human nature." Clients typically derive such notions of human nature from their perceptions of dominant sexual and gender norms within Western Europe and North America—particularly the United States—that they regard as a land of free and uninhibited sexual expression. Clients receive these messages through mass media, which serve as raw cultural materials that clients and others refine into complex concepts only tangentially related to the raw materials themselves. In so doing, hostess bar patrons romanticize sexual expression arising from natural instinct and free of the constraints they regard as inhibiting self-expression in other aspects of their personal and professional lives.

Clientelism and hostess bar patronage

The Chinese system of clientelism requires entrepreneurs to foster favorable social connections (*guanxi*) that will facilitate access to resources controlled by an authoritarian political system. This system is fraught with risks that far exceed changing market conditions and competition from rivals by comprising the unenforceability of contracts, a mercurial legal-regulatory system, and state agents' arbitrary exercise of power. Such considerable risks necessitate careful selection of business partners through observations regarding their trustworthiness, business acumen, and moral character. Hostess bars provide an ideal setting for men to make such assessments about one another because they provide an atmosphere that encourages excessive amounts of alcohol, food, and sexual consumption. With inhibitions reduced and the formality typically associated with business transactions suspended by the introduction of sex and alcohol, hostess bars offer potential business partners the opportunity to break down social barriers that remain firmly in place in office or other traditional settings.

Social conviviality is essential to the cultivation of *guanxi*'s symbolic capital, which, in turn, is necessary for businessmen's economic survival. Economic reliance on a bureaucracy of distributors to dispense resources and enforce the law necessitates the cultivation of *guanxi*, in addition to economic capital, to ensure business success. Lavish gifts, banquets, and favours to political officials and other powerful actors are normative aspects of doing business in China because they create indebtedness and obligation. Through the practice of *guanxi*, businessmen increase their likelihood of receiving operating licenses and other commercial requirements from a network of influential figures, including tax collectors, traffic and civil police officers, and the wholesale or retail enterprises that supply them with goods or buy goods that they produce. *Guanxi* effectively personalizes the otherwise impersonal market relations through the cultivation of instrumental social relationships that subvert state regulations.

Clientelism imposes many and varied risks for all concerned because of its reliance on extralegal transactions, agreements, and social alliances rather than contracts that specify the terms of a given business exchange. Parties to client–patron relationships inevitably face incentives to betray or terminate the association, which to outsiders might indicate that such relationships are short-lived and unstable. Yet the opposite is true, as client–patron relationships often enjoy considerable longevity because of the time that each party to the relationship takes to appraise the other's character and intention, the social bonding that ensues, and the resulting trust that cements the bond by dis-incentivizing the temptation to betray the other.

Cultivating *guanxi* in a hostess bar setting involves conveyance of multiple unspoken social cues in which a host who hopes to establish a clientelist relationship conveys his deference and lower social status relative to his prospective business partner. In the hostess bar this conveyance takes on routinized forms that rely heavily upon women's performance of sexual labor in particular ways. When the hostesses file into the karaoke room for selection, the host urges the highest status prospective business partner to select the most beautiful hostess. The prospective partner often declines the offer as a sign of courtesy, which requires the host to employ the services of the hostess he deems the most beautiful and talented singer. The host always partners with the hostess who dominant cultural norms regard as the least beautiful. The host's choice of bar is likewise an indicator of the esteem in which he holds the prospective business partner.

The host's performance of deference through significant financial outlays to ensure the most pleasurable experience for the prospective business partner continues throughout the night. He will instruct his prospective business partner's hostess to serve him with great enthusiasm, often by privately confiding to her the importance of this business relationship and promising her a higher fee if the evening is a success. He will also urge his own hostess to propose a toast to his prospective business partner, often by saying something to her along the lines of, "This is my big brother. He is a very powerful, reliable, and responsible man. I respect him very much. Go and propose a toast to big brother for me!"

During this performance, the host must maintain self-control in order to prove himself to his prospective business partner as a rational, reliable, and trustworthy person with business competence. The host must spend exorbitant amounts of money on hostesses in order to prove his wealth and raise his status in the eyes of his prospective business partners. Yet he must remain mindful of the ways in which he does so in order to avoid his actions being perceived by his prospective partners as driven by excessive desire, as such impulses could later prove dangerous in an established business partnership. While the host must demonstrate the ability to drink alcohol, sing karaoke, and join in convivial sociality, how he interacts with the hostesses carries the most weight. Dominant cultural norms, as well as the clients who are immersed within them, regard hostesses as "beautiful poisonous snakes" who must be controlled to demonstrate power, reliability, and self-control (*xuanya lema*, literally "to rein in at the precipice").

Patronizing hostesses to cultivate *guanxi* is necessary but, like other aspects of establishing this essential business relationship, filled with dangers that depend upon each client's profession and other aspects of social identity. For representatives of the Chinese Communist Party or other state officials, public discovery of their hostess bar patronage may result in revocation of their party membership and the end of a political career. Yet visiting hostess bars is so normative among government workers that certain government units do no longer print business cards that police might later discover in the purses of hostesses arrested for prostitution. Hostesses may also use blackmail or threats to achieve a desired end, including the end to bad behavior through asserting something along the lines of, "I'll call so-and-so official and have you thrown in jail!" Fear of offending a well-connected hostess does not entirely shield against abusive behavior by clients, yet most hostess bar patrons cannot afford to ignore the possibility that a hostess could harm their careers; using pseudonyms or other fake identities is accordingly a common practice among both hostesses and hostess bar patrons.

Clients also fear hostesses as a result of mass media representations that caution urban men against associating with these rural temptresses who can easily destroy their professional futures. Popular culture routinely refers to hostesses as "red spiders" who are sexually attractive because they outwardly appear charming and seductive in their sexy, tight dresses, but are evil characters who routinely blackmail and murder their clients. "Beauties bring disasters" (*hongyan huoshui*), an imperial Chinese adage, warns men against patronizing hostess bars by evoking tales of entire Chinese dynasties ruined by indulgence in sensuality. Media also routinely report real accounts of political careers and lives destroyed by hostesses' "vicious brutality" and "evil, poisonous nature."

The perceived power that beautiful hostesses wield over men accordingly presents prospective business partners with a perfect opportunity to display their ability to remain calm and rational in the face of temptation. Clients routinely demonstrate their self-control by deliberately barking orders at hostesses and asserting to one another that hostesses are little more than playthings and tools of relaxation. Note how hostess bar patrons Chang and Shi assert their own sense of superior self-control relative to the hostesses they patronize:

> Chang: Men release pressure and cleanse their soul by patronizing hostesses. Women are the toys because men earn money and women spend the money. Women cannot control their desires, but men can. Women are emotional and irrational animals, whereas men are rational human beings.

> Shi: My relationship with my hostess–mistress is a master–slave one. She is very obedient. She comes when summoned and leaves when dismissed. She called me last night and said she wanted to see me. I told her I was too busy to see her. [I have countless hostesses I patronize but] I always forget their names. When they call me, I do not know which one it is. At the critical moment, I retreat and cut off our relationship.

Yet these demonstrations of authority relative to hostesses belie the fact that hostesses receive a great deal of money, access to resources, and other benefits as a result of their relationships with hostess bar clients. Nonetheless, maintaining the illusion of masculine control over hostesses is a critical aspect of cultivating clientelism and maintaining peer group respect. Men who fall in love with hostesses, have too many hostesses as sexual partners, or who behave in ways perceived as irresponsible with hostesses, quickly lose their business partners' (and others') respect.

Concluding thoughts

Men in urban China justify their patronage of hostess bars in ways that closely resemble the rationales offered by sex workers' clients globally. Yet clients of high-end hostess bars express a complex and multi-layered approach to hostess bar patronage that revolves around the establishment and maintenance of *guanxi*, the social bonds essential to business success in the environment of clientelism that characterizes urban China. By demonstrating their ostensible dominance over bar hostesses, whose low status as seductive rural migrant women positions them both as temptresses and as potentially destructive forces, hostess bar patrons are able to demonstrate their self-control, business acumen, and other character traits regarded as essential to a trustworthy business partner.

Far from being a helpless pawn in these transactions, hostesses fill an essential role in facilitating the establishment of *guanxi* through their sexual labor in ways designed to secure their and their family's economic independence. This circulation of economic and social capital between the state, male business partners, hostesses, and the rural families to whom hostesses send financial support, is a formidable economic engine with contemporary urban China. Critical engagement with the dynamics at work within hostess bar settings allows for tremendous insight not just into urban China's sex industry, but into the dealings that constitute business as usual for a wide range of actors.

Note

1 This chapter is partially derived from an article published in the *Journal of Contemporary China* on January 22, 2007, available online: https://doi.org/10.1080/10670560500331815.

Part VI
Third parties

37

Third parties

An introduction

Susan Dewey, Isabel Crowhurst, and Chimaraoke Izugbara

Introduction

Third parties are a polarizing topic of study because of the significant social stigma attached to the organization and management of commercial sexual exchanges and the widespread perception that third parties exploit and otherwise abuse sex workers. Key themes in existing literature include defining third parties, exploitation and abuse, labor practices, and stigmatization and marginalization through racist and/or xenophobic dominant cultural beliefs. Chapters in this section engage with these ongoing challenges while offering clear directions for future research.

Key themes in existing literature

Third parties, who are variously referred to in the literature as managers, facilitators, traffickers, and pimps, receive profits from the sexual labor of others in ways that vary according to sex industry venue, legal context, and socio-cultural norms in a given setting. Mass media, cultural context, and the ideological perspectives that frame research all influence definitions of the individuals and behaviors accorded third-party status (Davis, 2013). Like sex workers and their clients, third parties come from diverse backgrounds with a wide variety of previous experiences that inform their engagement with and approaches to sex workers. Third parties' treatment by the justice system also varies greatly. Some studies show that female third parties who have previously worked in the sex industry appear to receive significantly lower criminal penalties than their male peers (Roe-Sepowitz et al., 2015). Third parties often have previous experience with the sex industry, whether as sex workers or as current or former intimate partners of sex workers, and movements from sex worker to third-party manager can be fluid, particularly in settings where limited alternatives exist for earning a living due to undocumented status or limited proficiency in the local language (Goldenberg et al., 2017). Third parties accordingly have a wealth of lived experiences that inform their decision-making as they manage their workers, especially in highly competitive workplace settings where income is dependent on tips (Mount, 2018).

Third parties are often depicted as exploiters and abusers who profit from others' sexual labor and human suffering through sophisticated forms of psychological manipulation that trap sex workers into a cycle of indebtedness and violence (Reid, 2016). In this view, male third parties subjugate women through a process of mind control akin to those used by perpetrators in domestic violence relationships (Raphael, Reichert, & Powers, 2010; Schwartz, Williams, & Farley, 2007). Third parties are also widely regarding as demanding sex workers' earnings in exchange for limited or no protective or other services, thus exploiting women in uniquely pernicious ways (Brady, Biradavolu, & Blankenship, 2015).

Labor practices that inform and characterize relationships between third parties and sex workers vary tremendously by venue size, type, and management style even within the geographical confines of a single city (Büschi, 2014). Cooperation and force take particularly complex forms in criminalized third-party relationships, where facilitators and sex workers must evade police while attempting to generate profits (Morselli & Savoie-Gargiso, 2014). In many instances, third parties come into such a role through social networks characterized by socio-economic constraints and severely limited opportunities for upward mobility. These factors make partnering with a sex worker for economic reasons a highly desirable option that generally operates along a set of established, albeit informal, rules of conduct (Marcus et al., 2012; Zhang, 2011).

Like the sex workers whose labor they manage, third parties often struggle significantly with various forms of social marginalization. This can include racism and related police profiling (Hannem & Bruckert, 2017), and moral panics regarding migrant men who seek to sexually exploit local women for their own gain (Van San & Bovenkerk, 2013). Women who have previously worked in the sex industry, or who are from communities that familiarized them with labor practices within it, are also likely to work as third parties (Shen, 2016). Considerable economic constraints and poverty can result in diversification among third parties, with multiple recruiters, facilitators, or other actors profiting from sex workers' labor (Aral et al., 2003).

Such complex socio-economic forces prompt third parties to innovatively respond to police profiling and other threats to their business as they formulate new marketing strategies (Finn & Stalans, 2016). This form of individualistic economic success, despite significant socio-economic hindrances and institutional exclusion, have made third parties—particularly in the form of "the pimp"—a valorized cultural figure in mass media (Benson, 2012; Quinn, 2000; Staiger, 2005)

Chapter overview

Olivar (Chapter 38) examines the role of third parties in the daily operations of trans-border sex markets to argue that the sex trade's relational dynamics comprise a fractal system of alliances. Dziuban and Stevenson (Chapter 39) argue that applying a labor lens to the analysis of working conditions and third-party relationships in the sex industry emphasizes how criminalizing sex workers, their workplaces, third parties, and clients intensifies sex workers' vulnerability to exploitation. Fey (Chapter 40) analyzes relations between sex workers and third parties in the form of police, activists, and community residents to emphasize how these parties' perspectives directly influence the everyday life and working conditions of those in the sex industry.

Martin (Chapter 41) identifies a spectrum of exploitation at work within the nuanced interplay of decision-making, constraint, force, violence, struggle, and resilience within commercial sex markets, and analyzes young women's experiences while avoiding anti-trafficking narratives that reify racial and gender stereotypes that criminalize marginalized people. Churakova (Chapter 42) reflects on the ethical issues she confronted while working as a counselling psychologist at the International Organization for Migration (IOM) Rehabilitation Center for survivors of human trafficking, located in Moscow, Russia.

Future directions

As is the case in most areas of sex industry research, existing work focuses on heteronormative commercial sex in which women are sellers and men are buyers. Very little is known about how third parties operate among or with men or transgender people who sell sex, or if individuals in these communities prefer to work independently. Since heteronormative third-party relationships generally reflect other forms of feminized labor in which men control and disproportionately benefit from women's work, it would be particularly interesting to explore whether gender roles play a significant part in decision-making about third-party relationships among transgender people and men who sell sex to men. Need exists for studies on the different uses to which sex workers put third parties, how some sex workers are able to leave third-party control and surveillance, and how third parties themselves relate to each other in the context of sex work. It would likewise be interesting to explore the processes by which an individual becomes a third party, including the diversity of labor and professional advancement strategies involved in doing so. For instance, further research could explore how third parties with significant sex work experience differ from those who do not have such experience in terms of their operating practices, engagement with police, and level of respect they receive from their sex worker employees.

Third parties are usually conceptualized as individuals with little to no consideration of the institutional actors that purport to provide security or otherwise benefit sex workers, including police, government bureaucrats, and advocacy groups. Technology continues to rapidly transform the delivery of commercial sexual services through websites and online platforms that allow advertising and charge high fees in ways that eliminate the need for a traditional third party but nonetheless profit from sex workers' labor. Such explorations would likely open avenues of inquiry that illuminate what has traditionally been a poorly understood area of the sex industry, even in studies that promote a sex worker rights stance.

References

Aral, Sevgi, St. Lawrence, Janet, Tikhonova, Lilia, Safarova, Emma, Parker, Kathleen, Shakarishvili, Anna, and Ryan, Caroline. 2003. The Social Organization of Commercial Sex in Moscow, Russia. *Sexually Transmitted Diseases* 30: 39–45.

Benson, Josef. 2012. Myths About Pimps: Conflicting Images of Hypermasculine Pimps in U.S. American Hip-Hop and Bisexual Pimps in the Novels of Donald Goines and Iceberg Slim. *Journal of Bisexuality* 12(3): 429–441.

Brady, David, Biradavolu, Monica, and Blankenship, Kim. 2015. Brokers and the Earnings of Female Sex Workers in India. *American Sociological Review* 80(6): 1123–1149.

Büschi, Eva. 2014. Sex Work and Violence: Focusing on Managers in the Indoor Sex Industry. *Sexualities* 17: 724–741.

Davis, Holly. 2013. Defining "Pimp": Working Towards a Definition in Social Research. *Sociological Research Online* 18(1): 1–26.

Finn, Mary and Stalans, Loretta. 2016. How Targeted Enforcement Shapes Marketing Decisions of Pimps: Evidence of Displacement and Innovation. *Victims & Offenders: An International Journal of Evidence-based Research, Policy, and Practice* 11(4): 578–599.

Goldenberg, Shira, Krusi, Andrea, Zhang, Emma, Chettiar, Jill, and Shannon, Kate. 2017. Structural Determinants of Health Among Im/Migrants in the Indoor Sex Industry: Experiences of Workers and Managers/Owners in Metropolitan Vancouver. *PLoS One* 12(1): 1–18.

Hannem, Stacey and Bruckert, Chris. 2017. "I'm Not a Pimp, But I Play One on TV": The Moral Career and Identity Negotiations of Third Parties in the Sex Industry. *Deviant Behavior* 38(7): 824–836.

Marcus, Anthony, Horning, Amber, Curtis, Ric, Sanson, Jo, and Thompson, Efram. 2012. Conflict and Agency in Young Sex Worker/Pimp Relations: Implications for Trafficking Victims Protection Policy. *Annals of the American Academy of Political and Social Science* 653(1): 225–246.

Morselli, Carlo and Savoie-Gargiso, Isa. 2014. Coercion, Control, and Cooperation in a Prostitution Ring. *Annals of the American Academy of Political and Social Science* 653(1): 247–265.

Mount, Liz. 2018. "Behind the Curtain": Strip Clubs and the Management of Competition for Tips. *Journal of Contemporary Ethnography* 47(1): 60–87.

Quinn, Eithne. 2000. Who's the Mack? The Performativity and Politics of the Pimp Figure in Gangster Rap. *Journal of American Studies* 34(1): 115–134.

Raphael, Jody, Reichert, Jessica, and Powers, Mark. 2010. Pimp Control and Violence: Domestic Sex Trafficking of Chicago Women and Girls. *Women and Criminal Justice* 20(1): 89– 104.

Reid, Joan. 2016. Entrapment and Enmeshment Schemes Used by Sex Traffickers. *Sexual Abuse: A Journal of Research and Treatment* 28(6): 491–511.

Roe-Sepowitz, Dominique, Gallagher, James, Risinger, Marcus, and Hickle, Kristine. 2015. The Sexual Exploitation of Girls in the United States: The Role of Female Pimps. *Journal of Interpersonal Violence* 30(16): 2814–2830.

Schwartz, Harvey, Williams, Jody, and Farley, Melissa. 2007. Pimp Subjugation of Women by Mind Control. In *Prostitution and Trafficking in Nevada: Making the Connections*, edited by Farley, Melissa, 49–84. San Francisco, CA: Prostitution Research and Education.

Shen, Anqi. 2016. Motivations of Women Who Organized Others for Prostitution: Evidence from a Female Prison in China. *Criminology & Criminal Justice* 16(2): 214–232.

Staiger, Annegret. 2005. "Hoes Can Be Hoed Out, Players Can Be Played Out, But Pimp Is for Life": The Pimp Phenomenon as Strategy of Identity Formation. *Symbolic Interaction* 28(3): 407–428.

Van San, Marion and Bovenkerk, Frank. 2013. Secret Seducers: True Tales of Pimps in the Red Light District of Amsterdam. *Crime, Law and Social Change* 60(1): 67–80.

Zhang, Sheldon. 2011. Woman Pullers: Pimping and Sex Trafficking in a Mexican Border City. *Crime, Law and Social Change* 56(5): 509–528.

38

Multiplicity and demonic alliances

An anthropological approach to the problem of third parties in prostitution

José Miguel Nieto Olivar

Introduction

While I was writing this chapter, I was in communication with two friends who I have known for many years through my research. One of them, a former street sex worker in Porto Alegre, Brazil, told me how happy she was to have recently met up once again with her ex-husband, who she called, with genuine admiration and love, "the last real pimp of the century." The other friend, a sex worker in the Amazonian borderlands between Brazil, Colombia, and Peru, shared with me how much she missed her former lover Carmen/Carmelo,[1] the deceased owner/manager of the brothel where she worked and "the only person who said 'I love you' to me in my life." This article brings both of these women together by emphasizing the complex relationships that occur between those who sell sex and the third parties who manage their sexual labor.

This chapter looks at third parties in the specific configuration of the sex markets I investigated between 2011 and 2015 in Tabatinga, a transborder city along the Amazonian frontier between Brazil, Colombia, and Peru.[2] It is the result of an ethnographic approach to "prostitution"[3] and sexual economies (Cabezas 2009; Piscitelli 2007, 2016) the interests of which do not lie in de-constructing meanings, but in tracing the paths of actors and networks (Latour 2008). Following the approach introduced by Kempadoo (2004), who proposes a tension between sex work and transactional sex, and drawing from my own work (Olivar 2013, 2016a, 2016b), this contribution does not go beyond "prostitution"; to the contrary, it implies diving into it – and into procurement – as a controversial, and disputed social *thing* and a complex range of relationships.[4]

Regarding pimping and procurement, there still exists an empirical lack of knowledge, limited analyses, and significant stigmas, all of which contribute to making "the pimp" the perfect embodiment of all exploitation and abuse (Blanchette & Silva 2017; Davis 2013; Dewey & Epler 2015). What little critical analysis exists often casts pimps as rational figures who function as third parties, managers of the sex industry, or people who benefit or profit from the women who engage in sex work.[5] But this approach, in which third parties are generally understood as a sort of external, coercive force, does not seem to reflect the reality of sex markets, nor does it enrich our analysis of this generally overlooked and misrepresented actor.

Blanchette and Silva (2017, 28) make explicit the limits of the prostitute–pimp–john triad by exposing "a whole galaxy of people who profit from and/or manage sex work," and a wide typology of Brazilian third parties that do not match up with the "classic" pimp figure nor with the structural position of the third party. Dewey and Epler (2015, 145) take a similar perspective to Blanchette and Silva (2017) in their adoption of the formula "men who benefit from the sex work of women"; however, the explanation of a street-based sex worker they interviewed enhances the complexity of their analysis: "Rent, drugs, food, kids . . . that's my pimp" (Dewey & Epler 2015, 147). Here we see *crack* portrayed as a pimp in this widened sense of the word, born from lived experience.

In the context of the broader field of sex work research into third parties, this chapter points out the need to empirically and theoretically deal with the moral burden of the pimp and how this construction of a "monster" liberally transforms our views of third parties and what they do. Here I follow the suggestion made by Blanchette and Silva (2017), interrogating the emic concept of pimp and the institutional elaborations of this personage as a "monster" or a "devil." The chapter also emphasizes the need to construct an approach that is more focused on relational flows, power tensions, and multiplicity, rather than on identities and fixed positions in a commercial structure. I want to call into question the very notion of "third parties." I believe that instead of thinking about subjects, we must think in terms of geometries of intimate relationships, connections, and derivations (Strathern 1991).

In order to propose a displacement in the problematic approaches towards pimps and pimping that currently dominate the literature, I adopt the anthropological concept of *demonic alliances* (Deleuze and Guattari 2008; Viveiros de Castro 2007). This concept allows us to mark socially structuring relationships, not by basing them on alliances of kinship and (re)production (a classical theme in anthropology), which are conceptually linked to norms (Butler 2004), but upon the profusion of multiple, lateral alliances that are conceptually linked to seduction, hunting, and sorcery, among other things. Demonic has to do here with difference, multiplicity, *illicit unions*, or *abominable loves* (Deleuze & Guattari 2008, 29). All of these things are the sexual desires and practices that, for Gayle Rubin (1999), operate beyond the threshold of acceptability in the moral logic of kinship and heterosexual, reproductive, and contractual conjugality. Relations of prostitution and of procurement, in their emic rhetoric of "war" and "hunting,"[6] can be compared to managing multiplicity and micro-alliances in other areas of human endeavor.

To achieve my goals, I describe the findings of my ethnographic investigations into the main forms trans-border sex markets take in Tabatinga, Brazil. I locate two key moments when "procurement" (i.e. "pimping") makes an appearance and end the chapter by looking for a thick descriptive approach in my exploration of an actual "procuress." Via this route, I hope to make explicit some analytical approaches for the anthropological problem of third parties in commercial sex.

Babado: *sexual economies, multiplicity, and the absence of pimps*

Between 2011 and 2015, I met several young Brazilian men and women (cis and trans-), many of them between 15 and 18 years old, who engaged in "*babado*" in Tabatinga. "*Fazer babado*" is the local name for "turning a trick"; that is, engaging in relations that we might call *transactional sex* (Hunter 2002) or *tactical sex* (Cabezas 2009), which are considered prostitution by a great number of people, locally and internationally. The young people I worked with agreed that "sexual exploitation" – to quote the term used by a local NGO in all its public presentations – is best described as what happens when they make an "old faggot" keep buying beer and food all night long for the entire gang, without anything sexual taking place afterwards. "Exploitation" is also what young *travesti* use to describe their petty *debarés* (minor thefts) from clients who temporarily lose consciousness as a result of drink, drugs, or sexual excitement.[7]

The young people engaged in *babado* drift through the streets, bars, and pubs at night. They dance at parties, they exchange messages via cell phones, they ride motorcycles, and appropriate the territory around street corners in ever-mutating groups. Some travel all the way to neighboring cities, where they cruise the streets with different degrees of familiarity and pleasure, in a space that became a trans-border region at about the same time as they were becoming gay and trans "Brazilians." They have sex in motels, hotels, and other discreet spots across the city, mainly on the Brazilian side of the border. Sexual intercourse, particularly with adult men, is intimately related to money for these youths, in the form of payments, presents, or "collaborations," in ways similar ways to those shown by Hunter (2002), Cabezas (2009), Piscitelli (2007, 2013), and Groes-Green (2013) among others. Among themselves, however, either as lovers or as friends, sex does not necessarily imply an exchange of money.

These youths do not engage in *babado* out of need, or as a way to find boyfriends or spouses.[8] Time and again, they would tell and show me that they did it for mere enjoyment (*curtição*).[9] Enjoyment of what? Sex, of course, but also of adventure, being part of a gang, having the ability to make money, enjoying the power of their transformed bodies that embody multiple – and even simultaneous – sexes and sexualities. *Babado* and *curtição* are urban nocturnal practices that intensively produce affection, money, and what I call demonic alliances. My interlocutors also enjoy what they view as my bizarre interest in listening to their stories: I, as a man, am always suspected of being an closeted older gay and a possible abominable love.

The money produced by *babado* and *debarés* within the framework of enjoyment is mainly transformed into beer and barbecues, new shoes and clothes, make-up and hair treatments, and into presents for friends and relatives. In this way, what my interlocutors earn is spent on building their "growing"[10] social lives and on enjoying life, as well as on social, family, and affective relationships. In this way, everyone within the closest networks and circle of related connections (Carsten 2004) profits or benefits from the *babado*, because *babado* and the money derived from it are relational multipliers.

But there is even more to all this. From 2012 on, some of the young men and women who I knew through my ethnographic investigations began to participate more actively in the Afro-indigenous Brazilian religion of Umbanda. In fact, they were guided in this process by one of their own: a poor gay and ex-*travesti* 23-year-old who had become a *Pai de Santo* (a spiritual guide and leader in Afro-indigenous Brazilian religions). This young *Pai de Santo* built his home and a religious temple (a *terreiro*) on a squatted patch of land on the outskirts of Tabatinga.

It is important to understand, in this context, that Afro-indigenous religions involve possession of priests and followers by the spirits and that the religious rituals are strongly embodied in this fashion. This means that the money from *babado* is also transformed into presents, clothes, accessories, beer, wine, and cigarettes for the spiritual entities of Umbanda, and in raising money for the materials to build the temple. This relationship implies intense bodily transactions with deities who use, penetrate, and form practitioners' bodies. It also implies tense negotiations where matter and spirit, bodies and goods, heads and feet, animals, humans, and entities intersect with each other, multiply, uncover, and expand into one another (Birman 2005; Fry 1986). Both the temple's entities and the *Pai de Santo* can hardly be described as pimps, procurers, or even third parties in these transactions because of the inseparability of the roles and relationships that are forged within the temple's sacred space. How can roles in these sorts of relationships be separated when, for example, the entity in question is not necessarily material but may only exist in the head of the young person who is possessed in the ceremony? As a trans "girl" [*menina*, in Portuguese] once told me, money is transformed into affect and care in the Pai de Santos' *terreiro* and also into *axé*, the divine substance of spiritual/material gift and counter-gift, which is essential to the worldview of Afro-indigenous Brazilian religions. Money, affect, care, sex, and *axé* shape these youths' lives through alliances and instances of becoming, constituting large, holistic networks of relatedness.

The young people of Tabatinga had no procurer or figure that could be identified as a "pimp" when they were involved in enjoyment, *curtição*, through their work. All their close acquaintances were potential mediators/procurers who could earn tips from their sex-working friends or from the men/clients if they helped facilitate a meeting or transaction. And Tabatinga whorehouse owners, of course, also made their tips. These figures, however, played a small role in this very open, fluid, and informal trans-border sex market. Carmelo, my friend and owner of a prostitution business in Tabatinga, always spoke wryly about "*los mariquitas*" (literally the "little faggots"). To Carmelo, they were volatile and ephemeral private procurers, in the service of the women who worked for her, yet always eager to scam the women by "fooling around" on their motorcycles. Such is "procurement" in this scenario: it comprises mutual and multiple mediations that are an integral part of the collective production of this complex intersection of economy, sexuality, and "delinquency." As men from both sides of the border explained to me: "all you have to do is sit outside a school and wait. You make an offer to a girl and even if she turns you down, she still might know someone who'll be willing."

This scene rolled merrily along for most of my fieldwork, largely unnoticed and uncommented by authorities on both sides of the border city. Then Jenny happened.

The fabrication of Jenny, the *proxeneta* (madam)

In November 2012, on the Colombian side of the trans-border city of Leticia (generally described as being the best organized and safest city in the region), a *proxeneta* (a female pimp or madam) was said to have been arrested and imprisoned for "selling under-age girls." As usual, the arrest was broadcast in spectacular form by the local radio stations, exposing names, neighborhoods, and links. The culprit was Jenny: a 16-year-old "madam" who lived with her mother in a poor neighborhood. Jenny's arrest and imprisonment came in the form of an ostentatious police operation which took place outside her school and was witnessed by some 1,000 people, including students, school officials, and teachers. Jenny had apparently been reported by the father of one of the girls she had "sold," who was also her friend and schoolmate. The father had caught his daughter with gifts and money that she could provide no explanation for. Pressed, the young woman stated that Jenny had allegedly facilitated a sexual encounter with a man, a Colombian army sergeant, in a hotel in Tabatinga.

Incarcerated at a youth detention center, Jenny became a "perpetrator," in the terminology of the police, social workers, and other public servants of the State. To the school principal, who I had the chance to talk to, Jenny's arrest "set an example" for many other girls at the school who also have their own "schemes" or who, like Jenny, have "sold" others. For Ángela, a former civil servant of the Colombian Institute of Family Welfare (ICBF – Instituto Colombiano de Bienestar Familiar), Jenny was nothing but a scapegoat to satisfy demands that the government had to deal with cases of sexual exploitation of children and teenagers.

Over a year later, Jenny was released from prison. She tried to go back to her old school but the atmosphere there became unbearable for her and she had to give up her studies. Her mother said she now smoked, drank, and swore in a way she had never done before her arrest and imprisonment. Shortly after her release, Jenny, the 16-year-old *proxeneta* who had been tried and jailed for the sake of protecting children's and teenager's rights, started going out with a young man. He also had a criminal record (for drug dealing) and Jenny soon became pregnant.

When I talked to Jenny one afternoon in 2016 at her mother's house, she exposed the same sort of logic that I had come to know well in my nights of fieldwork. Jenny explained that she was not a procuress or anything similar. She had not sold her friends. "That guy was my friend. He wanted to meet my mates and I put them in touch with one another."[11]

Just as the youngsters in Tabatinga did and do, Jenny had sexual intercourse with adult men who gave her money or gifts. It was not a secret to her schoolmates, nor to the taxi drivers I spoke to who had transported her to her encounters and often mediated these. Many of the men Jenny used to see were in the military or were police officers. Jenny would also "put them in touch" with her friends. Although Jenny spent a year in prison, deprived of freedom and under investigation, no criminal organization, adult pimping, nor any profiting network was ever found. Jenny is from a poor family, headed by a hardworking mother who did not ask Jenny for money. The money that Jenny made in her adventures (which was increased by the cash she made when she introduced her male "mates" to her female friends) helped at home, but was mainly spent by Jenny as a means to enjoy her nights out, to buy pretty clothes, to show off her goods and her entourage, all of which would have otherwise been far beyond her reach. Nevertheless, these sorts of expenditures create flows of bodies and capital, however small: "the finances of village women," in the words of an old woman who, in 2011, explained the gender and sexual domains of the cocaine economy to me. In other words, the flows of trans-border currency seem to successfully fulfill the function of producing Jenny as a desirable, autonomous, and sexually legitimate woman in her own context. As Kempadoo (2004: 74–75) shows in the case of Jamaica, in some contexts and moments (both inside and outside of sex work), having sex for free can be viewed as absurd, illogical, or even immoral.

Such is "procurement": for the authorities, it *must* exist. The existence of a pimp, of a monster (Lowenkron 2012), of a clearly identified and morally marked third party becomes necessary for the political construction of sexual exploitation and of the category of the innocent victim. This is especially the case when a multiplicity of mediations slip in between moral categories that strongly depend on victims and victimizers. Procurement is an indefinite construct and a fantasy framing that allows subjects to be disciplined and marginalized and that facilitates the forced materialization of arbitrary projects and figments of the imagination regarding relationships, sexualities, money, and prostitution (Olivar 2016c).

Carmelo's brothel: women, houses, and families

Inside a poor house in the city of Quibdó, in the Afro-Colombian Pacific region, two girls live with their maternal grandmother on the monthly remittances sent by their mother. Thanks to these remittances, the mother can afford for both of her daughters to live under the same roof, rather than separately at their respective paternal grandmothers. It has also freed the grandmother from the burdensome daily work of obtaining food, allowing her to stay at home and look after the girls who are now in their teens. The money that crosses the international border, through the Amazon, and over the Andes to land in the poorest state of Colombia – the state with that country's largest Black population – comes from the mother's sex work.

I have known the mother, Flor, since 2012, when she arrived from Quibdó at the Leticia airport, immediately heading to Tabatinga to work and live in Carmelo's house. This is a truly trans-border-*artesanal* Colombian brothel in Tabatinga, complete with a red light over the front door. Carmen was a Colombian, a lesbian white woman with (in her words) very traditional gender notions and a traditionally masculine style of gender. She was, therefore, known to herself and others as Carmelo. She has managed a small brothel in Leticia since the 1990s, but in 2009 she was arrested for the "sexual exploitation" of a 17-year-old girl who used to work with her. After nine months in prison, Carmelo was released without conviction, and she decided to re-open her house, this time on the Brazilian side of town (Tabatinga), which she saw as a more permissive location. It was in that red-light house (*el bombillo rojo*), that I first met Carmen/Carmelo in 2011 and where I did my fieldwork until November 2015, when she had to be hospitalized in Bogotá, Colombia.

In December 2014, a year prior to her death, Carmelo had been the target of a Brazilian military police operation aimed at defending the borders and promoting national integration. This was publicized by the regional media as the rescue of Colombian victims of human trafficking (Olivar 2016a). Transcending certain fantasies and realities regarding sexual commerce, however, Carmelo was neither an exploiter nor a powerful agent of the transnational and trans-border sex "mafias."

Carmelo depended on contacts between several Colombian cities. Carmelo would invite women, put money together to buy their tickets, and wait for them with her scooter at Leticia airport. She then put them in a taxi she paid for and would send them to her house in Tabatinga, where the women lived and worked. As is the case with practically all Colombians who live, regularly visit, and work in Tabatinga, none of these women would need any migration documents, or even need to register their entry in Brazil. Carmelo's house, where she herself lived and carried out her business, was in the words of a Brazilian health official, "a hut falling to pieces." Unlike many women working for her, she never built a life of luxury and comfort for herself; she never managed to accumulate money and become rich.

Working in the red-light house, women earn what they collectively decide they will charge. The minimum price for a trick used to be approximately U.S.$20, but no part of that money went to Carmelo or even passed through her hands. She earns money from the men by renting out the rooms for the tricks (U.S.$5 for 20/30 minutes) and selling beverages.

Carmelo used to manage the house alone and I saw many women leave without paying her back for the tickets that she had bought for them. I saw many women move elsewhere, to work at more comfortable or convenient brothels. Representing such forms of sexual commerce as "young girls being forced into prostitution" or as "human trafficking" for the sake of the demands of national integration and defense, suits specific moral-political demands and the fantasies of the border better than it does the local realities as they are apparent in such markets. Rather than a patriarchal institution for the imprisonment and exploitation of women, Carmelo's house was the setting for an intensive circulation of economies and affects where gifts, doubts, and debts became highly collaborative. This circulation took place around her business/house, and it was sustained by the solid management of good food and housing, of two old scooters, of long-term friendships with men, and of privy information as to where women could be recruited.

As a mediator, Carmelo was a nodal agent of a certain *demonic system*. A system that hundreds of women endorsed and contributed to – indeed, to which they had willingly traveled thousands of kilometers several times in their lives in order to participate in. Within this system, according to these women's own testimony, they had orgiastic nights, made great friends, found husbands, had children, shared amazing stories, learned a new language (Portuguese), and learned about drugs, borders, money, and, of course, work. This system of collaborations, debt, emotional blackmail, and claims, of work demands and domestic femininity, implied women's voluntary commitment to the maintenance of the house's ever-precarious and self-managed conditions.

One of the women who was part of the circulations generated by this system was Flor.

Through the translations resulting from Flor's relational work (Zelizer 2005), the money coming from cocaine (the main regional economy), timber, fishing, tourism, social benefits, trade in goods and services, and the salaries of state servants from all three surrounding countries is captured and sent to Quibdó. There, it is morally transformed into ceramic floor tiling, toys, school, maternal love, and kinship obligations. But at the border, part of that money inevitably implicates demonic alliances such as cocaine, hard liquor, silicone, anesthesia, scalpels, condoms, motorbike and airplane fuel, make-up, whorehouse clothes, and the body: sweat, saliva, and vaginal fluids. All of this allows Flor to continue choosing and construing specific ways of being a Black traveling woman, a daughter, a lover, a worker, a mother. It allows her to deal with snarls of *becoming-a-whore* and to manage her time, her money, and the limits of her body (Olivar 2016b). The mother and the traveler exploit the sex worker and profit from her. And here we arrive at two important points: the "procuress" is the sex worker herself (in a system of "internal relations of persons or positions),[12] and the sex workers collectively exercise (Foucault 1980) the labor of the "procuress" . . . even to the point of becoming "bosses" of one another.

This can be exemplified with an ethnographic image: the daily scene that occurred when Carmelo would try to get the women to cater to and please men, to "work well." Here one would see the fierce and collective resistance of the women, who only rose from their seats at the very moment they wished, or when the other women pressured them to do so. On the other hand, one would also see the extremely tiresome work of the aging and lonely Carmelo, going up and down on her scooter, carrying water, fixing holes in the brothel's ever-precarious ceiling, charging – as a man – the men money, trying to get love or sexual gifts from a younger woman, and – as a woman –managing the women's sex work, and constantly carrying out her agreed upon obligations as a domestic laborer by cooking and cleaning.

It is within this system of engendered material translations that the meta-connective actions and knowledge of the "procurer" become fundamental. It is for this very reason that Carmelo's body and engendered relational configuration (Strathern 1990; see note 12), as well as those of other "pimps" in other sexual markets (and of the "little faggots" that alarm Carmelo), are so important. Mediation is embodied. Two of the four brothels in Tabatinga between 2011 and 2015 were run by heterosexual couples and two by transgender persons, one of them being Carmelo. It seems that in a world in which "there ain't no real pimps out there no more" (Dewey & Epler 2015), the most effective mediator is not an external hyper-masculine devil, but a person capable of incorporating in themselves same-sex and cross-sex relations with both (engendered) sides of the prostitution relationship. Is it possible that the new devil "pimp" is in fact a queer cyborg?[13]

If Flor can be seen as a translator, Carmelo created and managed a framework of tensions where translations conflicted regarding the demonic nature of alliances that made up the framework. She did so by creating home, collaboration, and care. Despite all the tensions and struggles of administrating a brothel full of women without the full exercise of hierarchical power and without techniques of oppression and exploitation, Carmelo was always described by those who worked with/for her as a good person. She was remembered by most of the women for her concern and for taking care of them (not "protecting," in the masculine pimp sense), for the ease with which she fell in love, and for her kind heart.

And yet, Carmelo died alone in December 2015 at a public hospital in Bogotá, Colombia.

In love, relatedness, sex, and money, transactions are not as common as derivations, *formative associations* (McClintock 1995), co-creations, and transformations. Both gender and generational trajectories mark this process. As Carmelo grew older performing a butch lesbian style of gender, she had to invest more and more time, energy, and money to keep her girlfriend, but institutionalized sex work was becoming ever more weaker, in terms of the circulations it could produce, in contrast with the several forms of *babado*. Since the closure of her business in Leticia in 2009 (which occurred as part of a lover's spat with her jealous ex-partner, causing Carmelo to spend nine months in prison), Carmelo had transitioned into a time of sexual-affective-economic decadence. Between 2011 and 2015 she had at least two love affairs with women (40 and 30 years younger than her) working at her house, which ended in sexual-affective-economic suffering. As she got older, Carmelo gradually lost money and energy. She lost her power. As a boss, s/he was becoming a lonely "old man" loving young women and needing ever more the help and care of others.

Finally, Carmelo's system was interrupted at the end of 2015 when she became weaker, was hospitalized, and lost her cell-phone and scooters. While in the clutches of the public health system, the state had declared her to be, officially and only, a woman: frail, precarious, and aged. Her girlfriend left her and by then most of the female sex workers with whom she had years of friendship had moved out of town. The landlady and three of the women who were working for her at the time abandoned her in the hospital and appropriated her business, taking over its name, place, and even some of the furniture and electrical appliances before her death.

When I came across Flor in 2016 at another Colombian brothel in Tabatinga, she greeted me euphorically asked me to treat her to a shot of *aguardiente*.[14] We talked about Carmelo's death and about the good feelings we both had for her. Flor then told me about her travels and about the big money she made in the brothels on the island of San Andrés. She talked about the men who wanted her, who helped her so much, and for whom she feels so much.[15] She also told me about the excellent and regulated work conditions on the island, and how, on her last trip – and despite all the money she sent to her mother – she still made enough to pay for a plastic surgery operation in Colombia.

The memories of Carmen, the liquor I paid for, the increased amount of money her mother had asked for, the elegant men who paid for her family and surgery (not to mention the trans-border brothel's profits), to the Caribbean islands that regulate sex work and the human rights and police officers that struggle against human trafficking in the borderlands . . . all of this (including Flor's telling me her life story as part of my work, which the Brazilian state of São Paulo finances and that allows me to pay for Colombian *aguardientes* sold off-license in this Colombian whorehouse in Tabatinga) is implicated in the circulation flows of money, affect, and bodies that are blithely labeled "prostitution" or even "trafficking." It is all a function of so-called "third parties" that are many times in no way properly third parties. Thinking about Carmelo, her house, and her position as a "madam" thus implies that we think on all those nodules – those places, people, and affects, those networks of bodies, money, transformations, houses, and ever-multiplying and mutating alliances.

Concluding thoughts

I have followed in the present chapter the analytical tradition of challenging social knowledge about "prostitution," and about the relationships between the realms of sexuality, economy, morality, family, and affect. I have attempted to approach these by adding new elements to the collective process of knowledge construction. Alongside the idea of formative associations (McClintock 1995), I have articulated a relational anthropological perspective inspired by such authors as Strathern, Latour, and Viveiros de Castro, which has proven productive in imagining a constructive, multi-agentic and relational approach to the networks and mesh-works through which money, sexuality, affection, bodies, and relationships are created.

Within such a theoretical approach, I have suggested the image of demonic alliances (Viveiros de Castro 2002) as a fertile analogy to think about prostitution and procurement in a grammar of relations, transformations, multiplicity, and networks. For this, I presented some partial fragments from ethnography, focusing on the material forms of prostitution and third-party participation in a trans-border urban territory. The marginalized experiences of the participation of underage people in the sexual markets expose the absence of the pimp in these relationships and points to the difficulty of thinking about the prostitution relationship as a mathematical "story problem" that necessarily contains two or three *parties* or *variables*. The evidence collected during my ethnographic fieldwork is dramatic in two ways: first, in its portrayal of the diluted, ambiguous, and fractal multiplicity of agents mediating, shaping, and profiting from the *babado* economy. These agents are not just men, but women and trans-people; agents connected through several relationships, and who are both human and non-human, profane and religious. Second, this absence of clear-cut third parties becomes evident in the desperate actions of state power as it searches for, catches, or fabricates pimps and traffickers.

I also looked at Carmelo's brothel, trying to plunge directly into the pimp system of relations. In this way, I tried to place pimping or procurement within a problematic twist, as a super-intensification of the formative nets that create and sustain the commercialization of sex.

As has been put forth by Blanchette and Silva (2017) in their work about pimps in the United States and Brazil, procurement constitutes a kind of dangerous border territory in the field of political (and even academic) discussions about sex work and sex markets. It is "the devil." To bring procurement into the analytical light means inviting a third party into a relationship that we barely tolerate and understand as "necessarily" involving only two individuals: the prostitute and the client. It implies intensifying the presence of money via profit, commerce, and the hierarchical administration of relationships. "Procurement" thus appears as a sort of deformed and monstrous doppelganger of the sort of prostitution that is celebrated as feminist, autonomous, libertarian, and pro-union.

But the construct of a "third party" seems impossible as well. As procuress, Carmelo – in her *dividual* (and therefore non-singular) body, was a great and ever-spreading entity, working her way into other people and tools. She had far more than two eyes. She was always dependent on the bodies of workers and lovers and she therefore embodies and multiplies the network of demonic alliances and transformations that she helped create and mediate. The procurement relationship(s), as expressed in the life of Carmelo, make obvious the impossibility of a mathematics of individuals and established *parties* (second or third), rendering the alliances created in prostitution even more *anti-natural*.

Finally, the experiment I have presented here is part of a continuing collective effort to renew and displace theoretical frameworks and positions already established in the anthropological understanding of prostitution.[16] Those displacements can emerge from intimate/affective relationships, from meticulous fieldwork, and from the respect researchers should give to both the ordinary and spectacular dimensions of sex workers' actions, intellectual elaborations, aesthetic creations, and political inventions. I believe that these theoretical and conceptual displacements are necessary in order to understand and give resonance to the creative and radical potency that prostitution already has. Looking at the particular case of third parties, I believe that by following sexual cash flows "inside" and alongside payments and gifts, and deepening our knowledge about more-or-less institutionalized spaces of sexual commerce, we can offer up important reflections on the inclusive-disjunctive characteristics of sex work and perhaps even challenge its long standing demonic reputation in Western culture.

Notes

1 I will use both the feminine (Carmen) and masculine (Carmelo) Spanish forms of this person's name, as they were used in her life and in our relationship. Readers will thus see the two alternating from time to time. All other names except Carmen/Carmelo's, have been changed, as well as any information that could allow for the identification of my interlocutors.

2 Tabatinga (Brazil) connects to Leticia (Colombia) and the Peruvian island of Santa Rosa on the Amazon River, forming a triple trans-border city. See Zárate (2008), Aponte-Mota (2011); Olivar, Cunha, and Rosa (2015); Albuquerque and Paiva (2015) for more studies on commercial sex formations in this region. In other works, I develop analyses about the effects of the human trafficking struggle on this borderland (Olivar 2016a).

3 Much has been said regarding the proper term for those who exchange sex for money. In the English-speaking world, people who support the decriminalization or regulation of the sale of sex tend to refer to it as "sex work." Those who wish to abolish it or who support its criminalization (whole or in part) call it "prostitution" or even "rape," "slavery," "human trafficking," or other emotionally charged terms. As an anthropologist allied with Brazil's prostitute rights movement, For the purposes of the present article, I generally use "prostitution" as this is the socially constructed term that has been employed to pigeonhole most of my interlocutors.

4 Brazilian anthropologists have developed diverse analyses on/around *cafetinagem* (pimping) from diverse empirical fields: Fonseca (2004), Tedesco (2008), Tavares (2014), Patriarca (2015), Blanchette and Silva (2017).

5 See Blanchette and Silva (2017) for a general overview on how pimps are portrayed.

6 War (*guerra*), as in "war clothes" or "war names," or "battle" is an emic term used to describe both prostitution and relations with Police or the State. Hunt [*caçar*, in Portuguese], as used in "go out to hunt clients," or "to wear clothes for hunting" is used in a similar fashion. (Olivar, 2016b).

7 For the analysis of participation of adolescents and children in "prostitution," see outstanding work by Montgomery (2001) and Mai (2007).

8 See Nick Mai's (2007) analyses about mobility, work, dealing with potential third parties, and the meanings of sexual transactions between young errant men in Europe.

9 In his research with young women in Mozambique engaged in transactional sex, Groes-Green (2013) finds that they are called "*curtidoras*" (the one who enjoys). The transactional sex in that case is hardly linked with kinship logics of filiation and patronage.

10 "Growing" in the sense of transforming, generally from male to female.

11 Dewey and Epler (2015, 146) explain "collegial relationships between women" as a form of third-party participation capable of transforming friendship in a suspicion of pimping.

12 Here I follow British anthropologist Marilyn Strathern's (1990, 1991) conceptual system regarding relational and fractal sociality, gender in non-essential, performative, and relational *dividual* terms (cross-sex and same-sex relations), difference, and a whole critique of the notion of the individual among other things. Note that *dividual* does not mean two terms in relation, but a socially imagined binary logic that creates relations, differences, and people in a fractal way.

13 For bisexual pimping and the myth of hypermasculinity, see Benson (2012); for a feminist/gender discussion about the relative disappearance of "real pimps," and the butch lesbian woman as a typical pimp in present day Rio de Janeiro, see Blanchette and Silva (2017).

14 A Colombian alcoholic beverage made of distilled sugarcane, very popular and cheap.

15 About "help" and "program" as alternate sexual and economic possibilities, and about transnational sex markets from Brazil, see Piscitelli (2013, 2016). About sex work and mobility in the Caribbean, see Kempadoo (2004) and Cabezas (2009).

16 I would like to thank Susan Dewey and Thaddeus Blanchette for all the work and care put in to the editing of this chapter. I would like to thank Adriana Piscitelli, Claudia Fonseca, Thaddeus Blanchette, Ana Paula Silva, Laura Murray, Sonia Correa, Aline Tavares, Leticia Tedesco, Soraya Simões, and all the Brazilian scholars of different centers with whom in continuing labor we share knowledge, experiences, and affects about prostitution. In this sense, the Center for Gender Studies PAGU at the State University of Campinas (Unicamp), the Brazilian Interdisciplinary Association of AIDS and the Sexuality Policy Watch, and the Prostitution Watch (Federal University of Rio de Janeiro) are powerful think tanks about prostitution and sexual markets and economies. I would like to thank Kamala Kempadoo, Amalia Cabezas, and Cecilia Varela, too. Finally, and with love, nothing of this Brazilian effervescence on sex work would be possible without the intellectual and political shining of Gabriela Leite (the Whore Queen who died in 2013). Thanks Gabriela and everyone linked to the Brazilian Sex Workers Network (Rede Brasileira de Prostitutas) and other sex workers organizations, for everything I learnt.

References

Albuquerque, J.L. and Paiva, Luiz Fábio. 2015. Entre nacoes e legislações: algumas práticas de "legalidade" e "ilegalidade" na tríplice fronteira amazônica (Brasil, Colômbia, Peru). *Revista Ambivalências*, 3(5): 115–148.

Aponte-Mota, Jorge. 2011. *Leticia y Tabatinga: transformación de un espacio urbano en la Amazonia*. Master's dissertation. Leticia: Universidad Nacional de Colombia.

Benson, J. 2012. Myths about pimps: conflicting images of hypermasculine pimps in U.S. American hip-hop and bisexual pimps in the novels of Donald Goines and Iceberg Slim. *Journal of Bisexuality*, 12: 429–441.

Birman, Patricia. 2005. Transes e Transas: sexo e gênero nos cultos afro-brasileiros, um sobrevôo. *Revista de Estudos Feministas*, 13(2): 403–414.

Blanchette, Thaddeus and Silva, Ana. 2017. Sympathy for the devil: pimps, agents, and third parties involved in the sale of sex in Rio de Janeiro. In A. Horning and A. Marcus (eds.), *Third party sex work and pimps in the age of anti-trafficking*. New York: Springer, 15–47.

Butler, J. 2004. *Undoing gender*. New York, London: Routledge.

Cabezas, Amalia. 2009. *Economies of desire: sex and tourism in Cuba and the Dominican Republic*. Philadelphia: Temple University.

Carsten, Janet. 2004. Gender, bodies and kinship. In Janet Carsten (ed.) *After kinship*. Cambridge: Cambridge University Press, 57–82.

Davis, H. 2013. Defining "pimp": working towards a definition in social research. *Sociological Research Online*, 18(1): 1–15.

Deleuze, G. and Guattari, F. 2008. *Mil Platôs: capitalismo e esquizofrenia vol. 3*. São Paulo: Editora 34.

Dewey, Susan and Epler, Rhett. 2015. "Ain't no real pimps out there no more": characterizations of men who facilitate women's sex work activities in Denver, Colorado. *Wagadu*, 14: 135–152.

Fonseca, Claudia. 2004. A morte de um gigolô: fronteiras da transgressão e sexualidade nos dias atuais. In Gregori e Carrara Piscitelli (org.), *Sexualidades e saberes: convenções e fronteiras*. Rio de Janeiro: Garamond, 257–281.

Foucault, M. 1980. *Power/knowledge*. New York: Pantheon House.

Fry, Peter. 1986. Male homossexuality and spirit possession in Brazil. *Journal of Homosexuality*, 11: 137–153.

Groes-Green, Christian. 2013. "To put men in a bottle": eroticism, kinship, female power, and transactional sex in Maputo, Mozambique. *American Ethnologist*, 40(1): 102–117.

Hunter, M. 2002. The materiality of everyday sex: thinking beyond "prostitution." *African Studies*, 61: 99–120.

Kempadoo, Kamala. 2004. *Sexing the Caribbean: gender, race and sexual labour*. New York/London: Routledge.

Latour, Bruno. 2008. *Reensamblando lo social: una introducción a la teoria del actor-red*. Buenos Aires: Manantial.

Lowenkron, Laura. 2012. *O Monstro contemporâneo: a construção social da pedofilia em múltiplos planos*. Doctoral dissertation. Rio de Janeiro: National Museum/Federal University of Rio de Janeiro.

McClintock, Anne. 1995. *Imperial leather: race, gender and sexuality in the colonial contest*. London: Routledge.

Mai, Nick. 2007. *Young and minor migrants' errant mobility and involvement in sex work within the EU*. London: Institute for the study of European transformations (ISET).

Montgomery, Heather. 2001. *Modern Babylon? Prostituting children in Thailand*. London: Berghahn Books.

Olivar, José Miguel. 2013. *Devir puta: políticas da prostituição de rua na experiência de quatro mulheres militantes*. Rio de Janeiro: UERJ/CLAM.

Olivar, José Miguel. 2016a. Exploring traffic and exploitation on the Brazilian international border in the Amazon. *Social and Economic Studies*, 65(4): 57–86.

Olivar, José Miguel. 2016b. A feast of men: sexuality, kinship and predation in the practices of female prostitution in downtown Porto Alegre. In Susanne Hofmann and Adi Moreno (eds.) *Intimate economies: bodies, emotions and sexualities on the global market*. New York: Palgrave Macmillan, 111–134.

Olivar, José Miguel. 2016c. ". . . o que eu quero para minha filha": rumos de (in)definição da exploração sexual no Brasil. *Mana*, 22(2): 435–468.

Olivar, José Miguel, Cunha, Flávia, and Rosa, Patrícia. 2015. "Presenças e mobilidades transfronteiriças entre Brasil, Peru e Colômbia: o caso da "migração peruana na Amazônia brasileira." *Revista TOMO*, 26: 123–163.

Patriarca, Leticia. 2015. *As corajosas: etnografando experiências travestis na prostituição*. Master's dissertation. São Paulo: State University of São Paulo.

Piscitelli, Adriana. 2007. Shifting boundaries: sex and money in the north-east of Brazil. *Sexualities*, 10: 489–500.

Piscitelli, Adriana. 2013. *Trânsitos: brasileiras nos mercados transnacionais do sexo*. Rio de Janeiro: CLAM/Eduerj.

Piscitelli, Adriana. 2016. Sexual economies, love and human trafficking – new conceptual issues. *cadernos pagu*, 17: e16475.

Rubin, Gayle. 1999. Thinking sex: notes for a radical theory of the politics of sexuality. In P. Parker and R.G. Aggleton (eds.), *Culture, society and sexuality reader*. New York: Routledge, 143–178.

Strathern, Marilyn. 1990. *The gender of the gift: problems with women and problems with society in Melanesia.* Berkeley, CA: University of California Press.

Strathern, Marilyn. 1991. *Partial connections.* Sabage, MD: Rowman & Littlefield.

Tavares, Aline. 2014. *A organização da Zona: notas etnográficas sobre relações de poder na zona de prostituição Jardim Itatinga, Campinas-SP.* Master's dissertation. Campinas (Brazil): State University of Campinas.

Tedesco, Letícia. 2008. *Explorando o negócio do sexo: uma etnografia sobre as relações afetivas e comerciais entre prostitutas e agenciadores em Porto Alegre.* Master's dissertation. Porto Alegre: Federal University of Rio Grande do Sul.

Viveiros de Castro, Eduardo. 2002. *A inconstância da alma selvagem.* São Paulo: Cosac Naify.

Zárate Botía, Carlos. 2008. *Silvícolas, siringueros y agentes estatales: el surgimiento de una sociedad transfronteriza en la amazonia de Brasil, Perú y Colombia 1880–1932.* Leticia: Universidad Nacional de Colombia.

Zelizer, Viviana. 2005. *The purchase of intimacy.* Princeton, NJ: Princeton University Press.

39

Reflecting on labour exploitation in the sex industry

Agata Dziuban and Luca Stevenson

Introduction

In recent decades, labour exploitation in late capitalist societies has received a fair share of academic attention (Piketty 2014; Standing 2011; Weeks 2011). The specificity and dynamic of labour exploitation in the sex industry is, however, still largely overlooked in scholarly research.[1] This uneven distribution of analytical care results from a variety of factors, including the lack of recognition of sex work as a form of labour, the widespread criminalisation of sexual commerce and the absence of any internationally binding standards to help determine what constitutes fair or exploitative working conditions in the sex industry (EMPOWER 2016; ICRSE 2016a; Wagenaar, Amesberger and Altink 2017; x:talk 2010). In this chapter we propose that what significantly constrains discussions about the exploitation to which sex workers are subjected is the growing popularity of an abolitionist standpoint that depicts sex work as "sexual exploitation" rather than economic activity or work.

With this argument, this chapter aims to engage in the debate about labour exploitation in the sex industry by challenging abolitionist notions of sex work as "sexual exploitation", and, in turn, reflecting on the complex dynamic shaping relationships between sex workers and those third parties who organise, facilitate and profit from sex workers' work. While defining labour exploitation as labour arrangements that enable third parties to take unfair advantage of sex workers (ICRSE 2016a), we focus on some of the exploitative workplace practices occurring in the sex industry – contingent and casual labour arrangements, lack of access to labour-related protections and benefits, hazardous working conditions and severe wage manipulations. These practices have been identified in the course of community consultations with sex workers and sex worker-led organisations in Europe and Central Asia by the International Committee on the Rights of Sex Workers in Europe (ICRSE). We also argue that some of the key factors contributing to the labour exploitation experienced by sex workers in Europe and Central Asia are the criminalisation of sex workers, their workplaces, third parties and clients and the resulting exclusion of sex workers from employment legislation and protection. Finally, we explore the different ways that sex workers and their collectives across Europe and Central Asia attempt to counter labour exploitation and unfair workplace practices to which they are subjected.

Shifting the frame: from sexual exploitation to labour exploitation

The dominant neo-abolitionist perspective frames sex work as inherently oppressive, violent and exploitative (ICRSE 2016a, 2017; see also Beloso 2012; Hardy 2013; Wagenaar et al. 2017). This approach, heavily influenced by the radical current of second-wave feminism, considers sex work a paradigmatic expression of male domination and gender-based violence. According to abolitionist thinkers such as Kate Millet, Carole Pateman, Catharine MacKinnon, Andrea Dworkin and Sheila Jeffreys, the institution of "prostitution" is rooted in and contributes to the reproduction of patriarchy as it inevitably involves the appropriation and commodification of women's bodies and sexuality for the pleasure and benefit of men (Dworkin 1993; Jeffreys 1997; MacKinnon 1993; Millet 1975; Pateman 1988). US neo-abolitionist Kathleen Barry, author of the famous *Prostitution of Sexuality* and co-founder of the neo-abolitionist Coalition Against Trafficking in Women (CATW), goes even further to state that sex work constitutes the ultimate form of "sexual exploitation" by reducing women providing sexual services to "bodily parts", "sex objects" or "sexual tools" and deprives them of their personhood and individuality (Barry 1995). In this interpretative framework, prostitution is perceived as an "objective harm", a direct violation of women's rights to dignity, autonomy and bodily integrity, and as a dehumanising and objectifying abuse to which no woman could ever truly consent (Barry 1995; Dworkin 1993; Raymond 2013).

Neo-abolitionist writings often define prostitution as a form of "sexual exploitation", "sexual slavery", rape, sexual abuse or as a form of trafficking in human beings. Those terms are frequently used interchangeably and without any clear definitions or references, obscuring discussions about sex work, as well as about sex workers' experiences and realities. Campaigns led by abolitionists usually conflate or directly equate voluntary prostitution with forced prostitution, child commercial sexual exploitation, trafficking in human beings or sexual slavery (EWL 2006, 2012, 2014; Foundation Scelles 2016; Nordic Model Now et al. 2016). For example, the European Parliament's *Report on Sexual Exploitation and Prostitution And Its Impact on Gender Equality* (also known as the *Honeyball Report*) defined prostitution as "a form of slavery incompatible with human dignity and fundamental human rights (Honeyball 2014: 6), a definition adopted as a non-binding resolution by the European Parliament in 2014 (Scaramuzzino and Scaramuzzino 2015).

This conflation of sex work with sexual exploitation, slavery and violence, central to the neo-abolitionist argument, has been subjected to detailed critique by sex workers' collectives, different human rights, anti-trafficking or health organisations, as well as by researchers and academics working in the field of sex work studies (Amnesty International 2016a, 2016b; Bell 1994; Sanders, O'Neill and Pitcher 2009; Scoular 2015; Showden 2011; Weitzer 2011; Walkowitz et al. 2017). While none of these actors deny the existence of abuse, violence and trafficking in the sex industry, they point out that reducing prostitution to violence and sexual exploitation as per the neo-abolitionist perspective not only victimises sex workers as passive and deprived of agency and essentialises and universalises their experiences and realities, but makes invisible the different forms of violence and exploitation to which sex workers might be subjected by police and other state and non-state actors under criminalisation (Andrijasevic 2007; Bernstein 2010; Doezema 2010; FitzGerald 2010; Hahn and Holzscheiter 2013; NSWP, 2011; Zatz 1997).

Simultaneously, for more than four decades, sex workers and their local collectives, national organisations, regional and global networks have demanded that sex work be recognised as a legitimate form of labour and that sex workers, like many other workers, ought to be afforded labour rights in order to tackle violence and exploitation in the workplace (Berg 2014; Chateauvert 2014; Ditmore 2006, 2011; Gall 2012; Hardy 2010; Jenness 1990; Kempadoo and

Doezema 1998; Pheterson 1989, 1993; Schaffauser 2014; Stevenson and Dziuban 2018). By framing sex work as work – as a form of sexual, intimate and emotional labour and income-generating activity – sex worker collectives insist that sexual commerce should be viewed through the lens of labour and problematised primarily as belonging to the realm of economic reality. This focus on "sex work as work" rather than "sexual exploitation" or gender-based violence involves a critical analysis of the different factors shaping sex workers' working conditions, labour arrangements and the internal economies of the sex industry. It also helps to situate sex workers' labour realities in the wider field of analysis of exploitative workplace practices that take place under capitalism, and it has allowed for the development of a more nuanced understanding of labour exploitation within the sex industry (Berg 2014; EMPOWER 2016; ICRSE 2016a; NSWP 2015).

Conceptualising sex work as work and exploitation in the sex industry as labour exploitation – and not sexual exploitation – allows us to redefine the ways of problematising conditions under which sex workers perform their labour. It also conditions the understanding of a social justice perspective as one that strives not towards the eradication of prostitution, as abolitionists demand, but towards an improvement of labour conditions and a collective struggle against exploitation in sexual commerce. Most importantly, this perspective demands that we critically engage with the different labour and workplace relationships that are constitutive of the sex industry.

Although often captured in the stereotypical dual figures of the (vulnerable, battered and passive) prostitute and (unscrupulous, abusive and violent, and often racialised) pimp (NSWP 2013; Pheterson 1993), sex workers' relationships with "third parties", that is, with those who organise and profit from their work, are frequently quite complex and vary considerably across different contexts and sectors of the sex industry. Unlike the stigmatising and reductionist notion of a "pimp", the category of third parties refers to a vast array of individuals and entities who play a key role in organising and managing sexual commerce, handling transactions between sex workers and their clients, or providing other ancillary services that support the sex industry (Bruckert and Law 2013; ICRSE 2016a; NSWP 2013, 2015; Sanders 2008).[2] These different third-party relationships play a key role in determining arrangements in which sex workers perform their work, allowing workers different levels of autonomy and control over their labour conditions or workplace practices. Very often those labour-related relationships also allow third parties to impose unjust and exploitative working conditions and take unfair advantage of sex workers' labour, income, time and skills.

Labour exploitation in the sex industry: examples from Europe and Central Asia

Labour exploitation is a multifaceted phenomenon expressed in a vast array of workplace arrangements and practices that worsen sex workers' bargaining position vis-à-vis third parties and significantly limit the amount of control they can exercise over their labour, earnings and the conditions in which they perform their work. We highlight four distinct yet interrelated and mutually constitutive exploitative workplace practices reported by sex workers across Europe and Central Asia during community consultations on labour exploitation, which were conducted by the ICRSE in 2015 and 2016: job insecurity and precariousness, lack of labour-related benefits, hazardous working conditions and economic exploitation.[3]

Since sex work is not recognised as legitimate work in most European and Central Asian countries, a significant proportion of sex workers are pushed outside of the formal labour market and forced to perform their labour in the so-called grey or underground economy.

While working in criminalised and/or concealed work settings, sex workers are deprived of protections associated with legally recognised employment and become particularly dependent on third parties who organise and capitalise on their work. In order to secure their profits, sustain their businesses and avoid legal liability, third parties tend to shift potential risks on to workers by offering unfavourable employment options and maximising workers' flexibility. As a result, a significant number of sex workers in Europe perform their labour without any employment contracts, while others sign bogus contracts that conceal the type and character of the services involved (for more detailed arguments, see ICRSE 2015a, 2016a, 2017). It is also not uncommon for sex workers to register as self-employed but nevertheless engage in work arrangements that closely resemble labour under "typical" employment relationships. Unsurprisingly, these unfavourable and unclear contractual relations often translate into highly precarious, unstable and intermittent labour arrangements and uncertainty with respect to the expected workload, continuity of employment, stability of income and overall job security.

An unclear employment status and precarious working conditions (ILO 2012; Standing 2011) leave sex workers with very few, if any, means to safeguard their labour rights in the workplace (ICRSE 2016a). As reported by sex work collectives in most of the European countries where sex work is criminalised and not recognised as work, sex workers have very little access to welfare benefits and to those work-related provisions that are typically secured by labour law and/or bound up with standard employment relationships. Hence in most contexts sex workers do not receive benefits such as health and social insurance, accident sick leave, pensions, compensations, parental leave or paid holiday leave and thus have to bear the costs that follow from these excluded provisions themselves (ICRSE 2015a, 2016a, 2016b; see also TAMPEP 2009). As a consequence,

> deprived of this welfare safety net, sex workers may experience greater economic and existential vulnerability and thus resolve to perform their work while tired, sick, menstruating or pregnant when they are in precarious circumstances or being pressured by third parties.
> *(ICRSE 2016a, 10)*

Moreover, lack of access to these various labour-related benefits and protections increases sex workers' vulnerability to unfair and exploitative workplace practices, which include, but are not limited to, arbitrary termination of employment, wage manipulations or no overtime pay. Such lack of access also deprives sex workers of the means to challenge exploitation at work, including the ability to bring cases of exploitation to labour courts, unionise and/or bargain collectively.

As a result, sex workers throughout the world often perform their labour in unfavourable or hazardous work environments where they have little control over occupational health and safety risks. Sex workers have reported that some of the most widespread hazardous workplace practices include lack of access to safer sex equipment (such as condoms and lubricants) and high-quality sanitary amenities, excessive or constantly changing working hours and pressure to work while ill or provide services to an uncomfortably large number of clients during a single shift. Similarly, while aiming to protect and increase their own profits rather than sex workers' safety and well-being, third parties rarely invest in the implementation of effective anti-violence and security procedures in sex work venues. Thus, safety measures such as the employment of security staff, surveillance cameras, "ugly mugs" schemes to identify abusive clients, alert systems, panic buttons or any other tools that could be used when threats of abuse occur, are not sufficiently present in workplaces across Europe and Central Asia (for more details, see ICRSE 2016a).

An absence of the labour safeguards and the criminality of work environments are some of the key factors shaping internal economies of the sex industry (Sanders 2008; see also Brents and Sanders 2010; Sanders and Hardy 2012). These often result in the unfair organisation of work-place economies within which managers, venue owners, agents and other third parties providing sex workers with auxiliary services (Sanders 2008) secure their profit via economic exploitation by taking unjust advantage of sex workers' incomes. Many sex work venues, including brothels, massage parlours, saunas and lap-dance clubs, oblige sex workers to pay high commissions to third parties. These commissions, set arbitrarily by those who manage venues and organise sex workers' labour, are deducted from sex workers' earnings and can range from 15% to even up to 70%. Often, they are also supplemented with additional payments including entry fees, room rental fees, house fees, charges for drinks or food and tips to different third parties, including receptionists or drivers. It is not uncommon for sex work businesses to increase their earnings through internal fining systems subjecting sex workers to financial punishments for various "offences", such as being late, taking a day off, chastising or confronting rude clients or using a mobile phone while at work (ICRSE 2016a). This is not to say that exploitation does not take place outside of the managed sector. Sex workers working independently are also subjected to economic exploitation by various third parties facilitating their work, including landlords who provide spaces for sex work, drivers, agents or webmasters publishing sex work advertisements. Any of these persons might impose exorbitant charges on sex workers, thus unfairly capitalising on their dependent situation.

While one's vulnerability to various forms of exploitation and the extent of wage manipulation may vary significantly across countries, sectors of the sex industry and third party relationships, they are strongly correlated with sex workers' own vulnerabilities, legal status, economic condition and social positionality. All of these factors affect sex workers' bargaining position and their level of reliance on third parties providing auxiliary services. This is particularly evident in the case of single mothers, working-class women, LGBT* people, people who use illicit drugs, ethnic minorities, people of colour and undocumented migrants – many of whom experience discrimination or have limited access to more formal sectors of the economy (ICRSE 2015a, 2015b, 2016a, 2016b, 2016c, 2017).

Correlation between criminalisation and exploitation

As has been widely recognised and documented globally, sex workers' realities are often impacted by exploitation, violence and abuse (Deering et al. 2014; ICRSE 2015a; Sanders 2016; SWAN 2009). And while the exploitative practices to which sex workers are subjected result from asymmetrical and unjust third-party relationships, the scope and forms of labour exploitation as experienced by sex workers also vary across countries, and are shaped by the broader labour market, the local social environment and the different sectors of the industry. It is also important to acknowledge that, in many cases, the forms of exploitation are triggered – if not made possible – by laws that criminalise sex work, sex workers and their work environments.

The criminalisation of sex work often involves the criminalisation of some or all actors involved in sex work, including sex workers, clients and third parties. Forcing sex workers underground, into informal or underground economies, remote areas, isolated places, or hostile social environments, exposes them to policing, harassment, and violence, and significantly limits sex workers' access to justice. Criminalisation weakens sex workers' bargaining position in relation to other actors such as clients, the police and a variety of third parties. Therefore, laws, at least as theoretically conceived and developed to protect sex workers (or protect women from prostitution itself), are often among the key factors creating an environment susceptible of exploitation.

In particular, laws that frame all third-party relationships as criminal activity, irrespective of actual exploitation, coercion, violence or the specificity of their relation with sex worker(s), often achieve the opposite of their intended effect. Laws against procuring, managerial involvement in sex work, brothel keeping, facilitating sex work or living off the earnings of sex workers, implemented in most of the European and Central Asian countries, mean that anyone facilitating, managing or organising the work of other(s) is at risk of criminal liability. As a result, those who might not be deterred by the normative aspect of the law – and who are more prone to not respect other laws, and engage in criminal activity, including violence and coercion – are more likely to choose this line of work. By placing the management of sex work outside of the law, society increases the reliance of sex workers on third parties who might prioritise their own interests over sex workers' safety, well-being and good working conditions.[4]

It is also crucial to realise that laws addressing third-party involvement are very often used against sex workers who work in collective arrangements, sharing expenses such as rent and bills with other sex workers rather than paying managers, venue owners or other third parties. Sex workers who perform their labour together for safety and/or company are considered criminals and often prosecuted, fined, imprisoned or, in the case of migrants, deported. This, in turn, discourages sex workers from forming workers' collectives and operating in exploitation-free work environments, and pushes them into the managed sector, where unjust workplace practices are more common. This has been denounced as one of the most problematic consequences of criminalisation of third parties for and by sex workers in many countries (ICRSE 2015a, 2016a).

Another key adverse effect of the criminalisation of sex work is that it directly deprives sex workers of the protections against unfair labour arrangements afforded to other workers. Exclusion from protections offered by employment legislation denies sex workers access to labour rights and other protections granted to workers operating in the formal economy, although the increasing prevalence of precarious employment further limits protections offered to all workers. Unable to benefit from labour laws and employment codes, sex workers have very limited options to resolve workplace conflicts, report exploitative labour practices, seek redress when unfairly dismissed or experiencing discrimination at work and when subjected to harassment and abuse by their employers, agents or managers. Due to the criminalised environment in which they are forced to operate (and to other factors such as lack of documents for migrants), the sex workers' abilities to bargain collectively, organise strikes or in any other way insist on measures that could protect them from exploitation is extremely limited. This maintains and exacerbates the power asymmetry between sex workers and third parties.

Migrant sex workers' capacity to organise against exploitation in Europe is also significantly restricted due to a combination of repressive migration laws, anti-trafficking policies and laws criminalising sex work. Intensified border controls and restrictions on opportunities for legal migration increase sex workers' dependency on third parties, who often arrange their travel and facilitate employment upon arrival in the country of destination. Third parties tend to capitalise on this dependency by increasing debts, remunerations and commissions, which results in a greater workload and more exploitative and unfair workplace practices for migrant sex workers (Agustín 2007; Andrijasevic 2010; ICRSE 2016a, 2016b; Modupe-Oluwa Baye and Heumann 2014). While many states and non-governmental organisations claim to address the vulnerabilities of migrants in the sex industry by introducing anti-trafficking policies and "rehabilitation" programmes, little is being done to genuinely empower undocumented migrant sex workers through legal recognition, such as access to labour rights and other welfare benefits. Instead, police raids conducted in the name of rescuing victims of trafficking from sex industry venues often result in migrant sex workers' deportation, even when they have the required documents, as has been the case for Romanian sex workers in the UK.[5] Undocumented migrant sex workers can also be threatened with arrest and deportation when they attempt to challenge or report exploitative workplace practices but refuse to identify themselves as victims of trafficking or fail to meet the respective trafficking victim criteria in a given country (ICRSE 2016a, 2016b).

It is not uncommon for sex workers to ironically refer to the government as their "pimp". Numerous street protests include signs and placards denouncing the hypocrisy of the state that, on the one hand, condemns and represses sex work while benefiting from it on the other through taxation. In some European countries where sex work or some of its aspects are criminalised and sex work is not recognised as legitimate employment, sex workers are still required to pay taxes and their unreported income is subjected to tax readjustment. In other countries of the region, criminalisation triggers economic violence and exploitative practices by the police and other law enforcement agencies. These usually manifest themselves in fines for various (non-criminal) offences, including public indecency, vagrancy, loitering, hooliganism, or lack of proper documents. It has also been reported that in some parts of the region, law enforcement officers extort money, sexual services, bribes, and other goods from sex workers when conducting police raids, sweep-ups and "cleansing" actions (see for example SWAN 2009).

Sex workers against exploitation

Sex workers in Europe and globally have organised for years to address exploitation in the sex industry, as well as to tackle diverse factors – including the criminalisation of sex work and the social and economic marginalisation of sex workers – that make this exploitation possible (EMPOWER 2016; Gall 2006, 2012; ICRSE 2016a). While recognising that sexual labour is often performed in unjust, exploitative and hazardous conditions, sex worker rights activists in Europe have also been developing strategies for organising against exploitation by developing their own collectives and unions, educating each other about labour rights, enhancing sex workers' access to the justice system, advocating against the criminalisation of their labour and work settings, and protesting against labour reforms and increasingly precarious working environments for all workers.

Community-led collectives across Europe and Central Asia have spearheaded unionisation among sex workers in order to advocate for the recognition of sex workers' labour rights and to address exploitation. While collaboration with mainstream trade unions has not always been as successful as hoped (see Gall 2006, 2012), some organisations, such as the French sex worker-led collective STRASS (Syndicat du Travail Sexuel formed in 2009), have established themselves as autonomous sex worker labour unions, actively campaigning for fair working conditions in the sex industry, promoting collectively operated workplaces, and organising against structural factors that contribute to sex workers' vulnerabilities to exploitation. Like many other sex worker organisations in the region, STRASS also attempts to forge alliances with the labour movement and various workers' organisations in a common struggle against exploitation and the precaritisation of labour in the global capitalist economy (Stevenson and Dziuban 2018). One of the most recent STRASS projects aimed at improving sex workers' work-related safety and health consists of establishing "mutual insurance" that allows sex workers to contribute to a collective insurance that will then provide them with necessary support if they face illness or are unable to work (Personal communication with STRASS).[6]

Moreover, numerous sex worker collectives in the European region attempt to tackle exploitative practices in the sex industry by empowering sex workers operating in different venues to demand fairer and safer working conditions. Many community-led organisations provide their peers with work-related health and safety education, preventive materials, and advice. Some collectives, including Silver Rose in Russia or STAR-STAR in Macedonia, engage with managers, controllers, or owners of sex work businesses and settings to improve working conditions and implement occupational health and safety provisions for sex workers (ICRSE 2016a; NSWP 2014). Collectivo Hetaira in Spain and Hydra in Germany have, in turn, launched peer education projects to enhance sex workers' capacities to negotiate and bargain with agents and employers (Autres Regards 2012). The sex worker organisation PROUD in the Netherlands provides community members with information on their labour rights, tax obligations and workers' benefits, such as paid sick leave. Finally, some community-led projects, including the Italian Committee for the Civil Rights of Prostitutes, combat forced labour and exploitation in the sex industry by providing support services to persons who have been trafficked into the sex industry (ICRSE 2015a, 2016a).

Numerous sex worker-led collectives across Europe attempt to challenge exploitation in the industry by advocating for the recognition of sex work as labour and granting sex workers with the same labour rights and protections as other workers operating in the formal economy. In France, Italy, Kazakhstan, Northern Ireland, Norway, Ukraine and many other European countries, community organisations participate in demonstrations on International Workers Day, develop informational campaigns, engage in political lobbying at national and regional levels and provide state officials, medical personnel or representatives of law enforcement agencies with sensitising trainings on sex workers' occupational needs and concerns. Some sex workers' organisations also engage in transnational consultations on labour-related issues led by international governing bodies, such as the International Labour Organisation, to ensure that sex workers' perspectives and sex worker-specific labour concerns are included in diverse resolutions and reports, most recently on what defines "violence at work".[7] Co-constructing normative discourses on what constitutes work and what constitutes violence therefore takes place simultaneously at the grassroots level, at the level of pan-regional and global institutions, in street protests and strikes and in the development of international resolutions.

Many sex workers' collectives in the region recognise that sex workers' vulnerabilities to exploitation and unfair treatment at work are closely linked with severe barriers they must face when attempting to assert their rights in the justice system. This creates a climate of impunity for exploitative third parties and others, including the police, who profit from the situation. As a consequence, many sex worker-led organisations in the region provide legal support and take up actions to facilitate sex workers' access to justice when exploitation occurs. Kirmizi Semsiye (Red Umbrella Sexual Health and Human Rights Association) in Turkey, Sex Work Polska in Poland or STRASS in France, for instance, cooperate closely with trusted and sensitised lawyers who help sex workers bring exploitation-related cases to court. Some collectives, like Hydra in Berlin, Germany, have established emergency legal aid funds for which sex workers can apply when they need to hire a lawyer or cover the costs of a trial. Others, such as Silver Rose in Russia (NSWP 2014), enhance sex workers' legal literacy through "Know your rights" workshops, and publish fact sheets, usually in numerous languages, detailing sex work- and labour-related laws. The English Collective of Prostitutes (ECP) in the UK[8] and SCOT-PEP in Scotland[9] have developed "bust cards" that inform sex workers about how to protect themselves when faced with police raids or charges, such as "brothel keeping" if they work together for safety.

Finally, it is worth noting that while the slogan "sex work is work" has become prominent in the sex workers' rights movement, few sex workers and their organisations argue that "sex work is like any other job". In fact, many recognise that sex work often results from social marginalisation, exclusion from the labour market, and a lack of other employment options. Therefore, their advocacy for decriminalisation and self-organisation against exploitation is combined with political demands for social and economic changes that would enable those who do not want to work in the sex industry to leave it. Numerous sex worker organisations, such as Sex Workers

Open University (now Sex Workers Advocacy and Resistance Movement) or ECP in the UK, STRASS in France, or ICRSE, address sex workers' precarity and vulnerability by exposing the structural factors that economically disempower people and leave them with few job opportunities outside of the sex industry (see, for example, SWOU 2014). These organisations actively engage in debates about how to effectively tackle the rising economic inequality created by austerity measures and to safeguard people with more viable employment options so as to give them the power to resist against exploitative working conditions once they enter the sex industry. A minimum wage, universal basic income, universal childcare, secure housing and the inclusion of migrant and trans workers into the formal labour market are but a few of the numerous demands that have been put forward by sex worker collectives in the region. While sex worker rights activists are often depicted by neo-abolitionists as the "privileged few who chose their work" or as "happy hookers", it is worth reasserting that a large number of sex workers' collectives are united under banners such as "abolish poverty not prostitution" and key principles of their activism involve struggle against the economic and gender inequalities, racism and xenophobia, and repressive migration controls that limit people's opportunities in the labour market (ICRSE 2015a, 2015b, 2016a, 2016b, 2016c; Schaffauser 2014; Stevenson and Dziuban 2018).

Conclusions

The problem of exploitation experienced by sex workers, as well as the need to develop effective strategies to challenge it, are serious concerns for those who consider sex work as work as much as they are for neo-abolitionists and anti-prostitution feminists. The radical differences between how the sex industry's opponents and sex workers frame the sex industry – as a form of exploitation or a form of labour – translate into equally radical disagreement over the solutions to exploitation. Constructing prostitution as a form of sexual exploitation (or "sexual slavery"), the neo-abolitionists regard the elimination of prostitution itself as the only way to combat the exploitation experienced by sex workers. Those who acknowledge that sex work is a form of labour – including the vast majority of sex-worker led organisations and ourselves – recognise, in turn, that although exploitation occurs in the sex industry (as it does in other labour markets), it is not inherent to sex work. Yet exploitative workplace practices and unfair work arrangements faced by sex workers do not derive from some inner qualities of sexual labour, but rather result from unjust and asymmetrical labour and employment relations under which sex workers are forced to operate. Only by problematising these practices and arrangements, and doing so through the framework of labour rights and labour exploitation – by building parallels between sex work and other forms of work (Hardy 2013, 53) – can we gain a better understanding of exploitation in sexual commerce and, thus, guard sex workers against work in degrading and exploitative conditions.

This understanding has to be based also on a more rigorous examination of the impact of oppressive legal frameworks on sex workers' rights, safety and health (see, for example, Deering et al. 2014; Levy 2015; Sanders 2016; Shannon et al. 2015). Such examination has recently inspired increased scholarly engagement with the harms of criminalisation, one that takes into account sex workers' calls for decriminalisation and has been endorsed by global health and human rights organisations, such as the United Nations Joint Programme on HIV (UNAIDS), the World Health Organisation (WHO), Human Rights Watch (HRW) and Amnesty International (AI). What is required as well, however, is a more nuanced investigation of the ways in which various legal frameworks, policies and regulations governing sex work translate into unfair and exploitative conditions of work for people selling sexual services.

When criminalised and denied legal recognition as workers, sex workers are left with little means to challenge power imbalances at work, to defend themselves against exploitative practices, seek redress, self-organise and bargain collectively for better working conditions. It is for this reason that research that examines sex workers' labour conditions and policies shaping sex workers' labour realities needs to be developed and evaluated with the direct involvement of sex workers and sex worker communities.

Notes

1 Some of the few exceptions are: Bruckert and Law (2013), Cruz (2013), Modupe-Oluwa Baye and Heuman (2014), Sanders (2008), Sanders and Hardy (2012) and x:talk (2010).
2 These may include, but are not limited to, an online escort agency manager in London, a madam owning a massage parlour in rural Portugal, an older transgender 'tutor' in Albania, a landlord renting premises to a sex worker in Malmo, Sweden, a telephonist in one of the Warsaw brothels in Poland, a bouncer in a gay sauna in Rome or a webmaster managing a sex-ad website in France.
3 In the course of these consultations, made possible due to the funding offered by the Open Society Foundation and Red Umbrella Fund, numerous representatives of sex worker-led organisations across the European and Central Asian region were invited to share their expertise on the issue of exploitation through in-depth interviews (conducted in person or via Skype). Additionally, ICRSE staff members have analysed respective resources (including statements, reports and leaflets) developed by their member organisations. Results of these consultations were discussed more extensively in ICRSE's community report *Exploitation: Unfair Labour Arrangements and Precarious Working Conditions in the Sex Industry* (2016a).
4 Similarly, it can be argued that one of the effects of criminalising clients is that a large number of 'law abiding citizens', i.e. 'good clients', stopped using sex workers' services. As a result, many sex workers are now forced to accept more violent and/or abusive clients who are not deterred by the law. This makes sex workers more dependent on the 'bad clients' from whom the law was designed to protect them.
5 www.theguardian.com/uk-news/2016/may/01/romanian-sex-workers-challenge-uk-immigration-policy.
6 http://strass-syndicat.org/mutuelle-sante-et-prevoyance-pour-les-travailleurses-du-sexe-une-premiere-en-france.
7 See, for example, www.scot-pep.org.uk/news/scot-peps-response-ilo-consultation-violence-and-harassment-workplace.
8 http://prostitutescollective.net/know-your-rights.
9 www.scot-pep.org.uk/sex-workers-toolkit/law.

References

Agustín, Laura. 2007. *Sex at the Margins: Migration, Labour Markets and the Rescue Industry*. London: Zed Books.
Amnesty International. 2016a. *Criminalization of Sex Work in Norway Executive Summary: The Human Cost of "Crushing" the Market*. Available at: www.amnesty.org/download/Documents/EUR3641302016ENGLISH.PDF [Accessed on 7 January 2018].
Amnesty International. 2016b. *Decision on State Obligations to Respect, Protect, and Fulfil the Human Rights of Sex Worker: The International Council Decision*. Available at: www.amnesty.org/en/documents/pol30/4062/2016/en [Accessed on 7 January 2018].
Andrijasevic, Rutvica. 2007. Beautiful Dead Bodies: Gender, Migration and Representation. *Feminist Review* 86: 24–44.
Andrijasevic, Rutvica. 2010. *Migration, Agency and Citizenship in Sex Trafficking*. Basingstoke: Palgrave Macmillan.
Autres Regards. 2012. *Capacity Building and Awareness Raising: A European Guide with Strategies for the Empowerment of Sex Workers*. INDOORS Project. Available at: http://tampep.eu/documents/capacity_building&awareness_raising-Indoors_2.pdf [Accessed on 7 January 2018].
Barry, Kathleen. 1995. *The Prostitution of Sexuality*. New York: New York University Press.
Bell, Shannon. 1994. *Reading, Writing, and Rewriting the Prostitute Body*. Bloomington, IN: Indiana University Press.

Beloso, Brooke M. 2012. Sex, Work, and the Feminist Erasure of Class. *Signs: Journal of Women in Culture and Society* 38(1): 47–70.

Berg, Heather. 2014. Working for Love, Loving for Work: Discourses of Labor in Feminist Sex Work Activism. *Feminist Studies* 40(3): 693–721.

Bernstein, Elizabeth. 2010. Militarized Humanitarianism Meets Carceral Feminism: The Politics of Sex, Rights, and Freedom in Contemporary Antitrafficking Campaigns. *Signs: Journal of Women in Culture and Society* 36(1): 45–72.

Brents, Barbara and Sanders, Teela. 2010. Mainstreaming the Sex Industry: Economic Inclusion and Social Ambivalence. *Journal of Law and Society* 37(1): 40–60.

Bruckert, Chris and Law, Tuulia. 2013. *Beyond Pimps, Procurers and Parasites: Mapping Third Parties in the Incall/Outcall Sex Industry*. Ottawa: SSHRC. Available at: www.nswp.org/sites/nswp.org/files/ManagementResearch%20%284%29.pdf [Accessed on 7 January 2018].

Chateauvert, Melinda. 2014. *Sex Workers Unite: A History of the Movement from Stonewall to SlutWalk*. Boston, MA: Beacon Press.

Cruz, Katy. 2013. Unmanageable Work, (Un)liveable Lives: The UK Sex Industry, Labour Rights and the Welfare State. *Social and Legal Studies* 22(4): 465–488.

Deering, K., Amin, A., Shoveller, J., Nesbitt, A., Garcia-Morena, C., Duff, P., Aregento, E. and Shannon, K. 2014. A Systematic Review of the Correlates of Violence Against Sex Workers. *American Journal of Public Health* 104(5): 42–54

Ditmore, Melissa. 2006. *Encyclopedia of Prostitution and Sex Work*. Santa Barbara, CA: Greenwood.

Ditmore, Melissa. 2011. *Prostitution and Sex Work*. Santa Barbara, CA: Greenwood.

Doezema, Jo. 2010. *Sex Slaves and Discourse Masters: The Construction of Trafficking*. New York: Zed Books

Dworkin, Andrea. 1993. Prostitution and Male Supremacy. *Michigan Journal of Gender and Law* 1(1): 1–12.

EMPOWER. 2016. *Moving Towards Decent Work: Sex Worker Community Research on Decent and Exploitation in Thailand*. Available at: www.nswp.org/sites/nswp.org/files/Moving%20Toward%20Decent%20Work%2C%20EMPOWER%20-%20April%202016.pdf [Accessed on 7 January 2018].

EWL. 2006. *The Links Between Prostitution and Sex Trafficking: A Briefing Handbook*. Available on: www.catwinternational.org/Content/Images/Article/175/attachment.pdf [Accessed on 7 January 2018].

EWL. 2012. *Brussels' Call*. Available at: www.womenlobby.org/IMG/pdf/brussels_call_en_with_logos_4_dec_2012.pdf?2135/c7749b54d09d66dc5f18fc639bfb6e908b6dc374 [Accessed on 7 January 2018].

EWL. 2014. *18 Myths on Prostitution*. Available at: www.womenlobby.org/IMG/pdf/prostitution_myths_final_ewl.pdf?3513/adf2a4e692356c85e7aa8b35cfd34e7f1be9aa7e [Accessed on 7 January 2018].

FitzGerald, Shannon A. 2010. Biopolitics and the Regulation of Vulnerability: The Case of the Female Trafficked Migrant. *International Journal of Law in Context* 6(3): 277–294.

Foundation Scelles. 2016. *Prostitution: Exploitation, Persecution, Repression*. Available at: www.fondationscelles.org/pdf/RM4/1_Book_Prostitution_Exploitation_Persecution_Repression_Fondation_Scelles_ENG.pdf [Accessed on 7 January 2018].

Gall, Gregor. 2006. *Sex Worker Union Organizing: An International Study*. London: Palgrave Macmillan.

Gall, Gregor. 2012. *An Agency of Their Own: Sex Worker Union Organizing*. Winchester: Zero Books.

Hahn, Kristina and Holzscheiter, Anna. 2013. The Ambivalence of Advocacy: Representation and Contestation in Global NGO Advocacy for Child Workers and Sex Workers. *Global Society* 27(4): 497–520.

Hardy, Kate. 2010. Incorporating Sex Workers into the Argentine Labour Movement. *International Labor and Working-Class History* 77(1): 89–108.

Hardy, Kate. 2013. Equal to Any Other, But Not the Same as Any Other: The Politics of Sexual Labour, the Body and Intercorporeality. In C. Walkowitz, R.L. Cohen, T. Sanders and K. Hardy, eds, *Body/Sex/Work: Intimate, Embodied and Sexualized Labour*. London: Palgrave Macmillan, pp. 43–58.

Honeyball, Mary. 2014. *Report on Sexual Exploitation and Prostitution and Its Impact on Gender Equality* (2013/2103(INI)). Committee on Women's Rights and Gender Equality, European Parliament. Available at: www.europarl.europa.eu/sides/getDoc.do?pubRef=-//EP//NONSGML+REPORT+A7-2014-0071+0+DOC+PDF+V0//EN [Accessed on 7 January 2018].

ICRSE. 2015a. *Structural Violence: Social and Institutional Oppression Experienced by Sex Workers in Europe*. Available at: www.sexworkeurope.org/sites/default/files/userfiles/files/ICRSE%20CR%20StrctrlViolence-final.pdf [Accessed on 7 January 2018].

ICRSE. 2015b. *Underserved. Overpoliced. Invisibilised. LGBT Sex Workers Do Matter*. Available at: www.sexworkeurope.org/sites/default/files/resource-pdfs/icrse_briefing_paper_october2015.pdf [Accessed on 7 January 2018].

ICRSE. 2016a. *Exploitation: Unfair Labour Arrangements and Precarious Working Conditions in the Sex Industry*. Available at: www.sexworkeurope.org/sites/default/files/userfiles/files/ICRSE_Exploitation%20 Report_April2016_04_final.pdf [Accessed on 7 January 2018].

ICRSE. 2016b. *Surveilled. Exploited. Deported. Rights Violations Against Migrant Sex Workers in Europe and Central Asia*. Available at: www.sexworkeurope.org/sites/default/files/resource-pdfs/icrse_briefing_ paper_migrants_rights_november2016.pdf [Accessed on 7 January 2018].

ICRSE. 2016c. *Feminism Needs Sex Workers, Sex Workers Need Feminism: Towards a Sex Worker Inclusive Women's Rights Movement*. Available at: www.sexworkeurope.org/sites/default/files/userfiles/files/ ICRSE_Briefingpaper_woman%27s right_March2016__05.pdf [Accessed on 7 January 2018].

ICRSE. 2017. *Understanding Sex Work As Work: A Brief Guide for Labour Rights Activists*. Available at: www. sexworkeurope.org/sites/default/files/userfiles/files/ICRSE_labour%20campaigning_April2017_ PRINT.pdf [Accessed on 7 January 2018].

ILO. 2012. *From Precarious Work to Decent Work: Outcome Document to the Workers' Symposium on Policies and Regulations to combat Precarious Employment*. ILO: Geneva. Available at: www.ilo.org/wcmsp5/groups/ public/---ed_dialogue/---actrav/documents/meetingdocument/wcms_179787.pdf [Accessed on 7 January 2018].

Jeffreys, Sheila. 1997. *The Idea of Prostitution*. Melbourne: Spinifex Press.

Jenness, Valerie. 1990. From Sex as Sin to Sex as Work: COYOTE and the Reorganization of Prostitution as a Social Problem. *Social Problems* 37(3): 403–420.

Kempadoo, Kemala and Doezema, Jo, eds. 1998. *Global Sex Workers: Rights, Resistance, and Redefinition*. New York: Routledge.

Levy, Jay. 2015. *Criminalising the Purchase of Sex: Lessons from Sweden*. London: Routledge.

MacKinnon, Catharine. 1993. Prostitution and Civil Rights. *Michigan Journal of Gender & Law* 1(1): 13–31.

Millet, Kate. 1975. *The Prostitution Papers*. St. Albans: Paladin.

Modupe-Oluwa Baye, Enze and Heumann, Silke. 2014. Migration, Sex Work and Exploitative Labor Conditions: Experiences of Nigerian Women in the Sex Industry in Turin, Italy, and Counter-Trafficking Measures. *Gender, Technology and Development* 18(1): 77–105.

Nordic Model Now et al. 2016. *Joint Submission to the UN Women consultation on "sex work, the sex trade and prostitution"*. Available at: https://nordicmodelnow.org/2016/10/16/submission-to-the-un-women-consultation-on-sex-work-the-sex-trade-and-prostitution/ [Accessed on 7 January 2018].

NSWP. 2011. *Sex Work Is Not Trafficking*. Available at: www.nswp.org/sites/nswp.org/files/SW%20is%20 Not%20Trafficking.pdf [Accessed on 7 January 2018].

NSWP. 2013. *If My Boss Is Criminalised, I Can't Keep Condoms with Me at Work: Briefing Paper*. Available at: www.nswp.org/sites/nswp.org/files/thirdparties3_0.pdf [Accessed on 7 January 2018].

NSWP. 2014. *Good Practices in Sex Worker-Led HIV Programming: Europe Regional Report*. Available at: www.nswp.org/sites/nswp.org/files/Regional%20Europe.pdf [Accessed on 7 January 2018].

NSWP. 2015. "Sex Work Is Work". *Research for Sex Work* 14. Available at: www.nswp.org/sites/nswp. org/files/R4SW%202015_issue14_PDFV_0.pdf [Accessed on 7 January 2018].

Pateman, Carole. 1988. *Sexual Contract*. Cambridge, MA: Polity Press.

Pheterson, Gail. 1993. The Whore Stigma: Female Dishonor and Male Unworthiness. *Social Text* 37: 39–94.

Pheterson, Gail. 1989. *A Vindication of the Rights of Whores*. Seattle: Seal Press.

Piketty, Thomas. 2014. *Capital in the Twenty-First Century*. Cambridge, MA: Belknap Press of Harvard University.

Raymond, Janice G. 2013. *Not a Choice, Not A Job: Exposing the Myths About Prostitution and the Global Sex Trade*. Dulles: Potomac Books.

Sanders, Teela. 2008. Selling Sex in the Shadow Economy. *International Journal of Social Economics* 35(10): 704–716.

Sanders, Teela. 2016. Inevitably Violent? Dynamics of Space, Governance, and Stigma in Understanding Violence against Sex Workers. In Austin Sarat, ed., *Problematizing Prostitution: Critical Research and Scholarship*, Special Issue of *Studies in Law, Politics and Society*, 71: 93–114.

Sanders, Teela and Hardy, Kate. 2012. Devalued, Deskilled and Diversified: Explaining the Proliferation of the Strip Industry in the UK. *British Journal of Sociology* 63(3): 513–531.

Sanders Teela, O'Neill, Maggie and Pitcher, Jane. 2009. *Prostitution: Sex Work, Policy and Politics*. London: Sage.

Scaramuzzino, Roberto and Scaramuzzino, Gabriella. 2015. Sex Workers' Rights Movement and the EU: Challenging the New European Prostitution Policy Model. In Hakan Johansson and Sara Kalm, eds,

EU Civil Society: Patterns of Cooperation, Competition and Conflict. Palgrave Studies in European Political Sociology. London: Palgrave Macmillan, pp. 137–154.

Schaffauser, Thierry. 2014. *Les luttes des Putes*. Paris: La fabrique.

Shannon, K., Strathdee, S.A., Goldenberg, S.M., Duff, P., Mwangi, P., Rusakova, M. Reza-Paul, S., Lau, J., Deering, K., Pickles, M.R. and Bolly, M.C. 2015. Global epidemiology of HIV Among Female Sex Workers: Influence of Structural Determinants. *Lancet* 385(9962): 55–71.

Scoular, Jane. 2015. *The Subject of Prostitution: Sex Work, Law and Social Theory*. London: Routledge.

Showden, Clarisa. 2011. *Choices Women Make: Agency in Domestic Violence, Assisted Reproduction, and Sex Work*. Minneapolis, MN: University of Minnesota Press.

Stevenson, Luca and Dziuban, Agata. 2018. Silent No More: Self-Determination and Organisation of Sex Workers in Europe. In Synnove Jahnsen and Hendrik Wagenaar, eds, *Assessing Prostitution Policies in Europe*. London: Routledge, pp. 376–392.

Standing, Guy. 2011. *The Precariat: The New Dangerous Class*. London: Bloomsbury.

SWAN. 2009. *Arrest the Violence: Human Rights Violations Against Sex Workers in 11 Countries in Central and Eastern Europe and Central Asia*. Available at: www.opensocietyfoundations.org/sites/default/files/arrest-violence-20091217.pdf [Accessed on 7 January 2018].

SWOU. 2014. *SWOU Statement on Poverty, Sex Work and the Swedish Model: "Poverty Is Objectifying, Demanding and Coercive"*. Available at: www.swarmcollective.org/blog/statement-on-poverty-sex-work-and-the-swedish-model-poverty-is-objectifying-demeaning-and-coercive1 [Accessed on 7 January 2018].

TAMPEP. 2009. *Sex Work, Migration, Health: A Report on the Intersection of Legislation and Policies Regarding Sex Work, Migration and Health in Europe*. Available at: http://tampep.eu/documents/Sexworkmigrationhealth_final.pdf [Accessed on 7 January 2018].

Wagenaar, Hendrik, Amesberger, Helga and Altink, Sietske. 2017. *Designing Prostitution Policy: Intention and Reality in Regulating the Sex Trade*. Chicago: University of Chicago Press.

Weeks, Kathy. 2011. *The Problem with Work: Feminism, Marxism, Antiwork Politics, and Postwork Imaginaries*. Durham, NC: Duke University Press.

Weitzer, Ronald. 2011. *Legalizing Prostitution: From Illicit Vice to Lawful Business*. New York: New York University Press.

Walkowitz, Carol, Cohen, Rachel. L., Sanders, Teela and Hardy, Kate, eds. 2017. *Body/Sex/Work: Intimate, Embodied and Sexualized Labour*. London: Palgrave Macmillan.

x:talk. 2010. *Human Rights, Sex Work and the Challenge of Trafficking*. Available at: www.xtalkproject.net/wp-content/uploads/2010/12/reportfinal1.pdf [Accessed on 7 January 2018].

Zatz, Noah. 1997. Sex Work/Sex Act: Law, Labour, and Desire in Constructions of Prostitution, *Signs: Journal of Women in Culture and Society* 22(2): 277–307.

40

Protection through repression?

Theorising everyday police interactions with sex workers in Geneva

Mira Fey

Introduction

> *Nous, on est là pour que les prostituées puissent travailler dans de bonnes conditions.* [We are there so that prostitutes can work in good conditions.]
>
> *(Interview with Geneva vice squad, 24 October 2016)*

> *Il faut bien comprendre que chaque fois qu'on fait des lois, des règlements, dans cette optique de protéger les personnes qui exercent le métier de travailleuse du sexe, c'est toujours pour contrôler, c'est toujours dans un esprit d'encadrement, donc répressif. Mais, au fond du cœur de chacun d'entre eux, ils [les policiers] veulent les [les travailleuses du sexe] protéger quand même.* [One must understand that every time we make laws and rules, always to protect people who exercise sex work, this is always to control, always in a spirit of supervision, therefore repressive. Still, at the bottom of each [police officer's] heart, they still want to protect [sex workers].
>
> *(Interview with Aspasie, a sex worker support organisation, 25 April 2017)*

Third parties organising and managing transactional sexual exchanges take on different forms, among other factors depending on the legal framework of the respective country. These frameworks specify how prostitution[1] is regulated by state institutions such as the police (the third party under consideration here) and which role police officers assume vis-à-vis sex workers – punitive, protective, or somewhere in between as I argue for the case of Geneva, Switzerland. In this chapter, I first briefly discuss the existing literature on policing prostitution and its short-comings before turning to my analysis of the implementation of the Geneva prostitution law through everyday interactions between police and sex workers. While the law and its directives appear to clearly and unambiguously specify rights and responsibilities of sex workers and determine their protection as the main goal of policing prostitution, practices employed by police officers often focus largely on controlling measures through which officers hope to also ensure a safe working environment for sex workers. Other parties such as influential stakeholders in the city can affect regulations more easily than sex worker support organisations, which effectively leads to a situation where police officers have to narrowly navigate between enforcing the interests of public morality on the one hand and ensuring freedom and protection of sex workers on the other, at the expense of those migrant street sex workers most at risk of violence and exploitation. This raises the general questions of who regulates those who police and regulate sex workers, and whose interests are prioritised when policing prostitution. I return to these questions in the conclusion after discussing the findings of my research in Geneva, Switzerland within the context of regulated prostitution more broadly.

Policing prostitution

Generally, most research on sex work is carried out in countries where prostitution is prohibited as criminalization is the most prevalent worldwide,[2] thereby determining what we know about the influence of legal frameworks on people in prostitution and their relation to state institutions such as the police (Weitzer 2014). However, trust in police is notoriously low among sex workers operating in such prohibitionist frameworks because they are directly targeted, at risk of being arrested, and potentially abused by police officers. Consequently, sex workers are often more than reluctant to report violence and harassment (Armstrong 2017a). Therefore, when looking at police as third parties in prostitution, most of the research looking at police officers focuses on how policing negatively affects sex workers (Benson and Matthews 1995; Larsen 1996; Penfold et al. 2004; Matthews 2005; Hubbard 2006; Kinnell 2013). Researchers show how individual police officers might informally mitigate risks of violence, especially for street sex workers, without receiving formal orders to do so and without linkage to a specific legal framework (Campbell 2014; McKeganey and Barnard 1996, 2006; Sanders 2001, 2004a, 2004b). Another focus has been the role police take on when facing competing demands of community members of red-light districts and sex workers (Hubbard 1998; Kingston 2013; O'Neill and Pitcher 2010; Pitcher 2006; Sagar 2004). Most of this research uses interviews with sex workers as their main source. Consequently, police practices are not studied through observations, but rather through their own statements and sex workers' experiences.

Within regulatory frameworks where police could potentially take on a more positive role towards sex workers because these regulations include specified rights and responsibilities for people in prostitution, police officers faced resistance to their changed involvement in prostitution from other third parties such as pimps or brothel owners, as Wagenaar (2006) describes for the case of the Netherlands. Moreover, regular inspections of brothels and enforced taxation as part of the new regulations also changed the demographics towards fewer Dutch and more immigrant sex workers (Daalder 2007). In the German context, police officers were slow to adapt their behaviour to the legal change in 2001. Since policing is organised by municipality, there is great divergence between police practices in different parts of Germany, and sex workers cannot rely on the same treatment by different officers in different cities (Pates 2012). Indeed, researchers found through observations of bureaucrats at work that treatment of sex workers is more subject to individual characteristics of the police officer or case worker than determined by the law and the directives extracted from it (Leser et al. 2017; Vorheyer 2014). Ethnographic research on policing red-light districts in Germany highlights the importance of everyday patrols for the officers to gather an understanding of the situation for sex workers to gain trust yet does not describe how the cultivation of such trust affects sex workers' risks (Howe 2017). Still, most of this research carried out within criminalised regulatory frameworks focuses on difficulties for third parties such as the police in penetrating the intricacies of the sex industry after legal change, but does not analyse the interactions between police and sex workers themselves. Armstrong's in-depth study of the effects of decriminalisation in New Zealand is an exemplary exception here since she concentrates specifically on these interactions after legal change. Still, her findings are mostly applicable to this unique legal setting and also rely heavily on interviews with sex workers instead of making use of participant observation of police practices (Armstrong 2010, 2017a).

Generally, there is very little research on prostitution in Switzerland. The only studies to date connected with policing red-light districts have been carried out by Klauser (2007) who examined the effect of CCTV surveillance on the perception of (in-) security. There are some studies on migration patterns within the sex industry more largely (Thievent 2010) and more specifically on the situation of migrant sex workers in Geneva (Glardon 2004), but these have been carried out before the adoption of the Geneva prostitution law in 2009 and do not look at the effects of the regulatory framework on interactions between police officers and sex workers.

The research

Most existing research on police as third parties organising and managing transactional sexual exchanges still focuses on sex workers as the main actors or concentrates on police officers through the use of interviews rather than participant observation. The interactions between the two remain understudied, especially within a regulatory framework that arguably has the greatest potential for both *protective* and *controlling* aspects of everyday police practices towards sex workers. This regulatory setting is the focus of my research on the Geneva red-light district. During the course of 22 months, I used ethnographic methods such as direct and participant observation and semi-structured and informal interviews with police officers, social workers, and sex workers to understand how the Geneva prostitution law is translated into everyday police practices, and how these practices affect sex workers. Specifically, I focus on how police officers understand their role, how they perform this understanding in practice, and which effects this has for sex workers. Given that *protection* is one of the main goals of the law, which tools do police officers have to effectively implement protection, and ultimately, who is protected from what?

The case of Geneva

In late 2009, Geneva, the second-largest Swiss city and one of its 26 cantons, adopted LProst, the most comprehensive prostitution law within Switzerland because it includes mandatory registration for sex workers, specified regulations for brothels, and a specialised prostitution unit within the Judiciary Police responsible for enforcing the implementation. As a federal state and a direct democracy, it regulates health care, welfare, law enforcement, public education, and taxation separately by cantons, and citizens have greater influence on legislation through popular initiatives (Kriesi and Trechsel 2008). The federal state implemented a very general law on prostitution in 1986 that simply states that within Switzerland, prostitution is legal, but contradicts "good manners". Each canton has the authority to adopt further legislation to regulate prostitution, but no canton can prohibit it. Thus, some cantons passed specific regulations, such as Geneva, Zürich, and Vaud, while others such as Luzern decided through specific rulings not to do so. Geneva and Zürich also established specific vice squads in the Judiciary Police tasked with implementing regulations pertaining to prostitution and issues potentially disturbing public order such as drug dealing or begging.[3]

Findings

LProst: directives of the Geneva prostitution law

In order to understand how the Geneva regulatory framework affects interactions between police and sex workers and which different factors influence which aspects of the law are prioritised over others, I first offer an interpretation of the legal text. The Geneva prostitution law, adopted in December 2009, states three main goals (my translation, my interpretation in italics): (1) guaranteeing that the people who prostitute themselves are not victims of trafficking, threats, violence, pressure, or exploitation, or that no one is benefiting from their distress or dependence (*protection of sex workers*); (2) assuring that means for prevention and promotion of health and professional reorientation are in place (*protection of public health and morals*); (3) regulating places, hours, and modalities of prostitution (*control of sex workers, protection of public space*; État de Genève, art. 1, 2009). Within the law, prostitution is defined as "the activity of a person who will deliver sexual acts to a specific or unspecific number of clients for a fee"; sexual assistants for people with disability are excluded from the law (État de Genève, art. 2, 2009). It is important to note that this is formulated gender neutrally and includes sex workers and clients of any gender.

The remainder of the law first describes the responsibilities of sex workers: in order to be able to work, they have to be at least 18 years old, possess valid residence and working permits, and register with the prostitution unit, specifically established for upholding the law (État de Genève, art. 4, 2009). The data to be collected by the prostitution unit is then specified in detail (État de Genève, art. 4a, 2009). The following articles describe how different types of prostitution (public/street, brothel, escorts) are regulated, which controls by the unit they are subjected to, and which restrictions apply (État de Genève, art. 6–21, 2009). Additionally, collaboration with relevant NGOs are mentioned, focusing on health, social aspects, and professional reorientation (État de Genève, art. 22–24, 2009). The final articles of the law state that amendments might be added at any point and lay out the specifications of the application of the law (État de Genève, art. 25–29, 2009).

The legal text itself points to a shortcoming: While the first goal stresses the outcome of protection from violence and exploitation, the rest of the regulations do not mention how this should be achieved other than through repressive measures such as registration and control of permits and establishments. The articles on cooperation with NGOs are very short in comparison to the directives on registration and control. Further, they do not detail what such cooperation could look like or if this could be connected to improved protection of people in prostitution. This shortcoming of stressing protection as the goal, but lacking specific directives for its implementation other than through controlling measures, can be found in regulatory texts in several other countries as well, for example in the recent update of the German prostitution law that now also includes mandatory registration. By virtue of its title alone (*Prostituiertenschutzgesetz*, "prostitution protection law"), it claims protection for sex workers, but the directives and regulations largely specify more mechanisms of control for sex workers and additional rules brothel owners need to follow (Dalka 2017). A focus on control in order to protect was also one of the main criticisms members of the sex worker support organisation *Aspasie* stressed in several interviews and informal talks I had with them. Specifically, they argue that aspects of the Geneva law led to decreased safety of sex workers compared to the situation before the legal change in 2009.

According to the regulations, an apartment used for prostitution is defined as a *brothel* as soon as more than one sex worker uses it. This means that this apartment then has to be registered as entertainment facility under commercial law, which makes it effectively impossible for two sex workers to share an apartment for work. A social worker employed with *Aspasie* since the 1990s told me in an interview that this aspect led to greater insecurity and financial struggles for sex workers as they now either work alone in their apartments without being able to look out for each other, or have to rent over-priced rooms in brothels, thereby risking financial exploitation. She stressed that when the law was drafted and *Aspasie* consulted, she and other employees had already advised against this clause for above-mentioned reasons, but were ignored. Since the adoption of the law, *Aspasie* has been unsuccessfully advocating for reversing this regulation. Police claim that the clause prevents financial exploitation of one sex worker by another. However, according to *Aspasie* and sex workers I talked with, this is a rare occurrence in comparison to the general applicability of extortionist prices brothel owners charge sex workers for the rooms they rent there (generally around 100 CHF/$ per day according to police, sex workers, *Aspasie*, and the prices I have seen in brothels). This example shows that certain directives have directly decreased security for independent sex workers by limiting their possibilities to protect each other without a third party present. Instead, they now have to directly rely on police for protection from violence in case they decide to work alone and are assaulted at work. In case they work in brothels, they have to rely on police for protection from financial exploitation as officers are ordered to check rental receipts sex workers should receive. This should nominally help prevent extortion by brothel owners, but prices are standardised and non-negotiable around Geneva, so sex workers in brothels have no option but to accept them. Here, we see already that in policing prostitution, control mechanisms are used to provide protection instead of achieving this through including protective directives in the law or allowing sex workers to protect each other.

Moreover, the experience about the law-making process described by *Aspasie* also uncovers limitations of Swiss democracy; while they were included as advisers, their reservations were ignored.[4] Instead, influential stakeholders, here wealthy residents living next to the street-walking area, have been more successful in amending LProst: located at a main street close to the old town of Geneva, street sex workers stood night after night next to some of the most expensive apartments in the city centre. Even though there are very few residents in these mansion-like houses, these are highly influential citizens of Geneva who collected around 20 signatures to create a no-tolerance zone next to their houses and restricted the street-walking area to a small part of the main street. On the surface, used condoms and syringes found on a playground and next to a church nearby in the mornings were used as arguments for this restriction. The residents were successful in 2014 when Pierre Maudet, Justice Minister of the canton of Geneva, approved the amendment of the law (Roselli 2016). Since then, street sex workers outside the small authorised part of the Boulevard Helvéthique first receive a warning and then a fine that increases with repeated offence. While Ivan Caputo, head of the prostitution unit, did not explicitly confirm that wealth and influence of those residents was a strong reason for the success of their demands leading to the amendment, he nodded affirmatively when I put forth this idea. This incident highlights that important stakeholders are highly influential parties also in Switzerland for change in prostitution regulations and thereby police behaviour, just as it has been the case in the United States (Farrell and Cronin 2015, p. 215).

Factors affecting the translation of law into police directives

The analysis of the legal text of the Geneva prostitution law already reveals shortcomings toward the implementation of the first goal of the protection of sex workers, and the prioritisation of demands for amendments by influential stakeholders instead of those made by sex worker organisations uncover existing bias within the regulation of prostitution in Geneva. However, there is still potential room for the head of the prostitution unit in the Judiciary Police to translate the law into directives to effectively protect sex workers while also serving the interests of public morality. Here, I describe the composition of the prostitution unit and then analyse attitudes towards gender within the unit I gathered through interviews and observations to understand how these attitudes influence the policing of prostitution in Geneva. During the time of my field research, there were only seven officers in the unit: Ivan Caputo, head of the prostitution unit, and six officers, responsible for registering all new sex workers and controlling some 150 brothels, several escort agencies, and the street-walking area while also combating sex trafficking – a near impossible task for those seven police officers. The officers range from around 25 to 45 years in age. Most of them are married and have children. Mr. Caputo stressed in one interview that having a stable personal life was an important criterion for being considered for the unit, in order to avoid potential damages to the reputation of the unit and its officers resulting from officers getting drunk and socialising after work in bars frequented by sex workers. In the unit, there was one female officer and one black officer originally from the Congo. All but one officer of the unit had either migrated to Switzerland as young children or had parents who were not born in Switzerland.[5]

Both gender composition and origin of officers were aspects I addressed in several interviews and during patrols with different officers. They all stressed that the origin, race, or ethnicity of the officer was of no relevance for their work and was disregarded during the selection of officers. However, with regard to gender, Mr. Caputo said that he preferred not "too many" women in the unit since they switched the pairing of the officers for the patrol on a daily basis, and he stated that it might not be safe for two female officers to go on patrol without a male officer. Thus, if there were more than one or maybe two women in the unit, it would be difficult to pair them with the male officers while avoiding pairing two women. At the same time, he also stressed that the work of the unit was not exposed to a lot of physical threats or danger, and that they rarely used their guns. This contradiction suggests an implicit gender understanding leading the daily activities of the unit, through orders given by Mr. Caputo, the head of the unit.

This understanding was further underlined when I asked about the gender composition of sex workers in Geneva. I had to ask several times about the possibility of male sex workers – at first, Mr. Caputo only mentioned transgender women. He only specified after repeated enquiry that there are virtually no male sex workers registered in Geneva. For the approximately 10,000 women who registered since the adoption of the law in 2009, only around 50 men registered.[6] At the same time, *Aspasie* has one employee (out of a dozen employees totally) solely responsible for male sex work, highlighting a divergence in the assessment of the gender composition of sex workers in Geneva between the police and *Aspasie*.[7] Consequently, the work of the prostitution unit really is understood by the police officers as mostly about protecting and controlling *women* in prostitution, and since the unit is mostly composed of men (and should remain that way according to Mr. Caputo), this means masculine protection of *women* considered as in need of protection from *male* clients, from financial exploitation by *male* pimps or brothel owners, from trafficking by *male* traffickers.[8] This description was stated repeatedly by Mr. Caputo and during patrols. For instance, during my first patrol with two male officers, we went to the street-walking area at the Boulevard Helvéthique where *Aspasie*'s partner association *Boulevard* works from a bus to provide counselling and hand out condoms. One of the officers said that the police work and the work done by the social workers is both concerned with *protecting* sex workers, but while *Aspasie* is more concerned with the social aspect of this, the prostitution unit is tasked with *protection from violence* and what he called *"repression"*, meaning control of registrations and other parts of the regulation. When talking about the violence sex workers might need protection from, he used the gendered expression *filles*, "girls" in English, for sex workers. This term was almost exclusively used to refer to sex workers in all interactions I had with members of the prostitution unit. In contrast to that, *Aspasie* employees generally use the term *travailleurs de sexe*/sex workers or *femmes*/women, and employees of *SOS* Femmes, an organisation assisting women exiting prostitution, solely use *femmes*/women. This divergence underlines the perception officers have of these women as childlike, weaker, and in need of protection. When speaking about perpetrators of violence, these were generally referred to as men, clients, pimps, or traffickers. Brawls between sex workers were mentioned in interviews with police officers, but only in passing and as a matter for the general police, not the prostitution unit. In connection with Mr. Caputo's explanation of why there should be few women in the prostitution unit and his understanding of the gender composition of sex workers in Geneva in contrast to *Aspasie*'s, these gendered terminologies used by him and his officers show that the aforementioned gender-neutrally formulated regulations in Geneva are interpreted by police officers as *masculinist protection* of *women (girls)* from *male violence*. By doing so, clear categories of who protects (men) which victims (weak female girls) are constructed that facilitate an implementation of the protection of certain sex workers; those in need of protection or worthy of such are already pre-defined and exclude part of the prostitution population in Geneva such as male sex workers or also transgender sex workers, if these are not easily perceived as "weak girls". This is in line with research on German bureaucrats who favour "devote, suitable victims" of sex trafficking over women who might contradict police officers as subservient victims fit more easily into categories outlined by anti-trafficking regulations and thus facilitate their implementation (Leser et al. 2017, p. 25).

Translating directives into practice

As stressed above, directives on how to implement protection of sex workers are missing from LProst, so it is interesting to have a closer look at how police use the directives and connected already gendered orders given by Mr. Caputo in everyday practice to fulfil their understanding of their role as police officers in interactions with sex workers. When observing the interactions between police officers and sex workers on patrol, I focused on analysing repeated sequences of practices and sex workers' reactions to those. The explicit tasks during the patrol are: to verify whether sex workers have registered with the prostitution unit, whether they have a valid working permit (and therefore also legal status in Switzerland), and if in a brothel or apartment, to check the rental receipts the sex workers should have received. I observed in total 20 sets of interactions between pairs of police officers and different sex workers in the street-walking area, in commercial brothels, and in apartments used for prostitution. Here, I found that apart from these written directives, the pairs of officers followed specific scripts of practices when interacting with sex workers. While one of the two asks for relevant documents and then checks registration, working and residence permits, the other one generally exchanged pleasantries and jokes with the sex worker and asked questions about their well-being. This relaxed the atmosphere. In interactions with sex workers who already knew the specific officers, these exchanges also pointed to familiarity and mutual trust as the officers did not always ask for documents, especially when they knew the sex worker had a residence permit in Switzerland. Some sex workers addressed officers in these situations to notify them of problems they had with brothel owners and others; the officers made follow-up appointments with them to file the incident at the police station, thereby demonstrating the issue is taken seriously. The officers generally speak in a calm, friendly tone, bend their body to level their heads at the same height as the sex worker. During my participant observation, I witnessed few check-ups where documents were missing, but in those cases, the officers remained friendly and reminded the sex worker to renew the permit or otherwise face a fine.

The sex workers on the other hand differed more in their behaviour towards the officers. While all complied to show their documents, some wanted to resume work quickly and did not engage in small talk, others joked or even flirted with the officers. This was often connected to their previous familiarity with the officers, the type of prostitution they engaged in, but also to their country of origin: those who engaged least in small talk were the Romanians and Hungarians working predominantly in the street-walking area. According to members of the prostitution unit, *Aspasie*, and *SOS Femmes*, these women are the youngest and most likely among all sex workers in Geneva to have pimps and be in a situation of force and exploitation, financially at least or even sexually (Aspasie 2016; SOS Femmes 2016). They generally do not stay in Geneva for long periods of time, which is connected to the 90 days they are permitted to work in Switzerland without a residence permit. These 90 days are then often divided into much briefer stays. Consequently, there are few repeated interactions between those sex workers and police officers, preventing an establishment of trust through familiarity. In their countries of origin, sex workers are actively prosecuted and often abused by police, which further explains why those women who often lack knowledge of French or English do not approach police in situations of distress. In my observation of registrations at the police station, a young Hungarian woman I translated for had no idea for what purpose she was presenting documents to the police that had been arranged for her by men bringing her to Geneva as she told me in broken German. *Aspasie* and *SOS Femmes* confirmed that this was a common situation. Not being able to actually assist these women, the social workers struggled as much as police officers to establish trust in young street sex workers from Hungary and Romania. Even when they were not accompanied by men, the young women observed each other and did not speak freely about their situation. Additionally, the anti-trafficking measures implemented by police are targeting perpetrators instead of focusing on protecting victims. There are no safe houses reserved for trafficking victims. The organisations I talked to stressed the lack of victim and witness protection as the main reason why there are very few women coming forth to report trafficking and exploitation.

These observations reveal that police officers follow not only the written directives related to control, but also a script of practices to induce familiarity and trust in sex workers through repeated interactions. This seems to function with those sex workers staying for longer periods of time in Geneva, but fails with those populations most at risk of being victims of exploitation. While they possess the necessary documents to register and pass check-ups by the police, they do not open up to officers or social workers. This makes effective protection very difficult. This aspect points to an inherent short-coming in the Geneva prostitution law and its interpretation by the prostitution unit: by reducing the explicit purpose of their interactions with sex workers to registration and check-ups of documents used to implicitly create familiarity and trust, they open up possibilities to traffickers and others exercising force over specific vulnerable sex workers to comply with these administrative steps while preventing the creation of trust through closely observing each step these women take. The implicit practices officers use to establish familiar relations with sex workers are not operable in this case. Since there are no written directives to fall back on when informal scripts of practices fail, police officers are unable to convince victims of exploitation, abuse, and trafficking to rely on them in situations of distress. Here, we witness a transferal of attitudes towards the police originating from a prohibitionist legal setting to Geneva's regulatory framework, largely because police officers still follow explicit patterns of control. Additionally, the gendered understanding of policing and sex workers predominant in the prostitution group also aggravates this difficulty further as the understanding of *men* exercising control over *women* either as protectors or aggressors fits to the attitudes guiding previous gender relations of the young Hungarians and Romanians. Thus, these young women most at risk of being victims of exploitation are the least protected by the prostitution unit due to the inherent shortcomings of the legal text, the gendered interpretation of policing by the head of the unit, and because implicit practices fall short with this population due to their attitudes towards police stemming from previous experiences under a prohibitionist legal framework. Armstrong also details that those sex workers most at risk of violence and exploitation, migrant street sex workers, are largely those with the least trust in the police because they have, also historically, been subjected to "criminalisation and poor treatment", including being issued the infamous Anti-Social Behaviour Orders (ASBO) in the UK (Armstrong 2017a, 572) and being prohibited from exercising sex work with temporary working visas even in the generally more favourable context of decriminalised sex work in New Zealand (Armstrong 2017b). Again, this police treatment of those most vulnerable within the larger field of prostitution is connected with the visibility of street sex workers, public morality taking offence, and a resulting public demand to ban those workers from certain areas, home to families and/or affluent residents. This has been amply documented and analysed in the more restrictive context of the UK (e.g. Hubbard 1998, 2004) and the EU more generally (Hubbard et al. 2008), but also holds up, as shown here, in the Geneva setting where police are tasked to protect sex workers from exploitation and also understand their role as *protecting women from violence*, but lack the necessary tools and practices to effectively do so with those migrant street sex workers most vulnerable to violence and exploitation.

Conclusion

Which role do police officers take in organising and managing transactional sexual exchanges in a regulatory setting such as Geneva, Switzerland? How do they implement a law that stresses protection of sex workers from violence and exploitation as one of its main goals without specifying how this protection is to be achieved? As demonstrated here, the analysis of the implementation of the regulatory framework in Geneva reveals a bias within legislative processes towards favoring influential stakeholders demanding the upholding of public morality by displacing street sex workers from affluent residential areas. Advice on how to better protect vulnerable sex workers given by experts such as sex worker organisations is not implemented, a situation all too common in various countries across different legal settings. Even though police officers understand their role as protective, the directives they receive are regulated by wealthy residents rather than by those who they are tasked to protect. Additionally, when translating these directives into practice, the police officers are operating within certain limitations: by understanding their task largely as *male protection* of *women/girls* from *male violence/exploitation*, they essentially restrict those to be protected to female sex workers who fit this categorisation, and exclude male and transgender sex workers. Moreover, by relying on repeated interactions with sex workers and the use of informal scripts of practice to create trust relations, these are only established with those sex workers with whom police officers are able to interact frequently. Migrant street sex workers from Romania and Hungary who only stay in the area for brief amounts of time and lack trust in police officers and social workers before arriving in Switzerland are largely excluded from any protection through established trust relations. At the same time, they are those sex workers most affected by the demands for public order and morality coming from wealthy residents along the street-walking area.

This regrettable outcome of those migrant street sex workers most at risk of being subjected to violence and exploitation simultaneously also representing those least protected by police and most affected by demands for public order by influential stakeholders connects well with the existing body of literature on sex workers' vulnerabilities and potential for police protection. Even within the often applauded context of decriminalised prostitution in New Zealand, migrants holding temporary working visas are prohibited from participating in this safer exercising of sex work (Armstrong 2017b). Thus, while recent prostitution legislation recognises a need for the protection of sex workers and the creation of a safe working environment, much is left to be desired. Not only are specific protective measures rarely outlined in the legal text and recommendations by sex worker organisations largely ignored, leading to a focus on *protection through control* by police officers; additionally, vulnerable migrant sex workers are often excluded from any kind of protection, either directly through prohibition as in New Zealand, or indirectly as in the here outlined case of Geneva.

Notes

1 Here, I use *transactional sexual exchange, prostitution*, and *sex work* interchangeably to denote a situation in which buyer and seller both agree on the transaction of sexual services in exchange for money. While certain conditions might restrict agency or choice of the seller, most labour relations in the current economic system include such elements of force. Still, this transactional sexual exchange is to be strictly separated from trafficking for the purpose of sexual exploitation, which is subjected to international law, specified in the UN Protocol to Prevent, Suppress, and Punish Trafficking in Persons, especially Women and Children, entered into force in 2003 (UN General Assembly 2000).

2 I focus on Europe, North America, and Oceania here because trust in police is generally higher in these settings, especially among the dominant majority, which increases the potential for constructive relations between sex workers and police officers (Barker et al. 2008). Among minority populations in these areas such as communities of colour in the United States, trust in police is at least contested as the recent rise of the Black Lives Matter movement indicates. Here, interactions between police officers and sex workers belonging to minority groups are subject to such unstable levels of confidence, depending on previous experiences with police officers among other factors (Jackson and Bradford 2010; Sampson and Bartusch 1998; Weitzer and Tuch 2005). In other settings where the police are generally not regarded as a reliable institution, especially within marginalised populations, it is even less likely for sex workers to address police officers in situations of violence and abuse, given that officers are often perpetrators of such incidences themselves there (Biradavolu et al. 2009; Decker et al. 2015; Fick 2006).

3 Prostitution, drug dealing and consumption, and other similar issues connected with deviant behaviour are often subjected to specific legislation termed *morality policy*. This labeling stems from the fact that the issue is discussed emotionally rather than in a rational manner, that lay opinions are prioritised over experts' statements, and that facts based on policy research are ignored (Knill 2013; Meier 1999; Mooney 1999; Schmitt et al. 2013). Vice squads are in place to symbolically police deviants rather than effectively change behaviour (Weitzer 2010; Wagenaar and Altink 2012).

4 This mirrors legislative processes in other European countries that changed parts of their respective regulations in recent years such as Germany and the Netherlands where sex worker organisations were consulted (often after huge efforts on their parts to be included), but their recommendations largely ignored (Outshoorn 2012; BesD 2017). Currently, only in the case of New Zealand have sex worker organisations and their policy recommendations been taken seriously and implemented into regulation, leading to the decriminalisation of prostitution and improved protection of sex workers (Armstrong 2017a).

5 Overall, around 50% of the population of Geneva are not originally from Switzerland; even more have parents born outside of Switzerland (Office Cantonale de la Statistique 2015). Being a Swiss citizen is, however, one of the few requirements to join the police force. Still, this composition of the prostitution unit in terms of countries of origin is nothing particularly surprising in Geneva.

6 This is the absolute number of all sex workers who registered since 2009, but does not reflect the active participants in the Geneva sex industry. Currently, there are around 800–1,000 active sex workers, most of which are migrants, according to both the police evaluation and *Aspasie*'s statistics. This is linked to the fact that sex workers leaving Geneva are not automatically de-registered, but have to request to be deleted from the registry. During registration, they are informed of how to go about this, but very few actually undergo this step. The high number of overall registered sex workers in Geneva also stems from high spatial flexibility and limited days per year migrant sex workers who are not residents of Switzerland are permitted to work.

7 *Aspasie*'s annual report 2016 describes issues faced by men in prostitution in Geneva in detail, stating that most of these are young men from Eastern Europe or West Africa who occasionally engage in providing sexual services for financial remuneration as a last resort if other informal means of income such as drug dealing or begging fall short. Thus, they do not consider themselves as sex workers and generally do not register with the police (Aspasie 2016). Unfortunately, I was not able to interview any male sex workers due to a lack of time from *Aspasie*'s side.

8 This masculinist understanding of police tasks as mostly "male" work, potentially dangerous and requiring tough handling, is well described by Herbert (2001) who conducted an extensive ethnography of police units in Los Angeles. He stresses that while "softer" community policing shows better results in dealing with residents and fighting neighbourhood crime, most male police officers prefer to refrain from such tactics. These more social worker-type tasks are considered feminine and contradict their self-image as tough police *men*.

References

Armstrong, L. 2010. Out of the shadows (and into a bit of light): Decriminalisation, human rights and street-based sex work in New Zealand. In Hardy, K., Kingston, S., and Sanders, T., eds, *New Sociologies of Sex Work*, 39–58. Aldershot: Ashgate.

Armstrong, L. 2017a. From law enforcement to protection? Interactions between sex workers and police in a decriminalized street-based sex industry. *British Journal of Criminology*, 57(3): 570–588.

Armstrong, L. 2017b. Decriminalisation and the rights of migrant sex workers in Aotearoa/New Zealand: Making a case for change. *Women's Studies Journal*, 31(2): 69–76.

Aspasie. 2016. *Rapport annuel*. Geneva, Switzerland: Aspasie.

Barker, V., Giles, H., Hajek, C., Ota, H., Noels, K., Lim, T.S., and Somera, L. 2008. Police–civilian interaction, compliance, accommodation, and trust in an intergroup context: International data. *Journal of International and Intercultural Communication*, 1(2): 93–112.

Benson, C. and Matthews, R. 1995. Street prostitution: Ten facts in search of a policy. *International Journal of the Sociology of Law*, 23(4): 395–415.

Biradavolu, M.R., Burris, S., George, A., Jena, A., and Blankenship, K.M. 2009. Can sex workers regulate police? Learning from an HIV prevention project for sex workers in southern India. *Social Science & Medicine*, 68(8): 1541–1547.

Campbell, R. 2014. Not getting away with it: Linking sex work and hate crime in Merseyside. In Chakraborti, N. and Garland, J., eds, *Responding to hate crime: The case for connecting policy and research*. 55–71. Bristol, UK: Policy Press.

Daalder, A.L. 2007. *Prostitution in the Netherlands since the lifting of the brothel ban*. The Hague: Boom Juridische uitgevers.

Dalka, K. 2017. Prostituiertenschutzgesetz: Maximale Verunsicherung der Frauen. *Frankfurter Rundschau*. [online] Available at: www.fr.de/politik/meinung/leitartikel/prostituiertenschutzgesetz-maximale-verunsicherung-der-frauen-a-1416009 [Accessed 15 February 2018].

BesD. 2017. *Das ProstituiertenSchutzGesetz*. [online] Available at: https://berufsverband-sexarbeit.de/index.php/sexarbeit/gesetze-2/prostschg [Accessed 15 February 2018].

Decker, M.R., Crago, A.L., Chu, S.K., Sherman, S.G., Seshu, M.S., Buthelezi, K., Dhaliwal, M., and Beyrer, C. 2015. Human rights violations against sex workers: Burden and effect on HIV. *Lancet*, 385(9963): 186–199.

État de Genève 2009. Loi sur la prostitution (Lprost). *Grand Conseil de la République et canton de Genève*. Available at: www.ge.ch/legislation/rsg/f/s/rsg_I2_29.html [Accessed 15 February 2017].

Farrell, A. and Cronin, S. 2015. Policing prostitution in an era of human trafficking enforcement. *Crime, Law and Social Change*, 64(4–5): 211–228.

Fick, N. 2006. Enforcing fear: Police abuse of sex workers when making arrests. *South African Crime Quarterly*, 16: 27–33.

Glardon, M.J. 2004. Les travailleuses migrantes sur le marché du sexe à Genève. *Femmes en mouvement. Genre, migrations et nouvelle division internationale du travail, Genève, IUED, les colloques genre*. Geneva, Switzerland: Graduate Institution of Geneva.

Herbert, S. 2001. "Hard charger" or "station queen"? Policing and the masculinist state. *Gender, Place and Culture: A Journal of Feminist Geography*, 8(1): 55–71.

Howe, C. 2017. Sozialraum: Flanierende Polizeiarbeit im Quartier. In Scheffer, T., Howe, C., Kiefer, E., Negnal, D., and Porsché, Y., eds, 2017. *Polizeilicher Kommunitarismus: Eine Praxisforschung urbaner Kriminalprävention*, 77–104. Frankfurt: Campus Verlag.

Hubbard, P. 1998. Community action and the displacement of street prostitution: Evidence from British cities. *Geoforum*, 29(3): 269–286.

Hubbard, P. 2004. Cleansing the metropolis: Sex work and the politics of zero tolerance. *Urban studies*, 41(9): 1687–1702.

Hubbard, P. 2006. Out of touch and out of time? The contemporary policing of sex work. In Campbell, R. and O'Neill, M., eds, *Sex work now*. 1–32. Abingdon: Routledge.

Hubbard, P., Matthews, R., and Scoular, J. 2008. Regulating sex work in the EU: Prostitute women and the new spaces of exclusion. *Gender, Place & Culture*, 15(2): 137–152.

Jackson, J. and Bradford, B. 2010. What is trust and confidence in the police? *Policing: A Journal of Policy and Practice*, 4(3): 241–248.

Kingston, S. 2013. *Prostitution in the community: Attitudes, action and resistance*. Abingdon, UK: Routledge.

Kinnell, H. 2013. *Violence and sex work in Britain*. Abingdon, UK: Routledge.

Klauser, F.R. 2007. Difficulties in revitalizing public space by CCTV: Street prostitution surveillance in the Swiss city of Olten. *European Urban and Regional Studies*, 14(4): 337–348.

Knill, C. 2013. The study of morality policy: Analytical implications from a public policy perspective. *Journal of European Public Policy*, 20(3): 309–317.

Kriesi, H. and Trechsel, A.H. 2008. *The politics of Switzerland: Continuity and change in a consensus democracy*. Cambridge, UK: Cambridge University Press.

Larsen, E.N. 1996. The effect of different police enforcement policies on the control of prostitution. *Canadian Public Policy/Analyse de Politiques*, 40–55.

Leser, J., Pates, R., and Dölemeyer, A. 2017. The emotional Leviathan: How street-level bureaucrats govern human trafficking victims. *Digithum*, 19: 19–36. McKeganey, N.P. and Barnard, M. 1996. *Sex work on the streets: Prostitutes and their clients*. Buckingham, UK: Open University Press.

McKeganey, N.P. and Barnard, M. 2006. Street prostitution in Scotland: The views of working women. *Drugs: Education, Prevention and Policy*, 13(2): 151–166.

Matthews, R. 2005. Policing prostitution: Ten years on. *British Journal of Criminology*, 45(6): 877–895.

Meier, K.J. 1999. Drugs, sex, rock, and roll: A theory of morality politics. *Policy Studies Journal*, 27(4): 681–695.

Mooney, C.Z. 1999. The politics of morality policy: Symposium editor's introduction. *Policy Studies Journal*, 27(4): 675–680.

Office Cantonale de la Statistique 2015. *Bilan démographique selon l'origine et le sexe*. Available at: www.ge.ch/statistique/domaines/01/01_02_2/tableaux.asp#11 [Accessed 11 February 2017].

O'Neill, M. and Pitcher, J. 2010. Sex work, communities, and public policy in the UK. In Ditmore, M., Levy, A., and Willman, A., eds, *Sex work matters: Exploring money, power and intimacy in the sex industry, 2003–2018*. London: Zed books.

Outshoorn, J. 2012. Policy change in prostitution in the Netherlands: From legalization to strict control. *Sexuality Research and Social Policy*, 9(3): 233–243.

Pates, R. 2012. Liberal laws juxtaposed with rigid control: An analysis of the logics of governing sex work in Germany. *Sexuality Research and Social Policy*, 9(3): 212–222.

Penfold, C., Hunter, G., Campbell, R., and Barham, L. 2004. Tackling client violence in female street prostitution: Inter-agency working between outreach agencies and the police. *Policing & Society*, 14(4): 365–379.

Pitcher, J. ed. 2006. *Living and working in areas of street sex work: From conflict to coexistence*. Bristol, UK: Policy Press.

Roselli, S. 2016. Le nombre des prostituées a explosé à Genève! *Tribune de Genève*. [online]. Available at: www.tdg.ch/geneve/actu-genevoise/nombre-prostituees-explose/story/15598917 [Accessed 10 September 2017].

Sagar, T. 2004. Street watch: Concept and practice: Civilian participation in street prostitution control. *British Journal of Criminology*, 45(1): 98–112.

Sampson, R.J. and Bartusch, D.J. 1998. Legal cynicism and (subcultural?) tolerance of deviance: The neighborhood context of racial differences. *Law and Society Review*, 32(4): 777–804.

Sanders, T. 2001. Female street sex workers, sexual violence, and protection strategies. *Journal of sexual aggression*, 7(1): 5–18.

Sanders, T. 2004a. A continuum of risk? The management of health, physical and emotional risks by female sex workers. *Sociology of Health & Illness*, 26(5): 557–574.

Sanders, T. 2004b. The risks of street prostitution: Punters, police and protesters. *Urban Studies*, 41(9): 1703–1717.

Schmitt, S., Euchner, E.M., and Preidel, C. 2013. Regulating prostitution and same-sex marriage in Italy and Spain: The interplay of political and societal veto players in two catholic societies. *Journal of European Public Policy*, 20(3): 425–441.

SOS Femmes. 2016. *Rapport d'activité*. Available at: www.sosfemmes.ch/content/files/A3_SOS-femmes_rapportAnnuel2016_web.pdf [Accessed 14 September 2017].

Thievent, R. 2010. Temporal dimensions of cabaret dancer's circular migration to Switzerland. In Hardy, K., Kingston, S., and Sanders, T., eds, *New sociologies of sex work*, 149–165. Farnham, UK: Ashgate.

UN General Assembly. 2000. Protocol to prevent, suppress and punish trafficking in persons, especially women and children, supplementing the United Nations convention against transnational organized crime. *General Assembly Resolutions*, *55*: 25.

Vorheyer, C. 2014. *Prostitution und Menschenhandel als Verwaltungsproblem: eine qualitative Untersuchung über den beruflichen Habitus*. Bielefeld: transcript Verlag.

Wagenaar, H. 2006. Democracy and prostitution: Deliberating the legalization of brothels in the Netherlands. *Administration & Society*, *38*(2): 198–235.

Wagenaar, H. and Altink, S. 2012. Prostitution as morality politics or why it is exceedingly difficult to design and sustain effective prostitution policy. *Sexuality Research and Social Policy*, *9*(3): 279–292.

Weitzer, R. 2010. The mythology of prostitution: Advocacy research and public policy. *Sexuality Research and Social Policy*, *7*(1): 15–29.

Weitzer, R. 2014. Sex work, gender, and criminal justice. In Gartner, R. and McCarthy, B., eds, *The Oxford handbook of gender, sex, and crime*, 15–24. Oxford: Oxford University Press.

Weitzer, R. and Tuch, S.A. 2005. Determinants of public satisfaction with the police. *Police Quarterly*, *8*(3): 279–297.

41

Sex trading in neighbourhood context

Facilitation, violence, and the spectrum of young women's exploitation

Lauren Martin

Introduction

Commercial sex markets vary widely across and within global regions and countries, although in many of these contexts the provision of commercial sexual services often occurs alongside many documented harms, including violence, exploitation, criminalization, and stigmatization (Rekart 2005). Specific local contexts – including the legal status of commercial sex, regional economic inequalities, and oppressions based on gender, age, race, ethnicity, and socio-economic status – shape the experiences of people who trade or sell sex. Hence the specific dynamics surrounding child sex tourism in Thailand are very different from those in legal brothels staffed by adult providers in Germany, just as high-end escort services and street-based sex trading in the United States, South Africa, or Brazil all present their own challenges within particular socio-legal settings. Yet despite such diversity, dominant scholarly and activist perspectives on the global sex industry are split into a fundamental disagreement regarding whether commercial sex is legitimate work or a form of exploitation that is growing worldwide (Doezema 2005; Limoncelli 2009; Weitzer 2014). Conceptual conflict and disagreement about practice are compounded by a dearth of scholarly empirical research on traffickers and other intermediaries and how they function in practice within specific contexts (Gozdziak 2012; Weitzer 2014).

Globally, social and economic inequalities push people into the sex industry as a result of "economic disparities between sending and receiving countries, conflict and militarization, structural adjustment policies, [and] the worldwide growth of informal work" (Limoncelli 2009, 266). Research on commercial sex within the Unites States shows that patterns of racial segregation and disparities coupled with other forms of intersectional oppression create similar push patterns on a smaller geographic scale within local-level commercial sex markets (Martin et al. 2014). Thus, anti-trafficking and prevention of exploitation in commercial sex can be seen as part of a global movement for social and economic justice.

Yet many scholars note conceptual slippage in global anti-trafficking efforts that conflate trafficking victims with people seeking better economic opportunities through commercial sex or people choosing commercial sex as a form of work. Critics of anti-trafficking discourses and practices point to a "master narrative" of trafficking that has three primary elements: conflation of all commercial sex with trafficking, amounting to a "moral panic"; recycling of racially coded nineteenth-century tropes about "white slavery" that rely on a dyad of the violent pimp/ trafficker and the helpless, naive white victim in need of rescue; and reliance on arrest and incarceration of sex buyers, third parties, and many providers of sexual services, often in ways that disproportionately impact people of colour and poor people (Bernstein 2010; Doezema 2005; Musto 2013).

While the goal of both global movements – anti-trafficking and sex worker rights – is to minimize harms and violence against people in commercial sex, the pathway envisioned to achieve this goal is vastly different. Anti-trafficking efforts often view commercial sex itself as violence against women and accordingly emphasize the need to end forced commercial sex, constrained choice, and violence resulting from commercial sex. The sex worker rights movement seeks to liberalize and legitimize the commercial sex markets through decriminalization as a way to reduce harm and ensure the protection of sex workers' human rights (Doezema 2005; Limoncelli 2009).

Such profound ideological differences raises an as-yet-unanswered question for those of us who are deeply concerned with the well-being of young women involved in commercial sex: how can we take seriously the violence and marginalization experienced by people involved in commercial sex, yet remain critical of hyperbole, moral panic, racial stereotypes, and carceral logic within anti-trafficking efforts? I suggest, as scholars increasingly do, that one way to accomplish this goal involves paying close attention to local context in order to prevent conceptual slippage, over-generalization, and stereotyped discourse and narrative. This is best accomplished by emphasizing young women's descriptions of their nuanced experiences with these phenomena, as they themselves experience them, while rooted in everyday life. This chapter accordingly explores the lives of young women aged 24 and under who are involved in the sex trade in the Northside neighbourhood of Minneapolis, Minnesota, a medium-sized US city. Adult prostitution is illegal in Minnesota, although federal and state law regards minors under 18 who trade or sell sex as victims of commercial sexual exploitation (MDH 2018).

I begin by describing the neighbourhood, in which I have conducted more than a decade of community-based research with people involved in the sex trade, residents, police, service providers, advocates, community leaders, faith leaders, and others. Then, from the perspective of young women and people close to them, I describe the dynamics of manipulation, sexual harassment, and violence against girls and young women in neighbourhood hotspots known as "the smuts". Perpetrators are male and female peers, third parties, and potential sex buyers from outside of the neighbourhood. Finally, I argue that this case study (the local) situates how social and structural inequalities (the global) fuel involvement in commercial sex and trafficking within the lived realities of real young women. Context allows us to see the nuanced interplay of decision-making, constraint, force, violence, struggle, and resilience without over-generalizing.

Community-based research on the Northside

For over a decade I have conducted collaborative research in the Near-North and Camden neighbourhoods of Minneapolis, colloquially known as "the Northside". The Northside has 63,410 residents, which is 15% of Minneapolis' population (Minnesota Compass 2017). Minneapolis Police Department arrest records indicate that this neighbourhood features the highest number of police-identified individuals identified in pimping and trafficking-related investigations. Young people and others in the neighbourhood concur that Northside is home to third parties, but they also suggest that higher-paid leaders of more tightly organized trafficking operations live elsewhere (Martin et al. 2014). Some 71% of Northside residents are people of colour, with 41% African American, 13% Asian, and 8% Latino/a, in a city where the majority of residents are white (Minnesota Compass 2017). Neighbourhood challenges include intergenerational poverty, community violence, police violence, mass incarceration, homelessness, and disparities in education and health outcomes relative to the rest of the city, among others (Metropolitan Council 2014). Many residents are fiercely proud of the Northside and resist easy categorization of the neighbourhood based on these deficits; instead these residents emphasize its strengths, activism, and resistance to oppression. Goetz (2017), an expert on residential segregation in the United States, recently remarked that "neighborhoods [sic] simultaneously embody many different and often contrasting realities". This important caveat embraces divergent experiences of the same places without over-generalizing.

My understanding and analysis of young women's experiences in commercial sex is based on mixed-methods data from four different studies. The foundational study used community-based participatory research, including participant-observation and ethnographic methods, in the Northside beginning in 2005 (Martin 2013). Two participatory projects in youth-serving agencies involved young people in co-creation of research on commercial sex in the neighbourhood. The first involved focus groups with homeless young women (N = 24) and interviews with staff (N = 14) in a homeless youth drop-in centre in 2015 (Fogel et al. 2016). The second involved a team of six young people who experienced sexual exploitation and serve on an agency's advisory group; our team assisted them to develop and conduct their own study with their peers in 2016, including surveys (N = 45) and focus groups (N = 31) (UROC and The Link 2016). The final study combined stakeholder interviews of adults (N = 89) with a review of all cases of juveniles involved in prostitution and sex trafficking investigated by the Minneapolis Police Department (N = 79) from 2008 to 2014, and criminal background information on individuals involved in these cases including prior charges and police contact as victims of crime (Martin et al. 2014). Police data included a wide range of documents such as initial police reports, interview transcripts, evidence logs, and investigative notes. Data from the four studies were re-analysed in their original format of interview transcripts, database, and field notes. Research was approved by the University of Minnesota's Institutional Review Board.

These combined data evince diverse perspectives on young women's involvement in commercial sex in the neighbourhood. I also conferred with key people in the neighbourhood who have lifelong and deep contextual knowledge of the sex trade to fact check and see how this data resonates with their experiences. These conversations helped to fine tune the analysis. This cyclical process of analysis is part of community-based research and the recognition of multiple forms of expertise (Stringer 2014).

Sex trading and third parties in the Northside

The smuts

Young people and others described many small block areas in the Northside as "hot spots" for young people in the sex trade that are nearby but distinct from several known strolls for street-based prostitution primarily with adults trading sex, although some youth work there too. Some young people call these hot spots "the smuts". While they did not know the origin of the term, some said it was a "dirty" word. The smuts were described as deeply rooted in poverty and as places where young women are sexually exploited in low-end rental housing and abandoned houses repurposed for parties, drugs, and sex; as well as being a locale for recruiting, controlling, and holding young female victims of sex trafficking. The young women living (or "staying" as it was termed) in the smuts were described as both from the local neighbourhood and across the US state of Minnesota. The draw or pull of the smuts was a place to stay with parties, drugs, and "guys", meaning third parties who profit from women's sexual labour. For example, a street outreach worker interviewed in 2013 described it like this:

> I would say even if the girls weren't from the smuts, that's where the parties are and that's where their guys [who facilitate their involvement in prostitution] live. So, there's some combination of something in there that this is happening . . . she don't have to be from the smuts, but she ends up in the smuts . . . The smut[s] is, yeah, it's the product of poverty. So, it's definitely a magnet [for illicit and criminalized forms of business].

Language around third-party facilitation of commercial sex in this neighbourhood is fraught and often not aligned with terms in state and federal statutes. The statutes refer to a pimp as someone who promotes prostitution and a trafficker as someone who compels a person to participate in prostitution or commercial sex. Many in the neighbourhood do use the term pimp to describe a manipulative or violent third party, but young people and those close to them also referred to them as guys, boyfriends, or daddies. Pimp is perceived as a derogatory and racially coded term that is often used in hindsight to describe a past relationship or is used to describe someone else's exploitative situation. Young women rarely referred to their current boyfriend, child's father, or the other family member as a pimp.

Many on the Northside described how the physical built environment shapes the smuts following centuries of policy and housing discrimination against people of colour in the United States (Metropolitan Council 2014; O'Connor 1999). In the 2008 recession, the Northside "emerged as one of the prominent foreclosure hotspots in the region because of the prevalence of targeted, predatory marketing of high-cost subprime loans to prospective homeowners of color" (Metropolitan Council 2014, 14). Families of colour made up the majority of households displaced by foreclosure (Allen 2009; Ireland 2010). A 2010 tornado further destroyed Northside housing stock. The combination of foreclosures, absentee landlords, and the tornado created blocks within the Northside with abandoned, run-down and unregulated properties (Matsen 2012) that contributed to a physical infrastructure conducive to small-scale drug trafficking, prostitution, and related hustles some people in the smuts use to make a living. One Northside youth worker interviewed in 2014 said:

> They [landlords] don't care how you're making the money. You know, it's not a big deal. And I know the landlord is fully aware of what they got going on . . . [T]here's definitely a lot of trap houses [where people exchange sex and drugs for cash] in North Minneapolis, too. Just because there was more of a foreclosure rate over there.

Residents used several terms to describe the houses that define the smuts. "Trap house" is a widespread term across the United States, particularly in hip-hop. The term describes houses, often in a state of abandonment, where small-scale drug dealing and commercial sex commonly take place. Violence is common in such settings, due in part to the extra-judicial problem solving and deeply rooted gender inequalities that characterize the illicit drug and prostitution economies, with multiple perpetrator rapes referred to as a "train party" (or "t-roller") and the location where commonly they take place as a "breakdown station".

Interviewees described attending violent, sex-based parties in the smuts, both at trap houses and elsewhere, with male participants ranging in age from teens to forties and young women who were primarily in their early to late teens. Some parties were described as "orchestrated" by older men in the neighbourhood for the benefit of younger men. The pattern was clear. Party organizers invited only a few young women to a party that turned out to be a pre-planned multiple-perpetrator rape (Edinburgh et al. 2014; Martin et al. 2014). Young women were given drugs and alcohol and also threatened with weapons and physically restrained. According to people we interviewed, many of the young men who attended these parties were also not aware of what was going to happen, although some parties charged a fee for the males attending, and others were a reward for gang involvement or as a show of status and power. These parties function to "break down" girls, by being sexually assaulted, and also "break in" boys, who perpetrate this violence, since all young men in attendance are expected and pressured to take part in forcible sex.

The girls who are victims in these places were described as "breakdowns" with their peers concluding that they "wanted to be broke down". Parties, trap houses, and breakdowns create a cascade of bullying, shame, trauma, and humiliation with the girls labelled as whores or THOTs ("that hoe over there"). Many young women were not aware they were being invited to this kind of party. Thus, their first experience of a "breakdown" was not consensual and was described as setting the stage for the sex trade through a combination of shame, traumatization, and needing to meet basic needs, as well as putting them in proximity to people who use coercion and force to compel involvement in commercial sex.

The smuts shape how many young people living in the Northside navigate their neighbourhood. Young women described fear of violent retribution, rape, and kidnapping in retaliation for leaving a man who used to be their "pimp", daddy, or boyfriend who promoted, forced, and profited from their involvement in prostitution. So they avoid the smuts to avoid being found. According to many youth and adults I have known in the neighbourhood, young people have a mental map of where they can and cannot travel within the neighbourhood based on the location of "guys" who facilitate women's sexual labour, gangs, and "breakdown stations". Neighbourhood residents not involved in commercial sex are often unaware of these spatial complexities. In many ways there are two realities living side by side.

Neighbourhood-based sexual harassment and assault

Parties and breakdowns happen within a larger context of sexual harassment, sexualized comments, and sexual assault. Young women described a stream of sexualized commentary on their bodies, come-ons, solicitation for commercial sex, and attempts at casual sexual hook-ups in homeless shelters, drop-in centres, the streets, and other places in and near the smuts. One young person described a seemingly constant male gaze as young people seek services:

> If you were a teen girl and you walked in here [youth program], you walk through those doors and immediately all the guys in there is either looking at you or three or four is about to approach you. You can see it in their face.

In a focus group, several young women imitated how their male peers talk to them on a regular basis. Speaking in deep voices some young women said: "bro, look at that up in here!" "bro, I want to hit that, bro!" "She a THOT bro". "You want a cigarette? Come suck this dick. There's it right there." As quoted in a publication about our community-based research, "You want to hit my blunt [smoke marijuana]? You know what to do" (Fogel et al. 2016, 156).

In addition to sexual comments, constant sexual pressure, and the threat of sexual assault from male peers, young women described frequent solicitation from potential sex buyers. One young woman described:

> In the summertime, [interjection from another young person: "yeah, you got your shorts on"] I seen a man personally come up to me, "you know what you can get paid for that body? Just standing in a photo shoot. We're doing a private photo shoot, here's my card, you can make $600 just for showing up."

Many described sex buyers who drive through the neighbourhood looking for young women on the streets, in parks, homeless shelters, and more (Martin et al. 2014). A recent study exploring who purchases sex in Minnesota found that most sex buyers are white men of means (Martin et al. 2017). In the Northside, buyers purchase sex mostly from young women of colour living in poverty. Some of these men also display highly predatory behaviour similar to how neighbourhood men who profit from women's sexual labour identify potential young women to target (Martin et al. 2014).

Survival sex or trading sex for basic needs such as a place to stay, food, and clothes was described as common in the smuts. Many young people who stay in the smuts are homeless or precariously housed, have run away from home, and lack very basic needs. They are often disconnected from their families, their communities and formal government support systems such as school, welfare, health care and more. One young woman said "everyone" in this situation talks about whether or not to trade sex, "like every girl that's going through stuff who is homeless or doesn't have anywhere to go or doesn't have any money. They just don't have nothing. They don't have anything." Whether or not a young person decides or is forced to trade sex for basic needs, the conversation, possibility and option is there (Fogel et al. 2016).

Sex trafficking and facilitation in the smuts

The neighbourhood context of sexual harassment, sexual violence, and survival sex is part of a broader context that suffuses the sexual exploitation of neighbourhood young women. A seasoned police investigator who works closely with runaway and missing children echoed a common understanding in the neighbourhood that trading sex to meet basic needs is connected to longer-term involvement in prostitution and third-party facilitation and trafficking through what he describes as a "gateway":

> I think entering into survival sex is a gateway. It's a big gateway. Once you cross that bridge you're much more likely to get exploited as a sex trafficking victim because you've already looked at sex as a commercial exchange. You're using it to get something that you need. Not want necessarily – but you have to have. You have to have food. You have to have a place to sleep. Okay. This – you know, when your body is treated as a currency. That opens a door to somebody exploiting it. "Okay, well, you did this for a place to sleep, now maybe you can do it and make $300."

The shift of young women from survival sex to involvement in the formal commercial sex market typically involves third-party "facilitation" of some kind, which can include force, manipulation, violence, knowledge exchange, and material support (Curtis et al. 2008; Marcus et al. 2014; Martin et al. 2014). People who facilitate youth involvement in commercial sex include peers, neighbourhood men who may or may not self-identify as "pimps", and sex buyers.

Most of the young women who have participated in our research highlight the central role of peers in connecting them to more formal aspects of commercial sex. Peers are a source of knowledge about how to post advertisements online, who is organizing higher-paying parties with wealthy men, and other ways to access higher-paying customers. Peers also were described as using manipulation, shame, and fear to recruit on behalf of pimps. Some peers were described as acting in the role of an abuser, using violence and emotional manipulation to compel involvement in commercial sex. Thus, young people described peer relationships that included support, manipulation, and violence. Peer relationships can also be seen as a source of resilience and strength in which young people are trying hard to survive and support each other (Dank et al. 2015). Peers were described as working together for comradery, support, and safety. An outreach worker and community advocate said:

> One girl is already in it [commercial sex] and she might have some friends and she might build what they call "teams" [of women who sell sex together] [. . .] So, at some point she can become a renegade [working the street independently], maybe do it on her own if she isn't already, and find some other girls to do it with to have on their team.

One young woman described her experience of providing "protection" for a friend, which suggests the limits of peer support in the face of imminent violence:

> I was in the [hotel] room with her, but I hid in the bathroom. She was doing it on Backpage [online advertising forum]. I'm just in the bathroom but I can't do shit, but I'm in there to make sure shit don't go down. And when the dude [sex buyer] came in, put the gun to her face and took all her money, but I wasn't going to run the fuck out there. [Interjection from peer:] yeah, because you're not going to put your life in danger.

Many had similar stories to this young woman describing how her friend recruited her to turn over her prostitution earnings to her friend's boyfriend. It was described as typical for men who took such money, in exchange for offers of work, protection, or other services (irrespective of whether they planned to fulfil these promises), to make a pitch for commercial sex that downplays the kinds of sex acts that would be required by claiming, for example, that the promised income generation opportunity would just involve massage or dancing.

> My friend's boyfriend kind of influenced her on doing it and then she tried to influence me, and came to me saying, "oh, you don't have to have sex with him [the sex buyer], you just have to massage him or give him a hand job or stuff like that."

Most young women said they were pressured or forced to perform a wide range of sexual acts, including penetrative sex in all forms, sexual activities they regarded as disturbing or unclean because they involved human waste, and sex acts accompanied by violence (Fogel et al. 2016; Martin et al. 2017).

While some peers facilitate commercial sex as an attempt to help and support their friends to meet basic needs, others were described as blatantly manipulative, exploitative, and harmful. What seems like a friend, may actually be a front for an older person identified as a "pimp" or boyfriend. A staff member at a key youth services agency near the smuts said: "What is more of a trend now is more refined peer-to-peer recruiting . . . The newest innovation in recruiting, is teaching young girls how to recruit on behalf of the pimps." This kind of peer recruiting should be seen within a context of constrained and highly limited options for basic survival for many young women and their peers. Also, a young person acting on behalf of a third party who benefits from women's sexual labour can also be conditioned by violence, fear, and need for approval.

Many people in the neighbourhood described this as a common scenario. Minneapolis Police Department data and other interviews provide context about "boyfriends" who "influence" young women to engage in commercial sex. Most are significantly older, in their thirties and forties, and have many young girlfriends whom they also encourage and compel to participate in the commercial sex market. For these men, as well as some family-based operations, women's sexual labour is their primary source of income. Like young women involved in commercial sex, this may also be a function of highly reduced and constrained socio-economic options described above. These traffickers will alternate violence with care, love, and concern in order to build a bond that they use to facilitate sex trafficking, sharing similarities to situations of domestic violence (Martin et al. 2014; Reid 2016). Boyfriend-facilitators, on the other hand, may be roughly the same age as the young women. Some young women described such men as a better source of protection than their peers; one young woman described the men's work as follows:

> He gets paid for his service, protecting you, promoting you, keeping the product right, getting the hair done, getting the nails done. [Interjection from another youth: buying shoes, clothes]. Getting you waxed. Little things that ensure the product is right – that's his product.

The promise of protection, care, and concern comes with very real potential for violence and control from such men, including verbal violence, humiliation, put-downs, threat of violence with weapons, physical restraint, drug-induced assault, and sexual and physical assault (Martin et al. 2014). Within this complexity, some young women tried to make distinctions between good and bad third-party facilitators, "Madams and daddies are okay, but a pimp is going to take all your money." For this young woman, third parties that are helpful in managing and supporting commercial sex as a business were termed madams and daddies; whereas she viewed a pimp as a sort of illegitimate manager. But these terms were contested in the neighbourhood and often contingent of time and relationship.

Young people and others in the neighbourhood described third parties as sources of information about how commercial sex works. For example, a probation officer told us about a young woman from a family-based operation that sexually exploited minor girls for a profit. She was trafficked by her family and experienced violence and force as well as being provided drugs. At age 16 she was a skilled recruiter of young girls. Eventually:

> She got sick and tired [of him . . .] he cut her off of the drugs and wasn't giving her money anymore. So, she's like immediately like "F this." And she took all the girls that she recruited and took off. And then she started basically running those girls.

A street outreach worker discussed the difficulties girls and young women who trade sex for money independently have navigating more lucrative sex industry forms on their own.

> So even if initially they [young women] are thinking, "yeah, I can do this on my own." But how long can that be? Especially if she's stuck in it and she's seeing her friend [working for a third party] making twice as much, because this guy is kind of handling her business versus her.

While deploying manipulation and perpetrating violence, many third parties also provide connection to higher-end and better-paying sex buyers. Young women under 18, on their own, are not able to rent a hotel room and may not have access to transportation and other material supports necessary for involvement in commercial sex. With an adult third party, young women from or "staying" in the smuts are able to access and trade sex in many market segments across the Twin Cities and beyond, including through online escort advertisements, high-end parties in homes and hotels (including informal stripping and fetish activities), party buses, and more (Martin et al. 2014, 2017).

Most third parties are men, with fewer women involved in facilitating young women's sexual labour, and there are notable differences in their management tactics. The data suggests that pimps who are men often use sexual violence as a control tactic. Older women pimps and female peers were also described as manipulative and sometimes verbally and physically violent, but not typically using sexual violence the way that male facilitators do, as one young woman noted:

> And females are starting to be like that too, females aren't going to give a fuck about your feelings because "you didn't give a fuck about mine when you hurt me", you know what I'm saying? That's how people start to not care and just be selfish and start taking advantage of other people.

Young women and others suggested that being under the control of a third party who profits from their sexual labour is not necessarily a constant state, but rather may be best viewed as a phase or experience within a range of exploitation behind how young people staying in the smuts are involved in commercial sex (Martin et al. 2014). Young women described efforts to avoid such individuals but this was described as difficult due to force and manipulation, the potential for higher earnings while working with an experienced facilitator and, also because third parties also purchase sex buyers as a way to recruit new women to work for them.

The research described here did not interview people who self-identified as "pimps" or "traffickers", so I cannot describe relationships and market involvement from their point of view, nor can I explain how or why they are involved in pimping or trafficking. However, law enforcement data sheds some light on their background and experience: between 2008 and 2014, the Minneapolis Police Department investigated 39 cases involving a pimp or trafficker with 50 people identified as pimps or traffickers; mostly men (43) with a majority being African American men (37). Of the 7 women, 4 were Black and 3 were white. The men ranged in age from 14 to 55, women from 18–39. Of those arrested 18 (36%) had previous police contacts as a crime victim, runaway, or missing person. For women, 4 out of the 7 had previous records of victimization. The numbers are small, and this data is certainly incomplete, but it suggests the potential role of prior victimization in how people become involved in facilitating young women's sexual labour, particularly in ways that involve violence and exploitation (Nichols 2016).

Why does the Northside matter? Reflections and conclusions

Close attention to neighbourhood-level conditions that shape, push, and pull young people into commercial sex surfaces a spectrum of gender-based exploitation and violence against young women. This co-occurs alongside a wide variety of third-party involvement in the facilitation of commercial sex that resists easy generalization. Mutual support among peers, struggles to survive, and knowledge-sharing live in close proximity to coercion, force, and violence. Further, seeing young women in context shows them as full human beings making decisions about their lives, trying to better their situation, making ends meet, and surviving. All of this should be seen within the context of racism, housing segregation, poverty, and marginalization.

A dichotomy between force and choice seems a false dichotomy when placed in a context because in understanding lived experience we can visualize the complex ways that decision-making for these young women happens within a harmful and exploitative context that is shaped by structural inequality and disparities. From the perspective of young women in the smuts, being "pimped" is not a permanent state. Rather, it may best be understood as a moving or recurring phase in a spectrum of exploitation as young women seek ways to survive. Third-party facilitators are not all-controlling orchestrators, but their actions provide an infrastructure for sex trading and trafficking in the smuts. They provide access to higher-paying and wider market segments than what young people can access through survival sex in the neighbourhood. And they also fuel the broader context of sexual harassment, assault, and violence against young women through street culture, solicitation, violence in relationships, and strategic use of parties that involve drugs and multiple-perpetrator rape.

The smuts do not exist in a vacuum. These conditions are created and shaped by public policy and structural inequalities, the intersectional impacts of gender, race, and place in the longstanding US history of racial and socio-economic discrimination and segregation. The structural violence of living through homelessness, poverty, racism, and sexism causes much pain and suffering that is dehumanized and dehumanizing (Martin 2015). The society that in many ways has abandoned young people is dominated by institutions, government entities, an economy, and more that systematically privileges white people over people of colour. Most people who purchase sex from young people in the smuts are white men with significantly more financial resources than the young women, or those who facilitate the purchase and sale of their sexual labour.

Why does this matter in a global context? Weitzer argues that any attempt to create a macro or global picture of the sex industry is fundamentally flawed because we do not yet have enough strong empirical data about the wide variety of local contexts. He suggests that microstudies of smaller geographic areas can lead to more accurate and deeper understanding of the sex trade with "potential to identify trafficking 'hot spots' for targeted deployment of enforcement resources" (Weitzer 2014, 15). The Northside illuminates how some of the global themes around trafficking – individual decision-making (a re-frame of "choice"), force, resistance, struggle, violence, poverty, and survival – manifest in specific places. The case study also shows the role of local (in this case, neighbourhood) context in shaping experiences. Young women's experiences in the smuts are not necessarily immediately generalizable outside of their context, but knowing about their lives, struggles, and decision-making allow for deeper understanding and comparisons. Focus on context helps us resist generalization and conflation, but still be able to see the multiple forms of violence – structural, economic, interpersonal – that shape Northside young people's involvement in commercial sex. Others living in similar contexts may have similar experiences. Finally, this case study demonstrates the importance of visualizing people within the context of their lives, rather than as abstractions.

References

Allen, Ryan. 2009. The unraveling of the American dream: Foreclosures in the immigrant community of Minneapolis. Accessed online 11 November 2017. www.hhh.umn.edu/people/rallen/pdf/unraveling_american_dream.pdf.

Bernstein, Elizabeth. 2010. Militarized humanitarianism meets carceral feminism: The politics of sex, rights and freedom in contemporary antitrafficking campaigns. *Signs* 36(1): 45–71.

Curtis, Ric, Karen Terry, Meredith Dank, Kirk Dombrowski, and Bilal Khan. 2008. *The commercial sexual exploitation of children in New York City.* Accessed 15 October 2017. www.ncjrs.gov/pdffiles1/nij/grants/225083.pdf.

Dank, Meredith, Jennifer Yahner, Kuniko Madden, Isela Banuelos, Lilly Yu, Andrea Ritchie, Mitchyll Mora, and Brendan Conner. 2015. *Surviving the streets of New York: Experiences of LGBTQ youth, YMSM, and YWSW engaged in survival sex.* Accessed 15 November 2017. www.urban.org/sites/default/files/publication/42186/2000119-Surviving-the-Streets-of-New-York.pdf.

Doezema, Jo. 2005. Now you see her, now you don't: Sex workers at the UN trafficking protocol negotiation. *Social & Legal Studies* 14: 61–89.

Edinburgh, Laurel, Julie Pape-Blabolil, Scott Harpin, and Elizabeth Saewyc. 2014. Multiple perpetrator rape among girls evaluated at a hospital-based child advocacy center: Seven years of reviewed cases. *Child Abuse & Neglect* 38: 1540–1551.

Ireland, Mark. 2010. Bending toward justice: An empirical study of foreclosures in one neighborhood three years after impact and a proposed framework for a better community. Accessed 20 November 2017. www.kirwaninstitute.osu.edu/reports/2010/02_2010_BendingTowardJustice_ForeclResponse_Ireland.pdf.

Fogel, Katie, Lauren Martin, Bob Nelson, Marney Thomas, and Carolyn Porta. 2016. 'We're automatically sex in men's eyes, we're nothing but sex . . .': Young adult perceptions of sexual exploitation. *Journal of Child and Adolescent Trauma* 10(2): 151–160.

Goetz, Edward. 2017. Your "opportunity" map is broken. Here are some fixes. *Shelterforce: The Voice of Community Development.* Accessed 17 November 2017. https://shelterforce.org/2017/11/16/your-opportunity-map-is-broken-here-are-some-fixes.

Gozdziak, Elzbieta. 2012. Children trafficked to the United States: Myths and realities. *Global Dialogue* 14: 1–12.

Limoncelli, Stephanie. 2009. The trouble with trafficking: Conceptualizing women's sexual labor and economic human rights. *Women's Studies International Forum* 32: 261–269.

Marcus, Anthony, Amber Horning, Ric Curtis, Jo Sanson, and Efram Thompson. 2014. Conflict and agency among sex workers and pimps: A closer look at domestic minor sex trafficking. *ANNALS* 653: 225–246.

Martin, Lauren. 2013. Sampling and sex trading: Lessons on research design from the street. *Journal of Action Research* 11(3): 220–235.

Martin, Lauren. 2015. Sex and sensibilities: Doing action research while respecting even inspiring dignity. In Hilary Bradbury, ed., *The Sage handbook of action research*, 3rd ed., 505–511. London: Sage.

Martin, Lauren, Christina Melander, Harshada Karnik, and Corelle Nakamura. 2017. Mapping the demand: Sex buyers in the state of Minnesota. Accessed 2 February 2018. https://uroc.umn.edu/sites/uroc.umn.edu/files/FULL%20REPORT%20Mapping%20the%20Demand.pdf.

Martin, Lauren, Alexandra "Sandi" Pierce, Stephen Peyton, Ana Isabel Gabilondo, and Girija Tulpule. (2014). *Mapping the market for sex with minor trafficked girls in Minneapolis.* Accessed 2 November 2017. https://uroc.umn.edu/sites/uroc.umn.edu/files/MTM_Full%20Report_2014.pdf.

Matsen, Jeff. 2012. Rethinking revitalization: A data-driven approach to addressing the foreclosure crisis. Presentation to CIC Impact Summit. Accessed 20 November 2017. www.neighborhoodindicators.org/library/catalog?partner=128&page=2.

Metropolitan Council. 2014. Choice, place and opportunity. Section five: Racially concentrated areas of poverty in the region. Accessed 25 November 2017. https://metrocouncil.org/Planning/Projects/Thrive-2040/Choice-Place-and-Opportunity/FHEA/FHEA-Sect-5.aspx.

Minnesota Compass. 2017. Weber-Camden neighborhood and Near-North neighborhood. Accessed 25 November 2017. www.mncompass.org/profiles/communities/minneapolis/near-north and www.mncompass.org/profiles/communities/minneapolis/camden.

Minnesota Department of Health (MDH). 2018. Safe Harbor Minnesota. Accessed 4 February 2018. www.health.state.mn.us/injury/topic/safeharbor/.

Musto, Jennifer. 2013. Domestic minor sex trafficking and the detention-to-protection pipeline. *Dialectical Anthropology* 37: 257–276.

Nichols, Andrea. 2016. *Sex trafficking in the United States: Theory, research, policy, and practice.* New York: Columbia University Press.

O'Connor, Alice. 1999. Swimming against the tide: A brief history of federal policy in poor communities. In Ronald Ferguson and William Dickens, eds, *Urban problems and community development*, 77–138. Washington, DC: Brookings Institute.

Reid, Joan. 2016. Entrapment and enmeshment schemes used by sex traffickers. *Sexual Abuse: A Journal of Research and Treatment* 28(6): 491–511.

Rekart, Michael. 2005. Sex-work harm reduction. *Lancet* 366: 2123–34.

Stringer, Earnest. 2014. *Action research*, 4th ed. Thousand Oaks, CA: Sage.

UROC and The Link. 2016. Youth participatory action research: Creating a marketing intervention for the prevention of sexual exploitation among youth populations at high risk for trafficking. Accessed 2 November 2017. https://uroc.umn.edu/sites/uroc.umn.edu/files/The%20Link%20and%20UROC%20YPAR%20Report%20FINAL%20April%202016.pdf#overlay-context=sextrafficking.

Weitzer, Ronald. 2014. New directions in research on human trafficking. *ANNALS*. 65: 6–24.

42

Supporting female survivors of sex trafficking in Russia

Ethical challenges and dilemmas faced by a counselling psychologist

Irina Churakova

Introduction

In 2007 I worked as counselling psychologist at the International Organization for Migration (IOM) Rehabilitation Centre (RC) for survivors of human trafficking, located in Moscow, Russia, on a project funded by the European Commission and the US government. My responsibilities included working out and implementing the concept of psychological rehabilitation, psychological assessment, daily patients' monitoring, individual psychological counselling sessions and group psychotherapy work with human trafficking survivors. From May to December 2007, I attended to 78 clients in the programme and conducted 280 individual psychotherapy sessions and 50 group format trainings with them. The full programme of individual and group psychological counselling and rehabilitation at the RC was three weeks long. Each patient usually benefited from two to five individual counselling sessions as well as several psychotherapy group sessions, depending on the length of their stay at the centre.

In this contribution I discuss some of the ethical, professional and legal issues surrounding the complex provision of psychological counselling of female survivors of sex trafficking that I encountered in the course of my service.

Ethics in counselling psychology and ethical reasoning

Ethics, or moral philosophy, seeks to establish guidelines by which human character, relations and actions may be judged as good or bad, right or wrong. What is considered as an "ethical" practice varies between professions and cultures and changes over time. In relation to psychology, ethics is a codified set of values that apply to counselling practice (Woolfe, Dryden and Strawbridge, 2003). At the heart of counselling psychology is the relationship between the practitioner and the client – the person or persons for whom the practitioner is working. Because the quality of the relationship carries within itself an expression of its values, a good understanding of ethical behaviour and practice is of fundamental importance. This applies equally to the relationship with therapy clients, supervisees, trainees, employees, colleagues, other professionals and with employing organizations. In this respect, the ethical issues that arise in our profession should draw our attention and encourage counselling psychologists to ask questions of themselves, of their practice and of their professional relationships.

Despite the guidance offered by the British Psychological Society (BPS) and other professional bodies, rarely are there simple answers to the ethical questions that arise in counselling psychology. An ethical dilemma exists whenever there are "good but contradictory ethical reasons to take conflicting and incompatible courses of action" (Woolfe et al., 2003, 615). However, ethics is about more than resolving dilemmas; it is about a way of being, of inter-relating and of practising.

For a counselling psychologist, professional ethics represent at least three basic tasks. The first is acknowledging the reality and importance of the individuals whose lives we affect with our professional actions. The second is understanding the nature of the professional relationship and professional interventions. The third is being accountable for our behaviour (Pope and Vasquez, 2001).

Also crucial in understanding the underpinning of ethical professional practice is ethical reasoning, which operates at two levels. The intuitive level represents the immediate response of the individual's moral conscience, whereas the critical-evaluative level sheds light, refines and guides moral reasoning. The critical-evaluative level comprises three hierarchically related sub-levels. These are: *rules* – specific laws and codes of conduct; *principles* – universally applied values of equal merit; and *theories* – philosophical ideas about the nature and meaning of human existence. It is proposed that, because these three levels are interrelated, the solution to an ethical problem, which is difficult at one level, may be clearer at another level (Woolfe et al., 2003).

The BPS has identified five moral principles underlining the ethical decisions that must be taken by the counselling psychologist in their daily life and work. They are:

1 *Autonomy* – unconditional regard for the client, the maximization of the client's informed choice and their right to choose their own destiny, the intrinsic worth of each person and the right to self-fulfilment or even heteronomy, i.e. putting the other before oneself.
2 *Beneficence* – an obligation, a duty of care, to benefit the clients through the interventions.
3 *Non-maleficence* – "do no harm" or "do the least harm".
4 *Justice* – fairness in ensuring equality of access to training and services, particularly for people from minority groups.
5 *Fidelity* – faithfulness and loyalty, trustworthy and exact communication with clear boundaries and respect for the individual's autonomy expressed through good contracting, informed consent, and confidentiality.

The BPS suggests that because the counselling psychologist is a tool in the therapeutic process, it is important that her or his "principle ethics" should be integrated with "virtue ethics". The main four virtues for psychologists as outlined by Longman (1998) are:

1 *Prudence* – thinking carefully before taking action, avoiding risks, unpleasantness, difficulties.
2 *Integrity* – strength and firmness of character or principle, honesty, trustworthiness.
3 *Respectfulness* – feeling or showing respect, admiration, good intent and honour to something or somebody.
4 *Benevolence* – having or showing a wish to do good and help others.

The first two (prudence and integrity) are reflected in practitioners' behaviour and attitude, the second two (respectfulness and benevolence) are evidenced in the relationships with others.

In working through ethical decisions and dilemmas, which often occur in counselling with survivors of trafficking, the key is to be able to make well-reasoned decisions based on the evidence available. A number of models for making ethical decisions have been suggested, drawing from the ethical reasoning outlined above. Their common elements as summarized by Woolfe et al. (2003) are:

- Take time to clarify the elements of the dilemma from several different, and preferably opposing, perspectives.
- Consult as widely as possible in the time available, study professional codes and seek the views of supervisors, managers (if relevant), and legal advisors, giving information on a need-to-know or in-principle basis.
- Consider alternative courses of action and their consequences not only for the people immediately concerned but also for those close to them.
- Choose what appears to be the best opinion, but be prepared to review it in the light of new evidence.
- Check the outcome and review the process for further learning.

While scholars who study sex work likely all face ethical dilemmas that entail making decisions based on the principles outlined above as part of their research, not all have chosen to write about these difficulties. There are a number of reasons for this, including the reality that discussion of ethical dilemmas might be perceived as opening a door to criticize the researcher's moral principles or standards (Dewey and Zheng, 2013, 4). In what follows I discuss some of the challenges my colleagues at the RC and I faced in the provision of support to victims of sex trafficking. Before doing so, and to provide some context to the life stories of the individuals we encountered and worked with, I briefly outline some of their life trajectories.

Experiences and challenges at the IOM Rehabilitation Centre

The lives of the survivors I encountered in my work at the RC had been often extremely difficult and painful. In the case of one female survivor, for example, she was 9 when her mother had become an alcoholic and started neglecting her children. The young girl starved and had nothing suitable to wear at school where she was bullied and also faced the hostility of other children's parents. At the age of 15 the young woman was raped by her boyfriend, stopped going to school after that, and did not complete her education. Never receiving support or protection from law enforcement agencies, she went to live with a 32-year-old man who abused her and often beat her violently. She tried to commit suicide several times and eventually fled from her abusive partner but ended up with people who became her sex traffickers.

Another survivor I encountered had been a bright pupil in elementary school, greatly enjoying her studies until her mother got re-married and became an alcoholic. The young girl and her brother were often left unattended and beaten up by their mother. When she reached adolescence, the survivor was sexually harassed by her stepfather. As a result, she behaved aggressively at school, had no respect for teachers or students, and was seen as the "leader" of other young troublemakers. The school administration was not interested in understanding the girl's family situation and did not stop her from leaving education.

Yet another survivor had been brought up in a family where both parents were alcoholics. As a result, the young girl and her brother often experienced violence at the hands of their father. When still at elementary school the siblings ran away from home and lived in poor conditions with other neglected and drug-addicted young people. The survivor was raped by her peers when she was approximately 8 years of age, and the violence continued for several years, until she was first sexually trafficked at 12 years old. Finally, the last case is that of a survivor who came from Ukraine. She had run away from home looking for a better life in Moscow, but at the age of 16 she was recruited into prostitution. The young woman had a difficult relationship with her parents, whom, she became convinced, were not her real biological parents. Her mother kept looking for her and eventually found her in Moscow three years later when she was able to set her free from her exploiters.

The cases presented above reveal stories of women who have not chosen to enter prostitution, rather, they were forced into it as victims of sex trafficking. The survey we carried out at the RC reveals that of the 78 female survivors of sex trafficking we came in contact with, none of them had actually planned to work in the sex industry, nor were they aware that they would be forced into prostitution by their traffickers. The latter searched specifically for "naïve" young girls, they deceived them by promising them jobs as waitresses, cleaners, baby-sitters, either in Russia or abroad and preyed in particular on young women with difficult family situations, knowing that they could be more easily manipulated. According to data obtained in the course of the study, 25.64% of the victims of human trafficking (VOTs) were recruited into prostitution at the age of 15–17; 53.85% between the ages of 18–20; 12.82% between the ages of 21–25; and 7.69% were older when they were recruited, between the ages of 26–32. As for the duration of the exploitation period, 19.23% of the VOTs were involved in sex trafficking for 0.5 years or less; 55.13% from 0.5 to 1 year; 19.23% from 1 to 2 years; and 6.41% from 2 to 3 years. The average period of exploitation in prostitution, based on self-reporting, is 1.22 years. As far as the methods of recruitment, 70.5% of the survivors were recruited through personal contact, i.e. friends and peers; 18% through ads in the media and the Internet; 6.4% ran away from home and ended up in vulnerable situations that made them easy prey of sex traffickers; and 1.3% were sold directly by their relatives.

Psychological care and support of survivors of trafficking at the IOM RC was based on patients' psychological needs and aimed at giving the survivors new opportunities for a better future. In the atmosphere of psychological comfort and safety at the centre, the staff, including myself, worked on stimulating the psychological, spiritual and other resources of our clients, drawing on their unique life experiences, creativity, power of logical reasoning and motivation. As professionals we did our best to provide comprehensive support to the survivors, being aware that the difficulties they encountered were part of a long healing journey. During these processes we faced notable professional challenges as counselling psychologists. Drawing on IOM guidelines on the ethical treatment of victims of trafficking informed by the principles outlined earlier, we ensured that in our provision of services we always considered what is in the best interest of each individual, whatever their circumstances (IOM, 2007).

In doing so we also faced ethical dilemmas and challenges in our daily activities, which we addressed and tried to resolve on a case-by-case basis, and by always keeping the survivor's interest as our main target. For instance, at one point the RC hosted Aliona, a 15-year-old girl, for whom it was illegal to reside in the facility due to the project's own rules and restrictions vis-à-vis unaccompanied minors. Aliona was from Moldova, she had lost her documents and did not have any connection with her family, having ran away from the orphanage where she had grown up. On her way to Moscow she met and fell in love with a 23-year-old man and broke the RC rules many times to meet him, until he was threatened with a legal suit for sexual exploitation of a minor. In addition to managing her "unruly" behaviour, we also had to deal both with the fact that, as a minor, and as per IOM rules, Aliona should not have resided in the RC facilities and that she should have been sent back to her country of origin, Moldova. However, based on our professional judgement, we decided that it was in Aliona's best interest to stay in Russia. For some time she was accommodated in a state shelter for children, while we did our best to liaise with the Moldovan diplomatic mission to produce her documents. During this time, we had to face a number of legal challenges and ethical dilemmas. We had to ask ourselves: how can we ensure that Aliona remains safely and legally in Russia without breaking the law? How can we help her recover her documents when her country of origin is reluctant to recognize her as a citizen? Who will pay for her stay in the shelter during the process of document retrieval? To address these issues, we proceeded with determination to ensure that Aliona was treated as humanely as possible and we were eventually able to surmount all the hurdles that her case presented.

Other challenges we faced pertained to the relationship between the survivors and their own children. As many survivors had had difficult upbringings and relationships with their parents, they had low self-esteem and did not believe that they could be good parents themselves. Therefore, when they had children they often preferred to give them up for adoption. As one of the young women told me: "It's better for my son to be living in a good foster family, than in a bad natural one." In one case in particular, a survivor from Chechnya gave her firstborn son to a good friend of her family to be raised and taken care of. As care providers, we had to evaluate what would happen if the young woman changed her mind, and wanted to take the child back, given that the "adoption" had been unofficial. We had to ask whether the interests of the foster family and of the child would be considered in this eventuality. Often, the answers to these questions were not straightforward. In another case, two survivors who had been rescued by the police and went through rehabilitation at the RC, expected, after going through the programme, to go back home and take their children back with them. Their children had been under the care of their grandmothers who objected to giving the children back to their mothers. According to Russian legislation, however, a mother has priority over all relatives in the upbringing of her birth children. In dealing with these cases, we had to evaluate whether the children would be willing to move with the mothers, or whether they would rather stay with their grandmothers. How would the survivors be able to provide for their children? The difficulty in such cases was for us to facilitate taking a decision that would benefit all parties involved, an approach that we strove to take by ensuring everyone's well-being. Other difficult decisions we had to make concerned possible crimes committed, or criminal acts planned by the survivors. In each of the cases we encountered we had to evaluate the seriousness of the possible crime or intention to commit it and whether we had a responsibility to report it to the authorities.

To conclude it is important to emphasize that in dealing with these challenges I grew and developed not only professionally but also personally. Having direct experience of the complex and painful experiences of the survivors I encountered had a profound impact on my own life. After my studies, I thought I was ready to face any challenge in my profession, but coming from a privileged background had not really prepared me for the emotional difficulties I would have to face when dealing on a daily basis with the survivors and their stories. Their resilience, however, and desire to rebuild their lives was inspirational and an important aspect in directing my professional choices to ensure the well-being of these women.

My experience is not unique, and there are many others who operate as counselling psychologists and in other positions with victims of sex trafficking facing similar challenges to the ones I faced at RC. The discussion presented here shows how ethical guidelines and case-by-case decisions are important factors in ensuring targeted and sensitive provision of services to this vulnerable population.

References

Dewey S. and Zheng T. 2013. *Ethical Research with Sex Workers: Anthropological Approaches*. London: Springer.

IOM. 2007. *Direct Assistance for Victims of Trafficking*. Switzerland: IOM.

Longman A.W. (ed.). 1998. *Longman Dictionary of English Language and Culture*. London: Pearson Education.

Pope K.S. and Vasquez M.J.T. 2001. *Ethics in Psychotherapy and Counselling: A Practical Guide*. Hoboken, NJ: John Wiley & Sons.

Woolfe R., Dryden W. and Strawbridge S. (eds). 2003. *Handbook of Counselling Psychology*. London: Sage.

Part VII
Cultural representations

43

Cultural representations

An introduction

Susan Dewey, Isabel Crowhurst, and Chimaraoke Izugbara

Introduction

Literary, artistic, cinematic, and other cultural products have historically represented sex workers and the industry of which they are a part by mobilizing dominant cultural perceptions of commercial sex for particular socio-political, rights-based, religious, or other purposes. Key themes in existing research are sex work as metaphor, sex workers' artistic representations, historical shifts in modes of representation, and moving beyond the reproduction of inequalities in cultural representations of the sex industry. Chapters in this section engage with these aspects while offering clear directions for future research.

Key themes in existing literature

Cultural studies, art history, and numerous other academic disciplines have long emphasized the importance of critically engaging with how particular communities, social issues, or locales are represented in dominant cultural forms such as art, literature, and mass media. Studying the representation of red-light areas in tourist and other promotional literature, for instance, provides tremendous insight into how such representations differentially construe gender, race, class in conjunction with citizenship and other rights (Chapuis, 2016). In many cases, sex work—particularly prostitution—functions as a metaphor for social issues deemed particularly pressing in the historical or contemporary contexts and often has little to do with sex industry realities. These concerns have historically included moral panics about the deterioration of social life and the long-term consequences of women's participation in the workforce (Bryan-Wilson, 2012; Clayson, 2003).

Cultural representations can also shed light on the intersections of race, class, and gender that inform women's decision-making processes vis-à-vis commercial sex in extremely complex and often conflicted ways (Springer, 2015). Yet these representations may also fall into well-trodden terrain in portraying women in sex work as innocent victims of personal hardship, as calculating businesswomen, or sexual adventuresses, as often occurs in world cinema representations of women in prostitution (Campbell, 2006). Mass media, particularly journalism, further reinforces these deeply rooted stereotypes by focusing on prostitution as evidence of a decline in morality, product of abusive and/or dysfunctional childhoods, replete with violence and exploitation, and as a public nuisance (Van Brunschot, Sydie, & Krull, 1999).

Sex industry workers actively resist such negative and often inaccurate representations of their lives by creating their own artistic products that provide emic perspectives on a wide array of venue types and experiences within particular sex industry forms (Red Umbrella Project, 2013; Sterry, 2009). Memoirs by well-educated and highly paid escorts now form their own literary genre in Western Europe and North America, often by depicting commercial sex as a liberating, lucrative, and independent alternative to routinized occupations that offer little room for creativity or upward mobility (Attwood, 2010). Many researchers have successfully included arts-based methods to creatively engage with sex workers and facilitate the co-production of knowledge in ways that are meaningful to all participants (Capous-Desyllas, 2013; Schuler, 2017).

Historical shifts in modes of representation are somewhat evident in studies of how such representations have changed over time as well as what they reveal about a particular historical context. Historians note that studying prostitution is a powerful means by which to understand dominant concerns about gender, sexuality, and a host of other issues in a given historical period (Gilfoyle, 1999). Such studies have emphasized the important role sex workers played in mixed-gender sociality in newly independent states as women in prostitution navigated complex regulations designed to surveille them and extract money from their earnings (Campos, 2017). Analyses of significant shifts in cultural representations of male sex workers in academic research note major changes from nineteenth-century understandings of male sex work as an identity problem, to mid-century associations with economic exploitation by older men, and the subsequent construction of male prostitution as a public health crisis in the 1980s with the advent of the HIV/AIDS pandemic (Scott, 2003).

Cultural representations may reproduce inequalities that are likewise evident in policy, law, or social services approaches to sex work even as they contest or complicate dominant perceptions about the sex industry. Powerful gender ideologies underlie cultural representations of the sex industry in ways that directly impact social services provision and other assistance measures by positioning sex workers as victim/criminals in need of simultaneous punitive sanctions and therapeutic assistance (Majic, 2014). Among men who sell sex to other men in street contexts, studies focus on aggressively masculine youth that ostensibly require habilitation into middle-class sensibilities while ignoring the significant harms and compromised gender identities the men routinely face as they form networks of support designed to subvert their extreme socio-economic constraints (Kaye, 2007). Such approaches deny sex workers' agency and the potential for meaningful social change through alternative dominant cultural representations that more accurately represent their lives (McCracken, 2013).

Mass media concerns about sex trafficking, the exploitation of undocumented migrants, and other social concerns related to the sex industry have historically been used to justify stronger border controls and thereby improve public order and public health (Stenvoll, 2002). Clearly established dichotomies of perpetrators and victims in public anti-trafficking campaigns replicate historically long-standing exercises of power over women's bodies as a means to alleviate widespread public anxiety regarding migration, public disorder, and related social concerns (Andrijasevic, 2007). Yet alternatives do exist in the form of counter-narratives in which filmmakers or producers of other cultural products immerse themselves in the lives of those they seek to represent and do so in open-ended ways that much more accurately reflect the uncertainties and ambiguities that characterize real life (Plambech, 2016).

Chapter overview

Sambai and Simatei (Chapter 44) examine the construction of "the prostitute" in six African works of fiction and the accompanying popular cultural attitudes towards sex workers that these works seek to either affirm or subvert. Murray and colleagues (Chapter 45) present the results of a participatory photography project designed to challenge stigmatizing discourses about the sex industry through the circulation of poetic and artistic narratives that connect sex workers' daily lives with their rights. Preston (Chapter 46) examines how contemporary literature disrupts dominant epistemologies by illuminating the queerness of sex work and its affective and interior worlds, with a particular focus on how abject bodies in urban space confront borders of race, gender, sexuality, and class. Adesina (Chapter 47) examines the historical trajectories of Nigeria's sex industry, particularly as it relates to colonialism, poverty, necessity, livelihood options, local and international trade, and the role of the family. Skilbrei and Ystehede (Chapter 48) argue that representations of prostitution symbolize broader social concerns by analyzing changes in representations, from the 1880s until the present, of Jack the Ripper's murders of women in prostitution. Jeffreys and colleagues (Chapter 49) analyze two case studies of hostile public treatment directed at sex worker activists to argue that such hostility functions as a public shaming ritual that reminds sex workers of their outsider status. Lennon and Liamputtong (Chapter 50) explore how media continue to represent sex workers as a threat to the community moral fabric through advancing stigmatizing and discriminatory discourses that tacitly endorse violence against sex workers. Finally, although positioned in Part VIII on Technologies, Starr and Francis' contribution (Chapter 57) is of great relevance also to the analysis of cultural representations. Here the authors focus on the "whore gaze" and how through it sex workers' self-representations, enabled by new communication technologies, can break out the passivity so prevalent in mainstream cinematic and representational frameworks.

Future directions

A vast majority of literature on cultural representations of the sex industry focuses on the Global North, particularly North America, to the exclusion of the enormous body of related work produced in the Global South. Sex workers regularly feature as characters in movies produced in the burgeoning cinematic industries of Nigeria and India, which produce thousands of films annually that are distributed regionally as well as to diaspora populations worldwide. For instance, Indian cinema has featured the seductive "vamp" as a stock figure since the inception of the South Asian film industry, where the first actresses were the daughters of tawaif, Mughal courtesans who were displaced from their livelihood following the advent of the British Empire.

Empirical engagement with cultural representations should aspire to achieve greater geographic diversity with respect to the Global South, including studies of how sex workers use art to advance their rights. Likewise, a significant body of literature on current urban life in sub-Saharan Africa frequently includes sex workers as central or otherwise important characters, yet no one has yet systematically engaged with this literature. The same is true in regions of the world outside of Europe and North America, from which the bulk of critical media studies on this topic have emerged.

References

Andrijasevic, Rutvica. 2007. Beautiful Dead Bodies: Gender, Migration and Representation in Anti-Trafficking Campaigns. *Feminist Review* 86: 24–44.

Attwood, Feona. 2010. Call-Girl Diaries: New Representations of Cosmopolitan Sex Work. *Feminist Media Studies* 10(1): 109–112.

Bryan-Wilson, Julia. 2012. Dirty Commerce: Art Work and Sex Work Since the 1970s. *differences* 23(2): 71–112.

Campbell, Russell. 2006. *Marked Women: Prostitutes and Prostitution in the Cinema*. Madison, WI: University of Wisconsin Press.

Campos, Camila Pastor de Maria. 2017. Performers or Prostitutes? Artistes During the French Mandate over Syria and Lebanon, 1921–1946. *Journal of Middle East Women's Studies* 13(2): 287–311.

Capous-Desyllas, Moshoula. 2013. Representations of Sex Workers' Needs and Aspirations: A Case for Arts-Based Research. *Sexualities* 16(7): 772–787.

Chapuis, Amandine. 2016. Touring the Immoral: Affective Geographies of Visitors to the Amsterdam Red Light District. *Urban Studies* 54(3): 616–632.

Clayson, Hollis. 2003. *Painted Love: Prostitution in the French Art of the Impressionist Era*. Los Angeles, CA: Getty Publications.

Gilfoyle, Timothy. 1999. Prostitutes in History: From Parables of Pornography to Metaphors of Modernity. *American Historical Review* 104(1): 117–141.

Kaye, Kerwin. 2007. Sex and the Unspoken in Male Street Prostitution. *Journal of Homosexuality* 53(1/2): 37–73.

McCracken, Jill. 2013. *Street Sex Workers' Discourse: Realizing Change Through Agential Choice*. New York: Routledge.

Majic, Samantha. 2014. Beyond "Victims-Criminals": Sex Workers, Nonprofit Organizations, and Gender Ideologies. *Gender & Society* 28(3): 463–485.

Plambech, Sine. 2016. The Art of the Possible: Making Films on Sex Work Migration and Human Trafficking. *Anti-Trafficking Review* 7. www.antitraffickingreview.org/index.php/atrjournal/article/view/206.

Red Umbrella Project. 2013. *Prose and Lore: Memoir Stories About Sex Work-Issue 2*. New York: New York Foundation.

Schuler, Greta. 2017. "At Your Own Risk": Narratives of Migrant Sex Workers in Johannesburg. *Urban Forum* 28(1): 27–42.

Scott, John. 2003. A Prostitute's Progress: Male Prostitution in Scientific Discourse. *Social Semiotics* 13(2): 179–199.

Springer, Jennifer Thorington. 2015. Constructing Radical Black Subjectivities: Survival Pimping in Austin Clarke's *The Polished Hoe*. *Frontiers: A Journal of Women Studies* 36(2): 169–191.

Stenvoll, Dag. 2002. From Russia with Love: Newspaper Coverage of Cross Border Prostitution in Northern Norway 1990–2001. *European Journal of Women's Studies* 9(2): 143–162.

Sterry, David, ed. (2009). *Hos, Hookers, Call Girls, and Rent Boys: Professionals Writing on Life, Love, Money, and Sex*. Berkeley, CA: Soft Skull Press.

Van Brunschot, Erin, Sydie, Rosalind, and Krull, Catherine. 1999. Images of Prostitution: The Prostitute and Print Media. *Women and Criminal Justice* 10(4): 47–72.

44

Pleasures of the flesh

The image of the prostitute in African literature

Caroline Sambai and Peter Simatei

Introduction

Though seldom the main character, the prostitute is a familiar figure in African literature. She emerges as a multi-faceted icon, a figure whose identity is shaped by a confluence of complex socio-economic conditions and who, as a literary trope, serves as a vehicle for a large variety of objectives: "from moral reflections and social criticism to saucy entertainment" (Schönfeld 2000, 1). African literature reveals a diversity of depictions of the figure of the prostitute. As a woman, her identity is brought out as fluid and ambiguous while this same identity's socially constructed nature and performativity clearly emerges, especially in fiction written by women authors. In these works of fiction by women, prostitutes who are "represented both as sexual victims and sexual agents" (Ruiz 2012, 8) are given agency to articulate and perform identities that are alternative to dominant representations of the prostitute as a deviant character. Ruiz argues that prostitutes and other women who try to become "visible," engage in this kind of gender performativity in order to contest "the place and authority of the masculine position" and reclaim "Black women's bodies, deviant bodies and colonized bodies as producers of knowledge and speaking subjects through their identities" (Ruiz 2012, 8).

Yet in writings by men, such as David Maillu's *After 4.30* (1975), Charles Mangua's *Son of Woman* (1986), or Major Mwangi's *Going Down River Road* (2001), the prostitute often appears as the index of decadence in society. Such categories are problematized in women's writings, where the prostitute appears as a complex character that transcends the naturalized stereotype of the prostitute. Bessie Head's short story "Life" is named after its female protagonist, a prostitute from Botswana who performs her complex and multiple identities in Johannesburg as "singer, beauty queen, advertising model, and prostitute", an affirmation that disrupts the dichotomies of good and bad, moral and immoral, or mother and prostitute, a binary often manifested in male-authored texts. Yet the irony in Life's emancipation narrative is that when she returns to Botswana she ends up again in the patriarchal enclosure of marriage and can no longer control her body and enjoy her sexuality. In fact, she is brutally murdered by her husband after he accuses her of infidelity. Life's infidelity is a protest against the monotony of marriage and the routine that her new role as a traditional wife demands of her; it is a violation of traditional roles that reinforce control over women's bodies and personal freedoms. For this violation, Life pays with her life.

Female writers, including Oludhe Macgoye and Genga-Idowu, conceal or camouflage the activities of the prostitute in order "to project prostitution as a career and as a productive economic activity like any other" (Muriungi 2004, 286). Such camouflage, "gives prostitution a human face and revises the portrayal of the prostitute as it is cast in writings by other artists in Kenya, especially the male writers" (Muriungi 2004, 287). The portrayal of prostitution as empowering, as granting economic freedom to female characters and enabling them to create their own private spaces is a theme that runs through most novels authored by women but it also manifests itself in those male-authored texts that treat the prostitute as part of societal degeneration and corruption who equally needs transformation into a "better woman." But women writers do not present the prostitute as the pure embodiment of virtue. Like in many significant works of literature, the prostitute remains a locus of conflicting discourses and perspectives on prostitution but are somewhat liberated from being objects of masculine desire.

Generally in African literature, and especially by male authors, the portrayal of the prostitute follows two broad patterns. First, there are texts, mostly in the sub-genre of popular fiction, that construct the character of the prostitute in order to fulfill the artistic objective that Schönfeld (2000) calls "saucy entertainment." In such fictions there is a confluence of prostitution, crime, and drunkenness expressed in a grammar of sexual explicitness bordering on pornography. In this drama the prostitute is a repugnant villain and a master of deceit with a tendency to petty crime and alcoholism. She is a helpless victim of fate and is not given a voice to articulate her story and memory but is instead condemned for the vice of prostitution. Just like the decadent urban space she occupies, the prostitute is often treated as a degenerate character, a seductress, who tricks and degrades the men and, to borrow from McCombs, epitomizes "not only mechanical sex but also the mechanized greed of a corrupt capitalist economic system" (McCombs 1986, 217). Examples in this genre include David Maillu's *After 4.30* and *The Broken Drum* and Charles Mangua's *Son of Woman*.

In Maillu's *After 4.30* Emili Katango the prostitute is the irredeemable victim of male predation and violence. She is sexually exploited by her boss. Pregnant and abandoned she does not have the means—as a secretary she earns a meagre salary—to take care of herself and her illegitimate son and she decides to engage in prostitution to augment her income. She is vulgar and comes to enjoy what she calls "overworking men":

> I like the way I sweat men
> with this!
> A man is like a sheep,
> You see
> When he's inside you
> You can tell him anything on earth
> Call him a pig
> A swine
> A warthog
> Or sweetheart
> and he will reply you, yes, yes.
> (After 4.30, 5)

Maillu's representation of Katango is a good example of a disempowering narrative that uses the prostitute's body to inscribe male gratification and phallic politics and ends in the pornographization of the female body. Accorded no perspective of her own about her condition and denied an independent subjectivity, Katango's ability to exercise agency on the margins of social life is severely curtailed. For Maillu, "prostitution (is) an ugly sexual encounter" (Muriungi 2004, 291) and prostitutes are "filthy bitches with decaying cunts whose character-istic trademarks are vulgarity and obscenity" (Maillu 1975, 8). This dismal view of prostitution in which prostitutes are seen as a cause of decay in society continues in Maillu's other novels, notably *Broken Drum* where women are regarded as parasites and fleas.[1]

However, and as we pointed out earlier, a number of male novelists go beyond this sordid image and stereotype of the prostitute and instead problematize the whole phenomenon of prostitution by engaging its social and political implications. For example, in her text, *Song of Malaya* (1988) Okot p'Bitek uses a prostitute to laugh at society's hypocrisy towards prostitu-tion. The prostitute in *Song of Malaya*—Malaya is Swahili for prostitute and is the name sex workers are called in East Africa—is the main character and the narration is from her point of view. The prostitute here is more of the "whore-with-a-heart-of-gold" type who embodies kindness and warmth and who believes that her trade benefits society immensely.

In this text, Okot p'Bitek gives voice to prostitutes to challenge the discriminatory rules tar-geted against them by both the society and the state. In fact the prostitute in this text proceeds to demonstrate that prostitution serves a basic need and names the different type of people that secretly visit her for fulfillment of sexual pleasure. With bitter irony she condemns the hypocrisy of state agents that visit her at night for sex then turn against her during the day pretending to enforce state laws against prostitution:

> But you/Big Chief,
> Why do you look at me
> As if I were a bunch
> Of hornets?
> Why do you hiss
> Like a frightened cobra
> And bark at me
> As if I were
> A thief?
> Why, Baba . . .
> Was it not you
> Three nights ago?
> Or was it four months ago?
> Do you not remember
> Bursting into my house
> Forcing me down
> And tearing my knickers . . . As if I were unwilling?
> (p'Bitek 1988, 36)

This burst of sexual violence collapses into impotence and, with a sense of irony, the prostitute laughs at the impotence and the worthlessness of these wielders of state power:

> Oh-ha-ya-ya!
> But you were drunk,
> You could not finish . . .
> You feigned sleep,
> Snoring like a pregnant hippo . . .
> (p'Bitek 1988, 52)

In *Song of Malaya*, sex work is sanitized, the sex it involves is presented as therapeutic to the many working-class people hankering for some pleasurable relief from their dreary work routines. The prostitute in p'Bitek's text who projects herself as the spokeswoman of her fellow sex workers, takes us through the list of the clients she welcomes into her house. There is a "vigorous young sailor" returning ashore with a time bomb "pulsating in (his) loins," a homebound soldier, a reprieved murderer, a prisoner and a detainee about to be released with "granaries full to overflow . . ." (*Song*, 127–128). All of them find refuge, solace, and fulfillment in the prostitute who welcomes them with her warm hands. They include people of different races (drunken Sikhs, Indian vegetarians, and a "thick-skinned white miner") and professions, (engineers, factory workers, etc). Once in a while she catches a schoolboy in her net:

> All my thanks
> To you
> Schoolboy lover,
> I charge you
> No fee
> That shy smile
> On your face,
> And . . . Oh! I feel ten years
> Younger . . .
> Hey! Listen . . .
> Do not let the
> Teacher know
> He was here
> Last night!

The prostitute has no regret for being a *sex worker*. She actually urges her fellow sex workers to take pride in their work and to disregard the hypocritical moral police—priests, bishops, parliamentarians, and other state officials—who condemn them but are themselves the drive behind prostitution.

Such attempts to write the prostitute into the material and social inequities of postcolonial societies have received criticism from feminist scholars who argue that male authors merely deploy prostitutes as tropes for narrating their ideological projects.[2] Cyprian Ekwensi's *Jagua Nana* (1975), and Ngũgĩ wa Thiong'o's *Petals of Blood* (1977) are good illustrations of this assertion.

Jagua Nana, the protagonist in Cyprian Ekwensi's novel by the same name, is perhaps the most well known prostitute in African literature, probably because Ekwensi's novel was the first to feature a prostitute as its main character who is fully realized and credible and from whose perspective most events are viewed. In *Jagua Nana*, Ekwensi has constructed a complex character, who conflates the many characteristics, both positive and negative, that society attributes to prostitutes and that has been mirrored generally in modern literature throughout the world. Jagua Nana has been referred to as the "matriarch and archetypal prostitute of African literature" because "she embodies all the attributes of the prostitute in modern literature" (Nwahunanya 2011, 342).

Unlike other characters that are driven into prostitution by poverty and related social conditions Jagua Nana's journey begins initially as a revolt against what she considers the boredom of married life. Married to a rich businessman simply referred to as the Coal City man, Jagua would soon discover that the man's conservative and stingy lifestyle did not suit her restless and adventurous spirit. She refuses to adapt herself to his humdrum life and quits:

But he never took her to parties, and would not dress well, for fear the money would leak away. In no way did his ideas of living attract her. She found that she had obeyed her parents but now they were not there to see her misery and they would never understand her longing, the hot thirst for adventure in her blood. She refused to adapt herself to his humdrum life and she wondered how she had been able to remain with him as she did for over three years.

(Jagua, 167)

Jagua Nana becomes a prostitute by choice and she is not therefore a victim. She has autonomy over her own body. She understands her decision as a rebellion against patriarchal institutions like marriage that appear to limit her freedom to choose the kind of lifestyle she desires. Nana's action is a revolt against patriarchal values of the good woman, who is submissive in her role as wife and mother. But the fact that she arrives at this decision after three years of a childless marriage and after her husband decides to marry another woman also suggests that Jagua Nana quits the marriage out of frustrations with her personal life. However, the narrator's reference to "the hot thirst for adventure in her blood" seems to imply that Jagua Nana suffers an innate proclivity for prostitution, and that this may as well be a major drive in her longing for freedom outside marriage.

Nana's longing for Lagos and the glamorous life it promises is also framed in similar terms as if to suggest that her response to the lures of Lagos is structured by something deeply rooted in her female nature rather than a desire founded on socio-economic conditions. Nana wanted to be part of Lagos "where the girls were glossy, worked in offices like the men, danced, smoked, wore high-heeled shoes and narrow slacks, and were 'free' and 'fast' with their favours" (*Jagua* 167–168). She is attracted by what she hears about the people in Lagos who "did not have to go to bed at eight o'clock. Anyone who cared could go roaming the streets or wandering from one night spot to the other right up till morning" (*Jagua* 167–168).

In Lagos, Jagua Nana's search for pleasure is fulfilled. She is aware of the awesome power she wields over men and exploits it fully for her sexual and material satisfactions. She is quite seductive and although she is cast as the exploitative *femme fatale*, the author redeems her by endowing her with admirable qualities especially in her relations with the people whose friendship she values. She shows genuine love for Freddie, the young teacher, and as Emmanuel Obiechina 1987, 12) has noted, Nana is a character "full of vitality, warmth and humaneness . . . Her faults are many but in spite of them she remains likeable, even lovable, because she is never mean or contemptible." These positive attributes redeem Jagua Nana and turn her prostitution into an act of subversion of the dominant social order. However, since the world of the prostitute is linked with the corrupt and criminal politics of postcolonial Nigeria, Nana's world collapses as soon as she is lured into politics by Uncle Taiwo, one of her clients. Yet even in this particular case, Jagua Nana is empowered by the author and comes out more as an actor than a mere victim of the happenings. She articulates a candid opinion of politics, warning Freddie not to engage in it and thinks politics is a "game for dog. And in dis Lagos, is a rough game. De roughest game in de whole world. Is smelly and dirty and you too clean an' sweet" (*Jagua*, 137). The link of prostitution to political corruption is a predominant feature in African literature and Ekwensi, like most other African writers, is using prostitution as a trope to narrate the decay of post-independent political systems in Nigeria.

While in Ekwensi's *Jagua Nana*, the reasons that lead to Jagua Nana's prostitution is treated with a measure of ambiguity, in Ngũgĩ wa Thiong'o's *Petals of Blood* the prostitute is clearly the product of the contradictions of a capitalist society run by a neocolonial political class. Unlike Jagua Nana who becomes a prostitute by choice, Wanja, the prostitute in Ngũgĩ's novel, is the unwilling victim of the sexual abuse by this new class of comprador bourgeoisie whose appetite for both sex and wealth is part of their culture of conspicuous consumption and is symptomatic of the decadence characterizing their lifestyles as a ruling class. While still in school Wanja is seduced and gets pregnant by Kimeria, one of her father's friends and a former colonial home guard, an occurrence that severely restricts her choices in life. She dumps the baby in a latrine and begins her adult life as a barmaid then makes the choice to enter prostitution and invests the proceeds in a transport business and a brothel that she names Sunshine Lodge. Wanja comes to understand her own prostitution as mirroring the political prostitution of the elite, making a choice to participate in the "eat or be eaten" culture. She shocks Munira to the core when, as she yields to his persistent seduction, she tells him:

> No, Mwalimu. No free things in Kenya. A hundred shillings on the table if you want high-class treatment.
> This is New Kenya. You want it, you pay for it, for the bed and the light and my time and the drink that I shall later give you and the breakfast tomorrow. And all for a hundred shillings. For you. Because of old times. For others it will be more expensive.
>
> *(Petals, 279)*

Wanja does not use prostitution merely for economic advancement; it is her weapon for revenge against Kimeria and his two fellow capitalist exploiters, Chui and Mzigo. They are the directors of the local branch of foreign-owned Theng'eta Breweries who have manipulated county licensing laws in order to appropriate the right for Theng'eta drink from Wanja including property bequeathed to her by her grandmother. Wanja understands her revenge as personal—against the injustices done to her by Kimeria—but she is also seeking revenge for the downtrodden workers and peasants whose sufferings she understands as being created by the exploitative policies of the neocolonial class exemplified by Kimeria, Chui, and Mzigo.

Kimeria, who made his fortune as a Home Guard transporting bodies of Mau Mau killed by the British, was still prospering,

> Kimeria, who had ruined my life and later humiliated me by making me sleep with him during our journey to the city . . . this same Kimeria was one of those who would benefit from the new of Ilmorog. Why? Why? I asked myself why? Why? Had he not sinned as much as me? That's why one night I fully realized this law. Eat or you are eaten.
>
> *(Petals, 293)*

It is this epiphany that leads Wanja to open a brothel and to also sell sex. She justifies her "exploitation" of the girls she has recruited into the brothel by arguing that they were being exploited anyway,

> I have hired young girls . . . it was not hard . . . I promised them security . . . and for that . . . they let me trade their bodies . . . what is the difference whether you are sweating it out on a plantation, in a factory, or lying on your back anyway?
>
> *(Petals, 293)*

In her case, prostitution is the "only way I can get my own back on Chui, Mzigo and Kimeria" (*Petals*, 250). Wanja justifies prostitution as merely another type of work and, as in the case of p'Bitek's *Song of Malaya*, moral policing fails given the decadence of the very people seeking to enforce the law.

If in *Jagua Nana* prostitution is framed as a form of subversion of patriarchal social order, Wanja in *Petals of Blood* perceives it as an act of resistance, first through acquiescence with oppressive forces but later by joining a progressive group of patriots—Munira, Karega, and

Abdulla—to confront what now becomes clearly identified as a tyrannical neocolonial order represented by their tormentors, namely, Chui, Mzigo, and Kimeria. In a sense then, Ngũgĩ's portrayal of Wanja is positive to the extent that she makes her an "agent(s) of a radical politics." and even turning her "energies into instruments of political insurgency" (Gikandi 2000, 156). In Wanja, and as demonstrated by a number of scholars (Gikandi 2000; Stratton 1990), Ngũgĩ narrates the postcolonial history of Kenya, paralleling her story with the main political phases the nation has gone through. But Wanja does not outgrow her prostitute identity even when she transforms into a subject conscious of her exploitation and oppression.

In many instances therefore, prostitution in general is treated in African literature as a product of the ruptures wrought on African societies by colonial culture and economy; an outcome of urban decadence and of the unfinished project of modernity. The bodies of prostitutes become a locus of varied discourses ranging from those that conscript them to the service of patriarchal or nationalist ideologies to those, especially female writers, who feel it is their work to offer a positive image of the prostitute.

Notes

1 For more on this see Kurtz (1988).
2 Stratton (1990), for example, has argued that, "The trope elaborates a gendered theory of nationhood and of writing, one that excludes women from the creative production of the national polity or identity and of literary texts. Instead, woman herself is produced or constructed by the male writer as an embodiment of his literary/political vision" (51). She further argues that, "In these texts, prostitution is not related to the female social condition in patriarchal societies. Rather it is a metaphor for men's degradation under some non-preferred socio-political system—a metaphor which encodes women as agents of moral corruption, as sources of moral contamination in society" (53).

References

Ekwensi, Cyprian. 1975. *Jagua Nana*. Ibadan: Heinemann

Gikandi, Simon. 2000. *Ngũgĩ wa Thiong'o*. Cambridge, UK: Cambridge University Press.

Kurtz, Roger. 1988. *Urban Obsessions, Urban Fears: The Postcolonial Kenyan Novel*. New York: Africa World Press.

McCombs, Nancy. 1986. *Earth Spirit, Victim, or Whore? The Prostitute in German Literature, 1880–1925*. Frankfurt: Peter Lang.

Maillu, David. 1975. *After 4.30*. Nairobi: Comb Books.

Maillu, David. 1991. *The Broken Drum*. Nairobi: Jomo Kenyatta Foundation and Maillu Publishing House.

Mangua, Charles. 1986. *Son of Woman*. Nairobi: Heinemann.

Muriungi, Colomba. 2004. "The "Sweet Pepper:" Prostitution Declosetted in Kenyan Women's Writing." *InterText* 4(2): 285–312.

Mwangi, Major. 2001. *Going Down River Road*. Nairobi: East African Educational Publishers.

Ngũgĩ, wa Thiong'o. 1977. *Petals of Blood*. Nairobi: East African Educational Publishers.

Nwahunanya, Chinyere. 2011. "Jagua Nana's Children: The Image of the Prostitute in Post-Colonial African Literature." In *The Perspectives of Language and Literature: Essays in Honour of R.U. Uzoezie*, edited by N. Ezenwa-Ohaeto and Ifeyinwa J. Ogbazi, 339–355. Imo, Nigeria: Rex Charles & Patrick.

Obiechina, E.N. 1987. "Ekwensi as Novelist." *The Essential Ekwensi: A Literary Celebration of Cyprian Ekwensi's Sixty-Fifth Birthday*, edited by E.N. Emenyonu, 152–164. Ibadan: Heinemann Educational Books.

p'Bitek, Okot. 1988. *Song of Malaya*. Nairobi: Heinemann.

Ruiz, Maria Isabel Romero, ed. 2012. *Women's Identities and Bodies in Colonial and Post-Colonial History and Literature*. Newcastle upon Tyne, UK: Cambridge Scholars Publishing.

Schönfeld, Christiane. 2000. "Introduction." In *Commodities of Desire: The Prostitute in Modern German Literature*, edited by Christiane Schönfeld, 1–19. New York: Camden House.

Stratton, Florence. 1990. "Periodic Embodiments: A Ubiquitous Trope in African Men's Writing." *Research in African Literatures* 21(1): 111–126.

45

Shifting gazes and challenging discourses about sex work and mega-events in Brazil

Laura Murray, Ana Paula da Silva, Angela Donini, and Cristiane Oliveira

Introduction

Moral panics surrounding prostitution and mega-sporting events in the mass media have become an unfortunate and inseparable pair. Rio de Janeiro is a case in point. The city hosted two mega-sporting events back to back: the 2014 World Cup and the 2016 Olympic Games. Leading up to both events, the mass media's dominant narratives warned of increases in sex tourism, cross-border trafficking and landscapes of shame, violence and deception. Headlines called on readers to save children at risk of being sold and to save (or at least pity) sex workers forced to serve sex-hungry tourists. In the images that accompany these stories, sex workers' faces are often blurred, covered and hidden from the camera, disconnecting the image from its protagonists' history and tying it to the journalist's narrative.

One of the most significant barriers to changing the social imaginary about prostitution has been the systematic production of victimizing images of prostitution that erase sex workers' subjective realities and often obscure or sensationalize contexts and histories. Urban landscapes are often presented as not belonging to sex workers and red-light districts as void of life, transformed from spaces of work into universalized identities of exploitation and desperation. In other words, a discourse emblematic of the dynamics of modernity and coloniality (Quijano 2000) that pushes towards criminalization and exclusion. Authors have examined this relationship in terms of colonial portraits of prostitution (Alloula 1986) and more recently, trafficking (Agustín 2007; Andrijasevic 2007; Blanchette et al. 2013; Brown et al. 2010). While there is an important body of literature about sex work, moral panics and mega-events (Bonthuys 2012; GAATW 2007; Richter et al. 2012), there is less that specifically examines the role of images in fuelling these anxieties.

Urban "clean-up" projects as part of the mega-event preparation have been closely related to and imbricated in the moral panics surrounding prostitution (Kennelly and Watt 2011; Silk 2014). Rio de Janeiro experienced a series of urban clean-up projects, especially prior to the World Cup, that violently affected sex workers and displaced vulnerable population groups on a large scale. Prostitution is not a crime in Brazil and sex work is a recognized profession, yet all third-party involvement remains illegal, creating ample opportunity for the police to stage strategic crackdowns and enforcement of the country's ambiguous laws (Blanchette and da Silva 2016; Murray 2014). Displacements related to the World Cup and Olympic Games are rooted in gentrification processes that began well before the mega-events (Leite 1993), yet since 2000 have been more directly focused on tourist areas such as Copacabana as part of broader securitization of Brazilian urban politics (Amar 2009). Such sanitization and securitization processes have forced sex workers off the streets and closed brothels as part of efforts to rid the city of undesirable populations and demonstrate Brazil's potential for hosting mega-events. As da Silva and Blanchette (2005) observe, the closure of the extremely popular Help club in 2010 in Copacabana was an emblematic culmination of these processes and occurred after the city had been chosen to host both the World Cup and the Olympic Games.

Help's closure marked the beginning of a ferocious process of gentrification involving the installation of museums, hotels and plazas throughout downtown Rio – where the majority of sex work establishments are concentrated – transforming the areas where sex workers do business into construction sites and heavily policed tourist zones. This culminated in a police operation unprecedented in scale and violence in Brazil's recent democracy during which more than 400 sex workers were violently evicted from a building in Niterói, a city across the bay from Rio de Janeiro, in the month prior to the 2014 World Cup. Sex workers, activists and ally politicians denounced in the state legislature, Niterói City Council and state and federal secretariats of human rights, the rapes, robberies and physical violence that occurred during the raid (Murray 2014). As Murray (2014) notes, the entire operation was declared completely illegal by the Rio de Janeiro public defender's office, yet at the time of writing this chapter, three and half years later, no one has been held accountable for the extensive violence and illegality of the raid.

The sex worker movement in Rio de Janeiro was born out of fighting such police violence and gentrification processes (Leite 2009). From very early on, the movement challenged cultural representations of sex workers and worked with artists and musicians to attract media attention to their alternative narratives. In 1987, for example, Gabriela Leite led the then recently formed sex worker movement in a protest, joined by prominent actors, singers and writers, against the removal of the Vila Mimosa red-light district from its original location. Although the Vila Mimosa was eventually moved (twice – our work is focused on its second location), the movement continues to use cultural means such as fashion and the media to subvert dominant stereotypes about prostitution. *Daspu* (meaning: belonging to the "whores"), the clothing line founded by the sex worker rights organization Davida in 2005, is perhaps the most well known example of this activism for its provocative and playful use of fashion and the catwalk as a place to resignify prostitution (Lenz 2008).

It is within this complex context of vibrant cultural activism contrasted with police repression and urban clean-up campaigns that our project, *What You Don't See: Prostitution as We See It*, sought to create a counter-discourse to moral panics surrounding prostitution and vindicate sex workers' right to the city. Implemented in partnership with sex worker rights organizations in Rio de Janeiro, it is an artistic, poetic and political project that documented various meanings of sex work through the use of photography and audio diaries of working and living in Rio de Janeiro during a mega-event. It involved the production of a website with a virtual exhibition[1] and a gallery exhibition that opened in December 2017 in Rio de Janeiro and is scheduled for national and international circulation. The project takes inspiration from the experiences of research–activist collaborations in other global contexts that look specifically at the relationship between sex workers' daily lives and the urban environments in which they live, such as the photographic exhibition, *Our Lives, Our Spaces: Views of Women in a Red-Light District*, by sex workers in South Korea (Cheng 2013) and the *Working the City* and *Volume 44* projects with migrant sex workers in South Africa (Oliveira 2016). Our project, like these, prioritizes forms of knowledge production in which sex workers are knowledge co-producers and not research objects.

In this chapter we provide an overview of the project methodology and then focus on the Vila Mimosa red-light district as an example of how sex workers' images expose stark contrasts between mass media representations of sporting mega-events and their own. All of the images shared are by photographers in the Vila Mimosa. Rather than droves of sex-hungry tourists, images of waiting and frustrated expectations dominate. The mega-events appear through the military tanks and barriers that made it difficult to get to work. Consistent with the project experiences in South Africa and South Korea, we found that everyday images of cooking, caring for pets, going to work, waiting for clients and studying for exams show a range of subjectivities and diversities so often erased in mainstream media. We discuss participants' evaluations of the process, in particular how they paid more attention to detail in their surroundings and valued the opportunity to share a variety of aspects of their life to directly confront prejudice. We conclude reflecting on questions of representation and power that our project confronts but does not fully resolve, and suggest ways forward for more politically oriented and effective research.

The process

What You Don't See: Prostitution as We See It is part of a broader research project entitled *The Impacts of Sporting Mega-Events on Sexual Commerce in Rio de Janeiro* implemented by the Prostitution Policy Watch (PPW), a research–activist collaborative project based at the Institute of Research and Urban and Regional Planning at the Federal University of Rio de Janeiro (IPPUR/UFRJ). PPW carried out extensive ethnographic research during the 2014 World Cup (Beijo da Rua 2014) and for the Olympic Games designed a project with two components. One component included ethnographic research conducted in prostitution areas throughout Rio de Janeiro by 12 student researchers, 4 anthropologists, and 2 international researchers. The participatory photography component, which is the focus of this chapter, included 2 project coordinators, 3 sex worker field coordinators and 16 participants who worked in diverse areas of Rio de Janeiro's sex industry. The visual team also included 2 professional photography instructors, 2 filmmakers who edited a video about the process and a visual artist who created the project website and assisted in curatorial processes.

This chapter is co-authored by the coordinators of the visual component (Laura Murray and Angela Donini), the ethnography project coordinator responsible for the Vila Mimosa, Ana Paula da Silva, and the Vila Mimosa field coordinator, Cristiane Oliveira (pseudonym). Cristiane has worked for over a decade in the Vila Mimosa and in a variety of state and non-governmental HIV prevention and anti-trafficking projects in the area. As part of the project *Red-Light Rio*,[2] a partner of the PPW, she kept a diary of her daily life during the World Cup that inspired the expansion and continuation of the diary during the Olympic Games. Ana Paula da Silva is the current co-president of Davida, a PPW researcher since its founding, and has conducted ethnographic research on the Rio de Janeiro sexual economies, with a focus on sex tourism, trafficking and how race, class and gender intersect in these fields since 2004. Angela Donini is also a member of Davida and has studied issues of sexuality, gender and representation since 2003. A professor of philosophy and filmmaker, her work has focused on the politics of representation, feminism, epistemologies and art. Both Angela Donini and Laura Murray directed films about Gabriela Leite, *Corpos que Escapam* (*Bodies that Escape*) (2015) and *A Kiss for Gabriela* (2013), respectively, and worked together on the interviews with Gabriela available on the *Kiss for Gabriela* YouTube channel. Laura Murray is originally from the United States but has worked in Brazil as researcher, activist and filmmaker since 2004. She is also a member of Davida and the PPW and her ethnographic research has focused on the politics of sex work activism, sexuality, HIV/AIDS and the state.

The project team began organizing in March of 2016 and started recruiting participants in June and July of the same year. A total of 16 cis-gender and transgender women were recruited from four red-light districts of Rio de Janeiro: Vila Mimosa, Copacabana, Centro and the Barra da Tijuca (the centre of Olympics activity). Participants worked in brothel, street and online forums and covered the full economic spectrum of Rio de Janeiro's sexual economies. They received the same research stipend as the PPW student researchers and the original project design contemplated digital cameras for each person. Yet a combination of an economic crisis[3] and participants' perception that their mobile phone cameras would be more dynamic and discreet than a camera led to mobile phones being the primary forms of image capture used by the project.[4]

The project team formed three WhatsApp groups based on the areas coordinated by each sex worker field coordinator. WhatsApp groups facilitated more direct sharing and communication of images and audios between participants. In Brazil, WhatsApp is an extremely popular and widely used application due to its extremely low cost compared to phone calls. While there were commonalities among the groups in terms of the types of sex work, not all of the participants knew one another prior to the project. Even though they shared similar work environments, each participant brought different perspectives and experiences to each group. The groups were used as a space to share images of day-to-day life, and ended up also being an important forum of support through affirmative comments about new hair styles/clothes, clients, and provided support amid frustration caused by the lack of work (see Figure 45.1).

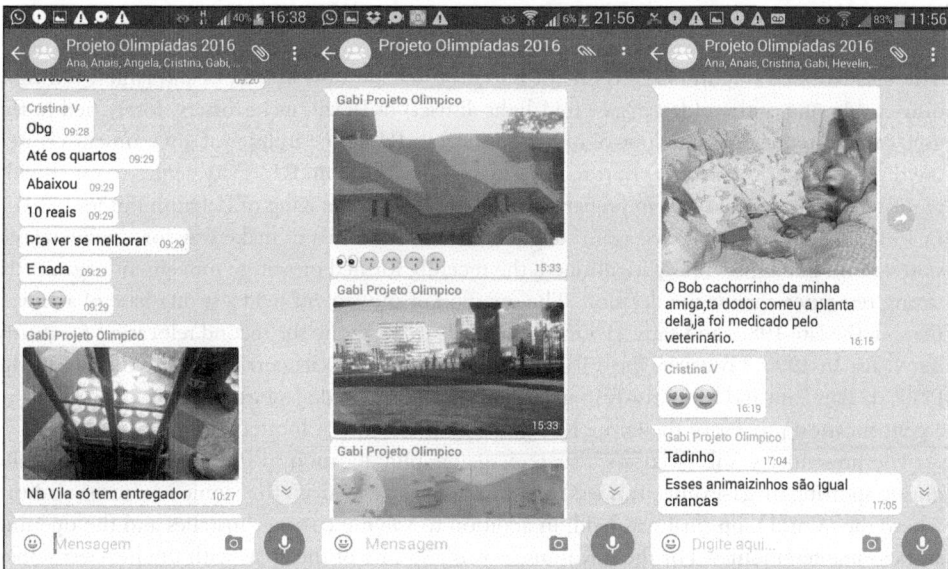

Figure 45.1 WhatsApp screenshots from the Vila Mimosa group. In the first one, Cristina says, "The room price was lowered to R$10 to see if it [the movement of clients] improves and nothing." To which Gabi replies, "In the Vila there's only a delivery guy." The text in the last WhatsApp image states, "Bob, my friend's little dog, is sick because he ate her plant, he's been medicated by the veterinarian." Gabi responded, "Poor guy. These little animals are like children."

Photography instructors also participated in the groups, providing feedback on images and sharing photos to inspire compositions.

Participants shared over 1,500 photos and thousands of audio and text messages through the WhatsApp groups before, during and after the Olympic and Paralympic Games (July–October 2016). Two small group photography trainings were held with each group in addition to meetings every two weeks to select the participants' favourite images for the website and discuss the site's layout and title. Each participant has an individual page on the website to highlight their unique perspectives with individualized backgrounds and images selected by them (Figure 45.2). The title of the project and website, *O Que Você Não Vê* (*What You Don't See*), came from one of the participants and was voted on by all through a poll on WhatsApp. The project team organized a workshop with all participants to review and finalize the website and make a final selection of the photographs to be printed for the gallery exhibition that opened in December 2017.

The project passed through the Ethics Board review at the Rio de Janeiro Federal University – Macae and all participants signed consent forms that authorized the use of the images and audios shared through the project's WhatsApp groups. In addition, they also signed authorizations for the video and audio registers recorded for the project video. They retain full rights to their images and the work shared on the website is protected through a Creative Commons No-Derivatives-Non-Commercial International License. Through these processes, we sought to experiment other ways of producing knowledge with what we understand to be more ethical forms of image production and dissemination. We also recognize that power hierarchies inherent in the research process crosscut our work and in our conclusion discuss what this might mean for our project and also similar participatory projects.

Vila Mimosa

The Vila Mimosa (Figure 45.3) is one of Rio de Janeiro's most notorious and largest red-light districts. As one of the oldest *zonas*[5] (red-light district) in Brazil, its history is closely tied to the government repression and control of prostitution in Rio. The municipal government created the district in the 1920s in an effort to relocate prostitution from Rio's city centre to one highly regulated and contained area in preparation for a visit from the King of Belgium (Simoes 2010). In 1987, the government once again sought to relocate the Vila to make way for a radio-television station, but as previously mentioned, the recently formed prostitute movement organized a strong resistance against the decision. The sex worker movement held a strong base of activism there in the late 1980s and early 1990s that was able to postpone the second relocation for nearly ten years. In 1996, however, the Vila Mimosa was moved to its current location between the Praça da Bandeira and São Cristóvão neighbourhoods in Rio de Janeiro's North Zone as part of a gentrification process of the entire Mangue area where it was located.

The present-day Vila occupies a strategic geographic location in Rio de Janeiro, especially during sporting mega-events. It is less than a kilometre away from the iconic Maracanã stadium where the World Cup final was held, in addition to Olympic soccer matches and the opening and closing ceremonies. For these reasons, it was also one of the areas with the heaviest police and military presence during the games (as seen in Figure 45.1).

The activism in the new Vila reorganized with the formation of an association of sex workers and business owners called AMOCAVIM. The association promotes social activities and courses with sex workers, organizes the area's commerce and negotiates improvements with local power brokers. During the World Cup, the organization sponsored the anti-trafficking

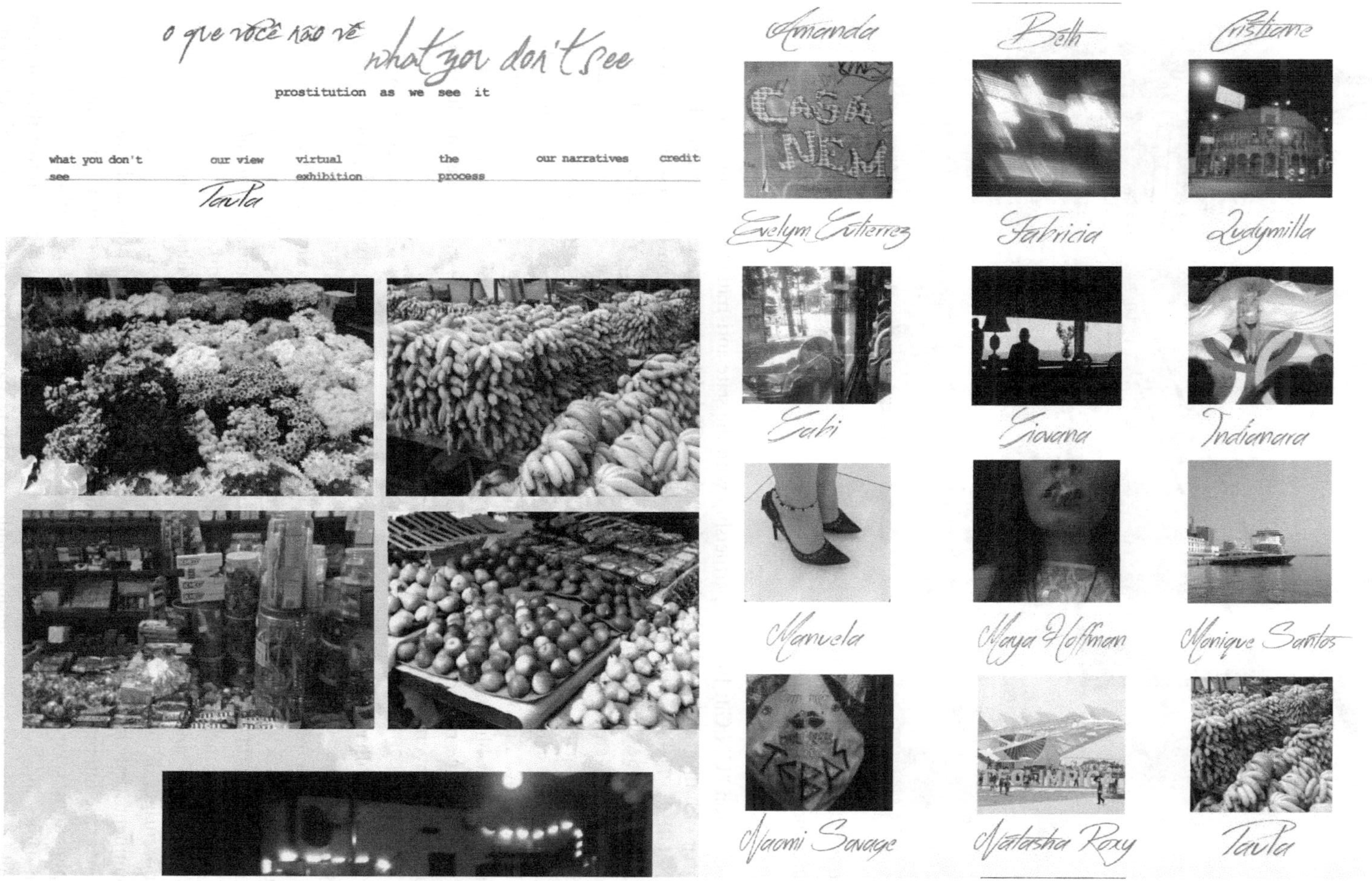

Figure 45.2 The webpage "Our View" of the *What You Don't See* website: each participant has their own page that can be viewed by clicking their name and/or image (right); Paula's personal page with her images taken throughout the project (left).

Figure 45.3 The Vila Mimosa.
Source: Photo by Fabricia Ferraz.

intervention "UN Gift Box" in partnership with the state anti-trafficking committee, state sec-
retariat of human rights and the United Nations Global Initiative to Fight Human Trafficking
(UN.GIFT). The life-sized cardboard box was decorated like a colourful present covered with
promises such as "Get to know the world and make good money". Yet when people entered
the box, they were confronted with grim photographs and horrific stories of human trafficking.
Aside from targeted state interventions such as these (that reinforce the trafficking narratives),
municipal and state authorities have largely abandoned Vila Mimosa. As observed by anthropologist Soraya Simões in her ethnography about the *zona* (2010), the precarious nature of
many of the establishments combined with the lower socio-economic status of the women who
work there have turned it into a preferred target of international sensationalist media sources
denouncing poverty and the "harms of the sex industry".

During the 2016 Olympic Games, images of Rio de Janeiro's sexscapes (Brennan 2004)
showed two different cultural representations of sex work deeply cross-cut by race, class and
sexuality divides. On one hand, circulating images of the city's tourist areas reinforced ideas
of Brazil as one of the global sex tourism routes and "child sex trafficking epidemics". While
some of the articles mentioned sex workers' disappointment with the low numbers of clients
during the World Cup, they also reinforced trafficking narratives and *international* exploitation
of Brazilian women. There was also the occasional story of a sex worker hoping to find "a way
out of our life" and referring to the games as an "opportunity" (Williams 2016). On the other
hand, images of the Vila Mimosa built on the World Cup once again showed stories of disappointment, desperation and cheap bargains. Rather than an area of hope and expectations for
money, the international press portrayed the Vila Mimosa as landscapes of poverty and *national*
exploitation. One article, which we will not cite to avoid giving it any visibility, circulated the
real names and faces of sex workers in the Vila Mimosa after promising them that their images
would not appear publicly, causing undue stress by revealing their occupations to family members in other Brazilian states. After the threat of legal action, the journalist blurred the women's

images, which, however, had already circulated widely and been picked up by other online media. *What You Don't See* participants in the Vila Mimosa began documenting their daily lives in the weeks before the Olympics opening ceremonies within this context.

What You Don't See

The images produced during the *What You Don't See* project show a life in process, with happiness, jokes, hopes, frustrations and friendships. In this sense, the images shared throughout the Olympic Games by sex workers in the Vila Mimosa highlight how the mainstream media narrative is developed mostly independently of the subjects involved. In their photographs, the Olympics appeared merely as a backdrop to daily life. On television, behind a cat and cleaning supplies, on billboards looking out from the bus on the way to work, and as part of the Rio de Janeiro beach landscape on a day off. The Olympics presence was felt through the difficulties it created in getting to work due to its intense military presence. Gabi titled one of her photographs of the tanks (seen in the WhatsApp conversation in Figure 45.1), "War", a telling title of how the relationship established between the state and the population whose lives were deeply affected by the securitization of the city during the games.

Women expressed frustration with the lack of clients through countless images of the *vila vazia* (empty Vila Mimosa). Figure 45.4 shows a compilation of such images, a combination of the empty streets and hallways of the Vila and selfies of their bodies in positions of waiting. Audios shared in the group also discussed the difficulties and deception with the slower "movement" in the *zona* than expected. As Gabi shared:

> Good morning friends, I'm watching the news, and getting goose bumps. The city centre, shops, etc. were waiting for the Olympics. With the negative movement now, they're all desperate too. It's not only us, but businesses throughout Rio de Janeiro, and Brazil.

Figure 45.4 Photos of the "Vila Vazia" that participants selected to show emptiness and waiting.

Source: Photos by Fabricia, Cristiane and Cristiane (from left to right).

While contrary to the women's expectations, their experiences were consistent with what has happened in other countries that hosted the Olympic Games and other sporting mega-events (Richter et al. 2012). In this sense the media hype surrounding client increases and the economic argument that the Games would be good for Brazil only served to increase the height of expectations from which the country has fallen, hard, since.[6] Audiofiles and images shared expressing frustration with the lack of clients were often followed by messages of hope, support and persistence. As Cristiane stated in an audiofile accompanied by a picture of her laying on her bed and watching television:

> I'm at home now. I've been on the street all day, and only had two clients. The *zona* is horrible ... But you cannot give up. Tomorrow is a new day. But for now, I need to rest a little bit.

Messages like, *força amiga* (be strong, friend) were common, in addition to positive reinforcements about the images and experiences shared. Several of the latter, such as the screenshot in Figure 45.1 of the deliveryman, depicted all that was being done to try and improve the "movement" in the *zona*. Suffering only appeared in the title of one image, which was of notebooks from one of the women's night university course.

Narratives of daily life were the subject of the overwhelming majority of the photos shared through the WhatsApp groups, with images of cooking, getting ready, going to work, at school and at work. Transmitting a sense of the different spaces that sex workers occupy throughout the day, the images show lives full of activities. While waiting, several documented the bars where they work, such as Fabricia's photo (Figure 45.5), which she titled "Work". Paula's webpage (Figure 45.2) is full of the colours of the fruit and vegetable market and the stands selling snacks and work supplies in the Vila. Pets were also common protagonists of the images, and frequently shared with the intention of lightening the mood of frustration. Paula's picture of her cat Shakira in Figure 45.6 shows her climbing into her bag on her way to work. Her audio shared with the image jokes about Shakira wanting to go work in the *zona*.

Figure 45.5 Work.

Source: Photo by Fabricia Ferraz.

Figure 45.6 Paula's cat Shakira climbing into her bag. Audio shared when sending the photo: "Good morning loves, how's everything? I'm sending a picture of Shakira for you to see her. Shakira wants to go to the *zona* to work too, she's always getting into my bag. Kisses, til soon and ciao!"

Source: Photo by Paula.

The relational aspect of the photos and ways in which they were shared also counter images of dominant media narratives in which sex workers are often portrayed as being exposed and alone. Brazilian clients tend to be invisible in media representations of sex work, even in areas like the Vila Mimosa where they make up the overwhelming majority. The women's images with men in the *zona* show relationships of affection and ties that go beyond money and sex. This is seen, for example, in Figure 45.7, a photograph of Gabi sharing a cup of coffee and which she had titled "Coffee friend". Another one of Gabi's photographs showed an image of her client's foot with a cane next to it, and was sent with the following audio: "He helps me whenever he can but he is very sick and he doesn't have much money so he rarely comes, but with great sacrifice, he still does help."

Many of the images, such as Gabi's photograph of her client's foot and the photos from the market on Paula's page, are details of daily interactions. In our conversations in the bi-weekly meetings and workshops, many sex workers mentioned how participating in the project changed how they viewed their surroundings. As Paula stated:

> I think its cool because you start to pay more attention to things. Now you pay attention to things that you didn't pay any attention to. Things that didn't exist to me, that had nothing to do with anything, now they exist.

The name of the project captures this element that Paula calls attention to in terms of bringing into existence elements of daily life that otherwise were invisible, both to the participants and the broader public who looks at the images. Zones of abandonment (Biehl 2005) and exclusion were replaced with colour, silhouettes, waiting, studying, the beach and pets; adding some light and humour to a sporting event and city that were anything but mega and far from lucrative.

Figure 45.7 Coffee friend.
Source: Photo by Gabi.

At the workshop in which we finalized the website, one participant expressed concern about all the photographs that showed Rio de Janeiro cityscapes, stating, "Wait a minute, we're saying that it's what you don't see, but a lot of these are images that people see all the time." Another one of the participants stopped her and said, "That's the point, it's for people to see prostitution and us as also being a part of these images." Similarly, at one of our workshops to plan the gallery hanging, a participant looked at all of the photographs selected for printing and commented that she was surprised at how few of the photos were of prostitution contexts. As a group, they decided to arrange the photos moving from those that more directly represented prostitution (photos in a motel room, condoms in a wallet) to the more daily scenes of the market and beach as a way to visually connect the narratives and show prostitution as part of daily life.

Reflections on collaboration and participation

At the time of finalizing this chapter for publication, the website had been up for less than six months and the gallery exhibition had just opened. Our experience thus far has been similar to Cheng's and Oliveira's observations regarding the circulation of sex workers' photographs in South Korea and South Africa; both found that the everyday aspects of women's lives had the largest impact on confronting the stigma around prostitution (Cheng 2013; Oliveira 2016). The public visiting the exhibition has commented that the photos show that the women are like "everybody else". At the same time, for the participants, having their everyday lives displayed in a gallery also evoked strong emotion. Paula, for example, teared up at seeing her cat's picture in a small picture frame at the headboard of the exhibition's bed installation.

The images reinforced not only the normalcy of their daily routines, but also sex workers' place in a city that systematically does more to erase, rather that support, them. The affirmation of sex workers' right to the city contrasted with the ways in which the Brazilian sex industry was simultaneously erased and exposed during recent mega-events. As Robert Lancaster (2011) notes, the media often uses anonymous snapshots of lives to illustrate predetermined narratives of victimization that are then often used to justify punitive state intervention to control dissident sexualities. This unfortunate, and internationally prevalent, dynamic is perhaps what most connects the project to contexts beyond Brazil.

We also found that the inclusion of diverse contexts of sex work provided a platform among participants for reflection and exchanges about different aspects of the sex industry. Other similar projects have tended to focus on specific geographical areas or types of sex work. Yet in our experience, the inclusion of a diverse group of sex workers in terms of gender, work environments and urban geographies allowed a broad look at the sex industry in Rio de Janeiro, forming links between these contexts through the WhatsApp groups and collective curatorial processes. The WhatsApp groups facilitated an exchange of information about work possibilities and also a space for collective frustrations and exasperation at the slow "movement". We found that when it comes to mega-events in particular, there were more commonalities than differences within Rio's diverse sex markets, especially as sex workers circulated throughout the city in search of clients. In this sense, *What You Don't See* contributes to the important body of research on exploring the differences between distinct prostitution contexts, and expands it by providing insights on the relationships and overlaps between different kinds of sex work in the context of international events.

We hope that our project contributed and continues to contribute to alternative narratives about sex work, yet are conscious of its limitations and that it alone of course is not enough. As Cheng (2013) states, "Putting the tools of representation" into sex workers' hands is a critical first step. Yet as Cheng and many who work with visual methodologies for research caution (Packard 2008; Oliveira 2016), these approaches do not erase power differences between researchers and participants. Even in projects where human rights might be the focus, photography can risk neutralizing various dimensions of people's lives thus potentially creating and expanding gulfs between people and their communities. As Oliveira notes, there are also potentially invasive aspects of such projects that must be recognized. While they do not replicate the victimizing and "bodies without a face" aesthetic common in the mass media, the images are personal and show sex workers' daily lives, asking, as Oliveira states (2016, 276), "people to engage with their lived experiences in ways that many of us might find invasive [if] the roles were reversed".

What You Don't See is a contribution and provocation to sex work research to use more of the artistic and cultural forums that sex worker activists and cultural producers have been so brilliantly using since the global movement's emergence (Delacoste and Alexander 1998; Leigh 2004). We would accordingly like to close by stating that we regard this project as not only being a call for more participatory and representative research methods, but also about facilitating political change. The participants' decision to use, on the exhibition poster and invitation, a photograph that they saw as having an activist and political stance for sex workers' rights (Figure 45.8) is illustrative of this aspect of the project.

Connecting *What You Don't See* to broader political movements, organizations and discourses for sex worker rights, similar to the *Working the City* and *Volume 44* projects, was key. The project was produced through a research–activist collaboration that defends sex workers' rights. The coordinators were all sex worker activists, with ties to the organized sex worker movement in Rio de Janeiro and Brazil more broadly. All of the project coordinators – for both the visual and ethnographic component of the broader research project – are active members of Davida. At the same time, we also sought to offer flexible and creative ways to amplify

Figure 45.8 Photo by Evelym Guiterrez.

participation and the number and diversity of sex workers' voices in a way that was protective of their privacy. The project design thus offered ways to form part of a political project for sex worker rights – photography, audio and the use of pseudonyms – through which sex workers could express themselves without having to necessarily disclose their identity. At the same time, others, such as Beth, saw it as an opportunity to more directly communicate with others about their lives and chose to use their real names and include identifiable images:

> I never participated in something like this so it was very constructive for me to express myself. Because it's not only the photos, it also gave me the chance to speak directly to people about what I am doing. So, it gave me more self-confidence with respect to what I do.

Beth's quote illustrates what we see as this project's critical contributions. Sex workers' images and narratives, communicated directly to the public through the online and exhibition format, rebuke the idea that sex work is bad for sex workers and provide a critical counterpoint to victimizing discourses. They debunk dominant myths about prostitution and mega-events, demonstrate the fallacy of moral panics and show, once again, that it is the stigma surrounding prostitution, and not sex work itself, that is harmful to sex workers.

Notes

1 https://whatyoudontsee.hotglue.me (in English), www.oquevcnaove.com (Portuguese).
2 http://redlightr.io.
3 Rio de Janeiro has suffered a deep economic and political crisis since shortly after the 2014 World Cup, a result of a state crisis exacerbated by a national political and economic crisis that has resulted in severe budget cuts for the country's public educational system and public research fund. The Rio de Janeiro State Research Fund (FAPERJ) approved a grant for the Prostitution Policy Watch at the end of 2015 for our Olympics research, at the time of finalizing this chapter (January 2018), the award had still not been transferred.
4 Several participants in the beginning used cameras donated through an Internet campaign until alternative funding came through to purchase mobile phones for those who didn't have them.
5 *Zona* in Portuguese is a neighbourhood, but it is also used in popular language to designate red-light districts.
6 In 2017, Rio de Janeiro declared bankruptcy and the governor responsible for the Olympic planning was convicted and sentenced to jail for corruption on charges related to bribes received from the construction companies responsible for the Olympics' infrastructure. In addition, the broader ethnographic research project found that there were no reported cases of child exploitation or trafficking linked to the Olympic Games during the event (Beijo da Rua 2017).

References

Alloula, Malek. 1986. *The colonial harem*. Minneapolis: University of Minnesota.
Amar, Paul. 2009. Operation princess in Rio de Janeiro: Policing "sex trafficking", stregthening worker citizenship, and the urban geopolitics of security in Brazil. *Security Dialogue*, 40: 513–541.
Andrijasevic, Rutvica. 2007. Beautiful dead bodies: Gender, migration and representation in anti-trafficking campaigns. *Feminist Review*, 86: 24–44.
Agustín, Laura. 2007. *Sex at the margins: Migration, labour markets and the rescue industry*. London: Zed Books.
Beijo da Rua. 2014. *World Cup 2014 special edition* [Online]. Rio de Janeiro: Davida. Available: https://issuu.com/prudha/docs/beijo_preview_final3/1 [Accessed 10/10 2017].
Biehl, Joao. 2005. *Vita: Life in a zone of social abandonment*. Berkeley: University of California Press.
Blanchette, Thaddeus and Ana Paula da Silva. 2016. Brazil has its eye on you: Sexual panic and the threat of sex tourism in Rio de Janeiro during the FIFA World Cup. *Brasiliana*, 4: 411–454.
Blanchette, Thaddeus, Ana Paula da Silva and Andressa Raylane Bento. 2013. The myth of Maria and the imagining of sexual trafficking in Brazil. *Dialectical Anthropology*, 37(2): 195–227.
Bonthuys, Elsje. 2012. The 2010 football World Cup and the regulation of sex work in South Africa. *Journal of Southern African Studies*, 38: 11–29.
Brennan, Denise. 2004. *What's love got to do with it? Transnational desires and sex tourism in the Dominican Republic*. Durham: Duke University Press.
Brown, William, Dina Iordanova and Leshu Torchin. 2010. *Moving people, moving images: Cinema and trafficking in the new Europe*. London: St Andrews Film Studies.
Cheng, Sealing. 2013. Private lives of public women: Photos of sex workers (minus the sex) in South Korea. *Sexualities*, 16: 30–42.
da Silva, Ana Paula and Thaddeus Blanchette. 2005. Nossa senhora da Help: Sexo, turismo, e deslocamento transnacional em Copacabana. *Cadernos Pagu*, 25: 249–280.
Delacoste, Frederique and Priscilla Alexander (eds.) 1998. *Sex work: Writings by women in the sex industry*. San Francisco: Cleis Press.
GAATW 2007. *Collateral damages: The impact of anti-trafficking measures on human rights around the world*. Bangkok: GAATW.
Kennelly, Jacqueline and Paul Watt. 2011. Sanitizing public space in the Olympic host cities: The spatial experiences of marginalized youth in 2010 Vancouver and 2012 London. *Sociology*, 45: 765–781.
Lancaster, Roger N. 2011. *Sex panics and the punitive state*. Berkeley: University of California Press.
Leigh, Carol. 2004. *Unrepentant whore*. San Francisco: Last Gasp.
Leite, Gabriela. 2009. *Filha, mae, avo e puta: A historia de uma mulher que deidiu ser prostituta*. Rio de Janeiro: Objetiva.
Leite, Juçara. 1993. *A república do mangue: Controle policial e prostituição no Rio de Janeiro 1954–1974*. Master's dissertation, Universidade Federal Fluminense.
Lenz, Flavio. 2008. *Daspu: Moda sem vergonha*. Rio de Janeiro: Objetivo.

Murray, Laura. 2014. Victim management and the politics of protection: Between "fazer direito" and "direitinho". *Revista Artemis*, XVIII: 28–41.

Oliveira, Elsa. 2016. Empowering, invasive or a little bit of both? A reflection on the use of visual and narrative methods in research with migrant sex workers in South Africa. *Visual Studies*, 31: 260–278.

Packard, Josh. 2008. "I'm going to show you what its really like out here": The power and limitation of participatory visual methods. *Visual Studies*, 23: 63–77.

Quijano, Aníbal. 2000. Coloniality of power and eurocentrism in Latin America. *International Sociology*, 15: 215–232.

Richter, Marlise, Stanley Luchters, Ndlovu Dudu, Marleen Temmerman and Matthew Francis Chersich. 2012. Female sex work and international sport events – no major changes in demand or supply of paid sex during the 2010 soccer World Cup: A cross-sectional study. *BMC Public Health*, 12. https://doi.org/10.1186/1471-2458-12-763.

Silk, Michael. 2014. The London 2012 Olympics: The cultural politics of urban regeneration. *Journal of Urban Cultural Studies*, 1: 273–293.

Simoes, Soraya Silveira. 2010. *Vila mimosa: Etnografia da cidade cenografica da prostitucao carioca*. Rio de Janeiro: Editora da UFF.

Williams, David. 2016. Exclusive – "I want to win Olympic gold for sex": Rio escort wants to use games to find a boyfriend "just like Julia Roberts in Pretty Woman". *Daily Mail*, 4 August.

46

Fictions of selling sex

New literatures of queer sex work

Patrick Preston

Rough-trade, rent boys, escorts, and hustlers have often appeared in twentieth- and twenty-first-century gay male writing, frequently characterized as any combination of desperate, infected, dangerous, abused, addicted, and morally suspect. Often these figures linger at the peripheries of fiction (Hollinghurst 1998), or are occasional fixations in the diaries of canonical gay writers (White 2005); spectral presences lacking depth or dialogue. Male commercial sex has often been exaggeratedly eroticized in cultural productions: fetishizing race, class, youth (Arnott 2007; Thomas 2015), or hyper-masculine physiologies (White 2016). A recurrent trope in these representations is the voyeuristic gaze at the male sex worker from afar, and a first- or third-person narration of the client perspective (Benderson 2006; Greenwell 2016). Literary representations of male sex work have rarely managed to break or escape these reductive caricatures, which have done little to unpick the moral censure of sex work as dangerous and damaging, or to elaborate the complexities and contingencies of selling sex.[1]

Neel Mukherjee's novel, *A Life Apart* (2010), disrupts dominant configurations of male sex work, narrating the story of Ritwik, a young man who moves from India to England in the 1990s to begin an English Literature degree. The novel details Ritwik's move across continents, his shifts from adolescent to undergraduate, and, when he quits university, to undocumented migrant, sex worker, and unpublished writer in London. This chapter argues that *A Life Apart* inverts the hegemonic gaze at the 'rent boy' from afar in literature by narrating the affective experience of an abject body in urban space. Ritwik's everyday urban encounters emphasize the multiple, embedded stigmas that affect his life. The space of the novel illuminates his felt responses to the city, and his use of imaginative play as a creative strategy to cope with the quotidian experience of exclusion. This representation of Ritwik's 'life apart' usefully elaborates the intersectional experience of a queer, non-white, migrant sex worker, complicating reductive assessments of how gender, migration, and trafficking manifest in commercial sex; and revealing the plurality and *queerness* of doing sex work. I use 'queer' both to connote same-sex desire and the inherently unstable relationship between sex, gender, and sexuality. As Edelman (2004, 17) writes: "queerness can never define an identity; it can only ever disturb one".

There is a need for progressive discourses of commercial sex in the humanities, where studies of non-normative sexualities are regularly trivialized and where the discussion of sex work is often a polarizing one. While some queer historiography has discussed male sex work (Reay 2010), literary research in this field is rare. Existing studies of *A Life Apart* have explored migration and queerness while overlooking commercial sex (Ray 2016). In the social sciences, despite a burgeoning discourse of sex work, studies of male and non-heterosexual workers remain few (Walby 2012, Aggleton and Parker 2015). Furthermore, the sociological and the literary are yet to be brought into productive conversation regarding commercial sex. This chapter argues that new literatures of queer sex work cleave this ground, opening up a space for criticality that moves beyond stigma and glimpses the dynamic ways in which sex work manifests across time and space, and between bodies that cannot be contained within heteronormative categories of identity. Building on the call from Smith et al. (2015, 3) for "multidimensional and multidisciplinary voices" in sex work debates, I argue that the speculative arena of the literary can usefully further sociological insights into sex work, and vice versa. Emerging from my own intersectional experience of research and sex work, I recuperate the voice of a sex worker within critical discourse, working against the assumption that those writing about it are not also *doing* it.

Working on the streets of King's Cross, Ritwik gets to know Zafar, who becomes his most regular client. Over the course of the novel, the two meet at various points, in hotel rooms, at Zafar's home, or in his car. Zafar becomes increasingly interrogative about Ritwik's work with other clients, stressing the challenges this commercial relationship presents to both actors. In their interactions, each character emphasizes the multiple performances involved in sex work, and how these are variously subverted and reproduced. Zafar plays out an erotic fantasy of caring for Ritwik, but his gestures of affection are quickly replaced by a *retreat* after sex,

> into an impenetrable world of introspection after each time. It is as if Ritwik starts fading for Zafar during the sex and disappears completely afterwards. It is as unintimate as physical contact gets and is always preceded and followed by a shower . . . to sluice off ritually not only semen, sweat, the touch of another body – there is no saliva, for Zafar never kisses – but also the bigger intangibles that he perceives to come with this paid sex.
>
> *(Mukherjee 2010, 347)*

This extract stresses the passage of time, through words such as 'fading', 'during', 'after', and 'preceded and followed'; emphasizing the dynamism of sex work, which is not a static act but a mobile practice that changes over time. Moments of commercial intimacy are experienced personally, and differently, by their actors. Ritwik and Zafar's bodies, sensations, thoughts, and feelings are shifting and becoming, rather than resolutely formed. Zafar's enthusiasm and affection before sex are quickly substituted by awkwardness and dismissal afterwards. His behaviour is erratic, and his gestures are part of a fragile erotic performance, pivoting from exaggerated tenderness to post-coital coldness as shame creeps over him. Through his perception of these shifts in Zafar's mood, Ritwik develops skills of self-preservation, maintaining an emotional distance and critical perspective, while simultaneously performing pliancy to satisfy his client: "Zafar remains resolutely locked in his own, limited needs. The taking type, rather than the giving, Ritwik thinks as he concentrates on timing and almost botches it up" (Mukherjee 2010, 338).

Rather than pursuing his own sexual abandon, Ritwik manages the encounter, carefully organizing its timings through his bodily movements to bring Zafar to orgasm quickly. While Zafar is 'locked into' a hurried pursuit of pleasure, the reader is privileged with access to Ritwik's thought process through the extended narration of this scene, illuminating the experience of sex as something banal and unremarkable. For all his sullen arrogance in the novel, the reader is not invited to judge Zafar negatively because of his *purchase* of sex. Rather, the narrative reveals the use of these moments of contact, which allow Zafar to express same-sex desire and indulge fantasies in a space free from moralizing reprieve or violent retaliation. Avenatti and Jones (2015, 91) have argued that consensual sex work can function as a form of therapy for clients, offering "a supportive space" for the exploration of "bodies, sexuality, relationships and identity in ways that are not accessible in the mainstream".

Indeed, Zafar demonstrates an emotional vulnerability as he navigates the tension between his felt desires and a deep-seated anxiety toward same-sex intimacy, which holds him back from kissing and spurs him to shower away the traces of another man from his skin. Shame provokes his cold evasiveness after sex, and his showering ritual exposes a fragile myth of cleansing as he seeks to wash away the physical – and mental – residues of the encounter and restore some prelapsarian state of heteronormative respectability. The effort to 'sluice' away the mixture of fluids from their commingled bodies – the blend of sweat and semen gathered uneasily on the surface of his skin – is telling of the stigma attached to the bodies of sex workers and also to queer men and migrants in the time of AIDS – pathologized as vectors of disease and contamination, and constructed as the source of an epidemiological crisis (Scott 2003). For Zafar, these fluids carry a risk of infection and even death. Yet, for all the washing away, a tension remains here, in the paradox of 'intangibles' '*perceive[d]*'. Sex cannot be decoded, and resists the seductions of knowingness. There is something queer about sex, in its resistance to narrative coherence and representation. Rather than explaining away its contingencies, Mukherjee points instead to the 'bigger intangibles' of chaotic and ultimately unreadable subjectivity.

While Zafar ignores Ritwik after sex, the novel sustains focus on Ritwik's inner world. Ritwik's life, while *apart*, is located at the centre of the novel, insisting upon the reader's attention. And as time passes in the novel, the cumulative effects of sex work on Ritwik's everyday life are unfurled: the capacity of rude clients to engender introspection and melancholy, and the coping mechanisms Ritwik develops to manage these experiences. Rather than simply showing the reader the commercial sex act, *A Life Apart* dwells on life beyond sex. Work is neither all encompassing nor an essential determinant of Ritwik's being. But it can and does spill over into other parts of his life, refuting the possibility of a neat separation between work and 'private' life, and revealing how each can seep into the other in complex ways.

In its detailing of Ritwik's life beyond work, *A Life Apart* narrates Ritwik's regular *unpaid* sex. As a student, Ritwik frequents a local cottage and cruising ground, picking up men for a thrill, a feeling of risk, a rush of adrenaline. Ritwik mostly finds these men unappealing. A man he cruises is, "just too unattractive, not what he wants, but the game has begun". They travel in the man's car – a journey of suspicion and agitation that gives Ritwik a "kick in his insides". He does not seek simple erotic gratification from an attractive sexual partner, but a heightened affective state, a physiological rush, often mixed with disgust. Any pleasure of sex is interrupted by Ritwik's anxieties and shame around his own queerness, a product of virulent homophobic cultural narratives. Further, these men commonly fetishize Ritwik's youth and race, emphasizing the persistence of narrow identity categories that fail to capture the complexity of a life: misapprehensions that leave Ritwik feeling marginalized. This depiction of Ritwik's *unpaid* sex life also serves as a comment *on* sex work. The assumption that sex work is unpleasant or ugly often serves a mythic corollary that unpaid sex is inevitably enjoyable, sacred, and/or intimate. Mukherjee dispels this normative fiction, cataloguing Ritwik's bad sex across the novel, paid and unpaid: characterized by contradictory and shifting feelings, ambivalence, shame, stimulation, or frustration at being compulsively fetishized. The sex he is paid for is not dissimilar to that which he seeks out in his leisure time. Indeed, it is a casual hook-up that initially – and accidentally – leads him to sex work: when a stranger mistakes Ritwik for a sex worker and leaves money by his bed after sex. Following this, Ritwik *chooses* to continue sex working, both on the street and also setting up meetings from his phone, reflecting the multiple forms that sex work takes, and the incidental and casual ways in which it sometimes arises.[2] Such encounters stress Ritwik's agency: his willing entrance into commercial sex and competent management of his working conditions.

This journey into sex work challenges the common and erroneous conflation of migration, trafficking, and sex work. Rather than escaping from desperate victimhood, Ritwik's motivation for leaving India is largely a longing for sex with men, as well as the pursuit of an English Literature degree. Mai and King (2009, 297) note that migrants and others "on the move" are "sexual beings expressing, wanting to express, or denied the means to express, their sexual identities". The trafficked workers who appear in *A Life Apart* are not those being paid for sex, but the casual workers Ritwik meets, those working on building sites who are kept in check by "the general atmosphere of fear and intimidation". Mukherjee draws a comparison between these precarious and casual labour forms and Ritwik's own work: intimate labour offers higher pay and flexible hours, affords Ritwik the time to write, and offers a space in which to express same-sex intimacy while pulling at the boundaries of identity and normative gender roles. These benefits set Ritwik apart from the experience of trafficking. Living illegally in London – without a national insurance number, bank account, or fixed address – sex work carries more tangible benefits for Ritwik than the other employment forms that he is offered.

Ritwik carries an abiding unease about the bodies of other sex workers, gazing at the women working around him in King's Cross through a narrow essentializing lens. He sees "remnants of human beings", constructing female bodies as corporeal *waste* in a no-go zone of the city. Yet this is a zone where Ritwik also lingers, and he benefits (unconsciously) from his proximity to these women: "It was only because they were out in the open that Ritwik didn't feel threatened by any potential violence" (Mukherjee 2010, 327). On the street, Ritwik is seen, and can see other workers, a visibility that tempers his anxiety. These bodies are looking out for one another, whether consciously or incidentally. Shunned as a 'fucking queer', and viewing these women as abject bodies, Ritwik is blind to the kinship bond that emerges unwittingly on the street simply through the proximity of these – mutually but differently – *other* bodies: an underlying, unspoken form of care that manifests as they dwell together in city space. A critical distance is opened up here between Ritwik's phobic gaze, the disembodied, anonymous narrator, and the reader. The reader is not persuaded into endorsing Ritwik's viewpoint, but rather to witness the contradictions and *construction* of the morality myths to which he subscribes.

Ritwik repeats the narratives he has consumed since arriving in the UK: sensational media discourses and overheard conversations. His anxiety is stoked by living in a strange country of, "psychopathic serial killers, of thousands of AIDS-infected people, of twisted criminals the papers write about almost every day" (Mukherjee 2010, 49). Mukherjee highlights the power of writing to shape feeling towards, and orientation away from, marginal bodies. A discarded *Daily Mail* on the London Underground carries an anti-immigrant headline, feeding Ritwik's own sense of unbelonging. His essentialist gaze is a cultural construct: an inherited imaginary. Ironically, Ritwik's own body becomes inscribed with these same indices – criminality, disease, danger – that he ascribes to others. What the novel plays with here are the multiple misreadings of identity in quotidian life. Misogyny, homophobia, and racism are all performed in the text, but rendered self-consciously by the author. Ritwik's reductive gaze is *staged* to highlight its contradictions. The responses he elicits – and has to others – foreground the common and often wounding assumptions made when race, gender, sexuality, class, nation, or work are regarded as essential determinants of identity. *A Life Apart* underscores the ambivalent feelings produced by these configurations as they are persistently mapped on to bodies from afar, as well as the difficulty of reformulating relationships outside of these models in everyday life.

Ritwik's essentialism extends to his racist and, "deep-etched prejudices about the unenlightened habits and attitudes of the Arab male". He equates Zafar's ethnicity with sexual primitivity: the will to dominate a passive erotic object. The narrator describes how Zafar also adopts the "role of imperious master", invoking a power dynamic of colonizer and colonized as he seeks to buy Ritwik out of selling sex on the streets of Kings Cross. However, the encounters between these men are not simply an exploitative and one-sided exercise of power. These meetings are not static, nor readable as the triumph of active over passive partner, but instead involve shifting dynamics, tensions, and a range of emotions and simultaneous sensations that cannot be neatly deciphered.

A Life Apart is a novel of multiple migrations: transnational and local, material and imagined, and across and between identity categories during (and outside of) sex work. For instance, in Ritwik's performance of a younger self, which leaves Zafar's illusion about his age unpricked, or when carrying wigs and high-heels in his rucksack on his way to visit a client who seeks a feminized partner. These multiple performances, and the casual, self-conscious adoption and discarding of different masks in different places and times, demonstrates the mutability of these identity categories, and signals the inevitable, unreadable gaps or excesses that exist in the interstices between and beyond them. *A Life Apart* depicts the experience of living *apart* from whiteness and heteronormativity or 'homonormativity' (Duggan 2002). But it also depicts life as a series of parts: a series of distinct *pieces*, and also a series of dramatic parts *played* – variations of self that can be conjured and dramatized.

Ritwik inhabits a world rarely rendered in detail on the page in literature. He lingers in liminal spaces, embodying, enacting, and reflecting on his work. In doing so, the narrative perspective is shifted away from hegemonic modes of representation – a client's-eye view – to emphasize Ritwik's personal, felt, interior world. Rather than an object to be consumed or looked at, he becomes the reader's lens on to the world around him. The reader is invited into spaces that Ritwik's clients will never know: his streams of consciousness and physiological sensations as he goes about his work. The revelation of his thought process details a fluctuating relationship with his work, and the sensate and affective minutiae of selling sex. The body of the 'rent boy' in literature is thus recalibrated, as the text shifts to an occupation with how Ritwik feels the fabric of the city around him as he moves through it. Giving, "a dismal blow-job, his back against a dark wall on Gifford Street, his knees on wet grit", Ritwik feels a 'rush' of feelings, the 'fear' of standing on the street in a queer, non-white body. It is a description rich in corporeality and affect: grit scraping hard against skin stretched over cartilage and bone, bricks against his back, the taste of a stranger's dick, and the rush of panic. As the surfaces of the city rub against his body, the sensory seeps into the text. The reader conjures these physiological/ imaginative responses to the street: the affective experience of a marginal body dwelling in urban 'space-time' (Massey 2005). Kings Cross becomes a dynamic, lived space, with bodies simultaneously and divergently passing through, going about their sex and work. In this, *A Life Apart* glimpses the ordinariness of men selling sex to men from the street, further complicating the notion that this is solely women's work. These scenes of queer sex work accrete over the course of the novel, such that labour becomes a repetitive motif in the text, emphasizing its banality. And after the event of reading, these images linger in the mind as memories, an affective trace that invites the reader's own critical reflections on sex work. The time and space of *A Life Apart*, its psychic and geographic landscapes, have the potential to produce a lasting impression on the reader, impacting upon imaginaries and discourses of queer sex work.

Ritwik has few avenues to express his thoughts and feelings around work. He does not disclose his sex work to his landlady or friends. Rather, *writing* offers Ritwik a vital mode of reflecting on sex, work, and feeling. Ritwik is writing his own novel within the novel, about a character called Miss Gilby, an English woman who moves to Calcutta to teach English to local women, at the turn of the twentieth century – a satiric subversion of the canonical norm of white Westerners depicting colonial culture in literature. Writing his own prose within *A Life Apart*, Ritwik stages literature's deconstructive play with identity. Although Miss Gilby is not an explicitly sexualized character, or a sex worker, her feelings often parallel Ritwik's experience: of being isolated and feeling other in a new and often hostile city. Ritwik and Miss Gilby are both displaced figures. Gilby is "a stranger in a family of strangers". Both are attacked in public for straying into forbidden urban territories. And both register a transgressive sense of freedom acquired through transnational migration. Gilby's "first touching of Indian soil . . . in a crucial and inexplicable way, had done something to her . . . had given her a sense of freedom, of dissidence even" (Mukherjee 2010, 28). For Ritwik, fiction functions as a site of personal expression unavailable at work or elsewhere, and a solitary and uninterrupted practice. Travelling queerly across time and place, Ritwik invents another body and another self to reflect his own experience of falling outside of social expectations:

> Miss Gilby feels a tightening in her chest . . . ignoring hundreds of years of refinement and social norms and rules, rules, rules, she moves over to Bimala, sits beside her, touches her shoulder . . . Bimala bursts into tears while Miss Gilby leaves her hand on the woman's sobbing, heaving shoulder. Hot tears drop like candle wax on to the paper she has been writing on . . . Miss Gilby notes one smudging drop on the inverted word 'learning' . . . about to spread out . . . and start disfiguring.
>
> *(Mukherjee 2010, 321)*

There is a queerness to this scene, the erotics of which are subtly suggested by sensory language: the lingering touch that brings forth 'hot tears'. Ritwik's own novel is charged with the underlying desire of Miss Gilby for her student, Bimala. Theirs is a commercial, same-sex relationship, and Ritwik writes the heightened tension as the two sit alone, in a moment of forbidden intimacy that contradicts 'rules, rules, rules'. This scene at once represents an *inscription* of meaning as words are written on the page, and the scene of meaning's undoing as Bimala's tears fall on to the page, penetrating the text and 'disfiguring' these words, in a symbolic defeat of affect over linguistic representation. 'Inversion' is a loaded term in conversations of same-sex desire, conjuring late nineteenth-century sexological discourses of 'sexual inversion', which pathologized same-sex intimacy (Havelock-Ellis and Symonds, 1897). Yet 'learning' is disfigured here, in a scene that subverts heteronormative respectability, emphasized by its occurrence in the private and rigidly gendered space of the *andamarhal*, the secluded and segregated area of the house where women live separately from men. This story glimpses a queerness, paralleling Ritwik's sex work in the present with its emphasis on transgression, tension, and non-normative desire. Ritwik writes a story of taboo, shame, and prohibition, which offers a metaphor for his own experience, and a mode of expressing queer tensions, in and out of work.

Gilby is a fiction created *by* Ritwik: an imperfect copy, mimicking her creator. Paradoxically, she is both palimpsest and retrospective construct – a queer figure, returned to the past from the present. Ritwik's fiction is an emotional landscape that offers him a hybrid space of belonging when facing a material reality of displacement and illegality. His backwards-looking narrative turns away from a precarious future and day-to-day reality, dwelling nostalgically on Calcutta. It is a queer form of nostalgia, which invents as much as it recollects. By drawing parallels between colonial Calcutta in 1905 and his sense of disorientation in 1990s London, Ritwik emphasizes the persistence of discrimination in the present, and the uneven access of (un)certain bodies to urban space based upon race, gender, class, sexuality, and/or work. This storytelling is a means of dwelling on the history of the city of his childhood, and on the inequalities that he confronts in the present.

Sanders (2005, 325) has identified the "emotional management strategies" used by female sex workers as "pragmatic, symbolic, and psychological defence mechanisms to manage the tensions of selling sex". I want to queer, and extend, this definition here. Ritwik deploys his own (creative) emotional management strategy as a means of coping and working through the tensions of selling sex. The sustained narration of Ritwik's life illuminates how such strategies extend – spatially, temporally, and imaginatively – beyond work, into other arenas of everyday life. Writing as 'emotional management strategy' becomes a pleasurable and creative act. The irregular hours and financial rewards of Ritwik's labour afford him the time and solitude to write and to reflect on work: a practice of separating the self from work. Ritwik's emotional management strategy is a queer one, navigated on the page, pulling at the seams of identity, working through isolation and expressing a yearning to transcend the strictures of heteronormativity that constrain and condemn his own life.

These acts of writing emphasize the lack of a stable public space available for sex workers to share and give voice to their experiences, stressing the commonplace shaming and silencing of our lives by a phobic majoritarian culture. A queer, migrant, male sex worker, Ritwik must conceal his work to avoid violent recrimination and further exclusion. But in response to this silencing, he tactically turns to the written word as a tool of expression: his creative output exists as, and *insists* upon, his own archive of feeling. Yet, by queering time, and utilizing invention, he sidesteps *autobiography*, and thus avoids the deterministic search for traces of trauma in the childhoods and adolescences of sex workers – the will to catalogue our lives as indexes of failure and abuse. Playing with identification, representation, and voice, he resists the disciplinary scrutiny of sex workers' life stories.

Ritwik's play with invention and artistic license is a poststructuralist challenge to essentialism, pointing instead to multiple modes of identification or non-identification. Rather than knowability and objectivity, the slipperiness of the text avoids determinacy. In this, Ritwik's meta-text stages the queer potentiality of literature, as it evades certainty and calls into question the very search for it; and the potential of literature as a site of creative exploration of/in the everyday life of a sex worker. This mode of literary invention invokes the recent writing of male sex workers (Wojnarowicz 1991; Cox 2008; Reed 2014), which use the page as a canvas of expression, often blurring the border between fiction and memoir in representing the experience of selling sex. These modes of writing usefully complicate the narrow lens through which sex work is often figured, and the tropes of disease, disorder, and duplicity often attached to our lives and labour. Throughout the twentieth century and to today, a dominant discourse has perpetuated (mis)understandings of male sex work. Avoiding the familiar tropes of vulnerable teenagers, pliable rough-trade, or opportunistic hustlers, Mukherjee turns from this persistent (predominantly upper-/middle-class) reduction of male sex workers to their physiognomy, instead elaborating the intersectional experience of one man, which is, inevitably, different from the experiences of others. Representing contingency, plurality, non-normativity – and *banality* – at the scene of everyday life, *A Life Apart* interrogates common miscalculations of sex work based upon panic, fear, disgust, voyeurism, and intrigue. It is a portrait that avoids condemning, glamourizing, or fetishizing the life of a male sex worker, and one that expands the terms of discussion of what our work might mean, and what it might not.

New literatures of sex work join recent sociological research in illuminating difference and working against the reproduction of stigma and violence. Literary forms can hold up static ideas and reductive modes of signification in order to demonstrate their constructed-ness. And the speculative field of literary criticism can helpfully inform the sociological by opening up a space of unknowingness and contingency, presenting an epistemological challenge to the empirical. These new literatures extend out into culture, beyond the academy, through discourse, publishing and re-publishing,[3] across multiple planes of everyday life: spatially, temporally, imaginatively, and affectively. While fiction may not tangibly impact upon policy, it possesses a softer power that can permeate the everyday: inspiring, troubling, or displacing preconceived understandings of intimate labour. *A Life Apart* elaborates the transformational potential of cultural production to shift discourses of sex work – in critical and popular contexts – helping to unravel the narrow terms through which sex work is so often configured, and by which queer sex work is so often overlooked.

Notes

1 Texts that elaborate the inner worlds of queer sex workers are few, and often overlooked. They include David Wojnarowicz's (1991) memoirs of 1980s New York life, Daniel A. Cox's novel, *Shuck* (2008), and Jeremy Reed's (2014) autobiographic poems of selling sex in 1980s London.
2 Internet escorting is not a part of this experience, given the novel's setting in the early to mid 1990s, prior to mass digitization.
3 *A Life Apart* was initially published in India as *Past Continuous* (Mukherjee 2008).

References

Aggleton, P. and R. Parker, eds. 2015. *Men Who Sell Sex: Global Perspectives*. Abingdon: Routledge.
Arnott, Jake. 2007. *Johnny Come Home*. London: Sceptre.
Avenatti, C. and E. Jones. 2015. Kinks and Shrinks: The Therapeutic Value of Queer Sex Work. In N. Smith, K. Pilcher, and M. Laing, eds, *Queer Sex Work*, 88–95. Abingdon: Routledge.
Benderson, Bruce. 2006. *The Romanian*. London: Snowbooks.
Cox, Daniel. A. 2008. *Shuck*. Vancouver: Arsenal Pulp Press.
Duggan, Lisa. 2002. The New Homonormativity: The Sexual Politics of Neoliberalism. In R. Castronovo and D. Nelson, eds, *Materializing Democracy: Toward a Revitalized Cultural Politics*, 175–194. Durham, NC: Duke University Press.
Edelman, Lee. 2004. *No Future: Queer Theory and the Death Drive*. Durham, NC: Duke University Press.
Greenwell, Garth. 2016. *What Belongs To You*. Croydon: Picador.
Havelock-Ellis, H. and J.A. Symonds. 1897. *Studies in the Psychology of Sex, Volume 1: Sexual Inversion*. London: Wilson & Macmillan.
Hollinghurst, Alan. 1988/1998. *The Swimming Pool Library*. Berkshire, UK: Vintage.
Mai, N. and R. King. 2009. Love, Sexuality and Migration: Mapping the Issue(s). *Mobilities* 4: 295–307.
Massey, Doreen. 2005. *For Space*. London: Sage.
Mukherjee, Neel. 2008. *Past Continuous*. London: Macmillan.
Mukherjee, Neel. 2010. *A Life Apart*. London: Corsair.
Ray, Shakuntala. 2016. Forbidden Tastes: Queering the Palate in Anglophone Indian Fiction. *Feminist Review* 114(1): 17–32.
Reay, Barry. 2010. *New York Hustlers: Masculinity and Sex in Modern America*. Manchester, UK: Manchester University Press.
Reed, Jeremy. 2014. *The Glamour Poet Versus Francis Bacon, Rent and Eyelinered Pussycat Dolls*. Exeter, UK: Shearsman Books.
Sanders, Teela. 2005. 'It's Just Acting': Sex Workers' Strategies for Capitalizing on Sexuality. *Gender, Work and Organization* 12(4): 319–342.
Smith, N., K. Pilcher, and M. Laing. 2015. Being, Thinking and Doing 'Queer' in Debates about Commercial Sex. In N. Smith, K. Pilcher, and M. Laing, eds, *Queer Sex Work*, 1–9. Abingdon: Routledge.
Scott, John. 2003. A Prostitute's Discourse: Male Prostitution in Scientific Discourse. *Social Semiotics* 13(2): 179–199.
Thomas, A.J. 2015. *Young Lad On Old Street*. Hertfordshire, UK: Red Page Publishing.
Walby, Kevin. 2012. *Touching Encounters: Sex, Work, & Male-For-Male Internet Escorting*. Chicago: University of Chicago Press.
White, Edmund. 2005. *My Lives*. St Ives, UK: Bloomsbury.
White, Edmund. 2016. *Our Young Man*. London: Bloomsbury.
Wojnarowicz, David. 1991. *Close To The Knives: A Memoir of Disintegration*. New York: Vintage. Tet et officabo. Dolorum auta quunt.

47

State and cross-border sex trade in colonial and post-colonial Nigeria

Oluwakemi Abiodun Adesina

English capital has come in and built the railways and constructed the harbours and cleared the channels . . . it has built roads and towns and established markets; it has introduced banks and a convenient currency; it has exploited minerals . . . the result is an enormous expansion of trade, in which the natives performed their part and reaped their reward.

(McPhee 1926, 104)

Introduction

Following contact with Europe in the fifteenth century, Africa experienced large-scale socio-economic changes. The slave trade not only increased the level of commerce between the two continents, it also resulted in the availability of new goods and services and engendered behaviours throughout Africa. In many parts of Africa, European commercial activities were concentrated along the coasts. The rise of mullato populations, mostly along coastal areas, is evidence that the interactions between Europeans and Africans during these early periods also sometimes involved sex. How much of the latter form of exchange occurred and how it was organized have not been studied in any systematic fashion. However, we know that the next phase of European presence in Africa – colonialism – generated new social and economic structures that massively redefined consumption and values in Africa as a whole.

The colonial roots of sex trade in Nigeria

Colonial rule significantly shaped the foundations of what became known as the sex trade in Africa. Colonialism emphasized wage labour, initiated massive inevitable changes in social relationships, including the local organization of gender, work, and exchanges (Lindsay 2003). The sex industry in Nigeria developed rapidly within this context, facilitated by port towns and military camps (NAI/Ondo Prof 1/3, 71). Furthermore, with the entrenchment of the cash economy, destruction of subsistence farming, and expansions in colonial economic spaces and activities, many people, particularly men, sought employment in the new cities, mines, or other places where they could earn wages. Limited housing for migrants, weak social networks, and

485

the uncertainties surrounding movement into new environments forced most migrant workers, mainly adult men, to move without their families. In these new environments, labourers experimented with new networks, associations, and liaisons. Within these contexts, sex workers also stepped in to provide sexual services to migrant workers who were mainly men (Lindsay 2003, 5). Several authors have written about the sex trade involving Nigerians in and outside the country over time and most authors have examined the poverty factor as explanations for the persistent subscription to sex trade – locally and internationally. It is instructive to note that central to this phenomenon are also women's sexuality, issues of sex rights as human rights, sex work abolitionism, and more, as discussed below.

This contribution examines the intersections of international sex work in colonial and post-colonial Nigeria. I argue that international sex work in these two eras, though separated by several decades, shares several similarities and responded to forms of economic globalization and entrenched patterns of lack of opportunities for women. While colonial and post-colonial governments have responded to the alleged menace posed by this industry, by blaming the culture of the people and developing impractical laws and policies, I contend that similar factors related to the marginalization of women and the masculinization of economies in the two different periods account for the waves of sex work that developed during these times. Naneen's (1991) description of sex trade involving Nigerians in the colonial Gold Coast is useful in understanding the organization and operations of trans-border sex trade, its reliance on cultural networks to move and settle, and the perceptions of the host community of Nigerian sex workers. While Naneen and other scholars like Aderinto (2012, 2015) focus mainly on issues that emanated during colonial administration – as they pointed to the drivers, dynamics, strategies of recruitments, the types of anxieties they inspired, and public/state responses to them – this work interrogates the connections between the trans-border sex trade across the decades while laying emphasis on the reliance by families on women's sexuality for survival during periods of economic crisis.

The origins of international sex trade in colonial Nigeria

In Nigeria, the pace of urbanization quickened after World War II (1939–1945). The war had a direct impact on urbanization because it rapidly increased labour requirements in African cities. In Nairobi, White (1990, 147) states that "in 1939, there were said to be 41,000 Africans in the city [Nairobi]; in 1941 their civilians were estimated at 70,000 and in 1944 at 66,500". The situation in Nairobi also resonated in Lagos. From available statistics about this period in Nigeria, there was a population explosion in Nigerian cities. The end of the Depression and post-World War II elicited both an economic and population expansion in the city of Lagos as migrants came in search of wage labour in the services of the railway and road construction. The war attracted an increased number of non-Africans (colonial officers and military personnel) to African cities, which entailed an increase in the employment of African domestic help (White, 1990). Most often, the female domestic help transmuted into sex workers. White (1990) has established the linkage between the increase in military population and prostitution:

> [A] large military presence expands the demand for prostitution and a wide range of temporary relationships: prostitutes provide companionship for men otherwise denied women friends, relieve the grim boredom of barracks life, and provide a social life that does not remove men from their working units.
>
> *(White 1990, 147)*

White's observation of the workings of prostitution in Kenya mirrored its organization in Nigeria, hence Aderinto's (2012, 72) assertion that "the Nigerian story of military [and] prostitution is not totally different from what [is] obtained in Europe or other parts of the British Empire".

Colonial urbanization provided the metaphorical breeding ground that enabled the sex industry to flourish. Media reports about the sex trade in colonial Nigeria were already common by the 1930s. Sensational newspaper editorials and headlines such as "Street Indecencies", "Save the Future Mothers" and "Girl Hawkers Morals" depicted widespread anxiety related to prostitution (Aderinto 2015). One newspaper article during this period described the activities of girls in the city of Lagos who sold common wares in the daytime and sex at night. Earnings from sex work complemented profits from their daytime licit trades. The behaviour of these girls led to the first major public outcry against child prostitution in Nigeria (White 1932). The colonial government responded by criminalizing street trading by young people (Isamah et al. 2002, 64), launching the "girl-hawking war" in Lagos to curb the menace of child prostitution and other juvenile crimes in the colony of Lagos (NAI/ComCol I/2844, 79; Blaize 1944).

However, by the 1940s, prostitution in colonial Nigeria had assumed new dynamics, increasingly becoming a major cause of concern for the Colonial Office in Nigeria. An important dimension of this phase in the history of sex work in Nigeria was the high-level involvement of women from the Cross River region in the trade. The Cross River area covers the Obubra Division in the Ogoja Province of the Eastern Region of colonial Nigeria. The Cross River region is drained by four major rivers, namely, Cross, Calabar, Kwa Iboe, and Imo (Udoka 1995). It sits very close to the historic ports of Calabar, Lagos, and Port Harcourt. The Cross River occupied a very important position for the commercial empire of Europe, where trade in export goods and the distribution of imported foreign luxury articles took place (Afigbo 1972). As a historical port area, Cross River hosted long-distance travellers, traders, fortune seekers, runaways, hustlers, migrants, and other groups of people who "multiplied the demand for prostitutes and greatly increased the monetary prices" (NAI/Ondo Prof 1/3, 8). The District Officer of Ibom, Mr. Mallinson, thought differently. He attributed the involvement of these women in the sex industry to the "lax local marriage customs" (NAE/OG: 120/54, 1) of the people for whom it was customary that a couple lived together for a considerable period without paying the mandatory bridewealth. In such cases, they could leave one another at will and move on to stay with other partners. To colonial officials and missionaries who were more concerned about the morality of such cohabitations, such arrangements were indistinguishable from "harlotry" (NAE/OG: 120/54, 1). Thus, they called for the tightening of the marriage system but soon realized that "the chief trouble was that the public opinion did not effectively condemn prostitution" (NAE/OG: 120/54, 6). So-called lax marriage customs may have deliberately aimed to enable women to participate in the lucrative trade in sex. Parpart (2001, 277) reminds us that in Zambia:

> Since copperbelt housing was tied to employment, which was predominantly for African men, the easiest way to acquire housing was to live with a man. For settled married women, this was no problem, but women without partners had more difficulty. The temporary mine marriage emerged as a solution. These relationships endured any period from a few days to many years. Since location managers did not require proof of marriage, any self-proclaimed couple could acquire housing. One woman had been able to remain in one house by being the "wife" of three different contract miners. Other women "changed hands four and five times respectively".

One sex worker interviewed by the Colonial Office had left her "husband". The District Officer (DO) wrote: "she admits she has recently lived the life of a harlot and prefers it" (NAE/OG: 120/54, 1). This corroborated the suspicion of the colonial officers that this was a deliberate custom that encouraged the money-spinning sex trade.

The Cross River–Gold Coast cross-border sex work trade

Women from the Cross River basin in Nigeria were also the earliest known cross-border sex workers in Nigeria. Records also indicate that some of their activities qualify as trafficking. Between 1935 and 1945 (NAE/B: 503/22, 1), several women in the area moved to the Gold Coast (present day, Ghana) to work near the gold mines as sex workers. There are, however, conflicting accounts of why and how the massive entry of women into international sex trade took roots in Cross River. Clan heads interviewed during the 1930s (NAE/OB: 503/22, 1) argued that the "white man" was responsible for the exodus of women to the Gold Coast for prostitution. Soldiers deployed to the Cross River region reportedly had the tendency to mistreat and humiliate local young men, forcing them to take refuge in the bushes. This was said to have resulted in the dearth of eligible local men and the surplus of young women. Liaisons that soon began between white men and the local women became the basis on which prostitution would later thrive (NAE/OB: 503/6, 1).

The emergence of a colonial factory in the 1930s at the coastal town of Afunatam in Cross River particularly attracted several male workers from Calabar and other coastal towns into Cross River. These men, earning wages, became a new pool of clients to the sex workers. The closure of the factory a few years later led to the departure of these migrant male workers, many of whom moved to different towns with their Cross River women (NAE/OB: 503/6, 2). Folklore holds that the women who went away with these migrant men notified the women back home of emerging opportunities in their new locations. According to reports received by the District Officer of Obubra from the clan heads of Obubra,

> these women notified their stay-at-home sisters of the joys and plentitude of prostitutions and one by one our women have departed to obtain their share of the wages of sin. Thus, is the exodus of our women – the potential mothers of our clan.
>
> *(NAE/OB: 503/6, 2)*

One can make the point that sex workers who left home for whatever reason, to the Gold Coast, offered networks and information on opportunities for other women back home in Cross River. These pioneers would also often return home with their spoils to the envy and admiration of their counterparts back home. Reports also exist of third parties emerging to facilitate and organize, for a fee, the recruitment of women from Cross River and adjoining areas, to manage their travel to the Gold Coast, ensure their safe passage, and support them to settle in the Gold Coast.

Cross River women sex workers in the Gold Coast was a major cause for concern in colonial times. Records indicate that it was common for women in the region to simply wander off to join the sex industry in the Gold Coast (NAE/OG: 1201/61, 13). By the early 1940s, sex trade in this region became highly profitable and very well organized. The trade was so prevalent that there was hardly a family in the Obubra Division that did not have an interest in it, particularly in the Bahumunu, Afunatam, and Bansara areas of the Division (NAE/OB: 503/22, 1). The District Officer of the Obubra Division, Captain J.T. Jewell, alleged that families, relatives, and even husbands in the Bahumunu Clan subscribed to the trade and sponsored women to join it.

Some husbands in the Cross River area also reportedly encouraged their wives to join sex work. In many instances, such women remitted their earnings back home to their husbands as letters and telegrams. Husbands used these remittances for family upkeep and to establish family businesses and built homes. Debates exist on whether such men saw the trade as an immediate opportunity and means to increase their household incomes or envisaged their wives' inevitable entry into the trade (NAE/OB: 503/6, 3–4).

Retired sex workers played the role of consultants. They provided new entrants with information regarding the modes of operation, clientele, accommodation, and transportation (NAE/OB: 503/22, 1). By the early 1940s, communities such as Ediba and Akunakuna had achieved media notoriety and were considered "responsible for the management of the trade" (Naneen 1991, 61). Over 80% of the sex workers who went to the Gold Coast settled in Accra and its environs. Kumasi, Secondi, and Tamale were other popular destinations. The popularity of sex workers from Nigeria during the period led citizens of the Gold Coast to believe that all "Nigerian women were harlots and that (it) is a recognised custom in Nigeria" (Naneen 1991, 60).

Communities of practising Nigerian sex workers in the Gold Coast were quite well organized and had in place a system for the receiving, welcoming, hosting, familiarizing, and socializing of newly arriving sex workers (Naneen 1991). Newly arriving women took shelter in the stranger's quarters, usually in the company of other women from the same clan. In these rented apartments, four to six women lived and worked together, sometimes receiving their clients at home (Naneen 1991). As the numbers of the sex workers and competition grew, pimps (usually young semi-educated boys) emerged and often doubled as accounts clerks/servants. Most often, pimps were chosen from back home and were usually the sex workers' family or clan members.

As stated by Naneen, Colonial documents attest to the systematic organization and profitable nature of the industry. In the Gold Coast, the clientele of Nigerian sex workers included sailors, military personnel, miners, and plantation workers (NAE/OB: 503/22). According to colonial records:

> [T]he principal point is that all the time she is acting as a member of a properly organized society and I am told . . . that these societies are now so affluent that they are building special quarters for their members and in addition providing legal assistance when necessary. That it is extremely profitable, there is no doubt at all. I talked with one lady who wished to change eighty pounds in currency notes and she had not been long away, and that by no means represented her total capital.
>
> *(NAE/OB: 503/22, 2)*

The remittances to family members were also remarkable. The District Officer, Obubra Division stated in 1941 that: "The continuous demand for Post Offices in places like Usumutong is almost solely due to the fact the people want the facilities for keeping in touch with their itinerant gold mines – the whole population battens on them" (NAE/OB: 503/22, 2).

Trans-national sex work in contemporary Nigeria

Cross River women's trans-national sex trade anticipated a pattern of international prostitution that emerged in twentieth-century Nigeria. Dominated by women from Edo state in mid-western Nigeria, this new wave of international prostitution started circa the 1980s. Elsewhere, I located the roots of the trans-national sex trade in modern Nigeria in the economic crisis caused by Structural Adjustment Programme (SAP) introduced by the Nigerian government in 1986 (Adesina 2006). As in Nigeria, the introduction of SAP, an economic policy that the

World Bank and the International Monetary Fund (IMF) forced many developing countries to adopt, was immediately accompanied by significant social, cultural, and economic changes. The policy was characterized by reduced government public spending, massive monetary devaluation, and the embargo on employment in the public sector, among others (Kwanashie 1996, 69; Adesina 2002, 76). These policies engendered widespread crisis and hardship that forced people into whatever activities and job they could do to earn a living. Research indicates that during the SAP era, the number of sex workers in Nigeria rose steeply (Ihonvbere and Ekekwe 1988, 280). This was the context that inspired the present boom in transnational prostitution in contemporary Nigeria. Currently, Europe, particularly Italy, is the major destination of sex workers from Nigeria.

Extant accounts of this thriving sex trade point to a complexity and scale that are reminiscent of Cross River/Gold Coast sex trade. Today, many Nigerian women and girls reach Italy by sea, supported by pervasive access to information technology, enterprising local and international third parties, a ready market of clients in Europe, and the ease of international mobility. This current form of trans-national sex trade in Nigeria has inspired discourses related to femininity, culture, family life, women, nationhood, development, and international diplomacy. While some commentators have called attention to the parallels between the current international sex trade in Nigeria and the slave trade (Gansler 2017; Taub 2017), others have described the trade as a major commentary on the failure of international laws and the waning capacity of the contemporary Nigerian state to protect its citizens (Robinson 2002). Other views have highlighted the trade as exemplifying the erosion of traditional Nigerian sexual morality and family values, the dominant role of global capitalism, and the emerging power of trans-national sexual markets (Correa 2015). However, one report commissioned by the United Nations emphasized the demand and supply side of the trade, noting that the fear of HIV/AIDS has rendered drug-addicted northern European girls unattractive on the local prostitution market and that Nigerian girls from Edo State largely filled the demand (Taub 2017).

The response of the Nigerian state to the transnational sex trade has been, at best, chaotic and unsystematic, characterized by legislation and policies that are flawed, ineffective, and impractical. Perhaps more than anything else, the crisis of strategy facing the Nigerian state finds expression in how it both blames Edo culture for the phenomenon and tries to mobilize it to address the transnational sex trade. The potent mix of factors, including pervasive poverty, gender inequality, and lack of opportunities that drives international sex migration is often glossed over as the state increasingly focuses on culture and spiritualism as key explanatory variables. The age-long Edo cultural practice of securing important contracts with an oath, administered by a juju priest, has particularly been targeted by the Nigerian state. In local parlance, only by complying with the terms of such oaths can parties be saved from their fatal repercussions. Sex traffickers reportedly use the practice of oath-taking to promote compliance among migrating women. Thus, as Ebegbulem (2018) reports, following pressure from the Nigerian state:

> The Benin Monarch, Oba Ewuare 11, placed a curse on perpetrators of human trafficking in Edo state as well as native doctors who administer oath of secrecy on victims, asserting that the gods of Benin Kingdom would destroy those involved in the illicit trade. The Monarch who assembled all his chiefs, Enogie, Edionwere, priests of different deities in Benin and native doctors at his palace, with a view to unleash different curses on the perpetrators, regretted that the oath of secrecy administered on the victims had been encouraging the illegal trade and warned all native doctors to shun the act and join hands with the palace to attract development and progress to the kingdom and not encouraging human trafficking. Addressing the native doctors and his chiefs, the monarch said, "it has been reported

that the traffickers would first take their victims to native doctors to swear an oath that they would not disclose the names of their traffickers and sponsors. Your power is to fight for . . . progress . . . and not to be used for the destruction of our young people." The monarch who also invoked his power as the spiritual leader of Benin kingdom nullified all the oaths of secrecy administered on all victims of human trafficking and urged them to speak out and seek assistance. From the statistics available, most of those being trafficked and the sponsors are from Edo state, and it is shameful that people who already have jobs would sell all they have and give to sponsors just to go to Europe. Those who traffic people to Italy, Germany and other countries first take them to Libya where they are enslaved. I urge you all to tell those who took the oath of secrecy to speak up, we will protect them. We need to start arresting those involved because this is a crime against God and humanity. It is modern day slavery. From today, we no longer want to hear of human trafficking in Benin. I hope those who have been involved in this illegal trade will stop from today. All native doctors who have administered oath of secrecy on victims of human trafficking should also tell those they administered such oath on to speak out. I am appealing to all native doctors to stop administering such oaths on trafficked victims and all such oaths are hereby nullified. No native doctor should do any charm for any potential illegal migrant to cross international border. Those who did it before now are forgiven and whoever does it from today will face the wrath of our ancestors, the monarch warned.

The report continues:

The palace chief priests representing different deities had earlier prepared the relevant rituals used to fight such evil acts in the society. The chiefs were all dressed in red attire with each of them executing their duties as custom provided . . . the sacrifices made were specially targeted at human traffickers and cultists . . . Oba Ewuare 11 was present as all the chief's priests in the kingdom performed their greetings before carrying out their duties. The event was attended by all the different groups in the palace of the Oba which was a clear indication that the matter was a serious one. It was learnt that sacrifices were made in different shrines in the Kingdom prior to the palace event with a view to ensure that anyone involved in human trafficking in any part of the state would be caught like a chicken.

Meanwhile, the Zonal Commander of the National Agency for the Prohibition of Trafficking in Persons, NAPTIP, Mr. Nduka Nwanwenne, described the Oba's intervention as a significant milestone in the war against human trafficking and illegal migration. According to him,

before now, victims of human trafficking rarely opened up to give evidence in court because of the oath they have taken. They are afraid and believe that the oath will have effect [sic] on them as the native doctors who administered such oaths have their personal items like fingernails, pubic hair, menstrual pads, pants, photographs, etc. Now that those oaths have been nullified by the monarch, our power of prosecution has been enhanced and we can now rescue more victims.

(Ebegbulem 2018)

Obaseki, Governor of Edo state governor, on his part, said:

The state government has adopted a multi-pronged approach which includes a law, aggressive campaigns at markets and across the broad spectrum of the media, stakeholder engagements, partnerships with the National Agency for Prohibition of Trafficking in Persons (NAPTIP) and international governments and bodies, in tackling the menace.

(Ebegbulem 2018)

The recurring reference to traffickers in the report is important. Popular narratives suggest that a highly organized network of traffickers is to blame for the transnational sex migration in Nigeria. Sex migrants are widely viewed to be victims lured into the trade with promises of decent work in Europe. Traffickers are constituted as part of a vicious and powerful network with connections in "cities in Europe, Asia, and America. It involves trickery and deception, inducement, fetish objects, intimidation, manipulation, abduction, exploitation, and sexploitation" (Eghagha 2017). Traffickers reportedly often include Nigeria-based retired or older sex workers called madams, hustlers, and sometimes, high-ranking members of the society. Foreign-based Nigerians are also frequently mentioned as traffickers. They support migrating women with networks, travel documents, and information on routes, among other things. According to a newspaper report of a prostitution ring that was uncovered in Belgium,

> The police revealed that the man at the centre of the ring lives in Germany and goes by the name pastor and he is believed to be a Nigerian. Further reports . . . revealed that the "girls", usually operate in Brussels and in Antwerp; a port city frequented by sailors from all over the world. The girls were either brought in through ships or planes in Amsterdam, from where they are sent to other parts of the European Union (EU), including Italy, Germany, and the Netherlands.

The report continues:

> [T]he Nigerian women entered these countries with forged passports given to them by the "pastor", who allegedly had a close connection in Brussels and Lagos to arrange the deal. The victims, in some cases were said to have fallen prey of the promises made by the ring that they would be taken through Europe and given lucrative jobs, such as modelling, waitress[es], and even as actresses and singers, only to realise on arrival that they were in debt to the men, who then sold them off for about $25,000.

(Salami 1996, 1; Adesina 2006, 14)

As was the case with the Gold Coast rush, information flow between Nigerian sex workers in Europe and their home communities also contributes to the current boom in international sex migration. News of fortunes made by migrant Nigerian women in Europe regularly filters home to the admiration and envy of local communities. Today, there are streets in Edo states named after retired migrant sex workers. Visitors in the major Edo city of Benin are also often shown big buildings erected by Europe-based women and girls. The widespread perception that migration is an escape route from poverty has become entrenched and a bane of state efforts to address the international sex trade. Ben Taub (2017) writes that

> women were sending back word of well-compensated employment as hairdressers, dressmakers, housekeepers, nannies, and maids, but the actual nature of their work in Italy remained hidden, and so parents urged their daughters to take out loans to travel to Europe and lift the family out of poverty. In time, sex workers became madams; from Italy, they employed recruiters, transporters, and document forgers in Nigeria.

Taub (2017) further notes that "as families of migrant women replaced ramshackle houses of mud and wood with walled-off properties" and "lists of expensive assets – cars, furniture, generators – purchased with remittances from Europe were included in obituaries, envious neighbours took note". Taub (2017) also highlights the important role of local churches in Nigeria, where "Pentecostal ministers, preaching a gospel of prosperity, extolled the benefits of migration".

Conclusion

This contribution on sex trade in colonial and contemporary Nigeria reveals clear intersections in the dynamics of the trade, strategies of recruitment, reliance on cultural networks, and the types of anxieties they inspired in the public and state responses to them. As in colonial times, the contemporary response of the Nigerian state to the trans-national sex trade has been, at best, untidy and disorganized, characterized by legislation and policies that are flawed, ineffective, and unworkable.

Though separated by several decades, cross-border sex work in both periods were driven by the economic marginalization of women, and facilitated by networks, the success stories of migrant sex workers, and the support from family members. The reponse of both the colonial and post-colonial government in Nigeria to cross-borders in these two eras was similar. The Nigerian state blamed local culture and focused attention on working with authorities in sending communities and receiving countries to control the movement of women. The state in both periods has also given little attention to addressing the socio-economic marginalization issues that triggered women's entry into cross-border sex trade.

References

Aderinto, Saheed. 2012. Of Gender, Race, and Class: The Politics of Prostitution in Lagos, Nigeria. *Frontiers* Vol. 33, No. 3, pp. 71–92.

Aderinto, Saheed. 2015. *When Sex Threatened the State: Illicit Sexuality, Nationalism, and Politics in Colonial Nigeria, 1900–1958.* Chicago: University of Chicago Press.

Adesina, Olutayo Charles. 2002. Growth and Change in the Ibadan Underground Foreign Exchange Market During Devaluation. In Jane I. Guyer, LaRay Denzer, and Adigun Agbaje, eds, *Money Struggles and City Life: Devaluation in Ibadan and Other Urban Centers in Southern Nigeria, 1986–1996.* Portsmouth, NH: Heinemann, pp. 75–91.

Adesina, Oluwakemi. 2006. Between Culture and Poverty: The Queen Mother Phenomenon and the Edo International Sex Trade. *JENDA: A Journal of Culture and African Women Studies* No. 8. www.africaknowledgeproject.org/index.php/jenda/article/view/127. Accessed 27 July 2018.

Afigbo, A.E. 1972. Trade and Politics on the Cross River, 1895–1905. *Transactions of the Historical Society of Ghana* Vol. 13, No. 1 (June), p. 26.

Blaize, Olayemi C. 1944. Moral Dangers in the Community. *Daily Times,* 24 November.

Correa, S. 2015. Emerging Powers, Sexuality and Human Rights: "Fumbling Around the Elephant?" www.sxpolitics.org/wp-content/uploads/2015/09/workingpaper-11.pdf. Accessed 18 April 2018.

Ebegbulem, S. 2018. "Our Gods Will Destroy You": Oba of Benin Curse Human Traffickers. *Vanguard.* www.vanguardngr.com/2018/03/gods-will-destroy-oba-benin-curse-human-traffickers. Accessed 27 July 2018.

Eghagha, H. 2017. What Are Edo Girls Doing in Italy? *Guardian.* https://guardian.ng/opinion/what-are-edo-girls-doing-in-italy. Accessed 18 April 2018.

Gansler, K. 2017. *The New Ways of Nigeria's Human Trafficking.* www.dw.com/en/the-new-ways-of-nigerias-human-traffickers/a-41167914. Accessed 18 April 2018.

Ihonvbere, J.O. and Ekekwe, E.N. 1988. Dependent Capitalism, Structural Adjustment and Democratic Possibilities in Nigeria's Third Republic. *Africa Spectrum* Vol. 23, No. 3, p. 280.

Isamah, A.N. and Rasidi A. Okunola. 2002. Family Life Under Economic Adjustment: The Rise of Child Breadwinners, in Jane I. Guyer, LaRay Denzer, and Adigun Agbaje, eds, *Money Struggles and City Life*. Portsmouth, NH Heinemann, pp. 26–39.

Kwanashie, Mike. 1996. Macroeconomic Policy: Monetary, Fiscal, Banking and Financial Institutions. In Akin Fadahunsi and Tunde Babawale, eds, *Nigeria: Beyond Structural Adjustment: Towards a Popular Democratic Development Alternative*. Lagos: Third World Forum (Nigeria Network and the Friedreich Ebert Foundation), pp. 69–87.

Lindsay, L.A. 2003. *Working with Gender: Wage Labour and Social Change in Southwestern Nigeria*. Portsmouth: NH, Heinemann.

Mcphee, A. 1926. *The Economic Revolution in British West Africa*. London: Routledge.

Naneen, B.B.B. 1991. Itinerant Gold Mines: Prostitution in the Cross-River Basin of Nigeria, 1930–1950. *African Studies Review* Vol. 34, No. 2 (September), p. 61.

National Archives Enugu (NAE)/OB: 503/6 *Prostitutes in Obubra Division*, pp. 3 and 4.

NAE/OB: 503/22 *Cross River Harlots*, p. 2.

NAE/OG: 1201/54 *Emigration of Cross River Eomen for Prostitution*, p. 1.

NAE/OG: 1201/61 *Matrimonial Problems at Ediba Town*, p. 13.

National Archives Ibadan (NAI)/ComCol I/2844, *Child Prostitution in Lagos, 1942–46*, pp. 79, 86.

NAI/OndoProf 1/3, *Social Welfare in the Colony and Protectorate*, pp. 8 and 79.

Parpart J.L. 2001. ""Wicked Women" and "Respectable Ladies": Reconfiguring Gender on the Zambian Copperbelt, 1936–1964" in D.L. Hodgson and S.A. McCurdy, *"Wicked" Women and the Reconfiguration of Gender in Africa*. Portsmouth, NH: Heinemann, pp. 275 and 277.

Robinson, M. 2002. Recommended Principles and Guidelines on Human Rights and Human Trafficking. www.ohchr.org/Documents/Publications/Commentary_Human_Trafficking_en.pdf. Accessed 18 April 2018.

Salami A. 1996. Nigerian Prostitution ring in Belgium uncovered. *Third Eye*, 18 December, p. 10.

Sogidi. 1935. Save the Future Mothers, 21 September.

Taub, B. 2017. The Desperate Journey of a Trafficked Girl. www.newyorker.com/magazine/2017/04/10/the-desperate-journey-of-a-trafficked-girl. Accessed 18 April 2018.

Udoka, I.A. 1995. The Shipping Industry in the Lower Cross River Region, Nigeria: 1865–1955. *Trans African Journal of History* Vol. 24. p. 205.

White, L. 1990. *The Comforts of Home: Prostitution in Colonial Nairobi*. Chicago and London: University of Chicago Press, pp. 147 and 148.

White, L. 1932. Editorial Note: Street Indecencies. *Lagos Daily News*, 27 May.

48

"Down on whores"

Considering representations of Jack the Ripper's victims

May-Len Skilbrei and Per Jørgen Ystehede

Introduction

> This book is dedicated to Polly Nicholls, Annie Chapman,
> Liz Stride, Kate Eddowes, and Marie Jeannette Kelly.
> You and your demise: of these things alone are we certain.
> Goodnight, ladies.
>
> *(Moore & Campbell, 1999)*

> The death of a beautiful woman is, unquestionably, the most poetical topic in the world, and equally is it beyond doubt that the lips best suited for such topic are those of a bereaved lover.
>
> *(Poe, 1846)*

The case of Jack the Ripper, an unknown assailant who murdered multiple women in London's Whitechapel district beginning in 1888, has attracted significant and enduring interest throughout the world. Polly Nicholls, Annie Chapman, Liz Stride, Kate Eddowes, and Marie Jeannette Kelly, the five women that the significant canon of work related to these murders generally regards as "his" victims, had earned at least some of their income from prostitution. This fact was central to how the case was presented at the time, and also in how it is represented today. One reason why the five women's involvement in prostitution has been so central is that one of the speculations about why the murders took place and who the murderer was is linked to a formulation in one of the many letters received by the police, supposedly penned by the Ripper: "I am down on whores and I shan't quit ripping [murdering] them till I do get buckled [arrested]" (quoted in Walkowitz, 1982, 551).

Ever since their lives and violent deaths first entered the public sphere, Nicholls, Chapman, Stride, Eddowes, and Kelly have been associated with prostitution in different settings and mediums. Representations of the victims take various forms that often dehumanize them. The often-mentioned fact that the five women were involved in prostitution may take part in legitimizing such representations which include graphic depictions in drawings and pictures on the front pages of London newspapers in 1888, and later in books, theatrical productions, and in films.

In this chapter, we explore the depictions in media, art, and popular culture of the lives and violent deaths of Nicholls, Chapman, Stride, Eddowes, and Kelly. While there were speculations of more victims at the time, the murders of these five women are generally thought to have been committed by the unknown attacker known only as Jack the Ripper. We are not preoccupied with Jack the Ripper as a person but with representations of the five women referred to as "whores" in the letter mentioned above. To accomplish this goal, we have collected material that depicts and describes the women and we will examine how they are represented in examples from various mediums from the 1880s, the decade in which all five women died, until the present. While these representations indisputably express shifting cultural norms surrounding femininity, here we are most interested in how prostitution and women involved in it are represented and represent broader social concerns.

Approaching the canon: attempting to get a grip on the Ripper literature

The rise of the fame of Jack the Ripper may in part be explained by the fact that it corresponded with the rise of the news media and the growing popularization of crime news at the end of the nineteenth century (Wood, 2016; see also Curtis, 2001). It was at this time that crime reporting found its form and its mass distribution became possible. But there is reason to believe that also other characteristics of nineteenth-century London are relevant to understand the great attention the case drew and the direction it took. The nineteenth century saw rapid urbanization, rural–urban migration and industrialization – not only in the UK but throughout western Europe. This shifted demographics in cities like London, but there were clear patterns in how this affected local communities within the cities. The Whitechapel area was itself very much the home of what historian Gertrude Himmelfarb (1983) has coined the gothic poor. How poverty and the poor were understood was also shifting. Early in the century, poverty was seen as part of divine will, a natural order and condition of life and society. By the mid nineteenth century, poverty was becoming redefined as a social problem, not least linked to fears about social unrest and revolution. Areas like Whitechapel became associated with danger and squalor, but also entertainment and loose morals, a playground for male elites. Jack the Ripper came to loom large in the moral imagination of the turn of the century, and this needs to be seen in light of fears at the time about how society was developing. The Ripper case drew wide attention at the time, and the coverage then, and later, was highly speculative and sensationalist. While the case and its circumstances were indeed shocking in and of themselves, there is reason to believe that news about it also served another purpose, and as such can be seen as the ultimate example of how crime news not only entertains but also tell moral tales and helps audiences make sense of the world. As Wood (2016, 305) describes its function, crime news "contributed to a process of 'sense-making' in the context of mass urban 'modernity' in the late nineteenth and early twentieth centuries". While it is tempting to regard the media coverage of the Jack the Ripper case as a case of a moral panic and dismiss it as sensationalist, Mariana Valverde (2006, 1) reminds us to look also for what warranted the extraordinary attention.

In this chapter, we are particularly interested in how the interest in these five cases links to prostitution in particular ways. Some concerns are tied into the historical fabric of when they came into existence, while others persevere and, literally, "trickle down" to the present from the first blood of Polly Nichols that was spilled. To reference the blood of Nichols is not to sensationalize the event nor to dehumanize her as a victim. It is in part to convey a fact and in part an apt metaphor for the literature on, and the created image of the case. Nicholls, Chapman,

Stride, Eddowes, and Kelly are referred to in the literature as the canonical five Ripper victims, but what does that really mean? The label "canon" not only testifies to the huge amount of interest and study into this case. But it also conveys a number of problematic methodological, ethical, and historical assumptions: that not only some murders of women seem to deserve more scrutiny than others, but the adjective canonical, more often associated with Biblical scripture, also suggests a canonical gospel and kinship to faith rather than fact.

One of many interesting aspects of the "Ripper phenomenon" is, to paraphrase the beginning of Alan Moore's graphic novel about the case – *From Hell* – that the only thing one can be sure about is the demise of these women (Moore & Campbell, 1999). Who the Whitechapel murderer, as the media first called Jack the Ripper, was – if ever such a creature, or creatures, even existed – is all conjecture. What we know is that Nicholls, Chapman, Stride, Eddowes, and Kelly were murdered, but so were many other prostitutes and women working in other precarious labour sectors in nineteenth-century London (Bondeson, 2016). The rest of the story is, similar to Moore's graphic novel, an elaborate fiction.

Difficult as it is to separate facts from fiction in how the Ripper case and its victims have been depicted and described, it is more useful to look for types of representations and what they express. The literature on Jack the Ripper is enormous. A basic search on WorldCat – the world's largest online library – for Jack the Ripper results in more than 2,000 books and close to 700 articles, in addition to music (500+ entries), films (400+ entries) and audiotapes (200+). A Google search provides 10,700,000 results, Google scholar lists 655 entries just for 2017, Yahoo 210,000 results, and so on. Thus, initially it may be helpful, when navigating the overwhelming amount of information on Jack the Ripper, to try to provide some broad, general categories to begin understanding the Ripper phenomena.

We argue that the Ripper literature may, broadly speaking, be separated into two main types or perspectives, first the "whodunnit perspective", and second the "what-does-this-mirror" approach. The first, the "whodunnit perspective", is the domain of the Ripperologists engaged in the question of what the identity of Jack the Ripper was, whereas the latter, "what-does-this-mirror" approach, is work that takes this case as a starting point for the cultural and criminological imagination (Young, 2011). In the following we will present and give some examples from each of these two categories, and then we turn to the question of how Jack the Ripper's five canonical victims are represented in these categories.

The "whodunnit perspective"

The first, largest, and most mainstream literature is the "whodunnit" perspective. In other words, representations of the Ripper case in literature and the media more broadly, sometimes referred to as Ripperologists, that try to find or discover the actual identity of Jack the Ripper. A typical description of the plight of the Ripperologist is illustrated by Ripperologist and amateur historian Mike Covell:

> Over seven years ago I started seriously researching and writing about "Jack the Ripper". It has been seven years of long hours spent at microfilm readers, computer screens, in local studies libraries, archives, and museums, studying, researching, writing, reading, travelling and trying to sort out the wheat from the chaff. Initially I started researching my home city's connection to the case [Hull in Yorkshire], where I discovered that no fewer than 14 suspects had links, I then started looking at the Hull press and how they covered the case. Eventually I was to go off on tangents and research and write about specific scares, suspects and victims. One such victim was Annie Chapman. What can be said or written about

Annie Chapman that has not already appeared previously? That was the question I asked recently, and my reply was, quite a lot actually. We know only of a handful of reports and primary sources regarding her life and untimely death at the hands of a serial killer known only as "Jack the Ripper", but there is always new material being discovered.

(Covell, 2014, p. 1)

Covell's "Ripperology bibliography" so far counts 11 monographs on the Ripper. His book on Annie Chapman, the second of the so-called canonical five Ripper victims, is just one example of the books on the Ripper where every detail seems to be of interest in the quest of finding proof for "their" theory on who Jack really was.[1] The list of suggestions of who Jack the Ripper was has been growing, if not yearly, certainly decennially, since the late 1880s. The police during the investigation named more than 10 people and the list has grown a lot since. Among the suspects have been authors such as Lewis Carroll (1832–1898), painters such as Walter Sickert (1860–1942), members of the Royal family such as the grandson of Queen Victoria Prince Albert Victor Edward (1864–1892), members of the House of Lords such as Lord Randolph Churchill (1849–1895), the father of Sir Winston Churchill (1874–1945), and recently, as of April 2017, member of the clergy and poet Francis Thompson (1859–1907). The number of suspects has grown so voluminously that there are even books dedicated solely to keeping track of and listing all the suspects (see for instance Russo, 2011). The list does not only include famous people, or people from high society, but also the middle and lower classes from all over the world. The list contains medical doctors, lawyers, butchers, chimneysweepers, members of the police, unemployed people from the urban poor, and foreigners and migrants ranging from Jews, Indians, Haitians to the Irish and the Russian and Italian Anarchists. The list includes both men and women, as well as people seen as more gender fluid.

The list of suspects and suggested motives reflects changes in analytical and scientific fashions when it comes to how to understand murder and prostitution, and also reflects developments in dominant popular cultural explanations for who could be the murderer. For instance, following World War II in the "whodunnit" approach one finds in the 1970s, 1980s, and early 1990s psychoanalysis as a popular framework to analyse and build a case regarding who the elusive Ripper might be. Here one finds a focus on the murder as resulting from various sets of sexual ailments. For instance, the criminologist David Abrahamsen argued that Jack the Ripper was not one but two people (Prince Albert Victor Edward and a manservant) who killed the women as a form of psychosexual response to – to use an euphemism of the nineteenth century – the love that dare not speak its name, the love between men (Abrahamsen, 1992).

With the rise of the popularity of the serial murder figure – a term coined in the late 1970s with the rise of so-called "criminal profiling" by US law enforcement agencies – Jack the Ripper became a popular case for criminal profilers to use as evidence to prove that serial killers actually exist (see especially Jenkins, 1994). After criminal profiling, finding the Ripper's DNA and using advances in forensic science has been a major focus. Especially widely focused on in the press has been the US crime reporter-cum-crime writer Patricia Cornwell – author of the Kay Scarpetta series and producer of the TV series *Bones* – who has spent a vast amount of money testing physical items from the time of the murders for DNA evidence. Cornwell supports the theory that the identity of Jack is Walter Sickert (see also Murray 2004), a modernist painter who also painted a series of images depicting the murder scenes. Both biographers of Sickert and Ripperologists who claim to have different findings and interpretations of the evidence have in turn counter-argued this claim. In her revised edition of her book on Jack the Ripper, Cornwell (2017, p. 488) describes confrontations with Ripperologists as follows:

When my book was released in the winter of 2002 and I headed to the UK for the publicity tour, I was baffled to hear reports from FBI friends that "Ripperologists are lying in wait for you" . . . Fire away my critics did, and my book tour in the UK was pretty damn awful. Afterward I described it to my publicists as "a ten-day deposition". I was attacked and probably did not handle it very well. In hindsight, I was just as guilty of assumptions and prejudices as the Ripperologists were. I completely dismissed their theories as fanciful and meritless, and they did mine.

The case of Jack the Ripper is arguably the world's most famous murder mystery and is also a profitable industry, especially for authors in the crime fiction and 'true crime' genres. The elusiveness of the killer's identity seems to be an enigma that is sufficiently intriguing so as not to cause people to lose interest in the case, but rather works to its advantage by sustaining the element of the unknown, of doubt. The case both seems to draw and invite the expert and the non-expert alike to be the detective. From *Jack the Ripper: The Casebook* (Jones, 2009) to the Jack the Ripper museum in Whitechapel, London, where the exhibit ends with leaving the question of the identity of the Ripper to the audience with signage that reads: "You get to answer the question and you get to decide".

From a "Jack of all trades" to a "Jack for all seasons": the "what-does-this-mirror" approach

The second, and more dominant in academic discourse, is what we have coined the "what-does-this-mirror" approach. In these representations of the Ripper case, the interest is not in who Jack the Ripper was as a person or what his true identity might have been. Rather the focus is often to use the case of Jack the Ripper as a point of departure to explore and examine other topics. The focus is on what the Jack the Ripper case may say about issues such as the British, nineteenth-century public views on sex, race, fallen women and street workers, gender politics, labour politics and conflicts, migrants and migration, urbanization, anti-Semitism, colonialism, and stereotypes of the Other in British society in particular or Western society and/or modernity in general (see e.g. Gilman, 1991). "Jack the Ripper" is treated in this literature more as a form of (Victorian) pastiche, a hodgepodge of cultural influences and trends, painting and shaping a series of images of the Ripper for different purposes and meaning productions. Basically, literally and metaphorically, providing a "Jack for all seasons", similar to the characterization Warwick and Willis (2007, 2) make in the introduction to a collection of selected articles on the case:

> the many true crime books on the Whitechapel murders, despite their often-declared intention to present only "the facts", that serve to perpetuate the myth of Jack the Ripper, and as [anthropologist] Roland Barthes says of myth, it: "transforms the reality of the world into an image of the world, History into Nature . . . myth has the task of giving an historical intention a natural justification". [. . . In writings on the] Whitechapel murders the historical truth of the deaths of the women and the conditions in which they lived become mere background to a mythological mystery.

Jack the Ripper is understood in the majority of these dominant cultural representations as a blank canvas for the public and/or private imagination to fill; the issue of who Jack was is almost of no or little relevance. To further contextualize these representations within the historical and cultural contexts that produced them, we now turn to representations of the five murdered women: Nicholls, Chapman, Stride, Eddowes, and Kelly.

"Jack's women" as accessories after the fiction

Predominantly, the victims of Jack the Ripper have received limited attention and interest as compared to the greater attention devoted to *either* the quest for the true identity of the Ripper *or* the cultural representations of the Ripper. This, however, is not to say that the victims have received scant attention per se. Not only have they been the subject of books, such as Covell's (2014) *Annie Chapman: Wife, Mother, Victim: The Life and Death of a Victim of Jack The Ripper*. They also became the focus of the controversy surrounding the opening of the Jack the Ripper museum in Whitechapel, London in 2015. In the application to the local council to establish the museum, the described intention was to

> recognise and celebrate the women of the East End who have shaped history, telling the story of how they have been instrumental in changing society. It will analyse the social, political and domestic experience from the Victorian period to the present day.
>
> (Docklands & East London Advertiser, *2015; see also Laite, 2015*)

As the opening date approached, it became clear that the project was not to present the long tradition of the area of the political protests of women, but rather to speculate on the victimization of women. Many critics found the new museum as merely disgraceful and exploitive. As one critic in the *Guardian*, a leading UK newspaper, put it:

> Certainly, someone killed five women with extreme savagery. But that person was not Jack the Ripper. Jack the Ripper is an invented villain, a figure of gothic melodrama who serves the purpose of making five murdered women also seem like inventions, mere accessories after the fiction . . . The women this man killed were real, as real as the murdered women we see in the headlines to this day. They deserve to be remembered with respect, not with self-interested manipulations and underhand deals.
>
> (Orr, 2015)

Far from being a museum for women's social history as its owner first claimed, the museum follows a traditional form of telling the Ripper story. From the time of the murders, newspapers and bulletins printed sensational details about what had happened to their bodies, and often included gruesome details, some based on eyewitness accounts, some based on the information the police gave, and some of the reporters' imagination of how a dead woman would look like (Walkowitz, 1992).

Though these perspectives are different, they highlight some dilemmas in their representations of the victims – of the canonical five Ripper victims. They both make the women mainly into accessories to the act of prostitution and the social meanings attached to it across different temporal and spatial contexts. The fact that the focus in these perspectives remains on the women's link to prostitution warrants some analysis.

On the women as accessories in the "whodunnit" perspective

In this kind of literature about the case, the murders and the victims are described as part of a speculation about who Jack the Ripper was. The *fin de siècle* rise of interest in the alienist (a former term for a person working in the area broadly defined as forensic psychiatry) and in psychology, as a science with privileged (scientific) access to the human soul, fed ideas about Jack the Ripper being an upper-class man who murdered prostitutes due to his suppressed sexuality

(Valverde, 2006). This framing was also widespread as the association between Robert Louis Stevenson's (1886) novel *The Strange Case of Dr Jekyll and Mr Hyde* and the Ripper case was made early on, not least because a play based on the book was showing in London at the time (Winter, 2016). To figure out who Jack was, many at the time of the murders and later have particularly focused on the victims' link to prostitution. This link was seen as what put the women at risk and the reason for why they were murdered. At the time, the journalist W.T. Stead was a central contributor to such speculations. In this case, but also in other pieces of his writing, he implicated upper-class men and their sexual exploitation of the lower classes, and the historian Judith Walkowitz (1982) demonstrates how this served as a starting point for local riots at the time.

On the women as accessories in the "what does-this-mirror" approach

Walkowitz (1982) draws the conclusion that a part of the power of the Ripper mythology is that the fate of the victims serves as a morality tale, as the Ripper can be seen as the punisher of female transgression. The idea at the time was that women belong in the private sphere, and when they venture out, even bringing something valued as private (sexuality) to the public market place, horrible things (rightfully) happen to them (for an analysis of the "fallen women" narrative in Victorian England, see Auerbach, 1982). That the murders were "justice served" was one of the narratives in the news media's coverage of the case at the time (Warkentin, 2011). In a fictional account published only three years after the murders, W.B. Lawson's *Jack the Ripper in New York* (1891), the character of Jack the Ripper serves the function of protecting chaste women from contamination and in effect creates an opposition between innocent women that should be protected and guilty ones that deserve punishment: "thus reinforcing gender roles that place women firmly within the domestic space, subordinate to men's power" (Warkentin, 2011, p. 11).

What the representation of the case mirrored in terms of the victims specifically and prostitution generally was different for the middle classes, for whom Whitechapel was associated with sin, compared to people residing in the area (Walkowitz, 1982). While the middle classes saw the murdered women as an expression of the immorality of the place and people there, those living in Whitechapel saw the women's fate and the representation of the women in newspapers as unjust: "To the Whitechapel poor, Annie Chapman and Mary Jane Kelly were not degraded outcasts, but members of their own class and community" (Walkowitz, 1982, 558).

While there was also sympathy with the victims outside Whitechapel, they were presented as reproachable due to prostitution. The representation also pointed to contemporary debates on women's rights, and some representations indicate that Jack the Ripper was also someone championing a righteous male wrath towards women. Walkowitz (1982) describes how the case at the time was taken to represent violence against women, also domestic violence, and that men were threatening women that the same fate as that of the Ripper's victims would befall upon them. Walkowitz writes (1982, 563): "I am not trying to argue that the Ripper episode directly increased sexual violence rather it covertly sanctioned male antagonism towards women and buttressed male authority over them". In effect, in Walkowitz' feminist reading, Jack the Ripper could be seen as a gothic man of reason. This is a point also further elaborated by Boyle (2005, 7) who emphasizes that violence is not a commonsense category, but may also be an ideological one:

> Men's violence against prostitute women is so pervasive, so normalised, that even this obviously aggressive act – hitting a woman on the head with a small brick – is not recognised as hostile, unusual or illegitimate. A feminist understanding of the crimes of Jack the Ripper and his successors therefore demands that we see the murders not as individual aberrations, but as the extreme end of a continuum of male violence.

That violence against women who sell sex is so often explained as a result of prostitution, can be seen as an expression of victim blaming. This point is made by Warkentin (2011) who has studied the earliest published fictional accounts of the case, the pulp fiction of the Victorian era, known as "penny dreadfuls" and "dime novels". She argues that the "Ripper's victims are represented as unruly women who are justly punished. Gender roles are firmly reestablished, and the criminal remains at large – an ominous warning to women to remain firmly and safely within feminine domestic space" (Warkentin, 2011, 14).

The case mirrored women's vulnerability as it evidenced how women who ventured into the public sphere, and were without a male protector, were possible targets of violent crimes. While this served as a special warning for poor women who on and off were making money out of prostitution, this also needs to be seen as a more general lesson learned at a time when also women of the upper echelons were seeking significant changes to a status quo that imposed significant limits on their basic human rights and freedoms, including the right to vote, to receive an education equal to their male peers, to labour rights, to marriage and divorce of their own free will, and to inheritance, which at that time generally only benefitted men.

Representations of the case also opened up class relations for critique. For instance, the stories reported by journalist W.T. Stead revealed the dissatisfaction felt among working-class citizens about how upper-class men subjected working-class neighbourhoods to deviance and acts they did not subject "their own" women to (Walkowitz 1992). The upper-class men who preyed upon poor women were interpreted through a psychological lens, and the degenerate rich men who remained undetected were thus a mirror for and critique of class relations and incipient conflicts at the time. While this interpretation upheld male ownership of women and women's sexuality, representations of the case drew attention to the living conditions of the victims and the squalor and poverty of London's East End.

"Down on whores": considering representations of Jack the Ripper's victims

We have no way of knowing whether the five women who were counted as Jack the Ripper's victims were targeted because they sold sex, were vulnerable to murder because they sold sex, or were counted as victims of the same murderer because they shared the trait of selling sex in Whitechapel and its vicinity. Today it is often assumed that Nicholls, Chapman, Stride, Eddowes, and Kelly were targeted *because* they sold sex. The notoriety of the case and the way it has continued to be part of popular culture means that it has become a standard reference to murders of people who sell sex, and assumed or convicted perpetrators in other series of murders against sex workers in contemporary times are also sometimes dubbed "ripper", most notably the "Yorkshire Ripper" (see for instance Boyle, 2005).

The case of Jack the Ripper is important because it highlights dilemmas involved in pointing to very real vulnerabilities of and harms towards women who sell sex. While it is important to identify vulnerabilities and harms, these may well serve sensationalist functions and contribute to further dehumanization and stigmatization of women associated with prostitution. In the "whodunnit" perspective the women are mainly used as moral legitimizations for speculations into the identity of a murderer. Also in the "what-does-this-mirror approach", Jack's canonical victims are used as part of meta-narratives were the focus is not on detailing individual suffering as in the case of the first perspective, but they remain instruments – tools – to paint pictures of whatever is fashionably believed to be the flipside of modern life.

Criminologists often state that images and other representations of crime are powerful because they speak to broader concerns in the sense that people do not only fear to be subjected to a particular crime but also to the chaos and lack of safety it involves (Valverde, 2006, p. 11).

According to Murray (2004, 52), the nineteenth-century interest in the case expressed fears and ambiguities in the face of modernity:

> The only thing to be revealed in the investigation of Jack the Ripper is ourself, and the one hundred and fifteen years of theorizing, investigation and myth stands as a testament to the latent desires and crisis that have lurked behind the facade of progress and reason that has driver modernity.

There is an added relevance to examining how the victims of Jack the Ripper were presented as this has served as a model for later representations of serial killers, what Valverde (2006, 130) calls "paradigm case": "The Jack the Ripper phenomenon can be regarded as a sort of paradigm case or original model for a whole series of representations of crime and criminals". The Ripper case is particularly suitable for this not only because it was spectacular, but also because it is open-ended: "A story with no closure, no final truth, and hence no privileged authority, is a richer site for the study of cultural constructions of criminality than one with a clear cut ending" (Valverde, 2006, 118).

It is useful for scholars of prostitution today to analyse how the special vulnerabilities of women involved in prostitution are dealt with at different times. While in the nineteenth century some feminists urged that the Ripper case should warrant protective measures for women in prostitution, including Josephine Butler (Walkowitz, 1982), these concerns were in the end channelled into law and order solutions, which increased the use of crackdowns (Curtis, 2001). Perhaps studying the Ripper case today could also inspire fictions that result in alternatives and potentials that take the vulnerabilities of women who sell sex and bring them out of the shadows.

Note

1 For an example of the countless discussions on the exact number of murder victims see for instance Jones (2009).

References

Abrahamsen, D. (1992). *Murder and Madness: The Secret Life of Jack the Ripper*. London: Donald I. Fine.
Auerbach, N. (1982). *Women and the Demon: The Life of a Victorian Myth*. Cambridge, MA: Harvard University Press.
Bondeson, J. (2016). *Rivals of the Ripper: Unsolved Murders of Women in Late Victorian London*. Stroud, UK: The History Press.
Boyle, K. (2005). *Media and Violence: Gendering the Debates*. London: Sage.
Cornwell, P. (2017). *Ripper: The Secret Life of Walter Sickert*. Seattle, WA: Thomas & Mercer.
Covell, M. (2014). *Annie Chapman – Wife, Mother Victim: The Life and Death of a Victim of Jack the Ripper*. Creativia.
Curtis, L. P. Jr. (2001). *Jack the Ripper and the London Press*. New Haven, CT: Yale University Press.
Docklands and East London Advertiser (2015). Museum in Cable St about Women and Suffragettes Turns Out to Be "Jack the Ripper", 28 July. www.eastlondonadvertiser.co.uk/news/heritage/museum-in-cable-st-about-women-and-suffragettes-turns-out-to-be-jack-the-ripper-1-4172863, retrieved 3 March 2018.
Gilman, S. L. (1991). *The Jew's Body*. London: Routledge.
Himmelfarb, G. (1983). *The Idea of Poverty*. New York: Alfred A. Knopf.
Jenkins, P. (1994). *Using Murder: The Social Construction of Serial Homicide*. New York: Aldine de Gruyter.
Jones, R. (2009). *Jack the Ripper: The Casebook*. London: Andre Deutsch.
Laite, J. (2015). Jack the Ripper's Victims Deserve to Be Commemorated. But Like This? *Guardian* 31 July. www.theguardian.com/commentisfree/2015/jul/31/jack-ripper-museum-victims-women, retrieved 3 March 2018.

Lawson, W.B. (1891). *Jack the Ripper in New York*. New York: Street & Smith.

Moore, A. and Campbell, E. (1999). *From Hell*. Mariatta, GA: Top Shelf Productions.

Murray, A. (2004). Jack the Ripper, the Dialectic of Enlightenment and the Search for Spiritual Deliverance in White Chappell, Scarlet Tracings. *Critical Survey* 16(1): 52–66.

Orr, D. (2015). Jack the Ripper Is an Invented Villain But His Victims Were Real: A Museum to These Crimes Is a Disgrace. *Guardian*, 7 August. www.theguardian.com/commentisfree/2015/aug/07/jack-the-ripper-museum-contemptuous-rip-off, retrieved 3 March 2018.

Poe, E.A. (1846). The Philosophy of Composition. *Graham's Magazine* 28 (4): 163–167.

Russo, S. (2011) *The Jack the Ripper Suspects: Persons Cited by Investigators and Theorists*. Jefferson, NC: McFarland & Co.

Stevenson, R.L. (1886). *The Strange Case of Dr. Jekyll and Mr. Hyde*. London: Longman Green & Co.

Valverde, M. (2006). *Law and Order: Images, Meanings, Myths*. Abingdon, UK: Routledge-Cavendish.

Walkowitz, J.R. (1982). Jack the Ripper and the Myth of Male Violence. *Feminist Studies* 8 (3): 542–574.

Walkowitz, J.R. (1992). *City of Dreadful Delight: Narratives of Sexual Danger in Late-Victorian London*. Chicago: University of Chicago Press.

Warkentin, E. (2011). A Bloody Pulp: Women in Two Early Fictionalizations of the Jack the Ripper Case. *CLUES: A Journal of Detection* 29 (1): 5–15.

Warwick, A. & Willis, M. eds. (2007). *Jack the Ripper: Media. Culture. History*. Manchester, UK: Manchester University Press.

Winter, S. A. (2016). "Two and the Same": Jack the Ripper and the Melodramatic Stage Adaption of *Strange Case of Dr Jekyll and Mr Hyde*. *Nineteenth Century Theatre and Film* 42 (2): 174–194. doi: 10.1177/1748372716645114.

Wood, J.C. (2016). Crime News and the Press. In Knepper, P. & Johansen, A. eds. *The Oxford Handbook of the History of Crime and Criminal Justice* (pp. 301–320). Oxford. Oxford University Press.

Young, J. (2011). *The Criminological Imagination*. New York: Polity.

49

Public encounters with whorephobia

Making sense of hostility toward sex worker advocates

Elena Jeffreys[1]

Introduction

This chapter builds upon a body of published work that critically interrogates the ongoing saga of "the sex wars", the feminist schism that first emerged in the 1980s over pornography. The dynamics at work in this schism have taken on numerous dimensions over time, and there are various explanations for this. Sociologist Crystal Jackson (2013, 190), in her research with the Desiree Alliance, a US network of sex workers and sex worker organisations, concluded: "It is clear that the feminist sex wars never went away, they just re-focused from pornography to sex trafficking". Elizabeth Bernstein (2010, 47) credits this trend to "a rightward shift on the part of many mainstream feminists and other secular liberals away from a redistributive model of justice and toward a politics of incarceration". In an effort to resolve the feminist crisis between those who regard the sex industry as inherently abusive and those who recognise sexual labour as legitimate work, sex workers and sex worker organisations demand that people "listen to sex workers" (Geymonat and Macioti, 2016; Jeffreys, Autonomy, Green and Vega, 2011).

Never before have the stakes been higher for sex workers. Journalist and former sex worker Melissa Gira Grant (2013, 33) explains: "legislators in many states have responded to the demands of feminist activists by boosting penalties for prostitution-related offenses and prioritizing enforcement". Militarised crackdowns against migrant sex workers routinely take place under the guise of preventing sex trafficking (Bernstein, 2010), and sex workers worldwide continue to face arrest, incarceration and stigmatisation for trying to make a living. Sex worker advocates continue to stand up in the public sphere to combat bad laws and the flawed ideological underpinnings that perpetuate them.

This chapter provides detailed analysis of two public events that purported to include sex workers as equal partners in dialogue yet instead marginalised sex worker voices. The case studies analysed in this chapter are exemplary of the ways in which sex worker advocates are shut down by audiences who present themselves as concerned allies. This self-presentation can take numerous forms, including the expression of concerns about sex workers' occupational health and safety or about women's rights more generally. These often give the impression of allegiance to the sex worker rights platform that recognises sexual labour as legitimate work. Yet, when sex workers discuss sex work as *work*, as a legitimate job or use language that would otherwise be applied to status quo ideas of employment, work and productivity, these audiences that purport to be allies quickly retreat. In response to ideas that normalise and legitimise sex work as a way to make a living, some audiences – including those that could be thought of as allies – invoke the disposition of morality policing and demonstrate a desire to prove themselves as more knowledgeable than sex worker advocates. This phenomenon has implications for the decriminalisation of sex work and creates challenges for sex workers and allies.

Case study 1: Lily Nutchada (Empower Foundation) presents to the School of Women's Studies at Chiang Mai University, Thailand (September 2014)

The Empower Foundation ("Empower") is Thailand's national sex worker organisation. Its leaders and staff are sex workers, and it has offices in a number of Thai cities and border towns including Bangkok, Maesai, Chiang Mai and Mukdaham. It has been operating for over 30 years and is engaged in promoting "rights and opportunities for sex workers" (Empower Foundation and Apisuk, 2015). Empower has been running high school diploma classes for sex workers for more than two decades as well as English and Thai language lessons (Sirorattanakul, 1997). It is also heavily involved in the response to HIV and sexually transmitted infections in Thailand as well as migrant rights. Empower describes its work as "making sex worker issues understandable, visible and important to policy makers and wider society" (Empower Foundation, 2012). Examples of its advocacy include campaigning for a minimum wage and improved work conditions for sex workers (Sakboon, 1996) and speaking out against the forced HIV testing of sex workers (Empower Foundation, 2012, 13).

In September 2014, Lily Nutchada, then a leader and peer educator with Empower, spoke at a formal academic event organised by her Empower colleague Chatchalawan Muangjan as part of the Department of Women's Studies Master of Arts Program at the Chiang Mai University campus in Nimmanhaemin. About 15 Empower members and their families, supporters, peer educators and other Empower leaders attended. To collect data as part of my own PhD research on sex worker organisations' autonomy from funders, I too was present. The session was in Thai. Liz Hilton, an Empower volunteer, sat next to me and translated the session into English, whispering into my ear while I took notes. What follows is not a word-for-word translation of the presentation but a summary drawn from my detailed notes of the translation into English that Hilton gave me while the presentation was occurring. I took note of the body language of all those who were present and the design of the physical space. I also confirmed the accuracy of my notes by debriefing with Nutchada after the event, and I gave Hilton a copy of my notes to check for possible mistakes.

Empower leaders put in a substantial amount of time and effort to meaningfully authenticate Empower in the space in which the presentation was taking place. Prior to the audience's arrival, Muangjan installed a replica of the Can Do Bar, an autonomous sex worker-run bar located in the Empower Chiang Mai Centre. Nutchada spoke from the installation as a means of providing audience members with a clear sense of this sex industry venue as a work environment. Installation items included the Can Do Bar banner, a vase of flowers and the popular board game "Connect 4"; items that typically might be found at many bars in Thailand and in fact came from the Can Do Bar that morning. Empower merchandise for sale was set up in the centre of the room. Their considerable efforts were a visual attempt to normalise the sex indus-try for the audience, especially those who attended the event with preconceived, and potentially flawed, assumptions about it.

The Empower entourage sat together in chairs on one side of the space, the open-air section of the classroom. Nutchada and Muangjan stood at the "bar", on the threshold of the open-air and covered sections of the room, ready to speak once everyone was seated. The indoor section of the classroom had a dozen chairs facing outwards, with two teachers, two visiting academics and five students in attendance. As such, sex workers and their families were seated directly fac-ing the university audience.

Muangjan introduced Nutchada and then sat on a step very near her. Nutchada began her presentation by explaining the diversity of work options and employment mobility that she – and by implication, her sex worker colleagues – experience within the sex industry, gently introducing positive ideas about sex work that were in opposition to status quo notions of sex work as oppressive:

> We all work for something. We don't work for free. When you go to university you have a plan about what you want to do in one year, two years or five years. Working as a sex worker is the same. We work for money, and we have a plan.

Nutchada described the importance of worker solidarity among sex workers by emphatically stating, "We are stronger together". She picked up a bunch of toothpicks from the "bar" to vividly demonstrate her point: "If you pick up one toothpick and try to break it, it is easy. But pick up a few in a group and you cannot break them, even with two hands". Nutchada, draw-ing on her own personal knowledge of sex work, then refuted the common stereotype that sex workers fuel corruption. To address this, Nutchada said:

> We don't pay police bribes because we like to support corruption. We pay because if we don't pay we are unable to work. So, we pay bribes just so we can work – we don't get anything special in return for the bribe.

This, and other points made by Nutchada during the presentation, were expressed from a sex worker point of view. She used the term "we" instead of "them", and she referred to her own personal experiences often.

At the end of the presentation there was time allocated for questions. The first question was asked by a visiting lecturer from Melbourne University: "Why, if sex workers like you are so proud, don't you tell Social Security [government pension plan] or your doctor about what you do [for a living]?" I observed that Nutchada and members of the Empower entourage immedi-ately became uncomfortable. They began shifting in their seats and looking knowingly at each other with concern. The lecturer's question was based upon negative assumptions about sex workers being maliciously secretive, "hiding" for the purpose of rorting Thai tax systems, and these assumptions contribute to the stereotype that sex workers in Thailand are corrupt. The Empower members also recognised the question as perpetrating oppressive ideas about sex work and disease by implying that sex workers lie to medical staff. The question suggested that sex workers deliberately avoid health testing or diagnosis. The question also challenged the veracity of Nutchada's presentation, suggesting that lack of disclosure to certain parties is proof that Thai sex workers do not take pride in the work they perform because they do not openly articulate their work to others. Nutchada answered the question with another personal anecdote, once again situating sex work in the context of labour:

When I go to the hospital, sick, they check my temperature. They don't ask me what job I do. Just like with Social Security. I make my payment each month, and so does my boss. And like you, Social Security doesn't ask what job I do. I'm not ashamed – they [Social Security officers] have come to my workplace and seen where I work, but the details of my job are not of interest to them. When you go to the hospital with a cut or broken arm, do they ask you your job? No, they tend to your cut or broken arm, they don't need to know your job. It doesn't mean sex workers are ashamed, it just means that we have a job like any other person. We don't need to tell people unless it's about our work.

This answer by Nutchada draws upon universal concepts of privacy and confidentiality. She was appealing to the personal experience of audience members, trying to draw parallels for the purpose of building understanding and empathy. Nutchada again, positioned sex work as work by drawing a comparison between sex workers and people in other jobs.

The next question from an audience member was similar to the first and again questioned the accuracy of Nutchada's claim that most sex workers take pride in their profession: "You say you want to be treated like other workers, but you also say you wouldn't agree with sex worker registration. Registration would make more people think of you as legitimate workers, so why do you disagree?" Nutchada answered: "Give me one actual benefit that I as a sex worker would receive from being registered, and of course I would consider it". The Melbourne University academic immediately spoke up again, more urgently this time, in support of the person asking the previous question: "The student just wants you to be accepted as a real worker, they support you. Why are you angry?" The student added, with her voice slightly louder this time: "Don't you care about violence against women? Registration will help stop it".

The event began to take on a confrontational tone that, unfortunately, began to cleave all participants into the room into all too familiar camps that either supported sex work as a legitimate form of labour, like Nutchada and her Empower peers, or regarded the sex industry as inherently violent and/or immoral and in need of government oversight, like the student and the visiting lecturer. A sex worker seated in the open-air area facing the student spoke up loudly to declare: "Sex workers don't want special registration, and if you listen to what we are saying we do work just like other forms of work . . . Why would I register for special protection that I don't actually need?" This statement was completely ignored by both the student and lecturer who had asked the questions. The student instead spoke over the sex worker and said very loudly: "Sex workers should get jobs teaching sex education to young people, don't you think that's a great idea?" Then more sex workers in the open-air area were trying to answer, while the members of the university audience shook their heads with disdain at the sex worker entourage. The atmosphere had quickly degenerated into one ridden with all the usual conflicts surrounding sex work.

A sex worker advocate sitting among the other sex worker attendees stood up as if to quieten everyone and, attempting to restore order through reason, made a small speech of her own:

Sex workers are fighting for rights, and you want us to be responsible for young people's sexual education as well? Like we don't have enough to do? I'm worried about young people's education, but you have to campaign for that yourselves – you are the young people; this is about your lives. Today Nutchada has given a very important presentation and you shouldn't discount what she has said. You can't ignore what Empower has been saying for over the last 30 years!

After this loud interjection I noticed some sex workers were now looking around at each other, visibly upset. There was quiet murmuring among the sex worker group. I observed that the dynamic occurring at this event was familiar to the Empower members present and perhaps emblematic of Empower's everyday experience in its work combating oppression and promoting sex worker pride and human rights. Nutchada had spoken optimistically from personal experience, promoted sex worker pride, situated her stories within the workplace and, when questioned, deployed universal human rights arguments to urge the audience to consider sex work differently. The presentation had received a hostile response.

As the props were being packed up and everyone was standing and preparing to leave, I felt a distinct atmosphere of superiority or victory coming from the university audience, as if the academics and students thought they had "caught out" Natchada for lying or otherwise misrepresenting her and her peers' work. None of the university audience members approached any of the sex workers present to ask questions or otherwise engage in dialogue, instead they chose to leave as if the ideological differences between them were so deeply rooted as to preclude meaningful conversation.

Back at the Can Do Bar that afternoon I debriefed with Natchada after the presentation and found out that Empower presents this lecture every few years and that the hostility is always the same. Natchada was quite upset but also very philosophical about it. She said to me that the people in the university seem to always "follow stupid". Natchada said that before attending university people would think for themselves, and then the longer they studied and the more important they became in academia, the more they would "follow stupid". She said that even when she was standing there, explaining her life experiences from her heart, they couldn't hear her because they "follow stupid". Natchada said that even if they knew that they were wrong, they were still convinced they could be correct if only they tried harder to "follow stupid". Natchada repeated this phrase to me over and over. In her experience as a sex worker advocate for many years, she had observed a repetitive singular mindset: that the sex industry is bad. Natchada believes that this mindset to "follow stupid" is so entrenched among women's studies academic audiences that there is literally no tactic able to break it. Even so, she expressed to me her intention of continuing to advocate to these audiences because "Empower can't give up".

Case study 2: Jules Kim (Scarlet Alliance) interviewed on Australian Broadcasting Corporation's *Lateline* (March 2015)

Scarlet Alliance, the Australian Sex Workers Association ("Scarlet"), is a peak membership body for sex workers and sex worker organisations in Australia. Formed in 1998, the issues the organisation advocates for include the decriminalisation of sex work (Fawkes, 2014), the decriminalisation of HIV (Matthews, 2008), and the rights of migrant workers (Scarlet Alliance, 2003). Its membership includes sex worker organisations and groups across Australia, funded and unfunded, as well as individual sex workers. Owners and operators are not eligible for Scarlet membership because of the disproportionate power that bosses have in all industries. If a sex worker is employed in a role as receptionist, or boss, their membership of Scarlet is suspended. Once no longer in that role they are eligible to re-join. As such, the structure of the organisation is protected from being influenced by the needs of brothel owners or ancillary staff. This is one of the ways Scarlet ensures the organisation is able to genuinely reflect sex worker interests.

Lateline was a popular 60-minute evening long-form news program produced five nights a week by the Australian Broadcasting Corporation for almost three decades. Each show typically included a few interviews, often with politicians, and some investigative journalism around issues deemed particularly relevant in Australia and internationally. Scarlet Alliance representatives, including myself, have appeared on *Lateline* a number of times to discuss issues related to the sex industry. In March 2015, *Lateline* host Emma Alberici interviewed Jules Kim, then manager of the Scarlet Alliance Migration Project, a national peer-led program of support, advocacy, policy analysis and resource production in four languages (Thai, Chinese, Korean and English). Alberici opened the interview by asking Kim about the Scarlet position on sex work law reform, the subject of that particular *Lateline* episode:

Alberici: So what evidence is there to show that legalised prostitution is safer?

Kim: Okay, I think it's important to make that distinction between decriminalisation and what's called legalisation. Now decriminalisation, I think people often think that it means no regulation, but it actually means a whole lot of government regulation. So it is being recognised internationally by many bodies, increasingly by the United Nations, International Labour Organisation, World Health Organisation and within the Australian Government's HIV and STI strategies as the best-practice approach for the health, safety and rights of sex workers. And all the evidence has shown that it does result in better outcomes, not just for sex workers but for the general community. Now . . .

Alberici: But do you accept that sex work can be harmful to women?

Kim: Well, I think the issue here as well is we are seeing a situation with [the Australian state of] Victoria that doesn't work, and we've always maintained that licensing doesn't work, and what they call legalisation, it doesn't work because it doesn't go far enough. It legalises very small sections of the sex industry, and so that it creates a system that is basically unworkable for the majority of the sex industry.

Alberici: Do you believe we should be getting rid of sex work altogether?

Kim: Absolutely not. I think it is a legitimate occupational choice that some people make.

Alberici: Women who find this work empowering or in any way a positive experience must surely be in a minority, a significant minority?

Kim: Look, I would say to you that most people that, I mean, people that find their work empowering or [a] positive experience are probably in the minority. I mean it's . . . people have to work, that's a fact of life.

Alberici: But you paint this as a no-alternative strategy?

Kim: It is not a no-alternative. Absolutely some people make choices to become sex workers.

Alberici: I find it incredibly hard to believe that a young woman, as we saw that woman say in that piece [a video clip played earlier in the show that featured interviews with an ex-sex worker], I find it very hard to believe that any woman would aspire to be a prostitute?

Kim: Yes of course. I think the reason that you find it so hard to believe is because sex work, the only narrative that we ever hear is the overwhelmingly negative one. Sex work is like any other work, there are good and bad jobs, there's good and bad clients, there's good and bad employers, like any job, but unlike any other job, we only ever hear the negative stories. Now the vast majority of . . . [sex] workers in Australia working everyday aren't experiencing those negative situations.

Kim speaks confidently about decriminalisation and describes sex work as a job. Alberici questions the validity of this argument, saying "I find it incredibly hard to believe". By disbelieving that anyone would aspire to sex work, Alberici pathologises sex workers as actively doing something that makes no logical sense to her. It is Alberici's job to ask Kim difficult questions, and as a journalist this is expected of her. It is surprising how abruptly Alberici cut off Kim's responses, however, never allowing her to answer. It is also unusual for journalists to raise their own opinion in such a combative manner. By the third question, Alberici has personally expressed disbelief at Kim's articulation of national policy positions formed by sex workers, without ever letting her respond. I propose this level of hostility would not be perpetrated upon many of Alberici's guests. Kim responds by explaining that victimising discourses heard in the public sphere are not representative and should not be the main source of information about sex work. Kim is challenging dominant ideas about the victimisation of sex workers.

Alberici then refers to some Australian research and questions Kim about migrant sex workers' level of English proficiency:

Alberici: Well, let's look at the statistics and the evidence from studies and the Kirby Institute report from the University of New South Wales [in Sydney, Australia] showed that 46% of sex workers rated their English language skills as fair or poor, so how can they properly negotiate conditions with clients?

Kim: Now, I will give you another statistic. Now, English level wasn't related to education level. Because if somebody . . .

Alberici: No, but if you can just go to my question.

Kim: Yeah, sure, okay.

Alberici: Now if you can't understand your conversation with your client . . .

Kim: They didn't say they couldn't understand.

Alberici: Well, I'm presuming that most clients in Australia would speak English.

Kim: No. No but . . .

Alberici: If that isn't well understood between the client and the sex workers then they are immediately at a disadvantage, aren't they?

Kim: Yes, but I feel like by implication you're saying that if somebody doesn't have good English skills that they somehow have less agency, or [are] somehow more of a victim or somehow have less ability to negotiate and that's certainly not the case.

Alberici: Is it not the case that they're less able to negotiate if they can't speak the same language as the client?

Kim: They didn't say they couldn't speak the same language.

Alberici: Fair or poor, is fairly indicative of a lack of ability to speak a language.

Kim: Um, okay I will give you another example. If you go into a restaurant, for example, and the person serving behind the counter . . .

Alberici: It's not the same.

Kim: . . . has fair or poor.

Alberici: It's not the same.

The research Alberici refers to is not listed or named on the *Lateline* website, but the specific nature of the information Alberici uses to characterise it allows me to reasonably assume that it is *The Sex Industry in New South Wales: A Report to the NSW Ministry of Health* report (2012) published by the Kirby Institute, an inter-disciplinary research centre specialising in blood-borne and sexually transmitted viruses, attached to the University of New South Wales. The research found that almost half of the respondents born in non-English speaking countries rated their English language skills as "fair or poor" (ibid., 17). The report does not suggest that this means sex workers have difficulty negotiating with clients at work. After making that conclusion herself, Alberici then questions Kim's understanding of the impact of English-speaking skills on a sex worker's ability to negotiate with clients. Kim responds by describing this idea in the context of other forms of hospitality work outside the sex industry. Alberici does not accept this comparison and instead emphatically states that sex work is *different*.

Kim's interview was marketed by *Lateline* as covering laws and models of sex industry regulation. The Kirby report is in favour of the decriminalisation of sex work:

> The NSW Government's legislative reforms of 1979 and 1995 should be endorsed. These reforms that decriminalised adult sex work have improved human rights, removed police corruption, netted savings for the criminal justice system and enhanced the surveillance, health promotion and safety of the NSW sex industry. International authorities regard the NSW regulatory framework as best practice. Contrary to early concerns, the NSW sex industry has not increased in size or visibility, and sex work remains stigmatised.
>
> (The Sex Industry in New South Wales, *2012, p. 9*)

Alberici, or her producer, has ignored this very clear endorsement of Kim's argument. Instead, one small piece of data was misrepresented by *Lateline* to be proof of the opposite:

Alberici: Let's go to another research paper. RMIT [Royal Melbourne Institute of Technology] health research has identified mental health as a big concern among prostitutes, finding that all participants in their study gave some indication that sex work constituted a major risk to their self-esteem?

Kim: Absolutely, because the stigma and discrimination around sex work is so great, it's still so significant and there is still . . . I mean, Scarlet Alliance has been advocating for years for anti-discrimination protection for sex workers, but they don't exist.

This research was not named by *Lateline*, and I have been unable to find anything that resembles what Alberici describes, although I do not doubt that it exists. Stigma and shame attached to sex work is a huge burden on mental health. The stress of hiding one's job, living a double life, lying to protect one's family and loved ones and living in fear of discrimination and prejudice; all of these factors impact an individual's self-esteem. Kim refers to the stigma and discrimination *surrounding* sex work, refuting (by omission) that sex work itself causes low self-esteem. Alberici does not seem to pick up this nuance. Instead, she moves on quickly and asks Kim another pithy question, with reference to more research. By listing numerous research articles, Alberici is positioning herself as highly knowledgeable on the topic and also mobilising "facts" in support of her argument that the sex industry is inherently harmful to women. This line of argument becomes particularly evident when Alberici begins to discuss the trafficking of women into sex work:

Alberici: What about the link between prostitution and trafficking?

Kim: There . . . I'm not sure what you . . . I don't think there has proven to be a link between sex work and trafficking.

Alberici: The London School of Economics reported last year that legalisation of prostitution in the Netherlands, Germany and New Zealand found subsequent growth in

> demand had led to increases in human tracking [*sic*] or coercion of people into the industry and the report called this the dark side of globalisation.
>
> *Kim:* The UN Special Rapporteur of Trafficking who came to Australia on her country visit, to . . . on . . . a couple of years ago stated that she found that there was no link between sex work and trafficking. Sex work in itself is not inherently violent or exploitative, and migration for sex work is not trafficking.
>
> *Alberici:* I'm so sorry, we have to leave it there, thank you for coming in, Jules Kim.
>
> *Kim:* Thank you.

Lateline did not cite the research to which Alberici referred, yet like the first study Alberici mentions, the specific details provided allows me to reasonably assume it is the work of Cho, Dreher and Neumayer (2013), titled "Does legalised prostitution increase human trafficking?" reported as "Legalised prostitution increases human trafficking" on the London School of Economics blog (Meegan, 2012).[2] The research was a *theoretical* analysis of 150 countries and did not include a case study of New Zealand (where sex work is decriminalised). The authors were comparing the strength of two hypotheses in their study. The first hypothesis, that legalisation would be likely to lead to a higher number of "reported" cases of trafficking, was found to be more likely than the second, that "legal" workers would replace trafficked workers (Cho et al., 2013, 67, 69, 75). Their statistical modeling found that if the "scale" of the sex industry expanded under legalisation, so too would the number of *reported* cases of trafficking. To be clear, the researchers did not collect any original data that would suggest this is the case. Cho, Dreher and Neumayer additionally acknowledged they found no "smoking gun" and were concerned that their findings might lead people to overlook the "potential benefits" of law reform, namely improved working conditions for sex workers (ibid., 76). The *Lateline* team clearly did not read the research itself, only the accompanying (and inaccurate) blog post. What is relevant here is that *Lateline* chose to refer to research that it perceived would assist Alberici to position herself as more knowledgeable than the Scarlet Alliance representative.

Discussion

The two case study examples of hostility against sex worker leaders are from actors who would otherwise be thought of as allies for the simple reason that they invited sex worker advocates to speak openly about their work in a public forum: women's studies academics, university students and a journalist on a public broadcaster. Sex worker leaders enter these spaces willingly and voluntarily, and even actively pursue the opportunity to engage in this public advocacy. In these examples the hostile actors *sought* the advocates' presence. Why then such hostility?

Morality policing

Explicit public disclosure, sex worker registration and becoming sex education therapists were three unsolicited policy suggestions proposed by women's studies academics and students to Empower in the first case study example. Each includes an element of morality policing. Pressure to disclose implies that sex workers should be more *truthful*. To be registered with the state implies that sex workers should be more *compliant*. To stop sex work and become an educator instead implies sex workers could become more *socially useful*. These suggestions only make sense if sex workers are liars, renegades and socially useless. When an Empower member challenged these ideas, they were chided for not being more appreciative of the students' good intentions.

Concern trolling

Hostility framed as genuine concern is a common tactic used in social justice debates. It has earned a specific term: concern trolling. Analysis of the phenomena, and the term itself, comes from self-identified "geek feminists", women involved in online spaces and active in gaming, programming, anime, futurism, science fiction, comics and new technology. These women work in industries dominated by men, and as such experience intense and varied sexism, which has informed their analysis. The website *Geek Feminism Wiki* describes concern trolling as behaviour conducted by: "a person who participates in a debate posing as an actual or potential ally who simply has some concerns they need answered before they will ally themselves with a cause. In reality they are a critic" (Geek Feminism, n.d.). I suggest that in the context of this behaviour towards sex workers there is another element: feigned concern for the well-being of sex workers, as if sex workers are unable to look out for our own well-being. Or perhaps these hostile, would-be allies actually are concerned and really believe that sex workers need suggestions for life improvement. Neither motivation is very kind.

Strategic use of research data to undermine sex worker leaders' validity

Deployment of research or data that undermines sex worker advocacy messages is not an uncommon method. Reaching for sources of information that are considered "higher" or more "empirical" than the word and actual lived experiences of sex worker leaders is a classic way to undermine and dismiss sex worker advocacy. There is vastly more compelling evidence to endorse sex worker advocacy messages than not; however, in the case studies documented here this does not seem to have mattered. Rather than a debate about evidence, it appears that these examples of hostility towards sex worker advocates are struggles about validity of voice, not about strength of argument. The strategic use of research for the purpose of invalidating sex workers' voices implicitly suggests that sex workers cannot be knowledgeable.

Implications for decriminalisation

Lily Nutchada and Jules Kim advocate for decriminalisation. Their advocacy is a product of decades of detailed sex worker movement discussion and is based on thousands and thousands of sex workers' experiences. Had the audiences in the above examples heard what Nutchada and Kim were saying, they would have learnt that sex workers have the solutions to questions of sex work law reform. The message "sex work is work" and the demands for decriminalisation were instead ignored by audiences who chose to "follow stupid".

Conclusion

Hostility towards sex worker advocates is distinctive. Sex workers argue that we need to be listened to. However, in this chapter's case studies the actors *are* listening but obviously not hearing. They are responding with well thought-out strategies to challenge sex worker advocacy messages, as if sex workers could not possibly develop the solutions themselves. What do these hostile audiences gain from morality policing, concern trolling and undermining sex workers' voices? These actors invite sex workers to advocate in public spaces and simultaneously keep them from having a secure platform. Their hostility serves as a reminder of sex workers' status as outsiders in public discourse and functions as a stigmatising ritual of public shaming repeated time and again across the world. Even when faced with this hostility, sex workers will not be silenced!

Notes

1 This chapter would not have been possible without the support and advocacy of Lily Nutchada (Empower Foundation, Thailand) and Jules Kim (Scarlet Alliance, Australian Sex Workers Association). Many thanks to Fiona Bucknall and Janelle Fawkes for editing and feedback.
2 The publication date for the journal article is January 2013 even though it was released earlier, thus the apparent discrepancy in dates.

References

Bernstein, Elizabeth. 2010. Militarized humanitarianism meets carceral feminism: The politics of sex, rights, and freedom in contemporary antitrafficking campaigns. *Signs* 36(1): 45–71.
Cho, Seo-Young, Axel Dreher and Eric Neumayer. 2013. Does legalized prostitution increase human trafficking? *World Development* 41 (January): 67–82. https://doi.org/10.1016/j.worlddev.2012.05.023.
Empower Foundation. 2012. Working with the Global Fund to fight AIDS, tuberculosis and malaria. In Laura Agustín, ed., *Research for Sex Work* 13: 13–14. Edinburgh: Network of Sex Work Projects.
Empower Foundation and Apisuk Chantawipa. 2015. Letter in support of Amnesty International's "Draft policy on sex workers' human rights" San Francisco: SWOP. Available at: www.swopusa.org/wp-content/uploads/2015/08/amnesty.pdf [Accessed 1 January 2018].
Fawkes, Janelle. 2014. Sex work legislation stands in the way of Australia's commitments: Decriminalisation for sex workers' health, safety and rights. *HIV Australia*, 12(2): 22–24.
Geek Feminism. n.d. Concern trolling. *Geek Feminism Wiki*. Available at: http://geekfeminism.wikia.com/wiki/Concern_troll [Accessed 1 January 2018].
Geymonat, Giulia Garafalo and P.G. Macioti (eds). 2016. Sex workers speak: Who listens? *Open Democracy*. Available at: www.opendemocracy.net/beyond-slavery-themes/sex-workers-speak [Accessed 1 January 2018].
Gira Grant, Melissa. 2013. The war on sex workers. *Reason Foundation* 44(9): 31–36.
Jackson, Crystal. 2013. *Sex worker rights organizing as social movement unionism: Responding to the criminalization of work.* PhD thesis. Las Vegas: University of Nevada.
Jeffreys, Elena, Audry Autonomy, Jane Green and Christian Vega. 2011. Listen to sex workers. *Interface: A Journal for and About Social Movements* 3(2): 271–287.
Lateline. 2015, 13 March. *Lateline.* Sydney: Australian Broadcasting Corporation. Available at: www.abc.net.au/lateline/content/2015/s4197616.htm [Accessed 1 January 2018].
Matthews, Kane. 2008. *The national needs assessment of sex workers who live with HIV.* Newtown: Scarlet Alliance. Available at: www.scarletalliance.org.au/library/hiv-needsassessment08 [Accessed 1 January 2018].
Meegan, Joe. 2012. Legalised prostitution increases human trafficking. *London School of Economics News and Media* (blog). Available at: www.lse.ac.uk/website-archive/newsAndMedia/newsArchives/2012/12/Legalised-prostitution-increases-human-trafficking.aspx [Accessed 1 January 2018].
Sakboon, M. 1996. Prostitution Bill is not the answer to the problem. *The Nation* Bangkok, Thailand. April 9 1996.
Scarlet Alliance. 2003. *Submission to the Parliamentary Joint Committee on the Australian Crime Commission.* Newtown: Scarlet Alliance. Available at: www.scarletalliance.org.au/library/traff_sub03/file_view [Accessed 1 January 2018].
Sirorattanakul, Tanida. 1997, 18 February. Empowering sex workers. *Bangkok Post*, section: Outlook.
The Sex Industry in New South Wales: A Report to the NSW Ministry of Health. 2012. Sydney: Kirby Institute, University of New South Wales. 978-0-646-56721-1. Available at: https://kirby.unsw.edu.au/report/nsw-sex-industry-report-2012 [Accessed 4 January 2018].

50

Two women, two murders

Stigmatized media representations of violence against sex workers

Rachel Lennon and Pranee Liamputtong

Stigma, discrimination, and sex work

For decades, stigma researchers and activists have used the concept of stigma to understand the myriad ways in which sex workers face socioeconomic exclusion, violence, and other forms of marginalization. Countless researchers across a wide variety of academic fields have built upon Erving Goffman's original (1963) articulation of this concept by emphasizing stigma's complex and multidimensional nature to note that stigmatization entails very real adverse effects at both the individual and structural levels in the form of socioeconomic marginalization, institution-alization of discriminatory norms through law and public policy, and adverse health outcomes (Benoit et al. 2018; Evans-Lacko et al. 2012; Hatzenbuehler and Link 2014).

Structural stigma is generally enforced through laws and regulation, making it a powerful social determinant of inequality alongside other social determinants. For many sex workers worldwide, structural stigma creates a vicious cycle in which policymakers outlaw their income generating activities on the grounds that they are inherently harmful to society, creating a climate that legitimizes their social exclusion and numerous forms of violence committed against them (Hatzenbuehler 2013, 5). In turn, these structural stigmas are inextricably linked with the subordination of women and the idealized social norms of contemporary society in relation to female sexuality.

A wealth of research identifies the harmful consequences of stigma and associated discrimination for sex workers, including mental health problems, increased drug abuse, violence, and other deleterious effects (Benoit et al. 2015; Hatzenbuehler et al. 2013). While some researchers argue that limited theorization around the "whore stigma" inhibits possibilities for reducing its impacts, significant evidence indicates stigma's widespread and totalizing impacts on sex workers' health, safety, and well-being (Benoit et al. 2018, 2015). Researchers also suggest that criminalized models of sex work and enforcement-based approaches subject women to higher levels of violence, poorer health, stigma, and discrimination, all of which compromise sex workers' human rights (Bruckert and Hannem 2013; Krüsi et al. 2016; Lazarus et al. 2012). Some evidence from New Zealand's decriminalization of all sex work indicates that this approach results in safer working conditions and fewer incidents of violence (Armstrong 2010, 2017).

Media and structural stigma

The press can never quite decide whether murdered sex workers are tragic victims, like any woman targeted by a serial killer, or have chosen a lifestyle that means they are partly responsible for their deaths (Smith 2006, para. 5).

In an age where the Internet has precipitated a cultural shift in the communications and news media landscape, it is essential to grasp how these changes can impact society at large. We now live in an expansive community where the reach of the media can be global (Westerman et al. 2014). Individuals need not look far to have daily access to world news, and this global shrinkage presents media consumers, and society at large, with a new suite of problems by perpetuating bias through the presentation on misinformed issues and one-sided stories. As research suggests, people learn from the media regardless of whether its intention is educational or otherwise (Maier et al. 2014; Perse and Lambe 2017).

Historically, media discourses around sex work portray women involved in sex work as morally suspect vectors of disease and anti-social agents whose activities harm society (Farvid and Glass 2014). Such media narratives accordingly "educate" the public on sex work by concurrently serving as a conduit for stigma (Hallgrímsdóttiir et al. 2008). Media portrayals of the sex industry has the proclivity to influence public opinion in ways that foster sex worker's dehumanization as well as encouraging negative self-perceptions and internalized stigma among sex workers themselves. Media continuously conflates dominant cultural perceptions of sex work as an illegitimate and immoral activity with the personhood of women engaged in it. Ultimately, this practice intensifies existing self-beliefs of unworthiness for this population group and endorses existing and misinformed stereotypes (Benoit et al. 2015, 2018; Hallgrímsdóttiir et al. 2008; Lazarus et al. 2012).

These dominant cultural representations are further compounded by scholarly and media portrayals of illegal and clandestine sex work performed only by those who are marginalized, such as those struggling with addiction, undocumented status, or other significant social problems (Weitzer 2015). These narratives in mainstream media influence the daily interactions sex workers have with clients and the public as well as sex workers' abilities to influence the policy and legislative environments in which they live and work. Entrenched attitudes and beliefs in the public consciousness about sex workers also feature, and are exacerbated by, media narratives in ways that reinforce pervasive stigma. Media tends to play a major role in perpetuating sex worker stigma, particularly because such portrayals typically feature sensationalized accounts of the sex industry in a moralizing tone (Weitzer 2017). As a result, these chronicles tend to reduce the lives of women in sex work "to narratives of crime and legal policy" (Bungay et al. 2011, 19), thereby reinforcing negative stereotypes about sex workers (Benoit at al. 2018; Jeffrey and MacDonald 2006). Such narratives only heighten surveillance over sex workers, particularly those who work in public, by increasing the pressure for communities to check in on these distasteful and public nuisances and amplifying enacted stigmas such as harassment, assault, and abuse (Benoit et al. 2018).

These negative media portrayals are pervasive and global. Even in New Zealand, which is internationally lauded for its evidence-based prostitution policies, media representations focus on trafficking in minors and sex workers' victimization, and deviation from social norms and appropriate gender roles, with very little attention paid to their clients (Farvid and Glass 2014). Victimization and economic exploitation are common themes in US, as well as global, representations of the sex industry (Weitzer 2017). Researchers working with women involved in street sex work in Vancouver, Canada note that the women experience significant social marginalization due to dominant cultural representations of them as drug addicts engaged in immoral sexual acts (Krüsi et al. 2016). Overall, media reporting on street sex work empha-sizes individual sensationalized events rather than structural explanations, which obscures the everyday realities street-based sex workers face (Strega et al. 2014). In these and many more ways, media narratives both construct and reproduce social stigma for sex workers. A study that examined media portrayals of sex workers over time found that social stigmatization is sustained through asymmetrical power relations between sex workers and dominant culture, as is evident in the media's ability to dominate popular discourse and reveal little about issues of everyday concern to sex workers (Hallgrímsdóttiir et al. 2008).

We engage with and build upon this literature by contrasting media coverage of two murder cases in Australia: one in which the victim was a sex worker and the other in which the vic-tim's life circumstances conformed to dominant cultural expectations for women. Our analysis further engages with what researchers have identified as the "missing white woman syndrome," in which round-the-clock media coverage follows the disappearance of young females who qualify as "damsels in distresses" by race, class, and other relevant social variables (Liebler 2010). This media phenomenon features disproportionate attention paid to victims of crime who are conventionally attractive and relatively privileged with respect to their class and ethno-racial identities. Australian researchers likewise note stark disparities between reports of murdered women of Aboriginal descent compared to middle-class white women, with the latter three and a half times more likely to have media representation than their Aboriginal counterparts, whose deaths media reported using a detached tone in comparison with the more personalized and intimate accounts of the murdered white women's lives (Gilchrist 2010).

Such research findings indicate that media representations frequently bolster systemic and structural inequalities that devalue the lives of those that are considered the "other" based on gender, class, and race (Hatzenbuehler and Link 2014). This amorphousness is also directed at sex workers by rendering them as invisible and unworthy in the eyes of the media. This also mirrors the public preference for the "damsel in distress," the woman who is a "good girl," and inadvertently highlights the public's widespread stigmatization of and discrimination towards marginalized women.

The socio-legal climate surrounding sex work in Australia

Australia legislation on prostitution and other sex industry forms varies across states, territo-ries, and municipalities, with no unified legal or policy framework governing the sex industry. Laws, and their enforcement, vary significantly across Australia, with licensed brothels operat-ing legally in some areas and not others, and street-based sex work tolerated in some areas but actively policed and criminalized in others (Abel 2014; Harcourt et al. 2010). This widespread variance indicates conflicting public and structural sentiments toward the sex industry across Australia. Some scholars argue that any laws to regulate the sex industry function as neoliberal control mechanisms in dealing with ancillary issues associated with sex work, including organ-ized crime and police corruption (Sullivan 2010). Australian sex worker rights activist Elena Jeffreys, whose work also features in this Handbook (Chapter 49), describes dominant cultural attitudes toward sex work as:

> A reason to declare mothers unfit, by banks as a reason to refuse loans, by landlords as a reason to evict tenants, and by visa officials to deny certain countries. Sex workers who also have positions in the public service are told that they are not "upholding public standards" and in some states of Australia it is still against the law to serve alcohol to a "known prostitute."
>
> *(Jeffreys and MacDonald 2006, 113)*

Media descriptions of women in sex work as "prostitutes" is a reminder of the negativity that dominant culture associates with sex work, leading many scholars and activists alike to contend that the continued use of stigmatizing terminology implies that a woman's worth is measured by her conformity, particularly in terms of sexual behavior. Such representations may even play a role in supporting violence against sex workers:

> This stigma [of calling sex workers prostitutes] is far-reaching and arguably does more damage to women who work in sex work than the actual work. The stigma feeds into understandings of women that are violence-supporting and referring to victims of violence as "prostitutes" continues to "other" these women and locates them as somehow deserving: she knew the danger . . . Identifying victims of violent crimes as "prostitutes" has a distancing effect: it makes "normal" women feel safe.
>
> *(Smith 2013, 1)*

Media reports on the murders of women involved in sex work often feature cautionary tales about the supposed inherent risks of prostitution that assign blame to victims, rather than perpetrators, of violence. Simply put, these types of accounts imply that sex workers actively participate in their demise because of the dangerous lives they lead as sex workers, especially if the women also use illicit drugs. The dominant cultural message, as Smith (2013) notes, justifies violence against sex workers even when it takes extreme forms, such as murder. To understand the means by which this dominant cultural message receives widespread cultural endorsement and dissemination in the specific case of Australia, we compare the extremely divergent media coverage surrounding two murders by the same perpetrator, Adrian Bayley. One of the victims, Jill Meagher, was a newly married woman living with her husband, and the other, Tracy Connelly, worked the streets of Melbourne. As we shall see, media reported and represented their lives and deaths in strikingly different ways because of the fact that Tracy earned her living through prostitution and Jill did not.

Australian media representations of the Connelly and Meagher murders

> [M]assive outpouring of public grief, front page stories on every paper in the country, protest marches, candlelit vigil . . . oh, hang on, wait a minute, she was identified in the media as a "St Kilda [street-based] Prostitute" "Never mind."
>
> *(Gilmore 2013, para. 1)*

The capital city of the Australian state of Victoria, Melbourne does not regularly experience the levels of violent crime, particularly homicide, that are unfortunately commonplace in many other urban locales worldwide. Media accordingly devoted significant time and attention to covering two murders committed in 2012 and 2013. An unknown perpetrator murdered the first victim, 40-year-old Tracy Connelly, in July 2013, and Adrian Bayley perpetrated the second murder, of 29-year old Jill Meagher, in September 2012. The significant differences in the way that these murders were reported by the media rested on one fact: that Tracy Connelly was a "prostitute." Although Tracy Connelly's murder was also accompanied by a significant rise in media reporting about street-based sex work—which in turn facilitated greater public attention to and commentary about this issue—the reports continually and unforgivingly identified Tracy as a prostitute. Unlike Jill, Tracy's killer still has not been found. Her partner, Tony, found her, badly beaten and stabbed to death, in the Ford Econovan where they had been living. Adrian Bayley, Jill's killer, pursued Jill as she walked home in the early hours of September 22, 2012.

He raped and strangled her to death, dumping her body 50 kilometers from the crime scene. He had committed over two decades of violent offences against women. At the time of the murder he was on parole and had already served sentences for sex crimes. Significantly, all of the victims of his previous crimes were street-based sex workers in St. Kilda, a neighborhood well known for street prostitution and where Tracy Connelly also engaged in commercial sex. Bayley, who raped five street-based sex workers over a six-month period in 2000, was sentenced to eight years for trapping these women in his vehicle to repeatedly sexually assault them (Farnsworth 2015). Regardless of the extent of violence, several sex workers who were attacked by Bayley chose to remain anonymous due to their fear of repercussions and mistrust of local police and the criminal justice system as a whole. One media report noted: "amid the horrific revelations in the Bayley case was as many as 10 women, who were sex workers, who were too scared of Bayley or too distrustful of the justice system to make police statements against him" (Koubaridis 2015, para. 20).

Globally, sex workers often under-report sexual assault for fear of being "found out" and stigmatized by police, media, and others, as many sex workers believe that police and the justice system see them as unworthy of protection (Benoit et al. 2018). This type of structural discrimination leads to further violence as the public begins to believe that sex workers have all but given up their rights for protection because of their occupation as part of the "whore stigma" (Vanwesenbeeck 2017). The shame of this "whore stigma" leaves women further vulnerable to stigma and discrimination (Benoit et al. 2018; Lazarus 2012; Vanwesenbeeck 2017) and, perhaps worse still, enables perpetrators to harm sex workers with virtual impunity.

In a 2013 interview with the Australian Broadcasting Corporation, a major news media outlet in Australia, Jill Meagher's husband, Tom Meagher, described the structural stigma sex workers face as contributing to the impunity with which Bayley committed his crimes. Consider the following excerpt from the published version of the interview transcript:

> "I'm aware his previous victims in previous cases before Jill were sex workers, and I'll never be convinced that doesn't have something to do with the lenience of his sentence," he said. "Put it like this: if he'd raped five people like Jill that many times in that brutal a fashion, I don't think he would have served eight years in prison." He says that "sends a disturbing message. What it says to women is if we don't like what you do, you won't get justice . . . And what it says to people like Bayley is not 'don't rape,' but 'be careful who you rape.'"
>
> *(ABC News 2013, para. 16)*

Researchers have reached similar conclusions through systematic comparisons of public reactions to the murders of Jill Meagher, an "ideal victim" because of her conformity to gender socio-sexual norms, and Joanna Martin, a 65-year old Australian grandmother who worked as an escort and a stripper and whose body was found in October 2011 (Thompson and Louise 2014). This is commensurate with the theory of the "missing white woman syndrome," in which media portray women who are "sexually deviant" as deserving violence. Thompson and Louise (2014) note that media continuously personified Jill Meagher as the epitome of innocence whereas Tracy Connelly and Joanna Martin received media treatment that focused on their involvement in prostitution. One journalist rather disturbingly attributed the significant public sympathy accorded to the former, rather than the latter, as the result of "a natural attraction to the brown-eyed brunette who always seems to be beaming with the happiness of a newlywed" (Akerman 2013, para. 29).

These assertions are an unfortunate indication of the idealistic and dominant gender roles that are not only pervasive in Australia, but also internationally (Harris et al. 2011; Seymour 2017). Tracy Connelly's sexuality was placed on public display and her life was heavily scrutinized in a public space through media reports. Her character and personality, which attracted explicit support and love from her community and family before and after her death, was suffused with and reduced to stigmatized discourse surrounding her sex industry involvement. This is commensurate with numerous arguments that typical media representations of women victims needing attention are based on the assumption that the "good girls" are not sexual except within the socially sanctioned role of wife, which mobilizes women's sexuality solely for the purposes of reproduction (Dunn 2010, 106, cited in Mendes and Silva 2010). Regardless of the rhetoric and awareness raising of the media regarding stigma and discrimination at the time of Tracy's death, recent media discourse about street-based sex work demonstrates the ongoing sensationalistic language favored by writers. In the online news site news.com, the journalist provides an explicit, yet almost poetic description of a peer of Tracy Connelly. A provocative photograph exposing a breast accompanies the article and is captioned "A St. Kilda prostitute has spoken about live as a sex worker" with the following introductory paragraph:

It's just after 10pm on a Friday and the witching hour has begun along Melbourne's red-light mile. Street sex workers in the inner-city suburb of St. Kilda have come out to earn money and are selling services to strangers in cars. Over the next three hours the trade will sizzle along at a cracking pace, with customers in cars whisking women off the street as soon as they return from their last assignation. Seasoned street worker Renee is the prettiest on the street and is earning "$100 for sex, $50 for oral, no less" she tells news.com.au, on her patch outside a late-night shop. The temperature is dropping and Renee wears a red cardigan over her white mini-dress and long bare legs in high heels.

(Sutton 2017, paras. 1–5)

The language used throughout this introductory paragraph such as the trade sizzling along at a "cracking pace" and descriptions of the worker who "wears a red cardigan over her white mini-dress and long bare legs in high heels" provides a gendered stereotype of a sex worker with her bare legs and exposed breast, as well as indicating the attire of a typical "bad girl." The author also makes an exception for the worker stating that she is "pretty," which, when a woman faces violence and abuses drugs is irrelevant, yet provides an almost poetic version of the down and out street-based sex worker. The issue with this type of inference on sex workers is that it downplays the underlying issues that women face such as drug addiction, entrance into sex work and overall risk management strategies.

The sexuality of "bad girls" is construed as dirty, socially unacceptable, and in need of control or punishment. This social construction of "bad girls" effectively leaves no social place for these morally degenerate "bad girls" (Liebler 2010; Mendes and Silva 2010; O'Neil et al. 2008). This moral panic permeates media representations of women in sex work, whom media repeatedly categorizes as "the other" and as a menace to community integrity and values (O'Neill et al. 2008). Interestingly, the Sutton (2017) article ends with the following three sentences, which undermines the gravity of the murders of Tracy and of Jill:

Renee was working on St. Kilda's streets when Adrian Bayley was free roaming the streets.
   "I know his face, but he never picked me up," Renee said, making a last, tired joke, "should I take it personally?"
Renee drove off for the night, her work on St. Kilda's streets over for another week.

Yet not all journalists adopted this stigmatizing tone. Journalist Jane Gilmore, writing in 2013 for the media outlet *Kings Tribune*, titled her coverage of Tracy Connelly's death "Woman Brutally Murdered in Inner Melbourne." While this difference may seem minor, Gilmore's article analyzes its significant departure from terminology used in other media outlets by acknowledging that the title and content of a majority of Australian news media articles identified Tracy Connelly as a sex worker, which Gilmore regarded as an act of discrimination:

> *The Age, The Herald Sun, The Daily Telegraph, The Border Mail, The Australian, The Courier, Perth Now*, and every other news outlet that ran the story used a combination of "St. Kilda" [and] "Prostitute"—so we [readers] know that she wasn't even just a "prostitute," she was a street prostitute.
>
> *(Gilmore 2013, para. 4)*

Journalist Mia Freedman (2013) noted that Jill Meagher's photograph frequently featured in media coverage of her death in ways that humanized and made readers sympathize with her as well as her family's loss. Photographs of Tracy Connelly did not appear until much later in news coverage of her death, which meant that the public was unable to identify with her in the same way as they were with Jill Meagher:

> When the news broke that a woman had been murdered in St. Kilda, there wasn't much media coverage, there were no photos of the woman. The sole identifier the media used for the woman was her profession. She was a sex worker . . . The media coverage of Tracy's murder was perfunctory. There were no photographs of Tracy Connelly in the media . . . without seeing her as a person, it can be harder for people to connect and care. The media needs pictures. Without them, news coverage is tiny . . . I'd like to think the lack of empathy, the complete absence of public support, distress or even shock about the death of Tracy Connelly is because of the lack of photos, not because of her occupation. Very few victims are ever described by the way they support themselves . . . Tracy was a sex worker—that's what she did, not who she was.
>
> *(Freedman 2013, para. 8)*

Congruent with scholarly evidence indicating that media reports on violence against sex workers generally focus on specific negative themes such as culpability, risk, infection, and trafficking (Farvid and Glass 2014; Hallgrímsdóttir et al. 2008; Weitzer 2017), much of the media commentary on Tracy Connelly's life focused on her supposed knowledge of the danger she put herself in when she made the choice to exchange sex for money. As reported by the prominent Victorian newspaper *The Age* in its article "St Kilda prostitute brutally murdered":

> Tracy Connelly had walked St Kilda's red-light district for at least a decade and knew her work was dangerous. In 2005, her minder was run over by a man who was angry that she refused to get in his car, Ms Connelly once told a court.
>
> She tried to survive without sex work, but needed the money.
>
> *(Bucci and Lynch 2013, paras. 1–2)*

Commentary about the dangers and known risks that Tracy would have subjected herself to were indeed common themes across media narratives, as journalist Jane Gilmore further comments:

Tracy Connelly was a "St. Kilda Prostitute," there's some underlying sense that she, in some way, deserved what happened to her, she should have known better. The first three paragraphs of the story in [the popular Australian newspaper] *The Age* read as follows: "Tracy Connelly had walked St. Kilda's red-light district for at least a decade and knew her work was dangerous. Her Minder [a Minder is generally a male akin to a pimp] also was run over by a man who was so angry that she refused to get in his car, Ms Connelly once told a court . . . she tried to survive without sex work, but needed the money . . . What if instead of "St. Kilda Prostitute," the headings on all those articles had been "Tracy Connelly, brutally murdered in her home yesterday"?

(Gilmore 2013, para. 9)

Gilmore characterizes dominant cultural perceptions as implying that because Tracy was a sex worker, she somehow deserved to die a violent death. The implication of this belief, of course, is that violence against women who are not involved in selling sex is somehow worse. Gilmore uses irony to surmise public perceptions of Tracy's murder: "To begin with, 'normal people' are less likely to be murdered." As a sex worker, Tracy was not a person and she did not deserve the same entitlements that a woman murdered should.

Worldwide, media continues to perpetuate fear-based responses to the sex industry and identifies those within it as threats to society's moral fabric (Greer and Jewkes 2004; O'Neill et al. 2008). Historically, regulatory and legislative approaches to sex work have been reactive and dictated by public outcry, which is both reflected in and facilitated by particular types of media reports (O'Neill et al. 2008). Jill Meagher's death and the subsequent public outcry around the fact that Adrian Bayley had such an extensive history of violently assaulting women led to the enforcement of stricter measures governing the release and subsequent monitoring of incarcerated people with a history of violence in the Australian state of Victoria, where Melbourne is located. Tracy's death, and the assaults of many other women in sex work, sparked discussion of legislative reforms, although concerted discussion across the media following her death did begin to address a tendency for the media to further stigmatize sex workers by negatively influencing public opinion.

Discussion

Structural stigma has a significant and deleterious effect on marginalized groups, including sexual minorities, people with mental illness, and illicit drug users (Evans-Lacko et al. 2012; Hatzenbuehler and Link 2014). Sex workers are a marginalized group highly subjected to structural stigma in the form of policy and legislation that often criminalizes and/or stigmatizes their means of earning a living. The media plays a substantial role in exacerbating structural stigma through sensationalistic reports of street-based sex workers and the chaos and uncertainty underpinning their lives. This phenomenon is not unique to Australia and occurs worldwide (Benoit et al. 2015; Krüsi et al. 2016). Entrenched cultural belief systems, attitudes, gender roles, and theories of exploitation and victimization have all manifested through media commentary and narrative that further stigmatize and marginalize sex workers (Farvid and Glass 2014; Hallgrímsdóttiir et al. 2008; Lazarus et al. 2012).

This chapter employed a specific Australian case study to document the structural stigma that is pervasive in relation to the sex industry and replicated and facilitated within media representation of sex workers as deviant and blameworthy social pariahs. Our comparison of media responses to the murders of Jill Meagher, the happily married woman, and Tracy Connelly, the transgressive street-based sex worker, emphasizes the power of entrenched belief systems about women's sexuality and the partiality towards antiquated gender norms. Taken together, these cases emphasize how dominant cultural forms generate media and public sympathy generated for the victims of violence who meet gendered cultural expectations while tacitly legitimizing violence against sex workers.

References

ABC News. 2013. "Jill Meagher's husband Tom Meagher says justice system failed her and Adrian Bayley's sentence is a disgrace." *ABC News*. Retrieved 2017: www.abc.net.au/news/2013-06-19/tom-meagher-says-justice-system-failed-his-wife/4766620.

Abel, G.M. 2014. A decade of decriminalisation: Sex work "down under" but not underground. *Criminology & Criminal Justice* 14, 5, 580–592.

Akerman, P. 2013. The legacy of Jill Meagher. *The Australian*. Retrieved January 2018: www.theaustralian.com.au/news/inquirer/the-legacy-of-jill-meagher/news-story/121efd9a0ee165c9ca2c03c6003fccba?sv=ffa5cf36c4408d7179c63fd82e232aac.

Armstrong, L. 2010. Out of the shadows (and into a bit of light): Decriminalisation, human rights and streetbased sex work in New Zealand. In K. Hardy, S. Kingston, and T. Sanders, Eds., *New sociologies of sex work*, 39–59. Surrey, UK: Ashgate.

Armstrong, L. 2017. From law enforcement to protection? Interactions between sex workers and police in a decriminalised street-based sex industry. *British Journal of Criminology* 57, 3, 570–588.

Benoit, C., McCarthy, B., and Jansson, M. 2015. Stigma, sex work, and substance abuse: a comparative analysis. *Sociology of Health & Illness* 37, 3, 437–451.

Benoit, C., Smith, M., Jansson, M., Magnus, S., Flagg, J., and Maurice, R. 2018. Sex work and three dimensions of self-esteem: Self-worth, authenticity and self-efficacy. *Culture, Health & Sexuality* 20, 1, 69–83.

Bruckert, C. and Hannem, S. 2013. Rethinking the prostitution debates: Transcending structural stigma in systemic responses to sex work. *Canadian Journal of Law and Society* 28, 1, 43–63.

Bucci, N. and Lynch, J. 2013. St Kilda prostitute brutally murdered. *The Age*. Retrieved February 2018: www.theage.com.au/national/victoria/st-kilda-prostitute-brutally-murdered-20130722-2qewy.html.

Bungay, V., Halpin, M., Atchison, C., and Johnston, C. 2011. Structure and agency: Reflections from an exploratory study of Vancouver indoor sex workers. *Culture, Health & Sexuality* 13, 1, 15–29.

Evans-Lacko, S., Brohan, E., Mojtabai, R., and Thornicroft, G. 2012. Association between public views of mental illness and self-stigma among individuals with mental illness in 14 European countries. *Psychological Medicine* 42, 8, 1741–1752.

Farnsworth, S. 2015. Jill Meagher's killer Adrian Bayley had history of violent sex attacks: Parole board failed to take him off the streets. ABC News. Retrieved January 2018: www.abc.net.au/news/2013-06-11/violent-past-of-jill-meagher-killer-adrian-bayley-revealed/4745406.

Farvid, P. and Glass, L. 2014. "It isn't prostitution as you normally think of it. Its survival sex": Media representations of adult and child prostitution in New Zealand. *Women's Studies Journal* 28, 1, 47–67.

Freedman, M. 2013, August 2. Her name was Tracy and she was my friend. Mamamia. Retrieved January 2018: www.mamamia.com.au/remembering-tracy-connelly.

Gilchrist, K. 2010. "Newsworthy" victims? Exploring differences in Canadian local press coverage of missing/murdered Aboriginal and white women. *Feminist Media Studies* 10, 4, 373–390.

Gilmore, J. 2013, July 23. Woman brutally murdered in inner Melbourne. *Kingstribune*. Retrieved January 2018: www.kingstribune.com.

Goffman, E. 1963. *Stigma: Notes on the management of a spoiled identity*. New York: Simon & Schuster.

Greer, C. and Y. Jewkes. 2004 Extremes of otherness: Media images of social exclusion. *Social Justice: A Journal of Crime, Conflict and World Order* 32, 1, 20–31.

Hallgrímsdóttiir, H.K, Phillips, R., Benoit, C., and Walby. 2008. Sporting girls, streetwalkers, and inmates of houses of ill repute: Media narratives and the historical mutability of prostitution stigmas. *Sociological Perspectives* 51, 1, 119–138.

Harcourt, C., O'Connor, J., Egger, S., Fairley, C.K., Wand, H., Chen, M.Y., Marshall, L., Kaldor, J.M., and Donovan, B. 2010. The decriminalisation of prostitution is associated with better coverage of health promotion programs for sex workers. *Australian and New Zealand Journal of Public Health* 34, 5, 482–486.

Harris, M., Nilan, P., and Kirby, E. 2011. Risk and risk management for Australian sex workers. *Qualitative Health Research* 21, 3, 386–398.

Hatzenbuehler, M.L. and Link, B.G. 2014. Introduction to the special issue on structural stigma and health. *Social Science & Medicine* 103, 1–6.

Hatzenbuehler, M.L., Phelan, J.C., and Link, B.G. 2013. Stigma as a fundamental cause of population health inequalities. *American Journal of Public Health* 103, 5, 813–821.

Jeffrey, L.A. and MacDonald, G. 2006. "It's the money, honey": The economy of sex work in the Maritimes. *Canadian Review of Sociology* 43, 3, 313–327.

Koubaridis, A. 2015. Who killed sex worker Tracy Connelly? Retrieved January 2018: www.news.com.au/national/crime/who-killed-sex-worker-tracy-connelly/news-story/b009c61963bc0d40ac01c893a6efc1ce.

Krüsi, A., Kerr, T., Taylor, C., Rhodes, T., and Shannon, K. 2016. "They won't change it back in their heads that we're trash": The intersection of sex work-related stigma and evolving policing strategies. *Sociology of Health & Illness* 38, 7, 1137–1150.

Lazarus, L., Deering, K.N., Nabess, R., Gibson, K., Tyndall, M.W., and Shannon, K. 2012. Occupational stigma as a primary barrier to health care for street-based sex workers in Canada. *Culture, Health & Sexuality* 14, 139–150.

Liebler, C.M. 2010. Me(di)a culpa?: The "missing white woman syndrome" and media self critique. *Communications, Culture and Critique* 3, 549–565.

Maier, A., Gentile, D.A., Vogel, D.L., and Kaplan, S.A. 2014. Media influences on self-stigma of seeking psychological services: The importance of media portrayals and person perception. *Psychology of Popular Media Culture* 3, 4, 239–256.

Mendes, K. and Silva, K. 2010. Representations of sex workers. *Commentary and Criticism*, 10, 1, 99–116.

O'Neill, M., Campbell, R., Hubbard, P., Pitcher, J., and Scoular, J. 2008. Living with the other: Street sex work, contingent communities and degrees of tolerance. *Crime Media Culture* 4, 1, 73–93.

Perse, E.M. and Lambe, J. 2017. *Media effects and society* (2nd ed.). New York: Routledge.

Seymour, K. 2017. "Stand up, speak out and act": A critical reading of Australia's White Ribbon campaign. *Australian & New Zealand Journal of Criminology* 51, 2, 293–310.

Smith, J. 2006. Prostitutes deserve as much sympathy as any murder victim. *Guardian* (Australia) December, 12.

Smith, L. 2013. Dehumanising sex workers: What's "prostitute" got to do with it? *The Conversation.* Retrieved January 2018: http://theconversation.com/dehumanising-sex-workers-whats-prostitute-got-to-do-with-it-16444.

Strega, S., Janzen, C., Morgan, J., Brown, L., Thomas, R., and Carriére, J. 2014. Never innocent victims: Street sex workers in Canadian print media. *Violence Against Women* 20, 1, 6–25.

Sullivan, B. 2010. When (Some) prostitution is legal: The impact of law reform on sex work in Australia. *Journal of Law Reform and Society* 37, 1, 85–104.

Sutton, C. 2017. "He attacked me with a baseball bat": St. Kilda sex worker talks about the dangers of her job. News.com.au. Retrieved February 2018: www.news.com.au/lifestyle/real-life/news-life/he-attacked-me-with-a-baseball-bat-street-sex-worker-reveals-her-life-in-the-most-dangerous-job-in-australia/news-story/13f3cbc94c5875b8c5084a18aa3e8fd5.

Thompson, J. and Louise, R. 2014. Sexed violence and its (dis)appearances: Media coverage surrounding the murders of Jill Meagher and Johanna Martin. *Outskirts* 31, 1–10.

Vanwesenbeeck, I. 2017. Sex work criminalisation is barking up the wrong tree. *Archives of Sexual Behaviour* 46, 1631–1640.

Weitzer, R. 2015. Researching prostitution and sex trafficking comparatively. *Sex Research Social Policy* 12, 81–91.

Weitzer, R. 2017. Resistance to sex work stigma. *Sexualities* 1–13. https://doi.org/10.1177%2F1363460716684509.

Westerman, D., Spence, P.R., and Van Der Heide, B. 2014. Social media as information source: Recency of updates and credibility of information. *Journal of Computer-Mediated Communications* 19, 2, 171–183.

Part VIII
Technologies

51

Technologies

An introduction

Susan Dewey, Isabel Crowhurst, and Chimaraoke Izugbara

Introduction

New technologies have been facilitating new sex industry forms in ways that foster increased visibility and potentially increased surveillance of sex industry participants. Key themes in existing research are a focus on technology and: male and transgender sex workers in Western Europe and North America, online sex workers' needs, labor conditions, client fora, and regulation. Chapters in this section engage with these ongoing challenges while offering directions for future research.

Key themes in existing literature

Research in this area features a significant amount of work with male and transgender sex workers, although such work remains almost exclusively confined to Western Europe and North America. This literature emphasizes the possibilities for mutuality and friendship that online fora extend to men who have sex with men (Walby, 2012). It also explores how technology is increasingly normalizing male sex work by representing it as another online commodity for sale—by men and for men—rather than a "deviant" or criminal activity (MacPhail, Scott, & Minichiello, 2014). Likewise, technology provides a venue for transgender sex workers to successfully perform their bodies, gender, and sensuality in self-affirming ways (Vartabedian, 2017).

Ease of access through mobile phone, personal computer, tablet, or other means makes technology a potentially transformative means for sex workers to engage in activism and information-sharing, particularly in locales or regions where prostitution is criminalized and sex workers may risk arrest or community scorn if they advocate publically (Dennermalm, 2014; Izugbara, 2012). Online publishing through blogs and similar fora facilitates sex workers' engagement with hostile publics as they organize and gain support for their cause (Feldman, 2014). This is particularly important given that online sex workers face a very different set of issues than their peers who work on the street or in indoor venues and accordingly describe their needs as far more related to issues such as business and legal advice rather than basic information about safer sex (Parsons, Koken, & Bimbi, 2007). Internet technology also provides researchers with novel means to access sex industry participants who were previously considered "hard to reach" because of their indoor work, and to protect confidentiality more effectively through large-scale survey distribution that allows almost complete anonymity (Jenkins, 2010).

Labor conditions vary in online sex industry forms in ways strongly impacted by individuals' previous sex industry experiences, as those who have worked the street previously tend to regard prostitution as a full-time occupation, are more likely to agree to sex without a condom, and less likely to screen clients as thoroughly as their peers who have only worked indoors (Cunningham & Kendall, 2011). Online sex workers tend to have greater ethno-racial, class, and related privileges that allow them to maximize their profits, although their efforts to reduce associated risks are considerably mitigated by the possibility for filming, still photography, and other abusive practices by clients (Jones, 2015). Commercial interests that govern online sex industry fora remain geared to owners, operators, and clients rather than sex workers (Pajnik et al., 2016). While a majority of websites and online fora remain targeted at male clients by advertising women's sexual services (Castle & Lee, 2008), both male and female broadcasters in webcam work have been found to engage in performative interactions with audience members designed to maximize interest (Weiss, 2017).

Technology also creates opportunities for sex workers' clients to anonymously congregate, sharing information and advice about their experiences in various sex industry venues (Holt & Blevins, 2007). These sites frequently mention that clients prefer the affective displays associated with more conventional intimate relationships, including conversation, cuddling, and other behaviors that generally occur between non-paying intimate partners (Milrod & Monto, 2012). The sheer diversity of technology-mediated sex industry forms also presents significant challenges to regulation, policing, and other forms of government oversight (Sanders et al., 2018). Online sex workers typically work from home, where their activities are not readily visible to police or other state agents and stigmatization discourages formal registration with the state of the home as a sex industry venue (Hubbard & Prior, 2012), and most legal efforts to regulate prostitution focus exclusively on heteronormative commercial sexual exchanges (Ashford, 2009).

Chapter overview

Campbell and colleagues (Chapter 52) examine how sex workers use virtual spaces, social media, and other online platforms and applications to establish and cement professional and peer support networks, with some based around safety but equally around collegiate or social chat as well as advocacy. Strohmeyer and colleagues (Chapter 53) explore the use of web, mobile, and social media technologies co-designed with sex workers as elements of support service delivery to analyze the socio-technical, socio-ethical, and socio-cultural implications of the resulting digital ecologies.

Rand (Chapter 54) contends that neoliberalism, constrained labor markets, and rapid technological improvements in the area of technology-mediated sexual services have resulted in a highly diversified online sexual service provision market that gives simplified access to clients. Panchanadeswaran and colleagues (Chapter 55) engage with sex workers' use of mobile phone technology in India to argue that while such technologies present innumerable opportunities for personal gain and empowerment, they also raise critical concerns about sex workers' surveillance and safety. Selmi (Chapter 56) draws on her research with phone sex operators in Italy to analyze how they mobilize corporeal, sexual, and gender resources and make clients feel that the interaction is "real" in the conversational space created through the phone. In the final chapter of the Handbook, Starr and Francis (Chapter 57) explore how sex workers have constructed cinematic products about their daily lives, their work, and delivering services to their peers and for advocacy. Here, the focus is on communication technologies and how film and video production developments, and advances in mobile phone and digital technologies have enabled sex workers to represent their work from their unique perspectives.

Future directions

Literature on technology's role in the sex industry is predominantly concentrated in the Global North, which is quite puzzling given the frequency with which technologies such as mobile phones are used by sex workers in the Global South. Little is known about how sex workers use technology in the Global South, how the global circulation of sexual labor takes on unique forms through technology, and the uses to which this labor is put. Researchers have explored even less about how technology-mediated sex work relates to third-party exchanges and the potential for labor exploitation. Technology-assisted violence against sex workers is also poorly studied.

Great potential for intervention research exists in the area of how technology might facilitate harm reduction for sex workers, particularly in the area of access to health services but also in terms of the potential for activism and the formation of mutual aid collectivities. Technology-mediated sexual services also present the potential for social isolation, cyber-bullying, and sharing photos or other sexual content without permission. More work needs to explore the nuances of how these technologies are shaping the sex industry in complex ways.

References

Ashford, Chris. 2009. Male Sex Work and the Internet Effect: Time to Re-Evaluate the Criminal Law. *Journal of Criminal Law* 73(3): 258–280.

Castle, Tammy and Lee, Jennifer. 2008. Ordering Sex in Cyberspace: A Content Analysis of Escort Websites. *International Journal of Cultural Studies* 11(1): 107–121.

Cunningham, Scott and Kendall, Todd. 2011. Prostitution 2.0: The Changing Face of Sex Work. *Journal of Urban Economics* 69(3): 273–287.

Dennermalm, Nicklas. 2014. Resistance to the Swedish Model through LGBTQ and Sex Work Community Collaboration and Online Intervention. *Digital Culture & Education*. Available at: www.digitalcultureandeducation.com/uncategorized/dennermalm_html.

Feldman, Valerie. 2014. Sex Work Politics and the Internet: Carving Out Political Space in the Blogosphere. In *Negotiating Sex Work: Unintended Consequences of Policy and Activism*, edited by Carisa R. Showden and Samantha Majic, 243–266. Minneapolis, MN: University of Minnesota Press.

Holt, Thomas and Blevins, Kristine. 2007. Examining Sex Work from the Client's Perspective: Assessing Johns Using On-Line Data. *Deviant Behavior* 28(4): 333–354.

Hubbard, Phil and Prior, Jason. 2012. Out of Sight, Out of Mind? Prostitution Policy and the Health, Well-Being and Safety of Home-Based Sex Workers. *Critical Social Policy* 33(1): 140–159.

Izugbara, Chimaraoke. 2012. Client Retention and Health Among Sex Workers in Nairobi, Kenya. *Archives of Sexual Behavior* 41(6): 1345–1352.

Jenkins, Suzanne. 2010. New Technologies, New Territories: Using the Internet to Connect with Sex Workers and Sex Industry Organizers. In *New Sociologies of Sex Work*, edited by Kate Hardy, Sarah Kingston, and Teela Sanders, 91–108. Burlington, VT: Ashgate.

Jones, Angela. 2015. Sex Work in a Digital Era. *Sociology Compass* 9(7): 558–570.

MacPhail, Catherine, Scott, John, and Minichiello, Victor. 2014. Technology, Normalisation and Male Sex Work. *Culture, Health & Sexuality* 17(4): 483–495.

Milrod, Christine and Monto, Martin. 2012. The Hobbyist and the Girlfriend Experience: Behaviors and Preferences of Male Customers of Internet Sexual Service Providers. *Deviant Behavior* 33(10): 792–810.

Pajnik, Mojca, Kambouri, Nelli, Renault, Matthieu, and Sori, Iztok. 2016. Digitalising Sex Commerce and Sex Work: A Comparative Analysis of French, Greek and Slovenian Websites. *Gender, Place and Culture: A Journal of Feminist Geography* 23(3): 345–364.

Parsons, Jeffery, Koken, Juline, and Bimbi, David. 2007. Looking Beyond HIV: Eliciting Individual and Community Needs of Internet Escorts. *Journal of Homosexuality* 53(1– 2): 219–240.

Sanders, T., Scoular, J., Campbell, R., Pitcher, J., and Cunningham, S. 2018. *Internet Sex Work*. Basingstoke, UK: Palgrave Macmillan.

Vartabedian, Julieta. 2017. Bodies and Desires on the Internet: An Approach to Trans Women Sex Workers' Websites. *Sexualities*. https://doi.org/10.1177/1363460717713381.

Walby, Kevin. 2012. *Touching Encounters: Sex, Work, and Male-for-Male Internet Escorting*. Chicago, IL: University of Chicago Press.

Weiss, Benjamin. 2017. Patterns of Interaction in Webcam Sex Work: A Comparative Analysis of Female and Male Broadcasters. *Deviant Behavior*. doi: 10.1080/01639625.2017.1304803.

52

Technology-mediated sex work

Fluidity, networking and regulation in the UK

Rosie Campbell, Yigit Aydin, Stewart Cunningham, Rebecca Hamer, Kathleen Hill, Camille Melissa, Jane Pitcher, Jane Scoular, Teela Sanders and Matt Valentine-Chase

Introduction and research methods

While there has been no comprehensive research attempting to quantify the size and growth of the online sector of the UK sex industry, certain studies have undertaken small-scale analyses of particular websites advertising sexual services to present estimates of different groups of sex workers advertising online (Pitcher and Wijers 2014; Smith and Kingston 2015). The currently available mapping and research data suggests that online sex work is the largest sector of the commercial sex industry in the UK (Sanders et al. 2018) and is a major and developing market globally, with Internet and digital technology having reshaped the sex industry (Jones 2015). Yet it is a sector that has been less explored by researchers compared to street or brothel-based sex work.

This chapter draws on findings from a three-year participatory action research project, "Beyond the Gaze" (hereafter, BtG), which has used mixed methods to explore the working practices, safety and regulation of online sex markets in the UK. BtG has utilised a broad definition of Internet facilitated sex work:

> Sex workers based on their own, or in collectives, or working through an agency, who use the Internet to market or sell sexual services either directly through in-person services, such as interacting with clients in person through escorting, erotic massage, BDSM[1] or through online indirect services including online interactions like web camming.
>
> *(Sanders et al. 2017, 15)*

This definition purposefully distinguishes between those who work as escorts and/or BDSM specialists providing services to their clients in person (direct services), but who use the Internet for advertising and marketing, and sex workers who provide technology-mediated indirect services, like webcamming,[2] phone sex chat[3] or instant message.[4]

Internet Sex Work, the book based on BtG's findings (Sanders et al. 2018), details the landscape of Internet-based sex work in the UK with a focus on the micro-practices of sex work online, new sex markets that have emerged and how these markets are organised. The book examines new forms of crimes against sex workers facilitated by the online environment, the safety strategies utilised by online workers and the legal regulation of the sector. In this chapter, we focus on illustrating how the Internet has created new marketing strategies and shaped work patterns, particularly enabling flexible work with a high degree of mobility and fluidity over time, space and job roles. We explore how sex workers are using virtual spaces, social media and other online platforms and applications to establish and cement professional and peer support networks, some based around safety but equally around collegiate or social chat as well as advocacy and activism. We will conclude by overviewing how the governance of sex work, particularly through policing, currently intersects with the online sex work world in the UK. Drawing on data from extensive interviews with police from across 15 UK police forces, we overview how UK policing is in its infancy in terms of engaging with online markets and accessing the extensive information about the commercial sex industry that feature on website platforms. Yet sex trafficking and modern slavery[5] is the current focus within UK policing with respect to online commercial sex work markets, leading us to reflect on the extent to which police services address other crimes against sex workers and harms that exist online as identified by online sex workers.

Funded by the UK Economic and Social Research Council, BtG's overall aim was to understand how the Internet has shaped sex work, including the working practices in Internet-based sex markets within the broader processes of UK regulation and policing. BtG was a three-year project that commenced in September 2015, with fieldwork and data collection taking place between December 2015 and March 2017 and dissemination and impact activity taking place between September 2017 to September 2018. A participatory action research project with sex workers forming part of the research team, BtG used a mixed methods approach with key methodological strands comprising desk research to map online spaces where sex workers market and/or provide services, semi-structured interviews with 62 sex workers of all genders who use the Internet for their work, semi-structured interviews with 56 police representatives from police services across the UK and 21 individuals, including managers, webmasters or moderators of online advertising platforms/forums/safety schemes for sex workers, plus other experts on online regulation of commercial sexual services. Three online surveys were carried out: the first with 641 Internet-based sex workers, the second with 1,323 customers of sex workers using the Internet, and the third with 49 projects providing support to online sex workers.

These sex worker and customer surveys are the largest of their kind to be carried out to date in the UK and reveal the characteristics and regulation of contemporary sex work, particularly for independent escorts and webcammers. Ethical approval was obtained for the study and measures put in place to protect the anonymity of all participants and enable informed consent. Here we draw on data from the sex worker and police interviews, which at the time of writing constitute the most comprehensive study of UK policing of online commercial sex work markets, and also data from the sex worker survey. Among the respondents, nearly three-quarters (73.5%, n = 469) were female, 19.4% (n = 124) were male, 3% (n = 19) were transgender with transwomen in the majority (n = 17), 2.9% (n = 18) were non-binary or intersex. Over half of respondents were aged between 25 and 44, 36.8% (n = 236) were 25–34, 26.5% (n = 170) were 35–44, 20.4% (n = 131) were 18–24, only one respondent was under 18, 11.1% (n = 71) were 45–54 and 4.7% (n = 30) were 55 or over. The majority of respondents (87.2%, n = 559) were white, 5% (n = 32) were of mixed ethnicity, 2.7% (n = 17) were Asian/Asian British and the same number Black/Black British. Nearly 15% (n = 94) of respondents were of non-UK nationality.

Fluidity and postmodern online sex work

Internet-based sex markets have become pervasive (Sanders 2005, 2008), facilitated by computer-mediated communication through email, chat-rooms, social media forums and web-based advertising. As Ray (2007a) and others have noted, the Internet has had a substantial impact on the way in which independent sex workers, as well as escort agencies and sometimes massage parlours, advertise their services. Research about how the Internet is used within commercial sex transactions and marketing illustrates that digital technology has not only changed how sex workers and clients communicate with one another, but also their social relationships, with the development of 'cyber communities' of both sex workers and customers (Sharp and Earle 2003; Walby 2012; Pitcher 2015a). Cooper (2017) has noted the liminality of contemporary sex work spaces in terms of both its ambiguous legal status – with aspects of legality and illegality – and its occupation, often simultaneously, of physical and virtual space, particularly for online sex work. One of the characteristics of online sex work further highlighted by BtG is its fluid, liminal and mobile nature. The majority of sex workers who took part in the BtG survey (96% n = 615) worked in independent indoor sectors as independent sex workers/escorts, webcam workers or providers of sexual massage or BDSM services.

Many provided different forms of direct and indirect online sex work, moving between sectors according to need with flexibility facilitated by the Internet. Nearly three-fifths of independent sex workers/escorts undertook some other form of sex work, particularly BDSM (27.8%; n = 132), webcamming (26.8%; n = 127) and phone sex work (23.4%; n = 111). There was a substantial overlap between webcam and phone workers, with 59.8% (n = 152) of webcam workers also undertaking phone sex work. Half (n = 127) also worked in independent sex work/escorting. Other sex work jobs included adult film, modelling agency work, brothel work, exotic dance and street sex work. The maximum number of sectors worked in was nine, with the average (mean) number of sectors being two. Yet it was still more common for respondents to work in only one sector, as was the case for 41.7% of respondents (n = 267), particularly those based in independent sex work/escorting.

Online and digital technology has facilitated more mobile and flexible forms of sex work. Some survey respondents were highly mobile, moving geographically for work to provide services in different parts of the country. Some described how they travelled for work regularly, either to day appointments across their region of residence and/or to other regions, or staying in hotels or renting a property for work in the UK or other countries for a longer period. Such 'touring' has been further facilitated by the Internet's enabling sex workers to update their profile to include temporary locations, access marketing sites with national and international reach and make appointments. Some people worked for bursts of time rather than on a regular basis. Sanders et al. (2018) described how certain simple functionality of online advertising platforms and profiles enable this fluid interaction with the customer base, giving individuals more choice over when and where they work. Levels of control over their businesses were high given that a minority of sex workers in the BtG study pay a third party to assist them in any aspect of their work, with the exception of advertising platforms paid to market profiles. Working conditions were largely considered to be enhanced due to the possibilities offered by digital technologies.

Sanders et al. (2016) illustrated fluidity across sectors of the labour market for online sex workers in their survey of 240 online sex workers, among whom 45% did sex work alongside another job and 13% were current students. What we know about the demographics of work patterns also helps explain the increasingly fluid nature of sex work. Sex work is often not always the primary mode of work, and is often undertaken on a part-time or sporadic basis, with sex workers using the features of digital technology, particularly advertising, to manage their time and labour. Just over one-third (37%) of BtG interview participants combined sex work with employment in other areas of the labour market or with study, although 63% of interview participants reported that sex work was their only job. A total of 34% worked in other labour sectors ranging from health and social care (n = 5) to administration/clerical (n = 4), some working in more than one, and six were students.

Sanders et al. (2018) found that, for many online sex workers, online technology had provided greater control over their working conditions and an increased ability to develop their own businesses and brand online. In the BtG sex worker survey, 89.4% (n = 573) agreed or strongly agreed that the Internet enabled sex workers to decide where to work, or when to work, and 89.4% (n = 573) agreed that it allowed sex workers to work independently without having to rely on third parties (89.4%; n = 573). Yet some of the disadvantages of online sex worker included the increased number of hours spent managing their business online, the unpredictability of earnings as well as stigma and privacy issues, including the potential for crimes such as doxing and the misuse of information. We now turn to the marketing strategies utilised by online sex workers in the UK.

Online spaces and marketing strategies

Long gone are the days when sex workers relied on advertisements in the personal or classified columns of newspapers, contact magazines, cards in telephone boxes or other locations in lieu of making initial contact with customers on the street, in bars, hotels, lorry parks or other physical locations. A key impact of online and digital technology on sex work over the last 20 years is the emergence of new online spaces and digital mobile communication technology that sex workers can use to advertise, screen customers and arrange face-to-face or technologically mediated exchange of services (see Cunningham et al. 2017). Most of the previous research on how sex workers advertise on the Internet has been primarily based on content analysis of platforms and advertisements (Pruitt 2005; Castle and Lee 2008; Lee-Gonyea et al. 2009; Capiola et al. 2014). Tyler's (2014, 2016) is one of the few studies to combine content analysis with qualitative interviews with sex workers who advertise online, in this case by focussing on male sex workers in London. Audacia Ray, a US writer and sex work activist, writing in 2007 notes that for independent sex workers "the internet has opened up a vast new world of opportunity in which different marketing styles can be tried out cheaply and easily – and changed immediately if they fail" (Ray 2007b, 46).

Our quantitative and qualitative data confirmed that there has emerged a wide range of online spaces that Internet-based sex workers in the UK use to facilitate and market commercial sexual services. BtG has created a typology of 12 categories that capture such current spaces (Cunningham et al. 2017; Sanders et al. 2018). Across these varied online platforms, websites and applications different business models are adapted that shape how sex workers engage with these different technologies and spaces. Here we briefly discuss five of these to illustrate the diversity and the varied marketing strategies sex workers use.

Multi-service adult entertainment platforms are websites offering a range of different sex work services within the one site. Platform 1, the market-leading website in the UK, is an example of this model and was used in different ways by the vast majority of both BtG interview and survey participants. Platform 1 is also a key market leader for the vast majority of UK sex workers, especially cisgender female sex workers. Our survey results show that 93.4% (n = 436) of cis-female sex workers use Platform 1 to offer all kinds of services. Male sex workers use Platform 1 much less often[6] (33%, n = 41) yet transmen (100%, n = 2), transwomen (88.2%, n = 15) and non-binary people (76.5%, n = 13) in our survey also appear to use Platform 1 in consistent numbers – although the number of respondents to the BtG survey in these gender categories was so low that no firm conclusions can be drawn on the practices of these groups of sex workers.

Escort directories/advertising platforms are third-party websites that allow sex workers who offer in-person direct sex work to create profiles to advertise their services. Some are international, others focus on the national level and still others operate at a more local level. Some charge a fee while others offer free profile advertising. While some carry advertisements for sex workers of all genders, there was gender stratification and some were targeted at specific segments of the customer market, e.g. customers of female sex workers, customers of gay or bisexual male escorts, and customers of transgender sex workers. For example, 15.6% (n = 100) of our survey sample advertised on one particular site branded as for gay and bisexual escorts, which is one of the more popular sites for male sex workers advertising for male customers.

Another method utilised by some online sex workers for advertising involves an individual website where independent sex workers market themselves. This website is created and managed by the sex workers themselves or by web designers/IT specialists on their behalf. Just under a third (28.9%, n = 185) of those who responded to our survey stated that they had their own website. Only four respondents who exclusively provided technology-mediated indirect services had their own website, suggesting that personal websites are predominantly used by those offering in-person services whether that be escorting, BDSM or massage, either solely or in combination with other services. In terms of the advantages of having a personal website, some sex workers spoke about how this freed them from having to rely on escort advertising sites, especially those that dominate the market, which meant they did not have to pay regular fees to those or deal with any technical or administrative problems that they felt could be encountered. As well as reducing overall reliance on other forms of escort advertising, many of the interview participants talked about how advertising via their own website gave them more freedom to express themselves and be clear about the services they offer, as Kay, who provides escort services, noted:

> So, the two, there's two main benefits to having a website, really. One is that Platform 1 has lots of rules and regulations about what you can say and what you can't say, so I wanted my own site so that I could put exactly what I needed to put on it.

It was also clear from interviews with sex workers who operated their own personal websites that being able to develop strong 'branding' was a key advantage and reason for their site. Amber, a 25-year-old sex worker who provides escort, massage, BDSM and other services, talked about how her website enabled her to take advantage of her 'niche' and allowed her to 'differentiate [her]self' in a crowded market. Similarly, 38-year-old Liam, who provides erotic massage services, felt that creating a strong brand through his personal website proved lucrative in terms of attracting clients that were specifically interested in the type of service he offered:

> What I've found is that people who come through my website are people who are directly interested in the service that I offer . . . Whereas people who came through much more generic websites, like Platform 18 or Platform 21 will often say, "And can you also do this? Can you also do that? Can you give me this? Can you give me that? I want this, I want it next time." Whereas now I get, I would say, pretty much the clients that I want to see. You know, I've created a product that – and a business that is now – is now attracting the people that I want to attract.

The ability to more clearly and directly brand their service through a personal website was seen as a major benefit for those who had one.

Dating and hook-up platforms were another space where services could be advertised and contact made with customers (Ljungberg 2017). These formed into two categories: a minority with designated commercial advertising spaces where sex workers can advertise their services openly and a majority that have policies prohibiting advertising for paid sex yet still feature such advertisements. Use of dating and hook-up sites in this way was more common among male sex workers in the BtG study, indeed use of dating sites to sell sex has been addressed in previous work by Tyler (2016) who charts the changing ways in which male sex workers advertise their services since the advent of the Internet. Tyler noted that men who used dating sites to sell sex often do this opportunistically rather than setting out necessarily to build a business as a sex worker. This was reflected among some of our participants. Some respondents did not use any paid sex work advertising sites because of the expense involved and advertised exclusively on free platforms, including dating sites and classified sites.

Classified advertising platforms are online advertising spaces/forums that allow individuals to post user-generated advertisements for a range of goods and services. Some classified sites permit sex work advertising and have dedicated and separate space for these while others prohibit it altogether. The use of signs and codes was also evident in the covert use of classified sites by male sex workers. For male sex workers, advertising themselves as a masseur was identified as a key strategy for subverting the restrictive rules on classified sites prohibiting adult advertising. Talking about his advertising on a classified site that forbids adult advertising, Mac observed that he "advertised as body massage, so that way people think they're getting a whatsit and then you'll always get contacted and asked how much do you charge – and then when you turn up to the job they don't even want a body massage". Ruz, 27 years old and who provides escort services, echoes this when he describes how on classified sites he is "saying like 'masseur' but everybody knows anyway when they like message me. They always ask for extra and it's always included of course."

It was rare in our interviews with female sex workers for them to discuss covert use of dating and classified sites to advertise sexual services in the same way as male sex workers did. Platform 33, a classified site that forbids adult advertising, was used by 21% (n = 26) of the cisgender male sex workers who responded to our survey but just 4.5% (n = 21) of the cisgender female sex workers. Classified sites that permit open adult advertising were, however, used more by female sex workers, although in relatively low numbers according to the results of our survey. For example, just 15.6% (n = 73) of women who responded to our survey used Platform 32, a key UK-based classified site that permits adult advertising. There were also mixed opinions on the effectiveness of this advertising source among female sex workers. Jill, 53 years old and who provides escort, webcamming and other services, said that Platform 32 was the most important advertising source for her and she got more business from that site than any of the others. Lavy and Helen, both migrant sex workers, used Platform 32 as their only source of advertising and were satisfied with the level of business it brought them, yet this was a classified site that had a specific section for escorts that had been developed by the company and no covert presence was required. Other sex workers were more critical of classified sites and felt that they produced a lot of time wasters and 'low-quality' clients because, as 37-year old Eloise, who provides escort and erotic massage services, says,

> [T]hey're not really genuine guys looking for punt, but they're on there looking for a new car or a washing machine and then they think, oh, I'll just go in adult section that's on there and piss about, you know what I mean?

The reasons sex workers gave in qualitative interviews for adopting different marketing strategies were varied and decisions on how to engage with the Internet were influenced by a range of factors. These included practical considerations like financial outlay and privacy concerns but the study findings also show how structural factors such as migration status and educational background may also impact choices and decisions. A range of sex workers use social media platforms such as Twitter, Facebook, Instagram and Snapchat to market themselves and their services and to network with customers and peers and it is to this networking with other sex workers that we now turn.

Networking, peer support and advocacy

Online spaces have become vital for connectivity enabling sex workers to network and access peer support and advocacy. In the survey of sex workers, 61% of respondents (n = 391) strongly agreed and a further 19.7% (n = 126) tended to agree that the Internet gave them access to such networks and support. When survey participants were asked about the main websites or online platforms they used for advice or support, those identified by the highest proportion of respondents were sex worker forums. There are a number of forums utilised by sex workers for advice about how to make best use of specific online advertising platforms but where wider peer advice can be accessed. One particular forum (45.7%, n = 211) was most frequently identified in our survey when respondents were asked which online sources they use to access advice. Several sex worker-led forums have been established by UK sex workers to facilitate peer information-sharing and support. Sex workers can register, read threads that relate to issues they are interested in, and post requests for advice. The second online platform most identified for advice by 39% (n = 180) of respondents was one of the longest established and was the second most popular source identified by women in our survey (45.7%, n = 165). A forum more recently established, specifically for UK-based gay and bisexual male escorts and masseurs, was the most popular form of support for male sex workers in our survey by over a third (39.3%, n = 24). The type of sex work job individuals performed shapes forum use and in open-ended survey data and interviews respondents identified forums they utilised that were specifically for workers performing certain jobs, such as erotic dancers, webcammers and BDSM providers.

Forums play an important role in fulfilling the advice and support needs of a considerable section of Internet-based sex workers but use varies, with some workers using them regularly and others only more occasionally. The safety benefits of forum membership include information-sharing about customers, warnings and access to safety buddies. Other main benefits identified with respect to forum participation included combating the isolation of lone working, getting practical information from peers, a space to socialise with colleagues and a sense of community, plus providing a particularly useful resource for 'newbies' with little experience of sex work. Some sex workers choose not to participate in forums due to concerns about privacy and anonymity, a view that tensions and conflicts between sex workers could take place in these spaces or because they already had the information and support they required.

In our survey, 34% (n = 157) said they used Twitter and 16.2% (n = 75) used Facebook for advice and support. A key trend among online sex workers is the use of social media platforms and free messaging apps, such as Whatsapp, to form private groups for professional networking, support and sharing safety information. These groups varied in size: some had a large membership and geographical reach, others were smaller and localised or were formed by small groups of close colleagues or friends working in the sector. These closed online networks provided many of the same benefits of the established sex worker forums, including reducing the isolation experienced by independent lone workers. Some respondents saw these networks as more personalised spaces that gave the option for smaller networks to form. While we cannot explore this in any depth here, an important finding was that increased online connectivity between sex workers has continued to enable sex worker activism (Ray 2007a), with online platforms being utilised creatively by sex workers in the UK as a vehicle for advocacy and activism around sex worker rights and as a tool for collective and individual voices (Sanders et al. 2018).

Policing online sex work

Existing research on the policing of sex work has focused on the policing of sectors of the sex industry that have visible locations such as brothel-based sex work and street sex work (Feis-Bryce 2018). In the UK context, BtG was the first national study to focus specifically on the policing of Internet-enabled sex work (Sanders et al. 2018). One key finding was the majority of police participants were aware that sex markets had undergone changes in the past decade, but detailed knowledge of the nature and extent of these changes and of developments in Internet-based sex work was variable. Many police service areas identified their work on the policing of online commercial sex markets as in its infancy. Two key reasons were identified for this: that the policing of sex markets had historically been focused on more visible aspects of sex work, such as street-based work, often responsive to complaints or concerns raised, and also that a lack of resources limited the development of policing in this sector. Overwhelmingly, policing of online markets to date focused on female sex work and few police mentioned male sex work.

The two main ways that police services were engaging with online markets were in relation to their responses to sex trafficking and wider public protection agenda. The majority of police activities in relation to online platforms, which had or were taking place, were doing so within the sex trafficking policing portfolio. During the period BtG fieldwork was being carried out, sex trafficking emerged as a priority for national government with a number of initiatives to identify victims of trafficking coordinated by national policing entities, specifically the National Crime Agency, taking place, these involved forces throughout the UK. This meant that within local force areas a higher priority was being placed on policing modern slavery of all forms, including slavery within the sex industry. Generally, there was less awareness of the independent/voluntary nature of much online sex work and, with the focus on sex trafficking made salient, issues of labour protections and the safety of those sex working of their own volition a lower priority. Thus, for example, online intelligence-related searches and 'mappings' carried out by some police were primarily focused on issues related to safeguarding against sex trafficking, with assumptions sometimes made that migrant sex workers are by definition victims of trafficking. This picture may be contrasted with the voices of migrant sex workers interviewed for the BtG study, many of whom presented a diversity of reasons for engaging with sex work that were quite similar to those presented by UK nationals participating in the research.[7]

Moreover, police activities targeting sex trafficking and exploitation could impact the working practices of consensual sex workers and could have implications for their safety and privacy. A primary element of activities in relation to monitoring sex markets was the identification of certain indicators of vulnerability and exploitation. There was some consciousness among officers that certain indicators used by the police to identify trafficking or sexual exploitation might also identify sex workers who were not trafficked or otherwise exploited, although this was not the intention of specialist teams. The potential implications of police actions related to sex trafficking also involving those working of their own volition include disruption of sex workers' business, as well as stigmatisation and potential threats to their safety if they are forced to work differently or to move from their current premises because their privacy has been compromised or due to increased reluctance to trust and report crime to the police.

Within this wider public protection agenda and safeguarding work, some police consider online sex work specifically within the remit of policing 'vulnerability' (Brown and Sanders 2017) and identified that among online sex workers were those who experienced a number of vulnerabilities. This could include sex workers whose involvement in sex work meant that they were targeted by a range of individuals aiming to exploit and harm sex workers, making them a 'vulnerable' group, for some forces this did include targeted violent and other crimes against sex workers. Community development and liaison work with the online sex work community was less common, with few police services involved in targeted initiatives to build trust in the police among online sex workers, including increasing the level of crime reporting to the police among people working in this sector. Only a minority of police referred to specific cases of crimes against online sex workers, including digitally facilitated crimes such as online abuse, harassment and abuse that had been reported to them and investigated.

The large majority of police officers were of the view that crimes against Internet-based sex work were under-reported to them, which was confirmed by findings from the sex worker survey (Sanders et al. 2017). Only a minority of police pointed to approaches in which they had ongoing community development work with sex workers and projects to build trust to better facilitate reporting of crime or exploitation. Proactive work with the online sector beyond the sex trafficking agenda was rare, although one police service[8] stood out in terms of such work. This had been enabled by a government grant to develop policing in the online sector under a safeguarding approach that had a focus on developing more trusting and confidence in the police among sex workers to increase reporting of crime through specialist police liaison officers and work with local support projects.

Police interview participants acknowledged inconsistencies in the interpretation of laws relating to sex work and noted that a key concern was to ensure greater safety and protection for sex workers. There were mixed views about how sex work should be regulated, but there was general agreement among police interviewees that sex workers' safety and protection should be paramount. Only a small number of police participants felt there should be more stringent regulation of websites advertising sexual services. Others felt this could reduce cooperation between sex workers, police and websites, make it more difficult to identify and investigate those who exploit sex workers such as organised crime groups, driving the sector underground and possibly on to the Dark Net, making it even more challenging for police forces. Yet several police felt online advertising platforms should be more proactive in measures to safeguard against exploitation, trafficking and slavery. One of the issues raised by all groups of research participants including police officers was the way in which the UK laws relating to managing or assisting in the management of a brothel and 'controlling prostitution for gain' can be enforced in ways that may impact negatively on sex workers based collectively. The majority of officers identified the need for a more strategic approach to sex work that does not penalise sex workers or involve activities that make the sex industry even more hidden and hard to reach, creating a context in which levels of confidence in the police and reporting are more likely to increase.

Conclusion

In the UK and globally, online and digital technology has transformed the sex industry. Sanders et al. (2018) have illustrated how, among other things, these technologies have created new forms of advertising/marketing for adult services, new forms of commercial erotic labour, new business models for sex workers and third parties involved in the sex industry and new tools for sex workers to utilise as part of their safety repertoires. At the same time, the move online has created vehicles for digitally enabled forms of abuse and violence against sex workers, accordingly presenting new challenges for policing and wider regulation.

In this chapter we have described how new forms of sexual commerce, online sex work spaces, marketing strategies, working practices, professional networking and peer support have emerged during the last decade in the UK. These have been shaped by online and digital technologies. Future technological innovation, alongside other changing socio-political dynamics, will continue to reshape sex work in the UK and globally where markets will merge, flourish, diverge and change in a very fast-paced technologically oriented point in capitalism. Sanders et al. (2018) capture the dynamic nature of contemporary Internet-based sex work, such that

> developments will already be underway which morph and change the way the online sex industry operates, both from internal technology features to other statutory changes in policing, methods of regulation and even perhaps legal changes. Therefore, the digital sex markets are always in a state of flux, responding to the market, influenced by the political landscape and exploited by those intent on causing harm as well as by the ingenuity and creativeness of the 'tech savvy' sex workers who create new business spaces and opportunities within the shifting online terrain.
>
> *(Sanders et al. 2018, 163)*

We are eager to see what happens to the organisation of the sex industry in the next decade as new forms of technology, possibly ones that we have yet to imagine, alter the terrain of commercial sexual services, sexual behaviour and consumerism.

Notes

1 Bondage, domination, sado masochism – some sex workers are specialist providers of BDSM services working as, for example, dominatrices, submissives or other specialist roles. Note some of these can be provided in person and also indirectly mediated by digital technology.
2 In webcamming the models perform shows, often but not always including nudity or sexual content, in front of their webcams, which are then streamed to customers watching on their own personal devices (computers/tablets/phones).
3 Phone sex chat is not an innovation of the digital age but we classify it as a form of indirect Internet-based sex work because it has also evolved with technological innovations.
4 Instant messaging involves sex workers providing a text chat service to customers. It operates like text messaging where the sex worker and customer communicate via typed messages on their personal devices. Some adult platforms facilitate instant messaging and allow the sex worker and customer to receive messages from each other without having to share any contact information as the messages are sent through a facility on the website. Instant messaging is charged by the messages received from the sex worker and there are character limits per message.
5 'Modern slavery' was a policy priority for the UK government at the time of our research fieldwork and this was reflected in policing priorities and roles. For example, most police service areas had named strategic leads for modern slavery. The Modern Slavery Act 2015 encompasses all modern slavery offences in the UK including slavery, servitude, forced labour and human trafficking. It makes reference to specific laws on trafficking for sexual exploitation, introduced in the Sexual Offences Act 2003. In this chapter though we use the term sex trafficking to refer to trafficking for sexual exploitation and wider 'slavery' offences in the context of commercial sex. We have done this because this chapter is part of an international volume, which includes contributions from people working across many different linguistic and cultural contexts and this term is the most salient.
6 Platform 16 was found to be the market leading website for male sex workers with 76.6% (n = 96) of cis male survey respondents using this site.
7 Although it should be acknowledged that the survey and interviews may only have reached a small number of migrant workers and not those who may have experienced trafficking or modern slavery, who are harder to reach.

8 Within the UK context, England and Wales together are split into 43 separate areas for policing, referred to commonly as forces, constabularys or services. In addition, for the whole of the UK there are two further services, the Police Service of Northern Ireland and Police Scotland. In this chapter we are using the term police services.

References

Brown, K. and Sanders, T.L.M. (2017) 'Pragmatic, progressive, problematic: addressing vulnerability through a local street sex work partnership initiative', *Social Policy and Society*, 16 (3), 429–441.

Capiola, A., Griffith, J.D., Balotti, B., Turner, R. and Sharrah, M. (2014) 'Online escorts: the influence of advertised sexual orientation', *Journal of Bisexuality*, 14 (2), 222–235.

Castle, T. and Lee, J. (2008) 'Ordering sex in cyberspace: a content analysis of escort websites', *International Journal of Cultural Studies*, 11 (1), 107–121.

Cooper, E. (2017) 'On-Street, off-street and online: the dynamic liminalities of sex work'. Paper presented at the Displacing Sex Work Conference, 15 March, Aalborg University, Copenhagen.

Cunningham, S., Sanders, T., Scoular, J., Campbell, R., Pitcher, J., Hill, K., Valentine-Chase, M., Melissa, C., Aydin, Y. and Hamer, B. (2017) 'Behind the screen: commercial sex, digital spaces and working online', *Technology in Society*. www.sciencedirect.com/science/article/pii/S0160791X17302117.

Feis-Bryce, A. (2018) 'Policing sex work in Britain: a patchwork approach'. In Sanders, T. and Laing, M. (eds) *Policing the sex industry*, 19–37. London: Routledge.

Jones, A (2015) 'Sex work in a digital age', *Sociology Compass*, 9 (7), 558–570.

Lee-Gonyea, J.A., Castle, T. and Gonyea, N.E. (2009) 'Laid to order: advertising on the internet', *Deviant Behavior*, 30, 321–348.

Ljungberg, E. (2017) 'Liquid, invisible and always available? Sex work and mobile communication'. Paper presented at Displacing Sex Work Conference, 15 March, Aalborg University, Copenhagen.

Pitcher, J. and Wijers, M. (2014) 'The impact of different regulatory models on the labour conditions, safety and welfare of indoor-based sex workers', *Criminology & Criminal Justice*, 14 (5), 549–564.

Pitcher, J. (2015a) 'Direct sex work in Great Britain: reflecting diversity', *Graduate Journal of Social Sciences*, 11 (2), 76–100.

Pitcher, J. (2015b) 'Sex work and modes of self-employment in the informal economy: diverse business practices and constraints to effective working', *Social Policy and Society*, 14 (1), 113–123.

Pruitt, M.V. (2005) 'Online boys: male-for-male internet escorts', *Sociological Focus*, 38, 189–203.

Ray, A (2007a) *Naked on the internet: hook-ups, downloads and cashing in on Internet sexploration*. Emeryville, CA: Seal Press.

Ray, A. (2007b) 'Sex on the open market: sex workers harness the power of the internet'. In Jacobs, K., Janssen, M. and Pasquinelli, M. (eds) *C'lickme: a netporn studies reader*, 45–68. Amsterdam: Institute of Network Cultures.

Sanders, T. (2005) 'It's just acting: sex workers' strategies for capitalising on sexuality', *Gender, Work and Organization*, 14 (4), 319–342.

Sanders, T. (2008) *Paying for pleasure: men who buy sex*. Cullompton, UK: Willan.

Sanders, T., Connelly, L. and Jarvis-King, L. (2016) 'On our own terms: the working conditions of internet-based sex workers in the UK', *Sociological Research Online*, 21 (4), 15.

Sanders, Teela, Jane Scoular, Rosie Campbell, Jane Pitcher and Stewart Cunningham. 2017. *Internet sex work: beyond the gaze*. Cham, Switzerland: Palgrave Pivot.

Sanders, T., Scoular, J., Campbell, R., Pitcher, J. and Cunningham, S. (2018) *Internet sex work*. Basingstoke, UK: Palgrave Macmillan.

Sharp, K. and Earle, S. (2003) 'Cyberpunters and cyberwhores: prostitution on the internet'. In Jewkes, Y. (ed.) *Dot cons: crime, deviance and identity on the internet*, 36–52. Cullompton, UK: Willan Publishing.

Smith, N. and Kingston, S. (2015) *Policy-relevant report: statistics on sex work in the UK*. Birmingham and Lancaster, UK: Universities of Birmingham and Lancaster.

Tyler, A.P. (2014) 'Advertising male sexual services'. In Minichiello, V. and Scott, J. (eds) *Male sex work and society*, 82–105. York, UK: Harrington Park Press.

Tyler, A.P. (2016) *Men selling sex to men: representations, identities, and experiences in contemporary London*. PhD, London South Bank University.

Walby, K. (2012) *Touching encounters: sex, work, and male-for-male internet escorting*. Chicago, IL: University of Chicago Press.

53

Justice-oriented ecologies

A framework for designing technologies with sex work support services

Angelika Strohmayer, Mary Laing, and Rob Comber

Introduction

A decade of austerity in the UK has seen a reduction of funding in the charity sector, referred to in the UK as "the third sector." These funding cuts, alongside the neo-liberal policies of successive governments, have moved forward the ways in which digital technologies are discussed in relation to supporting and improving existing infrastructures and ways of working in the third sector. There has been a push towards digitalization, with funding available to develop technologies, and a growing space in the tech world for those who want to design with and for the third sector, matched with a lack of funding in the charity sector for sustaining existing technologies, up-skilling charity staff, or the purchase of smartphones, computers, software, or other technologies. This has resulted in significant gaps between the promise of digital technology and meeting the needs of charity organizations.

One specific challenge involves a lack of mutual understanding regarding what this kind of technology design and development work can look like, what it means, and how it can be done. This comes from both sides: charity staff may lack detailed understanding of the ways in which digital technologies are designed and developed, and technologists may lack an understanding of the complexity of the space they are aiming to innovate within. This mismatch in knowledge and understanding can lead to "technological solutionism" where technologies are seen as the simple solution to solving complex socio-technical or socio-cultural developments or as the "easy" replacement of (often vital) human interactions. This is problematic as it over-simplifies *wicked problems* (Buchanan 1992; Rittel and Webber 1973; Zimmerman, Forlizzi, and Evenson 2007) or problems that are (nearly) impossible to solve due to difficulties in recognizing incomplete, constantly changing, or contradictory requirements, but also because it often assumes all beneficiaries have technology skills and digital literacy, as well as access to technologies such as smart phones.

Rather than attempting to design simple solutions to complex concerns, we look beyond this simplistic model of technology design with and for charities in this chapter. Instead, we explore the complexity of sex work support services and the opportunities that arise through this to develop ways in which digital technologies can be designed *not to replace services, but rather to support* existing infrastructures for harm reduction. In doing this, we look beyond direct service delivery and explore the ways in which digital technologies are already being used in charities to better understand how new interventions can fit into existing ecologies. This provides us with windows of opportunity for innovative uses of digital technologies as well as their sustainable implementation. We have written elsewhere about how the use of digital technologies can support and facilitate social justice outcomes in these charities, urging researchers and designers working in this space to design not only for direct service delivery, but for multidimensional uses of harm reduction, sustainability, and wider advocacy implications in relation to, for example, stigma (Strohmayer, Laing, and Comber 2017).

In this chapter, we explore these considerations by discussing justice-oriented ecologies; where we see the spaces in which design work is carried out—in this case charities—as complex and evolving agents of justice. Based on this, we strive to work towards a more nuanced discourse of designing and developing digital technologies with and for charities for their service delivery and advocacy work. We do this by presenting and reflecting on two recent projects. By providing examples of justice-oriented ecologies that we have worked within and reflected on, we are then able to ask open and provocative questions surrounding the ethics, methodologies, and pragmatics of research, design, and development to reflect on these ecologies. We want to encourage others researching, designing, and working in these spaces to ask themselves these (and similar) questions when working with sex work support services and in cognate third-sector spaces.

Technologies and sex work support services

Technologies and digital infrastructures can provide new opportunities for charities to rethink organizational control (Tilson, Lyytinen, and Sørensen 2010) or potentials for justice (Strohmayer et al. 2017). Furthermore, technologies can themselves generate new infrastructure to challenge existing structures (Tilson et al. 2010). They are also scalable, and possess upward flexibility; meaning that with digital technologies we can imagine the creation of almost any application or service (ibid.).

There has been a growing body of literature in disciplines such as human–computer interaction (HCI) and social work, which addresses particular elements of digital infrastructures in charities, which are explored below. These projects have often focused on designing to support the delivery of a particular task within charities. For example, there has been some work carried out on digital feedback systems (Dow et al. 2016, 2017), improving infrastructures for communication between staff and service users of a shelter for homeless women (Le Dantec and Fox 2015), or the use of digital technologies as elements of service delivery in *Hollaback!* a charity fighting street harassment (Dimond et al. 2013). Others have looked at supporting the operational work of the third sector, for example, designing digital technologies for accounting and transparency with charities (Marshall, Kirk, and Vines 2016).

There is also a growing body of work exploring the ways in which sex workers themselves use digital technologies, with much of the recent literature focusing on sex workers who work online. This can include research exploring working conditions (Sanders, Connelly, and King 2016), but can also include work looking more broadly at the ways in which digital technologies have been incorporated by sex workers into their working lives (Jones 2015; Sanders et al. 2018). Others have explored the ways in which the use of digital technologies could affect policy or law (Ashford 2009; Cunningham and Kendall 2011). However, these literatures focus on the ways in which sex workers use technologies, rather than the design processes of these.

Work with sex work support services proves less diverse. Research has been carried out in India to design a phone broadcasting system for urban sex workers in Bangalore to improve an NGO's outreach work (Sambasivan, Weber, and Cutrell 2011), and another piece of work has been carried out in Zambia to collect the fingerprints of sex workers to make accessing personal health records simpler (Wall et al. 2015). This shows, that in instances when considering technology design and use in support services, these technologies can be seen as tools of informing sex workers about health concerns or even tracking them for personal health-related reasons. We argue that this is not enough: digital technologies that are designed with sex work support services should strive to support sex workers in more diverse ways where various levels of justice and harm reduction intersect and produce fertile grounds for innovation.

When reviewing the literatures surrounding the technology use of sex work support services and the literatures surrounding the evaluation and design of digital technologies for service delivery in charities more broadly, we learn that few examine charities as holistic entities or agents for justice. Too often the evaluation of existing, or design of novel, interventions and digital artefacts of service delivery is the focus of these projects leaving the wider roles technologies can play unexplored. Looking at charities as ecologies and exploring the social interactions and wider implications of technologies within these contexts, however, allows us to build more nuanced understandings of the charities, their service delivery, and ultimately the digital interventions that are developed with and within them.

Justice-oriented ecologies

In order for newly adopted technologies to be useful for service delivery and not to simply reinforce existing power imbalances to amplify exclusion (Toyama 2011), they need to be embedded in the service, to follow "just sustainabilities" (Dombrowski, Harmon, and Fox 2016) where attention is drawn to systemic rather than individual concerns, and be accessible for all (i.e. not furthering the digital divide). A shift towards the exploration of charities as ecologies that do not only provide (digital) services, but that are also agents of social and criminal justice (Bryce et al. 2015; Kam 2014; Strohmayer et al. 2017), would allow researchers to not only evaluate, but also design technologies and interventions that look beyond direct impacts such as, for example, cost savings in service delivery and towards wider justice implications of the digitally supported work charities carry out (Strohmayer et al. 2017). With this we mean that when we look beyond the most obvious places where technologies can be implemented, we begin to look for places where the implementation of these technologies become useful and meaningful for the sex work support service and their organizational (infra)structures. In turn, this means we begin to work with existing expertise, assets, and resources, which should then result in improvements for sex workers who are supported by these organizations.

To enable this kind of work, we use the framework of Information Ecologies (IEs) (Nardi and O'Day 1999). This framework was developed in HCI and describes a localized system of actors, values, technologies, and practices that help us better understand human activities alongside technologies within these localized systems. This means that instead of looking only at technologies, we explore the actions that occur in relation to these technologies within the complex ecology of relationships, actors, practices, and values. To be able to design technologies within these complex and interconnected ecologies requires immersion within the particular IE to provide "a local habitation" (Nardi and O'Day 1999, 55).

Adding to this framework the aforementioned view of seeing charities as agents of justice (Feis-Bryce 2015; Kam 2014) allows us to see charities that develop the use of digital technologies to facilitate a holistic change in their services. In such a justice-oriented ecology individuals, policies, and technologies work together to establish ecologies of service delivery, advocacy, and critiques of existing structures. Through this framework, we look at sex work support services as holistic ecologies providing pathways towards justice for sex workers. The work is underlined by a strong belief in social justice, an attempt to engage in projects that reframe "technologies in charities" into justice-oriented ecologies that aim to facilitate movements towards more socially just research spaces and worlds (Dombrowski et al. 2016; Fraser 2007; Strohmayer et al. 2017).

Furthermore, research that is conducted in this way should not only result in novel interactions with technologies that are meaningful to those involved in the process, but also that these interactions demand "new ways of accounting for difference in inequity at the societal scale" (Dombrowski et al. 2016)—that the technologies become *just*, or truly sustainable designs. We see potential for (co-)designing innovative ways in which digital technologies could support existing service delivery and organizational practices, for *useful* designs. Here we see *useful* as something that promotes and supports the sex work support service provider in their service delivery and sex worker rights advocacy. Below, we use this framework of justice-oriented ecologies and describe the ways in which we developed and deployed digital technologies with two charities in the UK.

Understanding the ecology

Throughout the rest of this chapter, we provide two examples of projects that use the framework of justice oriented-ecologies to design and deploy digital technologies with sex work support services. Both of these are examples of work that is taking place in ongoing collaborations between the sex work support services and us as researchers. We explore the ecologies within a national charity in the UK called National Ugly Mugs, as well as one of their members, a local project called Girls are Proud and Male Action Project (GAP/MAP) that works within a national charity called Changing Lives. Through the exploration of their ecologies we reflect on the ways in which they engage with digital technologies through their service delivery, dissemination of work, and in research collaborations with us as HCI researchers and designers.

When we started working with both of these charities, they were very open with us in discussing their expertise in service delivery as well as their lack of expert knowledge regarding certain digital technologies. In these discussions, however, they were often explicit in their curiosity and willingness to learn about technologies, and in some cases had told us how they had already started to do this. Both were curious and excited about the prospects of using digital technologies in more innovative ways and have started researching and using digital technologies beyond our collaborative projects with them.

As part of the research process, we wanted to not only provide the charities with technologies that they would be able to continue to use after we had finished the project, but we also wanted to ensure that charity staff had the skills and confidence to work with these (and other) technologies once we had left the field. As such, throughout the project, staff often asked us to help them with their use of these and other technologies—for example by helping them with website analytics, or answering questions they had about other types of technologies they had read or heard about—and we often asked them questions about the work they do and attended training they offered where this was available. Through this exchange of expertise, in which we shared our knowledge of digital technologies with them, and they shared their expertise in service delivery with us, we were able to build up mutual confidence in relation to technologies, service delivery, and the ways in which these two spaces can interact. Below, we provide an overview of these projects to first build an understanding of the research space to co-design technologies to fit within and support the existing justice-oriented ecologies.

National Ugly Mugs

National Ugly Mugs (NUM) is a charity whose aim is to end violence against sex workers. They do this by providing access to justice and protection for sex workers in the UK through a digitally facilitated peer-alerting system, training police and other service providers, and through consensual sharing of intelligence with police forces. We have been working with NUM since December 2015 to explore the ways in which they utilize digital technologies to facilitate their service delivery and advocacy work. We have done this through a comprehensive evaluation of their existing services (Strohmayer et al. 2017) where we carried out ethnographic fieldwork in the NUM office, formal interviews, and countless informal chats with each member of staff. We also exchanged phone calls, emails, text messages, direct messages on Twitter, and public tweets to discuss different elements of their service delivery and the process to redesign their website and digital systems. We also carried out work with some of their members, as well as sex workers who are not members but benefit from their services, such as by receiving NUM alerts through a charity that is a member of NUM. We carried out all of this work to better understand the charity and the role technology plays as part of their everyday interactions with members, police, funders, policymakers, academics, and others. This evaluation also enabled us to develop implications for design for the development of digital technologies with sex work support services (Strohmayer et al. 2017).

As part of this work, we designed a new digital system with NUM that incorporates disparate technologies and digital services they used—turning their initially fragmented software usage into a centralized system. This allowed us to support the existing ecology in a meaningful way, to support the work they are doing through judicious changes to their existing use of technology while simultaneously supporting existing structures, organizational policies, and ways of working. Here we want to focus on two ways in which the new digital infrastructure is able to support the existing ecology: efficiency and identity. With the changes we are implementing in the system, we support staff in being able to do their job more easily and without having to switch between many different digital services. With this, we hope to improve the digital technologies staff are using; making administrative tasks—such as the approval of new members—faster and easier to complete, which ultimately allows staff to have more time to work on service delivery, such as the following up on reports and the creation of alerts.

We help to provide a more holistic organizational identity via design work involved in the redevelopment of their online identity, including the use of color, symbols, and other illustrations that are used in the new system. This work brings together the advocacy and service delivery they perform, making clearer their role as an organization: one that aims to end violence

Figure 53.1   Examples of illustrations made for National Ugly Mugs.

against sex workers through harm reduction service delivery and advocacy. For example, in Figure 53.1 we provide three examples of the types of artwork we produced for the website: these include symbols of the sex worker rights movement and incorporate elements of care, solidarity, and service delivery, as well as activism, advocacy, and support.

Girls Are Proud/Male Action Project

One of the organizational members of NUM is Changing Lives, which administers the two previously mentioned projects Girls are Proud and Male Action Project (GAP/MAP). They provide services to support people engaged in sex work, survival sex, or experiencing sexual exploitation and work across a large conurbation in the North East of England. They use a people-focused approach to support men and women involved in sex work, and those exposed to survival sex and/or sexual exploitation. They do outreach and drop-in work, but also provide more structured support for individuals and groups.

We have been working with Changing Lives since the summer of 2016 to design a digital toolkit for emotional well-being with staff, volunteers, and their service users. Through meetings and discussions with staff, creative workshops with service users, and participation in parts of their service delivery we continue to build a nuanced understanding of the organization and their complexities of praxis and politics. Here we want to focus on one particular use of digital technology within this toolkit. GAP/MAP service users, staff, and other supporters organized the first Red Umbrella March to honour International Day to End Violence Against Sex Workers in the city. We wanted to support this action and through conversations with staff decided to facilitate the collection of localized experiences and voices of those who took part in the march. The first author, and another researcher from Open Lab, took part in the march and also took part in the service afterwards that was organized by GAP/MAP and their service users. It was here that we provided a reflexive activity for those who participated in the march. This activity was repeated in 2017 when the first author of this chapter attended both the march and commemorative service again, continuing to work on the archive.

We asked participants to decorate wooden umbrellas, place these on a plastic box, press a button, and then record their audio-message to the umbrella. With the help of radio-frequency identification (RFID) tags and a bespoke open-source audio-recording tool called JigsAudio (see http://jigsaudio.com for more information) we were able to map audio recordings to umbrellas (see Figure 53.2 for pictures of this process). This allows us to create a multimedia installation that brings together craft, technologies, and voices of those who identify either as sex workers, as engaged in survival sex, or having been sexually exploited. This creates a hybrid space where the physical and digital become one and interact with one another. The umbrellas and messages can be displayed in physical and digital ways: a screen can present the webpage that was developed to link the umbrellas, and stories can be exhibited next to the tangible artefacts created by our participants.

This reflexive activity started a process of creating a living activist archive (Ferris and Allard 2016). Describing this as a living activist archive, we use the term *living* to make clear that this is an activity that took place in December 2016 and 2017, but that will also hopefully continue to *live on* beyond then. To define the term *activist archive* we make use of two particular pieces of work: Ferris and Allard's sex work database (Ferris and Allard 2016) and Harris' account of archives and archivists in the context of South Africa's transition from apartheid to democracy (Harris 2002). Activist archives embrace and emphasize that archives are socially constructed spaces of struggle over meaning-making (Ferris and Allard 2016) and a "crucible of human experience, a battleground for meaning and significance, a babel of stories, a place and a space of complex and ever-shifting power-plays" (Harris 2002, 85).

Figure 53.2 Pictures taken at the production of the Red Umbrella Archive: the creation of umbrellas (top left), using JigsAudio (top right), and a picture of the website ready to use (bottom).

Particularly when placing an archive in a justice-oriented ecology, such archives can be a tool to operationalize "particular social justice objectives" (Ferris and Allard 2016, 192). With this we mean that we hope to use the artefacts and collection of stories as a tool for advocacy, for power shifts in expression of thought. Since this activity was placed in a context of service delivery of the charity, we forefront the voices of sex workers and other GAP/MAP service users. Similar to Ferris and Allard's sex work database, we see the umbrellas, recordings, and the website that was subsequently created as a translation of our activist intentions into tangible manifestations that are useful for service delivery (the production of these artefacts, and the potential use of these artefacts), but that can simultaneously be used as tools for advocacy through, for example, an exhibition or sharing elements on social media.

Working towards justice-oriented ecologies

Both of these charities, like many others, use mundane technologies (such as email, SMS and other messaging applications, and telephone services) to communicate with beneficiaries, other staff, or research collaborators. Yet they also engage in the use and development of novel technologies. As outlined above, they have taken part in projects that bring about changes in potential futures with digital technologies in their organizational contexts (Tilson et al. 2010), in service delivery, advocacy work, and ultimately justice-oriented ecologies. Here we want to take a brief sidestep to make clear we do not claim that it is or was only our work that "established" these justice-oriented ecologies the charities work within. We see our role here as supporters of these existing ecologies and hope to facilitate reflection to support movements towards improved praxis, reflection, technologies, and ultimately a more socially just world.

By working collaboratively with the charities, we strove to understand the ecology we were working in, reflect on this, and then introduce digital interventions that play a role in the charity beyond their immediate use. With this we mean that while the technologies are useful for the purpose they were designed for (either to streamline existing processes, or to develop a living activist archive), they can also be useful within the justice-oriented ecology in other ways. For example, with the redevelopment of the NUM website we emphasize the connection between their service delivery and advocacy work through the visual design work. In our project with GAP/MAP, producing umbrellas facilitates a novel way of collecting hyper-localized client voices and disseminating these in diverse spaces through the interactivity of the hybrid space that is created by the tangible artefacts (the umbrellas) and digital infrastructure (the website).

These wider uses of the technologies become particularly meaningful when looking more closely at the importance of just sustainabilities (Dombrowski et al. 2016). Both of the projects were developed in collaboration with the charities; the project choice, research methods, and use of digital technologies were developed in collaboration with staff and service users. This collaborative process allows us to reflect on the sustainability of these projects, and we were able to support the charities on their journeys to becoming more digitally aware and confident. This became particularly clear in our interactions with staff from GAP/MAP. When we first showed them JigsAudio they liked the idea but asked us to take charge of the activity; but after the event took place and many who took part in the march sat and ate together, one of the members of staff asked us whether we could give her some extra umbrellas and a spare JigsAudio so she could repeat the same activity the following year; in 2017, we carried out the activity again together. While our provision of materials can encourage the continuation of the building of this technology, we cannot provide materials for GAP/MAP to continue the activity indefinitely. Having said that, the project has turned into the development of a research relationship between Open Lab and GAP/MAP that continues in the shape of different types of projects as well as a more nuanced and creative understanding of digital technologies focusing on the ways in which they could be used in service delivery and as a tool to bridge this with advocacy work.

With this example, we mean to show that when engaging with charities as justice-oriented ecologies where the *interactions* surrounding technologies (rather than the technologies themselves) are the focus of the projects, we can achieve an integration of digital technologies in socio-technically complex spaces that allow for meaningful interactions, rather than technological solutionism. How this manifests in these two projects is yet to be seen, but by ensuring that the technologies are situated within and can be sustainably incorporated into the existing digital ecologies, we believe we have laid some of the groundwork for these just sustainabilities.

Reflecting on justice-oriented ecologies

Technologies in charities do not work independently of service delivery, but rather are part of an emerging justice-oriented ecology: technologies are introduced, adapted into, and developed within, the practices of the charities. Taking the justice-oriented ecologies and the importance of just sustainabilities (Dombrowski et al. 2016) within this into account allows us to ask questions not only about the ways in which charities themselves work within this framework, but also to change the ways in which we look at digital service delivery. Below we provide some questions that accompany us on our ongoing journey to developing new meanings of technologies in service delivery. We continue to rely on these in our continued work with NUM, GAP/MAP, and other sex work support services and hope they are valuable for others designing, researching, or working to design and deploy digital technologies with sex work support services, and charities more broadly as well. These questions are framed as open and provocative ethical, methodological, and pragmatic questions that we do not claim to have definitive answers to; we do however provide a brief discussion of the questions outlining the ways in which we dealt with them in the two examples outlined above.

- How genuinely meaningful and useful is the digital intervention for the service provider and their beneficiaries?
- How do we ensure sustainability of the project we are working on with charities; and how can they continue to be useful to the charities once we as researchers and designers have left the field?
- What role do we as researchers and designers play in facilitating digital skills development for charity staff and volunteers?

We worked very closely with the charities while developing the projects outlined above. In this way, we were able to embed ourselves (to different degrees and in different ways) and become more contextually aware of the charity, their existing practices and interests, as well as their availability of resources. Throughout this process the first author in particular functioned as a "critical friend" who was able to support the charity but simultaneously question (and sometimes critique) current practices to better understand the ways in which technologies could be useful. In this way, we were also able to design digital technologies that would be useful to the charity after we had left the field.

When taking into consideration the *use* of the technologies that we design and deploy with charities, we also need to consider what skills members of staff, volunteers, and beneficiaries already have. Coming back to the argument of the "critical friend" we ask what the role of the researcher is in relation to up-skilling participants in the use of technology. At the same time, we also question whether it is actually our role as researchers to help develop existing skills or to point out that, for example, using social media to facilitate discussions online is a digital skill that the organizations may already utilize.

We ensured that, as part of both of the projects, staff, volunteers, and members/service users of the charities had not used the technologies we decided to work with in our projects. Also, in both cases, the levels of detail needed to be able to efficiently use the technologies differed greatly. In relation to the NUM project, we need to ensure that we provide sufficient training (both in in-person and in written formats) for them to be able to use the technologies relatively quickly. Their new digital system for service delivery depends on our technologies, so we need to make sure we provide sufficient (and to a certain degree continued) support for them. The GAP/MAP project is slightly different, as JigsAudio is very easy and straightforward to use. Going through the process of recording an audio message to an umbrella once, is probably enough to understand the way the technology works. Where a training element becomes important however is in the move from the tangible artefacts to the digital archiving through the website. It is here that we again need to ensure that we provide sufficient written and verbal training to ensure they are confident enough to carry out this activity without our support.

Conclusions

In this chapter we aimed to look beyond digital technologies that are employed in sex work support services (or charities more broadly) as "silver bullets" to solving complex socio-cultural, socio-ethical, and socio-technical problems. Instead we draw on literatures from various disciplines to provide a novel way of exploring the potential uses of technologies in these spaces as justice-oriented ecologies. In this way we strive to work toward exploring the complexities of sex work support services to develop ways in which interactions with digital technologies can support existing infrastructures or modes of service delivery. In turn, this will benefit sex workers who are members or service users of these organizations in more nuanced and complex ways. We provide two examples of projects we are involved in that work in this way and include a brief discussion of reflexive questions. We ask these of ourselves, and want to encourage researchers, designers, and others working in this space to also ask themselves these (and other similar) questions.

We are very aware that digital infrastructures for different charities or support services vary greatly. Through our personal and academic experiences, we have heard of underfunding of digital technologies, and the lack of access and skills associated with novel devices, software, or interventions. It is exactly for this reason that we frame our work in the way we do. We hope that other technologists, charity staff, and researchers working in this space take into consideration the design of digital technologies in charities as a holistic process rather than parachuting in and out of the charities to deploy "shiny" technologies that do not integrate with existing practices. We would like to encourage researchers working with sex work support services to take into consideration the role their research can play when working with these charities, particularly in relation to supporting service delivery and advocacy work to ultimately support sex workers.

We do not claim to have developed a taxonomy of the types of technologies that should or should not be designed with sex work support services, rather we provide a framework that has been useful for us in working in this space. This framework allowed us to avoid building technologies that fall into the trap of technological solutionism, and rather facilitate holistic learning around potentials for digital interventions in charities that function as justice-oriented ecologies. We continue to work on these kinds of projects and through this also continue to develop our understanding of service delivery, advocacy, and digital technologies. We continue to learn of new ways in which these seemingly disparate spaces can intersect to create a more inclusive and holistic picture of "service delivery" with and for sex workers.

Finally, we want to take a step back from our discussions of technologies in sex work support services. The idea of justice-oriented ecologies we have discussed above stems from justice-oriented interaction design and HCI's information ecologies, and as such is focused on the interaction around technologies. At the same time however, it is also aimed at those working on interventions in sex work support services of any kind, not just digital ones. We believe that any intervention aimed at supporting sex workers can make use of exploring the research and design space (i.e. the charity or its service provision) as a justice-oriented ecology and the questions we provide in this chapter. As such, this chapter not only contributes to HCI literatures, but also to wider research surrounding the development of sex work support services.

We argue that future research and engagements that explore (digital) interventions in sex work support services should regard charities as justice-oriented ecologies that provide harm reduction services for sex workers. Furthermore, the collaborations that are built could be constructed as "effective alliances" (Ferris and Allard 2016, 192) between academia, charities, their service users, and other allies to continue to support and contribute to efforts of sex worker rights advocates to eliminate whore stigma, violence against, and the underlying marginalization of sex workers. In sum, anything placed in these justice-oriented ecologies should strive to work alongside charity staff, volunteers, beneficiaries, and supporters to make meaningful and useful contributions to stakeholders involved in the projects.

Acknowledgments

We would like to take this opportunity to thank our collaborators at National Ugly Mugs and Changing Lives, their beneficiaries, and volunteers in supporting the projects described in this chapter and their feedback on this manuscript. We would also like to say thank you to Janis Meissner for the invaluable support with the Red Umbrella Archives project, to Zander Wilson for allowing us to make use of his JigsAudio technology, and to Tom Nappey, Ed Jenkins, and Rob Anderson for the continued support through the design work with NUM. This research was funded through the EPSRC Centre for Doctoral Training in Digital Civics (EP/L016176/1). Some data may be accessible under appropriate agreement.

References

Ashford, Chris. 2009. "Male Sex Work and the Internet Effect: Time to Re-Evaluate the Criminal Law?" *Journal of Criminal Law* 73 (3): 258–280. doi:10.1350/jcla.2009.73.3.573.

Bryce, Alex, Rosie Campbell, Jane Pitcher, Mary Laing, Adele Irving, Josh Brandon, Kerri Swindells, and Sophie Safrazyan. 2015. "Male Escorting, Safety and National Ugly Mugs." In *Queer Sex Work*, edited by Mary Laing, Katy Pilcher, and Nicola Smith. Abingdon, UK: Routledge.

Buchanan, Richard. 1992. "Wicked Problems in Design Thinking." *Design Issues* 8 (2): 5. doi:10.2307/1511637.

Cunningham, Scott, and Todd D. Kendall. 2011. "Prostitution 2.0: The Changing Face of Sex Work." *Journal of Urban Economics* 69 (3): 273–287. doi:10.1016/j.jue.2010.12.001.

Dimond, Jill P., Michaelanne Dye, Daphne Larose, and Amy S. Bruckman. 2013. "Hollaback!" In *Proceedings of the 2013 Conference on Computer Supported Cooperative Work—CSCW '13*, 477. New York: ACM Press. doi:10.1145/2441776.2441831.

Dombrowski, Lynn, Ellie Harmon, and Sarah Fox. 2016. "Social Justice-Oriented Interaction Design: Outlining Key Design Strategies and Commitments." *Proceedings of the 2016 ACM Conference on Designing Interactive Systems*. ACM, 656–671. doi:10.1145/2901790.2901861.

Dow, Andy, John Vines, Rob Comber, and Rob Wilson. 2016. "ThoughtCloud." In *Proceedings of the 2016 CHI Conference on Human Factors in Computing Systems—CHI '16*, 3625–3636. New York: ACM Press. doi:10.1145/2858036.2858105.

Dow, Andy, John Vines, Toby Lowe, Rob Comber, and Rob Wilson. 2017. "What Happens to Digital Feedback? Studying the Use of a Feedback Capture Platform by Care Organisations." In *Proceedings of the 2017 CHI Conference on Human Factors in Computing Systems—CHI '17*, 5813–5825. New York: ACM Press. doi:10.1145/3025453.3025943.

Feis-Bryce, Alex. 2015. "Why the Third Sector Must Be Political." *Huffington Post*. www.huffingtonpost.co.uk/alex-feisbryce/third-sector-politics_b_7783312.html.

Ferris, Shawna, and Danielle Allard. 2016. "Tagging for Activist Ends and Strategic Ephemerality: Creating the Sex Work Database as an Activist Digital Archive." *Feminist Media Studies* 16 (2): 189–204. doi:10.1080/14680777.2015.1118396.

Fraser, Nancy. 2007. "Re-Framing Justice in a Globalizing World." In *(Mis)recognition, Social Inequality and Social Justice*, edited by Terry Lovell, 17–35. Abingdon, UK: Routledge.

Harris, Verne. 2002. "The Archival Sliver: Power, Memory, and Archives in South Africa." *Archival Science* 2 (1–2): 63–86. doi:10.1007/BF02435631.

Jones, Angela. 2015. "Sex Work in a Digital Era." *Sociology Compass* 9 (7): 558–570. doi:10.1111/soc4.12282.

Kam, Ping Kwong. 2014. "Back to the 'Social' of Social Work: Reviving the Social Work Profession's Contribution to the Promotion of Social Justice." *International Social Work* 57 (6): 723–740. doi:10.1177/0020872812447118.

Le Dantec, Christopher A., and Sarah Fox. 2015. "Strangers at the Gate." In *Proceedings of the 18th ACM Conference on Computer Supported Cooperative Work & Social Computing—CSCW '15*, 1348–1358. New York: ACM Press. doi:10.1145/2675133.2675147.

Marshall, Matthew, David S. Kirk, and John Vines. 2016. "Accountable: Exploring the Inadequacies of Transparent Financial Practice in the Non-Profit Sector." In *Proceedings of the 2016 CHI Conference on Human Factors in Computing Systems—CHI '16*, 1620–1631. New York,: ACM Press. doi:10.1145/2858036.2858301.

Nardi, Bonnie A., and Vicki L. O'Day. 1999. *Information Ecologies: Using Technology with Heart*. Boston, MA: Massachusetts Institute of Technology.

Rittel, Horst W.J., and Melvin M. Webber. 1973. "Dilemmas in a General Theory of Planning." *Policy Sciences* 4 (2): 155–169. doi:10.1007/BF01405730.

Sambasivan, Nithya, Julie Weber, and Edward Cutrell. 2011. "Designing a Phone Broadcasting System for Urban Sex Workers in India." In *Proceedings of the 2011 Annual Conference on Human Factors in Computing Systems—CHI '11*, 267. New York: ACM Press. doi:10.1145/1978942.1978980.

Sanders, Teela, Laura Connelly, and Laura Jarvis King. 2016. "On Our Own Terms: The Working Conditions of Internet-Based Sex Workers in the UK." *Sociological Research Online* 21 (4): 1–14. doi:10.5153/sro.4152.

Sanders, Teela, Jane Scoular, Rosie Campbell, Jane Pitcher, and Stewart Cunningham. 2018. *Internet Sex Work: Beyond the Gaze*. New York: Palgrave Macmillan. doi:10.1007/978-3-319-65630-4.

Strohmayer, Angelika, Mary Laing, and Rob Comber. 2017. "Technologies and Social Justice Outcomes in Sex Work Charities: Fighting Stigma, Saving Lives." In *Proceedings of the 2017 CHI Conference on Human Factors in Computing Systems—CHI '17*, 3352–3364. New York: ACM Press. doi:10.1145/3025453.3025615.

Tilson, David, Kalle Lyytinen, and Carsten Sørensen. 2010. "Research Commentary—Digital Infrastructures: The Missing IS Research Agenda." *Information Systems Research* 21 (4): 748–759. doi:10.1287/isre.1100.0318.

Toyama, Kentaro. 2011. "Technology as Amplifier in International Development." In *Proceedings of the 2011 iConference on—iConference '11*, 75–82. New York: ACM Press. doi:10.1145/1940761.1940772.

Wall, Kristin M., William Kilembe, Mubiana Inambao, Yi No Chen, Mwaka Mchoongo, Linda Kimaru, Yuna Tiffany Hammond, et al. 2015. "Implementation of an Electronic Fingerprint-Linked Data Collection System: A Feasibility and Acceptability Study among Zambian Female Sex Workers." *Globalization and Health* 11 (1): 27. doi:10.1186/s12992-015-0114-z.

Zimmerman, John, Jodi Forlizzi, and Shelley Evenson. 2007. "Research Through Design as a Method for Interaction Design Research in HCI." In *Proceedings of the SIGCHI Conference on Human Factors in Computing Systems—CHI '07*, 493. New York: ACM Press. doi:10.1145/1240624.1240704.

54

Selling sexual services in the digital age

Flexible work opportunities for the self-employed entrepreneur or precarious unregulated labour?

Helen Rand

Introduction

Transmitted to customers on devices such as smart phones, laptops and tablets, technology-mediated services are rapidly changing the way many people in Britain access services in a number of industries, from ride-sharing to food delivery, and increasingly also the ways in which many people find work, from cleaning and construction work to professional work such as lawyers and accountants.[1] In the sex industry, technology-mediated services have made a significant impact on both customers and providers of sexual services. Technology-mediated sexual services include indirect services that have been around since the 1980s such as telephone sex, as well as services that have developed with the increased use of smart phones and fast Internet connections such as text messages (SMS), instant messaging (IM) and live video streaming, also known as webcamming (see Table 54.1).[2]

With a focus on Britain, this chapter will explore how the neoliberalisation of the economy and the labour market has benefitted from rapid technology developments and has ultimately enabled the growth in digital sexual service provision. It will then demonstrate the diversification of the online sex market, as technology is expanding and simplifying access to available services, often through the use of digital platforms. For sex workers who have access to an Internet connection and a laptop, creating a viable, money-making online profile is easy with almost instant access to customers through digital platforms. Providers of technology-mediated sexual services can offer a diversity of goods and services to meet the variety of demands from the market. In this chapter, I argue that the new technological forms of the sex industry are part of the so called 'gig economy' and the precarity associated with this form of on-demand labour are heightened because of the stigma and imposed morality associated with selling sexual services.

This chapter draws on a virtual ethnography (Domínguez et al. 2007; Hine 2000) of technology-mediated sexual services that took place from September 2015 to May 2016. During this period I engaged with the world of technology-mediated sexual services through observations of recruitment websites, advice-seeking forums (forums specifically for sex workers and forums that included threads on sex work), client review sites and digital platforms that facilitated the sale of technology-mediated sexual services. Through observations and textual analysis I was able to understand how this section of the sex industry was developing. This led me to focus my online observations on one particular platform that currently dominates the online sex market in Britain, I will refer to this platform as Grown Up Gigs. In August 2017, with colleagues at the University of Essex, data was extracted from Grown Up Gigs to establish the prevalence and demographics of those providing technology-mediated sexual services. Further data collection involved qualitative interviews with 19 technology-mediated sexual service providers, 5 clients of technology-mediated sexual services and a representative from a UK-based sex worker-led advocacy organisation. A year after the initial interviews, I conducted follow-up interviews with 5 providers of technology-mediated sexual services to gain further information for the generation of detailed case studies. The providers interviewed ranged from 23–62 years in age. The majority (n = 13) of sexual services providers were female, five were males and one person self-identified as having a fluid gender. To the best of my knowledge all those who took part in the study were consensually providing sexual services and had the economic capital to afford accommodation and a reliable Internet connection.[3] All the clients interviewed for this research were male. Three brought services only from women, one brought services from women and men and the other only from men. Their age ranged from 34–60 years.

Technology-mediated sexual services in context

The ethos at the heart of neoliberal Britain is a more contemporary version of the Protestant ethic, which regards each and every individual as responsible for one's own fate. Contemporary and severe contractions of the welfare state and the expansion of the free market have actively pushed individuals, through shifts in dominant cultural ideals as well as massive cuts to various forms of social support, to become self-sufficient entrepreneurs who contribute to the state while requiring no support from it (Harvey 2007; Ong 2007). This cultural shift, alongside technological developments, has impacted labour markets and the organisation of work, including sex work. The result is that non-standard forms of work, such as temporary contracts, self-employment and part-time work, are increasing and as Beck (2000) predicted, work that is full-time, permanent, unionised and subject to state labour regulations is diminishing. The growth of non-standard forms of work and technological developments have led to what Guy Standing (2017, 211) refers to as 'platform capitalism', also known as the 'gig economy', whereby digital platforms match workers with those seeking services, acting as 'labour brokers'.

In line with these shifts in the organisation of labour, I approach the provision of technology-mediated sexual services as a form of online demand labour, as part of the so-called 'gig economy' where workers are paid for a particular task or 'gig' and are not employed by the platform or an individual beyond the time limit of the task. As a result the worker is not protected by labour laws. However, acting as a labour broker, digital platforms take a percentage of the fee paid to the worker, ranging from 10% to 30%, depending on the platform (Standing 2017). Facilitated by a digital platform, online demand labour takes place remotely where the client and the worker are connected virtually (iLabour Project 2017). When the customer 'demands' or requires a service they are able to instantly connect via technology to a worker who is willing and available to perform the task required. This includes clerical work, software development, data entry and customer services.

This is slightly different from another form of on-demand labour – local on-demand digital labour. This refers to piecemeal work facilitated by an online platform or app. In local on-demand labour, the platform connects a client with a local worker as and when services and tasks are required (iLabour Project 2017). For example, this includes home improvement tasks, car rides, food delivery and beauty services. In reference to sex work, one could describe escorting or direct sex work facilitated by a platform as local on-demand digital labour – as the service requires the client and the worker to meet. However, technology-mediated sexual services is a form of online demand labour, as the service takes place remotely, connected by the Internet and/or mobile technology (see Table 54.1).

Table 54.1 Typology of technology-mediated sexual services

Webcamming	Webcamming is a sexual performance that is transmitted online via a small camera that is either built in or attached to a computer. The explicit nature of the performance depends on the provider – ranging from partial nudity to full sexual intercourse with another person. It can be understood as an online peep show. Webcam performances are available in different online spaces including online platforms that offer a variety of sexual services, such as Grown Up Gigs. The business model adopted charges customers per minute to view the show either in a group scenario, where more than one customer pays per minute to view the show or a private show, where the customer pays more per minute for a more explicit or intimate performance. Webcam performances are also available on webcam only platforms. The platform provides an online space for the interaction between the customer and the webcam provider. These platforms commonly adopt a business model that is based on free performances with the customer paying 'tips' to encourage the webcam provider to take off more clothes, for example.
Telephone calls	Erotic telephone calls connect the provider and the customer either online using platforms or offline services using mobile technology. In both cases the customer pays per minute for the service. Offline services use premium rate phone numbers where the cost is added to the customers' telephone bill, as well as prepaid services from a mobile or landline. As a form of sex work available before the Internet these services still exist but are decreasing in popularity. Online platforms, such as Grown Up Gigs offer telephone services facilitated by the platform known as 'direct chat', as well as prepaid telephone calls that operate through a telephone connection or Skype.
Text messages/SMS	Similarly to telephone calls, text messages are between the customer and the provider connected via the Internet or mobile technology. The customer pays per text, often with a premium put on the first text message. Text services are available from businesses that only provide this service and operate using a premium rate text number. In addition, online platforms such as Grown Up Gigs offer text messages that are transmitted via the platform to the paying customer's mobile phone. The customer replies to the text from their mobile phone and pays for the service via the platform's payment system. The provider is paid per text and neither party is aware of their personal phone numbers. Text messages may include photographs.
Instant messages	Instant messages (IM) are similar to text messages for provider and customer in that the communication is in the written form, but are only available online. The interaction takes place via the online platform using a computer and is billed per minute rather than per text. Providers may offer text and IM services as a standalone service, however more commonly, text and IM services form part of a portfolio of sexual services and are used as a way to establish rapport, discuss a further potential transaction and use the communication as an opportunity to decide if the customer is 'safe' and authentic.

Here, I establish a connection between new forms of sex work and the 'gig economy', and I argue that sex workers are being silenced in current policy discussions on the risks (and opportunities) of the so called 'gig economy'. For example, a recent report commissioned by the British government, the Taylor Review (2017), found that 'gig work' attracted more men than women. By not including sex work(ers) in the discussion the findings of this report and other reports are omitting a significant section of those who provide online on-demand labour (for further examples of this exclusion see Chartered Institute of Personnel and Development 2017 and Balaram et al. 2017).

Risks and opportunities

Online demand labour is characterised by uncertain hours and unstable income with no career or wage progression because workers are only paid when the market needs them. 'Gig economy' workers have no contracts and no direct employer, yet workers are still beholden to code of conducts and working conditions set out by the platform (De Stefano 2016). The same precarity applies to providers of technology-mediated sexual services, who have no contract with the digital platform that facilitates the exchange, but pay a 30% fee for each transaction. The 'contract' is directly with the client for a bounded period of time, meaning that there is no guarantee of income as providers' capacity to sell their services is driven by market demands from clients. Anita (female, telephone and text provider, aged 52) explains that some days she operates at a deficit, she makes no money and ends up paying the platform to advertise her services. She has responded to this by generating new ways to make more money:

> I wasn't getting that many calls. Some days I was getting five calls and then other days, I don't get any calls. Some days I might not get nothing at all [income]. So just try to implement and make sure I am covering my costs basically. I have started selling things. Just underwear, knickers. Cos you have to pay. Do you know how much Grown Up Gigs charges!?

The goods Anita and others sell on the platform is subject to the same 30% transaction fee Grown Up Gigs charges on all transactions. In addition to selling goods on the platform, Anita uploads content to Grown Up Gigs and other platforms such as Twitter, to generate more interest in her profile. The marketing work Anita does is unpaid as she hopes it will generate an income in the future. Among the participants of this research, it was not uncommon for providers of technology-mediated sexual services to work more hours than they are actually paid for, if the hours spent on marketing, managing contacts and technological tasks were included. As Kirsty (female, webcam/phone/text/IM provider, aged 23) states, "literally I am working around the clock. Even though I am not sat in front of the computer I am still working on my phone. That can be hard sometimes."

In addition, working for a 'faceless' digital platform means there are unclear employer relations. Workers do not know the people behind the platform and communication between workers and the platform managers is limited. Therefore it is unclear to what extent the services the platform provide for their transaction fee – such as administrating the payment system, maintaining the technology, marketing and so on – can be relied upon in the long term. Some participants were concerned about the precarity of working for Grown Up Gigs observing that they could not rely on this as a stable form of income:

There was some kind of cyber attack. Apparently they didn't get through the fire walls so no personal details got released, but it was the equivalent to the site being hit a hundred thousand times a second I think. It is just like somebody was just targeting their site which actually made it go down for ten days I think. That could really mess you up. So that again made me think I can't rely on that. Another confirmation I cannot rely on it as permanent income, as your only source of income.

(Paul, male, webcam, phone provider and escort, aged 45)

Unpaid work-for-labour, large (and changeable) transactions fees and unclear employer relations are experiences common to many workers involved in the 'gig economy' (Standing 2017). However, it can be argued that the precarity of this labour is more extreme for those providing sexual services because of the known stigma and associated impact of stigma for those who sell sexual services (Sanders 2005), as well as the impact of stigma on individuals when and if they choose to leave the sex industry (see Bowen and Bungay 2015). Megan (female, webcam provider, aged 23) experienced direct discrimination because of her association with the sex industry. She was fired from her job while working in a school to gain experience after graduating because the head teacher had found out she was webcamming. Megan's work as a webcammer was seen as a character flaw rather than an economic activity, deeming her inappropriate to work with children. The risk of being 'outed' was a recurrent theme in the interviews with providers. For some, their work as providers of technology-mediated sexual services was secret, however the visible nature of the Internet means disclosure is a significant risk. Rachel (female, webcam provider and escort, aged 31) had been 'outed' because she has an online profile. She was recognised in the gym and at her parents wedding anniversary party. She explains:

It has happened twice. Once online, he said I saw you at the gym and I had been at that gym that morning so I blocked and deleted him. Also at my parents wedding anniversary and someone said hello Rachel. Luckily Rachel isn't my real name so I denied all knowledge. If it had got out it would have been reasonably contentious . . . I just had to brazen it out.

Rachel further reflected on the risks of stigma:

It could ruin your career. You have to really think about what the risks are if it all went wrong, whether it could do you over in the future. If you want to adopt children, you'll find it very difficult because you have to fully disclose. Or, if you want to work for the Ministry of Defence, you have to fully disclose everything you've been up to . . . You will have to really think about that to make sure that you're not ever going to regret things, because you, honestly, don't make enough money to do anything you're going to regret because no amount of money is enough money. And no one in that [sex work] gets lots of money.

The nature of the Internet means online content is uploaded fairly easily, quickly and with an instant global reach. As a result, maintaining privacy and controlling an online identity for many of the providers was a concern. The risk of capping – recording and posting images and videos without the permission of the sex worker (Jones 2015) – was particularly concerning for webcam providers. Kirsty (female, webcam, phone, text and IM provider, aged 23) is open with friends and family about her work because she had already been outed: "One of [my] friends found my profile online and all of the people who I was initially worried about seeing, they all knew. So it was like there is no need to hide it anymore". Kirsty said she feels she has limited/no control over her online identity, despite using strategies to take down images and videos that were uploaded without her consent. As she explained,

> On [webcam platform] you have people sat there all night recording you and then posting it online . . . Cos I am the copyright owner so I just filed with the DMCA [Digital Millennium Copyright Act] and they get it shut down within 48 hours, normally. I find out who owns the server of the website and then find the people and then email them directly. I have a formal DMCA letter off the website that is really . . . you know . . . I just put my initials at the end of it, and then usually they get shut down dead quick.

Kirsty was working many unpaid hours to keep on top of this. When I interviewed her a year later, she had resigned herself to the fact this was out of her control and expressed regretfully:

> I think I have just accepted it is just out of my hands. Once it is on the Internet it is pretty much on the Internet. There is nothing I can do about it so I have just accepted it. Otherwise I don't know I was pretty much just spending my whole life trying to get them took down.

The risk of being disclosed as a sex worker is not a new risk because of technological developments, but there are new risks associated with technology because of the comparative ease in accessing images, videos and even personal information online and distributing online content, often without the consent of the sex worker.

However, despite these unstable working conditions and specific risks associated with selling sexual services, providers benefit from the perceived convenience of working at home, exercising more control over their working hours than other forms of employment would likely offer to them, and generating a relatively good income in relation to alternative employment options, including other digital economy work opportunities.

> I am happy to keep doing this whilst I am getting paid. Other things, I just can sign in whenever I want. It just gives me so much freedom to do other things.
>
> *(Anita, female telephone and text provider, aged 52)*

> I work on my terms. Just me really. I manage myself. I am my own boss. Which I love. The money is the best thing of it all.
>
> *(Paula, female webcam provider and escort, aged 38)*

> It gives me flexibility and options to earn more. At least you are still earning something and you have the ability to earn more if you need to.
>
> *(Lucy, female, text provider, aged 43)*

> It's one part funsies and one part – well the real logic behind it is you tell me another way to generate a housing deposit in this fucking market. That's the main reason for my decision to go for it. That's actually it. It all boils down to financials.
>
> *(Joe, fluid gender, webcam provider and escort, aged 27)*

Diversification of sexual services

This chapter focuses on the UK's current market leading platform that offers a range of sexual goods and services, including local on-demand labour (direct sex work) and online demand labour (technology-mediated sexual services), but there is a diversity of online and offline spaces used to facilitate technology-mediated sexual services that use different business models to generate income. There are numerous global digital platforms that offer webcamming services that can be accessed in Britain. These platforms facilitate a space for the provider to perform, while customers watch the performance (often for free) and use online tokens to tip the provider to progress their performance. For example, once the provider has reached a certain amount of tips they may take off more clothes or perform a sex act. The platform takes a percentage of the tips, but it is unclear what percentage the platforms take from each show as performers earn a fixed amount per token (Sanders et al. 2017). Furthermore, there are websites and platforms that target specific customers, such as services for men buying services from men or niche services provided by women with specific body types, race, age and so on. In addition to these online spaces, telephone and text services are also available through mobile technology, providing customers with erotic services to their mobile or landline telephone.

Despite the availability of numerous online and offline spaces, Grown Up Gigs remains the most popular space to sell services. This (almost) monopoly control of the market is not uncommon in platform capitalism, as seen with Uber (Standing 2017). The dominance of Grown Up Gigs means providers of technology-mediated sexual services have little choice but to use the platform. Participants in my research gave a number of reasons for using Grown Up Gigs to generate work. First, the amount of customers instantly available to them was unparalleled to other platforms on the market: "If you want to escort or cam that is the go to site because it is just so well known" (Paula, webcam provider and escort aged 38). Similarly, Megan (female, glamour model and webcam provider, aged 23) performs on Grown Up Gigs as well as a niche site for glamour models where she charges more per minute, but as she explains:

> You could make double the money. But [the platform] isn't that big. But my prices are higher, because it is more like O my god! This girl has been in the papers and this magazine. But the foot traffic is not as much as Grown Up Gigs anyway.

Second, there was a sense that despite the high transaction fee, Grown Up Gigs provided some safety and protection. As Kirsty highlights with her experience of capping:

> It has taken me weeks to get all the videos down since I have been [on alternative webcam platform]. I never had any of that with Grown Up Gigs. It is more safe . . . I didn't realise it was happening until I did a Google search of my user name and then it was all – concentrate on getting the stuff taken down off Google and then going back on Grown Up Gigs. They [customers] are not allowed to do that on Grown Up Gigs. Their profiles get taken down. Grown Up Gigs is more steady [than the alternative webcam platform].
>
> *(Kirsty, female, webcam/phone/text/IM provider, aged 23)*

And lastly, the providers had control over pricing and services they offered, which meant they could diversify their portfolio and ultimately generate more income. The majority of the participants offered more than one service, and several sold goods in addition to services, such as films and videos, as well as erotic fiction and underwear. Grown Up Gigs facilitates the ability to offer multiple services and goods.

The infrastructure and the business model adopted by the different platforms and websites have an impact on how providers of technology-mediated sexual services develop their online presence. In the case of Grown Up Gigs, creating a profile on the platform is not unlike setting up a profile on mainstream social networking platforms, such as Facebook. The profile is self-created and self-edited. The provider simply creates a username, uploads several photographs and adds details such as geographic region, age, body type, hobbies and interests. The provider then chooses from a drop-down menu which services they will provide – webcam, phone, IM, text and/or escorting and sexual preferences, including BDSM, anal, oral, massage and so on. The process is ongoing with providers reporting that they regularly update their profiles, adding more online content in the form of videos, photographs and blog entries, as well as adding items to their online shop. Grown Up Gigs' business model incentivises providers to add more online content by moving the provider's profile up the search outcome and alerting clients each time new content is added. As Anita (female, telephone and text provider, aged 52) explained, Grown Up Gigs charges an additional fee to be on the front page, but if she adds a new blog entry or uploads new photos she is added to the main page for two hours. In addition, the clients that have added her to a 'hot list' are notified of new content on her page, which generates more traffic to her profile, and ideally more business.

Just as creating a profile is similar to mainstream activities, increasingly in the UK people are exchanging sexual content via smart phones, and computers for pleasure rather than as an economic activity (see Clue and Kinsey Institute global survey on 'sexting' 2017). Although this is often considered to be done mostly by adolescents, there is growing evidence to suggest that this is not only their domain (Klettke et al. 2014). This digital sexual activity is unprecedented and many social commentators have suggested that Western society is increasingly sexualised with ordinary people engaging in sexual confessions and voyeurism (McNair 2002), as well as making and circulating sexual images and texts (Attwood 2009). I suggest that the increasing normalisation of technology-mediated sex reduces the transgression attached to making a profit from this same activity. Sylvia (female, webcam, phone and text provider and escort, aged 60) created a profile on Grown Up Gigs not long after joining an over fifties dating site, which she describes as a "cattle market, awful, terrible thing. Offers for free sex from guys, all young guys. Length and breadth of country." Through this mobile app someone suggested to her that she could make money being an escort. She recalls the conversation:

> Look, he said, there is a name for it. Escorting. Enrol on Grown Up Gigs as [pseudonym] and see what happens. I said don't be ridiculous you know. Nobody is going to want an escort over 50. You are wrong he says. You are a really, really good age. So we talked a while and he sort of challenged me, so I was like I'll bloody show you now. Before I enrolled I had never heard of Grown Up Gigs. I enrolled on it. Created a profile, no pictures or anything. Straight away I got a job from a guy from Bristol who was travelling on business. I took my first job and it went extremely well. And I have been working ever since. It turned out to be good work.

As she continues, "it [selling sex] is basically, it is the same as what I do now [casual sex] but got paid for it."

Similarly, Calvin, (male, phone, webcam provider and escort, aged 41) who has been selling sexual services online for four years, described how he was selling a product – himself – on free dating apps in much the same way as he sold services on Grown Up Gigs. "Whether paid or not, I am still selling myself". After spending many years on dating apps/hook up sites he decided he should try to see if he could get paid for doing the same thing. He currently has profiles on several dating apps, but only advertises on Grown Up Gigs for commercial services. Technology can provide a straightforward crossover from non-commercial sexual activity to commercial sexual activity if a person is looking for this transition. The ease of creating a commercial online profile may encourage a broader demographic to engage in selling sexual services. In addition, there is less police scrutiny and reduced risk of arrest than other forms of sex work, as the following section explains.

Regulating technology-mediated sexual services

This section examines the current lack of specific regulation of technology-mediated sexual services. In England and Wales,[4] the act of buying and selling sex is not illegal although it is illegal to profit from a brothel. In 1957, the Wolfenden Report recommended that sexual matters between consenting adults taking place in private were not subject to criminal law. Consequently, regulating prostitution in England and Wales has mainly focused on incivility opposed to morality (Phoenix 2017). From a statutory perspective, sex work has traditionally been understood as problematic if it causes a public nuisance and disturbs the 'decency' of others. Therefore, legislation in England and Wales has historically targeted street-based sex work, criminalising the activities that surround selling sex – such as soliciting and kerb crawling – rather than the act itself. However, since the Criminal Justice and Immigration Act 2008 and Police and Crime Act 2009, the regulation and criminalisation of sex work and pornography have increased (Carline 2011).

For example, from the mid-1990s–2008 Britain witnessed a 'boom' in night-time entertainment venues, including erotic dance venues, in part because of a laissez-faire regulatory approach. Under the 2004 Licensing Act, erotic dance venues were able to operate without any additional requirements compared to other alcohol venues (Brents and Sanders 2010). This, alongside the introduction of American style bars offering lap dancing, led to a significant rise in erotic dance venues with 350 opening over the course of a decade (Colosi 2010), making the presence of erotic dance venues in city centres mainstream (Brents and Sanders 2010). A neoliberal policy of minimum state involvement allowed the market to flourish and made room for entrepreneurs to open many new erotic dance venues.

However – as noted in the literature on sex work – sex work is often open to moral panics and subsequent changes in policy directions (Bernstein 2007; Hubbard et al. 2008; O'Connell Davidson 2015). Feminist groups – such as Object (campaigning to end the objectification of women) and the Fawcett Society (aimed at promoting gender equality) – supported by local residents and MPs, opposed the proliferation of 'gentlemen clubs' in British city centres and campaigned to close them (Hubbard and Colosi 2015). This led to a change in licensing. In 2009, The Police and Crime Act singled out 'sexual entertainment venues' over other licensed venues. Local authorities can now stipulate how many 'sexual entertainment venues' they permit in their jurisdiction. If it is zero – which some local authorities have adopted – they can refuse all new licenses without explanation. The Act acknowledged the moral concerns of some, but did not ban erotic dance venues completely, allowing the market to still thrive and be profitable. As argued by Sealing Cheng (2012), this example captures one of the paradoxes of neoliberalism. The free market is considered amoral, promoting profit and entrepreneurship, but paradoxically, on the ground there is a moral, conservative agenda that singles out and delegitimises certain forms of labour, such as sex work.

Currently, technology-mediated sexual services and sex work facilitated by the Internet are largely unregulated. There is no specific regulation for technology-mediated sexual services, like there is in the Philippines for example where webcamming is criminalised (Cellan Jones 2012). However, in the UK, technology-mediated sexual services do not come under direct scrutiny from law enforcement agencies. It appears that the focus of policies to target visible forms (and spaces) of sex work has not entailed keeping abreast of digital developments in the sex industry

(Sanders et al. 2017). Even, the most recent reports from the British government fail to mention new forms of sex work, such as webcamming, or any other on the Internet (Sanders et al. 2017).

In contrast to this apparent silence, long-standing forms of technology-mediated sexual services (telephone and more recently text services) are legitimised by the regulation of a government body. The Office of Communication (OFCOM), a government regulatory body for the communications industries, oversees premium rate telephone lines,[5] including telephone sex lines. Telephone sex lines are regulated in the same manner as other premium rate numbers – for example, the caller must be over 18 and there is a time/cost limit for each call. Sex lines are singled out, but OFCOM attempts to legitimise this form of sex work, by distancing it from other forms of sex work. The 'code of practice' outlined by the government body specifies that the services must not promote or facilitate prostitution, thereby distinguishing telephone sex work from other forms of sex work. This legislation is outdated because this method of accessing telephone services is increasingly unpopular (Phonepayplus 2014) and the majority of the participants in this study offer direct sex work as well as indirect sexual services. Telephone, text, IM and webcamming are used as a way to 'promote and facilitate prostitution'. For example, Sarah (female, text, IM, phone, webcam provider and escort, aged 38) started providing erotic phone calls for a company that used premium rate phone numbers over five years ago. During this time she only provided telephone services and continued to work as a hairdresser as well. After two years she joined Grown Up Gigs, "When I heard about [Grown Up Gigs] and that I could set my own rates I went on that instead." She found she had more control of her hours and her income. With the telephone company she earned 25–55p per minute, the more hours she logged on the higher her per minute rate was. With Grown Up Gigs she was able to choose her hours and set her own rate at £1.50 per minute. From here she developed her sexual service portfolio.

> The phone chat started first, which kind of led on to the webcamming. A few of my, sort of, customers where in the area, asked me if I did escorting. At the time I didn't, but once I had a bit of rapport with these guys I went to see one of them. And that is really how it all started. Then I kind of progressed to the webcam and then to the escorting.

She has clients that purchase all of the services she offers.

> I have regulars on phone, webcam and escorting. There is a cross over. [A client] will look at me on cam, or if I am not on cam they will phone me up, or do the instant messaging. Couple of my webcammers are guys I go and escort with. There is a bit of crossover.

However, the Internet is viewed by the current government as space that threatens the moral standards of British society and they have taken legislative measures to restrict online content, block websites and control access to adult online content through the age verification process (Tait 2017). Grown Up Gigs and other businesses offering technology-mediated sexual services state they adhere to the definition of 'extreme pornography' given in the Criminal Justice and Immigration Act 2008 in their terms and conditions. Providers reported their profiles had been deactivated if the content they uploaded had violated the Act, further adding to the uncertainty of this work as an income-generating activity. For example, Sylvia (female, telephone, webcam provider and escort, aged 60) regularly writes blogs and uploads them to Grown Up Gigs, as a way to generate interest to her profile. On a number of occasions she has had her profile deactivated because she has included references to animals or "numbers relating to youth". As she explains:

There are certain words you cannot use . . . The computer scans everything so if [the] computer picks up on something they will shut you down automatically. I once wrote about the black horse in the Lloyds advert. And the computer assumed it was bestiality. Then they shut you down. Then you have to wait until a human being goes through it and puts it back up for you . . . The first time it happened I thought what the hell I have done wrong. There is a list of your sexual preferences and you select from their list. And one of the things on their list is xxx which I haven't ticked. I once licked a guy's arsehole and I showed it and put it on my video clips. It is against terms and conditions, you can't do such things but you are allowed to say it is a preference. It's bonkers.

Further legislation will come into effect in April 2018 in the form of the Digital Economy Act, which will implement an age verification process on all adult content websites and platforms. It is unclear how this will impact the working lives of those who provide technology-mediated sexual services, but it is likely to further stigmatise those who provide services labelling them as deviants and a 'risk to children' while simultaneously increasing profits for the owners of the platforms. Wilkinson (2017) recognises that the proliferation of free online porn has meant a decrease in profits in the porn industry. Reducing the number of sites and restricting content through stricter legislation could potentially solve the problem and reduce competition, thereby increasing profits for the few that are able to navigate the system. The concern of the current political agenda is based on morality rather than rights for (sex) workers in a socio-economic context in which workers are pushed further into precarity.

Conclusion

In the current political economy, technology has supported the development of online on-demand sex work through which sex workers can offer a portfolio of services from their own home. Access to this work is fairly straightforward – at least for those who can afford a laptop and an Internet connection – with no start-up fees, no previous experience or qualifications required. The work is not illegal and apparent risks are fairly low with regard to personal safety and criminality. In comparison to other forms of service work, a relatively good income can be generated with providers reporting the flexibility and control over hours and income as significant benefits to this work. However, paradoxically to the reported benefits of this work, like other forms of labour in the so called 'gig economy', providing technology-mediated sexual services is precarious because the income is uncertain and the worker is subject to changes imposed by online platforms. There are also additional risks associated with providing technology-mediated sexual services, such as the persistent impact that stigma has on those selling sexual services, like Megan's account shows; the lack of control of an online identity, as observed by Kristy; and the risk of disclosure, as experienced by Rachel.

Technological developments and radical changes in labour processes have given space for new online models of working. The rise of 'platform capitalism', a business model that extracts large fees from the worker to broker work, has not bypassed the sex industry. Drawing on an existing market – and expanding the market for sexual services – new sexual services (such as webcamming and instant messaging) and established forms of sex work (escorting, as well as technology-mediated sexual services such as telephone and text services) are digitally facilitated by platforms. The digital platforms take a significant, and often changeable fee to broker the sexual interaction between the customer and the sex worker. This work is largely unregulated as a form of (sexual) labour and sex workers are currently marginalised and silenced in political debates on the 'gig economy', reducing opportunities for workers to resist their exploitation, therefore adding to the precarity of their work.

Notes

1 It is difficult to be precise on how many people are currently engaged in work facilitated by technology, and specifically platforms, because the work is often temporary and short term, but the Chartered Institute of Personnel and Development (2017) estimates that 4% of the British working population are currently working in the so called 'gig economy' and a trend that is expected to grow.

2 It should be noted that smart phones are in common use in the UK. Recent commercial research suggests 85% of the adult population own a smart phone (Deloitte 2017). In addition, there is near universal Internet coverage in Britain, although broadband speeds vary significantly across the country (ONS 2017). Therefore, the ability to access technology-mediated services is open to the majority of the population.

3 Two participants reported having to terminate their work during periods of uncertainty, such as staying with a friend while looking for a new home.

4 Scotland and Northern Ireland have devolved powers from the UK's central government to create their own laws on matters of justice and policing. In June 2015, it became illegal to purchase sex in Northern Ireland under the *Human Trafficking and Exploitation Act*.

5 Premium rate telephone lines charge customers a significantly higher rate than an average phone call. Somewhere between 35p to £3.60 per minute. The cost of the call is added to the customer's telephone bill. When adult content telephone calls were first established this was the only way to purchase telephone sexual services.

References

Attwood, Feona. 2009. *Mainstreaming Sex: The Sexualization of Western Culture*. New York: I.B. Tauris.

Balaram, Brhmie, Josie Warden and Fabian Wallace-Stephens. 2017. 'Good Gigs: A Fairer Future for the UK's Gig Economy'. London: RSA. www.thersa.org/discover/publications-and-articles/rsa-blogs/2017/04/making-the-gig-economy-work-for-everyone.

Beck, Ulrich. 2000. *The Brave New World of Work*. Oxford: Polity.

Bernstein, Elizabeth. 2007. *Temporarily Yours: Intimacy, Authenticity, and The Commerce of Sex*. Chicago: University of Chicago Press.

Bowen, Raven and Vicky Bungay. 2015. 'Taint: An Examination of the Lived Experiences of Stigma and Its Lingering Effects for Eight Sex Industry Experts'. *Culture, Health & Sexuality* 18 (2): 186–199. https://doi.org/10.1080/13691058.2015.1072875.

Brents, Barbara G. and Teela Sanders. 2010. 'Mainstreaming the Sex Industry: Economic Inclusion and Social Ambivalence'. *Journal of Law and Society* 37 (1): 40–60. https://doi.org/10.1111/j.1467-6478.2010.00494.x.

Carline, Anna. 2011. 'Criminal Justice, Extreme Pornography and Prostitution: Protecting Women or Promoting Morality?' *Sexualities* 14 (3): 312–333. https://doi.org/10.1177/1363460711400810.

Cellan Jones, Rory. 2012. 'Philippines Outlaws Cybersex and "Cam Girls"'. BBC News. www.bbc.co.uk/news/technology-19659801.

Chartered Institute of Personnel and Development. 2017. 'To Gig or Not to Gig'. Survey Report. London: CIPD. www.cipd.co.uk/Images/to-gig-or-not-to-gig_2017-stories-from-the-modern-economy_tcm18-18955.pdf.

Cheng, Sealing. 2012. 'Embodying the Sexual Limits of Neoliberalism'. *Scholar & Feminist Online* 11.1–11.2. http://sfonline.barnard.edu/gender-justice-and-neoliberal-transformations/embodying-the-sexual-limits-of-neoliberalism.

Clue and Kinsey Institute. 2017. 'Technology and Modern Sexuality: Results from Clue and Kinsey's International Sex Survey'. *Medium* (blog), 9 August. https://medium.com/clued-in/sex-and-tech-survey-33d64ecc3eda.

Colosi, Rachela. 2010. '"Just Get Pissed and Enjoy Yourself": Understanding Lap-Dancing as "Anti-Work"'. In *New Sociologies of Sex Work*, edited by Kate Hardy, Sarah Kingston and Teela Sanders, 181–196. Farnham, UK and Burlington, VT: Ashgate.

Deloitte. 2017. www2.deloitte.com/us/en/pages/technology-media-and-telecommunications/articles/global-mobile-consumer-survey-us-edition.html.

De Stefano, Valerio. 2016. *The Rise of The 'Just-in-Time Workforce': On-Demand Work, Crowdwork and Labour Protection in the 'Gig-Economy'*. Conditions of Work and Employment Series 71. Geneva: International Labour Office.

Domínguez Figaredo, Daniel, Anne Beaulieu, Adolfo Estalella, Edgar Cruz, Bernt Schnettler and Rosie Read. 2007. 'Virtual Ethnography'. *Qualitative Social Research* 8 (3). https://papers.ssrn.com/abstract=2813530.

Harvey, David. 2007. *A Brief History of Neoliberalism*. Oxford: Oxford University Press.

Hine, Christine. 2000. *Virtual Ethnography*. London and Thousand Oaks, CA: Sage.

Hubbard, Phil and Rachela Colosi. 2015. 'Taking Back the Night? Gender and the Contestation of Sexual Entertainment in England and Wales'. *Urban Studies* 52 (3): 589–605. https://doi.org/10.1177/0042098013504006.

Hubbard, Phil, Roger Matthews and Jane Scoular. 2008. 'Regulating Sex Work in the EU: Prostitute Women and the New Spaces of Exclusion'. *Gender, Place & Culture* 15 (2): 137–152. https://doi.org/10.1080/09663690701863232.

The iLabour Project. 2017. http://ilabour.oii.ox.ac.uk.

Jones, Angela. 2015. 'Sex Work in a Digital Era: Sex Work in a Digital Era'. *Sociology Compass* 9 (7): 558–570. https://doi.org/10.1111/soc4.12282.

Klettke, Bianca, David J. Hallford and David J. Mellor. 2014. 'Sexting Prevalence and Correlates: A Systematic Literature Review'. *Clinical Psychology Review* 34 (1): 44–53. https://doi.org/10.1016/j.cpr.2013.10.007.

McNair, Brian. 2002. *Striptease Culture: Sex, Media and the Democratization of Desire*. London: Routledge.

O'Connell Davidson and Julia O'Connell. 2015. *Modern Slavery: The Margins of Freedom*. Basingstoke, UK: Palgrave Macmillan.

Office of National Statistics. 2017. 'Statistical Bulletin Internet Access – Households and Individuals: 2017'. www.ons.gov.uk/peoplepopulationandcommunity/householdcharacteristics/homeinternetandsocialmediausage/bulletins/internetaccesshouseholdsandindividuals/2017#things-you-need-to-know-about-this-release.

Ong, Aihwa. 2007. 'Neoliberalism as a Mobile Technology'. *Transactions of the Institute of British Geographers* 32 (1): 3–8.

Phoenix, Jo. 2017. 'Prostitution and Sex Work'. In *The Oxford Handbook of Criminology*, edited by Alison Liebling, Shadd Maruna and Lesley McAra, 685–703. Oxford: Oxford University Press.

Phonepayplus. 2014. 'The Future for Phone-Paid Digital Goods and Services'. Phonepayplus.

Sanders, Teela. 2005. *Sex Work: A Risky Business*. London: Routledge.

Sanders, Teela, Jane Scoular, Rosie Campbell, Jane Pitcher and Stewart Cunningham. 2017. *Internet Sex Work*. New York: Springer.

Standing, Guy. 2017. *The Corruption of Capitalism: Why Rentiers Thrive and Work Does Not Pay*. London: Biteback.

Tait, Amelia. 2017. 'The UK Has Now Entered a Draconian Era of Porn Prohibition'. www.newstatesman.com/science-tech/privacy/2017/05/uk-has-now-entered-draconian-era-porn-prohibition.

Taylor, Matthew. 2017. 'Good Work: The Taylor Review of Modern Working Practices'. London: RSA. www.gov.uk/government/publications/good-work-the-taylor-review-of-modern-working-practices.

Wilkinson, Eleanor. 2017. 'The Diverse Economies of Online Pornography: From Paranoid Readings to Post-Capitalist Futures'. *Sexualities* 20 (8): 981–998. https://doi.org/10.1177/1363460716675141.

55

Mobile phone technology

Opportunities and perils for female sex workers in India

Subadra Panchanadeswaran,[1] Ardra Manasi, Natalie Brooks-Wilson, Shubha Chacko, Michael Brazda, and Santushi Kuruppu

Introduction

The proliferation of communication technologies has impacted the sex work industry globally in significant ways. Technological development, particularly the Internet and Internet-mediated sex work has been a topic of study for many scholars in the past (Bernstein, 2007; Cunningham & Kendall, 2011; Jones, 2015; Minichiello, Scott, & Callander, 2013; Murphy & Venkatesh, 2006). Some researchers have specifically emphasized the role of telephones and pagers in enabling many sex workers to conduct business indoors, away from the "public gaze" because of the discretion that technology affords to some extent (Lee-Gonyea, Castle, & Gonyea, 2009). Researchers have examined phone-based client solicitation and impact on HIV risk behaviors (Mahapatra, Saggurti, Halli, & Jain, 2012; Navani-Vazirani et al., 2015), while others have underscored technology's facilitation of spatial mobility among sex workers (Aral, St. Lawrence, & Uskula, 2006). Public health interventions have effectively adopted mobile phone technology for women in the developing world and the positive spillovers of this find resonance in the sex work industry too. Some examples include dissemination of psychoeducational information for women living with or at risk for HIV/AIDS, such as female sex workers through the innovative use of telephone broadcasting systems (Sambasivan, Weber, & Cutrell, 2011), and the deployment of mobile phone technology as a data collection tool to elicit real-time information from female sex workers to inform the development of a public health surveillance system (Curioso et al., 2005). On the other hand, there is evidence of the vulnerabilities created by the use of technologies for sex workers including client violence, manipulation, and loss of income (Veena, 2007). Sex workers, activists, and scholars alike have become only too aware of the potentially costly compromises that arise from challenges to female sex workers' privacy owing to phone sharing, male-controlled access and monitoring, and women's fear of violence from male spouses/partners (GSMA 2012a, 2012b; Handapangoda & Kumara, 2013; Lemish & Cohen, 2005; Ojokoh, 2009; Panchanadeswaran, Unnithan, Chacko, Brazda, & Kuruppu, 2017; Pertierra, 2005; Sambasivan, Cutrell, Toyama, & Nardi, 2010).

There is little research on female sex workers' subjective journeys that encompass aspects related to acquisition, learning, and use of mobile phone technology in their personal lives as well as for sex work. In this chapter, we focus on how female sex workers in India have embraced technology and have been active agents in using mobile phone technology to navigate the complex terrain of brothel, street, and home-based sex work. Our work with female sex workers demonstrates the myriad ways that women use mobile phones to straddle the rapidly changing demands within sex work and also to achieve personal goals related to familial and social priorities.

Voices from the ground in India: evidence from a phenomenological exploration

We used a phenomenological approach to examine the holistic experiences of female sex workers with mobile phone technology in two geographical locations in India. The first was Kamathipura in Mumbai, which is known for mostly brothel-based sex workers. The second was Karnataka state, particularly Bengaluru city and the semi-urban and rural areas accessible from Bengaluru city. Access to the sex worker community was enabled through discussions and collaborations with local non-governmental organizations (NGOs), gatekeepers, and through the Karnataka Sex Workers Union. Over a period of five months from January through May 2015, we met 67 female sex workers through in-depth interviews and focus group discussions (for more details about methods and analysis details, please refer to Panchanadeswaran, et al., 2017; Panchanadeswaran, Unnithan, Chacko, Brooks-Wilson, Brazda, Kuruppu, under review). The meetings were held at the offices of the local collaborating non-governmental organizations (NGOs) where they came in regularly to access services and to socialize with other sex workers. In the semi-structured interviews and focus group discussions, we asked women about their experiences of first exposure to mobile phone technology, getting acclimated and learning about technology, and how they used mobile phones. We also explored their perceptions of technology's influence on the sex work industry and the ways in which technology had aided/hindered their work.

Mobile phones and the business of sex work

Female sex workers who live in brothels in Kamathipura in Mumbai generally migrated from other parts of the country. Hence staying connected with their families and often young children in their home towns or villages is very important for most sex workers and it was often this vital need that mobile phone technology met. In the case of the women we interviewed, brothel owners were often one of the first people that initiated them into using mobile phone technology. Fatima, a 22-year-old brothel-based sex worker who was a migrant from Kolkata explained: "Here, *gharwali* [brothel madam] suggested me to take a mobile phone so that I can contact my children and my family members. Then she purchased a mobile for me and then I gave her the money later on." For many other sex workers, clients were the early initiators to mobile phone technology. For the most part, this was predominantly to gain unmitigated direct access to female sex workers especially in the case of brothel-based sex workers, as a 25-year-old migrant from Kolkata noted: "It was a gift from a customer . . . I used to refill the talk time as he was a foreigner, from Saudi. He gifted me the mobile and left." Many women talked at length about the process of gradually adapting to the technology through many mediators, including the phone sellers at the local shops, intimate partners, children, neighbors, and peers in their social network. However, many female sex workers stated that their ease with mobile phone technology was self-taught. A confident 28-year-old migrant sex worker from Bangladesh asserted: "I learned it on my own. Does one need to be taught? When you use the mobile, you get to know . . . looking at people."

The women we spoke to repeatedly underscored their perceptions about the multifarious ways in which mobile phone technology had slowly but assuredly transformed the sex work industry in recent times. It was clear from our observations that in a megapolis like Mumbai and Bengaluru as well as small towns and rural areas, cell phones were pervasive and had become a key mode of soliciting new clients for many female sex workers. Even within a brothel setting, female sex workers effectively used their phones to earn additional income. Minna Bibi, a 30-year-old female sex worker from Kolkata with ten years of working in a brothel in Mumbai described women's efforts to get around the brothel owners' exploitative practices:

> Earlier, there used to be these *gharwalis* who would get lots of customers, they would have contacts. These women would call girls [female sex workers] and take more money from customers and pay the girls less . . . the customer sometimes tries to contact the girl directly, if they try to give their number. The *gharwalis* train the girls to not give or take contact numbers from the customers. [Then gradually] If they [clients] gave the number, I used to take it . . . and get it stored on my mobile by my close friends who knew how to read and write. They would call directly and also pay us directly . . . So, in this case, the mobile is very helpful.

Solicitation patterns through the use of phone-based apps also seemed commonplace as Deepti, another 25-year-old relatively new brothel-based sex worker from Telangana stated:

> Madam [brothel owner] sends photographs with our face, full profile photograph from top to toe. Shows what the girl looks like, her height, her skin color, her figure etc. to the customer via WhatsApp. The customer fixes up a time, price . . . and agrees to come.

We also realized clients used mobile phone technology to circulate female sex workers' names through their networks. Street- and home-based female sex workers in Karnataka state forcefully underscored the use of mobile phone technology and current clients in furthering their reach to newer untapped clients, as one of the participants in a focus group discussion in rural Karnataka stated:

> I wasn't used to mobiles. First I had a lover and I used to call him from a coin booth . . . he told me not to call from a coin booth [pay phone], I'll get you a mobile . . . then he started giving my number to others, one after the other. My number was spread everywhere in this way . . . the number spread [among prospective clients and] . . . due to this, it became a routine for me.

Women's narrations also revealed the ways in which mobile phone technology had enabled easy access to porn for individuals in the sex industry. It was also apparent from our interviews with female sex workers that this instant access to porn often dictated male clients' desire and demands for the type of sexual services. This is evident from the quotes below by street and home-based sex workers in rural Karnataka who participated in a focus group discussion in rural Karnataka:

> Recently, if anyone wishes to watch any dirty video [porn] or a blue film, they do something on the Internet and I've watched some videos on the mobile with them [clients].
>   They showed me the video on the phone and insisted on doing sex in the way they showed in the video . . . Even though I saw them, I told them I cannot do anything like that.

An aspect that came up regularly in our conversations with female sex workers during our meetings was the modality of payment for "talk time." Many women claimed that their insistence to clients to pay for the same resulted in clients' perceptions of unfettered access to women and resulting problems. This was particularly felt by the street-based female sex workers whom we met during the course of our work. Veena, a 32-year-old sex worker in rural Karnataka underscored her helplessness thus:

> They [clients] do get angry . . . [and ask]: I put balance for you, and when I call, why don't you answer the phone? There were people at home and that's why I didn't answer the phone. Another person says, how many times should I call you? Why don't you answer the phone? Have you become so smart? Have you become so proud?

Demands and expectations from clients such as these appeared to necessitate active client management by female sex workers, for which mobile phones were indispensable. Technology-induced pressures seemed to frustrate some female sex workers. Mangala, an articulate home-based sex worker in Bengaluru noted:

> Because of the mobile, this is the torture, when they [clients] need me, they keep on calling me asking me to come. Then I get very angry at them and on the phone. [I feel] why did I buy this phone? I should keep it away or throw it or switch it off and be silent. When I don't have the feeling for it [engaging in sex work], they still force me. Like calling me to come for five minutes or half an hour . . . I feel very angry at this phone.

However, responding and actively engaging with clients seemed inevitable if they did not want to lose clients to other peers given the stiff competition for clients aided by mobile phone technology for female sex workers across settings. Shoma, a brothel-based sex worker who had migrated from Assam ten years back talked about her vigilance: "If I'm not in front of him, and he sees someone else, he'll go . . . [with her]." and Tara Bibi, another street-based female sex worker explained: "If the business happens more for us then they [other female sex workers] become jealous and talk nonsense . . . they say to clients 'her health is not good' . . . this creates problems for us."

Technology-induced vulnerability and gains

Anonymity and safeguarding individual identity is a vital concern for most sex industry participants, particularly sex workers. Many of the female sex workers we spoke to readily acknowledged the intense vulnerabilities that stemmed from their lack of control over the ways in which clients used mobile phone technology. Clandestine filming and photography by clients were highlighted consistently as an omnipresent risk from mobile phone technology. This was particularly significant given the extent to which women zealously protected their identities. Aseema, a brothel-based sex worker who had migrated from Kolkata described an experience: "Once there was a girl in our area whose video was recorded and uploaded [on] the Internet . . . that incident alerted us and now we do not allow the customers to carry mobiles [inside the rooms]."

This kind of vigilance was commonplace among female sex workers that we interviewed. Based on their evaluation of the clients, they appeared to decide on the extent to which they used mobile phones to further the scope of their work. Veeramma, a 40-year-old street-based sex worker in Bengaluru with 20 years of experience in sex work talked about her decisions to cautiously share her mobile phone number with only a few trusted male clients:

People who come and say, *Janu* [sweetie], I'll give you more money . . . Yes, these are 5–6 people I know . . . Then there are some old customers, who've been coming for 4–5 years, I gave them my number. Not to the others.

For street-based female sex workers, the dangers stemming from mobile phone technology seemed particularly severe. Sadly, Mallika, a 26-year-old street-based sex worker in rural Karnataka described her harrowing experience of being violated and exploited by clients:

One client called me stating that you come to this place I will give you money of Rupees 5,000 (approximately $77), for one night . . . I was happy to go . . . When I went to the said place, he came with a car with 3–4 people . . . All three of them were doing unwanted things . . . one was clicking photos . . . I was screaming and howling . . . they tortured me, video-recorded everything. I pleaded with them and held their feet to give back the recording but they slapped me.

Only a few female sex workers, however, were able to speak about thwarting imminent risk by using advanced features on their phones like turning on the GPS to escape from dangerous situations/clients. From female sex workers' accounts, it was apparent that mobile phones posed formidable challenges in their efforts to keep their sex worker identities secret from their intimate partners. For almost all the women we spoke to, it was a complex game of using hidden phones, managing calls from clients, and drawing firm boundaries with persistent clients. However, female sex workers lamented that despite their best efforts, frictions with intimate partners were common as depicted in the following quote by a focus group discussion participant in Bengaluru:

The person who was with me had bought for me [mobile phones] . . . twice and he himself broke them . . . I used to get calls during night . . . I could not talk in front of him . . . he would get angry and ask who are these rascals, calling you? Though I had asked them not to call, they would call me . . . I had given the number to two or three people . . . I had told them that he would be home by seven . . . but even then they would call in the night . . . Then the fights between us would start.

Additionally, given the widespread criminalization of sex work in India, female sex workers reported many strategies to stay extremely vigilant with regard to police raids and arrests where seizing of mobile phones, especially the SIM cards to gain access to the details of clients, was extensively described, especially by street-based female sex workers.

The liabilities of mobile phone technology notwithstanding, female sex workers' narrations also highlighted the intangible benefits of their associations with regular and trusted clients. For many, mobile phones were the vital link to forging deep, long-lasting and meaningful friendships with some clients. And, despite the dynamics of competition arising out of soliciting clients through mobile phones, and female sex workers' need to guard their clientele to secure their livelihoods, we encountered some heartwarming stories about women looking out for each other. A 36-year-old home-based sex worker with over 12 years of experience in sex work talked about her protective instincts towards younger and newer female sex workers: "I tell the girls not to go to their place, but call the men over to their place. Giving them instructions regarding their safety is my duty and hence I do that." Mobile phone technology has undoubtedly enabled women's abilities to build extensive supportive networks and enhanced their capacities to reach out for help when in need. This was ably described by a 40-year-old street-based female sex worker who said: "During crisis situations, no matter where you are, even if they call at 1 or 2 am we communicate through the mobile phone, gather as a group and go and rescue the person." Mobile phone technology appeared to have significantly boosted female sex workers' connectedness with their families, friends, and children given the higher frequency of interactions and real-time information sharing. Phone-induced learning was an often repeated theme in our discussions with women, including literacy skills, as a participant in a focus group discussion in rural Karnataka happily described:

> I didn't know how to sign. I didn't know what A looked like and didn't know any spell-ings. I didn't go to school at all. Slowly I learnt this is A, B, C, D etc. . . . I've learnt this through the mobile.

Not surprisingly, female sex workers seemed to be enjoying the autonomy and the self-directed ways in which mobile phone technology and social media platforms such as WhatsApp had contributed to their uptake of newer skills to click pictures, capture special moments in videos, and share/view the same within their social networks. For many female sex workers, mobile phone technology served multiple emotional and instrumental needs, thus highlighting the indispensability of the instrument despite their acknowledgment of the downsides. A 28-year-old brothel-based sex worker in Mumbai who had migrated from a small village in West Bengal talked about her obsession with her mobile phone thus:

> I play games, listen to music, and watch videos. The mobile phone has both good and bad effects. I talk on my mobile and also take care of it. If something happens to it, then it would be a big problem for me. It is my life now. If the mobile get stolen, then I will be upset. I bought this big mobile only to show my sister and capture some memories through clicking a video.

Concluding thoughts

After listening to female sex workers' narrations from the field in India, we gauged the complex and multifaceted ways in which mobile phone technology intersects with sex work and how it may be justifiably perceived as both a boon and a bane. During the course of our engagement with sex workers, we gleaned that mobile phones have indeed significantly transformed the landscape of the sex work industry in terms of marketing/advertising of sex workers through social media, which has been shown to be common in the case of Internet-based marketing and customer reviews of female escorts (Castle & Lee, 2008), and now appears to be emerg-ing among brothel-, street- and home-based sex workers in India. In addition to changing norms around sexual services provision, a gradual trend of mobile phone-based client solicita-tion offers female sex workers opportunities to deepen their relationships with trusted clients and opens up newer avenues for client networks. Furthermore, similar to findings from other studies around the world (Handapangoda & Kumara, 2013; Lemish & Cohen, 2005; Livholts & Bryant, 2013; Murphy & Priebe, 2011; Pertrierra, 2005; Zainudeen, Iqbal, & Samarajiva, 2010), our conversations with female sex workers revealed the criticality of mobile phones in enhancing marginalized women's abilities to augment their incomes, exercise autonomy, and gain competency with technology by facilitating newer learnings, fostering new connections, and strengthening existing familial and social bonds.

On the other hand, smartphone features including audio, video, and tracking capabilities have placed sex workers in peril, by presenting significant risks to their privacy due to increased surveillance and risk of violence from clients, partners, brothel owners, state actors such as the police, and others in the sex industry in relative positions of power. Using technology consistently to safeguard sex workers from predatory clients may be a key imperative going forward (Feis-Bryce, 2017). Vital to these efforts would be the cautious use of technologies such as closed circuit television cameras that may be ostensibly used to enhance "community safety" but may, in fact contribute to further endanger sex workers and intensify their experiences of surveillance (Wright, Heynen, & van der Meulen, 2015). Another fallout of the mobile phone technology use, as Jones (2015) and Panchanadeswaran et al. (2017) have pointed out, has been the ways in which it has served to push sex workers further underground and increase their isolation, thereby heightening their invisibility and affecting their access to available services.

Given female sex workers' holistic experiences with mobile phone technology, we question any attempt to universalize the impact of technology on sex workers and the sex work industry. Central to this understanding would be the need to recognize the duality of increased autonomy for women along with the danger of violation of privacy and anonymity for sex workers. Here, it is also worth reflecting on the ways in which technology can further serve to criminalize sex workers in the Indian context, often leading to their marginalization and exploitation. In this context, it is critical to acknowledge the need for incorporating sex workers' voices in the development of technology-based policies and interventions. Mobile phone technology is clearly essential to sex workers' attempts to optimally navigate personal and professional relationships. In this light, we argue that female sex workers should be treated as active users of information and communication technologies and emphasize the need to refrain from any overtly paternalistic generalizations of viewing sex workers as mere passive actors and victims in the process.

Acknowledgments

We would like to thank all the participants for generous sharing their insights with us. We also thank the staff and leadership at Navjeevan, Mumbai, Aneka, Bengaluru, and the Karnataka Sex Workers' Union, and all the participant NGO personnel for their participation, commitment, and support to the study.

Note

1 Funding disclosure: Fulbright-Nehru Award for Academic and Professional Excellence to the first author.

References

Aral, S.O., St. Lawrence, J.S., & Uuskula, A. (2006). Sex Work in Tallinn, Estonia: The Sociospatial Penetration of Sex Work into Society. *Sexually Transmitted Infections*, 82, 348–353. doi: 10.1136/sti.2006.020677.

Bernstein, E. 2007. *Temporarily Yours: Intimacy, Authenticity, and the Commerce of Sex*. Chicago: University of Chicago Press.

Castle, Tammy & Jenifer Lee. 2008. Ordering Sex in Cyberspace: A Content Analysis of Female Escort Websites. *International Journal of Cultural Studies*, 11: 97–111.

Cunningham, S. & T. Kendall 2011. Prostitution 2.0: The Changing Face of Sex Work. *Journal of Urban Economics*, 69, 3: 273–287.

Curioso, W.H., Karras, B.T., Campos, P.E., Buendia, C., Holmes, K.K., & Kimball, A.M. (2005). Design and Implementation of Cell-Preven: A Real-Time Surveillance System for Adverse Events Using Cell Phones in Peru. *Amia Annual Symposium Proceedings Archive*, 176–180.

Feis-Bryce, A. (2017). "Ugly Mugs": The Technology Saving the Lives of Sex Workers. www.theguardian.com/voluntary-sector-network/2017/may/10/national-ugly-mugs-the-technology-saving-the-lives-of-sex-workers, accessed March 25, 2018.

GSMA mWomen (2012a). From GMSA mWomen Programme: A Framework for Designing the mWoman Business Case. www.gsma.com/mobilefordevelopment/wp-content/uploads/2013/01/GSMA_mWomen_Business_Case_Framework_Full_Report_-FINAL.pdf, accessed March 2, 2018.

GSMA mWomen (2012b). From Striving and Surviving: Exploring the Lives of Women at the Base of the Pyramid. www.gsma.com/mobilefordevelopment/wp-content/uploads/2013/01/GSMA_mWomen_Striving_and_Surviving-Exploring_the_Lives_of_BOP_Women.pdf, accessed March 2, 2018.

Handapangoda, W.S. & Kumara, A.S. (2013). The World at Her Fingertips? Examining the Empowerment Potential of Mobile Phones Among Poor Housewives in Sri Lanka. *Gender, Technology and Development*, 17, 3: 361–385. doi: 0.1177/0971852413498742.

Jones, A. (2015). Sex Work in a Digital Era. *Sociology Compass*, 9, 7: 558–570.

Lee-Gonyea, J.A., Castle, T., & Gonyea, N.E. (2009). Laid to Order: Advertising on the Internet. *Deviant Behavior*, 30: 321–348.

Lemish, D. & Cohen, A.A. (2005). On the Gendered Nature of Mobile Phone Culture in Israel. *Sex Roles*, 52, 7: 511–521. doi: 10.1007/s11199-005-3717-7.

Livholts, M. & Bryant, L. (2013). Gender and the Telephone: Voice and Emotions Shaping and Gendering Space. *Human Technology: An Interdisciplinary Journal on Humans in ICT Environments*, 9, 2: 157–170.

Mahapatra, B., Saggurti, N., Halli, S.S., & Jain, A.K. (2012). HIV Risk Behaviors Among Female Sex Workers Using Cell Phones for Client Solicitation in India. *Journal of Aids & Clinical Research*, S1, 14. doi: 10.4172/2155-6113.S1-014.

Minichiello, V., Scott, J., & Callander, D. 2013. New Pleasures and Old Dangers: Reinventing Male Sex Work. *Journal of Sex Research*, 50, 304: 263–275.

Murphy, A. & Venkatesh, S. 2006. Vice Careers: The Changing Contours of Sex Work in New York City. *Qualitative Sociology*, 29: 129–154.

Murphy, L.L. & Priebe, A.E. (2011). "My Co-Wife Can Borrow My Mobile Phone!" Gendered Geographies of Cell Phone Usage and Significance for Rural Kenyans. *Gender, Technology and Development*, 15, 1: 1–23. doi: 10.1177/097185241101500101.

Navani-Vazirani, N.S., Solomon, D., Krishnan, G., Heylen, E., Srikrishnan, A.K., Vasudevan, C.K., & Ekstrand, M.L. (2015). Mobile Phones and Sex Work in South India: The Emerging Role of Mobile Phones in Condom Use by Female Sex Workers in Two Indian States. *Culture, Health and Sexuality*, 17: 252–265. doi: 10.1080/13691058.2014.960002.

Ojokoh, B.A. (2009). Empowering Nigerian Women Using Information Technology: Practical Strategies. *EAF Journal*, 20, 1: 58.

Panchanadeswaran, S., Unnithan, A.M., Chacko, S., Brazda, M., Brooks-Wilson, N., & Kuruppu, S. (Under review). What Should We Know About Female Sex Workers' Use of Mobile Phone Technology? Lessons in Effective Engagement from India.

Panchanadeswaran, S., Unnithan, A.M., Chacko, S., Brazda, M., & Kuruppu, S. (2017). What's Technology Got To Do With It? Exploring the Impact of Mobile Phones on Female Sex Workers' Lives and Livelihood in India. *Gender, Technology & Development*, 21, 1–2: 152–167. doi 10.1080109718524.2017.1385318.

Pertierra, R. (2005). Mobile Phones, Identity and Discursive Intimacy. *Human Technology: An Interdisciplinary Journal on Humans in ICT Environments*, 1, 1: 23–44.

Sambasivan, N., Cutrell, E., Toyama, K., & Nardi, B. (2010, April). Intermediated Technology Use in Developing Communities. In *Proceedings of the SIGCHI Conference on Human Factors in Computing Systems* (pp. 2583–2592). Vancouver, BC: ACM.

Sambasivan, N., Weber, J., & Cutrell, E. (2011, May). Designing a Phone Broadcasting System for Urban Sex Workers in India. In *Proceedings of the SIGCHI Conference on Human Factors in Computing Systems* (pp. 267–276). Vancouver, BC: ACM.

Veena, N. (2007). Revisiting the Prostitution Debate in the Technology Age: Women Who Use the Internet for Sex Work in Bangkok. *Gender, Technology and Development*, 11: 97–107. doi:10.1177/097185240601100105.

Wright, J., Heynen, R., & van der Meulen, E. (2015). "It Depends On Who You Are, What You Are": Community Safety and Sex Workers' Experience with Surveillance. *Surveillance and Society*, 13, 2: 265–282.

Zainudeen, A., Iqbal, T., & Samarajiva, R. (2010). Who's Got the Phone? Gender and the Use of the Telephone at the Bottom of the Pyramid. *New Media & Society*, 12, 4: 549–566. doi: 10.1177/1461444809346721.

56

The ordinary nature of fantasy

Language, gender and sexuality in phone sex work

Giulia Selmi

Introduction

Phone sex is a kind of virtual sex work that entails sexually explicit behaviour where at least one of the participants engage in masturbation or sexual fantasies. However, customers of these services may call not only to have a sexual conversation, but also to fulfil some other needs such as a sense of nurturing, sympathy or other forms of emotional intimacy. In other words some clients call this kind of service to buy sex over the phone, while some others pay to find a sort of "virtual girlfriend".

Having been very popular and widespread in the 1980s and 1990s, in the twenty-first century it may seem to be an "old fashioned" form of sex work compared to contemporary popular forms of Internet-based sex work. However, I believe that exploring this form of commercial sex and its disembodied nature can be very fruitful to analyse how gender and sexuality come into play in sex work interactions.

Commercial phone sex services offer sexual or emotional experiences over the phone through premium rate calls during which certain services are provided and for which higher than normal call prices are charged. Unlike a normal call, part of the premium rate call charge is paid to the service provider, thus supplying businesses with their revenue. Sex workers do not have any direct economic transaction with customers but receive a salary from the sex phone company, which is commensurate to the length of the calls.

Phone sex work, therefore, occupies a "border area" of the sex industry, where sex is sold, but through technology without any direct involvement with the customer. Unlike other embodied forms of sex work, clients and workers don't touch each other, and unlike other forms of technology-mediated sex work like webcamming they do not see each other. In phone sex the interaction with the customers has to be translated into a narrative that can rely only on the voice and the mobilization of a shared cultural imaginary of sex, sexuality and gender between the interlocutors.

By virtue of the absence of the physical body (and its constraints), in the few empirical studies on the phone sex industry (Flower 1998; Hall 1995), as well as in some autobiographical texts written by phone sex workers themselves (Austin 2002), the experience of phone sex is often explained using the notion of fantasy: anonymity and the lack of visual exchange between the interlocutors should promote "a less self-conscious and [. . .] more imaginative presentation"

(Hall 1995, 188). Following Amy Flower's (1998) understanding, phone sex work could be imagined as a "fantasy factory" where phone sex operators play with sexuality and gender creating new narratives of sexual interaction where ordinary patterns of behaviour and relationships are subverted or challenged.

In this chapter I argue that rather than fantasies, what makes phone sex work interaction successful (both in economic and interactional terms) is the operators' professional ability to discursively mobilize suitable corporeal, sexual and gender resources and make clients feel that the interaction is "real" in the conversational space (Shotter 1993) created through the phone. Rephrasing Goffman's (1974) question about how individuals interpret and give meaning to interactional situations through socially shared and culture specific frames, if asked, "What is going on here?" (ibid., 46) the client should be able to answer "I am having sex with a woman with a determined body, determined erotic preferences and a determined biography who is, in turn, having sex with me". In order to create and maintain this "reality agreement" phone sex operators have to be able to voice gender (Mattley 2002) through a competent and strategic narrative that fits clients' cultural expectations of sexuality and gender. I explore this process of voicing gender by analysing the discursive micro-practices performed by the operators,[1] through which they create successful sexual and care stories for their clients, strategically managing dominant gender repertoires.[2]

Voicing sex, voicing care, voicing gender

At the beginning of every call the operators play the role of the "switchboard lady" or answer the phone pretending to be an employee of the phone company in charge of asking the costumer which kind of operator he wants to talk to. Alongside being a strategy to "gain minutes" of paid conversation, this initial screening is crucial to understand the cultural expectations of the customer concerning the sexual, bodily and gender features of the interlocutor he is paying to talk to (Selmi 2013b). If the customer is willing to talk to a young or an older woman this will not only change the pseudonym used by the operators, but also the kind of story and embodiment – in terms of body appearance, intimate biography and sexual competences – they will perform. The transcription of a call that follows helps explain this process:

[The phone rings, Lara answers by playing the switchboard lady. She puts the client on hold and tells me his name is Marco, he is 50, and is looking for a young woman. She resumes the conversation and introduces herself using a shrill, girlish voice.] *Hi honey I'm Silvia what's your name? / Marco what a nice name, where are you calling from? / Turin? What a nice city I'm from Milan / How do I look like? I'm slim and small, but I have huge tits, I'm a blonde with blue eyes. I'm wearing a little dress that would drive you crazy . . . and you? / Wow, you are a really handsome man. What do you do, Marco? / Oh you must be an important man then! / What do I do? I go to university sweetie, I study literature / Am I single? Of course I am sweetie, I'm too young to have a boyfriend! / You want to know if I'm naughty, honey? No I'm not, I'm a little girl, I don't know much about this stuff, you're making me blush / So you're a sex god? Oh my, honey / I learn fast though sweetie, tell me what you want me to do / Oh I'm really blushing, I have never done this / I swear honey you are the first / You have to teach me honey, because I really don't know where to start, I really needed to meet someone like you to start doing naughty things.* [The line breaks up, after few seconds the client calls back, Lara plays the switchboard operator and finally resumes the conversation as Silvia.] *Where were we, honey? / Oh my, sweetie, you need to teach me how to suck you because I don't know, what do I have to do? / I unbutton your trousers, real slow / oh my, dear, it's so big, I can see under the boxers my love, I didn't know it could be so*

*huge I'm almost scared honey and now what do I have to do / OK then I take your boxers off real
sweet and I look at it it's wonderful my love, really incredible / Yes you were right, now that I saw it
I don't think I can never do without it and now, love, what do I have to do? I don't know where to
put my hands.* [The line breaks up again, the client calls back and the conversation continues
on this register for two more calls.]

(Lara, Kappa centre)

Lara performs as a young woman who knows nothing about sex and also finds it embarrassing.
She uses a shrill, girlish voice that supports her narrative and self-presentation – beautiful, small,
blonde hair and blue eyes – that consolidates the client's expectation in aesthetic terms. To manage her performance, Lara uses the "cultural" hints provided by the client during the interaction
supporting his gendered sexual expectations. By positioning herself as an innocent, naïve and
powerless Lolita, she positions him as a skilled Don Juan able to seduce and possess her by repeatedly confirming his virility. She draws upon the available gendered sexual script for men and
women (Frith and Kitzinger 2001; Oliver and Hyde 1993) positioning both herself and the customer within a shared sexual narrative that forecasts men's infallibility and expertise to give sexual
pleasure and women's ability to respond adequately to the partner's stimulation (Wiederman
2005). This is achieved through the mobilization of an ecology of elements – tone of voice, body
description, age, sexual biography and personal interests – that translate the cultural expectation
of the customer via the conversational space created through the phone call. Obviously both the
identity and the intimate biography of Lara are a fantasy – meaning that they do not correspond
to her actual name, body appearance or biography and nor is she doing the actual activities she
is describing to the customer. However, to be believed (and therefore to guarantee an economic
reward for their activities) operators' performances have to be gender-based fantasies. In other
words, they have to mobilize what Connell (1987) has called the interactional repertoire of
emphasized femininity and, conversely, that of hegemonic masculinity.

These dominant cultural scenarios of gender and sexuality act as the background knowledge
operators reflexively mobilize to create the best performance for the customers. During fieldwork I recursively interviewed the operators to better understand how they developed their
stories and characters and how they choose which kind to perform for each customer. The
quotes that follow are an excerpt of these conversations.

C'mon, you too know what they have in mind, right? Don't you watch TV? Take Pamela
Anderson's breasts, the ass of Angelina Jolie, Arcuri's legs and here is the body you need.
They look for the woman they don't have as girlfriend or wife, and we perform the woman
who we would like to be. Wouldn't you like to have your ass like Angelina Jolie?

(Elisa, Lambda centre)

And what should I tell them, that I have hairy legs, small breasts and want to be an astro-
naut? Look, it doesn't work this way, they'll hang up on you. The tits, the nurse and the
desperate housewife work, the little girl too, but that's about it.

(Sara, Kappa centre)

Elisa's answer on the bodily appearance the characters have to have is reflexive of the mobilization
of precise and stereotyped aesthetic models of femininity, making reference to the appearance of
famous actresses or singers who have skinny bodies, long legs, curvy breasts and long hair, thereby
defining the mainstream cultural imaginary of the ideal feminine body (Bordo 1993; Chapkis
1986) that both clients and operators share. The question "Wouldn't you like to have your ass

like Angelina Jolie?" underlines the awareness of how the gendered mainstream bodily imaginary works as an "object of desire" for both men and women and defines the cultural codes through which it can be voiced in the phone call. Moreover, this imaginary is the one customers are willing to pay for. As Sara states, different gender performances – or those where the woman does not comply with gender stereotypes and expectations – do not work and what grants economic success to the phone calls is the ability to create stories and identities that draw exactly upon this gendered mainstream repertoire. Paradoxically, even if the absence of a visual exchange and face-to-face interaction could potentially promote more creative and less stereotypical sexual narratives, operators are highly aware that it is precisely the use of stereotypical feminine bodies and social identities that grant success to the performance and fit clients' expectations.

This happens not only when the conversation is explicitly sexual, but also with those clients who are not after a sexual encounter over the phone, but are rather seeking an emotional relationship. These are usually regular customers who call frequently and want to talk with the same "girl" in order to create bonds and intimacy with her. This is the case with Pasquale, a customer who had been calling regularly for years at the time of the fieldwork and who considered Beatrice his "virtual" girlfriend. Beatrice's fictional identity, as created by the operators,[3] is that of a southern Italian woman in her thirties who had emigrated to the north of Italy to work as cashier in a supermarket.

> [The telephone rings: it's Pasquale calling, an old customer looking for Beatrice. Sara plays the role of the switchboard lady, she puts him on hold for some second and then answers with a sweet and soft voice:] *Hello my love, how are you today? / I'm fine, I'm at home preparing dinner because I had the morning shift at work today. / What? I'm cooking some pasta and a roasted chicken and potatoes. / Yes, sure! I'll definitively cook them for you once we meet. I'll do a cake for you also my dear! What dessert do you like most sweetheart? / Oh . . . and what are your plans for today?"* [Pasquale talks for a couple of minutes and Sara holds the line to tell me he is telling her he went fishing with his mates and she comments, "My God, this sucks!" While Pasquale is talking the line breaks up, Pasquale calls back and the conversation continues.] *What were you saying honey? / Yes, I do love you darling, I love you so much. / Did you go to the doctor? Why? / Oh dear, what happened?* [She holds the line and tells me that in the last days he had the flu and a sore throat.] *Oh I wish I were there to cuddle you all night honey.* [The line breaks up, Pasquale calls back seven times and the conversation continues like this till the end].
>
> *(Sara, Kappa centre)*

The whole conversation is constructed around the customer's needs: Beatrice asks questions about what he has done during the day or about his health, while confirming intimacy and emotional bonds through a very soft and sweet voice and several terms of endearment. This time it is not the body appearance or the sexual biography that works as the gendered cultural code that grants authenticity to the call, but the stereotypic performance of the good wife. While the operator positions herself as the caring and sympathetic wife, the client is positioned as the husband in need of care and attention within a traditional script of heterosexual – hence heteronormative – relationships.

As in the previous example of Marco, with Pasquale the interaction is managed by constantly and reflexively "citing the gender norms" (Butler 1990, 1993). This process of continuously referring to well-known gender norms allows phone sex operators to be perceived as "real women" thus guaranteeing the performance's "fake authenticity" and cultural intelligibility. To be able to manage the conversations, then, what is key for the operators is not to what extent they are able to manage fantasies, nor is it about the extent to which their stories are or are not connected to their personal biography or identity, but rather how well they are able "to do the woman" (West and Zimmerman 1987) in the interactional space made available by the phone.

The story of Alessio is another example of this process. In one of the two erotic phone services where I did my fieldwork, two of the operators were men. They were originally hired to lead a gay line that, however, never took off, so after few months they worked under the identity of female operators. One of them, Alessio, who performs as a female operator, was the "best operator" at the time of my fieldwork there. This was established by an internal ranking that the manager did every month on the basis of the number of minutes of conversation that each employee had been able to have with clients. But apart from his highest formal ranking, Alessio's expertise was some sort of an organizational myth among his colleagues who told me several times that he was a master in "keeping them stuck to the phone". To manage the phone calls Alessio uses the same strategies of his colleagues. He creates fake identities to embody the gendered cultural expectations of the customers and he led the conversations drawing on the cultural hints customers give him. He identifies Sandra and Lucia as his best identities: Sandra is a 'well-born' girl who goes to college and who can turn into a *sex bomb* when needed; while Lucia is a divorced woman in her fifties with a passion for cooking and gardening. As seen before, also Alessio improvises on the scenarios he has constructed. He strategically modifies his voice – a voice, as he told me, "like Jessica Rabbit for Sandra" and a voice "like that of my mother" for Lucia. And he responds competently to the clients' expectations by "doing the woman" they want to talk to or have sex with. By mobilizing, in the conversational space, a choreography of elements coming from the available gender practices on femininity – a cultural, social, discursive and bodily repertoire available to individuals for being acted, asserted, performed and mobilized to manage interactions (Kessler and McKenna 1978) – Alessio succeeds in "passing as a woman" (Garfinkel 1967). His gender performances fit into the shared criteria of cultural intelligibility (Butler 1990) that are required to maintain the "reality agreement" that makes the conversation possible. Drawing again on Garfinkel (1967), we could say that Alessio – like the well-known Agnes in Garfinkel's research – is able to do the woman "better" because being a man offers him a privileged and more reflexive positioning for mobilizing the symbolic universes of gender. He is at the same time similar to and different from his colleagues. He is similar to them because he lives within the same cultural scenarios of gender and sexuality as they (and the customers) do; but he is different because he cannot count on an acquired femininity. This means that he has to monitor more reflexively and carefully his performance of femininity to make his female characters sound real and believable.

Conclusion

Lorber's (1993) theory on gender differences is based on the notion that individuals see the differences between men and women (and therefore consider them real and adequate) because they believe these differences to be biologically real. Drawing on this theory, we could say that within the space of an erotic phone call the customers see (and therefore consider real and adequate) the gender performances of the operators, when they correspond to what they believe a sexual or emotional relationship should be or how they believe a sexy woman or a caring woman should behave. When "seeing is believing" is not possible because the phone forces a disembodied interaction, "believing is seeing" becomes necessary to make a conversation successful.

Rather than a fantasy factory then, phone sex work can be depicted as an "ordinary factory" (Selmi 2012b): it is the ordinary and stereotypical nature of the gender and sexual performance that grants success to the interaction and, ultimately, that guarantees a profit to the operators. Operators' narratives are interactively created on the social and symbolic repertoire of the "emphasized femininity" (Connell 1987), a set of gender practices conforming to female subordination and oriented to comply with male desires, whether they are sexual or caring. According to Lakoff (1975) we could say that these narratives are "powerless" discourses or narratives that position (and reproduce) female subordination to male speech and desire. However, operators use this shared background knowledge reflexively and negotiate its stereotypical features to turn them into "powerful" narratives (Hall 1995) aimed at managing the conversation at their own economic advantage. Rather than the expression of subordination and powerlessness, operators' ability to strategically capitalize on sexuality and gender (Sanders 2005) echoes De Certeau's (1980) well-known distinction between strategies and tactics: they tactically use the mainstream gender repertoires to open up spaces for their individual economic advantage using exactly those gender strategies, i.e. the unequal and stereotyped feature of femininity and masculinity, which would position them in a subordinate and powerless position. Rather than sex objects, phone sex workers appear as "sex experts" (Bell 1994: 109) or as owners of erotic knowledge (Selmi 2013a) through which they negotiate the interaction with customers.

Notes

1 I use the term "operator" instead of sex workers and/or phone sex workers because this is what the workers call themselves. In order to cope with the high level of stigmatization in the industry, they strategically choose this term to avoid the "whore stigma" and to uphold claims for the professional nature of the service they provide (see Selmi 2012a).
2 The analysis presented in this chapter originates from fieldwork I carried out between May 2007 and September 2008 in two erotic call centres in Italy, one was small and home based (Kappa) and one was of medium size and office based (Lambda). Three women aged 25–45 work in the Kappa centre from 8 am to 12 pm with three shifts of five or six hours each, while the Lambda centre has 10 employees (8 women and 2 men) aged 20–55 working from 8 am to 12 pm on working days and 24 hours a day at weekends. Customers of the phone sex services were mainly men. During my fieldwork only one call by a women was made to the Lambda centre and all workers considered it an exception. Even if occasionally women can call the service, in fact, it is designed for male customers. I used a case study research strategy and qualitative data collection techniques and analysis. Data collection involved participant observation and interviews. Moreover, I audio-recorded nearly 15 hours of calls between the operators and their costumers. For privacy and ethical reasons, I recorded the operators' voices only: I did not want to record clients' voices without their explicit consent and it would have been impossible to gain consent without breaking the "reality agreement" on which phone sex work is built.
3 I use the plural because two operators perform Beatrice interchangeably and – according to them and to my observation – the customer does not notice the difference.

References

Austin, Miranda. 2002. *Phone Sex: Aural Thrills and Oral Skills.* Emeryville, CA: Greenery Press.
Bell, S. 1994. *Reading, Writing, and Rewriting the Prostitute Body.* Bloomington, IN: Indiana University Press.
Bordo, Susan. 1993. *Unbearable Weight: Feminism, Western Culture, and the Body.* Berkeley, CA: University of California Press.
Butler, Judith. 1990. *Gender Trouble: Feminism and the Subversion of Identity.* London and New York: Routledge.
Butler, Judith. 1993. *Bodies That Matter: On the Discursive Limits of "Sex".* London and New York: Routledge.
Chapkis, Wendy. 1986. *Beauty Secrets: Women and the Politics of Appearance.* Cambridge, MA: South End Press.
Connell, Raewyn. 1987. *Gender and Power: Society, the Person and Sexual Politics.* Stanford, CA: Stanford University Press.
de Certeau, Michel. 1980. *The Practice of Everyday Life.* Berkeley, CA: University of California Press.

Flower, Amy. 1998. *The Fantasy Factory: An Insider View of the Phone Sex Industry*. Philadelphia, PA: University of Pennsylvania Press.

Frith, Hannah and Kitzinger, Celia. 2001. Reformulating Sexual Script Theory: Developing a Discursive Psychology of Sexual Negotiation. *Theory and Psychology* 11: 209–232.

Garfinkel, Harold. 1967. Passing and the Managed Achievement of Sex Status in an "Inter-Sexed" Person. In Harold Garfinkel, *Studies in Ethnomethodology*, 116–185. New York: Prentice Hall.

Goffman, Erving. 1974. *Frame Analysis*. Cambridge, MA: Harvard University Press.

Hall, Kira. 1995. Lip Service on the Fantasy Line. In K. Hall and M. Bucholtz (eds) *Gender Articulated: Language and the Socially Constructed Self*, 183–216. London: Routledge.

Kessler, SusanJ. and McKenna, Wendy. 1978. *Gender: An Ethnomethodological Approach*. Chicago, IL: University of Chicago Press.

Lakoff, Robin T. 1975. *Language and Women's Place*. New York: Harper & Row.

Lorber, Judith. 1993. Believing Is Seeing: Biology as Ideology. *Gender & Society* 7(4): 568–581.

Mattley, Christine. 2002. Voicing Gender: The Performance of Gender in the Context of Phone Sex Lines. In P. Gagne and R. Tewskbury (eds) *Gendered Sexualities: Advances in Gender Research*, 79–102. London: Elsevier Science.

Oliver, Mary Beth and Hyde, Janet Shibley. 1993. Gender Differences in Sexuality: A Meta-Analysis. *Psychological Bulletin* 114: 29–51.

Sanders, T. 2005. "It's Just Acting": Sex Workers' Strategies for Capitalizing on Sexuality. *Gender, Work and Organisation* 12(4): 319–341.

Selmi, Giulia. 2012a. Dirty Talks and Gender Cleanliness: An Account of Identity Management Practices in Phone Sex Work. In Ruth Simpson, Natasha Slutskaya, Patricia Lewis and Heather Höpfl (eds) *Dirty Work: Concepts and Identities*, 113–125. London: Palgrave Macmillan.

Selmi, Giulia. 2012b. The Ordinary Factory: The Construction of (Hetero)sexuality in Phone Sex Work. In Antosa Silvia (ed.) *Gender and Sexuality: Rights, Language and Performativity*. Palermo: Aracne.

Selmi, Giulia. 2013a. From Erotic Capital to Erotic Knowledge: Body, Gender and Sexuality as Symbolic Skills in Phone Sex Work. In Carol Wolkowitz, Rachel Lara Cohen and Teela Sanders (eds) *Body/Sex/Work: Intimate, Embodied and Sexualized Labour*, 146–160. London: Palgrave Macmillan.

Selmi, Giulia. 2013b. The Absent Presence: Phone Sex Work, Bodily Practices and Representations. *Etnografia e ricerca qualitative*, 6: 407–422.

Shotter, John. 1993. *Conversational Realities: Constructing Life Through Language*. London: Sage.

West, Candace and Zimmerman, Don H. 1987. Doing Gender. *Gender and Society* 1: 125–151.

Wiederman, Michael W. 2005. The Gendered Nature of Sexual Scripts. *The Family Journal* 13: 496–502.

57

"I need $5 million"[1]

What sex workers making media tell you that no one else can

P.J. Starr and Sonyka Francis

Introduction

The depictions of sex work and sex workers have long been a subject of fascination in cinema and these cultural products produce a spectacle for audiences, reinforcing prevailing narratives that stigmatize and marginalize. Mainstream cinematic representation intertwines with melodramatic portrayals of "white slavery" and human trafficking, anchoring the portrayals of sex workers in panics about race, migration, and the moral nature of the nation (Vance 2011). As a result, an almost insatiable appetite exists globally for sex trafficking "melomentaries" that blur the lines between documentary and narrative films, contributing to policy shifts that oppress sex workers by a variety of means (Vance 2012).

The allure of melomentary is such that the majority of contemporary scholarship about cinematic representation of sex work focuses on the impact of the sex trafficking trope. Deconstructing and questioning the portrayal of human trafficking as "sex slavery" and "sex trafficking" is vital, and this chapter explores the degree to which sex worker-made media can decenter these narratives and mobilize resistance. However, the scope of inquiry is not limited to this framing, which is primarily in reaction to oppression. Efforts to decolonize representation cannot confine themselves to "rebutting the coloniser" (Chaudhuri 2016). Sex worker-created film, media, and cultural products thrive in their own right, stretching far beyond the truncated discussion forced by sex trafficking discourse, reaching into realms or personal actualization, performance, and cultural shifts.

We, the authors, speak from our experience as cultural creators, curators, and organizers in communities of sex workers, and from our research backgrounds in the arts and humanities. We explore how sex workers have constructed cinematic products about their daily lives, their work, delivering services to their peers and advocacy. These can be viewed as cultural processes that reclaim sex workers' stories and create space purely for the rights of sex workers, not necessarily limited by the constructions of historical representations of sex trafficking. Other films have been created that directly dialogue with stigmatizing media—such as Sangli Talkies (2010) reply to *Prostitutes of God*—challenging the impact of these melomentaries on their own turf. The media and films discussed specifically will be drawn from festivals and events curated by sex workers and include notes about how audiences have reacted to these screenings including research carried out at our curated events.

The whore gaze

Sex worker-made media is produced and controlled by people who have experience in sex work, which is any person of any gender who engages in sexual/erotic acts for remuneration. For one author, the process of curating a film program for MOMA/PS1 in March 2018—the labor of presenting a series of films about the experiences of sex workers in the context of "sex worker space" fantasized by a UK-based non-profit—sparked a series of observations about the nature of the "whore gaze" (Starr 2018). Developing this notion situates sex worker-made media in film theory about the power and pleasure of looking and opens the way to explore the usurping potential of the genre. The term whore is used to flag the transgressive nature of the creative pursuits under consideration.

In 1975 Laura Mulvey codified the "male gaze" in cinema, using a psychoanalytical framing to map out the ways in which men behind the camera, in film, and in the audience objectify, diminish, and pacify women. "The male gaze projects its phantasy on the female figure . . . women are simultaneously looked at and displayed, with their appearance coded for strong visual and erotic impact" (Mulvey 1975, 809–810). Her feminist analysis of classic Hollywood films, such as *Rear Window* (1954) and *To Have and Have Not* (1944), references a kind of universal "(passive) woman" as the "raw material for the (active) gaze of man." The elements of the sexual objectification of women in film are based on sex work as the "leit-motiff of erotic spectacle: from pin-ups to strip-tease" (Mulvey 1975, 810).

This othering of sex work and sex workers is part of the structure of whorephobia in representation. The prostitute (or whore) is a polyseme onto which cultural anxieties are projected, reflected, and amplified to the detriment of sex workers. Gail Pheterson has described the functioning of the "whore stigma" as cultural elements overlap, reinforce, and blend until the prostitute (always she), "becomes one who sells her honor by offering to hire her body for base gain or for an unworthy doing" (Pheterson 1993, 39). Because of the pervasive whore stigma in many forms of artistic representation, the prostitute stands in for a culture's decline, danger, disease, urban blight, immorality, and fated doom. Similarly, even though Mulvey (1975) is not concerned with the actual representation of sex workers in film, sex work and sex workers become the template of representation through which cisgendered, nonprostitute,[2] white women are oppressed.

In theory, any filmmaker—including nonprostitutes—could cast aside the whore stigma, reject melomentary, and create better representations. However, only the act of whores taking up the camera can explode the myth that to be a whore is to be the passive subject of the male gaze *and* the white (moralizing) feminist gaze. In beginning to think further about what is distinct about the whore gaze, the work of bell hooks (1992) provides a way to confront white feminist film theorizing of the male gaze and the "female gaze"[3] through the concept of the "oppositional gaze." The gaze is a "site of resistance," in particular in the form of the spectatorship of black women who have been constructed as "absence, that denies the 'body' of the black female so as to perpetuate white supremacy and with it a phallocentric spectatorship where the woman to be looked at and desired is white" (hooks 1992, 230). The whore gaze may be oppositional as sex workers see and decry their absence, silence, or twisted representation perpetuating whorephobia, transphobia, racism, xenophobia, and ageism. In addition to interrogating with the whore gaze, sex workers take up the camera to burst the bubble of the anti-prostitution/anti-porn feminists. A thread in this so-called feminist theorizing is that "prostituted women" are (or should be) silent because they are so broken and brainwashed. In this context, it remains a revolutionary act to be a whore and represent one's own life and community. In the sections below, the whore gaze is employed to make sex trafficking/white slavery narratives irrelevant and to reclaim space and narratives in service of sex worker rights.

The limited landscape of representation: trafficking and other discourses

The narrative of persons—particularly women—involved in the sex trade often depict lives needing intervention to bring the wayward to heel and to permanently punish the irredeemable whore. Downtrodden sex workers are broken by life's hardship, deserve pity, ridicule, do not have the intelligence to consent to encounters, and are denied full citizenship because they are not capable. These tropes are present in early twentieth-century films such as *The Street of Sorrow* (1927) that depicts the intertwined stories in the wake of World War I of "fallen women" who trade sex for food—one of whom is killed in a fire for her transgressions—and the narrow escape of a virtuous woman from both prostitution and starvation. In another archetype, money comes too easily, quickly, and plentifully as a result of sex work, priming the protagonist for her fate or possible redemption to marriage. For example, *Klute* (1971) features a high-class call girl who is saved just in time by a small-town cop who whisks her away to suburbia.

The anti-trafficking movement is currently positioned at the top of public manipulation using a web of imagery including public service announcements, television series, documentaries that blur the line between fact and fiction, and narrative films (see Andrijasevic 2007; Shah 2013; Vance 2011, 2012). The avalanche of these materials include, but are not limited to, *The Selling of Innocents* (1996), *Born Into Brothels* (2004), *Lilya 4-ever* (2002), the *Human Trafficking* miniseries (2005), *Prostitutes of God* (2010), *Eight Minutes* (2015), *Real Men Don't Buy Girls* (2011) campaign, and the *Taken* franchise (2008, 2012, 2014, 2017–present). The fetishization of the capturing of innocent/good women for "sex trafficking" is a tendency that has been present in the moving image for more than 100 years since the release of films such as *The Traffic in Souls* (1913), returning again and again in the service of influencing public opinion. These representations have no empirical relationship to the actual lives of people working in various aspects of sex work. As Carole Vance (2011, 940) explains this is no accident: the form deployed by these media products is eighteenth-century melodrama, a "compelling narrative of sexual danger, drama, sensation, furious action, wild applause, and most important, clearly identifiable victims, villains, and heroes . . . misdirecting the eye from complexity and contradiction, offering a simplified and emotionally gripping substitute." Svati Shah (2013) has also described how representations of sex trafficking flatten sex workers' experience and dismiss autonomy by refusing to consider sex work as a livelihood option, maintaining an exclusive focus on women and girls, ignoring men and transgendered people, containing a narrative arc that ends with the brothel "rescue" of women and girls, equating sex work with violence, and overlooking any organizing efforts among sex workers.

Today sex trafficking representations re-circulate in hourly updates via online publications and are recycled in new films and short online videos. Such is the power of the trafficking discourse that before any words are spoken, the scenario is immediately familiar to the audience through resonant visual representations. The April 14, 2012 edition of the *Inquisitr* startles with a large posed image of a woman staring at the audience. Her face displays anguish, accompanied by a black eye. A masculine body stands behind her with his hands at her neck, perhaps in a caress. Headlining this article is the statement that "1.9 Million People Are Victims of Sex Trafficking, Most Won't Be Rescued." They are "traded into sexual slavery." The depiction of a desperate, abused, angry, isolated, and sexualized victim elides sex trafficking with sexual labor, conveying that any woman engaged in sexual work must be doing so by force and dismisses any prospect of agency. A promotional photo for the film *Trafficked* (2017) starring Ashley Judd, depicts a woman with her back turned, long hair concealing her identity, with hands tied behind her back while her head hangs in shame. Money flowing beneath her to replace the lower half of her body, the supporting text above the image reads: "Last Year's Slave

Traders Made $100 Billion." The *New York Post*'s editorial piece "Inside New York's Silent Sex Trafficking Epidemic" (Gonen et al. 2018) leads with a close-up image of bound ankles. The spectator may notice that the toes of a victim representing the horrors of trafficking are perfectly pedicured with legs restrained by rope work with striking similarity to shibari knotting.[4] The sex trafficking documentary *Tricked* (2013) featuring anti-trafficking crusading columnist Nicholas Kristoff, displays a female figure with her back turned, bound by handcuffs. Her face is obscured not unlike the photographs used for online advertising by sex workers wishing to remain anonymous. The accompanying text next to her freshly groomed hair, perfect lingerie, and heels reads, "A Shocking Look Inside America's Sex Trade."

Bringing the whore gaze to bear on these representations reveals that sex trafficking representations not only deliberately misdirect the audience, they craftily create eroticized fantasies of "enslaved" women and girls. The sex trafficking media purveyors draw on both the male gaze and the feminist critique of the male gaze to enthrall audiences/spectators who may be either titillated and/or motivated to "rescue" fictionalized bound women. Thus looking at sex trafficking melomentaries and related forms is very pleasurable. Once seduced into these narratives, audiences are fed imagined statistics about the scope of the problem and urged to act. Millions of women and girls are trafficked globally each year. Depicted as sex slaves, these women and girls are reportedly forced to sleep with multiple men each night (10 men, 20 men, 30, etc). The income from this trade is estimated to be in the billions. Much has been written about the topic of faux trafficking numbers but the following sums it up best. In 2015, the *Washington Post* fact checkers honored "sex trafficking statistics" the "bushels of bogus" award writing bluntly that,

> There are *not* 300,000 children at risk for sexual exploitation. There are *not* 100,000 children in the sex trade. Human trafficking is *not* a $9.5 billion business in the United States. Girls do *not* become victims of sex trafficking at an average age of 13 years. The federal government has *not* arrested hundreds of sex traffickers.
>
> *(Kessler 2015)*

Media shapes public perception and sex trafficking representations have a concrete effect on sex workers' lives through policy and action. Much of what is portrayed in sensationalized depictions of sex workers' lives is untrue, in many cases wildly so. Since the "Pizzagate" related shooting at the Comet Ping Pong restaurant in the wake of false media reports of "child sex trafficking," it is brutally clear that such representations do lead to action (Gira Grant 2016). People can and do react to false media, especially when they are continually told by authority figures that they should take action. The entirely fictional film *Lilya 4-ever* (2002)—a melodrama in which an adolescent Russian girl kills herself after being tricked and forced into prostitution by a Swedish pimp—has been screened all over the world with the assistance of Sweden and the International Organization for Migration (IOM) in human rights and anti-trafficking campaigns, state department briefings, and NGOs (non-government organizations) trainings (Small 2012). The *Human Trafficking* Series (2005—current) in which a global sex slavery/trafficking ring is brought to justice by America's Immigration and Customs Enforcement (ICE) who also heroically rescue trafficked persons, is also an entirely fictional product developed by Lifetime Network in consultation with ICE, Equality Now, and the International Justice Mission, two anti-prostitution NGOs. The *Human Trafficking* series has been shown to policymakers in Washington, DC and has been used to publicize two federal anti-trafficking bills (Small, 2012). One analysis of the current epidemic of sex trafficking representation finds that it is bound up with the creation of new policies—in the United States for example the Victims of Trafficking and Violence Protection Act (TVPA) passed in the year 2000—with media coverage of trafficking spiking in 2005 and being in constant circulation ever since (Austin and Farrell 2017). This self-perpetuating system of "ending sexual slavery" connects hysteria over trafficking, celebrity, power, and ever-encroaching legislation and force directed at sex workers. For celebrities and people seeking public office, engagement in the trafficking discourse provides them with social capital, almost cynically at the expense of sex workers and all the communities affected by sex work criminalization (Queen and Saunders 2017).

Jamie Small (2012, 416) has noted that sex workers may have little recourse in challenging these representations effectively given that

> [l]acking extensive media platforms, sex workers and their allies may disagree with the accuracy of the filmic representations, but they do not have the global communication resources to tell their stories effectively to broad audiences. Their voices are lost in the channels of corporate media.

It may be that the business of anti-trafficking has "billions of dollars" and the most enduring cultural form, the melodrama, at its disposal to seek hegemony. However, "new media" and social media bring new factors into play with "more than a million hours of original video being uploaded, streamed, or shared online every day" (Eppink and Ullman 2018). In the following section, the visions and representations in film and related media that are created by sex workers are explored in terms of the whore gaze. Depictions of trafficking are a very real concern, but the whore gaze is not limited by them. The penetration of the discourse is such that sex worker advocates are almost always asked to comment on trafficking as a way of assuring the audience that sex worker rights will not stand in the way of preventing abuse. Speaking about trafficking becomes the only way that sex workers are allowed to have a voice. Sex workers may be compelled to say that they are against trafficking before saying anything else in order to avoid being cut out of the conversation or worse being framed as abusers themselves. The whore gaze rejects instructions to talk about trafficking. Asking sex workers how they feel about trafficking has undertones of judgment and conflation. It is also the wrong question to ask. How do sex workers feel about rape? The answer to this question is particularly important since sex workers know a great deal about who is judged as a "worthy victim" and sex workers fully know that having "too many" sex partners make a woman unworthy of concern. How do sex workers feel about unfair labor practices? How does any person feel about unfair labor practices? Particularly when they pertain to the things that everyone uses on a daily basis, from the clothes worn, to the food eaten, to the technology society relies on. If these questions seem unimportant when creating media involving sex workers then the disciplining of the sex trafficking framework has not yet been overcome.

Sex worker-created media

Historically in different cultural settings prostitution and sex work have been associated with the creation of art and culture (Howard 1994; Smith 2013). People in the sex trades have produced culture as writers, actors, performers, and dancers. Theatres, bars, festivals, and places of entertainment may also be places where sex workers ply their trade, meet and entertain their customers, mingling the creation of cultural representations with the business of sex as well. Much has been written about the appearance of sex workers in greatly recognized forms of art, but sex workers are not only muses. Nor do sex workers venture out solely to be seen. The whore gaze includes being a spectator. Sex workers come out to see, to be part of audiences and to consume culture. Being in certain spaces can be risky and sex workers' presence in cultural centers has caused moralists to panic. The theater in Tudor England was described as the "generall

Market of Bawderie" where good women could not be told apart from whores (Howard 1994, 78). In order to understand the whore gaze, research should not be limited to the products (texts, film, performance, clothing) but must also include an analysis of place, the spaces associated with this culture that are are often viewed by outsiders as transgressive, and the traditions, which reflect how sex workers are always in dialogue with history and defining the future.

Bringing history, place, and traditions back into the discussion is a radical act when speaking about sex work and representation. De-historicizing sex workers and places associated with sex work such as brothels and neighborhoods is a way of encapsulating descriptions of real, living people as if they were butterflies placed behind glass (see Shah (2013, 562) for her description of the way that brothels in Sonagachi are depicted in narrative films and documentaries such as *Born Into Brothels* as "a timeless world where nothing moves, backward or forward, and from which everyone must simply be removed.") These timeless depictions of prostitutes can then be put to other social use in ways that are rarely important for sex workers and often are quite harmful. De Villiers (2017, 22) further observes that filmmakers and creators of cultural products use "the figure of the sex worker to say something about social and economic changes," which reduces sex workers to metaphors in ways that have been mostly out of their control and to their detriment. What happens when sex workers say what they find important about themselves as a subject, and speak about the different audiences they may seek including but not limited to sex worker communities? In this sex workers are not a unitary category of people. Sex workers of privilege can "other" sex workers from oppressed communities and identities just as much as any anti-sex trafficking campaigner can. White privilege functions effectively to inscribe the voices of white/elite sex workers as the truthful ones. The gaze of cisgendered white women sex workers that is now occasionally included in mainstream representation, is Olympia's gaze,[5] dependent on oppressing blackness (Saini 2017). To fail to speak about and analyze how power and privilege operate within sex worker-created narratives is to dehistoricize and dehumanize real-life media creators under the banner of the prostitute or the whore and obscure some of the most important forces at work in sex worker art and culture.

The whore gaze is the reclamation of sex workers' stories and the creation of spaces for the rights of sex workers through film nights, film festivals, and events. A key activist in this process is Carol Leigh (also known as Scarlot Harlot), the founder of the Bay Area Sex Worker Film and Art Festival. In 1979 Carol Leigh coined the term sex work, as she sought a way to neutralize the terminology of the anti-prostitution feminists.[6] Some 20 years later, Carol traveled with her mother to attend a film festival organized by representatives of Danzine in Portland entitled Sex by Sex Workers. "My mother said, 'you should do this too,'" Leigh (2017) recalled. Soon after Leigh convened the first Sex Worker Film and Art Festival in San Francisco. "One of the goals of the project was bringing in various forms of sex workers' culture into the community. The other goal was to increase diverse representation of the sex worker in the movement" (Leigh 2017). While not the first or the only convention displaying sex worker-made media, the Bay Area Sex Worker Film and Festival is an enduring and iconic film event dedicated to the whore gaze. Festival curation questions structures of privilege among sex workers and film programming often includes films that interrogate the term "sex work" itself. The festival has became a place where local artists perform and films by and about sex workers from many parts of the globe bring together complex views on the lives of sex workers, organizing, and action. It is also an organizing space for sex workers with sex worker-only workshops and healing sessions.

The opportunity to show one's work in a space created by sex workers is revolutionary both personally and politically, providing a sense of belonging and legitimacy. Mariko Passion—a media maker and performance artist who has focused on the representation of the experiences of Asian sex workers—made a narrative short about her own experiences as stripper, a martial arts themed film called *1-900-Asian-Princess* that was shown at the Sex Worker Film and Art Festival in 2003.

> That was the beginning of of my time in the [sex worker rights] movement. I remember getting an award from Annie Sprinkle and Carol Leigh, it was the happiest moment of my life at that time . . . I wanted very strongly to be expressing my work through my art.
>
> *(Passion 2017)*

Luca of the Sex Worker Advocacy and Resistance Movement (SWARM) who has been pivotal in establishing film festivals as part of the Sex Worker Open University in the UK, concurs that,

> [the film festivals] were really powerful for sex workers who have made movies to be able to show their movies in a proper cinema with a big audience. We also thought it was a good tool for organizing sex workers because sex workers who were not involved in activism were attending the film festival and for them it was the first time they were involved in an event. This lead to them becoming more involved.
>
> *(Luca 2017)*

Luca traces back the roots of his own activism to a DVD set of short films created by sex workers.

> I was a sex worker for a while but I barely knew anyone, then I found this compilation made by a sex worker organization . . . a DVD with lots of short movies about sex work and it was the first time I had ever come across anything like that . . . I started in sex worker activism.
>
> *(Luca 2017)*

In India, a country that is home to sex worker organizations with memberships of 10,000s, sex workers have hosted some of the largest festivals in the world. Shohini Ghosh—an ally to sex workers—documented the Durbar Mahila Samanwaya Committee (DMSC) organized Millennium Milan Mela (the Millennium Carnival Meet) in the film *Tales of the Night Fairies* (2002). The event was attended by a "large number of sex workers from the Asia Pacific region, ordinary citizens and members of the city's intelligentsia . . . [and] included seminars, workshops, cultural programmes, games and open fora on contested issues around gender and sexuality" (BAYSWAN, n.d.). The Millennium Milan Mela in Calcutta is of global significance to sex workers because it also marks the moment of the founding of International Sex Worker Rights Day (Network of Sex Work Projects n.d.). The film *Tales of the Night Fairies* stands in stark contrast to *Born Into Brothels* critiqued above, giving voice to sex workers of all genders, bringing sex worker organizing to the forefront. The film effectively situates this organizing and the cultural representations of the Millennium Milan Mela in historical traditions and in constant dialogue with other cultural forms in India such as music, dance, and film. In 2012 another festival was held in Calcutta, the Sex Worker Freedom Festival, a global convention in reaction to the hosting of the International AIDS Conference in Washington, DC. Many sex workers and drug users could not attend the AIDS Conference due to immigration restrictions on these particular groups entering the United States. The Sex Worker Open University obtained a small amount of funding to attend and document the festival resulting in the short film *The Honey Bringer* (2012). Luca (2017) of SWARM was one of the film's producers and recalled that the conference was really a great opportunity to film with sex workers from all over the world, to ask people about their issues and their needs. The film is not just talking heads, we also used footage from the protests and from the performance nights.

Sex workers represent themselves as connected social and political beings through this documentation of conventions and performances, creating family albums of the people involved, remembering the important issues of the time period and the particular cultural forms used to celebrate and protest. These films date back to at least the 1980s and include *Outlaw Poverty, Not Prostitutes* (1991), a landmark video directed by Carol Leigh that documented the 1989 World Whores Summit in San Francisco. *Major!* (2015) is, among other things, a re-assertion of the pre-eminence in sex worker rights of trailblazing black transgender rights leader Miss Major-Gracy, whose "hooker rights" actions extend back to the 1960s. Social media has allowed for much more of this type of material to be produced with footage of protests on YouTube, for example "Sex Worker Activists Disrupt Special Session on US Congress and HIV" posted by the Red Umbrella Diaries in 2012 and Latin American public service announcements of strikes and protests (RedTraSex 2017), and live streaming of events on Facebook, Instagram, and other outlets. As film and video production has become more accessible globally sex workers have adapted their strategies, a trajectory of engagement between sex workers and emerging technologies that has been in train for centuries:

> Each generation of sex workers has had to invent and learn new skills that in earlier years were never imagined. We adapted to the end of slavery and the arrival of a cash economy. We keep track of world events, politics, economics, and sports to understand our customers. We learned about passports, visas, and travel. We used postcards, telegrams, pagers, emails, mobile phones, webcams, and now apps.
>
> *(Empower Foundation 2016, 60)*

Sex workers in the Global South have been early adopters of mobile phone technology, using encrypted messaging apps such as Whatsapp for the creation of art works and for organizing long before such technologies were even understood in many parts of Europe and the United States. However, access to communication technologies is uneven due to injustice, oppression, and marginalization. Street sex workers and indigenous sex workers continue to use older technologies effectively to overcome their marginalization (Jones 2018) and some styles of communication—such as Empower Thailand's sign language—provide secure forms in the context of heavy policing and border patrol (Laovilwanyakul 2018). Pre-existing forms are meshed with new media. The documentary *No Human Involved* (2016) records community members leaving chalked messages on the sidewalk to warn of impending raids. In Brazil "puta politics" deploys the pre-existing fascination of gazing upon whores to create a spectacle of performance for documentation and distribution on social media—such as in the case of DASPU fashion shows and when sex workers are arrested in advance of sporting mega events—to strategically "mobilise allies, media attention and state power in favour of prostitute rights" (Blanchette and Murray 2016). The melange of communication strategies allows sex workers to continue to be able to represent themselves even when avenues such as the Internet are abruptly restricted due to criminalization.[7]

Though the spectacle of whores congregating in public space draws the eye, many films documenting sex workers organizing are more intimate, recording a meeting to share a meal, a memorial, or condom outreach to folks to protect their health.[8] Sex workers work together collectively to ensure our access to education and health; to advocate for safe fair work; to increase society's understanding and acceptance; to maintain a strong united community; and to hold a space in society where we can stand up. This includes books, artworks, films and performances.

(Empower Foundation 2016, 60)

Mariko Passion (2017) explains how these forms of documentation and representation are both personal and political, saying, "I made a film about herpes, it was about my relationship as well. I wanted to get out there education about sex work and STDs." The short documentary film *What You Don't See* (2017) is simultaneously personal and collective through the rapid-fire screening of photos, recordings, and Whatsapp conversations among sex workers about the day-to-day impact of sporting "mega-events" in Rio. In the film, sex workers cook, eat, dress, dance, display their bodies, take a bus, observe their workplaces, watch the news, and share cat photos.

The whore gaze does not isolate sex worker protagonists except if it would make sense to depict them away from family and community networks, such as when a sex worker is with a customer. *Saviour Complex* (2008), a narrative short, displays surrealist interactions of a woman with three clients consecutively with the purpose of "punching a hole in the hooker with a heart of gold stereotype." She deflates her customers' desires without expression, luxuriating in a pile of money with a small smile after they have departed. In this portrayal being covered in money is an achievement, not a depiction of shame as in the images of *Trafficked* (2017). *All that Sheltering Emptiness* (2010) is a meditation on "arousal, and other routines in the life of a New York City callboy" as he navigates sexual boundaries with a customer that puts sexual violence in a very complicated context. These types of films are not intended to be pornographic though sex workers frequently create in that genre. Rather they are transgressive and challenging about sexuality, personal actualization, and play with the notion of who a whore is. These films often can only be fully understood by sex workers and may outrage or confuse mainstream audiences as they deliberately confound the male gaze and the feminist critique of the male gaze. Luca (2017) of SWARM responds to this saying,

when we do make our own films (about our own engagement in sex work), it can be more nuanced. Of course I love the films saying that sex work is work, explaining the situation is very important, but sometimes the films that are a bit more poetic can explore our relationship to our work, our relationship to clients.

Sex worker self-representation for the most part transcends and eschews the extremely limited field imagined in the "sex trafficking" genre. Remarkable examples exist, however, of sex worker-made films that engage with the trafficking discourse to dismantle the melomentary and skewer the histrionics of films such as *The Selling of Innocents, Prostitutes of the God* and their ilk. In 2012 the Empower Foundation of Thailand released a short narrative film made by sex workers in conjunction with a report exposing the impact of law enforcement, raids, and "rescues" on sex workers. *Last Rescue in Siam* (2012) taunts the melodramatic trafficking film narrative, playfully referencing the past as a flickering black and white silent film. The film deflates the notion of innocence, as well as the "timelessness" of brothels in "Siam," by opening with a bucolic close up of a fresh-faced woman who sleeps "when the sun goes down and the stars come out." The long shot reveals that she is not sleeping in a village as the viewer might suppose but in a bustling sex work venue, filmed at the Can Do Bar, a collectively owned sex worker bar in Chiang Mai. In the mold of "keystone cops," police, social workers, and an NGO plot in their "war room" to rescue these sex workers—who they incorrectly assume are children—only to be outwitted during their over-hyped heroic raid by sex workers using their skills as pole dancers and performers to escape. The one sex worker they do manage to capture subverts her rehabilitation where she is forced to be a seamstress by sewing a ladder to escape. The associated report released with the film underscores the message: "We have now reached a point in history where there are more women in the Thai sex industry who are being abused by anti-trafficking practices than there are women being exploited by traffickers" (Empower Foundation 2012, vi).

In *VAMP Responds to Betrayal of Prostitutes of God Film* (2010) outraged community members who unwittingly appeared without their consent in the film *Prostitutes of God* confront film-maker Sarah Harris with her transgressions and fabrications. "You portrayed me as a brothel owner when I told you I am a sex worker," explains one woman. The adult son of a sex worker explains that his mother used the money she earned to raise him. "Your analysis is wrong, and we do not agree with it . . . you have no right to malign our mothers as pimps, traffickers, agents." Several speakers challenge the filmmaker's inclusion of a young woman's HIV status in the film, violating her confidentiality. "O white woman you have insulted our Devi (Goddess) and our women," concludes a woman who identifies as a Devdasi. The Veshya Anyay Mukti Parishad (VAMP, Prostitutes' Collective Against Injustice) who produced the film note that,

> in the age of the Internet, women in countries far away who used to be the objects of white people's gaze with no right of reply now have access to the representations that are made of them, and the technological means to answer back.

Discussion: why should anyone care that sex workers make films?

The whore gaze breaks out of the passivity forced upon sex workers by the sex trafficking framework and certain elements of feminist film theory. In this chapter we have discussed contemporary festivals where films made by sex workers have been featured and we have reviewed specific films to begin to codify what the whore gaze means for people who are actually whores. Media made from, containing, and for the whore gaze—that is films made by sex workers about aspects of sex workers' existence for other sex workers and at times for broader audiences—is filled with details about place, history, and tradition. This subverts the idea of the prostitute who exists across time, culture, and space, who can be molded to represent something other. On a practical level because of budget constraints or simply because of community ties and the spaces available, films—such as *Last Rescue in Siam*—may be made in real brothels and sex work places, rather than imagined spaces. The tchotchkes caught in the frame might be real tchotchkes. The camera does not linger on a flickering red light bulb or a dark alleyway because that was what a set director somewhere thought might signify whoredom. Films from, containing, and for the whore gaze are very often about organizing, whether it be meeting to share a meal, or a rally of thousands of whores. Community members are shown as real people—not archetypes or anonymous bodies filmed from a distance—and as connected social and political beings. To be a sex worker means that a person must be interacting with others, it is part of the job, and the point of earning a livelihood is to be with others, to support children, to treasure pets, to visit parents, to go to the store or market, and to contribute to the economy. Films from, containing, and for the whore gaze can and do meditate on the nature of sexual interaction. This might be pornography and it also may be whores thinking about sex and personhood, adding new observations to theorizing. The whore gaze will skewer the man with the savior complex, the whore gaze will find solace in a customer's odd act of kindness. There may be orgasms or eye rolling, or both. Money will usually represent success, power, control, love, and not shame. Money may also signify nothing special because sex work is work, and people normally get paid for their work without putting too much emphasis on it in a film. The whore gaze will confront the colonizer including white women.

However, no matter if sex worker-made media is interesting, all the works mentioned above are far distant from Hollywood and mobilize almost no capital or funding. In order to think about why anyone should care about this media, bell hooks' (1992) observation that the gaze is a site of resistance provides a framework. Many in the rescue industries say they are concerned about the fate of whores. Sex workers want to be a part of this conversation, but they have been removed from it.

> Resisting anti-sex work rhetoric, which is often packaged as "anti-trafficking" work, is challenging. After all, sex workers are framed as voiceless victims, and by this circular logic anyone speaking out and for the recognition of sex work isn't actually a sex worker.
>
> *(Dlamini and Shackleton 2016, 73)*

Sex workers may be excluded from meetings and shut out by people who hold this view but they will not remain silent. The whore gaze circulates online, in classes, any place films are shown. The "bad girls" of EMPOWER are able to deflate the sex trafficking discourse and VAMP speaks directly back. In Brazil, the "prostitutes' movement has responded with a two-prong strategy: on the one hand, it is engaging in street politics, guerrilla theatre, and practical initiatives; on the other, it is entering the forums and institutions that sprung up around human trafficking" (Blanchette and Murray 2016).

Sex worker representation has value in and of itself and not simply as a counter-weight to sex trafficking hysteria. The whore gaze shifts what it is acceptable to represent in regards to desire, sex, money, and work. Nonprostitute filmmakers occasionally find it possible to come up with narratives in which "prostitutes are fully-realized characters" such as *Harlots* described by one of its creators, Moira Buffini, as a "whore's eye view" of the oldest profession (Blake 2017). Buffini "hired an all-female writing and directing staff" to bring *Harlots* to life, not yet publicly acknowledging if any sex workers were hired to engage in this labor. The founders of the whore gaze should reap the benefits of their experience, that is, be paid as artists, writers, consultants, and directors. However, it is not any cause for celebration that a series like *The Deuce* (2017) can claim to have consulted with sex workers in order to create a portrayal of white sex workers succeeding at the cost of sex workers of color, reinforcing racist stereotyping (Saini 2017). It is much more heartening that a lead character in *Queen Sugar* (2016), a black woman, demands $5 million in reparations and has a good portion of it handed over to sex workers. Indeed, $1 million for sex worker rights organizing seems to be an outlandish sum until we consider that a Swedish organization falsely received $4 million in donations to assist non-existent sex slaves in a far-off land (Asia Pacific Regional Correspondent 2017).

To conclude, media made by sex workers, filmmakers, and organizations are distinct in their handling of the "morality" of sex work and the humanity of sex workers. Overwhelmingly, this is predicated on the need to decriminalize sex work, to remove criminal sanctions, and to end stigma. However, for sex worker cultural creators this is not something to be contemplated endlessly. It simply is a necessity.

> [P]eople are still asking: "prostitution . . . good or bad? Legal, illegal, decriminalised . . . what is best?" The debate goes on and on while we are still providing for our families, building up the country, advising each government that comes along, trying to stand up with others all while continuing to work on top of a mountain of stigma and laws.
>
> *(Empower Foundation 2016, 64)*

Whores have been written out of cultural history, here we write them back in. All we need is $5 million to publicize our works. We have a voice, you are just not listening.

Notes

1   Charley succeeds in her $5 million blackmail scheme and proceeds to have $1 million of it donated to a sex workers' rights organization (Mabry 2016). *Queen Sugar* displays the amount of work Black women do to dismantle social norms that are harmful to other women.
2   As per Pheterson (1993, 39).
3   A concept developed in response to the "male gaze" by feminist filmmakers to describe the distinct ways that women filmmakers gaze upon their female subjects and audience reaction to this work (Dirse 2013)
4   Shibari is a form of erotic bondage originating in Japan (Sebag-Montefiore 2016).
5   Édouard Manet's painting *Olympia* depicts a prostitute defiantly staring back at the spectator. Her gaze relies upon the presence of her black maid in the background, who is present but not to be seen and reinscribes the erotic whiteness of Olympia (O'Grady, 2003).
6   In the film *Red Umbrella Rights* (2017), Carol Leigh recounts that she was attending an "anti-porn/anti-prostitution conference with Andrea Dworkin as the main speaker" and went to a workshop that was called the "sex use industry." Leigh suggested that the workshop use the term sex work because "based on what the women do . . . the men use the services, but the women do the work" (Merryman 2017).
7   In April 2018, for example, the United States passed new legislation, a package of statutes including the *Stop Enabling Sex Traffickers Act* (SESTA) and *Allow States and Victims to Fight Online Sex Trafficking Act* (FOSTA), restricting online speech about sex work, causing closures of websites across the country, and affecting global communication as well.
8   For example, *Brigada Callejera De Apoyo A La Mujer "Elisa Martínez"* (2016) and *Remember the Living: Monica Forrester on Sisters in Spirit and Indigenous Sex Workers* (2012).

References

Andrijasevic, Rutvica. 2007. Beautiful Dead Bodies: Gender, Migration and Representation in Anti-Trafficking Campaigns. *Feminist Review* 86: 24–44.

Asia Pacific Regional Correspondent. 2017. Swedish NGO Under Investigation for Creating Fake "Rescue" Stories to Solicit Donations. *Network of Sex Work Projects*, August 28. www.nswp.org/news/swedish-ngo-under-investigation-creating-fake-rescue-stories-solicit-donations.

Austin, Rachel, and Amy Farrell. 2017. Human Trafficking and the Media in the United States." *Criminology and Criminal Justice.* Oxford Research Encyclopedias. New York: Oxford University Press. http://criminology.oxfordre.com/view/10.1093/acrefore/9780190264079.001.0001/acrefore-9780190264079-e-290.

BAYSWAN. n.d. "The Making of *Tales of the Night Fairies.*" www.bayswan.org/swfest/tales.html.

Blake, Meredith. 2017. "From 'The Handmaid's Tale' to 'I Love Dick,' the Female Gaze Is Thriving on Television." *Los Angeles Times*, May 5. www.latimes.com/entertainment/tv/la-et-st-female-gaze-television-20170505-htmlstory.html.

Blanchette, Thaddeus, and Laura Murray. 2016. The Power of Putas: The Brazilian Prostitutes' Movement in Times of Political Reaction. In P.G. Macioti and Giulia Garofalo Geymonat (Eds.), *Sex Workers Speak. Who Listens? (Beyond Trafficking and Slavery)*, 75–80. www.opendemocracy.net/beyond-slavery-themes/sex-workers-speak.

Brigada Callejera De Apoyo A La Mujer "Elisa Martínez." 2016. Mexico. www.sexworkerfest.com/videos/video_type/brigada-callejera-de-apoyo-a-la-mujer-elisa-martinez-ac.

Briski, Zana, and Ross Kauffman. 2004. *Born Into Brothels*. USA and India: THINKFilm.

Brown, Kevin. 2015. *Eight Minutes*. USA: A&E.

Carducci, Gina, and Mattilda Bernstein Sycamore. 2010. *All That Sheltering Emptiness*. USA. https://vimeo.com/209997150.

Carpenter, Alison and Giedroic, Coky. *Harlots*. UK: ITV Studios Global Entertainment. http://drama quarterly.com/battle-of-the-brothels.

Chaudhuri, Amit. 2016. The Real Meaning of Rhodes Must Fall. *Guardian*, March 16. www.theguardian.com/uk-news/2016/mar/16/the-real-meaning-of-rhodes-must-fall.

Cobban, William. 1996. *The Selling of Innocents. Associated Producers and Canadian Broadcasting Association.* www.imdb.com/title/tt3455118.

Dirse, Zoe. 2013. Gender in Cinematography: Female Gaze (Eye) behind the Camera. *Journal of Research in Gender Studies* 3 (1): 15–29.

Dlamini, Dudu, and Sally-Jean Shackleton. 2016. Sex Work Activism in South Africa: A Struggle for Visibility. In P.G. Macioti and G. Garofalo Geymonat (Eds.), *Sex Workers Speak. Who Listens? (Beyond Trafficking and Slavery)*, pp. 60–64. www.opendemocracy.net/beyond-slavery-themes/sex-workers-speak.

Donini, Angela, Flavia Viana, Laura Murray, Marina Calvancanti, and Tais Lobo. 2017. *What You Don't See*. Prostitution Policy Watch/Davida, Brazil. https://oquevcnaove.hotglue.me/?WhatYouDontSee.

Duguay, Christian. 2005. *Human Trafficking [Miniseries]*. USA: Lifetime Television.

Empower Foundation. 2012. *Hit and Run: Sex Worker's Research on Anti Trafficking in Thailand*. Thailand: Empower Foundation. www.empowerfoundation.org/sexy_file/Hit%20and%20Run%20%20RATSW%20Eng%20online.pdf.

Empower Foundation. 2016. We Don't Do Sex Work Because We Are Poor, We Do Sex Work to End Our Poverty. In P.G. Macioti and G. Garofalo Geymonat (Eds.), *Sex Workers Speak. Who Listens? (Beyond Trafficking and Slavery)*, pp. 60–64. www.opendemocracy.net/beyond-slavery-themes/sex-workers-speak.

Empower Studios. 2012. *Last Rescue in Siam*. Thailand: Bad Girl Films. www.sexworkerfest.com/videos/video_type/last-rescue-in-siam.

Eppink, Jason, and Sarah Ullman. 2018. The New Genres: Video in the Internet Age. *Museum of the Moving Image*. https://perma.cc/Y6QV-CGK4.

Ghosh, Shohini. 2002. *Tales of the Night Fairies*. San Francisco: Sex Worker Film and Art Festival.

Gira Grant, Melissa. 2016. Pizzagate and the Long Legacy of the Fabricated Sex Slave. *Pacific Standard*, December. https://psmag.com/news/pizzagate-and-the-long-legacy-of-the-fabricated-sex-slave#.7zncw4yha.

Gonen, Yoav, Shawn Cohen, Gabrielle Fonrouge, and Ruth Brown. 2018. Inside New York's Silent Sex Trafficking Epidemic. *New York Post*, April 16. https://nypost.com/2018/04/16/inside-new-yorks-silent-sex-trafficking-epidemic/.

Harris, Sarah. 2010. *Prostitutes of God*. India: VBS TV. www.telegraph.co.uk/expat/expatlife/8008562/Indias-prostitutes-of-God.html.

Havell, Clare, and Vincent Lee. 2012. *The Honey Bringer*. UK: Sex Worker Open University.

Hawks, Howard. 1944. *To Have and Have Not*. USA: Warner Bros.

Hitchcock, Alfred. 1954. *Rear Window*. USA: Paramount Pictures.

hooks, bell (1992). "The Oppositional Gaze: Black Female Spectator." In Amelia Jones, *The Feminism and Visual Cultural Reader*. New York: Routledge, pp. 94–105.

Howard, J. (1994). *The Stage and Social Struggle in Early Modern England*. London and New York: Routledge.

Inquistr. 2012. UN Report: 1.9 Million People Are Victims of Sex Trafficking, Most Won't Be Rescued, April 4. www.inquisitr.com/215448/un-report-1-9-million-people-are-victims-of-sex-trafficking-most-wont-be-rescued.

Jones, Monica. 2018. Shifting Media Representations from Rescue to Rights presented at the Sex Workers Speak: Communications technologies for Our Global Empowerment, Parallel Session, Commission on the Status of Women, New York, March 15.

Kessler, Glenn. 2015. Fact Checker: The Biggest Pinocchios of 2015. *Washington Post*, December 14, 2015. www.washingtonpost.com/news/fact-checker/wp/2015/12/14/the-biggest-pinocchios-of-2015/?noredirect=on&utm_term=.332fe32f4e74.

Laovilwanyakul, Thanta (Ping Pong). 2018. Media Strategies of EMPOWER Thailand presented at the Sex Workers Speak: Communications Technologies for Our Global Empowerment, Parallel Session, Commission on the Status of Women, New York, March 15.

Leigh, Carol. 1991. *Outlaw Poverty, Not Prostitutes*. San Francisco: Sex Worker Film and Art Festival. https://archive.org/details/OutlawPoverty_Pt2.

Leigh, Carol. 2017. Representation of Sex Work in Film and Festivals. Interview by P.J. Starr.

Loane Tucker, George. 1913. *The Traffic in Souls*. USA: Universal Film Manufacturing Company.

Luca. 2017. Sex Worker Advocacy and Resistance Movement: Representation of sex work in film and festivals. Interview by P.J. Starr.

Mabry, Tina. 2016. "Give Us This Day." *Queen Sugar*. USA: Oprah Winfrey Network.

Maggie's: Toronto Sex Workers Action Project. 2012. *Remembering the Living: Monica Forrester on Sisters in Spirit and Indigenous Sex Workers*. Toronto, Canada. www.sexworkerfest.com/videos/video_type/remember-the-living-monica-forrester-on-sisters-in-spirit-and-indigenous-sex-workers.

Merryman, Molly. 2017. *Red Umbrella Rights*. USA.

Moodysson, Lukas. 2002. *Lilya 4-ever*. Sweden: Sonet Film.

Mulvey, Laura. 1975. Visual Pleasure and Narrative Cinema. *Screen* 16 (3): 6–18.

Network of Sex Work Projects. n.d. "International Sex Worker Rights Day." www.nswp.org/event/international-sex-worker-rights-day.

O'Grady, Lorraine. 2003. "Olympia's Maid: Reclaiming Black Female Subjectivity." In Amelia Jones (Ed.) *The Feminism and Visual Cultural Reader*, 174–187. London: Routledge.

Ophelian, Annalise. 2015. *Major!* USA. www.missmajorfilm.com.

Pabst, G.W. 1927. *The Street of Sorrow*. USA: Sofar Films.

Pakula, Alan. 1971. *Klute*. USA: Warner Bros.

Passion, Mariko. 2017. The Revolution and Evolution of the Work of Mariko Passion. Interview by P.J. Starr.

Pelecanos, George, and David Simon. 2017. *The Deuce*. USA: HBO.

Pheterson, Gail. 1993. The Whore Stigma: Female Dishonor and Male Unworthiness. *Social Text* 37: 39–64.

Queen, Carol, and Penelope Saunders. 2017. California's Proposition 35 and the Trouble with Trafficking. In David Halperin and Trevor Hoppe (Eds.), *The War on Sex*, 323–346. Durham and London: Duke University Press.

Real Men Don't Buy Girls. 2011. Demi and Ashton Foundation. www.youtube.com/watch?v=uSSLv2PSu4c.

RedTraSex LAC. 2017. *8M RedTraSex 2017—Paro Internacional de Mujeres*. Latin America. www.youtube.com/watch?v=Ouk5Mc6NBYE.

Red Umbrella Diaries. 2016. *Sex Worker Activists Disrupt Special Session on US Congress and HIV*. https://perma.cc/7BJ3-8UVN.

Saini, Anna. 2017. The Representation of Sex Workers on Film/Video/Social Media. Interview by Sonyka Francis and P.J. Starr.

Sangli Talkies. 2010. *VAMP Responds to Betrayal by Prostitutes of God Film*. VAMP/SANGRAM, India. https://perma.cc/3YDU-2PBT.

Sebag-Montefiore, Clarissa. 2016. Shibari: Pushing Boundaries in the Ancient Japanese Practice of Knot Tying. *Guardian*, January 20. www.theguardian.com/stage/2016/jan/21/shibari-pushing-boundaries-in-the-ancient-japanese-practice-of-knot-tying.

Shah, Svati. 2013. Brothels and Big Screen Rescues. *Interventions: International Journal of Postcolonial Studies* 15 (4): 549–566.

Small, Jamie. 2012. Trafficking in Truth: Media, Sexuality, and Human Rights Evidence. *Feminist Studies* 38 (2): 415–443.

Smith, Ariel. 2008. *Saviour Complex*. Vtape, Toronto, Canada.

Smith, Jill Suzanne. 2013. *Berlin Coquette: Prostitution and the New German Woman, 1890–1933*. Ithaca: Cornell University Press.

Starr, P.J. 2016. *No Human Involved*. USA. www.nohumaninvolvedfilm.com

Starr, P.J. 2018. "The Whore Gaze (Preliminary)." Moral High Ground. April 23. http://moralhighground.tumblr.com/post/173232707815/the-whore-gaze-preliminary.

Vance, Carole. 2011. States of Contradiction: Twelve Ways to Do Nothing about Trafficking While Pretending To. *Social Research* 78(3): 933–948.

Vance, Carole. 2012. Innocence and Experience: Melodramatic Narratives of Sex Trafficking and Their Consequences for Law and Policy. *History of the Present* 2 (2): 200–218.

Wallace, Will. 2017. *Trafficked*. Worldwide: California Pictures. www.imdb.com/title/tt1720621.

Wasson, John Keith, and Jane Wells. 2013. *Tricked: The Documentary*. USA: First Run Features.

Villiers, Nicholas de. 2017. *Sexography*. Minneapolis: University of Minnesota Press.

Index